Writing and Reading Across the Curriculum

Ninth Edition

Laurence Behrens
University of California
Santa Barbara

Leonard J. Rosen
Bentley College

PEARSON
Longman

New York • San Francisco • Boston
London • Toronto • Sydney • Tokyo • Singapore • Madrid
Mexico City • Munich • Paris • Cape Town • Hong Kong • Montreal

To Bonnie, Michael, Amy, and Keiko—
and to L.C.R., Jonathan, and Matthew

Senior Sponsoring Editor: Virginia L. Blanford
Executive Marketing Manager: Megan Galvin-Fak
Senior Supplements Editor: Donna Campion
Production Manager: Charles Annis
Project Coordination, Text Design, and Electronic Page Makeup: Elm Street Publishing Services, Inc.
Cover Designer/Manager: John Callahan
Photo Researcher: Julie Tesser
Manufacturing Manager: Mary Fischer
Printer and Binder: Courier Corporation
Cover Printer: Lehigh Press, Inc.

For permission to use copyrighted material, grateful acknowledgment is made to the copyright holders on pp. 839–44, which are hereby made part of this copyright page.

Library of Congress Cataloging-in-Publication Data

Behrens, Laurence.
    Writing and reading across the curriculum/Laurence Behrens, Leonard J. Rosen.—9th ed.
        p. cm.
    Includes bibliographical references and index.
    ISBN 0-321-29100-X—ISBN 0-321-29115-8 (Exam copy)
    1. College readers. 2. Interdisciplinary approach in education—Problems, exercises, etc.
    3. English language—Rhetoric—Problems, exercises, etc. 4. Academic writing—Problems,
    exercises, etc. I. Rosen, Leonard J. II. Title.
PE1417.B396 2005
808'.0427—dc22

                                                                                            2004018222

Please visit our website at http://www.ablongman.com/behrens

ISBN 0-321-29100-X

4 5 6 7 8 9 10—CRS—07 06

Detailed Contents

Chapter 6
Analysis   165

Chapter 7
Locating, Mining, and Citing Sources   185

PART II
AN ANTHOLOGY OF READINGS   235

TECHNOLOGY/COMMUNICATION
Chapter 8
Cyberspace and Identity   237

PSYCHOLOGY
Chapter 9
Obedience to Authority   300

AMERICAN STUDIES
Chapter 10
What's Happening at the Mall?   375

FOLKLORE
Chapter 12
Fairy Tales: A Closer Look at Cinderella   539

LAW
Chapter 14
You, the Jury   733

Preface

When *Writing and Reading Across the Curriculum (WRAC)* was first published in 1982, it was—viewed from one angle—an experiment. We hoped to prove our hypothesis that both students and teachers would respond favorably to a composition reader organized by the kinds of focused topics that were typically studied in general education courses.

The response was both immediate and enthusiastic. Instructors found the topics in that first edition of *WRAC* both interesting and teachable, and students appreciated the links that such topics suggested to the courses they were taking concurrently in the humanities, the social sciences, and the sciences. Readers also told us how practical they found our "summary, synthesis, and critique" approach to writing college-level papers. In this edition, we have added the skill of analysis to the three writing skills that have anchored *WRAC* since its initial appearance.

In developing the eight subsequent editions of *WRAC*, we have been guided by the same principle: to retain the essential multidisciplinary character of the text while providing ample new material to keep it fresh and timely. Some topics have proved particularly enduring—our "Cinderella" and "Obedience" chapters have been fixtures of *WRAC* since the first edition. But we take care to make sure that a third to one-half of the book is completely new every time, both by extensively revising existing chapters and by creating new ones. Over nine editions, our discussion of rhetoric has expanded to seven chapters. While we have retained an emphasis on summary, critique, and synthesis (and, as indicated, have added a new emphasis on analysis), we continue to develop content on such issues as argumentation and online research and writing that addresses the issues and interests of today's classrooms.

STRUCTURE

Like its predecessors, the ninth edition of *Writing and Reading Across the Curriculum* is divided into two parts. Part I introduces the strategies of summary, critique, synthesis, analysis, and research. We take students step-by-step through the process of writing papers based on source material, explaining and demonstrating how summaries, critiques, syntheses, and analyses can be generated from the kinds of readings students will encounter later in the book—and throughout their academic careers. Part II consists of a series of subject chapters drawn from both academic and professional disciplines. Each subject is not only interesting in its own right but is also representative of the kinds of topics typically studied during the course of an undergraduate education. We also believe that students and teachers will discover connections among the thematic chapters of this edition that further enhance opportunities for writing, discussion, and inquiry.

CONTINUED FOCUS ON ARGUMENTATION

Part I of *Writing and Reading Across the Curriculum* is designed to prepare students for college-level assignments across the disciplines. The ninth edition continues the eighth edition's strengthened emphasis on the writing process and on argument, in particular. It provides coverage on the use of the World Wide Web for research and on citation of electronic sources. We continue to treat argument synthesis in a separate chapter, emphasizing the following:

- **The Elements of Argument: Claim, Support, Assumption.** This section adapts the Toulmin approach to argument to the kinds of readings that students will encounter in Part II of the book.

- **The Three Appeals of Argument:** *Logos, Ethos, Pathos.* This discussion may be used to analyze arguments in the readings that students will encounter in Part II.

- **Developing and Organizing the Support for Your Arguments.** This section helps students to mine source materials for facts, expert opinions, and examples that will support their arguments.

- **Annotated Student Argument Paper.** A sample student paper highlights and discusses argumentative strategies that a student writer uses in drafting and developing a paper.

RESEARCHING ONLINE

Students who look for sources beyond this book will as likely do so on the Web as in the library. For that reason, we retain our focus in this edition on online research. Chapter 7 addresses the following topics related to research:

- **Citing Online Sources.** Current MLA and APA conventions are discussed in detail.

- **The Benefits and Pitfalls of Conducting Research on the World Wide Web.** In student papers, Web sources make up an increasingly large proportion of "Works Cited" and "References" lists. It's convenient to find and use Web sources, but how reliable are they? We explain how instructors and students should address this new reality and why the Web as a research tool should be welcomed—but also why it should also be approached with caution.

PART I: NEW APPARATUS, TOPICS, READINGS, AND STUDENT PAPERS

New Apparatus, Chapters 1–7

Chapter 1: Summary, Paraphrase, and Quotation

As in the eighth edition, students are taken through the process of writing a summary of Barbara Graham's "The Future of Love: Kiss Romance Goodbye, It's Time for the Real Thing." We demonstrate how to annotate a source and divide it into sections, how to develop a thesis, and how to write and smoothly join section summaries. We also explain how to summarize narratives, illustrating our discussion with a summary of an article ("Virtual Love" by Meghan Daum) that appears later in Chapter 8. As in the eighth edition, students also learn three key skills:

- How to summarize figures and tables.
- How to paraphrase sources.
- How to quote sources.

Chapter 4: Explanatory Synthesis

Computers, Communication, and Relationships

As in the eighth edition, explanatory synthesis is now treated in a separate chapter. Thirteen brief selections on the topic of relationships begun online through e-mail and instant-messaging precede discussion of the planning and writing of a student paper. The first draft is accompanied by detailed instructor comments.

Chapter 5: Argument Synthesis

Volunteering in America

In Chapter 5 we offer a new argument synthesis, "Keeping Volunteering Voluntary," along with summaries and excerpts of several source materials for that paper. The argument synthesizes (among other sources) the work of William James, Plato's "Crito," and opinion pieces by various advocates and detractors of national service. While conceding that the government has a constitutional right to raise armies, the writer argues that an analogous right to compel young people to national, nonmilitary service has no basis either logically or morally.

Chapter 6: Analysis

We are pleased and excited to offer a major new chapter to Part I on writing analyses. The chapter opens with brief, competing analyses of *The Wizard of Oz* that demonstrate how, employing different analytical principles (one psychoanalytic and the other political), two writers can read very different meanings into the classic movie. Following an example analysis by Marie Winn that examines excessive television viewing as an addiction ("The Plug-in Drug"), we present a student example of analysis: an application of a theory by sociologist Randall Collins to living conditions in a college dormitory. We show students how to locate principles useful for conducting analyses, and we show how to write analyses themselves. Throughout Part II in the anthology, students will find ample occasions to practice this essential skill.

PART II: NEW THEMATIC CHAPTERS

As it has through the past eight editions, Part II of *Writing and Reading Across the Curriculum* provides students with opportunities to practice the skills of summary, synthesis, and critique—and now analysis—that they have learned in Part I. Two new chapters appear in the ninth edition of *WRAC*. Almost half of the reading selections in Part II are new to this edition.

Chapter 10: What's Happening at the Mall?

In this chapter we gather the work of a historian, an urban planner, a geographer, a sociologist, and scholars in American studies and comparative religion to investigate a fixture on the American landscape: the shopping mall. Malls are not only ubiquitous (45,000 of them as of 2003); they stand at the confluence of streams in American myth, race, class, business, gender, law, and design. As James Farrell, one of the authors in this chapter, puts it: Malls are "a place where we answer important questions: What does it mean to be human? What are people for? What is the meaning of things? Why do we work? What do we work for?" What's happening at the mall, it turns out, is important sociologically and culturally—but it is far from obvious. The selections gathered here will challenge students' commonplace views of malls. With this chapter we have tried to make the ordinary a bit strange (malls as religious centers?) and in the process provide ample occasion for thoughtful writing.

Chapter 13: New and Improved: Six Decades of Advertising

The centerpiece of this new chapter is a portfolio of forty-two full-page advertisements for cigarettes, liquor and beer, automobiles, food, and beauty and cleaning products that have appeared in popular American and British magazines since the mid-1940s. Advertisements are key indicators not only of our consumerism but also of our changing cultural values and our less variable human psychology. Students will find the new advertising chapter ideal for practicing their analysis skills. Prior to the portfolio, we offer several analytic tools that students can use to discern how advertisements operate: how they attempt to manipulate us, how they reveal our values and our sometimes hidden drives. One article identifies the fifteen basic appeals of advertising; two others consider the textual and graphics elements of the marketers' craft. Another summarizes the charges commonly leveled against advertising. A fascinating view of how marketers have presented five product categories over sixty years, this chapter will help students see themselves, culturally speaking, as products of a particular time and place.

PART II: REVISED THEMATIC CHAPTERS

Chapter 8: Cyberspace and Identity

E-mail and other forms of cybercommunication have so thoroughly insinuated themselves into our lives that we can hardly imagine life without them—an extraordinary development given that little more than a decade ago, the technology was not widely known beyond the scientific and engineering communities. That cybercommunication enhances—and distracts us from—our daily business is a given. Less clear though is the extent to which the technology has begun to alter our sense of self—an alteration that we explore in this chapter. Is the stockbroker who enters an online space to play one of the endless variants of *Dungeons and Dragons* the same starched professional she projects to her colleagues and clients at the office? When e-mailing a prospective date in an online club, how does a young man represent himself, knowing that he cannot be seen? In this edition, we add new selections on the phenomena of instant-messaging and blogging, as well as a new version of Michael Lewis's astounding story about a fifteen-year-old high school student who became a top legal expert on a major online information site.

Chapter 9: Obedience to Authority

The chapter that focuses on obedience continues to build on the profoundly disturbing Milgram experiments. Other selections in this chapter, such as Philip K. Zimbardo's account of his Stanford prison experiment and Solomon E. Asch's "Opinions and Social Pressure," have provided additional perspectives on the significance of the obedience phenomenon. This edition adds three articles: The chapter now opens with a selection on the Abu Ghraib (Iraq) prison scandal. Crispin Sartwell suggests that under certain circumstances we are all capable of committing acts of unspeakable evil. And Theodore Dalrymple maintains that blind disobedience to authority can be just as dangerous as blind obedience.

Chapter 11: Weight Debate

New to the eighth edition of *WRAC*, this chapter appeared at a time when the nation was just waking up to what the medical community was describing as an "epidemic" of obesity. Since that time the problem of unwanted weight gain has only intensified; we have, accordingly, retained the topic, cycling out three selections and adding three: an overview of America's problems with weight from *U.S. News and World Report*; updated statistics from the Centers for Disease Control; and an editorial from the journal *Science* on the ironies of our government's assigning one agency both to promote the interests of the food industry and to advise Americans on how to lose weight. This chapter offers students an opportunity to explore the place of food and weight, both in their own lives and in the broader cultural landscape.

Chapter 12: Fairy Tales: A Closer Look at Cinderella

This popular chapter includes variants of the Cinderella story along with the perspectives of a folklorist (Stith Thompson), two psychologists (Bruno Bettelheim and Jacqueline M. Schectman), a novelist (Judith Rossner), and a literary critic (Elisabeth Panttaja). New to this edition is a selection by Catherine Orenstein, who argues that the new genre of romance-based reality television succeeds because Americans love fantasy romances—as well as crass displays of "lies and manipulation." Our earliest models for such stories, she claims, are fairy tales. In "I Am Cinderella's Stepmother and I Know My Rights," novelist Judith Rossner humorously defends the much-maligned stepmother. Also new is Elisabeth Panttaja's analysis that Cinderella is not all that different, morally, than her stepsisters. Perhaps she is not especially worthy of the prince after all. This chapter helps students develop two basic skills: (1) the ability to analyze by applying elements of a theoretical reading to one or more variants of "Cinderella" and (2) the ability to think and write comparatively by reading multiple versions of the story and by developing criteria by which to clarify similarities and differences.

Chapter 14: You, the Jury

Debuting in the seventh edition of *WRAC*, "You, the Jury" places students in the role of juror by asking that they apply points of law to facts of a case in order to arrive at a just verdict. Students must argue for their verdict (no prior legal education is necessary), principally by demonstrating the skill of analysis. More broadly, thinking and writing about legal issues is an ideal approach to the principles of effective argument: students must provide support (the facts of the case) for their claim (their verdict), based on relevant assumptions or warrants (the laws). New to this chapter is a brief section on "Hot Coffee Spills" about (what else?) people who sue when they spill hot beverages on themselves.

ANCILLARIES

- **The Companion Web site (www.ablongman.com/behrens)** includes additional exercises, links, model papers and many more student resources. *Free.*

- **MyCompLab 2.0 Web Site www.mycomplab.com** offers exciting new resources in writing, grammar, and research that make this market-leading site even more useful for composition students and instructors. Included on this site are a practice bank of over 4,000 grammar exercises, a writing process tutorial, access to Longman's Tutor Center, and a wealth of other resources for student writers. *Available at www.ablongman.com.*

- **Longman Grammar and Documentation Study Card** (ISBN 0-321-29203-0) is a colorful study card packed with information, an eight-page guide to key grammar, punctuation, and documentation skills. Laminated for durability, this Study Card will provide students with a useful reference for years to come. *Available at www.ablongman.com.*

For the Instructor

- **The Instructor's Manual** for the ninth edition of *Writing and Reading Across the Curriculum* provides sample syllabi and course calendars, chapter summaries, classroom ideas for writing assignments, introductions to each set of readings, case outcomes for the legal readings, and answers to review questions. Included as well are tips on how to incorporate the textbook's companion Web site into the course material. ISBN 0-321-29099-2.

ACKNOWLEDGMENTS

We have benefited over the years from the suggestions and insights of many teachers—and students—across the country. We would especially like to thank: James Allen, *College of DuPage*; Chris Anson, *North Carolina State University*; Phillip Arrington, *Eastern Michigan University*; Anne Bailey, *Southeastern Louisiana University*; Carolyn Baker, *San Antonio College*; Joy Bashore, *Central Virginia Community College*; Nancy Blattner, *Southeast Missouri State University*; Mary Bly, *University of California, Davis*; Bob Brannan, *Johnson County Community College*; Paul Buczkowski, *Eastern Michigan University*; Jennifer Bullis, *Whatcom Community College*; Paige Byam, *Northern Kentucky University*; Susan Callendar, *Sinclair Community College*; Anne Carr, *Southeast Community College*; Jeff Carroll, *University of Hawaii*; Joseph Rocky Colavito, *Northwestern State University*; Michael Colonnese, *Methodist College*; James A. Cornette, *Christopher Newport University*; Timothy Corrigan, *Temple University*; Kathryn J. Dawson, *Ball State University*; Cathy Powers Dice, *University of Memphis*; Kathleen Dooley, *Tidewater Community College*; Judith Eastman, *Orange Coast College*; David Elias, *Eastern Kentucky University*; Susan Boyd English, *Kirkwood Community College*; Kathy Evertz, *University of Wyoming*; Bill Gholson, *Southern Oregon University*; Karen Gordon, *Elgin Community College*; Deborah Gutschera, *College of DuPage*; Lila M. Harper, *Central Washington University*; M. Todd Harper, *University of Louisville*; Kip Harvigsen, *Ricks College*; Michael Hogan, *Southeast Missouri State University*; Sandra M. Jensen, *Lane Community College*; Anita Johnson, *Whatcom Community College*; Mark Jones, *University of Florida*; Jane Kaufman, *University of Akron*; Rodney Keller, *Ricks College*; Walt Klarner, *Johnson County Community College*; Jeffery Klausman, *Whatcom Community College*; Alison Kuehner, *Ohlone College*; William B. Lalicker, *West Chester University*; Dawn Leonard, *Charleston Southern University*; Clifford L. Lewis, *U Mass Lowell*; Signee Lynch, *Whatcom Community College*; Krista L. May, *Texas A&M University*; Roark Mulligan, *Christopher Newport University*; Joan Mullin, *University of Toledo*; Stella Nesanovich, *McNeese State University*; Susie Paul, *Auburn University at Montgomery*; Aaron Race, *Southern Illinois University–Carbondale*; Nancy Redmond, *Long Beach City College*; Deborah Reese, *University of Texas at Arlington*; Priscilla Riggle, *Bowling Green State University*; Jeanette Riley, *University of New Mexico*; Robert Rongner, *Whatcom Community College*; Sarah C. Ross, *Southeastern Louisiana University*; Raul Sanchez, *University of Utah*; Rebecca Shapiro, *Westminster College*; Mary Sheldon, *Washburn University*; Philip Sipiora, *University of Southern Florida*; Joyce Smoot, *Virginia Tech*; Bonnie A. Spears, *Chaffey College*; Bonnie Startt, *Tidewater Community College*; R. E. Stratton, *University of Alaska–Fairbanks*; Katherine M. Thomas, *Southeast Community College*; Victor Villanueva, *Washington State University*; Jackie Wheeler, *Arizona State University*; Pat Stephens Williams, *Southern Illinois University at Carbondale*; and Kristin Woolever, *Northeastern University*.

We extend our gratitude to the following reviewers for their help in the preparation of this edition: Mark Brosamer, *Ohlone College*; Virginia Dumont-Poston, *Lander University*; Lynnell Edwards, *Concordia University*; Nikolai Endres, *Western Kentucky University*; Barbara Gross, *Rutgers NCAS*; Vicki Hill, *Brewton-Parker College*; Kacie Jossart, *University of North Dakota*; Jim Kenkel, *Eastern Kentucky University*; Malcolm Kiniry, *Rutgers University*; RoseAnn Morgan, *Middlesex County College*; David Moton,

Bakersfield College; Taunya Paul, *York Technical College;* Robert Francis Peltier, *Trinity College;* and Jan Thompson, *Landmark College.*

We thank Lucia Snowhill, reference librarian at the University of California at Santa Barbara, for her invaluable assistance in updating our section on "Locating Sources" in Chapter 7. Susan Messer also devoted long hours to updating our example citations in the latter part of that chapter. We would also like to acknowledge the invaluable assistance freely rendered to us by many people during and after the preparation of the law-oriented chapter, "You, the Jury." Amy Atchison, an attorney and law librarian at UCLA, provided numerous references, legal texts, and much-needed guidance through the legal research process. David Hricik, author of "The American Legal System" (page 742) and a professor at the Mercer University School of Law, also provided useful feedback. Leonard Tourney and Gina Genova, who teach legal writing courses at the University of California at Santa Barbara, provided valuable advice before and during the composition of this chapter. Our gratitude also to Lila Harper and her students at Central Washington University; Krista May and her students at Texas A&M University; Erik Peterson and his students at Central Washington University; and Sarah C. Ross and her students at Southeast Louisiana State University for helping us to field-test this chapter. The intelligent and perceptive comments of both instructors and students helped us make this chapter more focused and user friendly than it was when they received it.

A special thanks to our resourceful sponsoring editor, Ginny Blanford, along with Rebecca Gilpin and Charles Annis of Longman, for helping shepherd the manuscript through the editorial and production process. For the able work of Amber Allen of Elm Street Publishing Services, our photo researcher Julie Tesser, and Celeste Bates (for her expert help in securing permissions), we are most appreciative. Finally, a continued, heartfelt expression of gratitude to Joe Opiela, our longtime friend, supporter, and publisher.

Laurence Behrens
Leonard J. Rosen

A Note to the Student

Your sociology professor asks you to write a paper on attitudes toward the homeless population of an urban area near your campus. You are expected to consult books, articles, Web sites, and other online sources on the subject, and you are also encouraged to conduct surveys and interviews.

Your professor is making a number of assumptions about your capabilities. Among them:

- You can research and assess the value of relevant sources.
- You can comprehend college-level material, both print and electronic.
- You can use theories and principles learned from one set of sources as tools to better understand other sources (or events, people, places, or things).
- You can synthesize separate but related sources.
- You can intelligently respond to such material.

In fact, these same assumptions underlie practically all college writing assignments. Your professors will expect you to demonstrate that you can read and understand not only textbooks but also critical articles and books, primary sources, Internet sources, online academic databases, CD-ROMs, and other material related to a particular subject of study. For example: for a paper on the progress of the human genome project, you would probably refer to articles and Internet sources for the most recent information. Using an online database, you would find articles on the subject in such print journals as *Nature, Journal of the American Medical Association,* and *Bioscience,* as well as in leading newspapers and magazines. A Web search engine might lead you to a useful site called "A New Gene Map of the Human Genome" <http://www.ncbi.nlm.nih.gov/genemap99/> and the site of the "Human Genome Sequencing Department" at the Lawrence Berkeley National Laboratory <http://www.lbl.gov/>. You would be expected to assess the relevance of such sources to your topic and to draw from them the information and ideas you need. It's even possible that the final product of your research and reading may not be a conventional paper at all, but rather a Web site that you create to explain the science behind the human genome project, explore a particular controversy about the project, or describe the future benefits geneticists hope to derive from the project.

You might, for a different class, be assigned a research paper on the films of director Martin Scorsese. To get started, you might consult your film studies textbook, biographical sources on Scorsese, and anthologies of criticism. Instructor and peer feedback on a first draft might lead you to articles in both popular magazines (such as *Time*) and scholarly journals (such as *Literature/Film Quarterly*), a CD-ROM database, *Film Index International,* and relevant Web sites (such as the "Internet Movie Database" <http://us.imdb.com> and the Movie Review Query Engine <www.mrqe.com>).

These two example assignments are very different, of course; but the skills you need to work with them are the same. You must be able to research relevant sources. You must be able to read and comprehend these sources. You must be able to perceive the relationships among several pieces of source material. And you must be able to apply your own critical judgments to these various materials.

Writing and Reading Across the Curriculum provides you with the opportunity to practice the essential college-level skills we have just outlined and the forms of writing associated with them, namely:

- The *summary*
- The *critique*
- The *synthesis*
- The *analysis*

Each chapter of Part II of this book represents a subject from a particular area of the academic curriculum: Technology/Communication, Psychology, American Studies, Health Sciences, Folklore, Law, and Marketing/Advertising. These chapters, dealing with such topics as cyberspace and identity, obedience to authority, and shopping mall culture, illustrate the types of material you will study in your other courses.

The questions following the readings will allow you to practice typical college writing assignments. Review Questions help you recall key points of content. Discussion and Writing Suggestions ask you for personal, sometimes imaginative responses to the readings. The Synthesis Activities at the end of each chapter allow you to practice assignments of the type that are covered in detail in Part I of this book. For instance, you may be asked to *summarize* the Milgram experiment and the reactions to it, or to *compare and contrast* a controlled experiment to a real-life (or fictional) situation. Finally, Research Activities ask you to go beyond the readings in this book in order to conduct your own independent research on these subjects.

In this book, you'll find articles and essays written by physicians, literary critics, sociologists, psychologists, lawyers, folklorists, political scientists, journalists, and specialists from other fields. Our aim is that you become familiar with the various subjects and styles of academic writing and that you come to appreciate the interrelatedness of knowledge. Biologists, sociologists, and historians have different ways of contributing to our understanding of weight gain. Fairy tales can be studied by literary critics, folklorists, psychologists, and feminists. Human activity and human behavior are classified into separate subjects only for convenience. The novel you read in your literature course may be able to shed some light upon an assigned article from your economics course—and vice versa.

We hope, therefore, that your writing course will serve as a kind of bridge to your other courses and that as a result of this work you can become more skillful at perceiving relationships among diverse topics. Because it involves such critical and widely applicable skills, your writing course may well turn out to be one of the most valuable—and one of the most interesting—of your academic career.

LAURENCE BEHRENS
LEONARD J. ROSEN

How to Write Summaries, Critiques, Syntheses, and Analyses

Summary, Paraphrase, and Quotation

WHAT IS A SUMMARY?

The best way to demonstrate that you understand the information and the ideas in any piece of writing is to compose an accurate and clearly written summary of that piece. By a *summary* we mean a *brief restatement, in your own words, of the content of a passage* (a group of paragraphs, a chapter, an article, a book). This restatement should focus on the *central idea* of the passage. The briefest of all summaries (one or two sentences) will do no more than this. A longer, more complete summary will indicate, in condensed form, the main points in the passage that support or explain the central idea. It will reflect the order in which these points are presented and the emphasis given to them. It may even include some important examples from the passage. But it will not include minor details. It will not repeat points simply for the purpose of emphasis. And it will not contain any of your own opinions or conclusions. A good summary, therefore, has three central qualities: *brevity, completeness,* and *objectivity.*

CAN A SUMMARY BE OBJECTIVE?

Of course, the last quality mentioned above, objectivity, might be difficult to achieve in a summary. By definition, writing a summary requires you to select some aspects of the original and leave out others. Since deciding what to select and what to leave out calls for your personal judgment, your summary really is a work of interpretation. And, certainly, your interpretation of a passage may differ from another person's. One factor affecting the nature and quality of your interpretation is your *prior knowledge* of the subject. For example, if you're attempting to summarize an anthropological article and you're a novice in that field, then your summary of the article will likely differ from that of your professor, who has spent twenty years studying this particular area and whose judgment about what is more or less significant is undoubtedly more reliable than your own. By the same token, your personal or professional *frame of reference* may also affect your interpretation. A union representative and a management representative attempting to summarize the latest management offer would probably come up with two very different accounts. Still, we believe that in most cases it's possible to produce a reasonably objective summary of a passage if you make a conscious, good-faith effort to be unbiased and to prevent your own feelings on the subject from distorting your account of the text.

USING THE SUMMARY

In some quarters, the summary has a bad reputation—and with reason. Summaries often are provided by writers as substitutes for analyses. As students, many of us have summarized books that we were supposed to *review critically.* All the same, the summary does have a place in respectable college work. First, writing a summary is an excellent way to understand what you read. This in itself is an important goal of academic study. If you don't understand your source material, chances are you won't be able to refer to it usefully in an essay or research paper. Summaries help you understand what you read because they force you to put the text into your own words. Practice with writing summaries also develops your general writing habits, since a good summary, like any other piece of good writing, is clear, coherent, and accurate.

WHERE DO WE FIND WRITTEN SUMMARIES?

Here are a few types of writing that involve summary:

Academic Writing

- **Critique papers.** Summarize material in order to critique it.
- **Synthesis papers.** Summarize to show relationships between sources.
- **Analysis papers.** Summarize theoretical perspectives before applying them.
- **Research papers.** Take notes and report on research through summary.
- **Literature reviews.** Analyze work through brief summaries.
- **Argument papers.** Summarize evidence and opposing arguments.
- **Essay exams.** Demonstrate understanding of course materials through summary.

Workplace Writing

- **Policy briefs.** Condense complex public policy.
- **Business plans.** Summarize costs, relevant environmental impacts, and other important matters.
- **Memos, letters, and reports.** Summarize procedures, meetings, product assessments, expenditures, and more.
- **Medical charts.** Record patient data in summarized form.
- **Legal briefs.** Summarize relevant facts of cases.

Second, summaries are useful to your readers. Let's say you're writing a paper about the McCarthy era in the United States, and in part of that paper you want to discuss Arthur Miller's *The Crucible* as a dramatic treatment of the subject. A summary of the plot would be helpful to a reader who hasn't seen or read—or who doesn't remember—the play. Or perhaps you're writing a paper about the politics of recent humanitarian aid missions. If your reader isn't likely to be familiar with such groups as Doctors Without Borders, it would be a good idea to summarize the objectives and activities of such organizations at some early point in the paper. In many cases (an exam, for instance), you can use a summary to demonstrate your knowledge of what your professor already knows; when writing a paper, you can use a summary to inform your professor about some relatively unfamiliar source.

Third, summaries are required frequently in college-level writing. For example, on a psychology midterm, you may be asked to explain Carl Jung's theory of the collective unconscious and to show how it differs from Sigmund Freud's theory of the personal unconscious. You may have read about this theory in your textbook or in a supplementary article, or your instructor may have outlined it in his or her lecture. You can best demonstrate your understanding of Jung's theory by summarizing it. Then you'll proceed to contrast it with Freud's theory—which, of course, you must also summarize.

THE READING PROCESS

It may seem to you that being able to tell (or retell) in summary form exactly what a passage says is a skill that ought to be taken for granted in anyone who can read at high school level. Unfortunately, this is not so: For all kinds of reasons, people don't always read carefully. In fact, it's probably safe to say that usually they don't. Either they read so inattentively that they skip over words, phrases, or even whole sentences, or, if they do see the words in front of them, they see them without registering their significance.

When a reader fails to pick up the meaning and implications of a sentence or two, usually there's no real harm done. (An exception: You could lose credit on an exam or paper because you failed to read or to realize the significance of a crucial direction by your instructor.) But over longer stretches—the paragraph, the section, the article, or the chapter—inattentive or haphazard reading interferes with your goals as a reader: to perceive the shape of the argument, to grasp the central idea, to determine the main points that compose it, to relate the parts of the whole, and to note key examples. This kind of reading takes a lot more energy and determination than casual reading. But, in the long run, it's an energy-saving method because it enables you to retain the content of the material and to use that content as a basis for your own responses. In other words, it allows you to develop an accurate and coherent written discussion that goes beyond summary.

CRITICAL READING FOR SUMMARY

- *Examine the context.* Note the credentials, occupation, and publications of the author. Identify the source in which the piece originally appeared. This information helps illuminate the author's perspective on the topic he or she is addressing.
- *Note the title and subtitle.* Some titles are straightforward, whereas the meanings of others become clearer as you read. In either case, titles typically identify the topic being addressed and often reveal the author's attitude toward that topic.
- *Identify the main point.* Whether a piece of writing contains a thesis statement in the first few paragraphs or builds its main point without stating it up front, look at the entire piece to arrive at an understanding of the overall point being made.
- *Identify the subordinate points.* Notice the smaller subpoints that make up the main point, and make sure you understand how they relate to the main point. If a particular subpoint doesn't clearly relate to the main point you've identified, you may need to modify your understanding of the main point.
- *Break the reading into sections.* Notice which paragraph(s) make up the introduction, body, and conclusion of a piece. Break up the body paragraphs into sections that address the writer's various subpoints.
- *Distinguish between points, examples, and counterarguments.* Critical reading requires careful attention to what writers are *doing* as well as what they are *saying.* When a writer quotes someone else, or relays an example of something, ask yourself why this is being done. What point is the example supporting? Is another source being quoted as support for a point, or as a counterargument that the writer sets out to address?
- *Watch for transitions within and between paragraphs.* In order to follow the logic of a piece of writing, as well as to distinguish between points, examples, and counterarguments, pay attention to the transitional words and phrases writers use. Transitions function like road signs, preparing the reader for what's next.
- *Read actively and recursively.* Don't treat reading as a passive, linear progression through a text. Instead, read as though you are engaged in a dialogue with the writer: Ask questions of the text as you read, make notes in the margin, underline key ideas in pencil, put question or exclamation marks next to passages that confuse or excite you. Go back to earlier points once you finish a reading, stop during your reading to recap what's been presented so far, and move back and forth through a text.

HOW TO WRITE SUMMARIES

Every article you read will present a unique challenge as you work to summarize it. As you'll discover, saying in a few words what has taken someone else a great many can be difficult. But like any other skill, the ability to summarize

GUIDELINES FOR WRITING SUMMARIES

- *Read the passage carefully.* Determine its structure. Identify the author's purpose in writing. (This will help you distinguish between more important and less important information.) Make a note in the margin when you get confused or when you think something is important; highlight or underline points sparingly, if at all.
- *Reread the passage.* This time divide the passage into sections or stages of thought. The author's use of paragraphing will often be a useful guide. On the passage itself, *label* each section or stage of thought. *Underline* key ideas and terms. Write notes in the margin.
- *Write one-sentence summaries,* on a separate sheet of paper, of each stage of thought.
- *Write a thesis—a one- or two-sentence summary of the entire passage.* The thesis should express the central idea of the passage, as you have determined it from the preceding steps. You may find it useful to follow the approach of most newspaper stories—naming the *what, who, why, where, when,* and *how* of the matter. For persuasive passages, summarize in a sentence the author's conclusion. For descriptive passages, indicate the subject of the description and its key feature(s). (Note: In some cases, *a suitable thesis may already be in the original passage.* If so, you may want to quote it directly in your summary.)
- *Write the first draft of your summary* by (1) combining the thesis with your list of one-sentence summaries or (2) combining the thesis with one-sentence summaries *plus* significant details from the passage. In either case, eliminate repetition and less important information. Disregard minor details or generalize them (e.g., George H. W. Bush and Bill Clinton might be generalized as "recent presidents"). Use as few words as possible to convey the main ideas.
- *Check your summary against the original passage* and make whatever adjustments are necessary for accuracy and completeness.
- *Revise your summary,* inserting transitional words and phrases where necessary to ensure coherence. Check for style. *Avoid a series of short, choppy sentences.* Combine sentences for a smooth, logical flow of ideas. Check for grammatical correctness, punctuation, and spelling.

improves with practice. Here are a few pointers to get you started. They represent possible stages, or steps, in the process of writing a summary. These pointers are not meant to be ironclad rules; rather, they are designed to encourage habits of thinking that will allow you to vary your technique as the situation demands.

DEMONSTRATION: SUMMARY

To demonstrate these points at work, let's go through the process of summarizing a passage of expository material—that is, writing that is meant to inform and/or persuade. Read the following selection carefully. Try to identify its parts and understand how they work together to create an overall point.

The Future of Love: Kiss Romance Goodbye, It's Time for the Real Thing
Barbara Graham

Author of the satire Women Who Run with Poodles: Myths and Tips for Honoring Your Mood Swings *(Avon, 1994), Barbara Graham has written articles for* Vogue, Self, Common Boundary, *and other publications. She regularly contributes articles to the* Utne Reader, *from which this essay was taken.*

1   Freud and his psychoanalytic descendants are no doubt correct in their assessment that the search for ideal love—for that one perfect soulmate—is the futile wish of not fully developed selves. But it also seems true that the longing for a profound, all-consuming erotic connection (and the heightened state of awareness that goes with it) is in our very wiring. The yearning for fulfillment through love seems to be to our psychic structure what food and water are to our cells.

2   Just consider the stories and myths that have shaped our consciousness: Beauty and the Beast, Snow White and her handsome prince, Cinderella and Prince Charming, Fred and Ginger, Barbie and Ken. (Note that, with the exception of the last two couples, all of these lovers are said to have lived happily ever after—even though we never get details of their lives after the weddings, after children and gravity and loss have exacted their price.) Still, it's not just these lucky fairy tale characters who have captured our collective imagination. The tragic twosomes we cut our teeth on—Romeo and Juliet, Tristan and Iseult, Launcelot and Guinevere, Heathcliff and Cathy, Rhett and Scarlett—are even more compelling role models. Their love is simply too powerful and anarchic,

Barbara Graham, "The Future of Love: Kiss Romance Goodbye, It's Time for the Real Thing," *Utne Reader* Jan.–Feb. 1997: 20–23.

too shattering and exquisite, to be bound by anything so conventional as marriage or a long-term domestic arrangement.

3   If recent divorce and remarriage statistics are any indication, we're not as astute as the doomed lovers. Instead of drinking poison and putting an end to our love affairs while the heat is still turned up full blast, we expect our marriages and relationships to be long-running fairy tales. When they're not, instead of examining our expectations, we switch partners and reinvent the fantasy, hoping that this time we'll get it right. It's easy to see why: Despite all the talk of family values, we're constantly bombarded by visions of perfect romance. All you have to do is turn on the radio or TV or open any magazine and check out the perfume and lingerie ads. "Our culture is deeply regressed," says Florence Falk, a New York City psychotherapist. "Everywhere we turn, we're faced with glamorized, idealized versions of love. It's as if the culture wants us to stay trapped in the fantasy and does everything possible to encourage and expand that fantasy." Trying to forge an authentic relationship amidst all the romantic hype, she adds, makes what is already a tough proposition even harder.

4   What's most unusual about our culture is our feverish devotion to the belief that romantic love and marriage should be synonymous. Starting with George and Martha, continuing through Ozzie and Harriet right up to the present day, we have tirelessly tried to formalize, rationalize, legalize, legitimize, politicize, and sanitize rapture. This may have something to do with our puritanical roots, as well as our tendency toward oversimplification. In any event, this attempt to satisfy all of our contradictory desires under the marital umbrella must be put in historical context in order to be properly understood.

5   "Personal intimacy is actually quite a new idea in human history and was never part of the marriage ideal before the 20th century," says John Welwood, a Northern California–based psychologist and author, most recently, of *Love and Awakening*. "Most couples throughout history managed to live together their whole lives without ever having a conversation about what was going on within or between them. As long as family and society prescribed the rules of marriage, individuals never had to develop any consciousness in this area."

6   In short, marriage was designed to serve the economic and social needs of families, communities, and religious institutions, and had little or nothing to do with love. Nor was it expected to satisfy lust.

7   In *Myths to Live By*, Joseph Campbell explains how the sages of ancient India viewed the relationship between marriage and passion. They concluded that there are five degrees of love, he writes, "through which a worshiper is increased in the service and knowledge of his God." The first degree has to do with the relationship of the worshiper to the divine. The next three degrees of love, in order of importance, are friendship, the parent/child relationship, and marriage. The fifth and highest form is passionate, illicit love. "In marriage, it is declared, one is still possessed of reason," Campbell adds. "The seizure of passionate love can be, in such a context, only illicit, breaking in upon the order of one's dutiful life in virtue as a devastating storm."

8   No wonder we're having problems. The pressures we place on our tender unions are unprecedented. Even our biochemistry seems to militate against

long-term sexual relationships. Dr. Helen Fisher, an anthropologist at Rutgers University and author of *Anatomy of Love,* believes that human pair-bonds originally evolved according to "the ancient blueprint of serial monogamy and clandestine adultery" and are originally meant to last around four years—at least long enough to raise a single dependent child through toddlerhood. The so-called seven-year-itch may be the remains of a four-year reproductive cycle, Fisher suggests.

9   Increasingly, Fisher and other researchers are coming to view what we call love as a series of complex biochemical events governed by hormones and enzymes. "People cling to the idea that romantic love is a mystery, but it's also a chemical experience," Fisher says, explaining that there are three distinct mating emotions and each is supported in the brain by the release of different chemicals. Lust, an emotion triggered by changing levels of testosterone in men and women, is associated with our basic sexual drive. Infatuation depends on the changing levels of dopamine, norepinephrine, and phenylethylamine (PEA), also called the "chemicals of love." They are natural—addictive—amphetaminelike chemicals that stimulate euphoria and make us want to stay up all night sharing our secrets. After infatuation and the dizzying highs associated with it have peaked—usually within a year or two—this brain chemistry reduces, and a new chemical system made up of oxytocin, vasopressin, and maybe the endorphins kicks in and supports a steadier, quieter, more nurturing intimacy. In the end, regardless of whether biochemistry accounts for cause or effect in love, it may help to explain why some people—those most responsive to the release of the attachment chemicals—are able to sustain a long-term partnership, while thrillseekers who feel depressed without regular hits of dopamine and PEA are likely to jump from one liaison to the next in order to maintain a buzz.

10   But even if our biochemistry suggests that there should be term limits on love, the heart is a stubborn muscle and, for better or worse, most of us continue to yearn for a relationship that will endure. As a group, Generation Xers—many of whom are children of divorce—are more determined than any other demographic group to have a different kind of marriage than their parents and to avoid divorce, says Howard Markman, author of *Fighting for Your Marriage.* What's more, lesbians and gay men who once opposed marriage and all of its heterosexual, patriarchal implications now seek to reframe marriage as a more flexible, less repressive arrangement. And, according to the U.S. National Center for Health Statistics, in one out of an estimated seven weddings, either the bride or the groom—or both—are tying the knot for at least the third time—nearly twice as many as in 1970. There are many reasons for this, from the surge in the divorce rate that began in the '70s, to our ever-increasing life span. Even so, the fact that we're still trying to get love right—knowing all we know about the ephemeral nature of passion, in a time when the stigmas once associated with being divorced or single have all but disappeared—says something about our powerful need to connect.

11   And, judging from the army of psychologists, therapists, clergy, and other experts who can be found dispensing guidance on the subject, the effort to save—or reinvent, depending on who's doing the talking—love and marriage has

become a multimillion dollar industry. The advice spans the spectrum. There's everything from *Rules,* by Ellen Fein and Sherrie Schneider, a popular new book which gives 90's women 50's-style tips on how to catch and keep their man, to Harville Hendrix's *Getting the Love You Want,* and other guides to "conscious love." But regardless of perspective, this much is clear: Never before have our most intimate thoughts and actions been so thoroughly dissected, analyzed, scrutinized, and medicalized. Now, people who fall madly in love over and over are called romance addicts. Their disease, modeled on alcoholism and other chemical dependencies, is considered "progressive and fatal."

12   Not everyone believes the attempt to deconstruct love is a good thing. The late philosopher Christopher Lasch wrote in his final (and newly released) book, *Women and the Common Life:* "The exposure of sexual life to scientific scrutiny contributed to the rationalization, not the liberation, of emotional life." His daughter, Elisabeth Lasch-Quinn, an historian at Syracuse University and the editor of the book, agrees. She contends that the progressive demystification of passionate life since Freud has promoted an asexual, dispassionate, and utilitarian form of love. Moreover, like her father, she believes that the national malaise about romance can be attributed to insidious therapeutic modes of social control—a series of mechanisms that have reduced the citizen to a consumer of expertise. "We have fragmented life in such a way," she says, "as to take passion out of our experience."

13   Admittedly, it's a stretch to picture a lovesick 12th-century French troubadour in a 12-step program for romance addicts. Still, we can't overlook the fact that our society's past efforts to fuse together those historically odd bedfellows—passionate love and marriage—have failed miserably. And though it's impossible to know whether all the attention currently being showered on relationships is the last gasp of a dying social order—marriage—or the first glimmer of a new paradigm for relating to one another, it's obvious that something radically different is needed.

Read, Reread, Highlight

Let's consider our recommended pointers for writing a summary.

As you reread the passage, note in the margins of the essay important points, shifts in thought, and questions you may have. Consider the essay's significance as a whole and its stages of thought. What does it say? How is it organized? How does each part of the passage fit into the whole? What do all these points add up to?

Here is how the first few paragraphs of Graham's article might look after you had marked the main ideas, by highlighting and by marginal notations.

psychic   Freud and his psychoanalytic descendants are no doubt correct in their
importance   assessment that the search for ideal love—for that one perfect soulmate—
of love   is the futile wish of not fully developed selves. But it also seems true that
                      the longing for a profound, all-consuming erotic connection (and the

heightened state of awareness that goes with it) is in our very wiring. The yearning for fulfillment through love seems to be to our psychic structure what food and water are to our cells.

fictional, sometimes tragic examples of ideal love

Just consider the stories and myths that have shaped our consciousness: Beauty and the Beast, Snow White and her handsome prince, Cinderella and Prince Charming, Fred and Ginger, Barbie and Ken. (Note that, with the exception of the last two couples, all of these lovers are said to have lived happily ever after—even though we never get details of their lives after the weddings, after children and gravity and loss have exacted their price.) Still, it's not just these lucky fairy tale characters who have captured our collective imagination. The tragic twosomes we cut our teeth on—Romeo and Juliet, Tristan and Iseult, Launcelot and Guinevere, Heathcliff and Cathy, Rhett and Scarlett—are even more compelling role models. Their love is simply too powerful and anarchic, too shattering and exquisite, to be bound by anything so conventional as marriage or a long-term domestic arrangement.

difficulty of having a real relationship in a culture that glamorizes ideal love

If recent divorce and remarriage statistics are any indication, we're not as astute as the doomed lovers. Instead of drinking poison and putting an end to our love affairs while the heat is still turned up full blast, we expect our marriages and relationships to be long-running fairy tales. When they're not, instead of examining our expectations, we switch partners and reinvent the fantasy, hoping that this time we'll get it right. It's easy to see why: Despite all the talk of family values, we're constantly bombarded by visions of perfect romance. All you have to do is turn on the radio or TV or open any magazine and check out the perfume and lingerie ads. "Our culture is deeply regressed," says Florence Falk, a New York City psychotherapist. "Everywhere we turn, we're faced with glamorized, idealized versions of love. It's as if the culture wants us to stay trapped in the fantasy and does everything possible to encourage and expand that fantasy." Trying to forge an authentic relationship amidst all the romantic hype, she adds, makes what is already a tough proposition even harder.

contradictions of ideal love and marriage

What's most unusual about our culture is our feverish devotion to the belief that romantic love and marriage should be synonymous. Starting with George and Martha, continuing through Ozzie and Harriet right up to the present day, we have tirelessly tried to formalize, rationalize, legalize, legitimize, politicize, and sanitize rapture. This may have something to do with our puritanical roots, as well as our tendency toward oversimplification. In any event, this attempt to satisfy all of our contradictory desires under the marital umbrella must be put in historical context in order to be properly understood.

"personal intimacy" never considered part of marriage before 20th century

"Personal intimacy is actually quite a new idea in human history and was never part of the marriage ideal before the 20th century," says John Welwood, a Northern California–based psychologist and author, most recently, of *Love and Awakening.* "Most couples throughout history managed to live together their whole lives without ever having a conversation about what was going on within or between them. As long as family and society prescribed the rules of marriage, individuals never had to develop any consciousness in this area."

In short, marriage was designed to serve the economic and social needs of families, communities, and religious institutions, and had little or nothing to do with love. Nor was it expected to satisfy lust.

Divide Selection into Stages of Thought

When a selection doesn't contain sections with thematic headings, as is the case with "The Future of Love," how do you determine where one stage of thought ends and the next one begins? Assuming that what you have read is coherent and unified, this should not be difficult. (When a selection is unified, all of its parts pertain to the main subject; when a selection is coherent, the parts follow one another in logical order.) Look, particularly, for transitional sentences at the beginning of paragraphs. Such sentences generally work in one or both of the following ways: (1) they summarize what has come before; (2) they set the stage for what is to follow.

For example, look at the sentence that opens paragraph 10: "But even if our biochemistry suggests that there should be term limits on love, the heart is a stubborn muscle and, for better or worse, most of us continue to yearn for a relationship that will endure." Notice how the first part of this sentence restates the main idea of the preceding section. The second part of the transitional sentence announces the topic of the upcoming section: three paragraphs devoted to the efforts people make to attain, save, or reinvent romantic relationships.

Each section of an article generally takes several paragraphs to develop. Between paragraphs, and almost certainly between sections of an article, you will usually find transitions that help you understand what you have just read and what you are about to read. For articles that have no subheadings, try writing your own section headings in the margins as you take notes. Then proceed with your summary.

The sections of Graham's article may be described as follows:

Section 1: *Introduction*—a yearning for "fulfillment through love" pervades our culture, and that yearning is shaped by myths and romantic fantasies (paragraphs 1—3).

Section 2: *Marriage and love*—we expect passionate love to lead to happy, lifelong marriage. This is a relatively new and unique practice in human history (paragraphs 4—7).

Section 3: *Biochemistry and love*—love has a biochemical component, which complicates our abilities to sustain long-term relationships (paragraphs 8—9).

Section 4: *Marriage and love revisited*—many people are currently trying to preserve and/or reinvent marriage and love (paragraphs 10–12).

Section 5: *Conclusion*—the fusion of passionate love with the institution of marriage hasn't worked very well, and we need something "radically different" to replace it (paragraph 13).

Write a One- or Two-Sentence Summary of Each Stage of Thought

The purpose of this step is to wean you from the language of the original passage, so that you are not tied to it when writing the summary. Here are one-sentence summaries for each stage of thought in the five sections of "The Future of Love":

Section 1: Introduction—a yearning for "fulfillment through love" pervades our culture, and that yearning is shaped by myths and romantic fantasies (paragraphs 1–3).

As Americans, we crave romantic love; but we have unreal expectations based upon idealized images of love we learn from fantasies and fairy tales.

Section 2: Marriage and love—we expect passionate love to lead to happy, lifelong marriage. This is a relatively new and unique practice in human history (paragraphs 4–7).

We expect the passionate love of fairy tales to lead to "happily ever after" in the institution of marriage, and when this fails, we move on and try it again. Ironically, the idea that marriage should be based on love—rather than upon social and economic concerns—is a relatively recent practice in Western history.

Section 3: Biochemistry and love—love has a biochemical component, which complicates our abilities to sustain long-term relationships (paragraphs 8–9).

Biochemists are discovering that love and lust have hormonal causes, and their evidence suggests that our biological makeup predisposes us to seek the excitement of short-term relationships.

Section 4: Marriage and love revisited—many people are currently trying to preserve and/or reinvent marriage and love (paragraphs 10–12).

> Despite all the difficulties, we spend a lot of
> time analyzing the elements of relationships in
> order to preserve or perhaps reinvent marriage.
> We clearly want to make it work.

Section 5: Conclusion—the fusion of passionate love with the institution of marriage hasn't worked very well, and we need something "radically different" to replace it (paragraph 13).

> Because confining passionate love to the institu-
> tion of marriage hasn't worked very well, we need
> to revise our model for human relationships.

Write a Thesis: A One- or Two-Sentence Summary of the Entire Passage

The thesis is the most general statement of a summary (or any other type of academic writing—see Chapter 3 for a more complete discussion of thesis statements). It is the statement that announces the paper's subject and the claim that you or—in the case of a summary—another author will be making about that subject. Every paragraph of a paper illuminates the thesis by providing supporting details or explanations. The relationship of these paragraphs to the thesis is analogous to the relationship of the sentences within a paragraph to the topic sentence. Both the thesis and the topic sentences are general statements (the thesis being the more general) that are followed by systematically arranged details.

To ensure clarity for the reader, *the first sentence of a summary should begin with the author's thesis, regardless of where it appears in the article itself.* Authors may locate their thesis at the beginning of their work, in which case the thesis operates as a general principle from which details of the presentation follow. This is called a *deductive* organization: thesis first, supporting details second. Alternatively, authors may locate their thesis at the end of the work, in which case they begin with specific details and build toward a more general conclusion, or thesis. This is called an *inductive* organization—an example of which you see in "The Future of Love."

A thesis consists of a subject and an assertion about that subject. How can we go about fashioning an adequate thesis for a summary of "The Future of Love"? Probably no two proposed thesis statements for this article would be worded identically, but it is fair to say that any reasonable thesis will indicate that the subject is the current state of love and marriage in American society. How does Graham view the topic? What *is* the current state of love and marriage, in her view? Looking back over our section summaries, Graham's focus on the illusions of fairy tales and myths, the difference between marriage in the present day and its earlier incarnations, and the problems of divorce and "romance addiction" suggest she does not view the current state of affairs in an altogether positive light. Does she make a statement anywhere that pulls all this together? Her conclusion, in paragraph 13, contains her main idea:

"our society's past efforts to fuse together those historically odd bedfellows—passionate love and marriage—have failed miserably." Moreover, in the next sentence, she says "it's obvious that something radically different is needed." Further evidence of Graham's main point can be found in the complete title of the essay: "The Future of Love: Kiss Romance Goodbye, It's Time for the Real Thing." Mindful of Graham's subject and the assertion she makes about it, we can write a thesis statement *in our own words* and arrive at the following:

> The contemporary institution of marriage is in trouble, and this may be due to our unrealistic expectations that passionate love leads to lasting union; it may be time to develop a new model for love and relationships.

To clarify for our readers the fact that this idea is Graham's and not ours, we'll qualify the thesis as follows:

> In her article "The Future of Love: Kiss Romance Goodbye, It's Time for the Real Thing," Barbara Graham describes how our unrealistic expectations that passionate love leads to lasting union may be partly causing the troubled state of marriage today; thus she suggests we develop a new model for love and relationships.

The first sentence of a summary is crucially important, for it orients readers by letting them know what to expect in the coming paragraphs. In the example above, the sentence refers directly to an article, its author, and the thesis for the upcoming summary. The author and title reference also could be indicated in the summary's title (if this were a freestanding summary), in which case their mention could be dropped from the thesis. And lest you become frustrated too quickly, keep in mind that writing an acceptable thesis for a summary takes time—in this case, it took the three drafts, shown below, or roughly seven minutes to compose one sentence and another few minutes of fine-tuning after a draft of the entire summary was completed. The thesis needed revision because the first draft was too vague and incomplete; the second draft was more specific and complete, but left out the author's point about correcting the problem; the third draft was more complete, but it was cumbersome.

> **Draft 1:** Barbara Graham argues that our attempts to confine passionate love to the institution of marriage have failed.
> *(Too vague—the problem isn't clear enough)*

Draft 2: Barbara Graham ~~argues that our attempts to confine passionate love to the institution of marriage have failed.~~ describes how the contemporary institution of marriage is in trouble, and this may be due, she thinks, to our unrealistic expectations that passionate love will lead to lasting union. *(Incomplete—what about her call for a change?)*

Draft 3: In her article "The Future of Love: Kiss Romance Goodbye, It's Time for the Real Thing," Barbara Graham describes how ~~the contemporary institution of marriage is in trouble, and this may be due, she thinks, to~~ our unrealistic expectations that passionate love will lead to lasting union may be causing the troubles in the contemporary institution of marriage today, so she argues that perhaps it's time to develop a new model for love and relationships.
(Wordy)

Final: In her article "The Future of Love: Kiss Romance Goodbye, It's Time for the Real Thing," Barbara Graham suggests that because unrealistic expectations for romantic love may undermine marriage, we should develop a new model for love and relationships.

Write the First Draft of the Summary

Let's consider two possible summaries of the example passage: (1) a short summary, combining a thesis with one-sentence section summaries, and (2) a longer summary, combining a thesis, one-sentence section summaries, and some carefully chosen details. Again, realize that you are reading final versions; each of the following summaries is the result of at least two full drafts.

Summary 1: Combine Thesis Sentence with One-Sentence Section Summaries

In her article "The Future of Love: Kiss Romance Goodbye, It's Time for the Real Thing," Barbara Graham suggests that because unrealistic expectations for romantic love may undermine marriage, we should develop a new model for love and relationships. The existing model, and our craving for romantic love, is based heavily upon idealized images of love we learn from fantasies and fairy tales.

We expect the passionate love of fairy tales to lead to "happily ever after" in the institution of marriage, and when this fails, we move on and try it again. Ironically, the idea that marriage should be based on love—rather than upon social and economic concerns—is a relatively recent practice in Western history. While the romantic marriage ideal doesn't fit with tradition, biological evidence is mounting against it as well. Biochemists are discovering that love and lust have hormonal causes, and their evidence suggests that our biological makeup predisposes us to seek the excitement of short-term relationships.

Nonetheless, despite all the difficulties, we spend a lot of time analyzing the elements of relationships in order to preserve or perhaps reinvent marriage. We clearly want to make it work. Because confining passionate love to the institution of marriage hasn't worked very well, Graham ends by suggesting that we ought to revise our model for human relationships.

Discussion

This summary consists essentially of a restatement of Graham's thesis plus the section summaries, altered or expanded a little for stylistic purposes. The first sentence encompasses the summary of Section 1 and is followed by the summaries of Sections 2, 3, 4, and 5. Notice the insertion of a transitional sentence (highlighted) between the summaries of Sections 2 and 3, helping to link the ideas more coherently.

Summary 2: Combine Thesis Sentence, Section Summaries, and Carefully Chosen Details

The thesis and one-sentence section summaries can also be used as the outline for a more detailed summary. Most of the details in the passage, however, won't be necessary in a summary. It isn't necessary even in a longer summary of this passage to discuss all of Graham's examples—specific romantic fairy tales, ancient Indian views of love and passion, the specific hormones involved with love and lust, or the examples of experts who examine and write about contemporary relationships. It would be appropriate, though, to mention one example of fairy tale romance, to refer to the historical information on marriage as an economic institution, and to explain some of the biological findings about love's chemical basis.

None of these details appeared in the first summary, but in a longer summary, a few carefully selected details might be desirable for clarity. How do you decide which details to include? First, since the idea that love and marriage are not necessarily compatible is the main point of the essay, it makes sense to cite some of the most persuasive evidence supporting this idea. For example, you could mention that for most of Western history, marriage was meant "to serve the economic and social needs of families, communities, and religious institutions," not the emotional and sexual needs of individuals. Further, you might explain the biochemists' argument that serial monogamy based on mutual interests and clandestine adultery—not lifelong, love-based marriage—are the forms of relationships best serving human evolution.

You won't always know which details to include and which to exclude. Developing good judgment in comprehending and summarizing texts is largely a matter of reading skill and prior knowledge (see page 3). Consider the analogy of the seasoned mechanic who can pinpoint an engine problem by simply listening to a characteristic sound that to a less experienced person is just noise. Or consider the chess player who can plot three separate winning strategies from a board position that to a novice looks like a hopeless jumble. In the same way, the more practiced a reader you are, the more knowledgeable you become about the subject, and the better able you will be to make critical distinctions between elements of greater and lesser importance. In the meantime, read as carefully as you can and use your own best judgment as to how to present your material.

Here's one version of a completed summary, with carefully chosen details. Note that we have highlighted phrases and sentences added to the original, briefer summary.

(Thesis)

In her article "The Future of Love: Kiss Romance Goodbye, It's Time for the Real Thing," Barbara Graham suggests that because unrealistic expectations for romantic love may undermine marriage, we should develop a new model for love and relationships.

(Section 1, ¶s 1–3)

As Americans, we crave romantic love; but we have unreal expectations based upon idealized images of love we learn from fantasies and fairy tales such as "Beauty and the Beast" and "Cinderella." Tragedies such as Romeo and Juliet teach us about the all-consuming nature of "true love," and these stories are tragic precisely because the lovers never get to fulfill what we've been taught is the ideal: living happily ever after, in wedded bliss. The idea that romantic love should be confined to marriage is perhaps the biggest fantasy to which we subscribe. When we are unable to make this fantasy real—and it seems that this is often the case—we end that marriage and move on to the next one. The twentieth century is actually the first century in

(Section 2,
¶s 4–7)

Western history in which so much was asked of marriage. In earlier eras, marriage was designed to meet social and economic purposes, rather than fulfill individual emotional and sexual desires.

Casting further doubt on the effectiveness of the current model of marriage, biochemists are discovering how hormones and enzymes influence feelings of love and lust. It turns out that the "chemistry" a person newly in love often feels for another has a basis in fact, as those early feelings of excitement and contentment are bio-chemical in nature. When people jump from one relationship to the next, they may be seeking that chemical "rush." Further, these biochemical discoveries fit with principles of evolutionary

(Section 3,
¶s 8–9)

survival, because short-term relationships—and even adulterous affairs—help to more quickly propagate the species.

Nonetheless, despite such historical and biological imperatives, we don't seem interested in abandoning the pursuit of love and marriage. In order to preserve or perhaps reinvent marriage, we spend a lot of time scrutinizing and dissecting

(Section 4,
¶s 10–12)

the dynamics of relationships. Self-help books on the subject of love and relationships fill book-store shelves and top best-seller lists.

While some argue that such scrutiny ruins rather than reinvigorates love, perhaps our efforts to understand relationships can help us

(Section 5,
¶ 13)

to invent some kind of revised model for human relationships—since trying to confine passionate love to the institution of marriage clearly hasn't worked very well.

Discussion

Our final two suggested steps for writing summaries have two goals: (1) to check your summary against the original passage, making sure that you have included all the important ideas, and (2) to revise so that the summary reads smoothly and coherently.

The structure of this summary generally reflects the structure of the original—with one notable departure. As we noted earlier, Graham uses an inductive approach, stating her thesis at the end of the essay. The summary, however, states the thesis right away, then proceeds deductively to develop that thesis.

Compared to the first, briefer summary, this effort mentions fairy tales and tragedy; develops the point about traditional versus contemporary versions of marriage; explains the biochemical/evolutionary point; and refers specifically to self-help books and their role in the issue.

How long should a summary be? This depends on the length of the original passage. A good rule of thumb is that a summary should be no longer than one-fourth of the original passage. Of course, if you were summarizing an entire chapter or even an entire book, it would have to be much shorter than that. The summary above is about one-fourth the length of the original passage. Although it shouldn't be very much longer, you have seen (pages 17–18) that it could be quite a bit shorter.

The length as well as the content of the summary also depends on its *purpose*. Let's suppose you decided to use Graham's piece in a paper that dealt with the biochemical processes of love and lust. In this case, you might summarize *only* Graham's discussion of Fisher's findings, and perhaps the point Graham makes about how biochemical discoveries complicate marriage. If, instead, you were writing a paper in which you argued against attempts to redefine marriage, you would likely give less attention to the material on biochemistry. To help support your view, you might summarize Graham's points in paragraph 10 about the persistent desire for lasting union found among members of Generation X and evidenced in the high numbers of marriages and remarriages. Thus, depending on your purpose, you would summarize either selected portions of a source or an entire source, as we will see more fully in the chapters on syntheses.

EXERCISE 1.1

Individual and Collaborative Summary Practice

Turn to Chapter 9 and read Solomon A. Asch's article "Opinions and Social Pressure" (pages 306–12). Follow the steps for writing summaries outlined above—read, underline, and divide into stages of thought. Write down a one- or two-sentence summary of each stage of thought in Asch's article. Then, gather in groups of three or four classmates, and compare your summary sentences. Discuss the differences in your sentences, and come to some consensus about the divisions in Asch's stages of thought—and the ways in which to best sum these up.

As a group, write a one- or two-sentence thesis statement summing up the entire passage. You could go even further, and, using your individual summary sentences—or the versions of these your group revised—put together a brief summary of Asch's article, modeled upon the brief summary of Graham's essay on pages 17–18.

SUMMARIZING A NARRATIVE OR PERSONAL ESSAY

Narratives and personal essays differ from expository essays in several ways: they focus on personal experiences and/or views, they aren't structured around an explicitly stated thesis, and their ideas are developed more through the description of events or ideas than through factual evidence or logical explanation. A *narrative* is a story, a retelling of a person's experiences. That person and those experiences may be imaginary, as is the case with fiction, or they may be real, as in biography. In first-person narratives, you can't assume that the narrator represents the author of the piece, unless you know the narrative is a memoir or biography. In a *personal essay*, on the other hand, the narrator is the author. And while the writer of a personal essay may tell stories about his or her experiences, usually writers of such essays discuss thoughts and ideas as much as or more than telling stories. Personal essays also tend to contain more obvious points than do narratives. Summarizing personal essays or narratives presents certain challenges—challenges that are different from those presented by summarizing expository writing.

You have seen that an author of an expository piece (such as Graham's "The Future of Love") follows assertions with examples and statements of support. Narratives, however, usually are less direct. The author relates a story—event follows event—the point of which may never be stated directly. The charm, the force, and the very point of the narrative lie in the telling; generally, narratives do not exhibit the same logical development of expository writing. They do not, therefore, lend themselves to summary in quite the same way. Narratives do have a logic, but that logic may be emotional, imaginative, or plot-bound. The writer who summarizes a narrative is obliged to give an overview—a synopsis—of the story's events and an account of how these events affect the central character(s). The summary must explain the significance or *meaning* of the events.

Similarly, while personal essays sometimes present points more explicitly than do narratives, their focus and structure link them to narratives. Personal essays often contain inexplicit main points, or multiple points; they tend to *explore* ideas and issues, rather than make explicit *assertions* about those ideas. This exploratory character often means that personal essays exhibit a loose structure, and they often contain stories or narratives within them. While summarizing a personal essay may not involve a synopsis of events, an account of the progression of thoughts and ideas is necessary and, as with a narrative, summaries of personal essays must explain the significance of what goes on in the piece being summarized.

An example of a narrative essay appears in Chapter 8, where cyberspace and identity are discussed. In "Virtual Love" Meghan Daum, a freelance writer, describes her romantic experiences with a cyber-correspondent who called himself PFSlider. You may want to read this selection (pages 267–74) before proceeding further.

When summarizing a narrative or a personal essay, bear in mind the principles that follow, as well as those listed in the box on page 7.

To summarize events, reread the narrative and make a marginal note each time you see that an action advances the story from one moment to the next. The key here is to recall that narratives take place *in time*. In your summary, be sure to re-create for your reader a sense of time flowing. Name and describe the character(s) as well. (For our purposes, *character* refers to the person, real or fictional, about whom the narrative is written.) The trickiest part of the summary will be describing the connection between events and characters. Earlier (page 3) we made the point that summarizing any selection involves a degree of interpretation, and this is especially true of sum-

> ### HOW TO SUMMARIZE PERSONAL
> ### ESSAYS AND NARRATIVES
>
> - Your summary will *not* be a narrative, but rather the synopsis of a narrative or personal account. Your summary will likely be a paragraph at most.
> - You will want to name and describe the principal character(s) of the narrative and describe the narrative's main actions or events; or, in the case of the personal essay, identify the narrator and his or her relationship to the discussion.
> - You should seek to connect the narrative's character(s) and events: describe the significance of events for (or the impact of events on) the character(s), and/or the narrator.

marizing narratives and personal essays. What, in the case of Daum, is the significance of her narrative—or of any particular event she recounts? For example, what is the significance of the fact that she found it easier to communicate by e-mail than by phone? Or of her first physical meeting with Pete? Or of the couple's eventual breakup? Each of these events may be used to illustrate a particular point, and the events on which you choose to focus while summarizing a narrative will depend entirely on your purpose in using the narrative in the first place.

The general principles of summarizing narratives are similar to those of summarizing expository or persuasive passages. Make sure that you cover the major events, in the order in which they occurred (in line with your overall purpose, of course). Bring in details only to the extent that they support your purpose.

Here is a four-paragraph summary of Daum's article. (The draft is the result of two prior drafts.)

> In "Virtual Love" Meghan Daum describes her
> experience with an online romance that was
> sparked and nurtured by the mystery of cyberspace
> but that ultimately did not survive face-to-face
> contact in the physical world. Daum, a 26-year-
> old freelance writer living in New York City, was
> flattered when she received messages from
> PFSlider, a complete stranger living in Los
> Angeles who wrote to say that he admired various
> articles she had published. Intrigued, she
> responded, and the two struck up an e-mail
> correspondence. Never comfortable with phone
> conversations, Daum found in e-mail an ideal

means of communication. Initially, their messages
were casual and ironic, but Daum found herself
growing increasingly dependent on getting
messages from PFSlider.

Eventually, "Pete" (as she calls him) telephoned, and the two began talking by voice as
well as by e-mail. But e-mail was their preferred
mode of communication, and as they wrote one
another at all hours of the day and night, their
relationship became increasingly intense. E-mail
allowed her to be more open, honest, and romantic
than she could ever have been in person.

Finally, she and PFSlider met. Their first
date, though not a disaster, was disappointing.
What had made PFSlider so exciting on the computer
became ordinary in the physical world. After the
date, the two resumed the comforts and excitement
of their e-mail and phone correspondence until
Daum agreed to visit him in Los Angeles. Once
again, their meeting was disappointing: They
strained to make conversation, and she wished for
the purity of their cyberspace relationship.
During the next few days, as they visited spots in
Southern California, the relationship between Daum
and Pete withered and died. They had no arguments,
but in the real world they simply weren't connecting; there was no chemistry.

Even after Pete moved to New York for a
new job, they saw that there was no point in
continuing the relationship. Daum realized that
what had appealed to her most about her relationship with PFSlider was the courtship process
itself, but it was courtship as mystery,
courtship in the abstract, as represented by
cyberspace communication. In the real world of
physical objects, their relationship could not
survive. As she concludes, "our particular version of intimacy [was] now obscured by the
branches and bodies and falling debris that make
up the physical world."

For a shorter summary, simply omit some of the specific details (like Pete's
moving to New York). The briefest possible summary—one sentence long—
is represented by the first (thesis) sentence of the summary above:

In "Virtual Love" Meghan Daum describes her experience with an online romance that was sparked and

nurtured by the mystery of cyberspace but that
ultimately did not survive face-to-face contact in
the physical world.

SUMMARIZING FIGURES AND TABLES

In your reading in the sciences and social sciences, you will often find data
and concepts presented in nontext forms—as figures and tables. Such visual
devices offer a snapshot, a pictorial overview of material that is more quickly and clearly communicated in graphic form than as a series of (often complicated) sentences. Note that in essence, figures and tables are themselves
summaries. The writer uses a graph, which in an article or book is labeled as
a numbered "figure," to present the quantitative results of research as points
on a line or a bar, or as sections ("slices") of a pie. Pie charts show relative
proportions, or percentages. Graphs, especially effective in showing patterns,
relate one variable to another: for instance, income to years of education, or a
college student's grade point average to hours of studying.

In the following sections, we present a number of figures and tables from
two different sources, all related to romance and relationships. Figures 1.1, 1.2,
and 1.3 and Table 1.1 come from a study of the criteria used by participants on
television dating shows in the United States and Israel to pick dating partners.*
The categories are self-explanatory, although we should note that the category
"physical appearance" denotes features of height, weight, facial features, and
hair, while "sexual anatomy and bedroom behavior" refers to specifically
sexual features of physical appearance, as well as to "kissing technique," "fore-
play tactics," and the like. Figure 1.1 shows the criteria 266 American and Israeli
men chose as most important in selecting a dating partner. Study this pie chart.

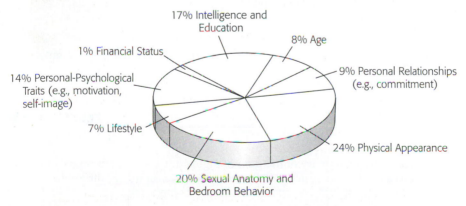

FIGURE 1.1   Categories Used by American and Israeli Males to Screen
Dating Candidates

---

* Amir Hetsroni, "Choosing a Mate in Television Dating Games: The Influence of Setting, Culture, and Gender," *Sex Roles* 42.1–2 (2000): 90–97.

Here is a summary of the information presented:

> Males rated the categories of "physical appearance" and "sexual anatomy and bedroom behavior" as most important to them. Nearly half the males in the sample, or 44%, rated these two categories, which both center on external rather than internal characteristics, as the most important ones for choosing a dating partner. Internal characteristics represented by the categories of "personal-psychological traits" and "intelligence and education" account for the next most important criteria, with a combined 31%. Males rated "relationship," "lifestyle," and "age" as nearly equal in their priorities; interestingly, a negligible 1% rated "financial status" as an important criterion when selecting a dating candidate.

Figure 1.2 shows, in percentages, how women rate dating criteria.

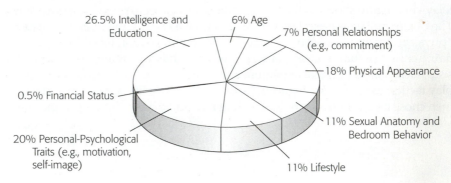

FIGURE 1.2 Categories Used by American and Israeli Females to Screen Dating Candidates

EXERCISE **1.2**

Summarizing Charts

Write a brief summary of the data in Figure 1.2. Use our summary of Figure 1.1 as a model, but structure and word your own summary differently.

Bar graphs are useful for comparing two sets of data. Figure 1.3 illustrates this with a comparison of categories males and females use to select dating partners.

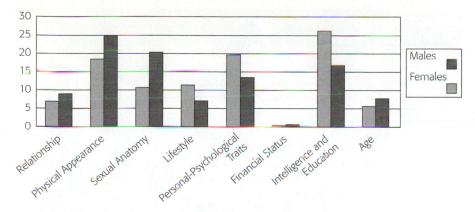

FIGURE 1.3 Comparison of Categories Used by American and Israeli Males and Females to Screen Dating Candidates

Here is a summary of the information in Figure 1.3:

> Males clearly differ from females in the criteria
> they use to select dating partners. Males in this
> sample focused on external characteristics such as
> "physical appearance" and especially "sexual anato-
> my and bedroom behavior" at significantly higher
> rates than did females. Conversely, females select-
> ed the internal characteristics of "lifestyle,"
> "personal-psychological traits," and "intelligence
> and education" at much higher rates than did males.
> However, less significant differences exist between
> males and females when rating the importance of
> "relationship," "financial status," and "age"; both
> male and female participants rated these three cri-
> teria as of lesser importance when selecting a
> dating partner.

A table presents numerical data in rows and columns for quick reference. If the writer chooses, tabular information can be converted to graphic information. Charts and graphs are preferable when the writer wants to emphasize a pattern or relationship; tables are used when the writer wants to emphasize numbers. While the previous charts and graphs combined the Israeli with the American data collected in the TV dating show study, Table 1.1 breaks down the percentages by sex and nationality, revealing some significant differences between the nationality groups. (*Note: n* refers to the total number of respondents in each category.)

Sometimes a single graph presents information on two or more populations, or data sets, all of which are tracked with the same measurements.

TABLE 1.1   Categories Used by American and Israeli Males and Females to Screen Dating Candidates

Category	American Males (%) (*n* = 120)	Israeli Males (%) (*n* = 146)	American Females (%) (*n* = 156)	Israeli Females (%) (*n* = 244)
Relationship	9.5	8.0	9.5	5.0
Physical appearance	18.5	30.0	12.0	22.0
Sexual anatomy and bedroom behavior	11.5	27.5	4.5	15.0
Lifestyle	9.0	6.0	11.0	11.5
Personal-psychological traits	20.0	8.0	27.0	15.0
Financial status	1.5	–	–	1.0
Intelligence and education	22.5	12.5	29.0	24.0
Age	7.5	8.0	7.0	6.0
TOTAL	100.0	100.0	100.0	100.0

Figure 1.4 comes from a study of 261 college students—93 males and 168 females. The students were asked (among other things) to rate the acceptability of a hypothetical instance of sexual betrayal by both a male and a female heterosexual romantic partner who has agreed to be monogamous. The graph plots the ways in which the gender of the transgressor played into the acceptability ratings given by male and female respondents. The researchers established mean values of 1 to 4 (indicating ratings of "totally unacceptable" to "totally acceptable"). A *mean* indicates the average of the ratings or scores given by a population or, in numerical terms, the sum of the scores divided by the number of scores. When respondents in the study were asked to assign a numerical rating of acceptability to instances of sexual betrayal, they chose numbers on a scale from 1 to 4, and these choices were averaged into mean acceptability ratings. None of the scores given by respondents in this study surpassed a mean acceptability rating of 2, but differences are evident between male and female ratings. The male respondents were more accepting of betrayal than the females, with an overall mean acceptability score of 1.63, whereas the females' mean score was 1.31.

A complete, scientific understanding of these findings would require more data, and statistical analysis of such data would yield precise information such as the exact numerical difference between male and female ratings. For example, in the original text of this study, the authors note that males were 11.6 times more accepting of sexual betrayal by male transgressors than were females. Even without such details, it is possible to arrive at a basic understanding of the data represented in the graph and to summarize this information in simple terms. Here is a summary of the information reported in this graph:

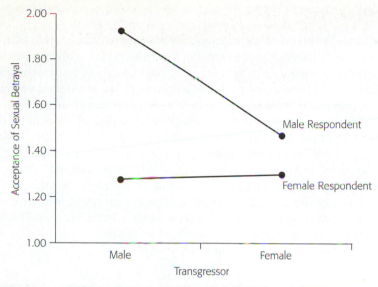

FIGURE 1.4 The Interaction of Sex of Respondent and Sex of Transgressor on the Acceptance of Sexual Betrayal

While males and females both rated sexual betrayal as unacceptable, males (with a mean rating of 1.63) were significantly more accepting overall than were females (with a mean rating of 1.31). Even more dramatic, however, is the difference between male and female ratings when the gender of the transgressor is factored in. Males rated male transgression as markedly more acceptable than female transgression, with approximate means of 1.90 for male transgressions and 1.43 for female transgressions. The males' ratings contrast sharply with those of females, who indicated a mean acceptability rating of approximately 1.25 for male transgressors, and 1.30 for female transgressors. Therefore, while both sexes found transgression by members of their own sex more acceptable than transgressions by the opposite sex, men were more accepting overall than women, and men believed male transgressors were significantly more acceptable than female transgressors. On the other hand, women found transgression overall less acceptable than males did, and women indicated far less difference in their ratings of male versus female transgressors than did the male respondents.

PARAPHRASE

In certain cases, you may want to *paraphrase* rather than summarize material. Writing a paraphrase is similar to writing a summary: It involves recasting a passage into your own words, so it requires your complete understanding of the material. The difference is that while a summary is a shortened version of the original, the paraphrase is approximately the same length as the original.

Why write a paraphrase when you can quote the original? You may decide to offer a paraphrase of material written in language that is dense, abstract, archaic, or possibly confusing. When you come across a passage that you don't understand, the temptation is strong to skip over it. Resist this temptation! Use a paraphrase as a tool for explaining to yourself the main ideas of a difficult passage. By translating another writer's language into your own, you can clarify what you understand and pinpoint what you don't. The paraphrase therefore becomes a tool for learning the subject.

The pointers below will help you write paraphrases.

HOW TO WRITE PARAPHRASES

- Make sure that you understand the source passage.
- Substitute your own words for those of the source passage; look for synonyms that carry the same meaning as the original words.
- Rearrange your own sentences so that they read smoothly. Sentence structure, even sentence order, in the paraphrase need not be based on that of the original. A good paraphrase, like a good summary, should stand by itself.

Let's consider an example. If you were investigating the ethical concerns relating to the practice of in vitro fertilization, you might conclude that you should read some medical literature. You might reasonably want to hear from the doctors who are themselves developing, performing, and questioning the procedures that you are researching. In professional journals and bulletins, physicians write to one another, not to the general public. They use specialized language. If you wanted to refer to a technically complex selection, you might need to write a paraphrase for the following selection.

In Vitro Fertilization: From Medical Reproduction to Genetic Diagnosis

Dietmar Mieth

[I]t is not only an improvement in the success-rate that participating research scientists hope for but, rather, developments in new fields of research in in vitro gene diagnosis and in certain circumstances gene therapy. In view of this, the French expert J. F. Mattei has asked the following question: "Are we forced to accept that in vitro fertilization will become one of the most compelling methods of genetic diagnosis?" Evidently, by the introduction of a new law in France and Sweden (1994), this acceptance (albeit with certain restrictions) has already occurred prior to the application of in vitro fertilization reaching a technically mature and clinically applicable phase. This may seem astonishing in view of the question placed by the above-quoted French expert: the idea of embryo production so as to withhold one or two embryos before implantation presupposes a definite "attitude towards eugenics." And to destroy an embryo merely because of its genetic characteristics could signify the reduction of a human life to the sum of its genes. Mattei asks: "In face of a molecular judgment on our lives, is there no possibility for appeal? Will the diagnosis of inherited monogenetic illnesses soon be extended to genetic predisposition for multi-factorial illnesses?"*

Like most literature intended for physicians, the language of this selection is somewhat forbidding to an audience of nonspecialists, who have trouble with phrases such as "predisposition for multi-factorial illnesses." As a courtesy to your readers and in an effort to maintain a consistent tone and level in your essay, you could paraphrase this paragraph of the medical newsletter. First, of course, you must understand the meaning of the passage, perhaps no small task. But, having read the material carefully (and perhaps consulting a dictionary), you might eventually prepare a paraphrase like this one:

> Writing in the *Newsletter of the European Network for Biomedical Ethics,* Dietmar Mieth reports that fertility specialists today want not only to improve the success rates of their procedures but also to diagnose and repair genetic problems before they implant fertilized eggs. Since the result of the in vitro process is often more fertilized eggs than can be used in a procedure, doctors may examine test-tube embryos for genetic defects and "withhold one or two" before implanting them. The practice of selectively implanting embryos raises concerns about eugenics and the rights of rejected embryos. On what genetic grounds will specialists distinguish flawed from healthy embryos and make a decision whether or not to implant? The appearance of single genes linked directly to specific, or "monogenetic," illnesses could be grounds for destroying an embryo. More complicated would be

---

* Dietmar Mieth, "In Vitro Fertilization: From Medical Reproduction to Genetic Diagnosis," *Biomedical Ethics: Newsletter of the European Network for Biomedical Ethics* 1.1 (1996): 45.

```
genes that predispose people to an illness but in
no way guarantee the onset of that illness. Would
these genes, which are only one factor in "multi-
factorial illnesses" also be labeled undesirable
and lead to embryo destruction? Advances in fer-
tility science raise difficult questions. Already,
even before techniques of genetic diagnosis are
fully developed, legislatures are writing laws gov-
erning the practices of fertility clinics.
```

We begin our paraphrase with the same "not only/but also" logic of the original's first sentence, introducing the concepts of genetic diagnosis and therapy. The next four sentences in the original introduce concerns of a "French expert." Rather than quoting Mieth, quoting the expert, and immediately mentioning new laws in France and Sweden, we decided (first) to explain that in vitro fertilization procedures can give rise to more embryos than needed. We reasoned that nonmedical readers would appreciate our making explicit the background knowledge that the author assumes other physicians possess. Then we quote Mieth briefly ("withhold one or two" embryos) to provide some flavor of the original. We maintain focus on the ethical questions and wait until the end of the paraphrase before mentioning the laws to which Mieth refers. Our paraphrase is roughly the same length as the original, and it conveys the author's concerns about eugenics. As you can see, the paraphrase requires a writer to make some decisions about the presentation of material. In many, if not most, cases, you will need to do more than simply "translate" from the original, sentence by sentence, to write your paraphrase.

Paraphrases are generally about the same length as (sometimes shorter than) the passages on which they are based. But sometimes clarity requires that a paraphrase be longer than a tightly compacted source passage. For example, suppose you wanted to paraphrase this statement by Sigmund Freud:

> We have found out that the distortion in dreams which hinders our understanding of them is due to the activities of a censorship, directed against the unacceptable, unconscious wish-impulses.

If you were to paraphrase this statement (the first sentence in the Tenth Lecture of his *General Introduction to Psychoanalysis*), you might come up with something like this:

```
It is difficult to understand dreams because they
contain distortions. Freud believed that these dis-
tortions arise from our internal censor, which
attempts to suppress unconscious and forbidden
desires.
```

Essentially, this paraphrase does little more than break up one sentence into two and somewhat rearrange the sentence structure for clarity.

Like summaries, then, *paraphrases* are useful devices, both in helping you to understand source material and in enabling you to convey the essence of this source material to your readers. When would you choose to write a summary instead of a paraphrase (or vice versa)? The answer to this question depends on your purpose in presenting your source material. As we've said, summaries are generally based on articles (or sections of articles) or books. Paraphrases are generally based on particularly difficult (or important) paragraphs or sentences. You would seldom paraphrase a long passage, or summarize a short one, unless there were particularly good reasons for doing so. (For example, a lawyer might want to paraphrase several pages of legal language so that his or her client, who is not a lawyer, could understand it.) The purpose of a summary is generally to save your reader time by presenting him or her with a brief and quickly readable version of a lengthy source. The purpose of a paraphrase is generally to clarify a short passage that might otherwise be unclear. Whether you summarize or paraphrase may also depend on the importance of your source. A particularly important source—if it is not too long—may rate a paraphrase. If it is less important, or peripheral to your central argument, you may choose to write a summary instead. And, of course, you may choose to summarize only part of your source—the part that is most relevant to the point you are making.

EXERCISE **1.3**

Paraphrasing

Locate three relatively complex, but brief, passages from readings currently assigned in your other courses. Paraphrase these passages, making the language more readable and understandable.

QUOTATION

A *quotation* records the exact language used by someone in speech or writing. A *summary,* in contrast, is a brief restatement in your own words of what someone else has said or written. And a *paraphrase* also is a restatement, although one that is often as long as the original source. Any paper in which you draw upon sources will rely heavily on quotation, summary, and paraphrase. How do you choose among the three?

Remember that the papers you write should for the most part be your own—your own language and certainly your own thesis, your own inferences, and your own conclusion. It follows that references to your source materials should be written primarily as summaries and paraphrases, both of which are built on restatement, not quotation. You will use summaries when you need a *brief* restatement, and paraphrases, which provide more explicit detail than summaries, when you need to follow the development of a source closely. When you quote too much, you risk losing ownership of your work: More easily than you might think, your voice can be drowned out by the voices of those you've quoted. So *use quotation sparingly,* as you would a pungent spice.

Nevertheless, *quoting just the right source at the right time can significantly improve your papers.* The trick is to know when and how to use quotations.

Choosing Quotations

You'll find that using quotations can be particularly helpful in several situations.

Quoting Memorable Language

Frequently, we quote when the source material is worded so eloquently or powerfully that to summarize or paraphrase it would be to sacrifice much of the impact and significance of the meaning. Here, for example, is historian John Keegan describing how France, Germany, Austria, and Russia slid inexorably in 1914 into the cataclysm of World War I:

> In the event, the states of Europe proceeded, as if in a dead march and a dialogue of the deaf, to the destruction of their continent and its civilization.*

No paraphrase could do justice to the power of Keegan's words, as they appear in his 1998 book, *The First World War*. You would certainly want to quote them in any paper dealing with the origins of this conflict.

WHEN TO QUOTE

- Use quotations when another writer's language is particularly memorable and will add interest and liveliness to your paper.
- Use quotations when another writer's language is so clear and economical that to make the same point in your own words would, by comparison, be ineffective.
- Use quotations when you want the solid reputation of a source to lend authority and credibility to your own writing.

Quotations can be direct or indirect. A *direct* quotation is one in which you record precisely the language of another. An *indirect* quotation is one in which you report what someone has said, although you are not obligated to repeat the words exactly as spoken (or written):

> **Direct quotation:** *Franklin D. Roosevelt said, "The only thing we have to fear is fear itself."*

> **Indirect quotation:** *Franklin D. Roosevelt said that we have nothing to fear but fear itself.*

---

* John Keegan, *The First World War* (New York: Vintage, 1998) 23.

The language in a direct quotation, which is indicated by a pair of quotation marks (" "), must be faithful to the language of the original passage. When using an indirect quotation, you have the liberty of changing words (although not changing meaning). For both direct and indirect quotations, *you must credit your sources*, naming them either in (or close to) the sentence that includes the quotation or in a parenthetical citation. (Note: We haven't included parenthetical citations in our examples here; see Chapter 7, pages 214–33 for specific rules on citing sources properly.)

Quoting Clear and Concise Language

You should quote a source when its language is particularly clear and economical—when your language, by contrast, would be wordy. Read this passage from a text by Patricia Curtis on biology:

> The honeybee colony, which usually has a population of 30,000 to 40,000 workers, differs from that of the bumblebee and many other social bees or wasps in that it survives the winter. This means that the bees must stay warm despite the cold. Like other bees, the isolated honeybee cannot fly if the temperature falls below 10°C (50°F) and cannot walk if the temperature is below 7°C (45°F). Within the wintering hive, bees maintain their temperature by clustering together in a dense ball; the lower the temperature, the denser the cluster. The clustered bees produce heat by constant muscular movements of their wings, legs, and abdomens. In very cold weather, the bees on the outside of the cluster keep moving toward the center, while those in the core of the cluster move to the colder outside periphery. The entire cluster moves slowly about on the combs, eating the stored honey from the combs as it moves.*

A summary of this paragraph might read as follows:

> ```
> Honeybees, unlike many other varieties of bee, are
> able to live through the winter by "clustering
> together in a dense ball" for body warmth.
> ```

A paraphrase of the same passage would be considerably more detailed:

> ```
> Honeybees, unlike many other varieties of bee
> (such as bumblebees), are able to live through the
> winter. The 30,000 to 40,000 bees within a honey-
> bee hive could not, individually, move about in
> cold winter temperatures. But when "clustering
> together in a dense ball," the bees generate heat
> by constantly moving their body parts. The cluster
> also moves slowly about the hive, those on the
> periphery of the cluster moving into the center,
> ```

---

* Patricia Curtis, "Winter Organization," *Biology*, 2nd ed. (New York: Worth, 1976) 822–23.

> those in the center moving to the periphery, and
> all eating honey stored in the combs. This nutri-
> tion, in addition to the heat generated by the
> cluster, enables the honeybee to survive the cold
> winter months.

In both the summary and the paraphrase we've quoted Curtis's "clustering together in a dense ball," a phrase that lies at the heart of her description of wintering honeybees. For us to describe this clustering in any language other than Curtis's would be pointless since her description is admirably brief and precise.

Quoting Authoritative Language

You will also want to use quotations that lend authority to your work. When quoting an expert or some prominent political, artistic, or historical figure, you elevate your own work by placing it in esteemed company. Quote respected figures to establish background information in a paper, and your readers will tend to perceive that information as reliable. Quote the opinions of respected figures to endorse some statement that you've made, and your statement becomes more credible to your readers.

Consider this discussion of space flight. Author David Chandler refers to a physicist and a physicist-astronaut:

> A few scientists—notably James Van Allen, discoverer of the Earth's
> radiation belts—have decried the expense of the manned space program
> and called for an almost exclusive concentration on unmanned scientif-
> ic exploration instead, saying this would be far more cost-effective.
>
> Other space scientists dispute that idea. Joseph Allen, physicist
> and former shuttle astronaut, says, "It seems to be argued that one
> takes away from the other. But before there was a manned space pro-
> gram, the funding on space science was zero. Now it's about $500
> million a year."

Note that in the first paragraph Chandler has either summarized or used an indirect quotation to incorporate remarks made by James Van Allen into the discussion on space flight. In the second paragraph, Chandler directly quotes his next source, Joseph Allen. Both quotations, indirect and direct, lend authority and legitimacy to the article, for both James Van Allen and Joseph Allen are experts on the subject of space flight. Note also that Chandler provides brief but effective biographies of his sources, identifying both so that their qualifications to speak on the subject are known to all:

> James Van Allen, *discoverer of the Earth's radiation belts,* . . .

> Joseph Allen, *physicist and former shuttle astronaut,* . . .

The phrases in italics are called *appositives*. Their function is to rename the nouns they follow by providing explicit, identifying detail. Any information about a person that can be expressed in the following sentence pattern can be made into an appositive phrase:

> James Van Allen is the *discoverer of the Earth's radiation belts*. He has decried the expense of the manned space program.

> James Van Allen, *discoverer of the Earth's radiation belts*, has decried the expense of the manned space program.

Appositives (in the example above, "discoverer of the Earth's radiation belts") efficiently incorporate identifying information about the authors you quote, while adding variety to the structure of your sentences.

Incorporating Quotations into Your Sentences

Quoting Only the Part of a Sentence or Paragraph That You Need

We've said that a writer selects passages for quotation that are especially *vivid and memorable, concise,* or *authoritative.* Now put these principles into practice. Suppose that while conducting research on college sports, you've come across the following, written by Robert Hutchins, former president of the University of Chicago:

> If athleticism is bad for students, players, alumni, and the public, it is even worse for the colleges and universities themselves. They want to be educational institutions, but they can't. The story of the famous half-back whose only regret, when he bade his coach farewell, was that he hadn't learned to read and write is probably exaggerated. But we must admit that pressure from trustees, graduates, "friends," presidents, and even professors has tended to relax academic standards. These gentry often overlook the fact that a college should not be interested in a full-back who is a half-wit. Recruiting, subsidizing, and the double educational standard cannot exist without the knowledge and the tacit approval, at least, of the colleges and universities themselves. Certain institutions encourage susceptible professors to be nice to athletes now admitted by paying them for serving as "faculty representatives" on the college athletic board.*

Suppose that in this entire paragraph you find a gem, a sentence with quotable words that will enliven your discussion. You may want to quote part of the following sentence:

> These gentry often overlook the fact that a college should not be interested in a fullback who is a half-wit.

---

* Robert Hutchins, "Gate Receipts and Glory," *Saturday Evening Post* 3 Dec. 1983: 38.

Incorporating the Quotation into the Flow of Your Own Sentence

Once you've selected the passage you want to quote, work the material into your paper in as natural and fluid a manner as possible. Here's how we would quote Hutchins:

> ```
> Robert Hutchins, former president of the University
> of Chicago, asserts that "a college should not be
> interested in a fullback who is a half-wit."
> ```

Note that we've used an appositive to identify Hutchins. And we've used only the part of the paragraph—a single clause—that we thought memorable enough to quote directly.

Avoiding Freestanding Quotations

A quoted sentence should never stand by itself—as in the following example:

> ```
> Various people associated with the university admit
> that the pressures of athleticism have caused a
> relaxation of standards. "These gentry often over-
> look the fact that a college should not be inter-
> ested in a fullback who is a half-wit." But this
> kind of thinking is bad for the university and even
> worse for the athletes.
> ```

Even if it includes a parenthetical citation, a freestanding quotation would have the problem of being jarring to the reader. Introduce the quotation with a *signal phrase* that attributes the source not in a parenthetical citation, but in some other part of the sentence—beginning, middle, or end. Thus, you could write:

> ```
> As Robert Hutchins notes, "These gentry often over-
> look the fact that a college should not be inter-
> ested in a fullback who is a half-wit."
> ```

Here's a variation with the signal phrase in the middle:

> ```
> "These gentry," asserts Robert Hutchins, "often
> overlook the fact that a college should not be
> interested in a fullback who is a half-wit."
> ```

Another alternative is to introduce a sentence-long quotation with a colon:

> ```
> But Robert Hutchins disagrees: "These gentry often
> overlook the fact that a college should not be
> interested in a fullback who is a half-wit."
> ```

Use colons also to introduce block quotations (as in the cases when we introduce long quotations in this chapter).

When attributing sources in signal phrases, try to vary the standard *states, writes, says,* and so on. Other, stronger verbs you might consider: *asserts, argues, maintains, insists, asks,* and even *wonders.*

EXERCISE **1.4**

Incorporating Quotations

Turn to the passage by Meghan Daum, "Virtual Love," pages 267–74, and find some sentences that you think make interesting points. Imagine you want to use these points in an essay you're writing on the opportunities and perils of online romance. Write five different sentences that use a variety of the techniques discussed thus far to incorporate whole sentences as well as phrases from "Virtual Love."

Using Ellipsis Points

Using quotations becomes somewhat complicated when you want to omit part of a quotation. Here's part of a paragraph from Henry David Thoreau's *Walden:*

> To read well, that is to read true books in a true spirit, is a noble exercise, and one that will task the reader more than any exercise which the customs of the day esteem. It requires a training such as the athletes underwent, the steady intention almost of the whole life to this object. Books must be read as deliberately and reservedly as they were written.*

Here is one way to quote the passage in part:

```
Reading  well  is  hard  work,  writes  Henry  David
Thoreau  in  Walden,  "that  will  task  the  reader  more
than  any  exercise  which  the  customs  of  the  day
esteem.  .  .  .  Books  must  be  read  as  deliberately
and  reservedly  as  they  were  written."
```

Whenever you quote a sentence but delete words from it, as we have done, indicate this deletion to the reader with three spaced periods—called an "ellipsis point"—in the sentence at the point of deletion. The rationale for using an ellipsis mark is that a direct quotation must be reproduced *exactly* as it was written or spoken. When writers delete or change any part of the quoted material, readers must be alerted so they don't think the changes were part of the original. When deleting an entire sentence or sentences from a quoted paragraph, as in the

---

* Henry David Thoreau, *Walden* (New York: Signet Classic, 1960): 72.

example above, end the sentence you have quoted with a period, insert the ellipsis, and continue the quotation.

If you are deleting the middle of a single sentence, use an ellipsis in place of the deleted words:

> ```
> "To read well . . . is a noble exercise, and one
> that will task the reader more than any exercise
> which the customs of the day esteem."
> ```

If you are deleting material from the end of one sentence through to the beginning of another sentence, add a sentence period before the ellipsis:

> ```
> "It requires a training such as the athletes under-
> went. . . . Books must be read as deliberately and
> reservedly as they were written."
> ```

If you begin your quotation of an author in the middle of his or her sentence, you need not indicate deleted words with an ellipsis. Be sure, however, that the syntax of the quotation fits smoothly with the syntax of your sentence:

> ```
> Reading "is a noble exercise," writes Henry David
> Thoreau.
> ```

Using Brackets to Add or Substitute Words

Use brackets whenever you need to add or substitute words in a quoted sentence. The brackets indicate to the reader a word or phrase that does not appear in the original passage but that you have inserted to avoid confusion. For example, when a pronoun's antecedent would be unclear to readers, delete the pronoun from the sentences and substitute an identifying word or phrase in brackets. When you make such a substitution, no ellipsis marks are needed. Assume that you wish to quote either of the underlined sentences in the following passage by Jane Yolen:

> Golden Press's *Walt Disney's Cinderella* set the new pattern for America's Cinderella. This book's text is coy and condescending. (Sample: "And her best friends of all were—guess who—the mice!") The illustrations are poor cartoons. And Cinderella herself is a disaster. She cowers as her sisters rip her homemade ball gown to shreds. (Not even homemade by Cinderella, but by the mice and birds.) <u>She answers her stepmother with whines and pleadings. She is a sorry excuse for a heroine, pitiable and useless.</u> She cannot perform even a simple action to save herself, though she is warned by her friends, the mice. She does not hear them because she is "off in a world of dreams."

Cinderella begs, she whimpers, and at last has to be rescued by—guess who—the mice!*

In quoting one of these sentences, you would need to identify to whom the pronoun *she* refers. You can do this inside the quotation by using brackets:

> ```
> Jane Yolen believes that "[Cinderella] is a sorry
> excuse for a heroine, pitiable and useless."
> ```

If the pronoun begins the sentence to be quoted, you can identify the pronoun outside the quotation and simply begin quoting your source one word later:

> ```
> Jane Yolen believes that in the Golden Press ver-
> sion, Cinderella "is a sorry excuse for a heroine,
> pitiable and useless."
> ```

Here's another example of a case where the pronoun needing identification occurs in the middle of the sentence to be quoted. Newspaper reporters must use brackets in these cases frequently when quoting sources, who in interviews might say something like this:

> After the fire they did not return to the station house for three hours.

A reporter wanting to use this sentence in an article would need to identify the pronoun:

> An official from City Hall, speaking on the condition that he not be identified, said, "After the fire [the officers] did not return to the station house for three hours."

You also will need to add bracketed information to a quoted sentence when a reference essential to the sentence's meaning is implied but not stated directly. An example:

> ```
> According to Robert Jastrow, a physicist and former
> official at NASA's Goddard Institute, "The proposi-
> tion [that computers will emerge as a form of life]
> seems ridiculous because, for one thing, computers
> lack the drives and emotions of living creatures."
> ```

The bracketed phrase clarifying "proposition"—"that computers will emerge as a form of life"—is the writer's summary of Jastrow's proposition, discussed prior to the quoted passage.

---

* Jane Yolen, "America's 'Cinderella,'" *Children's Literature in Education* 8 (1977): 22.

Using Brackets

Write your own sentences incorporating the following quotations. Use brackets to clarify information that isn't clear outside of its original context—and refer to the original sources to remind yourself of this context.

From the Robert Hutchins passage on college sports:
(a) *They* want to be educational institutions, but they can't.
(b) *These gentry* often overlook the fact that a college should not be interested in a fullback who is a half-wit.

From the Jane Yolen excerpt on Cinderella:
(c) *This book's* text is coy and condescending.
(d) *She* cannot perform even a simple action to save herself, though she is warned by her friends, the mice.
(e) She does not hear *them* because she is "off in a world of dreams."

Remember that when you quote any work, you are obligated to credit—or cite—that work properly; otherwise, you may be guilty of plagiarism. See pages 214–33 for guidance on citing sources.

WHEN TO SUMMARIZE, PARAPHRASE, AND QUOTE

Summarize
- To present main points of a lengthy passage (article or book)
- To condense peripheral points necessary to discussion

Paraphrase
- To clarify a short passage
- To emphasize main points

Quote
- To capture another writer's particularly memorable language
- To capture another writer's clearly and economically stated language
- To lend authority and credibility to your own writing

AVOIDING PLAGIARISM

Plagiarism is generally defined as the attempt to pass off the work of another as one's own. Whether born out of calculation or desperation, plagiarism is the least tolerated offense in the academic world. The fact that most plagiarism is unintentional—arising from ignorance of conventions rather than deceitfulness—makes no difference to many professors.

The ease of cutting and pasting whole blocks of text from Web sources into one's own paper makes it tempting for some to take the easy way out and avoid doing their own research and writing. But apart from the serious ethical issues involved, the same technology that makes such acts possible also makes it possible for instructors to detect them. Software marketed to instructors allows them to conduct Web searches, using suspicious phrases as keywords. The results often provide irrefutable evidence of plagiarism.

Of course, plagiarism is not confined to students. Recent years have seen a number of high-profile cases—some of them reaching the front pages of newspapers—of well-known scholars who were shown to have copied passages from sources into their own book manuscripts, without proper attribution. In some cases, the scholars maintained that these appropriations were simply a matter of carelessness, and that in the press and volume of work, they had lost track of which words were theirs and which were the words of their sources. But such excuses sounded hollow: These careless acts inevitably embarrassed the scholars professionally, disappointed their many admirers, and tarnished their otherwise fine work and reputations.

You can avoid plagiarism and charges of plagiarism by following the basic rules provided on page 44.

The following is an excerpt from an article by Richard Rovere on Senator Joseph P. McCarthy, along with several student versions of the ideas represented:

> McCarthy never seemed to believe in himself or in anything he had said. He knew that Communists were not in charge of American foreign policy. He knew that they weren't running the United States Army. He knew that he had spent five years looking for Communists in the government and that—although some must certainly have been there, since Communists had turned up in practically every other major government in the world—he hadn't come up with even one.*

One student wrote the following version of this passage:

> McCarthy never believed in himself or in anything he had said. He knew that Communists were not in charge of American foreign policy and weren't running the United States Army. He knew that he had spent five years looking for Communists in the government, and although there must certainly have been some there, since Communists were in practically every other

---

* Richard Rovere, "The Most Gifted and Successful Demagogue This Country Has Ever Known," *New York Times Magazine* 30 Apr. 1967: 192+.

```
major government in the world, he hadn't come up
with even one.
```

Clearly, this is intentional plagiarism. The student has copied the original passage almost word for word.

Here is another version of the same passage:

```
McCarthy knew that Communists were not running for-
eign policy or the Army. He also knew that although
there must have been some Communists in the gov-
ernment, he hadn't found a single one, even though
he had spent five years looking.
```

This student has attempted to put the ideas into her own words, but both the wording and the sentence structure still are so heavily dependent on the original passage that even if it *were* cited, most professors would consider it plagiarism.

In the following version, the student has sufficiently changed the wording and sentence structure, and she uses a signal phrase (a phrase used to introduce a quotation or paraphrase, signaling to the reader that the words to follow come from someone else) to properly credit the information to Rovere, so that there is no question of plagiarism:

```
According to Richard Rovere, McCarthy was fully
aware that Communists were running neither the gov-
ernment nor the Army. He also knew that he hadn't
found a single Communist in government, even after
a lengthy search (192).
```

And although this is not a matter of plagiarism, as noted above, it's essential to quote accurately. You are not permitted to change any part of a quotation or to omit any part of it without using brackets or ellipses (see pages 39–41).

RULES FOR AVOIDING PLAGIARISM

- Cite *all* quoted material and *all* summarized and paraphrased material, unless the information is common knowledge (e.g., the Civil War was fought from 1861 to 1865).
- Make sure that both the *wording* and the *sentence structure* of your summaries and paraphrases are substantially your own.

Critical Reading and Critique

2

CRITICAL READING

When writing papers in college, you are often called on to respond critically to source materials. Critical reading requires the abilities to both summarize and evaluate a presentation. As you have seen in Chapter 1, a *summary* is a brief restatement in your own words of the content of a passage. An *evaluation*, however, is a more difficult matter.

In your college work, you read to gain and *use* new information; but as sources are not equally valid or equally useful, you must learn to distinguish critically among them by evaluating them.

There is no ready-made formula for determining validity. Critical reading and its written equivalent—the *critique*—require discernment, sensitivity, imagination, knowledge of the subject, and above all, willingness to become involved in what you read. These skills cannot be taken for granted and are developed only through repeated practice. You must begin somewhere, though, and we recommend that you start by posing two broad categories of questions about passages, articles, and books that you read: (1) What is the author's purpose in writing? Does he or she succeed in this purpose? (2) To what extent do you agree with the author?

Question Category 1: What Is the Author's Purpose in Writing? Does the Author Succeed in This Purpose?

All critical reading *begins with an accurate summary*. Thus before attempting an evaluation, you must be able to locate an author's thesis and identify the selection's content and structure. You must understand the author's *purpose*. Authors write to inform, to persuade, and to entertain. A given piece may be primarily *informative* (a summary of the research on cloning), primarily *persuasive* (an argument on why the government must do something to alleviate homelessness), or primarily *entertaining* (a play about the frustrations of young lovers). Or it may be all three (as in John Steinbeck's novel *The Grapes of Wrath,* which revolves around migrant workers during the Great Depression). Sometimes, authors are not fully conscious of their purpose. Sometimes their purpose changes as they write. Also, more than one purpose can overlap: An essay may need to inform the reader about an issue in order to make a persuasive point. But if the finished piece is coherent, it will have a primary reason for having been written, and it should be apparent that the author is attempting primarily to inform, persuade, or entertain a particular audience. To identify this primary reason—this purpose—is your first job as a critical reader. Your

45

WHERE DO WE FIND WRITTEN CRITIQUES?

Here are a few types of writing that involve critique:

Academic Writing

- **Research papers.** Critique sources in order to establish their usefulness.
- **Position papers.** Stake out a position by critiquing other positions.
- **Book reviews.** Combine summary with critique.
- **Essay exams.** Demonstrate understanding of course material by critiquing it.

Workplace Writing

- **Legal briefs and legal arguments.** Critique previous rulings or arguments made by opposing counsel.
- **Business plans and proposals.** Critique other, less cost-effective approaches.
- **Policy briefs.** Communicate failings of policies and legislation through critique.

---

next job is to determine how successful the author has been. As a critical reader, you bring different criteria, or standards of judgment, to bear when you read pieces intended to inform, persuade, or entertain.

Writing to Inform

A piece intended to inform will provide definitions, describe or report on a process, recount a story, give historical background, and/or provide facts and figures. An informational piece responds to questions such as the following:

What (or who) is _____?

How does _____ work?

What is the controversy or problem about?

What happened?

How and why did it happen?

What were the results?

What are the arguments for and against _____?

To the extent that an author answers these and related questions and the answers are a matter of verifiable record (you could check for accuracy if you had the time and inclination), the selection is intended to inform. Having determined this, you can organize your response by considering three other criteria: accuracy, significance, and fair interpretation of information.

Evaluating Informative Writing

Accuracy of Information. If you are going to use any of the information presented, you must be satisfied that it is trustworthy. One of your responsibilities as a critical reader, then, is to find out if it is accurate. This means you should check facts against other sources. Government publications are often good resources for verifying facts about political legislation, population data, crime statistics, and the like. You can also search key terms in library databases and on the Web. Since material on the Web is essentially "self-published," however, you must be especially vigilant in assessing its legitimacy. In Chapter 7, which focuses on research, we provide a more detailed discussion of how you should approach Web sources. A wealth of useful information is now available on the Internet—but there is also a tremendous amount of misinformation, distorted "facts," and unsupported opinion.

Significance of Information. One useful question that you can ask about a reading is "So what?" In the case of selections that attempt to inform, you may reasonably wonder whether the information makes a difference. What can the person who is reading gain from this information? How is knowledge advanced by the publication of this material? Is the information of importance to you or to others in a particular audience? Why or why not?

Fair Interpretation of Information. At times you will read reports, the sole function of which is to relate raw data or information. In these cases, you will build your response on the two questions in category 1, introduced on page 45: What is the author's purpose in writing? Does she or he succeed in this purpose? More frequently, once an author has presented information, he or she will attempt to evaluate or interpret it—which is only reasonable, since information that has not been evaluated or interpreted is of little use. One of your tasks as a critical reader is to make a distinction between the author's presentation of facts and figures and his or her attempts to evaluate them. Watch for shifts from straightforward descriptions of factual information ("20 percent of the population") to assertions about what this information means ("*a mere* 20 percent of the population"), what its implications are, and so on. Pay attention to whether the logic with which the author connects interpretation with facts is sound. You may find that the information is valuable but the interpretation is not. Perhaps the author's conclusions are not justified. Could you offer a contrary explanation for the same facts? Does more information need to be gathered before firm conclusions can be drawn? Why?

Writing to Persuade

Writing is frequently intended to persuade—that is, to influence the reader's thinking. To make a persuasive case, the writer must begin with an assertion that is arguable, some statement about which reasonable people could disagree. Such an assertion, when it serves as the essential organizing principle of the article or book, is called a *thesis*. Here are two examples:

> Because they do not speak English, many children in this affluent land are being denied their fundamental right to equal educational opportunity.

> Bilingual education, which has been stridently promoted by a small group of activists with their own agenda, is detrimental to the very students it is supposed to serve.

Thesis statements such as these—and the subsequent assertions used to help support them—represent conclusions that authors have drawn as a result of researching and thinking about an issue. You go through the same process yourself when you write persuasive papers or critiques. And just as you are entitled to critically evaluate the assertions of authors you read, so your professors—and other students—are entitled to evaluate *your* assertions, whether they be encountered as written arguments or as comments made in class discussion.

Keep in mind that writers organize arguments by arranging evidence to support one conclusion and oppose (or dismiss) another. You can assess the validity of the argument and the conclusion by determining whether the author has (1) clearly defined key terms, (2) used information fairly, (3) argued logically and not fallaciously (see pages 49–54).

EXERCISE 2.1

Informative and Persuasive Thesis Statements

With a partner from your class, write one informative and one persuasive thesis statement for *three* of the following topics:

School prayer

Gun control

Sex education in schools

Grammar instruction in English class

Violent lyrics in music

Teaching computer skills in primary schools

Curfews in college dormitories

Course registration procedures

For example, for the topic *school prayer*, your informative thesis statement might read this way:

> Both advocates and opponents of school prayer frame their position as a matter of freedom.

Your persuasive thesis statement might be worded as follows:

> As long as schools don't dictate what kinds of prayers students should say, then school prayer should be allowed and even encouraged.

Don't worry about taking a position that you agree with or feel you could support. The exercise doesn't require that you write an essay at this point.

Evaluating Persuasive Writing

Read on pages 484–87 the argument "Too Much of a Good Thing," by Greg Crister, a recommendation to curtail the steep, recent rise in childhood obesity. We will illustrate our discussion on defining terms, using information fairly, and arguing logically by referring to Crister's argument. The example critique that follows these illustrations will be based on this same argument.

EXERCISE 2.2

Critical Reading Practice

Before continuing with the chapter's reading, look back at the Critical Reading for Summary box on page 6 of Chapter 1. Use each of the guidelines listed there to examine the essay by Greg Crister on pages 484–87. Note in the margins of the selection, or on a separate sheet of paper, the essay's main point, subpoints, and use of examples.

Persuasive Strategies

Clearly Defined Terms. The validity of an argument depends to some degree on how carefully an author has defined key terms. Take the assertion, for example, that American society must be grounded in "family values." Just what do people who use this phrase mean by it? The validity of their argument depends on whether they and their readers agree on a definition of "family values"—as well as what it means to be "grounded in" family values. If an author writes that in the recent past, "America's elites accepted as a matter of course that a free society can sustain itself only through virtue and temperance in the people" (Charles Murray, "The Coming White Underclass," *Wall Street Journal,* 20 Oct. 1993), readers need to know what, exactly, the author means by "elites" and by "virtue and temperance" before they can assess the validity of the argument. In such cases, the success of the argument—its ability to persuade—hinges on the definition of a term. So, in responding to an argument, be sure you (and the author) are clear on what exactly is being argued. Only then can you respond to the logic of the argument, to the author's use of evidence, and to the author's conclusions.

Crister supports his argument for launching a campaign to end overconsumption by stating that efforts to stigmatize "unhealthful behaviors . . . conform with what we know about effective health messages." While Crister does provide examples of what he considers "effective health messages," his definition of *effective* is open to debate. By what measures have "the campaign against unsafe sex and the campaign against smoking" been effective? The reader might well point to level HIV infection rates in the United States and continuing billion-dollar profits by tobacco companies and challenge Crister's definition of *effective*.

Fair Use of Information. Information is used as evidence in support of arguments. When you encounter such evidence, ask yourself two questions: (1) Is the information accurate and up-to-date? At least a portion of an argument becomes invalid if the information used to support it is inaccurate or out-of-date. (2) Has the author cited *representative* information? The evidence used in an argument must be presented in a spirit of fair play. An author is less than ethical who presents only evidence favoring his views when he is well aware that contrary evidence exists. For instance, it would be dishonest to argue that an economic recession is imminent and to cite only indicators of economic downturn while ignoring and failing to cite contrary (positive) evidence.

Crister uses the information he cites fairly and accurately: He presents statistics in paragraph 2 on the rise of childhood obesity; he refers to a published study in paragraph 6 to refute the assertion that "kids know when they are full"; and he cites studies again in paragraphs 8 and 9. However, Crister chooses not to use, let alone mention, other information that bears on the topic of weight gain. For example, he argues that we should create an antiobesity campaign that stigmatizes the behavior of those who lack the willpower to stop eating. The assumption: A lack of willpower is the primary reason people are obese. Whether or not this view is correct, a great deal of information (scientific studies included) suggests that other causes may be implicated in obesity. By not raising the possibility that genes or hormones, for instance, might play a role, information about which Crister is undoubtedly aware, he fails to present full and representative information on his chosen topic. True, the op-ed piece is a brief form, leaving not much room to develop an argument. Still, Crister leaves the impression that he has cited the most pertinent information on combating obesity when, in fact, he has disregarded a great deal of information.

Logical Argumentation: Avoiding Logical Fallacies

At some point, you will need to respond to the logic of the argument itself. To be convincing, an argument should be governed by principles of *logic*—clear and orderly thinking. This does *not* mean that an argument should not be biased. A biased argument—that is, an argument weighted toward one point of view and against others, which is in fact the nature of argument—may be valid as long as it is logically sound.

Several examples of faulty thinking and logical fallacies to watch for follow.

Emotionally Loaded Terms. Writers sometimes attempt to sway readers by using emotionally charged words—words with positive connotations to sway readers to their own point of view (e.g., "family values") or words with negative connotations to sway readers away from the opposing point of view. The fact that an author uses emotionally loaded terms does not necessarily invalidate the argument. Emotional appeals are perfectly legitimate and time-honored modes of persuasion. But in academic writing, which is grounded in logical argumentation, they should not be the *only* means of persuasion. You should be sensitive to *how* emotionally loaded terms are being used. In particular, are they being used deceptively or to hide the essential facts?

Crister's use of the word *gluttony* inserts an emotionally charged, moralizing tone into his argument. Gluttony is one of the "seven deadly sins" that, for centuries, people have been warned against committing, so destructive are they of character. Crister takes pains to say that he is no moralist ("no one should be stigmatized for being overweight"), but that claim is made false by his introduction of a "sin" into a discussion about public health. Crister operates with a value judgment that he does not fully want to own. Critical readers might legitimately object to the notion that overeating is a "sin" that ought to be stigmatized.

***Ad Hominem* Argument.** In an *ad hominem* argument, the writer rejects opposing views by attacking the person who holds them. By calling opponents names, an author avoids the issue. Consider this excerpt from a political speech:

> I could more easily accept my opponent's plan to increase revenues by collecting on delinquent tax bills if he had paid more than a hundred dollars in state taxes in each of the past three years. But the fact is, he's a millionaire with a millionaire's tax shelters. This man hasn't paid a wooden nickel for the state services he and his family depend on. So I ask you: Is *he* the one to be talking about taxes to *us*?

It could well be that the opponent has paid virtually no state taxes for three years; but this fact has nothing to do with, and is a ploy to divert attention from, the merits of a specific proposal for increasing revenues. The proposal is lost in the attack against the man himself, an attack that violates the principles of logic. Writers (and speakers) must make their points by citing evidence in support of their views and by challenging contrary evidence.

Faulty Cause and Effect. The fact that one event precedes another in time does not mean that the first event has caused the second. An example: Fish begin dying by the thousands in a lake near your hometown. An environmental group immediately cites chemical dumping by several manufacturing plants as the cause. But other causes are possible: A disease might have affected the fish; the growth of algae might have contributed to the deaths; or acid rain might be a factor. The origins of an event are usually complex and are not always traceable to a single cause. So you must carefully examine cause-and-effect reasoning when you find a writer using it. In Latin, this fallacy is known as *post hoc, ergo propter hoc* ("after this, therefore because of this").

> ## TONE
>
> Tone refers to the overall emotional effect produced by the writer's choice of language. Writers might use especially emphatic words to create a tone: A film reviewer might refer to a "magnificent performance" or a columnist might criticize "sleazeball politics."
>
> These are extreme examples of tone; but tone can be more subtle, particularly if the writer makes a special effort *not* to inject emotion into the writing. As we've indicated above in the section on emotionally loaded terms, the fact that a writer's tone is highly emotional does not necessarily mean that the writer's argument is invalid. Conversely, a neutral tone does not ensure an argument's validity.
>
> Note that many instructors discourage student writing that projects a highly emotional tone, considering it inappropriate for academic or preprofessional work. (One sure sign of emotion: the exclamation mark, which should be used sparingly.)

Crister claims in this argument that dietary restraint will help reduce childhood obesity. Readers familiar with the literature on obesity know that a debate exists concerning the causes of the condition. For instance, some obese people may eat as little as their thin friends do but still lose no weight. For them, it is clear, lack of willpower does not contribute to their weight problems. Genes and body chemistry may play causal roles, but Crister mentions no causes other than lack of willpower. Asserting that one cause leads to an effect—or failing to assert that multiple causes do—gives readers the right to question the logic of an argument.

Either/Or Reasoning. Either/or reasoning also results from an unwillingness to recognize complexity. If an author analyzes a problem and offers only two courses of action, one of which he or she refutes, then you are entitled to object that the other is not thereby true. Usually, several other options (at the very least) are possible. For whatever reason, the author has chosen to overlook them. As an example, suppose you are reading a selection on genetic engineering and the author builds an argument on the basis of the following:

> Research in gene splicing is at a crossroads: Either scientists will be carefully monitored by civil authorities and their efforts limited to acceptable applications, such as disease control; or, lacking regulatory guidelines, scientists will set their own ethical standards and begin programs in embryonic manipulation that, however well intended, exceed the proper limits of human knowledge.

Certainly, other possibilities for genetic engineering exist beyond the two mentioned here. But the author limits debate by establishing an either/or choice. Such limitation is artificial and does not allow for complexity. As a critical reader, be on the alert for either/or reasoning.

Hasty Generalization. Writers are guilty of hasty generalization when they draw their conclusions from too little evidence or from unrepresentative evidence. To argue that scientists should not proceed with the human genome project because a recent editorial urged that the project be abandoned is to make a hasty generalization. This lone editorial may be unrepresentative of the views of most individuals—both scientists and laypeople—who have studied and written about the matter. To argue that one should never obey authority because Stanley Milgram's Yale University experiments in the 1960s show the dangers of obedience is to ignore the fact that Milgram's experiment was concerned primarily with obedience to *immoral* authority. Thus, the experimental situation was unrepresentative of most routine demands for obedience—for example, to obey a parental rule or to comply with a summons for jury duty—and a conclusion about the malevolence of all authority would be a hasty generalization.

False Analogy. Comparing one person, event, or issue to another may be illuminating, but it may also be confusing or misleading. Differences between the two may be more significant than the similarities, and conclusions drawn from one may not necessarily apply to the other. A writer who argues that it is reasonable to quarantine people with AIDS because quarantine has been effective in preventing the spread of smallpox is assuming an analogy between AIDS and smallpox that (because of the differences between the two diseases) is not valid.

A false analogy can also be found in Crister's comparison between a proposed campaign to stigmatize obesity and "highly effective" campaigns that stigmatize unsafe sex and smoking (paragraph 4), which suggests that obesity is fundamentally similar to unsafe sex and smoking. Crister assumes that all three damaging behaviors have similar causes (i.e., lack of self-restraint) that can be addressed using similar means (campaigns to stigmatize). But if the analogy between obesity and smoking or unsafe sex breaks down because we find that their causes differ (and research is far from conclusive on the matter), then readers have no reason to agree with Crister that campaigns that reduce smoking and unsafe sex will help to reduce obesity.

Begging the Question. To beg the question is to assume as a proven fact the very thesis being argued. To assert, for example, that America is not in decline because it is as strong and prosperous as ever is not to prove anything: It is merely to repeat the claim in different words. This fallacy is also known as *circular reasoning*.

In one sense, when Crister advocates restraint to lower the incidence of obesity, he is doing an admirable job. He raises and rebuts two arguments against urging restraint on those who weigh too much (in paragraphs 3–7) and then argues directly that restraint is a successful strategy in combating obesity (in paragraphs 8–9). But Crister also assumes that lack of restraint alone is primarily the cause of obesity. Given the volume of compelling evidence (which he does not mention) that genes and other factors may play a role in weight gain, he would do well to argue—and not assume—that lack of restraint is a primary reason people gain weight. But he assumes the validity of this important point instead of proving it. He also assumes the validity of two lesser points: (1) that the campaigns against unsafe sex and smoking have been effective; and (2) that obesity is a condition comparable to unsafe sex and smoking and, thus, a condition that would benefit from campaigns to stigmatize unhealthy behaviors.

Non Sequitur. *Non sequitur* is Latin for "it does not follow"; the term is used to describe a conclusion that does not logically follow from a premise. "Since minorities have made such great strides in the past few decades," a writer may argue, "we no longer need affirmative action programs." Aside from the fact that the premise itself is arguable (*have* minorities made such great strides?), it does not follow that because minorities *may* have made great strides, there is no further need for affirmative action programs.

Oversimplification. Be alert for writers who offer easy solutions to complicated problems. "America's economy will be strong again if we all 'buy American,'" a politician may argue. But the problems of America's economy are complex and cannot be solved by a slogan or a simple change in buying habits. Likewise, a writer who argues that we should ban genetic engineering assumes that simple solutions ("just say 'no'") will be sufficient to deal with the complex moral dilemmas raised by this new technology.

For example, Crister does consider how causes other than lack of willpower may contribute to obesity. This is not to say that a lack of restraint plays no valid or even major role in weight gain. People can and should learn to say "no" to supersized fries. But to the extent Crister does not acknowledge other causes of obesity, he leaves himself open to the charge of oversimplification. His proposed "campaign against over-consumption" is one solution. It will not alone solve the obesity problem.

EXERCISE 2.3

Understanding Logical Fallacies

Make a list of the nine logical fallacies discussed in the last section. Briefly define each one in your own words. Then, in a group of three or four classmates, refer to your definitions and the examples we've provided for each logical fallacy. Collaborate with your group to find or invent examples for each of the fallacies. Compare your examples with those generated by the other groups in your class.

Writing to Entertain

Authors write not only to inform and persuade but also to entertain. One response to entertainment is a hearty laugh, but it is possible to entertain without laughter: A good book or play or poem may prompt you to reflect, grow wistful, become elated, get angry. Laughter is only one of many possible reactions. As with a response to an informative piece or an argument, your response to an essay, poem, story, play, novel, or film should be precisely stated and carefully developed. Ask yourself some of the following questions (you won't have space to explore all of them, but try to consider some of the most important): Did I care for the portrayal of a certain character? Did that character (or a group of characters united by occupation, age, ethnicity, etc.) seem overly sentimental, for example, or heroic? Did his adversaries seem too villainous or stupid? Were the situations believable? Was the action interesting or merely formulaic? Was the theme developed subtly or powerfully, or did the work come across as preachy or shrill? Did the action at the end of the work follow plausibly from what had come before? Was the language fresh and incisive or stale and predictable? Explain as specifically as possible what elements of the work seemed effective or ineffective and why. Offer an overall assessment, elaborating on your views.

Question Category 2: To What Extent Do You Agree or Disagree with the Author?

When formulating a critical response to a source, try to distinguish your evaluation of the author's purpose and success at achieving that purpose from your agreement or disagreement with the author's views. The distinction allows you to respond to a piece of writing on its merits. As an unbiased, evenhanded critic, you evaluate an author's clarity of presentation, use of evidence, and adherence to principles of logic. To what extent has the author succeeded in achieving his or her purpose? Still withholding judgment, offer your assessment and give the author (in effect) a grade. Significantly, your assessment of the presentation may not coincide with your views of the author's conclusions: You may agree with an author entirely but feel that the presentation is superficial; you may find the author's logic and use of evidence to be rock solid but at the same time may resist certain conclusions. A critical evaluation works well when it is conducted in two parts. After evaluating the author's purpose and design for achieving that purpose, respond to the author's main assertions. In doing so, you'll want to identify points of agreement and disagreement and also evaluate assumptions.

Identify Points of Agreement and Disagreement

Be precise in identifying points of agreement and disagreement with an author. You should state as clearly as possible what *you* believe, and an effective way of doing this is to define your position in relation to that presented in the piece. Whether you agree enthusiastically, disagree, or agree with reservations, you can organize your reactions in two parts: (1) summarize the author's position; and (2) state your own position and elaborate on your reasons for holding it. The elaboration, in effect, becomes an argument itself, and this is true regardless of the position you take. An opinion is effective when you support it by supplying evidence. Without such evidence, opinions cannot be authoritative. "I thought the article on inflation was lousy." Why?

"I just thought so, that's all." This opinion is worthless because the criticism is imprecise: The critic has taken neither the time to read the article carefully nor the time to explore his or her own reactions carefully.

EXERCISE 2.4

Exploring Your Viewpoints—in Three Paragraphs

Go to a Web site that presents short persuasive essays on current social issues, such as reason.com, opinion-pages.org, drudgereport.com, or Speakout.com. Or go to an Internet search engine and type in a social issue together with the word "articles," "editorials," or "opinion," and see what you find. Locate a selection on a topic of interest that takes a clear, argumentative position. Write one paragraph summarizing the author's key argument. Write two paragraphs articulating your agreement or disagreement with the author. (Devote each paragraph to a *single* point of agreement or disagreement.) Be sure to explain why you think or feel the way you do and, wherever possible, cite relevant evidence—from your reading, experience, or observation.

Explore the Reasons for Agreement and Disagreement: Evaluate Assumptions

One way of elaborating your reactions to a reading is to explore the underlying *reasons* for agreement and disagreement. Your reactions are based largely on assumptions that you hold and how these assumptions compare with the author's. An *assumption* is a fundamental statement about the world and its operations that you take to be true. A writer's assumptions may be explicitly stated; but just as often assumptions are implicit and you will have to "ferret them out"—that is, to infer them. Consider an example:

> *In vitro* fertilization and embryo transfer are brought about outside the bodies of the couple through actions of third parties whose competence and technical activity determine the success of the procedure. Such fertilization entrusts the life and identity of the embryo into the power of doctors and biologists and establishes the domination of technology over the origin and destiny of the human person. Such a relationship of domination is in itself contrary to the dignity and equality that must be common to parents and children.*

This paragraph is quoted from the February 1987 Vatican document on artificial procreation. Cardinal Joseph Ratzinger, principal author of the docu-

---

* From the Vatican document *Instruction on Respect for Human Life in Its Origin and on the Dignity of Procreation,* given at Rome, from the Congregation for the Doctrine of the Faith, 22 Feb. 1987, as presented in *Origins: N.C. Documentary Service* 16.40 (19 Mar. 1987): 707.

ment, makes an implicit assumption in this paragraph: No good can come of the domination of technology over conception. The use of technology to bring about conception is morally wrong. Yet thousands of childless couples, Roman Catholics included, have rejected this assumption in favor of its opposite: Conception technology is an aid to the barren couple; far from creating a relationship of unequals, the technology brings children into the world who will be welcomed with joy and love.

Assumptions provide the foundation on which entire presentations are built. If you find an author's assumptions invalid—that is, not supported by factual evidence—or if you disagree with value-based assumptions underlying an author's positions, you may well disagree with conclusions that follow from these assumptions. The author of a book on developing nations may include a section outlining the resources and time that will be required to industrialize a particular country and so upgrade its general welfare. Her assumption—that industrialization in that particular country will ensure or even affect the general welfare—may or may not be valid. If you do not share the assumption, in your eyes the rationale for the entire book may be undermined.

How do you determine the validity of assumptions once you have identified them? In the absence of more scientific criteria, you may determine validity by how well the author's assumptions stack up against your own experience, observations, reading, and values. A caution, however: The overall value of an article or book may depend only to a small degree on the validity of the author's assumptions. For instance, a sociologist may do a fine job of gathering statistical data about the incidence of crime in urban areas along the eastern seaboard. The sociologist also might be a Marxist, and you may disagree with the subsequent analysis of the data. Yet you may still find the data extremely valuable for your own work.

Readers will want to examine two assumptions at the heart of Crister's proposal to launch a campaign against overeating. The first is that lack of willpower alone causes, or primarily causes, obesity. While Crister does not directly assert this cause-and-effect relationship, he implies it by failing to mention other possible causes of obesity. If, for instance, genes or hormones are involved in the weight gain of some people, then it seems cruel to argue that their lack of willpower is somehow responsible—that if only they "tried harder" they could shed those unwanted pounds. Readers may also want to examine another of Crister's assumptions, that a moralizing tone is appropriate to a discussion of public health. Readers might take a different view, based on a very different assumption: that in combating problems in public health, we must deal with behaviors, not with attitudes and values associated with behaviors. Thus, in campaigns to reduce HIV infections, we would not speak of "sin" (as "gluttony" is a sin) but would instead focus strictly on reducing behaviors that spread infection. Readers are entitled to meet each of an author's assumptions with assumptions of their own; to evaluate the validity of those assumptions; and to begin formulating a critique, based on their agreement or disagreement.

CRITIQUE

In Chapter 1 we focused on summary—the condensed presentation of ideas from another source. Summary is key to much of academic writing because it relies so heavily on the works of others for support of claims. It's not going too far to say that summarizing is the critical thinking skill from which a majority of academic writing builds. However, most academic thinking and writing do not stop at summary; usually we use summary to restate our understanding of things we see or read. Then we put that summary to use. In academic writing, one typical use of summary is as a prelude to *critique*—a *formalized, critical reading of a passage.* It also is a personal response, but writing a critique is considerably more rigorous than saying that a movie is "great," or a book is "fascinating," or "I didn't like it." These are all responses, and, as such, they're a valid, even essential, part of your understanding of what you see and read. But such responses don't illuminate the subject for anyone—even you—if you haven't explained how you arrived at your conclusions.

Your task in writing a critique is to turn your critical reading of a passage into a systematic evaluation in order to deepen your reader's (and your own) understanding of that passage. Among other things, you're interested in determining what an author says, how well the points are made, what assumptions underlie the argument, what issues are overlooked, and what implications can be drawn from such an analysis. Critiques, positive or negative, should include a fair and accurate summary of the passage; they should also include a statement of your own assumptions. It is important to remember that you bring to bear an entire set of assumptions about the world. Stated or not, these assumptions underlie every evaluative comment you make; you therefore have an obligation, both to the reader and to yourself, to clarify your standards by making your assumptions explicit. Not only do your readers stand to gain by your forthrightness, but you do as well: In the process of writing a critical assessment, you are forced to examine your own knowledge, beliefs, and assumptions. Ultimately, the critique is a way of learning about yourself—yet another example of the ways in which writing is useful as a tool for critical thinking.

How to Write Critiques

You may find it useful to organize your critiques in five sections: (1) introduction, (2) summary, (3) assessment of the presentation (on its own terms), (4) your response to the presentation, and (5) conclusion.

The box opposite offers some guidelines for writing critiques. Note that they are guidelines, not a rigid formula. Thousands of authors write critiques that do not follow the structure outlined here. Until you are more confident and practiced in writing critiques, however, we suggest you follow these guidelines. They are meant not to restrict you, but rather to provide a workable sequence for writing critiques.

| **GUIDELINES FOR WRITING CRITIQUES** |

- *Introduce.* Introduce both the passage under analysis and the author. State the author's main argument and the point(s) you intend to make about it.

  Provide background material to help your readers understand the relevance or appeal of the passage. This background material might include one or more of the following: an explanation of why the subject is of current interest; a reference to a possible controversy surrounding the subject of the passage or the passage itself; biographical information about the author; an account of the circumstances under which the passage was written; or a reference to the intended audience of the passage.
- *Summarize.* Summarize the author's main points, making sure to state the author's purpose for writing.
- *Assess the presentation.* Evaluate the validity of the author's presentation, as distinct from your points of agreement or disagreement. Comment on the author's success in achieving his or her purpose by reviewing three or four specific points. You might base your review on one (or more) of the following criteria:

  Is the information accurate?

  Is the information significant?

  Has the author defined terms clearly?

  Has the author used and interpreted information fairly?

  Has the author argued logically?

- *Respond to the presentation.* Now it is your turn to respond to the author's views. With which views do you agree? With which do you disagree? Discuss your reasons for agreement and disagreement, when possible, tying these reasons to assumptions—both the author's and your own.
- *Conclude.* State your conclusions about the overall validity of the piece—your assessment of the author's success at achieving his or her aims and your reactions to the author's views. Remind the reader of the weaknesses and strengths of the passage.

DEMONSTRATION: CRITIQUE

The critique that follows is based on Greg Crister's "Too Much of a Good Thing," which appeared in the *Los Angeles Times* as an op-ed piece on July 22, 2001 (see pages 484–87) and which we have to some extent already begun to examine. In this formal critique, you will see that it is possible to agree with an author's main point or proposal, at least provisionally, but disagree with his or her method of demonstration, or argument. Critiquing a different selection, you could just as easily accept the author's facts and figures but reject the conclusion he or she draws from them. As long as you carefully articulate the author's assumptions and your own, explaining in some detail your agreement and disagreement, the critique is yours to take in whatever direction you see fit.

Let's summarize the preceding sections by returning to the core questions that guide critical reading. You will see how, when applied to Crister's argument, they help to set up a critique.

What Is the Author's Purpose in Writing?

As is the case with most editorials, Greg Crister's "Too Much of a Good Thing" is an argument. He wants readers to accept his proposal for resolving the obesity epidemic among children. Parents, Crister argues, should supervise what and how much their kids eat. Those who learn lessons of dietary restraint early on can avoid weight problems later in life.

Does the Author Succeed in This Purpose?

Crister takes a behavioral approach to the problem of obesity. To the extent that obesity is caused by undisciplined eating habits, his proposal is logical and convincing. But other studies show that not all causes of obesity are rooted in poor eating habits. Genetic makeup and hormone imbalances may also be at work. Crister makes no mention of these, and his analysis and proposed solution therefore seem limited. In addition, he adopts an antifat, judgmental tone in the essay that will likely offend people who are trying to lose weight. In sum, Crister is only partially successful in his argument.

To What Extent Do You Agree or Disagree with the Author?

Because Crister's analysis and proposed solution are based on the assumption that obesity has a single cause (poor eating habits), he opens himself to the objection that he has oversimplified the problem. Still, common sense suggests that overweight and obese people do contribute to their conditions by making unhealthy dietary choices. So Crister's suggestion that we teach children to eat moderately before they become obese is worth supporting— provided care is taken to acknowledge the nonbehavioral causes of obesity. Crister's moralistic tone gets in the way of an otherwise reasonable (if limited) argument. Of course, we might object to his tone but continue to find merit in his proposal.

The selections you will be likely to critique are those, like Crister's, that argue a specific position. Indeed, every argument you read is an invitation to agreement or disagreement. It remains only for you to speak up and justify your position.

*Model Critique**

A Critique of Greg Crister's
"Too Much of a Good Thing"

1   Citing statistics on the alarming increase in the
rates of childhood obesity, especially in the industrialized West, Greg Crister (<u>L.A. Times</u> Op-Ed, 22
July 2001) argues that parents can help avert obesity
in their own homes by more closely supervising the
diets of their children, serving reasonably sized
portions, and limiting snacks. Crister, who has
extensively researched obesity in his book <u>Fat Land:
How Americans Became the Fattest People in the World</u>
(Houghton Mifflin 2003), argues that through education we can create a leaner cultural norm, much as
the French did earlier in the century when faced with
a similar problem.

2   The stakes for maintaining a healthy body weight
couldn't be higher. Fully one-quarter of American
children through the age of eighteen "are overweight
or obese"—an "epidemic," according to the United
States Surgeon General (485). Not only are obese
individuals at increased risk for a wide range of
medical problems, but the nation as a whole will
absorb enormous costs for their obesity, "eventually
mak[ing] the battle against HIV/AIDS seem inexpensive" (485). Clearly we have good reason to fight the
rise of obesity, and Crister's suggestion that individual families become a battleground for that fight
makes perfect sense, as long as we realize that there
will be other battlegrounds (for example, the hospital, the pharmacy, and the genetics lab). We should
also take care that in "stigmatizing the unhealthful
behaviors that cause obesity" (485) we do not turn a
public health campaign into a moral crusade.

3   It takes no advanced degree in nutrition to
accept the claim that children (indeed, all of us)
should learn to eat in moderation. Apparently,
before the age of five the lesson isn't even needed.
Younger children, entirely on their own, will limit
how much food they eat at a meal regardless of the
amounts served. By five, however, they will eat
whatever is put before them. In a culture of the

---

* References to Crister are to his article as reprinted in *Writing and Reading Across the Curriculum.*

"supersized," high-fat, sugar-loaded, fast-food meal, such lack of restraint can lead to obesity. If we can teach children before their fifth birthday what counts as a reasonable portion, they might learn—for life—to eat in moderation. Crister cites other research to show that simple and yet profound dietary lessons, learned early, can make all the difference in averting a life spent battling the scale. He wisely gives parents an important role in teaching these lessons because parents, after all, teach all sorts of lessons. However, with statistics showing that roughly half of the adult population in this country is overweight or obese, Crister may want to urge parents to learn lessons about moderation themselves before attempting to become teachers for their children.

4   Crister's plan for combating the rise of childhood obesity through education is certainly reasonable, as far as it goes. But he focuses almost exclusively on behavioral factors when scientists have discovered that obesity has other, nonbehavioral causes (Gibbs). In labs across the world, researchers are identifying genes and hormones that influence weight gain. No one fully understands all the mechanisms by which overweight people, who may eat as little as their skinnier counterparts, gain or shed pounds. But it is clear that being fat is not simply about lacking willpower—that is, about "unhealthful behaviors" (485)—around food. Thus, we should not expect Crister's approach of teaching dietary moderation to work in every case. For many people, solutions to weight gain will be found both in new dietary behaviors and in medicines that come from labs where researchers study how the body burns and stores fat. To the extent that obesity is the result of a child's inability to say "no" to a supersized meal, we should teach restraint just as Crister advises. But his behavioral fix will not work for everyone, and parents should be instructed on what to do when teaching restraint alone fails to keep their children reasonably trim.

5   A more serious problem with Crister's argument is his use (twice) of the word "gluttony" and the judgmental attitude it implies. Early in the essay Crister argues that American parents need "to promulgate . . . dietary restraint, something our ancestors

knew simply as avoiding gluttony" (485). Gluttony was
one of the seven deadly sins (along with pride,
greed, envy, anger, lust, and sloth), which Christian
theologians have been denouncing for nearly 1,500
years (University) to little effect. While Crister
insists that "no one should be stigmatized for being
overweight," he advocates "stigmatizing the unhealthful behaviors that cause obesity" (485), assuming
that people distinguish between the sin and the
sinner. In practice, people rarely do. Crister does
little to distance himself from anti-fat bias after
introducing the bias-heavy term "gluttony" into the
essay—which is a mistake: The overweight and obese
have a hard enough time losing weight. They should
not have to suffer the judgments of those who suggest
"that thinness signals self-discipline and self-
respect, whereas fatness signals self-contempt and
lack of resolve" (Worley).

6   Given a proposal that is otherwise so sensible,
Crister doesn't need to complicate matters by inviting moral judgments. He is at his most convincing
when he makes a straightforward recommendation to
change the behavior of children based on sound scientific research. Effective dietary strategies can be
taught, and parents are the best teachers in this
case as long as they realize that teaching restraint
will be only one of several approaches and that judgments equating thinness with virtue should have no
place in our efforts. We face a difficult challenge
in meeting the growing problem of childhood obesity,
and for the most part Greg Crister suggests a reasonable and workable place to begin.

Works Cited

Crister, Greg. "Too Much of a Good Thing." Editorial. <u>Los Angeles
Times</u> 22 July 2001: B12

Gibbs, W. Wayt. "Gaining on Fat." <u>Scientific American</u> Aug. 1996:
46–52.

University of Leicester History of Art Department. "Seven Deadly
Sins." University of Leicester Web site 20 Dec. 2001. 2 Aug.
2002 <http://www.le.ac.uk/arthistory/seedcorn/faq-sds.html>.

Worley, Mary. "Fat and Happy: In Defense of Fat Acceptance."
National Association to Advance Fat Acceptance 22 Aug. 2002
<http://www.naafa.org>.

CRITICAL READING FOR CRITIQUE

- *Use the tips from Critical Reading for Summary on page 6:* Remember to examine the context; note the title and subtitle; identify the main point; identify the subpoints; break the reading into sections; distinguish between points, examples, and counterarguments; watch for transitions within and between paragraphs; and read actively.
- *Establish the writer's primary purpose in writing:* Is the piece primarily meant to inform, persuade, or entertain?
- *Evaluate informative writing. Use these criteria (among others):*

  Accuracy of information

  Significance of information

  Fair interpretation of information

- *Evaluate persuasive writing. Use these criteria (among others):*

  Clear definition of terms

  Fair use and interpretation of information

  Logical reasoning

- *Evaluate writing that entertains. Use these criteria (among others):*

  Interesting characters

  Believable action, plot, and situations

  Communication of theme

  Use of language

- *Decide whether you agree or disagree with the writer's ideas, position, or message:* Once you have determined the extent to which an author has achieved his or her purpose, clarify your position in relation to the writer's.

EXERCISE 2.5

Informal Critique of Sample Essay

Before reading the discussion of this model critique, write your own informal response to the critique. What are its strengths and weaknesses? To what extent does the critique follow the general guidelines for writing critiques that we outlined on page 59? To the extent it varies from the guidelines, speculate on why. Jot down some ideas for a critique that take a different approach to Crister's essay.

Discussion

- Paragraph 1 of the model critique introduces the selection to be reviewed, along with the author, and summarizes the author's main claim.

- Paragraph 2 provides brief background information. It sets a context that explains why the topic of obesity is important. The paragraph ends with the writer's thesis, offering qualified support for the proposal that parents should teach children to eat moderately.
- Paragraph 3 summarizes the argument of Crister's editorial. Note that the topic sentence expresses approval of the editorial's main (argumentative) thesis: Children should learn to eat in moderation.
- Paragraph 4 raises the first objection to Crister's argument, that he misrepresents the complexity of obesity by discussing only behavioral causes and solutions. The paragraph expresses qualified support for his position, but suggests that other, nonbehavioral ways of viewing the problem and other, nonbehavioral solutions should be explored.
- Paragraph 5 raises a significant disagreement with Crister's moralistic tone. The paragraph lays out the ways in which Crister is inappropriately judgmental.
- Paragraph 6, the conclusion, summarizes the overall position of the critique—to accept Crister's basic recommendation that parents teach dietary restraint to children, but to reject the moral judgments that make obese people feel inadequate.

Practice Critique

Select either of the following articles in Part II of this book:

"The Genocidal Killer in the Mirror," Crispin Sartwell (pages 362–63)

"Fat and Happy: A Defense of Fat Acceptance," Mary Ray Worley (pages 492–96)

Write a critique of the selected article, following the directions in this chapter for determining the author's purpose in writing the piece and for assessing the author's success in achieving that purpose.

For a somewhat more challenging assignment, try writing a critique of one of the following articles:

"Disobedience as a Psychological and Moral Problem," Erich Fromm (pages 356–61)

"'Cinderella': A Story of Sibling Rivalry and Oedipal Conflicts," Bruno Bettelheim, (pages 588–94)

Before writing your critique, consider the earlier discussions of evaluating writing in this chapter. Examine the author's use of information and persuasive strategies. Review the logical fallacies and identify any of these in the selection you've chosen to critique. First work out your ideas informally, perhaps producing a working outline. Then write a rough draft of your critique. Review the article—the subject of your critique—and revise your rough draft at least once before considering it finished.

3 Introductions, Theses, and Conclusions

WRITING INTRODUCTIONS

All writers, no matter how much they prepare, eventually have to face the question of writing an introduction. How to start? What's the best way to approach the subject? With high seriousness, a light touch, an anecdote? How best to engage the reader? Many writers avoid such agonizing choices by putting them off—productively. Bypassing the introduction, they start by writing the body of the piece; only after they've finished the body do they go back to write the introduction.

There's a lot to be said for this approach. Because you have presumably spent more time thinking and writing about the topic itself than about how you're going to introduce it, you are in a better position to begin directly with your presentation. And often, it's not until you've actually seen the piece on paper or screen and read it over once or twice that a natural way of introducing it becomes apparent. Even if there is no natural way to begin, you are generally in better psychological shape to write the introduction after the major task of writing is behind you and you know exactly what you're leading up to.

Perhaps, however, you can't operate this way. After all, you have to start writing *somewhere*, and if you have evaded the problem by skipping the introduction, that blank page may loom just as large whenever you do choose to begin. If this is the case, then go ahead and write an introduction, knowing full well that it's probably going to be flat and awful. Write whatever comes to mind, as long as you have a working thesis. Assure yourself that whatever you put down at this point (except for the thesis) "won't count" and that when the time is right, you'll go back and replace it with something that's fit for eyes other than yours. But in the meantime, you'll have gotten started.

The *purpose* of an introduction is to prepare the reader to enter the world of your paper. The introduction makes the connection between the more familiar world inhabited by the reader and the less familiar world of the writer's particular subject; it places a discussion in a context that the reader can understand.

You have many ways to provide such a context. We'll consider just a few of the most common.

Quotation

Here is an introduction to a paper on democracy:

"Two cheers for democracy" was E. M. Forster's not-quite-whole-hearted judgment. Most Americans would not agree. To them, our democracy is one of the glories of civilization. To one American in particular, E. B. White, democracy is "the hole in the stuffed shirt through which the sawdust slowly trickles . . . the dent in the high hat . . . the recurrent suspicion that more than half of the people are right more than half of the time" (915). American democracy is based on the oldest continuously operating written constitution in the world—a most impressive fact and a testament to the farsightedness of the founding fathers. But just how farsighted can mere humans be? In *Future Shock,* Alvin Toffler quotes economist Kenneth Boulding on the incredible acceleration of social change in our time: "The world of today . . . is as different from the world in which I was born as that world was from Julius Caesar's" (13). As we move into the twenty-first century, it seems legitimate to question the continued effectiveness of a governmental system that was devised in the eighteenth century; and it seems equally legitimate to consider alternatives.

The quotations by Forster and White help set the stage for the discussion of democracy by presenting the reader with some provocative and well-phrased remarks. Later in the paragraph, the quotation by Boulding more specifically prepares us for the theme of change that will be central to the paper as a whole.

Historical Review

In many cases, the reader will be unprepared to follow the issue you discuss unless you provide some historical background. Consider the following introduction to a paper on the film-rating system:

Sex and violence on the screen are not new issues. In the Roaring Twenties there was increasing pressure from civic and religious groups to ban depictions of "immorality" from the screen. Faced with the threat of federal censorship, the film producers decided to clean their own house. In 1930, the Motion Picture Producers and Distributors of America established the Production Code. At first, adherence to the Code was voluntary; but in 1934 Joseph Breen, newly appointed head of the MPPDA, gave the Code teeth. Henceforth all newly produced films had to be submitted for approval to the Production Code Administration, which had the power to award or withhold the Code seal. Without a Code seal, it was virtually impossible for a film to be shown anywhere in the United States, since exhibitors would not accept it. At about the same time, the Catholic Legion of Decency was formed to advise the faithful which films were and were not objectionable. For several decades the Production Code Administration exercised powerful control over what was portrayed in American theatrical films. By the 1960s, however, changing standards of morality had considerably weakened the Code's grip. In 1968, the Production

Code was replaced with a rating system designed to keep younger audiences away from films with high levels of sex or violence. Despite its imperfections, this rating system has proved more beneficial to American films than did the old censorship system.

The paper following this introduction concerns the relative benefits of the rating system. By providing some historical background on the rating system, the writer helps readers to understand his arguments. Notice the chronological development of details.

Review of a Controversy

A particular type of historical review is the review of a controversy or debate. Consider the following introduction:

> The *American Heritage Dictionary's* definition of civil disobedience is rather simple: "the refusal to obey civil laws that are regarded as unjust, usually by employing methods of passive resistance." However, despite such famous (and beloved) examples of civil disobedience as the movements of Mahatma Gandhi in India and the Reverend Martin Luther King, Jr., in the United States, the question of whether or not civil disobedience should be considered an asset to society is hardly clear cut. For instance, Hannah Arendt, in her article "Civil Disobedience," holds that "to think of disobedient minorities as rebels and truants is against the letter and spirit of a constitution whose framers were especially sensitive to the dangers of unbridled majority rule." On the other hand, a noted lawyer, Lewis Van Dusen, Jr., in his article "Civil Disobedience: Destroyer of Democracy," states that "civil disobedience, whatever the ethical rationalization, is still an assault on our democratic society, an affront to our legal order and an attack on our constitutional government." These two views are clearly incompatible. I believe, though, that Van Dusen's is the more convincing. On balance, civil disobedience is dangerous to society.*

The negative aspects of civil disobedience, rather than Van Dusen's article, are the topic of this paper. But to introduce this topic, the writer has provided quotations that represent opposing sides of the controversy over civil disobedience, as well as brief references to two controversial practitioners. By focusing at the outset on the particular rather than the abstract aspects of the subject, the writer hoped to secure the attention of her readers and to involve them in the controversy that forms the subject of her paper.

---

* Michelle Jacques, "Civil Disobedience: Van Dusen vs. Arendt," unpublished paper, 1993: 1. Used by permission.

From the General to the Specific

Another way of providing a transition from the reader's world to the less familiar world of the paper is to work from a general subject to a specific one. The following introduction begins a paper on improving our air quality by inducing people to trade the use of their cars for public transportation.

> While generalizations are risky, it seems pretty safe to say that most human beings are selfish. Self-interest may be part of our nature, and probably aids the survival of our species, since self-interested pursuits increase the likelihood of individual survival and genetic reproduction. Ironically, however, our selfishness has caused us to abuse the natural environment upon which we depend. We have polluted, deforested, depleted, deformed, and endangered our earth, water, and air to such an extent that now our species' survival is gravely threatened. In America, air pollution is one of our most pressing environmental problems, and it is our selfish use of the automobile that poses the greatest threat to clean air, as well as the greatest challenge to efforts to stop air pollution. Very few of us seem willing to give up our cars, let alone use them less. We are spoiled by the individual freedom afforded us when we can hop into our gas-guzzling vehicles and go where we want, when we want. Somehow, we as a nation will have to wean ourselves from this addiction to the automobile, and we can do this by designing alternative forms of transportation that serve our selfish interests.*

From the Specific to the General: Anecdote, Illustration

The following paragraph quotes an anecdote in order to move from the specific to a general topic:

> In an article on the changing American family, Ron French tells the following story:

>> Six-year-old Sydney Papenheim has her future planned. "First I'm going to marry Jared," she told her mother. "Then I'm going to get divorced and marry Gabby." "No, honey," Lisa Boettcher says, "you don't plan it like that." That's news to Sydney. Her mother is divorced and remarried, as is her stepdad. Her grandparents are divorced and remarried, as are enough aunts and uncles to field a team for "Family Feud." She gets presents from her stepfather's ex-wife. Her stepfather's children sometimes play at the house of her father. "You never know what is going to happen from day to day," says Sydney's stepdad, Brian

---

* Travis Knight, "Reducing Air Pollution with Alternative Transportation," unpublished paper, 1998: 1. Used by permission.

> Boettcher. "It's an evolution." It's more like a revolution, from
> Norman Rockwell to Norman Lear.*
>
> French continues on to report that by the year 2007, blended fam-
> ilies such as the Boettchers will outnumber traditional nuclear fami-
> lies. Yet most people continue to lament this change. We as a nation
> need to accept this new reality: The "till death do us part" version
> of marriage no longer works.[†]

The previous introduction went from the general (the statement that human
beings are selfish) to the specific (how to decrease air pollution); this one goes
from the specific (one little girl's understanding of marriage and divorce) to
the general (the changing American family). The anecdote is one of the most
effective means at your disposal for capturing and holding your reader's
attention. Speakers have long begun their general remarks with a funny,
touching, or otherwise appropriate story; in fact, there are plenty of books that
are nothing but collections of such stories, arranged by subject.

Question

Frequently, you can provoke the reader's attention by posing a question or a
series of questions:

> Are gender roles learned or inherited? Scientific research has estab-
> lished the existence of biological differences between the sexes, but the
> effect of biology's influence on gender roles cannot be distinguished
> from society's influence. According to Michael Lewis of the Institute
> for the Study of Exceptional Children, "As early as you can show me a
> sex difference, I can show you the culture at work." Social processes,
> as well as biological differences, are responsible for the separate roles
> of men and women.[‡]

Opening your paper with a question can be provocative, since it places readers in an active role: They begin by considering answers. *Are* gender roles
learned? *Are* they inherited? In this active role, they are likely to continue
reading with interest.

---

* Norman Lear (b. 1922): American television writer and producer noted for developing ground-
breaking depictions of the American family in the 1970s, such as *All in the Family, Sanford and Son,*
and *Maude.* Ron French, "Family: The D-Word Loses Its Sting as Households Blend," *Detroit News*
1 Jan. 2000, 17 Aug. 2000 <http://detnews.com/specialreports/2000/journey/family/
family.htm>.

[†] Veronica Gonzalez, "New Family Formations," unpublished paper, 1999: 1. Used by permission.

[‡] Tammy Smith, "Are Sex Roles Learned or Inherited?" unpublished paper, 1994: 1. Used by
permission.

Statement of Thesis

Perhaps the most direct method of introduction is to begin immediately with the thesis:

> Every college generation is defined by the social events of its age. The momentous occurrences of an era—from war and economics to politics and inventions—give meaning to lives of the individuals who live through them. They also serve to knit those individuals together by creating a collective memory and a common historic or generational identity. In 1979, I went to 26 college and university campuses, selected to represent the diversity of American higher education, and asked students what social or political events most influenced their generation. I told them that the children who came of age in the decade after World War I might have answered the Great Depression. The bombing of Pearl Harbor, World War II, or perhaps the death of Franklin Roosevelt might have stood out for those born a few years later. For my generation, born after World War II, the key event was the assassination of John F. Kennedy. We remember where we were when we heard the news. The whole world seemingly changed in its aftermath.*

This paper begins with a general assertion: that large-scale social events shape generations of college students. The advantage of beginning with a general thesis like this is that it immediately establishes the broader context and the point illustrated by the paper's subsequent focus on contemporary college students.

Stating your thesis in the first sentence of an introduction also works when you make a controversial argument. Stating a provocative point right away, such as "Democracy is dead," for a paper examining the problems plaguing representative government in current society, forces the reader to sit up and take notice—perhaps even to begin protesting. This "hooks" a reader, who is likely to want to find out how your paper will support its strong thesis. In the example paragraph above, the general thesis is followed by specific examples of social events and their effects on college students, which prepares the reader to compare the experiences of current college students with those of earlier generations.

One final note about our model introductions: They may be longer than introductions you have been accustomed to writing. Many writers (and readers) prefer a shorter, snappier introduction. The length of an introduction can depend on the length of the paper it introduces, and it is also largely a matter of personal or corporate style: there is no rule concerning the correct length of an introduction. If you feel that a short introduction is appropriate, use one. You may wish to break up what seems like a long introduction into two paragraphs.

---

* Arthur Levine, "The Making of a Generation," *Change* Sept.–Oct. 1993: 8.

EXERCISE **3.1**

Drafting Introductions

Imagine that you are writing a paper using the topic, ideas, and thesis you developed in the earlier exercises in this book. Choose one of the seven types of introductions we've discussed—preferably one you have never used before—and draft an introduction that would work to open a paper on this topic. Use our examples as models to help you draft your practice introduction.

WRITING A THESIS

A thesis is a one-sentence (and sometimes a two-sentence) summary of a paper's content. It is similar, actually, to a paper's conclusion (see pages 81–88) but lacks the conclusion's concern for broad implications and significance. Your thesis will be the product of your thinking; it therefore represents *your* conclusion about the topic on which you're writing, and therefore you have to have spent some time thinking (inventing) in order to arrive at the thesis that begins your actual paper.

For a writer in the drafting stages, the thesis establishes a focus, a basis on which to include or exclude information. For the reader of a finished product, the thesis anticipates the author's discussion. *A thesis, therefore, is an essential tool for both writers and readers of academic material.*

The previous sentence is our thesis for this section. Based on this thesis, we, as the authors, have limited the content of the section; and you, as the reader, will be able to form certain expectations about the discussion that follows. You can expect a definition of a thesis; an enumeration of the uses of a thesis; and a discussion focused on academic material. As writers, we will have met our obligations to you only if in subsequent paragraphs we satisfy these expectations.

The Components of a Thesis

Like any other sentence, a thesis includes a subject and a predicate, which consists of an assertion about the subject. In the sentence "Lee and Grant were different kinds of generals," "Lee and Grant" is the subject and "were different kinds of generals" is the predicate. What distinguishes a thesis from any other sentence with a subject and predicate is that *the thesis presents the controlling idea of the paper.* The subject of a thesis must present the right balance between the general and the specific to allow for thorough discussion within the allotted length of the paper. The discussion might include definitions, details, comparisons, contrasts—whatever is needed to illuminate a subject and carry on an intelligent conversation. (If the sentence about Lee and Grant were a thesis, the reader would assume that the rest of the paper contained comparisons and contrasts between the two generals.)

Bear in mind when writing theses that the more general your subject and the more complex your assertion, the longer your paper will be. For instance, consider the following sentence as the thesis for a ten-page paper:

> Meaningful energy conservation requires a shrewd application of political, financial, and scientific will.

You could not write an effective ten-page paper based on this thesis. The topic alone would require pages merely to carefully define what is meant by "energy conservation" and then by "meaningful." Energy can be conserved in homes, vehicles, industries, appliances, and power plants, and each of these areas would need consideration. Having accomplished this task, you would then have to turn your attention to the claim, which entails a discussion of how politics, finance, and science individually and collectively influence energy conservation. Moreover, the thesis asks you to argue that "shrewd application" of politics, finance, and science is required. Although this thesis may very well be accurate and compelling, it promises entirely too much for a ten-page paper.

Limiting the Scope of the Thesis

To write an effective thesis and thus a controlled, effective paper, you need to limit your subject and your claims about it. There are two strategies for achieving a thesis of manageable proportions: (1) start with a working thesis (this strategy assumes that you are familiar with your topic) and (2) begin with a broad area of interest and narrow it (this strategy assumes that you are unfamiliar with your topic).

Starting with a Working Thesis

Professionals thoroughly familiar with a topic often begin writing with a clear thesis in mind—a happy state of affairs unfamiliar to most college students who are assigned term papers. But professionals usually have an important advantage over students: experience. Because professionals know their material, are familiar with the ways of approaching it, are aware of the questions important to practitioners, and have devoted considerable time to study of the topic, they are naturally in a strong position to begin writing a paper. In addition, many professionals are practiced at invention; the time they spend listing or outlining their ideas helps them work out their thesis statements. Not only do professionals have experience in their fields, but they also have a clear purpose in writing; they know their audience and are comfortable with the format of their papers.

Experience counts—there's no way around it. As a student, you are not yet an expert and therefore don't generally have the luxury of beginning your writing tasks with a definite thesis in mind. Once you choose and devote time to a major field of study, however, you will gain experience. In the meantime, you'll have to do more work than the professional to prepare yourself for writing a paper.

But let's assume that you *do* have an area of expertise, that you are in your own right a professional (albeit not in academic matters). We'll assume that you understand your nonacademic subject—say, backpacking—and have been given a clear purpose for writing: to discuss the relative merits of backpack designs. Your job is to write a recommendation for the owner of a sporting-goods chain, suggesting which line of backpacks the chain should carry. Because you already know a good deal about backpacks, you may already have some well-developed ideas on the topic before you start doing additional research.

Yet even as an expert in your field, you will find that beginning the writing task is a challenge, for at this point it is unlikely that you will be able to conceive a thesis perfectly suited to the contents of your paper. After all, a thesis is a summary, and it is difficult to summarize a presentation yet to be written—especially if you plan to discover what you want to say during the process of writing. Even if you know your material well, the best you can do at the early stages is to formulate a *working thesis*—a hypothesis of sorts, a well-informed hunch about your topic and the claim to be made about it. Once you have completed a draft, you can evaluate the degree to which your working thesis accurately summarizes the content of your paper. If the match is a good one, the working thesis becomes the thesis. If, however, sections of the paper drift from the focus set out in the working thesis, you'll need to revise the thesis and the paper itself to ensure that the presentation is unified. (You'll know that the match between the content and thesis is a good one when every paragraph directly refers to and develops some element of the thesis.)

This same model will work when you must venture into academic territory, such as government or medieval poetry. The difference is that when approaching topics that are less familiar to you than something like backpacking, you will have to spend more time gathering data and brainstorming. Such labor prepares you to make assertions about your subject.

Choosing and Narrowing a Topic

Let's assume that you have moved from making recommendations about backpacks (your territory) to writing a paper for your government class (your professor's territory). Whereas you were once the expert who knew enough about your subject to begin writing with a working thesis, you are now the student, inexperienced and in need of a great deal of information before you can begin to think of thesis statements. It may be a comfort to know that your government professor would likely be in the same predicament if asked to recommend backpack designs. She would need to spend at least a few weeks, backpacking to become as experienced as you; and it is fair to say that you will need to spend several hours in the library before you are in a position to choose a topic suitable for an undergraduate paper.

Suppose you have been assigned an open-ended, ten-page paper in an introductory course on environmental science. Not only do you have to choose a subject, but you also have to narrow it sufficiently and formulate

your thesis. Where will you begin? We take the unusual case of an essentially directionless assignment to demonstrate how you can use invention strategies to identify topics of interest and narrow the scope of your paper.
Typically, your assignments will provide more guidance than "write a ten-
page paper." In that case, you can still apply the techniques discussed here,
though you will have less work to do.

So, how to begin thinking about your paper in environmental science?
First, you need to select broad subject matter from the course and become
knowledgeable about its general features. And if no broad area of interest
occurs to you, you can approach your task from other angles:

- Work through the syllabus or your textbook(s). Identify topics that
  sparked your interest.

- Review course notes and pay especially close attention to lectures that
  held your interest.

- Scan recent headlines for news items that bear on your coursework.

Usually you can make use of material you've read in a text or heard in a
lecture. The trick is to find a subject that is important to you, for whatever
reason. (For a paper in sociology, you might write on the subject of bullying
because of your own experience with school bullies. For an economics seminar, you might explore the factors that threaten banks with collapse because
your great-great-grandparents lost their life savings during the Great
Depression.) Whatever the academic discipline, try to discover a topic that
you'll enjoy exploring; that way, you'll be writing for yourself as much as for
your instructor.

Assume for your course in environmental science that you've settled on
the broad topic of energy conservation. At this point, the goal of your research
is to limit this subject to a manageable scope. A topic can be limited in at least
two ways. First, you can seek out a general article (perhaps an encyclopedia
entry, though these are not typically accepted as sources in a college-level
paper). A general article may do the work for you by breaking the larger topic
down into smaller subtopics that you can explore and, perhaps, limit even
further. Second, you can limit a subject by asking several questions about it:

Who?

Which aspects?

Where?

When?

How?

Why?

These questions will occur to you as you conduct your research and see the
ways in which various authors have focused their discussions. Having read
several sources on energy conservation and having decided that you'd like to

use them, you might limit the subject by asking *which aspects,* and deciding to focus on energy conservation as it relates to motor vehicles.

Certainly, "energy-efficient vehicles" offers a more specific focus than does "energy conservation." Still, the revised focus is too broad for a ten-page paper. (One can easily imagine several book-length works on the subject.) So again you try to limit your subject by posing additional questions, from the same list. In this case, you might ask which aspects of energy-efficient vehicles are possible and desirable and how auto manufacturers can be encouraged to develop them. In response to these questions, you may jot down such preliminary notes. For example:

- Types of energy-efficient vehicles

    All-electric vehicles

    Hybrid (combination of gasoline and electric) vehicles

    Fuel-cell vehicles

- Government action to encourage development of energy-efficient vehicles

    Mandates to automakers to build minimum quantities of energy-efficient vehicles by certain deadlines

    Additional taxes imposed on high-mileage vehicles

    Subsidies to developers of energy-efficient vehicles

Focusing on any *one* of these aspects as an approach to encouraging use of energy-efficient vehicles could provide the focus of a ten-page paper, and you do yourself an important service by choosing just one. To choose more would obligate you to too broad a discussion that would frustrate you: Either the paper would have to be longer than ten pages, or assuming you kept to the page limit, the paper would be superficial in its treatment. In both instances, the paper would fail, given the constraints of the assignment.

A certain level of judgment is involved in deciding whether a topic is too big or too small to generate the right number of pages. Judgment is a function of experience, of course, and in the absence of experience you will have to resort, at times, to trial and error. Still the strategies offered above (locate an article that identifies parts of a topic or pose multiple questions and identify parts) can guide you. Ultimately, you will be able to tell if you've selected an appropriate topic as you reread your work and answer this question: *Have I developed all key elements of the thesis in depth, fully?* If you have skimmed the surface, narrow the topic and/or the claim of your thesis and redraft the paper. If you have added filler to meet the assignment's page requirements, broaden the topic and/or claim and redraft the paper. In general, you will do well to spend ample time gathering data, brainstorming, gathering more data, and then brainstorming again in order to limit your subject before attempting to write about it. Let's take an example. Assume that you settle on the following as an appropriately defined topic for a ten-page paper:

Encouraging the development of fuel cell vehicles

The process of choosing an initial subject (invention) depends heavily on the reading you do (data gathering). The more you read, the deeper your understanding. The deeper your understanding, the likelier it will be that you can divide a broad and complex subject into manageable—that is, researchable—topics. In the example above, your reading in the online and print literature may suggest that the development of fuel-cell technology is one of the most promising approaches to energy conservation on the highway. So reading allows you to narrow the subject "energy conservation" by answering the initial questions—those focusing on *which aspects* of the general subject. Once you narrow your focus to "energy efficient vehicles," you may read further and quickly realize that this is a broad subject that also should be limited. In this way, reading stimulates you to identify an appropriate topic for your paper. Your process here is recursive—you move back and forth between stages of the process, each movement bringing you closer to establishing a clear focus *before* you attempt to write your paper.

EXERCISE 3.2

Practice Narrowing Topics

In groups of three or four classmates, choose one of the following and respond to the questions listed above for narrowing topics: Who? Which aspects? Where? When? How? Why? See if you can formulate a more narrow approach to the topic.

- Downloading music off the Internet
- College sports
- School violence
- Internet chat rooms
- America's public school system

Making an Assertion

A thesis statement is an assertion or claim you wish to make *about* your paper's topic. If you have spent enough time reading and gathering information, and brainstorming ideas about the assignment, you will be knowledgeable enough to have something to say about the subject, based on a combination of your own thinking and the thinking of your sources.

If you have trouble making an assertion, devote more time to invention strategies: Try writing your subject at the top of a page and then listing everything you now know and feel about it. Often from such a list you will discover an assertion that you then can use to fashion a working thesis. A good way to gauge the reasonableness of your claim is to see what other authors have asserted about the same topic. In fact, keep good notes on the views of others. These notes will prove a useful counterpoint to your own views as you write and think about your claim, and you may want to use them in your paper. Next, make several assertions about your topic, in order of increasing complexity, as in the following:

1. Fuel-cell technology has emerged as a promising approach to developing energy-efficient vehicles.

2. To reduce our dependence on nonrenewable fossil fuel, the federal government should encourage the development of fuel-cell vehicles.

3. The federal government should subsidize the development of fuel-cell vehicles as well as the hydrogen infrastructure needed to support them; otherwise, the United States will be increasingly vulnerable to recession and other economic dislocations resulting from our dependence on the continued flow of foreign oil.

Keep in mind that these are *working theses*. Because you haven't written a paper based on any of them, they remain *hypotheses* to be tested. You might choose one and use it to focus your initial draft. After completing a first draft, you would revise it by comparing the contents of the paper to the thesis and making adjustments as necessary for unity. The working thesis is an excellent tool for planning broad sections of the paper, but—again—don't let it prevent you from pursuing related discussions as they occur to you.

Using the Thesis to Plan a Structure

A working thesis will help you sketch the structure of your paper, since structure flows directly from the thesis. Consider, for example, the third thesis on fuel-cell technology:

> The federal government should subsidize the development of fuel-cell vehicles as well as the hydrogen infrastructure needed to support them; otherwise, the United States will be increasingly vulnerable to recession and other economic dislocations resulting from our dependence on the continued flow of foreign oil.

This thesis, compared to the mildly argumentative second statement and the explanatory first statement, is *strongly argumentative,* or *persuasive.* The economic catastrophes mentioned by the writer indicate a strong degree of urgency in the need for the solution recommended—federal subsidy of a national hydrogen infrastructure to support fuel cell vehicles. If a paper based on this thesis is to be well developed, the writer must make a commitment to explaining (1) why fuel-cell vehicles are a preferred alternative to gasoline-powered vehicles; (2) why fuel-cell vehicles require a hydrogen infrastructure (i.e., the writer must explain that fuel cells produce power by mixing hydrogen and oxygen, generating both electricity and water in the process); (3) why the government needs to subsidize industry in developing fuel-cell vehicles; and (4) how continued reliance on fossil fuel technology could make the country vulnerable to economic dislocations. This thesis therefore helps the writer plan the paper, which should include a section on each of these four topics. Assuming that the paper follows the organizational plan we've proposed, the working thesis would become the final thesis, on the basis of which a reader could anticipate sections of the paper to come. In a finished product, the thesis becomes an essential tool for guiding readers.

Note, however, that this thesis is still provisional. It may turn out, as you research or begin drafting, that the paper to which this thesis commits you will be too long and complex. You may therefore decide to drop the second clause of the thesis dealing with the country's vulnerability to economic dislocations and focus almost exclusively on the need for the government to subsidize the development of fuel-cell vehicles and of a hydrogen infrastructure, relegating the economic concerns to your conclusion (if at all). If you make this change, your final thesis would read as follows:

> The federal government should subsidize the development of fuel-cell vehicles, as well as the hydrogen infrastructure needed to support them.

This revised thesis makes an assertive commitment to the subject, although the assertion is not as complex as the original. Still, it is more assertive than the second proposed thesis:

> To reduce our dependence on nonrenewable fossil fuel, the federal government should encourage the development of fuel-cell vehicles.

Here we have a *mildly argumentative* thesis that enables the writer to express an opinion. We infer from the use of the words "should encourage" that the writer endorses the idea of the government promoting fuel-cell development. But a government that "encourages" development is making a lesser commitment than one that "subsidizes," which means that it allocates funds for a specific policy. So a writer who argues for mere encouragement takes a milder position than one who argues for subsidies. Note also the contrast between this second thesis and the first one, in which the writer is committed to no involvement in the debate and no government involvement whatsoever.

> Fuel-cell technology has emerged as a promising approach to developing energy-efficient vehicles.

This first of the three thesis statements is *explanatory,* or *informative.* In developing a paper based on this thesis, the writer is committed only to explaining how fuel-cell technology works and why it is a promising approach to energy-efficient vehicles. Based on this particular thesis, then, a reader would *not* expect to find the author strongly recommending, for instance, that fuel-cell engines replace internal combustion engines at some point in the near future. Neither does the thesis require the writer to defend

> ## HOW AMBITIOUS SHOULD YOUR THESIS BE?
>
> Writing tasks vary according to the nature of the thesis.
>
> - The *explanatory thesis* is often developed in response to short-answer exam questions that call for information, not analysis (e.g., "How does James Barber categorize the main types of presidential personality?").
> - The *mildly argumentative thesis* is appropriate for organizing reports (even lengthy ones), as well as essay questions that call for some analysis (e.g., "Discuss the qualities of a good speech").
> - The *strongly argumentative thesis* is used to organize papers and exam questions that call for information, analysis, *and* the writer's forcefully stated point of view (e.g., "Evaluate the proposed reforms of health maintenance organizations").
>
> The strongly argumentative thesis, of course, is the riskiest of the three, since you must unequivocally state your position and make it appear reasonable—which requires that you offer evidence and defend against logical objections. But such intellectual risks pay dividends, and if you become involved enough in your work to make challenging assertions, you will provoke challenging responses that enliven classroom discussions and your own learning.

a personal opinion; he or she need only justify the use of the relatively mild term "promising."

As you can see, for any topic you might explore in a paper, you can make any number of assertions—some relatively simple, some complex. It is on the basis of these assertions that you set yourself an agenda for your writing— and readers set for themselves expectations for reading. The more ambitious the thesis, the more complex will be the paper and the greater will be your readers' expectations.

To Review: A thesis (a one-sentence summary of your paper) helps you organize your discussion, and it helps your reader anticipate it. Theses are distinguished by their carefully worded subjects and predicates, which should be just broad enough and complex enough to be developed within the length limitations of the assignment. Both novices and experts typically begin the initial draft of a paper with a working thesis—a statement that provides writers with structure enough to get started but with latitude enough to discover what they want to say as they write. Once you have completed a first draft, however, you test the "fit" of your thesis with the paper that follows. When you have a good fit, every element of the thesis is developed in the paper. Discussions that drift from your thesis should be deleted, or the thesis changed to accommodate the new discussions.

Drafting Thesis Statements

After completing the group exercise where you narrowed a topic (Exercise 3.2, page 77), work individually or in small groups to draft three possible theses in relation to your earlier ideas. Draft one *explanatory thesis,* one *explanatory but mildly argumentative thesis,* and one *strongly argumentative thesis.*

WRITING CONCLUSIONS

One way to view the conclusion of your paper is as an introduction worked in reverse, a bridge from the world of your paper back to the world of your reader. A conclusion is the part of your paper in which you restate and (if necessary) expand on your thesis. Essential to many conclusions is the summary, which is not merely a repetition of the thesis but a restatement that takes advantage of the material you've presented. The *simplest conclusion is a summary of the paper,* but you may want more than this for the end of your paper. Depending on your needs, you might offer a summary and then build onto it a discussion of the paper's significance or its implications for future study, for choices that individuals might make, for policy, and so on. You might also want to urge the reader to change an attitude or to modify behavior. Certainly, you are under no obligation to discuss the broader significance of your work (and a summary, alone, will satisfy the formal requirement that your paper have an ending); but the conclusions of better papers often reveal authors who are "thinking large" and want to connect the particular concerns of their papers with the broader concerns of society.

Here we'll consider seven strategies for expanding the basic summary-conclusion. But two words of advice are in order. First, no matter how clever or beautifully executed, a conclusion cannot salvage a poorly written paper. Second, by virtue of its placement, the conclusion carries rhetorical weight. It is the last statement a reader will encounter before turning from your work. Realizing this, writers who expand on the basic summary-conclusion often wish to give their final words a dramatic flourish, a heightened level of diction. Soaring rhetoric and drama in a conclusion are fine as long as they do not unbalance the paper and call attention to themselves. Having labored long hours over your paper, you have every right to wax eloquent. But keep a sense of proportion and timing. Make your points quickly and end crisply.

Statement of the Subject's Significance

One of the more effective ways to conclude a paper is to discuss the larger significance of what you have written, providing readers with one more reason to regard your work as a serious effort. When using this strategy, you move from the specific concern of your paper to the broader concerns of the

reader's world. Often, you will need to choose among a range of signifi-
cances: A paper on the Wright brothers might end with a discussion of air
travel as it affects economies, politics, or families; a paper on contraception
might end with a discussion of its effect on sexual mores, population, or the
church. But don't overwhelm your reader with the importance of your
remarks. Keep your discussion well focused.

The following paragraphs conclude a paper on George H. Shull, a pioneer
in the inbreeding and crossbreeding of corn:

> . . . Thus, the hybrids developed and described by Shull 75 years ago
> have finally dominated U.S. corn production.
>
> The adoption of hybrid corn was steady and dramatic in the Corn
> Belt. From 1930 through 1979 the average yields of corn in the U.S.
> increased from 21.9 to 95.1 bushels per acre, and the additional value
> to the farmer is now several billion dollars per year.
>
> The success of hybrid corn has also stimulated the breeding of
> other crops, such as sorghum hybrids, a major feed grain crop in arid
> parts of the world. Sorghum yields have increased 300 percent since
> 1930. Approximately 20 percent of the land devoted to rice produc-
> tion in China is planted with hybrid seed, which is reported to yield
> 20 percent more than the best varieties. And many superior varieties
> of tomatoes, cucumbers, spinach, and other vegetables are hybrids.
> Today virtually all corn produced in the developed countries is from
> hybrid seed. From those blue bloods of the plant kingdom has come
> a model for feeding the world.*

The first sentence of this conclusion is a summary, and from it the reader can
infer that the paper included a discussion of Shull's techniques for the hybrid
breeding of corn. The summary is followed by a two-paragraph discussion
on the significance of Shull's research for feeding the world.

Call for Further Research

In the scientific and social scientific communities, papers often end with a
review of what has been presented (as, for instance, in an experiment) and the
ways in which the subject under consideration needs to be further explored.
If you raise questions that you call on others to answer, however, make sure
you know that the research you are calling for hasn't already been conducted.

This next conclusion comes from a sociological report on the placement
of the elderly in nursing homes.

> Our study shows a correlation between the placement of elderly citi-
> zens in nursing facilities and the significant decline of their motor and
> intellectual skills over the ten months following placement. What the
> research has not made clear is the extent to which this marked decline

---

* William L. Brown, "Hybrid Vim and Vigor," *Science* Nov. 1984: 77–78.

is due to physical as opposed to emotional causes. The elderly are referred to homes at that point in their lives when they grow less able to care for themselves—which suggests that the drop-off in skills may be due to physical causes. But the emotional stress of being placed in a home, away from family and in an environment that confirms the patient's view of himself as decrepit, may exacerbate—if not itself be a primary cause of—the patient's rapid loss of abilities. Further research is needed to clarify the relationship between depression and particular physical ailments as these affect the skills of the elderly in nursing facilities. There is little doubt that information yielded by such studies can enable health care professionals to deliver more effective services.

Notice how this call for further study locates the author in a large community of researchers on whom she depends for assistance in answering the questions that have come out of her own work. The author summarizes her findings (in the first sentence of the paragraph), states what the work has not shown, and then extends an invitation.

Solution/Recommendation

The purpose of your paper might be to review a problem or controversy and to discuss contributing factors. In such a case, it would be appropriate, after summarizing your discussion, to offer a solution based on the knowledge you've gained while conducting research. If your solution is to be taken seriously, your knowledge must be amply demonstrated in the body of the paper.

Here is a conclusion to a paper on problems in college sports:

(1) . . . The major problem in college sports today is not commercialism—it is the exploitation of athletes and the proliferation of illicit practices which dilute educational standards.

(2) Many universities are currently deriving substantial benefits from sports programs that depend on the labor of athletes drawn from the poorest sections of America's population. It is the responsibility of educators, civil rights leaders, and concerned citizens to see that these young people get a fair return for their labor both in terms of direct remuneration and in terms of career preparation for a life outside sports.

(3) Minimally, scholarships in revenue-producing sports should be designed to extend until graduation, rather than covering only four years of athletic eligibility, and should include guarantees of tutoring, counseling, and proper medical care. At institutions where the profits are particularly large (such as Texas A & M, which can afford to pay its football coach $280,000 a year), scholarships should also provide salaries that extend beyond room, board, and tuition. The important thing is that the athlete be remunerated fairly and have the opportunity to gain skills from a university environment without undue competition from a physically and psychologically demanding full-time job. This may well require that scholarships be extended over five or six years, including summers.

> (4) Such a proposal, I suspect, will not be easy to implement. The cur-
> rent amateur system, despite its moral and educational flaws, enables
> universities to hire their athletic labor at minimal cost. But solving the
> fiscal crisis of the universities on the backs of America's poor and
> minorities is not, in the long run, a tenable solution. With the support
> of concerned educators, parents, and civil rights leaders, and with the
> help from organized labor, the college athlete, truly a sleeping giant, will
> someday speak out and demand what is rightly his—and hers—a fair
> share of the revenue created by their hard work.*

In this conclusion, the author summarizes his article in one sentence: "The major problem in college sports today is not commercialism—it is the exploitation of athletes and the proliferation of illicit practices which dilute educational standards." In paragraph 2, he continues with an analysis of the problem just stated and follows with a general recommendation—that "concerned educators, parents, and civil rights leaders" be responsible for the welfare of college athletes. In paragraph 3, he makes a specific proposal, and in the final paragraph, he anticipates resistance to the proposal. He concludes by discounting this resistance and returning to the general point, that college athletes should receive a fair deal.

Anecdote

An anecdote is a briefly told story or joke, the point of which in a conclusion is to shed light on your subject. The anecdote is more direct than an allusion. With an allusion, you merely refer to a story ("Too many people today live in Plato's cave . . . "); with the anecdote, you actually retell the story. The anecdote allows readers to discover for themselves the significance of a reference to another source—an effort most readers enjoy because they get to exercise their creativity.

The following anecdote concludes a political-philosophical paper. First, the author includes a paragraph summing up her argument, and she follows that with a brief story.

> Ironically, our economy is fueled by the very thing that degrades our
> value system. But when politicians call for a return to "traditional
> family values," they seldom criticize the business interests that pro-
> mote and benefit from our coarsened values. Consumer capitalism
> values things over people; it thrives on discontent and unhappiness
> since discontented people make excellent consumers, buying vast
> numbers of things that may somehow "fix" their inadequacies. We buy
> more than we need, the economy chugs along, but such materialism is
> the real culprit behind our warped value systems. Anthony de Mello
> tells the following story:

---

* Mark Naison, "Scenario for Scandal," *Commonweal* (2004).

> Socrates believed that the wise person would instinctively lead a frugal life, and he even went so far as to refuse to wear shoes. Yet he constantly fell under the spell of the marketplace and would go there often to look at the great variety and magnificence of the wares on display.
>
> A friend once asked him why he was so intrigued with the allures of the market. "I love to go there," Socrates replied, "to discover how many things I am perfectly happy without."*

The writer chose to conclude the article with this anecdote. She could have developed an interpretation, but this would have spoiled the dramatic value for the reader. The purpose of using an anecdote is to make your point with subtlety, so resist the temptation to interpret. Keep in mind three guidelines when selecting an anecdote: It should be prepared for (readers should have all the information they need to understand it), it should provoke the reader's interest, and it should not be so obscure as to be unintelligible.

Quotation

A favorite concluding device is the quotation—the words of a famous person or an authority in the field on which you are writing. The purpose of quoting another is to link your work to theirs, thereby gaining for your work authority and credibility. The first criterion for selecting a quotation is its suitability to your thesis. But you should also carefully consider what your choice of sources says about you. Suppose you are writing a paper on the American work ethic. If you could use a line by comedian David Letterman or one by the current secretary of labor to make the final point of your conclusion, which would you choose and why? One source may not be inherently more effective than the other, but the choice certainly sets a tone for the paper. The following two paragraphs conclude a paper examining the popularity of vulgar and insulting humor in television shows, movies, and other popular culture:

> But studies on the influence of popular culture suggest that cruel humor serves as more than a release in modern society. The ubiquitous media pick up on our baser nature, exaggerate it to entertain, and, by spitting it back at us, encourage us to push the boundaries even further. As a result, says Johns Hopkins' Miller, "We're gradually eroding the kinds of social forms and inhibitions that kept [aggressive] compulsions contained."
>
> Before the cycle escalates further, we might do well to consider the advice of Roman statesman and orator Cicero, who wrote at the peak of the Roman empire: "If we are forced, at every hour, to watch or listen to horrible events, this constant stream of ghastly impressions

---

* Frances Wageneck, *Family Values in the Marketplace,* unpublished paper, 2000: 6. Used by permission.

will deprive even the most delicate among us of all respect for humanity."*

The two quotations used here serve different but equally effective ends. The first idea provides one last expert's viewpoint, then leads nicely into the cautionary note the writer introduces by quoting Cicero. The Roman's words, and the implied parallel being drawn between Rome and contemporary culture, are strong enough that the author ends there, without stepping in and making any statements of her own. In other cases, quotations can be used to set up one last statement by the author of a paper.

There is a potential problem with using quotations: If you end with the words of another, you may leave the impression that someone else can make your case more eloquently than you can. The language of the quotation will put your own prose into relief. If your own prose suffers by comparison—if the quotations are the best part of your paper—you'd be wise to spend some time revising. The way to avoid this kind of problem is to make your own presentation strong.

Question

Questions are useful for opening papers, and they are just as useful for closing them. Opening and closing questions function in different ways, however. The introductory question promises to be addressed in the paper that follows. But the concluding question leaves issues unresolved, calling on the readers to assume an active role by offering their own answers. Take a look at the following two paragraphs, written to conclude a paper on genetically modified (GM) food:

> Are GM foods any more of a risk than other agricultural innovations that have taken place over the years, like selective breeding? Do the existing and potential future benefits of GM foods outweigh any risks that do exist? And what standard should governments use when assessing the safety of transgenic crops? The "frankenfood" frenzy has given life to a policymaking standard known as the "precautionary principle," which has been long advocated by environmental groups. That principle essentially calls for governments to prohibit any activity that raises concerns about human health or the environment, even if some cause-and-effect relationships are not fully established scientifically. As Liberal Democrat MP [Member of Parliament] Norman Baker told the BBC: "We must always apply the precautionary principle. That says that unless you're sure of adequate control, unless you're sure the risk is minimal, unless you're sure nothing horrible can go wrong, you don't do it."
>
> But can any innovation ever meet such a standard of certainty— especially given the proliferation of "experts" that are motivated as

---

* Nina J. Easton, "The Meaning of America," *Los Angeles Times Magazine* 7 Feb. 1993: 21.

> much by politics as they are by science? And what about those mil-
> lions of malnourished people whose lives could be saved by trans-
> genic foods? [Is] the "precautionary principle" [really] so
> precautionary after all [?]*

Perhaps you will choose to raise a question in your conclusion and then answer it, based on the material you've provided in the paper. The answered question challenges a reader to agree or disagree with your response and thus also places the reader in an active role. The following brief conclusion ends a student paper entitled "Is Feminism Dead?"

> So the answer to the question "Is the feminist movement dead?" is
> no, it's not. Even if most young women today don't consciously iden-
> tify themselves as "feminists"—due to the ways in which the term
> has become loaded with negative associations—the principles of
> gender equality that lie at feminism's core are enthusiastically
> embraced by the vast number of young women, and even a large per-
> centage of young men.

Speculation

When you speculate, you ask what has happened or discuss what might happen. This kind of question stimulates the reader because its subject is the unknown.

The following paragraph concludes "The New Generation Gap" by Neil Howe and William Strauss. In this article, Howe and Strauss discuss the differences among Americans of various ages, including the "GI Generation" (born between 1901 and 1924), the "Boomers" (born 1943–1961), the "Thirteeners" (born 1961–1981), and the "Millennials" (born 1981–2000):

> If, slowly but surely, Millennials receive the kind of family protection
> and public generosity that GIs enjoyed as children, then they could
> come of age early in the next century as a group much like the GIs
> of the 1920s and 1930s—as a stellar (if bland) generation of rational-
> ists, team players, and can-do civic builders. Two decades from now
> Boomers entering old age may well see in their grown Millennial
> children an effective instrument for saving the world, while
> Thirteeners entering midlife will shower kindness on a younger gen-
> eration that is getting a better deal out of life (though maybe a bit less
> fun) than they ever got at a like age. Study after story after column
> will laud these "best damn kids in the world" as heralding a resur-
> gent American greatness. And, for a while at least, no one will talk
> about a generation gap.†

---

* "Frankenfoods Frenzy," *Reason* 13 Jan. 2000, 17 Aug. 2000 <http://reason.com/bi/bi-gmf.html>.

† Neil Howe and William Strauss, "The New Generation Gap," *Atlantic Monthly* Dec. 1992: 65.

Howe and Strauss thus conclude an article concerned largely with the apparently unbridgeable gaps of understanding between parents and children with a hopeful speculation that generational relationships will improve considerably in the next two decades.

EXERCISE 3.4

Drafting Conclusions

Imagine that you have written a paper using the topic, ideas, and thesis you developed in the earlier exercises in this chapter. Choose one of the seven types of conclusions we've discussed—preferably one you have never used before—and draft a conclusion that would work to end your paper. Use our examples as models to help you draft your practice conclusion.

Explanatory Synthesis

4

WHAT IS A SYNTHESIS?

A *synthesis* is a written discussion that draws on two or more sources. It follows that your ability to write syntheses depends on your ability to infer relationships among sources—essays, articles, and fiction as well as nonwritten sources such as lectures, interviews, and observations. This process is nothing new for you, since you infer relationships all the time—say, between something you've read in the newspaper and something you've seen for yourself, or between the teaching styles of your favorite and least favorite instructors. In fact, if you've written research papers, you've already written syntheses. In an *academic synthesis*, you make explicit the relationships that you have inferred among separate sources.

The skills you've already learned and practiced from the previous three chapters will be vital in writing syntheses. Clearly, before you're in a position to draw relationships between two or more sources, you must understand what those sources say; in other words, you must be able to *summarize* these sources. Readers will frequently benefit from at least partial summaries of sources in your synthesis essays. At the same time, you must go beyond summary to make judgments—judgments based, of course, on your *critical reading* of your sources: what conclusions you've drawn about the quality and validity of these sources, whether you agree or disagree with the points made in your sources, and why you agree or disagree.

Further, you must go beyond the critique of individual sources to determine the relationships among them. Is the information in source B, for example, an extended illustration of the generalizations in source A? Would it be useful to compare and contrast source C with source B? Having read and considered sources A, B, and C, can you infer something else—D (not a source, but your own idea)?

Because a synthesis is based on two or more sources, you will need to be selective when choosing information from each. It would be neither possible nor desirable, for instance, to discuss in a ten-page paper on the American Civil War every point that the authors of two books make about their subject. What you as a writer must do is select from each source the ideas and information that best allow you to achieve your purpose.

PURPOSE

Your purpose in reading source materials and then in drawing on them to write your own material is often reflected in the wording of an assignment. For instance, consider the following assignments on the Civil War:

WHERE DO WE FIND WRITTEN SYNTHESES?

Here are just a few of the types of writing that involve synthesis:

Academic Writing

- **Analysis papers.** Synthesize and apply several related theoretical approaches.
- **Research papers.** Synthesize multiple sources.
- **Argument papers.** Synthesize different points into a coherent claim or position.
- **Essay exams.** Demonstrate understanding of course material through comparing and contrasting theories, viewpoints, or approaches in a particular field.

Workplace Writing

- **Newspaper and magazine articles.** Synthesize primary and secondary sources.
- **Position papers and policy briefs.** Compare and contrast solutions for solving problems.
- **Business plans.** Synthesize ideas and proposals into one coherent plan.
- **Memos and letters.** Synthesize multiple ideas, events, and proposals into concise form.
- **Web sites.** Synthesize information from various sources to present in Web pages and related links.

American history: Evaluate the author's treatment of the origins of the Civil War.

Economics: Argue the following proposition, in light of your readings: "The Civil War was fought not for reasons of moral principle but for reasons of economic necessity."

Government: Prepare a report on the effects of the Civil War on Southern politics at the state level between 1870 and 1917.

Mass communications: Discuss how the use of photography during the Civil War may have affected the perceptions of the war by Northerners living in industrial cities.

Literature: Select two twentieth-century Southern writers whose work you believe was influenced by the divisive effects of the Civil War. Discuss the ways this influence is apparent in a novel or a group of

short stories written by each author. The works
should not be *about* the Civil War.

Applied technology:　Compare and contrast the technology of warfare
available in the 1860s with the technology available
a century earlier.

Each of these assignments creates for you a particular purpose for writing. Having located sources relevant to your topic, you would select, for possible use in a paper, only those parts that helped you in fulfilling this purpose. And how you used those parts, how you related them to other material from other sources, would also depend on your purpose. For instance, if you were working on the government assignment, you might possibly draw on the same source as another student working on the literature assignment by referring to Robert Penn Warren's novel *All the King's Men,* about Louisiana politics in the early part of the twentieth century. But because the purposes of these assignments are different, you and the other student would make different uses of this source. Those same parts or aspects of the novel that you find worthy of detailed analysis might be mentioned only in passing by the other student.

USING YOUR SOURCES

Your purpose determines not only what parts of your sources you will use but also how you will relate them to one another. Since the very essence of synthesis is the combining of information and ideas, you must have some basis on which to combine them. *Some relationships among the material in your sources must make them worth synthesizing.* It follows that the better able you are to discover such relationships, the better able you will be to use your sources in writing syntheses. Notice that the mass communications assignment requires you to draw a *cause-and-effect* relationship between photographs of the war and Northerners' perceptions of the war. The applied technology assignment requires you to *compare and contrast* state-of-the-art weapons technology in the eighteenth and nineteenth centuries. The economics assignment requires you to *argue* a proposition. In each case, *your purpose will determine how you relate your source materials to one another.*

Consider some other examples. You may be asked on an exam question or in instructions for a paper to *describe* two or three approaches to prison reform during the past decade. You may be asked to *compare and contrast* one country's approach to imprisonment with another's. You may be asked to *develop an argument* of your own on this subject, based on your reading. Sometimes (when you are not given a specific assignment) you determine your own purpose: You are interested in exploring a particular subject; you are interested in making a case for one approach or another. In any event, your purpose shapes your essay. Your purpose determines which sources you research, which ones you use, which parts of them you use, at which points in your essay you use them, and in what manner you relate them to one another.

TYPES OF SYNTHESES: EXPLANATORY AND ARGUMENT

In this and the next chapter we categorize syntheses into two main types: *explanatory* and *argument*. The easiest way to recognize the difference between these two types may be to consider the difference between a newspaper article and an editorial on the same subject. Most likely, we'd say that the main purpose of the newspaper article is to convey *information*, and the main purpose of the editorial is to convey *opinion* or *interpretation*. Of course, this distinction is much too simplified: Newspaper articles often convey opinion or bias, sometimes subtly, sometimes openly; and editorials often convey unbiased information, along with opinion. But as a practical matter, we can generally agree on the distinction between a newspaper article that primarily conveys information and an editorial that primarily conveys opinion.

We'll say, for the sake of convenience, that the newspaper article provides an explanation and that the editorial provides an argument. This is essentially the distinction we make between explanatory and argument syntheses.

As an example of the distinction, read the following paragraph:

> Researchers now use recombinant DNA technology to analyze genetic changes. With this technology, they cut and splice DNA from different species, then insert the modified molecules into bacteria or other types of cells that engage in rapid replication and cell division. The cells copy the foreign DNA right along with their own. In short order, huge populations produce useful quantities of recombinant DNA molecules. The new technology also is the basis of genetic engineering, by which genes are isolated, modified, and inserted back into the same organism or into a different one.[*]

Now read this paragraph:

> Many in the life sciences field would have us believe that the new gene splicing technologies are irrepressible and irreversible and that any attempt to oppose their introduction is both futile and retrogressive. They never stop to even consider the possibility that the new genetic science might be used in a wholly different manner than is currently being proposed. The fact is, the corporate agenda is only one of two potential paths into the Biotech Century. It is possible that the growing number of anti-eugenic activists around the world might be able to ignite a global debate around alternative uses of the new science— approaches that are less invasive, more sustainable and humane and that conserve and protect the genetic rights of future generations.[†]

---

[*] Cecie Starr and Ralph Taggart, "Recombinant DNA and Genetic Engineering," *Biology: The Unity and Diversity of Life* (New York: Wadsworth, 1998).

[†] Jeremy Rifkin, "The Ultimate Therapy: Commercial Eugenics on the Eve of the Biotech Century," *Tikkun* May–June 1998: 35.

Both of these passages deal with the topic of biotechnology, but the two take quite different approaches. The first passage came from a biology textbook, while the second appeared in a magazine article. As we might expect from a textbook on the broad subject of biology, the first passage is explanatory and informative; it defines and explains some of the key concepts of biotechnology without taking a position or providing commentary about the implications of the technology. Magazine articles often present information in the same ways; however, many magazine articles take specific positions, as we see in the second passage. This passage is argumentative or persuasive. Its primary purpose is to convey a point of view regarding the topic of biotechnology.

While each of these excerpts presents a clear instance of writing that is either explanatory or argumentative, it is important to note that the sources for these excerpts—the textbook chapter and the magazine article—contain elements of both explanation and argument. The textbook writers, while they refrain from taking a particular position, do note the controversies surrounding biotechnology and genetic engineering. They might even subtly reveal a certain bias in favor of one side of the issue, through their word choice, tone, and perhaps through devoting more space and attention to one point of view. Explanatory and argumentative writing are not mutually exclusive. The overlap in the categories of explanation and argument is also found in the magazine article: In order to make his case against genetic engineering, the writer has to explain certain elements of the issue. Yet, even while these categories overlap to a certain extent, the second passage clearly has argument as its primary purpose, whereas the first passage is primarily explanatory.

In Chapter 2 we noted that the primary purpose in a piece of writing is either informative, persuasive, or entertaining (or some combination of the three). Some scholars of writing argue that all writing is essentially persuasive, and even without entering into that complex argument, we've just seen how the varying purposes in writing do overlap. In order to persuade others of a particular position, we typically must also inform them about it; conversely, a primarily informative piece of writing must also work to persuade the reader that its claims are truthful. Both informative and persuasive writing often include entertaining elements, and writing intended primarily to entertain also typically contains information and persuasion. For practical purposes, however, it is possible—and useful—to identify the *primary* purpose in a piece of writing as informative/explanatory, persuasive/argumentative, or entertaining. Entertainment as a primary purpose is the one least often practiced in purely academic writing—perhaps to your disappointment!—but information and persuasion are ubiquitous. Thus, while recognizing the overlap between these categories, we distinguish in this and the following chapter between two types of synthesis writing: explanatory (or informative) and argument (or persuasive). Just as distinguishing the primary purpose in a piece of writing helps you to critically read and evaluate it, distinguishing the primary purpose in your own writing helps you to make the appropriate choices regarding your approach.

In this chapter we'll first present some guidelines for writing syntheses in general, then we'll proceed to focus on explanatory syntheses. In the next chapter, we'll discuss the argument synthesis.

HOW TO WRITE SYNTHESES

Although writing syntheses can't be reduced to a lockstep method, it should help you to follow the guidelines listed in the box below.

GUIDELINES FOR WRITING SYNTHESES

- *Consider your purpose in writing.* What are you trying to accomplish in your essay? How will this purpose shape the way you approach your sources?
- *Select and carefully read your sources,* according to your purpose. Then reread the passages, mentally summarizing each. Identify those aspects or parts of your sources that will help you fulfill your purpose. When rereading, *label* or *underline* the sources for main ideas, key terms, and any details you want to use in the synthesis.
- *Take notes on your reading.* In addition to labeling or underlining key points in the readings, you might write brief one- or two-sentence summaries of each source. This will help you in formulating your thesis statement and in choosing and organizing your sources later.
- *Formulate a thesis.* Your thesis is the main idea that you want to present in your synthesis. It should be expressed as a complete sentence. You might do some predrafting about the ideas discussed in the readings in order to help you work out a thesis. If you've written one-sentence summaries of the readings, looking these over will help you to brainstorm connections between readings and to devise a thesis.

  When you write your essay drafts, you will need to consider where your thesis fits in your paper. Sometimes the thesis is the first sentence, but more often it is *the final sentence of the first paragraph*. If you are writing an *inductively arranged* synthesis (see page 148), the thesis sentence may not appear until the final paragraphs. (See Chapter 3 for more information on writing an effective thesis.)
- *Decide how you will use your source material.* How will the information and the ideas in the passages help you fulfill your purpose?
- *Develop an organizational plan,* according to your thesis. How will you arrange your material? It is not necessary to prepare a formal outline. But you should have some plan that will indicate the order

THE EXPLANATORY SYNTHESIS

Many of the papers you write in college will be more or less explanatory in nature. An explanation helps readers understand a topic. Writers explain when they divide a subject into its component parts and present them to the reader in a clear and orderly fashion. Explanations may entail descriptions that recreate in words some object, place, emotion, event, sequence of events, or state of affairs. As a student reporter, you may need to explain an event—to relate when, where, and how it took place. In a science lab, you would

---

in which you will present your material and that will indicate the relationships among your sources.

- *Draft the topic sentences for the main sections.* This is an optional step, but you may find it a helpful transition from organizational plan to first draft.

- *Write the first draft of your synthesis,* following your organizational plan. Be flexible with your plan, however. Frequently, you will use an outline to get started. As you write, you may discover new ideas and make room for them by adjusting the outline. When this happens, reread your work frequently, making sure that your thesis still accounts for what follows and that what follows still logically supports your thesis.

- *Document your sources.* You must do this by crediting them within the body of the synthesis—citing the author's last name and page number from which the point was taken and by providing full citation information in a list of "Works Cited" at the end. Don't open yourself to charges of plagiarism! (See pages 42–44; see also Chapter 7 for more information on documenting sources.)

- *Revise your synthesis,* inserting transitional words and phrases where necessary. Make sure that the synthesis reads smoothly, logically, and clearly from beginning to end. Check for grammatical correctness, punctuation, spelling.

Note: The writing of syntheses is a recursive process, and you should accept a certain amount of backtracking and reformulating as inevitable. For instance, in developing an organizational plan (Step 6 of the procedure), you may discover a gap in your presentation that will send you scrambling for another source—back to Step 2. You may find that formulating a thesis and making inferences among sources occur simultaneously; indeed, inferences are often made before a thesis is formulated. Our recommendations for writing syntheses will give you a structure; they will get you started. But be flexible in your approach; expect discontinuity and, if possible, be comforted that through backtracking and reformulating you will eventually produce a coherent, well-crafted essay.

observe the conditions and results of an experiment and record them for review by others. In a political science course, you might review research on a particular subject—say, the complexities underlying the debate over gay marriage—and then present the results of your research to your professor and the members of your class.

Your job in writing an explanatory paper—or in writing the explanatory portion of an argumentative paper—is not to argue a particular point, but rather *to present the facts in a reasonably objective manner.* Of course, explanatory papers, like other academic papers, should be based on a thesis. But the purpose of a thesis in an explanatory paper is less to advance a particular opinion than to focus the various facts contained in the paper.

DEMONSTRATION: EXPLANATORY SYNTHESIS— COMPUTERS, COMMUNICATION, AND RELATIONSHIPS

To illustrate how the process of synthesis works, we'll begin with a number of short extracts from several articles on the same subject.

Suppose you were writing a paper on a matter that many computer users are discussing these days: the ways in which communication via computers (that is, computer-mediated communication, or CMC) is changing human patterns of interaction and relationships. Some writers and thinkers are excited about the world of possibilities opened up by this technological medium, while others are skeptical about whether the Internet will lead to more interaction and connection between people, or will harm the quality of such connections. Still others argue that this new mode of communication is likely to further isolate us from each other, and "real" human contact will become a rare and precious thing.

EXERCISE **4.1**

Exploring the Topic

Before reading what others have written on the subject of computers, communication, and relationships, write several paragraphs exploring what you know and what you think about this topic. You might focus your first paragraph on discussing your own experience with computer communication and relationships. How much have you used e-mail, instant messaging, and other Internet-related activity? How have these technologies affected your ability to communicate with others? What are some positive and negative impacts of such communication on relationships? In your second paragraph you might broaden the focus by discussing what you know about these issues in the world at large. What are some concerns people have about computers and their effects on communication? What do you think most interests journalists, professors, politicians, and businesspeople about computer communication and relationships?

Because this is a topic that bears upon a broader subject—the ways that computers and the Internet affect our lives—you decide to investigate what has been written on the subject, both in print and electronic texts. In the following pages we present excerpts from the kinds of articles your research might locate.

Note: To save space and for the purpose of demonstration, the following passages are brief excerpts only. In preparing your paper, naturally you would draw upon the entire articles from which these extracts were made. (The discussion of how these passages can form the basis of an explanatory synthesis resumes on page 107.)

Cyberspace: A New Frontier for Fighting Words
Sanjiv N. Singh

Sanjiv N. Singh holds a J.D. from the UCLA School of Law. The article from which this piece is excerpted appeared in the Rutgers Computer and Technology Law Journal, *in 1999.**

[T]he Internet has begun to transform the way in which people interact. Various mediums now exist that allow for cheap and almost instantaneous communication via computer. For example, e-mail is now an increasingly common way to communicate with family, friends, and acquaintances. . . . Technology research firms estimate that by the year 2001, fifty percent of the U.S. population will communicate via e-mail. . . .

Many colleges and graduate schools routinely provide students with, and in some cases require, use of e-mail accounts. As a result, significant segments of our population are being socialized in an environment where cyberspace communication is an encouraged form of establishing and confirming social engagements or simply corresponding with friends.

Social Relationships in Electronic Forums: Hangouts, Salons, Workplaces and Communities
Rob Kling

Rob Kling is a professor of Information Systems and Information Science in the School for Library and Information Science at the University of Indiana at Bloomington. He has

---

* Sanjiv N. Singh, "Cyberspace: A New Frontier for Fighting Words," *Rutgers Computer and Technology Law Journal* 25.2 (1999): 283.

*published numerous articles examining the impact of information technologies on orga-
nizations, the workplace, publishing and education, as well as on social life. His books
include* Computerization and Controversy: Value Conflicts and Social Choices *(1996), and*
Computers and Politics: High Technology in American Local Governments *(1982). The following reading is excerpted from an essay that appeared in* CMC Magazine.*

Enthusiasts for [Internet] forums argue that they are building new forms of community life (Rheingold, 1993). But other analysts observe that not every collection of people who happen to talk (or write) to each other form the sense
of trust, mutual interest, and sustained commitments that automatically deserve
to be labeled as communities (Jones, 1995). . . .

In the United States, communities seem to be deteriorating from a complex
combination of causes. In the inner cities of big urban centers, many people
fear street crime and stay off the streets at night. In the larger suburban and
post-suburban areas, many people hardly know their neighbors and "latch key"
children often have little adult contact after school. An African proverb which
says that "it takes a whole village to raise a child" refers to a rich community life
with a sense of mutual responsibility that is difficult to find in many new neighborhoods. Some advocates believe that computer technology in concert with
other efforts could play a role in rebuilding community life by improving communication, economic opportunity, civic participation, and education (Schuler,
1994; Civille, Fidelman, and Altobello, 1993).

Signs of Life in the USA
Sonia Maasik and Jack Solomon

*Sonia Maasik is a member of the Writing Program faculty at UCLA, and Jack Solomon is an
English professor at California State College, Northridge. In addition to their popular textbook
(from which this excerpt comes)* Signs of Life in the USA: Readings on Popular Culture for
Writers *(3rd edition, 2000), the two have also collaborated on* California Dreams and
Realities: Readings for Critical Thinkers and Writers *(1999).†*

The emerging outlines of the Web's global village have some people very excited and others worried. The worried contingent are concerned that the relationships people are building on the Net lack an essential core of humanity. The
unreal world of virtual culture, they believe, the world in which you can pretend

---

* Rob Kling, "Social Relationships in Electronic Forums: Hangouts, Salons, Workplaces and
Communities," *CMC Magazine* 22 July 1996, 4 Feb. 2000 <http://www.december.com/
cmc/mag/1996/jul/kling.html>.

† Sonia Maasik and Jack Solomon, eds., *Signs of Life in the USA: Readings on Popular Culture for
Writers,* 3rd ed. (Boston: Bedford Books, 2000).

to be just about anything, is being substituted for a social reality made up of real human beings. And such a world, based entirely on the transmission of electronic signals, is potentially a world in which human beings will be unable to conceive of others as human beings. When all interaction is electronic, they ask, where is the ground for true human empathy and relatedness?

Life at High-Tech U
Deborah Branscum

A contributing editor to Newsweek, *a columnist for* Fortune.com's *"Valley Talk," and a freelance technology writer, Deborah Branscum has written articles for a number of publications, including* Wired, New York Times, Infoworld, *and* Yahoo Internet Life. *She operates a Web site called MonsterBuzz.com and founded its affiliated BUZZ executive conference.* *

Some academics dismiss [e-mail] as an unhealthy substitute for human contact. But Stanford's Richard Holeton, who tracked e-mail discussions of first-year students in one dorm, found that 87 percent of their messages involved important social or critical dialogue. Those issues included "pornography, free speech, a potential grape boycott on campus and a sexual-harassment allegation," says Holeton. And the people who dominated dorm life in face-to-face encounters were not the same folks who ruled the e-mail debates. Electronic discourse, it seems, offered a voice to some students who might not otherwise be heard.

Instant Messaging Is In, Phones Out
Ellen Edwards

Ellen Edwards is a staff writer for the Washington Post. *This article appeared in the* Seattle Times *on 16 June 2003.* †

In what may be a permanent shift, kids are communicating online rather than by phone. And as they get older, when they do use the phone, it's more likely to be a cell, and even that may be for text messaging rather than talking. "I'm

---

* Deborah Branscum, "Life at High-Tech U," *Newsweek* 27 Oct. 1997: 78–80.

† Ellen Edwards, "Instant Messaging Is in, Phones Out," *Seattle Times,* 16 Jan. 2003.

absolutely certain instant messages will have a profound effect on relationships," says Georgetown University linguistics professor Deborah Tannen. "I just don't know what it will be. I think it will be as great or maybe greater than the invention of the telephone."

"The phone never rings in our home," says Gary Knell, the president and CEO of Sesame Workshop, which produces "Sesame Street." Knell has four children, ages 17, 15, 12 and 8. "I look, and they are holding IM conversations with 20 friends. All the arguments in our house are about computer access."

The computer gives kids scope. As they get older and more independent, the cell gives them mobility.

America Online, which provides the most-used instant messaging service through AOL subscriptions and its free AOL Instant Messaging service (AIM), estimates that by 2005 IMs will surpass e-mail as the primary way of communicating online. Right now 1.6 billion AOL and AIM IMs are sent every day. AOL is of course fueling the fire by adding extras that kids love, taking the IM smiley face signs to new levels with customized signatures, instant greetings that flash and dance across the screen and personalized "away" messages.

The theory of "away" messages, for those times when you are on the Internet but away from your computer, says Tannen, "is that you're always supposed to be available." When you're not, she says, the "away" message is your apology. "When I come home from school, I get on the Internet right away," says Lucy Bascom, a seventh-grader at Bethesda, Md.'s, Westland Middle School. Homework questions still are left to the phone, not IMs, she says. IMs may be closing in on phone chat, but the mechanism hasn't killed it completely.

"Sometimes it's simultaneous," says Lucy's dad, John Bascom, who says his 13-year-old daughter multi-tasks pretty effectively between the two. But IMing got so all-consuming for Lucy several years ago that her parents installed software to limit her online time. When she's on the phone, she says, she's usually talking to someone with whom she is also IMing. "It's really convenient to say things you wouldn't have the confidence to say on the phone," says Lucy. "There are no long awkward pauses when you are trying to think of a word."

Teens Bare Their Hearts with Instant Messages
Stanley A. Miller II

Stanley A. Miller II is a staff writer for the Milwaukee Journal Sentinel, *where this article first appeared on 26 June 2001.**

---

* Stanley A Miller II, "Teens Bare Their Hearts with Instant Messages," *Milwaukee Journal Sentinel,* 26 June 2001.

According to a study released late last week by the Pew Internet & American Life Project, a non-profit research group, 37% of teenagers said they have used instant messaging to write something they wouldn't have said in person.

"Sometimes it is easier to say what is in your heart online," a 17-year-old girl wrote in one of the study's online discussion groups. "You can type the words and hit send instead of freezing up in person. In the mornings I sometimes get love letters, and it makes me feel so good. I love hearing what my sweetie is thinking."

The report also found that 17% of teens using instant messaging said they used it to ask someone out, and 13% used it to break up with someone.

Sean Witzling, who will be a sophomore this fall at Shorewood High School, said he uses instant messaging every day, usually to coordinate social plans with his friends. Witzling said he's never asked a girl out using instant messaging, and he would never break up with one that way. "That would be too mean," he said.

Charles Giles Crosse IV, 15, thought it was mean when his girlfriend broke up with him about a year ago using instant messaging. The young couple were shooting messages back and forth about sports "when out of the blue she was like, 'oh yeah, by the way, I don't think we should see each anymore.' It came out of nowhere. I lost a lot of respect for that person."

Nick Eannelli, who will be a junior at Shorewood, said the method of communication is just too impersonal for that type of talk. Eannelli said he has never asked anyone out using instant messaging, but a friend of his did and was turned down. "I think it was more along the lines of my friend acting really strange," he said. "I think it was doomed to begin with. If you are going to do something personal, you should do it face to face."

The Pew study found there were no gender-based differences in who initiated instant-message breakups, with an equal number of boys and girls using the technology to end their relationships.

Teens' Instant-Messaging Lingo Is Evolving into a Hybrid Language
Stephanie Dunnewind

Stephanie Dunnewind is a staff writer for the Seattle Times, *where this article first appeared on 12 April 2003.**

As teens use it, instant messaging is full of acronyms (BRB equals "be right back"), words missing vowels and a complete lack of capitalization. It's like trying to read a sentence made of vanity license plates.

---

* Stephanie Dunnewind, "Teens' Instant-Messaging Lingo Is Evolving into a Hybrid Language," *Seattle Times,* 12 April 2003.

For example: "i wz gtin2d@ & now gota type it agen b patient!" equals, according to the Web site transL8it! (www.transl8it.com), "I was getting to that and now gotta type it again be patient!"

Instant messaging and chat lingo is shortened for speed since conversations are conducted in real time. If a friend is waiting for a response, you want to type it out as quickly as possible. For text messages on mobile devices, the number of characters that can fit in a transmission is limited, so the language is condensed.

"If your thumbs have got to carry the weight, you tend to do some abbreviations," explained Rob Mahowald, research manager for the Massachusetts-based IDC. "You quickly learn what shortcuts people are going to understand."

So the written language is stripped of everything unnecessary (punctuation, capitals, traditional spelling) until it's a bare, phonetic representation of how people talk.

"A Genuine Linguistic Revolution"

Some linguists argue that the Web language is a new entity, a hybrid of speech and writing. In an article on yourDictionary.com, one linguist called Net lingo "a genuine linguistic revolution." Others, however, note that it hasn't impacted language much outside the Internet yet. Teens say it's uncool to use IM acronyms in regular conversation.

"They are altering language to suit the technology," said David Silver, a University of Washington professor of communication who studies new media. Teens have also incorporated IM the same as teens have always used slang, as a way to separate themselves as a group, he said.

Nearly three-quarters of online teens use instant messaging, compared with less than half of adults, according to a 2000 survey by the Pew Internet & American Life Project.

"The strategic use of 'POS' 'parent over shoulder' is just brilliant," Silver said. "Say a teen is supposed to be doing homework but of course is on IM. A parent comes up and he quickly types 'POS' and sends it out. Suddenly everyone is talking about math homework."

Minding Your E-Manners: Over-use of Instant Messaging Can Be a Major Breach of Netiquette
Michelle Slatalla

Michelle Slatalla is a staff writer for the Gazette *(Montreal, Quebec), where this article first appeared on 25 September 1999.**

---

* Michelle Slatalla, "Minding Your E-Manners: Over-use of Instant Messaging Can Be a Major Breach of Netiquette," *New York Times* 25 Sep. 1999.

Unlike E-mail messages, which wait patiently for you to open them, an instant message is the electronic equivalent of a ringing phone because it pops up on the recipient's screen right away.

But somebody apparently forgot to ask instant-message users what they thought. Many of the features that make the service so appealing to teen-agers— its speed and the ability to see who else is online—has made it as welcome as a Friday afternoon meeting in many offices. . . .

Instant messages can be more annoying than other forms of electronic communication because they appear on screen as soon as they are sent. Recipients of voice mail, E-mail or faxes can acknowledge a message whenever it is convenient.

Just as you can turn off the ringer on your phone, you can turn off your instant messages, keeping everyone, or just certain people, from getting through. But just as with a phone that is never answered, people will wonder why you are not available for instant messages. Another strategy is to tell your computer to respond to instant messages by sending a message saying you will be back later, but that can also irritate people.

"It's the cyber-equivalent of someone walking into your office and starting up a conversation as if you had nothing better to do," said Jeanne Hinds, who publishes a Web page called Etiquette Hell, at www.thinds.com/jmh/ehell.

Hinds, whose site chronicles lapses in politeness, said instant messages violate the sense of private space.

"Even in the office, we think of our personal space as being a 5-foot radius around ourselves," she said. "Instant messages come blaring into the space, and it's an invasion."

Developing Personal and Emotional Relationships Via Computer-Mediated Communication
Brittney G. Chenault

Brittney G. Chenault holds a degree from the Graduate School of Library and Information Science at the University of Illinois, Urbana-Champaign. This article appeared in the online journal CMC Magazine *and has been widely read and quoted since its publication in 1998.**

The idea of a community accessible only via my computer screen sounded cold to me at first, but I learned quickly that people can feel passionately about e-mail and computer conferences. I've become one of them.

---

* Brittney G. Chenault, "Developing Personal and Emotional Relationships Via Computer-Mediated Communication," *CMC Magazine* May 1998, 20 Mar. 2000 <http://www.december.com/cmc/mag/1998/may/chenault.html>.

I care about these people I met through my computer . . . (Rheingold, 1993, p. 1). . . .

People meet via CMC every day, exchange information, debate, argue, woo, commiserate, and support. They may meet via a mailing list or newsgroup, and continue the interaction via e-mail. Their relationships can range from the cold, professional encounter, to the hot, intimate rendezvous. Rheingold describes people in virtual communities as using the words they type on screens to exchange pleasantries and argue, engage in intellectual discourse, conduct commerce, exchange knowledge, share emotional support, make plans, brainstorm, gossip, feud, fall in love, find friends and lose them, play games, flirt, create a little high art and a lot of idle talk.

Cyberspace Romances: Interview with Jean-François Perreault of *Branchez-vous*
John Suler

John Suler is a professor of psychology at Rider University in Lawrenceville, New Jersey, and a practicing psychologist. His publications include Contemporary Psychoanalysis *and* Eastern Thought *(1993) as well as the online hypertext book* The Psychology of Cyberspace. *This excerpt comes from that Web site and represents a comment made by Jean-François Perreault, a staff writer for* Branchez-vous, *an online magazine based in Quebec, Canada.**

My guess is that in a "true" romance on the Internet, the couple eventually will want to meet each other face-to-face. They may HAVE to meet each other for the relationship to fully develop and to be fully satisfying. For these people, the Internet simply was a way to meet each other. I say "simply" but this feature of the Internet shouldn't be underestimated. It is a POWERFUL way for people with compatible interests and personalities to find each other.

There are some people who may NOT want to meet the lover face-to-face. My guess is that these people prefer living with the fantasy that they have created (consciously or unconsciously) about the cyber-lover. . . . They may not want to meet each other face-to-face because the fantasy might be destroyed by the hard facts of reality. Who can say whether this is "wrong" or "dangerous"? Many people allow themselves the luxury of fantasy—either

---

* John Suler, "Cyberspace Romances: Interview with Jean-François Perreault of *Branchez-vous*," *The Psychology of Cyberspace,* 11 Dec. 1996, 7 Apr. 2000 <http://www.rider.edu/users/suler/psycyber/psycyber.html>.

through books, or TV, or movies. And most people don't confuse this fantasy with reality. A cyber-lover is just another type of "escape fantasy"—only it's much more interactive, and therefore much more exciting, than the more usual methods.

Click Here for Romance
Jennifer Wolcott

A staff writer for the Christian Science Monitor, *Jennifer Wolcott writes on a wide range of topics, including social issues, the arts, and popular culture.**

Online chat can sprout real-life romances that begin with surprisingly honest communication and realistic expectations, traits that many traditional relationships lack at first, according to an Ohio University sociologist who is studying relationships that begin in cyberspace. "I really feel the basis of these relationships is better and deeper than many real-life meetings because the couples are honest with each other in their writings," says Andrea Baker, assistant professor of sociology at Ohio University's Lancaster campus. . . . Baker's study suggests the written word tends to promote frank conversation in cyberspace, especially between couples who eventually want to meet face-to-face. Study participants said this immediate sincerity when meeting online was a pleasant switch from the typical blind date scenario. "Couples say this kind of honesty is absolutely necessary to forming a good relationship," Baker says. "In most cases, they are extremely honest and really cover the downsides as well as the upsides so there won't be any surprises when they meet." . . .

Honesty is what most appealed to California resident John Dwyer about the online approach. Disillusioned with the bar scene, he decided to give it a whirl. He posted a personal ad and photograph, got hundreds of responses, and eventually connected with Debbie. They married this past New Year's Eve—a year and a half after she answered his online ad. "If you are honest when talking online, you can strip away all the superficial stuff and really get to know someone," says Debbie. How did she know John was being honest? "I got a sense from the conversation whether it was real or contrived," she says. "I could tell after a while that he wasn't just someone trying to land a fish."

---

* Jennifer Wolcott, "Click Here for Romance," *Christian Science Monitor* 13 Jan. 1999, 23 Feb. 2000 <http://www.csmonitor.com/durable/1991/01/13/fp11s1-csm.shtml>.

> **You've Got Romance! Seeking Love Online:
> Net-Based Services Change the Landscape,
> If Not the Odds, of Finding the Perfect Mate**
> *Bonnie Rothman Morris*

Bonnie Rothman Morris is a journalist and screenwriter who writes frequently for the New York Times, *which is the source for this excerpt. Morris's screenplays include the comedies* Guy and Doll *and* Taking the Leap.*

Tom Buckley didn't have much use for a dating service, or so he thought. "I didn't need to pay a company to help set me up to get a date, a girlfriend, a fiancée, a wife," said Buckley, 30, a steel broker in Portland, Ore., who plays rugby in his spare time. But after a lonely Thanksgiving dinner where he was the only single adult at the family dinner table, Buckley signed up for a free week on Match.com. What ensued on the matchmaking service was an e-mail romance with Terri Muir, a schoolteacher on Vancouver Island in British Columbia. "Anybody who knew us would never have thought we would have gone down that road," Buckley said in a telephone interview. Reflecting on the couple's instant attraction, he said, "e-mail made it easier to communicate because neither one of us was the type to walk up to someone in the gym or a bar and say, 'You're the fuel to my fire.'"

Thirteen months after their first feverish exchanges, Buckley and Ms. Muir lied to their families and friends and sneaked away to Vancouver to meet for the first time. At their wedding one year later, they finally told the tale of how they had met to their 100 guests. More and more single people, used to finding everything else on the Internet, are using it to search for love. More than 2,500 Web sites for adults are now devoted to matchmaking, said Daniel Bender, founder of Cupid's Network, an Internet portal for personals sites. . . .

[Robert Spradling] struck up an online romance with a Ukrainian woman whom he had met on American Singles. The woman immediately asked him for money to pay the agency she was using to translate and send her romantic e-mails back to him. There are many such agencies in the former Soviet Union, Spradling said. Next she told Spradling she wanted to start her own matchmaking agency. Spradling, 42, an employee in the development office at Morehead State University in Kentucky, footed the bill for that, too. After sending her about $8,000, Spradling asked her to marry him, via e-mail. She said yes and invited him to Kiev. "When you meet somebody and you think you're in love, you never see any faults," said Spradling, who said the couple had made

---

* Bonnie Rothman Morris, "You've Got Romance! Seeking Love Online: Net-Based Services Change the Landscape, If Not the Odds, of Finding the Perfect Mate," *New York Times* 26 Aug. 1993.

wedding plans when he was visiting. After his return to the United States, Spradling never heard from her again. He's sworn off finding love through the Internet for now. . . . "I caution a lot of guys to be careful and keep their head and learn a lot about who they're dating online," Spradling said.

Online Dating Sheds Its Stigma as Losers.com
Amy Harmon

A graduate of the University of Michigan, Amy Harmon writes on technology issues for the New York Times, *where the article from which the following passage is excerpted first appeared on 29 June 2003.**

Online dating, once viewed as a refuge for the socially inept and as a faintly disrespectable way to meet other people, is rapidly becoming a fixture of single life for adults of all ages, backgrounds and interests. More than 45 million Americans visited online dating sites last month, up from about 35 million at the end of 2002, according to comScore Media Metrix, a Web tracking service. Spending by subscribers on Web dating sites has soared, rising to a projected $100 million or more a quarter this year from under $10 million a quarter at the beginning of 2001, according to the Online Publishers Association.

And despite the Web's reputation as a meeting ground for casual sex, a majority of the leading sites' paying subscribers now say that what they are looking for is a relationship.

Stories of deception persist. Many online daters turn out to be married, and it is taken for granted that everybody lies a little. But they are more often trumped by a pervasive dissatisfaction with singles bars, dates set up by friends and other accepted ways of meeting prospective mates.

Consider Your Purpose

Here, then, are brief selections from thirteen sources on computer-mediated communication. How do you go about synthesizing these sources?

First, remember that before considering the *how,* you must consider the *why.* In other words, what is your *purpose* in synthesizing these sources? You might use them for a paper dealing with a broader issue: the effects of

* Amy Harmon, "Online Dating Sheds Its Stigma as Losers.com," *New York Times* 29 June 2004.

computer technology on our daily lives. If this were your purpose, these sources would be used for only one section of your discussion, and the paper as a whole would advance an *argument* for a particular viewpoint about technology in modern society. Or, for a communications course you might consider the impact technology is having on communication, comparing this kind of communication with other forms of written communication and/or with face-to-face, verbal communication. The various excerpts would provide important examples of how communication is changing. Or, moving out of the academic world and into the commercial one, you might be a computer consultant preparing a brochure for a new Internet application or matchmaking Web site. In this brochure, you might want to address the personal uses to which people put these kinds of applications, or for the Web site, you would focus on the positive aspects of forming relationships on the Internet.

But for now let's keep it simple: You want to write a paper, or a section of a paper, that simply explains the impact the Internet is having on relationships between people so that those who may be interested, but who know little or nothing about these issues, will understand some aspects of the CMC phenomenon. Your job, then, is to write an *explanatory* synthesis—a synthesis that presents a focused overview of computer-mediated communication but does not advance your own opinion on the subject.

EXERCISE 4.2

Critical Reading for Synthesis

Look over the preceding readings and make a list of the ways they address the overall topics of computers, communication, and relationships. Make your list as specific and detailed as you can. Then write several lists grouping together the readings that deal with similar aspects of the overall topics. You might imagine that you were planning to write a very short synthesis on one small aspect of the broad topics; in this case, for different aspects of the topic, which readings would you use?

We asked one of our students, Alyssa Mellott, to read these passages and to use them as sources in a short paper on some of the issues surrounding CMC. We also asked her to write some additional comments describing the process of developing her ideas into a draft. We'll draw upon some of these comments in the following discussion.

Formulate a Thesis

The difference between a *purpose* and a *thesis* is a difference primarily of focus. Your purpose provides direction to your research and focus to your paper. Your thesis sharpens this focus by narrowing it and formulating it in the words of a single declarative statement. (Refer to Chapter 3 for additional discussion on formulating thesis statements.)

Since Alyssa's purpose in this case was to synthesize source material with little or no comment, her thesis would be the most obvious statement she could make about the relationship among these passages. By "obvious" we mean a statement that is broad enough to encompass the main points of all these readings. Taken as a whole, what do they *mean?* Here Alyssa describes the process she followed in coming up with a preliminary thesis for her explanatory synthesis:

> I began my writing process by looking over all the readings and noting the main point of each.
>
> Then I reviewed all of these points and identified the patterns in the readings. These I included underneath my list of main points:
>
> —Readings focus on Internet communication, or CMC.
>
> —Relationships affected by CMC: communal, long-distance, academic, romantic.
>
> —Some authors discuss positive views, others negative views, of CMC and relationships.
>
> Reviewing these points, I drafted a preliminary thesis:
>
>> The Internet is changing the ways people interact and form relationships.
>
> This was a true statement, but it sounded too vague and too obvious. It didn't adequately represent the specific kinds of interactions and relationships impacted by CMC or the concerns regarding technology and relationships. My next version followed:
>
>> Computers and the Internet create new ways for people to interact, but we have yet to see whether or not these new modes of communication will improve human interaction.
>
> This thesis was more comprehensive, but it was vague, and the last part seemed bland; it didn't reflect the strong feelings about the possible effects of CMC. I wanted my thesis to be more specific and a little more dramatic:

```
With so many computer users forming a variety of
online relationships, no one can deny that this new
technology is affecting our modes of communication;
however, reactions to these changes range widely
from excitement over our abilities to forge global
connections, to fear that such connections will
prove much less satisfying than old-fashioned human
interactions.
```

```
     Though long, this introduced the point of my
synthesis: people's mixed reactions to how CMC will
affect relationships. This working thesis would
help me structure my synthesis around specific
views on CMC. Now I proceeded to the next step in
writing—organizing my material.
```

Decide How to Use Your Source Material

The easiest way to deal with sources is to summarize them. But because you are synthesizing *ideas* rather than sources, you will have to be more selective than if you were writing a simple summary. You don't have to treat *all* the ideas in your sources, only the ones related to your thesis. Some sources might be summarized in their entirety; others, only in part. Look over your earlier notes or sentences discussing the topics covered in the readings, and refer back to the readings themselves. Focusing on some of the more subtle elements of the issues addressed by the authors, expand your earlier summary sentences. Write brief phrases in the margin of the sources, underline key phrases or sentences, or take notes on a separate sheet of paper or in a word processing file or electronic data filing program. Decide how your sources can help you achieve your purpose and support your thesis. For example, how, if at all, will you use the quotations by Rheingold contained in the passage by Chenault? How could you incorporate the personal experiences reported by some of the people who formed romantic attachments online?

Develop an Organizational Plan

An organizational plan is your map for presenting material to the reader. What material will you present? To find out, examine your thesis. Do the content and structure of the thesis (that is, the number and order of assertions) suggest an organizational plan for the paper? Expect to devote at least one paragraph of your paper to developing each section of this plan. Having identified likely sections, think through the possibilities of arrangement. Ask yourself: What information does the reader need to understand first? How do I build on this first section—what block of information will follow? Think of each section in relation to others until you have placed them all and have worked your way through to a plan for the whole paper.

Study your thesis, and let it help suggest an organization. Bear in mind that any one paper can be written—successfully—according to a variety of plans. Your job before beginning your first draft is to explore possibilities. Sketch a series of rough outlines: Arrange and rearrange your paper's likely sections until you develop a plan that both facilitates the reader's understanding and achieves your objectives as a writer. Think carefully about the logical order of your points: Does one idea or point lead to the next? If not, can you find a more logical place for the point, or are you just not clearly articulating the connections between the ideas?

Your final paper may deviate from your final plan, since in the act of writing you may discover the need to explore new material, to omit planned material, to refocus or to reorder your entire presentation. Still, a well-conceived plan will encourage you to begin writing a draft.

Summary Statements

Alyssa describes the process of organizing the material as follows.

> In writing summary statements, I noted the most important aspects of CMC and its effect on relationships:
>
> - An increasing number of people use the Internet to interact (Singh 97).
>
> - Advocates of CMC believe it could help improve community life by "improving communication, economic opportunity, civic participation, and education" (Kling 97—98).
>
> - Some fear the ways in which real human interaction is being taken over by "virtual culture" (Maasik and Solomon 98).
>
> - The Internet offers college students opportunities for meaningful discussions. It may be a useful outlet for otherwise quiet people (Branscum 99).
>
> - IM is a fast-growing mode of CMC. Teenagers love it, but others view it as frequently rude and intrusive (Edwards 99—100; Miller 100—101; Dunnewind 101—102; Slatalla 102—103).

- Via CMC, people form meaningful attachments (Rheingold qtd. in Chenault 103—104).

- CMC romances may or may not last; but CMC has enormous potential for bringing together people with similar interests (Perreault qtd. in Suler 104—105).

- Romances begun online can be more honest than those begun face-to-face (Wolcott 105).

- Online dating services get mixed reviews. Buyers must be cautious (Morris 106—107).

I tried to group some of these topics into categories that would have a logical order. First I wanted to report the rise in Internet use and its effect on relationships.
Next, I wanted to explain what Internet enthusiasts are so excited about.
I also wanted to explain the views of CMC's critics and to respond to those with some positive predictions.
Next, I intended to counter this optimistic view with words of caution from Internet skeptics about romantic relationships that begin online.
Finally, I planned to conclude with a short summary of the debate. I returned to my thesis:

> With so many computer users forming a variety of online relationships, no one can deny that this new technology is affecting our modes of communication; however, reactions to these changes range widely from excitement over our abilities to forge global connections, to fear that such connections will prove much less satisfying than old-fashioned human interactions.

Based on her thesis, Alyssa developed an outline for an eight-paragraph paper, including introduction and conclusion:

A. Introduction: explain the CMC debate.

B. Enthusiasm over the possibilities that the Internet provides for communication.

C. Skepticism about CMC relationships.

D. The growing popularity of IM.

E. Advantages of Internet relationships over old-fashioned relationships.

F. Specific example of an online relationship.

G. Words of caution and a negative example.

H. Conclusion: summing up.

Write the Topic Sentences

Option: Writing draft versions of topic sentences will get you started on each main idea of your synthesis and will help give you the sense of direction you need to proceed. Here are Alyssa's draft topic sentences for sections based on the thesis and organizational plan she developed. These sentences give an idea of the logical progression of the essay as a whole.

- An increasing number of people are becoming Internet users every day.

- Using the Internet to strengthen community life may sound like a good idea; however, skeptics warn that the quality of relationships formed through the Internet is not up to par with those formed through face-to-face human interactions.

- One of the fastest-growing forms of CMC is the instant message, or IM, which is a kind of cross between a telephone conversation and an e-mail exchange.

- Some contend that the Internet can provide certain advantages for communication that face-to-face human interactions cannot.

- Research indicates that at the start of a relationship, participants in Internet romances are often more honest and open with one another than their counterparts in traditional dating situations.

- With increasing numbers of people using Internet matchmaking services, skeptics remind us that people should exercise caution in getting to know people via CMC.

Write Your Synthesis

The first draft of Alyssa's explanatory synthesis follows below. Thesis and topic sentences are highlighted. Modern Language Association (MLA) documentation style, explained in Chapter 7, is used throughout. Note that for the sake of clarity, parenthetical references are to pages in *Writing and Reading Across the Curriculum*.

The comments and suggestions for revision made by Alyssa's instructor appear on the facing pages of this first draft.

Model Synthesis: First Draft

> ### Advantages and Disadvantages of Computer-Mediated Communication
> *Alyssa Mellott*
>
> 1 From the home, to the workplace, to the classroom, the Internet has clicked its way into our everyday lives. On any given day, research papers may be e-mailed to professors, ads are posted to sell just about anything, and arrangements to meet significant others for dinner and a movie can be made—all with the help of the Internet. In addition to providing us with such conveniences, computer-mediated communication (CMC) provides a medium for fostering new relationships. Whether you are looking for a business partner, fellow political enthusiasts, or a future spouse, the Internet can be a powerful tool for uniting people with similar interests. With so many computer users forming a variety of online relationships, no one can deny that this new technology is affecting our modes of communication; however, reactions to these changes range widely from excitement over our abilities to forge global connections, to fear that such connections will prove much less satisfying than old-fashioned human interactions.
>
> 2 An increasing number of people are becoming Internet users every day. It is estimated that by the year 2001, "fifty percent of the U.S. population will communicate via e-mail" (Singh 97). Is the growing popularity of the Internet as a form of communication and its effect on our modes of communication a positive trend? Champions of the Internet point out that in transforming the way people interact, the Internet has made communication faster, more efficient, and less expensive. Internet enthusiasts also feel that

Discussion and Suggestions for Revision

The following section summarizes the key points and suggestions for revision made during Alyssa's conference with her instructor. (For purpose of demonstration, these comments are likely to be more comprehensive than the selective comments provided by most instructors.)

Title and Paragraph 1

Your title could be more interesting and less mechanical. Your first paragraph introduces the subject with some good, specific examples, but you sound a bit too much like a proponent of the new technology, rather than a writer who is objectively presenting various positions on CMC's potential.

Your thesis statement could be shortened and tightened up. While it's good that you aim to specifically characterize the two overall positions regarding CMC, you end up oversimplifying things a bit.

Suggestions for Revision: Make the current title more interesting and less focused on a clear-cut set of oppositions.

In order to maintain an objective stance—since this essay is meant to be explanatory rather than argumentative—you might cut some of your examples here and get to the point sooner. You could then follow your introduction with a paragraph in which you develop some of the background points you raise in your current introduction—that the Internet has enormous potential for "uniting people with similar interests," as you say. You could refer to points from the readings to make your discussion more objectively explanatory.

Shorten your thesis statement by separating the two ideas you've currently joined with a semicolon: the first clause introduces the thesis you state in the second clause, so separating these ideas will help emphasize your essay's main point. More important, rephrase your thesis so that it more accurately characterizes the positions offered in the readings. For example, none of the readings emphasize the "global" dimension to the connections forged on the Internet, nor does the notion of "fear" that Internet relations will be "less satisfying than old-fashioned . . . interactions" adequately account for the negative views regarding CMC. Back up a bit and formulate a slightly less specific—and more comprehensive—statement.

Edit your use of passive voice—*who* e-mails papers to professors? Avoid clichéd phrases such as "on any given day. . . ."

Paragraph 2

This paragraph starts with a good background point about the prevalence of the Internet in our lives; then you shift to one of the key reasons some people are excited about CMC. The first idea does lead to the second, but could bear more development, as could your second point about CMC's community-building potential.

Suggestions for Revision: Consider splitting this paragraph in two. As suggested in the comments on paragraph 1, some of the points raised in your introduction

Internet forums "are building new forms of community life" (Kling 98). It has been suggested that CMC could play a role in "rebuilding [deteriorating] community life" in inner cities, suburban, and post-suburban areas of the United States. Kling quotes an African proverb, "it takes a whole village to raise a child," to express the need for a "rich community life" based on "mutual responsibility" that seems to be lacking in our modern neighborhoods (98). Some observers feel CMC can improve "communication, economic opportunity, civic participation, and education" (Kling 98).

3   Using the Internet to strengthen community life may sound like a good idea; however, skeptics warn that the quality of relationships formed through the Internet is not up to par with those formed through face-to-face human interactions. Analysts have observed that not everyone who communicates via the Internet forms "the sense of trust, mutual interest, and sustained commitments" that characterize communities (Kling 98). Others are concerned that the relationships people are building through the Internet "lack an essential core of humanity" (Maasik and Solomon 98). They feel that our social reality made up of real people is being taken over by a virtual culture. It is within this virtual culture that a danger exists for people to become "unable to conceive of others as human beings," resulting in an environment lacking in "human empathy and relatedness" (Maasik and Solomon 98). Similarly, some teachers consider e-mail to be "an unhealthy substitute for human contact" (Branscum 99).

4   One of the fastest-growing forms of CMC is the instant message, or IM, which is a kind of cross between a telephone and an e-mail conversation. Using IM, people carry on conversations in writing in real time. Increasingly, teenagers IM rather than phone or even e-mail one another (Edwards 99). America Online estimates that "by 2005 IMs will surpass e-mail as the primary way of communicating online" (Edwards 100). According to a recent study, "37% of teenagers said they have used instant messaging to write something they wouldn't have said in person" (Miller 100). The study reported that some even break up their romances through instant messages, though this is considered tacky. One youth said, "I lost a lot of

could be moved to a background paragraph—and the first two sentences in this current paragraph 2 would fit there. Look back over the readings for more ideas that would help you develop points about CMC's pervasiveness and its general, positive potential. After discussing that, you could begin a third paragraph focused upon the point about the Internet's potential for building communities. Spend more time defining "community" and explaining how, according to its advocates, CMC could replace lost community.

Edit your sentences—you have some repetitive and choppy sentence structures and passive constructions that could be rephrased in the active voice.

Paragraph 3

Paragraph 3 follows logically from paragraph 2, and you make a clear transition in your topic sentence. However, this paragraph's points would be stronger if you had explained the arguments about the Internet's community-building potential in the last paragraph.

In your effort to paraphrase points from the Maasik and Solomon reading, and to intersperse their quoted words with your own, you end up producing wordy and awkward sentences. Furthermore, when you paraphrase the authors in the sentence "They feel that our social reality . . . ," you haven't changed the wording enough to qualify as a legitimate paraphrase.

In the last sentence of this paragraph you throw in another reference that doesn't really add anything to your points. Why do you need this point?

Suggestions for Revision: Once you've developed your points further in paragraph 2, rework the points expressed by the "skeptics" in this paragraph to more clearly relate back to the ideas of community you've just discussed.

Consider dealing with the ideas from Maasik and Solomon in a block quote, or else rework your sentences to more smoothly incorporate their ideas without using their sentence structures and wording.

If you feel the added point in your last sentence is important, then clarify that importance; if it's really not necessary, then leave it out.

Paragraph 4

The sentences on breaking up romances by IM are interesting, but they seem to belong in a later part of the paper dealing with CMC romances. Here they may blur the focus. The same point applies to the sentences about IM lingo. While interesting, they don't directly relate to the thesis about the advantages and disadvantages of CMC communication.

Suggestions for Revision: Either relocate or simply drop the sentences dealing with the breakup of e-romances via IM; also drop the sentences that follow on IM lingo. Otherwise, just fix up surface problems, making passive phrases ("it can also be seen as rude and intrusive") active.

respect for that person," after his girlfriend broke up with him by IM (Miller 101). Teens have even created their own abbreviated lingo for IM communication: "I wz gtin2d@ & now gota type it agen b patient!" means "I was getting to that and now gotta type it again be patient!" BRB means "Be right back," and "POS" means "parent over shoulder," a phrase that is used just before the conversation changes direction to a more serious subject (Dunnewind 101–02). But while instant messaging is appealing and convenient, it can also be seen as rude and intrusive. According to reporter Michelle Slatalla, "Instant messages can be more annoying than other forms of electronic communication because they appear on screen as soon as they are sent. Recipients of voice mail, E-mail, or faxes can acknowledge a message whenever it is convenient" (103). As Jeanne Hinds, publisher of a Web site on "netiquette," notes, "It's the cyber-equivalent of someone walking into your office and starting up a conversation as if you had nothing better to do" (qtd. in Slatalla 103).

5   The argument has been taken a step further by some who contend that CMC can provide certain advantages to communication that face-to-face human interactions cannot. In a study of first-year college students, Stanford's Richard Holeton found that students who were ordinarily reserved were often the most active participants in Internet discussions (Branscum 99). Similarly, the Internet can serve as a way for people who are having trouble dating to find romantic partners. For instance, Tom Buckley met his wife after signing up with Match.com. Buckley noted that the Internet helped him to meet his wife because "neither one of us was the type to walk up to someone in the gym or a bar and say, 'You're the fuel to my fire'" (qtd. in Morris 106). Holeton's research and Tom Buckley's experience suggest that the Internet may provide an avenue of expression and opportunity for otherwise quiet or timid individuals.

6   Research indicates that at the start of a relationship, participants in Internet romances are often more honest and open with one another than their counterparts in traditional dating situations. Andrea Baker, assistant professor of sociology at Ohio University's Lancaster campus, who is studying romances that start over the Internet, reports that relationships that start online are "better and deeper" than traditional relationships because the

Paragraph 5

The topic sentence is confusing. You write, "The argument has been taken a step further . . . ," and this wording suggests that you're referring to the argument *against* CMC, since this is the last argument about which you've written. In actuality, however, you seem to be referring to the entire argument over CMC, not just one side of it. Other than that, this paragraph contains interesting points and good examples.

Suggestions for Revision: Change your opening sentence to more accurately reflect the paragraph's focus.

Paragraph 6

You do a nice job of extending the points made in your previous paragraph; however, your first sentence here doesn't make that relationship clear. By starting with "Research indicates . . . ," you imply that you're moving on to a new element of CMC, rather than adding to the last point.

Suggestions for Revision: Write a topic sentence that spells out how your new points relate to the last ones. You also might add a sentence that sums up your overall point at the end of the paragraph to help improve the logical "flow" between this paragraph and paragraph 7.

couples are honest in the words they write (qtd. in Wolcott 105). Like the participants in Baker's study, California resident John Dwyer found the sincerity present in online communication to be a pleasant change from more traditional dating scenes (Wolcott 105). After posting a personal ad on the Internet, Dwyer met his future wife, Debbie, who commented, "'If you are honest when talking online, you can strip away all the superficial stuff and really get to know someone'" (Wolcott 105).

7   With increasing numbers of people using Internet matchmaking services, skeptics remind us that people should exercise caution in getting to know people via CMC. After having his heart broken and his wallet drained by a romantic partner he met online, Robert Spradling has sworn off using the Internet to find love and warns others to "be careful and keep their head and learn a lot about who they're dating online" (qtd. in Morris 107).

8   Wouldn't it be nice if the saying was "What you read is what you get"? Anyone who has spent even five minutes playing with e-mail cannot deny that the enthusiasm surrounding the possibilities posed for communication by the Internet is warranted. Nevertheless, we must constantly be reminded that the computer screen poses as an effective poker face for those with insincere intentions.

Works Cited

Branscum, Deborah. "Life At High-Tech U." <u>Newsweek</u> 27 Oct. 1997: 78—80.

Dunnewind, Stephanie. "Call Them 'Generation Text': Teens' Instant-Messaging Lingo Is Evolving into a Hybrid Language." <u>Seattle Times</u> 12 Apr. 2003: E1+.

Edwards, Ellen. "IM Generation: Instant Messaging Is In, Phones Out." <u>Seattle Times</u> 16 June 2003: E4.

Kling, Rob. "Social Relationships in Electronic Forums: Hangouts, Salons, Workplaces and Communities." <u>CMC Magazine</u> July 1996:4. Feb. 2000 <http://www.december.com/cmc/ mag/1996/jul/ kling.html>.

Maasik, Sonia, and Jack Solomon, eds. <u>Signs of Life in the USA</u> Boston: Bedford Books, 1997.

Miller, Stanley A. "Passing Notes: Teens Bare Their Hearts with Instant Messages." <u>Milwaukee Journal Sentinel</u> 26 June 2001: 1M+.

Morris, Bonnie R. "You've Got Romance! Seeking Love Online: Net-Based Services Change the Landscape, If Not the Odds, of Finding the Perfect Mate." <u>New York Times on the Web</u> 26 Aug. 1999. 23 Feb. 2000 <http://www.nytimes.com/library/tech/yr/mo/circuits/ index.html>.

Paragraph 7

Again, you're lacking an effective transition here, one that makes clear the way these new points qualify or limit the positive assessments offered in paragraph 6. The Spradling story provides a nice counterpoint to the happy couple's experience in the last paragraph, but as a reader I don't get a complete picture of the actual events in Spradling's experience.

Suggestions for Revision: Write a better transitional sentence to open the paragraph. Slow down a little and tell Spradling's story more clearly. Review the reading by Suler: Is there a way in which a cyberlove relationship might apply to Spradling's difficulties in moving his romance from the online to the offline realm?

Paragraph 8

Your conclusion focuses too much on the last issue raised in your essay, while failing to bring a sense of closure to the essay by pulling together all the points of the essay.

Suggestions for Revision: Think about what all these points add up to. Yes, as your current conclusion states, the Internet can help people hide malignant intentions—but is this the whole story? Are people able to lie and conceal things in real life as well as in the virtual world? And what about your earlier points about community-building and human connection? Try to wrap things up more comprehensively, rather than focusing narrowly on the one issue of deceit.

Singh, Sanjiv N. "Cyberspace: A New Frontier for Fighting Words." Rutgers Computer and Technology Law Journal 25.2 (1999): 283.

Slatalla, Michelle. "Minding Your E-Manners: Over-use of Instant Messaging Can Be a Major Breach of Netiquette." Gazette (Montreal) 25 Sep. 1999: K2.

Wolcott, Jennifer. "Click Here for Romance." Christian Science Monitor 13 Jan. 1999. 23 Feb. 2000 <http://www.csmonitor.com/durable/1991/01/13/fp11s1-csm.shtml>.

Wright, Robert. "Will We Ever Log Off?" Time 21 Feb. 2000: 56–58./BIB/BIBSET

Revise Your Synthesis: Global, Local, and Surface Revisions

Many writers find it helpful to plan for three types of revision: (1) global, (2) local, and (3) surface. *Global revisions* affect the entire paper: the thesis, the type and pattern of evidence employed, the overall organization, the tone. A global revision may also emerge from a change in purpose. For example, the writer of this paper might decide to rewrite the draft focusing on the recent development of CMC rather than on the advantages and disadvantages of this form of communication.

Local revisions involve changes made within paragraphs: topic and transitional sentences; the type of evidence presented within a paragraph; evidence added, modified, or dropped within a paragraph; logical connections from one sentence or set of sentences within a paragraph to another.

Surface revisions deal with sentence style and construction, word choice, and errors of grammar, mechanics, spelling, and citation form.

Most of the comments and suggestions for revision offered for the preceding draft focus on local revision strategies, though the instructor has suggested a few (relatively minor) global revisions for the first paragraph (e.g., "Your thesis statement could be shortened and tightened"). Subsequent revision suggestions focus on rewriting topic sentences for clarity, splitting long paragraphs into shorter ones, providing additional evidence to support the point made in the topic sentence, dropping evidence not sufficiently supporting the paper's thesis, clarifying a narrative, and changing the focus of the concluding paragraph. A few suggestions focus on surface elements: editing for repetitive and choppy sentence structure, replacing passive sentences with active ones.

EXERCISE 4.3

Revising the Sample Synthesis

Try your hand at creating a final draft of the paper on pages 123–27 by following the revision suggestions above, together with using your own best judgment about how to improve the first draft. Make global, local, and surface changes. After trying your own version of the paper, compare it to the revised version of our student-produced paper below.

Revised Model Synthesis: Final Draft

Computer-Mediated Communication: New and Improved Human Relations or the End of Real Interaction?
Alyssa Mellott

1 From the home, to the workplace, to the classroom, the Internet has clicked its way into our everyday lives. Today's students can e-mail as file attachments their end-of-term papers to their professors and can then turn around and use e-mail to gather a group of friends for a party or to celebrate the term's completion. These online exchanges, called CMC (or computer-mediated communication), sound fairly commonplace at the turn of the millennium. But what we have yet to discover is how CMC might change both the ways we communicate and the quality of our relationships. While many praise CMC's potential to bridge barriers and promote meaningful dialogue, others caution that CMC is fraught with dangers.

2   Very soon, half of America will communicate via e-mail, according to analysts (Singh 97). We can only assume that figure will grow—rapidly—as children who have matured in the Internet era move on to college and into careers. With e-mail becoming an increasingly common form of communication, people are discovering and conversing with one another in a variety of ways that bring a new twist to old, familiar patterns. Using e-mail, people meet "to exchange pleasantries and argue, engage in intellectual discourse, conduct commerce, exchange knowledge, share emotional support, make plans, brainstorm, gossip, feud, [and] fall in love" (Chenault 104). That is, through e-mail people do what they have always done: communicate. But the medium of that communication has changed, which excites some people and concerns others.

3   Advocates argue that the Internet has not only made existing types of communication faster, more convenient, more efficient, and less expensive; it has also made possible "new forms of community life," such as chat rooms and discussion lists, in which people from all over the country and the world gather to share information and exchange points of view (Kling 98). CMC is potentially so powerful a medium

of exchange that some believe it can promote dialogue within communities that are declining. A community, after all, is built on people acting in the interests of their neighbors for the common good. Via e-mail, online newsgroups, and e-forums, neighbors will have new ways of looking out for one another (Kling 98).

4   Still, skeptics aren't convinced that electronic communication can provide the basis of lasting personal relationships, primarily because relationships initiated on a computer display lack immediacy and physical presence. What may be missing in the electronic village, say the critics, is "an essential core of humanity" (Maasik and Solomon 98):

> The unreal world of virtual culture . . . is being substituted for a social reality made up of real human beings. And such a world, based entirely on the transmission of electronic signals, is potentially a world in which human beings will be unable to conceive of others as human beings. When all interaction is electronic, [the critics] ask, where is the ground for true human empathy and relatedness? (Maasik and Solomon 98–99)

5   The fact that people communicate—via e-mail, snail (written) mail, or in person—does not guarantee that their exchanges lead to community. Members of a community trust and care for one another; they extend themselves and offer help (Kling 98). Critics of CMC argue that the supporters gloss over this important distinction when they assume that electronic forums are "building new forms of community life" (Kling 98). Talking, electronically or otherwise, marks only the beginning of a process. Community building is hard work and takes time.

6   One of the fastest-growing forms of CMC is the instant message, or IM, which is a kind of cross between a telephone and an e-mail conversation. Using IM, people carry on real time conversations in writing. Increasingly, teenagers IM rather than phone or even e-mail one another (Edwards 99). America Online estimates that "by 2005 IMs will surpass e-mail as the primary way of communicating online" (Edwards 100). According to a recent study, "37% of teenagers said they have used instant messaging to write something they wouldn't have said in person" (Miller 101). But while instant messaging is appealing and convenient, some users view it as potentially rude

and intrusive. According to reporter Michelle Slatalla, "Instant messages can be more annoying than other forms of electronic communication because they appear on the screen as soon as they are sent. Recipients of voice mail, E-mail, or faxes can acknowledge a message whenever it is convenient" (103). As Jeanne Hinds, publisher of a Web site on "netiquette," notes, "It's the cyber-equivalent of someone walking into your office and starting up a conversation as if you had nothing better to do" (qtd. in Slalatta 103).

7   Notwithstanding such concerns, proponents of CMC confidently point to examples in which the new technologies of communication bring people together in meaningful, healthy ways. In a study of first-year college students, researcher Richard Holeton of Stanford University found that students who were ordinarily reserved were often the most active participants in Internet discussions (Branscum 99). Similarly, the Internet can serve as a way for people who are having trouble dating to find partners. For instance, Tom Buckley of Portland, Oregon, met his wife after signing up with Match.com. Buckley noted that the Internet helped him to meet his wife because "neither one of us was the type to walk up to someone in the gym or a bar and say, 'You're the fuel to my fire'" (qtd. in Morris 106). Holeton's research and Buckley's experience suggest that the Internet may provide a way for otherwise quiet or timid individuals to express themselves.

8   Beyond simply providing a safe and lower-stress place to meet, the Internet may actually promote honest communication. An Ohio University sociologist, Andrea Baker, concluded from her research that individuals who begin their romance online can be at an advantage: Writing via e-mail can promote a "better and deeper" relationship than one begun in person because writing itself promotes a frank, honest exchange (qtd. in Wolcott 105). Certainly this was the experience of John Dwyer, a Californian who tired of meeting women in bars and decided instead to post an advertisement online. He eventually met the woman who would become his wife—Debbie—who said: "'If you are honest when talking online, you can strip away all the superficial stuff and really get to know someone'" (Wolcott 105). When it

works, CMC can promote a sincere exchange among those looking for lasting relationships.

9   Increasingly, Internet dating services are becoming an accepted way of meeting prospective romantic partners. As <u>New York Times</u> reporter Amy Harmon notes, "Online dating, once viewed as a refuge for the socially inept and as a faintly disrespectable way to meet other people, is rapidly becoming a fixture of single life for adults of all ages, backgrounds and interests" (107).

10   Skeptics are not so easily convinced, however. Show them an example of a relationship that blossomed online and they will point to another in which one party was betrayed emotionally or financially. Take, for instance, the experience of Robert Spradling. He met and formed a romantic attachment to a Ukrainian woman online. She encouraged the romance via e-mail and eventually asked for money to set up a business. He sent $8,000 and later, again online, asked her to marry him. She agreed, they met in Kiev, and after Spradling returned home, she disappeared—his money gone and his heart broken (Morris 106–07). Perhaps Spradling was one of the Internet romantics for whom it is wiser to avoid face-to-face meetings. That way, he could have enjoyed the interactive fantasy of a "cyber-lover" without ever having to ruin the fun with the uncomfortable truths of real life (Suler 104–05).

11   It is far from certain, then, that all or even most relationships begun online develop positively. Closer to the truth is that both online and offline, some relationships begin—and end—in deceit while others blossom. Experts do not yet know whether computer-mediated communication, because of its electronic format, alters relationships as they are forming or, rather, simply offers a new territory in which to find others. Time will tell. In the meantime, the advice that loved ones give us when we set off to find new friends—Be careful!—makes sense whether we are looking in the virtual world or down the street.

Works Cited

Branscum, Deborah. "Life at High-Tech U." <u>Newsweek</u> 27 Oct. 1997: 78—80.

Chenault, Brittney G. "Developing Personal and Emotional Relationships Via Computer-Mediated Communication." <u>CMC Magazine</u> May 1998. 20 Mar. 2000 <http://www.december.com/cmc/mag/1998/may/chenault.html>.

Edwards, Ellen. "IM Generation: Instant Messaging Is In, Phones Out." <u>Seattle Times</u> 16 June 2003: E4.

Harmon, Amy. "Online Dating Sheds Its Stigma as Losers.com." <u>New York Times</u> 29 June 2003: A1+.

Kling, Rob. "Social Relationships in Electronic Forums: Hangouts, Salons, Workplaces and Communities." <u>CMC Magazine</u> 22 July 1996. 4 Feb. 2000 <http://www.december.com/cmc/mag/1996/jul/kling.html>.

Maasik, Sonia, and Jack Solomon, eds. <u>Signs of Life in the USA</u>. Boston: Bedford Books, 1997.

Miller, Stanley A. "Passing Notes: Teens Bare Their Hearts with Instant Messages." <u>Milwaukee Journal Sentinel</u> 26 June 2001: 1M+.

Morris, Bonnie R. "You've Got Romance! Seeking Love Online: Net-Based Services Change the Landscape, If Not the Odds, of Finding the Perfect Mate." <u>New York Times on the Web</u> 26 Aug. 1999. 23 Feb. 2000 <http://www.nytimes.com/library/tech/yr/mo/circuits/index.html>.

Singh, Sanjiv N. "Cyberspace: A New Frontier for Fighting Words." <u>Rutgers Computer and Technology Law Journal</u> 25.2 (1999): 283.

Slatalla, Michelle. "Minding Your E-Manners: Over-use of Instant Messaging Can Be a Major Breach of Netiquette." <u>Gazette</u> (Montreal) 25 Sep. 1999: K2.

Suler, John. "Cyberspace Romances: Interview with Jean-François Perreault of <u>Branchez-vous</u>." <u>The Psychology of Cyberspace</u> 11 Dec. 1996. 7 Apr. 2000 <http://www.rider.edu/users/suler/psycyber/psycyber.html>.

Wolcott, Jennifer. "Click Here for Romance." <u>The Christian Science Monitor</u> 13 Jan. 1999. 23 Feb. 2000 <http://www.csmonitor.com/durable/1991/01/13/fp11s1-csm.shtml>.

CRITICAL READING FOR SYNTHESIS

- *Use the tips from Critical Reading for Summary presented in Chapter 1 (page 6).* Remember to examine the context; note the title and subtitle; identify the main point; identify the subpoints; break the reading into sections; distinguish between points, examples, and counterarguments; watch for transitions within and between paragraphs; and read actively and recursively.
- *Establish the writer's primary purpose.* Use some of the guidelines discussed in Chapter 2; is the piece primarily informative, persuasive, or entertaining? Assess whether the piece achieves its purpose.
- *Read to identify a key idea.* If you begin reading your source materials with a key idea or topic already in mind, read to identify what your sources have to say about the idea.
- *Read to discover a key idea.* If you begin the reading process without a key idea in mind yet, read to discover a key idea that your sources address.
- *Read for relationships.* Regardless of whether you already have a key idea, or whether you are attempting to discover one, your emphasis in reading should be on noting the ways in which the readings relate to each other, to a key idea, and to your purpose in writing the synthesis.

Argument Synthesis

5

WHAT IS AN ARGUMENT SYNTHESIS?

The explanatory synthesis, as we have seen, is fairly modest in purpose. It emphasizes the sources themselves, not the writer's interpretation. Because your reader is not always in a position to read your sources, this kind of synthesis, if well done, can be very informative. But the main characteristic of the explanatory synthesis is that it is designed more to *inform* than to *persuade*. As we have said, rather than arguing a particular point, the thesis in an explanatory synthesis focuses on an objective presentation of facts or opinions. As the writer of an explanatory synthesis, you remain, for the most part, a detached observer.

Recall the thesis our student devised for her final draft of the explanatory synthesis on computer-mediated communication in Chapter 4:

> While many praise CMC's potential to bridge barriers
> and promote meaningful dialogue, others caution that
> CMC is fraught with dangers.

This thesis summarizes the viewpoints people espouse in regard to CMC, arguing neither for nor against any one viewpoint.

In contrast to an explanatory thesis, an argumentative thesis is *persuasive* in purpose. Writers working with the same source material might conceive of and support opposing theses. So the thesis for an argument synthesis is a claim about which reasonable people could disagree. It is a claim with which—given the right arguments—your audience might be persuaded to agree. The strategy of your argument synthesis is therefore to find and use convincing *support* for your *claim*.

The Elements of Argument: Claim, Support, and Assumption

Let's consider the terminology we've just used. One way of looking at an argument is to see it as an interplay of three essential elements: claim, support, and assumption. A *claim* is a proposition or conclusion that you are trying to prove. You prove this claim by using *support* in the form of fact or expert opinion. Linking your supporting evidence to your claim is your *assumption* about the subject. This assumption—also called a *warrant*—is an underlying belief or principle about some aspect of the world and how it operates, as we discussed in Chapter 2. By nature, assumptions (which are often unstated) tend to be more general than either claims or supporting evidence.

For example, here are the essential elements of an argument advocating parental restriction of television viewing for their high school children:

Claim
High school students should be restricted to no more than two hours of TV viewing per day.

Support
An important new study and the testimony of educational specialists reveal that students who watch more than two hours of TV a night have, on average, lower grades than those who watch less TV.

Assumption
Excessive TV viewing adversely affects academic performance.

As another example, if we converted the thesis for our explanatory synthesis into a claim suitable for an argument synthesis, it might read as follows:

Computer mediated communication threatens to undermine human intimacy, connection, and ultimately community.

Here are the other elements of this argument:

Support
- While the Internet presents us with increased opportunities to meet people, these meetings are limited by geographical distance.
- People are spending increasing amounts of time in cyberspace: In 1998, the average Internet user spent over four hours per week online, a figure that has nearly doubled recently.
- College health officials report that excessive Internet usage threatens many college students' academic and psychological well-being.
- New kinds of relationships fostered on the Internet often pose challenges to preexisting relationships.

Assumptions

- The communication skills used and the connections formed during Internet contact fundamentally differ from those used and formed during face-to-face contact.
- "Real" connection and a sense of community are sustained by face-to-face contact, not by Internet interactions.

Arguments should be constructed logically, or rationally, so that assumptions link evidence (supporting facts and expert opinions) to claims. As we'll see, however, logic is only one component of effective arguments.

EXERCISE 5.1

Practicing Claim, Support, and Assumption

Devise two sets of claims with support and assumptions for each. First, devise a one-sentence claim addressing the positive impact (or potentially positive impact) of CMC on relationships—whether you personally agree with the claim or not. Then list the supports on which such a claim might rest and the assumptions that underlie these. Second, write a claim that states your own position on any debatable topic you choose. Again, devise statements of support and relevant assumptions.

The Three Appeals of Argument: *Logos, Ethos*, and *Pathos*

Speakers and writers have never relied upon logic alone in advancing and supporting their claims. More than 2,000 years ago, the Athenian philosopher and rhetorician Aristotle explained how speakers attempting to persuade others to their point of view could achieve their purpose by relying on one or more *appeals*, which he called *logos, ethos*, and *pathos*.

Since we frequently find these three appeals employed in political argument, we'll use political examples in the following discussion. But keep in mind that these appeals are also used extensively in advertising, legal cases, business documents, and many other types of argument.

Logos

Logos is the rational appeal, the appeal to reason. If speakers expect to persuade their audiences, they must argue logically and must supply appropriate evidence to support their case. Logical arguments are commonly of two types (often combined). The *deductive* argument begins with a generalization, then cites a specific case related to that generalization, from which follows a conclusion. A familiar example of deductive reasoning, used by Aristotle himself, is the following:

All men are mortal. (*generalization*)

Socrates is a man. (*specific case*)

Socrates is mortal. (*conclusion about the specific case*)

In the terms we've just been discussing, this deduction may be restated as follows:

Socrates is mortal. (*claim*)

Socrates is a man. (*support*)

All men are mortal. (*assumption*)

An example of a more contemporary deductive argument may be seen in President John F. Kennedy's address to the nation in June 1963 on the need for sweeping civil rights legislation. Kennedy begins with the generalizations that it "ought to be possible . . . for American students of any color to attend any public institution they select without having to be backed up by troops" and that "it ought to be possible for American citizens of any color to register and vote in a free election without interference or fear of reprisal." Kennedy then provides several specific examples (primarily recent events in Birmingham, Alabama) and statistics to show that this was not the case. He concludes:

> We face, therefore, a moral crisis as a country and a people. It cannot be met by repressive police action. It cannot be left to increased demonstrations in the streets. It cannot be quieted by token moves or talk. It is time to act in the Congress, in your state and local legislative body, and, above all, in all of our daily lives.

Underlying Kennedy's argument is the following reasoning:

All Americans should enjoy certain rights. (*assumption*)

Some Americans do not enjoy these rights. (*support*)

We must take action to ensure that all Americans enjoy these rights. (*claim*)

Another form of logical argumentation is *inductive* reasoning. A speaker or writer who argues inductively begins not with a generalization, but with several pieces of specific evidence. The speaker then draws a conclusion from this evidence. For example, in a 1990 debate on gun control, Senator Robert C. Byrd (D-VA) cites specific examples of rampant crime involving guns: "I read of young men being viciously murdered for a pair of sneakers, a leather jacket, or $20." He also offers statistical evidence of the increasing crime rate: "[I]n 1951, there were 3.2 policemen for every felony committed in the United States; this year [1990] nearly 3.2 felonies will be committed per every police officer." He concludes, "Something has to change. We have to stop the crimes that are distorting and disrupting the way of life for so many innocent, law-respecting Americans. The bill that we are debating today attempts to do just that."

Senator Edward M. Kennedy (D–MA) also used statistical evidence in arguing for passage of the Racial Justice Act of 1990, designed to ensure that minorities were not disproportionately singled out for the death penalty. Kennedy points out that between 1973 and 1980, 17 defendants in Fulton County, Georgia, were charged with killing police officers, but the only defendant who received the death sentence was a black man. Kennedy also cites statistics to show that "those who killed whites were 4.3 times more likely to receive the death penalty than were killers of blacks," and that "in Georgia, blacks who killed whites received the death penalty 16.7 percent of the time, while whites who killed received the death penalty only 4.2 percent of the time."

Of course, the mere piling up of evidence does not in itself make the speaker's case. As Donna Cross explains in "Politics: The Art of Bamboozling,"* politicians are very adept at "card-stacking." And statistics can be selected and manipulated to prove anything, as demonstrated in Darrell Huff's landmark book *How to Lie with Statistics* (1954). Moreover, what appears to be a logical argument may, in fact, be fundamentally flawed. (See Chapter 2 for a discussion of logical fallacies and faulty reasoning strategies.) On the other hand, the fact that evidence can be distorted, statistics misused, and logic fractured does not mean that these tools of reason can be dispensed with or should be dismissed. It means only that audiences have to listen and read critically—perceptively, knowledgeably, and skeptically (though not necessarily cynically).

Sometimes, politicians can turn their opponents' false logic against them. Major R. Owens (D–NY), attempted to counter what he took to be the reasoning on welfare adopted by his opponents:

Welfare programs create dependency and so should be reformed or abolished. (*assumption*)

Aid to Families with Dependent Children (AFDC) is a welfare program. (*support*)

AFDC should be reformed or abolished. (*claim*)

In his speech opposing the Republican welfare reform measure of 1995, Owens simply changes the specific (middle) term, pointing out that federal subsidies for electric power in the West and Midwest and farmers' low-rate home loan mortgages are, in effect, welfare programs. ("We are spoiling America's farmers by smothering them with socialism.") The logical conclusion—that we should reform or eliminate farmers' home loan mortgages—would clearly be unacceptable to many of those pushing for reform of AFDC. Owens thus suggests that opposition to AFDC is based less on reason than on lack of sympathy for its recipients.

---

* Donna Cross, "Politics: The Art of Bamboozling," *Word Abuse: How the Words We Use Use Us* (New York: Coward, 1979).

Using Deductive and Inductive Logic

Choose a college-related issue about which you are concerned. Write down a claim about this issue. Then write two paragraphs addressing your claim— one in which you organize your points deductively and one in which you organize them inductively. Some sample issues might include college admissions policies, classroom crowding, or grade inflation. Alternatively, you could base your paragraphs on a claim generated in Exercise 5.1.

Ethos

Ethos, or the ethical appeal, is based on the ethical nature of the person making the appeal, not on the ethical rationale for the subject under discussion. A person making an argument must have a certain degree of credibility: That person must be of good character, have sound sense, and be qualified to hold the office or recommend policy.

For example, Elizabeth Cervantes Barrón, running for senator from California as the peace and freedom candidate, begins her statement, "I was born and raised in central Los Angeles. I grew up in a multiethnic, multicultural environment where I learned to respect those who were different from me. . . . I am a teacher and am aware of how cutbacks in education have affected our children and our communities."

On the other end of the political spectrum, American Independent California gubernatorial candidate Jerry McCready also begins with an ethical appeal: "As a self-employed businessman, I have learned firsthand what it is like to try to make ends meet in an unstable economy being manipulated by out-of-touch politicians." Both candidates are making an appeal to *ethos*, based on the strength of their personal qualities for the office they seek.

L. A. Kauffman is not running for office but rather writing an article arguing against socialism as a viable ideology for the future. To defuse objections that he is simply a tool of capitalism, Kauffman begins with an appeal to *ethos*: "Until recently, I was executive editor of the journal *Socialist Review*. Before that I worked for the Marxist magazine, *Monthly Review*. My bookshelves are filled with books of Marxist theory, and I even have a picture of Karl Marx up on my wall."* Thus, Kauffman establishes his credentials to argue knowledgeably about Marxist ideology.

Conservative commentator Rush Limbaugh frequently makes use of the ethical appeal by linking himself with the kind of Americans he assumes his audiences to be (what author Donna Cross calls "glory by association"):

> In their attacks [on me], my critics misjudge and insult the American people. If I were really what liberals claim—racist, hatemonger, blowhard—I would years ago have deservedly gone into oblivion. The truth is, I provide information and analysis the media refuses to disseminate, information and analysis the public craves. People listen

---

* L. A. Kauffman, "Socialism No," *Progressive* 1 April 1993.

to me for one reason: I am effective. And my credibility is judged in the marketplace every day. . . . I represent America's rejection of liberal elites. . . . I validate the convictions of ordinary people.*

EXERCISE 5.3

Using Ethos

Return to the claim you used for Exercise 5.2, and write a paragraph in which you use an appeal to *ethos* to make a case for that claim.

Pathos

Speakers and writers also appeal to their audiences by use of *pathos*, an appeal to the emotions. Nothing is inherently wrong with using an emotional appeal. Indeed, since emotions often move people far more powerfully than reason alone, speakers and writers would be foolish not to use emotion. And it would be a drab, humorless world if human beings were not subject to the sway of feeling as well as reason. The emotional appeal becomes problematic only if it is the *sole* or *primary* basis of the argument. This imbalance of emotion over logic is the kind of situation that led, for example, to the internment of Japanese Americans during World War II or that leads to periodic political spasms to enact anti-flag-burning legislation.

President Reagan was a master of emotional appeal. He closed his first inaugural address with a reference to the view from the Capitol to the Arlington National Cemetery, where lie thousands of markers of "heroes":

> Under one such marker lies a young man, Martin Treptow, who left his job in a small-town barbershop in 1917 to go to France with the famed Rainbow Division. There, on the western front, he was killed trying to carry a message between battalions under heavy artillery fire. We're told that on his body was found a diary. On the flyleaf under the heading, "My Pledge," he had written these words: "America must win this war. Therefore, I will work, I will save, I will sacrifice, I will endure, I will fight cheerfully and do my utmost, as if the issue of the whole struggle depended on me alone." The crisis we are facing today does not require of us the kind of sacrifice that Martin Treptow and so many thousands of others were called upon to make. It does require, however, our best effort and our willingness to believe in ourselves and to believe in our capacity to perform great deeds, to believe that together with God's help we can and will resolve the problems which now confront us.

Surely, Reagan implies, if Martin Treptow can act so courageously and so selflessly, we can do the same. The logic is somewhat unclear, since the connection between Martin Treptow and ordinary Americans of 1981 is rather tenuous (as Reagan concedes); but the emotional power of Martin Treptow, whom reporters were sent scurrying to research, carries the argument.

---

* Rush Limbaugh, "Why I Am a Threat to the Left,"*Los Angeles Times*, 9 Oct. 1994, B5.

A more recent president, Bill Clinton, also used *pathos*. Addressing an audience of the nation's governors about his welfare plan, Clinton closed his remarks by referring to a conversation he had held with a welfare mother who had gone through the kind of training program Clinton was advocating. Asked by Clinton whether she thought that such training programs should be mandatory, the mother said, "I sure do." When Clinton asked her why, she said:

> "Well, because if it wasn't, there would be a lot of people like me home watching the soaps because we don't believe we can make anything of ourselves anymore. So you've got to make it mandatory." And I said, "What's the best thing about having a job?" She said, "When my boy goes to school, and they say, 'What does your mama do for a living?' he can give an answer."

Clinton uses the emotional power he counts on in that anecdote to set up his conclusion: "We must end poverty for Americans who want to work. And we must do it on terms that dignify all of the rest of us, as well as help our country to work better. I need your help, and I think we can do it."

EXERCISE 5.4

Using Pathos

Return to the claim you used for Exercises 5.2 and 5.3, and write a paragraph in which you use an appeal to *pathos* to argue for that claim.

DEMONSTRATION: DEVELOPING A SOURCE-BASED ARGUMENT SYNTHESIS— VOLUNTEERING IN AMERICA

To demonstrate how to plan and draft an argument synthesis, let's consider another subject. If you were taking an economics or sociology course, you might at some point consider the extent to which Americans volunteer— that is, give away their time freely—for causes they deem worthy. In a market economy, why would people agree to forgo wages in exchange for their labor? Are there other kinds of compensation for people who volunteer? Is peer pressure involved? Can a spirit of volunteerism be taught or encouraged? And, in light of the articles that follow and the example argument based on them, can the government—which has the constitutional right to compel military service—*compel* citizens to serve their communities (rendering their service something other than voluntary)?

Suppose, in preparing to write a short paper on volunteering, you located the following sources:

- "A New Start for National Service," John McCain and Evan Bayh
- "A Time to Heed the Call," David Gergen
- "Volunteering in the United States, 2003" Bureau of Labor Statistics, U.S. Department of Labor

- "Americorps Mission Statement"
- "National Service, Political Socialization, and Citizenship," Eric B. Gorham
- "Calls for National Service," Roger Landrum, Donald J. Eberly, and Michael W. Sherraden
- "The Moral Equivalent of War," William James
- "Crito," Plato
- "Keeping Alive the Spirit of National Service," Richard North Patterson
- "Rumsfeld: No Need for Draft; 'Disadvantages Notable,'" Kathleen T. Rhem
- "Politics and National Service: A Virus Attacks the Volunteer Sector," Bruce Chapman

We've provided excerpts for a few of these sources in the pages that follow and a summary of the others. As you read, carefully note the kinds of information and ideas you could draw upon to develop an *argument synthesis*. In preparing your papers, naturally you will draw upon entire articles and book chapters, not brief excerpts. (The discussion of how these passages can form the basis of an argument synthesis resumes on page 145.)

A New Start for National Service
John McCain and Evan Bayh

John McCain (R-AZ) and Evan Bayh (D-IN) are U.S. senators. This op-ed piece appeared in the New York Times *on 6 November 2001, a few weeks after the terrorist attacks of September 11.**

1   Since Sept. 11, Americans have found a new spirit of national unity and purpose. Forty years ago, at the height of the cold war, President John F. Kennedy challenged Americans to enter into public service. Today, confronted with a challenge no less daunting than the cold war, Americans again are eager for ways to serve at home and abroad. Government should make it easier for them to do so.

2   That is why we are introducing legislation to revamp national service programs and dramatically expand opportunities for public service.

3   Many tasks lie ahead, both new and old. On the home front, there are new security and civil defense requirements, like increased police and border patrol needs. We will charge the Corporation for National Service, the federal office that oversees national volunteer programs, with the task of assembling a plan that would put civilians to work to assist the Office of Homeland Security. The military will need new recruits to confront the challenges abroad, so our bill will also improve benefits for our service members.

---

* John McCain and Evan Bayh, "A New Start for National Service," Op-Ed, *New York Times*, 6 Nov. 2001.

4   At the same time, because the society we defend needs increased services, from promoting literacy to caring for the elderly, we [should] expand AmeriCorps and senior service programs to enlarge our national army of volunteers.

5   AmeriCorps' achievements have been impressive: thousands of homes have been built, hundreds of thousands of seniors given the care they need to live independently and millions of children tutored.

6   Since its inception in 1993, nearly 250,000 Americans have served stints of one or two years in AmeriCorps. But for all its concrete achievements, AmeriCorps has been too small to rouse the nation's imagination. Under our bill, 250,000 volunteers each year would be able to answer the call—with half of them assisting in civil defense needs and half continuing the good work of AmeriCorps.

7   We must also ask our nation's colleges to promote service more aggressively. Currently, many colleges devote only a small fraction of federal work-study funds to community service, while the majority of federal resources are used to fill low-skill positions. This was not Congress's vision when it passed the Higher Education Act of 1965. Under our bill, universities will be required to promote student involvement in community activities more vigorously. . . .

8   Public service is a virtue, and national service should one day be a rite of passage for young Americans. This is the right moment to issue a new call to service and give a new generation a way to claim the rewards and responsibilities of active citizenship.

A Time to Heed the Call
David Gergen

David Gergen is an editor-at-large for U.S. News & World Report, *in which this essay appeared on 24 December 2001. He has served as an advisor to presidents Nixon, Ford, Reagan, and Clinton and currently directs the Center for Public Leadership at the John F. Kennedy School of Government.**

1 How do we transform [our country's] new love of nation [following the events of September 11] into a lasting mission? How do we keep the flame alive? With imagination, we could do just that if we boldly call millions of young Americans to give at least a year of service to the nation. Remember FDR's Civilian Conservation Corps and the magnificent parks all those young people built in the wilderness? There are many parallel responsibilities today. Beefing up border operations, teaching kids in poor schools, helping out in hospitals—those are just a few. Add three months of physical training, with kids from Brooklyn mixing in with kids from Berkeley, and the results would be eye popping.

---

* David Gergen, "A Time to Heed the Call," *U.S. News & World Report*, 24 Dec. 2001, 60–61.

2   Giving something back. Voluntary service when young often changes people for life. They learn to give their fair share. Some 60 percent of alumni from Teach for America, a marvelous program, now work full time in education, and many others remain deeply involved in social change. Mark Levine, for example, has started two community-owned credit unions in Washington Heights, N.Y., for recent immigrants. Alumni of City Year, another terrific program, vote at twice the rates of their peers. Or think of the Peace Corps alumni. Six now serve in the House of Representatives, one (Christopher Dodd) in the Senate.

3   A culture of service might also help reverse the trend among many young people to shun politics and public affairs. Presidential voting among 18-to-29-year-olds has fallen over the past three decades from half to less than a third. In a famous poll of a year ago, some 47 percent said their regular source of political news was the late-night comedy shows. If the young were to sign up for national service, as scholar Bill Galston argues, that could lead to greater civic engagement. . . .

4   The best plan on offer today is one advanced by Sens. John McCain of Arizona, a Republican, and Democrat Evan Bayh of Indiana and given strong support by the Democratic Leadership Council. It would build on AmeriCorps, the volunteer program started by President Clinton, at first opposed and now embraced by many Republicans. AmeriCorps has achieved significant results but remains modest in size with about 50,000 volunteers. It has never enjoyed the panache of the Peace Corps—as many as 2 out of 3 Americans say they have never heard of the program. McCain and Bayh would expand AmeriCorps fivefold, to 250,000 volunteers a year, and channel half the new recruits into homeland-security efforts. The program would also open up more chances for seniors to serve—another important contribution. . . .

5   September 11 was a seminal moment for America. Everyone who lived through it will remember exactly where he or she was when the terrible news came. But the moment will pass unless we seize it and give it more permanent meaning. Fortunately, some already hear the call.

Volunteering in the United States, 2003
Bureau of Labor Statistics, U.S. Department of Labor

Every year, the Bureau of Labor Statistics (BLS) collects and analyzes patterns of volunteering in the United States. Following, in tabular form, is a summary of data collected from September 2002 to September 2003. According to the BLS, "Volunteers are defined as persons who did unpaid work (except for expenses) through or for an organization. [These data are based on] a monthly survey of about 60,000 households that obtains information on employment and unemployment among the nation's civilian noninstitutional population age 16 and over."*

---

* Bureau of Labor Statistics, "Volunteering in the United States, 2003" (Washington, DC: U.S. Department of Labor, 2003).

TABLE 5.A Volunteers by selected characteristics, September 2002 and 2003

(Numbers in thousands)

Characteristic	September 2002r			September 2003		
	Number	Percent of population	Median annual hours	Number	Percent of population	Median annual hours
Sex						
Total, both sexes	59,783	27.4	52	63,791	28.8	52
Men	24,706	23.6	52	26,805	25.1	52
Women	35,076	31.0	50	36,987	32.2	52
Age						
Total, 16 years and over	59,783	27.4	52	63,791	28.8	52
16 to 24 years	7,742	21.9	40	8,671	24.1	40
25 to 34 years	9,574	24.8	33	10,337	26.5	36
35 to 44 years	14,971	34.1	52	15,165	34.7	50
45 to 54 years	12,477	31.3	52	13,302	32.7	52
55 to 64 years	7,331	27.5	60	8,170	29.2	60
65 years and over	7,687	22.7	96	8,146	23.7	88
Educational attainment (1)						
Less than a high school diploma	2,806	10.1	48	2,793	9.9	48
High school graduate, no college (2)	12,542	21.2	49	12,882	21.7	48
Less than a bachelor's degree (3)	15,066	32.8	52	15,966	34.1	52
College graduates	21,627	43.3	60	23,481	45.6	60

(1) Data refer to persons 25 years and over.
(2) Includes high school diploma or equivalent.
(3) Includes the categories, some college, no degree; and associate degree.
r = revised. Estimates for 2002 have been revised to reflect the use of Census 2000-based population controls. See the Technical Note for additional information.

AmeriCorps Mission Statement

"AmeriCorps is a network of national service programs that engage more than 50,000 Americans each year in intensive service to meet critical needs in education, public safety, health, and the environment. AmeriCorps members serve through more than 2,100 non-profits, public agencies, and faith-based organizations. They tutor and mentor youth, build affordable housing, teach computer skills, clean parks and streams, run after-school programs, and help communities respond to disasters. Created in 1993, AmeriCorps is part of the Corporation for National and Community Service, which also oversees Senior Corps and Learn and Serve America. Together these programs engage more than 2 million Americans of all ages and backgrounds in service each year."* AmeriCorps' four-part mission involves "Getting Things Done," "Strengthening Communities," "Encouraging Responsibility," and "Expanding Opportunity."

National Service, Political Socialization, and Citizenship
Eric B. Gorham

This first chapter of Eric B. Gorham's National Service, Citizenship, and Political Education *(1992) defines national service "as a nation-wide program of community work that citizens, mostly young people, enter for one or two years. It is either voluntary or coercive, and employs participants in public sector or 'voluntary' sector jobs at subminimum wages. In the process, participants serve the needs of the nation, acquire job and life skills, and learn the essentials of American citizenship." Gorham goes on to trace the history of America's national service in the twentieth century, referring to William James's famous "Moral Equivalent of War," the initiatives of various presidents, beginning with Roosevelt, and various local initiatives like Seattle's Program for Local Service. According to Gorham, "Proponents [of national service] maintain that young people must learn citizenship, and either they argue that such programs inculcate this generally, or they have attached particular programs designed to increase the civic competence of young adults. Indeed, the rhetoric of citizenship . . . defends national service on moral and political grounds." In his book, Gorham argues that the language government uses to promote programs for national service betrays an effort to "reproduce a postindustrial, capitalist economy in the name of good citizenship." Eric Gorham is associate professor of political science at Loyola University, New Orleans.†*

---

* Institute for Future Work Force Development. "National AmeriCorps History." *Youth in Action AmeriCorps.* Northern Arizona University. 10 July 2003. 20 July 2003 <http://www4.nau.edu> Path: americorps; American History.

† For credit information on Gorham, see the "Works Cited" list on pp. 154–55.

Calls for National Service
Roger Landrum, Donald J. Eberly, and Michael W. Sherraden

The passage introduces the work of William James, who in a famous speech in 1906 essentially began America's conversation about national service in the twentieth century. The authors suggest that "James was clearly thinking only of young men and the image of Ivy League undergraduates. . . . He didn't consider the issue of constitutional limits on involuntary servitude. His recommendation of conscription was softened only by the concepts of collectivity and social sanctions. . . . Still, James succeeded in embedding a phrase, 'the moral equivalent of war,' in the national consciousness; he raised the fundamental issue of proper socialization of youth in the context of a democracy at peace; and he planted the idea of national service." The essay appears in a collection of scholarly commentaries on national service, edited by Sherraden and Eberly.*

The Moral Equivalent of War
William James

William James (1842–1910), an influential philosopher, psychologist, and professor at Harvard University, is best known for his works The Varieties of Religious Experience *(1902) and* The Principles of Psychology *(1890). "The Moral Equivalent of War," first delivered in 1906 as a speech at Stanford University and later published in 1910, became a seminal document in the national service movement. In the speech, James argues that the qualities of character that distinguish soldiers (for instance, self-discipline and regard for the common good) are important to developing and maintaining a civil society. James believes these qualities "can be bred without war" and lays out a "moral equivalent of war" for doing so. The essay, which is central to any understanding of the national service movement in the twentieth century, can be found at <http://www.emory.edu/EDUCATION/mfp/moral.html>.*

Crito
Plato

Socrates (c. 470 BCE–c. 399 BCE) was condemned to die by the authorities of Athens for "corrupting" its youth through his teachings. In a famous dialogue of Plato, Crito wishes to convince his friend and teacher to escape before the sentence (death by the drinking of hemlock, a poison) is to be carried out. Instead of running, Socrates explains to Crito the obligations of a citizen to the state. His reference to "the laws" and to "we" and "us" is to the authorities of Athens—and, by extension, to any governing body to which people freely give their allegiance.

---

* For credit information on Landrum, *et al.*, see the "Works Cited" list on pp. 154–55.

The excerpt here provides a flavor for Socrates' logic. The entire dialogue can be found at the Classic Literature Online Library, <http://www.greece.com/library/plato/crito_04.html>.

Socrates:

Then the laws will say: "Consider, Socrates, if this is true, that in your present attempt you are going to do us wrong. For, after having brought you into the world, and nurtured and educated you, and given you and every other citizen a share in every good that we had to give, we further proclaim and give the right to every Athenian, that if he does not like us when he has come of age and has seen the ways of the city, and made our acquaintance, he may go where he pleases and take his goods with him; and none of us laws will forbid him or interfere with him. Any of you who does not like us and the city, and who wants to go to a colony or to any other city, may go where he likes, and take his goods with him. But he who has experience of the manner in which we order justice and administer the State, and still remains, has entered into an implied contract that he will do as we command him. And he who disobeys us is . . . wrong."*

Keeping Alive the Spirit of National Service
Richard North Patterson

Richard North Patterson is a prolific novelist who lives in San Francisco and Martha's Vineyard. His books include Protect and Defend *(2001) and* Balance of Power *(2003). In an op-ed essay on national service appearing in the* Boston Globe *on 1 August 1999, he argues for congressional re-authorization of the AmeriCorps program as a way of restoring to American youth what he thinks was lost over the past several decades: "a common experience, a chance to serve, which cuts across the barriers of race, class, and education." In national service, Patterson sees "the chance for our young to make their best contribution to a stronger country and a better society."*

Rumsfeld: No Need for Draft; "Disadvantages Notable"
Kathleen T. Rhem

Kathleen Rhem writes for the American Forces Press Service. In an article posted on the DefenseLINK Web site on 7 January 2003, she cites senior Pentagon officials in reporting that the Unites States has no need for, and no plans to implement, a national military draft. The all-volunteer army, says the Chairman of the Joint Chiefs of Staff, is "efficient; it's effective; it's given the United States of America . . . a military that is second to none." The

---

* Plato, "Crito." *Classic Greek Literature Online*, 28 June 2004 <http://www.greece.com/library/plato/crito_04.html>.

Pentagon intends to keep its forces voluntary to maintain morale and readiness. In fact, forced military service, say the officials, has "notable disadvantages."

Politics and National Service:
A Virus Attacks the Volunteer Sector
Bruce Chapman

Bruce Chapman, former U.S. Ambassador to the U.N. organizations in Vienna and former senior fellow at the Hudson Institute, currently serves as president of the Discovery Institute of Seattle, Washington, a public policy center for studying national and international affairs. An early proponent of the all-volunteer army who dedicated many years to public service (as secretary of state for the State of Washington, former director of the U.S. Census Bureau, and as an aide to President Reagan), Chapman opposes all government involvement in volunteer programs, likening proposals for government-sponsored national service to the influenza virus. The excerpted selection that follows appears in a collection of essays, National Service: Pro & Con *(1990).**

1   Why does the national service virus keep coming back? Perhaps because its romance is so easy to catch, commanding a nostalgic imagination and evoking times when Americans were eager to sacrifice for their country. Claiming to derive inspiration from both military experience and the social gospel—if we could only get America's wastrel youth into at least a psychic uniform we might be able to teach self-discipline again and revive the spirit of giving—it hearkens back to William James's call for a "moral equivalent of war." But at the end of the twentieth century should we be looking to war for moral guidance?

2   True service is one of the glories of our civilization in the West, especially in the great independent (or volunteer) sector of American society. Inspiration for service in the West comes from the Bible in parable and admonition and is constantly restated in the long historical tradition of Judeo-Christian faith. Personal service is a freewill offering to God. This is very different from performance of an obligation to government, which is a tax on time or money.

3   True service, then, has a spiritual basis, even for some outside the Judeo-Christian tradition per se. Fulfillment of an obligation to government, in contrast, has a contractual basis unless it is founded on an outright commitment to a coercive utopianism. Either way, it is not true service. Nor can enrollment in a government-funded self-improvement project or acceptance of a government job be called true service. Indeed, when coercion or inducements are provided, as in the various national service schemes, the spirit of service is to that degree corrupted.

---

* Bruce Chapman, "Politics and National Service: A Virus Attacks the Volunteer Sector," Williamson M. Evers, ed. *National Service: Pro & Con* (Stanford: Hoover Institution Press, 1990) 133–44.

Consider Your Purpose

As with the explanatory synthesis, your specific purpose in writing an argument synthesis is crucial. What, exactly, you want to do will affect your claim, the evidence you select to support your claim, and the way you organize the evidence. Your purpose may be clear to you before you begin research, may emerge during the course of research, or may not emerge until after you have completed your research. (Of course, the sooner your purpose is clear to you, the fewer wasted motions you will make. On the other hand, the more you approach research as an exploratory process, the likelier that your conclusions will emerge from the sources themselves, rather than from preconceived ideas. For a discussion on locating and evaluating sources, see Chapter 7.)

Let's say that while reading these sources, your own encounters with a service organization (perhaps you help schoolchildren improve their literacy skills) have influenced your thinking on the subject. You find yourself impressed that so many people at the literacy center volunteer without being compelled to do so. You observe that giving time freely adds to the pleasures of volunteering, and to its significance as well. Meanwhile, perhaps your school is considering a service "requirement"—that is, a mandate that all students perform a given number of community service hours in order to graduate. The juxtaposition of "compelled" service with freely given service sparks in you an idea for a source-based paper.

You can understand and even sympathize with the viewpoints of educators who believe that while they have students in their clutches (so to speak), they have an opportunity to pass on an ethic of service. To students who would not volunteer time on their own, setting a graduation requirement makes sense. Yet you might regard "forced" volunteerism as a contradiction in terms that defeats the essential quality of volunteering: freely donated time. Perhaps you believe that time given freely to meet the needs of others is an act of selflessness that brings profound satisfaction. Your purpose in writing, then, emerges from these kinds of response to the source material.

Making a Claim: Formulate a Thesis

As we indicated in the introduction to argument synthesis, one useful way of approaching an argument is to see it as making a *claim*. A claim is a proposition, a conclusion that you are trying to prove or demonstrate. If your purpose is to demonstrate that the state should not compel people to serve their communities, then that is the claim at the heart of your argument. The claim is generally expressed in one-sentence form as a *thesis*. You draw *support* from your sources as you argue logically for your claim. At times, you may also argue by making appeals to *ethos* and *pathos* (see pages 131–36).

Of course, not every piece of information in a source is useful for supporting a claim. By the same token, you may draw support for your claim from sources that make entirely different claims. You may use as support for your own claim, for example, a sentiment expressed in William James's "On the Moral Equivalent of War," that values such as selfless concern for the common good, learned through service, "are absolute and permanent human goods." Yet while James called for "a conscription of the whole youthful population" to nonmilitary service projects, you may believe that service should be voluntary. Still, you could cite James and comment, where you think appropriate, on where you and he diverge.

Similarly, you might use one source as part of a *counterargument*—an argument opposite to your own—so that you can demonstrate its weaknesses and, in the process, strengthen your own claim. On the other hand, the author of one of your sources may be so convincing in supporting a claim that you adopt it yourself, either partially or entirely. The point is that *the argument is in your hands*: You must devise it yourself and must use your sources in ways that will support the claim expressed in your thesis.

You may not want to divulge your thesis until the end of the paper, to draw the reader along toward your conclusion, allowing the thesis to flow naturally out of the argument and the evidence on which it is based. If you do this, you are working *inductively*. Or you may wish to be more direct and *begin* with your thesis, following the thesis statement with evidence to support it. If you do this, you are working *deductively*. In academic papers, deductive arguments are far more common than inductive arguments.

Based on your own experience and reactions to reading sources, you may find yourself agreeing with Bruce Chapman's argument that compelled or monetarily induced service "corrupts" the experience of service. At the same time, you may find yourself unwilling to take Chapman's extreme stance that even modest stipends such as the ones earned while working for AmeriCorps and other government programs constitute "corruption." While you believe that government programs encouraging service are beneficial, you certainly don't want to see the federal government create a nonmilitary version of compulsory national service. After a few tries, you develop the following thesis:

> The impulse to expand service through volunteer programs like AmeriCorps, VISTA, and the Peace Corps is understandable, even praiseworthy. But as volunteerism grows and gains public support, we should resist letting its successes become an argument for *compulsory* national service.

Decide How You Will Use Your Source Material

Your claim commits you to (1) discussing the benefits of service in government-sponsored programs like AmeriCorps and VISTA, and (2) arguing that, benefits notwithstanding, there are good reasons not to make national service compulsory. The sources provide plenty of information and ideas—that is, evidence—that will allow you to support your claim. (You might draw on one universally available source, the U.S. Constitution, not included in the materials here.) William James and Plato, backed by contemporary commentators Eric Gorham and Roger Landrum, Donald Eberly, and Michael Sherraden, provide a philosophical and historical foundation for the paper. The statistics generated by the Department of Labor offer current, accurate information on volunteerism in America. The selections by David Gergen, Richard North Patterson, and Senators McCain and Bayh provide pro-service arguments, while the essay by Bruce Chapman provides a negative one.

Develop an Organizational Plan

Having established your overall purpose and your claim, having developed a thesis (which may change as you write and revise the paper), and having decided how to use your source materials, how do you logically organize your essay? In many cases, including this one, a well-written thesis will suggest an overall organization. Thus, the first part of your argument synthesis will define volunteerism and set a broad historical context, along with mention of a possible early attempt to make national service compulsory. The second part will argue that national service should *not* be made compulsory. Sorting through your material and categorizing it by topic and subtopic, you might arrive at the following outline:

```
   I. Introduction. Pervasiveness of volunteerism in
      America. Use Bureau of Labor Statistics data.
  II. The desire to "make more of a good thing." The
      McCain/Bayh "Call to Service Act." Thesis.
 III. Intellectual history of service:
      A. Recent history. Refer to William James.
         State that service need not be military.
      B. Ancient history. Refer to Plato. State that
         citizens owe the State an obligation.
  IV. Can the U.S. government compel citizens to
      service?
      A. Military service. Yes. Right granted by
         U.S. Constitution.
      B. Transition: military vs. civilian.
      C. Civilian service: No.
         1. Logical reason: public service is not
            analogous to military service.
         2. Moral reason: compelled or induced ser-
            vice (that is, with money) "corrupts"
            spirit of service.
            a. Concede point that "less pure" forms
               of service that pay stipends, such as
               AmeriCorps and VISTA, are beneficial.
```

> b. But state forcefully that compulsory (as opposed to minimally compensated) service does corrupt the spirit of service.

V. Conclusion:

> A. Government should expand opportunities to serve *voluntarily* (even with pay).
>
> B. It should resist the impulse to compel young people to serve.

Argument Strategy

The argument represented by this outline will build not only on evidence drawn from sources but also on the writer's assumptions. Consider the bare-bones logic of the argument:

> Voluntary service, paid or unpaid, promotes good citizenship and benefits the community. (*assumption*)
>
> People who have worked in volunteer programs have made significant contributions to community and public life. (*support*)
>
> We should support programs that foster volunteerism. (*claim*)

The crucial point about which reasonable people will disagree is the *assumption* that unpaid *and* paid volunteer service promote good citizenship. One source author, Bruce Chapman, makes a partial and extreme form of this assumption when he writes that financially rewarded service is "corrupted" (see page 144). A less-extreme assumption—the one guiding the model paper—is possible: Citizenship can be learned in a minimally paid environment such as AmeriCorps. The writer of the model paper agrees with Chapman, however, about another assumption: that nonmilitary service should never be forced on anyone.

Writers can accept or partially accept an opposing assumption by making a *concession*, in the process establishing themselves as reasonable and willing to compromise. In our example, the writer does exactly this (see paragraph 10 in the sample synthesis that follows) and uses as *supporting evidence* facts from David Gergen's report that many paid veterans of government-sponsored teaching programs learn about citizenship and continue to teach after their contracted time is up. By raising potential objections and making concessions, the writer blunts the effectiveness of *counterarguments*.

The *claim* of the example argument about service is primarily a claim about *policy*, about actions that should (or should not) be taken. An argument can also concern a claim about *facts* (Does X exist? Does X lead to Y? How can we define X?) or a claim about *value* (What is X worth?). You have seen that the present argument rests on an assumed definition of "service."

Depending on how you define the term, you will agree—or not—with the writer. Among the source authors, Bruce Chapman defines service one way (it is neither rewarded with money nor compelled), while David Gergen and Senators McCain and Bayh define it another (as work done with or without minimal pay to help others and reinforce core values). As you read the following paper, watch how the writer weaves these opposing views into the argument.

A well-reasoned argument will involve a claim primarily about fact, value, *or* policy. Secondary arguments are sometimes needed, as in the present example, to help make a case.

Draft and Revise Your Synthesis

The final draft of a completed synthesis, based on the above outline, follows. Thesis, transitions, and topic sentences are highlighted; Modern Language Association (MLA) documentation style, explained in Chapter 7, is used throughout. Note that for the sake of clarity, references in the following synthesis are to pages in *Writing and Reading Across the Curriculum*.

A cautionary note: When writing syntheses, it is all too easy to become careless in properly crediting your sources. Before drafting your paper, please review the section on avoiding plagiarism in Chapter 1 (pages 42–44) as well as the relevant sections on citing sources in Chapter 7 (pages 214–33).

Model Synthesis

Keeping Volunteering Voluntary

1 The spirit of volunteerism is alive and well in America. In 2002–2003, 28.8 percent of Americans, 16 and older, some 63.8 million, freely gave time to their communities (Bureau 140). Moved by a desire to serve others, more than one-quarter of us donate 52 hours a year, more than one full work-week, to building shelters, coaching Little League, caring for the elderly, teaching literacy, and countless other community minded pursuits (Bureau 140). Experts tell us that volunteerism builds character, teaches citizenship, and addresses unfulfilled national needs (Gorham 141).

2 Saying that nearly one in three Americans volunteer is another way of saying that just more than two in three do not. Given volunteering's benefits both to the individual and the community, it is little wonder that from time to time politicians propose to make more of a good thing. In this spirit, in November 2001 Senators John McCain (R-AZ) and Evan

Bayh (D-IN) introduced Bill S1274, the "Call to Service Act," which would dramatically increase the opportunities to serve in government-sponsored volunteer programs. "Public service is a virtue," write the senators in a *New York Times* op-ed piece not quite two months after the horrors of September 11, 2001. They believe that this "is the right moment to issue a new call to service and give a new generation a way to claim the rewards and responsibilities of active citizenship." The impulse to expand service through volunteer programs like AmeriCorps, VISTA, and the Peace Corps is understandable, even praiseworthy. But as volunteerism grows and gains public support, we should resist letting its successes become an argument for compulsory national service.

3   Senators McCain and Bayh do not call for compulsory service. Nonetheless, one can hear an echo of the word "compulsory" in their claim that "national service should one day be a rite of passage for young Americans." The word "should" suggests obligation, and the word "all" is clearly implied. It's not a stretch to imagine the senators and others at some point endorsing a program of compulsory service, an idea that has been around for nearly a century. In 1906, the philosopher William James called for "a conscription of the whole youthful population" to nonmilitary projects that would improve character (142). James, whom many consider the intellectual father of national service, admired the discipline and sacrifice of soldiers but thought it absurd that such "[m]artial virtues" as "intrepidity, contempt of softness, surrender of private interest, [and] obedience to command" should be developed only in the service of war. He imagined a "reign of peace" in which these qualities would "remain the rock upon which" peaceful states might be built (142).

4   In the early twentieth century, there were not nearly as many young people as today, both in the general public and in college (Landrum, Eberly, and Sherraden 142), and so the details of implementing a plan for national service may have seemed manageable. A hundred years later we might regard James's proposal as impractical or even illegal, but at the time he struck an important chord. His vision of learning what Senators McCain and Bayh call "the rewards and responsibilities of active citizenship" (138) through nonmilitary service in peace time (a "moral equivalent of war") entered our national

vocabulary and remains a part of it today (Landrum, Eberly, and Sherraden 142).

5   The question of what sort of service, or obligation, citizens owe a country is as old as civilization. In one of his famous dialogues, Plato records a conversation between Socrates, whom Athens had imprisoned and condemned to death for corrupting the city's youth with his teachings, and a friend who urges that he escape and save himself. Socrates argues that if he has accepted and enjoyed the privileges of citizenship, then he must also accept the judgment of the State. This is his obligation. According to Socrates, citizens obligate themselves to the State when they accept its benefits (143). But how is that obligation to be paid? Some twenty-four hundred years after Socrates accepted what he thought was his duty and drank a cup of hemlock, Americans pay their obligations to the government differently (thank goodness!): through taxes, jury duty, and obedience to laws passed by elected officials.

6   Can the government compel us to do more? Can it compel us, for instance, to military or nonmilitary service? The U.S. Constitution grants Congress the right to raise armies (Article 1, Section 8, Clause 14). The way Congress chooses to do this, however, reflects the needs of a particular time. During World War II and the Vietnam War, the government implemented a military draft. Today, for reasons of professionalism and morale, the Department of Defense prefers an all-volunteer army to an army of conscripts. The Chairman of the Joint Chiefs of Staff was recently reported to have said that the "country doesn't need a draft because the all-volunteer force works—in fact, the United States has the most effective military in the world precisely because it is all-volunteer" (Rehm 143—44).

7   The State has a constitutional right to draft young people into military service in times of military need, whether it chooses to exercise that right through an all-volunteer or a conscripted army. But does the State also have the right to require citizens to perform nonmilitary service? For example, because our libraries are understaffed, our parks overgrown, and many of our schoolchildren reading below grade level, should the State be able to require citizens to serve the unmet needs of the larger community? No—for both logical and moral reasons.

8   Military need is not logically equivalent to non-military need, mostly because we fulfill nonmilitary needs through the normal operations of government. When the State identifies work to be done for the common good, it taxes citizens and directs its employees to perform that work. The State might also put out bids and pay contractors to perform the work. This is how we build highways and libraries. If the State performs these basic functions poorly, it fails in its responsibilities. The remedy to this failure should not be the drafting of America's youth into national service for one or two years. The State could not honestly or reasonably call for national service as a means of improving the moral character of youth when its real need is to find cheap labor for cleaning streets and teaching third graders how to read. If the State lacks the money or competence to do its work well, then citizens should overhaul the system by electing new, more effective represen-tatives. If necessary, the legislature could raise taxes. But it should not use its own failures to jus-tify public service.

9   Nor could the State compel young people to national, nonmilitary service on moral grounds. We know that volunteerism promotes selflessness, a con-cern for community, and an appreciation of country (McCain and Bayh; Gergen; James; Patterson). Still, the essential quality of volunteerism is that it is time given freely. "True service," writes Bruce Chapman, "has a spiritual basis [rooted in the Judeo-Christian tradition]. . . . Fulfillment of an obligation to government, in contrast, has a contractual basis." Chapman argues that "performance of an obligation to government . . . is a tax on time or money." The spirit of service is "corrupted" when it is either forced or rewarded with money (144).

10   Chapman makes the extreme argument that volunteer programs that pay youth in room and board, health care, and tuition vouchers corrupt the spirit of giving. He ignores the financial realities of young people, many of whom, if they received no money for their service, would refuse to serve. And then they would lose the possibility of learning from programs that encourage civic participation and patriotism. That would be a shame, for the members of AmeriCorps, the Peace Corps, and VISTA, for instance, all receive a small stipend. They grow as

individuals and as citizens, learning life-long lessons. Former presidential advisor and journalist David Gergen describes this growth:

> Voluntary service when young often changes people for life. They learn to give their fair share. Some 60 percent of alumni from Teach for America, a marvelous program, now work full time in education, and many others remain deeply involved in social change. . . . Alumni of City Year, another terrific program, vote at twice the rates of their peers. Or think of the Peace Corps alumni. Six now serve in the House of Representatives, one (Christopher Dodd) in the Senate. (139)

Unquestionably, national programs for volunteers can benefit both the individuals serving and the communities served—even if those individuals receive a small stipend. So we don't have to accept Chapman's extreme position that even a hint of money "corrupts" the volunteer's spirit.

11   Still, as Chapman points out, volunteerism that is forced in any way, that turns the impulse to serve into an obligation, would corrupt. If the State required nonmilitary service for the "good" of the individual (and recall that it could not reasonably or honestly do so), the act of service would no longer be rooted in generosity. And it is the spirit of generosity, of one person's freely giving to another, that underlies all the good that volunteering achieves. Convert the essential generous impulse to an obligation, and the very logic for compelling service—to teach civic values—disappears. The State could no more expect those forced into service to have learned good citizenship or patriotism than we could expect a child whose parents order him to "make friends with Johnny" to have learned anything useful about friendship or to feel a special kinship with Johnny. Affection, citizenship, and patriotism don't work that way. They are freely given, or they are coerced. And if coerced, they are corrupt.

12   Without any incentive other than the good it would do their communities and their own hearts, 63.8 million Americans—more than one quarter of the country—volunteer. Could more people volunteer, specifically more young people? Yes, especially in light of the finding that young people in their early twenties volunteer the least, relative to all other age groups (Bureau 140). The McCain/Bayh "Call to Service Act"

deserves enthusiastic support, as does any effort to encourage service by people younger than 25. Those who serve while young turn out to be more involved with their communities over the course of their lives (Gergen; AmeriCorps), and such involvement can only benefit us all. Reasonable rewards such as tuition vouchers, minimal pay, health care, and room and board can give young people the safety net they need to experiment with serving others and in that way discover their own wellsprings of generosity.

13   So let's support McCain/Bayh and every such effort to encourage service. Ideally, enough programs will be in place one day to offer all high school and college graduates the option of serving their communities. "[T]oo often," writes Richard North Patterson, "we offer young people a vision of community which extends to the nearest shopping mall" (143). Government-sponsored programs for service can make us better than that, and we should promote volunteerism wherever and whenever we can. But we must guard against using the success of these programs as a pretext for establishing mandatory national or community service.

Works Cited

Bureau of Labor Statistics. "Volunteering in the United States, 2003." 18 Dec. 2003. 17 Jan. 2004 <http://www.bls.gov/news.release/volun.nr0.htm>.

Chapman, Bruce. "Politics and National Service: A Virus Attacks the Volunteer Sector." <u>National Service: Pro & Con</u>. Ed. Williamson M. Evers. Stanford, CA: Hoover Institution P, 1990. 133–44.

Constitution of the United States of America. The New York Public Library Desk Reference. New York: Webster's New World, 1989.

Corporation for National and Community Service. "AmeriCorps Mission." <u>AmeriCorps: Getting Things Done. Program Directory, Spring/Summer 1995</u>. Microfiche Y2N.21/29 10AM3. Washington, DC: GPO, 1995.

Gergen, David. "A Time to Heed the Call." <u>U.S. News & World Report</u> 24 Dec. 2001: 60–61.

Gorham, Eric B. "National Service, Political Socialization, and Citizenship." <u>National Service, Citizenship, and Political Education</u>. Albany: SUNY P, 1992. 5–30.

James, William. "The Moral Equivalent of War." <u>International Conciliation</u> 27 (Washington, DC: Carnegie Endowment for International Peace, 1910): 8-20.

Landrum, Roger, Donald J. Eberly, and Michael W. Sherraden. "Calls for National Service." <u>National Service: Social, Economic and Military Impacts</u>. Ed. Michael W. Sherraden and Donald J. Eberly. New York: Pergamon, 1982. 21–38.

McCain, John, and Evan Bayh. "A New Start for National Service." <u>New York Times</u> 6 Nov. 2001: A25.

Patterson, Richard North. "Keeping Alive the Spirit of National Service." <u>Boston Globe</u> 1 Aug. 1999: A19.

Plato, "Crito." <u>Classic Literature Online Library</u>. Trans. Benjamin Jowett. 17 July 2003 <http://www.greece.com/library/plato/crito_04.html>.

Rhem, Kathleen T. "Rumsfeld: No Need for Draft; 'Disadvantages Notable.'" <u>American Forces Information Service</u> 7 Jan. 2003. 17 July 2003 <http://www.dod.gov/news/Jan2003/n01072003_200301074.html>.

Discussion

The writer of this argument synthesis on compulsory national service attempts to support a *claim*—one that favors national service but insists on keeping it voluntary—by offering *support* in the form of facts (rates of volunteerism from the Bureau of Labor Statistics) and opinions (testimony of experts). However, since the writer's claim rests on a definition of "true service," its effectiveness depends partially upon the extent to which we, as readers, agree with the *assumptions* underlying that definition. (See our discussion of assumptions in Chapter 2, pages 56–57.) An assumption (sometimes called a *warrant*) is a generalization or principle about how the world works or should work—a fundamental statement of belief about facts or values. In this particular case, the underlying assumption is that "true service" to a community must be voluntary, never required. The writer makes this assumption explicit. Though you are under no obligation to do so, stating assumptions explicitly will clarify your arguments to readers.

Assumptions often are deeply rooted in people's psyches, sometimes deriving from lifelong experiences and observations and not easily changed, even by the most logical of arguments. People who learned the spirit of volunteerism early in life, perhaps through "required" activities in religious or public school, might not accept the support offered for the claim that required service would be illogical or "corrupted." But others might well be persuaded and might agree that programs to expand opportunities for national service should be supported, though service itself should never be compelled. A discussion of the model argument's paragraphs, along with the argument strategy for each, follows. Note that the writer avoids plagiarism by carefully attributing and quoting sources.

- **Paragraph 1:** The writer uses statistics to establish that a culture of volunteerism is alive and well in America.

  Argument strategy: In this opening paragraph, the writer sets up the general topic—volunteerism in America—and establishes that Americans volunteer in impressive numbers. The writer uses information from the Bureau of Labor Statistics to anticipate and deflect possible criticism from those who might say: "So few of us volunteer that we should require national service in order to promote citizenship and to build character."

- **Paragraph 2:** Here the writer sets a context for and introduces the McCain/Bayh proposal to expand national service. The writer then presents the thesis.

    Argument strategy: This paragraph moves in one direction with an inspiring call to service by Senators McCain and Bayh and then takes a sharp, contrasting turn to the thesis. The first part of the thesis, "as volunteerism grows and gains public support," clearly follows from (and summarizes) the first part of paragraph 2. The transition "But" signals the contrast, which sets up the warning. A contrast generates interest by creating tension, in this case prompting readers to wonder: "Why *should* we resist compulsory service?"

- **Paragraphs 3–5:** In these paragraphs, the writer discusses the intellectual history of service: first, the writing of William James in the early years of the past century, and next, Plato's account of a dialogue between Socrates and a student. The writer discusses their relevance to the issue at the center of this essay: service to the greater community.

    Argument strategy: At this point, the writer is *preparing* to offer reasons for accepting the claim that we must resist compulsory service. The goal of paragraphs 3–5 is to set a historical context for the essay by establishing service as a significant cultural norm in America and, more broadly, by showing that the notion of obligation to the State is fundamental to civil societies. The end of paragraph 5 makes a transition to modern-day America and begins to move from the preparation for argument to argument.

- **Paragraph 6:** This paragraph opens with two questions and sets up a key distinction in the essay between military and nonmilitary service. After raising the distinction, the writer devotes the paragraph to establishing the right of the American government to draft citizens into the army. A high-ranking military administrator is quoted to the effect that the all-volunteer army is a better fighting force than earlier, conscripted armies.

    Argument strategy: This paragraph begins moving the reader into the argument by introducing and discussing the first part of the distinction just presented: military service. The writer establishes that compulsory military service is constitutional and in keeping with the historical obligations that citizens owe the State. But even here, in a case in which the State has the clear authority to conscript people, the writer quotes a military official as saying that voluntary service is superior to compulsory service. The reader will find this strong preference for volunteerism continued in the second part of the essay devoted to nonmilitary service.

- **Paragraph 7:** This transitional paragraph raises the core question on which the argument hangs: Does the State have the right, as it does in military matters, to press citizens into nonmilitary, national service? The writer answers the question in the final sentence of this paragraph and, in so doing, forecasts the discussion that follows.

    Argument strategy: Here the writer sets up the second part of the paper, where reasons for accepting the claim will be presented. Up until this point, the writer has established that (1) volunteers can build character through service, (2) citizens owe a debt to the State, and (3) the State can legally collect on that debt by drafting citizens into the army in time of war. In this transition paragraph, the writer poses the question that will take the rest of the paper to answer. The question becomes an invitation to read.

- **Paragraphs 8–9:** In these two paragraphs, the writer answers—in the negative—the question posed in paragraph 7. The State does *not* have the right to press citizens into national service. Paragraph 8 offers a logical reason: that military and nonmilitary service are not equivalent. Paragraph 9 offers a moral reason: that coerced or compulsory service is "corrupted."

      Argument strategy: These paragraphs lay out the main reasons for accepting the claim that we should resist letting the successes of volunteerism become an argument for compulsory national service. The writer argues on two grounds—logical and moral—in an effort to build a strong case.

- **Paragraph 10:** Here the writer concedes a problem with the view (expressed by Chapman) in paragraph 9 that service that is either compelled or financially rewarded is corrupted. Allowing that this extreme position does not take into account the financial needs of young people, the writer endorses an alternate view, that minimal payment for service is legitimate. To support this more moderate position, the writer quotes David Gergen.

      Argument strategy: With this concession, the writer backs off an extreme view. The tactic makes the writer look both reasonable and realistic just prior to arguing very firmly, in the next paragraph, against compulsory service.

- **Paragraph 11:** Here the writer endorses one of Chapman's strongly held positions: forced service corrupts the spirit of volunteerism.

      Argument strategy: Here is the emotional core of the argument. The writer has previously argued that for logical reasons (paragraph 8) compulsory service must be rejected. The writer devotes three paragraphs to developing moral reasons, in the end endorsing Chapman's view. In paragraph 11, the writer uses an analogy for the first time: compelling service is equivalent to compelling a child to like someone. Neither works. The value of service rests on the offering of oneself freely to those in need.

- **Paragraphs 12–13:** The writer concludes by re-stating the claim—in two paragraphs.

> **Argument strategy:** These concluding paragraphs parallel the two-part structure of the thesis: Part 1 (paragraph 12), that volunteerism has many benefits and deserves support; Part 2 (paragraph 13), that we must resist the any effort to make service compulsory.

Other approaches to an argument synthesis would be possible, based on the sources provided here. One could agree with Bruce Chapman and adopt the extreme view against both compulsory and paid service. Such an argument would make no concessions of the sort found in paragraph 10 of the model synthesis. Another approach would be to argue that young people must be taught the value of service before they take these values on themselves, and that the best way to teach an ethic of service is to require a year or two of "compulsory volunteering." That which is required, goes the logic of this argument, eventually becomes second nature. We might make a parallel case about teaching kids to read. Kids may not enjoy practicing thirty minutes every night, but eventually they come to realize the joys and benefits of reading, which last a lifetime. Still another argument might be to focus on the extent to which Americans meet (or fail to meet) their obligations to the larger community. This would be a glass-half-full/half-empty argument, beginning with the statistic that one-quarter of Americans regularly volunteer. The half-full argument would praise current efforts and, perhaps, suggest policies for ensuring continued success. The half-empty argument would cite the statistic with alarm, claim that we have a problem of shockingly low volunteer rates, and then propose a solution. Whatever your approach to the subject, in first *critically examining* the various sources and then *synthesizing* them to support a position about which you feel strongly, you are engaging in the kind of critical thinking that is essential to success in a good deal of academic and professional work.

DEVELOPING AND ORGANIZING THE SUPPORT FOR YOUR ARGUMENTS

Experienced writers seem to have an intuitive sense of how to develop and present supporting evidence for their claims. This sense is developed through much hard work and practice. Less experienced writers wonder what to say first, and having decided on that, wonder what to say next. There is no single method of presentation. But the techniques of even the most experienced writers often boil down to a few tried and tested arrangements.

As we've seen in the model synthesis in this chapter, the key to devising effective arguments is to find and use those kinds of support that most persuasively strengthen your claim. Some writers categorize support into two broad types: *evidence* and *motivational appeals*. Evidence, in the form of facts, statistics, and expert testimony, helps make the appeal to *logos* or reason. Motivational appeals—appeals to *pathos* and *ethos*—are employed to get people to change their minds, to agree with the writer or speaker, or to decide upon a plan of activity.

Let's now look at some of the most common principles for using and organizing support for your claims.

Summarize, Paraphrase, and Quote Supporting Evidence

In most of the papers and reports you will write in college and the professional world, evidence and motivational appeals derive from summarizing, paraphrasing, and quoting material in the sources that either have been provided to you or that you have independently researched. (See Chapter 1 on when to summarize, paraphrase, and quote material from sources.) For example, in paragraph 10 of the model argument synthesis, you will find a block quotation from David Gergen used to make the point that minimally paid volunteer programs can provide lifelong lessons. You will also find several brief quotations woven into sentences throughout. In addition, you will find summaries and a paraphrase. In each case, the writer is careful to cite sources.

Provide Various Types of Evidence and Motivational Appeals

Keep in mind the appeals to both *logos* and *pathos*. As we've discussed, the appeal to *logos* is based on evidence that consists of a combination of *facts, statistics, and expert testimony*. In the model synthesis, the writer uses all of these varieties of evidence: facts (from David Gergen's article on how "[v]oluntary service . . . often changes people for life"); statistics (the incidence of volunteering in the United States); and testimony (from Eric Gorham, Bruce Chapman, David Gergen, Roger Landrum, Donald Rumsfeld, and William James). The model synthesis makes an appeal to *pathos* by engaging the reader's self interest: Certainly if the federal government were to institute compulsory national service, the lives of many readers would be touched. More explicitly, paragraph 11 makes a moral argument against compulsory service. Through analogy (compelling citizens to service is equivalent to ordering a child to like someone), the writer attempts to claim the reader's sympathy and respect for common sense. In effect, the writer says, responsible parents would never do such a thing; responsible governments shouldn't either. (Of course, readers could reject the analogy and the assumption about good parenting on which it rests. Some parents might very well push their children into friendships and believe themselves justified for doing so.)

Use Climactic Order

Organize by climactic order when you plan to offer a number of categories or elements of support for your claim. Recognize that some elements will be more important—and likely more persuasive—than others. The basic principle here is that you should *save the most important evidence for the end,* since whatever you have said last is what readers are likely to most remember. A secondary principle is that whatever you say first is what they are *next* most likely to remember. Therefore, when you have several reasons to support your claim, an effective argument strategy is to present the second most important, then one or more additional reasons, saving the most important reason for last. Paragraphs 8–11 of the model synthesis do exactly this.

Use Logical or Conventional Order

Using logical or conventional order means that you use as a template a preestablished pattern or plan for arguing your case.

One common pattern is describing or arguing a *problem/solution*. Using this pattern, you begin with an introduction in which you typically define the problem, then perhaps explain its origins, then offer one or more solutions followed by a conclusion.

Another common pattern is presenting *two sides of a controversy*. Using this pattern, you introduce the controversy and (if an argument synthesis) your own point of view or claim, then explain the other side's arguments, providing reasons why your point of view should prevail.

A third common pattern is *comparison-contrast*. In fact, this pattern is so important that we will discuss it separately in the next section.

The order in which you present elements of an argument is sometimes dictated by the conventions of the discipline in which you are writing. For example, lab reports and experiments in the sciences and social sciences often follow this pattern: *Opening* or *Introduction*, *Methods and Materials* [of the experiment or study], *Results*, *Discussion*. Legal arguments often follow the so-called IRAC format: *Issue*, *Rule*, *Application*, *Conclusion*.

Present and Respond to Counterarguments

When developing arguments on a controversial topic, you can effectively use *counterargument* to help support your claims. When you use counterargument, you present an argument *against* your claim, but then show that this argument is weak or flawed. The advantage of this technique is that you demonstrate that you are aware of the other side of the argument and that you are prepared to answer it.

Here is how a counterargument typically is developed:

    I. Introduction and claim

   II. Main opposing argument

  III. Refutation of opposing argument

  IV. Main positive argument

Use Concession

Concession is a variation of counterargument. As in counterargument, you present the opposing (or otherwise objectionable) viewpoint, but instead of demolishing that argument, you concede that it does have some validity and even some appeal, although your own argument is the stronger one. This concession bolsters your own standing—your own ethos—as a fair-minded person who is not blind to the virtues of the other side. (See paragraph 10 of the example synthesis for a variation of the concession argument.) You'll find that instead of making an *opposing* argument, the writer produces a supporting argument but views one part of it as flawed. The writer rejects that section (the extreme position that *any* form of compensation corrupts the spirit of volunteerism) and endorses the remaining sections. In terms of overall argument strategy, the result—the reader sees the writer as being reasonable—is the same as it would be if the writer used the more standard concession in which an opposing argument is viewed as having some merit. Here is an outline for a more typical concession argument:

   I. Introduction and claim

   II. Important opposing argument

   III. Concession that this argument has some validity

   IV. Positive argument(s)

Sometimes, when you are developing a counterargument or concession argument, you may become convinced of the validity of the opposing point of view and change your own views. Don't be afraid of this happening. Writing is a tool for learning. To change your mind because of new evidence is a sign of flexibility and maturity, and your writing can only be the better for it.

Avoid Common Fallacies in Developing and Using Support

In the section on critical reading in Chapter 2, we considered some of the criteria that, as a reader, you might use for evaluating informative and persuasive writing (see pages 47–54). We discussed how you might assess the accuracy, the significance, and the author's interpretation of the information presented. We also considered the importance in good argument of clearly defined key terms and the pitfalls of emotionally loaded language. Finally, we saw how to recognize such logical fallacies as either/or reasoning, faulty cause-and-effect reasoning, hasty generalization, and false analogy. As a writer, no less than as a critical reader, be aware of these common problems and try to avoid them.

Be aware, also, of your responsibility to cite source materials appropriately. When you quote a source, double- and triple-check that you have done so accurately. When you summarize or paraphrase, take care to use your own language and sentence structures (though you can, of course, also quote within these forms). When you refer to someone else's idea—even if you are not quoting, summarizing, or paraphrasing—give the source credit. By maintaining an ethical stance with regard to the use of sources, you take your place in and perpetuate the highest traditions of the academic community.

THE COMPARISON-AND-CONTRAST SYNTHESIS

A particularly important type of argument synthesis is built on patterns of comparison and contrast. Techniques of comparison and contrast enable you to examine two subjects (or sources) in terms of one another. When you compare, you consider *similarities*. When you contrast, you consider *differences*. By comparing and contrasting, you perform a multifaceted analysis that often suggests subtleties that otherwise might not have come to your (or your reader's) attention.

To organize a comparison-and-contrast argument, you must carefully read sources in order to discover *significant criteria for analysis*. A *criterion* is a specific point to which both of your authors refer and about which they may agree or disagree. (For example, in a comparative report on compact cars, criteria for *comparison and contrast* might be road handling, fuel economy, and comfort of ride.) The best criteria are those that allow you not only to account for obvious similarities and differences—those concerning the main aspects of your sources or subjects—but also to plumb deeper, exploring subtle yet significant comparisons and contrasts among details or subcomponents, which you can then relate to your overall thesis.

Organizing Comparison-and-Contrast Syntheses

Two basic approaches to organizing a comparison-and-contrast synthesis are available: organization by *source or subject* and organization by *criteria*.

Organizing by Source or Subject

You can organize a comparative synthesis by first summarizing each of your sources or subjects and then discussing significant similarities and differences between them. Having read the summaries and become familiar with the distinguishing features of each source, your readers will most likely be able to appreciate the more obvious similarities and differences. In the discussion, your task is to focus on both the obvious and subtle comparisons and contrasts—that is, on those that most clearly support your thesis.

Organization by source or subject is best saved for passages that can be briefly summarized. If the summary of your source or subject becomes too long, your readers might forget the points you made in the first summary as they are reading the second. A comparison-and-contrast synthesis organized by source or subject might proceed like this:

    I. Introduce the paper; lead to thesis.

    II. Summarize source/subject A by discussing its significant features.

    III. Summarize source/subject B by discussing its significant features.

    IV. Write a paragraph (or two) in which you discuss the significant points of comparison and contrast between sources or subjects A and B. Alternatively, begin comparison-contrast in section III upon introducing source or subject B.

End with a conclusion in which you summarize your points and, perhaps, raise and respond to pertinent questions.

Organizing by Criteria

Instead of summarizing entire sources one at a time with the intention of comparing them later, you could discuss two sources simultaneously, examining the views of each author point by point (criterion by criterion), comparing and contrasting these views in the process. The criterion approach is best used when you have a number of points to discuss or when passages or subjects are long and/or complex. A comparison-and-contrast synthesis organized by criteria might look like this:

I. Introduce the paper; lead to thesis.
II. Criterion 1
   a. Discuss what author A says about this point.
   b. Discuss what author B says about this point, comparing and contrasting B's treatment of the point with A's.
III. Criterion 2
   a. Discuss what author A says about this point.
   b. Discuss what author B says about this point, comparing and contrasting B's treatment of the point with A's.

And so on. Proceed criterion by criterion until you have completed your discussion. Be sure to arrange criteria with a clear method; knowing how the discussion of one criterion leads to the next will ensure smooth transitions throughout your paper. End by summarizing your key points and, perhaps, raising and responding to pertinent questions.

However you organize your comparison-and-contrast synthesis, keep in mind that comparing and contrasting are not ends in themselves. Your discussion should point somewhere: to a conclusion, an answer to "So what— why bother to compare and contrast in the first place?" If your discussion is part of a larger synthesis, point to and support the larger claim. If you write a stand-alone comparison-and-contrast, though, you must by the final paragraph answer the "why bother?" question.

EXERCISE 5.5

Comparing and Contrasting

Refer back to the readings on the compulsory national service controversy. Select two that take opposing sides, such as David Gergen's "A Time to Heed the Call" (pages 138–39) and Bruce Chapman's "Politics and National Service: A Virus Attacks the Volunteer Sector" (page 144). Identify at least two significant criteria for analysis—two specific points to which both authors refer and about which they agree or disagree. Then imagine you are preparing to write a short comparison-and-contrast paper and devise two outlines: the first organized by source and the second organized by criteria.

SUMMARY OF SYNTHESIS CHAPTERS

In this and the previous chapter, we've considered the two main types of synthesis: the *explanatory synthesis* and the *argument synthesis*. Although for ease of comprehension we've placed them into separate categories, these types are not, of course, mutually exclusive. Both explanatory syntheses and argument syntheses often involve elements of one another. Which approach you choose will depend upon your *purpose* and the method that you decide is best suited to achieve this purpose.

If your main purpose is to help your audience understand a particular subject, and in particular to help them understand the essential elements or significance of this subject, then you will be composing an explanatory synthesis. If your main purpose, on the other hand, is to persuade your audience to agree with your viewpoint on a subject, or to change their minds, or to decide upon a particular course of action, then you will be composing an argument synthesis.

In planning and drafting these syntheses, you can draw upon a variety of strategies: supporting your claims by summarizing, paraphrasing, and quoting from your sources; using appeal to *logos*, *pathos*, and *ethos*; and choosing from among strategies such as climactic or conventional order, counterargument, concession, and comparison-contrast that will best help you to achieve your purpose.

The strategies of synthesis you've practiced in these last two chapters will be dealt with again in Chapter 7, where we'll consider a category of synthesis commonly known as the research paper. The research paper involves all of the skills in summary, critique, and synthesis that we've discussed so far. We'll discuss approaches to locating and critically evaluating sources, selecting material from among them to provide support for your claims, and documenting your sources in standard professional formats.

But first, we need to examine analysis, another important strategy for academic thinking and writing. Chapter 6 will introduce you to a mode of thinking and writing that, like synthesis, draws upon various strategies you've been practicing as you move through *Writing and Reading Across the Curriculum*.

Analysis

6

WHAT IS AN ANALYSIS?

An *analysis* is an argument in which you study the parts of something to understand how it works, what it means, or why it might be significant. The writer of an analysis uses an analytical tool: a *principle* or *definition* on the basis of which an object, an event, or a behavior can be divided into parts and examined. Here are excerpts from two analyses of L. Frank Baum's *The Wizard of Oz:*

> At the dawn of adolescence, the very time she should start to distance herself from Aunt Em and Uncle Henry, the surrogate parents who raised her on their Kansas farm, Dorothy Gale experiences a hurtful reawakening of her fear that these loved ones will be rudely ripped from her, especially her Aunt (Em—M for Mother!).*

> [*The Wizard of Oz*] was originally written as a political allegory about grassroots protest. It may seem harder to believe than Emerald City, but the Tin Woodsman is the industrial worker, the Scarecrow [is] the struggling farmer, and the Wizard is the president, who is powerful only as long as he succeeds in deceiving the people.†

As these paragraphs suggest, what you discover through an analysis depends entirely on the principle or definition you use to make your insights. Is *The Wizard of Oz* the story of a girl's psychological development, or is it a story about politics? The answer is *both*. In the first example, psychiatrist Harvey Greenberg applies the principles of his profession and, not surprisingly, sees *The Wizard of Oz* in psychological terms. In the second example, a newspaper reporter applies the political theories of Karl Marx and, again not surprisingly, discovers a story about politics.

Different as they are, these analyses share an important quality: Each is the result of a specific principle or definition used as a tool to divide an object into parts to see what it means and how it works. The writer's choice of analytical tool simultaneously creates and limits the possibilities for analysis. Thus, working with the principles of Freud, Harvey Greenberg sees *The Wizard of Oz* in psychological, not political, terms; working with the theories of Karl Marx, Peter Dreier understands the movie in terms of the economic relationships among characters. It's as if the writer of an analysis who adopts one analytical tool puts on a pair of glasses and sees an object in a specific way. Another writer, using a different tool (and a different pair of glasses), sees the object differently.

---

* Harvey Greenberg, *The Movies on Your Mind* (New York: Dutton, 1975) 16.

† Peter Dreier, "Oz Was Almost Reality," *Cleveland Plain Dealer* 3 Sept. 1989.

WHERE DO WE FIND WRITTEN ANALYSES?

Here are just a few types of writing that involve analysis:

Academic Writing

- **Experimental and lab reports.** Analyze the meaning or implications of the study results in your Discussion section.
- **Research papers.** Analyze information in sources; apply theories to material being reported.
- **Process analysis.** Break down the steps or stages involved in completing a process.
- **Literary analysis.** Analyze characterization, plot, imagery, or other elements in works of literature.
- **Essay exams.** Demonstrate understanding of course material by analyzing data using course concepts.

Workplace Writing

- **Grant proposals.** Analyze the issues you seek funding for in order to address them.
- **Reviews of the arts.** Employ dramatic or literary analysis to assess artistic works.
- **Business plans.** Break down and analyze capital outlays, expenditures, profits, materials, and the like.
- **Medical charts.** Review patient symptoms and explore treatment options.
- **Legal briefs.** Break down and analyze facts of cases and elements of legal precedents; apply legal rulings and precedents to new situations.
- **Case studies.** Describe and analyze the particulars of a specific medical, social service, advertising, or business case.

At this point, you may be a bit skeptical. Are there as many analyses of *The Wizard of Oz* as there are people to read it? Yes, or at least as many analyses as there are analytical tools. This does not mean that all analyses are equally valid or useful. The writer must convince the reader. In creating an essay of analysis, the writer must organize a series of related insights, using the analytical tool to examine first one part and then another of the object being studied. To read Harvey Greenberg's essay on *The Wizard of Oz* is to find paragraph after paragraph of related insights—first about Aunt Em, then the Wicked Witch, then Toto, and then the Wizard. All these insights point to Greenberg's single conclusion that "Dorothy's 'trip' is a marvelous metaphor for the psychological journey every adolescent must make."* Without Greenberg's analysis, we prob-

---

* Harvey Greenberg, *The Movies on Your Mind* (New York: Dutton, 1975) 16.

ably would not have thought about the movie as a psychological journey. This is precisely the power of an analysis: its ability to reveal objects or events in ways we would not otherwise have considered.

The writer's challenge is to convince readers that (1) the analytical tool being applied is legitimate and well matched to the object being studied; and (2) the analytical tool is being used systematically to divide the object into parts and to make a coherent, meaningful statement about these parts and the object as a whole.

DEMONSTRATION OF ANALYSIS

The first example of analysis that follows was written by a professional writer; the second was written by a student in response to an assignment in his sociology class. Each example illustrates the two defining features of analysis just discussed: (1) a statement of an analytical principle or definition and (2) the use of that principle or definition in closely examining an object, behavior, or event. As you read, try to identify these features. An exercise with questions for discussion follows each example.

The Plug-In Drug
Marie Winn

Writer and media critic Marie Winn has been interested in the effect of television on both individuals and the larger culture. The following analysis of television viewing as an addictive behavior originally appeared in her book, The Plug-In Drug: Television, Computers, and Family Life *(2002). In this passage, she carefully defines the term* addiction *and then applies it systematically to the behavior under study.*

1   The word "addiction" is often used loosely and wryly in conversation. People will refer to themselves as "mystery-book addicts" or "cookie addicts." E. B. White wrote of his annual surge of interest in gardening: "We are hooked and are making an attempt to kick the habit." Yet nobody really believes that reading mysteries or ordering seeds by catalogue is serious enough to be compared with addictions to heroin or alcohol. In these cases the word "addiction" is used jokingly to denote a tendency to overindulge in some pleasurable activity.

2   People often refer to being "hooked on TV." Does this, too, fall into the light-hearted category of cookie eating and other pleasures that people pursue with unusual intensity? Or is there a kind of television viewing that falls into the more serious category of destructive addiction?

3   Not unlike drugs or alcohol, the television experience allows the participant to blot out the real world and enter into a pleasurable and passive mental state. To be sure, other experiences, notably reading, also provide a temporary respite

Marie Winn, *The Plug-In Drug: Television, Computers, and Family Life* (New York: Penguin, 2002).

from reality. But it's much easier to stop reading and return to reality than to stop watching television. The entry into another world offered by reading includes an easily accessible return ticket. The entry via television does not. In this way television viewing, for those vulnerable to addiction, is more like drinking or taking drugs—once you start it's hard to stop.

4   Just as alcoholics are only vaguely aware of their addiction, feeling that they control their drinking more than they really do ("I can cut it out any time I want—I just like to have three or four drinks before dinner"), many people overestimate their control over television watching. Even as they put off other activities to spend hour after hour watching television, they feel they could easily resume living in a different, less passive style. But somehow or other while the television set is present in their homes, it just stays on. With television's easy gratifications available, those other activities seem to take too much effort.

5   A heavy viewer (a college English instructor) observes:

> I find television almost irresistible. When the set is on, I cannot ignore it. I can't turn it off. I feel sapped, will-less, enervated. As I reach out to turn off the set, the strength goes out of my arms. So I sit there for hours and hours.

6   Self-confessed television addicts often feel they "ought" to do other things—but the fact that they don't read and don't plant their garden or sew or crochet or play games or have conversations means that those activities are no longer as desirable as television viewing. In a way, the lives of heavy viewers are as unbalanced by their television "habit" as drug addicts' or alcoholics' lives. They are living in a holding pattern, as it were, passing up the activities that lead to growth or development or a sense of accomplishment. This is one reason people talk about their television viewing so ruefully, so apologetically. They are aware that it is an unproductive experience, that by any human measure almost any other endeavor is more worthwhile.

7   It is the adverse effect of television viewing on the lives of so many people that makes it feel like a serious addiction. The television habit distorts the sense of time. It renders other experiences vague and curiously unreal while taking on a greater reality for itself. It weakens relationships by reducing and sometimes eliminating normal opportunities for talking, for communicating.

8   And yet television does not satisfy, else why would the viewer continue to watch hour after hour, day after day? "The measure of health," wrote the psychiatrist Lawrence Kubie, "is flexibility . . . and especially the freedom to cease when sated." But heavy television viewers can never be sated with their television experiences. These do not provide the true nourishment that satiation requires, and thus they find that they cannot stop watching.

EXERCISE 6.1

Reading Critically: Winn

Typically in analyses, authors first present their analytical principle in full and then systematically apply parts of the principle to the object or phenomenon under study. In her brief analysis of television viewing, Marie Winn pursues an alternate, though equally effective, strategy by *distributing* parts of her analytical principle across the essay. Locate where Winn defines key elements of addiction. Locate where she uses each element as an analytical lens to examine television viewing as a form of addiction.

In the first two paragraphs, how does Winn create a funnel-like effect that draws readers into the heart of her analysis?

Recall a few television programs that genuinely moved or stirred you to worthwhile reflection or action. To what extent does Winn's analysis describe your positive experiences as a television viewer? (Consider how Winn might argue that from within an addicted state, a person may feel "humored, moved or educated" but is in fact—from a sober outsider's point of view—deluded.) If Winn's analysis of television viewing as an addiction does *not* account for your experience, does it follow that her analysis is flawed? Explain.

The Coming Apart of a Dorm Society
Edward Peselman

Edward Peselman wrote the following paper as a first-semester sophomore, in response to the following assignment from his sociology professor:

Read Chapter 3, "The Paradoxes of Power," in Randall Collins's Sociological Insight: An Introduction to Non-Obvious Sociology *(2nd ed., 1992). Use any of Collins's observations to examine the sociology of power in a group with which you are familiar. Write for readers much like yourself: freshmen or sophomores who have taken one course in sociology. Use Collins as a way of learning something "non-obvious" about a group to which you belong or have belonged.*

The citations in this paper follow American Psychological Association (APA) format.

The Coming Apart of a Dorm Society
Edward Peselman

1 During my first year of college, I lived in a dormitory, like most freshmen on campus. We inhabitants of the dorm came from different cultural and economic backgrounds. Not surprisingly, we brought with us many of the traits found in people outside of college. Like many on the outside, we in the dorm sought personal power at the expense of others. The gaining and maintaining of power can be an ugly business, and I saw people hurt and in turn hurt others all for the sake of securing a place in the dorm's prized social order. Not until one of us challenged that order did I realize how fragile it was.

2   Randall Collins, a sociologist at the University of California, Riverside, defines the exercise of power as the attempt "to make something happen in society" (1992, p. 61). A society can be understood as something as large and complex as "American society"; something more sharply defined—such as a corporate or organizational society; or something smaller still—a dorm society like my own, consisting of six 18-year-old men who lived at one end of a dormitory floor in an all-male dorm.

3   In my freshman year, my society was a tiny but distinctive social group in which people exercised power. I lived with two roommates, Dozer and Reggie. Dozer was an emotionally unstable, excitable individual who vented his energy through anger. His insecurity and moodiness contributed to his difficulty in making friends. Reggie was a friendly, happy-go-lucky sort who seldom displayed emotions other than contentedness. He was shy when encountering new people, but when placed in a socially comfortable situation he would talk for hours.

4   Eric and Marc lived across the hall from us and therefore spent a considerable amount of time in our room. Eric could be cynical and was often blunt: He seldom hesitated when sharing his frank and sometimes unflattering opinions. He commanded a grudging respect in the dorm. Marc could be very moody and, sometimes, was violent. His temper and stubborn streak made him particularly susceptible to conflict. The final member of our miniature society was Benjamin, cheerful yet insecure. Benjamin had certain characteristics which many considered effeminate, and he was often teased about his sexuality—which in turn made him insecure. He was naturally friendly but, because of the abuse he took, he largely kept to himself. He would join us occasionally for a pizza or late-night television.

5   Together, we formed an independent social structure. Going out to parties together, playing cards, watching television, playing ball: These were the activities through which we got to know each other and through which we established the basic pecking order of our community. Much like a colony of baboons, we established a hierarchy based on power relationships. According to Collins, what a powerful person wishes to happen must be achieved by controlling others. Collins's observation can help to define

who had how much power in our social group. In the
dorm, Marc and Eric clearly had the most power.
Everyone feared them and agreed to do pretty much
what they wanted. Through violent words or threats of
violence, they got their way. I was next in line: I
wouldn't dare to manipulate Marc or Eric, but the
others I could manage through occasional quips.
Reggie, then Dozer, and finally Benjamin.

6   Up and down the pecking order, we exercised control through macho taunts and challenges. Collins
writes that "individuals who manage to be powerful
and get their own way must do so by going along with
the laws of social organization, not by contradicting
them" (p. 61). Until mid-year, our dorm motto could
have read: "You win through rudeness and intimidation." Eric gained power with his frequent and brutal
assessments of everyone's behavior. Marc gained power
with his temper—which, when lost, made everyone run
for cover. Those who were not rude and intimidating
drifted to the bottom of our social world. Reggie was
quiet and unemotional, which allowed us to take
advantage of him because we knew he would back down
if pressed in an argument. Yet Reggie understood that
on a "power scale" he stood above Dozer and often
shared in the group's tactics to get Dozer's food
(his parents were forever sending him care packages).
Dozer, in turn, seldom missed opportunities to take
swipes at Benjamin, with references to his sexuality.
From the very first week of school, Benjamin could
never—and never wanted to—compete against Eric's
bluntness or Marc's temper. Still, Benjamin hung out
with us. He lived in our corner of the dorm, and he
wanted to be friendly. But everyone, including
Benjamin, understood that he occupied the lowest spot
in the order.

7   That is, until he left mid-semester. According to
Collins, "any social arrangement works because people
avoid questioning it most of the time" (p. 74). The
inverse of this principle is as follows: When a
social arrangement is questioned, that arrangement
can fall apart. The more fragile the arrangement (the
flimsier the values on which it is based), the more
quickly it will crumble. For the entire first semester, no one questioned our rude, macho rules and
because of them we pigeonholed Benjamin as a wimp. In
our dorm society, gentle men had no power. To say the
least, ours was not a compassionate community. From a

distance of one year, I am shocked to have been a
member of it. Nonetheless, we had created a mini-
society that somehow served our needs.

8   At the beginning of the second semester, we found
Benjamin packing up his room. Marc, who was walking
down the hall, stopped by and said something like:
"Hey buddy, the kitchen get too hot for you?" I was
there, and I saw Benjamin turn around and say: "Do
you practice at being such a _____, or does it come
naturally? I've never met anybody who felt so good
about making other people feel lousy. You'd better
get yourself a job in the army or in the prison
system, because no one else is going to put up with
your _____." Marc said something in a raised voice.
I stepped between them, and Benjamin said: "Get out."
I was cheering.

9   Benjamin moved into an off-campus apartment with
his girlfriend. This astonished us, first because of
his effeminate manner (we didn't know he had a girlfriend) and second because none of the rest of us had
been seeing girls much (though we talked about it
constantly). Here was Benjamin, the gentlest among
us, and he blew a hole in our macho society. Our
social order never really recovered, which suggests
its flimsy values. People in the dorm mostly went
their own ways during the second semester. I'm not
surprised, and I was more than a little grateful.
Like most people in the dorm, save for Eric and Marc,
I both got my lumps and I gave them, and I never felt
good about either. Like Benjamin, I wanted to fit in
with my new social surroundings. Unlike him, I didn't
have the courage to challenge the unfairness of what
I saw.

10   By chance, six of us were thrown together into a
dorm and were expected, on the basis of proximity
alone, to develop a friendship. What we did was sink
to the lowest possible denominator. Lacking any real
basis for friendship, we allowed the forceful, macho
personalities of Marc and Eric to set the rules,
which for one semester we all subscribed to—even
those who suffered.

11   The macho rudeness couldn't last, and I'm glad it
was Benjamin who brought us down. By leaving, he
showed a different and a superior kind of power. I
doubt he was reading Randall Collins at the time, but
he somehow had come to Collins's same insight: As
long as he played by the rules of our group, he suffered because those rules placed him far down in the

dorm's pecking order. Even by participating in pleasant activities, like going out for pizza, Benjamin
supported a social system that ridiculed him. Some
systems are so oppressive and small-minded that they
can't be changed from the inside. They've got to be
torn down. Benjamin had to move, and in moving he
made me (at least) question the basis of my dorm
friendships.

Reference

Collins, R. (1992). *Sociological insight: An introduction to non-
obvious sociology* (2nd ed.). New York: Oxford University Press.

EXERCISE **6.2**

Reading Critically: Peselman

What is the function of paragraph 1? Though Peselman does not use the word
sociology, what signals does he give that this will be a paper that examines the
social interactions of a group? Peselman introduces Collins in paragraph 2.
Why? What does Peselman accomplish in paragraphs 3–4? How does his use
of Collins in paragraph 5 logically follow the presentation in paragraphs 3–4?
The actual analysis in this paper takes place in paragraphs 5–11. Point to
where Peselman draws on the work of Randall Collins, and explain how he
uses Collins to gain insight into dorm life.

HOW TO WRITE AN ANALYSIS

Consider Your Purpose

Whether you are assigned a topic to write on or are left to your own devices,
you inevitably face this question: What is my main idea? Like every paper, an
analysis has at its heart an idea you want to convey. For Edward Peselman, it
was the idea that a social order based on flimsy values is not strong enough
to sustain a direct challenge to its power, and thus will fall apart eventually.
From beginning to end, Peselman advances this one idea: first, by introducing readers to the dorm society he will analyze; next, by introducing principles of analysis (from Randall Collins); and finally, by examining his dorm
relationships in light of these principles. The entire set of analytical insights
coheres as a paper because the insights are *related* and point to Peselman's
single idea.

Peselman's paper offers a good example of the personal uses to which
analysis can be put. Notice that Peselman gravitated toward events in his life
that confused him and about which he wanted some clarity. Personal topics
can be especially fruitful for analysis when you know the particulars well and

can provide readers with details. You view the topic with some puzzlement, and, through the application of your analytical tool, you may come to understand it. When you select topics to analyze from your experience, you provide yourself with a motivation to write and learn. When you are motivated in this way, you spark the interest of readers.

Using Randall Collins as a guide, Edward Peselman returns again and again to the events of his freshman year in the dormitory. We sense that Peselman himself wants to know what happened in that dorm. He writes, "I saw people hurt and in turn hurt others all for the sake of securing a place in the dorm's prized social order." Peselman does not approve of what happened, and the analysis he launches is meant to help him understand.

Locate an Analytical Principle

When you are given an assignment that asks for analysis, use two specific reading strategies to identify principles and definitions in source materials.

- **Look for a sentence that makes a general statement about the way something works.** The statement may strike you as a rule or a law. The line that Edward Peselman quotes from Randall Collins has this quality: "[A]ny social arrangement works because people avoid questioning it most of the time." Such statements are generalizations, conclusions to sometimes complicated and extensive arguments. You can use these conclusions to guide your own analyses as long as you are aware that for some audiences, you will need to re-create and defend the arguments that resulted in these conclusions.

- **Look for statements that take this form: "X" can be defined as (or "X" consists of) the following: A, B, and C.** The specific elements of the definition—A, B, and C—are what you use to identify and analyze parts of the object being studied. You've seen an example of this approach in Marie Winn's multipart definition of addiction (pages. 167–68), which she uses to analyze television viewing. As a reader looking for definitions suitable for conducting an analysis, you might come across Winn's definition of addiction and then use it for your own purposes, perhaps to analyze the playing of video games as an addiction.

Essential to any analysis is the validity of the principle or definition being applied, the analytical tool. Make yourself aware, both as writer and reader, of a tool's strengths and limitations. Pose these questions of the analytical principles and definitions you use: Are they accurate? Are they well accepted? Do *you* accept them? What are the arguments against them? What are their limitations? Since every principle or definition used in an analysis is the end product of an argument, you are entitled—even obligated—to challenge it. If the analytical tool is flawed, then the analysis that follows from it will be flawed also.

The following excerpt is from *Sociological Insight* by Randall Collins; Edward Peselman uses a key sentence from this material as an analytical tool in his paper on power relations in his dorm (see page 171). The sentence that Peselman will use in his paper has been underlined.

1 Try this experiment some time. When you are talking to someone, make them explain everything they say that isn't completely clear. The result, you will discover, is a series of uninterrupted interruptions:

A: Hi, how are you doing?
B: What do you mean when you say "how"?
A: You know. What's happening with you?
B: What do you mean, "happening"?
A: Happening, you know, what's going on.
B: I'm sorry. Could you explain what you mean by "what"?
A: What do you mean, what do I mean? Do you want to talk to me or not?

2 It is obvious that this sort of questioning could go on endlessly, at any rate if the listener doesn't get very angry and punch you in the mouth. But it illustrates two important points. First, virtually everything can be called into question. We are able to get along with other people not because everything is clearly spelled out, but because we are willing to take most things people say without explanation. Harold Garfinkel, who actually performed this sort of experiment, points out that there is an infinite regress of assumptions that go into any act of social communication. Moreover, some expressions are simply not explainable in words at all. A word like "you," or "here," or "now" is what Garfinkel calls "indexical." You have to know what it means already; it can't be explained.

3 "What do you mean by 'you'?"

4 "I mean *you, you!*" About all that can be done here is point your finger.

5 The second point is that people get mad when they are pressed to explain things that they ordinarily take for granted. This is because they very quickly see that explanations could go on forever and the questions will never be answered. If you really demanded a full explanation of everything you hear, you could stop the conversation from ever getting past its first sentence. The real significance of this for a sociological understanding of the way the world is put together is not the anger, however. It is the fact that people try to avoid these sorts of situations. They tacitly recognize that we have to avoid these endless lines of questioning. Sometimes small children will start asking an endless series of "whys," but adults discourage this.

6 In sum, any social arrangement works because people avoid questioning it most of the time. That does not mean that people do not get into arguments or disputes about just what ought to be done from time to time. But to have a dispute already implies there is a considerable area of agreement. An office manager may dispute with a clerk over just how to take care of some business letter, but they at any rate know more or

less what they are disputing about. They do not get off into a . . . series of questions over just what is meant by everything that is said. You could very quickly dissolve the organization into nothingness if you followed that route: There would be no communication at all, even about what the disagreement is over.

7   Social organization is possible because people maintain a certain level of focus. If they focus on one thing, even if only to disagree about it, they are taking many other things for granted, thereby reinforcing their social reality.

The statement that Peselman has underlined—"any social arrangement works because people avoid questioning it most of the time"—is the conclusion of an argument that takes Collins, using the example of repeated questioning of terms, several paragraphs to develop. Peselman agrees with the conclusion and uses it in paragraph 7 of his paper. Observe that for his own purposes Peselman does *not* reconstruct Collins's argument. He selects *only* Collins's conclusion and then imports that into his paper. Once he identifies in Collins a principle he can use in his analysis, he converts the principle into questions that he then directs to his topic: life in his freshman dorm. Two questions follow directly from Collins's insight:

1. What was the social arrangement in the dorm?
2. How was this social arrangement questioned?

Peselman clearly defines his dormitory's social arrangement in paragraphs 3–6 (with the help of another principle borrowed from Collins). Beginning with paragraph 7, he explores how one member of his dorm questioned that arrangement:

> That is, until he left mid-semester. According to Collins, "any social arrangement works because people avoid questioning it most of the time" (p. 74). The inverse of this principle is as follows: when a social arrangement is questioned, that arrangement can fall apart. The more fragile the arrangement (the flimsier the values on which it is based), the more quickly it will crumble. For the entire first semester, no one questioned our rude, macho rules and because of them we pigeonholed Benjamin as a wimp. In our dorm society, gentle men had no power. To say the least, ours was not a compassionate community. From a distance of one year, I am shocked to have been a member of it. Nonetheless, we had created a mini-society that somehow served our needs.

Formulate the Argument

An analysis is an argument with two components. The first component states and establishes the writer's agreement with a certain principle or definition.

Part 1 of the Argument

This component of the argument essentially takes the following form:

> **Claim 1:** Principle X (or definition X) is valuable.

Principle X can be a theory as encompassing and abstract as the statement that *myths are the enemy of truth.* Principle X can be as modest as the definition of a term—for instance, "addiction" or "comfort." As you move from one subject area to another, the principles and definitions you use for analysis will change, as these assignments illustrate:

Sociology: Write a paper in which you place yourself in American society by locating both your absolute position and relative rank on each single criterion of social stratification used by Lenski and Lenski. For each criterion, state whether you have attained your social position by yourself or if you have "inherited" that status from your parents.

Literature: Apply principles of Jungian psychology to Hawthorne's "Young Goodman Brown." In your reading of the story, apply Jung's principles of the *shadow, persona*, and *anima*.

Physics: Use Newton's second law ($F = ma$) to analyze the acceleration of a fixed pulley, from which two weights hang: m_1 (.45 kg) and m_2 (.90 kg). Explain in a paragraph the principle of Newton's law and your method of applying it to solve the problem. Assume that your reader is not comfortable with mathematical explanations: do not use equations in your paragraph.

Finance: Using Guidford C. Babcock's "Concept of Sustainable Growth" [*Financial Analysis* 26 (May–June 1970): 108–14], analyze the stock price appreciation of the XYZ Corporation, figures for which are attached.

The analytical tools to be applied in these assignments change from discipline to discipline. Writing in response to the sociology assignment, you would use sociological principles developed by Lenski and Lenski. In your literature class, you would use principles of Jungian psychology; in physics, Newton's second law; and in finance, a particular writer's concept of "sustainable growth." But whatever discipline you are working in, the first part of your analysis will clearly state which (and whose) principles and definitions you are applying. For audiences unfamiliar with these principles, you will need to explain them; if you anticipate objections, you will need to argue that they are legitimate principles capable of helping you as you conduct an analysis.

Part 2 of the Argument

In the second component of your argument, you *apply* specific parts of your principle or definition to the topic at hand. Regardless of how it is worded, this second argument in an analysis can be rephrased to take the following form:

> **Claim 2:** By applying Principle (or definition) X, we can understand ___*(topic)*___ as ___*(conclusion based on analysis).*___

This is your thesis, the main idea of your analytical essay. Fill in the first blank with the specific object, event, or behavior you are examining. Fill in the second blank with your conclusion about the meaning or significance of this object, based on the insights made during your analysis. The second claim of Marie Winn's analysis can be rephrased as follows:

GUIDELINES FOR WRITING ANALYSIS

Unless you are asked to follow a specialized format, especially in the sciences or the social sciences, you can present your analysis as a paper by following the guidelines below. As you move from one class to another, from discipline to discipline, the principles and definitions you use as the basis for your analyses will change, but the following basic steps will remain the same:

- *Create a context for your analysis.* Introduce and summarize for readers the object, event, or behavior to be analyzed. Present a strong case about why an analysis is needed: Give yourself a motivation to write, and give readers a motivation to read. Consider setting out a problem, puzzle, or question to be investigated.
- *Introduce and summarize the key definition or principle that will form the basis of your analysis.* Plan to devote the first part of your analysis to arguing for the validity of this principle or definition *if* your audience is not likely to understand it or if they are likely to think that the principle or definition is *not* valuable.
- *Analyze your topic.* Systematically apply elements of this definition or principle to parts of the activity or object under study. You can do this by posing specific questions, based on your analytic principle or definition, about the object. Discuss what you find part by part (organized perhaps by question), in clearly defined sections of the essay.
- *Conclude by stating clearly what is significant about your analysis.* When considering your essay as a whole, what new or interesting insights have you made concerning the object under study? To what extent has your application of the definition or principle helped you to explain how the object works, what it might mean, or why it is significant?

By applying a multipart definition, we can understand *television view-ing* as *an addiction.*

Develop an Organizational Plan

The writing of first draft will benefit enormously if you plan out the logic of your analysis. Turn key elements of your analytical principle or definition into questions and then develop the paragraph-by-paragraph logic of the paper.

Turn Key Elements of a Principle or Definition into Questions

Prepare for an analysis by developing questions based on the definition or principle you are going to apply, and then by directing these questions to the activity or object to be studied. The method is straightforward: State as clear-ly as possible the principle or definition to be applied. Divide the principle or definition into its parts and, using each part, develop a question. For example, Marie Winn develops a multipart definition of addiction, each part of which is readily turned into a question that she directs at a specific behav-ior: television viewing. Her analysis of television viewing can be understood as *responses* to each of her analytical questions. Note that in her brief analy-sis, Winn does not first define addiction and then analyze television view-ing. Rather, *as* she defines aspects of addiction, she analyzes television viewing.

Develop the Paragraph-by-Paragraph Logic of Your Paper

The following paragraph from Edward Peselman's essay illustrates the typi-cal logic of a paragraph in an analytical essay:

> Up and down the pecking order, we exercised con-trol through macho taunts and challenges. Collins writes that "individuals who manage to be powerful and get their own way must do so by going along with the laws of social organization, not by con-tradicting them" (p. 61). Until mid-year, our dorm motto could have read: "You win through rudeness and intimidation." Eric gained power with his fre-quent and brutal assessments of everyone's behav-ior. Marc gained power with his temper—which, when lost, made everyone run for cover. Those who were not rude and intimidating drifted to the bottom of our social world. Reggie was quiet and unemotion-al, which allowed us to take advantage of him because we knew he would back down if pressed in an argument. Yet Reggie understood that on a "power scale" he stood above Dozer and often shared in the group's tactics to get Dozer's food

> (his parents were forever sending him care
> packages). Dozer, in turn, seldom missed opportu-
> nities to take swipes at Benjamin, with references
> to his sexuality. From the very first week of
> school, Benjamin could never—and never wanted to—
> compete against Eric's bluntness or Marc's temper.
> Still, Benjamin hung out with us. He lived in our
> corner of the dorm, and he wanted to be friendly.
> But everyone, including Benjamin, understood that
> he occupied the lowest spot in the order.

We see in this example paragraph the typical logic of analysis:

- *The writer introduces a specific analytical tool.* Peselman quotes a line from Randall Collins:

  > "[I]ndividuals who manage to be powerful and get
  > their own way must do so by going along with the
  > laws of social organization, not by contradicting
  > them."

- *The writer applies this analytical tool to the object being examined.* Peselman states *his* dorm's law of social organization:

  > Until mid-year, our dorm motto could have read:
  > "You win through rudeness and intimidation."

- *The writer uses the tool to identify and then examine the meaning of parts of the object.* Peselman shows how each member (the "parts") of his dorm society conforms to the laws of "social organization":

  > Eric gained power with his frequent and brutal
  > assessments of everyone's behavior. Marc gained
  > power with his temper—which, when lost, made
  > everyone run for cover. Those who were not rude
  > and intimidating drifted to the bottom of our
  > social world. . . .

An analytical paper takes shape when a writer creates a series of such paragraphs and then links them with an overall logic. Here is the logical organization of Edward Peselman's paper:

- Paragraph 1: Introduction states a problem—provides a motivation to write and to read.
- Paragraph 2: Randall Collins is introduced—the author whose work will provide principles for analysis.
- Paragraphs 3–4: Background information is provided—the cast of characters in the dorm.
- Paragraphs 5–9: The analysis proceeds—specific parts of dorm life are identified and found significant, using principles from Collins.

CRITICAL READING FOR ANALYSIS

- *Read to get a sense of the whole in relation to its parts.* Whether you are clarifying for yourself a principle or definition to be used in an analysis, or reading a text that you will analyze, understand how parts function to create the whole. If a definition or principle consists of parts, use these to organize sections of your analysis. If your goal is to analyze a text, be aware of its structure: note the title and subtitle; identify the main point and subordinate points and where they are located; break the material into sections.
- *Read to discover relationships within the object being analyzed.* Watch for patterns. When you find them, be alert—for you create an occasion to analyze, to use a principle or definition as a guide in discussing what the pattern may mean:

  > In fiction, a pattern might involve responses of characters to events or to each other, recurrence of certain words or phrasings, images, themes, or turns of plot, to name a few.

  > In poetry, a pattern might involve rhyme schemes, rhythm, imagery, figurative or literal language, and more.

  Your challenge as a reader is first to see a pattern (perhaps using a guiding principle or definition to do so) and then to locate other instances of that pattern. By reading carefully in this way, you prepare yourself to conduct an analysis.

- Paragraphs 10–11: Summary and conclusion are provided—the freshman dorm society disintegrated for reasons set out in the analysis. A larger point is made: Some oppressive systems must be torn down.

Draft and Revise Your Analysis

You will usually need at least two drafts to produce a paper that presents your idea clearly. The biggest changes in your paper will typically come between your first and second drafts. No paper that you write, including an analysis, will be complete until you revise and refine your single compelling idea: your analytical conclusion about what the object, event, or behavior being examined means or how it is significant. You revise and refine by evaluating your first draft, bringing to it many of the same questions you pose when evaluating any piece of writing, including these:

- Are the facts accurate?
- Are my opinions supported by evidence?

- Are the opinions of others authoritative?
- Are my assumptions clearly stated?
- Are key terms clearly defined?
- Is the presentation logical?
- Are all parts of the presentation well developed?
- Are dissenting points of view presented?

Address these same questions on the first draft of your analysis, and you will have solid information to guide your revision.

Write an Analysis, Not a Summary

The most common error made in writing analyses—which is *fatal* to the form—is to present readers with a summary only. For analyses to succeed, you must *apply* a principle or definition and reach a conclusion about the object, event, or behavior you are examining. By definition, a summary (see Chapter 1) includes none of your own conclusions. Summary is naturally a part of analysis; you will need to summarize the object or activity being examined and, depending on the audience's needs, summarize the principle or definition being applied. But in an analysis, you must take the next step and share insights that suggest the meaning or significance of some object, event, or behavior.

Make Your Analysis Systematic

Analyses should give the reader the sense of a systematic, purposeful examination. Marie Winn's analysis illustrates the point: She sets out specific elements of addictive behavior in separate paragraphs and then uses each, within its paragraph, to analyze television viewing. Winn is systematic in her method, and we are never in doubt about her purpose.

Imagine another analysis in which a writer lays out four elements of a definition but then applies only two, without explaining the logic for omitting the others. Or imagine an analysis in which the writer offers a principle for analysis but directs it to only a half or a third of the object being discussed, without providing a rationale for doing so. In both cases, the writer would be failing to deliver on a promise basic to analyses: Once a principle or definition is presented, it should be thoroughly and systematically applied.

Answer the "So What?" Question

An analysis should make readers *want* to read. It should give readers a sense of getting to the heart of the matter, that what is important in the object or activity under analysis is being laid bare and discussed in revealing ways. If when rereading the first draft of your essay, you cannot imagine readers saying, "I never thought of ____ this way," then something may be seriously wrong. Reread closely to determine why the paper might leave readers flat and exhausted, as opposed to feeling that they have gained new and important insights. Closely reexamine your own motivations for writing. Have *you* learned anything significant through the analysis? If not, neither will readers, and they will turn away. If you have gained important insights through your analysis, communicate them clearly. At some point, pull together your related insights and say, in effect: "Here's how it all adds up."

Attribute Sources Appropriately

In an analysis the nature of the form dictates that you work with one or two sources and apply insights from those to some object or phenomenon you want to understand more thoroughly. The strength of an analysis derives mostly from *your* application of a principle or definition. You will have fewer sources to cite in an analysis than in a synthesis. Nevertheless, take special care to cite and quote, as necessary, the one or two sources you use throughout the analysis.

ANALYSIS: A TOOL FOR UNDERSTANDING

As this chapter has demonstrated, analysis involves applying principles as a way to probe and understand. With incisive principles guiding your analysis, you will be able to pose questions, observe patterns and relationships, and derive meaning. Do not forget that this meaning will be only one of several possible meanings. Someone else, possibly you, using different analytical tools could observe the same phenomena and arrive at very different conclusions regarding meaning or significance. We end the chapter, therefore, as we began it: with the two brief analyses of *The Wizard of Oz.* The conclusions expressed in one look nothing like the conclusions expressed in the other, save for the fact that both seek to interpret the same movie. And yet we can say that both are useful, both reveal meaning:

> At the dawn of adolescence, the very time she should start to distance herself from Aunt Em and Uncle Henry, the surrogate parents who raised her on their Kansas farm, Dorothy Gale experiences a hurtful reawakening of her fear that these loved ones will be rudely ripped from her, especially her Aunt (Em—M for Mother!).*

> [*The Wizard of Oz*] was originally written as a political allegory about grass-roots protest. It may seem harder to believe than Emerald City, but the Tin Woodsman is the industrial worker, the Scarecrow [is] the struggling farmer, and the Wizard is the president, who is powerful only as long as he succeeds in deceiving the people.†

---

* Harvey Greenberg, *The Movies on Your Mind* (New York: Dutton, 1975) 16.

† Peter Dreier, "Oz Was Almost Reality," *Cleveland Plain Dealer* 3 Sept. 1989.

You have seen in this chapter how it is possible for two writers, analyzing the same object or phenomenon but applying different analytical principles, to reach vastly different conclusions about what the object or phenomenon may mean or why it is significant. *The Wizard of Oz* is both an inquiry into the psychology of adolescence and a political allegory. What else the classic film may be awaits revealing with the systematic application of other analytical tools. In the same way, the insights you gain as a writer of analyses depend entirely on your choice of tool and the subtlety with which you apply it.

Locating, Mining, and Citing Sources

7

SOURCE-BASED PAPERS

Summaries, critiques, and analyses are generally based on only one or two sources. Syntheses, by contrast (and by definition), are based on multiple sources. But whatever you call the final product, the quality of your paper will be directly related to your success in locating and using a sufficient quantity of relevant, significant, reliable, and up-to-date sources.

Research involves many of the skills we have been discussing in this book. It requires you to (1) locate and take notes on relevant sources; (2) organize your findings; (3) summarize, paraphrase, or quote these sources accurately and ethically; (4) critically evaluate them for their value and relevance to your subject; (5) synthesize information and ideas from several sources that best support your own critical viewpoint; and (6) analyze subjects for meaning and significance.

The model argument synthesis in Chapter 5, "Keeping Volunteering Voluntary" (pages 149–55) is an example of a research paper that fulfills these requirements.

THE RESEARCH QUESTION

Research handbooks generally advise students to narrow their subjects as much as possible, as we discussed in Chapter 3. A ten-page paper on the modern feminist movement would be unmanageable. You would have to do an enormous quantity of research (a preliminary computer search of this subject would yield several thousand items), and you couldn't hope to produce anything other than a superficial treatment of such a broad subject. You could, however, write a paper on a contemporary feminist response to a particular social issue, or the relative power of some current feminist political organizations. It's difficult to say, however, how narrow is narrow enough. (A literary critic once produced a twenty page article analyzing the first paragraph of Henry James's *The Ambassadors*.)

Perhaps more helpful as a guideline on focusing your research is to seek to answer a particular question, a *research question*. For example, how did the Clinton administration respond to criticisms of bilingual education? To what extent is America perceived by social critics to be in decline? What factors led to the WorldCom collapse? How has the debate over genetic engineering evolved during the past decade? To what extent do contemporary cigarette ads perpetuate sexist attitudes? Or how do contemporary cigarette ads differ in message and tone from cigarette ads in the 1950s? Focusing on questions such as these and approaching your research as a way of answering such questions is probably the best way to

---

WHERE DO WE FIND WRITTEN RESEARCH?

Here are just a few types of writing that involve research:

Academic Writing

- **Research papers.** Research an issue and write a paper incorporating the results of that research.
- **Literature reviews.** Research and review relevant studies and approaches to a particular science or social-science topic.
- **Experimental reports.** Research previous studies in order to refine—or show need for—your current approach; conduct primary research.
- **Case studies.** Conduct both primary and secondary research.
- **Position papers.** Research approaches to an issue in order to formulate your own approach.

Workplace Writing

- Reports in business, science, engineering, social services, medicine
- Market analyses
- Business plans
- Environmental impact reports
- Legal research: memoranda of points and authorities

---

narrow your subject and ensure focus in your paper. The essential answer to this research question eventually becomes your *thesis,* which we discussed in Chapter 3; in the paper, you present evidence that systematically supports your thesis.

EXERCISE 7.1

Constructing Research Questions

Moving from a broad topic or idea to formulation of precise research questions can be challenging. Practice this skill by working with small groups of your classmates to construct research questions about the following topics (or come up with some topics of your own). Write at least one research question for each topic listed, then discuss these topics and questions with the other groups in class.

Racial or gender stereotypes in television shows

Drug addiction in the U.S. adult population

Global environmental policies

Employment trends in high-technology industries

U.S. energy policy

LOCATING SOURCES

Once you have a research question, you want to see what references are available. You'll begin with what we call "preliminary research," in which you familiarize yourself quickly with the basic issues and generate a preliminary list of sources. This effort will help you refine your research question and conduct efficient research once you move into the stage that we call "focused research."

PRELIMINARY RESEARCH

You can go about finding preliminary sources in many ways; some of the more effective ones are listed in the box below. We'll consider a few of these suggestions in more detail.

Consulting Knowledgeable People

When you think of research, you may immediately think of libraries, print, and Web material. But don't neglect a key reference—other people. Your *instructor* probably can suggest fruitful areas of research and some useful sources. Try to see your instructor during office hours, however, rather than immediately before or after class, so that you'll have enough time for a productive discussion.

Once you get to the library, ask a *reference librarian* which reference sources (e.g., bibliographies, specialized encyclopedias, periodical indexes, statistical almanacs) you need for your particular area of research. Librarians won't do your research for you, but they'll be glad to show you how to research efficiently and systematically.

TYPES OF RESEARCH DATA

Primary Sources

- Data gathered directly using research methods appropriate to a particular field
  Sciences: experiments, observations
  Social sciences: experiments, surveys, interviews
  Humanities: close reading/observation and interpretation

Secondary Sources

- Information and ideas collected or generated by others who have performed their own primary and/or secondary research
  Library research: books, periodicals, etc.
  Online research

WRITING THE RESEARCH PAPER

Here is an overview of the main steps involved in writing research papers. Keep in mind that, as with other writing projects, writing such papers is a recursive process. For instance, you will gather data at various stages of your writing, as the list below illustrates.

Developing the Research Question
- **Find a subject.** Decide what subject you are going to research and write about.
- **Develop a research question.** Formulate an important question that you would like to answer through your research.

Locating Sources
- **Conduct preliminary research.** Consult knowledgeable people, general and specialized encyclopedias, overviews and bibliographies in recent books, the *Bibliographic Index*, and subject heading guides.
- **Refine your research question.** Based on your preliminary research, brainstorm about your topic and ways to answer your research question. Sharpen your focus, refining your question and planning the sources you'll need to consult.
- **Conduct focused research.** Consult books, electronic databases, general and specialized periodicals, biographical indexes, general and specialized dictionaries, government publications, and other appropriate sources. Conduct interviews and surveys as necessary.

Mining Sources
- **Develop a working thesis.** Based on your initial research, formulate a working thesis that attempts to respond to your research question.
- **Develop a working bibliography.** Keep track of your sources, either on paper or electronically, including both bibliographic information

---

You can also glean vital primary information from people when you interview them, ask them to fill out questionnaires or surveys, or have them participate in experiments. We'll cover this aspect of research in more detail below.

Encyclopedias

Reading an encyclopedia entry about your subject will give you a basic understanding of the most significant facts and issues. Whether the subject is American politics or the mechanics of genetic engineering, the encyclopedia article—written by a specialist in the field—offers a broad overview that may and key points about each source. Make this bibliography easy to sort and rearrange.

- **Evaluate sources.** Attempt to determine the veracity and reliability of your sources; use your critical reading skills; check *Book Review Digest;* look up biographies of authors.
- **Take notes from sources.** Paraphrase and summarize important information and ideas from your sources. Copy down important quotations. Note page numbers from sources of this quoted and summarized material.
- **Develop a working outline and arrange your notes according to your outline.**

Drafting; Citing Sources

- **Write your draft.** Write the preliminary draft of your paper, working from your notes, according to your outline.
- **Avoid plagiarism.** Take care to cite all quoted, paraphrased, and summarized source material, making sure that your own wording and sentence structure differ from those of your sources.
- **Cite sources.** Use in-text citations and a Works Cited or References list, according to the conventions of the discipline (e.g., MLA, APA, CSE).

Revising (Global and Local Changes)

- **Revise your draft.** Consider global, local, surface revisions. Check that your thesis still fits with your paper's focus. Review topic sentences and paragraph development and logic. Use transitional words and phrases to ensure coherence. Make sure that the research paper reads smoothly and clearly from beginning to end.

Editing (Surface Changes)

- **Edit your draft.** Check for style, combining short, choppy sentences and ensuring variety in your sentence structures. Check for grammatical correctness, punctuation, and spelling.

---

serve as a launching point to more specialized research in a particular area. The article may illuminate areas or raise questions that you feel motivated to pursue further. Equally important, the encyclopedia article frequently concludes with an *annotated bibliography* describing important books and articles on the subject.

Encyclopedias have certain limitations, however. First, most professors don't accept encyclopedia articles as legitimate sources for academic papers. You should use encyclopedias primarily to familiarize yourself with (and to select a particular aspect of) the subject area and as a springboard for further research. Also, because new editions of encyclopedias appear only once every

LOCATING PRELIMINARY SOURCES

- Ask your instructor to recommend sources on the subject.
- Scan those sections in your textbooks offering suggestions for further reading. Ask your college librarian for useful reference tools in your subject area.
- Read an encyclopedia article on the subject and use the bibliography following the article to identify other sources.
- Read the introduction to a recent book on the subject and review that book's bibliography to identify more sources.
- Consult the annual *Bibliographic Index* (see page 192 for details).
- Use an Internet search engine to explore your topic. Type in different keyword or search term combinations and browse the sites you find for ideas and references to sources you can look up later (see the box on pages 198–99 for details).

NARROWING THE SUBJECT VIA RESEARCH

If you need help narrowing a broad subject, try one or more of the following:
- Search by subject in an electronic database to see how the subject breaks down into components.
- Search the subject heading in an electronic periodical catalog, such as *InfoTrac,* or in a print catalog such as the *Readers' Guide to Periodical Literature.*
- Search the *Library of Congress Subject Headings* catalog (see Subject-Heading Guides, pages 192–93, for details).

five or ten years, the information they contain—including bibliographies—may not be current. Current editions of the *Encyclopaedia Britannica* and the *Encyclopedia Americana,* for instance, may not include information about the most recent developments in biotechnology. Some encyclopedias are now also available online—*Britannica Online,* for example—and this may mean, but not guarantee, that information is up to date.

Some of the most useful general encyclopedias include the following:

Academic American Encyclopedia

Encyclopedia Americana

New Encyclopaedia Britannica (or Britannica Online)

Keep in mind that the library also contains a variety of more *specialized encyclopedias*. These encyclopedias restrict themselves to a particular disciplinary area, such as chemistry, law, or film, and are considerably more detailed in their treatment of a subject than are general encyclopedias. Here are examples of specialized encyclopedias:

Social Sciences

Encyclopedia of Education

Encyclopedia of Psychology

West's Encyclopedia of American Law

International Encyclopedia of the Social and Behavioral Sciences

Humanities

Encyclopedia of American History

Dictionary of Art

Encyclopedia of Religion and Ethics

Film Encyclopedia

The New Grove Encyclopedia of Music

Science and Technology

Encyclopedia of Life Sciences

Encyclopedia of Electronics

Encyclopedia of Artificial Intelligence

Encyclopedia of Physics

McGraw-Hill Encyclopedia of Environmental Science

Van Nostrand's Scientific Encyclopedia

Business

Encyclopedia of Banking and Finance

International Encyclopedia of Economics

EXERCISE **7.2**

Exploring Specialized Encyclopedias

Go to the reference section of your campus library and locate several specialized encyclopedias within your major or area of interest. Look through the encyclopedias, noting their organization, and read entries on topics that interest you. Jot down some notes describing the kinds of information you find. You might also use this opportunity to look around at the other materials available in the reference section of the library, including the *Bibliographic Index* and the *Book Review Digest*.

Overviews and Bibliographies in Recent Books

If your professor or a bibliographic source directs you to an important recent book on your subject, skim the introductory (and possibly the concluding) material to the book, along with the table of contents, for an overview of key issues. Look also for a bibliography, works cited, and/or references list. These lists are extremely valuable resources for locating material for research. For example, Robert Dallek's 2003 book *An Unfinished Life: John Fitzgerald Kennedy, 1917–1963* includes a seven-page bibliography of reference sources on President Kennedy's life and times.

Keep in mind that authors are not necessarily objective about their subjects, and some have particularly biased viewpoints that you may unwittingly carry over to your paper, treating them as objective truth.* However, you may still be able to get some useful information out of such sources. Alert yourself to authorial biases by looking up the reviews of your book in the *Book Review Digest* (described below). Additionally, look up biographical information on the author (see the section on biographical indexes, pages 205–06), whose previous writings or professional associations may suggest a predictable set of attitudes on the subject of your book.

Bibliographic Index

The *Bibliographic Index* is a series of annual volumes that enables you to locate bibliographies on a particular subject. The bibliographies referred to in this reference book generally appear at the end of book chapters or periodical articles, or they may themselves be book or pamphlet length. Browsing through the *Bibliographic Index* in a general subject area may give you ideas for further research in particular aspects of the subject, along with particular references.

Subject-Heading Guides

Seeing how a general subject (e.g., education) is broken down in other sources also could stimulate research in a particular area (e.g., bilingual primary education in California). In the subsequent sources, general subjects are analyzed into secondary subject headings, similar to the way that chapter titles in a book's table of contents represent subcomponents of a general subject (indicated in the book title). To locate such sets of secondary subject headings, consult the following sources:

---

* Bias is not necessarily bad. Authors, like any other people, have certain preferences and predilections that influence the way they view the world and the kinds of arguments they make. As long as they inform you of their biases, or as long as you are aware of them and take them into account, you can still use these sources judiciously. (You might gather valuable information from a book about the Watergate scandal, even if it were written by former president Richard Nixon or one of his top aides, as long as you make proper allowance for their understandable biases.) Bias becomes a potential problem only when it masquerades as objective truth or is accepted as such by the reader. For suggestions on identifying and assessing authorial bias, see the material in Chapter 2 on persuasive writing (pages 47–54) and evaluating assumptions (pages 56–57).

An electronic database

An electronic or print periodical catalog (e.g., *InfoTrac, Readers' Guide, Social Science Index*)

The Library of Congress Subject Headings catalog

The *Propaedia* volume of the *New Encyclopaedia Britannica* (1998)

Once you've used these kinds of tools to narrow your scope to a particular subject and research question (or set of research questions), you're ready to undertake more focused research.

FOCUSED RESEARCH

Your objective now is to learn as much as you can about your particular subject. Only then will you be qualified to make an informed response to your research question. This means that you'll have to become something of an expert on the subject—or if that's not possible, given time constraints, you can at least become someone whose critical viewpoint is based solidly on the available evidence. In the following pages we'll suggest how to find sources for this kind of focused research. In most cases, your research will be *secondary* in nature, based on (1) books; (2) electronic databases; (3) general and specialized periodicals; (4) specialized reference sources; and (5) the World Wide Web. In certain cases, you may gather your own *primary* research, using (6) interviews, surveys, structured observation, or content/textual analysis.

Books

Books are useful in providing both breadth and depth of coverage of a subject. Because they generally are published at least a year or two after the events treated, they also tend to provide the critical distance that is sometimes missing from journal articles. Conversely, this delay in coverage also means that the information you find in books will not be as current as information you find in journals. And, of course, books may also be shallow, inaccurate, outdated, or hopelessly biased; for help in making such determinations, see *Book Review Digest,* discussed below. You can locate relevant books through the electronic or card catalog. When using this catalog, you may search in four ways: (1) by *author,* (2) by *title,* (3) by *subject,* and (4) by *keyword.* Entries include the call number, publication information, and frequently a summary of the book's contents. Larger libraries use the Library of Congress cataloging system for call numbers (e.g., E111/C6); smaller ones use the Dewey Decimal System (e.g., 970.015/C726).

Book Review Digest

Perhaps the best way to determine the reliability and credibility of a book you may want to use is to look it up in the *Book Review Digest* (also available online and issued monthly and cumulated annually). These volumes list (alphabetically by author) the most significant books published during the year, supply a brief description of each, and most important, provide excerpts from (and references to) reviews. If a book receives bad reviews, you don't necessarily have to avoid it (the book may still have something useful to offer, and the review itself may be unreliable). But you should take any negative reaction into account when using that book as a source.

Electronic Databases

Much of the information that is available in print—and a good deal that is not—is also available in electronic form. Almost certainly, your library card catalog has been computerized, allowing you to conduct searches much faster and more easily than in the past. Increasingly, researchers access magazine, newspaper, and journal articles and reports, abstracts, and other forms of information through *online databases* (many of them on the Internet) and through databases on *CD-ROMs*. One great advantage of using databases (as opposed to print indexes) is that you can search several years' worth of different periodicals at the same time.

Online databases—that is, those that originate outside your computer—are available through international, national, or local (e.g., campus) networks. The largest such database is DIALOG, which provides access to more than 300 million records in more than 400 databases, ranging from sociology to business to chemical engineering. Another large database is LexisNexis (like DIALOG, available only through online subscription). *LexisNexis Academic* provides access to numerous legal, medical, business, and news sources. In addition to being efficient and comprehensive, online databases are generally far more up-to-date than print sources. If you have an Internet connection from your own computer, you can access many of these databases—including those available through commercial online services such as CompuServe and America Online—without leaving your room.

Access to online databases often requires an account and a password, which you may be able to obtain by virtue of your student status. In some cases, you will have to pay a fee to the local provider of the database, based on how long you are online. But many databases will be available to you free of charge. For example, your library's computers may offer access to magazine and newspaper databases, such as Expanded Academic ASAP, InfoTrac, EbscoHost, and National Newspaper Index, as well as to the Internet itself.

The *World Wide Web* offers graphics, multimedia, and hyperlinks to related material in numerous sources. To access these sources, you can either browse (i.e., follow your choice of paths or links wherever they lead) or type in a site's address.

To search for Web information on a particular topic, try using one of the more popular search engines:

Google: http://www.google.com
Yahoo: http://www.yahoo.com

AltaVista: http://altavista.com

WebCrawler: http://webcrawler.com

SearchCom: http://www.search.com

Lycos: http://www.lycos.com

Review the "Help" and "Advanced Search" sections of search engines to achieve the best results. (See the box on pages 198–99 for some general tips on searching online.)

Many databases and periodical indexes are also available online. Among the most useful are the *Readers' Guide to Periodical Literature* (index only), *New York Times* (available full-text online), *Film Index International* (index only), *PAIS International* (index only), and *America: History and Life* (index only). Other standard reference sources include the *Statistical Abstract of the United States* (full text), *The Encyclopaedia Britannica* (full text—called *Britannica Online*), *Bibliography of Native North Americans* (index only), *Environment Reporter* (full text), and *National Criminal Justice Reference Service* (index with some links to full text). Of particular interest is *InfoTrac*, which (if you are in a participating library or have a password) provides access to more than 1,000 general interest, business, government, and technological periodicals. In recent years, CD-ROM (compact disk-read only memory) indexes and databases have given way to online versions.

Keep in mind, however, that while electronic sources make it far easier to access information than do their print counterparts, they often do not go back more than fifteen years. For earlier information, therefore (e.g., the original reactions to the Milgram experiments of the 1960s), you would have to rely on print indexes.

EXERCISE 7.3

Exploring Electronic Sources

Use your library's Internet connection (or your home computer if you have Internet access) to access a search engine or academic/professional database. Select a topic/research question of interest to you, review the box on using keywords and Boolean logic to refine online searches (pages 198–99) and try different combinations of keywords and Boolean operators to see what sources you can find for your topic. Jot down notes describing the kinds of sources you find and which terms seem to yield the best results. Effective searching on the Internet takes practice; you'll save time when conducting research if you have a good sense of how to use these search strategies.

The Benefits and Pitfalls of the World Wide Web

In the past few years, the World Wide Web has become not just a research tool but a cultural phenomenon. The pop artist Andy Warhol once said that in the future everyone would be famous for 15 minutes. He might have added that everyone would also have a personal Web site. People use the Web not just to look up information but to shop, to make contact with long-lost friends and relatives, to grind their personal or corporate axes, and to advertise themselves and their accomplishments.

The Web makes it possible for people sitting at home, work, or school to gain access to the resources of large libraries and explore corporate and government databases. In her informative book *The Research Paper and the World Wide Web*, Dawn Rodrigues quotes Bruce Dobler and Harry Bloomberg on the essential role of the Web in modern research:

> It isn't a matter anymore of using computer searches to locate existing documents buried in some far-off library or archive. The Web is providing documents and resources that simply would be too expensive to publish on paper or CD-ROM.
>
> Right now—and not in some distant future—doing research without looking for resources on the Internet is, in most cases, not really looking hard enough. . . . A thorough researcher cannot totally avoid the Internet and the Web.*

And indeed, Web sites are increasingly showing up as sources in both student and professional papers. But like any other rapidly growing and highly visible cultural phenomenon, the Web has created its own backlash. First, as anyone who has tried it knows, for many subjects, systematic research on the Web is rarely possible. For all the information that is available on the Internet, a great deal more is not and never will be converted to digital format. One library director has estimated that only about 4,000 of 150,000 published scholarly journals are available online, and many of these provide only partial texts of relatively recent articles in the paper editions. The *New York Times* is available on the Web, but the online edition includes only a fraction of the content of the print edition, and online versions of the articles generally are abridged. Also, you must often pay for access to such articles. If you are researching the rise of McCarthyism in America during the early 1950s or trying to determine who else, since Stanley Milgram, has conducted psychological experiments on obedience, you are unlikely to find much useful information for your purpose on the Web.

Moreover, locating what *is* available is not always easy, since there's no standardized method—like the Library of Congress subheading and call number system—of cataloging and cross-referencing online information. The tens of thousands of Web sites and millions of Web pages, together with the relative crudity of search engines such as Yahoo, Google, AltaVista, and WebCrawler, have made navigating an ever-expanding cyberspace an often daunting and frustrating procedure.

Second, it is not a given that people who do research on the Web will produce better papers as a result. As quoted by Stephen R. Knowlton, David Rothenberg, a professor of philosophy at New Jersey Institute of Technology,

---

* Dawn Rodrigues, *The Research Paper and the World Wide Web* (Upper Saddle River, NJ: Prentice Hall, 1997).

believes that "his students' papers had declined in quality since they began using the Web for research."* Neil Gabler, a cultural critic, writes:

> The Internet is such a huge receptacle of rumor, half-truth, misinformation and disinformation that the very idea of objective truth perishes in the avalanche. All you need to create a "fact" in the web world is a bulletin board or chat room. Gullible cybernauts do the rest.[†]

Another critic is even blunter: "Much of what purports to be serious information is simply junk—neither current, objective, nor trustworthy. It may be impressive to the uninitiated, but it is clearly not of great use to scholars."[‡]

Of course, print sources are not necessarily objective or reliable either, and in Chapter 2 we discussed some criteria by which readers may evaluate the quality and reliability of information and ideas in *any* source (page 47). Web sources, however—particularly self-published Web pages—present a special problem. In most cases, material destined for print has to go through one or more editors and fact-checkers before being published, since most authors don't have the resources to publish and distribute their own writing. But anyone with a computer and a modem can "publish" on the Web; furthermore, those with a good Web authoring program and graphics software can create sites that, outwardly at least, look just as professional and authoritative as those of the top academic, government, and business sites. These personal sites will appear in search-engine listings—generated through keyword matches rather than through independent assessments of quality or relevance—and uncritical researchers who use their information as a factual basis for the claims they make in their papers do so at their peril.

The Internet has also led to increased problems with plagiarism. Many college professors complain these days about receiving work copied directly off of Web sites. Such copying runs the gamut from inadvertent plagiarism of passages copied and pasted off the Web into notes and then transferred verbatim to papers, to intentional theft of others' work, pasted together into a document and claimed as the student's own. In one recent case, an instructor reports that she received a student paper characterized by a more professional writing style than usual for that student. The instructor typed a few keywords from the paper into an Internet search engine, and one of the first sources retrieved turned out to be a professional journal article from which the student had copied whole passages and pasted them together to create a "report." This student received an "F" in the course and was referred to a university disciplinary committee for further action.

---

* Steven R. Knowlton, "Students Lost in Cyberspace," *Chronicle of Higher Education* 2 Nov. 1997: 21.

† Neil Gabler, "Why Let Truth Get in the Way of a Good Story?" *Los Angeles Times* "Opinion," 26 Oct. 1997: 1.

‡ William Miller, "Troubling Myths About On-Line Information," *Chronicle of Higher Education* 1 Aug. 1997: A44.

USING KEYWORDS AND BOOLEAN LOGIC TO REFINE ONLINE SEARCHES

You will find more—and more relevant—sources on Internet search engines and library databases if you carefully plan your search strategies. *Note: Some search engines and online databases have their own systems for searching, so review the "Help" section of each search engine, and use "Advanced Search" options where available. The following tips are general guidelines, and their applicability in different search engines may vary somewhat.*

- Identify multiple keywords: Write down your topic and/or your research question, then brainstorm synonyms and related terms for the words in that topic/question.

  Sample topic: Political activism on college campuses.

  Sample research question: What kinds of political activism are college students involved in today?

  Keywords: Political activism; college students.

  Synonyms and related terms: politics; voting; political organizations; protests; political issues; universities; colleges; campus politics.

- Conduct searches using different combinations of synonyms and related terms.
- Find new terms in the sources you locate and search with these.
- Use quotation marks around terms you want linked: "political activism."
- Use Boolean operators to link keywords: The words AND, OR, and NOT are used in Boolean logic to combine search terms and get more precise results than using keywords alone.

The Internet sometimes proves a very tempting source from which to lift materials. But not only is such activity ethically wrong, it is also likely to result in serious punishment, such as permanent notations on your academic transcript or expulsion from school. One thing all students should know is that while cheating is now made easier by the Internet, the converse is also true: Instructors can often track down the sources for material plagiarized from the Internet just as easily as the student found them in the first place. (Easier, in fact, because now instructors can scan papers into software or Internet programs that will search the Web for matching text.) For more on plagiarism, see the section devoted to this subject in Chapter 1 (pages 42–44).

We certainly don't mean to discourage Web research. Thousands of excellent sites exist in cyberspace. The reference department of most college and

> **AND:** Connecting keywords with AND narrows a search by retrieving only sources that contain *both* keywords:
>
> *political activism AND college students*
>
> **OR:** Connecting keywords with OR broadens a search by retrieving all sources that contain at least one of the search terms. This operator is useful when you have a topic/keyword for which there are a number of synonyms. Linking synonyms with OR will lead you to the widest array of sources:
>
> *political activism OR protests OR political organizing OR voting OR campus politics*
>
> *college OR university OR campus OR students*
>
> **AND** and **OR:** You can use these terms in combination, by putting the OR phrase in parentheses:
>
> *(political activism OR protests) AND (college OR university)*
>
> **NOT:** Connecting keywords with NOT (or, in some cases, AND NOT) narrows a search by excluding certain terms. If you want to focus upon a very specific topic, NOT can be used to limit what the search engine retrieves; however, this operator should be used carefully as it can cause you to miss sources that may actually be relevant:
>
> *college students NOT high school*
>
> *political activism NOT voting*

university libraries will provide lists of such sites, arranged by discipline, and the most useful sites also are listed in the research sections of many handbooks. Most people locate Web sites, however, by using search engines and by "surfing" the hyperlinks. And for Web sources, more than print sources, the warning *caveat emptor*—let the buyer beware—applies.

Evaluating Web Sources

In their extremely useful site on evaluating web resources (http://www2.widener.edu/Wolfgram-Memorial-Library/webevaluation/webeval. htm), reference librarians Jan Alexander and Marsha Tate offer some important guidelines. First, they point out, it's important to determine what *type* of Web page you are dealing with. Web pages generally fall into six categories, each with a different purpose: (1) entertainment, (2) business/marketing, (3) reference/information, (4) news, (5) advocacy of a particular point of view or program, (6) personal page. The purpose of the page—informing, selling, persuading, entertaining—has a direct bearing on the objectivity and reliability of the information presented.

Second, when evaluating a Web page, you should apply the same general criteria as are applied to print sources: (1) accuracy, (2) authority, (3) objectivity, (4) currency, and (5) coverage. As we've noted, when assessing the *accuracy* of a Web page, it's important to consider the likelihood that its information has been checked by anyone other than the author. When assessing the *authority* of the page, consider the author's qualifications to write on the subject and the reputability of the publisher. In many cases on the Web, it's difficult to determine not just the qualifications, but the very identity of the author. When assessing the *objectivity* of a Web page, consider the bias on the part of the author or authors and the extent to which they are trying to sway their readers' opinions. Many Web pages passing themselves off as informational are in fact little more than "infomercials." When assessing the *currency* of a Web page, you should determine whether the content is up-to-date and whether the publication date is clearly labeled. Many Web pages lack clearly indicated dates. And even if a date is provided, it may be difficult to tell whether the date indicates when the page was written, when it was placed on the Web, or when it was last revised. Finally, when assessing the *coverage* of a Web page, consider which topics are included (and not included) in the work and whether the topics are covered in depth. Depth of coverage has generally not been a hallmark of Web information.

Other pitfalls of Web sites: Reliable sites may include links to other sites that are inaccurate or outdated, so users cannot rely on the link as a substitute for evaluating the five criteria just outlined. Web pages are also notoriously unstable, frequently changing or even disappearing without notice.

Perhaps most serious, the ease with which it is possible to surf the Net can encourage intellectual laziness and make researchers too dependent on Web resources. Professors are increasingly seeing papers largely or even entirely based on information in Web sites. While Web sources are indeed an important new source of otherwise unavailable information, there is usually no substitute for library or primary research, such as interviews or field study. The vast majority of printed material in even a small college library—much of it essential to informed research—does not appear on the Web, nor is it likely to in the immediate future. Much of the material you will research in the next few years remains bound within covers. You may well learn of its existence in electronic databases, but at some point you'll have to walk over to a library shelf, pull out a book, and turn printed pages.

Above all, remember that you must apply the critical reading skills you've been practicing throughout this textbook to all your sources—no matter what types they are or where you found them (see Chapter 2 for coverage of critical reading).

Practice Evaluating Web Sources

To practice applying the evaluation criteria discussed in the section above on Web sources, go to an Internet search engine and look for sources addressing a topic of interest to you (perhaps following completion of Exercise 7.3, page 195). Try to locate one source representing each of the six types of Web pages (i.e., entertainment, business/marketing, reference/information, news, advocacy, and personal). Print out the main page of each of these sources and bring the copies to class. In small groups of your classmates look over the sites each student found. For each site, make note of (1) accuracy, (2) authority, (3) objectivity, (4) currency, and (5) coverage.

General Periodicals

Because many more periodical articles than books are published every year, you are likely (depending on the subject) to find more information in periodicals than in books. By general periodicals, we mean the magazines and newspapers that are generally found on newsstands, such as the *New York Times*, *Newsweek*, or the *New Republic*. By their nature, general periodical articles tend to be more current than books. The best way, for example, to find out about the federal government's current policy on Social Security reform is to look for articles in periodicals and newspapers. However, periodical articles may have less critical distance than books, and like books, they may become dated, to be superseded by more recent articles. Let's first look at the use of magazines from a research perspective.

Magazines

General periodicals (such as *Time*, the *New Republic*, and the *Nation*) are intended for nonspecialists. Their articles, which tend to be highly readable, may be written by staff writers, freelancers, or specialists. But usually they do not provide citations or other indications of sources, and so are of limited usefulness for scholarly research.

The most well-known general index to this kind of material is the *Readers' Guide to Periodical Literature*, an index of articles that have appeared in several hundred general-interest magazines and a few more specialized magazines such as *Business Week* and *Science Digest*. Articles in the *Readers' Guide* are indexed by author, title, and subject.

Another general reference for articles is the *Essay and General Literature Index*, which indexes essays (sometimes called book articles) contained in anthologies.

Increasingly, texts and abstracts of articles are available on online databases. These texts may be downloaded to your computer or e-mailed to you.

Newspapers

News stories, feature stories, and editorials (even letters to the editor) may be important sources of information. Your library certainly will have the *New York Times* index, and it may have indexes to other important newspapers, such as the *Washington Post, Los Angeles Times, Chicago Tribune, Wall Street Journal*, and *Christian Science Monitor.* Newspaper holdings will be on microfilm, CD-ROM, or online. You will need a micro-printer/viewer to get hard copies if you are using microfilm.

Note: Because of its method of cross-referencing, the *New York Times* index may at first be confusing. Suppose that you want to find stories on bilingual education during a given year. When you locate the "Bilingual education" entry, you won't find citations but rather a "*See also* Education" reference that directs you to seven dates (August 14, 15, and 17; September 11; October 20, 29, and 30) under the heading of "Education." Under this major heading, references to stories on education are arranged in chronological order from January to December. When you look up the dates you were directed to, you'll see brief descriptions of these stories on bilingual education.

Specialized Periodicals

Many professors will expect at least some of your research to be based on articles in specialized periodicals or "scholarly journals." So instead of (or in addition to) relying on an article from *Psychology Today* (which would be considered a general periodical even though its subject is somewhat specialized) for an account of the effects of crack cocaine on mental functioning, you might also rely on an article from the *Journal of Abnormal Psychology.* If you are writing a paper on the satirist Jonathan Swift, in addition to a recent reference that may have appeared in the *New Yorker,* you may need to locate a relevant article in *Eighteenth-Century Studies.* Articles in such journals normally are written by specialists and professionals in the field, rather than by staff writers or freelancers, and the authors will assume that their readers already understand the basic facts and issues concerning the subject. Other characteristics of scholarly journals: they tend to be heavily researched, as indicated by numerous footnotes/endnotes and references; they are generally published by university presses; most of the authors represented are university professors; the articles, which have a serious, formal, and scholarly tone, are generally peer-reviewed by other scholars in the field.

To find articles in specialized periodicals, you'll use specialized indexes—that is, indexes for particular disciplines. You may also find it helpful to refer to *abstracts.* Like specialized indexes, abstracts list articles published in a particular discipline over a given period, but they also provide summaries of the articles listed. Abstracts tend to be more selective than indexes, since they consume more space (and involve considerably more work to compile); but, because they also describe the contents of the

articles covered, they can save you a lot of time in determining which articles you should read and which ones you can safely skip. Don't treat
abstracts alone as sources for research; if you find useful material in an
abstract, you need to locate the article to which it applies and use that as
your source of information.

A list of some of the more commonly used specialized periodical indexes
and abstracts in the various disciplines follows below.*

Social Science

Anthropological Index

Education Index

Index to Legal Periodicals

Psychological Abstracts (online as *PsycInfo*)

Public Affairs Information Service (PAIS)

Social Science Index

Sociological Abstracts

Women's Studies Abstracts

ERIC (Educational Resources Information Center)

Social SciSearch

Worldwide Political Science Abstracts

Humanities

America: History and Life

Art Index

Essay and General Literature Index

Film/Literature Index

Historical Abstracts

Humanities Index

International Index of Film Periodicals

*MLA International Bibliography of Books and Articles on Modern Languages and
Literature*

Music Index

Religion Index

Year's Work in English Studies

Arts and Humanities Citation Index

---

* *Note:* The format (print, online, or CD-ROM) of these databases will vary by library. Online
databases (as opposed to their print counterparts) are enhanced by more flexible search capa-
bility and, in some cases, by links to the full text.

MLA Bibliography
Philosophers' Index
Historical Abstracts

Science and Technology Indexes

Applied Science and Technology Index
Biological Abstracts
Chemical Abstracts
Engineering Index
General Science Index
Index to Scientific and Technical Proceedings (ceased publication in 1999)

Science and Technology

Aerospace and High Technology Database
Agricola (agriculture)
Biosis Previews (biology, botany)
Chemical Abstracts (chemistry)
Compendex (engineering)
Environment Abstracts
INSPEC (engineering)
MathSciNetPubMed (medical)
ScienceCitation Index
SciSearch

Business Indexes

Business Index
Business Periodicals Index
Economic Titles/Abstracts
Wall Street Journal *Index*

Business Databases

ABI/INFORM (index with access to some full text)
EconLit (index only)
STAT-USA (full text)
Standard and Poor's News (full text)

Law Databases

LexisNexis (full text)
Westlaw (full text)

Exploring Specialized Periodicals

Visit your campus library and locate the specialized periodical indexes for your major or area of interest (ask a reference librarian to help you). Note the call numbers for specialized periodicals (also called academic journals) in your field, and visit the periodical room or section of the library, where recent editions of academic journals are usually housed. Locate the call numbers you've noted, and spend some time looking through the specialized periodicals in your field. The articles you find in these journals represent some of the most recent scholarship in your field—the kind of scholarship many of your professors are busy conducting. Write half a page or so describing some of the articles you find interesting, and explain why.

Biographical Indexes

To look up information on particular people, you can use not only encyclopedias but an array of biographical sources. You can also use these biographical sources to alert yourself to potential biases on the part of your source authors, as such biases may be revealed by other work these authors have done and details of their backgrounds. A brief selection of biographical indexes follows.

Living Persons

Contemporary Authors: A Biographical Guide to Current Authors and Their Works

Current Biography

International Who's Who

Who's Who in America

Persons No Longer Living

Dictionary of American Biography

Dictionary of National Biography (Great Britain)

Dictionary of Scientific Biography

Who Was Who

Persons Living or Dead

Biography Almanac

McGraw-Hill Encyclopedia of World Biography

Webster's Biographical Dictionary

Dictionaries

Use dictionaries to look up the meaning of general or specialized terms. Here are some of the most useful dictionaries:

General

Merriam–Webster's Collegiate Dictionary

Oxford English Dictionary

Webster's New Collegiate Dictionary

Webster's Third New International Dictionary of the English Language

Social Sciences

Black's Law Dictionary

Dictionary of the Social Sciences

McGraw-Hill Dictionary of Modern Economics

Humanities

Dictionary of American History

Dictionary of Films

Dictionary of Philosophy

Harvard Dictionary of Music

McGraw-Hill Dictionary of Art

Science and Technology

Computer Dictionary and Handbook

Condensed Chemical Dictionary

Dictionary of Biology

Dorland's Medical Dictionary

Business

Dictionary of Advertising Terms

Dictionary of Business and Economics

Mathematical Dictionary for Economics and Business Administration

McGraw-Hill Dictionary of Modern Economics: A Handbook of Terms and Organizations

Other Sources/Government Publications

Besides those already listed, you have many other options and potential sources for research. Here are only some of your options: For statistical and other basic reference information on a subject, consult a *handbook* (such as *Statistical Abstracts of the United States*). For current information on a subject as of a given year, consult an *almanac* (such as *World Almanac*). For annual updates of information, consult a *yearbook* (such as *The Statesman's Yearbook*). For maps and other geographic information, consult an *atlas* (such as *New*

CRITICAL READING FOR RESEARCH

- *Use all the critical reading tips we've suggested thus far.* The tips contained in the boxes Critical Reading for Summary on page 6, Critical Reading for Critique on page 64, Critical Reading for Synthesis on page 128, and Critical Reading for Analysis on page 181 are all useful for the kinds of reading used in conducting research.
- *Read for relationships to your research question.* How does the source help you formulate and clarify your research question?
- *Read for relationships between sources.* How does each source illustrate, support, expand upon, contradict, or offer an alternative perspective to those of your other sources?
- *Consider the relationship between your source's form and content.* How does the form of the source—specialized encyclopedia, book, article in a popular magazine, article in a professional journal—affect its content, the manner in which that content is presented, and its relationship to other sources?
- *Pay special attention to the legitimacy of Internet sources.* Consider how the content and validity of the information on the Web page may be affected by the purpose of the site. Assess Web-based information according to the five criteria suggested by Alexander and Tate (see pages 199–200): (1) accuracy; (2) authority; (3) objectivity; (4) currency; and (5) coverage.

York Times Atlas of the World). Often, simply browsing through the reference shelves for data on your general subject—such as biography, public affairs, psychology—will reveal valuable sources of information. And of course, much reference information is available on government sites on the Web.

In addition to all their other holdings, many libraries keep pamphlets in a *vertical file* (i.e., a file cabinet). For example, a pamphlet on global warming might be found in the vertical file rather than in the library stacks. Such material is accessible through the *Vertical File Index* (a monthly subject-and-title index to pamphlet material).

Finally, note that the U.S. government regularly publishes large quantities of useful information. Some indexes to government publications include the following:

American Statistics Index
Congressional Information Service
The Congressional Record
Information U.S.A.

GUIDELINES FOR CONDUCTING INTERVIEWS

- Become knowledgeable about the subject before the interview so that you can ask intelligent questions. Prepare most of your questions beforehand.
- Ask "open-ended" questions designed to elicit meaningful responses, rather than "forced choice" questions that can be answered with a word or two, or "leading questions" that presume a particular answer. For example, instead of asking "Do you think that male managers should be more sensitive to women's concerns for equal pay in the workplace?" ask, "To what extent do you see evidence that male managers are insufficiently sensitive to women's concerns for equal pay in the workplace?"
- Ask follow-up questions to elicit additional insights or details.
- If you record the interview (in addition to or instead of taking notes), get your subject's permission, preferably in writing.

Interviews and Surveys

Depending on the subject of your paper, some or all of your research may be conducted outside the library. In conducting such primary research, you may perform experiments in science labs or make observations or gather data in courthouses, city government files, shopping malls (if you are observing, say, patterns of consumer behavior), the quad in front of the humanities building, or in front of TV screens (if you are analyzing, say, situation comedies or commercials, or if you are drawing on documentaries or interviews—in which cases you should try to obtain transcripts or tape the programs).

You may also want to *interview* your professors, your fellow students, or other individuals knowledgeable about your subject. Additionally, or alternatively, you may wish to conduct *surveys* via *questionnaires*. When well prepared and insightfully interpreted, such tools can produce valuable information about the ideas or preferences of a group of people.

MINING SOURCES

Having located your sources (or at least having begun the process), you'll proceed to "mining" them—that is, extracting from them information and ideas that you can use in your paper. To keep track of these sources, you'll need to compile a working bibliography so that you know what information you have and how it relates to your research question. Of course, you'll need to take notes on your sources and evaluate them for reliability and relevance.

GUIDELINES FOR CONDUCTING SURVEYS AND DESIGNING QUESTIONNAIRES

- Determine your *purpose* in conducting the survey: what kind of *information* you seek, and *whom* (i.e., what subgroup of the population) you intend to survey.
- Decide whether you want to collect information on the spot or have people send their responses back to you. (You will get fewer responses if they are sent back to you, but those you do get will likely be more complete than surveys conducted on the spot.)
- Devise and word questions carefully so that they (1) are understandable and (2) do not reflect your own biases. For example, if you are conducting a survey on attitudes toward capital punishment and you ask, "Do you believe that the state should endorse legalized murder?" you've loaded the question to influence people to answer in the negative.
- Devise short-answer or multiple-choice questions; open-ended questions encourage responses that are difficult to quantify. (You may want to leave space, however, for "additional comments.") Conversely, "yes" or "no" responses or rankings on a 5-point scale are easy to quantify.
- It may be useful to break out the responses by as many meaningful categories as possible—for example, gender, age, ethnicity, religion, education, geographic locality, profession, and income.

And you should develop some kind of outline—formal or informal—that allows you to see how you are going to subdivide and organize your discussion and, thus, at what points you'll be drawing on relevant sources. In doing this you are engaging in a process that has identifiable stages. For an extended discussion of this writing process, see Chapter 3.

THE WORKING BIBLIOGRAPHY

As you conduct your research, keep a *working bibliography*—that is, a compilation of bibliographic information on all the sources you're likely to use in preparing the paper. Note full bibliographic information on each source you consider. If you're meticulous about this during the research process, you'll be spared the frustration of having to go back to retrieve information—such as the publisher or the date—just as you're typing your final draft.

Now that library catalogs and databases are available online, it's easy to copy and paste your sources' (or potential sources') bibliographic information into a document, or to e-mail citations to yourself for cutting and pasting later. A more traditional but still very efficient way to compile bibliographic information is on 3" × 5" note cards. (Note that certain software programs allow you to create sortable electronic records.) Using any of these methods, you can easily add, delete, and rearrange individual bibliographic records as your research progresses. Whether you keep bibliographic information on note cards or in a document, be sure to record the following:

- The author or editor (last name first) and, if relevant, the translator
- The title (and subtitle) of the book or article
- The publisher and place of publication (if a book) or the title of the periodical
- The date and/or year of publication; if periodical, volume and issue number
- The edition number (if a book beyond its first edition)
- The inclusive page numbers (if article)
- The specific page number of a quote or other special material you might paraphrase

You also may want to include the following:

- A brief description of the source (to help you recall it later in the research process)
- The library call number (to help you relocate the source if you haven't checked it out)
- A code number, which you can use as a shorthand reference to the source in your notes

Your final bibliography, known as "Works Cited" in Modern Language Association (MLA) format and "References" in American Psychological Association (APA) format, consists of the sources you have actually summarized, paraphrased, or quoted in your paper. When you compile the bibliography, arrange your sources alphabetically by authors' last names.

Here is an example of a working bibliography notation or record for a book:

> Gorham, Eric B. *National Service, Political Socialization, and Political Education.* Albany: SUNY P, 1992.
>
> Argues that the language government uses to promote national service programs betrays an effort to "reproduce a postindustrial, capitalist economy in the name of good citizenship." Chap. 1 provides a historical survey of national service.

Here is an example of a working bibliography record for an article:

> Gergen, David. "A Time to Heed the Call." *U.S. News & World Report* 24 Dec. 2001: 60-61.
>
> Argues that in the wake of the surge of patriotism that followed the September 11 terrorist attacks, the government should encourage citizens to participate in community and national service. Supports the McCain-Bayh bill.

Here is an example of a working bibliography record for an online source:

> Bureau of Labor Statistics. "Table 1: Volunteers by Selected Characteristics, September 2002 and 2003." 18 Dec. 2003. Accessed 17 Jan. 2004. <http://www.bls.gov/news.release/volun.t01.htm>. Provides statistical data on volunteerism in the U.S.

Some instructors may ask you to prepare—either in addition to or instead of a research paper—an *annotated bibliography*. This is a list of relevant works on a subject, with the contents of each briefly described or assessed. The sample bibliography records shown could become the basis for two entries in an annotated bibliography on national service. Annotations differ from *abstracts* in that annotations do not claim to be comprehensive summaries; they indicate, rather, how the items may be useful to the researcher.

Note-Taking

People have their favorite ways of note-taking. Some use use legal pads or spiral notebooks; others type notes into a laptop computer, perhaps using a database program. Some prefer 4" × 6" cards for note-taking. Such cards have some of the same advantages as 3" × 5" cards for working bibliographies: They can easily be added to, subtracted from, and rearranged to accommodate changing organizational plans. Also, discrete pieces of information from the same source can easily be arranged (and rearranged) into subtopics—a difficult task if you have taken three pages of notes on an article without breaking the notes down into subtopics.

Whatever your preferred approach, we recommend including the following along with the note itself:

- A topic or subtopic label, corresponding to your outline (see below)
- A code number, corresponding to the number assigned the source in the working bibliography
- A page reference at end of note

Here is a sample note record for the table "Volunteers by Selected Characteristics, September 2002 and 2003" by the Bureau of Labor Statistics (bibliographic record above):

> *"Pervasiveness of Volunteerism" (A)*   7
>
> *Shows that 28.8 percent of Americans age 16 and older, 63.8 million in all, devote time to community service.*

Here is a notecard for the periodical article by Gergen (see bibliography note on page 211):

> *"Beneficial paid volunteer programs" (D3 C(1))*   12
>
> *Both the community and the individual benefit from voluntary service programs. Cites Teach for America, Alumni of City Year, Peace Corps as programs in which participants receive small stipends and important benefits. (60) "Voluntary service when young often changes people for life. They learn to give their fair share." (60).*

Both note records are headed by a topic label followed by the tentative location in the paper outline where the information may be used. The number in the upper-right corner corresponds to the bibliography note. The note itself in the first record uses *summary*. The note in the second record uses *summary* (sentence 1), *paraphrase* (sentence 2), and *quotation* (sentence 3). Summary is used to condense important ideas treated in several paragraphs in the sources; paraphrase (with relevant page number), for the important detail on specific programs; quotation (again with relevant page number), for particularly incisive language by the source authors. For general hints on when to use each of these three forms, see Chapter 1, page 42.

At this point we must stress the importance of using quotation marks around quoted language *in your notes.* Making sure to note the difference between your own and quoted language will help you avoid unintentionally using someone else's words or ideas without crediting them properly. Such use, whether intentional or unintentional, constitutes plagiarism—a serious academic offense—something that professors don't take lightly; you don't want to invite suspicion of your work, even unintentionally. See the discussion of plagiarism on pages 42–44 for more details.

Evaluating Sources

Sifting through what seems like a formidable mountain of material, you'll need to work quickly and efficiently; you'll also need to do some selecting. This means, primarily, distinguishing the more important from the less important (and the unimportant) material. Draw on your critical reading

---

GUIDELINES FOR EVALUATING SOURCES

- Skim the source. With a book, look over the table of contents, the introduction and conclusion, and the index; zero in on passages that your initial survey suggests are important. With an article, skim the introduction and the headings.
- Be alert for references in your sources to other important sources, particularly to sources that several authors treat as important.
- Other things being equal, the more recent the source, the better. Recent work usually incorporates or refers to important earlier work.
- If you're considering making multiple references to a book, look up the reviews in the *Book Review Digest* or the *Book Review Index*. Also, check the author's credentials in a source such as *Contemporary Authors* or *Current Biography*.

---

skills to help you determine the reliability and relevance of a source. See the box on Critical Reading for Research on page 207, and review Chapter 2, particularly the sections on evaluating informative writing (page 47) and evaluating persuasive writing (pages 49–54). The hints in the box above may also simplify the task.

Arranging Your Notes: The Outline

Using your original working thesis (see Chapter 3 on theses)—or a new thesis that you have developed during the course of data-gathering and invention—you can begin constructing a *preliminary outline*. This outline indicates the order in which you plan to support your thesis.

Some people prefer not to develop an outline until they have more or less completed their research. At that point they will look over their note records, consider the relationships among the various pieces of evidence, possibly arrange notes or cards into separate piles, then develop an outline based on their perceptions and insights about the material. Subsequently, they rearrange and code the note records to conform to their outline—an informal outline indicating just the main sections of the paper and possibly one level below that. Thus, the model paper on national service (see Chapter 5) could be informally outlined as follows:

```
Intro: Pervasiveness of volunteerism in America;
       Thesis: We should not turn the success of
       volunteerism in America into an argument
       for compulsory national service.
Intellectual history of public service: James,
       Plato
```

```
Can government compel citizens to public service?
      Military service: yes, in time of war
      Civilian service: no—logical, legal,
      moral reasons
Conclusion: Government should expand
      opportunities for public service, but
      should not compel such service.
```

Such an outline will help you organize your research and should not be unduly restrictive as a guide to writing.

The *formal outline* (a multileveled plan with Roman and Arabic numerals, capital and small lettered subheadings) may still be useful, not so much as an exact blueprint for composition—although some writers do find it useful for this purpose—but rather as a guide to revision. That is, after you have written your draft, outlining it may help you discern structural problems: illogical sequences of material; confusing relationships between ideas; poor unity or coherence; sections that are too abstract or underdeveloped. Many instructors also require that formal outlines accompany the finished research paper.

The formal outline should indicate the logical relationships in the evidence you present. But it may also reflect the general conventions of a particular academic field. Thus, after an *introduction,* papers in the social sciences often proceed with a description of the *methods* of collecting information, continue with a description of the *results* of the investigation, and end with a *conclusion.* Papers in the sciences often follow a similar pattern. Papers in the humanities generally are less standardized in form. In devising a logical organization for your paper, ask yourself how your reader might best be introduced to the subject, be guided through a discussion of the main issues, and be persuaded that your viewpoint is a sound one.

Formal outlines are generally of two types: *topic outlines* and *sentence outlines.* In the topic outline, headings and subheadings are indicated by words or phrases—as in the informal outline above. In the sentence outline, each heading and subheading is indicated in a complete sentence. Both topic and sentence outlines generally are preceded by the thesis.

You'll find a formal topic outline of the national service paper in Chapter 5 on pages 147–48.

CITING SOURCES

When you refer to or quote the work of another, you are obligated to credit or cite your source properly. There are two types of citations—in-text citations and full citations at the end of a paper—and they work in tandem.

If you are writing a paper in the humanities, you probably will be expected to use the Modern Language Association (MLA) format for citation. This format is fully described in the *MLA Handbook for Writers of Research Papers,* 6th ed. (New York: Modern Language Association of America, 2003). A paper in the social sciences will probably use the American Psychological Association (APA) format. This format is fully described in the *Publication Manual of the American Psychological Association,* 5th ed. (Washington, DC: American Psychological Association, 2001).

In the following section, we will focus on MLA and APA styles, the ones you are most likely to use in your academic work. Keep in mind, however, that instructors often have their own preferences. Some require the documentation style specified in *The Chicago Manual of Style,* 15th ed. (Chicago: University of Chicago Press, 2003). This style is similar to APA style, except that publication dates are not placed within parentheses. Instructors in the sciences often follow the Council of Science Editors (CSE) format (formerly Council of Biology Editors). Or they may prefer a number format: Each source listed on the bibliography page is assigned a number, and all text references to the source are followed by the appropriate number within parentheses (and sometimes brackets). Some instructors like the old MLA style, which calls for footnotes and endnotes. Check with your instructor for the preferred documentation format if this is not specified in the assignment or indicated in class.

IN-TEXT CITATION

The general rule for in-text citation is to include only enough information to alert the reader to the source of the reference and to the location within that source. Normally, this information includes the author's last name and the page number (plus the year of publication, if using APA guidelines). But if you have already named the author in the preceding text, just the page number is sufficient.

Content Notes

Occasionally, you may want to provide a footnote or an endnote as a *content note*—one that provides additional information bearing on or illuminating, but not directly related to, the discussion at hand, as in this example:

TYPES OF CITATIONS

- Citations that indicate the source of quotations, paraphrases, and summarized information and ideas. These citations—generally limited to author's last name, relevant page number, and publication date of source—appear *in text,* within parentheses.
- Citations that appear in an alphabetical list entitled "Works Cited" or "References" *following the paper.* These citations provide full bibliographical information on the source.

> [1] Equally well-known is Forster's distinc-
> tion between story and plot: In the former, the
> emphasis is on sequence ("the king died and then
> the queen died"); in the latter, the emphasis is
> on causality ("the king died and then the queen
> died of grief").

Notice the format: The first line is indented five spaces or one-half inch and the note number is raised one-half line. A single space from there, the note begins. Subsequent lines of the note are flush with the left margin. If the note is at the bottom of the page (a footnote), it is placed four lines below the text of the page, and the note itself is single-spaced. Double spaces are used between notes. Content notes are numbered consecutively throughout the paper; do not begin renumbering on each page. Most word-processing programs have functions for inserting consecutive footnotes, formatting them, and placing them in the appropriate position on your pages.

FULL CITATIONS

In MLA format, your complete list of sources, with all information necessary for a reader to locate a source, is called "Works Cited." (It should begin on a new page.) In APA format, the list of sources is called "References." Entries in such listings should be double-spaced, with second and subsequent lines of each entry indented (a "hanging indent")—five spaces or one-half inch. In both styles, a single space follows the period. For comparison of MLA and APA citation styles, here are two samples of journal citations. Citation of books and other sources follow slightly different guidelines:

Sample MLA Full Citation (for a journal article)

Haan, Sarah C. "The 'Persuasion Route' of the Law:

Advertising and Legal Persuasion." <u>Columbia Law

Review</u> 100 (2000): 1281–326.

Sample APA Full Citation (for a journal article)

Haan, S. C. (2000). The "persuasion route" of the

law: Advertising and legal persuasion. *Columbia

Law Review, 100,* 1281–1326.

The main differences between MLA and APA styles are these: (1) In MLA style, the date of the publication of a book follows the name of the publisher; in APA style, the date is placed within parentheses following the author's name. (2) In APA style, only the initial of the author's first name is given, and only the first word (and any proper noun) of the book or article title is capitalized. The first letter of the subtitle (after a colon in a title) is also capitalized. In MLA style, the author's full name is given, and all words following the first word of the title (except articles and prepositions) are capitalized. (3) In APA style (unlike MLA style), quotation marks are not used around journal/magazine article titles. (4) APA style (unlike MLA style) requires the use of "p." and "pp." in in-text citations to indicate page numbers of periodical articles. (5) In APA format, titles of books and journals are italicized, as are the punctuation that follows and the volume (but not issue) numbers; MLA requires underlining for book and journal titles. (6) When citing books, both MLA and APA rules dictate that publishers' names should be shortened; thus, "Random House" becomes "Random"; "William Morrow" becomes "Morrow." However, MLA style uses a more extensive system of abbreviations for publishers' names.

Note: The hanging indent (second and subsequent lines indented) is the recommended format for both MLA and APA style references.

Provided below are some of the most commonly used citations in MLA and APA formats. For a more complete listing, consult the *MLA Handbook,* the APA's *Publication Manual,* or whichever style guide your instructor has specified. Please note that achieving conformance to either citation system requires precision and attention to detail, down to every keystroke and punctuation mark.

MLA STYLE

In-Text Citation

Here are sample in-text citations using the MLA system:

> From the beginning, the AIDS antibody test has been "mired in controversy" (Bayer 101).

Notice that in the MLA system no date and no punctuation come between the author's name and the page number within the parentheses. Notice also that the parenthetical reference is placed *before* the final punctuation of the sentence, because it is considered part of the sentence.

If you have already mentioned the author's name in the text—in a *signal phrase*—it is not necessary to repeat it in the citation:

> According to Bayer, from the beginning, the AIDS antibody test has been "mired in controversy" (101).

In MLA format, you must supply page numbers for summaries and paraphrases, as well as for quotations:

```
According to Bayer, the AIDS antibody test has been

controversial from the outset (101).
```

Use a block, or indented form, for quotations of five lines or more. Introduce the block quotation with a full sentence followed by a colon. Indent one inch or ten spaces (that is, double the normal paragraph indentation). Place the parenthetical citation *after* the final period:

```
Robert  Flaherty's  refusal  to  portray  primitive

people's  contact  with  civilization  arose  from  an

inner conflict:

    He had originally plunged with all his heart into

    the role of explorer and prospector; before Nanook,

    his own father was his hero. Yet as he entered the

    Eskimo world, he knew he did so as the advance guard

    of industrial civilization, the world of United

    States Steel and Sir William Mackenzie and railroad

    and mining empires. The mixed feeling this gave him

    left his mark on all his films. (Barnouw 45)
```

Again, were Barnouw's name mentioned in the sentence leading into the quotation, the parenthetical reference would be simply (45).

Usually parenthetical citations appear at the end of your sentences; however, if the reference applies only to the first part of the sentence, the parenthetical information is inserted at the appropriate point *within* the sentence:

```
While Baumrind argues that "the laboratory is not

the place to study degree of obedience" (421),

Milgram asserts that such arguments are groundless.
```

At times, you must modify the basic author/page number reference. Depending on the nature of your source(s), you may need to use one of the citation formats below.

Quoted Material Appearing in Another Source

```
(qtd. in Garber 211)
```

An Anonymous Work

> ("Obedience" 32)

Two Authors

> (Bernstein and Politi 208)

A Particular Work by an Author, When You List Two or More Works by That Author in the List of Works Cited

> (Toffler, <u>Wave</u> 96–97)

Two or More Sources as the Basis of Your Statement

> (Butler 109; Carey 57)

In-Text Citation of Electronic Sources (MLA)

Web sites, CD-ROM data, and e-mail generally do not have numbered pages. Different browsers may display and printers may produce differing numbers of pages for any particular site. You should therefore omit both page numbers and paragraph numbers from in-text citations to electronic sources, unless these page or paragraph numbers are provided within the source itself. For in-text citations of electronic sources, MLA prefers that you cite the author's name in the sentence rather than in a parenthetical, where possible. In APA style, use parentheses for citation of author's name and the year of publication as you would when citing print material.

Examples of MLA Citations in List of Works Cited

Books (MLA)

One Author

> Fahs, Alice. <u>The Imagined Civil War: Popular</u>
>
> <u>Literature of the North and South, 1861–1865</u>.
>
> Chapel Hill: U of North Carolina P, 2003.

Note: MLA convention dictates abbreviating the names of university presses (e.g., Oxford UP for Oxford University Press or the above for University of North Carolina Press). Commercial publishing companies are also shortened by dropping such endings as "Co.," or "Inc." The *MLA Handbook* includes a list of abbreviations for publishers' names.

Two or More Books by the Same Author

Gubar, Susan. <u>Critical Condition: Feminism at the</u>

<u>Turn of the Century</u>. New York: Columbia UP, 2000.

---. <u>Racechanges: White Skin, Black Face in American</u>

<u>Culture</u>. New York: Oxford UP, 1997.

Note: For MLA style, references to works by the same author are listed in alphabetical order of title.

Two Authors

Gerson, Allan, and Jerry Adler. <u>The Price of</u>

<u>Terror</u>. New York: Harper, 2003.

More than Three Authors

Burawoy, Michael, et al. <u>Global Ethnography: Forces,</u>

<u>Connections, and Imaginations in a Postmodern</u>

<u>World</u>. Berkeley: U of California P, 2000.

Book with an Editor and No Author

Dean, Bartholomew, and Jerome M. Levi, eds. <u>At the</u>

<u>Risk of Being Heard: Identity, Indigenous</u>

<u>Rights, and Postcolonial States</u>. Ann Arbor: U

of Michigan P, 2003.

Later Edition

Whitten, Phillip. <u>Anthropology: Contemporary</u>

<u>Perspectives</u>. 8th ed. Boston: Allyn, 2001.

Selection from an Anthology

Hardy, Melissa. "The Heifer." <u>The Best American</u>

<u>Short Stories</u>. Ed. Sue Miller. Boston:

Houghton, 2002. 97—115.

Note: Include page numbers of a selection drawn from an anthology.

Government Publication

National Institute of Child Health and Human

Development. Closing the Gap: A National

Blueprint to Improve the Health of Persons with

Mental Retardation. Washington: GPO, 2002.

United States. Cong. House. Committee on Government

Reform. Interim Report of the Activities of the

House Committee on Government Reform. 107th

Cong. 1st sess. Washington: GPO, 2001.

Periodicals (MLA)

Continuous Pagination Throughout Annual Cycle

Binder, Sarah. "The Dynamics of Legislative

Gridlock, 1947–1996." American Political

Science Review 93 (1999): 519—31.

Separate Pagination Each Issue

O'Mealy, Joseph H. "Royal Family Values: The

Americanization of Alan Bennett's The Madness

of King George III." Literature/Film Quarterly

27.2 (1999): 90—97.

Monthly Periodical

Davison, Peter. "Girl, Seeming to Disappear."

Atlantic Monthly May 2000: 108—11.

Signed Article in Weekly Periodical

Gladwell, Malcolm. "The New-Boy Network." New

Yorker 29 May 2000: 68—86.

Unsigned Article in Weekly Periodical

"GOP Speaker Admits 'Exaggerations.' " <u>New Republic</u>
   14 Aug. 2000: 10–11.

Signed Article in Daily Newspaper

Vise, David A. "FBI Report Gauges School Violence
   Indicators." <u>Washington Post</u> 6 Sept. 2000: B1+.

Unsigned Article in Daily Newspaper

"The World's Meeting Place." <u>New York Times</u> 6 Sept.
   2000: A11.

Review

Barber, Benjamin R. "The Crack in the Picture
   Window." Rev. of <u>Bowling Alone: The Collapse
   and Revival of American Community</u>, by Robert D.
   Putnam. <u>Nation</u> 7 Aug. 2000: 29–34.

Interview Conducted by the Researcher

Emerson, Robert. Personal interview. 10 Oct. 2002.

Electronic Sources (MLA)

According to guidelines in the *MLA Handbook,* the following information
should be included when crediting electronic sources:

1. *Name of the author, editor, compiler, or translator* (if given)
2. *Title* of the work, with quotation marks if something other than a book;
   underlined if it is a book
3. Information, if any, about *print publication*
4. Information about electronic publication, including title of the Internet
   site or name of any organization or institution sponsoring the site
5. *Access information,* including
   a. the date of electronic publication or latest update, if available
   b. the researcher's date of access
   c. the URL (in angle brackets < >)

If the URL of the exact document is extremely long and complex, making
transcription errors possible, provide instead the URL of the relevant search

page or home page. From there, using other publication facts given in the citation, readers should be able to locate the cited document. URLs should include the access-mode identifier—*http, ftp, gopher,* or *telnet.* Enclose URLs in angle brackets (< >). When a URL continues from one line to the next, break it only after a slash. Do not add a hyphen.

Because few standards currently exist for those who post publications on the Internet, you may not necessarily be able to find or supply all the desired information. Thus you may simply settle for what is available while aiming for comprehensiveness. Formatting conventions are illustrated by the models below.

An Entire Internet Site for an Online Scholarly Project or Database

> The *Piers Plowman Electronic Archive.* Ed. Robert
>
> Adams et al. 2003. Society for Early English
>
> and Norse Electronic Texts, University of
>
> Virginia Institute for Advanced Technology in
>
> the Humanities. 15 July 2003
>
> <http://www.iath.virginia.edu/seenet/piers/
>
> piersmain.html>.

Note: The information presented is (1) title of site, project, or database; (2) name of the editor of project or site; (3) electronic publication information, including date of electronic publication or latest update and name of sponsoring institution; and (4) date of access and URL.

A Personal Home Page or Professional Site

> Winter, Mick. <u>How to Talk New Age</u>. 28 July 2003
>
> <http://www.well.com/user/mick/newagept.html>.

Note: In addition to date of access (shown here), the citation should include the date of last update, if given.

An Online Book

> Smith, Adam. <u>The Wealth of Nations</u>. Oxford: Oxford
>
> UP, 1985. The Adam Smith Institute. 2001. 15
>
> July 2003 <http://www.adamsmith.org/smith/
>
> won-intro.htm>.

A Part of an Online Book

Smith, Adam. "Of the Division of Labour." <u>The
Wealth of Nations</u>. Oxford: Oxford UP, 1985. The
Adam Smith Institute. 2001. 15 July 2003
<http://www.adamsmith.org/smith/won-b1-c1.htm>.

An Article in a Scholarly Journal

Epstein, Paul. "The Imitation of Athena in the
Lysistrata of Aristophanes." <u>Animus</u> 7 (2002).
16 July 2003 <http://www.swgc.mun.ca/animus/
current/epstein7.htm>.

An Unsigned Article in a Newspaper or on a Newswire

"Verizon to Rehire 1,100 Laid-off Workers." <u>AP
Online</u> 16 July 2003. 18 July 2003
<http://www.nytimes.com/aponline/technology/
AP-Verizon-Jobs.html>.

A Signed Article in a Newspaper or on a Newswire

Vartabedian, Ralph. "Columbia's Crew Lived after
Radio Calls Ended." <u>Chicago Tribune</u> 16 July
2003. 20 July 2003
<http://www.chicagotribune.com/technology/
la-nashuttle16jul16,1,1997210.story?coll=
chi-news-hed>.

An Article in a Magazine

Kim, Jimin. "When Cell Phones Meet Camcorders."
<u>Forbes</u> 16 July 2003. 12 Aug. 2003
<http://www.forbes.com/home/2003/07/16/
cx_jk_0716tentech.html>.

An E-Mail Communication

```
Mendez, Michael R. "Re: Solar power." E-mail to

    Edgar V. Atamian. 11 Sept. 2003.

Armstrong, David J. E-mail to the author. 30 Aug.

    2003.
```

An Online Posting

For online postings, discussion groups, or synchronous communications, cite a version stored as a Web file, if one exists, so that your readers can more easily find your sources. Label sources as needed (e.g., online posting, online defense of dissertation, etc., with neither underlining nor quotation marks).

```
Flanders, Julia. "Mentoring in Humanities

    Computing." Online posting. 8 May 2003.

    Humanist Discussion Group. 16 July 2003

    <http://lists.village.virginia.edu/

    lists_archive/Humanist/v17/0001.html>.
```

Synchronous Communication

```
Mendez, Michael R. Online debate. "Solar Power

    Versus Fossil Fuel Power." 3 Apr. 2000.

    CollegeTownMOO. 3 Apr. 2000

    <telnet://next.cs.bvc.edu.7777>.
```

Downloaded Computer Software

```
Quicktime. Vers. 6.3. 16 July 2003

    <http://www.apple.com/quicktime/download/>.
```

APA STYLE

In-Text Citation

Here are sample in-text citations using the APA system:

```
Much research shows that rather than inducing any

lasting changes in a child's behavior, punishment
```

> "promotes only momentary compliance"(Berk, 2002,
>
> p. 383).

Note: In the APA system, there is a comma between the author's name, the date, and the page number, and the number itself is preceded by "p." or "pp." Note also that the parenthetical reference is placed *before* the final punctuation of the sentence.

If you have already mentioned the author's name in the text, it is not necessary to repeat it in the citation:

> According to Berk (2002), much research shows that
> rather than inducing any lasting changes in a
> child's behavior, punishment "promotes only momen-
> tary compliance"(p. 383).

> According to Berk, much research shows that rather
> than inducing any lasting changes in a child's
> behavior, punishment "promotes only momentary com-
> pliance"(2002, p. 383).

When using the APA system, provide page numbers only for direct quotations, not for summaries or paraphrases. If you do not refer to a specific page, simply indicate the date:

> Berk (2002) asserted that many research findings
> view punishment as a quick fix rather than a long-
> term solution to behavior problems in children.

For quotations of forty words or more, use block (indented) quotations. In these cases, place the parenthetical citation *after* the period:

> Various strategies exist for reducing children's
> tendency to view the world in a gender-biased
> fashion:

> > Once children notice the vast array of gender
> > stereotypes in their society, parents and teachers
> > can point out exceptions. For example, they can

> arrange for children to see men and women pursuing
> nontraditional careers. And they can reason with
> children, explaining that interests and skills, not
> sex, should determine a person's occupation and
> activities. (Berk, 2002, p. 395)

Again, were Berk's name mentioned in the sentence leading into the quotation, the parenthetical reference in APA style would be simply (2002, p. 395).

If the reference applies only to the first part of a sentence, the parenthetical reference is inserted at the appropriate points *within* the sentence:

> Shapiro (2002, p. 32) emphasizes the idea that law
> firms are "continually in flux," while Sikes focus-
> es on their stability as institutions.

At times you must modify the basic author/page number reference. Depending on the nature of your source(s), you may need to use one of the citation formats below.

Quoted Material Appearing in Another Source

> (as cited in Garber, 2000, p. 211)

An Anonymous Work

> ("Obedience," 2003, p. 32)

Two Authors

> (Striano & Rochat, 2000, p. 257)

Two or More Sources as the Basis of Your Statement

> (Ehrenreich 2001, p. 68; Hitchens, 2001, p. 140)

Note: Entries are arranged in alphabetical order of surname.

In-Text Citation of Electronic Sources (APA)

As noted earlier, Web sites, CD-ROM data, and e-mail generally do not have numbered pages (unless they are PDF reproductions of print material). If paragraph numbers are visible in the source, you can use them instead of page numbers for in-text citations. If the document has headings but no page or paragraph numbers, cite the heading and the number of the paragraph following it.

Citation to an Electronic Source with Headings

(Kishlansky, 2002, Conclusion section, paragraph 2)

Examples of APA Citations in List of References

Books (APA)

One Author

Fahs, Alice. (2003). *The imagined civil war:*
Popular literature of the north and south,
1861–1865. Chapel Hill: University of North
Carolina Press.

Two or More Books by the Same Author

Gubar, S. (1997). *Racechanges: White skin, black*
face in American culture. New York: Oxford
University Press.

Gubar, S. (2000). *Critical condition: Feminism at*
the turn of the century. New York: Columbia
University Press.

Note: For APA style, references to works by the same author are listed in chronological order of publication, earliest first. Use the author's name in all entries.

Two Authors

Gerson, A., & Adler, J. (2003). *The price of*
terror. New York: Harper.

Note: In APA format, the "and" between names of two authors is indicated by an ampersand (&).

More than Three Authors

Burawoy, M., Blum, J. A., George, S., Gille, Z.,
Gowan, T., Haney, L., et al. (2000). *Global*

ethnography: *Forces, connections, and*

imaginations in a postmodern world. Berkeley:

University of California Press.

Note: If there are more than six authors, list only the first six, followed by *et al.*

Book with an Editor and No Author

Dean, B., & Levi, J. M. (Eds.). (2003). *At the risk*

of being heard: Identity, indigenous rights,

and postcolonial states. Ann Arbor: University

of Michigan Press.

Later Edition

Whitten, P. (2001). *Anthropology: Contemporary*

perspectives (8th ed.). Boston: Allyn & Bacon.

Selection from an Anthology

Halberstam, D. (2002). Who we are. In S. J. Gould

(Ed.), *The best American essays 2002* (pp.

124—136). New York: Houghton Mifflin.

Government Publication

National Institute of Child Health and Human

Development. (2002). *Closing the gap: A*

national blueprint to improve the health of

persons with mental retardation. Washington,

DC: U.S. Government Printing Office.

Caring for children act of 2003: Report of the

Senate Committee on Health, Education, Labor,

and Pensions, S. Rep. No. 108-37 (2003).

Periodicals (APA)

Continuous Pagination Throughout Annual Cycle

```
Tomlins, C. L. (2003). In a wilderness of tigers:

    Violence, the discourse of English colonizing,

    and the refusals of American history.

    Theoretical Inquiries in Law, 4, 505—543.
```

Note: Inclusive page numbers are indicated in full, unlike in MLA format which permits elisions: e.g., 505–43.

Separate Pagination Each Issue

```
O'Mealy, J. H. (1999). Royal family values: The

    Americanization of Alan Bennett's The Madness

    of King George III. Literature/Film Quarterly,

    27(2), 90—97.
```

Monthly Periodical

```
Davison, P. (2000, May). Girl, seeming to

    disappear. Atlantic Monthly, 285, 108—111.
```

Signed Article in Weekly Periodical

```
Gladwell, M. (2000, May 29). The new-boy network.

    New Yorker, 68—86.
```

Unsigned Article in Weekly Periodical

```
Spain and the Basques: Dangerous stalemate. (2003,

    July 5). Economist, 368, 44—45.
```

Signed Article in Daily Newspaper, Discontinuous Pages

```
Vise, D. A. (2000, September 6). FBI report gauges

    school violence indicators. Washington Post,

    pp. B1, B6.
```

Unsigned Article in Daily Newspaper

> The world's meeting place. (2000, September 6). *New*
>
> *York Times*, p. A11.

Review

> Barber, B. R. (2000, August 7). The crack in the
>
> picture window. [Review of the book *Bowling*
>
> *alone: The collapse and revival of American*
>
> *community*]. Nation, 29–34.

Note: Some weekly magazines do not have volume numbers, in which case, include only the date and page numbers in your reference.

Electronic Sources (APA)

The basic information needed to cite electronic sources using APA documentation style includes the following:

1. *Name of the author* (if given)
2. *Date* of publication, update, or retrieval
3. *Document title, description, and/or source*
4. The *URL*, or Internet address (the most crucial element)

The APA *Publication Manual* recommends that writers check the URLs regularly, while drafting a paper and before submission, as the location of documents sometimes changes. As with MLA citations, include as much pertinent information as is available to help your reader find the source, such as volume and issue numbers if available.

The general APA format for online periodical sources is as follows:

> Author, I. (date). Title of article. *Name of Periodical. Volume* and issue number (if available). Retrieved month, day, year, from source

For online sources, do not add periods or other punctuation immediately following URLs. Also, if you need to continue a URL across lines, break the URL after a slash or before a period. Do not use a hyphen. An extra hyphen or period may prevent a reader from accessing the source.

An Article in an Internet-Only Scholarly Journal

> Sheehan, K. B., & Hoy, M. G. (1999). Using e-mail to
>
> survey Internet users in the United States:

```
Methodology and assessment [Electronic version].

Journal of Computer-Mediated Communication,

4(3). Retrieved August 14, 2001, from

http://www.ascusc.org/jcmc/vol4/issue3/

sheehan.html
```

Note: The APA guidelines distinguish between Internet articles that are based on a print source, and those that appear in Internet-only journals. When an Internet article is reproduced from a print source, simply follow the usual journal article reference format, and include the phrase "Electronic version" in brackets following the title of the article. In such a case, you don't need to include the URL or date retrieved from the Internet.

Stand-Alone Document with Author and Date

```
Winter, M. (2003) How to talk new age. Retrieved

July 25, 2003, from http://www.well.com/user/

mick/newagept.html
```

Note: When no date of publication is given, indicate this with "n.d." (no date) in parentheses where the date usually would appear. If no author is identified, begin the reference with the document title.

An Unsigned Article in a Newspaper or on a Newswire

```
Verizon to rehire 1,100 laid-off workers. (2003, 16

July). AP Online. Retrieved July 18, 2003, from

http://www.nytimes.com/aponline/technology/

AP-Verizon-Jobs.html
```

A Signed Article in a Newspaper or on a Newswire

```
Vartabedian, R. (2003, 16 July). Columbia's crew

lived after radio calls ended. Chicago Tribune.

Retrieved July 20, 2003, from

http://www.chicagotribune.com/technology/

lanashuttle16jul16,1,1997210.story?coll=

chi-news-hed
```

An Article in a Magazine

    Kim, J. (2003, July 16). When cell phones meet
        camcorders. *Forbes*. Retrieved August 12, 2003,
        from http://www.forbes.com/home/2003/07/16/
        cx_jk_0716tentech.html

An Abstract

    Eliaphson, N., & Lichterman, P. (2003). Culture in
        interaction. *American Journal of Sociology*.
        Abstract retrieved October 25, 2003, from
        http://www.journals.uchicago.edu/AJS/journal/
        issues/v108n4/040241/brief/040241.abstract.html

Electronic Copy of a Periodical Article Retrieved from a Database

    Bergeron, L. R. (2002). Family preservation: An
        unidentified approach in elder abuse
        protection. *Families in Society, 83*, 547–556.
        Retrieved July 28, 2003, from XanEdu Research
        Engine, ProQuest.

For online postings or synchronous communications, the APA recommends referencing only those sources that are maintained in archived form. However, archived discussions or postings are rarely peer-reviewed, are not generally regarded as having scholarly content, and are not archived for very long, so APA advises that you cite them with care in formal works. APA also advises against using nonarchived postings, as they are not retrievable by your readers. If you do choose to include sources that are not archived—and this includes e-mail communications between individuals—the APA suggests citing them as personal communications in the text of your work, but leaving them out of the references list.

An Anthology
of Readings

Cyberspace and Identity

A cartoon in the *New Yorker* a few years ago showed two dogs sitting near a computer. One dog says to the other, "On the Internet, nobody knows you're a dog." That's as succinct a statement as one can make about the benefits and the drawbacks of electronic communication. On the one hand, the Internet is a great democratizer: everyone is equal because anyone can publish anything. On the other hand, if anyone can publish anything, then for all we know, some of the material we read online might be written by "dogs."

The speed with which the Internet has become an essential medium of personal, business, and professional communication is truly breathtaking. Virtually unknown to the general public little more than a decade ago, e-mail and instant messaging are now so ubiquitous that it's hard to imagine how we ever got along without them. (Quite well, thank you, skeptics will respond.) Many people obsessively check their e-mail ten or more times a day. We appear to measure our worth and status according to how many people (and canines) are sending us messages. We are daily bombarded with megabytes of spam and other useless communications. On the other hand, the Internet provides many with lifelines to family and friends. In Times Square, New York, an all-night Internet café provides immigrants with inexpensive means of staying in touch with loved ones in their home countries. On the AskMe.com Web site, people who need answers to questions in any of hundreds of categories can get free advice from "experts." (Let the buyer beware, however: as an article reprinted at the end of this chapter demonstrates, experts are not always what they appear to be.)

Is the Internet a truly new mode of communication, or is it just an electronic hybrid of the conventional letter and the telephone conversation? The 1999 movie *You've Got Mail* delighted audiences with the very contemporary situation of a couple enjoying an e-mail relationship that was more intense than the relationships they were simultaneously experiencing with their live-in lovers. The comic mileage was generated by the fact that in real life they actually knew and detested each other. Is this kind of situation only possible because of the distinctive nature of e-mail? Significantly, *You've Got Mail* was a remake of a 1940 Ernst Lubitsch film called *The Shop Around the Corner*. The latter film was also remade in 1949 as an MGM musical, *In the Good Old Summertime*, and in the 1960s as a Broadway show, *She Loves Me*. In the first three versions, the lovers are pen pals who work side by side in the same shop but don't know the identities of their correspondents. More recently, of course, when few people write personal letters, the same situation calls for a new mode of communication—though one sharing certain essential features of the old mode of communication.

As some of the writers in this chapter point out, cybercommunication is a mixed blessing—if not an actual curse. Increasingly, employers monitor their employees' e-mail, or install software to block instant messaging; and they sometimes impose penalties (even to the point of firing people) for inappropriate use of company e-mail facilities. A spouse going through a divorce or custody proceeding may obtain a warrant to search the e-mail of the other spouse, in an attempt to find incriminating evidence. The veil of anonymity provided by the Internet can expose people to vicious "flaming" attacks—abusive, sometimes threatening messages. And because "nobody knows you're a dog," people can pretend to be what they are not. For some, assuming alternate identities can be a healthy form of play and self-development; for others, it can be a mode of perpetrating deception or even criminal fraud.

A fascinating recent case of such e-deception involved the online magazine *Slate*. In February 2002 an individual named Robert Klingler, who claimed to be the North American head of BMW, sent an e-mail to one of the magazine's editors, proposing to write a series of five diary entries for *Slate* about his activities as a top-level executive of a major automobile manufacturer. *Slate* took Klingler up on his offer and the first two entries appeared in the magazine. Deputy editor Jack Shafer recounts what happened next:

> When *Slate* readers pointed out to the editors that neither Google.com nor Nexis searchers produced any hits for a "Robert Klingler and the automobile industry," we assumed the worst and took the entries down from the site. A phone call to the European auto company in question confirmed that no "Robert Klingler" worked for them.*

Subsequent efforts to track down and contact "Robert Klingler" proved unsuccessful. Meanwhile, *Slate*, with egg on its face, ruefully admitted that it had been duped, apologized to its readers, candidly posted all of the evidence on its site, and promised "greater vigilance in the future."†

In this chapter, we will explore the interrelationship between cybercommunication (both in its private and its public forums, including e-mail and "blog" sites) and identity—what we generally think of as our essential self, that unique core of personhood and personality that makes each person different from anyone else. But what is a "true" identity? Is it the self that we create for ourselves over the years and project to the world at large—our families, our friends, our coworkers, the general public? Is it the self to which

---

* Jack Shafer, "*Slate* Gets Duped," *Slate* 5 March 2002. <http://slate.msn.com/?id=2062867>.

† See the above selection by Shafer for additional links to the "Klingler" affair, including Shafer's subsequent (12 March 2002) investigative article, "Who Is 'Robert Klingler'?: On the Trail of the Man Who Duped *Slate*," as well as Klingler's diary entries and readers' responses to the imbroglio.

we retreat when we are alone, perhaps fantasizing about operating in some alternate universe? Is it some combination of these? Under what circumstances is our "true" identity (assuming there is such a thing) most likely to emerge? And, to pose one of the central questions of this chapter: How has the Internet, with its new modes of communication, allowed us to develop new ways of creating—or obliterating—identity?

Some writers think that the Internet offers fertile fields of play for experimenting with our identities. Even so simple an act as choosing a screen name for ourselves—BadBarry, Icequeen, Coolsurferdude, Beachbunny—attaches a label to a particular aspect of our identity (or one that may not previously have existed); and when we create alternate screen names, we create alternate identities, each of which may have a distinctive personality, each of which we may explore and develop in e-mail, instant messages, electronic bulletin boards, chat rooms, online gaming, and other arenas of the Internet.

The selections in this chapter broaden and deepen the phenomenon introduced in the brief selections presented in Chapter 4 for the model explanatory synthesis on computer-mediated communication (CMC). In "We've Got Mail—Always," Andrew Leonard surveys the revolution wrought by e-mail and considers some of its benefits and drawbacks. The technical aspects of e-mail—just how does a message get from sender to recipient?—are engagingly outlined by John Dyson in "Journey of an E-Mail." In "The End of History" Fred Kaplan reports on many historians' concern that the ephemeral nature of e-mail, combined with the decline of letters, will leave their future colleagues with precious few records to draw upon when reporting key events of the twenty-first century.

The next several pieces explore relatively new and popular phenomena in cyberspace: instant messaging and blogging. In "I Think, Therefore IM," Jennifer Lee explains how teachers are often baffled by the abbreviated *lingua franca* students began using in their e-mails and instant messages and are now transferring to their academic papers. Another new cyberphenomenon, the Weblog, is introduced by John C. Dvorak in "The Blog Phenomenon." And in "The Intimacy of Blogs," Michael Snider takes note of several of the more interesting blog sites.

"A Shared Sadness," by Russ Parsons, shows the coming together of a small online community when one of their members faces major surgery. The next piece explores the phenomenon of online romances (a subject introduced in the CMC readings by Suler, Wolcott, and Morris in Chapter 4): in "Virtual Love," Meghan Daum writes of her own experience with a passionate e-mail affair. Next, sociologist Sherry Turkle explains how creating and experimenting with multiple identities on the Internet can be psychologically healthy. Two examples of this kind of identity-creation follow. In "Boy, You Fight Like a Girl," Alex Pham discusses why gender-switching is so popular among online gamers. And in "The 15-Year-Old Legal Whiz," Michael Lewis recounts how a teenager with no legal training became the top legal expert on a widely used information Web site.

We've Got Mail—Always
Andrew Leonard

We begin this chapter with a broad survey of the e-mail revolution. Andrew Leonard's first sentence introduces his basic approach: "Is e-mail a blessing or a curse?" He goes on to illustrate areas in which it is one or the other—or both at once. Leonard begins and ends with his own experiences, but in the course of the article, he covers many areas of contemporary life in which e-mail has changed the way that we communicate with one another. This article first appeared as part of a special issue of Newsweek *devoted to computers, dated 20 September 1999. Leonard is a contributing editor for* Newsweek *and a senior technology correspondent of the online magazine* Salon.com.

1   Is e-mail a blessing or a curse? Last month, after a week's vacation, I discovered 1,218 unread e-mail messages waiting in my IN box. I pretended to be dismayed, but secretly I was pleased. This is how we measure our wired worth in the late 1990s—if you aren't overwhelmed by e-mail, you must be doing something wrong.

2   Never mind that after subtracting the stale office chitchat, spam, flame wars, dumb jokes forwarded by friends who should have known better and other e-mail detritus, there were perhaps seven messages actually worth reading. I was doomed to spend half my workday just deleting junk. E-mail sucks.

3   But wait—what about those seven? A close friend in Taipei I haven't seen in five years tells me he's planning to start a family. A complete stranger in Belgium sends me a hot story tip. Another stranger offers me a job. I'd rather lose an eye than lose my e-mail account. E-mail rocks!

4   E-mail. Can't live with it, can't live without it. Con artists and real artists, advertisers and freedom fighters, lovers and sworn enemies—they've all flocked to e-mail as they would to any new medium of expression. E-mail is convenient, saves time, brings us closer to one another, helps us manage our ever-more-complex lives. Books are written, campaigns conducted, crimes committed—all via e-mail. But it is also inconvenient, wastes our time, isolates us in front of our computers and introduces more complexity into our already too-harried lives. To skeptics, e-mail is just the latest chapter in the evolving history of human communication. A snooping husband now discovers his wife's affair by reading her private e-mail—but he could have uncovered the same sin by finding letters a generation ago.

5   Yet e-mail—and all online communication—is in fact something truly different; it captures the essence of life at the close of the 20th century with an authority that few other products of digital technology can claim. Does the pace of life seem ever faster? E-mail simultaneously allows us to cope with that acceleration and contributes to it. Are our attention spans shriveling under barrages of new, improved forms of stimulation? The quick and dirty e-mail is made to order for those whose ability to concentrate is measured in nanoseconds. If we accept that the creation of the globe-spanning Internet is one of the most important technological innovations of the last half of this century, then we must

give e-mail—the living embodiment of human connection across the Net—pride of place. The way we interact with each other is changing; e-mail is both the catalyst and the instrument of that change.

6   The scope of the phenomenon is mind-boggling. Worldwide, 225 million people can send and receive e-mail. Forget about the Web or e-commerce or even online pornography: e-mail is the Internet's true killer app—the software application that we simply must have, even if it means buying a $2,000 computer and plunking down $20 a month to America Online. According to Donna Hoffman, a professor of marketing at Vanderbilt University, one survey after another finds that when online users are asked what they do on the Net, "e-mail is always No. 1."

7   Oddly enough, no one planned it, and no one predicted it. When research scientists first began cooking up the Internet's predecessor, the Arpanet, in 1968, their primary goal was to enable disparate computing centers to share resources. "But it didn't take very long before they discovered that the most important thing was the ability to send mail around, which they had not anticipated at all," says Eric Allman, chief technical officer of Sendmail, Inc., and the primary author of a 20-year-old program—Sendmail—that still transports the vast majority of the world's e-mail across the Internet. It seems that what all those top computer scientists really wanted to use the Internet for was as a place to debate, via e-mail, such crucially important topics as the best science-fiction novel of all time. Even though Allman is now quite proud that his software helps hundreds of millions of people communicate, he says he didn't set out originally to change the world. As a systems administrator at UC Berkeley in the late '70s, he was constantly hassled by computer-science researchers in one building who wanted to get their e-mail from machines in another location. "I just wanted to make my life easier," says Allman.

8   Don't we all? When my first child was born in 1994, e-mail seemed to me some kind of Promethean gift perfectly designed to help me cope with the irreconcilable pressures of new-fatherhood and full-time freelance writing. It saved me time and money without ever requiring me to leave the house; it salvaged my social life, allowed me to conduct interviews as a reporter and kept a lifeline open to my far-flung extended family. Indeed, I finally knew for sure that the digital world was viscerally potent when I found myself in the middle of a bitter fight with my mother—on e-mail. Again, new medium, old story.

9   My mother had given me an e-mail head start. In 1988, she bought me a modem so I could create a CompuServe account. The reason? Her younger brother had contracted a rapidly worsening case of Parkinson's disease. He wasn't able to talk clearly, and could hardly scrawl his name with a pen or pencil. But he had a computer, and could peck out words on a keyboard. My mom figured that if the family all had CompuServe accounts, we could send him e-mail. She grasped, long before the Internet became a household word, how online communication offered new possibilities for transcending physical limitations, how as simple a thing as e-mail could bring us closer to those whom we love.

10   It may even help us find those whom we want to love in the first place. Jenn Shreve is a freelance writer in the San Francisco Bay Area who keeps a close eye on the emerging culture of the new online generation. For the last couple

of years, she's seen what she considers to be a positive change in online dating habits. E-mail, she argues, encourages the shy. "It offers a semi-risk-free environment to initiate romance," says Shreve. "Because it lacks the immediate threat of physical rejection, people who are perhaps shy or had painful romantic failures in the past can use the Internet as a way to build a relationship in the early romantic stages."

11   But it's not just about lust. E-mail also flattens hierarchies within the bounds of an office. It is far easier, Shreve notes, to make a suggestion to your superiors and colleagues via e-mail than it is to do so in a pressure-filled meeting room. "Any time when you have something that is difficult to say, e-mail can make it easier," she says. "It serves as a buffer zone."

12   Of course, e-mail's uses as a social lubricant can be taken to extremes. There is little point in denying the obvious dark side to the lack of self-constraint encouraged by e-mail. Purveyors of pornography rarely call us on the phone and suggest out loud that we check out some "hot teen action." But they don't think twice about jamming our e-mail boxes full of outrageously prurient advertisements. People who would never insult us face to face will spew the vilest, most objectionable, most appalling rhetoric imaginable via e-mail or an instant message, or in the no-holds-barred confines of a chat room.

13   Cyberspace's lapses in gentility underscores a central contradiction inherent in online communication. If it is true that hours spent on the Net are often hours subtracted from watching television, one could argue that the digital era has raised the curtains on a new age of literacy—more people are writing more words than ever before! But what kind of words are we writing? Are we really more literate, or are we sliding ever faster into a quicksand of meaningless irrelevance, of pop-cultural triviality—expressed, usually, in lowercase letters—run amok? E-mail is actually too easy, too casual. Gone are the days when one would worry over a letter to a lover or a relative or a colleague. Now there's just time for that quick e-mail, a few hastily cobbled together thoughts written in a colloquial style that usually borders on unedited stream of consciousness. The danger is obvious: snippy comments to a friend, overly sharp retorts to one's boss, insults mistakenly sent to the target, not the intended audience. E-mail allows us to act before we can think—the perfect tool for a culture of hyperstimulation.

14   So instead of creating something new, we forward something old. Instead of crafting the perfect phrase, we use a brain-dead abbreviation: IMHO for In My Humble Opinion, or ROTFLMAO, for Rolling On The Floor Laughing My A— Off. Got a rumor? E-mail it to 50 people! Instant messaging and chat rooms just accentuate the casual negative. If e-mail requires little thought, then instant messaging—flashing a message directly onto a recipient's computer monitor—is so insubstantial as to be practically nonexistent.

15   E-mail, ultimately, is a fragile thing, easy to forge, easy to corrupt, easy to destroy. A few weeks ago a coworker of mine accidentally and irretrievably wiped out 1,500 of his own saved messages. For a person who conducts the bulk of his life online, such a digital tragedy is akin to erasing part of your own memory. Suddenly, nothing's left. It is comforting to think that, if preserved in a retrievable way, all the notes the world is passing back and forth today

constitute a vast historical archive, but the opposite may also be true. Earlier this summer, I visited some curators at the Stanford University Library who are hard at work compiling a digital archive of Silicon Valley history. They bemoaned a new, fast-spreading corporate policy that requires the deletion of all corporate e-mails after every 60 or 90 days. As Microsoft and Netscape have learned to their dismay, old e-mails, however trivial they seem when they are written, can and will come back to haunt you. It is best, say the lawyers, to just wipe them all out.

16   Still, e-mail is enabling radically new forms of worldwide human collaboration. Those 225 million people who can send and receive it represent a network of potentially cooperating individuals dwarfing anything that even the mightiest corporation or government can muster. Mailing-list discussion groups and online conferencing allow us to gather together to work on a multitude of projects that are interesting or helpful to us—to pool our collective efforts in a fashion never before possible. The most obvious place to see this collaboration right now is in the world of software. For decades, programmers have used e-mail to collaborate on projects. With increasing frequency, this collaboration is occurring across company lines, and often without even the spur of commercial incentives. It's happening largely because it can—it's relatively easy for a thousand programmers to collectively contribute to a project using e-mail and the Internet. Perhaps each individual contribution is small, but the scale of the Internet multiplies all efforts dramatically.

17   Meanwhile, now that we are all connected, day and night, across time zones and oceans and corporate firewalls, we are beginning to lose sight of the distinction between what is work and what is play.

18   Six years after I logged onto CompuServe for the first time, I went to Australia for three weeks. Midway through my visit, I ended up in Alice Springs, a fraying-at-the-edges frontier town about a thousand miles away from anywhere in the middle of the great Australian outback. An exotic place, nestled among the oldest mountain remnants of the world, where flocks of parrots swoop and flutter through the downtown shopping district. But instead of wandering through the desert seeking out wallabies and feral camels, I found myself dialing long distance to a friend's University of Melbourne Internet account, and transferring from there via a telnet program to my own account at the Well in San Francisco. Once on the Well, I checked my mail to see if a fact checker for *Wired* magazine had any fresh queries for me concerning a story I had recently submitted.

19   I was on the job—in large part because I had an e-mail address and had made the Devil's bargain with the wired world. As I listened for the sound of the modem connecting in Alice Springs, I felt in the pit of my stomach that I had lost control over some valuable part of my life. Your employer will refrain from calling you at 11:30 at night, but not from sending an inquiring, hectoring, must-be-promptly-answered-as-soon-as-you-log-on e-mail. E-mail doesn't just collapse distance, it demolishes all boundaries. And that can be, depending on the moment, either a blessing or a curse.

Review Questions

1. Summarize some of the ways that e-mail can be, as Leonard puts it, either a "blessing or a curse."

2. What was the original purpose of the people who invented e-mail?

3. How does Leonard inject himself into his discussion of e-mail?

Discussion and Writing Suggestions

1. What part does e-mail play in your own life? Explain how you have experienced some of the e-mail "blessings" and "curses" to which Leonard refers, illustrating your account with relevant anecdotes.

2. Many people bemoan the e-mail revolution, complaining that it has replaced letter-writing, which they see as a superior form of communication. Consider the advantages and disadvantages of e-mail communication versus those of communication by letter and by telephone. Begin by creating a table, with rows for e-mail, letter-writing, and telephone calls, and with columns for advantages and disadvantages. Develop this table into a short paper. In your discussion consider particular situations that illustrate the benefits and drawbacks of each form of communication.

3. According to freelance writer Jenn Shreve, e-mail "offers a semi-risk-free environment to initiate romance." To what extent have you found this to be true, either in your own experience or the experience of others you know? Why "semi-risk-free," as opposed to "risk-free"?

4. Leonard notes that "E-mail allows us to act before we can think." Recount an occasion when you have written an e-mail message in the heat of anger (or passion), pushed the "Send" button "in haste" and then "at leisure" regretted sending your words. What was the aftermath? Did the incident change how you wrote and sent e-mail in the future?

5. One of the ways that e-mail changes its users, according to Leonard, is to reduce their "gentility" when communicating with others, particularly others they don't know personally. To what extent has e-mail changed the way you think about yourself, changed your concept of your own identity? For example, when you send e-mail messages to particular individuals, do you, in effect, redefine yourself or reconstruct yourself according to the type of person you would like to be, to those individuals? By the same token, do the e-mail messages you receive from certain people imply a certain "you"—one who may be somewhat different from the "you" that exists apart from e-mail? Why do you think e-mail is a good tool for bringing about these redefinitions and reconstructions of your self?

Journey of an E-Mail
John Dyson

Every day, we operate and depend upon a multitude of technical devices without having the foggiest idea how they work. Forget high-tech computers: how many of us could explain the operation of a radio, a telephone, a light bulb, the electric motor that powers our fan? How many of us could give an accurate and coherent account of the internal workings of a low-tech device like a flush toilet?

The main job of a science writer is to explain to nontechnically inclined people how the technology that we take for granted works. In the following selection, freelance writer John Dyson explains just what happens when we click "Send" on our e-mail screen.

1   Doug and Julie Young raise Dandie Dinmont terriers. They also publish a newsletter for fellow lovers of the breed. Not too long ago they wanted a picture of Mr. D, our family pet.

2   I could have sent the photo by ordinary mail, but that would have taken at least four days. Instead, sitting down at the computer in my den overlooking London's River Thames, I sent an e-mail. I typed in an address, young@monti-zard.com, composed a short message, then attached a photograph I'd scanned into my PC. Finally I clicked Send. Mr. D instantly vanished from my screen—headed to a farmhouse in rural Ohio.

3   Along with more than 150 million others around the world, I use e-mail all the time and can't imagine living without it. How it actually works, of course, was a mystery. So one day I decided to find out. Mounting my bicycle, I pedaled off to follow my dog through cyberspace.

4   The first stop was a brick office plaza between a canal and an elevated highway in Brentford, west London. This was one of the homes of Cable & Wireless, the company that connects my computer to the Internet by telephone lines.

5   Escorted through security checks and card-swipe doors, I entered a brightly lit, windowless room with rows of fridge-size metal cabinets called racks, containing computers the size of TV sets, each costing as much as a car. In an adjoining control room, engineers, some of whom were wearing earrings, were monitoring rows of complicated numbers on video screens. As the racks tend to look the same, engineers give them names. "This is Marvin," said Jason Semple, pointing to one. "He's your postbox."

6   A burly 27-year-old, Semple hooked a finger over the spine of what looked like one of scores of videocassettes on a shelf. He slid out a circuit board glittering with tiny gold wires and silver connectors.

7   "When your PC dials our number, it's answered by one of these modems," Semple explained. "It checks your name and password with another computer, then asks what you want."

8   My computer had replied, "I've got mail."

9   Next, Mr. D was fed into a "mail server"—a bunch of computers filling five racks. One read my e-mail's destination and checked another, which stored Internet addresses like a gigantic phone directory.

10   The Cable & Wireless directory could do ten look-ups a second. It didn't find montizard.com, so it asked a bigger directory, storing ten million addresses in Europe and Africa. That didn't work either, so it asked one of 13 core directories (ten in the United States, two in Europe, one in Japan) holding every Internet address in the world.

11   Back came the answer: "Send mail to BuckeyeNet." This is the company connecting the Youngs to the Internet. BuckeyeNet's Internet address—209.41.2.152—was clipped like a dog tag to Mr. D's collar.

12   Next, something bizarre happened. Imagine a postal clerk who chops your letter into little bits and puts them in separate envelopes. This is done to every e-mail. All the bits and bytes representing Mr. D were instantly divided among about 120 packets. Every one was stamped with BuckeyeNet's address, plus my own address, so the jigsaw puzzle could be reassembled at the other end.

13   But they didn't go all at once. Instead, a single packet was sent off like a scout car, to knock on the door of BuckeyeNet, say hello and make a connection. The first stop was a gateway router, which would help the scout car find the way.

14   Picture the Internet as 65,000 interstate highways crisscrossing the globe and connected to smaller roads and streets. Like a cop with a walkie-talkie on every crossroad, the router learns the fastest way to get an e-mail to its destination. It knows all the routes and, by talking with other "cops" down the road every half-minute, it discovers where the delays are—say, heavy telephone traffic or a cut cable.

15   A Cable & Wireless router sent Mr. D's hello packet across London to the company's transmission center in Docklands, where another router fed it into the stream of e-mail packets heading for the westerly tip of Cornwall, the nearest part of England to America.

16   All this happened in four milliseconds—like a lightning flash.

17   I took a decidedly slower train to Cornwall and went to Porthcurno, a cliff-top village. There, in a barn-size room, is the base station of the transatlantic Gemini cable.

18   Take a hair-thin fiber of glass, wrap it in a protective jacket, then incorporate it with others in a rubbery protective tube. This is fiber-optic cable, known in the trade as pipe.

19   A flashing laser at one end fires digital on/off signals along the fiber. At about 120,000 miles a second—more than half the speed of light—they zip to the other end.

20   "It's the high-tech equivalent of two kids signaling each other with flashlights," explained Dave Shirt, operations director. With pretty quick fingers, I'd say: the lasers flash ten billion times a second.

21   Mr. D's packet next jostled for elbowroom with a torrent of transatlantic electronic traffic—equivalent to 100,000 closely typed pages every second, or

400,000 simultaneous phone calls. Think that's a lot? At present six parallel lanes of traffic hurtle along every glass fiber. Newly laid cables will soon have 128 lanes, preparing for the explosion of Internet traffic when every movie ever made could be available online.

22   I returned to London, hopped a plane to New York and rented a car, then picked up Mr. D's trail again on a long, flat beach in Manasquan, N.J., where the Gemini cable comes ashore. Next the e-mail zipped along poles and beside railroad tracks before flashing into 60 Hudson Street, in downtown Manhattan. Time taken from London: approximately 40 milliseconds, or one-tenth of a blink of the eye.

23   This 22-floor art-deco building is a "telco hotel" where telephone companies own or rent space for equipment so they can connect to one another more easily. The scout packet was switched into high-capacity "fat pipes" crossing the continent. It also hit what engineers call ATM—asynchronous transfer mode.

24   Now Mr. D was diced yet again into dozens of identically sized cells which flashed through the back of a telephone exchange in West Orange, N.J., just west of New York.

25   But from there the cells had a really wild ride, zipping through pipe beside railroad tracks, into and out of Philadelphia, up the Ohio Valley, through Cleveland and into another telephone exchange at Willow Springs, outside Chicago. Here the bits came together, and the original packet was restored. It all took a fraction of a second.

26   Barely pausing for a breath, so to speak, the scout packet next raced through Chicago and Detroit, before landing in a building in Columbus, Ohio—headquarters of Fiber Network Solutions. There I met the company's co-founder, Kyle Bacon, a laid-back 27-year-old wearing two gold earrings.

27   Bacon, who used to duck classes to work on his university's computer system, helped set up a network that controls Internet pipes so businesses and industry have to pay the company to open the tap. That was three years ago. Now the company employs 45 people, and Bacon drives a silver BMW whose license plate reads FAT PIPE.

28   A router in the company switched Mr. D into a skinny pipe running direct to the home of BuckeyeNet—then a two-room office with a dirt parking lot, some five miles from rural Lancaster. BuckeyeNet has over a thousand clients and 13 computers. By way of comparison, the biggest Internet-access provider in the world, America Online, has some 19 million subscribers and servers covering football fields of floor space.

29   Dressed in shorts and, naturally, sporting a gold earring, Jonathan Sheline, 27, told me he'd set up the company after leaving the Army, where he'd served hitches in the infantry and counterintelligence. In just 18 months his net was one of the largest in the town. Our friends the Youngs are among its $17.95-a-month clients.

30   BuckeyeNet's mail server unwrapped Mr. D's scout packet, which carried a message. "Helo," it said. "I am j.dyson at cwcom.net." "Helo" means *hello* in a computer language called Simple Mail Transfer Protocol (SMTP).

31   BuckeyeNet's mail server sent an acknowledgment to London, which took one-tenth of a second to arrive. Next the two computers negotiated the connection. Their conversation, using codes as well as plain text, went like this.

32   Ohio: Okay, I'm listening. SMTP is spoken here.

33   London: I have mail from j.dyson at cwcom.net.

34   Ohio: Pleased to meet you.

35   London: I've got mail for montizard.com.

36   Ohio (checking list of clients): Okay, I can handle that.

37   London: I'm ready to send data.

38   Ohio: Start mail input.

39   From London, five packets hit the road. If any crashed or failed to arrive, the Ohio dispatcher would let London know and they'd be sent again. When this bunch arrived, Ohio said: "I got the first five, give me five more."

40   Despite all the messages Ping-Ponging across the Atlantic, the last bit of Mr. D straggled into BuckeyeNet's server less than half a minute after I had originally clicked Send. For me it had been nine hours in the air, four hours waiting for a connection and an hour and a half in cars. And my luggage was left behind. But Mr. D still had to go the last five miles.

41   When I arrived in their old farmhouse on nearly five acres outside Rushville, Doug and Julie Young were making breakfast for 35 dogs, 30 ferrets, two llamas and a parrot. Julie had an armful of cans, bowls and milk cartons, difficult to carry because they were all different sizes.

42   Meanwhile, from a big paper bag, Doug filled a container with pellets of dog food—the perfect metaphor for understanding why e-mails are minced and shredded into packets and cells. Like pellets, they pour more easily and therefore travel much faster.

43   A big, jovial man of 51, Doug uses e-mail to talk with breeders all over the world. When he clicked Get Mail, the BuckeyeNet server checked his mailbox and forwarded its contents down the phone line. The stream of bits materialized into Mr. D gazing imperially out of the screen from his kitchen chair, not a bit ruffled after his 4000-mile dash.

Review Questions

1. How did Dyson's own server computer in West London know where to send his message?

2. Why are e-mail messages chopped into numerous electronic pieces (or "packets") before they are transmitted?

3. What is SMTP?

Discussion and Writing Suggestions

1. Write a summary (one or two paragraphs) of the process Dyson describes without using any of the specifics: personal or place

names. Your summary should represent a general description of how a piece of e-mail makes its way from sender to recipient.

2. Discuss the ways in which Dyson attempts to make what is essentially a complex process intelligible and interesting to his readers. To what extent do you think he succeeds?

3. To what extent were you surprised by the mechanics of e-mail routing, as explained by Dyson? Before you read this article, what did you imagine happened when you hit the "send" button to transmit your e-mail message to its intended recipient(s)?

4. Think of a technical or scientific process that you understand reasonably well, but that many other people don't. Using Dyson's article as a model, describe what happens in a way that removes some of the mystery from the process, without unduly simplifying it. Examples: What happens when you turn the ignition key in your car? What happens when rain or snow starts falling? How do insects pollinate plants? How is beer or wine made? What happens when you push down the flush lever of a toilet?

The End of History
Fred Kaplan

One of the most basic qualities of digital communication is its impermanence. It's true, as many caution, that the average user can't permanently delete compromising or potentially embarrassing messages by simply hitting the Delete key. Lawyers, armed with subpoenas and aided by technical experts, can recover supposedly deleted messages documenting illicit romances and other unethical or unwise activities, to the consternation of the indiscreet sender. Still, such recovery is not an easy or common practice, and it remains the case that multitudes of messages that previously helped to form the historical record—letters, memos, reports, and so on—no longer exist because of the medium on which they were created.

The short shelf life of electronic documents poses a serious problem for historians, who, years later, attempt to locate documents through which they can construct historical narratives. These historical narratives can be viewed as a collective identity: We discover or rediscover who we are by studying and reflecting on what we did. We define ourselves as a people or as a culture ("America is a generous country," "The U.S. too often tries to impose its will on other countries," etc.) by referring to the historical record—a record constructed out of perishable documents. In the following article, Fred Kaplan addresses the problem of digital deletion of what may become the historical record.

Kaplan is a columnist and jazz critic for the online magazine Slate. *His work has also appeared in such magazines and newspapers as the* New Yorker, Atlantic Monthly, Harper's, New York Times, Boston Globe, Guardian (London), *and* Ottawa Citizen. *This piece was first posted in the 4 June 2003 issue of* Slate.

1   When tomorrow's historians go to write the chronicles of decision-making that led to Gulf War II [2003], they may be startled to find there's not much history to be written. The same is true of Clinton's war over Kosovo, Bush Sr.'s Desert Storm, and a host of other major episodes of U.S. national security policy. Many of the kinds of documents that historians of prior wars, and of the Cold War, have taken for granted—memoranda, minutes, and the routine back-and-forth among assistant secretaries of state and defense or among colonels and generals in the Joint Chiefs of Staff—simply no longer exist.

2   The problem is not some deliberate plot to conceal or destroy evidence. The problem—and it may seem churlish to say so in an online publication—is the advent of e-mail.

3   In the old days, before the mid-to-late 1980s, Cabinet officials and their assistants and deputy assistants wrote memos on paper, then handed them to a secretary in a typing pool. The secretary would type it on a sheet of paper backed by two or three carbon sheets, then file the carbons. Periodically, someone from the national archive would stop by with a cart and haul away the carbons for posterity.

4   Nobody does this today. There are no typing pools to speak of. There are few written memos.

5   Eduard Mark, a Cold War historian who has worked for 15 years in the U.S. Air Force historian's office, has launched a one-man crusade to highlight, and repair, this situation. He remembers an incident from the early '90s, when he was researching the official Air Force history of the Panama invasion, which had taken place only a few years earlier. "I went to the Air Force operations center," Mark says. "They had a little Mac computer on which they'd saved all the briefings. They were getting ready to dump the computer. I stopped them just in time, and printed out all the briefings. Those printouts I made are the only copies in existence."

6   That was a decade ago, when computers were not yet pervasive in the Pentagon and many offices still printed important documents on paper. The situation now, Mark says, is much worse.

7   Almost all Air Force documents today, for example, are presented as PowerPoint briefings.* They are almost never printed and rarely stored. When they are saved, they are often unaccompanied by any text. As a result, in many cases, the briefings are incomprehensible.

8   The new, paperless world has encouraged a general carelessness in official record-keeping. Mark says that J5, the planning department of the Joint Chiefs of Staff, does not, as a rule, save anything. When I talked with Mark on the phone Tuesday, he said he had before him an unclassified document, signed by the Air Force chief of staff and the secretary of the Air Force, ordering the creation of a senior steering group on "transformation" (the new buzzword for making military operations more agile and more inter-service in nature). The document was not dated.

9   Mark has personal knowledge of the situation with the Air Force. However, officials and historians in other branches of the national-security bureaucracy say, on background, that the pattern is pretty much the same across the board.

---

* PowerPoint is a software program used to prepare presentations. it allows for the creation and display—generally projected—of textual and graphic information.

10   Certain high-level documents are usually (but, even then, not always) saved—memos that cross the desks of the president, Cabinet secretaries, and military chiefs (the Air Force and Army chiefs of staff, and the chief of naval operations). But beneath that level, it's hit and miss, more often miss.

11   An enterprising historian writing about World Wars I or II can draw on the vast military records at the National Archive, as well as letters from Churchill, Roosevelt, de Gaulle, and others. (Who writes letters anymore?) Those chronicling the Cold War or the Vietnam War can plumb the presidential libraries of Truman, Eisenhower, Kennedy, Johnson, and Ford (less so of Nixon because it's a privately funded library), and find plenty of illuminating memos written to and from not just Cabinet officers, such as John Foster Dulles, Robert McNamara, and Dean Rusk, but the crucial sub-Cabinet officials and security advisers, such as Andrew Goodpaster, Walt Rostow, John McNaughton, McGeorge Bundy, and George Ball.

12   Twenty years from now, if someone went looking for similar memos by Paul Wolfowitz, Richard Perle, Richard Armitage, and Elliott Abrams on, say, the Bush administration's Middle East policies, not many memos would be found because they don't exist. Officials today e-mail their thoughts and proposals. Perhaps some individuals have been fastidious about printing and saving their e-mails, but there is no system in place for automatically doing so.

13   Robert Caro, author of the revealingly massive and detailed biographies of Lyndon Johnson and Robert Moses, often advises aspiring historians, "Turn every page." What to do, though, if there aren't any pages to turn?

Review Questions

1. Why, according to Kaplan, is "e-mail wrecking our national archive"?

2. In what area of activity does Kaplan find most of his examples?

3. Upon what kind of documents did historians of the past—for example, those studying World War I or II—rely in researching their books and articles?

Discussion and Writing Suggestions

1. To what extent do you consider what Kaplan describes to be a serious problem? What do you foresee as some of the consequences of not having a relatively complete written record of military, government, business, and other activities, as a result of the ephemeral nature of e-mail communication?

2. Examine one or more of your history textbooks, focusing on a particular subject—for example, the Civil War, the Russian Revolution, the Great Depression. On what kinds of documentary and other evidence does the historical narrative appear to be based? (See if

the narrative is footnoted and check the footnote references.) What parts of this narrative might be missing if the documents on which they were based had been destroyed or were not available? How might the loss of such documentary evidence have affected the way that we view the event today?

3. Describe an instance in your own life when the loss or premature deletion of an e-mail message has caused you inconvenience, or worse.

I Think, Therefore IM
Jennifer Lee

From time immemorial teachers have been distressed over violations of standard English form in student papers. But student e-mail can generate an entirely new level of dismay. Many writers (and not just students) assume that it is unnecessary, in e-mail messages, to capitalize words such as "I" (or any other words, for that matter), to punctuate, or—the subject of the following article—even to use complete words. In her article in Chapter 4 on "Teens' Instant-Messaging Lingo" (pages 101–02), Stephanie Dunnewind quotes the following sentence: "I wz gtin2d@ & now gota type it agen b patient!" Increasingly, such lingo is employed not only in e-mail but also in papers. Like screen names, cyberlingo is a way of expressing identity, both individually ("How creative can I be in devising abbreviations and new words?") and collectively ("I am part of a community that uses such language as a matter of course"). In the following selection Jennifer Lee, a New York Times *staff writer, considers this phenomenon. Lee's piece first appeared in the 19 September 2002 issue of the* Times.

1   Each September Jacqueline Harding prepares a classroom presentation on the common writing mistakes she sees in her students' work.

2   Ms. Harding, an eighth-grade English teacher at Viking Middle School in Guernee, Ill., scribbles the words that have plagued generations of schoolchildren across her whiteboard:

There. Their. They're.

Your. You're.

To. Too. Two.

Its. It's.

This September, she has added a new list: u, r, ur, b4, wuz, cuz, 2.

3   When she asked her students how many of them used shortcuts like these in their writing, Ms. Harding said, she was not surprised when most of them raised their hands. This, after all, is their online lingua franca: English adapted for the spitfire conversational style of Internet instant messaging.

Jennifer Lee, "I Think, Therefore IM," *New York Times*, 19 September 2002.

4   Ms. Harding, who has seen such shortcuts creep into student papers over the last two years, said she gave her students a warning: "If I see this in your assignments, I will take points off."

5   "Kids should know the difference," said Ms. Harding, who decided to address this issue head-on this year. "They should know where to draw the line between formal writing and conversational writing."

6   As more and more teenagers socialize online, middle school and high school teachers like Ms. Harding are increasingly seeing a breezy form of Internet English jump from e-mail into schoolwork. To their dismay, teachers say that papers are being written with shortened words, improper capitalization and punctuation, and characters like &, $ and @.

7   Teachers have deducted points, drawn red circles and tsk-tsked at their classes. Yet the errant forms continue. "It stops being funny after you repeat yourself a couple of times," Ms. Harding said.

8   But teenagers, whose social life can rely as much these days on text communication as the spoken word, say that they use instant-messaging shorthand without thinking about it. They write to one another as much as they write in school, or more.

9   "You are so used to abbreviating things, you just start doing it unconsciously on schoolwork and reports and other things," said Eve Brecker, 15, a student at Montclair High School in New Jersey.

10   Ms. Brecker once handed in a midterm exam riddled with instant-messaging shorthand. "I had an hour to write an essay on *Romeo and Juliet,*" she said. "I just wanted to finish before my time was up. I was writing fast and carelessly. I spelled 'you' 'u.' " She got a C.

11   Even terms that cannot be expressed verbally are making their way into papers. Melanie Weaver was stunned by some of the term papers she received from a 10th-grade class she recently taught as part of an internship. "They would be trying to make a point in a paper, they would put a smiley face in the end," said Ms. Weaver, who teaches at Alvernia College in Reading, PA. "If they were presenting an argument and they needed to present an opposite view, they would put a frown."

12   As Trisha Fogarty, a sixth-grade teacher at Houlton Southside School in Houlton, Maine, puts it, today's students are "Generation Text."

13   Almost 60 percent of the online population under age 17 uses instant messaging, according to Nielsen/NetRatings. In addition to cellphone text messaging, Weblogs and e-mail, it has become a popular means of flirting, setting up dates, asking for help with homework and keeping in contact with distant friends. The abbreviations are a natural outgrowth of this rapid-fire style of communication.

14   "They have a social life that centers around typed communication," said Judith S. Donath, a professor at the Massachusetts Institute of Technology's Media Lab who has studied electronic communication. "They have a writing style that has been nurtured in a teenage social milieu."

15   Some teachers see the creeping abbreviations as part of a continuing assault of technology on formal written English. Others take it more lightly, saying that it is just part of the larger arc of language evolution.

16 "To them it's not wrong," said Ms. Harding, who is 28. "It's acceptable because it's in their culture. It's hard enough to teach them the art of formal writing. Now we've got to overcome this new instant-messaging language."

17 Ms. Harding noted that in some cases the shorthand isn't even shorter. "I understand 'cuz,' but what's with the 'wuz'? It's the same amount of letters as 'was,' so what's the point?" she said.

18 Deborah Bova, who teaches eighth-grade English at Raymond Park Middle School in Indianapolis, thought her eyesight was failing several years ago when she saw the sentence "B4 we perform, ppl have 2 practice" on a student assignment.

19 "I thought, 'My God, what is this?'" Ms. Bova said. "Have they lost their minds?"

20 The student was summoned to the board to translate the sentence into standard English: "Before we perform, people have to practice." She realized that the students thought she was out of touch. "It was like 'Get with it, Bova,'" she said. Ms. Bova had a student type up a reference list of translations for common instant-messaging expressions. She posted a copy on the bulletin board by her desk and took another one home to use while grading.

21 Students are sometimes unrepentant.

22 "They were astonished when I began to point these things out to them," said Henry Assetto, a social studies teacher at Twin Valley High School in Elverson, Pa. "Because I am a history teacher, they did not think a history teacher would be checking up on their grammar or their spelling," said Mr. Assetto, who has been teaching for 34 years.

23 But Montana Hodgen, 16, another Montclair student, said she was so accustomed to instant-messaging abbreviations that she often read right past them. She proofread a paper last year only to get it returned with the messaging abbreviations circled in red.

24 "I was so used to reading what my friends wrote to me on Instant Messenger that I didn't even realize that there was something wrong," she said. She said her ability to separate formal and informal English declined the more she used instant messages. "Three years ago, if I had seen that, I would have been 'What is that?'"

25 The spelling checker doesn't always help either, students say. For one, Microsoft Word's squiggly red spell-check lines don't appear beneath single letters and numbers such as u, r, c, 2 and 4. Nor do they catch words which have numbers in them such as "l8r" and "b4" by default.

26 Teenagers have essentially developed an unconscious "accent" in their typing, Professor Donath said. "They have gotten facile at typing and they are not paying attention."

27 Teenagers have long pushed the boundaries of spoken language, introducing words that then become passe with adult adoption. Now teenagers are taking charge and pushing the boundaries of written language. For them, expressions like "oic" (oh I see), "nm" (not much), "jk" (just kidding) and "lol" (laughing out loud), "brb" (be right back), "ttyl" (talk to you later) are as standard as conventional English.

28 "There is no official English language," said Jesse Sheidlower, the North American editor of the *Oxford English Dictionary*. "Language is spread not

because anyone dictates any one thing to happen. The decisions are made by the language and the people who use the language."

29   Some teachers find the new writing style alarming. "First of all, it's very rude, and it's very careless," said Lois Moran, a middle school English teacher at St. Nicholas School in Jersey City.

30   "They should be careful to write properly and not to put these little codes in that they are in such a habit of writing to each other," said Ms. Moran, who has lectured her eighth-grade class on such mistakes.

31   Others say that the instant-messaging style might simply be a fad, something that students will grow out of. Or they see it as an opportunity to teach students about the evolution of language.

32   "I turn it into a very positive teachable moment for kids in the class," said Erika V. Karres, an assistant professor at the University of North Carolina at Chapel Hill who trains student teachers. She shows students how English has evolved since Shakespeare's time. "Imagine Langston Hughes's writing in quick texting instead of 'Langston writing,' " she said. "It makes teaching and learning so exciting."

33   Other teachers encourage students to use messaging shorthand to spark their thinking processes. "When my children are writing first drafts, I don't care how they spell anything, as long as they are writing," said Ms. Fogarty, the sixth-grade teacher from Houlton, Maine. "If this lingo gets their thoughts and ideas onto paper quicker, the more power to them." But during editing and revising, she expects her students to switch to standard English.

34   Ms. Bova shares the view that instant-messaging language can help free up their creativity. With the help of students, she does not even need the cheat sheet to read the shorthand anymore.

35   "I think it's a plus," she said. "And I would say that with a + sign."

Review Questions

1. What are the main features of "instant-messaging language"?

2. What reasons are most frequently offered for the ever-more-frequent use of this language?

3. What objections do some teachers (and others) have to instant-messaging language?

Discussion and Writing Suggestions

1. Do you engage in what teacher Jacqueline Harding calls "this new instant-messaging language" in e-mail communications with your friends and family? Have you used such language in your school-work or in e-mails to teachers? If so, what has been the reaction? How do you think teachers should handle the use of such language? To what extent do you view instant-messaging lingo—or instant-messaging itself—as an expression of your identity? Lee quotes several people in her article: With whom do you most agree? Why?

2. MIT professor Judith S. Donath says (paragraph 14) that students "have a social life that centers around typed communication." To what extent do you agree with this comment?

3. Several people quoted for this article point to a difference between formal and informal uses of language. To what extent do you recognize such a distinction? Which types of written communications are best expressed in informal language? In formal language? What do you see as the main advantages and disadvantages of each type of language?

The Blog Phenomenon
John C. Dvorak

Blogs, or Weblogs—public online diaries—are only the most recent examples of proliferating cyberspace phenomena. That is to say, blogging is the latest way that people, in their infinite resourcefulness and ingenuity, have devised to communicate with one another. Blog sites are the latest way of announcing to the world: "I am here. My thoughts and my doings are interesting to the rest of the world." In the following selection, computer guru John C. Dvorak explains and offers reasons for this new online development. Dvorak writes on technology and software issues for PC Magazine, *and he is the author of numerous books on personal computing and software, including* Hypergrowth: The Rise and Fall of Osborne Computer Corporation *(1984, with Adam Osborne) and* Dvorak's Guide to Desktop Telecommunications *(1992, with Nick Anis). This article first appeared in* PC Magazine *on 26 February 2002.*

1   A recent overlooked Web trend—overlooked by the mainstream media, at least—is the proliferation of public diaries, generically referred to as Blogs. The term originated from "WeB log" and was further promoted by pyra.com as a Blog at its www.blogger.com site, although www.pita.com is considered the original source of easy-to-use Web logging. People who "Blog" are called Bloggers, and right now there are hundreds, thousands of Blogs on the Net.

2   The vanity page is dead; long live the Blog. The vanity Web page has lost momentum. People who posted one have already done so, and the growth has slowed. Most are uninteresting and uninspired. Cat pictures dominate too many of them. A Blog is the next iteration, and most vanity site mavens have gravitated toward these things. Serious vanity site developers have gone into posting hobby or special-interest sites, having learned by experience how to make an attractive Web page. This is, indeed, progress.

3   And the universe of these diaries can even be searched at various specialty search sites, such as www.blogfinder.com.

4   Generally speaking, these postings are fascinating, since they often have serious elements of Hyde Park corner blather, besides blatant exhibitionism and obvious self-indulgence. And whatever you think of them, you'll admit that they are much more interesting than the static vanity site from years ago.

5   One of the best examples you'll find on the Web of a homebrew special-interest site is the stunning Jacob's Bugatti Pages at www.homestead.mac.com/

bugatti/jacob. If you have a hobby and want to make the Web part of that hobby, then look no further than Jacob's for inspiration. But if you just want to pontificate and talk about yourself, start a Blog.

6   Blogging goes beyond software posting and uses an entire system that allows for easy creation. With a Blog there is no coding to do. The Blog is usually more attractive than sloppy HTML* done by an amateur, and by nature it demands updating so that the material is kept current. People can't resist updating the diary and apologize if they don't do it—as if anyone really cares. You have to be dedicated to a Web site to keep it current. Not so the Blog; it's more addictive. And hobbyist Blogs have emerged. For example, some people like to watch a lot of movies and review them. They see a movie and immediately post their comments. Some of these homebrew reviewers are better than the pros.

7   Still, with the few hobbyist exceptions, Blogs are mostly personal diaries. Here's where the sociology comes in. Why, exactly, do people want to have other people read these ramblings? Many are incriminating! Ask a Web log addict why he or she does it and you'll get a range of answers that tend towards the "because it's easy" or "because it's fun!" bromides. I think there are deeper reasons. Here are a few obvious possibilities:

- *Ego gratification.* Some people need to be the center of attention. It makes them feel good about themselves to tell the world what important things they've been doing and what profound thoughts they've been having. Curiously, while this looks like the most obvious reason for a Web log, I think it's probably the least likely reason, since it's too trite and shallow.
- *Antidepersonalization.* When people begin to think that they are nothing more than a cog in the wheel of society, they look for any way to differentiate themselves. The Web log proves they are different. Just read it. You'll see.
- *Elimination of frustration.* Day-to-day life, especially in the city, is wrought with frustration, and the Web log gives people the ability to complain to the world. You get to read a lot of complaining in these logs. If you think I'm a complainer, oh boy!
- *Societal need to share.* As a cynic who gets paid to write, I have a hard time with this explanation. But it seems some people genuinely like to "share," and this is one way.
- *Wanna-be writers.* A lot of people want to be published writers. Blogs make it happen without the hassle of getting someone else to do it or having to write well—although there is good writing to be found. Some is shockingly good. Most of it is miserable. I expect to see those Open Learning classes around the country offering courses in Blog writing.

8   Whatever the reason for the Blog phenomenon, it's not going to go away anytime soon. The main positive change: far fewer cat pictures!

---

* HyperText Mark-Up Language is a system of "tags" (rather than a computer "language") that instructs the Web browser how to format and display text and graphics.

Review Questions

1. What is a "blog"?

2. Why are blogs tending to replace personal ("vanity") Web pages, according to Dvorak?

3. What are the main reasons cited by Dvorak for the rise and proliferation of blogs?

Discussion and Writing Suggestions

1. Examine some blogs (e.g., <www.blogfinder.com>, <www.blogtree. com>). Locate and review some of the blogs referenced both in this article and in Michael Snider's article, which follows next. To what extent do you find such sites interesting and worth posting? To what extent to you regard them as mere "vanity" or "ego gratification" projects? Cite specific examples to support your conclusions.

2. To what extent do you agree that blogs are "not going to go away anytime soon"? Have you read—or did you regularly read—blogs before reading this article? Have you posted your own? Which (if any) of the reasons for creating blogs discussed by Dvorak toward the end of his article do you find most persuasive?

3. Examine some blog sites from the perspective of how the writers present themselves to the world. What kind of people are they, based upon not only their words but also on their choice of subjects, their distinctive "voices," and the appearance of their sites? To what extent do you like their attitude about the things they write about? To what extent do you agree with their opinions? To what extent would you like to meet them or even have dinner with them? To what extent do you detect indications that their personas are created, that they are hiding behind masks?

4. In a subsequent article written for *PC Magazine* almost two years after this one, Dvorak, in a more pessimistic mood, noted two significant developments since he wrote "The Blog Phenomenon." One was the "wholesale abandonment of blog sites" by writers who could not be bothered to keep them up. The other was the "casual co-opting of the blog universe by Big Media." In the latter category he noted the emergence of numerous professional blog sites created by large firms such as the *Washington Post* and MSNBC. To what extent do you agree that the early enthusiasm for blogs may have been overheated? To what extend will personal blogs continue to play a significant role in the cyberspace universe of e-mail, instant messages, and the Web?

The Intimacy of Blogs
Michael Snider

In the previous selection, John C. Dvorak explains the phenomenon of blogs. In the follow-ing article, Michael Snider, a columnist for Macleans, *a Canadian (print) magazine, focuses on some of the people who have created Weblogs and discusses why they felt impelled to create their sites. Plain Layne, Rambling Rhodes, and Gudy Two Shoes: these are only three of the thousands of individuals who, through their Web sites, attract a new kind of audience. Call it ego gratification, call it therapy, call it identity creation, call it literature, Web logs are in (for now). This article first appeared in the 15 September 2003 issue of* Macleans.

1   When Plain Layne suddenly pulled her site down in early June, a little corner of the blogosphere went nuts. Instead of the 26-year-old Minnesotan's poignant daily entries on her Weblog, an on-line journal, a blunt one-line message greet-ed visitors: "Take very good care of you." No more honestly introspective nar-ratives of her life. No more unbridled entries detailing the search for her birth parents, sessions with her therapist or her disappointing love affair with Violet, the stubby-tongued Dragon Lady. Comments flooded cyberspace. "Her sur-prising, unannounced departure is sending me and my overactive imagination into a frenzy of worry," wrote Gudy Two Shoes on his own Weblog. "If she's gone then I wish her well," posted Intellectual Poison. "She got me started with this whole blogging thing, something that I am truly grateful for." And Daintily Dirty asked, "Are the relationships we create by our blogging of any value?"

2   That's a good question. It turned out that Plaine Layne, aka Layne Johnson, wasn't gone for good. She'd just had a week during which she moved into a new house and witnessed the birth of her surrogate little sister's baby before getting her site back up (*http://plainlayne.dreamhost.com*). But the reaction from her readers was genuine. One of the prime reasons people blog is to make connections with others, and when Plain Layne went missing, it was like a neighbour had just up and moved in the middle of the night, with no for-warding address.

3   Weblogs are independent Web sites usually operated by a single person or by a small group of people. They serve as frequently updated forums to discuss whatever the blogger wants to discuss. Unmonitored, each blogger is author, editor and publisher, beholden solely to his or her own whims and desires. There are political blogs, media blogs, gay blogs, sports blogs, war blogs, anti-war blogs, tech blogs, photo blogs—hundreds of thousands of blogs, actually (estimates are as high as two million). "Blogging is not people wasting other people's time talking about the minutiae of their lives," says Joe Clark, 38, a Toronto author who operates several blogs. "The thing that's attractive about reading Weblogs is that you know there is one human being or a group of human beings behind them."

4   Free and easy-to-use publishing programs with names like Blogger, Movable Type and Live Journal spurred the phenomenon. Now, anyone with a computer

and an Internet connection can set up their own blog with relative ease. Paul Martin blogs, journalists blog, pundits, critics and social misfits blog. And what can you find there? Well, imagine standing in front of a library of gargantuan magazine racks loaded with glossy covers with everything from newsweeklies to girlie mags.

5   Blogs break down into two very general groups: linking blogs and personal online journals. Political blogs like Glenn Reynolds' *Instapundit.com*, media blogs like Jim Romenesko's Poynter Online (*www.poynter.org/medianews*), or tech blogs like *slashdot.com* are of the former kind. They're link-driven sites that connect readers to theme-related news stories and sometimes add a little commentary along with it. A personal blog is more like a diary entry or column in a daily newspaper, *a la* Rebecca Eckler of the *National Post* or Leah McLaren of the *Globe and Mail*—all about "me and what I think." Writers recount events in their lives—sometimes very private ones—and air their thoughts to a public audience.

6   Reasons vary. Sometimes, the practice is therapeutic. For some, like Ryan Rhodes, who runs Rambling Rhodes (*http://ramblingrhodes.blogspot.com*), blogging has some functional purposes. Rhodes, from Rochester, Minn., is news editor for an IBM publication called *eServer Magazine* but also writes humour columns for some local newspapers. He figured blogging would be a good writing exercise that might offer him instant feedback from readers. "I like knowing the stuff I write is being read," says Rhodes, "and I like it when it hits someone in a positive way and they tell me, so I can use it later for my column."

7   Personal blogs are famous for breaking usual standards of disclosure, revealing details considered by some to be very private. Dan Gudy, a 29-year-old Berliner, kept a diary when he was a teenager but gave it up, unhappy with the results. "My first experience was a total failure," says Gudy. "It was only myself talking about myself and I do that enough." But last year, when he created his site, Gudy Two Shoes (*http://gudy.blogspot.com*), the self-described introvert discovered that blogging opened a release valve. "I had to deal with some problems at the time and somehow needed to let it out. Part of me asked, why not use a blog for that?" Now, Gudy blogs about the books he reads and bike-riding through the German countryside. He also blogs about his sex life with his wife. "People can talk about what a nice bike ride they had or what a nice meal they had, but why can't they talk about what a nice f— they had last night?"

8   For many, that very willingness to discuss intimate details is one of the most alluring facets of blogging. "Your Weblog becomes an exterior part of you," says Clark, "so you can have some distance from your feelings, even though you're putting them out for everyone to read. But then all your readers are right up close and they know you because you're writing directly to them." In turn, readers can offer their own feedback: personal blogs frequently allow them to comment after each post, with something as easy as clicking a link that opens a pop-up box where they can add their own two cents' worth. "When I first started blogging," writes Daintily Dirty (*http://www.blogdreams.blogspot.com*), an anonymous 32-year-old blogger who chatted with *Macleans* via instant messenger, "I had no idea what I was getting into with the personal nature of the interactions. But the connections you find are what keep you coming back."

9   Layne Johnson's readers can attest to that. An excellent narrative writer who opens her soul to her readers, Plain Layne's daily entries regularly receive dozens of comments. "I hopped from one blog to the next and somewhere found Plain Layne," says Gudy. "What made me stay was her brutal honesty and intimacy of sharing, her very beautiful way of writing." Rhodes echoes the sentiment. "Layne is digital crack," he says. "Hands down, as far as I've read, she's got the best personal blog. I have to read her every day."

10   Johnson politely turned down a request for an interview, explaining her blogging is a personal exercise that's meant to be cathartic. And somehow, that's the way it should be. Plain Layne does her talking, or typing, on her blog. "I think the hardest thing about sharing your life on-line is that at some point you discover people know you," Johnson wrote in a June post. "They know you from the inside out, the way your mind works, what makes you laugh or cry, your hopes and fears." It's clear to see she uses her blog as an outlet, a place to dump her anxiety and frustration in a search for identity and understanding. It's also a place of amusement and mirth, with stories of stupefying office meetings and uproarious golf outings, all told with a flair and talent that would make some "me" columnists envious.

11   Blogs might seem too revealing for people who prefer their diaries to remain private. But more and more strangers are inviting millions of other strangers into their lives, with a willingness to share just about anything, finding their own shelf space on the world's most accessible magazine rack, open to anyone who cares to pick up a copy. Welcome to the blogosphere.

Review Questions

1. What is the rhetorical function of Snider's opening anecdote about Plain Layne?

2. How does Snider categorize the two general groups of blogs?

3. What are the main uses of blogging, according to Snider?

Discussion and Writing Suggestions

1. Have you or someone you know created a blog? If so, describe its contents and its format.

2. Check out Plain Layne <http://plainlayne.dreamhost.com>, Rambling Rhodes <ramblingrhodes.blogspot.com>, Gudy Two Shoes <gudy.blogspot.com>, or another site mentioned by Snider. Write a one- to two-page report on what you find, describing the site. What kind of personality appears to be authoring the site?

3. Examine a particular blog site and assess it, providing analysis and evaluation, and offering suggestions for its improvement.

A Shared Sadness
Russ Parsons

Most e-mail messages are private communications between a sender and one or more specifically designated recipients. Increasingly popular, however, are public electronic forums, such as chat groups, bulletin boards, newsgroups, the Usenet, and "Multi-User Domains" (MUDs). These groups, or electronic communities, are generally organized around particular personal or professional interests—e.g., Shakespeare studies, cancer survival, environmental issues, online romance. In these forums, to which users generally register or subscribe, senders post messages that can be read by all members of the group, and to which any member can respond. New and old members can also read discussion "threads" that transpired among members of the group days or even months ago.

In the following article, Los Angeles Times *staff writer Russ Parsons recounts one such discussion thread concerning a person he had never met, but whose fate touched him, and many others, deeply. Parsons's article offers another perspective on how electronic communication has helped foster new ways of relating to one another, has helped create new communities of like-minded individuals. "A Shared Sadness" first appeared in the* Los Angeles Times *on 7 August 1998.*

1   People who haven't spent much time there seem to imagine cyberspace as their own private nightmare brought to life. To some people it is a scary place, full of predators of one stripe or another. To some it is a virtual Gomorrah, a RAM-charged peep show catering to unimaginable perversions.

2   Others fear it as a cold place, a place of separation peopled only by the lonely, locked in their own little worlds. Though they may talk to one another, do they communicate?

3   "What about a sense of community?" asked a friend of mine the other day. "What about things like communication on shared subjects other than the narrow topics at hand, those things that provide the glue that transforms a group of people into a community?" (He is a professor, and he does talk that way.)

4   So I told him about Gary Holleman. Gary helped start one of the Internet discussion groups, or chat lists, I belong to. A chat list, for the uninitiated, is kind of like an ongoing letter dedicated to a specific topic. If you have something to say about that topic, you e-mail your comment to a central computer, which then forwards it to everyone else on the list. If they have something to add, they can either respond to you privately or send another message back to the central computer.

5   You can find a chat list for just about any special interest imaginable. I belong to five: one devoted to mysteries, one for wine, one for the organization Slow Food, one for cookbooks and another—the one Holleman started—for chefs and cooks.

6   There are a couple of hundred people who are on the list: not all of them are chefs and cooks. Some are culinary students or work in related fields. Some are merely curious eavesdroppers (called lurkers).

7   Conversations—that is the only way to describe them—cover everything from practical matters like Alto-Sham slow cookers (from context, I gather that this is a kind of steam oven used in production kitchens) to a rather heated philosophical argument about whether cooking is an art or a craft. At any one time, several of these topics (called threads) are happening at the same time.

8   One day early last October, in the midst of these workaday discussions, there was a note titled "Gary Holleman's Broken Heart." In it, with surprising wit and panache (we're talking chefs, remember?), Gary, a corporate chef who did product research and development, informed us that he had suddenly learned he needed some heart surgery.

9   *As you may or may not know, I recently found out that I need some spare parts for my heart—an operation that my doctors perform every day and is analogous to a medical "slam-dunk." However, for my friends, family and especially me, the prospects are somewhat more intimidating.*

10   The problem, he wrote, began at lunch at a food conference in Portland, Ore.:

11   *"The mean age of the population is gradually moving upward, and with it a new concern for fat-free, heart-healthy foods," the luncheon speaker from Noble Assn. said as he discussed food trends for the late 1990s. The woman next to me was full of questions for me about the Internet. I heard neither the speaker nor my lunch partner. My heart felt as if it were jumping through my chest. I was sure I had taken on a cartoonish figure [and that] everyone in the room could see my heart beating two feet in front of my body. In fact, I was worried my heart had invaded the personal space of the gentleman across the table.*

12   The problem recurred the next morning. He called his doctor back home in Minnesota and was told to go immediately to a cardiologist. There he learned that he had a leaky heart valve and would need to have open-heart surgery within a couple of weeks. Since the nearest major medical center was in Fargo, N.D., that's where he headed.

13   *I was stunned. The doctor says I have a four-plus aortic insufficiency (on a scale of one to four, four being the worst). While over the past year I had been unable to keep up my 15–20-miles-a-week jogging schedule, I had no idea that the problem was a lack of oxygen due to a broken heart. I thought I was just getting old.*

14   After a couple of days of tests, he was told there was a complication: He also had an enlarged aortic artery that might have to be replaced as well.

15   *"While not technically difficult, this would be a much more complex operation," Dr. Damle said with his beautiful East Indian accent. Complex means longer. And slightly more risk, I assume.*

16   To keep everyone updated on his progress, Gary created a small mailing list that he would post to regularly. If we sent him a note, he'd add our names.

17   I didn't know Gary and, to be perfectly honest, his name hadn't registered from his postings in the past. His was a face in the crowd of postings that comes through my computer every day—someone I saw every day but never thought much about.

18   But I was touched by the hopeful, funny tone of the note. It was a nice piece of writing. I sent him a note, telling him so and suggested that when it was all over, he should collect these essays for a book. That got me on the list.

19   The next day another missive arrived.

20   *Can a heartbroken man in Minnesota find happiness in a Fargo operating room? Read on.*

21   *"Allergic to any foods?" the intake nurse asked as she diligently filled out the proper forms.*

22   *"No, but I am a vegetarian. Ovolacto," I replied.*

23   *"A chef AND a vegetarian?"*

24   *An hour later the food arrived. A splendid vegetarian feast—sort of. One cup of hot, canned, diced beets. Another cup of hot, canned, diced beets. One scoop of instant mashed potatoes (I recognize the flavor: NIFDA Red Label). Another scoop of instant mashed potatoes.*

25   There was worse news than lunch, though.

26   *The CT scan is in, and the results are clear. I have an aortic aneurysm. "The walls of the aortic artery are weak and enlarged. I am sure that is what is causing the failure of the valve," said Dr. Damle.*

27   *The word "aneurysm" was not what I wanted to hear. It means, in Damle's words, that "we have increased the magnitude of the operation significantly." This means more risk, and, as I think it, he says it.*

28   Gary sounded more upbeat after the weekend.

29   *The "rose-colored glasses" in pill form prescribed by my surgeon, also known as antianxiety medicine, are working well. I know this for several reasons:*

30   *(1) I just traveled 500 miles round-trip over 24 hours with three of my teens and my wife, and I still think I have had an absolutely marvelous weekend. We went to visit my four grandkids. Yes, at 42 years old I am too young for either heart surgery or grandkids, but I am blessed with both. However, I don't think there is a correlation.*

31   *(2) I also know the antianxiety medicine is working because I have forgotten what I had anxiety about in the first place.*

32   Well, not entirely. He told of talking with one of his kids over lunch.

33   *"So, did your mother tell you there has been a change in plans for the operation? I need more extensive surgery."*

34   *"Yeah, I guess I heard. But it's still routine surgery, right?"*

35   *It's always a hard thing to know, much less tell someone else, just how risky an operation is. There is always balance—honesty and plain talk countered by hope, comfort and matter-of-factness.*

36   *"Well, yes, routine . . . I guess." How routine can open-heart surgery get, I wonder?*

37   *"Oh, that's good."*

38   *"But you know when we talked before, I said it was a slam-dunk medical procedure? Well, now it's more like a three-point shot."*

39   *I see the panic in his eyes. He is remembering how well I play basketball. In fact, I am remembering how well I play basketball. Thinking quickly, I add, "But, uh, Michael Jordan is taking the three-point shot!" The concern fades from his face, and we eat our salads in silence.*

40   The next post was full of news of the next day's surgery. It turns out that because of the location of the aneurysm, the surgery was going to be even more complex to avoid starving the brain of blood.

41   *The risk here is substantial. It's starting to feel more like a half-court shot by a random spectator trying to win a million dollars. I exaggerate. The doctor I have chosen is the finest doctor in North Dakota for this type of operation. (OK, I admit it. There aren't that many doctors in N.D., but Damle is excellent.)*

42   Getting ready for the surgery, he and his wife, Lois, rented a suite in a hotel across the street from the hospital. Since there was a kitchen, why not fix dinner? It had to be better than hospital food.

43   *My only disappointment making dinner was a result of the apparent dearth of fresh basil in Fargo, N.D. We went to Hornbacher's grocery store—the biggest in town—only to find REALLY shabby looking herbs, none of which resembled basil. I inquired at the checkout counter.*

44   *"Where is the best produce section in town?" I asked the checkout person. She thought for a moment, as if it were a trick question. "Uh, here?"*

45   *"Excuse me, I don't THINK so. Not in a MILLION YEARS! Your herbs look like they are left over from the floods of '97! They look like they went THROUGH the floods!" I could feel my blood pressure rising. And then I remember that I forgot to take my midday antianxiety pill.*

46   *And that brings me to the night before the dawn that has consumed my thoughts for the last two weeks. The blood tests are in. The doctor is ready. My family is by my side. I have my Ambien sleeping pills. And from reading the flood of e-mail I have received, I know my friends are thinking of me and praying for me. It is not generally my nature to try and attract attention (in the grocery store, from my friends or God for that matter), but I am indeed comforted and joyful over the love and affection that has been uploaded to my little port on the Net. Thank you, God bless you all. I'll key you soon.*

47   The next day, in order to keep calls to the family at a minimum, a member of the chat list was designated to act as go-between. I checked in every hour to see how Gary was doing.

48   There were constant updates. First:

49   *The surgery is taking longer than expected, but that's not necessarily a bad sign.*

50   Then:

51   *I have just spoken with the nurse's station, and Gary has been returned to surgery. I am hoping things are going well, but this may be the time to start praying.*

52   It got worse.

53   *Gary is in very, very critical condition. Please stop what you are doing for just a moment and pray however and to whomever you do it.*

54   By 4, it seemed a corner had been turned.

55   *Gary is out of surgery. His heart is being supported by a left ventricular assist device. He is much improved. He is currently in intensive care and will be in the recovery room soon.*

56   But at 5:

57   *I just spoke with Lois. Gary has been taken back into surgery for the third time. She does not know for what. We all continue to hope and pray.*

58   A couple of minutes later:

59   *I just spoke to Gary's brother Michael, and Gary's condition has taken an unforeseen turn toward critical.*

60   After that, a maddening silence. I found things to straighten up around my desk, staying late and doing busy work in between logging on to check for news. Finally, just after 7:

61   *Gary Holleman left us half an hour ago. We all loved him.*

62   Messages flew back and forth as the news spread. It seemed everyone had been doing just what I had been doing—staying close to the computer to check in. The next day—Oct. 22, 1997—was declared a day of silence in Gary's honor. We took up a collection for his children and—this being cyberspace, again—someone added a tribute section to his home page where anyone who wanted could write a note about Gary. (If you want to visit, it's still up: *http://www.churchstreet.com/co/gary.htm*)

63   Just like anyplace else, we grieved for a friend we'd lost and knew that our little community had been changed forever.

Review Questions

1. What is a chat list?

2. Summarize "A Shared Sadness." Avoid direct quotations, but try to convey the sense of the changing circumstances of Holleman's condition, particularly once he undergoes surgery.

Discussion and Writing Suggestions

1. Discuss the significance of the title "A Shared Sadness." In your discussion consider how Parsons uses the word "community." What kind of community developed in the wake of Holleman's illness and surgery? How was this virtual community different from what we generally think of as a "community"? How would you characterize the distinctive identity of the members of the community that followed the news of Holleman's changing condition?

2. Many people who have read this article have found it unusually touching. Given that thousands of people die of heart disease every year, which aspects of "A Shared Sadness" make the story of this particular death so moving?

3. The Web site on Gary Holleman referred to in this article no longer exists, but other sites devoted to Holleman do. (You can conduct a search to find them on Google.com.) Read some of the postings by those who knew Holleman, either in person, or through the chat list, and write a short account of what you find.

4. Have you ever been in the waiting room or been waiting at home while someone you know underwent major surgery? Describe your reactions and the reactions of others around you, or others you were in contact with, as the surgery approached, and as news of its progress filtered out. To what extent were your reactions similar to those of Parsons and his virtual community?

Virtual Love
Meghan Daum

Star vehicles like You've Got Mail *aside, the popular media abounds with stories—some inspirational, some cautionary—about online romances. In a typical pattern, couples first meet one another in public chat rooms, then retire to private spaces for one-on-one e-mail conversations, then at some point, perhaps, "progress" to cybersex. (In no small number of cases, one or both parties are already married, and the discovery of the online romance by the outraged spouse leads to divorce. Question: Does engaging in an online, entirely text-based romance constitute infidelity to one's spouse or significant other?) Many of these relationships remain at a virtual level; in other cases, couples begin communicating by telephone, and then, perhaps, decide to meet one other in person. Some of these stories have happy endings; most don't. Disappointment seems almost a given: even in those cases not involving outright fraud or misrepresentation (a male representing himself as female, a 50-year-old married woman representing herself as a 30-year-old single, a request by one party to the other for "travel expenses"), the reality is seldom able to match the expectation raised by the intoxication of an idealized cyberromance.*

Online dating originates not only in special-interest chat rooms but also in numerous matchmaking sites on the Web, like Matchmaker.com, AmericanSingles.com, Altmatch.com, CatholicSingles.com, and ThirdAge.com. One site, Match.com, takes credit for about a thousand weddings that have resulted from couples meeting at its site. In the following article, the author describes how she met her partner in yet another way: when he unexpectedly e-mailed her after reading some of her published work. The progress of this relationship is detailed in "Virtual Love." Meghan Daum is a freelance writer whose articles have appeared in such magazines as Harper's, Vogue, *and the* New Yorker. *This article first appeared in the 25 August–1 September 1997 issue of the* New Yorker.

1   It was last November; fall was drifting away into an intolerable chill. I was at the end of my twenty-sixth year, and was living in New York City, trying to support myself as a writer, and taking part in the kind of urban life that might be construed as glamorous were it to appear in a memoir in the distant future. At the time, however, my days felt more like a grind than like an adventure: hours of work strung between the motions of waking up, getting the mail, watching TV with my roommates, and going to bed. One morning, I logged on to my America Online account to find a message under the heading "is this the real meghan daum?" It came from someone with the screen name PFSlider. The body of the message consisted of five sentences, written entirely in lowercase letters, of perfectly turned flattery: something about PFSlider's admiration of

some newspaper and magazine articles I had published over the last year and a half, something about his resulting infatuation with me, and something about his being a sportswriter in California.

2   I was engaged for the thirty seconds that it took me to read the message and fashion a reply. Though it felt strange to be in the position of confirming that I was indeed "the real meghan daum," I managed to say, "Yes, it's me. Thank you for writing." I clicked the "Send Now" icon, shot my words into the void, and forgot about PFSlider until the next day, when I received another message, this one headed "eureka."

3   "wow, it is you," he wrote, still in lowercase. He chronicled the various conditions under which he'd read my few-and-far-between articles—a boardwalk in Laguna Beach, the spring-training pressroom for a baseball team that he covered for a Los Angeles newspaper. He confessed to having a crush on me. He referred to me as "princess daum." He said he wanted to have lunch with me during one of his two annual trips to New York.

4   The letter was outrageous and endearingly pathetic, possibly the practical joke of a friend trying to rouse me out of a temporary writer's block. But the kindness pouring forth from my computer screen was bizarrely exhilarating, and I logged off and thought about it for a few hours before writing back to express how flattered and "touched"—this was probably the first time I had ever used that word in earnest—I was by his message.

5   I am not what most people would call a computer person. I have no interest in chat rooms, newsgroups, or most Web sites. I derive a palpable thrill from sticking a letter in the United States mail. But I have a constant low-grade fear of the telephone, and I often call people with the intention of getting their answering machines. There is something about the live voice that I have come to find unnervingly organic, as volatile as live television. E-mail provides a useful antidote for my particular communication anxieties. Though I generally send and receive only a few messages a week, I take comfort in their silence and their boundaries.

6   PFSlider and I tossed a few innocuous, smart-assed notes back and forth over the week following his first message. Let's say his name was Pete. He was twenty-nine, and single. I revealed very little about myself, relying instead on the ironic commentary and forced witticisms that are the conceit of so many E-mail messages. But I quickly developed an oblique affection for PFSlider. I was excited when there was a message from him, mildly depressed when there wasn't. After a few weeks, he gave me his phone number. I did not give him mine, but he looked it up and called me one Friday night. I was home. I picked up the phone. His voice was jarring, yet not unpleasant. He held up more than his end of the conversation for an hour, and when he asked permission to call me again I granted it, as though we were of an earlier era.

7   Pete—I could never wrap my mind around his name, privately thinking of him as PFSlider, "E-mail guy," or even "baseball boy"—began phoning me two or three times a week. He asked if he could meet me, and I said that that would be O.K. Christmas was a few weeks away, and he told me that he would be

coming back East to see his family. From there, he would take a short flight to New York and have lunch with me.

8   "It is my off-season mission to meet you," he said.

9   "There will probably be a snowstorm," I said.

10   "I'll take a team of sled dogs," he answered.

11   We talked about our work and our families, about baseball and Bill Clinton and Howard Stern and sex, about his hatred for Los Angeles and how much he wanted a new job. Sometimes we'd find each other logged on simultaneously and type back and forth for hours.

12   I had previously considered cyber-communication an oxymoron, a fast road to the breakdown of humanity. But, curiously, the Internet—at least in the limited form in which I was using it—felt anything but dehumanizing. My interaction with PFSlider seemed more authentic than much of what I experienced in the daylight realm of living beings. I was certainly putting more energy into the relationship than I had put into many others. I also was giving Pete attention that was by definition undivided, and relishing the safety of the distance between us by opting to be truthful instead of doling out the white lies that have become the staple of real life. The outside world—the place where I walked around avoiding people I didn't want to deal with, peppering my casual conversations with half-truths, and applying my motto "Let the machine take it" to almost any scenario—was sliding into the periphery of my mind.

13   For me, the time on-line with Pete was far superior to the phone. There were no background noises, no interruptions from "call waiting," no long-distance charges. Through typos and misspellings, he flirted maniacally. "I have an absurd crush on you," he said. "If I like you in person, you must promise to marry me." I was coy and conceited, telling him to get a life, baiting him into complimenting me further, teasing him in a way I would never have dared to do in person, or even on the phone. I would stay up until 3 A.M. typing with him, smiling at the screen, getting so giddy that when I quit I couldn't fall asleep. I was having difficulty recalling what I used to do at night. It was as if he and I lived together in our own quiet space—a space made all the more intimate because of our conscious decision to block everyone else out. My phone was tied up for hours at a time. No one in the real world could reach me, and I didn't really care.

14   Since my last serious relationship, I'd had the requisite number of false starts and five-night stands, dates that I wasn't sure were dates, and emphatically casual affairs that buckled under their own inertia. With PFSlider, on the other hand, I may not have known my suitor, but, for the first time in my life, I knew the deal: I was a desired person, the object of a blind man's gaze. He called not only when he said he would call but unexpectedly, just to say hello. He was protected by the shield of the Internet; his guard was not merely down but nonexistent. He let his phone bill grow to towering proportions. He told me that he thought about me all the time, though we both knew that the "me" in his mind consisted largely of himself. He talked about me to his friends, and admitted it. He arranged his holiday schedule around our impending date. He managed

to charm me with sports analogies. He didn't hesitate. He was unblinking and unapologetic, all nerviness and balls to the wall.

15   And so PFSlider became my everyday life. All the tangible stuff fell away. My body did not exist. I had no skin, no hair, no bones. All desire had converted itself into a cerebral current that reached nothing but my frontal lobe. There was no outdoors, no social life, no weather. There was only the computer screen and the phone, my chair, and maybe a glass of water. Most mornings, I would wake up to find a message from PFSlider, composed in Pacific time while I slept in the wee hours. "I had a date last night," he wrote. "And I am not ashamed to say it was doomed from the start because I couldn't stop thinking about you."

16   I fired back a message slapping his hand. "We must be careful where we tread," I said. This was true but not sincere. I wanted it, all of it. I wanted unfettered affection, soul-mating, true romance. In the weeks that had elapsed since I picked up "is this the real meghan daum?" the real me had undergone some kind of meltdown—a systemic rejection of all the savvy and independence I had worn for years, like a grownup Girl Scout badge.

17   Pete knew nothing of my scattered, juvenile self, and I did my best to keep it that way. Even though I was heading into my late twenties, I was still a child, ignorant of dance steps and health insurance, a prisoner of credit-card debt and student loans and the nagging feeling that I didn't want anyone to find me until I had pulled myself into some semblance of an adult. The fact that Pete had literally seemed to discover me, as if by turning over a rock, lent us an aura of fate which I actually took half-seriously. Though skepticism seemed like the obvious choice in this strange situation, I discarded it precisely because it was the obvious choice, because I wanted a more interesting narrative than cynicism would ever allow. I was a true believer in the urban dream: the dream of years of struggle, of getting a break, of making it. Like most of my friends, I wanted someone to love me, but I wasn't supposed to need it. To admit to loneliness was to smack the face of progress, to betray the times in which we lived. But PFSlider derailed me. He gave me all of what I'd never even realized I wanted.

18   My addiction to PFSlider's messages indicated a monstrous narcissism, but it also revealed a subtler desire, which I didn't fully understand at the time. My need to experience an old-fashioned kind of courtship was stronger than I had ever imagined. And the fact that technology was providing an avenue for such archaic discourse was a paradox that both fascinated and repelled me. Our relationship had an epistolary quality that put our communication closer to the eighteenth century than to the impending millennium. Thanks to the computer, I was involved in a well-defined courtship, a neat little space in which he and I were both safe to express the panic and the fascination of our mutual affection. Our interaction was refreshingly orderly, noble in its vigor, dignified despite its shamelessness. It was far removed from the randomness of real-life relationships. We had an intimacy that seemed custom-made for our strange, lonely times. It seemed custom-made for me.

19   The day of our date, a week before Christmas, was frigid and sunny. Pete was sitting at the bar of the restaurant when I arrived. We shook hands. For a split

second, he leaned toward me with his chin, as if to kiss me. He was shorter than I had pictured, though he was not short. He struck me as clean-cut. He had very nice hands. He wore a very nice shirt. We were seated at a very nice table. I scanned the restaurant for people I knew, saw none, and couldn't decide how I felt about that.

20   He talked, and I heard nothing he said. I stared at his profile and tried to figure out whether I liked him. He seemed to be saying nothing in particular, but he went on forever. Later, we went to the Museum of Natural History and watched a science film about storm chasers. We walked around looking for the dinosaurs, and he talked so much that I wanted to cry. Outside, walking along Central Park West at dusk, through the leaves, past the yellow cabs and the splendid lights of Manhattan at Christmas, he grabbed my hand to kiss me and I didn't let him. I felt as if my brain had been stuffed with cotton. Then, for some reason, I invited him back to my apartment. I gave him a few beers and finally let him kiss me on the lumpy futon in my bedroom. The radiator clanked. The phone rang and the machine picked up. A car alarm blared outside. A key turned in the door as one of my roommates came home. I had no sensation at all—only a clear conviction that I wanted Pete out of my apartment. I wanted to hand him his coat, close the door behind him, and fight the ensuing empti-ness by turning on the computer and taking comfort in PFSlider.

21   When Pete finally did leave, I berated myself from every angle: for not kiss-ing him on Central Park West, for letting him kiss me at all, for not liking him, for wanting to like him more than I had wanted anything in such a long time. I was horrified by the realization that I had invested so heavily in a made-up charac-ter—a character in whose creation I'd had a greater hand than even Pete him-self. How could I, a person so self-congratulatingly reasonable, have been sucked into a scenario that was more akin to a television talk show than to the relatively full and sophisticated life I was so convinced I led? How could I have received a fan letter and allowed it to go this far?

22   The next day, a huge bouquet of FTD flowers arrived from him. No one had ever sent me flowers before. I forgave him. As human beings with actual flesh and hand gestures and Gap clothing, Pete and I were utterly incompatible, but I decided to pretend otherwise. He returned home and we fell back into the computer and the phone, and I continued to keep the real world safely away from the desk that held them. Instead of blaming him for my disappointment, I blamed the earth itself, the invasion of roommates and ringing phones into the immaculate communication that PFSlider and I had created.

23   When I pictured him in the weeks that followed, I saw the image of a plane lifting off over an overcast city. PFSlider was otherworldly, more a concept than a person. His romance lay in the notion of flight, the physics of gravity defiance. So when he offered to send me a plane ticket to spend the weekend with him in Los Angeles I took it as an extension of our blissful remoteness, a three-dimensional E-mail message lasting an entire weekend.

24   The temperature on the runway at J.F.K. was seven degrees Fahrenheit. Our DC-10 sat for three hours waiting for deicing. Finally, it took off over the frozen city, and the ground below shrank into a drawing of itself. Phone calls were made, laptop computers were plopped onto tray tables. The recirculating air

dried out my contact lenses. I watched movies without the sound and told myself that they were probably better that way. Something about the plastic interior of the fuselage and the plastic forks and the din of the air and the engines was soothing and strangely sexy.

25   Then we descended into LAX. We hit the tarmac, and the seat-belt signs blinked off. I hadn't moved my body in eight hours, and now I was walking through the tunnel to the gate, my clothes wrinkled, my hair matted, my hands shaking. When I saw Pete in the terminal, his face seemed to me just as blank and easy to miss as it had the first time I'd met him. He kissed me chastely. On the way out to the parking lot, he told me that he was being seriously considered for a job in New York. He was flying back there next week. If he got the job, he'd be moving within the month. I looked at him in astonishment. Something silent and invisible seemed to fall on us. Outside, the wind was warm, and the Avis and Hertz buses ambled alongside the curb of Terminal 5. The palm trees shook, and the air seemed as heavy and palpable as Pete's hand, which held mine for a few seconds before dropping it to get his car keys out of his pocket. He stood before me, all flesh and preoccupation, and for this I could not forgive him.

26   Gone were the computer, the erotic darkness of the telephone, the clean, single dimension of Pete's voice at 1 A.M. It was nighttime, yet the combination of sight and sound was blinding. It scared me. It turned me off. We went to a restaurant and ate outside on the sidewalk. We strained for conversation, and I tried not to care that we had to. We drove to his apartment and stood under the ceiling light not really looking at each other. Something was happening that we needed to snap out of. Any moment now, I thought. Any moment and we'll be all right. These moments were crowded with elements, with carpet fibers and automobiles and the smells of everything that had a smell. It was all wrong. The physical world had invaded our space.

27   For three days, we crawled along the ground and tried to pull ourselves up. We talked about things that I can no longer remember. We read the Los Angeles *Times* over breakfast. We drove north past Santa Barbara to tour the wine country. I felt like an object that could not be lifted, something that secretly weighed more than the world itself. Everything and everyone around us seemed imbued with a California lightness. I stomped around the countryside, an idiot New Yorker in my clunky shoes and black leather jacket. Not until I studied myself in the bathroom mirror of a highway rest stop did I fully realize the preposterousness of my uniform. I was dressed for war. I was dressed for my regular life.

28   That night, in a tiny town called Solvang, we ate an expensive dinner. We checked into a Marriott and watched television. Pete talked at me and through me and past me. I tried to listen. I tried to talk. But I bored myself and irritated him. Our conversation was a needle that could not be threaded. Still, we played nice. We tried to care, and pretended to keep trying long after we had given up. In the car on the way home, he told me that I was cynical, and I didn't have the presence of mind to ask him just how many cynics he had met who would travel three thousand miles to see someone they barely knew.

29   Pete drove me to the airport at 7 A.M. so I could make my eight-o'clock flight home. He kissed me goodbye—another chaste peck that I recognized from

countless dinner parties and dud dates. He said that he'd call me in a few days when he got to New York for his job interview, which we had discussed only in passing and with no reference to the fact that New York was where I happened to live. I returned home to frozen January. A few days later, he came to New York, and we didn't see each other. He called me from the plane taking him back to Los Angeles to tell me, through the static, that he had got the job. He was moving to my city.

30   PFSlider was dead. There would be no meeting him in distant hotel lobbies during the baseball season. There would be no more phone calls or E-mail messages. In a single moment, Pete had completed his journey out of our mating dance and officially stepped into the regular world—the world that gnawed at me daily, the world that fostered those five-night stands, the world where romance could not be sustained, because so many of us simply did not know how to do it. Instead, we were all chitchat and leather jackets, bold proclaimers of all that we did not need. But what struck me most about this affair was the unpredictable nature of our demise. Unlike most cyber-romances, which seem to come fully equipped with the inevitable set of misrepresentations and false expectations, PFSlider and I had played it fairly straight. Neither of us had lied. We'd done the best we could. Our affair had died from natural causes rather than virtual ones.

31   Within a two-week period after I returned from Los Angeles, at least seven people confessed to me the vagaries of their own E-mail affairs. This topic arose, unprompted, in the course of normal conversation. I heard most of these stories in the close confines of smoky bars and crowded restaurants, and we all shook our heads in bewilderment as we told our tales, our eyes focused on some point in the distance. Four of these people had met their correspondents, by traveling from New Haven to Baltimore, from New York to Montana, from Texas to Virginia, and from New York to Johannesburg. These were normal people, writers and lawyers and scientists. They were all smart, attractive, and more than a little sheepish about admitting just how deeply they had been sucked in. Mostly, it was the courtship ritual that had seduced us. E-mail had become an electronic epistle, a yearned-for rule book. It allowed us to do what was necessary to experience love. The Internet was not responsible for our remote, fragmented lives. The problem was life itself.

32   The story of PFSlider still makes me sad, not so much because we no longer have anything to do with each other but because it forces me to see the limits and the perils of daily life with more clarity than I used to. After I realized that our relationship would never transcend the screen and the phone—that, in fact, our face-to-face knowledge of each other had permanently contaminated the screen and the phone—I hit the pavement again, went through the motions of everyday life, said hello and goodbye to people in the regular way. If Pete and I had met at a party, we probably wouldn't have spoken to each other for more than ten minutes, and that would have made life easier but also less interesting. At the same time, it terrifies me to admit to a firsthand understanding of the way the heart and the ego are snarled and entwined like diseased trees that have folded in on each other. Our need to worship somehow fuses with our

need to be worshipped. It upsets me still further to see how inaccessibility can make this entanglement so much more intoxicating. But I'm also thankful that I was forced to unpack the raw truth of my need and stare at it for a while. It was a dare I wouldn't have taken in three dimensions.

33   The last time I saw Pete, he was in New York, three thousand miles away from what had been his home, and a million miles away from PFSlider. In a final gesture of decency, in what I later realized was the most ordinary kind of closure, he took me out to dinner. As the few remaining traces of affection turned into embarrassed regret, we talked about nothing. He paid the bill. He drove me home in a rental car that felt as arbitrary and impersonal as what we now were to each other.

34   Pete had known how to get me where I lived until he came to where I lived: then he became as unmysterious as anyone next door. The world had proved to be too cluttered and too fast for us, too polluted to allow the thing we'd attempted through technology ever to grow in the earth. PFSlider and I had joined the angry and exhausted living. Even if we met on the street, we wouldn't recognize each other, our particular version of intimacy now obscured by the branches and bodies and falling debris that make up the physical world.

Discussion and Writing Suggestions

1. Daum remarks that, contrary to what she had previously assumed about cybercommunication, her e-mail correspondence with Pete was "anything but dehumanizing. My interaction with PFSlider seemed more authentic than much of what I experienced in the daylight realm of living beings. I was certainly putting more energy into the relationship than I had put into many others" (paragraph 12). To what extent have you experienced this same reaction to virtual correspondence (if not virtual romance)? How do you account for this phenomenon?

2. To what extent do you see the problems that developed between Daum and PFSlider a result of the new identities that each had created for the other in an effort to nurture and sustain their relationship? To what extent did the Internet make the creation of such identities possible—in a way that, for example, phone conversations, letters, or earlier face-to-face meetings, might have made less easy?

3. Daum writes that PFSlider told her that "he thought about me all the time, though we both knew that the 'me' in his mind consisted largely of himself" (paragraph 14). What do you think she means? In what sense did they "both" know this? Do you think that this statement would have been less true had Pete and she first encountered one another face-to-face? Or if they had first made contact by letter and telephone rather than by e-mail?

4. Daum notes that as her virtual relationship developed, "the real me had undergone some kind of meltdown—a systematic rejection of all the savvy and independence I had worn for years, like a grownup Girl Scout badge" (paragraph 16). Why do you think this happened? To what extent do your own experiences or those of others you know bear out this phenomenon? To what extent is the Internet (as opposed to the power of new romance, virtual or old-fashioned) the key factor in causing such a "meltdown"?

5. How do you account for the particular way in which Daum's relationship developed, both before and after she and Pete physically met? Consider, in particular, Daum's reflections to herself (paragraph 21) immediately after their first date. Was the relationship doomed from the start, because of the unrealistic expectations that each had developed, or might people different from these particular two have been able to sustain their relationship over the long term? To what extent does Daum's case provide a general lesson about online romances?

6. Daum remarks (paragraph 30) that her affair with Pete "died from natural causes rather than virtual ones." And she concludes (paragraph 34) that her and Pete's "particular version of intimacy [was] now obscured by the branches and bodies and falling debris that make up the physical world." What do you think she means by these statements? What were the "natural causes"? What are the "branches and bodies and falling debris"?

Cyberspace and Identity
Sherry Turkle

What we think of as our identity is generally our unique inner self—that core personality that makes us different from our friends, our brothers or sisters, even our identical twin. Not only do we like to think of our identity as unique, but we also see it as unified and whole. People who have multiple personalities, like those we read about in the cases of The Three Faces of Eve or Sybil, are clinical aberrations. Increasingly, however, this view of the unitary self is being challenged. We have long known that personalities can fragment; but it is only recently that the concept of fragmented or "decentered" selves has been seen not only as normal but actually as psychologically healthy. Certainly, in some extreme cases, the personality can fragment to the point where the individual cannot function normally (particularly if one personality is not aware of the existence of the others). But if Superman and his alternate identity Clark Kent can healthfully coexist in the same body, then why not DrJane and Hellraiser as two different screen names of a single Internet subscriber? It is not that one side of the self excludes the other; it is rather that both (or in fact several) sides are aspects of the same individual, and there is no reason why one cannot "cycle through" the various sides of oneself while remaining a balanced, functioning member of society.

In the following article, sociologist Sherry Turkle explores this concept of multiple identity, as it has been fostered by the development of cyberspace communication. Turkle did her undergraduate work at Radcliffe College and earned a joint doctorate in sociology and personality psychology from Harvard University in 1976. A licensed clinical psychologist, Turkle is Professor of the Sociology of Science in the Program in Science, Technology, and Society at the Massachusetts Institute of Technology. One of the most highly regarded authorities in the field, Turkle has written numerous articles on computer technologies and virtual communities in such periodicals as the Utne Reader, Sociological Inquiry, Social Research, Sciences, American Prospect, Signs, *and* Daedalus. *Her books include* Psychoanalytic Politics: Jacques Lacan and Freud's French Revolution *(1981),* The Second Self: Computers and the Human Spirit *(1984), and* Life on the Screen: Identity in the Age of the Internet *(1995). In 1995 she was selected by* Newsweek *as one of the "50 For the Future: the Most Influential People to Watch in Cyberspace." Turkle has been featured on the cover of* Wired *(April 1996) and* Technology Review *(February/March 1996). She has also been profiled in* Scientific American *(April 1998) and the* New York Times *(18 June 1998). This article, originally entitled "Looking Toward Cyberspace: Beyond Grounded Sociology: Cyberspace and Identity," first appeared in* Contemporary Sociology *in November 1999.*

1   We come to see ourselves differently as we catch sight of our images in the mirror of the machine. Over a decade ago, when I first called the computer a "second self" (1984), these identity-transforming relationships were most usually one-on-one, a person alone with a machine. This is no longer the case. A rapidly expanding system of networks, collectively known as the Internet, links millions of people together in new spaces that are changing the way we think, the nature of our sexuality, the form of our communities, our very identities. In cyberspace, we are learning to live in virtual worlds. We may find ourselves alone as we navigate virtual oceans, unravel virtual mysteries, and engineer virtual skyscrapers. But increasingly, when we step through the looking glass, other people are there as well.

2   Over the past decade, I have been engaged in the ethnographic and clinical study of how people negotiate the virtual and the "real" as they represent themselves on computer screens linked through the Internet. For many people, such experiences challenge what they have traditionally called "identity," which they are moved to recast in terms of multiple windows and parallel lives. Online life is not the only factor that is pushing them in this direction; there is no simple sense in which computers are causing a shift in notions of identity. It is, rather, that today's life on the screen dramatizes and concretizes a range of cultural trends that encourage us to think of identity in terms of multiplicity and flexibility.

Virtual Personae

3   In this essay, I focus on one key element of online life and its impact on identity: the creation and projection of constructed personae into virtual space. In cyberspace, it is well known, one's body can be represented by one's own textual description: The obese can be slender, the beautiful plain. The fact that self-presentation is written in text means that there is time to reflect upon and edit one's "composition," which makes it easier for the shy to be outgoing, the "nerdy" sophisticated. The relative anonymity of life on the screen—one has the choice of being known only by one's chosen "handle" or online name—gives people the chance to express often unexplored aspects of the self. Additionally,

multiple aspects of self can be explored in parallel. Online services offer their users the opportunity to be known by several different names. For example, it is not unusual for someone to be BroncoBill in one online community, ArmaniBoy in another, and MrSensitive in a third.

4   The online exercise of playing with identity and trying out new identities is perhaps most explicit in "role playing" virtual communities (such as Multi-User Domains, or MUDs) where participation literally begins with the creation of a persona (or several); but it is by no means confined to these somewhat exotic locations. In bulletin boards, newsgroups, and chat rooms, the creation of personae may be less explicit than on MUDs, but it is no less psychologically real. One IRC (Internet Relay Chat) participant describes her experience of online talk: "I go from channel to channel depending on my mood. . . . I actually feel a part of several of the channels, several conversations . . . I'm different in the different chats. They bring out different things in me." Identity play can happen by changing names and by changing places.

5   For many people, joining online communities means crossing a boundary into highly charged territory. Some feel an uncomfortable sense of fragmentation, some a sense of relief. Some sense the possibilities for self-discovery. A 26-year-old graduate student in history says, "When I log on to a new community and I create a character and know I have to start typing my description, I always feel a sense of panic. Like I could find out something I don't want to know." A woman in her late thirties who just got an account with America Online used the fact that she could create five "names" for herself on her account as a chance to "lay out all the moods I'm in—all the ways I want to be in different places on the system."

6   The creation of site-specific online personae depends not only on adopting a new name. Shifting of personae happens with a change of virtual place. Cycling through virtual environments is made possible by the existence of what have come to be called "windows" in modern computing environments. Windows are a way to work with a computer that makes it possible for the machine to place you in several contexts at the same time. As a user, you are attentive to just one of windows on your screen at any given moment, but in a certain sense, you are a presence in all of them at all times. You might be writing a paper in bacteriology and using your computer in several ways to help you: You are "present" to a word processing program on which you are taking notes and collecting thoughts, you are "present" to communications software that is in touch with a distant computer for collecting reference materials, you are "present" to a simulation program that is charting the growth of bacterial colonies when a new organism enters their ecology, and you are "present" to an online chat session where participants are discussing recent research in the field. Each of these activities takes place in a "window," and your identity on the computer is the sum of your distributed presence.

7   The development of the windows metaphor for computer interfaces was a technical innovation motivated by the desire to get people working more efficiently by "cycling through" different applications, much as time-sharing computers cycle through the computing needs of different people. But in practice, windows have become a potent metaphor for thinking about the self as a multiple, distributed, "time-sharing" system.

8   The self no longer simply plays different roles in different settings—something that people experience when, for example, one wakes up as a lover; makes breakfast as a mother; and drives to work as a lawyer. The windows metaphor suggests a distributed self that exists in many worlds and plays many roles at the same time. The "windows" enabled by a computer operating system support the metaphor, and cyberspace raises the experience to a higher power by translating the metaphor into a life experience of "cycling through."

Identity, Moratoria, and Play

9 Cyberspace, like all complex phenomena, has a range of psychological effects. For some people, it is a place to "act out" unresolved conflicts, to play and replay characterological difficulties on a new and exotic stage. For others, it provides an opportunity to "work through" significant personal issues, to use the new materials of cybersociality to reach for new resolutions. These more positive identity effects follow from the fact that for some, cyberspace provides what Erik Erikson ([1950]1963) would have called a "psychosocial moratorium," a central element in how he thought about identity development in adolescence. Although the term moratorium implies a "time out," what Erikson had in mind was not withdrawal. On the contrary, the adolescent moratorium is a time of intense interaction with people and ideas. It is a time of passionate friendships and experimentation. The adolescent falls in and out of love with people and ideas. Erikson's notion of the moratorium was not a "hold" on significant experiences but on their consequences. It is a time during which one's actions are, in a certain sense, not counted as they will be later in life. They are not given as much weight, not given the force of full judgment. In this context, experimentation can become the norm rather than a brave departure. Relatively consequence-free experimentation facilitates the development of a "core self," a personal sense of what gives life meaning that Erikson called "identity."

10   Erikson developed these ideas about the importance of a moratorium during the late 1950s and early 1960s. At that time, the notion corresponded to a common understanding of what "the college years" were about. Today, 30 years later, the idea of the college years as a consequence-free "time out" seems of another era. College is pre-professional, and AIDS has made consequence-free sexual experimentation an impossibility. The years associated with adolescence no longer seem a "time out." But if our culture no longer offers an adolescent moratorium, virtual communities often do. It is part of what makes them seem so attractive.

11   Erikson's ideas about stages did not suggest rigid sequences. His stages describe what people need to achieve before they can move ahead easily to another developmental task. For example, Erikson pointed out that successful intimacy in young adulthood is difficult if one does not come to it with a sense of who one is, the challenge of adolescent identity building. In real life, however, people frequently move on with serious deficits. With incompletely resolved "stages," they simply do the best they can. They use whatever materials they have at hand to get as much as they can of what they have missed.

Now virtual social life can play a role in these dramas of self-reparation. Time in cyberspace reworks the notion of the moratorium because it may now exist on an always-available "window."

Expanding One's Range in the Real

12 Case, a 34-year-old industrial designer happily married to a female co-worker, describes his real-life (RL) persona as a "nice guy," a "Jimmy Stewart type like my father." He describes his outgoing, assertive mother as a "Katharine Hepburn type." For Case, who views assertiveness through the prism of this Jimmy Stewart/Katharine Hepburn dichotomy, an assertive man is quickly perceived as "being a bastard." An assertive woman, in contrast, is perceived as being "modern and together." Case says that although he is comfortable with his temperament and loves and respects his father, he feels he pays a high price for his own low-key ways. In particular, he feels at a loss when it comes to confrontation, both at home and at work. Online, in a wide range of virtual communities, Case presents himself as females whom he calls his "Katharine Hepburn types." These are strong, dynamic, "out there" women who remind Case of his mother, who "says exactly what's on her mind." He tells me that presenting himself as a woman online has brought him to a point where he is more comfortable with confrontation in his RL as a man.

13   Case describes his Katharine Hepburn personae as "externalizations of a part of myself." In one interview with him, I used the expression "aspects of the self," and he picked it up eagerly, for his online life reminds him of how Hindu gods could have different aspects or subpersonalities, all the while being a whole self. In response to my question "Do you feel that you call upon your personae in real life?" Case responded:

> Yes, an aspect sort of clears its throat and says, "I can do this. You are being so amazingly conflicted over this and I know exactly what to do. Why don't you just let me do it?" . . . In real life, I tend to be extremely diplomatic, non-confrontational. I don't like to ram my ideas down anyone's throat. [Online] I can be, "Take it or leave it." All of my Hepburn characters are that way. That's probably why I play them. Because they are smart-mouthed, they will not sugarcoat their words.

In some ways, Case's description of his inner world of actors who address him and are able to take over negotiations is reminiscent of the language of people with multiple-personality disorder. But the contrast is significant: Case's inner actors are not split off from each other or from his sense of "himself." He experiences himself very much as a collective self, not feeling that he must goad or repress this or that aspect of himself into conformity. He is at ease, cycling through from Katharine Hepburn to Jimmy Stewart. To use analyst Philip Bromberg's language (1994), online life has helped Case learn how to "stand in the spaces between selves and still feel one, to see the multiplicity and still feel a unity." To use computer scientist Marvin Minsky's (1987) phrase, Case feels at ease cycling through his "society of mind," a notion of identity as distributed and heterogeneous. Identity, from the Latin *idem*, has been used habitually to refer to the sameness between two qualities. On the Internet, however, one can be many, and one usually is.

An Object to Think with for Thinking About Identity

14 In the late 1960s and early 1970s, I was first exposed to notions of identity and multiplicity. These ideas—most notably that there is no such thing as "the ego," that each of us is a multiplicity of parts, fragments, and desiring connections—surfaced in the intellectual hothouse of Paris; they presented the world according to such authors as Jacques Lacan, Gilles Deleuze, and Felix Guattari. But despite such ideal conditions for absorbing theory, my "French lessons" remained abstract exercises. These theorists of poststructuralism spoke words that addressed the relationship between mind and body, but from my point of view had little to do with my own.

15   In my lack of personal connection with these ideas, I was not alone. To take one example, for many people it is hard to accept any challenge to the idea of an autonomous ego. While in recent years, many psychologists, social theorists, psychoanalysts, and philosophers have argued that the self should be thought of as essentially decentered, the normal requirements of everyday life exert strong pressure on people to take responsibility for their actions and to see themselves as unitary actors. This disjuncture between theory (the unitary self is an illusion) and lived experience (the unitary self is the most basic reality) is one of the main reasons why multiple and decentered theories have been slow to catch on—or when they do, why we tend to settle back quickly into older, centralized ways of looking at things.

16   When, 20 years later, I used my personal computer and modem to join online communities, I had an experience of this theoretical perspective which brought it shockingly down to earth. I used language to create several characters. My textual actions are my actions—my words make things happen. I created selves that were made and transformed by language. And different personae were exploring different aspects of the self. The notion of a decentered identity was concretized by experiences on a computer screen. In this way, cyberspace becomes an object to think with for thinking about identity—an element of cultural bricolage.

17   Appropriable theories—ideas that capture the imagination of the culture at large—tend to be those with which people can become actively involved. They tend to be theories that can be "played" with. So one way to think about the social appropriability of a given theory is to ask whether it is accompanied by its own objects-to-think-with that can help it move out beyond intellectual circles.

18   For example, the popular appropriation of Freudian ideas had little to do with scientific demonstrations of their validity. Freudian ideas passed into the popular culture because they offered robust and down-to-earth objects to think with. The objects were not physical but almost-tangible ideas, such as dreams and slips of the tongue. People were able to play with such Freudian "objects." They became used to looking for them and manipulating them, both seriously and

not so seriously. And as they did so, the idea that slips and dreams betray an unconscious began to feel natural.

19   In Freud's work, dreams and slips of the tongue carried the theory. Today, life on the computer screen carries theory. People decide that they want to interact with others on a computer network. They get an account on a commercial service. They think that this will provide them with new access to people and information, and of course it does. But it does more. When they log on, they may find themselves playing multiple roles; they may find themselves playing characters of the opposite sex. In this way, they are swept up by experiences that enable them to explore previously unexamined aspects of their sexuality or that challenge their ideas about a unitary self. The instrumental computer, the computer that does things for us, has revealed another side: a subjective computer that does things *to* us as people, to our view of ourselves and our relationships, to our ways of looking at our minds. In simulation, identity can be fluid and multiple, a signifier no longer clearly points to a thing that is signified, and understanding is less likely to proceed through analysis than by navigation through virtual space.

20   Within the psychoanalytic tradition, many "schools" have departed from a unitary view of identity, among these the Jungian, object-relations, and Lacanian. In different ways, each of these groups of analysts was banished from the ranks of orthodox Freudians for such suggestions, or somehow relegated to the margins. As the United States became the center of psychoanalytic politics in the mid-twentieth century, ideas about a robust executive ego began to constitute the psychoanalytic mainstream.

21   But today, the pendulum has swung away from that complacent view of a unitary self. Through the fragmented selves presented by patients and through theories that stress the decentered subject, contemporary social and psychological thinkers are confronting what has been left out of theories of the unitary self. It is asking such questions as, What is the self when it functions as a society? What is the self when it divides its labors among its constituent "alters"? Those burdened by posttraumatic dissociative disorders suffer these questions; I am suggesting that inhabitants of virtual communities play with them. In our lives on the screen, people are developing ideas about identity as multiplicity through new social *practices* of identity as multiplicity.

22   With these remarks, I am not implying that chat rooms or MUDs or the option to declare multiple user names on America Online are causally implicated in the dramatic increase of people who exhibit symptoms of multiple-personality disorder (MPD), or that people on MUDs have MPD, or that MUDding (or online chatting) is like having MPD. I am saying that the many manifestations of multiplicity in our culture, including the adoption of online personae, are contributing to a general reconsideration of traditional, unitary notions of identity. Online experiences with "parallel lives" are part of the significant cultural context that supports new theorizing about nonpathological, indeed healthy, multiple selves.

23   In thinking about the self, *multiplicity* is a term that carries with it several centuries of negative associations, but such authors as Kenneth Gergen (1991), Emily Martin (1994), and Robert Jay Lifton (1993) speak in positive

terms of an adaptive, "flexible" self. The flexible self is not unitary, nor are its parts stable entities. A person cycles through its aspects, and these are themselves ever-changing and in constant communication with each other. Daniel Dennett (1991) speaks of the flexible self by using the metaphor of consciousness as multiple drafts, analogous to the experience of several versions of a document open on a computer screen, where the user is able to move between them at will. For Dennett, knowledge of these drafts encourages a respect for the many different versions, while it imposes a certain distance from them. Donna Haraway (1991), picking up on this theme of how a distance between self states may be salutory, equates a "split and contradictory self" with a "knowing self." She is optimistic about its possibilities: "The knowing self is partial in all its guises, never finished, whole, simply there and original; it is always constricted and stitched together imperfectly; and therefore able to join with another, to see together without claiming to be another." What most characterizes Haraway's and Dennett's models of a knowing self is that the lines of communication between its various aspects are open. The open communication encourages an attitude of respect for the many within us and the many within others.

24   Increasingly, social theorists and philosophers are being joined by psychoanalytic theorists in efforts to think about healthy selves whose resilience and capacity for joy comes from having access to their many aspects. For example, Philip Bromberg (1994) insists that our ways of describing "good parenting" must now shift away from an emphasis on confirming a child in a "core self" and onto helping a child develop the capacity to negotiate fluid transitions between self states. The healthy individual knows how to be many but to smooth out the moments of transition between states of self. Bromberg says: "Health is when you are multiple but feel a unity. Health is when different aspects of self can get to know each other and reflect upon each other." Here, within the psychoanalytic tradition, is a model of multiplicity as a state of easy traffic across selves, a conscious, highly articulated "cycling through."

From a Psychoanalytic to a Computer Culture?

25 Having literally written our online personae into existence, they can be a kind of Rorschach test. We can use them to become more aware of what we project into everyday life. We can use the virtual to reflect constructively on the real. Cyberspace opens the possibility for identity play, but it is very serious play. People who cultivate an awareness of what stands behind their screen personae are the ones most likely to succeed in using virtual experience for personal and social transformation. And the people who make the most of their lives on the screen are those who are able to approach it in a spirit of self-reflection. What does my behavior in cyberspace tell me about what I want, who I am, what I may not be getting in the rest of my life?

26   As a culture, we are at the end of the Freudian century. Freud, after all, was a child of the nineteenth century; of course, he was carrying the baggage of a very different scientific sensibility than our own. But faced with the challenges

of cyberspace, our need for a practical philosophy of self-knowledge, one that does not shy away from issues of multiplicity, complexity, and ambivalence, that does not shy away from the power of symbolism, from the power of the word, from the power of identity play, has never been greater as we struggle to make meaning from our lives on the screen. It is fashionable to think that we have passed from a psychoanalytic culture to a computer culture—that we no longer need to think in terms of Freudian slips but rather of information processing errors. But the reality is more complex. It is time to rethink our relationship to the computer culture and psychoanalytic culture as a proudly held joint citizenship.

References

Bromberg, Philip. 1994. "Speak that I May See You: Some Reflections on Dissociation, Reality, and Psychoanalytic Listening." *Psychoanalytic Dialogues* 4 (4): 517–47.

Dennett, Daniel. 1991. *Consciousness Explained.* Boston: Little, Brown.

Erikson, Erik. [1950] 1963. *Childhood and Society,* 2nd ed. New York: Norton.

Gergen, Kenneth. 1991. *The Saturated Self-Dilemmas of Identity in Contemporary Life.* New York: Basic Books.

Haraway, Donna. 1991. "The Actors are Cyborg, Nature Is Coyote, and the Geography Is Elsewhere: Postscript to 'Cyborgs at Large'." In *Technoculture,* edited by Constance Penley and Andrew Ross. Minneapolis: University of Minnesota Press.

Lifton, Robert Jay. 1993. *The Protean Self: Human Resilience in an Age of Fragmentation.* New York: Basic Books.

Martin, Emily. 1994. *Flexible Bodies: Tracking Immunity in American Culture from the Days of Polio to the Days of AIDS.* Boston: Beacon Press.

Minsky, Martin. 1987. *The Society of Mind.* New York: Simon & Schuster.

Turkle, Sherry. [1978] 1990. *Psychoanalytic Politics: Jacques Lacan and Freud's French Revolution.* 2nd ed. New York: Guilford Press.

————1984. *The Second Self: Computers and the Human Spirit.* New York: Simon & Schuster.

————1995. *Life on the Screen: Identity in the Age of the Internet.* New York: Simon & Schuster.

Review Questions

1. As she draws upon the ideas of psychologist Erik Erikson, how does Turkle examine the implications of creating multiple cyber-personalities on the Internet?

2. For Turkle, how did the Internet help support the theory that the "unitary self" is an illusion?

3. What is the basis of the analogy between Freud's theories about dreams and slips of the tongue and people assuming multiple identities on the Internet?

Discussion and Writing Suggestions

1. For Turkle, one of the most exciting—and healthy—aspects of the Internet is that it allows us to create and explore multiple personas and personalities for ourselves. To what extent have you experienced this sense of creation and re-creation of yourself as you communicate with individuals and groups in various cybercontexts?

2. Turkle discusses Case, the man who cycles between his "Katherine Hepburn" and "Jimmy Stewart" personas. What is the significance of this phenomenon? Turkle argues that this "collective self" phenomenon is different from multiple personality disorder, in that there is unity in multiplicity. To what extent do you agree?

3. Turkle writes, "In our lives on the screen, people are developing ideas about identity as multiplicity through new social *practices* of identity as multiplicity" (paragraph 21). Write a paper using this sentence as a thesis. Develop specific examples from your own experience or the experiences of people you know.

4. Turkle argues that there is a difference between people who have multiple personality disorder (MPD) and people who assume multiple personalities or who explore multiple aspects of themselves on the Internet. What is the difference? To what extent do you agree with Turkle's ideas on this point?

5. Turkle contends that we need "a practical philosophy of self-knowledge, one that does not shy away from issues of multiplicity, complexity, and ambivalence, that does not shy away from the power of symbolism, from the power of the word, from the power of identity play" (paragraph 26). Assuming that you agree, how should a philosophy of such self-knowledge be fostered? Do schools have a role here? Or do adolescents need to develop such awareness on their own?

Boy, You Fight Like a Girl
Alex Pham

In the previous article, Sherry Turkle discusses how people on the Net are able to "cycle" through multiple personas. This phenomenon is exemplified in a particular Internet subculture: online gaming. In "Boy, You Fight Like a Girl," Los Angeles Times staff writer Alex Pham discusses the penchant of many online gamers for gender-switching—and the reactions they encounter. This article first appeared in the Los Angeles Times on 17 May 2001.

1   In her flowing crimson cape, thigh-high leather boots and metal-studded red leather bustier, Cardinal is a bow-and-arrow-toting *femme fatale.*

2   But not only is Cardinal not real—she's a character in the popular computer game "Ultima Online"—she's not really female. Cardinal is the alter-ego of Kenn Gold, a 33-year-old former Army sergeant with thorny green-and-black tattoos covering both of his muscular arms.

3   As one of the thousands of online gamers who play characters of the opposite gender, Gold created Cardinal as a tactical move: Female characters generally get treated better in the male-dominated world of virtual adventuring. Yet he was unprepared for the shock of seeing the world through a woman's eyes.

4   "I can't even begin to tell you how funny it is to watch guys trip all over themselves and be dumb," Gold said. "It's very amusing to see them try to be really sophisticated and cool, when they're turning out to be just the opposite."

5   Changing genders has long been a piece of online role-playing games—part juvenile mischievousness, part theatrical posing and part psychological release. But as the genre explodes—online games now attract hundreds of thousands of players—it's prompted a blossoming of cross-gender experimentation and created sexually amorphous virtual worlds that some revel in and others curse.

6   Men find they must constantly brush off unwanted advances, and their female characters are not taken as seriously. But they also find it easier to chat with other players and escape the relentless competition among male characters.

7   The story is the same for women who play men to avoid cheesy pick-up lines. They discover that moving among predominantly male groups involves participating in constant one-upmanship. And as their male characters move up the ranks, they fear losing the respect of other players if their true gender is discovered.

8   Online adventures are one of the fastest-growing segments of the computer game market, with titles such as "EverQuest," "Asheron's Call" and "Ultima Online." And it's not just kids with nothing better to do. Teachers, nurses, construction workers and accountants create alter-egos and join with others to explore virtual realms and slay imaginary beasts.

9   In "EverQuest," the most popular of the games with more than 360,000 subscribers, players spend an average of 20 hours a week online. Players call it "EverCrack" because it's so addictive. Much of the allure is the ability to put mundane daily life aside and pretend to be something they're not—an elf, a woodsman, a knight.

10   The ultimate challenge: to be another gender. Although some gamers swap genders to explore their own sexuality—a tiny fraction are cross-dressers in real life—the vast majority do it as a test of skill.

11   "There's a long history of this as a performance genre," said Henry Jenkins, director of comparative media studies at the Massachusetts Institute of Technology. "There is Glenda Jackson who plays Hamlet. Dustin Hoffman played Tootsie. It's a great challenge, a way to show virtuosity."

Virtual Experience Can Have Real Ramifications

12 Encouraging the make-believe are online avatars—the graphic representation of a player's character. Scantily clad females are impossibly thin and full-bosomed. Males are muscular and rendered in heroic proportions. As a result, the contrast

between avatar and player can be striking, even when gamers are playing their own gender.

13   In "EverQuest," only 20% of subscribers are female, but 40% of avatars are. Even accounting for the number of women who play male characters, that amounts to roughly half the female characters in "EverQuest" being played by men such as Gold.

14   This might be fun and games, but as any serious player of such adventures will attest, online experiences—with their power to make people laugh, cry or become angry—can have real-life consequences.

15   "It certainly makes you more aware of how men treat women," said Ralph Koster, 29, who has played a female character for years in an early online text-based game, "LegendMUD." "You're more aware that there are a lot of gendered interactions that we don't recognize as such. It makes you think more about what you're saying and how you're sending subtle messages without being aware of it."

16   For instance, "if you're a female character, just something as innocent as smiling might get read wrong." And if a male character tries to help a female character, it's assumed he wants something. Often, he does.

17   Mark Wight, a 28-year-old heavy-equipment operator from Ramona, Calif., said he wanted to hook his female character, Cytarack, into a hunting group so she could gain experience and advance in the game.

18   "There was this one guy who traveled halfway across the game's virtual continent to hunt with her, but it seemed he was more interested in other things," Wight said, explaining that some players engage in online "cybersex" with each other—basically a modern twist on phone sex in which acts are described in real-time chat. "I don't play her anymore because people get other ideas. Many adults play because they're looking for somebody on the other side."

19   In his Mission Viejo apartment, Gold jockeys two computers as he maneuvers Cardinal around "Ultima Online's" virtual realm. He chain smokes Camels, surrounded by stacks of "X-Men" comic books and an exhaustive collection of "Star Trek" video tapes.

20   In the Army, Gold commanded a Black Hawk helicopter maintenance crew. These days, he's a graduate student in English at Cal State Fullerton, where he teaches freshman composition.

21   At this moment, however, he is Cardinal, a spell-casting huntress on horseback with a mane of pink hair, leather gloves and black tights.

22   Gold confesses that he has another female character—this one in "EverQuest"—whom he declines to name because no one knows she is played by a man. His character is a longtime member of a "guild," a band of players who agree to play together.

23   Many of his band would be upset, explained Gold, who spends about 35 hours each week playing "EverQuest" and "Ultima Online." "They'd feel they couldn't trust me anymore. I'd be ostracized. These are guys who think they're worldly, and it scares them to think that there are women they're interested in who may actually be guys."

24   The deception cuts both ways. Louise, a 44-year-old Sacramento house painter who declined to give her last name, plays a male character and is the

leader of her "EverQuest" guild. She said she fears that if the members of her guild were to discover not only her gender but her age, she would lose their respect.

25   "Some of them are teenage boys," Louise said. "I don't think they'd take it too well. There's a belief that women can't be aggressive. But that's not true at all. I love to be aggressive. It gives me a real adrenaline rush."

26   In daily life, though, she is shy. It is only when she slips into a role-playing mode that Louise says she can fully express her aggressive nature without fear of being belittled.

27   But because online relationships can be as intense as their real-world counterparts, there is the potential to wreak psychological havoc.

Emboldened Under Veil of Online Anonymity

28 Gold five years ago attended an online wedding involving two characters in a game called "Meridian 59." Once the vows were exchanged, the bride declared that she was actually a man and that the two had had cybersex, humiliating the groom in front of their virtual guests. It was all a revenge plot the "bride" had devised because the groom had killed another of the player's characters months earlier in the game.

29   What makes such behavior possible, of course, is the anonymous nature of the Web. Online players are less accountable for their words and, therefore, less inhibited with their expressions.

30   "The Internet makes you bolder," said Rick Hall, a game producer at Origin Systems, the company that created "Ultima Online." "If you're the type of guy who wouldn't approach a girl in real life, you can do it online. And if you get shot down, who cares."

31   Similarly, anonymity gives people the freedom to emphasize a particular personality trait or mood they would stifle in real life. Many players maintain a stable of characters they can pull out to match their mood.

32   Geoffrey Zatkin, a senior game designer for the company that wrote "EverQuest," rotates between three characters—a male fencer, a male rogue and a female druid. Each represents a facet of his identity. The fencer is witty, the rogue aloof and the druid outgoing. Zatkin plays the female character when feeling chatty.

33   For Ramin Shokrizade, playing female characters allows him to escape the competitiveness that pervades the male culture.

34   "Among power gamers, it gets to be very competitive," said Shokrizade, 35, an exercise trainer and math and science tutor in Palm Desert who says he plays online role-playing games an average of 80 hours a week. "If you're female, they don't do that with you. I enjoy chatting with other players and helping people out. I've been a track coach for 15 years, so I'm used to helping people. This is just a way of practicing what I know."

35   Still, Shokrizade was surprised at how differently he was treated as a female character.

36   "It was strange," he said. "If you don't mind being in a supportive role, life is a lot easier for you. You're not expected to be in a leadership role."

37   Players who wish to escape gender constraints online ironically find themselves in a medium that, if anything, reinforces sexual stereotypes.

38   "Females tend to get in groups faster, but we get harassed," said Aaron Harvey, a 26-year-old freelance Web designer from Ventura who plays a female gnome in "EverQuest." "People are constantly trying to pick us up. I've been offered [more powerful weaponry] for cybersex, which I turn down rather quickly."

39   Often, players who gender-swap online are reluctant to talk about their reasons.

40   "It's not something you would talk about or be proud of," said Pavel Curtis, who developed a well-known text-based online community called LambdaMOO when he was a researcher at Xerox's Palo Alto Research Center. "Society doesn't see it as a healthy form of experimentation. At best, it's seen as duplicitous. At worst, it's sick and perverted."

41   Such strongly held views underscore how important gender identity is to people—even online, where physical appearances are not supposed to matter.

42   "We tailor our actions based on who we think we're talking to," said Amy Bruckman, assistant professor in the College of Computing at Georgia Tech in Atlanta. "Because these factors shape our interactions, we're often uncomfortable when we don't know these cues on age, race and gender."

43   As a result, much effort goes into spotting fakes. The clues cited by players are telling indications of how people perceive gender. Bruckman recalled a time when she tried to pass as a male character but was instantly pegged as an impostor. How? "It was just my style of speaking. I used long sentences with lots of adjectives, which is seen as stereotypic of females," Bruckman said.

44   "Everybody, it seems, needs to know," Koster said. "It's like a void that needs to be filled, and it's deeply ingrained in our culture. There's this notion that the Internet will give us this utopia where gender, age and race don't matter. The idea that we'll all be disembodied floating lights just ain't gonna happen."

Discussion and Writing Suggestions

1. Do you or anyone you know engage in online gaming? To what extent can you confirm the kinds of behavior Pham discusses in "Boy, You Fight Like a Girl"—particularly, gender switching and the reaction to gender switching? What is your take on this phenomenon?

2. What kind of gender stereotypes are revealed in the experiences of people who engage in gender-switching while participating in online games? To what extent do you think such gender stereotyping is aggravated by the very experience of participating in such games? That is, to what extent might the anonymity of the Internet make sexists of people who, in their "real world" interpersonal relations, generally behave with more tolerance and sensitivity? To what extent (on the other hand) might online gaming attract people with sexist mindsets?

3. How does the type of online behavior discussed in Pham's article tie into Dyson's observations on Internet anonymity and Turkle's discussion of multiple personas? To what extent are Dyson, on the one hand, and Turkle, on the other, likely to regard gender-switching during online gaming as psychologically healthy?

4. Amy Bruckman recalls that she tried to pass as a male while playing online games, but was immediately spotted because of her "style of speaking." In general, do you believe that males and females have different styles of speaking (or writing)? If so, what characterizes these different styles? Do you think you are likely to be successful in passing yourself off as a member of the opposite sex?

   You might try an experiment along these lines: divide a group of people into an equal number of males and females. Have some in each group adopt personas in which they switch genders. Have people write an anonymous series of notes to one another, asking and answering questions, devising a system by which the notes are transmitted from one person to another. (E-mailing would work only if anonymity can be maintained; otherwise, notes would have to be written on paper.) Have writers attempt to determine the actual genders of their anonymous correspondents. Ask those people who successfully determined the gender of their correspondents (as opposed to just guessed correctly) what were the "giveaways."

The 15-Year-Old Legal Whiz
Michael Lewis

The last few selections have focused on how people create new identities for themselves on the Internet—or perhaps more accurately, how they create new aspects of themselves as they communicate online. In particular, Sherry Turkle focused on the creation of new selves as an exploration of different personas. And in the introduction to this chapter, we described the "Robert Klingler" affair, in which an individual claiming to be the North American head of a major European automobile manufacturer succeeded in getting a couple of his "Diary" entries published in the online magazine Slate *before the editors realized that they had been taken in by a skillful con artist.*

In the following article, Michael Lewis, a contributing editor for the New York Times Magazine, *details the fascinating account of how a 15-year-old with no legal training posed as an expert attorney on the Web—and not only got away with it but was confirmed in his expert status, both by his "clients" and by actual, practicing attorneys! That this is possible raises questions not only about the special status of the law as an elite profession, but also about how the Internet tends to make anyone with a little knowledge into an authority. This article first appeared in the* New York Times Magazine *on 15 July 2001 and, as adapted below, appears in Lewis's book* Next: The Future Just Happened *(2001).*

1   In the summer of 2000, in a desert town called Perris, halfway between Los Angeles and Palm Springs, lived a 15-year-old boy named Marcus Arnold. His parents had immigrated to Perris from Belize, by way of South-Central L.A. Why anyone would move to Perris from anywhere was not immediately clear. Perris was one of those non-places that America specializes in creating. One day it was a flat hazy stretch of sand and white rock beneath an endless blue sky; the next some developer had laid out a tract of 25,000 identical homes; and the day after that it was teeming with people who were there, mainly, because it was not someplace else.

2   Marcus lived with his parents and his twin brother in a small brick house. A great big bear of a boy, Marcus was six feet tall and weighed maybe 200 pounds. He did not walk but lumbered from the computer to the front door, then back again. The computer squatted on a faux antique desk in the alcove between the dining room and the living room, which were as immaculately kept as showrooms in a model home. It was the only computer in the house, he said. In theory, the family shared it; in practice, it belonged to him. He now needed as much time on it as he could get, as he was a leading expert on AskMe.com. His field was the law.

3   The blue screen displayed the beginning of an answer to a question on AskMe.com Marcus had bashed out before I arrived:

> Your son should not be in jail or on trial. According to Miranda versus Arizona the person to be arrested must be read his rights before he was asked any questions. If your son was asked any questions before the reading of his rights he should not be in prison. If you want me to help you further write me back on this board privately.

4   The keyboard vanished beneath Marcus's jumbo hands and another page on AskMe.com popped up on the screen. Marcus wanted to show me the appallingly weak answer to a question that had been offered by one of the real lawyers on the site. "I can always spot a crummy attorney," he said. "There are people on the Web site who have no clue what they're talking about, they are just there to get rankings and to sell their services and to get paid." Down went his paws, out of sight went the keyboard, and up popped one of Marcus's favourite Web sites. This one listed the menus on death row in Texas. Photographs of men put to death by the state appeared next to hideous lists of the junk food they'd ordered for their last meals.

5   Marcus had stumbled upon AskMe.com late in the spring of 2000. He was studying for his biology exam and looking for an answer to a question. He noticed that someone had asked a question about the law to which he knew the answer. Then another. A thought occurred: why not answer them himself? To become an official expert he only needed to fill in a form, which asked him, among other things, his age. He did this on June 5—a day enshrined in Marcus's mind. "I always wanted to be an attorney since I was, like, 12," he said, "but I couldn't do it because everyone is going to be, 'like, what? Some 12-year-old kid is going to give me legal advice?'"

6   "They'd feel happier with a 15-year-old?"

7   He drew a deep breath and made a face that indicated that he took this to be a complicated question. "So when I first went on AskMe," he said, "I told everybody I was 20, roughly about 20, and everyone believed me." Actually, he claimed to be 25. To further that impression he adopted the handle "LawGuy 1975."

8   Once he became an expert, Marcus's career took on a life of its own. The AskMe rankings were driven by the number of questions the expert answered, the speed of his replies, and the quality of those replies, as judged by the recipients, who bestowed on them a rating of between one and five stars. By July 1 Marcus was ranked number 10 out of 150 or so experts in AskMe.com's criminal law division, many of whom were actual lawyers. As he tells it, that's when he decided to go for the gold. "When I hit the top 10 I got some people who were like, 'Congratulations, blah blah blah.' So my adrenaline was pumping to answer more questions. I was just, like, 'You know what, let me show these people I know what I'm doing'." He needed to inspire even more people to ask him questions, and to reply to them quickly, and in a way that prompted them to reward him with lots of stars. To that end he updated the page that advertised his services. When he was done it said:

9   I am a law expert with two years of formal training in the law. I will help anyone I can! I been involved in trials, legal studies and certain forms of jurisprudence. I am not accredited by the state bar association yet to practise law . . . sincerely, Justin Anthony Wyrick, Jr.

10   "Justin was the name I always wanted—besides mine," Marcus said. Justin Anthony Wyrick Jr. had a more authoritative ring to it, in Marcus's opinion, and in a lot of other people's, too. On one day Marcus received and answered 110 questions.

11   The more questions Marcus answered, the more people who logged onto the boards looking for legal advice wanted to speak only to him. In one two-week stretch he received 943 legal questions and answered 939. When I asked him why he hadn't answered the other four, a look of profound exasperation crossed his broad face. "Traffic law," he said. "I'm sorry, I don't know traffic law." By the end of July he was the No. 3 rated expert in criminal law on AskMe.com. Beneath him in the rankings were 125 licensed attorneys and a wild assortment of ex-cops and ex-cons. The next youngest person on the board was 31.

12   In a few weeks Marcus had created a new identity for himself: legal wizard. School he now viewed not so much as preparation for a future legal career as material for an active one. He investigated a boondoggle taken by the local school board and discovered it had passed off on the taxpayer what to him appeared to be the expenses for a private party. He brought that, and a lot more, up at a public hearing. Why grown-up people with grown-up legal problems took him seriously was the great mystery Marcus didn't much dwell on— except to admit that it had nothing to do with his legal training. He'd had no legal training, formal or informal. On the top of the Arnold family desk was a thin dictionary, plus stacks and stacks of court cases people from AskMe who had come to rely on Marcus's advice had mimeographed and sent to him, for his review. (The clients sent him the paperwork and he wrote motions, which the clients then passed on to licensed attorneys for submission to a court.) But there was nothing on the desk, or in the house, even faintly resembling a book

about the law. The only potential sources of legal information were the family computer and the big-screen TV.

13 "Where do you find books about the law?" I asked.

14 "I don't," he said, tap-tap-tapping away on his keyboard. "Books are boring. I don't like reading."

15 "So you go on legal Web sites?"

16 "No."

17 "Well, when you got one of these questions did you research your answer?

18 "No, never. I just know it."

19 "You just know it."

20 "Exactly."

21 The distinct whiff of an alternate reality lingered in the air. It was just then that Marcus's mother, Priscilla, came through the front door. She was a big lady, tee-tering and grunting beneath jumbo-sized sacks of groceries. A long box of donuts jutted out of the top of one.

22 "Hi Marcus, what you doing?" she said, gasping for breath.

23 "Just answering questions," he said.

24 "What were you answering?" she asked, with real pleasure. She radiated pride.

25 "I got one about an appellate bond—how to get one," he said. "Another one about the Supreme Court. A petition to dismiss something."

26 "We got some chili cheese dogs here."

27 "That's cool."

28 "Where did you acquire your expertise?" I asked.

29 "Marcus was born with it!" shouted Priscilla. Having no idea how to respond, I ignored her.

30 "What do you mean?" Marcus asked me. He was genuinely puzzled by my question.

31 "Where does your information come from?"

32 "I don't know," he said. "Like, I really just don't know."

33 "How can you not know where knowledge comes from?" I asked.

34 "After, like, watching so many TV shows about the law," he said, "it's just like you know everything you need to know." He gave a little mock shiver. "It's scary. I just know these things."

35 Again Priscilla shouted from the kitchen. "Marcus has got a gift!"

36 She shouted from the kitchen: "Marcus had his gift in the womb. I could feel it."

37 "What do you think these people would have done if you weren't there to answer their questions?" I asked Marcus.

38 "They would have paid an attorney," he said. But as he said it his big grin van-ished and a cloud shadowed his broad, open face. It may well have been that he was recalling the public relations fiasco that followed the discovery by a hun-dred or so licensed attorneys on AskMe.com the true identity of the new expert moving up their ranks. In any case, he lifted his giant palms toward me in the manner of the Virgin Mary resisting the entreaties of the Holy Spirit, and said, "Look, I'm not out there to take business from other people. That's not my job."

39 "But you think that legal expertise is overrated?"

40   "Completely."

41   Once Marcus attained his high rankings on AskMe.com, a lot of people he didn't really know began to ask for his phone number and his fee structure. For the first time, his conscience began to trouble him. He decided it was time to come clean with his age. To do this he changed his expert profile. Where it had read "legal expert," it now read "15-year-old intern attorney expert." A few hours after he posted his confession, hostile messages came hurtling toward him. A few of them came from his "clients," but most came from the lawyers and others who competed with him for rankings and prizes and publicity. A small war broke out on the message boards, with Marcus accusing the lawyers of ganging up on him to undermine his number three ranking and the lawyers accusing Marcus of not knowing what he was talking about. The lawyers began to pull up Marcus's old answers and bestow on them lowly one-star ratings— thus dragging down his average. (At the time, third parties could score expert answers; after the incident AskMe.com changed its policy.) Then they did something even worse: asked him detailed questions about the finer points of the law. When he couldn't supply similarly detailed answers, they laid into him. Marcus's replies to the e-mail lashings read less like the work of a defense attorney than of a man trying to talk his torturers into untying him:

42   "I am reporting your abusive response, for it hurts my reputation and my dignity as an expert on this board."

43   "Please don't e-mail me threats."

44   "You really are picking on me."

45   "Leave me alone! I am not even a practising attorney!"

46   "Please, I beg of you, stop sending me letters saying that you'll be watching me, because you are scaring my parents."

47   "I really just want to be friends."

48   "Can't we just be friends?"

49   To which Marcus's wittiest assailant replied, "In your last two posts you've ended by asking that I be your friend. That's like the mortally wounded gladiator asking to be friends with the lion."

50   On the one hand, the whole episode was absurd—Marcus Arnold was a threat to no one but himself and, perhaps, the people who sought his advice. To practice law you still needed a license, and no 15-year-old boy was going to be granted one. At the same time, Marcus had wandered into an arena live with combustible particles. The Internet had arrived at an embarrassing moment for the law. The knowledge gap between lawyers and non-lawyers had been shrinking for some time, and the Internet was closing it further.

51   Legal advice was being supplied over the Internet, often for free—and it wasn't just lawyers doing the supplying. Students, cops, dicks, even ex-cons went onto message boards to help people with their questions and cases. At the bottom of this phenomenon was a corrosively democratic attitude toward legal knowledge. "If you think about the law," the past chairman of the American Bar Association, Richard S. Granat, told the *New York Times,* in an attempt to explain the boom in do-it-yourself Internet legal services, "a large component is just information. Information itself can go a long way to help solve legal problems."

52   Marcus had been publicly humiliated by the real lawyers, but it didn't stop him from offering more advice. Then the clients began to speak. With pretty much one voice they said: Leave the kid alone! A lot of people seemed to believe that any 15-year-old who had risen so high in the ranks of AskMe.com legal experts must be some kind of wizard. They began to seek him out more than ever before; they wanted his, and only his, advice. In days Marcus's confidence was fully restored. "You always have your critics," he said. "I mean, with the real lawyers, it's a pride issue. They can't let someone who could be their son beat them. Plus they have a lot more time than I do. I'm always stretched for time. Six hours a day of school, four hours of homework, sometimes I can't get on line to answer the questions until after dinner."

53   Marcus's ranking rebounded. Two weeks after he disclosed his age, he was on the rise; two weeks later he hit No. 1. The legal advice he gave to a thousand or so people along the way might not have withstood the scrutiny of the finest legal minds. Some of it was the sort of stuff you could glean directly from Judge Judy; more of it was a simple restating of the obvious in a friendly tone. Marcus didn't have much truck with the details; he didn't handle complexity terribly well. But that was the whole the point of him—he didn't need to. A lot of what a real lawyer did was hand out simple information in a way that made the client feel served, and this Marcus did well. He may have had only the vaguest idea of what he was talking about and a bizarre way of putting what he did know. But out there in the void, they loved him.

Review Questions

1. How did Marcus Arnold's legal career start, according to Lewis?
2. How did Marcus rapidly climb in the AskMe rankings?
3. From what sources did Marcus get the answers he was providing to people who asked him questions about the law?
4. What, for Lewis, is the chief lesson of Marcus's success as a legal expert?
5. How did Marcus Arnold fall—and then rise again?

Discussion and Writing Suggestions

1. In an earlier version of this article, Lewis wrote that role theorists claim that "we have no 'self' as such. Our selves are merely the masks we wear in response to the social situations in which we find ourselves. The Internet had offered up a new set of social situations, to which people had responded by grabbing for a new set of masks." To what extent do you agree with this assertion? Support your response with illustrations from your own experience or the

experiences of people you know. Relate your comments at some point to Lewis's discussion of Marcus Arnold.

2. To what extent do you approve of what Marcus Arnold did? Do you think that he is a healthy or an unhealthy symptom of what is happening on the Internet? To what extent would you be prepared to seek legal advice from Arnold?

3. In an earlier version of this article, Lewis argued that Marcus "was using the Internet the way adults often use their pasts." But since young people like Marcus do not have much of a past, they turn to the future and "imagine themselves into some future adult world." To what extent do you think that this theory accounts for the fascination of many young people for the Internet—i.e., that it provides a means of fantasizing about their lives in the future?

4. Go to <www.AskMe.com>, find a category and subcategory with which you are reasonably familiar, and browse through the answers to questions that some of the experts have provided. How good are their answers? Could you have provided better ones? (Try a few.) Do the more reliable and complete answers appear to come from experts who—according to their own description of their qualifications and credentials—have had the most training and experience?

SYNTHESIS ACTIVITIES

1. Write an article for a newsmagazine exploring the various facets of the Internet revolution. Use the selection by Leonard as a model for survey articles of this type, but avoid using more than one or two of Leonard's own examples. Draw upon not only Leonard but also Lee, Dvorak, Snider, Parsons, Turkle, Pham, and Lewis, as well as some of the brief selections on computer-mediated communication (CMC) in Chapter 4 (pages 97–108). Focus in particular on how the Internet provides a means of exploring and defining aspects of our identity. Keep the article relatively objective—that is, it should essentially take the form of an *explanatory* synthesis—but don't be afraid of venturing mildly argumentative assessments of the e-mail phenomenon or the directions in which our Internet culture is headed.

2. Argue that the net effects of the cyberrevolution are positive—*or* that they are negative. In formulating your argument, acknowledge and explain that e-mail has both positive and negative aspects, but assert that on balance, the positive outweighs the negative (or vice versa) in terms of how e-mail has affected both private and public discourse. Draw upon as many articles and selections in this chapter (and in the CMC section of Chapter 4) as will be helpful in supporting your case.

3. How has the Internet changed the way we think about identity? Draw upon the selections in the latter part of the chapter—Daum, Dyson, Lee, Dvorak, Snider, Turkle, Pham, and Lewis—to explore this topic. Consider such matters as (1) the identity or identities we create when we send messages; (2) the implied identities of those who send us messages; (3) the relationship or conflict between our actual identity and our implied identity or identities (see, especially, Turkle on this subject); (4) the relationship between our physical selves and our implied selves.

4. In her article "Cyberspace and Identity," Sherry Turkle points out that starting in the 1960s, many people who studied identity concluded that "there is no such thing as 'the ego,' that each of us is a multiplicity of parts, fragments, and desiring connections" (paragraph 14). Similarly, in an earlier version of his article on 15-year-old legal expert Marcus Arnold, Michael Lewis noted some recent ideas about the self promulgated by role theorists, who argue that "we have no 'self' as such. Our selves are merely the masks we wear in response to the social situations in which we find ourselves. The Internet had offered up a new set of social situations, to which people had responded by grabbing up a new set of masks."

   Using either the statement by Turkle or the statement by Lewis as an analytical principle, discuss particular anecdotes and events recounted in some of the selections in this chapter. Most of the authors represented in the chapter have something to say on this matter; but focus, in particular, on Leonard, Lee, Snider, Parsons, Daum, Pham, and Lewis.

5. Daum's experience with online romance is common, if not universal. While some lucky souls do indeed find their future mates over the Internet, most who attempt online romance find that the relationships burn brightly for awhile and then smolder and die—particularly, once the parties actually meet.

   Why should this be so? What accounts for the eventual failure of so many online romances? Aren't we expressing our "true" selves in e-mail messages? Or are the selves we project simply idealized versions of our selves that cannot survive in the "real world"? To what extent is there an inherent conflict, a tension, between our physical selves and our cyberselves? In your response, draw not only upon Daum and other selections in this chapter, but also upon some of the short readings on online romance (e.g., Suler, Wolcott, and Morris) in Chapter 4.

6. Reread the final paragraph (paragraph 34) of Daum's article, "Virtual Love." Reflecting on the course of her relationship with PFSlider, she writes, "The world had proved to be too cluttered and fast for us, too polluted to allow the thing we'd attempted through technology ever to grow in the earth." Consider this thought, and extract an analytical principle that can be applied in other contexts.

For example, what is she saying about romance? What is she saying about technology? What does she mean by "cluttered and fast" and "polluted"? (Note also the "branches and bodies and falling debris that make up the physical world" in the paragraph's final sentence.) Write an analysis of some situation or set of situations outside of this article, using the principle you infer from Daum's paragraph. You might want to bring in particular examples from other articles in the chapter, such as those by Leonard, Dvorak, Snider, Turkle, Pham, and Lewis.

7. The e-mail revolution appears to have changed some of the rules of communication, often for the worse. One of the more unpleasant developments of the new medium is "flaming"—the sending of abusive, insulting, sometimes vicious messages, or even threats, to another with whom one may have a minor disagreement. Considerably less serious, but still annoying to many e-mail recipients, is the tendency of some writers not to use punctuation or capital letters, indeed not to bother proofreading (or even signing) their messages at all. While some believe that e-mail messages do not require strict adherence to stylistic conventions, others take issue. In *The Elements of E-Mail Style*, authors David Angell and Brent Heslop assert, "Using all lower-case letters is annoying for the recipient and can result in your message being misunderstood or not read at all."*

    Do you regard such disregard of conventions, intentional or not, as breaches of communication etiquette or are they simply part of the distinctive nature of e-mail culture? Attempt to explain these and perhaps other negative features of Internet communication, drawing upon some of the selections that you have read in this chapter and in the CMC readings in Chapter 4.

8. In a piece entitled "The Return of the Word," Adam Gopnik writes, "E-mail has succeeded brilliantly for the same reason that the videophone failed miserably: what we actually want from our exchanges is the minimum human contact commensurate with the need to connect with other people. 'Only connect.' Yes, but *only* connect."† What do you think Gopnik means? Why "*only* connect"? Just what kind of contact do we crave, do we need from our Internet correspondents? In your response, draw upon some of the following selections: Leonard, Dvorak, Snider, Parsons, Daum, Turkle, Pham, and Lewis.

---

* David Angell and Brent Heslop, *The Elements of E-Mail Style: Communicate Effectively via Electronic Mail* (Reading, MA: Addison-Wesley, 1994).

† Adam Gopnik, "The Return of the Word," *New Yorker*, 6 December 1999. The quotation "Only connect" is from *Howards End* (1910) by E. M. Forster.

RESEARCH ACTIVITIES

1. Explore some aspect of online romance. What services are available for people who want to find love on the Internet? What are the benefits and drawbacks of using such services? What are the special thrills and the hazards of seeking love online? How is online romance similar to and different from the old-fashioned kind? What happens when two people who have met and fallen in love (or lust) online meet in person? Begin your research by reviewing some of the selections in this chapter that focus on these matters, and then pursue the matter further by seeking additional sources. (Note in particular an article by Jennifer Egan, "Love in the Time of No Time," which appeared in the 23 November 2003 issue of the *New York Times Magazine*.)

2. One of the most popular offshoots of e-mailing is "instant messaging," a process that allows people to have e-mail exchanges in real time, one that represents a kind of hybrid between the letter (in that messages are written) and the telephone (in that an exchange takes place over a relatively brief, unbroken period of time). Write an article for a newsmagazine exploring the phenomenon of instant messaging—how it got started, why it has become so popular, how it became a legal issue (when America Online initially refused to license its instant-messaging software), where it seems headed.

3. As Andrew Leonard explains in "We've Got Mail—Always," e-mail was invented in the late 1960s when scientists in different locations who used the Arpanet, the predecessor of the Internet, sought to develop a way of sharing resources and information with one another. Write a report on the early history of e-mail, focusing on the period before 1990 when it became a mass phenomenon. Who were the main players? What were the key moments? What were the technical challenges? At what point did it become apparent that e-mail was going to have far broader applications than was originally conceived?

4. Like anything else, e-mail has a significant legal dimension. Of increasing concern to employees is the privacy of their e-mail and the extent to which employers can monitor their e-mail and use it against them. Employers have been known to send fake e-mails to employees pretending to be other employers offering more lucrative or prestigious jobs. Employees who responded favorably were deemed disloyal and subsequently denied promotion. In 2000, civil libertarians became alarmed when the FBI revealed that it was using a software program called Carnivore to monitor all e-mail passing through a particular Internet Service Provider (ISP), ostensibly in an attempt to catch terrorists, drug dealers, and child pornographers. During a divorce proceeding, one spouse may obtain a court order to search the e-mail records of the other spouse

for incriminating information about extramarital affairs. Explore some of the ways that e-mail monitoring and searching has been used against people, along with some of the ways that civil libertarians and others have been resisting activities in court.

5. Visit some chat rooms or electronic bulletin boards and "lurk" over the ongoing electronic communications—that is, read what others are writing without announcing your own presence. Visit forums on a variety of subjects. For example, if you are a member of America Online, you'll find chat rooms available on numerous subjects. If you read electronic publications like Slate.com or Salon.com, you can trace discussion threads in which readers react to articles that have been published. Report on what you find. What tentative conclusions can you draw about the types of communication that occur in such places? Categorize the types of comments made. What appear to be the effects of anonymity? To what extent do you detect that writers are creating personas for themselves, identities that may be different from what they are like in person?

6. Conduct a survey about e-mail use. Try to keep the group you survey relatively homogenous (e.g., undergraduates) and organize that group by subcategories (e.g., class standing, major, gender, whether an individual has her or his own computer or must use college equipment). Develop a questionnaire, as well as a set of interview questions, exploring such issues as the main purposes of sending e-mail messages, the average length of messages, how often e-mail is checked, and the use of chat rooms and electronic bulletin boards. Write a report based on your findings. Use tables and graphs or charts to summarize your data. Use standard social science format for developing your report: an *introduction*, a section on *methods* of gathering data, a section on *results*, a *discussion* of the results, and a *conclusion*.

7. Visit AskMe.com and browse through the questions and answers by various "experts" in one of the numerous categories listed. It's best to select a category—whether movies, computer software, or refinishing cabinets—with which you have some "expert" knowledge, yourself. Notice how many of the responses have been rated (on a scale of one to five stars) by the questioner and by other experts. Assess the quality of the responses, based on your own knowledge of the subject, and compare them with the ratings posted. Write a report, possibly for a magazine like *Consumer Reports*, assessing the quality of information provided by particular experts in this area on AskMe.com.

9

Obedience to Authority

Would you obey an order to inflict pain on another person? Most of us, if confronted with this question, would probably be quick to answer: "Never!" Yet if the conclusions of researchers are to be trusted, it is not psychopaths who kill noncombatant civilians in wartime and torture victims in prisons around the world but rather ordinary people following orders. People obey. This is a basic, necessary fact of human society. As psychologist Stanley Milgram has written, "Obedience is as basic an element in the structure of social life as one can point to. Some system of authority is a requirement of all communal living."

The question, then, is not, "Should we obey the orders of an authority figure?" but rather, "To what *extent* should we obey?" Each generation seems to give new meaning to these questions. During the Vietnam War, a number of American soldiers followed a commander's orders and murdered civilians in the hamlet of My Lai. In 1987 former White House military aide Oliver North was prosecuted for illegally diverting money raised by selling arms to Iran—considered by the U.S. government to be a terrorist state—to fund the anticommunist Contra (resistance) fighters in Nicaragua. North's attorneys claimed that he was following the orders of his superiors. And, although North was found guilty,* the judge who sentenced him to perform community service (there was no prison sentence) largely agreed with this defense when he called North a pawn in a larger game played by senior officials in the Reagan administration. In the 1990s the world was horrified by genocidal violence in Rwanda and in the former nation of Yugoslavia. These were civil wars, in which people who had been living for generations as neighbors suddenly, upon the instigation and orders of their leaders, turned upon and slaughtered one another.

Finally, in April 2004, the world (particularly, the Muslim world) was horrified by accounts—and graphic photographs—of the degrading torture and humiliation of Iraqi prisoners at the hands of American soldiers in a Baghdad prison. Among the questions raised by this incident: Were these soldiers obeying orders to "soften up" the prisoners for interrogation? Were they fulfilling the roles of prison guards they thought were expected of them? Were they abusing others because, given the circumstances, they could? President Bush asserted that this kind of abuse "does not reflect the nature of the American people." But as the Milgram and Zimbardo experiments in this chapter demonstrate, we are likely to be unpleasantly surprised by revelations of just what our "nature" really is—not only as Americans but, more fundamentally, as human beings.

---

* In July 1990, North's conviction was overturned on appeal.

In less dramatic ways, conflicts over the extent to which we obey orders surface in everyday life. At one point or another, you may face a moral dilemma at work. Perhaps it will take this form: The boss tells you to overlook File X in preparing a report for a certain client. But you're sure that File X pertains directly to the report and contains information that will alarm the client. What should you do? The dilemmas of obedience also emerge on some campuses with the rite of fraternity or sports-related hazing. Psychologists Janice Gibson and Mika Haritos-Fatouros have made the startling observation that whether the obedience in question involves a pledge's joining a fraternity or a torturer's joining an elite military corps, the *process* by which one acquiesces to a superior's order (and thereby becomes a member of the group) is remarkably the same:

> There are several ways to teach people to do the unthinkable, and we have developed a model to explain how they are used. We have also found that college fraternities, although they are far removed from the grim world of torture and violent combat, use similar methods for initiating new members, to ensure their faithfulness to the fraternity's rules and values. However, this unthinking loyalty can sometimes lead to dangerous actions: Over the past 10 years, there have been countless injuries during fraternity initiations and 39 deaths. These training techniques are designed to instill obedience in people, but they can easily be a guide for an intensive course in torture.
>
> 1. *Screening to find the best prospects:*
>   - Normal, well-adjusted people with the physical, intellectual, and, in some cases, political attributes necessary for the task.
> 2. *Techniques to increase binding among these prospects:*
>   - Initiation rites to isolate people from society and introduce them to a new social order, with different rules and values.
>   - Elitist attitudes and "in-group" language, which highlight the differences between the group and the rest of society.
> 3. *Techniques to reduce the strain of obedience:*
>   - Blaming and dehumanizing the victims, so it is less disturbing to harm them.
>   - Harassment, the constant physical and psychological intimidation that prevents logical thinking and promotes the instinctive responses needed for acts of inhuman cruelty.
>   - Rewards for obedience and punishments for not cooperating.
>   - Social modeling by watching other group members commit violent acts and then receive rewards.
>   - Systematic desensitization to repugnant acts by gradual exposure to them, so they appear routine and normal despite conflicts with previous moral standards.*

---

* Janice T. Gibson and Mika Haritos-Fatouros, "The Education of a Torturer," *Psychology Today* November 1986. Reprinted with permission from *Psychology Today Magazine.* Copyright 1986 Sussex Publishers, Inc.

Many of these processes appear to have been at work in the Iraqi prison scandal.

In this chapter, you will explore the dilemmas inherent in obeying the orders of an authority. First, you will learn more about the Abu Ghraib prison scandal from a *U.S. News & World Report* article in which Marianne Szegedy-Maszak asks: "Was it conditions at [the Iraqi prison] or perverse human nature that led to these atrocities?" Next, psychologist Solomon E. Asch describes an experiment he devised to demonstrate the powerful influence of group pressure upon individual judgment. Psychologist Stanley Milgram then reports on his own landmark study in which he set out to determine the extent to which ordinary individuals would obey the clearly immoral orders of an authority figure. The results were shocking, not only to the psychiatrists who predicted that few people would follow such orders but also to many other social scientists and people—some of whom applauded Milgram for his fiendishly ingenious design, some of whom bitterly attacked him for unethical procedures. We include one of these attacks, a scathing review by psychologist Diana Baumrind. Another, and later, perspective on the reaction to Milgram's experiment is provided by British writer Ian Parker in his essay "Obedience."

Next, Philip K. Zimbardo reports on his famous (and controversial) Stanford Prison experiment, which eerily anticipates the brutality of young American soldiers at the Abu Ghraib prison. In Zimbardo's experiment, volunteers exhibited astonishingly convincing and obedient attitudes as they play-acted at being prisoners and guards. Three essays conclude the chapter. In "Disobedience as a Psychological and Moral Problem," psychoanalyst and philosopher Erich Fromm discusses the comforts of obedient behavior. In "The Genocidal Killer in the Mirror," Crispin Sartwell draws on the recent history of genocide to shake our belief that under similar circumstances we would behave honorably. Finally, in "Just Do What the Pilot Tells You," British physician Theodore Dalrymple reminds us that obedience to authority is not always a bad thing; in fact, routine *dis*obedience to authority can be just as dangerous as unthinking obedience.

The Abu Ghraib Prison Scandal: Sources of Sadism
Marianne Szegedy-Maszak

In January 2004, a military investigator in Baghdad found on his cot a disk containing images of horrific physical abuse and humiliation committed by American military guards against Iraqi detainees at Abu Ghraib prison. A whistleblower, who (along with his family) was subsequently placed in protective custody because of death threats, found the images so disturbingly at odds with standards of military conduct and basic decency that he reported the abuse, which quickly grew into an international scandal. President Bush strongly condemned the "disgraceful conduct by a few American troops who dishonored our country and disregarded our values." Others, recalling abuses in Vietnam and Nazi Germany, wondered whether the military's culture of obedience and the extreme circumstances of war can turn otherwise decent people into agents of terror. At stake are the questions at the heart of this chapter: What if these "few" American soldiers weren't monsters? What if they were typical men and women who, caught in the wrong circumstances, found themselves committing atrocities? Faced with similar pressures, might the most ordinary person (of any nation) be capable of heinous acts?

At press time (August 2004), criminal charges had been brought against seven enlisted soldiers from the 372nd Military Police Company. Specialist Jeremy C. Sivits pleaded guilty and was sentenced to a year in prison; he is now cooperating with authorities in building the case against the other defendants. Pfc. Lynndie England, prominent in many of the photos (including one that shows her dragging a naked Iraqi man on a leash), will face trial at Fort Bragg, NC. The other five await hearings in Iraq and Germany, and their attorneys have already indicated that they will employ a "following orders" defense. An investigative report by a panel chaired by Maj. Gen. George Fay (which some critics have labeled a "whitewash"), due for release at the end of August, names some officers from the 205th Military Intelligence Brigade as bearing culpability for what happened. The commander of this unit, Col. Thomas Pappas, was reprimanded for failing to assure that his officers followed the Geneva Conventions at Abu Ghraib. Additionally, a separate Pentagon investigation chaired by former CIA director James Schlesinger is expected to criticize Secretary of Defense Donald Rumsfeld and his senior aides, though the Schlesinger report is prohibited from entering into "matters of personal responsibility."

In "Sources of Sadism," which first appeared in the 24 May 2004 edition of U.S. News & World Report, Marianne Szegedy-Maszak explores some of the reasons psychologists have offered to explain how American soldiers (at least one of whom was college-aged at the time of the abuses) could have knowingly degraded and tortured Iraqi detainees. The author refers directly to two experiments you will read about at some length in this chapter: Philip Zimbardo's Stanford Prison Experiment and Stanley Milgram's experiments in obedience.

If you have not yet seen the Abu Ghraib photos and wish to do so (be warned—they are disturbing), you can readily find them on the Internet.

1   Those hoping to see a flicker of anger or remorse or conscience on the faces of the American soldiers photographed tormenting Iraqi prisoners in Abu Ghraib are likely to be disappointed. Evidence of how these young recruits apparently became gleeful sadists can be found in neither their faces nor their biographies.

2   While many theories have been advanced about the forces that tragically came together at Abu Ghraib—inadequate training, overzealous intelligence gathering, failure of leadership—none can adequately account for the hardening of heart necessary for such sadism. So the question is: Are there particular conditions in Iraq today that might shed light on why these soldiers committed these unconscionable acts?

3   The usual points of reference in psychology are two classic studies that attempted to explore the capacity for evil residing in "normal" people. In 1971, Stanford psychologist Philip Zimbardo created a simulated prison and randomly assigned students to be either guards or prisoners. With astonishing speed,

the "guards" indulged in forms of torture and humiliation not unlike those horrifying us today. This followed on earlier experiments by Yale psychologist Stanley Milgram on obedience to authority. Milgram recruited volunteers to participate in what he described as a study on learning. An actor sat in a chair that students believed was wired with electricity. Each time this actor would give an incorrect answer, the students would be directed by Milgram to deliver a larger shock. As the subject in the electric chair seemed to suffer more and more, 2 out of 3 of the unwitting students administered shocks that would have been lethal in real life.

4   These experiments demonstrate that Everyman is a potential torturer. But what relevance does that have to Baghdad today? Robert Okin, a professor of psychiatry at the University of California-San Francisco who has worked with victims of torture, says that while there are lessons to be learned from these studies, the particulars of the soldiers' life in Abu Ghraib also need to be taken into account. In Iraq, Okin says, the abuse became "an inexcusable way of working off their rage, anxiety about their own safety, and their sense of helplessness."

5   The anxiety and helplessness are exacerbated by difficult living conditions and constant danger—including the unfavorable odds of 450 military guards overseeing 7,000 often hostile prisoners. Then there is the issue of sex: One of the least discussed aspects of the occupation in Iraq has been the lack of a reliable local brothel where male soldiers are able to unwind. Experts have long appreciated the fact that sexual activity can often be a way of relieving the anxiety of war.

6   Abu Ghraib also has three traits that psychologist Herbert Kelman has described as necessary for torture: authorization, routinization, and dehumanization. To translate the jargon, authorization means that someone with power needs to say that extreme measures are acceptable. (Pfc. Lynndie England said in an interview last week that her superiors said, "Hey, you're doing great; keep it up.")

7   Authorization leads to routinization, a kind of division of labor. In Nazi Germany, for example, one person had responsibility for writing the orders to deport the Jews, someone else for shaving their heads, and so on. The guards at Abu Ghraib were told they were merely "softening up" the prisoners for interrogation. Such parceling out of responsibility, says Boston psychiatrist Jonathan Shay, "seems to tantalize someone's moral compass, making it possible to do things that might be personally distasteful."

8   Dehumanization follows. In Vietnam the enemy became "slopes," and in Iraq they're "towel heads." Covering prisoners' faces with hoods, Okin adds, makes it possible for the soldiers "to sever any empathic human connection with them."

9   The protected walls of Abu Ghraib made it an island where conventional morality no longer applied. When these soldiers testify at court-martial, perhaps their testimony will contribute to the psychological theories on blind obedience to authority. However, Okin says, "The ethical questions just don't go away; horror doesn't go away by being able to explain it." And indeed, as the explanations always fall short, the horror continues to loom large.

Review Questions

1. What are the "usual points of reference in psychology" for abuses like those that occurred at Abu Ghraib?

2. According to Herbert Kelman, what conditions are necessary for a person to commit acts of torture?

3. How might the circumstances that soldiers faced in Iraq have contributed to the events at Abu Ghraib?

4. What are the limits of psychological explanations of torture, according to Szegedy-Maszak?

Discussion and Writing Suggestions

1. How did you respond when the Abu Ghraib prison scandal broke? (If you were not aware of the scandal, consider the factors that may have kept the news from reaching you.)

2. Read "The Abu Ghraib Timeline," compiled by the Associated Press in May 2004 <http://www.scvhistory.com/scvhistory/signal/iraq/abughraib-timeline.htm>. What do you learn from the timeline about the U.S. military's and the U.S. government's response to reports of abuse?

3. A former commander of the Army Reserve unit implicated in the Abu Ghraib abuse (the 372nd MP Company) and now an attorney with the federal government, James D. Villa, wrote the following in an op-ed essay for the *Washington Post* on 12 May 2004: "Various people, including the families of some of the soldiers in question, have said that the soldiers were not given appropriate training to run a detention facility and had inadequate support to do their jobs. While these statements may be true, in what Army field manual can one locate the section about stacking naked prisoners like cordwood, or affixing collars to their necks? Is special training needed to show a soldier that this sort of thing is contemptible and contrary to any standards of decency?" Your comments?

4. To what extent do you feel that the harsh conditions soldiers faced in Iraq either excuse the abuse of Iraqi prisoners or make you more understanding of that abuse?

5. Szegedy-Maszak writes that the "protected walls of Abu Ghraib made it an island where conventional morality no longer applied." What is it about being on a metaphorical island (that is, being cut off from the influence of others) that invites people to abandon conventional morality? In your own experience, can you identify "island-like" moments in which conventional morality seemed no longer to apply?

6. At least several of those involved in the Abu Ghraib abuse were of college age. Do you regard them as moral monsters—as isolated bad apples? How different are they from ordinary Americans, particularly ordinary Americans in stressful conditions?

Opinions and Social Pressure
Solomon E. Asch

In the early 1950s, Solomon Asch (b. 1907), a social psychologist at Rutgers University, conducted a series of simple but ingenious experiments on the influence of group pressure upon the individual. Essentially, he discovered, individuals can be influenced by groups to deny the evidence of their own senses. Together with the Milgram experiments of the next decade (see the selections that follow here), these studies provide powerful evidence of the degree to which individuals can surrender their own judgment to others, even when those others are clearly in the wrong. The results of these experiments have implications far beyond the laboratory: they can explain a good deal of the normal human behavior we see every day— at school, at work, at home.

1 That social influences shape every person's practices, judgments, and beliefs is a truism to which anyone will readily assent. A child masters his "native" dialect down to the finest nuances; a member of a tribe of cannibals accepts cannibalism as altogether fitting and proper. All the social sciences take their departure from the observation of the profound effects that groups exert on their members. For psychologists, group pressure upon the mind of the individual raises a host of questions they would like to investigate in detail.

2 How, and to what extent, do social forces constrain people's opinions and attitudes? This question is especially pertinent in our day. The same epoch that has witnessed the unprecedented technical extension of communication has also brought into existence the deliberate manipulation of opinion and the "engineering of consent." There are many good reasons why, as citizens and as scientists, we should be concerned with studying the ways in which human beings form their opinions and the role that social conditions play.

3 Studies of these questions began with the interest in hypnosis aroused by the French physician Jean Martin Charcot (a teacher of Sigmund Freud) toward the end of the 19th century. Charcot believed that only hysterical patients could be fully hypnotized, but this view was soon challenged by two other physicians, Hyppolyte Bernheim and A. A. Liébault, who demonstrated that they could put most people under hypnotic spell. Bernheim proposed that hypnosis was but an extreme form of a normal psychological process which became known as "suggestibility." It was shown that monotonous reiteration of instructions could induce in normal persons in the waking state involuntary bodily changes such as swaying or rigidity of the arms, and sensations such as warmth and odor.

4   It was not long before social thinkers seized upon these discoveries as a basis for explaining numerous social phenomena, from the spread of opinion to the formation of crowds and the following of leaders. The sociologist Gabriel Tarde summed it all up in the aphorism: "Social man is a somnambulist."

5   When the new discipline of social psychology was born at the beginning of this century, its first experiments were essentially adaptations of the suggestion demonstration. The technique generally followed a simple plan. The subjects, usually college students, were asked to give their opinions or preferences concerning various matters; some time later they were again asked to state their choices, but now they were also informed of the opinions held by authorities or large groups of their peers on the same matters. (Often the alleged consensus was fictitious.) Most of these studies had substantially the same result: confronted with opinions contrary to their own, many subjects apparently shifted their judgments in the direction of the views of the majorities or the experts. The late psychologist Edward L. Thorndike reported that he had succeeded in modifying the esthetic preferences of adults by this procedure. Other psychologists reported that people's evaluations of the merit of a literary passage could be raised or lowered by ascribing the passage to different authors. Apparently the sheer weight of numbers or authority sufficed to change opinions, even when no arguments for the opinions themselves were provided.

6   Now the very ease of success in these experiments arouses suspicion. Did the subjects actually change their opinions, or were the experimental victories scored only on paper? On grounds of common sense, one must question whether opinions are generally as watery as these studies indicate. There is some reason to wonder whether it was not the investigators who, in their enthusiasm for a theory, were suggestible, and whether the ostensibly gullible subjects were not providing answers which they thought good subjects were expected to give.

7   The investigations were guided by certain underlying assumptions, which today are common currency and account for much that is thought and said about the operations of propaganda and public opinion. The assumptions are that people submit uncritically and painlessly to external manipulation by suggestion or prestige, and that any given idea or value can be "sold" or "unsold" without reference to its merits. We should be skeptical, however, of the supposition that the power of social pressure necessarily implies uncritical submission to it: independence and the capacity to rise above group passion are also open to human beings. Further, one may question on psychological grounds whether it is possible as a rule to change a person's judgment of a situation or an object without first changing his knowledge or assumptions about it.

8   In what follows I shall describe some experiments in an investigation of the effects of group pressure which was carried out recently with the help of a number of my associates. The tests not only demonstrate the operations of group pressure upon individuals but also illustrate a new kind of attack on the problem and some of the more subtle questions that it raises.

9   A group of seven to nine young men, all college students, are assembled in a classroom for a "psychological experiment" in visual judgment. The experimenter informs them that they will be comparing the lengths of lines. He shows two large white cards [see Figure 1]. On one is a single vertical black line—the standard whose length is to be matched. On the other card are three vertical lines of various lengths. The subjects are to choose the one that is of the same length as the line on the other card. One of the three actually is of the same length; the other two are substantially different, the difference ranging from three quarters of an inch to an inch and three quarters.

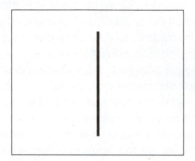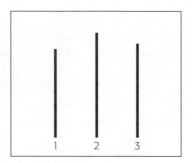

FIGURE 1   Subjects were shown two cards. One bore a standard line. The other bore three lines, one of which was the same length as the standard. The subjects were asked to choose this line.

10   The experiment opens uneventfully. The subjects announce their answers in the order in which they have been seated in the room, and on the first round every person chooses the same matching line. Then a second set of cards is exposed; again the group is unanimous. The members appear ready to endure politely another boring experiment. On the third trial there is an unexpected disturbance. One person near the end of the group disagrees with all the others in his selection of the matching line. He looks surprised, indeed incredulous, about the disagreement. On the following trial he disagrees again, while the others remain unanimous in their choice. The dissenter becomes more and more worried and hesitant as the disagreement continues in succeeding trials; he may pause before announcing his answer and speak in a low voice, or he may smile in an embarrassed way.

11   What the dissenter does not know is that all the other members of the group were instructed by the experimenter beforehand to give incorrect answers in unanimity at certain points. The single individual who is not a party to this pre-arrangement is the focal subject of our experiment. He is placed in a position in which, while he is actually giving the correct answers, he finds himself unexpectedly in a minority of one, opposed by a unanimous and arbitrary majority with respect to a clear and simple fact. Upon him we have brought to bear two opposed forces: the evidence of his senses and the unanimous opinion of a group of his peers. Also, he must declare his judgments in public, before a majority which has also stated its position publicly.

12   The instructed majority occasionally reports correctly in order to reduce the possibility that the naive subject will suspect collusion against him. (In only a few cases did the subject actually show suspicion; when this happened, the experiment was stopped and the results were not counted.) There are 18 trials in each series, and on 12 of these the majority responds erroneously.

13   How do people respond to group pressure in this situation? I shall report first the statistical results of a series in which a total of 123 subjects from three institutions of higher learning (not including my own Swarthmore College) were placed in the minority situation described above.

14   Two alternatives were open to the subject: he could act independently, repudiating the majority, or he could go along with the majority, repudiating the evidence of his senses. Of the 123 put to the test, a considerable percentage yielded to the majority. Whereas in ordinary circumstances individuals matching the lines will make mistakes less than 1 per cent of the time, under group pressure the minority subjects swung to acceptance of the misleading majority's wrong judgments in 36.8 per cent of the selections.

15   Of course individuals differed in response. At one extreme, about one quarter of the subjects were completely independent and never agreed with the erroneous judgments of the majority. At the other extreme, some individuals went with the majority nearly all the time. The performances of individuals in this experiment tend to be highly consistent. Those who strike out on the path of independence do not, as a rule, succumb to the majority even over an extended series of trials, while those who choose the path of compliance are unable to free themselves as the ordeal is prolonged.

16   The reasons for the startling individual differences have not yet been investigated in detail. At this point we can only report some tentative generalizations from talks with the subjects, each of whom was interviewed at the end of the experiment. Among the independent individuals were many who held fast because of staunch confidence in their own judgment. The most significant fact about them was not absence of responsiveness to the majority but a capacity to recover from doubt and to reestablish their equilibrium. Others who acted independently came to believe that the majority was correct in its answers, but they continued their dissent on the simple ground that it was their obligation to call the play as they saw it.

17   Among the extremely yielding persons we found a group who quickly reached the conclusion: "I am wrong, they are right." Others yielded in order "not to spoil your results." Many of the individuals who went along suspected that the majority were "sheep" following the first responder, or that the majority were victims of an optical illusion; nevertheless, these suspicions failed to free them at the moment of decision. More disquieting were the reactions of subjects who construed their difference from the majority as a sign of some general deficiency in themselves, which at all costs they must hide. On this basis they desperately tried to merge with the majority, not realizing the longer-range consequences to themselves. All the yielding subjects underestimated the frequency with which they conformed.

18   Which aspect of the influence of a majority is more important—the size of the majority or its unanimity? The experiment was modified to examine this

question. In one series the size of the opposition was varied from one to 15 persons. The results showed a clear trend. When a subject was confronted with only a single individual who contradicted his answers, he was swayed little: he continued to answer independently and correctly in nearly all trials. When the opposition was increased to two, the pressure became substantial: minority subjects now accepted the wrong answer 13.6 per cent of the time. Under the pressure of a majority of three, the subjects' errors jumped to 31.8 per cent. But further increases in the size of the majority apparently did not increase the weight of the pressure substantially. Clearly the size of the opposition is important only up to a point.

19   Disturbance of the majority's unanimity had a striking effect. In this experiment the subject was given the support of a truthful partner—either another individual who did not know of the prearranged agreement among the rest of the group, or a person who was instructed to give correct answers throughout.

20   The presence of a supporting partner depleted the majority of much of its power. Its pressure on the dissenting individual was reduced to one fourth: that is, subjects answered incorrectly only one fourth as often as under the pressure of a unanimous majority. The weakest persons did not yield as readily. Most interesting were the reactions to the partner. Generally the feeling toward him was one of warmth and closeness; he was credited with inspiring confidence. However, the subjects repudiated the suggestion that the partner decided them to be independent.

21   Was the partner's effect a consequence of his dissent, or was it related to his accuracy? We now introduced into the experimental group a person who was instructed to dissent from the majority but also to disagree with the subject. In some experiments the majority was always to choose the worst of the comparison lines and the instructed dissenter to pick the line that was closer to the length of the standard one; in others the majority was consistently intermediate and the dissenter most in error. In this manner we were able to study the relative influence of "compromising" and "extremist" dissenters.

22   Again the results are clear. When a moderate dissenter is present the effect of the majority on the subject decreases by approximately one third, and extremes of yielding disappear. Moreover, most of the errors the subjects do make are moderate, rather than flagrant. In short, the dissenter largely controls the choice of errors. To this extent the subjects broke away from the majority even while bending to it.

23   On the other hand, when the dissenter always chose the line that was more flagrantly different from the standard, the results were of quite a different kind. The extremist dissenter produced a remarkable freeing of the subjects; their errors dropped to only 9 percent. Furthermore, all the errors were of the moderate variety. We were able to conclude that dissents *per se* increased independence and moderated the errors that occurred, and that the direction of dissent exerted consistent effects.

24   In all the foregoing experiments each subject was observed only in a single setting. We now turned to studying the effects upon a given individual of a change in the situation to which he was exposed. The first experiment exam-

ined the consequences of losing or gaining a partner. The instructed partner began by answering correctly on the first six trials. With his support the subject usually resisted pressure from the majority: 18 of 27 subjects were completely independent. But after six trials the partner joined the majority. As soon as he did so, there was an abrupt rise in the subjects' errors. Their submission to the majority was just about as frequent as when the minority subject was opposed by a unanimous majority throughout.

25   It was surprising to find that the experience of having had a partner and of having braved the majority opposition with him had failed to strengthen the individuals' independence. Questioning at the conclusion of the experiment suggested that we had overlooked an important circumstance; namely, the strong specific effect of "desertion" by the partner to the other side. We therefore changed the conditions so that the partner would simply leave the group at the proper point. (To allay suspicion it was announced in advance that he had an appointment with the dean.) In this form of the experiment, the partner's effect outlasted his presence. The errors increased after his departure, but less markedly than after a partner switched to the majority.

26   In a variant of this procedure the trials began with the majority unanimously giving correct answers. Then they gradually broke away until on the sixth trial the naive subject was alone and the group unanimously against him. As long as the subject had anyone on his side, he was almost invariably independent, but as soon as he found himself alone, the tendency to conform to the majority rose abruptly.

27   As might be expected, an individual's resistance to group pressure in these experiments depends to a considerable degree on how wrong the majority was. We varied the discrepancy between the standard line and the other lines systematically, with the hope of reaching a point where the error of the majority would be so glaring that every subject would repudiate it and choose independently. In this we regretfully did not succeed. Even when the difference between the lines was seven inches, there were still some who yielded to the error of the majority.

28   The study provides clear answers to a few relatively simple questions, and it raises many others that await investigation. We would like to know the degree of consistency of persons in situations which differ in content and structure. If consistency of independence or conformity in behavior is shown to be a fact, how is it functionally related to qualities of character and personality? In what ways is independence related to sociological or cultural conditions? Are leaders more independent than other people, or are they adept at following their followers? These and many other questions may perhaps be answerable by investigations of the type described here.

29   Life in society requires consensus as an indispensable condition. But consensus, to be productive, requires that each individual contribute independently out of his experience and insight. When consensus comes under the dominance of conformity, the social process is polluted and the individual at the same time surrenders the powers on which his functioning as a feeling and thinking being depends. That we have found the tendency to conformity in our

society so strong that reasonably intelligent and well-meaning young people are willing to call white black is a matter of concern. It raises questions about our ways of education and about the values that guide our conduct.

30   Yet anyone inclined to draw too pessimistic conclusions from this report would do well to remind himself that the capacities for independence are not to be underestimated. He may also draw some consolation from a further observation: those who participated in this challenging experiment agreed nearly without exception that independence was preferable to conformity.

Review Questions

1. What is "suggestibility"? How is this phenomenon related to social pressure?

2. Summarize the procedure and results of the Asch experiment. What conclusions does Asch draw from these results?

3. To what extent did varying the size of the majority and its unanimity affect the experimental results?

4. What distinction does Asch draw between consensus and conformity?

Discussion and Writing Suggestions

1. Before discussing the experiment, Asch considers how easily people's opinions or attitudes may be shaped by social pressure. To what extent do you agree with this conclusion? Write a short paper on this subject, drawing upon examples from your own experience or observation or from your reading.

2. Do the results of this experiment surprise you? Or do they confirm facts about human behavior that you had already suspected, observed, or experienced? Explain, in two or three paragraphs. Provide examples, relating these examples to features of the Asch experiment.

3. Frequently, the conclusions drawn from a researcher's experimental results are challenged on the basis that laboratory conditions do not accurately reflect the complexity of human behavior. Asch draws certain conclusions about the degree to which individuals are affected by group pressures based on an experiment involving subjects choosing matching line lengths. To what extent, if any, do you believe that these conclusions lack validity because the behavior at the heart of the experiment is too dissimilar to real-life situations of group pressure on the individual? Support your opinions with examples.

4. We are all familiar with the phenomenon of "peer pressure." To what extent do Asch's experiments demonstrate the power of peer pressure? To what extent do you think that other factors may be at work? Explain, providing examples.

5. Asch's experiments, conducted in the early 1950s, involved groups of "seven to nine young men, all college students." To what extent do you believe that the results of a similar experiment would be different today? To what extent might they be different if the subjects had included women, as well, and subjects of various ages, from children, to middle-aged people, to older people? To what extent do you believe that the social class or culture of the subjects might have an impact upon the experimental results? Support your opinions with examples and logical reasoning. (Beware, however, of overgeneralizing, based upon insufficient evidence.)

The Perils of Obedience
Stanley Milgram

In 1963, a Yale psychologist conducted one of the classic studies on obedience. Stanley Milgram designed an experiment that forced participants either to violate their conscience by obeying the immoral demands of an authority figure or to refuse those demands. Surprisingly, Milgram found that few participants could resist the authority's orders, even when the participants knew that following these orders would result in another person's pain. Were the participants in these experiments incipient mass murderers? No, said Milgram. They were "ordinary people, simply doing their jobs." The implications of Milgram's conclusions are immense.

Consider these questions: Where does evil reside? What sort of people were responsible for the Holocaust, and for the long list of other atrocities that seem to blight the human record in every generation? Is it a lunatic fringe, a few sick but powerful people who are responsible for atrocities? If so, then we decent folk needn't ever look inside ourselves to understand evil since (by our definition) evil lurks out there, in "those sick ones." Milgram's study suggested otherwise: that under a special set of circumstances the obedience we naturally show authority figures can transform us into agents of terror.

The article that follows is one of the longest in this book, and it may help you to know in advance the author's organization. In paragraphs 1–11, Milgram discusses the larger significance and the history of dilemmas involving obedience to authority; he then summarizes his basic experimental design and follows with a report of one experiment. Milgram organizes the remainder of his article into sections, which he has subtitled "An Unexpected Outcome," "Peculiar Reactions," "The Etiquette of Submission," and "Duty Without Conflict." He begins his conclusion in paragraph 108. If you find the article too long or complex to complete in a single sitting, then plan to read sections at a time, taking notes on each until you're done. Anticipate the article that immediately follows this one: It reviews Milgram's work and largely concerns the ethics of his experimental design. Consider these ethics as you read so that you, in turn, can respond to Milgram's critics.

Stanley Milgram (1933–1984) taught and conducted research at Yale and Harvard universities and at the Graduate Center, City University of New York. He was named Guggenheim Fellow in 1972–1973 and a year later was nominated for the National Book Award for Obedience to Authority. *His other books include* Television and Antisocial Behavior *(1973),* The City and the Self *(1974),* Human Aggression *(1976), and* The Individual in the Social World *(1977).*

1   Obedience is as basic an element in the structure of social life as one can point to. Some system of authority is a requirement of all communal living, and it is only the person dwelling in isolation who is not forced to respond, with defiance or submission, to the commands of others. For many people, obedience is a deeply ingrained behavior tendency, indeed a potent impulse overriding training in ethics, sympathy, and moral conduct.

2   The dilemma inherent in submission to authority is ancient, as old as the story of Abraham, and the question of whether one should obey when commands conflict with conscience has been argued by Plato, dramatized in *Antigone,* and treated to philosophic analysis in almost every historical epoch. Conservative philosophers argue that the very fabric of society is threatened by disobedience, while humanists stress the primacy of the individual conscience.

3   The legal and philosophic aspects of obedience are of enormous import, but they say very little about how most people behave in concrete situations. I set up a simple experiment at Yale University to test how much pain an ordinary citizen would inflict on another person simply because he was ordered to by an experimental scientist. Stark authority was pitted against the subjects' strongest moral imperatives against hurting others, and with the subjects' ears ringing with the screams of the victims, authority won more often than not. The extreme willingness of adults to go to almost any lengths on the command of an authority constitutes the chief finding of the study and the fact most urgently demanding explanation.

4   In the basic experimental design, two people come to a psychology laboratory to take part in a study of memory and learning. One of them is designated as a "teacher" and the other a "learner." The experimenter explains that the study is concerned with the effects of punishment on learning. The learner is conducted into a room, seated in a kind of miniature electric chair; his arms are strapped to prevent excessive movement, and an electrode is attached to his wrist. He is told that he will be read lists of simple word pairs, and that he will then be tested on his ability to remember the second word of a pair when he hears the first one again. Whenever he makes an error, he will receive electric shocks of increasing intensity.

5   The real focus of the experiment is the teacher. After watching the learner being strapped into place, he is seated before an impressive shock generator. The instrument panel consists of thirty level switches set in a horizontal line. Each switch is clearly labeled with a voltage designation ranging from 15 to 450 volts. The following designations are clearly indicated for groups of four switches, going from left to right: Slight Shock, Moderate Shock, Strong Shock, Very Strong Shock, Intense Shock, Extreme Intensity Shock, Danger: Severe Shock. (Two switches after this last designation are simply marked XXX.)

6   When a switch is depressed, a pilot light corresponding to each switch is illuminated in bright red; an electric buzzing is heard; a blue light, labeled "voltage energizer," flashes; the dial on the voltage meter swings to the right; and various relay clicks sound off.

7   The upper left-hand corner of the generator is labeled SHOCK GENERATOR, TYPE ZLB, DYSON INSTRUMENT COMPANY, WALTHAM, MASS. OUTPUT 15 VOLTS—450 VOLTS.

8   Each subject is given a sample 45-volt shock from the generator before his run as teacher, and the jolt strengthens his belief in the authenticity of the machine.

9   The teacher is a genuinely naive subject who has come to the laboratory for the experiment. The learner, or victim, is actually an actor who receives no shock at all. The point of the experiment is to see how far a person will proceed in a concrete and measurable situation in which he is ordered to inflict increasing pain on a protesting victim.

10   Conflict arises when the man receiving the shock begins to show that he is experiencing discomfort. At 75 volts, he grunts; at 120 volts, he complains loudly; at 150, he demands to be released from the experiment. As the voltage increases, his protests become more vehement and emotional. At 285 volts, his response can be described only as an agonized scream. Soon thereafter, he makes no sound at all.

11   For the teacher, the situation quickly becomes one of gripping tension. It is not a game for him; conflict is intense and obvious. The manifest suffering of the learner presses him to quit; but each time he hesitates to administer a shock, the experimenter orders him to continue. To extricate himself from this plight, the subject must make a clear break with authority.*

12   The subject, Gretchen Brandt,† is an attractive thirty-one-year-old medical technician who works at the Yale Medical School. She had emigrated from Germany five years before.

13   On several occasions when the learner complains, she turns to the experimenter coolly and inquires, "Shall I continue?" She promptly returns to her task when the experimenter asks her to do so. At the administration of 210 volts, she turns to the experimenter, remarking firmly, "Well, I'm sorry, I don't think we should continue."

14   EXPERIMENTER: The experiment requires that you go on until he has learned all the word pairs correctly.

15   BRANDT: He has a heart condition. I'm sorry. He told you that before.

16   EXPERIMENTER: The shocks may be painful but they are not dangerous.

17   BRANDT: Well, I'm sorry, I think when shocks continue like this, they *are* dangerous. You ask him if he wants to get out. It's his free will.

18   EXPERIMENTER: It is absolutely essential that we continue. . . .

---

* The ethical problems of carrying out an experiment of this sort are too complex to be dealt with here, but they receive extended treatment in the book from which this article is adapted.

† Names of subjects described in this piece have been changed.

19   BRANDT: I'd like you to ask him. We came here of our free will. If he wants to continue I'll go ahead. He told you he had a heart condition. I'm sorry. I don't want to be responsible for anything happening to him. I wouldn't like it for me either.

20   EXPERIMENTER: You have no other choice.

21   BRANDT: I think we are here on our own free will. I don't want to be responsible if anything happens to him. Please understand that.

22   She refuses to go further and the experiment is terminated.

23   The woman is firm and resolute throughout. She indicates in the interview that she was in no way tense or nervous, and this corresponds to her controlled appearance during the experiment. She feels that the last shock she administered to the learner was extremely painful and reiterates that she "did not want to be responsible for any harm to him."

24   The woman's straightforward, courteous behavior in the experiment, lack of tension, and total control of her own action seem to make disobedience a simple and rational deed. Her behavior is the very embodiment of what I envisioned would be true for almost all subjects.

An Unexpected Outcome

25 Before the experiments, I sought predictions about the outcome from various kinds of people—psychiatrists, college sophomores, middle-class adults, graduate students, and faculty in the behavioral sciences. With remarkable similarity, they predicted that virtually all subjects would refuse to obey the experimenter. The psychiatrists, specifically, predicted that most subjects would not go beyond 150 volts, when the victim makes his first explicit demand to be freed. They expected that only 4 percent would reach 300 volts, and that only a pathological fringe of about one in a thousand would administer the highest shock on the board.

26   These predictions were unequivocally wrong. Of the forty subjects in the first experiment, twenty-five obeyed the orders of the experimenter to the end, punishing the victim until they reached the most potent shock available on the generator. After 450 volts were administered three times, the experimenter called a halt to the session. Many obedient subjects then heaved sights of relief, mopped their brows, rubbed their fingers over their eyes, or nervously fumbled cigarettes. Others displayed only minimal signs of tension from beginning to end.

27   When the very first experiments were carried out, Yale undergraduates were used as subjects, and about 60 percent of them were fully obedient. A colleague of mine immediately dismissed these findings as having no relevance to "ordinary" people, asserting that Yale undergraduates are a highly aggressive, competitive bunch who step on each other's necks on the slightest provocation. He assured me that when "ordinary" people were tested, the results would be quite different. As we moved from the pilot studies to the regular experimental series, people drawn from every stratum of New Haven life came to be employed in the experiment: professionals, white-collar workers, unemployed persons, and industrial workers. *The experiment's total outcome was the same as we had observed among the students.*

28   Moreover, when the experiments were repeated in Princeton, Munich, Rome, South Africa, and Australia, the level of obedience was invariably somewhat *higher* than found in the investigation reported in this article. Thus one scientist in Munich found 85 percent of his subjects to be obedient.

29   Fred Prozi's reactions, if more dramatic than most, illuminate the conflicts experienced by others in less visible form. About fifty years old and unemployed at the time of the experiment, he has a good-natured, if slightly dissolute, appearance, and he strikes people as a rather ordinary fellow. He begins the session calmly but becomes tense as it proceeds. After delivering the 180-volt shock, he pivots around in his chair and, shaking his head, addresses the experimenter in agitated tones:

30   PROZI: I can't stand it. I'm not going to kill that man in there. You hear him hollering?

31   EXPERIMENTER: As I told you before, the shocks may be painful, but . . .

32   PROZI: But he's hollering. He can't stand it. What's going to happen to him?

33   EXPERIMENTER (*his voice patient, matter-of-fact*): The experiment requires that you continue, Teacher.

34   PROZI: Aaah, but unh, I'm not going to get that man sick in there—know what I mean?

35   EXPERIMENTER: Whether the learner likes it or not, we must go on, through all the word pairs.

36   PROZI: I refuse to take the responsibility. He's in there hollering!

37   EXPERIMENTER: It's absolutely essential that you continue, Prozi.

38   PROZI (*indicating the unused questions*): There's too many left here. I mean, Jeez, if he gets them wrong, there's too many of them left. I mean, who's going to take the responsibility if anything happens to that gentleman?

39   EXPERIMENTER: I'm responsible for anything that happens to him. Continue, please.

40   PROZI: All right. (*Consults list of words.*) The next one's "Slow—walk, truck, dance, music." Answer, please (*A buzzing sound indicates the learner has signaled his answer.*) Wrong. A hundred and ninety-five volts. "Dance." (*Zzumph!*)

41   LEARNER (*yelling*): Let me out of here! My heart's bothering me! (*Teacher looks at experimenter.*)

42   EXPERIMENTER: Continue, please.

43   LEARNER (*screaming*): Let me out of here! You have no right to keep me here! Let me out of here, my heart's bothering me, let me out!

44   PROZI (*shakes head, pats the table nervously*): You see, he's hollering. Hear that? Gee, I don't know.

45   EXPERIMENTER: The experiment requires . . .

46   PROZI (*interrupting*): I know it does, sir, but I mean—hunh! He don't know what he's getting in for. He's up to 195 volts! (*Experiment continues, through 210 volts, 225 volts, 240 volts, 255 volts, 270 volts, at which point Prozi, with evident relief, runs out of word-pair questions.*)

47   EXPERIMENTER: You'll have to go back to the beginning of that page and go through them again until he's learned them all correctly.

48   PROZI: Aw, no. I'm not going to kill that man. You mean I've got to keep going up with the scale? No sir. He's hollering in there. I'm not going to give him 450 volts.

49   EXPERIMENTER: The experiment requires that you go on.

50   LEARNER: Ohhh. I absolutely refuse to answer anymore. (*Shouting urgently now.*) Let me out of here! You can't hold me here! Get me out. Get-me-out-of-here!

51   EXPERIMENTER: Continue. The next word is "Green," please.

52   PROZI: "Green—grass, hat, ink, apple." (*Nothing happens. No answering buzz. Just gloomy silence.*)

53   PROZI: I don't think he is going to answer.

54   EXPERIMENTER: If the learner doesn't answer in a reasonable time, about four or five seconds, consider the answer wrong. And follow the same procedures you have been doing for wrong answers. Say, "Wrong," tell him the number of volts, give him the punishment, read him the correct answer. Continue, please.

55   PROZI: "Green—grass, hat, ink, apple." Answer, please. (*More silence. Subject just sits there.*)

56   EXPERIMENTER: Go on with the procedure, please.

57   PROZI: Three hundred and fifteen volts. The answer is "ink." (*Zzumph!*)

58   LEARNER: Ohh. Ooohh.

59   PROZI (*relieved to hear response*): Next one . . .

60   LEARNER: I absolutely refuse to answer.

61   PROZI: You got to. You get a shock if you don't answer. (*Experiment continues with learner refusing to answer, and finally, failing even to grunt or groan. At 375 volts, the subject stands up.*)

62   PROZI: I think something's happened to that fellow in there. I don't get no answer. He was hollering at less voltage. Can't you check in and see if he's all right, please?

63   EXPERIMENTER: (*with same detached calm*): Not once we've started. Please continue, Teacher.

64   PROZI (*sits down, sighs deeply*): "Cool—day, shade, water, paint." Answer, please. Are you all right in there? Are you all right?

65   EXPERIMENTER: Please continue, Teacher. Continue, please. (*Subject pushes lever. Zzumph!*)

66   PROZI (*swiveling around in his chair*): Something's happened to that man in there. (*Swiveling back.*) Next one. "Low—dollar, necklace, moon, paint." (*Turning around again.*) Something's happened to that man in there. You better check on him, sir. He won't answer or nothing.

67   EXPERIMENTER: Continue. Go on, please.

68   PROZI: You accept all responsibility?

69   EXPERIMENTER: The responsibility is mine. Correct. Please go on. (*Subject returns to his list, starts running through words as rapidly as he can read them, works through to 450 volts.*)

70   PROZI: That's that.

71   EXPERIMENTER: Continue using the 450 switch for each wrong answer. Continue, please.

72   PROZI: But I don't get anything!

73   EXPERIMENTER: Please continue. The next word is "white."

74   PROZI: Don't you think you should look in on him, please?

75   EXPERIMENTER: Not once we've started the experiment.

76   PROZI: What if he's dead in there? (*Gestures toward the room with the electric chair.*) I mean, he told me he can't stand the shock, sir. I don't mean to be rude, but I think you should look in on him. All you have to do is look in on him. All you have to do is look in the door. I don't get no answer, no noise. Something might have happened to the gentleman in there, sir.

77   EXPERIMENTER: We must continue. Go on, please.

78   PROZI: You mean keep giving him what? Four-hundred-fifty volts, what he's got now?

79   EXPERIMENTER: That's correct. Continue. The next word is "white."

80   PROZI (*now at a furious pace*): "White—cloud, horse, rock, house." Answer, please. The answer is "horse." Four hundred and fifty volts. (*Zzumph!*) Next word, "Bag—paint, music, clown, girl." The answer is "paint." Four hundred and fifty volts. (*Zzumph!*) Next word is "Short—sentence, movie . . ."

81   EXPERIMENTER: Excuse me, Teacher. We'll have to discontinue the experiment.

Peculiar Reactions

82 Morris Braverman, another subject, is a thirty-nine-year-old social worker. He looks older than his years because of his bald head and serious demeanor. His brow is furrowed, as if all the world's burdens were carried on his face. He appears intelligent and concerned.

83   When the learner refuses to answer and the experimenter instructs Braverman to treat the absence of an answer as equivalent to a wrong answer, he takes his instruction to heart. Before administering 300 volts he asserts officiously to the victim, "Mr. Wallace, your silence has to be considered as a wrong answer." Then he administers the shock. He offers half-heartedly to change places with the learner, then asks the experimenter, "Do I have to follow these instructions literally?" He is satisfied with the experimenter's answer that he does. His very refined and authoritative manner of speaking is increasingly broken up by wheezing laughter.

84   The experimenter's notes on Mr. Braverman at the last few shocks are:

> Almost breaking up now each time gives shock. Rubbing face to hide laughter. Squinting, trying to hide face with hand, still laughing. Cannot control his laughter at this point no matter what he does. Clenching fist, pushing it onto table.

85   In an interview after the session, Mr. Braverman summarizes the experiment with impressive fluency and intelligence. He feels the experiment may have been designed also to "test the effects on the teacher of being in an essentially sadistic role, as well as the reactions of a student to a learning situation that was authoritative and punitive." When asked how painful the last few shocks administered to the learner were, he indicates that the most extreme category on the scale is not adequate (it read EXTREMELY PAINFUL) and places his mark at the edge of the scale with an arrow carrying it beyond the scale.

86   It is almost impossible to convey the greatly relaxed, sedate quality of his conversation in the interview. In the most relaxed terms, he speaks about his severe inner tension.

87   EXPERIMENTER: At what point were you most tense or nervous?

88   MR. BRAVERMAN: Well, when he first began to cry out in pain, and I realized this was hurting him. This got worse when he just blocked and refused to answer. There was I. I'm a nice person, I think, hurting somebody, and caught up in what seemed a mad situation . . . and in the interest of science, one goes through with it.

89   When the interviewer pursues the general question of tension, Mr. Braverman spontaneously mentions his laughter.

90   "My reactions were awfully peculiar. I don't know if you were watching me, but my reactions were giggly, and trying to stifle laughter. This isn't the way I usually am. This was a sheer reaction to a totally impossible situation. And my reaction was to the situation of having to hurt somebody. And being totally helpless and caught up in a set of circumstances where I just couldn't deviate and I couldn't try to help. This is what got me."

91   Mr. Braverman, like all subjects, was told the actual nature and purpose of the experiment, and a year later he affirmed in a questionnaire that he had learned something of personal importance: "What appalled me was that I could possess this capacity for obedience and compliance to a central idea, i.e., the value of a memory experiment, even after it became clear that continued adherence to this value was at the expense of violation of another value, i.e., don't hurt someone who is helpless and not hurting you. As my wife said, 'You can call yourself Eichmann.'* I hope I deal more effectively with any future conflicts of values I encounter."

The Etiquette of Submission

92 One theoretical interpretation of this behavior holds that all people harbor deeply aggressive instincts continually pressing for expression, and that the experiment provides institutional justification for the release of these impulses. According to this view, if a person is placed in a situation in which he has complete power over another individual, whom he may punish as much as he likes, all that is sadistic and bestial in man comes to the fore. The impulse to shock the victim is seen to flow from the potent aggressive tendencies, which are part of the motivational life of the individual, and the experiment, because it provides social legitimacy, simply opens the door to their expression.

93   It becomes vital, therefore, to compare the subject's performance when he is under orders and when he is allowed to choose the shock level.

94   The procedure was identical to our standard experiment, except that the teacher was told that he was free to select any shock level on any of the trials. (The experimenter took pains to point out that the teacher could use the high-

* *Adolf Eichmann* (1906–1962), the Nazi official responsible for implementing Hitler's "Final Solution" to exterminate the Jews, escaped to Argentina after World War II. In 1960, Israeli agents captured him and brought him to Israel, where he was tried as a war criminal and sentenced to death. At his trial, Eichmann maintained that he was merely following orders in arranging murders of his victims.

est levels on the generator, the lowest, any in between, or any combination of levels.) Each subject proceeded for thirty critical trials. The learner's protests were coordinated to standard shock levels, his first grunt coming at 75 volts, his first vehement protest at 150 volts.

95   The average shock used during the thirty critical trials was less than 60 volts—lower than the point at which the victim showed the first signs of discomfort. Three of the forty subjects did not go beyond the very lowest level on the board, twenty-eight went no higher than 75 volts, and thirty-eight did not go beyond the first loud protest at 150 volts. Two subjects provided the exception, administering up to 325 and 450 volts, but the overall result was that the great majority of people delivered very low, usually painless, shocks when the choice was explicitly up to them.

96   This condition of the experiment undermines another commonly offered explanation of the subjects' behavior—that those who shocked the victim at the most severe levels came only from the sadistic fringe of society. If one considers that almost two-thirds of the participants fall into the category of "obedient" subjects, and that they represented ordinary people drawn from working, managerial, and professional classes, the argument becomes very shaky. Indeed, it is highly reminiscent of the issue that arose in connection with Hannah Arendt's 1963 book, *Eichmann in Jerusalem.* Arendt contended that the prosecution's efforts to depict Eichmann as a sadistic monster was fundamentally wrong, that he came closer to being an uninspired bureaucrat who simply sat at his desk and did his job. For asserting her views, Arendt became the object of considerable scorn, even calumny. Somehow, it was felt that the monstrous deeds carried out by Eichmann required a brutal, twisted personality, evil incarnate. After witnessing hundreds of ordinary persons submit to the authority in our own experiments, I must conclude that Arendt's conception of the banality of evil comes closer to the truth than one might dare imagine. The ordinary person who shocked the victim did so out of a sense of obligation—an impression of his duties as a subject—and not from any peculiarly aggressive tendencies.

97   This is, perhaps, the most fundamental lesson of our study: ordinary people, simply doing their jobs, and without any particular hostility on their part, can become agents in a terrible destructive process. Moreover, even when the destructive effects of their work become patently clear, and they are asked to carry out actions incompatible with fundamental standards of morality, relatively few people have the resources needed to resist authority.

98   Many of the people were in some sense against what they did to the learner, and many protested even while they obeyed. Some were totally convinced of the wrongness of their actions but could not bring themselves to make an open break with authority. They often derived satisfaction from their thoughts and felt that—within themselves, at least—they had been on the side of the angels. They tried to reduce strain by obeying the experimenter but "only slightly," encouraging the learner, touching the generator switches gingerly. When interviewed, such a subject would stress that he had "asserted my humanity" by administering the briefest shock possible. Handling the conflict in this manner was easier than defiance.

99   The situation is constructed so that there is no way the subject can stop shocking the learner without violating the experimenter's definitions of his own competence. The subject fears that he will appear arrogant, untoward, and rude if he breaks off. Although these inhibiting emotions appear small in scope alongside the violence being done to the learner, they suffuse the mind and feelings of the subject, who is miserable at the prospect of having to repudiate the authority to his face. (When the experiment was altered so that the experimenter gave his instructions by telephone instead of in person, only a third as many people were fully obedient through 450 volts.) It is a curious thing that a measure of compassion on the part of the subject—an unwillingness to "hurt" the experimenter's feelings—is part of those binding forces inhibiting his disobedience. The withdrawal of such deference may be as painful to the subject as to the authority he defies.

Duty Without Conflict

100 The subjects do not derive satisfaction from inflicting pain, but they often like the feeling they get from pleasing the experimenter. They are proud of doing a good job, obeying the experimenter under difficult circumstances. While the subjects administered only mild shocks on their own initiative, one experimental variation showed that, under orders, 30 percent of them were willing to deliver 450 volts even when they had to forcibly push the learner's hand down on the electrode.

101   Bruno Batta is a thirty-seven-year-old welder who took part in the variation requiring the use of force. He was born in New Haven, his parents in Italy. He has a rough-hewn face that conveys a conspicuous lack of alertness. He has some difficulty in mastering the experimental procedure and needs to be corrected by the experimenter several times. He shows appreciation for the help and willingness to do what is required. After the 150-volt level, Batta has to force the learner's hand down on the shock plate, since the learner himself refuses to touch it.

102   When the learner first complains, Mr. Batta pays no attention to him. His face remains impassive, as if to dissociate himself from the learner's disruptive behavior. When the experimenter instructs him to force the learner's hand down, he adopts a rigid, mechanical procedure. He tests the generator switch. When it fails to function, he immediately forces the learner's hand onto the shock plate. All the while he maintains the same rigid mask. The learner, seated alongside him, begs him to stop, but with robotic impassivity he continues the procedure.

103   What is extraordinary is his apparent total indifference to the learner; he hardly takes cognizance of him as a human being. Meanwhile, he relates to the experimenter in a submissive and courteous fashion.

104   At the 330-volt level, the learner refuses not only to touch the shock plate but also to provide any answers. Annoyed, Batta turns to him, and chastises him: "You better answer and get it over with. We can't stay here all night." These are the only words he directs to the learner in the course of an hour. Never again does he speak to him. The scene is brutal and depressing, his hard, impassive face showing total indifference as he subdues the screaming learner and gives him shocks. He seems to derive no pleasure from the act itself, only quiet satisfaction at doing his job properly.

105   When he administers 450 volts, he turns to the experimenter and asks, "Where do we go from here, Professor?" His tone is deferential and expresses his willingness to be a cooperative subject, in contrast to the learner's obstinacy.

106   At the end of the session he tells the experimenter how honored he has been to help him, and in a moment of contrition, remarks, "Sir, sorry it couldn't have been a full experiment."

107   He has done his honest best. It is only the deficient behavior of the learner that has denied the experimenter full satisfaction.

108   The essence of obedience is that a person comes to view himself as the instrument for carrying out another person's wishes, and he therefore no longer regards himself as responsible for his actions. Once this critical shift of viewpoint has occurred, all of the essential features of obedience follow. The most far-reaching consequence is that the person feels responsible *to* the authority directing him but feels no responsibility *for* the content of the actions that the authority prescribes. Morality does not disappear—it acquires a radically different focus: the subordinate person feels shame or pride depending on how adequately he has performed the actions called for by authority.

109   Language provides numerous terms to pinpoint this type of morality: *loyalty, duty, discipline* all are terms heavily saturated with moral meaning and refer to the degree to which a person fulfills his obligations to authority. They refer not to the "goodness" of the person per se but to the adequacy with which a subordinate fulfills his socially defined role. The most frequent defense of the individual who has performed a heinous act under command of authority is that he has simply done his duty. In asserting this defense, the individual is not introducing an alibi concocted for the moment but is reporting honestly on the psychological attitude induced by submission to authority.

110   For a person to feel responsible for his actions, he must sense that the behavior has flowed from "the self." In the situation we have studied, subjects have precisely the opposite view of their actions—namely, they see them as originating in the motives of some other person. Subjects in the experiment frequently said, "If it were up to me, I would not have administered shocks to the learner."

111   Once authority has been isolated as the cause of the subject's behavior, it is legitimate to inquire into the necessary elements of authority and how it must be perceived in order to gain compliance. We conducted some investigations into the kinds of changes that would cause the experimenter to lose his power and to be disobeyed by the subject. Some of the variations revealed that:

- *The experimenter's physical presence has a marked impact on his authority.* As cited earlier, obedience dropped off sharply when orders were given by telephone. The experimenter could often induce a disobedient subject to go on by returning to the laboratory.
- *Conflicting authority severely paralyzes action.* When two experimenters of equal status, both seated at the command desk, gave incompatible orders, no shocks were delivered past the point of their disagreement.
- *The rebellious action of others severely undermines authority.* In one variation, three teachers (two actors and a real subject) administered a test and shocks. When the two actors disobeyed the experimenter and refused to

go beyond a certain shock level, thirty-six of the forty subjects joined their disobedient peers and refused as well.

112   Although the experimenter's authority was fragile in some respects, it is also true that he had almost none of the tools used in ordinary command structures. For example, the experimenter did not threaten the subjects with punishment—such as loss of income, community ostracism, or jail—for failure to obey. Neither could he offer incentives. Indeed, we should expect the experimenter's authority to be much less than that of someone like a general, since the experimenter has no power to enforce his imperatives, and since participation in a psychological experiment scarcely evokes the sense of urgency and dedication found in warfare. Despite these limitations, he still managed to command a dismaying degree of obedience.

113   I will cite one final variation of the experiment that depicts a dilemma that is more common in everyday life. The subject was not ordered to pull the lever that shocked the victim, but merely to perform a subsidiary task (administering the word-pair test) while another person administered the shock. In this situation, thirty-seven of forty adults continued to the highest level on the shock generator. Predictably, they excused their behavior by saying that the responsibility belonged to the man who actually pulled the switch. This may illustrate a dangerously typical arrangement in a complex society: it is easy to ignore responsibility when one is only an intermediate link in a chain of action.

114   The problem of obedience is not wholly psychological. The form and shape of society and the way it is developing have much to do with it. There was a time, perhaps, when people were able to give a fully human response to any situation because they were fully absorbed in it as human beings. But as soon as there was a division of labor things changed. Beyond a certain point, the breaking up of society into people carrying out narrow and very special jobs takes away from the human quality of work and life. A person does not get to see the whole situation but only a small part of it, and is thus unable to act without some kind of overall direction. He yields to authority but in doing so is alienated from his own actions.

115   Even Eichmann was sickened when he toured the concentration camps, but he had only to sit at a desk and shuffle papers. At the same time the man in the camp who actually dropped Cyclon-b into the gas chambers was able to justify *his* behavior on the ground that he was only following orders from above. Thus there is a fragmentation of the total human act; no one is confronted with the consequences of his decision to carry out the evil act. The person who assumes responsibility has evaporated. Perhaps this is the most common characteristic of socially organized evil in modern society.

Review Questions

1. Milgram states that obedience is a basic element in the structure of social life. How so?

2. What is the dilemma inherent in obedience to authority?

3. Summarize the obedience experiments.

4. What predictions did experts and laypeople make about the experiments before they were conducted? How did these predictions compare with the experimental results?

5. What are Milgram's views regarding the two assumptions bearing on his experiment that (1) people are naturally aggressive and (2) a lunatic, sadistic fringe is responsible for shocking learners to the maximum limit?

6. How do Milgram's findings corroborate Hannah Arendt's thesis about the "banality of evil"?

7. What, according to Milgram, is the "essence of obedience"?

8. How did being an intermediate link in a chain of action affect a subject's willingness to continue with the experiment?

9. In the article's final two paragraphs, Milgram speaks of a "fragmentation of the total human act." To what is he referring?

Discussion and Writing Suggestions

1. Milgram writes (paragraph 2): "Conservative philosophers argue that the very fabric of society is threatened by disobedience, while humanists stress the primacy of the individual conscience." Develop the arguments of both the conservative and the humanist regarding obedience to authority. Be prepared to debate the ethics of obedience by defending one position or the other.

2. Would you have been glad to have participated in the Milgram experiments? Why or why not?

3. The ethics of Milgram's experimental design came under sharp attack. Diana Baumrind's review of the experiment typifies the criticism; but before you read her work, try to anticipate the objections she raises.

4. Given the general outcome of the experiments, why do you suppose Milgram gives as his first example of a subject's response the German émigré's refusal to continue the electrical shocks?

5. Does the outcome of the experiment upset you in any way? Do you feel the experiment teaches us anything new about human nature?

6. Comment on Milgram's skill as a writer of description. How effectively does he portray his subjects when introducing them? When re-creating their tension in the experiment?

7. Mrs. Braverman said to her husband: "You can call yourself Eichmann." Do you agree with her? Explain.

8. Reread paragraphs 29 through 81, the transcript of the experiment in which Mr. Prozi participated. Appreciating that Prozi was debriefed—that is, was assured that no harm came to the learner— imagine what Prozi might have been thinking as he drove home after the experiment. Develop your thoughts into a monologue, written in the first person, with Prozi at the wheel of his car.

Review of Stanley Milgram's Experiments on Obedience
Diana Baumrind

Many of Milgram's colleagues saluted him for providing that "hard information" about human nature. Others attacked him for violating the rights of his subjects. Still others fault- ed his experimental design and claimed he could not, with any validity, speculate on life out- side the laboratory based on the behavior of his subjects within.

In the following excerpted review, psychologist Diana Baumrind excoriates Milgram for "entrapping" his subjects and potentially harming their "self-image or ability to trust adult authorities in the future." In a footnote at the end of this selection (page 331), we summa- rize Milgram's response to Baumrind's critique.

Diana Baumrind is a psychologist who, when writing this review, worked at the Institute of Human Development, University of California, Berkeley. The review appeared in American Psychologist *shortly after Milgram published the results of his first experiments in 1963.*

1   . . . The dependent, obedient attitude assumed by most subjects in the experi- mental setting is appropriate to that situation. The "game" is defined by the experimenter and he makes the rules. By volunteering, the subject agrees implicitly to assume a posture of trust and obedience. While the experimental conditions leave him exposed, the subject has the right to assume that his secu- rity and self-esteem will be protected.

2   There are other professional situations in which one member—the patient or client—expects help and protection from the other—the physician or psycholo- gist. But the interpersonal relationship between experimenter and subject addi- tionally has unique features which are likely to provoke initial anxiety in the subject. The laboratory is unfamiliar as a setting and the rules of behavior ambiguous compared to a clinician's office. Because of the anxiety and passiv- ity generated by the setting, the subject is more prone to behave in an obedi- ent, suggestible manner in the laboratory than elsewhere. Therefore, the laboratory is not the place to study degree of obedience or suggestibility, as a function of a particular experimental condition, since the base line for these phenomena as found in the laboratory is probably much higher than in most

other settings. Thus experiments in which the relationship to the experimenter as an authority is used as an independent condition are imperfectly designed for the same reason that they are prone to injure the subjects involved. They disregard the special quality of trust and obedience with which the subject appropriately regards the experimenter.

3   Other phenomena which present ethical decisions, unlike those mentioned above, *can* be reproduced successfully in the laboratory. Failure experience, conformity to peer judgment, and isolation are among such phenomena. In these cases we can expect the experimenter to take whatever measures are necessary to prevent the subject from leaving the laboratory more humiliated, insecure, alienated, or hostile than when he arrived. To guarantee that an especially sensitive subject leaves a stressful experimental experience in the proper state sometimes requires special clinical training. But usually an attitude of compassion, respect, gratitude, and common sense will suffice, and no amount of clinical training will substitute. The subject has the right to expect that the psychologist with whom he is interacting has some concern for his welfare, and the personal attributes and professional skill to express his good will effectively.

4   Unfortunately, the subject is not always treated with the respect he deserves. It has become more commonplace in sociopsychological laboratory studies to manipulate, embarrass, and discomfort subjects. At times the insult to the subject's sensibilities extends to the journal reader when the results are reported. Milgram's (1963) study is a case in point. The following is Milgram's abstract of his experiment:

> This article describes a procedure for the study of destructive obedience in the laboratory. It consists of ordering a naive S to administer increasingly more severe punishment to a victim in the context of a learning experiment.* Punishment is administered by means of a shock generator with 30 graded switches ranging from Slight Shock to Danger: Severe Shock. The victim is a confederate of E. The primary dependent variable is the maximum shock the S is willing to administer before he refuses to continue further.† 26 Ss obeyed the experimental commands fully, and administered the highest shock on the generator. 14 Ss broke off the experiment at some point after the victim protested and refused to provide further answers. The procedure created extreme levels of nervous tension in some Ss. Profuse sweating, trembling, and stuttering were typical expressions of this emotional disturbance. One unexpected sign of tension—yet to be explained—was the regular occurrence of nervous laughter, which in some Ss developed into uncontrollable seizures. The variety of interesting behavioral

---

* In psychological experiments, *S* is an abbreviation for *subject*; *E* is an abbreviation for *experimenter*.

† In the context of a psychological experiment, a *dependent variable* is a behavior that is expected to change as a result of changes in the experimental procedure.

dynamics observed in the experiment, the reality of the situation for the S, and the possibility of parametric variations* within the framework of the procedure point to the fruitfulness of further study [p. 371].

5   The detached, objective manner in which Milgram reports the emotional disturbance suffered by his subjects contrasts sharply with his graphic account of that disturbance. Following are two other quotes describing the effects on his subjects of the experimental conditions:

> I observed a mature and initially poised businessman enter the laboratory smiling and confident. Within 20 minutes he was reduced to a twitching, stuttering wreck, who was rapidly approaching a point of nervous collapse. He constantly pulled on his earlobe, and twisted his hands. At one point he pushed his fist into his forehead and muttered: "Oh God, let's stop it." And yet he continued to respond to every word of the experimenter, and obeyed to the end [p. 377].

> In a large number of cases the degree of tension reached extremes that are rarely seen in sociopsychological laboratory studies. Subjects were observed to sweat, tremble, stutter, bite their lips, groan, and dig their fingernails into their flesh. These were characteristic rather than exceptional responses to the experiment.
> One sign of tension was the regular occurrence of nervous laughing fits. Fourteen of the 40 subjects showed definite signs of nervous laughter and smiling. The laughter seemed entirely out of place, even bizarre. Full-blown, uncontrollable seizures were observed for 3 subjects. On one occasion we observed a seizure so violently convulsive that it was necessary to call a halt to the experiment. . . [p. 375].

Milgram does state that,

> After the interview, procedures were undertaken to assure that the subject would leave the laboratory in a state of well being. A friendly reconciliation was arranged between the subject and the victim, and an effort was made to reduce any tensions that arose as a result of the experiment [p. 374].

It would be interesting to know what sort of procedures could dissipate the type of emotional disturbance just described. In view of the effects on subjects, traumatic to a degree which Milgram himself considers nearly unprecedented in sociopsychological experiments, his casual assurance that these tensions were dissipated before the subject left the laboratory is unconvincing.

6   What could be the rational basis for such a posture of indifference? Perhaps Milgram supplies the answer himself when he partially explains the subject's destructive obedience as follows, "Thus they assume that the discomfort caused the victim is momentary, while the scientific gains resulting from the experiment

---

* *Parametric variation* is a statistical term that describes the degree to which information based on data for one experiment can be applied to data for a slightly different experiment.

are enduring" [p. 378]. Indeed such a rationale might suffice to justify the means used to achieve his end if that end were of inestimable value to humanity or were not itself transformed by the means by which it was attained.

7   The behavioral psychologist is not in as good a position to objectify his faith in the significance of his work as medical colleagues at points of breakthrough. His experimental situations are not sufficiently accurate models of real-life experience; his sampling techniques are seldom of a scope which would justify the meaning with which he would like to endow his results; and these results are hard to reproduce by colleagues with opposing theoretical views. Unlike the Sabin vaccine,* for example, the concrete benefit to humanity of his particular piece of work, no matter how competently handled, cannot justify the risk that real harm will be done to the subject. I am not speaking of physical discomfort, inconvenience, or experimental deception per se, but of permanent harm, however slight. I do regard the emotional disturbance described by Milgram as potentially harmful because it could easily effect an alteration in the subject's self-image or ability to trust adult authorities in the future. It is potentially harmful to a subject to commit, in the course of an experiment, acts which he himself considers unworthy, particularly when he has been entrapped into committing such acts by an individual he has reason to trust. The subject's personal responsibility for his actions is not erased because the experimenter reveals to him the means which he used to stimulate these actions. The subject realizes that he would have hurt the victim if the current were on. The realization that he also made a fool of himself by accepting the experimental set results in additional loss of self-esteem. Moreover, the subject finds it difficult to express his anger outwardly after the experimenter in a self-acceptant but friendly manner reveals the hoax.

8   A fairly intense corrective interpersonal experience is indicated wherein the subject admits and accepts his responsibility for his own actions, and at the same time gives vent to his hurt and anger at being fooled. Perhaps an experience as distressing as the one described by Milgram can be integrated by the subject, provided that careful thought is given to the matter. The propriety of such experimentation is still in question even if such a reparational experience were forthcoming. Without it I would expect a naive, sensitive subject to remain deeply hurt and anxious for some time, and a sophisticated, cynical subject to become even more alienated and distrustful.

9   In addition the experimental procedure used by Milgram does not appear suited to the objectives of the study because it does not take into account the special quality of the set which the subject has in the experimental situation. Milgram is concerned with a very important problem, namely, the social consequences of destructive obedience. He says,

> Gas chambers were built, death camps were guarded, daily quotas of corpses were produced with the same efficiency as the manufacture of appliances. These inhumane policies may have originated in the mind of a single person,

---

* The Sabin vaccine provides immunization against polio.

> but they could only be carried out on a massive scale if a very large number
> of persons obeyed orders [p. 371].

But the parallel between authority-subordinate relationships in Hitler's Germany and in Milgram's laboratory is unclear. In the former situation the SS man or member of the German Officer Corps, when obeying orders to slaughter, had no reason to think of his superior officer as benignly disposed towards himself or their victims. The victims were perceived as subhuman and not worthy of consideration. The subordinate officer was an agent in a great cause. He did not need to feel guilt or conflict because within his frame of reference he was acting rightly.

10   It is obvious from Milgram's own description that most of his subjects were concerned about their victims and did trust the experimenter, and that their distressful conflict was generated in part by the consequences of these two disparate but appropriate attitudes. Their distress may have resulted from shock at what the experimenter was doing to them as well as from what they thought they were doing to their victims. In any case there is not a convincing parallel between the phenomena studied by Milgram and destructive obedience as the concept would apply to the subordinate-authority relationship demonstrated in Hitler's Germany. If the experiments were conducted "outside of New Haven and without any visible ties to the university," I would still question their validity on similar although not identical grounds. In addition, I would question the representativeness of a sample of subjects who would voluntarily participate within a noninstitutional setting.

11   In summary, the experimental objectives of the psychologist are seldom incompatible with the subject's ongoing state of well being, provided that the experimenter is willing to take the subject's motives and interests into consideration when planning his methods and correctives. Section 4b in *Ethical Standards of Psychologists* (APA, undated) reads in part:

> Only when a problem is significant and can be investigated in no other way
> is the psychologist justified in exposing human subjects to emotional stress
> or other possible harm. In conducting such research, the psychologist must
> seriously consider the possibility of harmful aftereffects, and should be pre-
> pared to remove them as soon as permitted by the design of the experi-
> ment. Where the danger of serious aftereffects exists, research should be
> conducted only when the subjects or their responsible agents are fully
> informed of this possibility and volunteer nevertheless [p. 12].

From the subject's point of view procedures which involve loss of dignity, self-esteem and trust in rational authority are probably most harmful in the long run and require the most thoughtfully planned reparations, if engaged in at all. The public image of psychology as a profession is highly related to our own actions, and some of these actions are changeworthy. It is important that as research psychologists we protect our ethical sensibilities rather than adapt our personal standards to include as appropriate the kind of indignities to which Milgram's subjects were exposed. I would not like to see experiments such as Milgram's proceed unless the subjects were fully informed of the dangers of serious aftereffects and his correctives were clearly shown to be effective in restoring their state of well being.*

References

American Psychological Association (n.d.). *Ethical standards of psychologists: A summary of ethical principles.* Washington, DC: APA.

Milgram, S. (1963). Behavioral study of obedience. *Journal of Abnormal and Social Psychology. 67,* 371–378.

---

* Stanley Milgram replied to Baumrind's critique in a lengthy critique of his own [From Stanley Milgram, "Issues in the Study of Obedience: A Reply to Baumrind," *American Psychologist* 19, 1964, pp. 848–851]. Following are his principal points:

• Milgram believed that the experimental findings were in large part responsible for Baumrind's criticism. He writes:

Is not Baumrind's criticism based as much on the unanticipated findings as on the method? The findings were that some subjects performed in what appeared to be a shockingly immoral way. If, instead, every one of the subjects had broken off at "slight shock," or at the first sign of the learner's discomfort, the results would have been pleasant, and reassuring, and who would protest?

• Milgram objected to Baumrind's assertion that those who participated in the experiment would have trouble justifying their behavior. Milgram conducted follow-up questionnaires. The results, summarized in Table 1, indicate that 84 percent of the subjects claimed they were pleased to have been a part of the experiment.

TABLE 1 Excerpt from Questionnaire Used in a Follow-up Study of the Obedience Research

Now That I Have Read the Report, and All Things Considered . . .	Defiant	Obedient	All
1. I am very glad to have been in the experiment	40.0%	47.8%	43.5%
2. I am glad to have been in the experiment	43.8%	35.7%	40.2%
3. I am neither sorry nor glad to have been in the experiment	15.3%	14.8%	15.1%
4. I am sorry to have been in the experiment	0.8%	0.7%	0.8%
5. I am very sorry to have been in the experiment	0.0%	1.0%	0.5%

Note—Ninety-two percent of the subjects returned the questionnaire. The characteristics of the nonrespondents were checked against the respondents. They differed from the respondents only with regard to age; younger people were overrepresented in the nonresponding group.

• Baumrind objected that studies of obedience cannot meaningfully be carried out in a laboratory setting, since the obedience occurred in a context where it was appropriate. Milgram's response: "I reject Baumrind's argument that the observed obedience does not count because it occurred where it is appropriate. That is precisely why it *does* count. A soldier's obedience is no less meaningful because it occurs in a pertinent military context."

• Milgram concludes his critique in this way: "If there is a moral to be learned from the obedience study, it is that every man must be responsible for his own actions. This author accepts full responsibility for the design and execution of the study. Some people may feel it should not have been done. I disagree and accept the burden of their judgment."

Review Questions

1. Why might a subject volunteer for an experiment? Why do subjects typically assume a dependent, obedient attitude?

2. Why is a laboratory not a suitable setting for a study of obedience?

3. For what reasons does Baumrind feel that the Milgram experiment was potentially harmful?

4. For what reasons does Baumrind question the relationship between Milgram's findings and the obedient behavior of subordinates in Nazi Germany?

Discussion and Writing Suggestions

1. Baumrind contends that the Milgram experiment is imperfectly designed for two reasons: (1) The laboratory is not the place to test obedience; (2) Milgram disregarded the trust that subjects usually show an experimenter. To what extent do you agree with Baumrind's objections? Do you find them all equally valid?

2. Baumrind states that the ethical procedures of the experiment keep it from having significant value. Do you agree?

3. Do you agree with Baumrind that the subjects were "entrapped" into committing unworthy acts?

4. Assume the identity of a participant in Milgram's experiment who obeyed the experimenter by shocking the learner with the maximum voltage. You have just returned from the lab, and your spouse asks you about your day. Compose the conversation that follows.

Obedience
Ian Parker

As Ian Parker points out, Milgram's experiment became "the most cited, celebrated—and reviled—experiment in the history of social psychology." Parker also explains, however, that for Milgram himself the experiment was a mixed blessing: it would both "make his name and destroy his reputation."

Milgram was fascinated by the Asch experiment, but when all was said and done, this experiment was only about lines. He wondered if it were possible "to make Asch's conformity experiment more humanely significant." Milgram's breakthrough, his "incandescent moment," came when he asked himself "Just how far would a person go under the experimenter's orders?" We have seen the results in the experiment he describes and discusses in an earlier selection.

In the following selection, Ian Parker, a British writer who lives in New York, focuses on both the immediate and the long-term reaction to Milgram's experiments among both the general public and Milgram's professional colleagues and also of the effect of the experiment upon the experimenter himself. This selection is excerpted from an article that Parker wrote for the Autumn 2000 issue of Granta. *Parker writes regularly for the* New Yorker *and has also written for* Human Sciences, History of the Human Sciences, Political Studies, *and* Human Relations.

1   Milgram had a world exclusive. He had caught evil on film. He had invented a kind of torture machine. But it was not immediately clear what he should do with his discovery. When he began the study, he had no theory, nor was he planning to test another man's theory. His idea had sprung from contemplation of Solomon Asch, but the "incandescent" moment at Princeton was a shift away from theory into experimental practice. He had had an idea for an experiment. Now, he was in an odd situation: he had caused something extraordinary to happen, but, technically, his central observation counted for nothing. With no provocation, a New Haven man had hit a fellow citizen with 450 volts. To the general observer, this will come as a surprise, but it is not a social scientific discovery, as Edward E. Jones, the distinguished editor of the *Journal of Personality,* made clear to Milgram when he declined the invitation to publish Milgram's first paper. "The major problem," Jones wrote to Milgram, "is that this is really the report of some pilot research on a method for inducing stress or conflict . . . your data indicate a kind of triumph of social engineering . . . we are led to no conclusions about obedience, really, but rather are exhorted to be impressed with the power of your situation as an influence context." The *Journal of Abnormal and Social Psychology* also rejected the paper on its first submission, calling it a "demonstration" rather than an experiment.

2   Milgram had described only one experimental situation. When he resubmitted the paper to the same journal, he now included experimental variables, and it was publishable. In the rewrite, Milgram put the emphasis on the way in which differences in situation had caused differences in degrees of obedience: the closer the learner to the teacher, the greater the disobedience, and so on. These details were later lost as the experiment moved out of social psychology into the larger world. But it could hardly have happened otherwise. The thought that people were zapping each other in a Yale laboratory is bound to be more striking than the thought that zapping occurs a little less often when one is looking one's victim in the eye. The unscientific truth, perhaps, is that the central comparison in Milgram's study is not between any two experimental variables: it is between what happened in the laboratory, and what we thought would happen. The experimental control in Milgram's model is our hopelessly flawed intuition.

3   "Somehow," Milgram told a friend in 1962, "I don't write as fast or as easily as I run experiments. I have done about all the experiments I plan to do on Obedience, am duly impressed with the results, and now find myself acutely constipated." Milgram found it hard to knock the experiment into social scientific shape. It would be another decade before he incorporated his findings into a serious theory of the sources of human obedience. When he did so, in the

otherwise absorbing and beautifully written book *Obedience to Authority* (1974), his thoughts about an "agentic state"—a psychological zone of abandoned autonomy—were not widely admired or developed by his peers, not least because they were so evidently retrospective. Most readers of *Obedience to Authority* are more likely to take interest in the nods of acknowledgment made to Arthur Koestler's *The Ghost in the Machine,* and to Alex Comfort, the English anarchist poet, novelist, and author of *The Joy of Sex.* Most readers will take more pleasure—and feel Milgram took more pleasure—in the novelistic and strikingly unscientific descriptions of his experimental subjects. ("Mrs Dontz," he wrote, "has an unusually casual, slow-paced way of speaking, and her tone expresses constant humility; it is as if every assertion carries the emotional message: 'I'm just a very ordinary person, don't expect a lot from me.' Physically, she resembles Shirley Booth in the film *Come Back, Little Sheba.*")

4   But while Milgram was struggling to place his findings in a proper scientific context, they seemed to have found a natural home elsewhere. Stanley Milgram—a young social psychology professor at the start of his career—appeared to be in a position to contribute to one of the late twentieth century's most pressing intellectual activities: making sense of the Holocaust. Milgram always placed the experiments in this context, and the figure of Adolf Eichmann, who was seized in Buenos Aires in the spring of 1960, and whose trial in Jerusalem began a year later, loomed over his proceedings. (In a letter that urged Alan Elms to keep up the supply of experimental volunteers, Milgram noted that this role bore "some resemblance to Mr. Eichmann's position.") The trial, as Peter Novick has recently written in *The Holocaust in American Life,* marked "the first time that what we now call the Holocaust was presented to the American public as an entity in its own right, distinct from Nazi barbarism in general." When Milgram published his first paper on the obedience studies in 1963, Hannah Arendt's articles about the trial had just appeared in the *New Yorker,* and in her book, *Eichmann in Jerusalem,* and they had given widespread currency to her perception about "the banality of evil." Milgram put Eichmann's name in the first paragraph of his first obedience paper, and so claimed a place in a pivotal contemporary debate. His argument was this: his study showed how ordinary people are surprisingly prone to destructive obedience; the crimes of the Holocaust had been committed by people obeying orders; those people, therefore, could now be thought ordinary. The argument had its terrifying element and its consoling element: according to Milgram, Americans had to see themselves as potential murderers; at the same time we could understand Nazis to be no more unusual than any New Haven guy in a check shirt.

5   It may seem bizarre now: Milgram returned to ordinary Nazis their Nuremberg defense, nicely polished in an American laboratory. But the idea struck a chord, and news quickly spread of Milgram's well-meaning, all-American torturers. "Once the [Holocaust] connection was in place," said Arthur G. Miller, a leading Milgram scholar, "then the experiments took on a kind of a larger-than-life quality." Milgram's work was reported in the *New York Times* (65% IN TEST BLINDLY OBEY ORDER TO INFLICT PAIN), and the story was quickly picked up by *Life, Esquire,* ABC television, UPI, and the British press. The fame of the experiments

spread, and as the Sixties acquired their defining spirit, Holocaust references were joined by thoughts of My Lai; this was a good moment in history to have things to say about taking orders. By the time Milgram had published his book and released a short film of the experiment, his findings had spread into popular culture, and into theological, medical, and legal discussions. Thomas Blass, a social psychologist at the University of Maryland, Baltimore County, who is preparing a Milgram biography, has a large collection of academic references, including a paper in the context of accountancy ethics. (Is it unthinking obedience that causes accountants to act unlawfully on behalf of clients?) Outside the academy, Dannie Abse published an anti-Milgram play, *The Dogs of Pavlov,* in 1973, and two years later, in America, CBS broadcast a television movie, *The Tenth Level,* that made awkward melodrama out of the obedience experiments, and starred William Shatner as a spookily obsessed and romantically disengaged version of Professor Milgram. ("You may know your social psychology, Professor, but you have a lot to learn about the varieties of massage.") Peter Gabriel sang "We Do What We're Told (Milgram's 37)" in 1986. And there would be more than a whiff of Milgram in the 1990 episode of *The Simpsons,* "There's No Disgrace Like Home," in which the family members repeatedly electrocute one another until the lights across Springfield flicker and dim. Last year, "The Stanley Milgram Experiment"—a comedy sketch duo—made its off-off-Broadway debut in New York. Robbie Chafitz, one of the pair, had been startled and amused by the Milgram film as a teenager, and had always vowed to use the name one way or another. Besides, as he told me, "anything with electricity and people is funny."

6   But however celebrated the experiments became, there was a question they could never shake off. It was an ethical issue: had Stanley Milgram mistreated his subjects? Milgram must have seen the storm coming, at least from the moment when Herbert Winer marched into his office, talking of heart attacks. In the summer of 1962, other subjects recorded their feelings about the experiment in response to a questionnaire sent out by Milgram along with a report explaining the true purpose of the experiment. Replies were transferred on to index cards and are now held—unpublished and anonymous—at Yale. "Since taking part in the experiment," reads one card, "I have suffered a mild heart attack. The one thing my doctor tells me that I must avoid is any form of tension." Another card: "Right now I'm in group therapy. Would it be OK if I showed this report to [the] group and the doctors at the clinic?"

7   Since then, the experiment has been widely attacked from within the profession and from outside. To many, Milgram became a social psychological demon; Alan Elms has met people at parties who have recoiled at the news that he was a Milgram lieutenant. The psychologist Bruno Bettelheim described Milgram's work as "vile" and "in line with the human experiments of the Nazis." In his defense, Milgram would always highlight the results of post-experimental psychological studies—which had reported "no evidence of any traumatic reactions"—and the fact of the debriefings in Linsly-Chittenden Hall, in which care had been taken to give obedient subjects reasons not to feel bad about themselves. They were told to remember, for example, that doctors routinely hurt people in a thoroughly good cause. (Alan Elms wonders if this debriefing was

too effective, and that subjects should have been obliged to confront their actions more fully.)

8   But Milgram never quite won the ethical argument. And the controversy was immediately damaging to his career. Someone—perhaps a Yale colleague, according to Thomas Blass—quickly brought the experiment to the attention of the American Psychological Association, and Milgram's application for APA membership was delayed while the case against him was considered. Today, although the APA is happy to include Milgram's shock generator in a traveling psychology exhibition, it is careful to describe the experiments as "controversial" in its accompanying literature. As the APA points out, modern ethical guidelines (in part inspired by Milgram) would prevent the obedience studies from being repeated today.

9   The controversy followed him. In 1963 Milgram left Yale for Harvard. He was happy there. This is where his two children were born. And when a tenured job came up, he applied. But he needed the unanimous support of his colleagues, and could not secure it. He was blackballed by enemies of the obedience work. (According to Alexandra Milgram, her husband once devised a board game based on the tenure of university professors.) The late Roger Brown, a prominent Harvard psychologist, told Thomas Blass that there had been those in the department who thought of Milgram as "sort of manipulative, or the mad doctor. They felt uneasy about him."

10   So in 1967 Stanley Milgram left Harvard to become head of the social psychology programme in the psychology department in the Graduate Center of the City University of New York (CUNY). In one sense, it was a promotion; he was a full professor at thirty-three. "But after Yale and Harvard, it was the pits," said Milgram's friend and fellow social psychologist, Philip Zimbardo. "Most people I know who didn't get tenure, it had a permanent effect on their lives. You don't get to Yale or Harvard unless you've been number one from kindergarten on, you've been top—so there's this discontinuity. It's the first time in your life you've failed. You're Stanley Milgram, and people all over the world are talking about your research, and you've failed." Milgram was the most cited man in social psychology—Roger Brown, for example, considered his research to be of "profound importance and originality"—yet in later life, he was able to tell Zimbardo that he felt under-appreciated.

11   The ethical furor preyed on Milgram's mind—in the opinion of Arthur G. Miller, it may have contributed to his premature death—but one of its curious side effects was to reinforce the authenticity of his studies in the world outside psychology departments. Among those with a glancing knowledge of Milgram, mistreatment of experimental subjects became the only Milgram controversy. The studies remained intellectually sound, a minor building block of Western thought, a smart conversational gambit at cocktail parties. "People identified the problem with Milgram as just a question of ethics," says Henderikus Stam, of the University of Calgary in Canada, who trained as a social psychologist, but who lost faith and is now a psychological theoretician and historian. "So in a way people never got beyond that. Whereas there's a deeper epistemological question, which is: what can we actually know when we've done an

experiment like that, what are we left with? What have we learned about obedience?"

12   Within the academy, there was another, quieter, line of criticism against Milgram: this was methodological. In a paper in 1968 the social psychologists Martin Orne and Charles Holland raised the issue of incongruity, pointing out that Milgram's subjects had been given two key pieces of information: a man in apparent danger, and another man—a man in a lab coat—whose lack of evident concern suggested there was no danger. It seemed possible that obedient subjects had believed in the more plausible piece of information (no danger), and thus concluded, at some conscious or semi-conscious level, that the experiment was a fake, and—in a "pact of ignorance"—been generous enough to role-play for the sake of science. In other words, they were only obeying the demands of amateur dramatics.

13   Perhaps forgetting that people weep in the theatre, Milgram's response was to argue that the subjects' signs of distress or tension—the twitching and stuttering and racing heartbeats—could be taken as evidence that they had accepted the experiment's reality. He also drew upon the questionnaire he had sent out in 1962, in which his volunteers—now entirely in the know—had been asked to agree with one of five propositions, running from, "I fully believed the learner was getting painful shocks" to "I was certain the learner was not getting the shocks." Milgram was pleased to note that three-quarters of the subjects said they believed the learner was definitely or probably getting the shocks. (He added, reasonably, "It would have been an easy out at this point to deny that the hoax had been accepted.")

14   Herbert Winer reports that he was fully duped, and Alan Elms told me that, watching through the mirror during the summer of 1961, he saw very little evidence of widespread disbelief. But it is worth pointing out that Milgram could have reported his questionnaire statistics rather differently. He could have said that only fifty-six per cent accepted his first proposition: "I fully believed the learner was getting painful shocks." Forty-four per cent of Milgram's subjects claimed to be at least partially unpersuaded. (Indeed, on his own questionnaire, Winer said he had some doubts.) These people do not have much of a presence in Milgram's writings, but you catch a glimpse of them in the Yale Library index cards. One reads: "I was quite sure 'grunts and screams' were electrically reproduced from a speaker mounted in [the] students' room." (They were.) "If [the learner] was making the sounds I should have heard the screams from under the door—which was a poorly fit [*sic*] thin door. I'm sorry that I didn't have enough something to get up and open this door. Which was not locked. To see if student was still there." On another card: "I think that one of the main reasons I continued to the end was that . . . I just couldn't believe that Yale would concoct anything that would be [as] dangerous as the shocks were supposed to be." Another subject had noticed how the experimenter was watching him rather than the learner. Another hadn't understood why he was not allowed to volunteer to be the learner. And another wrote, "I had difficulty describing the experiment to my wife as I was so overcome with laughter—haven't had such a good laugh since the first time I saw the 4 Marx Bros—some 25 years ago."

15   For an experiment supposed to involve the undeserved torture of an innocent Irish-American man, there was a lot of laughter in Yale's Interaction
Laboratory. Frequently, Milgram's subjects could barely contain themselves as
they moved up the shock board. ("On one occasion," Milgram later wrote, "we
observed a seizure so violently convulsive that it was necessary to call a halt to
the experiment.") Behind their one-way mirror, Milgram and Elms were at times
highly amused. And when students are shown the Milgram film today, there
tends to be loud laughter in the room. People laugh, and—despite the alleged
revelation of a universal heart of darkness—they go home having lost little faith
in their friends and their families.

16   According to Henderikus Stam, the laughter of the students, and perhaps that
of the subjects, is a reasonable response to an absurd situation. It's a reaction
to the notion that serious and complex moral issues, and the subtleties of
human behaviour, can reasonably be illuminated through play-acting in a university laboratory. The experiment does nothing but illuminate itself. "What it
does is it says, 'Aren't we clever?' If you wanted to demonstrate obedience to
authority wouldn't you be better showing a film about the Holocaust, or news
clips about Kosovo? Why do you need an experiment, that's the question? What
does the experiment do? The experiment says that if we really want to know
about obedience to authority we need an abstract representation of that obedience, removed from all real forms of the abuse of authority. But what we then
do is to use that representation to refer back to the real historical examples."

17   What happens when we refer back to historical examples? Readers of *Hitler's
Willing Executioners,* Daniel Jonah Goldhagen's study of the complicity of ordinary German citizens in the Holocaust, will learn within one paragraph of a
German policeman, Captain Wolfgang Hoffmann, a "zealous executioner of
Jews," who "once stridently disobeyed a superior order that he deemed morally objectionable." The order was that he and members of his company should
sign a declaration agreeing not to steal from Poles. Hoffmann was affronted that
anyone would think the declaration necessary, that anyone would imagine his
men capable of stealing. "I feel injured," he wrote to his superiors, "in my sense
of honour." The genocidal killing of thousands of Jews was one thing, but plun-
dering from Poles was another. Here was an order to which he was opposed,
and which he felt able to disobey.

18   Goldhagen is impatient with what he calls "the paradigm of external compulsion," which sets the actions of the Holocaust's perpetrators in the context of
social-psychological or totalitarian state forces. His book aims to show how the
crimes of the Holocaust were carried out by people obeying their own consciences, not blindly or fearfully obeying orders. "If you think that certain people
are evil," he told me, "and that it's necessary to do away with them—if you hate
them—and then someone orders you to kill them, you're not carrying out the
deed only because of the order. You're carrying it out because you think it's right.
So in all those instances where people are killing people they hate—their enemies
or their perceived enemies—then Milgram is just completely inapplicable."

19   Goldhagen wonders if the Milgram take on the Holocaust met a particular
need, during the Cold War, for America's new German allies "to be thought well
of." He also wonders if, by robbing people of their agency, "of the fact that they're

moral beings," the experiment tapped into the kind of reductive universalism by which, he says, Americans are easily seduced—the belief that all men are created equal, and in this case equally obedient. Goldhagen has no confidence in the idea that Milgram was measuring obedience at all. The experimental conditions did not properly control for other variables, such as trust, nor did they allow for the way decisions are made in the real world—over time, after consultation. Besides, said Goldhagen, in a tone close to exasperation, "people disobey all the time! Look around the world. Do people always pay all their taxes? Do what their bosses tell them? Or quietly accept what any government decides? Even with all kinds of sanctions available, one of the greatest problems that institutions face is to get their members to comply with rules and orders." Milgram's findings, he says, "are roundly, repeatedly and glaringly falsified by life."

20   In the opinion of Professor Stam, this comes close to defining the problems of social psychology itself. It is a discipline, he says, that makes the peculiar claim that "if you want to ask questions about the social world, you have to turn them into abstract technical questions." The Milgram experiment, he says, "has the air of scientificity about it. But it's not scientific, it's . . . *scientistic.*"

21   And there is Milgram's problem: he devised an intensely powerful piece of tragicomic laboratory theatre, and then had to smuggle it into the faculty of social science. His most famous work—which had something to say about trust, embarrassment, low-level sadism, willingness to please, exaggerated post-war respect for scientific research, the sleepy, heavy-lidded pleasure of being asked to *take part,* and, perhaps, too, the desire of a rather awkward young academic to secure attention and respect—had to pass itself off as an event with a single, steady meaning. And that disguise has not always been convincing. It's odd to hear Arthur G. Miller—one of the world's leading Milgram scholars—acknowledge that there have been times when he has wondered, just for a moment, if the experiments perhaps mean nothing at all.

22   But the faculty of social psychology is not ready to let Milgram go. And there may be a new way to rescue the experiments from their ungainly ambiguity. This is the route taken by Professors Lee Ross and Richard E. Nisbett (at Stanford and the University of Michigan respectively), whose recent synthesis of social psychological thinking aims to give the subject new power. According to Professor Ross, the experiments may be "performance," but they still have social psychological news to deliver. If that is true, then we can do something that the late professor was not always able to do himself: we can make a kind of reconciliation between the artist and the scientist in Stanley Milgram.

23   Ross and Nisbett find a seat for Stanley Milgram at social psychology's high table. They do this slyly, by taking the idea of obedience—Milgram's big idea—and putting it quietly to one side. When Ross teaches Milgram at Stanford, he makes a point of giving his students detailed instructions on how to prepare for the classes—instructions that he knows will be thoroughly ignored. He is then able to stand in front of his students and examine their disobedience. "I asked you to do something that's good for you rather than bad for you," he tells them. "And I'm a legitimate authority rather than an illegitimate one, and I actually have power that the Milgram experimenter doesn't have. And yet you didn't obey. So the study can't just be about obedience." What it is primarily about, Ross tells his students—

and it may be about other things too—is the extreme power of a situation that has been built without obvious escape routes. (As Herbert Winer said: "At no time was there a pause or a break when anything could be raised. . . .") "There was really no exit," Ross told me, "there was no channel for disobedience. People who were discomforted, who wanted to disobey, didn't quite know how to do it. They made some timid attempts, and it got them nowhere. In order to disobey they have to step out of the whole situation, and say to the experimenter, 'Go to hell! You can't tell me what to do!' As long as they continue to function within that relationship, they're asking the experimenter for permission not to give shocks, and as long as the experimenter denies them that permission, they're stuck. They don't know how to get out of it." Ross suspects that things would have turned out very differently given one change to the situation. It's a fairly big change: the addition of a prominent red button in the middle of the table, combined with a clearly displayed notice signed by the "Human Subjects' Committee" explaining that the button could be pressed "by any subject in any experiment at any time if he or she absolutely refuses to continue."

24   According to Ross and Nisbett (who are saying something that Milgram surely knew, but something he allowed to become obscured), the Obedience Experiments point us towards a great social psychological truth, perhaps *the* great truth, which is this: people tend to do things because of where they are, not who they are, and we are slow to see it. We look for character traits to explain a person's actions—he is clever, shy, generous, arrogant—and we stubbornly underestimate the influence of the situation, the way things *happened to be* at that moment. So, if circumstances had been even only subtly different (if she hadn't been running late; if he'd been *told* the film was a comedy), the behaviour might have been radically different. Under certain controlled circumstances, then, people can be induced to behave unkindly: to that extent, Milgram may have something to say about a kind of destructive obedience. But under other circumstances, Professor Ross promised me, the same people would be nice. Given the correct situation, he said, we could be led to do "terrifically altruistic and self-sacrificing things that we would never have agreed to before we started."

25   So the experiment that has troubled us for nearly forty years (that buzzing and howling), and which caused Milgram to have dark thoughts about America's vulnerability to fascism, suddenly has a new complexion. Now, it is about the influence of *any* situation on behaviour, good or bad: "You stop on the highway to help someone," Professor Ross said, "and then the help you try to give doesn't prove to be enough, so you give the person a ride, and then you end up lending them money or letting them stay in your house. It wasn't because that was the person in the world you cared about the most, it was just one thing led to another. Step by step."

26   That's the Milgram situation. "We can take ordinary people," Ross said, "and make them show a degree of obedience or conformity—or for that matter altruism or bravery, whatever—to a degree that we would normally assume you would only see in the rare few. And that's relevant to telling us what we're capable of making people do, but it also tells us that when we observe the world, we are often going to be making an attribution error, because lots of times, the

situational factors have been opaque to us, and therefore we are making erroneous inferences about people. The South African government says, 'Can we deal with this fellow Mandela?' and the answer is, 'No, he's a terrorist.' But a social psychologist would say, 'Mandela, in *one* context, given *one* set of situations, was a terrorist.'" According to Ross, that's the key lesson of social psychology; that's how the discipline can be useful in education, the work place, and law. "Our emphasis," he says, "should be on creating situations that promote what we want to promote, rather than searching endlessly for the right person. Don't assume that people who commit atrocities are atrocious people, or people who do heroic things are heroic. Don't get overly carried away; don't think, because you observed someone under one set of discrete situational factors, that you know *what they're like,* and therefore can predict what they would do in a very different set of circumstances."

27   It's hard not to think of Stanley Milgram in another set of circumstances—to imagine the careers he did not have in films or in the theatre, and to wonder how things would have turned out if his work had appeared at another time, or had been read a little differently. It may now be possible to place the Obedience Experiments somewhere near the center of the social psychological project, but that's not how it felt in the last years of Milgram's life. He had failed to secure tenure at Harvard. Disappointed, he moved to New York, assuming he would soon be leaving again, to take up a post at a more glamorous institution. But he was still at CUNY seventeen years later, at the time of his premature death. "He had hoped it would be just for five years," Alexandra Milgram told me, "But things got much more difficult to move on to other places. You were glad to have what you had. And he was happy to do the work that he did. I don't think he was as happy at the university as he was at, say, Harvard, but he was a very independent person: he had his ideas, he had his research."

28   The research pushed Milgram into a kind of internal exile. Confirming his reputation as social psychology's renegade, he pursued work that, although often brilliantly conceived and elegantly reported, could look eccentric and old-fashioned to colleagues, and that ran the risk of appearing to place method ahead of meaning. "It would flash and then burn out," says Professor Miller, "and then he'd go on to something else." He sent his (young, able-bodied) students on to the New York subway to ask people to give up their seats. He co-wrote a paper about *Candid Camera*'s virtues as an archive for students of human behaviour. Pre-empting the play *Six Degrees of Separation,* he studied the "small world" phenomenon, investigating the chains of acquaintance that link two strangers. He took photographs of rail commuters and showed them to those who travelled on the same route, to explore the notion of the "familiar stranger." In an expensive, elaborate, and ultimately inconclusive experiment in 1971, he explored the links between antisocial acts seen on television and similar acts in real life by getting CBS to produce and air two versions of a hit hospital drama, *Medical Center.* He asked students to try to give away money on the street. He tested how easy it was for people to walk between a pavement photographer and his subject. And when he was recuperating from one of a series of heart attacks, he made an informal study of the social psychology of being a hospital patient. He was only fifty-one when he died.

29   Once, shortly before the Obedience Experiments had begun, Milgram had written from Yale about his fear of having made the wrong career move. "Of course," he told a friend, "I am glad that the present job sometimes engages my genuine interests, or at least, a part of my interests, but there is another part that remains submerged and somehow, perhaps because it is not expressed, seems most important." He described his routine: pulling himself out of bed, dragging himself to the lecture room "where I misrepresent myself for two hours as an efficient and persevering man of science . . . I should not be here, but in Greece shooting films under a Mediterranean sun, hopping about in a small boat from one Aegean isle to the next." He added, in a spirit of comic self-laceration, "Fool!"

Review Questions

1. Why was Milgram's article rejected when it was first submitted for publication? What did Milgram do to ensure its professional acceptability?

2. What does Parker mean when he says (paragraph 5) that "Milgram returned to ordinary Nazis their Nuremberg defense, nicely polished in an American laboratory"?

3. In what sense did his obedience experiments ruin Milgram's career?

4. Based on what you have read about Daniel Jonah Goldhagen, explain the meaning of the title of his book, *Hitler's Willing Executioners*.

5. What does Henderikus Stam mean when he charges that Milgram's experiment is "not scientific, it's . . . scientistic"?

Discussion and Writing Suggestions

1. Parker charts the course of the Milgram experiments working their way into popular consciousness—from magazine articles to TV dramas, to episodes of *The Simpsons*. Why do you think that the obedience experiments, more than thousands of other social science experiments, performed during the 1960s, made such an indelible impact, even outside the profession of social psychology?

2. Parker focuses in part upon the ethical problems with Milgram's experiments. To what extent do you believe that these experiments were unethical? To what extent does Milgram's chief rejoinder— that his surveys taken after the fact show that the vast majority of his subjects suffered no permanent ill effects—effectively rebut the ethical objections?

3. One theory about why many of Milgram's subjects behaved as they did—going all the way to the top of the shock register—is that they

did not really believe that the subjects were being shocked; they simply went along with the experimenter because they did not think it possible that a prestigious institution like Yale would be a party to inflicting harm on people. To what extent do you find this theory plausible?

4. Parker notes that not only did many of Milgram's subjects laugh during the experiments and later, in recounting it to others, but many students also laugh when they watch Milgram's film ("Obedience") in class. If you saw the film, did you laugh when you saw it? Did others? Attempt to account for this apparently incongruous reaction.

5. How necessary was Milgram's experiment? Parker notes that many have argued that if we want to learn about the power of authority to compel obedience, all we need do is study the numerous historical examples (the Holocaust being the one most often cited) of obedience to malign authority. To what extent do the results of Milgram's experiments add anything to what we already know about obedience from actual historical events?

6. Parker includes the following quotation from Daniel Jonah Goldhagen, author of *Hitler's Willing Executioners*: "If you think that certain people are evil . . . and that it's necessary to do away with them—if you hate them—and then someone orders you to kill them, you're not carrying out the deed only because of the order. You're carrying it out because you think it's right" (paragraph 18). In other words, people who commit evil acts do so less because they feel compelled to obey external authority figures than because they are following their own consciences, their own sense of who is the enemy. To what extent do you find that this theory accounts for many of the evil acts in the world?

7. Parker cites Ross's theory that an important reason that so many of Milgram's subjects were fully obedient is that they had no "escape route"—the experimenter never gave them time or opportunity to call a halt to the experimental procedure. To what extent do you find this theory plausible? Would a "red button" to stop the experiment likely have led to a different set of results?

8. Lee Ross and Richard E. Nisbet believe that the main factor determining the obedience of Milgram's subjects was not the *character* of the subjects, but rather the *situation*—that given a different situation (i.e., a situation not involving a carefully controlled laboratory experiment), the same subjects who were so obedient might have behaved very differently. To what extent do you find this theory plausible? Can you think of examples in which people will behave in different ways in different situations?

The Stanford Prison Experiment
Philip G. Zimbardo

As well known—and as controversial—as the Milgram obedience experiments, the Stanford Prison Experiment (1973) raises troubling questions about the ability of individuals to resist authoritarian or obedient roles, if the social setting requires these roles. Philip G. Zimbardo, professor of psychology at Stanford University, set out to study the process by which prisoners and guards "learn" to become compliant and authoritarian, respectively. To find subjects for the experiment, Zimbardo placed an advertisement in a local newspaper:

Male college students needed for psychological study of prison life. $15 per day for 1–2 weeks beginning Aug. 14. For further information & applications, come to Room 248, Jordan Hall, Stanford U.

The ad drew seventy-five responses. From these Zimbardo and his colleagues selected twenty-one college-age men, half of whom would become "prisoners" in the experiment, the other half "guards." The elaborate role-playing scenario, planned for two weeks, had to be cut short due to the intensity of subjects' responses. This article first appeared in the New York Times Magazine *(8 April 1973).*

In prison, those things withheld from and denied to the prisoner become precisely what he wants most of all.
> —Eldridge Cleaver, "Soul on Ice"

Our sense of power is more vivid when we break a man's spirit than when we win his heart.
> —Eric Hoffer, "The Passionate State of Mind"

Every prison that men build / Is built with bricks of shame, / And bound with bars lest Christ should see / How men their brothers maim.
> —Oscar Wilde, "The Ballad of Reading Gaol"

Wherever anyone is against his will that is to him a prison.
> —Epictetus, "Discourses"

1   The quiet of a summer morning in Palo Alto, Calif., was shattered by a screeching squad car siren as police swept through the city picking up college students in a surprise mass arrest. Each suspect was charged with a felony, warned of his constitutional rights, spread-eagled against the car, searched, handcuffed, and carted off in the back seat of the squad car to the police station for booking.

2   After fingerprinting and the preparation of identification forms for his "jacket" (central information file), each prisoner was left isolated in a detention cell to wonder what he had done to get himself into this mess. After a while, he was

blindfolded and transported to the "Stanford County Prison." Here he began the process of becoming a prisoner—stripped naked, skin-searched, deloused, and issued a uniform, bedding, soup, and towel.

3   The warden offered an impromptu welcome:

4   "As you probably know, I'm your warden. All of you have shown that you are unable to function outside in the real world for one reason or another—that somehow you lack the responsibility of good citizens of this great country. We of this prison, your correctional staff, are going to help you learn what your responsibilities as citizens of this country are. Here are the rules. Sometime in the near future there will be a copy of the rules posted in each of the cells. We expect you to know them and to be able to recite them by number. If you follow all of these rules and keep your hands clean, repent for your misdeeds, and show a proper attitude of penitence, you and I will get along just fine."

5   There followed a reading of the 16 basic rules of prisoner conduct, "Rule Number One: Prisoners must remain silent during rest periods, after lights are out, during meals, and whenever they are outside the prison yard. Two: Prisoners must eat at mealtimes and only at mealtimes. Three: Prisoners must not move, tamper, deface, or damage walls, ceilings, windows, doors, or other prison property. . . . Seven: Prisoners must address each other by their ID number only. Eight: Prisoners must address the guards as 'Mr. Correctional Officer.' . . . Sixteen: Failure to obey any of the above rules may result in punishment."

6   By late afternoon these youthful "first offenders" sat in dazed silence on the cots in their barren cells trying to make sense of the events that had transformed their lives so dramatically.

7   If the police arrests and processing were executed with customary detachment, however, there were some things that didn't fit. For these men were now part of a very unusual kind of prison, an experimental mock prison, created by social psychologists to study the effects of imprisonment upon volunteer research subjects. When we planned our two-week-long simulation of prison life, we sought to understand more about the process by which people called "prisoners" lose their liberty, civil rights, independence, and privacy, while those called "guards" gain social power by accepting the responsibility for controlling and managing the lives of their dependent charges.

8   Why didn't we pursue this research in a real prison? First, prison systems are fortresses of secrecy, closed to impartial observation, and thereby immune to critical analysis from anyone not already part of the correctional authority. Second, in any real prison, it is impossible to separate what each individual brings into the prison from what the prison brings out in each person.

9   We populated our mock prison with a homogeneous group of people who could be considered "normal-average" on the basis of clinical interviews and personality tests. Our participants (10 prisoners and 11 guards) were selected from more than 75 volunteers recruited through ads in the city and campus newspapers. The applicants were mostly college students from all over the United States and Canada who happened to be in the Stanford area during the summer and were attracted by the lure of earning $15 a day for participating in a study of prison life. We selected only those judged to be emotionally stable, physically healthy, mature, law-abiding citizens.

10   The sample of average, middle-class, Caucasian, college-age males (plus one Oriental student) was arbitrarily divided by the flip of a coin. Half were randomly assigned to play the role of guards, the others of prisoners. There were no measurable differences between the guards and the prisoners at the start of the experiment. Although initially warned that as prisoners their privacy and other civil rights would be violated and that they might be subjected to harassment, every subject was completely confident of his ability to endure whatever the prison had to offer for the full two-week experimental period. Each subject unhesitatingly agreed to give his "informed consent" to participate.

11   The prison was constructed in the basement of Stanford University's psychology building, which was deserted after the end of the summer-school session. A long corridor was converted into the prison "yard" by partitioning off both ends. Three small laboratory rooms opening onto this corridor were made into cells by installing metal barred doors and replacing existing furniture with cots, three to a cell. Adjacent offices were refurnished as guards' quarters, interview-testing rooms, and bedrooms for the "warden" (Jaffe) and the "superintendent" (Zimbardo). A concealed video camera and hidden microphones recorded much of the activity and conversation of guards and prisoners. The physical environment was one in which prisoners could always be observed by the staff, the only exception being when they were secluded in solitary confinement (a small, dark storage closet, labeled "The Hole").

12   Our mock prison represented an attempt to simulate the psychological state of imprisonment in certain ways. We based our experiment on an in-depth analysis of the prison situation, developed after hundreds of hours of discussion with Carlo Prescott (our ex-con consultant), parole officers, and correctional personnel, and after reviewing much of the existing literature on prisons and concentration camps.

13   "Real" prisoners typically report feeling powerless, arbitrarily controlled, dependent, frustrated, hopeless, anonymous, dehumanized, and emasculated. It was not possible, pragmatically or ethically, to create such chronic states in volunteer subjects who realize that they are in an experiment for only a short time. Racism, physical brutality, indefinite confinement, and enforced homosexuality were not features of our mock prison. But we did try to reproduce those elements of the prison experience that seemed most fundamental.

14   We promoted anonymity by seeking to minimize each prisoner's sense of uniqueness and prior identity. The prisoners wore smocks and nylon stocking caps; they had to use their ID numbers; their personal effects were removed and they were housed in barren cells. All of this made them appear similar to each other and indistinguishable to observers. Their smocks, which were like dresses, were worn without undergarments, causing the prisoners to be restrained in their physical actions and to move in ways that were more feminine than masculine. The prisoners were forced to obtain permission from the guard for routine and simple activities such as writing letters, smoking a cigarette, or even going to the toilet; this elicited from them a childlike dependency.

15   Their quarters, though clean and neat, were small, stark, and without esthetic appeal. The lack of windows resulted in poor air circulation, and persistent odors arose from the unwashed bodies of the prisoners. After 10 P.M. lockup, toilet priv-

ileges were denied, so prisoners who had to relieve themselves would have to urinate and defecate in buckets provided by the guards. Sometimes the guards refused permission to have them cleaned out, and this made the prison smell.

16   Above all, "real" prisons are machines for playing tricks with the human conception of time. In our windowless prison, the prisoners often did not even know whether it was day or night. A few hours after falling asleep, they were roused by shrill whistles for their "count." The ostensible purpose of the count was to provide a public test of the prisoners' knowledge of the rules and of their ID numbers. But more important, the count, which occurred at least once on each of the three different guard shifts, provided a regular occasion for the guards to relate to the prisoners. Over the course of the study, the duration of the counts was spontaneously increased by the guards from their initial perfunctory 10 minutes to a seemingly interminable several hours. During these confrontations, guards who were bored could find ways to amuse themselves, ridiculing recalcitrant prisoners, enforcing arbitrary rules, and openly exaggerating any dissension among the prisoners.

17   The guards were also "deindividualized": They wore identical khaki uniforms and silver reflector sunglasses that made eye contact with them impossible. Their symbols of power were billy clubs, whistles, handcuffs, and the keys to the cells and the "main gate." Although our guards received no formal training from us in how to be guards, for the most part they moved with apparent ease into their roles. The media had already provided them with ample models of prison guards to emulate.

18   Because we were as interested in the guards' behavior as in the prisoners', they were given considerable latitude to improvise and to develop strategies and tactics of prisoner management. Our guards were told that they must maintain "law and order" in this prison, that they were responsible for handling any trouble that might break out, and they were cautioned about the seriousness and potential dangers of the situation they were about to enter. Surprisingly, in most prison systems, "real" guards are not given much more psychological preparation or adequate training than this for what is one of the most complex, demanding, and dangerous jobs our society has to offer. They are expected to learn how to adjust to their new employment mostly from on-the-job experience, and from contacts with the "old bulls" during a survival-of-the-fittest orientation period. According to an orientation manual for correctional officers at San Quentin, "the only way you really get to know San Quentin is through experience and time. Some of us take more time and must go through more experiences than others to accomplish this; some really never do get there."

19   You cannot be a prisoner if no one will be your guard, and you cannot be a prison guard if no one takes you or your prison seriously. Therefore, over time a perverted symbiotic relationship developed. As the guards became more aggressive, prisoners became more passive; assertion by the guards led to dependency in the prisoners; self-aggrandizement was met with self-deprecation, authority with helplessness, and the counterpart of the guards' sense of mastery and control was the depression and hopelessness witnessed in the prisoners. As these differences in behavior, mood, and perception became more evident to all, the need for the now "righteously" powerful guards to rule

the obviously inferior and powerless inmates became a sufficient reason to support almost any further indignity of man against man:

20 Guard K: "During the inspection, I went to cell 2 to mess up a bed which the prisoner had made and he grabbed me, screaming that he had just made it, and he wasn't going to let me mess it up. He grabbed my throat, and although he was laughing I was pretty scared. . . . I lashed out with my stick and hit him in the chin (although not very hard), and when I freed myself I became angry. I wanted to get back in the cell and have a go with him, since he attacked me when I was not ready."

21 Guard M: "I was surprised at myself . . . I made them call each other names and clean the toilets out with their bare hands. I practically considered the prisoners cattle, and I kept thinking: 'I have to watch out for them in case they try something.' "

22 Guard A: "I was tired of seeing the prisoners in their rags and smelling the strong odors of their bodies that filled the cells. I watched them tear at each other on orders given by us. They didn't see it as an experiment. It was real and they were fighting to keep their identity. But we were always there to show them who was boss."

23 Because the first day passed without incident, we were surprised and totally unprepared for the rebellion that broke out on the morning of the second day. The prisoners removed their stocking caps, ripped off their numbers, and barricaded themselves inside the cells by putting their beds against the doors. What should we do? The guards were very much upset because the prisoners also began to taunt and curse them to their faces. When the morning shift of guards came on, they were upset at the night shift who, they felt, must have been too permissive and too lenient. The guards had to handle the rebellion themselves, and what they did was startling to behold.

24 At first they insisted that reinforcements be called in. The two guards who were waiting on stand-by call at home came in, and the night shift of guards voluntarily remained on duty (without extra pay) to bolster the morning shift. The guards met and decided to treat force with force. They got a fire extinguisher that shot a stream of skin-chilling carbon dioxide and forced the prisoners away from the doors; they broke into each cell, stripped the prisoners naked, took the beds out, forced the prisoners who were the ringleaders into solitary confinement, and generally began to harass and intimidate the prisoners.

25 After crushing the riot, the guards decided to head off further unrest by creating a privileged cell for those who were "good prisoners" and then, without explanation, switching some of the troublemakers into it and some of the good prisoners out into the other cells. The prisoner ringleaders could not trust these new cellmates because they had not joined in the riot and might even be "snitches." The prisoners never again acted in unity against the system. One of the leaders of the prisoner revolt later confided:

26 "If we had gotten together then, I think we could have taken over the place. But when I saw the revolt wasn't working, I decided to toe the line. Everyone settled into the same pattern. From then on, we were really controlled by the guards."

27   It was after this episode that the guards really began to demonstrate their inventiveness in the application of arbitrary power. They made the prisoners obey petty, meaningless, and often inconsistent rules, forced them to engage in tedious, useless work, such as moving cartons back and forth between closets and picking thorns out of their blankets for hours on end. (The guards had previously dragged the blankets through thorny bushes to create this disagreeable task.) Not only did the prisoners have to sing songs or laugh or refrain from smiling on command; they were also encouraged to curse and vilify each other publicly during some of the counts. They sounded off their numbers endlessly and were repeatedly made to do pushups, on occasion with a guard stepping on them or a prisoner sitting on them.

28   Slowly the prisoners became resigned to their fate and even behaved in ways that actually helped to justify their dehumanizing treatment at the hands of the guards. Analysis of the tape-recorded private conversations between prisoners and of remarks made by them to interviewers revealed that fully half could be classified as nonsupportive of other prisoners. More dramatic, 85 percent of the evaluative statements by prisoners about their fellow prisoners were uncomplimentary and deprecating.

29   This should be taken in the context of an even more surprising result. What do you imagine the prisoners talked about when they were alone in their cells with each other, given a temporary respite from the continual harassment and surveillance by the guards? Girl friends, career plans, hobbies or politics?

30   No, their concerns were almost exclusively riveted to prison topics. Their monitored conversations revealed that only 10 percent of the time was devoted to "outside" topics, while 90 percent of the time they discussed escape plans, the awful food, grievances or ingratiating tactics to use with specific guards in order to get a cigarette, permission to go to the toilet, or some other favor. Their obsession with these immediate survival concerns made talk about the past and future an idle luxury.

31   And this was not a minor point. So long as the prisoners did not get to know each other as people, they only extended the oppressiveness and reality of their life as prisoners. For the most part, each prisoner observed his fellow prisoners allowing the guards to humiliate them, acting like compliant sheep, carrying out mindless orders with total obedience, and even being cursed by fellow prisoners (at a guard's command). Under such circumstances, how could a prisoner have respect for his fellows, or any self-respect for what *he* obviously was becoming in the eyes of all those evaluating him?

32   The combination of realism and symbolism in this experiment had fused to create a vivid illusion of imprisonment. The illusion merged inextricably with reality for at least some of the time for every individual in the situation. It was remarkable how readily we all slipped into our roles, temporarily gave up our identities, and allowed these assigned roles and the social forces in the situation to guide, shape, and eventually to control our freedom of thought and action.

33   But precisely where does one's "identity" end and one's "role" begin? When the private self and the public role behavior clash, what direction will attempts to impose consistency take? Consider the reactions of the parents, relatives, and

friends of the prisoners who visited their forlorn sons, brothers, and lovers during two scheduled visitors' hours. They were taught in short order that they were our guests, allowed the privilege of visiting only by complying with the regulations of the institution. They had to register, were made to wait half an hour, were told that only two visitors could see any one prisoner; the total visiting time was cut from an hour to only 10 minutes, they had to be under the surveillance of a guard, and before any parents could enter the visiting area, they had to discuss their son's case with the warden. Of course they complained about these arbitrary rules, but their conditioned, middle-class reaction was to work within the system to appeal privately to the superintendent to make conditions better for their prisoners.

34   In less than 36 hours, we were forced to release prisoner 8612 because of extreme depression, disorganized thinking, uncontrollable crying, and fits of rage. We did so reluctantly because we believed he was trying to "con" us—it was unimaginable that a volunteer prisoner in a mock prison could legitimately be suffering and disturbed to that extent. But then on each of the next three days another prisoner reacted with similar anxiety symptoms, and we were forced to terminate them, too. In a fifth case, a prisoner was released after developing a psychosomatic rash over his entire body (triggered by rejection of his parole appeal by the mock parole board). These men were simply unable to make an adequate adjustment to prison life. Those who endured the prison experience to the end could be distinguished from those who broke down and were released early in only one dimension—authoritarianism. On a psychological test designed to reveal a person's authoritarianism, those prisoners who had the highest scores were best able to function in this authoritarian prison environment.

35   If the authoritarian situation became a serious matter for the prisoners, it became even more serious—and sinister—for the guards. Typically, the guards insulted the prisoners, threatened them, were physically aggressive, used instruments (night sticks, fire extinguishers, etc.) to keep the prisoners in line, and referred to them in impersonal, anonymous, deprecating ways: "Hey, you," or "You [obscenity], 5401, come here." From the first to the last day, there was a significant increase in the guards' use of most of these domineering, abusive tactics.

36   Everyone and everything in the prison was defined by power. To be a guard who did not take advantage of this institutionally sanctioned use of power was to appear "weak," "out of it," "wired up by the prisoners," or simply a deviant from the established norms of appropriate guard behavior. Using Erich Fromm's definition of sadism, as "the wish for absolute control over another living being," all of the mock guards at one time or another during this study behaved sadistically toward the prisoners. Many of them reported—in their diaries, on critical-incident report forms, and during post-experimental interviews—being delighted in the new-found power and control they exercised and sorry to see it relinquished at the end of the study.

37   Some of the guards reacted to the situation in the extreme and behaved with great hostility and cruelty in the forms of degradation they invented for the prisoners. But others were kinder; they occasionally did little favors for the prisoners, were reluctant to punish them, and avoided situations where prisoners were being harassed. The torment experienced by one of these good guards is obvious in his perceptive analysis of what if felt like to be responded to as a "guard":

38   "What made the experience most depressing for me was the fact that we were continually called upon to act in a way that just was contrary to what I really feel inside. I don't feel like I'm the type of person that would be a guard, just constantly giving out [orders] . . . and forcing people to do things, and pushing and lying—it just didn't seem like me, and to continually keep up and put on a face like that is just really one of the most oppressive things you can do. It's almost like a prison that you create yourself—you get into it, and it becomes almost the definition you make of yourself, it almost becomes like walls, and you want to break out and you want just to be able to tell everyone that 'this isn't really me at all, and I'm not the person that's confined in there—I'm a person who wants to get out and show you that I am free, and I do have my own will, and I'm not the sadistic type of person that enjoys this kind of thing.'"

39   Still, the behavior of these good guards seemed more motivated by a desire to be liked by everyone in the system than by a concern for the inmates' welfare. No guard ever intervened in any direct way on behalf of the prisoners, ever interfered with the orders of the cruelest guards, or ever openly complained about the subhuman quality of life that characterized this prison.

40   Perhaps the most devastating impact of the more hostile guards was their creation of a capricious, arbitrary environment. Over time the prisoners began to react passively. When our mock prisoners asked questions, they got answers about half the time, but the rest of the time they were insulted and punished— and it was not possible for them to predict which would be the outcome. As they began to "toe the line," they stopped resisting, questioning and, indeed, almost ceased responding altogether. There was a general decrease in all categories of response as they learned the safest strategy to use in an unpredictable, threatening environment from which there is no physical escape—do nothing, except what is required. Act not, want not, feel not, and you will not get into trouble in prisonlike situations.

41   Can it really be, you wonder, that intelligent, educated volunteers could have lost sight of the reality that they were merely acting a part in an elaborate game that would eventually end? There are many indications not only that they did, but that, in addition, so did we and so did other apparently sensible, responsible adults.

42   Prisoner 819, who had gone into an uncontrollable crying fit, was about to be prematurely released from the prison when a guard lined up the prisoners and had them chant in unison, "819 is a bad prisoner. Because of what 819 did to prison property we all must suffer. 819 is a bad prisoner." Over and over again. When we realized 819 might be overhearing this, we rushed into the room where 819 was supposed to be resting, only to find him in tears, prepared to go back into the prison because he could not leave as long as the others thought he was a "bad prisoner." Sick as he felt, he had to prove to them he was not a "bad" prisoner. He had to be persuaded that he was not a prisoner at all, that the others were also just students, that this was just an experiment and not a prison and the prison staff were only research psychologists. A report from the warden notes, "While I believe that it was necessary for *staff* [me] to enact the warden role, at least some of the time, I am startled by the ease with which I could turn off my sensitivity and concern for others for 'a good cause.'"

43   Consider our overreaction to the rumor of a mass escape plot that one of the guards claimed to have overheard. It went as follows: Prisoner 8612, previously released for emotional disturbance, was only faking. He was going to round up a bunch of his friends, and they would storm the prison right after visiting hours. Instead of collecting data on the pattern of rumor transmission, we made plans to maintain the security of our institution. After putting a confederate informer into the cell 8612 had occupied to get specific information about the escape plans, the superintendent went back to the Palo Alto Police Department to request transfer of our prisoners to the old city jail. His impassioned plea was only turned down at the last minute when the problem of insurance and city liability for our prisoners was raised by a city official. Angered at this lack of cooperation, the staff formulated another plan. Our jail was dismantled, the prisoners, chained and blindfolded, were carted off to a remote storage room. When the conspirators arrived, they would be told the study was over, their friends had been sent home, there was nothing left to liberate. After they left, we would redouble the security features of our prison making any future escape attempts futile. We even planned to lure ex-prisoner 8612 back on some pretext and imprison him again, because he had been released on false pretenses! The rumor turned out to be just that—a full day had passed in which we collected little or no data, worked incredibly hard to tear down and then rebuilt our prison. Our reaction, however, was as much one of relief and joy as of exhaustion and frustration.

44   When a former prison chaplain was invited to talk with the prisoners (the grievance committee had requested church services), he puzzled everyone by disparaging each inmate for not having taken any constructive action in order to get released. "Don't you know you must have a lawyer in order to get bail, or to appeal the charges against you?" Several of them accepted his invitation to contact their parents in order to secure the services of an attorney. The next night one of the parents stopped at the superintendent's office before visiting time and handed him the name and phone number of her cousin who was a public defender. She said that a priest had called her and suggested the need for a lawyer's services! We called the lawyer. He came, interviewed the prisoners, discussed sources of bail money, and promised to return again after the weekend.

45   But perhaps the most telling account of the insidious development of this new reality, of the gradual Kafkaesque metamorphosis of good into evil, appears in excerpts from the diary of one of the guards, Guard A:

46   *Prior to start of experiment:* "As I am a pacifist and nonaggressive individual. I cannot see a time when I might guard and/or maltreat other living things."

47   *After an orientation meeting:* "Buying uniforms at the end of the meeting confirms the gamelike atmosphere of this thing. I doubt whether many of us share the expectations of 'seriousness' that the experimenters seem to have."

48   *First Day:* "Feel sure that the prisoners will make fun of my appearance and I evolve my first basic strategy—mainly not to smile at anything they say or do which would be admitting it's all only a game. . . . At cell 3 I stop and setting my voice hard and low say to 5486, 'What are you smiling at?' 'Nothing, Mr. Correctional Officer.' 'Well, see that you don't.' (As I walk off I feel stupid.)"

49   *Second Day:* "5704 asked for a cigarette and I ignored him—because I am a non-smoker and could not empathize. . . . Meanwhile since I was feeling empathetic towards 1037, I determined not to talk with him. . . . After we had count and lights out [Guard D] and I held a loud conversation about going home to our girl friends and what we were going to do to them."

50   *Third Day (preparing for the first visitors' night):* "After warning the prisoners not to make any complaints unless they wanted the visit terminated fast, we finally brought in the first parents. I made sure I was one of the guards on the yard, because this was my first chance for the type of manipulative power that I really like—being a very noticed figure with almost complete control over what is said or not. While the parents and prisoners sat in chairs, I sat on the end of the table dangling my feet and contradicting anything I felt like. This was the first part of the experiment I was really enjoying. . . . 817 is being obnoxious and bears watching."

51   *Fourth Day:* ". . . The psychologist rebukes me for handcuffing and blindfolding a prisoner before leaving the [counseling] office, and I resentfully reply that it is both necessary security and my business anyway."

52   *Fifth Day:* "I harass 'Sarge' who continues to stubbornly overrespond to all commands. I have singled him out for the special abuse both because he begs for it and because I simply don't like him. The real trouble starts at dinner. The new prisoner (416) refuses to eat his sausage . . . we throw him into the Hole ordering him to hold sausages in each hand. We have a crisis of authority; this rebellious conduct potentially undermines the complete control we have over the others. We decide to play upon prisoner solidarity and tell the new one that all the others will be deprived of visitors if he does not eat his dinner. . . . I walk by and slam my stick into the Hole door. . . . I am very angry at this prisoner for causing discomfort and trouble for the others. I decided to force-feed him, but he wouldn't eat. I let the food slide down his face. I didn't believe it was me doing it. I hated myself for making him eat but I hated him more for not eating."

53   *Sixth Day:* "The experiment is over. I feel elated but am shocked to find some other guards disappointed somewhat because of the loss of money and some because they are enjoying themselves."

54   We were no longer dealing with an intellectual exercise in which a hypothesis was being evaluated in the dispassionate manner dictated by the canons of the scientific method. We were caught up in the passion of the present, the suffering, the need to control people, not variables, the escalation of power, and all the unexpected things that were erupting around and within us. We had to end this experiment: So our planned two-week simulation was aborted after only six (was it only six?) days and nights.

55   Was it worth all the suffering just to prove what everybody knows—that some people are sadistic, others weak, and prisons are not beds of roses? If that is all we demonstrated in this research, then it was certainly not worth the anguish. We believe there are many significant implications to be derived from this experience, only a few of which can be suggested here.

56   The potential social value of this study derives precisely from the fact that normal, healthy, educated young men could be so radically transformed under

the institutional pressures of a "prison environment." If this could happen in so short a time, without the excesses that are possible in real prisons, and if it could happen to the "cream-of-the-crop of American youth," then one can only shudder to imagine what society is doing both to the actual guards and prisoners who are at this very moment participating in that unnatural "social experiment."

57   The pathology observed in this study cannot be reasonably attributed in pre-existing personality differences of the subjects, that option being eliminated by our selection procedures and random assignment. Rather, the subjects' abnormal social and personal reactions are best seen as a product of their transaction with an environment that supported the behavior that would be pathological in other settings, but was "appropriate" in this prison. Had we observed comparable reactions in a real prison, the psychiatrist undoubtedly would have been able to attribute any prisoner's behavior to character defects or personality maladjustment, while critics of the prison system would have been quick to label the guards as "psychopathic." This tendency to locate the source of behavior disorders inside a particular person or group underestimates the power of situational forces.

58   Our colleague, David Rosenhan, has very convincingly shown that once a sane person (pretending to be insane) gets labeled as insane and committed to a mental hospital, it is the label that is the reality which is treated and not the person. This dehumanizing tendency to respond to other people according to socially determined labels and often arbitrarily assigned roles is also apparent in a recent "mock hospital" study designed by Norma Jean Orlando to extend the ideas in our research.

59   Personnel from the staff of Elgin State Hospital in Illinois role-played either mental patients or staff in a weekend simulation on a ward in the hospital. The mock mental patients soon displayed behavior indistinguishable from that we usually associate with the chronic pathological syndromes of acute mental patients: Incessant pacing, uncontrollable weeping, depression, hostility, fights, stealing from each other, complaining. Many of the "mock staff" took advantage of their power to act in ways comparable to our mock guards by dehumanizing their powerless victims.

60   During a series of encounter debriefing sessions immediately after our experiment, we all had an opportunity to vent our strong feelings and to reflect upon the moral and ethical issues each of us faced, and we considered how we might react more morally in future "real-life" analogues to this situation. Year-long follow-ups with our subjects via questionnaires, personal interviews, and group reunions indicate that their mental anguish was transient and situationally specific, but the self-knowledge gained has persisted.

61   By far the most disturbing implication of our research comes from the parallels between what occurred in that basement mock prison and daily experiences in our own lives—and we presume yours. The physical institution of prison is but a concrete and steel metaphor for the existence of more pervasive, albeit less obvious, prisons of the mind that all of us daily create, populate, and perpetuate. We speak here of the prisons of racism, sexism, despair, shyness, "neurotic hang-ups," and the like. The social convention of marriage, as

one example, becomes for many couples a state of imprisonment in which one partner agrees to be prisoner or guard, forcing or allowing the other to play the reciprocal role—invariably without making the contract explicit.

62   To what extent do we allow ourselves to become imprisoned by docilely accepting the roles others assign us or, indeed, choose to remain prisoners because being passive and dependent frees us from the need to act and be responsible for our actions? The prison of fear constructed in the delusions of the paranoid is no less confining or less real than the cell that every shy person erects to limit his own freedom in anxious anticipation of being ridiculed and rejected by his guards—often guards of his own making.

Review Questions

1. What was Zimbardo's primary goal in undertaking the prison experiment?

2. What was the profile of the subjects in the experiments? Why is this profile significant?

3. Zimbardo claims that there is a "process" (paragraphs 2, 7) of becoming a prisoner. What is this process?

4. What inverse psychological relationships developed between prisoners and guards?

5. What was the result of the prison "riot"?

6. Why did prisoners have no respect for each other or for themselves?

7. How does the journal of Guard A illustrate what Zimbardo calls the "gradual Kafkaesque metamorphosis of good into evil"? (See paragraphs 45–54.)

8. What are the reasons people would voluntarily become prisoners?

9. How can the mind keep people in jail?

Discussion and Writing Suggestions

1. Reread the four epigraphs to this article. Write a paragraph of response to any one of them, in light of Zimbardo's discussion of the prison experiment.

2. You may have thought, before reading this article, that being a prisoner is a physical fact, not a psychological state. What are the differences between these two views?

3. In paragraph 8, Zimbardo explains his reasons for not pursuing his research in a real prison. He writes that "it is impossible to separate what each individual brings into the prison from what the prison brings out in each person." What does he mean? And how does this distinction prove important later in the article? (See paragraph 58.)

4. Zimbardo reports that at the beginning of the experiment each of the "prisoner" subjects "was completely confident of his ability to endure whatever the prison had to offer for the full two-week experimental period" (paragraph 10). Had you been a subject, would you have been so confident, prior to the experiment? Given what you've learned of the experiment, do you think you would have psychologically "become" a prisoner or guard if you had been selected for these roles? (And if not, what makes you so sure?)

5. Identify two passages in this article: one that surprised you relating to the prisoners and one that surprised you relating to the guards. Write a paragraph explaining your response to each. Now read the two passages in light of each other. Do you see any patterns underlying your responses?

6. Zimbardo claims that the implications of his research matter deeply—that the mock prison he created is a metaphor for prisons of the mind "that all of us daily create, populate, and perpetuate" (paragraph 61). Zimbardo mentions the prisons of "racism, sexism, despair, [and] shyness." Choose any one of these and discuss how it might be viewed as a mental prison.

7. Reread paragraphs 61 and 62. Zimbardo makes a metaphorical jump from his experiment to the psychological realities of your daily life. Prisons—the artificial one he created and actual prisons—stand for something: social systems in which there are those who give orders and those who obey. All metaphors break down at some point. Where does this one break down?

8. Zimbardo suggests that we might "choose to remain prisoners because being passive and dependent frees us from the need to act and be responsible for our actions" (paragraph 62). Do you agree? What are the burdens of being disobedient?

Disobedience as a Psychological and Moral Problem
Erich Fromm

Erich Fromm (1900–1980) was one of the twentieth century's distinguished writers and thinkers. Psychoanalyst and philosopher, historian and sociologist, he ranged widely in his interests and defied easy characterization. Fromm studied the works of Freud and Marx closely, and published on them both, but he was not aligned strictly with either. In much of his voluminous writing, he struggled to articulate a view that could help bridge ideological and personal conflicts and bring dignity to those who struggled with isolation in the industrial world. Author of more than thirty books and contributor to numerous edited collections and journals, Fromm is best known for Escape from Freedom *(1941),* The Art of Loving *(1956), and* To Have or To Be? *(1976).*

In the essay that follows, first published in 1963, Fromm discusses the seductive comforts of obedience, and he makes distinctions among varieties of obedience, some of which he believes are destructive, and others, life affirming. His thoughts on nuclear annihilation may seem dated in these days of post–Cold War cooperation, but it is worth remembering that Fromm wrote his essay just after the Cuban missile crisis, when fears of a third world war ran high. (We might note that despite the welcome reductions of nuclear stockpiles, the United States and Russia still possess, and retain battle plans for, thousands of warheads.) And in the wake of the 9/11 attacks, the threat of terrorists acquiring and using nuclear weapons against the United States seems very real. On the major points of his essay, concerning the psychological and moral problems of obedience, Fromm remains as pertinent today as when he wrote some forty years ago.

1   For centuries kings, priests, feudal lords, industrial bosses, and parents have insisted that *obedience is a virtue* and that *disobedience is a vice.* In order to introduce another point of view, let us set against this position the following statement: *human history began with an act of disobedience, and it is not unlikely that it will be terminated by an act of obedience.*

2   Human history was ushered in by an act of disobedience according to the Hebrew and Greek myths. Adam and Eve, living in the Garden of Eden, were part of nature; they were in harmony with it, yet did not transcend it. They were in nature as the fetus is in the womb of the mother. They were human, and at the same time not yet human. All this changed when they disobeyed an order. By breaking the ties with earth and mother, by cutting the umbilical cord, man emerged from a prehuman harmony and was able to take the first step into independence and freedom. The act of disobedience set Adam and Eve free and opened their eyes. They recognized each other as strangers and the world outside them as strange and even hostile. Their act of disobedience broke the primary bond with nature and made them individuals. "Original sin," far from corrupting man, set him free; it was the beginning of history. Man had to leave the Garden of Eden in order to learn to rely on his own powers and to become fully human.

3   The prophets, in their messianic concept, confirmed the idea that man had been right in disobeying; that he had not been corrupted by his "sin," but freed from the fetters of pre-human harmony. For the prophets, *history* is the place where man becomes human; during its unfolding he develops his powers of reason and of love until he creates a new harmony between himself, his fellow man, and nature. This new harmony is described as "the end of days," that period of history in which there is peace between man and man, between man and nature. It is a "new" paradise created by man himself, and one which he alone could create because he was forced to leave the "old" paradise as a result of his disobedience.

4   Just as the Hebrew myth of Adam and Eve, so the Greek myth of Prometheus sees all human civilization based on an act of disobedience. Prometheus, in stealing the fire from the gods, lays the foundation for the evolution of man. There would be no human history were it not for Prometheus' "crime." He, like Adam and Eve, is punished for his disobedience. But he does not repent and ask for forgiveness. On the contrary, he proudly says: "I would rather be chained to this rock than be the obedient servant of the gods."

5   Man has continued to evolve by acts of disobedience. Not only was his spiritual development possible only because there were men who dared to say no to the powers that be in the name of their conscience or their faith, but also his intellectual development was dependent on the capacity for being disobedient—disobedient to authorities who tried to muzzle new thoughts and to the authority of long-established opinions which declared a change to be nonsense.

6   If the capacity for disobedience constituted the beginning of human history, obedience might very well, as I have said, cause the end of human history. I am not speaking symbolically or poetically. There is the possibility, or even the probability, that the human race will destroy civilization and even all life upon earth within the next five to ten years. There is no rationality or sense in it. But the fact is that, while we are living technically in the Atomic Age, the majority of men—including most of those who are in power—still live emotionally in the Stone Age; that while our mathematics, astronomy, and the natural sciences are of the twentieth century, most of our ideas about politics, the state, and society lag far behind the age of science. If mankind commits suicide it will be because people will obey those who command them to push the deadly buttons; because they will obey the archaic passions of fear, hate, and greed; because they will obey obsolete clichés of State sovereignty and national honor. The Soviet leaders talk much about revolutions, and we in the "free world" talk much about freedom. Yet they and we discourage disobedience—in the Soviet Union explicitly and by force, in the free world implicitly and by the more subtle methods of persuasion.

7   But I do not mean to say that all disobedience is a virtue and all obedience is a vice. Such a view would ignore the dialectical relationship between obedience and disobedience. Whenever the principles which are obeyed and those which are disobeyed are irreconcilable, an act of obedience to one principle is necessarily an act of disobedience to its counterpart and vice versa. Antigone is the classic example of this dichotomy. By obeying the inhuman laws of the State, Antigone necessarily would disobey the laws of humanity. By obeying the latter, she must disobey the former. All martyrs of religious faiths, of freedom, and of science have had to disobey those who wanted to muzzle them in order to obey their own consciences, the laws of humanity, and of reason. If a man can only obey and not disobey, he is a slave; if he can only disobey and not obey, he is a rebel (not a revolutionary); he acts out of anger, disappointment, resentment, yet not in the name of a conviction or a principle.

8   However, in order to prevent a confusion of terms an important qualification must be made. Obedience to a person, institution, or power (heteronomous obedience) is submission; it implies the abdication of my autonomy and the acceptance of a foreign will or judgment in place of my own. Obedience to my own reason or conviction (autonomous obedience) is not an act of submission but one of affirmation. My conviction and my judgment, if authentically mine, are part of me. If I follow them rather than the judgment of others, I am being myself; hence the word *obey* can be applied only in a metaphorical sense and with a meaning which is fundamentally different from the one in the case of "heteronomous obedience."

9   But this distinction still needs two further qualifications, one with regard to the concept of conscience and the other with regard to the concept of authority.

10   The word *conscience* is used to express two phenomena which are quite distinct from each other. One is the "authoritarian conscience" which is the internalized voice of an authority whom we are eager to please and afraid of displeasing. This authoritarian conscience is what most people experience when they obey their conscience. It is also the conscience which Freud speaks of, and which he called "Super-Ego." This Super-Ego represents the internalized commands and prohibitions of father, accepted by the son out of fear. Different from the authoritarian conscience is the "humanistic conscience"; this is the voice present in every human being and independent from external sanctions and rewards. Humanistic conscience is based on the fact that as human beings we have an intuitive knowledge of what is human and inhuman, what is conducive of life and what is destructive of life. This conscience serves our functioning as human beings. It is the voice which calls us back to ourselves, to our humanity.

11   Authoritarian conscience (Super-Ego) is still obedience to a power outside of myself, even though this power has been internalized. Consciously I believe that I am following *my* conscience; in effect, however, I have swallowed the principles of *power;* just because of the illusion that humanistic conscience and Super-Ego are identical, internalized authority is so much more effective than the authority which is clearly experienced as not being part of me. Obedience to the "authoritarian conscience," like all obedience to outside thoughts and power, tends to debilitate "humanistic conscience," the ability to be and to judge oneself.

12   The statement, on the other hand, that obedience to another person is *ipso facto* submission needs also to be qualified by distinguishing "irrational" from "rational" authority. An example of rational authority is to be found in the relationship between student and teacher; one of irrational authority in the relationship between slave and master. Both relationships are based on the fact that the authority of the person in command is accepted. Dynamically, however, they are of a different nature. The interests of the teacher and the student, in the ideal case, lie in the same direction. The teacher is satisfied if he succeeds in furthering the student; if he has failed to do so, the failure is his and the student's. The slave owner, on the other hand, wants to exploit the slave as much as possible. The more he gets out of him the more satisfied he is. At the same time, the slave tries to defend as best he can his claims for a minimum of happiness. The interests of slave and master are antagonistic, because what is advantageous to the one is detrimental to the other. The superiority of the one over the other has a different function in each case; in the first it is the condition for the furtherance of the person subjected to the authority, and in the second it is the condition for his exploitation. Another distinction runs parallel to this: rational authority is rational because the authority, whether it is held by a teacher or a captain of a ship giving orders in an emergency, acts in the name of reason which, being universal, I can accept without submitting. Irrational authority has to use force or suggestion, because no one would let himself be exploited if he were free to prevent it.

13   Why is man so prone to obey and why is it so difficult for him to disobey? As long as I am obedient to the power of the State, the Church, or public opinion, I feel safe and protected. In fact it makes little difference what power it is that I am obedient to. It is always an institution, or men, who use force in one form

or another and who fraudulently claim omniscience and omnipotence. My obedience makes me part of the power I worship, and hence I feel strong. I can
make no error, since it decides for me; I cannot be alone, because it watches
over me; I cannot commit a sin, because it does not let me do so, and even if
I do sin, the punishment is only the way of returning to the almighty power.

14   In order to disobey, one must have the courage to be alone, to err, and to
sin. But courage is not enough. The capacity for courage depends on a person's
state of development. Only if a person has emerged from mother's lap and
father's commands, only if he has emerged as a fully developed individual and
thus has acquired the capacity to think and feel for himself, only then can he
have the courage to say "no" to power, to disobey.

15   A person can become free through acts of disobedience by learning to say
no to power. But not only is the capacity for disobedience the condition for freedom; freedom is also the condition for disobedience. If I am afraid of freedom,
I cannot dare to say "no," I cannot have the courage to be disobedient. Indeed,
freedom and the capacity for disobedience are inseparable; hence any social,
political, and religious system which proclaims freedom, yet stamps out disobedience, cannot speak the truth.

16   There is another reason why it is so difficult to dare to disobey, to say "no"
to power. During most of human history obedience has been identified with
virtue and disobedience with sin. The reason is simple: thus far throughout
most of history a minority has ruled over the majority. This rule was made necessary by the fact that there was only enough of the good things of life for the
few, and only the crumbs remained for the many. If the few wanted to enjoy
the good things and, beyond that, to have the many serve them and work for
them, one condition was necessary: the many had to learn obedience. To be
sure, obedience can be established by sheer force. But this method has many
disadvantages. It constitutes a constant threat that one day the many might
have the means to overthrow the few by force; furthermore there are many
kinds of work which cannot be done properly if nothing but fear is behind the
obedience. Hence the obedience which is only rooted in the fear of force
must be transformed into one rooted in man's heart. Man must want and
even need to obey, instead of only fearing to disobey. If this is to be achieved,
power must assume the qualities of the All Good, of the All Wise; it must
become All Knowing. If this happens, power can proclaim that disobedience
is sin and obedience virtue; and once this has been proclaimed, the many can
accept obedience because it is good and detest disobedience because it is
bad, rather than to detest themselves for being cowards. From Luther to the
nineteenth century one was concerned with overt and explicit authorities.
Luther, the pope, the princes, wanted to uphold it; the middle class, the workers, the philosophers, tried to uproot it. The fight against authority in the State
as well as in the family was often the very basis for the development of an
independent and daring person. The fight against authority was inseparable
from the intellectual mood which characterized the philosophers of the
enlightenment and the scientists. This "critical mood" was one of faith in
reason, and at the same time of doubt in everything which is said or thought,
inasmuch as it is based on tradition, superstition, custom, power. The principles *sapere aude* and *de omnibus est dubitandum*—"dare to be wise" and "of

all one must doubt"—were characteristic of the attitude which permitted and furthered the capacity to say "no."

17   The case of Adolf Eichmann [see note, page 320] is symbolic of our situation and has a significance far beyond the one in which his accusers in the courtroom in Jerusalem were concerned with. Eichmann is a symbol of the organization man, of the alienated bureaucrat for whom men, women and children have become numbers. He is a symbol of all of us. We can see ourselves in Eichmann. But the most frightening thing about him is that after the entire story was told in terms of his own admissions, he was able in perfect good faith to plead his innocence. It is clear that if he were once more in the same situation he would do it again. And so would we—and so do we.

18   The organization man has lost the capacity to disobey, he is not even aware of the fact that he obeys. At this point in history the capacity to doubt, to criticize, and to disobey may be all that stands between a future for mankind and the end of civilization.

Review Questions

1. What does Fromm mean when he writes that disobedience is "the first step into independence and freedom"?

2. Fromm writes that history began with an act of disobedience and will likely end with an act of obedience. What does he mean?

3. What is the difference between "heteronomous obedience" and "autonomous obedience"?

4. How does Fromm distinguish between "authoritarian conscience" and "humanistic conscience"?

5. When is obedience to another person *not* submission?

6. What are the psychological comforts of obedience, and why would authorities rather have people obey out of love than out of fear?

Discussion and Writing Suggestions

1. Fromm suggests that scientifically we live in the twentieth century but that politically and emotionally we live in the Stone Age. As you observe events in the world, both near and far, would you agree? Why?

2. Fromm writes: "If a man can only obey and not disobey, he is a slave; if he can only disobey and not obey, he is a rebel (not a revolutionary)" (paragraph 7). Explain Fromm's meaning here. Explain, as well, the implication that to be fully human one must have the freedom to both obey and disobey.

3. Fromm writes that "obedience makes me part of the power I worship, and hence I feel strong" (paragraph 13). Does this statement

ring true for you? Discuss, in writing, an occasion in which you felt powerful because you obeyed a group norm.

4. In paragraphs 15 and 16, Fromm equates obedience with cowardice. Can you identify a situation in which you were obedient but, now that you reflect on it, were also cowardly? That is, can you recall a time when you caved in to a group but now wish you hadn't? Explain.

5. Fromm says that we can see ourselves in Adolf Eichmann—that as an organization man he "has lost the capacity to disobey, he is not even aware of the fact that he obeys." To what extent do you recognize yourself in this portrait?

The Genocidal Killer in the Mirror
Crispin Sartwell

Upon first learning of such experiments as those conducted by Asch, Milgram, and Zimbardo, many of us are apt to shake our heads at the obedient participants, confident that we would behave differently—that is, independently and ethically—under the same circumstances. But how can we be so sure? In this essay on the phenomenon that novelist Joseph Conrad called the "heart of darkness," Crispin Sartwell reviews recent history to help persuade us that we should not be so smug about our own capacity to resist corrupt authority and to commit heinous acts. Among Sartwell's books are The Art of Living: Aesthetics of the Ordinary in World Spiritual Traditions *(1995),* Obscenity, Anarchy, Reality *(1996),* Act Like You Know: African-American Autobiography and White Identity *(1998), and* Extreme Virtue: Truth and Leadership in Five Great American Lives *(2003). The following essay appeared as an op-ed column in the* Los Angeles Times *on 11 April 2004.*

1   Ten years ago this month, the Hutu government of Rwanda mobilized its citizenry into a killing machine and started stacking corpses toward the sky. It's been 30 years since the Cambodian killing fields, 40 since the start of the Cultural Revolution, 60 since the height of the Nazi Holocaust, 100 since the Belgians started murdering Congolese, 500 since the beginnings of the African slave trade and the systematic annihilation of the native peoples of the Western Hemisphere.

2   There are various things we ought to have learned from the history of genocide. One, surely, is that no problem is as profound and no evil as prevalent as state power: The rise of genocide coincides with the rise of the modern political state, and every single one of these events is inconceivable without the bland bureaucracy of death.

3   But another is this: We—and by this I mean you and I—are deeply evil. I would like to believe that I am too good, too smart, too decent to hop on the genocide bandwagon. But I know better. It's obvious, and it's a familiar point, that average Germans, average Hutus, average Americans have been mobilized for genocide. I am not profoundly different than these people, and

if you think you are, then you are either a moral hero or you are profoundly self-deluded.

4   Are you a moral hero? The qualities that are needed to recruit a person to genocide are widely shared.

- *Deference to authority.* This would be the state, the experts—under normal conditions. Ponder, perhaps, how you react to a school principal or a police officer or a president. Do you often believe what the authorities tell you just because they are authorities?
- *Response to social consensus.* People are herd animals; they seek to associate themselves with a consensus of their acquaintances. If you hate being excluded by a clique, or dress in terms of trends, you are responding in this way.
- *Willingness to respond to people as members of groups, and to expect groups, overall, to display certain qualities.* I might not want to do this, but I do. I know a lot about gay people, for example: How they talk, where they live, what they do.
- *Desire for your own security and that of your family and friends, to the extent you are willing to make moral compromises to preserve it.* These are qualities found in greater or lesser degree in everyone, and they're more than enough. You, like me, are a genocidal killer, only you (probably), like me, haven't had the opportunity to display your enthusiasm. Your goodness, like mine, has little to do with who you are and everything to do with the social conditions you happen to find yourself in.

5   In Rwanda, the Hutu government claimed falsely that it was under attack from Tutsis—a claim repeated incessantly on the state-run radio—and mobilized the population into "civilian self-defense forces." It created squads dedicated to "obligatory labor for the public good" and armed them with firearms or machetes. It rewarded those who were zealous killers with houses or cars, punished those who hesitated and killed those who sheltered the intended victims. Just two months later, 800,000 people were dead.

6   Hitler didn't kill 6 million Jews, or King Leopold 10 million Africans. They used a bureaucracy and a media machine and, finally, people just like me and you. They mobilized a society. I remember staring at Rwanda on my television, reading about Cambodia in my newspaper as the killing continued. I shook my head and did absolutely nothing—basically the same approach taken by the world in each instance. I fear that if the same thing were happening in my town to people "not like me" in some identifiable way, I would take the same approach.

7   Many decent people have.

Review Questions

1. What links the historical events cited by Sartwell in the first paragraph of this column?

2. According to Sartwell, what two main things should we have learned from the history of genocide?

3. By what institutional means did leaders and governments accomplish their genocidal purposes, according to Sartwell?

Discussion and Writing Suggestions

1. To what extent do you agree with Sartwell that "no problem is as profound and no evil as prevalent as state power"?

2. Sartwell asks, "Are you a moral hero?" and then invites us to answer the bulleted questions that follow. Did you attempt to address such questions? Discuss your provisional responses. To what extent do you agree with Sartwell's assumption that "we . . . are deeply evil"? To what extent to you take issue with it?

3. Sartwell makes the following, radical claim: "Your goodness, like mine, has little to do with who you are and everything to do with the social conditions you happen to find yourself in." In other words, goodness is not an innate quality. It is a social, learned quality. Do you agree?

Just Do What the Pilot Tells You
Theodore Dalrymple

Most of the readings in this chapter have illustrated the dangers of unthinking obedience to either individual or group authority. But we don't mean to suggest that disobedience is always the best, the wisest, the most moral, or the most logical choice. As even Stanley Milgram acknowledged at the beginning of his article, "Some system of authority is a requirement of all communal living, and it is only the person living in isolation who is not forced to respond, with defiance or submission, to the commands of others" (page 314). Were we to routinely defy the authority of parents, teachers, police officers, employers, clients, etc., what we call civilization could not continue to function. We would be living in a Darwinian world where only the strong would survive. The law would not provide authority, but it would also not provide protection. In fact, we need to obey most orders that we are given for our own safety and welfare.

In the following article first published in the July 5, 1999, New Statesman, Theodore Dalrymple, a British physician, reminds us of those occasions when we should do what we are told. "Blind disobedience to authority," he observes, "is no more to be encouraged than blind obedience." In the course of his discussion Dalrymple attempts to find a reasonable balance between these two poles.

1 Some people think a determined opposition to authority is principled and romantic.

2   It is a quarter of a century since the psychologist Stanley Milgram published his masterpiece, *Obedience to Authority.* It is one of the few books of academic psychological research that can be read with as much pleasure as a novel and which suggest almost as much about the human condition as great literature. Only someone who had no interest whatever in the genocidal upheavals of our century could fail to be gripped, and horrified, by it.

3   Milgram asked ordinary people to come to the psychology laboratories of Yale University to take part in an experiment to determine the effects of punishment on learning. The subjects were told to deliver electric shocks of increasing severity, from 15 to 450 volts, whenever a man who was supposed to learn pairs of words made a mistake. In fact the man was an actor who received no shocks at all, but who simply acted as if he had.

4   Milgram discovered that about two-thirds of his subjects (who were probably representative of the population as a whole) were quite prepared to give a complete stranger electric shocks that they believed to be painful, dangerous and even possibly fatal, despite the stranger's screams of protest, simply because they were told by someone apparently in authority—the psychologist overseeing the experiment—that the test had to go on.

5   By a series of clever manipulations, Milgram proved that it was obedience to authority that led people to behave in this fashion, rather than, say, the unleashing of a latent sadistic urge to inflict pain on people. Although Milgram was restrained in his discussion of the significance of his findings, he nevertheless suggested that they helped to explain how, in certain circumstances, even decent people might become torturers and killers.

6   It is not difficult to see how someone might draw anarchist or anti-authority conclusions from Milgram's horrifying experimental results. Indeed the title alone sometimes seems to produce this effect. As I was re-reading it, after an interval of 20 years, on a plane to Dublin, the woman next to me—a social worker in a Dublin hospital—said: "I've always been against all authority."

7   "All?" I asked.

8   "All," she replied. "We've suffered a lot in Ireland from the authority of the Catholic Church."

9   "What about the pilot of this aircraft?" I asked. "I assume you would prefer him to continue to fly it, rather than, say, for me to take over, and that were I to attempt to do so, he should exert his authority over me as captain?"

10   She readily agreed that in this instance his authority was necessary, though only for a short time, and was legitimate because she had granted it to him. I pointed out that even the brief authority that she had been so kind as to bestow upon him actually depended upon a whole chain, or network, of other authority, such as licensing boards, medical examiners and so forth, upon whose competence, honesty and diligence she could not possibly pronounce. She was not against all authority, therefore: on the contrary, she trusted much of it implicitly, even blindly. And necessarily so in a complex, technologically advanced society.

11   But her initial response to the question of obedience to authority was far from unusual. She probably thought a blanket opposition to authority was a heroic moral stance, indeed the only possible decent attitude towards it. To oppose authority is always romantic and principled, to uphold it prosaic and cowardly.

12   Yet civilization requires a delicate balance between stability and change. Neither mulish support for what exists simply because it already exists nor Bukharinite opposition* to it for much the same reason is a sufficient guide to action. Disobedience to authority is not inherently more glorious than obedience. It rather depends on the nature of the orders given or the behaviour demanded. As Milgram himself wrote, "Some system of authority is a requirement of all communal living. . . ."

13   The psychological advantage to a person of decrying authority altogether and of adopting a mental attitude of invariant opposition is that it allows him to think himself virtuous without having to engage with the necessary, messy compromises of real life.

14   Like many another young doctor, I came across the problem of authority early in my career. I worked for a physician who was far more dedicated to the welfare of her patients than I knew that I should ever be, and whom I esteemed greatly both as a doctor and as a person; yet it seemed to me that in her zeal to help her patients, to leave no stone unturned on their behalf, she often carried the investigation and treatment of moribund patients far beyond what common sense dictated. Alas, this entailed suffering, for medical investigations are often uncomfortable or painful. In my opinion, unnecessary and fruitless hardship was inflicted upon patients in their last days of life; and it fell to my lot to inflict it.

15   I was, of course, only obeying orders. I sometimes questioned those orders, but in the end I obeyed them. I was a young and inexperienced man; I knew a fiftieth as much medicine as my superior and had a thousandth of her experience. She was haunted by the fear of not doing all that could be done to save a life, while I was haunted by the unpleasantness of taking another useless blood test from a dying patient. I was never sure in any individual case that she, not I, was right.

16   Besides, I believed that the interests of patients were served by the existence of a hierarchy among doctors. Someone had to take ultimate responsibility for the care of patients, and if junior doctors were to disobey their superiors every time they disagreed with them, the system would fall apart. Clearly a point might be reached in which it was a junior doctor's duty to disobey, but there was no general rule to guide him in the estimation of when that point had come. The exercise of judgement was, and will always remain, necessary.

17   The social worker's attitude towards authority was, in practice, far more nuanced than she admitted, but there is nevertheless a danger in the disjunction between her attitude in theory and her attitude in practice. For the idea that revolt against authority is everywhere and always a noble stance is one that can soon be communicated to people who are prepared to take it literally.

18   For example, teachers tell me that if they mention to parents that their children are misbehaving, sometimes in grotesquely antisocial ways, the parents will turn unpleasant—towards the teachers, who in this instance represent authority. Recently I met a stepfather who was sent to prison for attacking a

---

*Nikolai Bukharin, a theoretician of the Russian Revolution of 1917, became the editor of the official revolutionary newspaper *Pravda* and subsequently, a member of the ruling Politboro. Originally allied with Stalin, Bukharin differed with the Stalinist majority on the pace of agricultural collectivization and industrialization; his position became that of the "right oppsition." Dismissed from his posts, Bukharin was eventually tried for treason and executed.

teacher who complained about his stepson. The security men in my hospital tell me that when they catch a boy stealing a car in the hospital grounds and return him to his parents, the parents start shouting—at the security men, who again represent authority. Indeed some security men now refuse to take the car thieves home, for fear of parental violence directed at them.

19   Blind disobedience to authority is no more to be encouraged than blind obedience. It is far from pleasant when encountered. Among my patients are quite a number who admit to having always had "a problem with authority." They confess it coyly, as if it were a sign of spiritual election, when it is no such thing: it is, rather, a sign of unbridled egotism. Unable to apply themselves at school, they are unable to take orders at work, and their personal relationships are almost always stormy and violent. They accept no rules, not even the informal ones that grow up between people who live closely together. For people who have a problem with authority, their whim is law. The only consideration that moderates their conduct is the threat of superior, but essentially arbitrary, violence by others.

20   It is not difficult to guess the kind of parental upbringing that results in a problem with authority. Discipline in the home is without principle or consistency, but is rather experienced by the child as the arbitrary expression of the brute power of others over himself. The conduct that on one occasion results in a slap results on another occasion in a Mars bar. The child therefore learns that discipline is an expression not of a rule that has a social purpose, but of a stronger person's momentary emotional state. He therefore comes to the conclusion that the important determinants of a relationship with others are first how you feel, and second what you can get away with by virtue of your comparative strength. Nothing else is involved.

21   To such a person, all human relationships are essentially expressions of power. An order given by another person is thus a threat to his ego, because following orders is submission to power and nothing else: there can be no other reason for it. The distinction between service and slavery collapses. To obey is to extinguish your existence as an autonomous being.

22   While obedience to authority has its dangers—as this century above all others testifies—disobedience to authority likewise has its dangers. There are hidden ironies in Milgram's great work, a work that has generally been taken as a tract against obedience to authority.

23   His experimental design depended upon deceiving his experimental subjects, upon his not asking for their informed consent to take part in his experiments. Had Milgram applied modern ethical standards to the conduct of his experiments, they could never have been performed at all, and we should never have been horrified by their results.

24   Against this, Milgram might urge two considerations. First, that the experimental subjects retrospectively approved of their participation, once they had been fully informed of the experiment's purpose and design. But this does not in the least answer the ethical objection.

25   Second, that the knowledge gained from the experiments was so important that it was worth a little light deception of the subjects to obtain it. This argument turns upon the estimation by somebody—in this case, Milgram himself—that the light was worth the candle: in short, it depends upon our old friend, authority.

Review Questions

1. As a young physician, how did Dalrymple find himself conflicted over obeying authority?

2. What kind of problems does Dalrymple find with "[b]lind disobedience to authority"?

3. What, theorizes Dalrymple, is the usual cause of some people's problem with authority figures?

Discussion and Writing Suggestions

1. To what extent do you agree with Dalrymple about the dangers of routine disobedience to authority? Support your response with examples from your reading, or from your own observation or experience.

2. On the one hand, Dalrymple suggests, one should always defer to the authority of an airline pilot. On the other hand, it was immoral for subjects to obey the authority figure in the Milgram experiment. In less obvious cases than these, is it possible to suggest guidelines for people to use in determining whether particular orders, or orders from particular types of people, should be obeyed or disobeyed? What kinds of orders require the exercise of moral or logical judgment on the part of the person receiving the orders? Is it possible to devise a test—perhaps a series of steps ("If . . . then . . .) that would help people to determine whether it is rational and/or moral to obey authority? (Test these guidelines against some of the experimental procedures reported in this chapter. Test them also against the personal anecdote that Dalrymple tells about the time that he worked with a more experienced physician.)

3. To what extent do you agree with Dalrymple that people who have problems with authority are likely to have been subject to arbitrary discipline from parents or parental figures during their childhoods? To what extent do you agree that people who routinely defy authority are displaying "unbridled egotism"?

SYNTHESIS ACTIVITIES

1. Compare and contrast the Asch and the Milgram experiments, considering their separate (1) objectives, (2) experimental designs and procedures, (3) results, and (4) conclusions. To what extent do the findings of these two experiments reinforce one another? To what extent do they highlight different, if related, social phenomena? To what extent do their results reinforce those of Zimbardo's prison experiment?

2. Milgram writes that "perhaps the most fundamental lesson of our study [is that] ordinary people, simply doing their jobs, and without any particular hostility on their part, can become agents in a terrible destructive process." Using this statement as a principle, analyze several situations recounted in this chapter, and perhaps some outside this chapter, of which you are aware because of your studies, your reading, and possibly even your own experience. Draw upon not only Milgram himself, but also Asch, Zimbardo, Fromm, and Sartwell.

3. The writer Doris Lessing has argued that children need to be taught how to disobey so they can recognize and avoid situations that give rise to harmful obedience. If you were the curriculum coordinator for your local school system, how would you teach children to disobey responsibly? What would be your curriculum? What homework would you assign? What class projects? What field trips? One complicated part of your job would be to train children to understand the difference between *responsible* disobedience and anarchy. What is the difference?

   Take up these questions in a paper that draws on both your experiences as a student and your understanding of the selections in this chapter. Points that you might want to consider in developing the paper: defining overly obedient children; appropriate classroom behavior for responsibly disobedient children (as opposed to inappropriate behavior); reading lists; homework assignments; field trips; class projects.

4. A certain amount of obedience is a given in society. Stanley Milgram and others observe that social order, civilization itself, would not be possible unless individuals were willing to surrender a portion of their autonomy to the state. Allowing that we all are obedient (we must be), define the point at which obedience to a figure of authority becomes dangerous.

   As you develop your definition, consider the ways you might use the work of authors in this chapter and their definitions of acceptable and unacceptable levels of obedience. Do you agree with the ways in which others have drawn the line between reasonable and dangerous obedience? What examples from current stories in the news or from your own experience can you draw on to test various definitions?

5. Describe a situation in which you were faced with a moral dilemma of whether or not to obey a figure of authority. After describing the situation and the action you took (or didn't take), discuss your behavior in light of any two readings in this chapter. You might consider a straightforward, four-part structure for your paper: (1) your description; (2) your discussion, in light of source A; (3) your discussion, in light of source B; and (4) your conclusion—an overall appraisal of your behavior.

6. Erich Fromm equates disobedience with courage: "In order to disobey, one must have the courage to be alone, to err, and to sin." Novelist Doris Lessing makes much the same statement by equating obedience with shame: "among our most shameful memories is this, how often we said black was white because other people were saying it." Using such statements as principles for analysis, examine an act of obedience or disobedience in your own life and determine the extent to which, following Fromm or Lessing, you now consider it courageous or shameful. Having completed this part of your analysis, conclude by reassessing your behavior. Write one or more paragraphs on whether or not you would behave similarly if given a second chance in the same situation.

7. Discuss the critical reaction to the Milgram experiments. Draw upon Baumrind and Parker, as well as Milgram himself, in summarizing both the ethical and procedural objections to the experiments. Following these summaries, develop your own critique, positive or negative, bringing in Milgram himself, where appropriate.

8. In his response to Diana Baumrind, Stanley Milgram makes a point of insisting that follow-up interviews with subjects in his experiments show that a large majority were pleased, in the long run, to have participated. (See Table 1 in the footnote to Baumrind, page 331.) Writing on his own postexperiment surveys and interviews, Philip Zimbardo writes that his subjects believed their "mental anguish was transient and situationally specific, but the self-knowledge gained has persisted" (paragraph 60). Why might they *and* the experimenters nonetheless have been eager to accept a positive, final judgment of the experiments? Develop a paper in response to this question, drawing on the selections by Milgram, Zimbardo, and Baumrind.

9. Develop a synthesis in which you extend Baumrind's critique of Milgram (and possibly, the critiques of others, as discussed by Parker) to the Stanford Prison Experiment. This assignment requires that you understand the core elements of Baumrind's critique; that you have a clear understanding of Zimbardo's experiment; and that you systematically apply elements of the critique(s), as you see fit, to Zimbardo's work. In your conclusion, offer your overall assessment of the Stanford Prison Experiment. To do this, you might answer Zimbardo's own question in paragraph 55: "Was [the experiment] worth all the suffering?" Or you might respond to another question: Do you agree that Zimbardo is warranted in extending the conclusions of his experiment to the general population?

10. In response to the question "Why is man so prone to obey and why is it so difficult for him to disobey?" Erich Fromm suggests that obedience lets people identify with the powerful and invites feel-

ings of safety. Disobedience is psychologically more difficult and requires an act of courage (see paragraphs 13 and 14). Solomon Asch notes that the tendency to conformity is generally stronger than the tendency to independence. And in his final paragraph, Philip Zimbardo writes that a "prison of fear" keeps people compliant and frees them of the need to take responsibility for their own actions. In a synthesis that draws on these three sources (and perhaps others, such as Sartwell), explore the interplay of *fear* and its opposite, *courage,* in relation to obedience. To prevent the paper from becoming too abstract, direct your attention repeatedly to a single case, the details of which will help to keep your focus. This case may be based upon a particular event from your own life or the life of someone you know.

11. To what extent are young people particularly prone to obedience? In developing your response, draw on Zimbardo, Brooks, and Szegedy-Maszak (several of the soldiers implicated in the Abu Ghraib scandal were college-age), as well as on your own outside reading, observations, and experience. If the Zimbardo experiment were conducted today, do you think that the results would be about the same as they were in the early 1970s?

12. Theodore Dalrymple writes that "civilisation requires a delicate balance between stability and change"—between (he implies) obedience, which maintains the status quo, and disobedience, which promotes change. Use this statement as an analytical principle to examine issues of stability and change in one small, contained example of a civilization: a group to which you have belonged and know intimately. This group could be a school-based or church-based club, a musical collaboration, a sports team, or a collection of employees at a workplace. In your analysis, examine the interplay of members' obedience and disobedience in the progress or dissolution of the group. The fruits of your examination will be a thesis by which you organize your subsequent writing.

13. How different are the American soldiers involved in the Abu Ghraib abuse from ordinary Americans? (Another way to pose the question: how likely would you or your neighbor be, under the same circumstances the soldiers faced, to commit similar acts?) Do you regards these soldiers as President Bush did, as a "disgraceful . . . few . . . who dishonored our country and disregarded our values"? To what extent do you see them as more representative of ordinary Americans? In a well-developed paper that draws on the Szegedy-Maszak article about Abu Ghraib and on the selections by Asch, Zimbardo, Milgram, and Fromm, argue that the soldiers who committed the abuses were a "disgraceful few" or, by contrast, more typical of other Americans than we feel comfortable admitting. The heart of your response will turn on your

understanding of "where" morality is located: within individuals, who carry and apply a consistent moral code wherever they go; or within the situations in which individuals find themselves and must make decisions.

RESEARCH ACTIVITIES

1. When Milgram's results were first published in book form in 1974, they generated heated controversy. The reactions reprinted here (by Baumrind and Parker) represent only a very small portion of that controversy. Research other reactions to the Milgram experiments and discuss your findings. Begin with the reviews listed and excerpted in the *Book Review Digest;* also use the *Social Science Index*, the *Readers' Guide to Periodical Literature*, and newspaper indexes to locate articles, editorials, and letters to the editor on the experiments. (Note that editorials and letters are not always indexed. Letters appear within two to four weeks of the weekly magazine articles to which they refer, and within one to two weeks of newspaper articles.) What were the chief types of reactions? To what extent were the reactions favorable?

2. Milgram begins his article "Obedience to Authority" with a reference to Nazi Germany. The purpose of his experiment, in fact, was to help throw light on how the Nazi atrocities could have happened. Research the Nuremberg war crimes tribunals following World War II. Drawing specifically on the statements of those who testified at Nuremberg, as well as those who have written about it, show how Milgram's experiments do help explain the Holocaust and other Nazi crimes. In addition to relevant articles, see Telford Taylor, *Nuremberg and Vietnam: An American Tragedy* (1970); Hannah Arendt, *Eichmann in Jerusalem: A Report on the Banality of Evil* (1963); Richard A. Falk, Gabriel Kolko, and Robert J. Lifton (eds.), *Crimes of War* (1971).

3. Obtain a copy of the transcript of the trial of Adolf Eichmann—the Nazi official who carried out Hitler's "final solution" for the extermination of the Jews. Read also Hannah Arendt's *Eichmann in Jerusalem: A Report on the Banality of Evil,* along with the reviews of this book. Write a critique both of Arendt's book and of the reviews it received.

4. The My Lai massacre in Vietnam in 1969 was a particularly egregious case of overobedience to military authority in wartime. Show the connections between this event and Milgram's experiments. Note that Milgram himself treated the My Lai massacre in the epilogue to his *Obedience to Authority: An Experimental View* (1974).

5. Investigate the court-martial of Lt. William Calley, convicted for his role in the My Lai massacre. Discuss the question of whether President Nixon was justified in commuting his sentence. Examine

in detail the dilemmas the jury must have faced when presented with Calley's defense that he was only following orders.

6. Research the Watergate break-in of 1972 and the subsequent cover-up by Richard Nixon and members of his administration, as an example of overobedience to authority. Focus on one particular aspect of Watergate (e.g., the role of the counsel to the president, John Dean, or why the crisis was allowed to proceed to the point where it actually toppled a presidency). In addition to relevant articles, see Robert Woodward and Carl Bernstein, *All the President's Men* (1974); Leon Jaworski, *The Right and the Power: The Prosecution of Watergate* (1976); *RN: The Memoirs of Richard Nixon* (1978); John Dean, *Blind Ambition* (1976); John Sirica, *To Set the Record Straight: The Break-in, the Tapes, the Conspirators, the Pardon* (1979); Sam Ervin, *The Whole Truth: The Watergate Conspiracy* (1980); John Ehrlichman, *Witness to Power: The Nixon Years* (1982).

7. In April 2004, news broke of the systematic abuse, including beatings and sexual humiliation, by American military police, of Iraqi "detainees" at Baghdad's Abu Ghraib prison. The scandal was intensified—as was outrage in the Muslim world—by graphic photographs that the soldiers had taken of these activities. A high-level American inquiry uncovered some of the following abuses:

> Punching, slapping, and kicking detainees; jumping on their naked feet . . . positioning a naked detainee on a MRE Box, with a sandbag on his head, and attaching wires to his fingers, toes, and penis to simulate electric torture . . . having sex with a female detainee. . . . Using military working dogs (without muzzles) to intimidate and frighten detainees, and in at least one case biting and severely injuring a detainee. . . . Breaking chemical lights and pouring the phosphoric liquid on detainees. . . . Beating detainees with a broom handle and a chair. . . . Sodomizing a detainee with a chemical light and perhaps a broom stick.

In the days following, many commentators noted the similarities between the Abu Ghraib's guards' behavior and the behavior of some of the subjects in the Milgram and Zimbardo experiments. Zimbardo himself, in an op-ed piece in the *Boston Globe*, wrote:

> The terrible things my guards [at Stanford] did to their prisoners were comparable to the horrors inflicted on the Iraqi detainees. My guards repeatedly stripped their prisoners naked, hooded them, chained them, denied them food or bedding privileges, put them into solitary confinement, and made them clean toilet bowls with their bare hands. . . . Over time, these amusements took a sexual turn, such as having the prisoners simulate sodomy on each other. . . . Human behavior is much more under the control of situational forces than most of us recognize or want to acknowledge. In a situation that implicitly gives permission for suspending moral values, many of us can be morphed into creatures alien to our usual natures.

Research the Abu Ghraib scandal; then write a paper comparing and contrasting what happened in the Baghdad prison with what happened in Zimbardo's Stanford prison experiment—and possibly also in Milgram's electric shock experiments. Focus not only on what happened, but also on *why* it may have happened.

8. Examine conformity as a social phenomenon (and a particular manifestation of obedience to group authority) in some particular area. For example, you may choose to study conformity as it exists among school children, adolescent peer groups, social clubs or associations, or businesspeople. You may want to draw upon your sociology or social psychology textbooks and such classic studies as William H. Whyte's *The Organization Man* (1956) or David Riesman's *The Lonely Crowd* (1950), or focus upon more recent books and articles, such as Rosabeth Moss Kantor's *A Tale of "O": On Being Different in an Organization* (1980) and John Goldhammer's 1996 book *Under the Influence: The Destructive Effects of Group Dynamics* (1996). You may also find enlightening some fictional treatments of conformity, such as Sinclair Lewis's *Babbitt* (1922), Sloan Wilson's *The Man in the Gray Flannel Suit* (1950), and Herman Wouk's *The Caine Mutiny: A Novel of World War II* (1951). What are the main factors creating the urge to conform among the particular group you are examining? What kind of forces may be able to counteract conformity?

9. At the outset of his article, Stanley Milgram refers to imaginative works revolving around the issue of obedience to authority: the story of Abraham and Isaac; three of Plato's dialogues, "Apology," "Crito," and "Phaedo"; and the story of Antigone (dramatized by both the fifth-century B.C. Athenian Sophocles and the twentieth-century Frenchman Jean Anouilh). Many other fictional works deal with obedience to authority—for example, George Orwell's *1984* (1949), Herman Wouk's novel *The Caine Mutiny* (and his subsequent play *The Caine Mutiny Court Martial*), and Shirley Jackson's "The Lottery." Check with your instructor, with a librarian, and with such sources as the *Short Story Index* to locate other imaginative works on this theme. Write a paper discussing the various ways in which the subject has been treated in fiction and drama. To ensure coherence, draw comparisons and contrasts among works showing the connections and the variations on the theme of obedience to authority.

What's Happening at the Mall? 10

Perhaps you think the answer to this chapter's opening question is obvious. After all, we Americans frequent shopping centers more than we do houses of worship. Each month of the year 2001, nearly 200 million of us shopped at a mall and bought fully one-half of the nation's consumer goods (excluding cars and car parts), some $1.8 trillion worth. So what's happening at the mall? We shop, which is hardly news. Yet if leading scholars and cultural critics can be believed, we do much, much more, often unaware of a larger drama being staged in which we play a significant part. As the historian and American Studies scholar James J. Farrell observes:

> Shopping centers are constructed of steel and concrete, bricks and mortar, but they are also made of culture. Indeed, culture is about the only thing they *can* be made of. . . . They're a place where we answer important questions: What does it mean to be human? What are people for? What is the meaning of things? Why do we work? What do we work for? And what, in fact, are we shopping for? Like colleges and churches, malls provide answers to these critical questions.

So we may go to malls to buy designer jeans or the latest electronic gear, but because malls are where we also go to see and be seen, to judge, to learn, and to buy both what we want as well as what we need, in visiting the mall we are participating in a larger cultural phenomenon—likely without realizing it.

Geographers describe shopping centers as "built environments" in which the engine of mass production capitalism meets you, the end-consumer. Consider the matchup: on entering the mall, you come face-to-face with billions of dollars invested in product design, manufacturing, advertising, and distribution—not to mention additional millions devoted to making the mall itself an appealing space in which to shop. Management knows that, on average, you will spend $71.04 on your 3.2 visits per month and devotes considerable energy to tuning your experience. From employing broad strategies like corridor designs that direct pedestrian flow past the maximum number of stores, to narrow ones like selecting background music to create just the right ambience for your visit, mall owners strive to provide a satisfying, stimulating experience—and they employ retail science to aid the process: Have you ever considered why the metal chairs in most food courts lack padding? Management has. Comfortable chairs encourage leisurely meals and discourage shopping. Make chairs *uncomfortable* and customers will return to the stores more quickly. Whether or not you recognize these strategies, they exist and management employs them.

The shopping mall has become so commonplace a fixture on the retail landscape that we overlook its relatively new arrival as a building type. In the post–World War II years, the Eisenhower administration initiated the construction of thousands of miles of highways to promote interstate commerce just as automobiles became widely available. By the millions, Americans followed the highways out of town, abandoning the city and its problems for homes in the safer, cleaner, less-expensive suburbs. Visionary architect Victor Gruen understood that the rapidly expanding suburbs lacked not only opportunities for shopping but also spaces that fostered the spirited give and take of community life. A carefully designed structure might achieve both, Gruen reasoned, a place in which to meet, stroll, and talk—as people had in markets for thousands of years—as well as a place in which to shop. Gruen set to work. Mindful of the way that automobiles choked traditional shopping districts, he relegated cars to parking lots, away from the stores, thereby creating inside his shopping centers pedestrian promenades reminiscent of the grand arcades of nineteenth-century Europe. He also improved the shopping experience by carefully controlling the mix of retail tenants. Because the center was (and continues to be) private property, management could exclude bars and pool halls and other businesses that, in its view, detracted from its image of upbeat consumerism. Gone, too, were vagrants and the homeless, who may have enjoyed constitutional protections on Main Street but who were considered trespassers at the mall. And finally, implementing a technical solution that had been impractical before the 1950s, Gruen enclosed his centers to protect shoppers from the elements. His centrally heated and cooled buildings created a spring–like shopping environment, year-round.

One-half of Gruen's vision proved prophetic. In the fifty years following the debut of his innovative Southdale Center in Edina, Minnesota, developers opened 45,000 other centers across the country (the number includes open air, enclosed, and strip malls). However, developers eventually abandoned Gruen's call to merge community and commercial functions in a single, town-like shopping environment. If the appearance of community could enhance sales, mall management would offer community services. But if the noisy and sometimes rude exercise of community threatened business, management would protect its profits by barring, for example, picketers. Court cases followed that raised questions of how free free-speech ought to be in America's new public (though legally private) gathering places. Thus the mall emerged on the American scene with a mixed identity as both a commercial and a community space, an identity that remains fractured to this day. Victor Gruen lived long enough to see the profit motive overtake the needs of community in the design and management of shopping centers, and he left America for Europe deeply disappointed.

Meanwhile malls have grown ever larger and more extravagant, with especially ambitious ones offering lavish entertainment. Restaurants, movie theaters, amusement parks, and water parks attract and *keep* crowds for extended periods. As a building type, the mall has become so dominant that public venues have begun incorporating mall-like features. Attend a special exhibit at your local museum and the exit will likely funnel you into a gift shop. Catch a plane to visit a friend, and you will find the airport looking every bit like a mall, with wide pedestrian boulevards opening onto storefronts. Malls, and elements of mall design, are everywhere.

Historians, geographers, religious studies experts, architects, psychologists, anthropologists, sociologists, and cultural critics all study what goes on (and does not go on) in shopping centers, and all have something to say about their significance in our lives. Some lament how the rise of malls correlates with a loss of authentic human interaction in our marketplaces; some celebrate the business savvy—the confluence of big money, design expertise, and management know-how—needed to make shopping dependably safe and pleasant; some see in mostly white suburban malls evidence of a troubling segregation; some warn that the shift of town centers from public to private spaces endangers our democracy; some savor the excitement of the modern market; and some see in our malls a new, "sacred" space where we gather to find order in an otherwise chaotic world.

In reading the nine selections that follow, you will learn more about these perspectives. And because you have almost certainly shopped in malls, you will bring direct experience to your reading and writing on the topic. The chapter opens with a selection from *One Nation Under Goods*, in which American Studies scholar James J. Farrell asks, "why should we think about malls" in the first place, aside from their obvious function as places to shop. (His answer: malls attract crowds, and if we want to understand American culture, we must go where the people are.) The next two selections set the emergence of shopping centers in a broad historical context. Laura Paquet provides a social history of shopping from ancient times to the present. Geographer Richard Francaviglia then suggests the ways in which Walt Disney's Main Street USA, his idealized recreation of late nineteenth- and early twentieth-century small-town Main Streets, became a prototype for modern mall design.

The readings continue with Victor Gruen's "Shopping Towns USA." One of the most influential shopping mall developers of the twentieth century, Gruen explains how the expanding automobile culture after World War II gave rise to the American suburb and the need for shopping centers that would provide "in modern community life [what] the ancient Greek Agora, the Medieval Market Place and our own Town Squares provided in the past." Writing in 1960, he envisioned shopping malls becoming important social as well as commercial centers. Writing thirty-three years later on the opening of the Mall of America, the nation's largest, David Guterson delivers grim news (as far as Gruen is concerned): Today, malls offer "only a desolate substitute for the rich, communal lifeblood of the traditional marketplace." But Ira Zepp, Jr., a professor of religious studies, regards malls in a more positive light, seeing in them a "sacred space" that fulfills "our need for order and orientation," much as houses of worship have in earlier times. His thesis that we can find spiritual comfort in shopping malls may seem a stretch for some, but the argument is well reasoned.

The chapter ends with historical, sociological, and psychological analyses of malls. Historian Lizabeth Cohen explores the ways in which mall development has perpetuated America's class and racial divisions. In recounting the battles of developers to exclude undesirable elements (for example, political protesters and the homeless) from malls, Cohen finds a threat to the "shared public sphere upon which our democracy depends." Sociologist George Lewis, writing in the *Journal of Popular Culture,* claims that management may publicly promote the *idea* of the mall as a community space but privately discourages the emergence of real communities. Even so, authentic communities of elders and teens manage to form at the mall, their priority being to socialize, not shop. Finally, in a chapter from his classic book *The Malling of America,* William Kowinski writes humorously but pointedly on "mallaise," a zombielike mental state that can overtake unwary shoppers.

Some authors in this chapter indict mall culture; others celebrate it. Your goal in reading and writing on this topic will be to challenge and clarify your own thinking. And you may, after working with this material, come to regard the most ordinary of activities, shopping at the mall, in a strange, new light.

Shopping for American Culture
James J. Farrell

Our discussion of malls and their place in American culture opens with "Shopping for American Culture," the introduction to James J. Farrell's One Nation Under Goods: Malls and the Seductions of American Shopping *(Smithsonian Books, 2003). Farrell, a historian, directs the American Studies program at St. Olaf College. Unapologetic in his enjoyment of malls (unlike several others in the chapter), he writes: "I love malls. I love them for all the obvious reasons. I love the color and the crowds. . . . I love people watching: seeing the wonder of children's eyes and the animated conversations of teenagers." If we want to understand American culture, says Farrell, we must study life at America's shopping malls, for malls express our consumer culture, revealing us to ourselves.*

1 Malls are an American cultural phenomenon. The United States now has more shopping centers than high schools, and in the last forty years, shopping center space has increased by a factor of twelve. By 2000, there were more than forty-five thousand shopping malls with 5.47 billion square feet of gross leasable space in the United States. Currently, America's shopping centers (most of which are strip malls) generate more than a trillion dollars in annual sales. Not counting sales of cars and gasoline, that's slightly more than half of the nation's retail activity. The International Council of Shopping Centers (ICSC) reported that in 2000, America's shopping centers served 196 million Americans a month and employed more than 10.6 million workers, about 8 percent of the nonfarm workforce in the country. We go to malls 3.2 times a month and spend an average of $71.04 each time (a one-third increase in

TABLE 10.1 Shopping Centers in the United States				
	1970	1980	1990	2000
Number of shopping centers	11,000	22,100	36,500	45,000
Total leasable sales area (billions of square feet)	1.49	2.96	4.39	5.57
Retail sales in shopping centers (billions of dollars)	82.0	305.4	681.4	1,136.0
Employment in shopping centers (millions of people)	2.49	5.28	8.60	10.69

Source: Data from ICSC, *Scope.* (*Scope* is a publication of the International Council of Shopping Centers, Inc., New York, N.Y.; reprinted by permission.)

spending from 1995 to 2000). Shopping centers also support our state and city governments, generating $46.6 billion in sales taxes, almost half of all state tax revenue (see Table 10.1).[1]

2   Shopping is such a common part of America's pursuit of happiness that we usually take shopping centers for granted. But although malls are usually places of consumer forgetfulness, they can inspire a sense of thoughtfulness. It's no particular problem if we come back from the mall empty-handed, but it should be a deep disappointment if we come back empty-headed.[2]

3   But why should we think about malls?

4   Quite simply, because Americans go to malls. We may not like the malling of America, but if we want to understand Americans, we have to look for them where they are, not where we think they ought to be. We need to follow Americans to the mall and see what they're doing because shopping centers can reveal cultural patterns that we don't usually see. In some ways, culture is what happens when we are not paying attention. When we are fully conscious of our choices, they are likely to express our individual values and preferences, but when we're going about our daily business with little thought about what we're doing, we act according to the habits of our hearts, and those habits are shaped as much by culture as by character.[3]

5   Malls are a great place for the pleasures of shopping, but they're an even better place for the pleasures of thinking, in part because they help us think about the cultural contours of shopping. Shopping is, etymologically, the process of going to shops to purchase goods and services. According to Webster, a shop is a small retail store; the word comes from a root that denoted the booths or stalls of the marketplace. The verb *to shop* appeared in the late eighteenth century; by the late twentieth century, shopping had become a way of life. Measured in constant dollars, the average American of today consumes twice as many goods and services as the average American of 1950 and ten times as much as a counterpart from 1928. On average, we each consume more than one hundred pounds of materials a day. Shopping, it seems, might be more American than apple pie.[4]

6   Sometimes shopping is a utilitarian act. We need a shirt or a suitcase, and we go to the mall to get it. Sometimes, though, shopping is intrinsically pleasurable,

and we go to the mall to just do it. Shopping itself can be therapeutic, even fun, whether or not anything ends up in the shopping bag. So an exploration of malls can help us think about what we have in mind—as well as what we don't have in mind—when we are shopping.[5]

7   When we get home from the mall, we tell the family, "I was shopping." It sounds simple. Yet shopping is a complex act, or, more precisely, a complex interaction. It's not just a matter of choosing items and paying for them, it's an act of desire that is shaped individually and culturally, an interaction with shops and with a complex infrastructure of production and distribution. It's an act of conscience in which our own values interact with commercial and cultural values. Shopping requires a biological being to enter an architectural space outfitted with commercial art and designed to sell artifacts manufactured and distributed in a market economy. Shopping centers are built of solid materials, but the spaces are also socially constructed and regulated by political entities. Our malls reflect and affect personal perceptions, social norms, religious beliefs, ethical values, cultural geography, domestic architecture, foreign policy, and social psychology. And the artifacts within shopping centers are equally complex, synthesizing material form and symbolic meaning. Shopping is no simple task.

8   Malls are a good place to think about retailing and retail culture, an important subset of American commercial culture. Because we are consumers, we think we know how consumption works, but we don't usually pay attention to how consumption is *produced.* In malls of America, consumption is not just happenstance. It's carefully planned and programmed. To be informed consumers, therefore, we need information not just about the products we buy but also about the spaces—architectural and social—where we buy them.

9   Malls are America's public architecture, a primary form of public space, the town halls of the twentieth and twenty-first centuries. Sociologist Mark Gottdiener contends that the mall "has become the most successful form of environmental design in contemporary settlement space." The late nineteenth century was known for its train stations and department stores. In the early twentieth century it was skyscrapers and subways. Mid-twentieth-century Americans created suburban forms, including subdivisions, malls, and office parks. The late twentieth century was an era of malls and airports, and the airports increasingly looked like malls.[6]

10   Malls are also art galleries, carefully crafted collections of commercial art. To the connoisseur, they offer an unending display of artful design, including product design, package design, retail design, visual merchandising, sculpture, and architecture. The artists we find in museums often challenge our conceptions of ourselves and unsettle our sense of society. The artists who exhibit their skills in the museums we call malls, on the other hand, tend to reinforce our sense of ourselves, producing a commercial art that makes malls more popular than museums in American culture. But even people who have taken courses in art appreciation don't always take time to appreciate the creativity of commercial art.

11   Malls are also outstanding museums of contemporary American material culture. In them, we find a huge collection of the artifacts that help us make sense of our world. And as in most museums, reading these artifacts can help us read the culture.

12   Indeed, as cultural institutions, malls perform what Paul Lauter calls "cultural work," a term that describes "the ways in which a book or other kind of 'text'—a movie, a Supreme Court decision, an advertisement, an anthology, an international treaty, a material object—helps construct the frameworks, fashion the metaphors, create the very language by which people comprehend their experience and think about their world." In short, malls help teach us the common sense of our culture. If we look closely at malls, we will soon be looking inside our own heads. So it is partly the purpose of this book to explain this social construction of common sense—the way we teach each other, both explicitly and implicitly, the common sense of our culture.[7]

13   Understanding a single act of shopping means understanding the culture in which it occurs. When we go to the mall looking for jeans, we find ourselves embedded in a cultural fabric that fits us like a pair of jeans. Shopping centers are constructed of steel and concrete, bricks and mortar, but they are also made of culture. Indeed, culture is about the only thing they *can* be made of. Retailers routinely use our cultural values to stimulate sales. Shopping centers reinforce these values even as they distract us from other American values—justice, equality, democracy, and spirituality—that might also animate our lives.[8]

14   As this suggests, malls are a manifestation of popular philosophy. They're a place where we answer important questions: What does it mean to be human? What are people for? What is the meaning of things? Why do we work? What do we work for? And what, in fact, are we shopping for? Like colleges and churches, malls provide answers to these critical questions. Like colleges, malls are places where we make statements about the good, the true, and the beautiful. Like churches, they are places where we decide what is ultimately valuable and how we will value it. And malls are places where we act out, and institutionalize, our values.[9]

15   As the local outlet of the new world order, malls can teach us a great deal about the central institutions of our American lives. Malls are the intersection of manufacturing and merchandising, nature and culture, home and away, love and money. At the mall, we can see the market at work, and we can contemplate what it means to live in a society shaped by the powerful institutions of commercial capitalism. American individualism often makes it hard for Americans to understand institutions and the prescriptions and patterns that structure our lives. We forget that when we walk into a mall, we walk into a market full of *cultural* questions and controversies. Anthropologists Mary Douglas and Baron Isherwood contend that "consumption is the very arena in which culture is fought over and licked into shape." Malls, therefore, are one place where we make significant decisions both as individuals and as a society.[10]

16   Yet if we want to understand malls, we must examine them within a broader framework. The mall makes sense in the flow of our whole lives, as we compare and contrast it to what we experience every day. The mall, for example, tells us immediately that it's not home and it's not work. It's an architecture of pleasure, not of comfort or efficiency. Shopping is what academics would call an "intertextual experience," an activity that only makes sense if we know how to read many different cultural "texts": ads, stores, mannequins, clothes, logos, race, class, gender, and sexuality. And the mall's complexities are multiplied by its customers.

17   There are many malls in America, and each mall is many things to many people. Architecturally, a mall is singular, but sociologically, psychologically, and culturally, it's plural. Each store is a variety store, not just because it sells a variety of products but because it evokes different responses from a variety of people. Each of us brings our own cognitive map to the mall, so it's a different place to a mother and her child, to a mall worker and a mall walker. It's different if we're different in any way—and we all are. Malls mean different things to women and men, to blacks and whites, to gay people and their heterosexual friends, to teenagers and senior citizens. The mall looks and feels different to poor people than it does to the affluent. Although the mall may try to be all things to all people, it succeeds mainly by being different things to different people. It's possible to speak truthfully about an American consumer culture, but if we look closely, we'll see that we are a consumption society with many different and interconnected consumer cultures.[11]

. . .

18   . . . We often go to malls to buy things we don't have—a pair of pants, a toaster, a new lamp, a book, or a CD. Yet we also go to buy more important things—an identity, a secure sense of self, a set of social relationships, a deeper sense of community, an expression of who we are and who we would like to be. We go to shopping centers with the unfulfilled needs of our American lives, so the mall's attractions are one way of studying the deficiencies of American life. We can use the things we carry *at* the mall to help us understand the things we carry *to* the mall. We can use the mall to make sense of our everyday life.

19   This book is the story of the stories we tell at the mall. Whatever else they may be, shopping centers are places where we tell stories about ourselves—about who we are and what we value. In the plot to separate us from our money, malls are also plotted. They tell stories—about business, about shoppers, about work and leisure, about good and evil, about American culture(s). Stores, and not just bookstores, are full of stories. Victoria's Secret is a romance novel about sex, seduction, and desire, about bodies and beauty, about femininity and masculinity. Sportsmart is the sports page of the mall, telling stories about striving and success. Abercrombie & Fitch combines adventure stories with coming-of-age stories. The Gap started by telling stories about the generation gap, but now their stories are about "cool" characters and their "casual" lives. The stories of progress at Radio Shack are often futuristic fantasies, and Hot Topic tells stories about individualism and conformity, dissent and deviance. The Rainforest Café spins adventure yarns and nature stories. The department stores tell stories about abundance and choice. All of the retailers tell stories about "the good life" and about America. All of the *things* in the mall also have a story. Each artifact is a story of nature becoming culture, of raw material (com)modified to make it meaningful to Americans. At the mall, it's always story time, and, at least according to the publicity, there's almost always a happy ending.

20   This book is the story of all those stories. It's a storybook.

21   It's also my story. It's a story by me, of course, but it's also a story about me, because I'm one of the people I'm writing about. I'm not a power shop-

per, but I love malls. I love them for all the obvious reasons. I love the color and the crowds. I love looking at commercial art, because it is, in fact, beautiful. I love people watching: seeing the wonder of children's eyes and the animated conversations of teenagers. I like the oasis of pedestrianism in a car culture: I like walking, and I like to walk in malls. But I also love malls because in them, as geographer Jon Goss says, "I have learned a great deal about myself: about my humanity, the values and beliefs of 'my' culture, and my intimate desires."[12]

22   I appreciate malls more now than I did at the beginning of my research. When you look closely at their complexity, especially the intricate coordination needed to produce each day's consumption, it's a miracle that they work as well as they do. I have come to understand that shopping centers are part of a huge conspiracy, a conspiracy of customer satisfaction. The people who work in malls genuinely want to please the people who shop in malls. So I appreciate the ways that shopping center professionals study Americans to see just what, in fact, will please us, and I appreciate the many pleasures that are to be found at the mall, whether or not we ever buy anything.

23   But I also appreciate the ways that a shopping center can be a "social trap," an institution in which the sum total of perfectly good behavior is not so good. Still, my main complaint is not primarily with malls but with a larger commercial culture that characterizes us mainly as consumers. My main argument is with an America that sells itself short by buying into the cluster of values expressed so powerfully in our malls.[13]

Notes

1. International Council of Shopping Centers (ICSC), "Scope USA," at the ICSC web site, www.icsc.org; John Fetto, "Mall Rats," *American Demographics* 24 (March 2002): 10; Judith Ann Coady, "The Concrete Dream: A Sociological Look at the Shopping Mall" (Ph.D. diss., Boston University, 1987), 720; Ira G. Zepp Jr., *The New Religious Image of Urban America: The Shopping Mall as Ceremonial Center,* 2d ed. (Niwot: University Press of Colorado, 1997), 10.

2. As my colleague Eric Nelson says, malls "are the last place anyone would go to think seriously. There is nothing, however, that demands more serious thought." Eric Nelson, *Mall of America: Reflections of a Virtual Community* (Lakeville, Minn.: Galde Press, 1998), 152.

3. Zepp, *New Religious Image,* 10.

4. John C. Ryan and Alan Durning, *Stuff: The Secret Lives of Everyday Things* (Seattle: Northwest Environment Watch, 1997), 4–5.

5. Barry J. Babin, William R. Darden, and Mitch Griffin, "Work and/or Fun: Measuring Hedonic and Utilitarian Shopping Value," *Journal of Consumer Research* 20 (March 1994): 646–47.

6. Mark Gottdiener, "Recapturing the Center: A Semiotic Analysis of Shopping Malls," in *The City and the Sign: An Introduction to Urban Semiotics,* ed. Mark Gottdiener and Alexandros Ph. Lagopoulos (New York: Columbia University Press, 1986), 291.

7. Paul Lauter, *From Walden Pond to Jurassic Park: Activism, Culture, and American Studies* (Durham N.C.: Duke University Press, 2001), 11.

8. Leon G. Schiffman and Leslie Lazar Kanuk, *Consumer Behavior*, 5th ed. (Englewood Cliffs, N.J.: Prentice Hall, 1994), 437.

9. Jon Goss, "Once-upon-a-Time in the Commodity World: An Unofficial Guide to Mall of America," *Annals of the Association of American Geographers* 89 (March 1999): 47.

10. Mary Douglas and Baron Isherwood, *The World of Goods* (New York: Basic Books, 1979), 57.

11. Elizabeth Chin, *Purchasing Power: Black Kids and American Consumer Culture* (Minneapolis: University of Minnesota Press, 2001), 12–13.

12. Goss, "Once-upon-a-Time," 49.

13. David Orr, *Ecological Literacy: Education and the Transition to a Postmodern World* (Albany: State University of New York Press, 1992), 5.

Review Questions

1. According to Farrell, why should anyone think seriously about shopping centers?
2. In what ways can malls be understood as "cultural institutions"?
3. Farrell claims that the mall is "a place where we answer important questions." What are these questions?
4. How do shopping malls "tell stories"?
5. Why does Farrell appreciate malls?

Discussion and Writing Suggestions

1. Of the statistics concerning shopping centers that Farrell cites in paragraph 1 and Table 10.1, which do you find most striking? Why?

2. In paragraph 7 Farrell makes a series of provocative claims in developing the assertion that "shopping is a complex act, or, more precisely, a complex interaction." Choose any of the sentences in paragraph 7 that follow this assertion and then write for five minutes in response. Share your insights with others who have read the selection.

3. Reread paragraph 14 and select one of the questions that Farrell claims is raised by mall culture. Write two paragraphs in response: First, explain what you think Farrell means in posing the question. (For example, explain how malls help us to investigate "What does it mean to be human?") Second, discuss the validity of the question in relation to malls. (For instance, discuss how reasonable it seems to contemplate what it means to be human in a shopping mall.)

4. Farrell writes (paragraph 14): "Like churches, [malls] are places we decide what is ultimately valuable and how we will value it." Your comments?

5. Farrell suggests (in paragraph 16) that elements of shopping malls can be "read" like a "text" for meaning. How can one find clues to understanding American culture in advertisements? Store layouts? Mannequins? Clothes? Logos?

6. Do you agree with Farrell (paragraph 18) that we go to malls in search of "an identity, a secure sense of self, a set of social relationships, a deeper sense of community, an expression of who we are and who we would like to be"? How can these things be bought?

A Social History of Shopping
Laura Paquet

In the selection that follows, Laura Paquet presents an overview of shopping from ancient times to modern, opening with a little-known fact: The first street dedicated to shopping that could be closed off from a town at night appeared not in twentieth-century America but 3,600 years ago in the Mesopotamian city of Ur. Paquet is a Canadian journalist and travel writer who has published in numerous publications in Canada, the United States, and Europe, including National Geographic Traveler *and* Travel Canada. *The following selection first appeared in her book* The Urge to Splurge: A Social History of Shopping *(ECW Press, 2003).*

> *If you were looking for an analogy for the modern mall you would have to go back to the walled cities of Italy and France. Like San Gimignano or Les Baux de Provence, the mall offers the ancient trifecta of enclosure, protection, and control. The analogy is not with a well-policed downtown but with a small, thoroughly fascist medieval city-state.*
>
> —James B. Twitchell, *Lead Us Into Temptation,* 1999

1   We tend to think of malls as modern creations, spawned by the same post-war wave that gave us Levittown, transistor radios, and Tang.* And, yes, America's first fully enclosed, climate-controlled shopping mall *was* an invention of the Eisenhower era: the Southdale Shopping Center opened in suburban Minneapolis in 1956. However, it wasn't the world's first building to shelter a number of retailers under one weatherproof roof—not by a long shot.

---

* Shopping Malls as we know them today came of age in the same era as *Levittown, transistor radios,* and *Tang,* products of America's economic boom following World War II when the ingenuity and science that had been channeled to the military was turned to the civilian sector. In 1947 in *Levittown,* NY, and 1951 in Levittown, PA, the Levitt brothers built inexpensive, pre-fabricated housing on as assembly-line basis in huge, suburban tracts. In 1954, Texas Instruments and Regency Electronics invented mass-market electronics with the release of the first *transistor radios.* What made the radios so appealing was that (unlike vacuum tube models) they were portable. In the 1960s, *Tang,* an instant, citrus-based beverage (add water and stir) that had accompanied astronauts on every Gemini and Apollo mission, became a heavily marketed drink to a consumer market fascinated with space travel.

2   Like so many things about city life, the mall as we know it evolved in stages. By about 1600 BC, in the Mesopotamian city of Ur, someone had come up with the idea of separating a street of shops from the rest of town with doors that were closed at night. Historians think that shoppers may have been able to take shelter from the elements under a series of awnings as well.

3   That's pretty much as far as the enclosed shopping promenade evolved for more than a millennium. But then the ancient Greeks came along, with their penchant for marketplaces. Unlike today's malls, where political rabble-rousing is very strongly discouraged, these marketplaces were centers of debate and discussion. In fact, one of the major Greek schools of philosophy, stoicism, was named for the *stoa,* a large roofed structure that was open to an outdoor square on one side but walled on the other three. Stoas served various functions, but many were used as marketplaces. By the fifth century BC, the Greek city of Miletus (now in Turkey) boasted an L-shaped market stoa fronting on the harbor, its prominent placement proof of the importance residents and visitors placed on trade.

4   Flash forward 500 years to the days when Trajan was emperor of the Roman Empire (AD 98–117). In a move that sounds eerily like the activities of the urban renewal zealots of the 1960s, Trajan decided that Rome's crowded jumble of streets and small buildings should be replaced with grand buildings and a more formal plan. Down came thousands of homes and shops, and up went the massive Forum.

5   Just as shopping malls and major sports stadiums tend to sprout next to each other today, a series of markets was built next to the Forum. The ones nearest the stadium were multi-story buildings terraced into the side of the Quirinal hill. But just beyond them was the Aula Traiana, a two-story market with a vaulted roof. The ruins today look oddly familiar, with large square shop doorways marching methodically down each side of a central corridor, and a second story of shops lining a gallery that runs the length of the hall. Add a Sunglass Hut kiosk and a food court, and you could be in a very early prototype of your local shopping center.

That's, Like, Totally Bazaar, Dude

6   The next move in "mall" development would take place in the Middle East, where some unremembered shopkeeper hit on the idea of building a roof between his shop and the one across the street. Others followed suit, sometimes covering multiple connected streets. The result was called a bazaar or souk.

7   One twelfth-century observer described a Jerusalem souk known as the Street of Herbs, which had divided itself into sections by commodity. "At the top of the street is a place where they sell fish. And behind the market where they sell the fish is a very large place on the left hand where cheese, chicken and eggs are sold. On the right hand of this market are the shops of the Syrian gold workers."[1]

8   These souks shared a few traits with their modern, enclosed counterparts, such as a labyrinthine floor plan, and diverse but segregated uses. In the fif-

teenth century, builders in Constantinople (today's Istanbul) would begin building the mega-souk, the Mall of America of its day: the Grand Bazaar, also known
as the Covered Market.

9   The bazaar started as a small warehouse in the 1400s and evolved along
a series of actual streets, which were gradually roofed. Today, more than
3,300 shops line the 60-odd "streets" of the Grand Bazaar. While some of the
historic divisions of individual streets have been superseded by new types
of commerce (I doubt that souvenir t-shirts, for example, were a big seller
during the reign of Suleyman the Magnificent in the 1500s), you can still find
gemstones on Jewelers' Street, and silver teakettles, carpets, and leather
goods in their own domains.

10   Even though the bazaar is now a massive tourist trap, alive with touts and
pickpockets, I discovered on a trip in 1999 that it has a charm the average North
American mall can't match.

11   The vaulted roof shimmers in jewel tones of blue, red, and gold through the
rather gloomy lighting. An old man sits cross-legged in a courtyard in front of his
carpets. Stall after stall displays open bowls of fragrant cardamom and cinna-
mon. And instead of neon signs and blaring loudspeakers, most shops have a
personable young man (and they are almost always men) whose sole job is to
engage shoppers in conversation, using some of the most transparent ruses
ever devised.

12   "You are going the wrong way!" one cried out as I passed him. I stopped,
startled. It was entirely possible that he was right. I'd been wandering the twisty
interior streets for half an hour, fascinated and utterly lost.

13   Seeing that he had caught my attention, he crowed, "This is the right way for
you!" Delightedly, he pointed toward his small shop, and I couldn't resist taking
a peek. Years later, it occurred to me that I could have used the services of
someone like him when I was trying to funnel people to my book signing.
Maybe there is something to this Wal-Mart greeter business, after all.

Throwing Good Shillings After Bad

14 For centuries, the vast majority of customers shopped on streets that were by
turns muddy, windy, rainy, and dirty. But retailers across Europe were beginning
to discover the advantages of setting up shop inside large buildings that already
attracted crowds of the wealthy and powerful, such as castles, palaces and merchants' exchange buildings. In the 1500s, the nave of St. Paul's Cathedral in
London was home to a number of small entrepreneurs, and it was a popular
place for wealthy townspeople to show off their new clothes. Visitors to such
public buildings could usually buy toys, books, sewing supplies, and other small
items from makeshift stalls.

15   More established shopkeepers were initially wary of setting up business in
communal buildings. When Sir Thomas Gresham, a London financier, built the
Royal Exchange in 1568, he designed it as a facility for both traders (on the
main floor) and shopkeepers (in the two upper galleries). However, shopkeepers who were used to living above their stores—where they could keep a
close eye on the premises and thwart attempted burglaries—were not thrilled

about the idea of shops they couldn't guard overnight. Moreover, the thought of sharing the same building with so many competitors made them nervous.

16   The retail areas of the building were virtually empty for three years, until Gresham offered tenants a year's free rent if they agreed to move in. The shopkeepers who took him up on his offer wouldn't regret it; once it was full, the exchange prospered and spurred many other rich men to open similar enterprises. In 1676, the Exeter Exchange on the Strand in London was built solely to house market stalls.

The Palais Royal: Flush with Shopping

17 These seventeenth-century market buildings had some things in common with the modern mall, but shopping trends would soon take another turn that would send shoppers back outdoors.

18   Glazing techniques in the eighteenth century allowed shopkeepers to build large store windows, where they could set up elaborate displays that customers could not easily disturb (unlike a pile of goods on a market stall table). London streets such as Pall Mall and the Strand, with their spacious sidewalks, were soon lined with bow-fronted shops, which shoppers found much more enticing than simple stalls.

19   By the late 1700s, visitors from all over the world were marvelling at the pleasant, organized nature of London's shopping streets. "A stranger . . . appreciates the sidewalks made of broad stones, running down both sides of the streets, whereon he is safe from the terrifying rush of carts and coaches as if he were in his own room; for no wheel dares to encroach even a finger's breadth upon the footpath," wrote Carl Philip Moritz, a German who visited England in the 1780s. "Especially in the Strand, where one shop jostles another and people of very different trades often live in the same house, it is surprising to see how from bottom to top the various houses often display large signboards with painted letters."

20   However, one problem remained: shoppers didn't like browsing in the wind, rain, and hot sun. The solution to that problem would come from a city that had more pressing reasons than most others to solve it: Paris.

21   Unlike London, late eighteenth-century Paris was not a pleasant place to stroll. The streets—long before Baron Haussmann would develop the city's famous boulevards—were narrow, and few had sidewalks. Window shopping was a muddy and rather dangerous pursuit.

22   Then, in 1780, the Duke of Chartres had an inspired idea. Like modern English lords, who open their homes to tourists in order to pay their taxes, the duke needed money and decided to commercialize his residence. Luckily, he lived in the Palais Royal, so he had a prime bit of real estate to play with.

23   On the surface, his plan wasn't terribly revolutionary: he decided to enclose the palace's back garden on three sides with residential buildings, each with a colonnaded row of shops on the ground floor.

24   Similar squares existed throughout Europe, from the Piazza San Marco in Venice to Covent Garden in London. But the Palais Royal—with its prestigious location in the heart of Paris, and its use of the latest building materials and techniques—brought together the right elements at the right, prosperous time.

25   Instead of market stalls, the colonnades sheltered permanent, elegant shops. Each shop had a glazed window, perfect for displaying the luxury goods that the growing middle class coveted and the rich upper class could afford. The covered walkway in front of the shops opened not to a square full of traffic, as in Covent Garden, but to a festive park.

26   Like the Greeks' L-shaped stoa overlooking the harbor at Miletus, the colonnade of the Palais Royal allowed shoppers to move easily from outdoor space to enclosed space. It protected them from rain and snow, while allowing breezes to cool them in the heat of summer. In the garden court, fountains, trees, and concerts provided diversion for weary buyers.

27   The place was an immediate hit.

28   Like today's largest malls, the Palais Royal boasted many amenities besides shops, including cafés, social clubs, a currency exchange, hotels, concert rooms, theaters, and a waxworks. The three stories of apartments above the shops attracted the equivalent of today's loft owners—artists and single men—as well as a fair number of prostitutes, who had the sense to live where society gathered.

Sex and Bloody Revolution: At a Mall Near You!

29 The Palais Royal was not a cheap place to shop, which only added to its allure. Unlike people who browsed for ribbons and toys in the makeshift stalls of the previous century's exchanges, shoppers in the purpose-built Palais Royal chose largely from luxuries: jewelry, finely tailored clothes, marble objects, furniture, paintings, and similar items. In addition, they could avoid the hassle of bargaining, since the shopkeepers were the first in Paris to adopt fixed prices for their goods. Perhaps because the resulting prices were so high, the fixed-price trend wouldn't take wide hold in Paris for another six or seven decades.

30   The high prices didn't stop the crowds from coming. The Palais was *the* place to shop, flirt, gamble, and discuss big ideas. In fact, in a bit of brutal irony for the Palais' noble developer, the complex was one of the flashpoints for the French Revolution. On July 12, 1789, a riot against the city's royal troops began in the Palais' gardens and engulfed the city; two days later, a mob stormed the Bastille.

31   But even the intrigues and danger of the Revolution couldn't shake the hold the Palais had on the people of Paris. It remained a hotbed of gossip and social life. In 1790 a Russian visitor, N. M. Karamzin, observed:

> Everything that can be found in Paris (and what cannot be found in Paris) is in the Palais Royal . . . Here are assembled all the remedies for boredom and all the sweet banes for spiritual and physical health, every method of swindling those with money and tormenting those without it, all means of enjoying and killing time. One could spend an entire life, even the longest, in the Palais Royal, and as in an enchanting dream, dying, say "I have seen and known all."[2]

32   What wouldn't the developers of today's malls give for that kind of press?

33   However, success was a double-edged sword for the Palais Royal. During and after the Napoleonic Wars, its colonnades were magnets for off-duty soldiers looking for amusement. Customers became more interested in gambling and amorous liaisons, and less interested in buying goods. When the Duke of

Chartres's son, Louis Philippe, outlawed both prostitution and gambling on his property in 1837, the Palais' fortunes tumbled.

Arcades Uneaten by Pac-Man Machines

34 What the duke and his son had failed to foresee was the advantages of a completely enclosed shopping space. Colonnades let in light and fresh air, but they also admitted bugs and snow. Future developers would solve these problems with an innovation that was at once both obvious and ingenious.

35 In London and Milan, in Naples and in Paris itself, architects simply replaced the outer pillars of the colonnade with a solid wall or with a second row of facing shops. By doing so, they cut off the colonnade's extensive, permeable access to the outdoors. But while that meant that shoppers had fewer entry points, it also meant better protection from the elements—and better control over the resulting space. The result was the instantly popular shopping arcade.

36 English architectural critic Ralph Redivivus, writing in 1839, was as excited about the arcade concept as Karamzin had been about the Palais Royal half a century earlier:

> As far as possible convenience is concerned most assuredly nothing could be devised more suitable to such a climate as ours . . . than a covered street which bids defiance to the humours of the atmosphere, and where one may lounge and look at shopwindows, though the rain should come down in torrents, or though an August sun should broil people as they walk along in the open streets.[3]

37 Generally, in these days before electric light, arcades had glass roofs or skylights to decrease the need for candles or gaslight—a design element that caused maintenance headaches for the arcades' owners until the glass technology improved in the late nineteenth century.

38 Some arcades, following the pattern of the Grand Bazaar in Istanbul, were merely roofed versions of existing streets. Many others, such as London's Burlington Arcade, were enclosed spaces from their inception. Like the colonnades that had preceded them, these planned arcades drew heavily on classical ideas of regularity and order. Unlike the typically chaotic city street, they presented shoppers with a tidy environment of uniform windows and doors. And although they were enclosed, they were conceived as "streets" of a sort, often built between existing buildings and giving pedestrians an additional route between two other thoroughfares.

Snooty Shopping, U.K. Edition

39 Arcades were the last major form of enclosed, multiple-vendor shopping space to take root before the climate-controlled mall burst onto the scene in the twentieth century. But both arcades and their cousins, the colonnades, continued to evolve in the intervening years.

40 The fortunes of arcades rose or fell based on the fortunes of the streets that surrounded them. Closed off as they were, they usually withered if commerce moved elsewhere. Some of those that survived, such as the Burlington Arcade, pinned their hopes on the carriage trade.

41   From the day it opened in 1819, the Burlington Arcade has positioned itself as an elegant and exclusive shopping destination. Critics, of course, have always found its wares foolish. As journalist Augustus Sala noted dryly in 1859: "I don't think there is a shop in its *enceinte** where they sell anything that we could not do without. Boots and shoes are sold there, to be sure, but what boots and shoes? Varnished and embroidered and be-ribboned figments, fitter for a fancy ball or a lady's chamber, there to caper to the jingling melody of a lute, than for serious pedestrianism."[4] Harsh words from a man whose love of fine china and rare books often led him into debt.

42   In the intervening years since Sala's era, the arcade has maintained its image as an upscale destination. In early 2003, its Web site fairly radiated snooty class.

43   "The Burlington Arcade provides a fashionable destination for wealthy domestic and overseas visitors to London and is a focal point amongst some of London's most famous retailing names," it proclaimed. "Fortnum and Mason, Simpsons and Aspreys together with an exciting selection of restaurant, café and food emporiums are all within close proximity providing a rare opportunity for retailers in Burlington Arcade to access a broad range of affluent custom."[5]

44   Hey, it takes a lot of profit to maintain a Grade II heritage property.

Snooty Shopping, U.S. Edition

45 The Burlington Arcade is neither the first nor the last shopping enclave to appeal to customers' sense of status. But the next buildings to do so successfully would not be built in the old world. For the next stage in the mall's evolution, it's time to cross the Atlantic.

46   The first planned shopping area in the United States was Market Square, built in the Chicago suburb of Lake Forest, Illinois, in 1916. Like the Palais Royal, it consisted of three low buildings surrounding a central park, although in this case streets rather than colonnaded walkways fronted the buildings.

47   Six years later, a developer in Kansas City, Missouri, took this idea one step further. Country Club Plaza was billed as the first major shopping development in the world to focus specifically on shoppers arriving by car. Developer J.C. Nichols didn't have much choice: the city's rail line didn't reach as far as his site on a largely undeveloped swamp.

48   Locals called the place "Nichols' Folly," but the developer had the last laugh— he had correctly hedged his bets on America's burgeoning love for the auto- mobile. Rather than a park, the Spanish-themed plaza with its red-tile roofs was built around a series of parking lots. But, like Market Square, it was a three-sided structure of low-slung buildings, and each shop had an external entrance.

49   Similar structures sprang up across the United States in subsequent decades, particularly in California. Efforts to promote the centers grew more flamboyant as the competition increased. In 1950, the Campus Drive-In shopping center in San Diego opened with a 50-foot neon majorette marking its entrance; the previous year, the new Town & Country Shopping Center in suburban Columbus, Ohio, had promoted night-time shopping by hiring a woman named Grandma Carver to dive 90 feet into a four-foot pool of flaming water set up in the parking lot.

---

* "An encircling fortification around a fort, castle, or town." [*American Heritage Dictionary*]

50   While they often offered drivers advantages over congested downtown shopping streets, these early malls shared one major disadvantage with their more traditional competitors: exposure to the elements. However, builders didn't have easy access to the technology needed to easily heat and cool a large, enclosed mall until the 1950s.

Oofta, by Golly! Cold-Weather Shopping in Minnesota

51 Weather wasn't such a major problem in sunny California and Texas, but in the cities of the Midwest, humid summers and icy winters discouraged shoppers from coming out to spend. It's no accident that America's first fully enclosed, climate-controlled shopping mall sprang up from the prairie in suburban Minneapolis.

52   To avoid building boilers for the 800,000-square-foot Southdale Shopping Center, architect Victor Gruen's Los Angeles-based firm developed a new kind of heat pump to heat and cool the mall, which opened in 1956. Like the developers of European arcades a century earlier, Southdale's builders realized that their enclosed space gave them a major advantage over their competitors, an advantage they promoted in a fact sheet published for the mall's opening:

> In a region which is often beset by inclement weather, the fact that Southdale [shoppers] will enjoy a perpetual springtime looms as an important drawing card. Every foot of the Center, including all shops, arcades and public areas, will be air-conditioned, completely free of snow, soot, or wilting heat.[6]

53   Another advantage the center had over many older malls was the fact that it boasted two department stores, Dayton's and Donaldsons. In a situation reminiscent of Thomas Gresham's struggles with the Royal Exchange four centuries earlier, it took the developer more than a year of negotiations before the two companies agreed to open under the same roof.

Malls, Kudzu, and Other Creeping Menaces

54 In less than half a century since Southdale was built, malls have changed and expanded beyond most developers' wildest dreams—and most critics' direst nightmares.

55   Eight years after Southdale opened, the U.S. boasted 7,600 malls. By 1972, the total had jumped to 13,174. But it was the greedy 1980s that were the golden age of the mall developer: 16,000 malls were built in that decade.

56   By the end of 2001, there were more than 45,000 malls in America—6,086 in California alone. And even though 95 percent of these centers were strip malls—structures in which a line of stores opens onto a street or parking lot—it was clear that Americans had embraced the concept of planned shopping centers with a vengeance.

57   However, the statistics hide another story: the bloom had started to fade from the shopping center rose, at least in the United States. The savings and loan crisis knocked the development industry for a loop in the early 1990s, and analysts began muttering nervously that many areas of the country had more retail space than they needed.

58   As a result, many developers changed their approach in the 1990s. Instead of building "ordinary" new malls, they either built over-the-top extravaganzas, or focused on upgrading and expanding their existing properties.

Mega-Oofta: The Mall of America and Its Canadian Cousin

59 Southdale's original 800,000 square feet—considered enormous at the time— would make the complex simply an average "regional center" these days, according to definitions published by the International Council of Shopping Centers. Perhaps that's why Southdale has ballooned to 1.7 million square feet—the most recent expansion added restaurants, a 16-screen movie theater, and a third-floor wing of teenybopper stores called Trendz on Top.

60   Of course, Southdale is in a peculiar situation. It's competing for customers with the Godzilla* of U.S. shopping centers: the 4.3-million-square-foot Mall of America, which opened in 1992 just six miles to the east. So much ink has been spilled on that complex that I won't add much to it here. You probably already know most of the mind-boggling details, such as the fact that the mall logs 600,000 to 900,000 visits *every week,* and that over a third of its customers come from more than 150 miles away. More than 2,500 couples have been married here. And apparently, if you took off the roof, nine Eiffel Towers could be crammed inside.

61   Even those facts pale beside the vital statistics of Mall of America's mother ship, the West Edmonton Mall. Built in four phases (so far), between 1981 and 1998, the 5.2-million-square-foot mall is home to more than 800 stores, a bungee-jumping facility, a submarine, an ice rink, a chapel, several aquariums, a hotel, the world's biggest indoor theme park . . . when you have a reputation to uphold as the world's largest mall, the list of attractions just keeps growing.

62   My first and last visit to WEM, as its developers call it, took place in the summer of 1986, just after the third phase opened. Along with other attractions, that expansion added the water park and two "theme streets," Bourbon Street and Europa Boulevard.

63   I was in Edmonton for a wedding. As the bride-to-be and I floated in the wave pool, waiting for the next artificial roller to crest over us, I thought about the place and what it all meant. Of course, I was only 21 at the time, so I didn't think terribly hard.

64   I remember being both fascinated and appalled by the sheer size of the place. As a third-year university student in the middle of acquiring a traditional liberal arts education, I felt compelled to be at least somewhat appalled. But as a young woman with a little money saved up from a summer job, I couldn't help but be transfixed by the number of opportunities to splurge.

65   What sticks with me to this day, however, was the unabashed artificiality of WEM. The developers had no compunctions about claiming that a visit to their

---

* *Godzilla,* star of 22 sci-fi movies from the Toho film company of Japan, is a skyscraper-sized, Tyrannosaurus-rex look-alike monster with atomic-fire breathing powers that periodically wrecks havoc on Japanese cities. At least one Godzilla film a few years back was made in America; all of the prior ones were known for their cheesy (albeit serviceable) special effects. "Godzilla" has entered the language to signify any large, overpowering force.

Bourbon Street was just as good—or better—than a trip to the real New Orleans. Better, of course, because it was safer, more predictable, and climate controlled.

The Theme Park Mall

66 Safety and artificiality have come to be the defining qualities of malls around the world. As city cores fell into scary disrepair, mall managers around the world touted the fact that their spaces were enclosed, patrolled, and secure. Look around any mall today, and within minutes you'll likely spot a security guard in quasi-police garb. Read promotional materials and you'll see frequent references to well-lit parking lots. Some shopping centers have capitalized on this aura of security to bring formerly public events, such as Halloween trick or treating—now known as "Malloween" in some malls—into their sanitized confines.

67   This focus on control annoys critics of shopping centers, and even makes shoppers who appreciate safety slightly uneasy. As I did at West Edmonton Mall, many others wonder whether this theme park atmosphere is healthy for us. As Daniel Miller and his British co-authors put it:

> When people yearn for a return to "personal service" or support current trends for opening up enclosed shopping centers to "natural light," we suggest that they are at least as concerned about the increasing artificiality of their social relationships (and in particular the perceived materialism of their children) as they are about the physical environment itself.[7]

68   If this sort of artifice is enough to bring people into the mall, getting them to stay requires an array of psychological trickery that would have amazed the Duke of Chartres.

You Can Head for the Check-out, But You Can Never Leave

69 Have you ever wondered why most malls have no windows to the outside world? That's easy. The architects want you to forget any other world even exists. The sight of trees, sunshine, and birds might encourage you to *leave the mall.* And, not surprisingly, shopping mall owners don't want you to do that.

70   Instead, they want you to stay inside as long as possible. The idea is to replicate the artificial feeling of a theater or a Hollywood sound stage, where shoppers can be the stars of their own show. The shopping center industry has even coined a term for the idea of shopping as theater—the "retail drama"—which William Severini Kowinski popularized in his fascinating 1985 book, *The Malling of America.**

71   In the retail drama, we are all indebted actors treading the shopping mall boards. The sales clerks and the other shoppers are all part of the cast. In the mall, the large rectangular doorways of each store, shaped like the proscenium arches of a traditional stage, add to the fantasy. We can enter a variety of stages, try on new "costumes" and touch new "props," which we can ultimately buy to fulfill our fantasies of who we are and who we want to become.

---

* A selection from Kowinski's *Malling of America* appears later in this chapter.

72 Blank, windowless walls aren't the only technique developers use to keep us immersed in our fantasies. Builders also do their best to ensure that we can't find our way out. Most of today's successful malls are designed more like ancient labyrinths than the long, straight corridor of the Burlington Arcade.

73 If you've ever become hopelessly lost in a mall, take comfort in the fact that you've been purposely led astray. It's known as the "Gruen effect," named after Southdale's architect. Basically, the intent is to force serious shoppers—the blinkered, intent folks who come to the mall with a shopping list and attitude—to see stores they wouldn't otherwise visit. Straight hallways and clear sightlines make it too easy to find your store, buy what you came for, and get out.

74 It's a peculiar concept. Many shoppers—like my husband, for example—find the idea of trolling through endless, confusing corridors so annoying that they avoid malls completely. Others, like me, spend half their time sighing in frustration as they try to decipher the rare mall maps.

75 I remember the first time I learned that the confusing nature of malls was no accident. I was taking a press tour of Bayshore—the very mall where, 16 years later, I'd be doing [a] book signing—and I noticed an escalator that ran from the ground floor directly up to the new third story. I naively asked why there weren't two sets of escalators: an up-and-down set between the first and second floors, and a second pair between the upper two stories.

76 The PR person giving the tour explained, without shame, that the one-way express escalator was designed to keep shoppers moving around the mall, even if they didn't really intend to.

77 I can testify that the escalator fulfils that function admirably. I've lost count of the times I've stepped onto it by mistake and watched the second-floor store I had hoped to reach pass me by like a desert mirage. As a result, I have to hike across half the mall to find a staircase, escalator, or elevator that will actually take me where I want to go.

78 This design strategy seems counterproductive. Yes, it makes me pass stores I didn't plan to see. But, trust me, I'm in no frame of mind to buy. Usually, I'm muttering unpleasant words under my breath as I hotfoot it down the corridors. Until, of course, I sprint by a display of discount books and something catches my eye.

79 All right, I admit it. I'm annoyed, but I still buy.

80 But with luck, this mall-as-maze idea will be one of the design trends to lose favor among shopping center architects. Such miracles do happen.

81 There are encouraging signs that change is in the wind. For instance, the wisdom of sealing off shoppers from the real world is now being questioned in Broomfield, Colorado. There, a new mall called FlatIron Crossing features "window walls" of clear glass that can even be rolled back to let in light and air when the weather permits. "We're trying to blur the lines of where outdoor and indoors start and stop," David School, one of the mall's developers, told a newspaper reporter in 1999.[8]

82 The builders of the stoa at Miletus, and the Duke of Chartres's architect at the Palais Royal, would recognize this idea. Just like the fashions sold in mall stores throughout the world, everything old eventually becomes new again in the world of shopping center design. And if bell-bottoms and platform shoes can be revived, nothing's impossible.

Notes

Particularly useful references for this chapter included Spiro Kostof's *A History of Architecture: Settings and Rituals,* Margaret MacKeith's *The History and Conservation of Shopping Arcades,* and Mark Girouard's *Cities and People.* The International Council of Shopping Centers provided valuable information on the history of the development of the modern American shopping center, as did the Web page of Steven Schoenherr, a history professor at the University of San Diego <history.sandiego.edu/gen/filmnotes/shoppingcenter.html>.

1. "At the top of the street," Arieh Sharon, *Planning Jerusalem,* London, Weidenfeld & Nicolson, 1973, quoted in Margaret MacKeith, *The History and Conservation of Shopping Arcades,* 9.

2. "Everything that can be found in Paris," N.M. Karamzin, *Letters of a Russian Traveler,* New York and Oxford, 1957, 215, quoted in Mark Girouard, *Cities and People,* 204.

3. "As far as possible convenience," Ralph Redivivus, *Civil Engineer and Architect's Journal,* March 1839, quoted in Margaret MacKeith, *The History and Conservation of Shopping Arcades,* 1.

4. "I don't think there is a shop," Augustus Sala, quoted in Alison Adburgham, *Shopping in Style,* 102.

5. "The Burlington Arcade provides," <http://www.burlington-arcade.co.uk>.

6. "In a region which is often beset," Southdale Shopping Center fact sheet, 1956, <http://www.southdale.com>.

7. "When people yearn for a return," Daniel Miller, Peter Jackson, Nigel Thrift, Beverley Holbrook, and Michael Rowlands, *Shopping, Place and Identity,* xi.

8. "We're trying to blur the lines," David Scholl, quoted in Jeanie Straub, "Regional shopping mall's design banks on meshing indoors, outdoors," *Boulder County Business Report,* December 17, 1999.

Review Questions

1. Laura Paquet both explains and argues in this selection. Review her work and note where she uses each approach.

2. Trace the evolution of shopping malls, from ancient times to present.

3. Which of the shopping centers Paquet discusses was initially built in the 1400s and has remained in use until the present day?

4. How did glazing techniques for producing glass and the construction of sidewalks affect London's shopkeepers in the late eighteenth century?

5. Architecturally, what were the main differences and similarities among the Palais Royal, the Burlington Arcade, and Southdale Center (the first modern mall)?

6. In the 1990s, what motivation did mall developers have to upgrade new and existing properties? Why was building an "ordinary" mall no longer an appealing prospect?

7. How do mall developers attempt to keep customers in the mall for as long as possible?

Discussion and Writing Suggestions

1. Reread the epigraph to this selection, by James B. Twitchell, comparing the modern mall to a fascistic medieval city-state. In your view, does the comparison hold?

2. Characterize the tone of Paquet's writing in this selection and offer quotations to support your view.

3. Is there any sense in which you view shopping malls differently, having read Paquet's selection? Does your learning that the origins of the modern mall can be traced back thousands of years affect your view of malls and what people do in them today? Explain.

4. In paragraph 31, reread N. M. Karamzin's account of the Palais Royal, the exclusive shopping district in Paris. Apply Karamzin's description, part-by-part, to a modern mall. How well does his account describe what one finds today?

5. Paquet writes that both the Palais Royal in Paris (1780) and the Burlington Arcade in London (1839) sold luxury items that appealed to relatively wealthy customers. These earlier forms of the shopping center aimed to attract an upscale clientele. In your experience with modern malls, to what extent do you find a similar targeting of customers? Are some malls geared especially to the wealthy? To the middle class? To the poor? How can you tell?

6. Paquet concludes with this statement: "Just like the fashions sold in mall stores throughout the world, everything old eventually becomes new again in the world of shopping center design." What does she mean?

Main Street Revisited
Richard Francaviglia

What models did developers turn to when creating the modern American shopping mall? In this next selection, Richard Francaviglia argues that Walt Disney played a key role. His romanticized "Main Street USA," a re-creation of small-town America's shopping district for his new theme park, Disneyland, set the standard for carefully designed and managed shopping environments. Main Street USA, moved indoors to a climate-controlled environment, became the modern shopping mall. A geographer and historian, Francaviglia directs the Center for Greater Southwestern Studies and the History of Cartography at the University of Texas, Arlington. This selection appeared in his book Main Street Revisited: Time, Space, and Image-

Building in Small-Town America *(University of Iowa Press, 1996), which won the J. B. Jackson Prize for conveying "the insights of professional geography in language that is interesting and attractive to a lay audience."*

1   Main Street USA . . . fits into the genre of intensely designed and orchestrated space/place. On every inch of Disney's Main Street USA, from the public square to the Plaza, architecture, street furniture, and all aspects of the streetscape are historically themed and carefully engineered. It is this sense of "history" that nearly overwhelms the visitor. All of the street lights are patterned after the "whiteway" lights that lined Main Streets in the early twentieth century. The park benches, wrought iron railings, plantings—everything on Main Street is carefully designed to convey a feeling of the late Victorian period. Even the trees and bushes are carefully sculpted and tended. On Main Street USA, most visitors imbibe the ambience of the past, but they are in fact participating in something far more elementary; their attitudes and perceptions are being shaped through a type of social engineering. This leads to the fourteenth axiom of Main Street development.* *Main Street is essentially a stage upon which several types of human dramas are performed simultaneously, each character or actor in the drama having a designated role that is dependent on his or her relationship to the "set."* Whether one stands behind the counter or in front of a store window brings with it different expectations. Disney was the ultimate merchant on Main Street, and visitors to Main Street USA are the ultimate customers.

2   In Disney's Main Street USA, architecture becomes the façade that creates the impression that all was right with the world in the small town at the turn of the century; it implies that commerce (and merchants) thrive along Main Street, and that society and a community are working together in harmony. Of course, Disney's Main Street does not feature those inevitable services that indicate the other, or darker, side of life. There are no funeral parlors, pool halls, or bars. It should come as no surprise that Disney created small-town America as it *should* have been. His Main Street mirrors a pre-adolescent period free from the change and turmoil that characterizes much of life. . . .

3   What concerns, even infuriates, historians and scholars most about Walt Disney is that he created an abstracted image that it is so tempting to confuse with reality. Disney masterfully abstracted his experiences in [one of his hometowns] *Marceline* and worked with his designers to capture the essences of other towns to produce a small-town image that has nearly universal appeal. In so doing, Disney intuitively knew that *all* planned townscapes—including those Main Streets created in the eighteenth and nineteenth centuries—were in a sense engineered to create effects. Even the vistas down Main Street USA were carefully designed to have significant features (the Railroad Station and Sleeping Beauty's Castle), or, as Disney himself is reported to have said, there should be a "wienie at the end of every street.". . .

---

* Throughout the book from which this selection was taken, Francaviglia draws broad lessons, what he sees as fundamental truths, about the evolution of Main Streets across America during the 19th and 20th centuries. Main Street's being a "stage upon which . . . human dramas are performed" is one such axiom. You will notice that James Farrell uses much the same language to discuss what goes on in shopping malls, earlier in the chapter.

4   At symbolic levels, Disney's engineering of the small-town environment in Main Street USA is revealing because he so beautifully captured the essence of the romanticism of the small town. Disney himself was moved by the originals, and shaped them into an icon that affects the way we will view its "real" counterparts. To the general public, Main Street USA in Disneyland was very credible in that it featured towers and architectural turrets where they seemed logical, and even though the trim was fairly lavish, it was subdued enough to remind one of Main Streets in the relatively prosperous period during the "McKinley Era"* at about the turn of the century.

5   Students of urban design know that Disney possessed an element of genius in that he carefully designed this Main Street to have an intersection about halfway between the public square and the plaza. That intersection provides a node of activity where merchants have materials on display outside and where towers can form visual exclamation points for the architecture. Looking down one of these side streets, one sees trees that convey the feeling that the commercial streetscape is yielding to a residential area. But in reality, the trees seen behind that intersection on Main Street are the trees of Jungleland, so close is the juxtaposition between one "world" of Disneyland and another. The entire Disneyland theme park is magnificently engineered into only about ninety-six acres of space, which is smaller than the area encompassed within the city limits of most American towns! In world history, few places this small have had such a powerful effect on so many people.

6   In keeping with his ability to create magic through place, Disney used night to his advantage. Because Main Street USA is experienced at night as well as during the daytime, Disney provided marvelous rim-lighting on the buildings. Incandescent bulbs were strung along all of the cornices to convey a very stylized and ornate appearance, enabling the architecture and the streetscape to "shine" at night as well as in the daytime. The Main Street electrical parade runs through the area at night, and Main Street at night provides a kind of visual excitement that was rarely, perhaps never, actually seen in the small towns of America. Rim-lighting of this kind was, however, common in pavilions and the grand buildings of expositions. Like many of Disney's creations, rim-lighting in this context brings a touch of the exotic or even whimsical to Main Street, rather reminding one more of the festive environments of parks and fairs than the Main Street of the typical American small town. Historian and social critic Jon Weiner recently noted that "Disneyland's Main Street is a fiction; the real Main Streets of real small towns at the turn of the century were not so nice"[1]—an understatement borne out by architectural historians and historical geographers. And yet, as architect Paul Goldberger accurately noted, Disney produced "a kind of universally true Main Street—it's better than the real Main Street of the turn of the century ever could be."[2] That Disney's Main Street seems so universally beautiful comes as less of a surprise when one realizes that Walt Disney was rather sophisticated and widely travelled: in fact, Tivoli Gardens in Copenhagen, Denmark, was said to have greatly impressed Walt Disney in 1952—a seminal year in the early designs of

---

* William McKinley (1843–1901), the 25th President of the United States (1897–1901), was assassinated while in office.

Disneyland.[3] Disney and his designers reportedly were impressed by an exhibit called "Yesteryear's Main Street" at the Museum of Science and Industry in Chicago, which was sponsored by General Motors.[4] Disney's Main Street, which, according to WED (which stands for Walter Elias Disney) imagineering historian David Mumford, "is actually a typical representation of a Walt Disney imagineering project, since it represents a collaborative effort by many creative people,"[5] was thus inspired by many places. . . .

7   If this description of [Main Street USA] sounds familiar, and it should indeed, that is because it has in fact become the model of the typical American shopping mall, where the visitor or shopper leaves the car in the parking lot and enters an environment that is climatically controlled, and where the real world is left outside. In malls, as in Disney's Main Streets, every aspect of design and circulation is carefully orchestrated (Fig. 10.1). This should come as no surprise, for many of the designers of shopping centers and malls in the United States

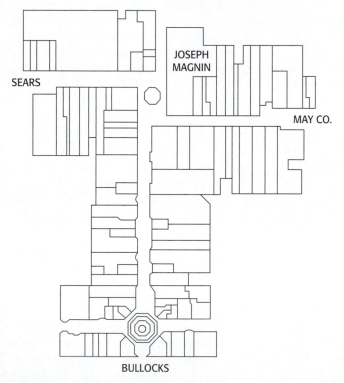

FIGURE 10.1   The Mall as Main Street. This diagram of the South Coast Plaza Shopping Center, a mall in Costa Mesa, California, reveals many of the same design elements seen in Disneyland's Main Street USA—notably an important intersection of four radiating axes (bottom) and a linear thoroughfare running into another point of decision-making where a carousel is positioned (upper center). The similarities are more than coincidental, as many shopping center designers have studied Disney's Main Street. Computer graphic based on a 1975 map in a kiosk at the mall.

have visited Disney's parks in order to develop a much better understanding of how people move through, appreciate, and patronize a retail environment.[6]

8   It is ironic that Walt Disney, who was politically conservative and espoused rugged individualism, actually produced an environment that embodies such nearly total social engineering and control. According to architectural critic Jane Holtz Kay, Disney's Main Street and shopping malls embody both "public persona" and "private autocracy."[7] The autocratic control of theme parks, of course, is linked to safety and security, and is perhaps one reason why shopping centers are highly successful, and highly criticized by those who feel that such places are "contrived." Malls, too, are able to control behavior using their "private" status. As William Kowinski succinctly stated in his classic article entitled "The Malling of America":

> Malls are designed for Disney's children. Stores are pressed close together; they have small low façades. In fact, everything about malls is minimized . . . the mall is laid out with few corners and no unused space along store rows so that there are no decisions to make—you just flow on.[8] *

9   Few can deny the attractiveness of mall environments to a generation of retail shoppers drawn to the relative serenity and the climate control of the shopping center. That such malls are a current incarnation of Main Street is borne out by the flourishing social life and the persistence of marketing and craft fairs within today's shopping centers. The relative visual uniformity of shopping centers from coast to coast should not be particularly surprising; they, like Disney's Main Street, are archetypal environments of popular culture. This has caused architectural critics to blast the lack of "imagination" of their creators while, ironically, reflecting nostalgically on the days of the *real* American town in, perhaps, the 1880s when, critics contend, there was far greater "individuality."

10   In reality, of course, this was not the case; as we have seen, by the 1880s Victorian-era Main Streets had developed into highly standardized forms. Their major architectural components could—like McDonald's—be found from coast to coast. That scholars lament the standardization of the mall while praising the architectural integrity of historic Main Streets reveals the power of nostalgia in affecting even the most educated of our citizens. Whatever else one may say about the typical shopping center, it is an abstracted reincarnation of Main Street, where pedestrians have the right of way over vehicular traffic, where *all* store façades are attractive and where all of the merchants agree to maintain regular hours and carefully control their signage and sales pitches—techniques which avoid the appearance of haphazard or eccentric individualism.

11   Sociologists have long known that people visit shopping centers for far more than commercial reasons. More than twenty years ago, when Edward Tauber insightfully stated that "not all shopping motives, by any means, are even related to the product,"[9] he introduced the concept of "sociorecreational shopping." Several very revealing articles over the last dozen or more years have shown that shopping centers are important places of social interaction where people may wind up meeting future spouses and friends; where families go simply to stroll, to see people and to be seen by them; where young people go to "hang

---

* A selection from Kowinski's *Malling of America* appears later in this chapter.

out" and socialize. Whereas academicians may condemn this type of behavior as manipulated or inauthentic, it is in fact one of the major reasons why commercial and marketing towns have existed for centuries. This may be stated as the fifteenth axiom of Main Street development: *Despite its market-driven businesses, Main Street is primarily a social environment.* Main Street is an integral element in the "collective consciousness," as geographer Alan Baker used the term, to refer to landscape creation and perception that is linked to a national identity.[10]

Notes

1. Jon Weiner, "Tall Tales and True," *Nation* 258, no. 4: 134.

2. Paul Goldberger, in Judith Adams, *The American Amusement Park Industry:* 98.

3. Arline Chambers, "The Architecture of Reassurance: Designing the Disney Theme Parks," "Disney Chronology" (unpublished paper), p. 5.

4. Andrew Lainsbury, personal communication with author, July 13, 1995.

5. Letter from David Mumford to Jack and Leon Janzen, November 13, 1992, reproduced in Jack E. Janzen, "MAIN STREET . . . Walt's Perfect Introduction to Disneyland": 30.

6. Richard Francaviglia, "Main Street Revisited."

7. Jane Holtz Kay, "When You Stimulate a Star," *Landscape Architecture,* June 1990: 54.

8. *New Times,* May 1, 1978: 33.

9. Edward Tauber, "Sociorecreational Shopping," *Human Behavior* 2, no. 4; reproduced in *Intellectual Digest* 4, no. 3 (November 1973): 38.

10. Alan R. H. Baker, "Collective Consciousness and the Last Landscape: National Ideology and the Commune Council of Mesland (Loir-et-Cher) as Landscape Architect during the 19th Century," chapter 12 in *Ideology and Landscape in Historical Perspective,* edited by Alan Baker and Gideon Biger: 255–88.

Review Questions

1. Describe the ways in which Disney's Main Street USA is a carefully controlled environment.

2. What impression does Disney's street create for the visitor, according to Francaviglia?

3. What is the critics' chief complaint about this street?

4. In what ways does mall design borrow from Disney's Main Street USA?

5. Why is the placement of an intersection important to the success of Main Street USA as well as to the typical shopping mall?

Discussion and Writing Suggestions

1. If you have visited Disneyland or Disneyworld, describe your experiences on Main Street USA. Did the street impress you as it did

Francaviglia? To what extent do you find shopping mall design similar in key respects to the design of Main Street USA?

2. "Whatever else one may say about the typical shopping center, it is an abstracted reincarnation of Main Street, where pedestrians have the right of way over vehicular traffic, where *all* store facades are attractive and where all of the merchants agree to maintain regular hours and carefully control their signage and sales pitches—techniques which avoid the appearance of haphazard or eccentric individualism" (paragraph 10). To what extent do you agree that these aims are desirable?

3. In paragraph 11, quoting another author, Francaviglia introduces the term "sociorecreational shopping." Define the term and relate it to your own experiences as a mall shopper.

4. This selection is excerpted from a book-length study of America's Main Streets. Throughout the longer work, Francaviglia offers a number of "axioms" regarding his subject. You find two of these axioms in this selection. See paragraph 1: "Main Street is essentially a stage upon which several types of human dramas are performed simultaneously." An *axiom* is a statement that is universally recognized as true. Do you agree that Francaviglia's statement is beyond dispute?

5. Following question 4, Francaviglia offers a second axiom in this selection. See paragraph 11: "Despite its market-driven businesses, Main street is primarily a social environment." Do you agree that Francaviglia's statement is beyond dispute?

Shopping Towns USA
Victor Gruen and Larry Smith

Victor Gruen (born Viktor Grüenbaum, 1903–1980) is the American architect credited with creating the modern shopping mall. Born and trained in Vienna, he fled the Nazi occupation and moved to New York in 1938, where he worked as an architect before opening his own firm in 1951 in Los Angeles. Gruen believed that shopping centers would promote the interests not only of businesses but also of suburbanites, who lived in vast, culturally isolated developments that lacked the community focus of urban neighborhoods. Shopping centers could become community centers, argued Gruen, and in the process promote American values. Gruen is credited with building the first fully enclosed, air-conditioned shopping mall in Edina, Minnesota, in 1956. Ultimately, he returned to Europe, disappointed that other mall developers pursued profits more than they did community development. The following selection, in which Gruen articulates his vision for shopping centers, appears as the "Prologue" in Shopping Towns USA (Reinhold Publishing, 1960).

1 Buying and selling is as old as mankind. Prehistoric man exchanged the deer he had slain for a necklace of pretty shells. The modern housewife acquires a package of frozen food in exchange for some round pieces of metal. Gratification of

needs and desires motivates both transactions. Only the conditions under which they take place have changed.

2   A condition of most important consequence, of course, was the introduction of the middleman—the merchant—who turned barter into commerce. He carried the work produced by others from place to place, established trade routes and trading posts, founded country stores and merchant states. Wherever he settled he became an integral, invigorating part of urban life.

3   In the Greece of antiquity the merchant spread his wares under the colonnades of the *Stoa,* a building especially designated for his activity. The *Stoa* was as important in the *Agora,* or city square, as the *Bouleuterion* where the political representatives met, or the *Ecclesiasterion,* designed for public meetings. The Temple was nearby. Citizens strolling in the square discussed the topics of the day, transacted their business, did their marketing, while philosophers, poets, and entertainers argued, recited and performed. Court trials were held there. Banquets were spread. The *Agora* was the center of city life, and in this colorful, lively, dynamic environment commerce had its share.

4   This integration of human activities was a universal pattern. Its existence was guaranteed in ancient Rome where wheeled traffic was banished from the city's forum when vehicles threatened to crowd out the humans.

5   The medieval city market square was the city's center, not only geographically but socially and commercially, religiously and culturally. The City Hall and Guild Halls were placed there. The Cathedral, the merchants' and craftsmen's stalls and stores surrounded it. The open center area became in turn the market place, the fair ground and the entertainment center for the citizenry.

6   That genius of the Renaissance, Leonardo da Vinci, recognized the threat to human values of life when they become isolated. He designed a City Center for the convenience and pleasure of the people, confining wheeled vehicles to an underground road.

7   Our own New England and Midwest towns are witness to the basic town square concept which our forefathers brought with them from Europe. It persisted here well into the nineteenth century.

8   The advent of the Industrial Revolution radically changed the organization and character of cities. Thousands of factories were built in the midst of towns and cities. The city grew into a crazy quilt of packed humanity. The industrial slum became the new pattern of the city.

9   Life in the city soon became intolerable and those who could afford it led the march to the suburbs. The exodus increased its tempo with the advent of the interurban, elevated and subway trains and became a rout with the emergence of the automobile.

10   The automobile was the means by which the last vestige of community coherence was destroyed. So long as suburban dwellers traveled in vehicles that ran on tracks, new communities had a central point—the railway stop—to build around. As the cities stretched out along the tentacles of railroad lines, shops, churches, and community buildings sprang up around the railroad station; the size of residential areas was automatically controlled by the walking distance from the station. Such subcenters are still clearly recognizable in the Greater London Area.

11   When the automobile emerged as a means of private mass transportation, the final urban explosion took place. Automobiles, free of steel rails or overhead

wires, could move at will in every direction. They provided complete freedom of movement to the individual driver and made him independent of public transportation. So, with the automobile came a dispersal of population that followed no pattern whatever.

12   To accommodate the flood of humans seeking escape from the intolerable conditions of the city, mass housing builders tore up the ground, chopped down the trees, and removed swiftly and cynically every vestige of what the people had come to find. Modern suburbia was born, in which there were neither the values of a rural community nor those of an urban environment.

13   But people must live somewhere and suburbia grew. According to a report of the United States Census Bureau, suburbs grew seven times as fast as central cities in the years 1950 to 1954. The population of metropolitan areas in 1950 was 83,796,000; 95,304,000, in 1954. Within incorporated city areas an increase of 3.8 percent occurred; 27.8 percent in suburban communities of the metropolitan area. In 1957 a population census was taken in New York City in an attempt to obtain additional state aid by proving increased population. To the great surprise of city government it was found that the combined total population of the five boroughs had decreased from 7,891,957 in 1950 to 7,795,417—or 1.2 percent—at a time when the population of the Greater Metropolitan Area was increasing dramatically.

14   As the spreading continued with increasing speed, distances between places of residence and the central city grew by leaps and bounds.

15   In spite of this, public transportation faced the threat of annihilation. The inroads that private automobile traffic had made on public transportation is indicated by figures of a study made by the Westchester County Association. It showed that despite a population increase during the years 1949 to 1954 of 15.5 percent, the number of railroad commuters decreased during the same period by 16.3 percent.

16   Throughout the United States, the growth was so fast and frenzied that purely practical matters—construction of roads, highways, drainage and sewage, power and gas lines—lagged years behind; but any serious attempt at adequate planning of properly situated schools, shopping facilities, community centers and churches was nonexistent. Row upon row of identical houses set in an empty countryside proved to be less than the Heaven its settlers had bargained for. Suburbia had become an arid land inhabited during the day almost entirely by women and children and strictly compartmentalized by family income, social, religious, and racial background.

17   A psychiatrist of the United States Department of Health, Leonard J. Duhl, believes that this matriarchal pattern of suburbia sets up mental health hazards. Labeling it a "Feminine World," he describes it as a place where people are keeping up with the Joneses, where conformity is considered a necessity and where children have only limited experiences and are not exposed to broader environmental influences.*

---

* For more on the "Feminine World" of the suburbs that Gruen introduces here, see Lizabeth Cohen, "From Town Center to Shopping Center: The Reconfiguration of Community Market Places in Postwar America" in the *American Historical Review*, 101 (4), October 1996, particularly pp. 1072–1077. A portion of Cohen's article appears later in this chapter.

18   Critics of City Planning are equally concerned. Christopher Tunnard and Henry Hope Reed, in their book *American Skyline,* have this to say about suburbia:

> How different this is from our earlier American tradition which allowed people of all classes to mingle together as they still do in communities where people live as well as work. Something of this mixture is healthier for democracy which will surely suffer if residential suburbs continue to refuse public housing projects, business firms, industry and rest camps. Without these they will remain smug, lacklustre backwaters.

19   Many others, trained to apprehend the private and public dangers inherent in our unplanned suburban growth, are increasingly concerned. Charles Abrams, Chairman of the New York State Commission Against Discrimination, points out that: "The suburbs and their quest for status are shaping the American personality of the future as the frontier once shaped the American personality of the past."

20   Since suburbia is undoubtedly having a serious effect on the personality of our entire urban life, it is natural that its influence should be felt by the segment of human activity that is of primary concern to us here: the marketing of goods for the gratification of human needs and desires. In this amorphous conglomeration—suburbia—the merchant has had difficulty in finding a logical way to integrate his activities with the local scene.

21   Stores, which followed their customers into the suburbs, were no longer provided with obvious predetermined locations such as near railway stations. For the customer no longer emerged at defined points; he and his automobile were everywhere.

22   Under these circumstances the best bet seemed to be store locations on highways over which shoppers would have to travel on their way back and forth to the city. As the number of highway stores increased, more people stopped their cars along the curb and parking space became available only for a cash premium—a new type of hitching post, the parking meter, had made its appearance. Because the shortage and cost of curb parking tended to slow down sales, merchants arranged for off-street car storage areas, at first behind and later on in front of their stores.

23   Business grew and so did automobile traffic. Consequently, serious traffic congestion appeared on the highways, so serious that drivers began to avoid them by using alternate routes. When these roads inevitably attracted new stores and new congestion, super highways and freeways were constructed at tremendous cost in order to promote an easy flow of traffic.

24   In the meantime, residential areas surrounding congested traffic carriers, or facing the unsightly service facilities of stores, became undesirable. The original owners and tenants moved out and only those who could not afford or were not permitted to live in the more desirable places moved in. Soon stores found themselves surrounded by residential areas of reduced buying power.

25   As customers were siphoned off from the roads along which merchants had settled, partly by neighborhood deterioration, partly by the use of new freeways, a wild scramble for new locations started. Merchandising outlets were built in freshly created suburban areas still farther removed. Here, within a few years,

merchants encountered a repetition of the undesirable conditions from which they had tried to escape. The need for farsighted, comprehensive planning finally became urgently apparent.

26   Planning is needed not only to bring order, stability, and meaning to chaotic suburbia; it is necessary in order to establish a strong logical framework within which individual merchandising enterprises can flourish and provide crystallization points for suburbia's community life.

27   Some members of the business community have, in the past, resisted the concept of comprehensive planning. They regarded it as interference with individual initiative and free enterprise. It has been labeled by some as "undemocratic." But planning, properly understood and exercised, does not result in fixed patterns, in authoritarianism, in regimentation, or in the suppression of individualism.

28   No democratic society can flourish without law and order which, when applied to the physical environment, necessitates planning. In a complex and highly mechanized society environmental planning safeguards the basic human rights. By providing the best conditions for physical and mental health, it protects *life*. By establishing barriers against anarchy and the infringements of hostile natural and man-made forces, it protects *liberty*. By the creation of a humane environment it invites and encourages the *pursuit of happiness*.

29   When environmental planning is applied to the designing of new commercial facilities, many conditions must be analyzed, criteria weighed, requirements met, and problems solved. These all involve in various ways and to varying degrees the needs and desires of the shopper. It is deeply significant that the term is "shopping center," not "selling center." This indicates clearly that the wishes and desires of the shopper take priority over those of the seller. (An earlier term, "parking center," failed to catch on.)

30   The basic need of the suburban shopper is for a conveniently accessible, amply stocked shopping area with plentiful and free parking. This is the purely practical need for which the shopping center was originally conceived and which many centers most adequately fulfill. Good planning, however, will create additional attractions for shoppers by meeting other needs which are inherent in the psychological climate peculiar to suburbia. By affording opportunities for social life and recreation in a protected pedestrian environment, by incorporating civic and educational facilities, shopping centers can fill an existing void. They can provide the needed place and opportunity for participation in modern community life that the ancient Greek *Agora*, the Medieval Market Place and our own Town Squares provided in the past.

31   That the shopping center can fulfill this perhaps subconscious but nonetheless urgent need of suburbanites for the amenities of urban living, is convincingly proved in a large number of centers. In such centers, pedestrian areas are filled with teeming life not only during normal shopping hours, but on Sundays and holidays when people windowshop, promenade, relax in the garden courts, view exhibits and patronize the restaurants.

32   All age groups are provided for. Auditoriums are booked to capacity. Meeting rooms are busy with civic and cultural affairs. Dance schools, music schools, and ice skating rinks attract teen-agers; amusement centers are popular with children.

33   Such a planning concept also results in an upgrading of the residential area surrounding the center. It not only protects surrounding communities from

blight but actually raises their desirability and consequently their property values.

34   If the shopping center becomes a place that not only provides suburbanites with their physical living requirements, but simultaneously serves their civic, cultural and social community needs, it will make a most significant contribution to the enrichment of our lives.

Review Questions

1. How did the increased use of the automobile contribute to the need for shopping centers?

2. Why did some merchants initially resist the concept of a carefully planned shopping center?

3. Aside from providing access to well-stocked stores and plenty of free parking, what attractions do shopping centers offer suburban communities?

4. In what ways did the rapid growth of suburbia in the 1950s fail to create for new suburbanites the promised "Heaven" they were hoping for?

5. In what ways had suburbia become a "Feminine World," according to Gruen?

Discussion and Writing Suggestions

1. In paragraph 28, Gruen offers a vigorous defense of centrally planned shopping centers, arguing that retail development, just like democracy, demands law and order. We gain the free exercise of life, liberty, and happiness, he suggests, through maintaining order. How convinced are you by Gruen's defense of centralized shopping center design?

2. In what sense can it be said that Gruen believed his shopping centers could save America from the curse of suburbia? In developing an answer, see especially paragraphs 16–20.

3. Gruen states (in paragraph 31) that "the shopping center can fulfill [a] subconscious but nonetheless urgent need of suburbanites for the amenities or urban living." What are these needs? To what extent do you believe that people living in the suburbs have them?

4. Reread the final paragraph of this selection. Gruen was a visionary who believed that shopping centers could meet "civic, cultural, and social community needs," as well as the commercial needs of suburbanites. Are you sympathetic to this vision? In your experience, to what extent do shopping centers today meet his standards?

5. In the first five paragraphs, Gruen conducts a very brief historical tour of shopping. In the context of the overall selection, why does

he begin in this way? In developing your answer, pay close attention to his conclusion.

Enclosed. Encyclopedic. Endured: One Week at the Mall of America
David Guterson

In 1993 journalist and novelist David Guterson, on assignment for Harper's *magazine, spent a week in the recently opened Mall of America. As you will discover, Guterson approached the mall with a skeptical eye, both fascinated with and wary of its massive scale. Guterson agrees with James Farrell that one can take the pulse of American culture by spending time in malls. But what Guterson sees is cause for alarm. A contributing editor to* Harper's, *Guterson has most notably written a collection of short stories,* The Country Ahead of Us, the Country Behind *(Vintage, 1996) and the novel* Snow Falling on Cedars, *which won the 1995 PEN/Faulkner Award.*

1   Last April, on a visit to the new Mall of America near Minneapolis, I carried with me the public-relations press kit provided for the benefit of reporters. It included an assortment of "fun facts" about the mall: 140,000 hot dogs sold each week, 10,000 permanent jobs, 44 escalators and 17 elevators, 12,750 parking places, 13,300 short tons of steel, $1 million in cash disbursed weekly from 8 automatic-teller machines. Opened in the summer of 1992, the mall was built on the 78-acre site of the former Metropolitan Stadium, a five-minute drive from the Minneapolis–St. Paul International Airport. With 4.2 million square feet of floor space—including twenty-two times the retail footage of the average American shopping center—the Mall of America was "the largest fully enclosed combination retail and family entertainment complex in the United States."

2   Eleven thousand articles, the press kit warned me, had already been written on the mall. Four hundred trees had been planted in its gardens, $625 million had been spent to build it, 350 stores had been leased. Three thousand bus tours were anticipated each year along with a half-million Canadian visitors and 200,000 Japanese tourists. Sales were projected at $650 million for 1993 and at $1 billion for 1996. Donny and Marie Osmond had visited the mall, as had Janet Jackson and Sally Jesse Raphael, Arnold Schwarzenegger, and the 1994 Winter Olympic Committee.* The mall was five times larger than Red Square[†] and twenty times larger than St. Peter's Basilica;[‡] it incorporated 2.3 miles of hallways and

---

* Celebrities Donnie and Marie Osmond, part of a Salt Lake City based family entertainment team, were best known for three television variety shows that aired on prime time between 1976 and 1981. Sally Jesse Raphael is a talk show host whose programs aired between 1985 and 2002. Arnold Schwarzenegger needs no introduction.

[†] *Red Square* is the central square in the ancient center of Moscow, near the Kremlin, where during the Communist Soviet era military parades were held on May 1st.

[‡] Built in the 16th century in the Italian Renaissance style, *St. Peter's Basilica* is the great church of Vatican City.

almost twice as much steel as the Eiffel Tower. It was also home to the nation's largest indoor theme park, a place called Knott's Camp Snoopy.

3   On the night I arrived, a Saturday, the mall was spotlit dramatically in the manner of a Las Vegas casino. It resembled, from the outside, a castle or fort, the Emerald City or Never-Never Land,* impossibly large and vaguely unreal, an unbroken, windowless multi-storied edifice the size of an airport terminal. Surrounded by parking lots and new freeway ramps, monolithic and imposing in the manner of a walled city, it loomed brightly against the Minnesota night sky with the disturbing magnetism of a mirage.

4   I knew already that the Mall of America had been imagined by its creators not merely as a marketplace but as a national tourist attraction, an immense zone of entertainments. Such a conceit raised provocative questions, for our architecture testifies to our view of ourselves and to the condition of our souls. Large buildings stand as markers in the lives of nations and in the stream of a people's history. Thus I could only ask myself: Here was a new structure that had cost more than half a billion dollars to erect—what might it tell us about ourselves? If the Mall of America was part of America, what was that going to mean?

5   I passed through one of the mall's enormous entranceways and took myself inside. Although from a distance the Mall of America had appeared menacing—exuding the ambience of a monstrous hallucination—within it turned out to be simply a shopping mall, certainly more vast than other malls but in tone and aspect, design and feel, not readily distinguishable from them. Its nuances were instantly familiar as the generic features of the American shopping mall at the tail end of the twentieth century: polished stone, polished tile, shiny chrome and brass, terrazzo floors, gazebos. From third-floor vistas, across vaulted spaces, the Mall of America felt endlessly textured—glass-enclosed elevators, neon-tube lighting, bridges, balconies, gas lamps, vaulted skylights—and densely crowded with hordes of people circumambulating in an endless promenade. Yet despite the mall's expansiveness, it elicited claustrophobia, sensory deprivation, and an unnerving disorientation. Everywhere I went I spied other pilgrims who had found, like me, that the straight way was lost and that the YOU ARE HERE landmarks on the map kiosks referred to nothing in particular.

6   Getting lost, feeling lost, being lost—these states of mind are intentional features of the mall's psychological terrain. There are, one notices, no clocks or windows, nothing to distract the shopper's psyche from the alternate reality the mall conjures. Here we are free to wander endlessly and to furtively watch our fellow wanderers, thousands upon thousands of milling strangers who have come with the intent of losing themselves in the mall's grand, stimulating design. For a few hours we share some common ground—a fantasy of infinite commodities and comforts—and then we drift apart forever. The mall exploits our acquisitive instincts without honoring our communal requirements, our eternal desire for discourse and intimacy, needs that until the twentieth century were traditionally met in our marketplaces but that are not met at all in giant shopping malls.

---

* The *Emerald City* and *Never-Never Land* are the exotic, imaginary destinations featured in *The Wizard of Oz* and *Peter Pan,* respectively.

7 On this evening a few thousand young people had descended on the mall in pursuit of alcohol and entertainment. They had come to Gators, Hooters, and Knuckleheads, Puzzles, Fat Tuesday, and Ltl Ditty's. At Players, a sports bar, the woman beside me introduced herself as "the pregnant wife of an Iowa pig farmer" and explained that she had driven five hours with friends to "do the mall party scene together." She left and was replaced by Kathleen from Minnetonka, who claimed to have "a real shopping thing—I can't go a week without buying new clothes. I'm not fulfilled until I buy something."

8   Later a woman named Laura arrived, with whom Kathleen was acquainted. "I *am* the mall," she announced ecstatically upon discovering I was a reporter. "I'd move in here if I could bring my dog," she added. "This place is heaven, it's a *mecca."*

9   "We egg each other on," explained Kathleen, calmly puffing on a cigarette. "It's like, sort of, an addiction."

10   "You want the truth?" Laura asked. "I'm constantly suffering from megamall withdrawal. I come here all the time."

11   Kathleen: "It's a sickness, It's like cocaine or something; it's a drug."

12   Laura: "Kathleen's got this thing about buying, but I just need to *be* here. If I buy something it's an added bonus."

13   Kathleen: "She buys stuff all the time; don't listen."

14   Laura: "Seriously, I feel sorry for other malls. They're so small and *boring."*

15   Kathleen seemed to think about this: "Richdale Mall," she blurted finally. She rolled her eyes and gestured with her cigarette. "Oh, my God, Laura. Why did we even *go* there?"

16 There is, of course, nothing naturally abhorrent in the human impulse to dwell in marketplaces or the urge to buy, sell, and trade. Rural Americans traditionally looked forward to the excitement and sensuality of market day; Native Americans traveled long distances to barter and trade at sprawling, festive encampments. In Persian bazaars and in the ancient Greek agoras the very soul of the community was preserved and could be seen, felt, heard, and smelled as it might be nowhere else. All over the planet the humblest of people have always gone to market with hope in their hearts and in expectation of something beyond mere goods—seeking a place where humanity is temporarily in ascendance, a palette for the senses, one another.

17   But the illicit possibilities of the marketplace also have long been acknowledged. The Persian bazaar was closed at sundown; the Greek agora was off-limits to those who had been charged with certain crimes. One myth of the Old West we still carry with us is that market day presupposes danger; the faithful were advised to make purchases quickly and repair without delay to the farm, lest their attraction to the pleasures of the marketplace erode their purity of spirit.

18   In our collective discourse the shopping mall appears with the tract house, the freeway, and the backyard barbecue as a product of the American postwar years, a testament to contemporary necessities and desires and an invention not only peculiarly American but peculiarly of our own era too. Yet the mall's varied and far-flung predecessors—the covered bazaars of the Middle East, the stately arcades of Victorian England, Italy's vaulted and skylit galleries, Asia's

monsoon-protected urban markets—all suggest that the rituals of indoor shopping, although in their nuances not often like our own, are nevertheless broadly known. The late twentieth-century American contribution has been to transform the enclosed bazaar into an economic institution that is vastly profitable yet socially enervated, one that redefines in fundamental ways the human relationship to the marketplace. At the Mall of America—an extreme example—we discover ourselves thoroughly lost among strangers in a marketplace intentionally designed to serve no community needs.

19   In the strict sense the Mall of America is not a marketplace at all—the soul of a community expressed as a *place*—but rather a tourist attraction. Its promoters have peddled it to the world at large as something more profound than a local marketplace and as a destination with deep implications. "I believe we can make Mall of America stand for all of America," asserted the mall's general manager, John Wheeler, in a promotional video entitled *There's a Place for Fun in Your Life*. "I believe there's a shopper in all of us," added the director of marketing, Maureen Hooley. The mall has memorialized its opening-day proceedings by producing a celebratory videotape: Ray Charles singing "America the Beautiful," a laser show followed by fireworks, "The Star-Spangled Banner" and "The Stars and Stripes Forever," the Gatlin Brothers, and Peter Graves. "Mall of America . . . ," its narrator intoned. "The name alone conjures up images of greatness, of a retail complex so magnificent it could only happen in America."

20   Indeed, on the day the mall opened, Miss America visited. The mall's logo—a red, white, and blue star bisected by a red, white, and blue ribbon—decorated everything from the mall itself to coffee mugs and the flanks of buses. The idea, director of tourism Colleen Hayes told me, was to position America's largest mall as an institution on the scale of Disneyland or the Grand Canyon, a place simultaneously iconic and totemic, a revered symbol of the United States and a mecca to which the faithful would flock in pursuit of all things purchasable.

21 On Sunday I wandered the hallways of the pleasure dome with the sensation that I had entered an M.C. Escher drawing*—there was no such thing as up or down, and the escalators all ran backward. A 1993 Ford Probe GT was displayed as if popping out of a giant packing box; a full-size home, complete with artificial lawn, had been built in the mall's rotunda. At the Michael Ricker Pewter Gallery I came across a miniature tableau of a pewter dog peeing on a pewter man's leg; at Hologram Land I pondered 3-D hallucinations of the Medusa and Marilyn Monroe. I passed a kiosk called The Sportsman's Wife; I stood beside a life-size statue of the Hamm's Bear, carved out of pine and available for $1,395 at a store called Minnesot-ah! At Pueblo Spirit I examined a "dream catcher"— a small hoop made from deer sinew and willow twigs and designed to be hung over its owner's bed as a tactic for filtering bad dreams. For a while I sat in front of Glamour Shots and watched while women were groomed and brushed for photo sessions yielding high-fashion self-portraits at $34.95 each. There was no

---

* *M.C. Escher* (1898–1972) was a printmaker famous for images that confused viewers' perceptions of geometric space, making (for instance) finite walkways into infinite loops from which people could never exit. For examples of his work, go to <http://www.mcescher.com/> and select "Gallery."

stopping, no slowing down. I passed Mug Me, Queen for a Day, and Barnyard Buddies, and stood in the Brookstone store examining a catalogue: a gopher "eliminator" for $40 (it's a vibrating, anodized-aluminum stake), a "no-stoop" shoehorn for $10, a nose-hair trimmer for $18. At the arcade inside Knott's Camp Snoopy I watched while teenagers played Guardians of the 'Hood, Total Carnage, Final Fight, and Varth Operation Thunderstorm; a small crowd of them had gathered around a lean, cool character who stood calmly shooting video cowpokes in a game called Mad Dog McCree. Left thumb on his silver belt buckle, biceps pulsing, he banged away without remorse while dozens of his enemies crumpled and died in alleyways and dusty streets.

22   At Amazing Pictures a teenage boy had his photograph taken as a body-builder—his face smoothly grafted onto a rippling body—then proceeded to purchase this pleasing image on a poster, a sweatshirt, and a coffee mug. At Painted Tipi there was wild rice for sale, hand-harvested from Leech Lake, Minnesota. At Animalia I, came across a polyresin figurine of a turtle retailing for $3,200. At Bloomingdale's I pondered a denim shirt with its sleeves ripped away, the sort of thing available at used-clothing stores (the "grunge look," a Bloomingdale's employee explained), on sale for $125. Finally, at a gift shop in Knott's Camp Snoopy, I came across a game called Electronic Mall Madness, put out by Milton Bradley. On the box, three twelve-year-old girls with good features happily vied to beat one another to the game-board mall's best sales.

23   At last I achieved an enforced self-arrest, anchoring myself against a bench while the mall tilted on its axis. Two pubescent girls in retainers and braces sat beside me sipping coffees topped with whipped cream and chocolate sprinkles, their shopping bags gathered tightly around their legs, their eyes fixed on the passing crowds. They came, they said, from Shakopee—"It's nowhere," one of them explained. The megamall, she added, was "a buzz at first, but now it seems pretty normal. 'Cept my parents are like Twenty Questions every time I want to come here. 'Specially since the shooting."

24   On a Sunday night, she elaborated, three people had been wounded when shots were fired in a dispute over a San Jose Sharks jacket. "In the *mall*," her friend reminded me. "Right here at megamall. A shooting."

25   "It's like nowhere's safe," the first added.

26   They sipped their coffees and explicated for me the plot of a film they saw as relevant, a horror movie called *Dawn of the Dead,* which they had each viewed a half-dozen times. In the film, they explained, apocalypse had come, and the survivors had repaired to a shopping mall as the most likely place to make their last stand in a poisoned, impossible world. And this would have been perfectly all right, they insisted, except that the place had also attracted hordes of the infamous living dead—sentient corpses who had not relinquished their attraction to indoor shopping.

27   I moved on and contemplated a computerized cash register in the infant's section of the Nordstrom store: "The Answer Is Yes!!!" its monitor reminded clerks. "Customer Service Is Our Number One Priority!" Then back at Bloomingdale's I contemplated a bank of televisions playing incessantly an advertisement for Egoïste, a men's cologne from Chanel. In the ad a woman on a wrought-iron balcony tossed her black hair about and screamed long and passionately; then there were many women screaming passionately, too, and

throwing balcony shutters open and closed, and this was all followed by a bottle of the cologne displayed where I could get a good look at it. The brief, strange drama repeated itself until I could no longer stand it.

. . .

28 On Valentine's Day last February—cashing in on the promotional scheme of a local radio station—ninety-two couples were married en masse in a ceremony at the Mall of America. They rode the roller coaster and the Screaming Yellow Eagle and were photographed beside a frolicking Snoopy, who wore an immaculate tuxedo. "As we stand here together at the Mall of America," presiding district judge Richard Spicer declared, "we are reminded that there is a place for fun in your life and you have found it in each other." Six months earlier, the Reverend Leith Anderson of the Wooddale Church in Eden Prairie conducted services in the mall's rotunda. Six thousand people had congregated by 10:00 A.M., and Reverend Anderson delivered a sermon entitled "The Unknown God of the Mall." Characterizing the mall as a "direct descendant" of the ancient Greek agoras, the reverend pointed out that, like the Greeks before us, we Americans have many gods. Afterward, of course, the flock went shopping, much to the chagrin of Reverend Delton Krueger, president of the Mall Area Religious Council, who told the *Minneapolis Star Tribune* that as a site for church services, the mall may trivialize religion. "A good many people in the churches," said Krueger, "feel a lot of the trouble in the world is because of materialism."

29 But a good many people in the mall business today apparently think the trouble lies elsewhere. They are moving forward aggressively on the premise that the dawning era of electronic shopping does not preclude the building of shopping-and-pleasure palaces all around the globe. Japanese developers, in a joint venture with the [developers of Canada's West Edmonton Mall], are planning a $400 million Mall of Japan, with an ice rink, a water park, a fantasy-theme hotel, three breweries, waterfalls, and a sports center. We might shortly predict, too, a Mall of Europe, a Mall of New England, a Mall of California, and perhaps even a Mall of the World. The concept of shopping in a frivolous atmosphere, concocted to loosen consumers' wallets, is poised to proliferate globally. We will soon see monster malls everywhere, rooted in the soil of every nation and offering a preposterous, impossible variety of commodities and entertainments.

30   The new malls will be planets unto themselves, closed off from this world in the manner of space stations or of science fiction's underground cities. Like the Mall of America and West Edmonton Mall—prototypes for a new generation of shopping centers—they will project a separate and distinct reality in which an "outdoor café" is not outdoors, a "bubbling brook" is a concrete watercourse, and a "serpentine street" is a hallway. Safe, surreal, and outside of time and space, they will offer the mind a potent dreamscape from which there is no present waking. This carefully controlled fantasy—now operable in Minnesota—is so powerful as to inspire psychological addiction or to elicit in visitors a catatonic obsession with the mall's various hallucinations. The new malls will be theatrical, high-tech illusions capable of attracting enormous crowds from distant points and foreign ports.

Their psychology has not yet been tried pervasively on the scale of the Mall of America, nor has it been perfected. But in time our marketplaces, all over the world, will be in essential ways interchangeable, so thoroughly divorced from the communities in which they sit that they will appear to rest like permanently docked spaceships against the landscape, windowless and turned in upon their own affairs. The affluent will travel as tourists to each, visiting the holy sites and taking photographs in the catacombs of far-flung temples.

31   Just as Victorian England is acutely revealed beneath the grandiose domes of its overwrought train stations, so is contemporary America well understood from the upper vistas of its shopping malls, places without either windows or clocks where the temperature is forever seventy degrees. It is facile to believe, from this vantage point, that the endless circumambulations of tens of thousands of strangers—all loaded down with the detritus of commerce—resemble anything akin to community. The shopping mall is not, as the architecture critic Witold Rybczynski has concluded, "poised to become a real urban place" with "a variety of commercial and noncommercial functions." On the contrary, it is poised to multiply around the world as an institution offering only a desolate substitute for the rich, communal lifeblood of the traditional marketplace, which will not survive its onslaught.

32   Standing on the Mall of America's roof, where I had ventured to inspect its massive ventilation units, I finally achieved a full sense of its vastness, of how it overwhelmed the surrounding terrain—the last sheep farm in sight, the Mississippi River incidental in the distance. Then I peered through the skylights down into Camp Snoopy, where throngs of my fellow citizens caroused happily in the vast entrails of the beast.

Review Questions

1. According to Guterson, what is one key difference between shopping places of old and modern malls?

2. What is the difference between a marketplace and a tourist attraction?

3. What has been America's "contribution" to the closed bazaar, according to Guterson?

4. Reread paragraphs 7–15, in which Guterson reports on an interview he conducted with several mall patrons. Characterize these interviewees. Why does Guterson include these conversations in the article? What point is he making (indirectly)?

5. Reread paragraphs 21–22, in which Guterson relates his experiences wandering "the hallways of the pleasure dome." By the end of paragraph 22, what impression has he created?

6. What predictions does Guterson make concerning modern mega-malls?

Discussion and Writing Suggestions

1. Having read Guterson's article, reflect for a moment on his title: "Enclosed. Encyclopedic. Endured." What do each of these words mean in relation to the article?

2. Guterson opens this article by citing some of the Mall of America's vital statistics. What effect do these statistics have on you?

3. Guterson makes a judgment in this selection about the Mall of America and, more broadly, about American culture. What is this judgment? As evidence for your answer, cite three or four sentences.

4. In paragraph 4, Guterson writes that the building of the Mall of America as a tourist attraction "raise[s] provocative questions, for our architecture testifies to our view of ourselves and to the condition of our souls." In paragraph 31 he makes a similar point, referring to Victorian England's nineteenth-century train stations. Explain Guterson's connection between architecture and the broader culture.

5. In paragraph 5, Guterson refers to fellow shoppers at the Mall of America as "other pilgrims." Speculate on his use of "pilgrims." Why does he not simply refer to these people as "shoppers"?

6. In paragraph 16, Guterson writes: "All over the planet the humblest of people have always gone to market with hope in their hearts and in expectation of something beyond mere goods—seeking a place where humanity is temporarily in ascendance." What does he mean? Is this your hope in going to the mall?

7. Guterson devotes paragraph 26 to a summary of the movie *Dawn of the Dead*. Speculate on his reasons for including the summary in this article.

The Shopping Mall as Sacred Space
Ira Zepp, Jr.

A professor emeritus of Religious Studies at Western Maryland College, Ira Zepp, Jr. has written what a book reviewer for the Los Angeles Times *calls a "profound and refreshing work that allows us to see a common place of contemporary life in an utterly unexpected way."* The New Religious Image of Urban America: The Shopping Mall as Ceremonial Center *(2nd ed., University Press of Colorado, 1997) examines the mall as a type of architecturally spiritual place that "centers" and orders the world, much as cathedrals do. It will be a stretch for some to regard the mall as a place to go to restore spiritual order; but Zepp is persuasive, grounding his argument in scholarship and in a rich, cross-cultural understanding of spiritual practices. You just may find yourself convinced.*

1 I believe one of the reasons malls have grown rapidly and their popularity increased is that they fulfill our need for order and orientation. Malling means centering. Yin-Fu Tuan, professor of geography at the University of Minnesota, says that "to be livable, nature and society must show order and display a harmonious relationship."[1] Or as philosopher of religion Paul Tillich said, we seek to "unify multiplicity."

The Nature of the Center

2 A theoretical framework from religious studies helps explain people's fondness for centeredness.* Human beings have always tried to center their lives and their world. Returning to the center has been a universal tendency, whether that center be a family reunion, a hometown, a native land, or a religious center such as Rome or Jerusalem.

3 This human propensity to design centers is illustrated by the prevalence of both circular construction and construction using such related shapes as hexagons, octagons, squares, and crosses. These geometric expressions reflect that same reality and have the same purpose: to incorporate all the dimensions of the earth—north, south, east, and west—the four corners of the world and the cardinal points of the compass.

4 The number four, incidentally, was a sacred number for many Native Americans precisely because of its all-embracing nature. The Native American shaman, Black Elk, observed that much of Indian activity—from drawing to dancing, to building their homes, whether tepee, hogan, or igloo—was done in a circle. The social and religious meeting place for the Navaho, a structure which connects this world with its place of origin, is the round ceremonial center called *kiva*.

5 This circular and cyclical activity was a reflection of the "power of the world" which worked in circles also; for example, the wind whirls, the seasons cycle, birds often fly concentrically, the sun and moon (both round) go and come in a circle. Everything tries to be round. The circularity of space for the Native American is also symbolized in the sacred hoop and the desire of every tribal member is to keep the hoop unbroken.

6 The inclusiveness of circular design echoes how we experience the world and perceive reality. These circles, squares, and crosses are a way of saying that the universe and, finally, our lives are symmetrical, well regulated, ordered, and under control.

7 The quadrilateral symbol, in whatever form, is a miniaturization of the world, a microcosm, a small picture of how we understand the larger universe to be. By this propensity to center, we are telling ourselves life is integrated and whole.

8 Centers are not only measured spatially and mathematically, they can be existential as well. The Quakers begin their silent meditation with the phrase "centering down"—that is, becoming stable, anchored, "together," to more easily get in touch with the cosmic center, the sources of stability and peace.

---

* It will be obvious to many readers that the following discussion is dependent on the seminal works of Mircea Eliade and Paul Wheatley. Their contributions to the history of religions and human geography, respectively, are indispensable.

9   Communities have always centered themselves. Sometimes they have a functional center, as in many towns and villages laid out in the nineteenth-century, where there is a literal meeting of the quadrants at the town center. For example, you cannot avoid them if you drive through Harvard Square in Cambridge, Massachusetts or Gettysburg, Pennsylvania.

10   Other communities have ritual or ceremonial centers, such as parks, groves, or recreational areas. In religious studies we call such an area an axis mundi, the axle or pole around which our world turns and without which our world would collapse. These areas are indispensable to our personal and communal life. These centers are either built as a result of a hierophany (manifestation of the holy) or by ritual construction. Shopping malls are examples of the latter—what Mircea Eliade, the renowned religious historian at the University of Chicago, calls "mythic geometry."

11   The geometric designs in the mall also tell a story about how we ultimately understand the world to be; they are a replication of the larger planet. We have said by this paradigmatic structure that our experience of the world is one of balance and harmony. We have traveled to the "center" and discovered unity.

12   Carl Jung, the famous Swiss psychologist, calls the circle an archetype, an original image found in the collective unconscious of humankind. The pictures precede obviously the formulation and foundation of the living religions, but have appropriated these designs for their symbolic art and much of the architecture of their house of worship; for example, Buddhist stupas, Islamic mosques, Christian cathedrals, and Jewish temples and synagogues. Secular versions would be the Athenian agora, the Roman forum, the Mexican zocala, and the Middle Eastern bazaar.

13   The nature of the center gives us a clue to why so much human activity, from children's games to religious art and architecture to shopping malls, is expressed by circularity.

14   By applying the typology of Wheatley's and Eliade's "mythic geometry" to malls, we find a remarkable conformity and similarity between the design of the average mall and their models of sacred space.

Center as Source of Power

15 The number of people who gravitate to them indicate that centers are places of empowerment. Travelers, pilgrims, tourists, and shoppers departing from a center, find themselves renewed and strengthened as a result of the energy found there. Even if physically exhausted, their spirits are uplifted.

16   The axis mundi—whether it be a state capital, a religious shrine, or a mall as the social and shopping center of a community—becomes, to paraphrase Wheatley, "the pivot of ontological transition at which divine power enters the world and diffuses through wider territory."[2]

17   In this reduced version of the world, in this cosmos on a small scale where all life—human and natural—meet, you experience power coming from six directions: the four cardinal points of the compass and the zenith and nadir. To use Wheatley's graphic phrase, it is "an architectural evocation of an axis mundi."

18　Wheatley suggests that it is through such a center of the world that cosmic power enters and is spread throughout the country. This diffusion of energy binds "periphery and center, province and capital, dependencies and metropolitan territory."[3] This dissemination of power also established a unity of time and space. A community sense was created and maintained.

19　Paul Wheatley has abundant evidence in his *Pivot of the Four Quarters* that one reason gateways to traditional communities were large and ostentatious, out of all proportion to their function, was that power flowed out of the center through these entrances at the cardinal points.

20　Mall entrances, reflecting other significant centers of power, are often quite impressive. Their distinctiveness serves more than aesthetic, decorative, or functional purposes.

21　It is also interesting to watch the mall's capacity to balance centripetal and centrifugal forces. People are obviously drawn to this center and, just as effectively, the center delivers them back to the world with newly acquired treasures and relationships, if not a new sense of well-being.

22　When we are at the center, we can get our bearing, orient ourselves again, and find our way out of life's disorders. We discover at the center a source of power; this mirror of the universe concentrates the generally available dynamism.

23　Even in the midst of crowds, people are aware that a degree of renewal is taking place. Malls, at their centers, strive to be places of vitality and energy.

24　Consequently, it is not accidental that most places we call centers attempt to re-invigorate or recharge human energy. At both the personal and social levels, we find communities making such sources of power available.

25　This idea is ingrained in our language: New Windsor Conference Center, Baltimore Civic Center, Washington Heights Medical Center, Carroll County Agricultural Center, Aberdeen Shopping Center, Adams County Senior Center, Harford Recreational Center, Hagerstown Counseling Center, any number of college student centers, and religious worship centers. And so it goes. We find the concept of "center" an appropriate description for a place of human empowerment, a group of people who deliver social services, and an organization whose purpose is to help, heal, or otherwise improve the world.

26　This is undoubtedly what mall developer James Rouse* has in mind when he uses the concept of center. His speeches and essays are replete with references to "center." He refers to the "design of the center," the "quality of the center," "little details of the center," and to "our center." Whatever else Rouse intends to convey, it is the human aspect of the center he wants to emphasize.

27　The center was originally understood to be where God and people and heaven and earth were connected. And power was generated there. We all know examples of these centers: the sacred mountains of Sinai and Zion, the cities of Benares and Mecca, the temples of St. Peter's in Rome and the

---

* Developer *James Rouse* (1915–1986) ranks as a legendary figure among 20th-century American urban planners. At various points in his career, he built shopping malls; a comprehensively planned suburban community (Columbia, MD) that he hoped would correct the "sterility" of the suburbs; and festival marketplaces (including Fanueil Hall in Boston and South Street Sea Port in New York) in an effort to revive depressed urban areas. He later created a foundation to address problems of affordable housing.

Mormons in Salt Lake City, Utah. Church altars, dining room tables, and scholars' desks can also be center of the sacred.

28   Such centers act as magnets. Their attractiveness is in direct proportion to
the power and meaning we find there. We make regular pilgrimages to these
special places to regain our identity, and to be reconnected, which, as I mentioned earlier, is the meaning of *re-ligare* (religion).

Center as Celestial Echo

29 Primitive people from Polynesia to Egypt to the British Isles were very careful in
the construction of their centers. They found it extremely important to have, as a
base for their center, a celestial or transcendent reference point and pattern. Eliade
stresses there was usually some celestial archetype which provided a model for
our earthly building and temporal construction, which would act as an axis mundi.
And this other-worldly or heavenly counterpart would represent the true and
authentic world. The heavenly Jerusalem, the historical Jerusalem, and the coming
Jerusalem are all reflections of a city already found in the mind of God.

30   Eliade summarizes the inclination we have to reflect transcendent patterns
in the construction of centers:

> Man constructs according to an archetype. Not only do his city and his temple
> have celestial models, the same is true of the entire region that he inhabits,
> with the rivers that water it, the fields that give him his food, etc. The map of
> Babylon shows the city at the center of a vast circular territory bordered by a
> river, precisely as the Sumerian envisaged Paradise. This participation by urban
> culture in an archetypal model is what gives them their reality and validity.[4]

In one form or another, heavenly models are reflected in earthly circularity.

31   Even the political centers of Paris, Washington, D.C., and the centers (cir-
cuses) of London are further examples. It is true, as well, of Dante's celestial
rose, the thousand-petaled Lotus of Buddhism, and the Tibetan Mandala.*

32   The design and layout of most modern shopping malls is a "secular" version
of this ancient prototype. Many malls are built in the form of a cross, with all
paths leading to the center. The cross here is, of course, not the Christian cross
or a sectarian image. It is fundamentally a human image, for it is another way
of drawing a circle.

---

* *Dante's celestial rose, the thousand-petaled Lotus of Buddhism,* and *the Tibetan Mandala* are all religious symbols involving circles and "centeredness," as Zepp puts it. In the third book of Dante's *Divine
Comedy, The Paradiso,* Dante ascends to the tenth and final heaven and, in a mystical vision, encounters
an emanation of God's love represented in a series of circles in the center of which is a cross--and in
the cross, a blooming rose. The *Lotus* in *Buddhism* is said to symbolize a person seeking enlightenment.
With roots that grow in murky water (self-ignorance), the Lotus plant sends a shoot upward, through darkness, toward the light (enlightenment)--at which point, nourished by the sun and air, it blossoms. Seen
from above, the Lotus blossom appears as a series of nested cups, or circles, of petals at the center of
which can be found the seeds. Each part of the flower, and plant, is related to a teaching in the Buddhist
tradition. The *Tibetan Mandala* is a form of impermanent religious art that serves as part of Tibetan
Buddhist meditation practice. Sometimes made of colored sand, they are arranged as a series of inter-
secting circles along a central axis.

FIGURE 10.2   Rose Window. Painton Cowen says that "every rose window is a symbol and image of the Creation and the created universe." Chartres' famous rose window is a triumph of geometry—an idealized model of the universe—circles within circles. Periphery and center are clearly depicted here. Dante's celestial rose and Buddha's thousand-petaled lotus are variations of this pattern. Photo of South Rose Window at Chartres, Paul Almasy/Corbis.

33   Knowing the frequency of circular patterns is more important than whether we know the engineer or architect's conscious and unconscious motivations for them. Circles in public buildings are symbols of welcome and inclusiveness, a way to make our non-private space more humanly accessible. The function of cardinal axiology, says Wheatley, is to assimilate and bring together all the surrounding territory—which is to say that the entire world meets in the center of every mall.

34   This sacred geometry can be seen in a representative sample of mall floor plans, gathered from across the country. And even in the malls which do not have a symmetrical design, a balance and harmony can be discerned in spite of the offcenteredness. White Flint Mall in Rockville, Maryland, is an example of this.

35   If there is not a pronounced interaction at the center of the mall as in Lancaster, Pennsylvania's Park City and Long Island's Smith Haven Mall, there may be a long corridor between rows of shops. In the center of the corridor may be a series of pools or flower gardens surrounded by trees and benches. Tampa Bay Center in Florida is a good illustration of this pattern. Or, in the absence of a large visible center, smaller centers (crosses or circles) may be placed intermittently along the walkway.

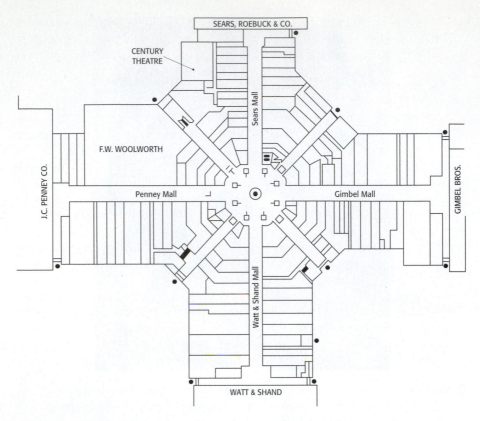

FIGURE 10.3 Park City, *Lancaster, PA*. This mall reflects the many circles of a rose window, the quadrilateral design of a mandala, and the floor plan of typical cathedral or basilica. The center in this mall is inescapable.

Center as Sign of Order

36 As humans we have a profound need to repudiate, if not escape, the disorder and brokenness of life, and to establish islands of stability as a counterpoint to chaos. The creation of a center is usually the way people resist disorder. We always seem to be in the process of ordering (cosmicizing)—that is, making a whole (cosmos) out of disintegration (chaos). Indeed, the words for world in Latin (*cosmos*) and in German (*Welt*) suggest that in this place life is ordered by meaning and purpose. It is a uni-verse.

37   Practical activities, even the routine operation of a shopping mall, take second place to our need to see ourselves related appropriately to our environment. The so-called practical activities may offend the gods or spirits of nature unless they are perceived to have their roles in a coherent world system.[5]

38   We could not live long in an asymmetrical, chaotic community. Jung wrote an excellent monograph entitled *The Mandala*. *Mandala* is the Sanskrit word for a circle, divided into four separate, equal sections. It is really a symbol of the universe and Jung said that it is also a picture of the self. He discovered, in his

clinical practice, that people of all ages who were emotionally disturbed or who were undergoing a certain degree of trauma, would often draw circular designs, presumably to reassure themselves that life is not radically ruptured. The innocent activity of our doodling often takes the shape of circles. At every level of human experience, the center must hold.

39   The re-creation of a center establishes order amidst chaos, serenity in turbulence, unity out of disparity, wholeness out of brokenness. The center, with all the paths leading to the middle, is a replication of the primordial world in all its harmony and pristine order.

40   Out of the disorder of the city and the disease of the suburbs arises the shopping mall and its perceived symmetry and tranquility. People come to this center feeling isolated, lonely, and anonymous. They need to be at ease, to belong, to center themselves again. Chaos will be cosmicized. Disorder will be ordered.

41   Again, the mathematical balance, so frequently found in malls, is a way of reinforcing that the world is ultimately safe. The enclosure, combined with architectural balance, engenders the sense of safety many people claim they find in the mall.

42   Wheatley, in his extraordinary study on urban communities—construction from Mexico to Burma—has shown how order integrates space at several significant levels, e.g., global (cosmic), state (political), capital (ceremonial), and temple (ritual).[6] I want to add to this list of levels the shopping mall, a combination of the ceremonial and the ritual. As a result of their centered nature, their capacity to reveal and to communicate stability, malls juxtapose themselves to the mundane world outside. The outside world's profane dimension, according to Eliade, has no mythical meaning, is not invested with prestige, and lacks an exemplary model.[7] Or as John E. Smith, head of the philosophy department of Yale University, says, "The profane stands over against the holy, not because it is sordid or 'unclean,' but because it is ordinary and harbors no mystery, nor calls forth the sense that beyond and beneath our life is a holy ground."

43   To the extent that the mall is space discontinuous from the trivial, ordinary world, it is understood to be potentially sacred. The sacred is always more real than the profane and therefore more powerful than the ordinary world. As Eliade says in his *Sacred and Profane,* whatever is designated as sacred participates in and releases power. This power, in turn, puts us next to reality, which is tantamount to Being itself. This archaic ontology is reflected in the design of most malls and experienced by those for whom the mall is "more than" a collection of shops. There is a sense in which the mall is a space thought to be more real, vital, and energizing than the run-of-the-mill pragmatic world beyond it.

44   Perhaps this is why there is within us a "nostalgia for paradise" (Eliade), a longing for the village, a yearning for home or hometown, where life was more real and animated. This "more than" characteristic is perceived in malls and presents us with a sense of welcome, stability, and centeredness in which we can share vicariously.

45   Many shopping malls, as the foregoing reveals, are designed to repeat a cosmogony, that is, to re-create an ordered world. This is not to be taken lightly. As intellectual and social historian Eric Voegelin says, "The analogical repetition is not an act of futile imitation, for in repeating the cosmos man participates, in the measure allowed to his existential limitations, in the creation of cosmic order itself."[8]

46   So the mall attempts to make the world a whole, to have it integrated, habitable, safe, and balanced. Eliade, from a lifetime of studying the human fascination with the sacred, concludes: "To the degree that ancient holy places, temples or altars lose their religious efficacy, people discover and apply other geomantic architecture or iconographic formulas which, in the end, sometimes astonishingly enough represent the same symbolism of the 'Center.'"[9]

47   I contend that the mall represents, for many contemporary people, a substitute for those ancient sacred centers. If churches, schools, and families (our three major institutions) fail us, we will seek other places to fulfill basic human needs. It is not accidental, therefore, that malls contain the same structures, objects, and symbols which gave ancient centers their rich human meaning. For, as Eliade emphasizes, "images, symbols, and myths are not irresponsible creations of the psyche; they respond to a need and fulfill a function, that of bringing to light the most hidden modalities of being. Consequently, the study of them enables us to reach a better understanding of man—of man 'as he is.'"[10]

Notes

1. Tuan, Yi-Fu, *Space and Place: The Perspective of Experience,* Minneapolis: University of Minnesota Press, 1977, p. 88.

2. Wheatley, Paul, *The Pivot of the Four Quarters,* Chicago: Aldine Publishing Co., 1972, p. 434.

3. *Ibid.,* p. 68.

4. Eliade, Mircea, *Cosmos and History: The Myth of the Eternal Return.* Trans. by William R. Trask. New York: Harper and Row Torchbook, 1959, p. 10.

5. Tuan, p. 88.

6. Wheatley, p. 53.

7. Eliade, p. 28.

8. Quoted in Wheatley, p. 57.

9. Eliade, Mircea, *Images and Symbols: Studies in Religious Symbolism,* New York: Sheed and Ward, 1969, p. 52.

10. Eliade, p. 12.

Review Questions

1. What is a "center" in the sacred sense that Zepp uses it?
2. Where do we find examples of centers both in religious and nonreligious settings?
3. What is the *axis mundi?*
4. Why, in the view of religious historian Paul Wheatley, are centers powerful places?
5. Why are malls often laid out as a cross?

6. According to Zepp, how can structures transmit the power of a center even if their architects do not consciously conceive of their designs as having cosmic significance?

7. Why do we seek out centers? In what sense can the mall as a center be considered sacred space?

Discussion and Writing Suggestions

1. Does the fact that shopping malls, like cathedrals, mosques, and synagogues, have centers persuade you that the purpose of "the center" in each setting is the same?

2. In paragraph 22, Zepp writes: "When we are at the center, we can get our bearing, orient ourselves again, and find our way out of life's disorders. We discover at the center a source of power." Have you ever felt energized or uplifted as a result of visiting the mall? Put another way, does the prospect of going to a mall excite you? At the mall is there any sense in which you find your bearings or renew your energy?

3. Trace how Zepp uses the work of religious scholars Wheatley and Eliade to advance his analysis that malls are sacred space.

4. In his final paragraph, Zepp writes: "I contend that the mall represents, for many contemporary people, a substitute for . . . ancient sacred centers." Read the rest of paragraph 47 and determine the extent to which you feel Zepp has made a compelling case. Are you convinced that shopping centers, quite aside from their status as places where you can buy things, meet a fundamental human need?

5. Write a dialogue between you and an adult relative about your going to the mall to hang out with friends. Your relative prefers that you don't. Try using Zepp's arguments in the dialogue. What will be your relative's response?

From Town Center to Shopping Center
Lizabeth Cohen

In the following article, which appeared in the American Historical Review *(October 1996), Lizabeth Cohen traces the "restructuring of the consumer marketplace" that followed America's population shift to the suburbs after World War II. Millions of people who had lived in the cities, walking to the corner store, faced an entirely new experience as shoppers once they moved to the suburbs. In their new homes, a trip to the store meant a ride in the car, likely to a shopping center where relations between store owner and customer had fundamentally changed. Cohen, a professor of history at New York University, studies the effects that the new mass-consumption society had on America. You will see that she identifies two developments, relating to segregation and free speech, that threaten our general welfare.*

1 When the editors of *Time* Magazine set out to tell readers in an early January 1965 cover story why the American economy had flourished during the previous year, they explained it in terms that had become the conventional wisdom of postwar America. The most prosperous twelve months ever, capping the country's fourth straight year of economic expansion, were attributable to the American consumer, "who continued spending as if there were no tomorrow." According to *Time*'s economics lesson, consumers, business, and government "created a nonvicious circle: spending created more production, production created wealth, wealth created more spending." In this simplified Keynesian* model of economic growth, "the consumer is the key to our economy." As R. H. Macy's board chair Jack Straus explained to *Time*'s readers, "When the country has a recession, it suffers not so much from problems of production as from problems of consumption." And in prosperous times like today, "Our economy keeps growing because our ability to consume is endless. The consumer goes on spending regardless of how many possessions he has. The luxuries of today are the necessities of tomorrow." A demand economy built on mass consumption had brought the United States out of the doldrums of the Great Depression and World War II, and its strength in the postwar period continued to impress those like retail magnate Straus whose own financial future depended on it.[1]

2   Although Straus and his peers invested great energy and resources in developing new strategies for doing business in this mass-consumption economy, historians have paid far less attention to the restructuring of American commercial life in the postwar period than to the transformation of residential experience. An impressive literature documents the way the expansion of a mass consumer society encouraged a larger and broader spectrum of Americans to move into suburban communities after the war.[2] Between 1947 and 1953 alone, the suburban population increased by 43 percent, in contrast to a general population increase of only 11 percent.[3] At an astonishing pace, the futuristic highways and mass-built, appliance-equipped, single-family homes that had been previewed at the New York World's Fair in 1939–1940 seemed to become a reality. Thanks to a shortage in urban housing, government subsidies in highway building and home construction or purchase, and pent-up consumer demand and savings, a new residential landscape began to take shape in metropolitan areas, with large numbers of people commuting into cities for work and then back to homes in the suburbs. (Increasingly as the postwar era progressed, suburbanites worked, not just lived, outside cities.)

3   Less explored by historians and slower to develop historically was the restructuring of the consumer marketplace that accompanied the suburbanization of residential life. New suburbanites who had themselves grown up in urban

---

* *John Maynard Keynes* (1883–1946) was an influential British economist for whom a school of economics (Keynesian) was named. Keynes advocated government intervention in the boom-and-bust business cycles of capitalism—especially in downturns, when government stimulus packages can lessen the effects of unemployment.

neighborhoods walking to corner stores and taking public transportation to shop downtown were now contending with changed conditions. Only in the most ambitious suburban tracts built after the war did developers incorporate retail stores into their plans. In those cases, developers tended to place the shopping district at the core of the residential community, much as it had been in the pre-war planned community of Radburn, New Jersey, and in the earliest shopping centers, such as Kansas City's Country Club Plaza of the 1920s. These precedents, and their descendents in early postwar developments in Park Forest, Illinois, Levittown, New York, and Bergenfield, New Jersey, replicated the structure of the old-style urban community, where shopping was part of the public space at the settlement's core and residences spread outward from there.[4] But most new suburban home developers made no effort to provide for residents' commercial needs. Rather, suburbanites were expected to fend for themselves by driving to the existing "market towns," which often offered the only commerce for miles, or by returning to the city to shop. Faced with slim retail offerings nearby, many new suburbanites of the 1940s and 1950s continued to depend on the city for major purchases, making do with the small, locally owned commercial outlets in neighboring towns only for minor needs.

4   It would not be until the mid-1950s that a new market structure appropriate to this suburbanized, mass-consumption society prevailed. Important precedents existed in the branch department stores and prototypical shopping centers constructed between the 1920s and 1940s in outlying city neighborhoods and in older suburban communities, which began the process of decentralizing retail dollars away from downtown. But now the scale was much larger. Even more significant, the absence or inadequacy of town centers at a time of enormous suburban population growth offered commercial developers a unique opportunity to reimagine community life with their private projects at its heart.[5]

5   By the early 1950s, large merchandisers were aggressively reaching out to the new suburbanites, whose buying power was even greater than their numbers.[6] The 30 million people that *Fortune* magazine counted as suburban residents in 1953 represented 19 percent of the U.S. population but 29 percent of its income. They had higher median incomes and homeownership rates, as well as more children fourteen and under than the rest of the metropolitan population, all indicators of high consumption.

6   Merchandisers also realized that postwar suburbanites were finally living the motorized existence that had been predicted for American society since the 1920s. As consumers became dependent on, virtually inseparable from, their cars, traffic congestion and parking problems discouraged commercial expansion in central business districts of cities and smaller market towns, already hindered by a short supply of developable space.[7] Reaching out to suburbanites where they lived, merchandisers at first built stores along the new highways, in commercial "strips" that consumers could easily reach by car. By the mid-1950s, however, commercial developers—many of whom owned department stores—were constructing a new kind of marketplace, the regional shopping center aimed at satisfying suburbanites' consumption *and* community needs. Strategically located at highway intersections or along the busiest thoroughfares, the regional shopping center attracted patrons living within half an hour's drive,

who could come by car, park in the abundant lots provided, and then proceed on foot (although there was usually some bus service as well). Here was the "new city" of the postwar era, a vision of how community space should be constructed in an economy and society built on mass consumption. Well-designed regional shopping centers would provide the ideal core for a settlement that grew by adding residential nodes off of major roadways rather than concentric rings from downtown, as in cities and earlier suburban communities. After spending several months in the late 1950s visiting these "modern-day downtowns," *Women's Wear Daily* columnist Samuel Feinberg was moved to invoke Lincoln Steffens's proclamation on his return from the Soviet Union in the 1920s: "I have seen the future and it works." [8]

7   This essay will analyze the larger social and political implications of the shift in community marketplace from town center to shopping center. Although I draw on national evidence, I pay special attention to the case of Paramus, New Jersey, a postwar suburb seven miles from the George Washington Bridge that sprouted virtually overnight in the vegetable fields of Bergen County and became the home of the largest shopping complex in the country by the end of 1957.[9] Within six months, R. H. Macy's Garden State Plaza and Allied Stores Corporation's Bergen Mall opened three quarters of a mile from each other at the intersection of Routes 4, 17, and the soon-to-be-completed Garden State Parkway. Both department store managements had independently recognized the enormous commercial potential of Bergen and Passaic counties; although the George Washington Bridge connected the area to Manhattan in 1931, the Depression and the war postponed major housing construction until the late 1940s. By 1960, each shopping center had two to three department stores as anchors (distinguishing it from many pre-war projects built around a single anchor), surrounded by fifty to seventy smaller stores. Attracting half a million patrons a week, these shopping centers dominated retail trade in the region.[10]

8   The Paramus malls have special significance because of their location adjacent to the wealthiest and busiest central business district in the nation. If these malls could prosper in the shadow of Manhattan, the success of their counterparts elsewhere should come as no surprise. Moreover, the Paramus case illuminates [two] major effects of shifting marketplaces on postwar American community life: in commercializing public space, they brought to community life the market segmentation that increasingly shaped commerce; [and] in privatizing public space, they privileged the rights of private property owners over citizens' traditional rights of free speech in community forums.

. . .

9   When planners and shopping-center developers envisioned [a] new kind of consumption-oriented community center in the 1950s, they set out to perfect the concept of downtown, not to obliterate it, even though their projects directly challenged the viability of existing commercial centers such as Hackensack, the political and commercial seat of Bergen County. It is easy to overlook this visionary dimension and focus only on the obvious commercial motives developers and investors shared. Of course, developers, department stores, and big investors such as insurance companies (who leapt at the promise of a huge return on the vast amounts of capital they controlled) were pursuing the enormous potential for profit in shopping-center development.[11] But they also

believed that they were participating in a rationalization of consumption and community no less significant than the way highways were improving transportation or tract developments were delivering mass housing.

10   The ideal was still the creation of centrally located public space that brought together commercial and civic activity. Victor Gruen, one of the most prominent and articulate shopping-center developers, spoke for many others when he argued that shopping centers offered to dispersed suburban populations "crystallization points for suburbia's community life." "By affording opportunities for social life and recreation in a protected pedestrian environment, by incorporating civic and educational facilities, shopping centers can fill an existing void."[12] Not only did Gruen and others promote the construction of community centers in the atomized landscape of suburbia, but in appearance their earliest shopping centers idealized—almost romanticized—the physical plan of the traditional downtown shopping street, with stores lining both sides of an open-air pedestrian walkway that was landscaped and equipped with benches.[13]

11   While bringing many of the best qualities of urban life to the suburbs, these new "shopping towns," as Gruen called them, also sought to overcome the "anarchy and ugliness" characteristic of many American cities. A centrally owned and managed Garden State Plaza or Bergen Mall, it was argued, offered an alternative model to the inefficiencies, visual chaos, and provinciality of traditional downtown districts. A centralized administration made possible the perfect mix and "scientific" placement of stores, meeting customers' diverse needs and maximizing store owners' profits. Management kept control visually by standardizing all architectural and graphic design and politically by requiring all tenants to participate in the tenants' association. Common complaints of downtown shoppers were directly addressed: parking was plentiful, safety was ensured by hired security guards, delivery tunnels and loading courts kept truck traffic away from shoppers, canopied walks and air-conditioned stores made shopping comfortable year 'round, piped-in background music replaced the cacophony of the street. The preponderance of chains and franchises over local stores, required by big investors such as insurance companies, brought shoppers the latest national trends in products and merchandising techniques. B. Earl Puckett, Allied Stores' board chair, boasted that Paramus's model shopping centers were making it "one of the first preplanned major cities in America."[14] What made this new market structure so unique and appealing to businessmen like Puckett was that it encouraged social innovation while maximizing profit.

12   Garden State Plaza and Bergen Mall provide good models for how shopping centers of the 1950s followed Gruen's prescription and became more than miscellaneous collections of stores. As central sites of consumption, they offered the full range of businesses and services that one would previously have sought downtown. They not only sold the usual clothing and shoes in their specialty and department stores—Sterns and J. J. Newberry at Bergen Mall, Bamberger's (Macy's New Jersey division), J. C. Penney's and Gimbels at Garden State Plaza—but also featured stores specifically devoted to furniture, hardware, appliances, groceries, gifts, drugs, books, toys, records, bakery goods, candy, jewelry, garden supplies, hearing aids, tires, even religious objects. Services grew to include restaurants, a post office, laundromat, cleaners, key store, shoe repair, bank, loan company, stock brokerage houses, barber shop, travel agency, real

estate office, "slenderizing salon," and Catholic chapel. Recreational facilities ranged from a 550-seat movie theater, bowling alley, and ice-skating rink to a children's gymnasium and playground.

13   Both shopping centers made meeting rooms and auditoriums available to community organizations and scheduled a full range of cultural and educational activities to legitimize these sites as civic centers, which also attracted customers. Well-attended programs and exhibitions taught shoppers about such "hot" topics of the 1950s and 1960s as space exploration, color television, modern art, and civics. Evening concerts and plays, ethnic entertainment, dances and classes for teenagers, campaign appearances by electoral candidates, community outreach for local charities: these were some of the ways that the Bergen Mall and Garden State Plaza made themselves indispensable to life in Bergen County. In sum, it was hard to think of consumer items or community events that could not be found at one or the other of these two shopping centers. (In the 1970s, a cynical reporter cracked that "the only institution that had not yet invaded" the modern shopping mall was the funeral home.) Furthermore, stores and services were more accessible than those downtown, as the centers were open to patrons from 10 a.m. to 9:30 p.m., at first four nights a week and by the 1960s, six nights a week. To a regional planner such as Ernest Erber, these postwar shopping centers helped construct a new kind of urbanism appropriate to the automobile age: the "City of Bergen," he named the area in 1960. The *New York Times* agreed, remarking of the Paramus commercial complex, "It lives a night as well as a day existence, glittering like a city when the sun goes down."[15]

14   When developers and store owners set out to make the shopping center a more perfect downtown, they aimed to exclude from this public space unwanted urban groups such as vagrants, prostitutes, racial minorities, and poor people. Market segmentation became the guiding principle of this mix of commercial and civic activity, as the shopping center sought perhaps contradictorily to legitimize itself as a true community center and to define that community in exclusionary socioeconomic and racial terms. The simple demographics of postwar America helped: when nine of the ten largest cities in the United States lost population between 1950 and 1960 while all metropolitan areas grew, three whites were moving out for every two non-whites who moved in, laying the groundwork for the racially polarized metropolitan populations of today.[16] In this way, suburbanization must be seen as a new form of racial segregation in the face of a huge wave of African-American migration from the South to the North during the 1950s.

15   Shopping centers did not exclude inadvertently by virtue of their suburban location. Rather, developers deliberately defined their communities through a combination of marketing and policing. Macy's reminded its stockholders in 1955 as it was building its first shopping center, the Garden State Plaza, "We are a type of organization that caters primarily to middle-income groups, and our stores reflect this in the merchandise they carry and in their physical surroundings."[17] It was this concern for "physical surroundings" that made the setting of the suburban shopping center appealing to retailers—and ultimately to customers. As Baltimore's Planning Council explained more explicitly than merchants ever would, "Greater numbers of low-income, Negro shoppers in Central Business District stores, coming at the same time as middle and upper income

white shoppers traveling to . . . segregated suburban centers, have had unfortunate implications [for downtown shopping]."[18]

16   Store selection, merchandise, prices, and carefully controlled access to suburban shopping centers supported the class and color line. A survey of consumer expenditures in northern New Jersey in 1960–1961 revealed that while 79 percent of all families owned cars, fewer than one-third of those with incomes below $3,000 did, and the low-income population included a higher percentage of non-white families than the average for the whole sample.[19] Although bus service was available for shoppers without cars, only a tiny proportion arrived that way (in 1966, a daily average of only 600 people came to the Garden State Plaza by bus compared to a mid-week daily average of 18,000 cars and a holiday peak of 31,000 cars, many carrying more than one passenger), and bus routes were carefully planned to serve non-driving customers—particularly women—from neighboring suburbs, not low-income consumers from cities such as Passaic, Paterson, and Newark.[20] Whereas individual department stores had long targeted particular markets defined by class and race, selling, for example, to "the carriage trade" at the upper end, shopping centers applied market segmentation on the scale of a downtown. In promoting an idealized downtown, shopping centers like Garden State Plaza and Bergen Mall tried to filter out not only the inefficiencies and inconveniences of the city but also the undesirable people who lived there.

. . .

17 Whereas, at first, developers had sought to legitimize the new shopping centers by arguing for their centrality to both commerce and community, over time they discovered that those two commitments could be in conflict. The rights of free speech and assembly traditionally safeguarded in the public forums of democratic communities were not always good for business, and they could conflict with the rights of private property owners—the shopping centers—to control entry to their land. Beginning in the 1960s, American courts all the way up to the Supreme Court struggled with the political consequences of having moved public life off the street and into the privately owned shopping center. Shopping centers, in turn, began to reconsider the desirable balance between commerce and community in what had become the major sites where suburbanites congregated.[21]

18   Once regional shopping centers like the Paramus malls had opened in the 1950s, people began to recognize them as public spaces and to use them to reach out to the community. When the Red Cross held blood drives, when labor unions picketed stores in organizing campaigns, when political candidates campaigned for office, when anti-war and anti-nuclear activists gathered signatures for petitions, they all viewed the shopping center as the obvious place to reach masses of people. Although shopping centers varied in their responses—from tolerating political activists to monitoring their actions to prohibiting them outright—in general, they were wary of any activity that might offend customers. A long, complex series of court tests resulted, culminating in several key Supreme Court decisions that sought to sort out the conflict between two basic rights in a free society: free speech and private property. Not surprisingly, the cases hinged on arguments about the extent to which the shopping center had displaced the traditional "town square" as a legitimate public forum.[22]

19   The first ruling by the Supreme Court was *Amalgamated Food Employees Union Local 590 vs. Logan Valley Plaza, Inc.* (1968), in which Justice Thurgood Marshall, writing for the majority, argued that refusing to let union members picket the Weis Markets in the Logan Valley Plaza in Altoona, Pennsylvania, violated the workers' First Amendment rights, since shopping centers had become the "functional equivalent" of a sidewalk in a public business district. Because peaceful picketing and leaflet distribution on "streets, sidewalks, parks, and other similar public places are so historically associated with the exercise of First Amendment rights," he wrote, it should also be protected in the public thoroughfare of a shopping center, even if privately owned. The Logan Valley Plaza decision likened the shopping center to a company town, which had been the subject of an important Supreme Court decision in *Marsh vs. Alabama* (1946), upholding the First Amendment rights of a Jehovah's Witness to proselytize in the company town of Chickasaw, Alabama, despite the fact that the Gulf Shipbuilding Corporation owned all the property in town. The "Marsh Doctrine" affirmed First Amendment rights over private property rights when an owner opened up his or her property for use by the public.[23]   The stance taken in Logan Valley began to unravel, however, as the Supreme Court became more conservative under President Richard Nixon's appointees. In *Lloyd Corp. vs. Tanner* (1972), Justice Lewis F. Powell, Jr., wrote for the majority that allowing anti-war advocates to pass out leaflets at the Lloyd Center in Portland, Oregon, would be an unwarranted infringement of property rights "without significantly enhancing the asserted right of free speech." Anti-war leaflets, he argued, could be effectively distributed elsewhere, without undermining the shopping center's appeal to customers with litter and distraction.[24]

20   The reigning Supreme Court decision today is *PruneYard Shopping Center vs. Robbins* (1980). The Supreme Court upheld a California State Supreme Court ruling that the state constitution granted a group of high school students the right to gather petitions against the U.N. resolution "Zionism Is Racism." The court decided that this action did not violate the San Jose mall owner's rights under the U.S. Constitution. But, at the same time, the court reaffirmed its earlier decisions in *Lloyd vs. Tanner* and *Scott Hudgens vs. National Labor Relations Board* (1976) that the First Amendment did not guarantee access to shopping malls, and it left it to the states to decide for themselves whether their own constitutions protected such access.

21   Since *PruneYard,* state appellate courts have been struggling with the issue, and mall owners have been winning in many more states than they have lost. Only in six states, California, Oregon, Massachusetts, Colorado, Washington, and most recently New Jersey, have state supreme courts protected citizens' right of free speech in privately owned shopping centers. In New Jersey, the courts have been involved for some time in adjudicating free speech in shopping centers. In 1983, the Bergen Mall was the setting of a suit between its owners and a political candidate who wanted to distribute campaign materials there. When a Paramus Municipal Court judge ruled in favor of the mall, the candidate's attorney successfully appealed on the familiar grounds that "there is no real downtown Paramus. Areas of the mall outside the stores are the town's public sidewalks." He further noted that the mall hosted community events and contained a meeting hall, post office, and Roman Catholic chapel. In this case, and

in another one the following year over the right of nuclear-freeze advocates to distribute literature at the Bergen Mall, free speech was protected on the grounds that the mall was equivalent to a town center.[25]

22   Such suits should be unnecessary (at least for a while) in New Jersey, because in a historic decision in December 1994 the New Jersey Supreme Court affirmed that the state constitution guaranteed free speech to opponents of the Persian Gulf War who wanted to distribute leaflets at ten regional malls throughout the state. Writing for the majority, Chief Justice Robert N. Wilentz confirmed how extensively public space has been transformed in postwar New Jersey:

> The economic lifeblood once found downtown has moved to suburban shopping centers, which have substantially displaced the downtown business districts as the centers of commercial and social activity . . . Found at these malls are most of the uses and activities citizens engage in outside their homes . . . This is the new, the improved, the more attractive downtown business district—the new community—and no use is more closely associated with the old downtown than leafletting. Defendants have taken that old downtown away from its former home and moved all of it, except free speech, to the suburbs.

Despite the New Jersey Supreme Court's commitment to free speech, it nonetheless put limits on it, reaffirming the regional mall owners' property rights. Its ruling allowed only the distribution of leaflets—no speeches, bullhorns, pickets, parades, demonstrations, or solicitation of funds. Moreover, the court granted owners broad powers to regulate leaflet distribution by specifying days, hours, and areas in or outside the mall permissible for political activity. Thus, although shopping centers in New Jersey and five other states have been forced to accommodate some political activity, they have retained authority to regulate it and are even finding ways of preventing legal leafletters from exercising their constitutional rights, such as by requiring them to have million-dollar liability policies, which are often unobtainable or prohibitively expensive. In many other states, shopping centers have been able to prohibit political action outright, much as they control the economic and social behavior of shoppers and store owners.[26]

23   An unintended consequence of the American shift in orientation from public town center to private shopping center, then, has been the narrowing of the ground where constitutionally protected free speech and free assembly can legally take place.

. . .

24 Mass consumption in postwar America created a new landscape, where public space was more commercialized [and] more privatized within the regional shopping center than it had been in the traditional downtown center. This is not to romanticize the city and its central business district. Certainly, urban commercial property owners pursued their own economic interests, [and] political activity in public spaces was sometimes limited. . . . Nonetheless, the legal distinction between public and private space remained significant; urban loitering and vagrancy laws directed against undesirables in public places have repeatedly been struck down by the courts, while privately owned shopping centers have been able to enforce trespassing laws.[27] Overall, an important shift from one kind of social order to another took place between 1950 and 1980, with

major consequences for Americans. A free commercial market attached to a rel-atively free public sphere (for whites) underwent a transformation to a more regulated commercial marketplace (where mall management controlled access, favoring chains over local independents, for example) and a more circum-scribed public sphere of limited rights. Economic and social liberalism went hand in hand and declined together.

25   Not by accident, public space was restructured and segmented by class and race in New Jersey, as in the nation, just as African Americans gained new pro-tections for their right of equal access to public accommodations. Although civil rights laws had been on the books in New Jersey since the late nineteenth cen-tury, comprehensive legislation with mechanisms for enforcement did not pass until the 1940s. With the "Freeman Bill" of 1949, African Americans were final-ly guaranteed equal access to schools, restaurants, taverns, retail stores, hotels, public transportation, and facilities of commercial leisure such as movie theaters, skating rinks, amusement parks, swimming pools, and beaches, with violators subject to fines and jail terms. Throughout the 1940s and 1950s, African-American citizens of New Jersey—and other northern states—vigilantly chal-lenged discrimination by private property owners. Yet larger structural changes in community marketplaces were under way, financed by private commercial interests committed to socioeconomic and racial segmentation. While African Americans and their supporters were prodding courts and legislatures to elim-inate legal segregation in public places, real-estate developers, retailers, and consumers were collaborating to shift economic resources to new kinds of seg-regated spaces.[28]

26   The landscape of mass consumption created a metropolitan society in which people were no longer brought together in central marketplaces and the parks, streets, and public buildings that surrounded them but, rather, were separated by class and race in differentiated commercial sub-centers. Moreover, all com-mercial sub-centers were not created equal. Over time, shopping centers became increasingly class stratified, with some like the Bergen Mall marketing themselves to the lower middle class, while others like the Garden State Plaza went upscale to attract upper middle-class consumers. If tied to international capital, some central business districts—such as New York and San Francisco—have prospered, although they have not been left unscarred from recent retail mergers and leveraged buy-outs. Other downtowns, such as Hackensack and Elizabeth, New Jersey, have become "Cheap John Bargain Centers" serving cus-tomers too poor and deprived of transportation to shop at malls. Even in larger American cities, poor urban populations shop downtown on weekends while the white-collar workers who commute in to offices during the week patronize the suburban malls closer to where they live. Some commercial districts have been taken over by enterprising, often newly arrived, ethnic groups, who have breathed new life into what would otherwise have been in decay, but they nonetheless serve a segmented market. Worst off are cities like Newark, once the largest shopping district in the state, which saw every one of its major department stores close between 1964 and 1992 and much of its retail space remain abandoned, leaving residents such as Raymond Mungin to wonder, "I don't have a car to drive out to the malls. What can I do?" Mass consumption was supposed to bring standardization in merchandise and consumption pat-

terns. Instead, diverse social groups are no longer integrated into central consumer marketplaces but rather are consigned to differentiated retail institutions, segmented markets, and new hierarchies.[29]

27 Finally, the dependence on private spaces for public activity and the more recent privatization of public space gravely threaten the government's constitutional obligations to its citizens. Not only freedom of speech and public assembly in shopping centers are at issue. Just recently, Amtrack's Pennsylvania Station in New York City tried to stave off two suits requiring it to respect constitutional rights guaranteed in public places: an effort by artist Michael Lebron to display a political message on the gigantic curved and lighted billboard that he had rented for two months, and a case brought by the Center for Constitutional Rights to force Amtrak to stop ejecting people from the station because they are homeless. When Jürgen Habermas theorized about the rise and fall of a rational public sphere, he recognized the centrality in the eighteenth and nineteenth centuries of accessible urban places—cafés, taverns, coffeehouses, clubs, meeting houses, concert and lecture halls, theaters, and museums—to the emergence and maintenance of a democratic political culture. Over the last half-century, transformations in America's economy and metropolitan landscape have expanded the ability of many people to participate in the mass market. But the commercializing, privatizing, and segmenting of physical gathering places that has accompanied mass consumption has made more precarious the shared public sphere upon which our democracy depends.[30]

Notes

I would like to acknowledge the skill and imagination of two research assistants, Deb Steinbach and Susan Spaet. My research was supported by grants from the National Endowment for the Humanities (1993), the American Council of Learned Societies (1994), and New York University (1993–1994). I am also grateful to several audiences who shared helpful reactions to versions of this article: the international conference "Gender and Modernity in the Era of Rationalization," Columbia University, September 1994; the conference "Significant Locales: Business, Labor, and Industry in the Mid-Atlantic Region," sponsored by the Center for the History of Business, Technology, and Society, Hagley Museum and Library, October 1994; the history department at George Washington University, February 1995; Tricia Rose's American Studies Colloquium, New York University, February 1995; the Historians of Greater Cleveland, May 1995; and my audience at Vassar College, November 1995. Individuals whose readings have especially helped me include Herrick Chapman, Michael Ebner, Ken Jackson, Richard Longstreth, Tricia Rose, Phil Scranton, David Schuyler, Sylvie Schweitzer, and two anonymous readers for the *AHR.*

1. "The Economy: The Great Shopping Spree," *Time* (January 8, 1965): 58–62 (and cover).

2. See Kenneth T. Jackson, *Crabgrass Frontier: The Suburbanization of the United States* (New York, 1985); Robert Fishman, *Bourgeois Utopias: The Rise and Fall of Suburbia* (New York, 1987); Joel Garreau, *Edge City: Life on the New Frontier* (Garden City, N.Y., 1991); William Sharpe and Leonard Wallock, "Bold New City or Built-Up 'Burb? Redefining Contemporary Suburbia," with comments by Robert Bruegmann, Robert Fishman, Margaret Marsh, and June Manning Thomas, *American Quarterly* 46 (March 1994): 1–61; Carol O'Connor, "Sorting Out Suburbia," *American Quarterly* 37 (Summer 1985): 382–94.

3. The Editors of *Fortune, The Changing American Market* (Garden City, N.Y., 1995), 76.

4. Ann Durkin Keating and Ruth Eckdish Knack, "Shopping in the Planned Community: Evolution of the Park Forest Town Center," unpublished paper in possession of author; Howard Gillette, Jr., "The Evolution of the Planned Shopping Center in Suburb and City," *American Planning Association Journal* 51 (Autumn 1985): 449–60; Daniel Prosser, "The New Downtowns: Commercial Architecture in Suburban New Jersey, 1920–1970," in Joel Schwartz and Daniel Prosser, *Cities of the Garden State: Essays in the Urban and Suburban History of New Jersey* (Dubuque, Iowa, 1977), 113–15; "Park Forest Moves into '52," *House and Home: The Magazine of Building* 1 (March 1952): 115–16; William S. Worley, *J. C. Nichols and the Shaping of Kansas City: Innovation in Planned Residential Communities* (Columbia, Mo., 1990); Richard Longstreth, "J. C. Nichols, the Country Club Plaza, and Notions of Modernity," *The Harvard Architecture Review, Vol. 5: Precedent and Invention* (New York, 1986), 121–32; William H. Whyte, Jr., "The Outgoing Life," *Fortune* 47 (July 1953): 85; Michael Birkner, *A Country Place No More: The Transformation of Bergenfield, New Jersey, 1894–1994* (Rutherford, N.J., 1994), 174–77; *Bergen Evening Record,* Special Foster Village Edition, August 10, 1949.

5. Jackson, *Crabgrass Frontier,* 255–61. On precedents in the pre–World War II period, see Richard Longstreth, "Silver Spring: Georgia Avenue, Colesville Road, and the Creation of an Alternative 'Downtown' for Metropolitan Washington," in *Streets: Critical Perspectives on Public Space,* Zeynep Celik, Diane Favro, and Richard Ingersoll, eds. (Berkeley, Calif., 1994), 247–57; Longstreth, "The Neighborhood Shopping Center in Washington, D.C., 1930–1941," *Journal of the Society of Architectural Historians* 51 (March 1992): 5–33; Longstreth, "The Perils of a Parkless Town," in *The Car and the City: The Automobile, the Built Environment, and Daily Urban Life,* Martin Wachs and Margaret Crawford, eds. (Ann Arbor, Mich., 1992), 141–53.

6. Editors of *Fortune, Changing American Market,* 78–80, 90. Also see "New Need Cited on Store Centers," *New York Times* (February 13, 1955): 7.

7. Richard Longstreth, "The Mixed Blessings of Success: The Hecht Company and Department Store Branch Development after World War II," Occasional Paper No. 14, January 1995, Center for Washington Area Studies, George Washington University.

8. Samuel Feinberg, "Story of Shopping Centers," *What Makes Shopping Centers Tick,* reprinted from *Women's Wear Daily* (New York, 1960), 1. For useful background on the development of regional shopping centers, see William Severini Kowinski, *The Malling of America: An Inside Look at the Great Consumer Paradise* (New York, 1985); Neil Harris, *Cultural Excursions: Marketing Appetites and Cultural Tastes in Modern America* (Chicago, 1990), 7, 76–77, 278–88; Margaret Crawford, "The World in a Shopping Mall," in Michael Sorkin, ed., *Variations on a Theme Park: The New American City and the End of Public Space* (New York, 1992), 3–30; Gillette, "Evolution of the Planned Shopping Center."

9. On the postwar growth of Paramus and Bergen County, see Raymond M. Ralph, *Farmland to Suburbia, 1920–1960,* Vol. 6, Bergen County, New Jersey History and Heritage Series (Hackensack, N.J., 1983), 62–71, 76–90; Catherine M. Fogarty, John E. O'Connor, and Charles F. Cummings, *Bergen County: A Pictorial History* (Norfolk, Va., 1985), 182–93; *Beautiful Bergen: The Story of Bergen County, New Jersey,* 1962; Patricia M. Ryle, *An Economic Profile of Bergen County, New Jersey* (Office of Economic Research, Division of Planning and Research, New Jersey Department of Labor and Industry, March 1980); League of Women Voters of Bergen County, *Where Can I Live in Bergen County: Factors Affecting Housing Supply* (Closter, N.J., 1972).

10. Feinberg, *What Makes Shopping Centers Tick*, 2, 94–102; Ralph, *Farmland to Suburbia*, 70–71, 84–85; Mark A. Stuart, *Our Era, 1960–Present*, Vol. 7, Bergen County, New Jersey History and Heritage Series (Hackensack, N.J., 1983), 19–22; Prosser, "New Downtowns," 119–20; Edward T. Thompson, "The Suburb That Macy's Built," *Fortune* 61 (February 1960): 195–200; "Garden State Plaza Merchant's Manual," May 1, 1957, and certain pages revised in 1959, 1960, 1962, 1963, 1965, 1969, Garden State Plaza Historical Collection.

11. On the financing of shopping centers and the great profits involved, see Jerry Jacobs, *The Mall: An Attempted Escape from Everyday Life* (Prospect Heights, Ill., 1984), 52.

12. Victor Gruen, "Introverted Architecture," *Progressive Architecture* 38, no. 5 (1957): 204–08; Victor Gruen and Larry Smith, *Shopping Towns USA: The Planning of Shopping Centers* (New York, 1960), 22–24; both quoted in Gillette, "Evolution of the Planned Shopping Center." For more on Gruen, see Kowinski, *Malling of America*, 118–20, 210–14; "Exhibit of Shopping Centers," *New York Times* (October 19, 1954): 42. Paul Goldberger recently profiled shopping-center builder Martin Bucksbaum in "Settling the Suburban Frontier," *New York Times Magazine* (December 31, 1995): 34–35.

13. Robert Bruegmann made the same point about the way the earliest design of sub-urban shopping centers resembled downtown shopping streets in a talk to the Urban History Seminar of the Chicago Historical Society, February 17, 1994.

14. Quoted in Feinberg, *What Makes Shopping Centers Tick*, 101. In addition to sources already cited on the control possible in a shopping center versus a downtown, see "Shopping Centers Get 'Personality,' " *New York Times* (June 29, 1958): 1.

15. Ernest Erber, "Notes on the 'City of Bergen,' " September 14, 1960, Box B, Ernest Erber Papers (hereafter, Erber), Newark Public Library (hereafter, NPL), Newark; "Paramus Booms as a Store Center," *New York Times* (February 5, 1962): 33–34; "The Mall the Merrier, or Is It?" *New York Times* (November 21, 1976): 62. For details on particular stores and activities at Bergen Mall and Garden State Plaza, see Feinberg, *What Makes Shopping Centers Tick*, 97–100; Fogarty, *et al.*, *Bergen County*, 189; Prosser, "New Downtowns," 119. Almost every issue of the *Bergen Evening Record* from 1957 and thereafter yields valuable material (in articles and advertisements) on mall stores, ser-vices, and activities. The discussion here is based particularly on issues from November 8, 13, and 19, 1957, January 8, 1958, June 10, 1959, and March 2, 1960. Also see "Shoppers! Mass Today on Level 1," *New York Times*, June 14, 1994; press release on Garden State Plaza's opening in the Historical Collection of Garden State Plaza, folder "GSP history"; "It Won't Be Long Now . . . Bamberger's, New Jersey's Greatest Store, Comes to Paramus Soon," promotional leaflet, stamped August 22, 1956, file "Bergen County Shopping Centers," Johnson Free Public Library, Hackensack, N.J.; "The Shopping Center," *New York Times* (February 1, 1976): 6–7.

For data on the allocation of shopping-center space in ten regional shopping cen-ters in 1957, see William Applebaum and S. O. Kaylin, *Case Studies in Shopping Center Development and Operation* (New York, 1974), 101. For evidence of the community orientation of shopping centers nationwide, see Arthur Herzog, "Shops, Culture, Centers—and More," *New York Times Magazine* (November 18, 1962): 34–35, 109–10, 112–14; in the *New York Times:* "A Shopping Mall in Suffolk Offering More Than Goods," June 22, 1970: 39; "Supermarkets Hub of Suburbs," February 7, 1971: 58; "Busy Day in a Busy Mall," April 12, 1972: 55. On the com-munity-relations efforts of branch stores, see Clinton L. Oaks, *Managing Suburban Branches of Department Stores* (Stanford, Calif., 1957), 81–83.

16. George Sternlieb, *The Future of the Downtown Department Store* (Cambridge, Mass., 1962), 10.

17. R. H. Macy & Company, *Annual Report* (New York, 1955). The *Times-Advocate,* March 14, 1976, argues that Bamberger's, Macy's store at the Garden State Plaza, was at the forefront of the chain's appeal to the middle to upper-income shopper. On market segmentation of shopping centers, also see William H. Whyte, Jr., *The Organization Man* (New York, 1956), 316–17; Jacobs, *The Mall,* 5, 12; and Albert Bills and Lois Pratt, "Personality Differences among Shopping Centers," *Fairleigh Dickinson University Business Review* 1 (Winter 1961), which distinguishes between the customers of the Bergen Mall and Garden State Plaza in socioeconomic terms. Crawford's "World in a Shopping Mall," in Sorkin, *Variations on a Theme Park,* discusses the sophisticated strategies that market researchers use to analyze trade areas and pitch stores to different kinds of customers, 8–9.

18. George Sternlieb, "The Future of Retailing in the Downtown Core," *AIP Journal* 24 (May 1963), as reprinted in Howard A. Schretter, *Downtown Revitalization* (Athens, Ga., 1967), 95, and quoted in Jon C. Teaford, *The Rough Road to Renaissance: Urban Revitalization in America, 1940–1985* (Baltimore, Md., 1990), 129.

19. United States Department of Labor, Bureau of Labor Statistics, "Consumer Expenditures and Income, Northern New Jersey, 1960–61," BLS Report No. 237–63, December 1963, Schomburg Center, New York Public Library, Clipping File "Consumer Expenses & Income-NJ."

20. "The Wonder on Routes 4 and 17: Garden State Plaza," brochure, file "Bergen County Shopping Centers," Johnson Free Public Library, Hackensack, New Jersey; "Notes on Discussion Dealing with Regional (Intermunicipal) Planning Program for Passaic Valley Area (Lower Portion of Passaic Co. and South Bergen," n.d., Box A, Folder 3, Erber, NPL; "Memorandum to DAJ and WBS from EE," November 22, 1966, Box B, Erber, NPL; National Center for Telephone Research (A Division of Louis Harris and Associates), "A Study of Shoppers' Attitudes toward the Proposed Shopping Mall in the Hudson County Meadowlands Area," conducted for Hartz Mountain Industries, February 1979, Special Collections, Rutgers University, New Brunswick, New Jersey.

21. Shopping centers retreated from promoting themselves as central squares and street corners not only because of the free speech issue but also to limit the loitering of young people. *New York Times:* "Supermarkets Hub of Suburbs," February 7, 1971: 58; "Coping with Shopping-Center Crises, Dilemma: How Tough to Get If Young Are Unruly," March 7, 1971: sect. 3, p. 1; "Shopping Centers Change and Grow," May 23, 1971: sect. 7, p. 1.

22. For a useful summary of the relevant court cases and legal issues involved, see Curtis J. Berger, "*PruneYard* Revisited: Political Activity on Private Lands," *New York University Law Review* 66 (June 1991): 633–94; also "Shopping Centers Change and Grow," *New York Times* (May 23, 1971): sect. 7, p. 1. The corporate shopping center's antagonism to free political expression and social action is discussed in Herbert I. Schiller, *Culture Inc.: The Corporate Takeover of Public Expression* (New York, 1989), 98–101.

23. On *Amalgamated vs. Logan Valley Plaza,* see "Property Rights vs. Free Speech," *New York Times* (July 9, 1972): sect. 7, p. 9; "Amalgamated Food Employees Union Local 590 v. Logan Valley Plaza," 88 S.Ct. 1601 (1968), *Supreme Court Reporter,* 1601–20; 391 US 308, U.S. Supreme Court Recording Briefs 1967, No. 478, microfiche; "Free Speech: Peaceful Picketing on Quasi-Public Property," *Minnesota Law Review* 53 (March 1969): 873–82. On *Marsh vs. State of Alabama,* see 66 S.Ct.

276, *Supreme Court Reporter,* 276–84. Other relevant cases between *Marsh vs. Alabama* and *Amalgamated vs. Logan Valley Plaza* are *Nahas vs. Local 905, Retail Clerks International Assoc.* (1956), *Amalgamated Clothing Workers of America vs. Wonderland Shopping Center, Inc.* (1963), *Schwartz-Torrance Investment Corp. vs. Bakery and Confectionary Workers' Union, Local No. 31* (1964); with each case, the Warren court was moving closer to a recognition that the shopping center was becoming a new kind of public forum.

24. "4 Nixon Appointees End Court's School Unanimity, Shopping Centers' Right to Ban Pamphleteering Is Upheld, 5 to 4," *New York Times* (June 23, 1972): 1; "Shopping-Center Industry Hails Court," *New York Times* (July 2, 1972): sect. 3, p. 7; "Lloyd Corporation, Ltd. v. Donald M. Tanner (1972)," 92 S.Ct. 2219 (1972), *Supreme Court Reporter,* 2219–37. The American Civil Liberties Union brief went to great lengths to document the extent to which shopping centers have replaced traditional business districts; see "Brief for Respondents," U.S. Supreme Court Record, microfiche, 20–29. See also People's Lobby Brief, U.S. Supreme Court Record, microfiche, 5.

    The Supreme Court majority wanted to make it clear that in finding in favor of the Lloyd Center, it was not reversing the Logan Valley decision, arguing for a distinction based on the fact that anti-war leafletting was "unrelated" to the shopping center, while the labor union was picketing an employer. The four dissenting justices, however, were less sure that the distinction was valid and that the Logan Valley decision was not seriously weakened by Lloyd. The important court cases between *Amalgamated vs. Logan Valley Plaza* and *Lloyd vs. Tanner* included *Blue Ridge Shopping Center vs. Schleininger* (1968), *Sutherland vs. Southcenter Shopping Center* (1971), and *Diamond vs. Bland* (1970, 1974).

25. Berger, *"PruneYard* Revisited"; Kowinski, *Malling of America,* 196–202, 355–59; "Shopping Malls Protest Intrusion by Protesters," *New York Times* (July 19, 1983): B1; "Opening of Malls Fought," *New York Times* (May 13, 1984): sect. 11 (New Jersey), 7; "Michael Robins v. PruneYard Shopping Center (1979)," 592 P. 2nd 341, *Pacific Reporter,* 341–51; "PruneYard Shopping Center v. Michael Robins," 100 S.Ct. 2035 (1980), *Supreme Court Reporter,* 2035–51; U.S. Supreme Court Record, *PruneYard Shopping Center vs. Robins* (1980), microfiche. The most important Supreme Court case between *Lloyd vs. Tanner* and *PruneYard* was *Scott Hudgens vs. National Labor Relations Board* (1976), where the majority decision backed further away from Logan Valley Plaza and refused to see the mall as the functional equivalent of downtown. "Scott Hudgens v. National Labor Relations Board," 96 S.Ct. 1029 (1976), *Supreme Court Reporter,* 1029–47.

26. "Court Protects Speech in Malls," *New York Times* (December 21, 1994): A1; "Big Malls Ordered to Allow Leafletting," *Star-Ledger* (December 21, 1994): 1; "Now, Public Rights in Private Domains," *New York Times* (December 25, 1994): E3; "Free Speech in the Mall," *New York Times* (December 26, 1994): 38; Frank Askin, "Shopping for Free Speech at the Malls," 1995, unpublished ms. in possession of the author.

27. "Amtrak Is Ordered Not to Eject the Homeless from Penn Station," *New York Times* (February 22, 1995): A1.

28. Article on passage of New Jersey Civil Rights Bill, *New York Times,* March 24, 1949; Marion Thompson Wright, "Extending Civil Rights in New Jersey through the Division Against Discrimination," *Journal of Negro History* 38 (1953): 96–107; State of New Jersey, Governor's Committee on Civil Liberties, "Memorandum on Behalf of Joint Council for Civil Rights in Support of a Proposed Comprehensive Civil Rights Act for New Jersey," 1948, II, B 8, Folder "Civil Rights, New Jersey, 1941–48," NAACP Papers, Library of Congress, Washington, D.C.; "Report of Legislative Committee, NJ State Conference of NAACP Branches," March 26, 1949, II, B 8, Folder "Civil Rights, New

Jersey, 1941–48," NAACP Papers. Other NAACP files on discrimination document the actual experiences of African Americans in New Jersey during the 1940s and 1950s.

29. "Closing of 'Last' Department Store Stirs Debate on Downtown Trenton," *Star-Ledger,* June 5, 1983; "Urban Areas Crave Return of Big Markets," *Star-Ledger,* July 17, 1984; "Elizabeth Clothier Mourns Demise of Century-Old Customized Service," *Sunday Star-Ledger,* January 10, 1988; "President's Report to the Annual Meeting Passaic Valley Citizens Planning Association." Box A, Folder 3.

30. Jürgen Habermas, *The Structural Transformation of the Public Sphere: An Inquiry into a Category of Bourgeois Society,* Thomas Burger trans., with Frederick Lawrence (Cambridge, Mass., 1989); Geoff Eley, "Nations, Publics, and Political Cultures: Placing Habermas in the Nineteenth Century," in Nicholas B. Dirks, Geoff Eley, and Sherry B. Ortner, eds., *Culture/Power/History: A Reader in Contemporary Social Theory* (Princeton, N.J., 1994), 297–335.

Review Questions

1. As people moved from cities to the suburbs, what changes occurred in their shopping patterns?

2. In the 1950s, how did the people who developed regional shopping centers plan to meet the needs of customers?

3. What two major effects followed from markets moving from town centers to shopping centers?

4. In what sense could the earliest developers of shopping centers be called visionaries?

5. In what sense was suburbanization a new form of racial segregation, according to Cohen?

6. How did developers seek to create in their shopping centers an "idealized downtown"?

7. Explain the legal battles that arose in connection with shopping centers.

8. The rise of the shopping center over the last 50 years has given many people access to the mass market, says Cohen. But this access has come at a price. What is that price?

Discussion and Writing Suggestions

1. Cohen argues that shopping centers gave rise to a new form of racial segregation in this country. In your own experience, have you observed or experienced segregation at a shopping center?

2. Reread paragraph 14 and explain the this passage: "Market segmentation became the guiding principle of [the shopping center's] mix of commercial and civic activity, as the shopping center sought perhaps contradictorily to legitimize itself as a true community center and to define that community in exclusionary socioeconomic

and racial terms." What was the mix of commercial and civic activity? What was contradictory about shopping center management's calling their centers "community centers"?

3. Reread paragraph 25 and comment on this passage: "While African Americans and their supporters were prodding courts and legislatures to eliminate legal segregation in public places, real-estate developers, retailers, and consumers were collaborating to shift economic resources to new kinds of segregated spaces." To what extent do you agree that suburban shopping malls constitute "segregated spaces"?

4. What evidence do you find from your own experience that shopping centers are "class stratified"—that is, some centers cater to the upper-middle class, some to the lower-middle class?

5. Have you seen any evidence that political activity (for instance, protesting or gathering of signatures for petitions) is any less welcome in a shopping center than it is on a city street? Write a descriptive paragraph or two describing the experience.

6. Interview an older acquaintance or relative, perhaps a grandparent, on how shopping has changed over the years. Does this person recall a time before the rise of shopping centers? What was better about shopping in the middle of the twentieth century versus shopping at the beginning of the twenty-first? What was worse?

Community Through Exclusion and Illusion
George Lewis

In this article, which first appeared in the Journal of Popular Culture *(Fall 1990), George Lewis investigates the extent to which shopping malls "really act as [a] social magnet, bringing people together in a true sense of community." Through public service programs and promotions, mall management would have us believe that its facilities function as town centers in the spirit that Victor Gruen had envisioned. But Lewis, a sociologist at the University of the Pacific, challenges that view, concluding that the groups that congregate in malls "seldom share the common ties and engage in the sort of social interactions necessary to forge a sense of 'we-ness.'" Lewis bases his insights on a study of two groups—elders and teenagers—at a New England shopping center.*

1   Everyday life in America, in the past three decades, has been critically affected by the evolution and spread of the shopping mall as the central concept in American retailing. These economic monoliths, evolving from the earlier retail form of the suburban shopping center, are now about far more than just shopping. People go to the modern mall for professional services, such as legal, medical or optical aid. There are fashion shows, art shows and musical performances in these climate controlled, air conditioned spaces. Restaurants, video arcades, movie theatres and even ice skating rinks and sand beaches with tanning lights focused upon them

are found in the contemporary enclosed mall. In a word, the regional shopping mall has become a kind of civic center, a point of attraction for millions of Americans, whether they choose to buy something there regularly or not.

. . .

Community In The Mall: Manufactured Illusion or Social Reality?

2   With all its promotions and public service programs, does the mall really act as this sort of social magnet, bringing people together in a true sense of community? The answer, if one is to define community as more than just the bringing together of demographically similar persons in one locale, is more apt to be negative than it is positive. Malls can, and do, lure and assemble *collectivities* and *crowds* of shoppers, but these groups seldom share the common ties and engage in the sort of social interactions necessary to forge a sense of "we-ness"—of community—from the raw social material of a crowd.

3   Jessie Bernard makes a crucial conceptual distinction here between "the community," which emphasizes *locale* as its most important and fundamental criterion, and "community," which emphasizes *common ties* and *interaction* as significant criteria in its conceptualization. "Community," then, is characterized not by locale, but by the *gemeinschaften* spirit of communal and primary relationships in which intimacy, sentiment, and a sense of belonging exist among individuals.[1]

4   Thomas Bender agrees, further defining community as characterized by close, usually face to face relationships. "Individuals are bound together by affective or emotional ties rather than by a perception of individual self-interest. There is a 'we-ness' in a community; one is a member."[2]

5   If this is the sort of social relationship one means by community, than it is difficult to find among customers at most shopping malls. Physically, malls are geared for high turnover. Chairs and benches in rest areas and food courts are unpadded in the seat—designed to be uncomfortable if sat in too long. The architecture of the mall itself, behind the colorful neon store logos and displays, is anonymous, uniform, predictable and plain. The corridors are wide and filled with hurrying customers. Security guards discourage loiterers and help to move foot traffic along. The muzak, if it exists, reinforces the image of the mall as a public space—a place where strangers encounter one another en route to their desired locations.

6   Most shoppers who frequent the mall, even if lured there by some promotional scheme, come alone or in small groups of two or three.[3] They are intent upon their business, focusing upon shopping and not upon interaction with other mall customers. For the most part, they do not know each other and they don't come to the mall on any regular, day-to-day basis. In short, the high turnover, volume of persons, and transiency that is a designed part of most malls works *against* the development and emergence of community within their walls.

7   This is understood by mall managers and developers. As one put it: "Having the *perception* of a community feeling does not mean that it actually exists. It is not the same thing. Perception is not necessarily reality."[4] So the important thing, from a marketing perspective, is to create the warm *illusion* of community, while at the same time quietly stacking the deck against its actual development. "We don't want the mall to be a community in any real sense, because

we'll attract people we don't want to. People who are not here to shop but are coming for some other purpose. It would upset our tenants who want to make money. We don't want anything to upset our tenants."

8   And yet, within this illusion, this false setting of community, the seeds of community have been planted. Ironically, among the very sorts of persons the managers and developers do not want to see attracted to the mall—the non-shoppers—have arisen fledgling forms of community, characterized by primary ties, face to face interaction, daily meeting and the development of social networks. These developing communities, or social worlds—one comprised mainly of retired persons and others over 65, and the other of teenagers—are the empirical focus of this paper. The data presented here were collected in June and July of 1988 in a series of unstructured interviews conducted in a large shopping center in New England. The interviews, which total over 200 hours of material, are one portion of a research effort undertaken by the Salt Center For Cultural Studies, in examining various facets of the impact of popular and mass culture on regional cultural forms.[5]

. . .

The Elderly

9   The mall is a central life setting for many elderly persons who frequent it on a regular basis. They walk back and forth, up and down the common area of the older wing of the mall (the "old mall"), greeting friends and acquaintances and sitting with them, visiting, in the sunken circular seating areas they have named the "north hole," "south hole," or "center hole." Some visit the mall every day, arriving when the doors are opened in the morning. Many stay all day, leaving in mid to late afternoon. A few will have a light dinner at one of the mall eateries before going home for the evening.

10   Many of these persons are retired, many widowed. They feel they have little else to fill their days. Their time in the mall usually conforms to set routines. They will be found in a specific seating area at a regular time, have coffee at the same restaurant at the same time, and leave the mall each day within 15 or 20 minutes of their leaving time the day before. This patterning of behavior is pervasive among the elderly and characterizes the nature of their social interaction at the mall.

11   Bert, for example, a 78-year-old retiree, comes to the mall every day of the week. "I come here at quarter of eleven and I leave at twenty minutes past one," he says matter-of-factly, as he sneaks a glance at his watch. "I do this every day. Every day except. . . ."

12   His two companions finish for him; "Five days a week. He's missed one day this year."

13   Bert resumes his own account. "And I have my lunch here at noontime." This is Bert's eleven o'clock stop, outside of Porteous, one of the large department-style anchor stores of the mall. He won't be here at eleven-thirty.

14   "I move every half hour. I go from here down to where the clock is. Then where the clock is, I go down in front of Woolworth's, then I come back again and go up there and take my bus by the front of JC Penney."

15   Linda, a mall custodian, noted that the elderly "would rather be at the mall than anywhere else. They probably know more about the place than I do.

Probably know more than security does, too. I know 'cause my father-in-law is one of 'em. He comes in twice a day, every day. Ya, he sets over in the old mall, then he comes down and sets by Porteous for a while, then over by McDonalds."

16   The controlled environment of the mall offers another benefit to the elderly— it is a safe and comfortable place to walk for exercise. As Jacobs has pointed[6] out, many malls have instituted some form of walking program for the elderly— though the impetus for these programs usually comes from outside the mall itself, as the elderly are most often perceived by mall management as a group who does very little, if any, buying and thus contributes quite minimally in pro- portion to their presence, to the economic life of the mall.

17   "We really don't want them to come here if they're not going to shop," a mall manager remarked. "They take up seats we would like to have available for shoppers." However, from a public relations standpoint, it is difficult for mall management to overtly discourage the elderly from using the mall for their own purposes. Conversely, management can sometimes be talked into the minimal support of programs such as walking-for-health, in hopes it shows off to the community of shoppers they do want to attract, the degree of social con- sciousness and responsibility they supposedly feel.

18   The mall studied here is no exception to this pattern. A local doctor and the YMCA spearheaded the senior walking program, which opened in the spring of 1987 and which is now jointly sponsored by the doctor, the Y and the mall. The program encourages the elderly to walk laps and to record their own progress. To date, there are over 300 walkers signed into this program.

19   For those participating, entrance to the mall can be as early as 6:00 a.m., when security unlocks the doors—a full 3 or 4 hours prior to the opening of most commercial establishments inside the mall.

20   Pat, a regular "miler" in the program, usually arrives by car a few minutes before six and waits until the glass doors are unlocked.

21   "Age first," Pat insists as he holds a door for his two companions. Inside the mall, silent mannequins observe the three men begin their daily laps. Pat, now eighty years old, decides to take a short cut.

22   "You cheated," accuses the security guard.

23   "No, *you're* cheatin'," Pat accuses. "You're supposed to unlock all these doors and you're talkin' instead. I gotta bum hip, and when you get to my age, you won't be walkin'!" He smiles and disappears down the corridor. Two women call out to him in disbelief.

24   "You were here before us!"

25   "That's right," Pat laughs. "You're gettin' lazy."

26   After his five miles of walking laps, Pat sits down at his favorite restaurant, just now opening for business. Coming to the mall, he says, "gets me out of the house. I wish they opened at five. Pretty soon I'll be meeting six or seven fellas I know. We talk, shoot the breeze. I just come out here to kill a little time, that's all. What am I going to do at home?"

27   He leans back to prop his elbow on the back of his chair. His eyes follow a woman in red high heels taking choppy steps past a boutique. "I was in busi- ness 65 years. Was in the meat business. Gave it to my son, my son gave it to his son. I don't know whether you ever heard of it—Pat's Meat Mart?"

28   Two elderly ladies in cotton skirts and sneakers walk past and wave to Pat. "Morning," he answers. These women he identifies as past customers of his, as he jokes with them. "I have a lot of customers, really I do . . . people know us, ya know."

29   He looks down and then away, as if he doesn't want to talk anymore. Then: "I was going to show you my darlin's picture." He pulls out his wallet and unfolds a fragile, yellowed newspaper clipping. "She was the nicest. Everybody loved her. They only make one like her. . . . I miss this one, I tell ya. I do, I really do. Oh, we were inseparable. I had her for 34 years. She died when she was 51, so—God wanted her. There's nothing I could do, ya know. That's the story of my life." A tight little smile.

30   "Where do ya want me to send the bill?" he asks, snapping back to the present.

31   Retired and living alone, many of these elderly seek the mall as a safe and neutral ground to keep up old job contacts—not just the more surface relationships with old customers, but more primary ties with workmates themselves. George, who worked for a large electrical plant until they "closed out" in 1983 and forced him into retirement, meets his work buddies every Friday in the mall for lunch. Over the five years he has done this, he notes, fewer and fewer are alive to attend. "Every month," he says, "the faces we used to see, they're thinnin' out, . . . thinnin' out. . . ."

32   Charlie comes to the mall to meet people and to avoid heat in the summer and cold in the winter. "Some people I meet here," he says, "I've known for forty years." The elderly congregate in knots and clusters, laughing and joking among themselves. Charlie flags down Bob and Irene in the crowd and gives them two coupons from the previous day's paper, good for money off at a mall fast food stand.

33   Connie complains of telephone sales people to the group—especially a seller of cemetery plots. "I told him I have my plot all picked out. I'm just sitting here waiting to go. He didn't call back." She continues, "Here (in the mall) we sit and talk about our illnesses, medications, diets. We have a lot of fun."

34   More than most social worlds, the world of the elderly in the mall takes its shape and character from the face to face relationships of the people who regularly are a part of it. For these elderly—most of whom are retired, who live alone, and are most probably widowed—there is now little or no need to expend energy, concern and time in the areas of career, job development, self-improvement, spousal relations, or even in family and community activities. Cut off from these concerns and ties, their status and power position in the larger society lowered, they find meaning in the construction and maintenance of networks of personal relationships with others like themselves.[7] These "personal communities," then, are not defined by a bounded area so much as they are a web-like network of personal relationships in which each person is selectively attached to a definite number of discrete persons. At the edges of this network are those persons, such as the servers in the restaurants, the custodians, and the security personnel, with whom relationships are affectively neutral, of a surface level, and usually joking in nature.

35   Harry sums it up. "It's hard being a senior citizen. Very hard. It's a monotonous life. You know, when you're constructive for a good many years and then you have to relax and do nothing—and you're alone—that's worse."

36   Tom, sitting beside Harry, points out that he has some pretty good friends at the mall. He continues; "Girls down in the food court. They all look for us. We don't come in, they ask everybody where we are. They think we're sick, or something."

37   Harry and Bert tip their heads in agreement. "They look out for us. We kid a lot with them and everything."

38   Harry takes it from there. "Well, you're seeing a face, you know. If you stayed at home and you're alone, you see nothing. No matter where you'd live, you'd see a car go by. But people, you don't see." Silence. Then, "So you come out here to see the living, more or less." He looks to his friends for reinforcement. "Am I right? I think so."

39   Tom jumps in. "But you make everything sound so *sad,* Harry. My Lord, it's not *that* bad. I come out here to see my friends. To get out of the house. That's all."

The Teens

40 Teenagers visit the mall on an almost daily basis. They arrive in groups or individually to meet their friends. A number work in the mall, usually at minimum wage, in the fast food establishments located, for the most part, in the "new wing" of the mall, built just three years ago. When they are off work, they "hang out" with other youths, who use the mall as a place for social gathering.

41   The mall is one of the few places teenagers can go in this society where they are—albeit reluctantly—allowed to stay without being asked to leave.[8] Many who frequent the mall don't go to school. Some also try to stay away from their homes, but they really don't have anywhere else they can be on their own. As Millison concluded, malls are much the suburban equivalent to the urban street corners where inner city kids congregate.[9] Suburban kids come to malls to look around, meet and make friends, stay away from home, and hang out—because there is nowhere else to go.

42   Paul, a security guard, explains. "We aren't allowed to harass the kids, and I know they gotta hang out somewhere. But we tell them to keep moving, especially around the seats and tables in the food service area. They know they have to keep moving. If they get too loud, or talk back, or are creating any kind of disturbance like that, then we clear them out. Troublemakers we identify, and we don't let them back in."

43   Calling themselves "mall rats" (males) and "mall bunnies" (female), the teens congregate in the new wing of the mall, the largest number of them arriving in the late afternoon. They wander around the different shops, playing video games in the arcade, smoking cigarettes, showing off their latest hair, makeup and clothing styles, and waiting for something, anything, to happen. Most of them will stay until nine-thirty or ten, when the stores close and the mall shuts down.

44   Derick, 15, his hands jammed into the pockets of his frayed cutoff jean shorts, admits that the mall is "a place to go before I have to go to work. I only work right across the street. I have nowhere else to hang out. Most of my friends hang out here."

45   Looking at the arcade in the adjacent wing of the mall, he gestures towards it with a quick nod of his head. "Go over there to play video games. Spend all my money. I don't like spending all my money, but it's there." He shrugs. "Fuck it."

46   Standing near Derick in the small knot of teenagers, Ed, 16, takes a long, slow drag off his cigarette and exhales out the corner of his mouth. "I just started coming on almost a daily basis last year, because it was something to do," he says. "You can come here anytime. It's pretty good, but if we didn't have anything, you'd probably get in more trouble than we would if we came here, so it kinda works out, you know. It's something to do and it kinda keeps you outa trouble."

47   As he says this, he scans the familiar row of neon lit food stalls. Shoppers rush by, but he appears calm and undisturbed, like his four friends standing nearby. They chatter noisily among themselves, making jokes, and playfully pushing each other around, only half aware, seemingly, of the bustle and motion of other people.

48   Nodding toward his friends, Ed goes on to explain the social networking that takes place in the mall. "I met all these people here. I've met lots of other people, too. One place where you can always find someone. If you know somebody, they know somebody else, they'll probably see 'em here, and you'll know them, then they'll know someone who is walking around and you know that person. So when you come here, you kinda build on people."

49   Some teens spend a great deal of time networking in the mall. For them, it is practically a second home. Tammy, age 14, says, "I used to come here every Saturday from eleven o'clock to nine-thirty, and just walk around with my friends, like Gina here, just walk around and check out the guys."

50   When roaming from shop to shop, playing video games, or cruising the strip becomes tiresome, teens usually migrate to the food court. Here they sit, talk, bum change, smoke cigarettes and try to avoid the attention of the security people, even as most of the activities they are engaged in will inevitably attract it.

51   The group gathers around a table, some standing, others sitting and talking. One of the girls breaks from her conversation to announce that Bob is coming. Bob has been kicked out of the mall for boisterous behavior and is not allowed in for another two months.

52   "Just about all of us have gotten kicked out at one time or another," Tony says in a matter of fact manner. "I was sitting down without anything to eat once, and like I didn't know the policy and he said, 'Move,' and I go, 'Why?' I ran my mouth a little too much. What I basically did was stand up for myself, but he didn't like that, so he just booted me for a couple months."

53   "Actually, I'm not supposed to be even in here. He said he's kicked me out forever, but I mean like I changed my hair style so he doesn't recognize me anymore."

54   Ed nods. "I changed mine and I changed my jacket. I used to wear a big leather jacket. I used to wear that all the time. That gave me away. But I've started wearing this jacket now with all my KISS pins on. And as long as I don't act up or do anything, they don't really care. See, I like it here so much I hafta come back."

55   Liz, 15, discusses relationships with the security guards in general. "Some days they can really get on us and other days they just won't come and like we'll be sitting down at the table and on busy days or on days they're not in a really good mood, they'll come over and tell us to move."

56   "They have no respect for mall rats," a boy standing on the edge of the group adds. "It's just days like that they can be real dinks."

57   And yet the mild harassment of the security guards is easily borne, especially when changing one's costume or haircut can many times be enough to erase identity in their eyes. Indeed, such treatment is better, for most, than the treatment they can expect elsewhere. And this relatively light scrutiny given them by the security guards also allows some teens to get away with minor interpersonal drug transactions, especially when the mall is crowded and busy.

58   "Other than The Beach, which is just like, 'deal it out on the streets,' I mean ya can get just about anything out here—pot, acid, hash, right here on Saturdays, when it is crowded."

59   "If you know the right people, you can pick up anything."

60   "And we pretty much know everybody here."

61   For some teens, the mall—with or without drugs—is an escape from home or school. Heather, 16, explains that she comes here "to get away from home, get away from problems 'cause I can't stay at home. Because of my nephew and my sister. They bother me. So I come to the mall." Slouching in her seat, she flips open the top of her red Marlboro box and counts her cigarettes. "School is no better. I go through a year of school, and they still put me through the next grade even if I'm failing. I like it, but it's not gonna get me through college if I do that. I don't care about partying. I just wanna get through school."

62   For Tiffany the mall has become a second home of sorts. At the age of thirteen she lives with Tony, another of the mall rats, and one other mall friend. "My mom kicked me out when I was eleven," she says with an edge of anger in her voice. "She's a bitch. I call her every day and she's just. . . ." Tiffany stops short as she shakes her head and rolls her eyes.

63   "I started going to foster homes and everything and I just quit. Now, I'm in State custody and I just. . . ." She stops again and laughs nervously and blushes. "Sorry about that," she says, apologizing to her friends, seeming to imply that she has become too personal, too emotional. Abruptly, she continues, "I don't do anything that they want me to do." She lets out a quick triumphant laugh.

64   "I swear to God if they came up to me and dragged me where I didn't want to go, I'd beat the crap right out of them. I would kill 'em. I got 'em twisted around my little finger. They don't mess with me." She growls, as she clenches her teeth and curls her small fist, pounding it lightly on the table.

65   Tony leans back and shakes his head slightly to part his long hair from his face. "I left home and I quit school and moved from, like, hotel to hotel for awhile with a Navy buddy and that wasn't a really good situation, 'cause we were getting kicked outta hotels and motels. We didn't have anywhere to go. So we went up to The Beach and when I went up there it's like there's a Burger King and an auto parts store and a Shop and Save and it's like . . . there was no mall. I was real glad to get back down here, 'cause it was, like, up there, it was boring the hell out of me."

66   The social world of these teens revolves around their contacts and time at the mall. Indeed, this world of the teenager is, in its larger sense, one of segregation from adults and the assumption of adult sexual, economic, and social roles. This segregation, and the relative lack of any clearly defined and socially supported roles for youth, help define the mall community of "rats and bunnies," especially those who have opted out, or been driven from, socially acceptable school and family settings.

67   These youths, disallowed entrance into the social world of adulthood, are attempting to forge meaning and community from their shifting networks of face to face peer relationships in the mall. And yet, unlike the elderly, theirs is a relatively unstable social system. Teens come and go and, more importantly, they do grow up. As a consequence, relationships rest almost entirely in present time and revolve around present circumstances. The past is seldom spoken of, or shared. "Best friends" at the mall may part ways next month, and not see each other again. This fluidity and change in social relationships is a socially uncertain part of the teen years which, for mall rats and bunnies, is also characterized by a lingering malaise concerning the world outside their fragile community—a malaise in which jealousy, mistrust and despair are prominent features. As Tony says:

68   "We are the mall rats. We are the mall. What the fuck else can I say?"

Conclusion: Community in the Mall

69 The American shopping mall has been bemoaned by critics for its impersonality, its uniformity, its total focus on meaningful interaction as rational and economic in nature. Where are the primary relations, the face to face interactions, the social networks that exist along with the economic transactions of the traditional marketplace, the local community, or even the urban village? This case study of one American mall suggests that, for shoppers in the mall, one does indeed need to look elsewhere for the primary interactive ties of community, no matter how cleverly mall management creates the *illusion* of community at the mall. In the end, it seems, this is a shared illusion—neither management nor shoppers are fooled by it, but both can *pretend* that they are creating or engaging in the meaningful and socially necessary relations of community.

70   Ironically, then, the real community ties that do exist in the mall have little to do with its economic function. The elder and the teen spend very little money there and do not frequent the mall for economic reasons. They are there, each day, to greet friends, to create and strengthen their meaningful, face to face primary relationships, to define themselves as a social world, whether it be one of "milers" or of "mall rats"—a community of kind to which they can give emotional support and from which they can draw a sense of self and group identity.

71   Mall management does not like to see such groups develop. They use mall space for other than economic purposes. These warm knots of community can and do disrupt the cool smooth flow of economic transaction. Group members take seats designed for shoppers. They create a focus in the mall that is not economic in nature.

72   Politically, however, it is hard—especially with the elderly—to ban, or even to overtly discourage their presence. But it can be contained and monitored by security personnel. And, especially with the teens, if it becomes too socially visible and disruptive, some members of the group can be ejected.

73   Why, then, under these less than ideal circumstances, do the elderly and teenagers use the mall as their locus of community? It seems likely there are at least five general social reasons for this choice. First, and probably most important, elders and teens both represent social groupings for whom our society provides little social space. The elderly, once they are retired especially, are cut off from the familiar and fulfilling world of work. Their income drops sharply. They

are likely to be treated more and more as children by both their families and their non-elderly acquaintances. If they are widowed and live at home, they have lost most of the primary face to face support they have relied on for most of their adult lives.[10]

74   Consequently, they have a need to seek out others in similar situations. The mall is a central, safe place to get to, and there is usually regularly scheduled mass transportation available for the benefit of the shoppers (when it most likely would *not* be available on any regular basis for, say, transport to a non-economically oriented center or meeting place, such as a park or activities center).

75   For the teens, caught as they are between the statuses of childhood and adulthood, there are few social spaces or physical places open where they can congregate and develop their own contacts and social networks.[11] Most often, their activity is too closely defined, monitored, and circumscribed for them to see it as their own (in institutions such as the family and the school). Or, if they do find a niche of their own—such as cruising Main Street or hanging out in a park or fast food parking lot—they are usually dispersed by the authorities, or caught in curfews, or both.

76   And when school and family settings become nonviable alternatives, teens really have very few places to go. Once again, the mall offers its lure. It is centrally located, easy to get to for those with or without their own transportation, seen as a "safe" place by parents, and may, for some, also be the location of their full- or part-time job (usually for minimum wage—but that is another bit of discrimination teens have to bear).

77   Second, the elderly and teens are, to a great extent, faceless persons to adult American society. They are categorized as "old people" or "kids," and, because of the unimportance of their marginal status, they tend to be overlooked as individuals, though they are stereotypically reacted to as members of groups. For both of these groups, this social reaction increases their need to affirm identity and to create meaningful community for themselves.[12]

78   It also means that, in the mall setting, the elderly are usually overlooked, are nearly invisible to the shoppers hurrying on their way. Being socially invisible, the elderly cannot get much in the way of shoppers and thus their presence, as disruption, is less likely to be an issue requiring action on the part of mall management.

79   For the teens, even the security guards who keep them under surveillance can easily be fooled by a simple change of hair style or jacket. The boisterous teen who is ejected from the mall easily "slips out" of his or her public identity and is back the next day or week, a unique *person* returning to his or her community, invisible in return even to the watching security guards.

80   Third, as alluded to in point one above, the mall is centrally located, easy to get to, safe and climate controlled. The amenities that exist there for the shoppers—restaurants, rest rooms, benches and seats—can also be used by the non-shopper, as long as mall management does not actively discourage such usage.

81   Fourth, for the elderly, discouragement could be dangerous, in a public relations sense. Conversely, the elderly can be used to advantage to further the mall's illusion of community by publicizing their support of community

programs such as that of walking-for-health. For the teens, many of them work in the fast food stores and do leave money in the video arcade and the record stores. Therefore they do have some economic links to some of the businesses operating in the mall. The mall rats and bunnies also provide a visually exciting and socially validating backdrop for these youth oriented businesses, for other youths and young adults who come to shop.

82   Finally, these communities seem, in general, to police themselves quite well. They are aware of their status in the eyes of mall management and attempt, each in their own distinctive way, to keep a low enough profile so their presence is tolerated.[13]

83   Ironically, then, and for these reasons, deep within the impersonal and concrete structure of the mall, cultural chains of belonging seem to have been forged. The sense of community, to such an extent denied these groupings of the elderly and the young, in the larger society, is being created and shared in the mall, while shoppers rush blindly past under lights of cold neon, across the polished sheen of endless tiled floors.

Notes

1. Jessie Bernard, *The Sociology of Community* (Glenview, Ill: Scott, Foresman, 1973), p. 3.

2. Thomas Bender, *Community and Social Change in America* (Baltimore: Johns Hopkins University Press, 1978), p. 7.

3. Chain Store Age Executive, "Why They Shop Some Centers," 1987, 54, 33.

4. Interview with mall marketing director, 1986.

5. The author served as Director of Research for this study. Interviews quoted in this paper were conducted by himself, SALT staff members Pamela Wood and Hugh French, and students Brett Jenks, Edite Pedrosa, Amy Rowe, Julie Maurer, Peter Lancia, Harry Brown, Amy Schnerr and Lou Brown. Original tapes and transcripts are on file at SALT CENTER, Kennebunkport, ME 04609.

6. Jerry Jacobs, *The Mall: An Attempted Escape From Every Day Life* (Prospect Heights, Ill: Waveland Press, 1984), pp. 27–32.

7. Robert Atchley, *Social Forces and Aging* (Belmont, CA: Wadsworth, 1985), pp. 56–58.

8. Bob Greene, "Fifteen: Young Men Cruising Shopping Malls," *Esquire,* 1982, 98, pp. 17–18; Kowinski, *op. cit.,* pp. 68–73.

9. Martin Millison, *Teenage Behavior In Shopping Centers,* International Council of Shopping Centers, 1976, p. 11.

10. Peggy Eastman, "Elders Under Siege," *Psychology Today,* 1984, January, p. 30.

11. Richard Flacks, *Youth and Social Change* (Chicago: Markham, 1971), p. 17.

12. *loc. cit.,* p. 223.

13. This includes relations between the two groups. The elderly mainly frequent the old wing of the mall, while the teens frequent the new wing. The elderly arrive very early and usually leave by late afternoon. The teens usually arrive in mid to late afternoon and stay until the mall closes.

Review Questions

1. In what sense have modern malls become "civic centers"?

2. What are the differences between "the community" and "community," according to Lewis? Why does he introduce this distinction early in the article?

3. What conditions at malls inhibit the growth of community?

4. For what reasons do elders come to the mall? How does mall management react to their presence?

5. Why do teenagers visit the mall?

6. What characteristics do the teenage community and the elderly community share when at the mall?

7. In what sense is the world of the mall a "shared illusion," according to Lewis?

8. What five reasons does Lewis give for teens and elders seeking out the mall as a place to build their communities?

Discussion and Writing Suggestions

1. Lewis quotes a mall manager saying: "Having the *perception* of a community feeling does not mean that it actually exists. It is not the same thing." Why would mall managers take the trouble to create an illusion that malls encourage community ties?

2. Why is it "ironic," according the Lewis, that malls have become the meeting place for actual communities?

3. In shopping malls you have visited, what evidence do you find of an elder's community similar to the one Lewis describes?

4. Read the account of Pat, a mall regular (paragraphs 20–29). What is your response to Pat's story?

5. Reread paragraphs 43–57. Based on your experience, how accurate is Lewis's description of what teenagers do at the mall?

6. One of the key investigative tools for a sociologist like Lewis is the personal interview. Reread those portions of the article devoted to interviews of the elderly and teenagers. How important are these interviews to the success of Lewis's argument? What, in your view, do they add to the selection?

7. Write several paragraphs describing one of your experiences as a "mall rat" or "mall bunny." Include an account of the teenagers who gather at the mall as well as a description of the mall itself (for example, discuss its location, its appearance, the type of customers it attracts). In a final paragraph describe the extent to which you think the people you have described form a community.

Mallaise: How to Know If You Have It
William Kowinski

William Kowinski's The Malling of America: An Inside Look at the Great Consumer Paradise *(William Morrow, 1985) has become a classic in the literature on the cultural impact of shopping centers. The following selection, which forms a chapter in* Malling, *is representative of Kowinski's tone throughout: ironic, playful, and pointed in its critique of malls and their effects. "Mallaise" is his attempt to name the disease that some people feel on being absorbed by the totality of the mall's environment. Perhaps you will recognize one or more of the symptoms.*

1   Malls make some people sick. Literally, sometimes. They feel feverish, their eyes glaze, their stomachs tumble, they fall down, they throw up.

2   Some people are just annoyed by one or another aspect of a mall, or a non-specific quality of a particular mall, or malls in general. "That mall makes me *sick!*" they say. Or "I don't like malls—I *hate* them." Malls make people angry. Some of these people are shoppers, but some are people who work in malls or even own mall stores.

3   Malls affect people. They're designed to. But in some ways, either by their nature or by a side effect caused by their main ingredients, they do things to people that people are unaware of or don't understand, but if they knew or understood, they probably wouldn't like it.

4   There are other more obvious things that happen to people in malls that they don't or wouldn't like. Crime, for instance.

5   This section of *The Malling of America* is about some of the negative aspects of malls that affect people and that people perceive. Does the mall make you tired? Set your nerves on edge? Do you find it difficult to concentrate? Do you feel the absence of certain phenomena—weather, for example, or civil liberties? Do you sometimes wonder if you are really as safe as mall management would like you to believe?

6   If you're a parent, do you fear for your children's ability to survive outside comfort control because they spend so much time in the mall? And if you're an adolescent, do you feel your horizons becoming limited to a hundred chain store-outlets and three anchor department stores? Or are you worried that this is precisely the world your parents do live in, and where they want you always to remain?

7   These are some of the symptoms of mallaise. Perhaps you have one or two, or know someone who does, or perhaps you want to be prepared, just in case. Then perhaps you should read on.

8   I had my first attack of *mal de mall* in Columbia, Maryland. I was in a restaurant in the Columbia Mall having coffee. The attack was characterized by feverishness, sudden fatigue, and high anxiety, all recurring whenever I glanced out at the mall itself. The thought of going out there again made me sweat and swoon, and I had to fight the hallucinatory certainty that when I left the restaurant I would be in Greengate mall, or maybe Woodfield, or Tysons Corner. Or *all* of them.

9   *Mal de mall,* or mall sickness, is one of the classifications of mallaise, the general term for physical and psychological disturbances caused by mall contact. I know because I made them all up. Among the symptoms I have personally observed or heard about from their victims are these:

10   *Dismallcumbobulation:* "I don't like to go to malls because I always get lost," a woman told me, "and that's embarrassing. I feel stupid. It makes me mad." The hyped-up overabundance of similar products plus the bland sameness of many mall environments make people feel lost even when they aren't. Even familiar malls relocate stores and reconfigure themselves, which adds to the feeling of a continuous featureless space. And the similarity of one mall to another is disorienting. You walk out of the Stuft Potato and you not only don't remember which way your car is, you might not remember what mall this is. There are other kinds of dismallcumbobulation: the loss of a sense of time as well as place, and forgetting one's purpose in coming to the mall— all of which can lead to apathy and hopelessness, loss of consciousness, or fainting. Some victims recommend deep-breathing exercises every fifteen minutes while at the mall.

11   *Inability to Relate to Others:* "It's impossible to talk to someone when you're shopping at the mall," a friend told me, explaining why she prefers to shop alone. "I notice it at the mall all the time—you see two people together but they aren't really talking to each other. They're talking, but they're staring off in different directions, and pretty soon they just wander away from each other." Among the possible effects of this symptom are disenchantment and divorce.

12   *Plastiphobia,* or the fear of being enclosed in a cocoon of blandness. "Suddenly I just stood still and looked around," a young man said. "I saw all the people and what we were all doing there, what we were spending our day doing, and I suddenly just couldn't wait to get out. I was in a plastic place with plastic people buying plastic products with plastic charge cards. I had to escape." Sometimes this reaction is accompanied by severe anxiety, alienation from the human race, and in at least one very severe case I know of, by all the usual manifestations of a drug overdose.

13   All of these, and their variations, are unfortunate side effects (or perhaps just extreme cases) of the main psychological effects that the mall intends. Excitement may become overstimulation; relaxation may drift into confusion and torpor. The combination is what I call the Zombie Effect.

14   There is, in fact, a fine line between the ideal mall shopper and the dismayed mall shopper, between mall bliss and mallaise, between the captivated shopper and the Zombie Effect. The best description of the Zombie Effect I've heard was Barbara Lambert's, which she imparted while we toured the malls of Chicagoland.

15   It hits you, Barbara said, when you're standing there naked, looking in the mirror of the dressing room. Your clothes are in a pile on the floor or draped over a chair. Maybe it's just a little cubicle with a curtain, and you can still hear the hum and buzz of the mall and the tiny timbres of Muzak. You're about to try something on, in an effortless repetition of what you've been doing since you came to the mall. And suddenly you realize *you've been here all day.* Time has in fact been passing while you've been gliding through store after store in

a tender fuzz of soft lights and soft music. The plash of fountains, the glow of people, but almost no intrusive sound has broken your floating—no telephone, no demands, nothing to dodge or particularly watch out for. Just a gentle visual parade of clothes, fabric tags, and washing instructions. Racks, displays, cosmetics, brisk signs, flowing greenery, and spasms of color in the dream light. An ice-cream cone, a cup of coffee. Other figures have glided by: walking models of the mall's products, or walking models of the weird. An old man who reminds you of your grandfather, sitting on a blond-wood bench under a potted palm. A woman who may or may not have been your best friend's other best friend in high school, striding by on strange shoes—or maybe that's a new style and yours are strange? You're looking at your naked image in a bare little room, and a little breeze touches you. Whatever you actually came here for is in the distant past. You've been floating here . . . for hours.

16   But that's the whole idea of this psychological structure: to turn off your mind and let you float; to create a direct and unfettered connection between eyeing and buying; and the more you do, the easier it becomes. Malls make for great eye/hand-on-credit-card co-ordination.

17   The way it's done is with a combination of peacefulness and stimulation. The environment bathes you in sweet neutrality with soft light, candied music, and all the amenities that reassure and please without grabbing too much individual attention. At the same time, the stores and products dance for you with friendly smiles and colorful costumes. The sheer number of products and experiences you pay for and their apparent variety are in themselves factors that excite and focus.

18   Once again, it's all a lot like television. TV lulls and stimulates simultaneously. The medium itself is familiar and comfortable and friendly; the programs can be interesting but it is not really by accident that they are not as compact, colorful, dramatic, or insistent as the commercials. Watching television we are everywhere and nowhere in particular, just as at the mall. Suddenly you might realize that you've been watching it all day, just floating for hours. And if you look at people watching television—especially their eyes—they look pretty much like mall shoppers: the Zombie Effect.

19   But these effects are all supposed to be pleasant and unconscious. When either the lulling or stimulating quality—or especially the combination and conflict between them—is strongly felt, then it's no longer pleasant. Overstimulation causes anxiety, and sometimes an intense focus on heavy-duty, no-nonsense, get-out-of-my-way shopping, or else a frenzied need to get out of there, fast and forever. The lulling and sense deprivation cause listlessness and confusion, and occasionally rebellion at being Muzaked into implacable mushy madness. The conflict of both going on at the same time can cause the sense of dislocation and exhaustion that is the clearest indicator of the Zombie Effect. The victim shuffles and mumbles, is distant or unduly preoccupied, doesn't listen, acts automatically, and not only can't remember where the car is parked but often doesn't care.

20   There are ancilliary symptoms and causes as well: headaches caused by guilt at buying too much; depression at not being able to buy everything; the walking emptiness caused by consistently emphasized, endless greed.

21   The cure for all forms of mallaise is theoretically simple: The victim leaves the mall. There are no laws requiring people to stay in the mall, or even to go there in the first place. It isn't anyone's civic, moral, spiritual, or intellectual duty. The mall may be the best place—or even the only place—to shop for certain products, but that doesn't mean the shopper has to stay there for hours. Nevertheless, it isn't always easy to leave.

22   For that is another aspect of the Zombie Effect: Victims stay for no good or apparent reason, and even beyond their conscious desire to be there. Shoppers mallinger partly because of the mall's psychological apparatus, its implicit promise of safety, sanctuary, and salvation. Of Nirvana! The Crystal City! A New Heaven on a New Earth! The mall hasn't become the most successful artificial environment in America for nothing.

23   With its real walls and psychological illusions, the mall protects against so many hazards and uncertainties that the mallaise sufferer may well mallinger a little longer to ponder the consequences of walking out. Such a person may fear trading the maladies of the Zombie Effect for the perils of mall withdrawal, which is characterized by shaking in downtown areas, fear of crossing streets, inordinate terror in the presence of rain or sunshine, confusion when actual travel is required between purchases, and the feeling of estrangement when wearing a coat.

24   I wish I could say that medical science is on top of this new set of malladies, but the truth is that it is scandalously behind the times. Right now, there may be many thousands of Zombie Effect sufferers, untreated and undiagnosed. If you find this hard to believe—well, have you been to the mall lately?

25   There is one more form of mallaise that is especially frustrating because it is not so simply cured, even theoretically. It is the state of being malcontented with what the mall offers and how it offers it. Sufferers will rail on about the same limited clothing styles reproduced in a hundred mall shops, or the same five movies shown in two dozen mall theaters—the only cinemas around. They will complain endlessly about fast-print outlets masquerading as bookstores, where clerks don't know anything more about books than what appears on the computer stock list. They will raise angry fists against the screening boxes calling themselves cinemas, with their dark and blurry unwatchable images on the screen, and cold and tinny sound.

26   These unfortunate mallcontents really have a problem, because in many places they don't have any alternative: If they want to shop for clothes, see a first-run movie, buy a new book or record, it's the mall or nothing.

27   They flail away at the promises the mall implies but does not keep. They are in a sense prisoners of the mall, if only because the mall's predominance has destroyed the alternatives they miss, even the imaginary ones.

Discussion and Writing Suggestions

1. At what point in this selection did you realize that Kowinski has a sense of humor? Work through the piece and mark what in your view are the funniest lines.

2. Through humor, Kowinski makes a number of penetrating observations about mall culture. Of the various maladies he catalogs (with tongue in cheek), which one seems the most insightful? Why?

3. Have you observed in yourself, a friend, or family member any symptoms of *mal de mall?* Describe your experience.

4. Kowinski compares mall shopping to television watching (see paragraph 18). Is the comparison apt, in your view?

5. In paragraph 16, Kowinski writes that the "whole idea of [the mall's] psychological structure [is] to turn off your mind and let you float; to create a direct and unfettered connection between eyeing and buying." Have you ever noticed that malls are designed to have a "psychological structure"? Explain.

6. In introducing the Zombie Effect (see paragraph 18), Kowinski writes: "Watching television we are everywhere and nowhere in particular, just as at the mall." Do you agree?

7. Kowinski gives the feeling of being lost in a mall a funny name: *dismallcumbobulation.* But he is making a serious point in noting the essential sameness of malls. Have you noticed how one mall often looks like others—with the same chain stores and repeating architectural features? One could shop at a mall in Louisville or in Buffalo and not be able to tell them apart. How do you respond to these similarities? Have you ever been dismallcumbobulated?

8. In paragraph 25, Kowinski may come closest to expressing his underlying view of malls than at any other point in the selection. Reread the paragraph and summarize what you take to be his general attitude toward malls.

SYNTHESIS ACTIVITIES

1. In an explanatory paper that draws on several selections in this chapter, explain to a time traveler from the sixteenth century, or a visitor from the remotest regions on present-day Earth, the phenomenon of shopping malls. Answer basic questions, such as: What is a mall? When did malls appear? Why? How are malls organized and managed? Discuss important factors that gave rise to malls: weather; transportation (development of cars and highways); and the growth of suburbs. Finally, without taking sides, explain the controversies sparked by malls.

2. In an exploratory paper, one in which you speculate more than argue, attempt to define the deep-seated appeal that shopping centers hold for many people. The selections by Zepp and Francaviglia should be helpful. In paragraph 44, Zepp suggests that we feel a nostalgia in shopping malls—a longing for home, for a simplified version of the world. In writing about Main Street USA (which

became a model design for malls), Francaviglia describes how Walt Disney re-created Main Street as it should have been, as simpler and more ordered than Main Streets actually were. Both authors attempt to explain the attraction of shopping malls. Working with these and one or two other authors in this chapter, explore the psychological (and if Zepp is to be believed, even spiritual) changes that can come over shoppers as they enter a mall.

3. James Farrell (paragraph 14) writes: "Like churches, [malls] are places where we decide what is ultimately valuable and how we will value it." Ira Zepp devotes considerable effort to understanding malls as sacred spaces. Working with these two authors and any others in the chapter who can contribute to the discussion, write an argument on the spiritual or religious dimensions of shopping malls. In this argument, you could discount the connection entirely, accept it, or accept it in part.

4. Lizabeth Cohen argues that malls built in the suburbs effectively shut out people who lived in the city and who could not afford a car—a development Cohen regards as a new expression of an old problem: racial and economic segregation. In your experience with shopping malls, what evidence do you find of either or both types of segregation? In developing a response, draw on the selections by Farrell (and his notion that malls tell "stories"); and Paquet (with her history of shopping centers in the eighteenth and nineteenth centuries appealing to wealthy clientele). Descriptions of your own experiences in malls could figure heavily into your paper.

5. Richard Francaviglia writes that "Sociologists have long known that people visit shopping centers for far more than commercial reasons" (paragraph 11). In a paper that draws on the work of Francaviglia, Gruen, Zepp, and Lewis as well as on your own experience, explain these noncommercial reasons for going to the mall.

6. Laura Paquet begins her selection by quoting an author who compares the modern mall to a fascistic medieval city-state. Francaviglia characterizes mall management as "autocratic." In a paper that draws on these two authors and also on Cohen and Guterson, answer this question: For customers, store owners, and mall management, what is gained and what is lost in rigorously controlling activities at the mall? Note that Victor Gruen, writing in 1960, argued (in paragraph 27) that carefully planning and controlling the retail space need *not* result in "authoritarianism, regimentation, or in the suppression of individualism."

7. Several authors in this chapter write on the layout of malls. Paquet relates the experience of getting lost. Francaviglia writes on the importance of intersections. Zepp writes about the significance of key design elements (such as circles). For Guterson, the mall feels like a giant prison. Given the work of these authors and

your experience at malls, write a paper examining the importance of mall design.

8. Use William Kowinski's concept of "mallaise" to analyze one or more of your visits to a mall. As independent evidence for mallaise, you might refer to the selections by Guterson (especially paragraph 5) and Paquet (especially paragraphs 59–82). The test of your analysis will be how successfully Kowinski's vocabulary helps you to see your shopping experience(s) in new and interesting ways.

9. Gruen (paragraphs 1–5) and Guterson (paragraphs 6, 16–18) fondly recall the bazaars and market places of old in which people came not only to buy but also to engage in the give and take of community life. Guterson (see especially paragraph 31) and Lewis (see paragraphs 1–7), particularly, claim that authentic community is difficult to find in modern shopping centers. If one finds community at all, it exists in spite of, not because of, management's efforts. What is your sense of shopping malls as a center of community life? Drawing on the views of authors in this chapter, develop your answer into an argument.

10. Guterson, Kowinski, Cohen, Lewis, and Paquet have found much to be critical of in shopping malls. By contrast, Farrell, Zepp, Francaviglia, and Gruen find much to recommend in malls. Given your experiences in malls, with which set of authors do you tend to agree? Do malls please you more than they disturb you, or vice versa? Draw on the authors in this chapter as you develop your answer in an argument.

11. In *Shopping Towns USA*, Victor Gruen envisioned shopping centers becoming the hub of suburban life. Centers would combine commercial space with public, civic space into "crystallization points" that would free suburbanites from traveling to the city to make major purchases. Moreover, shopping centers with their tightly controlled programs for design and management would make rational the previously haphazard method of locating stores in suburbia. Gruen did not live to see his vision fulfilled. Was his plan naive? Do you think the community function of shopping centers could coexist with the commercial function? Is there still hope for such a combination, or is the mall's effort best left to making money?

12. In the introduction to this chapter you will find a block quotation from James J. Farrell's book, *One Nation Under Goods*. Farrell claims that shopping centers are places where the culture answers fundamental questions about itself, such as: What does it mean to be human? What are people for? Reread the full list of questions, select *one*, and write a synthesis in which you argue that it is possible, or impossible, to answer such a question by studying shopping centers. In addition to using Farrell's selection, you might draw on the work of Paquet, Francaviglia, Gruen, Lewis, and Cohen.

13. Relate an experience you've had in a shopping center and analyze it in light of any of the reading selections in this chapter. How can the insights of one (or more) of the chapter's authors help you to understand your experience?

RESEARCH ACTIVITIES

1. Devote some time to viewing movies that are set, at least partially, in malls: You might consider the horror classic, George Romero's *Dawn of the Dead* (a sequel to *Night of the Living Dead*), *Mall Rats, Scenes from a Mall,* and *Fast Times at Ridgemont High.* Watch one or more of the movies several times, and then write a paper in which you "read" the director's vision of modern American life as it is expressed in shopping malls. As part of your research, you might draw on movie reviews. More ambitious projects will involve a comparative treatment of two or more movies.

2. Investigate and report on the types of data that social scientists collect in their efforts to help store owners boost sales. You might begin with a book like *Why We Buy: The Science of Shopping,* in which Paco Underhill (an anthropologist) relates how he conducts field studies of shoppers in the act of shopping. Others who investigate the purchasing habits of shoppers include sociologists, psychologists, and economists. The general topic, the "science of shopping," is very broad, and you will want to narrow the focus. Some possibilities: the design of store displays, the training of sales staff, the choice of background music, or the routing of customers through a retail space. This assignment stresses information, so you will be writing an explanatory synthesis.

3. Read William Kowinski's *Malling of America,* from which one selection in this chapter ("Mallaise") was excerpted. *Malling* has become something of a classic. After you read it, gather book reviews from around the country (check the *Book Review Digest*) and report on the book's reception.

4. Identify one shopping mall project about which you would like to learn more. The project may be a national destination mall, like the Mall of America, or a regional mall near your home. Based on newspaper and magazine articles, trace for readers the mall's progress from the permit process to the opening. How involved was the community in the process? Were there protests? Did the town or city government provide incentives for mall development? Did the developers rely on union labor? These are just of a few of the many questions you might explore in your research. Your goal is to tell the mall's story, from conception to design to building to occupancy.

5. Research the phenomenon of "dead" or "ghost" malls: facilities that are twenty years or older that have been left vacant. What are the

forces that drive malls to failure? (Possibilities: population trends; an anchor store's not renewing its lease; competition from new or neighboring malls.) How great a problem are vacant malls? How have communities repurposed them? In writing your paper, gather enough research to point out broad, industrywide trends and then, as a case study, illustrate these trends by relating the demise of a *particular* shopping mall.

6. Choose a shopping mall to visit three or four times over the course of several weeks. On your first visit, spend one hour watching people shop, and take notes. Later, review your notes and decide on a particular question you would like to explore on return visits. Pose that question as precisely as possible: it may concern a particular population at the mall (seniors, mothers with kids, fathers with kids, couples, teens, etc); a particular aspect of mall management (perhaps security, janitorial, or food services); mall architecture; traffic flow. Any of the readings in this chapter will help you to identify a particular question to pursue. Having framed the question, return to the mall for a series of one-hour visits in which you make and record observations. (Avoid shopping! Your focus is on gathering information.) Write a paper in which you report on your research. Include a description of the mall studied, a context for your question (a discussion of why the question is interesting), data that you recorded (albeit informally), and a discussion of what you discovered.

7. Research one of the predecessors of the modern mall, taking as your starting point the article in this chapter by Laura Paquet. Paquet discusses the Greek stoa, the Roman Forum, the Middle Eastern bazaar or souk, the Grand Bazaar of Constantinople, the Royal Exchange (London), the Palais Royal (Paris), or the arcades of London or Milan. The research paper that you write will be explanatory in nature. Assume that your audience is familiar with shopping malls but unfamiliar with the shopping venues throughout history that preceded the mall.

8. Reread paragraphs 17–23 in Lizabeth Cohen's article, "From Town Center to Shopping Center," and select for further research one of the Supreme Court cases she discusses concerning the limits to free speech in privately owned shopping centers. Locate the Supreme Court opinion and summarize it. Re-create for readers the conflict that led to the court case, and discuss (after your summary) the implications of the Court's decision on future protests at shopping centers. You might try conducting your research on the Internet, particularly if you have access to the LexisNexis database. Select "Federal Case Law" and, within this area, "Supreme Court" cases. Choose "Guided Search," as opposed to "Basic Search," so that you can use more keywords and combinations of keywords. Try such keywords as "free speech" OR "freedom of speech" AND "mall"

OR "privately owned shopping center*" and other such terms; and search for "all available dates." If you have the citation number for a case (like "485 U.S. 112"), you can directly input the citation (without the need for keywords) to retrieve the case.

9. Research differences in shopping patterns between men and women. You might focus on one or more of the following questions: Do men and women shop with different expectations about the speed of making purchases? Do either tend to shop for the sake of (that is, the pleasure of) shopping? Do women "look" more than men? Do either tend to regard shopping more as a social as opposed to functional, or necessary, activity? Do men more than women tend to be impulse shoppers? Locate carefully controlled studies when conducting your research.

Weight Debate

You may have heard of (or may be fighting!) the "Freshman 15"—the extra weight that first-year students gain when they settle down to endless helpings of high-calorie cafeteria food. More calories in than out (no time for exercise with all that studying—right?) is the basic equation for weight gain. And in record numbers, Americans—college students included—are packing on the pounds. The most recent figures indicate that 64 percent of American adults are overweight or obese and that 13 percent of children are overweight. By 2005, the poor diet and sedentary lifestyles associated with obesity may lead to more preventable deaths than tobacco use, according to one recently published study. At the same time that the majority of Americans are gaining unprecedented amounts of weight, an alarmingly high number of girls and young women are voluntarily starving themselves (sometimes to death) in an effort to achieve an idealized image of slenderness promoted by the media. Too many pounds and too few: America has a weight problem.

Open most newspapers or magazines and the chances are excellent that you will find advertisements featuring images of underweight models. The entertainment and advertising industries bombard us with streams of fit, toned actors who remind us, whether we agree or not, that thin is in. Whole industries have emerged to help us achieve this lean and hungry look, but recent statistics show that fewer and fewer of us are succeeding.

According to the Centers for Disease Control and the *Journal of the American Medical Association,* the number of Americans who are overweight or obese has reached epidemic proportions.* One in two American adults is overweight; one in five is obese. In this country we spend $75 billion annually in obesity-related medical expenses and lose another $42 billion in diminished productivity. Add to these amounts the $33 billion Americans spend trying to *lose* weight each year, and the magnitude of the problem begins to take shape. Lest you think being overweight or obese poses a problem only to those immediately concerned, think again: Medicaid and Medicare, funded by *your* tax dollars, paid $39 billion dollars in 2003 for people suffering from obesity-related illnesses: diabetes, heart disease, certain cancers, and gallbladder disease. That's federal money *not* spent on providing student loans, for instance.

Monetary losses associated with weight gain represent only the measurable portion of the problem. In a culture infatuated with youthful athleticism, the obese too often suffer from profound lack of self-esteem as friends, family, coworkers, and strangers unfairly equate being fat with flaws of character. And it is not as if the overweight and obese don't try to lose weight. Dieting is one of America's urgent pastimes: at any given moment, 29 percent of men and 44 percent of American

---

* In 2001, the U.S. Surgeon General published a "Call to Action to Prevent and Decrease Overweight and Obesity." You can find the full report along with comprehensive statistics on the state of America's weight at <http://www.surgeongeneral.gov/topics/obesity/>.

women are trying to lose weight. But diets—95 percent of them—do *not* work, according to recent studies; and so those who have every intention of thinning down find themselves doomed to a cycle of losing weight and, within months or a few years, gaining all or most of it back. At the other end of the scale, literally and figuratively, the psychological costs of monitoring one's weight are equally overwhelming to the nation's 7 to 10 million anorexics and bulimics. For well over a decade, physicians and therapists have sought to help their patients get the nutrition they need to thrive, but their conditions remain stubbornly resistant to change.

On the one hand, then, our culture pressures us to be thin, exacting a heavy price in self-esteem if we are not. On the other, competitive forces have led the food industry to invest millions in manipulating the flavors and textures of their goods so that we will buy and eat more. Couple this effort with clever advertising campaigns, super-sized portions, and bright packaging, and one wonders why every American isn't either overweight or terrified to eat anything at all.* Our culture makes us the object of a strange tug-of-war, urging us to consume while at the same time warning us to show no visible signs of consumption. As a result, some choose self-starvation; record numbers move in the other direction, eating all that good food even as they look miserably each morning at the bathroom scale. Whether too fat or too thin, at the end of the day Americans think constantly, even obsessively, about weight.

This chapter gathers some provocative articles and essays on being overweight and obese—that is, on being *fat.* We use this politically incorrect word neutrally, not pejoratively, following the usage of several authors whose work appears in the pages that follow.† The readings divide into two sections, the first a gathering of facts and figures, the second a series of commentaries. We open with a February 2004 cover story, "Rethinking Weight," from *U.S. News and World Report* in which senior writer Amanda Spake presents an overview of America's weight debate, calling our attention particularly to a question occupying many researchers: Should we consider obesity a disease, as we do alcoholism? (In July 2004, Medicare announced that it would cover the expenses related to obesity treatments. These include stomach surgery, diet programs, and behavioral and psychological counseling.) Following this overview, you will find an editorial by physicians Jeffrey P. Koplan and William H. Dietz from the the *Journal of the American Medical Association,* which begins with the claim that "Obesity is epidemic in the United States." Next we offer two tables summarizing data from a recent study by the Centers for Disease Control and Prevention on the prevalence of obesity among U.S. adults.

The second part of the chapter consists of readings that comment on our culture's preoccupation with thinness. We begin with an op-ed piece for the

---

* In early 2004, McDonald's decided to stop offering a "Supersize" option at its restaurants.

† The literature on anorexia nervosa and bulimia is so extensive that we could not represent it with any reasonably comprehensive coverage here. If you have an interest in these subjects, you will find many books and articles readily available in community as well as academic libraries, and also on the Web.

Los Angeles Times by Greg Crister, who argues that in order to reduce weight-related problems in this country we should stigmatize the behavior of unhealthy overeating, teaching children (especially) that "[e]ating too much food is a bad thing." Next comes a policy statement from the National Association to Advance Fat Acceptance (NAAFA) on the subject of "Dieting and the Diet Industry." Mary Ray Worley, a NAAFA member, writes of the debilitating self-hatred among fat people and of her life-changing decision to join "a growing number of people [who] believe it's possible to be happy with your body even if it happens to be fat." Roberta Seid follows with "Too 'Close to the Bone': The Historical Context for Women's Obsession with Slenderness." In a startlingly original critique, Seid examines the spiritual dimensions of our obsession with thinness as well as the historical changes that led to a new—and thinner—body ideal. Next, Hillel Schwartz argues that our culture is caught in the grip of a "despotism of slenderness." He imagines a fat "utopia" in which fat people accept themselves and are accepted by the culture at large. In an editorial that appeared in the journal *Science*, Marion Nestle, a professor in the Department of Nutrition and Food Studies at New York University, then offers insights into the politics of obesity. We conclude the chapter with a selection by Atul Gawande, writing in the *New Yorker*. A surgeon who assisted on a gastric-bypass, Gawande tells the story of Vincent Caselli, a Boston-area contractor whose efforts to lose weight proved so futile that he submitted to an increasingly popular surgical procedure that reduced his stomach to a one-ounce-sized pouch.

A note on statistics: Monthly, it seems, researchers are updating data on the incidence of overweight and obesity, and you will find discrepancies among articles on such basic information as the percentage of the U.S. adult population that is overweight or obese (the correct number, as of March 2004, is 64 percent). When citing statistics in your work, use those found in the most recent of this chapter's articles: the selection from *U.S. News and World Report* (February 2004) and the tables from the Centers for Disease Control (November 2003). If you can find even more current data (check the CDC website, <www.cdc.gov>, and type "obesity statistics" into the search box), so much the better. Changing statistics aside, the arguments you will find in this chapter on how we should be thinking about America's weight problems remain current.

Rethinking Weight
Amanda Spake

One sure sign that the obesity epidemic has caught the nation's attention is the increased number of articles devoted to the subject in the popular press. The following selection appeared as a cover story in the 9 February 2004 edition of U.S. News and World Report. *Amanda Spake is a senior writer for the magazine and has served both as a contributor to* Salon.com *and as an editor to the* Washington Post *magazine and* Mother Jones. *In this piece, Spake directs our attention to a central debate among obesity researchers: whether or not to classify obesity as a disease (just as alcoholism is classified as a disease). The*

*ultimate positions of the government and insurance companies in this debate will deter-
mine for tens of millions the levels of support they will receive in fighting to achieve a
healthy weight.*

1   Maria Pfisterer has never in her life been skinny. The Arlington, Texas, mother of
three was at her slimmest at age 18, when she married Fred, an Air Force
sergeant. But she was plump, not seriously fat. She first became seriously overweight at age 21, when she gained about 70 pounds during her first pregnancy. By the time she delivered her daughter Jordan, now 14, she was carrying
over 200 pounds on her 5-foot, 2-inch frame.

2   Over the past 14 years, Pfisterer has tried every weight-loss strategy imaginable: She has taken the (now banned) appetite-suppressing drug combo fen-
phen (she lost 60 pounds only to regain it during her second pregnancy). She
went on a doctor-prescribed and -supervised low-calorie diet (she lost 10 pounds
but regained it). She has been enrolled in Jenny Craig, Weight Watchers, Curves,
and a variety of quick-weight-loss fads. All resulted in a little lost and more
regained. She has taken antidepressants, reputed to have weight loss as a side
effect. They didn't for her. She would love to get into one of those intensive medical weight-loss programs, but she can't afford the $4,000-plus price tag. So she
does what she can. "If I lose weight, it seems like I always go back up to that same
197 to 202 range," she says. "I just don't know how to keep it off."

3   Pfisterer isn't alone. A majority of Americans—now 64 percent—are overweight or obese and struggling to conquer their expanding waistlines before
their fat overtakes their health and makes them sick or kills them. At the heart
of this obesity epidemic is a debate over whether obesity is a biological "disease" and should be treated like any other life-threatening illness—cancer, heart
disease—or whether it is simply a risk factor for those killers. The stakes are high
because the answer may determine who gets treated for obesity, what treatments are available, who pays for treatment, and, ultimately, who stays healthy.

4   New understandings of the biology of obesity are driving the debate. "I think
there's enough data now relating to mechanisms of food intake regulation that
suggest obesity is a biologically determined process," says Xavier Pi-Sunyer,
director of the Obesity Research Center at St. Luke's-Roosevelt Hospital in New
York City. And many national and international health organizations—from the
National Institutes of Health (NIH) to the World Health Organization—agree. The
WHO has listed obesity as a disease in its International Classification of Diseases
since 1979. In fact, the organization recently called on member states to adopt
programs to encourage a reduction of fat and sugar in the global diet. The recommendation did not sit well with the U.S. food industry or with some within
the Bush administration, who still maintain the obesity epidemic can be
reversed by individuals taking more personal responsibility and making better
lifestyle choices. Many health insurers agree. "For a wide number of people in
this country the question is: How do you motivate people to make changes in
diet and increase physical activity?" says Susan Pisano of the Health Insurance
Association of America.

5   The reason governments, insurance companies, and others still take such
positions, says Pi-Sunyer, is that "they are worried they will have to reimburse
doctors and patients for treatment. And now, you have such a huge number

of people needing treatment." On any given day, about 29 percent of men and 44 percent of women are trying to lose weight, and presumably a large percentage of those would love to be offered medically supervised treatment if it were covered in their health insurance plan.

6   Instead, they pay out of pocket for a $33 billion commercial diet industry—and keep getting fatter. The number of people who are severely obese—that is, those with a body mass index of 40 or above or who are more than 100 pounds overweight—is growing two times as fast as is obesity generally. From 1986 to 2000, the prevalence of Americans reporting a BMI of 40 or above quadrupled, from about 1 in 200 adults to 1 in 50. People who are severely obese generally have more weight-related illnesses and require more expensive treatments than do those who are merely "too fat."

7   **Fat's High Price** A new study by RTI International and the Centers for Disease Control and Prevention, published this month in the journal *Obesity Research,* shows that the nation is spending about $75 billion a year on weight-related disease. Type II diabetes, heart disease, hypertension, high cholesterol, gallbladder disease, osteoarthritis merely top the list. Almost 80 percent of obese adults have one of these conditions, and nearly 40 percent have two or more.

8   Healthcare costs for illnesses resulting from obesity now exceed those related to both smoking and problem drinking. About 325,000 deaths a year are attributed to obesity. The trend lines are only expected to get worse, since childhood obesity is also increasing rapidly.

9   Researchers are encouraged by the stance taken by the WHO and NIH, as well as the American Medical Association, the National Academy of Sciences, and the CDC. Says Yale psychologist Kelly Brownell: "The ramifications could be enormous—for opening up better treatments, and to some extent for social attitudes toward people with this problem. When alcoholism was declared a disease, it changed attitudes and reduced the stigma of blame."

10   And to be sure, there is no shortage of stigma and blame when it comes to obesity. Weight discrimination dates back to the early Christian church, which included "gluttony" as one of the seven deadly sins. Obesity was viewed as the outward manifestation of the "sin" of overindulgence. Most overweight adults have suffered ridicule, self-consciousness, or depression, particularly if they were obese as children or adolescents. Severely obese patients frequently report workplace discrimination. One woman told researchers: "They put my desk in the back office where no one could see me."

11   Prejudice against the obese stems from the widely held belief that getting fat—and certainly staying fat—results from a failure of willpower, a condition that could be remedied if obese people simply made a personal choice to eat less. But to most obesity experts this notion of personal choice is downright nutty. "Who would choose to be obese?" asks Rudolph Leibel, a Columbia University geneticist and a noted obesity researcher. "Telling someone they've decided to become obese is like saying, 'You've decided to give yourself a brain tumor.'"

12   Increasingly, researchers are demonstrating that obesity is controlled by a powerful biological system of hormones, proteins, neurotransmitters, and genes that regulate fat storage and body weight and tell the brain when, what, and how much to eat. "This is not debatable," says Louis Aronne, director of the

Comprehensive Weight Control Program at New York-Presbyterian Hospital and president-elect of the North American Association for the Study of Obesity.* "Once people gain weight, then these biological mechanisms, which we're beginning to understand, develop to prevent people from losing weight. It's not someone fighting 'willpower.' The body resists weight loss."

13   This wonder of natural chemical engineering evolved over centuries to protect humans against famine and assure reproduction of the species. "The idea that nature would leave this system to a matter of 'choice' is naive," says Arthur Frank, director of George Washington University's Weight Management Program. "Eating is largely driven by signals from fat tissue, from the gastrointestinal tract, the liver. All those organs are sending information to the brain to eat or not to eat. So, saying to an obese person who wants to lose weight, 'All you have to do is eat less,' is like saying to a person suffering from asthma, 'All you have to do is breathe better.' "

14   When Maria Pfisterer looks at her family, she sees her future—and it is frightening. Her father, a diabetic with congestive heart failure and hypertension, weighs nearly 400 pounds, and at age 60 he can scarcely move. Her older sister is also obese and suffers from hypertension. Both Maria and her sister worry they will eventually develop diabetes like their dad.

15   "My daughter Jordan is very heavy. She's struggling already with weight, and if she gets any more sedentary, I worry what will happen to her," says Pfisterer. "I'm trying to teach her to eat better and keep active. She's into dance, but she'll say, 'I'm the fattest kid there.' It breaks my heart."

16   Pfisterer herself says she does not eat a lot and is always on the go. "I don't eat half gallons of ice cream or bags of chips. But if I lose a little, I regain. I think genetics have a lot to do with it."

17 **Studies of Twins** Leibel, director of the division of molecular genetics at Columbia University College of Physicians and Surgeons, has spent a career documenting what Pfisterer knows intuitively. He says, "I believe there are strong genetic factors that determine susceptibility to obesity." Obesity does not result from a single gene, he explains, but rather a variety of genes that interact with environmental influences to increase one's chance of becoming obese. In studies of adult twins, who share many or all of the same genes, BMI,[†] body composition, and other measures of fatness appear to be 20 to 70 percent inherited.

18   Still, biology is not destiny. Overweight results from one thing: eating more food than one burns in physical activity. Genes simply facilitate becoming fat. "I think the primary problem is on the food intake side," Leibel adds. "There are multiple genes involved in that intake process, and there is good reason to believe that nature and evolution have selected for ingestion of large amounts of food."

19   But even when limitless food is available, not everyone gets fat. In a series of studies of adult twins in Quebec who ate a high-calorie diet designed to produce weight gain, results between sets of twins were vastly different. Some twin

---

* *The North American Association for the Study of Obesity* is later referred to by its acronym *NAASO*. See the organization's Web site at <http://www.naaso.org/>.

† *BMI*, or Body Mass Index, is a ratio of weight in relation to height and one measure of fatness. See page 478 for a BMI chart.

pairs gained three times as much weight and fat as others. "We know there are genetic factors," says Jules Hirsch, professor emeritus at Rockefeller University, "but obesity may be a multistep process." Hirsch says an overabundance of fat cells leading to obesity may be the result of gene-environmental interactions that occur in infancy or in utero, leading to vastly different responses to food in adulthood. The story of the offspring of women who survived the Dutch winter famine of 1944–45 may be a case in point. Babies born to women who suffered severe undernutrition early in their pregnancies tended to have more fat and become obese more readily as adults. But the offspring of women who were undernourished late in pregnancy tended to be leaner and have less fat as adults. Clearly, says Hirsch, there is a great deal more to learn about how obesity develops.

20   Even scientists who basically accept that obesity is a sophisticated biological problem feel that treatment has to consider the powerful roles of social organization and psychology. Take the case of the bottomless soup bowls.

21   University of Illinois nutrition and marketing professor Brian Wansink sat student volunteers in front of bowls of tomato soup in his lab and told them they were involved in a "taste test." Some of the students' bowls were normal. The others had bowls that automatically refilled from a hidden tube in the bottom. The students with the bottomless bowls ate an average of about 40 percent more soup before their brain told them they were full. "Biology has made us efficient at storing fat," says Wansink. "But obesity is not just biology; it's psychology. We're not good at tracking how much we eat. So we use cues—we eat until the plate is empty, or the soup is gone, or the TV show is over."

22   Indeed, research shows that people eat more in groups and with friends than they do when dining alone. Simply eating with one other person increases the average amount eaten at meals by 44 percent. Meals eaten with large groups of friends tend to be longer in duration and are as much as 75 percent bigger that those eaten alone. Eating with someone, suggests John DeCastro, the author of these studies, probably leads to relaxation and a "disinhibition of restraint."

23   Viewing obesity principally as a biological disease worries Wansink because he fears it will remove personal control and shift blame to someone else. But doctors who treat overweight patients say that thinking of obesity as a disease would simply make more treatment available. Most obesity programs rely on personal responsibility to put into action behavioral techniques designed to achieve greater control over biology. "Most of our treatment is still based on modifying choice," says GWU's Frank. "But underneath it all you've got to recognize why it is so difficult to eat less and lose weight. It doesn't make it easier, but it takes it out of the world of willful misconduct."

24 **Frauds** The biggest dilemma overweight people face is the world of largely mediocre, misleading, useless, or downright dangerous devices, diet programs, supplements, and drugs promoted to reduce fat. "The treatment of obesity is littered with a history of abuses," says NAASO's Aronne. "Every infomercial out there about weight is damaging people because it's giving them an unrealistic view of what can be done." Most university- and hospital-based weight-loss programs produce a 10 percent loss of body weight in six months. This is more than enough to reduce the incidence of Type II diabetes by 58 percent and

lower blood pressure in borderline hypertensives. But it is not enough to make a fat person as thin as a Hollywood celebrity. Coverage of obesity by health insurers might bring science and sanity to the chaos of weight loss, where, as Aronne puts it, "ethical treatments are competing in an unethical marketplace."

25   But clinicians acknowledge that weight-loss successes are modest. "To be frank, a lot of the treatment has not been very effective," says Pi-Sunyer. He points out that there are currently two drugs approved for long-term treatment of obesity, sibutramine and orlistat. Their effect is modest, and their cost is high, about $100 a month. "So for people to pay that amount, they would like to see more impressive results." Two drugs approved for treating epilepsy, topiramate and zonisamide, are being tested to treat obesity, but the jury is still out on them. "So that's an out for the insurers," says Pi-Sunyer. They can say, 'Unless you have a treatment that takes weight off and keeps it off, then why pay for it?' It would be a much stronger argument if we had a more proven treatment."

26   What's standing in the way? Basically funding for research. The American Obesity Association reports that NIH funding for research on obesity is less than one sixth that spent on AIDS. "Given the nature of the problem and the side effects," says Pi-Sunyer, "we're spending a pittance."

27   The health insurance industry argues that obesity treatments can't be covered because there is no evidence of effectiveness. Critics counter that the same argument could apply to a lot of complicated diseases. "We don't have a good way of treating Alzheimer's disease," says GWU's Frank, "and we don't have a particularly good way of treating AIDS either. We have a health insurance system based on illness, not treatment effectiveness. Why should obesity be the one disease that's subjected to this cost-effectiveness standard?"

28   About half of the $75 billion yearly price tag for obesity is covered by taxpayers in Medicare and Medicaid funds. These government health plans are debating right now whether the plans should cover obesity treatment. Currently, only in cases of severe obesity will government and some private insurers reimburse doctors for surgery to reduce girth.

29   But not always. Samantha Moore, a 26-year-old Maine woman who weighs nearly 400 pounds, was recently turned down a third time for gastric bypass surgery. Even though she has been dieting all her life, her insurer denied surgery because she has not made enough "medically supervised" attempts at weight loss. Does the insurer pay for medically supervised weight loss? "No," says Moore. "It's shocking to me that the insurance company keeps saying, essentially, 'You're not sick enough to get this surgery.' I think they're putting off a decision because if I wait much longer, I'll be too sick to get the surgery."

30 **Fat or Fit?** Not all scientists agree that labeling obesity "a disease" will improve the situation for people like Pfisterer or Moore. Stephen Ball, an exercise physiologist at the University of Missouri, says, "If we call obesity a disease, then anything that reduces one's fatness or lowers BMI would be a successful treatment, such as liposuction or a very low-calorie diet, where we know these are not healthy. By the same token, if you don't lose weight with an exercise program but your blood glucose becomes normal, cholesterol improves, then that could

be considered a failure, because it didn't reduce weight. Fitness is a more important indicator of health outcomes than fatness."

31 Indeed, Steven Blair at the Cooper Institute in Dallas has shown that cardio-vascular fitness as measured on a treadmill test is a better predictor of mortal-ity and illness than BMI. "I'm convinced . . . that people who are active or fit but in a high BMI group have lower death rates from all causes—cancer, heart dis-ease, diabetes—than the sedentary and unfit in the normal or lean BMI cate-gory. Even among women in our study with BMIs of 37, 20 percent did well enough on the treadmill test to be considered fit. We're obsessed with weight, but where has that gotten us?"

32 Ultimately, if better and more accessible treatments are not offered to obese Americans, the cost not only of obesity but of treatment and health insurance will escalate. The number of people undergoing surgery doubled from 2001 to 2003, in part because people are becoming more obese but also because many want medical help with weight loss and can't find any other treatment health insurers will cover.

33 Frustrated with her options and limited ability to pay for treatment, about six months ago Maria Pfisterer began to explore the possibility of gastric bypass surgery. She is not 100 pounds overweight, and her BMI is not over 40—gen-erally the criteria physicians use for evaluating candidates who would benefit from surgery. Gastric bypass surgery is an irreversible procedure in which the size of the stomach is reduced and the small intestine is bypassed to produce rapid weight loss in people whose fat is putting their lives in danger. Recovery is long, complication rates are high, side effects are bothersome, and it's major surgery—people die from it. But Pfisterer learned through obesity-help.com, a Web site offering advice to the obese, that her insurer might pay for surgery, given her family history.

34 "For people like me, who are considered on the low end for surgery, there are other options that might be better," she says. "But I can't take advantage of them unless health insurance starts to pay for them."

Review Questions

1. What debate lies at the center of the obesity epidemic, and what is its significance?

2. Why did the Bush administration object to the World Health Organization's classification of obesity as a "disease" and recom-mendation that people eat less fat and sugar?

3. What motivation do insurers have for *not* regarding obesity as a disease? Currently, what is the insurance industry's response to coverage for weight-loss treatments?

4. Identify some of the more important obesity-related statistics that Spake cites in this article.

5. What do obesity researchers believe about the claim that obese people lack the willpower to lose weight?

6. What adaptive use has storing fat had in human history?

7. What do studies of twins suggest about the interplay between genetic makeup and environment in causing obesity?

8. What roles do social organization and psychology play in gaining weight, according to obesity studies?

9. In what ways can consumers be confused by the various treatments for obesity, some medically approved, some not?

10. Summarize the argument that it is possible to be fat but fit.

Discussion and Writing Suggestions

1. Did any of the obesity related statistics in this article surprise you? Which ones? Why?

2. "'Who would choose to be obese?' asks Rudolph Leibel, a Columbia University geneticist and a noted obesity researcher. 'Telling someone they've decided to become obese is like saying, "You've decided to give yourself a brain tumor." ' " Your response?

3. Reread paragraphs 30 and 31. How difficult would it be for you, considering cultural stereotypes, to regard an active but obese person as "fit"? Explain your response.

4. Spake writes: "Weight discrimination dates back to the early Christian church, which included 'gluttony' as one of the seven deadly sins. Obesity was viewed as the outward manifestation of the 'sin' of overindulgence." What evidence of this "early Christian" thinking do you see in evidence today? Do you detect any sense in which obese people are regarded as morally flawed?

5. To what extent are Spake's remarks concerning weight discrimination and prejudice against the obese (see paragraphs 10–11) applicable to those who are overweight (but not obese)?

6. Discuss evidence you have seen of weight discrimination and prejudice. To spark your thinking on the subject, you might read a relevant case (*Russell v. Salve Regina*) in Chapter 14 (pages 762–64), concerning a nursing student who sued her college, which had harassed her and forced her to withdraw from school, for intentional infliction of emotional distress, breach of contract, invasion of privacy, and discrimination.

7. Review the references to Maria Pfisterer throughout the article, in paragraphs 1–3, 14–16, and 33–34. To what use is Spake putting these references in the article?

Caloric Imbalance and Public Health Policy
Jeffrey P. Koplan, MD, MPH and
William H. Dietz, MD, PhD

On 27 October 1999, the Journal of the American Medical Association (JAMA), one of the country's most prestigious medical journals, devoted an entire issue to obesity—a publication decision that demanded the attention of the American public. Articles in this issue reported on the increased mortality and disease risk associated with obesity. Working with data that had been recently gathered by the Centers for Disease Control and Prevention (CDC) in Atlanta, Koplan and Dietz open their editorial with a brief, dramatic statement. In 2001, the U.S. Surgeon General, David Satcher, amplified the urgency of their editorial in his Call to Action to Prevent and Decrease Overweight and Obesity. It is now commonplace to see the words obesity and epidemic in the same sentence.

1   Obesity is epidemic in the United States. More than 50% of U.S. adults are now overweight, based on a body mass index (BMI)[1] of 25 kg/m² or more.[2] Furthermore, 22% of the U.S. adult population is obese, based on a BMI of 30 kg/m2 or more, equivalent to approximately 13.5 kg (30 lb) overweight. Three percent of U.S. adults have a BMI of 40 kg/m² or more, which represents a weight excess of approximately 45 kg (100 lb). Blacks and Hispanics are disproportionally affected. As the study by Mokdad and colleagues in this issue of *The Journal*[3] clearly demonstrates, the increase in the prevalence of obesity has been rapid. No area of the country has been spared.

2   Obesity is not simply a cosmetic disorder. Approximately 60% of overweight 5- to 10-year-old children already have 1 associated biochemical or clinical cardiovascular risk factor, such as hyperlipidemia, elevated blood pressure, or increased insulin levels, and 25% have 2 or more.[4] As Must and colleagues[5] demonstrate in their article, the risk factors observed in children will become chronic diseases in adults. Almost 80% of obese adults have diabetes, high blood cholesterol levels, high blood pressure, coronary artery disease, gallbladder disease, or osteoarthritis, and almost 40% have 2 or more

---

[1] Your Body Mass Index is your weight in kilograms divided by the square of your height in meters. See the BMI chart immediately following this editorial. [editors]

[2] Flegal KM, Carroll MD, Kuczmarski RJ, Johnson CL. Overweight and obesity in the United States: prevalence and trends, 1960–1994. *Int J Obesity,* 1998;22:39–47.

[3] Mokdad AH, Serdula MK, Dietz WH, Bowman BA, Marks JS, Koplan JP. The spread of the obesity epidemic in the United States, 1991–1998. *JAMA.* 1999;282:1519–1522.

[4] Freedman DS, Dietz WH, Srinivasan SR, Berenson GS. The relation of overweight to cardiovascular risk factors among children and adolescents: the Bogalusa Heart Study. *Pediatrics.* 1999;103:1175–1182.

[5] Must A, Spadano J, Coakley EH, Field AE, Colditz G, Dietz WH. The disease burden associated with overweight and obesity. *JAMA.* 1999;282:1523–1529.

of these comorbidities. Based on the study by Allison and colleagues,[6] only smoking exceeds obesity in its contribution to total mortality rates in the United States. A recent estimate suggesting that the direct and indirect costs of obesity in the United States approximated 10% of the national health care budget[7] underscores why the nation can no longer afford to ignore obesity as a major medical problem.

3   Genes related to obesity are clearly not responsible for the epidemic of obesity because the gene pool in the United States did not change significantly between 1980 and 1994. However, comparison of the differences in BMI in children and adolescents on a percentile by percentile basis indicates that the changes in BMI were limited to the upper half of the BMI distribution; the mean BMI increased by substantially more than the median.[8] These observations suggest either that 50% of children and adolescents had obesity susceptibility genes that were acted on by environmental changes, or that environmental changes only affected 50% of the population.

4   The human body, like any system, obeys the laws of thermodynamics. An excess of energy intake over expenditure leads to storage of energy in the form of fat. What may have developed as an evolutionary response to periods of famine and sparse foodstuffs has become a burden with negative health consequences in contemporary society. Only during the last several decades has an imbalance of energy intake and output occurred for a large proportion of the American population.

5   Between surveys conducted from 1977 through 1978 and 1994 through 1996, reported daily energy intakes increased from 9404 (2239) to 10 311 kJ (2455 kcal) in men and from 6443 (1534) to 6913 kJ (1646 kcal) in women.[9,10] Innumerable environmental changes that foster eating more frequently have occurred: the availability of more food and foods with higher energy content, the growth of the fast food industry, the increased numbers and marketing of snack foods, and an increased time for socializing along with a custom of socializing with food and drink. In a parallel development, opportunities in daily life to burn energy have diminished: children watch more television daily, physical education has been markedly reduced in our schools, many neighborhoods lack sidewalks for safe walking, the workplace has become

---

[6] Allison DB, Fontaine KR, Manson JE, Stevens J, VanItallie TB. Annual deaths attributable to obesity in the United States. *JAMA.* 1999;282:1530–1538.

[7] Wolf AM, Colditz GA. Current estimates of the economic costs of obesity in the United States. *Obesity Res.* 1998;6:97–106.

[8] Troiano RP, Flegal KM. Overweight children and adolescents: description, epidemiology, and demographics. *Pediatrics.* 1998;101(suppl):497–504.

[9] Federation of American Societies for Experimental Biology, Life Sciences Research Office. *Third Report on Nutrition Monitoring in the United States.* Vol 2. Washington, DC: U.S. Government Printing Office; 1995.

[10] Frazao E. *America's Eating Habits: Changes and Consequences.* Washington, DC: U.S. Dept of Agriculture; 1999. Information Bulletin AIB–750.

increasingly automated, household chores are assisted by labor saving machinery, and walking or bicycling has been replaced by automobile travel for all but the shortest distances.

6   Public health and clinical strategies to address the obesity epidemic must begin with weight maintenance for the adult population, weight loss for the obese, and increased physical activity for all. Weight maintenance for the obese as well as the nonobese will prevent further increases in the prevalence and the severity of obesity and also will prevent new cases of obesity in those who currently have weights within the healthy range. Modest weight losses of 5% to 10% of body weight improve glucose tolerance, hyperlipidemia, and blood pressure in obese adults.[11] Because physical activity may prevent obesity, improve obesity-associated comorbidities,[12] reduce mortality,[13,14] and have beneficial effects on a variety of other chronic diseases,[15] strategies to increase physical activity must be implemented for the entire population. Implementation of these strategies will require a shift in emphasis from a cosmetic ideal weight for height to an acceptable weight for health.

7   The time has come to develop a national comprehensive obesity prevention strategy that incorporates educational, behavioral, and environmental components analogous to those already in place for tobacco use. For example, the decline in tobacco use not only reflects an increased awareness of the health consequences of its use but also reflects a broad social strategy to reduce exposure. Prevention of tobacco use includes health warnings on cigarette packages, creation of tobacco-free spaces in restaurants and public buildings, enforcement of laws that prohibit tobacco sales to minors, and taxes that make cigarettes expensive.

8   Solutions to the obesity epidemic will differ from those that have reduced tobacco use. In contrast to tobacco use, energy intake derives from multiple foods rather than a single product. Furthermore, people can choose not to smoke, whereas they cannot easily choose not to eat without adverse health consequences. As in the case of tobacco users, obese individuals must not become the target of discrimination but should be seen as persons with a chronic health condition in need of support and treatment. Nonetheless, without comprehensive population-based efforts to prevent and treat obesity, the prevalence of obesity and its expensive associated diseases and mortality are likely to continue to

---

[11] National Institutes of Health. *Clinical Guidelines on the Identification, Evaluation, and Treatment of Overweight and Obesity in Adults.* Bethesda, Md: National Institutes of Health; 1998. Publication 98–4083.

[12] U.S. Department of Health and Human Services. *Physical Activity and Health: A Report of the Surgeon General.* Atlanta, Ga: Centers for Disease Control and Prevention; 1996.

[13] Lee CD, Blair SN, Jackson AS. Cardiorespiratory fitness, body composition, and all-cause and cardiovascular disease mortality in men. *Am J Clin Nutr.* 1999;69:373–380.

[14] Wei M, Kampert JB, Barlow CE, et al. Relationship between low cardiorespiratory fitness and mortality in normal-weight, overweight, and obese men. *JAMA.* 1999;282:1547–1553.

[15] Powell KE, Carperson CJ, Koplan JP, Ford ES. Physical activity and chronic disease. *Am J Clin Nutr.* 1989;49:999–1006.

increase. Like rickets, pellagra, goiter, and dental caries, the most effective solutions to the obesity epidemic are likely environmental. However, in contrast to single-nutrient deficiency diseases, which can be addressed by nutrient fortification, environmental solutions to obesity will be more complex.

9   Because obesity has not been the focus of major preventive efforts, a desperate need exists for research to identify effective interventions and programs to prevent obesity. Several promising directions are already apparent. As Robinson[16] demonstrates in this issue of *The Journal,* reduced television viewing by children slows rates of weight gain. A recent school-based intervention that focused on increased physical activity, increased fruit and vegetable consumption, reduced consumption of high-fat foods, and reduced inactivity significantly reduced obesity prevalence in preadolescent girls.[17] One successful experimental approach to make fruits and vegetables or other nutritious foods more competitive is to offer more diverse, attractive, and less-expensive alternatives to high energy value foods in vending machines and cafeteria lines.[18] Schools also provide one of the few supervised locations where children can be physically active. The significant health benefits associated with physical activity and the reduced opportunities for children to be active make restoration of daily physical education in schools a priority. Nonetheless, some communities lack the facilities or have chosen not to support physical education programs.

10   In response to the high costs of health care associated with obesity and inactivity, a number of major corporations have initiated effective programs that include weight loss and increased physical activity.[19] However, given the economics and dynamics of the small- to medium-sized workplaces in which 50% of the U.S. workforce is employed, broader dissemination of such programs may be limited. With relatively high turnover of members in managed care plans and uncertain cost recovery of investments in diet and exercise programs whose benefits may not be apparent for a year or two, managed care plans may be less motivated to institute such health promotion programs. The health and financial benefits, such as reduced workdays lost to illness or reduced health care costs, are increasingly supported by data but will require wide acceptance by employers and health plans before workers become the focus of activities promoting healthful diets and levels of physical activity.

11   Because work-site physical activity programs will not be an option for many adults, changes in the community environment to promote physical activity may offer the most practical approach to prevent obesity or reduce its comorbidities.

---

[16] Robinson TN. Reducing children's television viewing to prevent obesity: a randomized controlled trial. *JAMA.* 1999;282:1561–1567.

[17] Gortmaker SL, Peterson K, Wiecha J, et al. Reducing obesity via a school-based interdisciplinary intervention among youth: Planet Health. *Arch Pediatr Adolesc Med.* 1999;153:409–418.

[18] French SA, Story M, Jeffery RW, et al. Pricing strategy to promote fruit and vegetable purchase in high school cafeterias: *J Am Diet Assoc.* 1997;97:1008–1010.

[19] Tully S. America's healthiest companies. *Fortune.* 1995;131:98–106.

Restoration of physical activity as part of the daily routine represents a critical goal. As recent studies have shown, physical activity need not be vigorous or continuous to produce health benefits.[20,21,22] Changes that promote physical activity may be as mundane as improving the location and appearance of stairwells or as complex as the redesign of communities. In many parts of the United States, community infrastructure to support physical activity already exists, such as sidewalks and bicycle trails, and work-sites, schools, and shopping areas in close proximity to residential areas. Such infrastructure makes walking or bicycling to school, to work, or to shop part of daily physical activity. In these areas, strategies to promote physical activity may be easier to implement than in communities that lack such infrastructure.

12   Automobile trips that can be safely replaced by walking or bicycling offer the first target for increased physical activity in communities. Recent data indicate that approximately 25% of all trips are less than 1 mile, and 75% of these are by car[23] (Paul Schimek, oral communication, September 14, 1999). Reliance on physical activity as an alternative to car use is less likely to occur in many cities and towns unless they are designed or retro-fitted to permit walking or bicycling. The location of schools, work sites, and shopping areas near residential areas will require substantial changes in community or regional design. Several incentives may promote such changes. Alternatives to automobiles will reduce air pollution as well as increase physical activity. Community recreation areas or facilities may promote physical activity during leisure time. Such facilities clearly improve the desirability of communities. For example, a recent survey of new home buyers indicated that almost all of the amenities that made communities desirable places to live were features that promoted physical activity, such as walking and jogging trails, outdoor swimming pools, playgrounds, and parks.[24]

13   People in the United States are proud of the nation's magnificent geography and enjoy exploration of and adventures in it. U.S. mythology is filled with images of vigorous physicality and glorified hard work—cowboys, farmers, longshoremen, miners, and athletes. Most U.S. citizens value the image of physically active presidents—from the boxing and hunting of Teddy Roosevelt to the swimming of Franklin Delano Roosevelt, the touch football of John Kennedy,

[20] Dunn AL, Marcus BH, Kampert JB, Garcla ME, Kohl HW III, Blair SN. Comparisons of lifestyle and structured interventions to increase physical activity and cardiorespiratory fitness. *JAMA.* 1999;281:327–334.

[21] Andersen RE, Wadden TA, Bartlett SJ, Zemel B, Verde TJ, Franckowiak SC. Effects of lifestyle activity vs. structured aerobic exercise in obese women. *JAMA.* 1999;281:335–340.

[22] Manson JE, Hu FB, Rich-Edwards JW, et al. A prospective study of walking as compared with vigorous exercise in the prevention of coronary heart disease in women. *N Engl J Med.* 1999;341:650–658.

[23] Schimek P. Unpublished calculations from 1995 Nationwide Personal Transportation Survey. U.S. Department of Transportation, Federal Highway Administration, Research and Technical Support Center. Lanham, Md: Federal Highway Administration; 1997.

[24] Fletcher J. Is this Disneyland? no, the new suburbs. *Wall Street Journal.* June 4, 1999:W12.

TABLE 11.1 Body Mass Index Chart

Height (inches)	19	20	21	22	23	24	25	26	27	28	29	30	31	32	33	34	35	36
									Body Weight (pounds)									
58	91	96	100	105	110	115	119	124	129	134	138	143	148	153	158	162	167	172
59	94	99	104	109	114	119	124	128	133	138	143	148	153	158	163	168	173	178
60	97	102	107	112	118	123	128	133	138	143	148	153	158	163	168	174	179	184
61	100	106	111	116	122	127	132	137	143	148	153	158	164	169	174	180	185	190
62	104	109	115	120	126	131	136	142	147	153	158	164	169	175	180	186	191	196
63	107	113	118	124	130	135	141	146	152	158	163	169	175	180	186	191	197	203
64	110	116	122	128	134	140	145	151	157	163	169	174	180	186	192	197	204	209
65	114	120	126	132	138	144	150	156	162	168	174	180	186	192	198	204	210	216
66	118	124	130	136	142	148	155	161	167	173	179	186	192	198	204	210	216	223
67	121	127	134	140	146	153	159	166	172	178	185	191	198	204	211	217	223	230
68	125	131	138	144	151	158	164	171	177	184	190	197	203	210	216	223	230	236
69	128	135	142	149	155	162	169	176	182	189	196	203	209	216	223	230	236	243
70	132	139	146	153	160	167	174	181	188	195	202	209	216	222	229	236	243	250
71	136	143	150	157	165	172	179	186	193	200	208	215	222	229	236	243	250	257
72	140	147	154	162	169	177	184	191	199	206	213	221	228	235	242	250	258	265
73	144	151	159	166	174	182	189	197	204	212	219	227	235	242	250	257	265	272
74	148	155	163	171	179	186	194	202	210	218	225	233	241	249	256	264	272	280
75	152	160	168	176	184	192	200	208	216	224	232	240	248	256	264	272	279	287
76	156	164	172	180	189	197	205	213	221	230	238	246	254	263	271	279	287	295

TABLE 11.2 Body Mass Index Chart

Height (inches)	37	38	39	40	41	42	43	44	45	46	47	48	49	50	51	52	53	54
									Body Weight (pounds)									
58	177	181	186	191	196	201	205	210	215	220	224	229	234	239	244	248	253	258
59	183	188	193	198	203	208	212	217	222	227	232	237	242	247	252	257	262	267
60	189	194	199	204	209	215	220	225	230	235	240	245	250	255	261	266	271	276
61	195	201	206	211	217	222	227	232	238	243	248	254	259	264	269	275	280	285
62	202	207	213	218	224	229	235	240	246	251	256	262	267	273	278	284	289	295
63	208	214	220	225	231	237	242	248	254	259	265	270	278	282	287	293	299	304
64	215	221	227	232	238	244	250	256	262	267	273	279	285	291	296	302	308	314
65	222	228	234	240	246	252	258	264	270	276	282	288	294	300	306	312	318	324
66	229	235	241	247	253	260	266	272	278	284	291	297	303	309	315	322	328	334
67	236	242	249	255	261	268	274	280	287	293	299	306	312	319	325	331	338	344
68	243	249	256	262	269	276	282	289	295	302	308	315	322	328	335	341	348	354
69	250	257	263	270	277	284	291	297	304	311	318	324	331	338	345	351	358	365
70	257	264	271	278	285	292	299	306	313	320	327	334	341	348	355	362	369	376
71	265	272	279	286	293	301	308	315	322	329	338	343	351	358	365	372	379	386
72	272	279	287	294	302	309	316	324	331	338	346	353	361	368	375	383	390	397
73	280	288	295	302	310	318	325	333	340	348	355	363	371	378	386	393	401	408
74	287	295	303	311	319	326	334	342	350	358	365	373	381	389	396	404	412	420
75	295	303	311	319	327	335	343	351	359	367	375	383	391	399	407	415	423	431
76	304	312	320	328	336	344	353	361	369	377	385	394	402	410	418	426	435	443

BMI Tables. To use these tables, find your height in the left-hand column. Move across to a given weight. The number at the top of the column is your BMI.

the jogging of Jimmy Carter and Bill Clinton, the wood-splitting and horseback riding of Ronald Reagan, and the golf and horseshoe tossing of George Bush. Similar role models are needed for women and minorities.

14   However, despite the pervasive conceptual preference for being lean and active, the environments and behaviors that have been developed make both characteristics difficult to achieve. Far too many people appear to have accepted the determinants of the problems of overweight and inactivity, and rely on "treatments" in the forms of myriad ineffective diet remedies and nostrums. As with many health issues, it is essential to emphasize prevention as the only effective and cost-effective approach. There is a particular need to focus on children and adolescents whose excess weight and sedentary lifestyle will form the basis for a lifetime of preventable morbidity and increased premature mortality.

15   Obesity, overweight, and a sedentary lifestyle are serious health issues now and will only worsen without thoughtful and scientifically based interventions that address societal and individual attitudes and behaviors and their environmental context. Physicians and other health care professionals, elected officials, educators, employers, and parents need to recognize the magnitude and impact of this major health problem and provide the will and energy to correct it through preventive approaches. In the past 25 years, several newer areas have been incorporated as targets for clinical and public health concern, such as tobacco control and injury prevention. It is now time to promote weight control and physical activity.[25]

Review Questions

1. What percentage of Americans is overweight, and what percentage is obese? What is the source of these data?

2. What is the relationship between obesity and general health, according to the authors?

3. Why, according to the authors, can the United States "no longer afford to ignore obesity as a major medical problem"?

4. What causes obesity?

5. What are the authors' recommendations for combating the epidemic of obesity?

6. Why will environmental strategies play an especially important role in the fight against obesity, and in what ways will these strategies prove complex?

7. The authors urge readers to accept prevention as an approach to obesity, as opposed to treatment. Why?

[25] Acknowledgments: We thank Martha Katz, MA, Steve Gortmaker, PhD, and Tom Robinson, MD, for their comments and suggestions.

Discussion and Writing Suggestions

1. Scan the footnotes of this article from the *Journal of the American Medical Association.* For what sorts of statements do the authors cite sources? Generally, how dependable do you find the information in this editorial?

2. What elements of the editorial identify it *as* an editorial? (You might reflect on the editorials you read in newspapers.) To what extent does the piece by Koplan and Dietz fit the same genre of writing?

3. The authors review a good deal of information in their discussion of "caloric imbalance." Do you find that the authors are *not* discussing any elements of being overweight or obese that you consider to be important?

4. Koplan and Dietz use the highly charged word "epidemic" in their article. Physicians use this word to denote a specific set of circumstances. Look up "epidemic" in a dictionary and discuss the ways in which the rising incidence of obesity compels the authors to use this word.

5. The authors state that their recommendations for reducing obesity "will require a shift in emphasis from a cosmetic ideal weight for height to an acceptable weight for health" (paragraph 6). What forces are at work in the culture that help to define and promote a cosmetically ideal weight? What success do you envision for moving Americans away from such an ideal?

6. The authors are calling for a major national mobilization against obesity that is reminiscent of the mobilization against tobacco use. To what extent do you feel that the authors have made the case in this editorial for such a broadscale, expensive, and extended campaign? Have they convinced you that obesity poses a major health risk to the well-being of the nation?

Prevalence of Obesity Among U.S. Adults, by Characteristics and by State
Centers for Disease Control and Prevention

The Centers for Disease Control and Prevention (CDC) published a report entitled "U.S. Obesity Trends in Adults from 1991–2001," from which a broad conclusion emerged: "The prevalence of obesity among U.S. adults increased to 20.9 percent in 2001, a 5.6 percent increase in 1 year and a 74 percent increase since 1991." On its Web site, the CDC describes itself as "the lead federal agency for protecting the health and safety of people—at home and abroad, providing credible information to enhance health decisions, and promoting health through strong partnerships." As such, the CDC is charged with devising and implementing strategies for preventing disease. The first stage in developing a strategy, of course, is to understand the extent of a problem, which the CDC attempted to do with its study. Note that Dr. Jeffrey Koplan, lead author of the JAMA editorial immediately preceding these tables, was a former director of the CDC. The two tables below are from the 2002 study. To see complete data, go to the CDC Web site at <http://www.cdc.gov/nccdphp/dnpa/obesity/>.

Prevalence of Obesity Among U.S. Adults, by Characteristics

1 In 2000, the prevalence of obesity among U.S. adults was 19.8 percent, which reflects a 61 percent increase since 1991.

2 In 2000, 38.8 million American adults met the classification of obesity, defined as having a body mass index, BMI score of 30 or more.

3 Between 2000 and 2001 obesity prevalence climbed from 19.8 percent of American adults to 20.9 percent of American adults.

TABLE 11.3   1991–2001 Prevalence of Obesity Among U.S. Adults, by Characteristics

Characteristics	Percent Obese BRFSS data by year:[*]					
	1991	1995	1998	1999	2000	2001
Total	12.0	15.3	17.9	18.9	19.8	20.9
Gender						
Men	11.7	15.6	17.7	19.1	20.2	21.0
Women	12.2	15.0	18.1	18.6	19.4	20.8
Age groups						
18–29	7.1	10.1	12.1	12.1	13.5	14.0
30–39	11.3	14.4	16.9	18.6	20.2	20.5
40–49	15.8	17.9	21.2	22.4	22.9	24.7
50–59	16.1	21.6	23.8	24.2	25.6	26.1
60–69	14.7	19.4	21.3	22.3	22.9	25.3
<70	11.4	12.1	14.6	16.1	15.5	17.1
Race, ethnicity						
White, non Hispanic	11.3	14.5	16.6	17.7	18.5	19.6
Black, non Hispanic	19.3	22.6	26.9	27.3	29.3	31.1
Hispanic	11.6	16.8	20.8	21.5	23.4	23.7
Other	7.3	9.6	11.9	12.4	12.0	15.7
Educational Level						
Less than High School	16.5	20.1	24.1	25.3	26.1	27.4
High school degree	13.3	16.7	19.4	20.6	21.7	23.2
Some college	10.7	15.1	17.8	18.1	19.5	21.0
College or above	8.0	11.0	13.1	14.3	15.2	15.7
Smoking status						
Never smoked	12.0	15.2	17.9	19.0	19.9	20.9
Ex-smoker	14.0	17.9	20.9	21.5	22.7	23.9
Current smoker	9.9	12.3	14.8	15.7	16.3	17.8

[*] Behavioral Risk Factor Surveillance System.

TABLE 11.4   Obesity Prevalence Among U.S. Adults by State. BRFSS Data by Year*

State Obesity	1991	1995	1998	1999	2000	2001
Alabama	13.2	18.3	20.7	21.8	23.5	23.4
Alaska	13.1	19.2	20.7	19.2	20.5	21.0
Arizona	11.0	12.8	12.7	11.6	18.8	17.9
Arkansas	12.7	17.3	19.2	21.9	22.6	21.7
California	10.0	14.4	16.8	19.6	19.2	20.9
Colorado	8.4	10.00	14.0	14.3	13.8	14.4
Connecticut	10.9	11.9	14.7	14.5	16.9	17.3
Delaware	14.9	16.2	16.6	17.1	16.2	20.0
District of Columbia	15.2	n/a	19.9	17.9	21.2	19.9
Florida	10.1	16.5	17.4	17.9	18.1	18.4
Georgia	9.2	12.6	18.7	20.7	20.9	22.1
Hawaii	10.4	10.4	15.3	15.3	15.1	17.6
Idaho	11.7	13.8	16.0	19.5	18.4	20.0
Illinois	12.7	16.4	17.9	20.2	20.9	20.5
Indiana	14.8	19.6	19.5	19.4	21.3	24.0
Iowa	14.4	17.2	19.3	20.9	20.8	21.8
Kansas	n/a	15.8	17.3	18.5	20.1	21.0
Kentucky	12.7	16.6	19.9	21.1	22.3	24.2
Louisiana	15.7	17.4	21.3	21.5	22.8	23.3
Maine	12.1	13.7	17.0	18.9	19.7	19.0
Maryland	11.2	15.8	19.8	17.6	19.5	19.8
Massachusetts	8.8	11.1	13.8	14.3	16.4	16.1
Michigan	15.2	17.7	20.7	22.1	21.8	24.4
Minnesota	10.6	15.0	15.7	15.0	16.8	19.2
Mississippi	15.7	18.6	22.0	22.8	24.3	25.9
Missouri	12.0	18.0	19.8	20.8	21.6	22.5
Montana	9.5	12.6	1.7	14.7	15.2	18.2
Nebraska	12.5	15.7	17.5	20.2	20.6	20.1
Nevada	n/a	13.3	13.4	15.3	17.2	19.1
New Hampshire	10.4	14.7	14.7	13.8	17.1	19.0
New Jersey	9.7	14.2	15.2	16.8	17.6	19.0
New Mexico	7.8	12.7	14.7	17.3	17.8	18.8
New York	12.8	13.3	15.9	16.9	17.2	19.7
North Carolina	13.0	16.5	19.0	21.0	21.3	22.4
North Dakota	12.9	15.6	18.7	21.2	19.8	19.9
Ohio	14.9	17.2	19.5	19.8	21.0	21.8
Oklahoma	11.9	13.0	18.7	20.2	19.0	22.1
Oregon	11.2	14.7	17.8	19.6	21.0	20.7
Pennsylvania	14.4	16.1	19.0	19.0	20.7	21.4
Rhode Island	9.1	12.9	16.2	16.01	16.8	17.3
South Carolina	13.8	16.1	20.2	20.2	21.5	21.7
South Dakota	12.8	13.6	15.4	19.0	19.2	20.6
Tennessee	12.1	18.0	18.5	20.1	22.7	22.6
Texas	12.7	15.0	19.9	21.1	22.7	23.8
Utah	9.7	12.6	15.3	16.3	18.5	18.4
Vermont	10.0	14.2	14.4	17.2	17.7	17.1
Virginia	10.1	15.2	18.2	18.6	17.5	20.0
Washington	9.9	13.5	17.6	17.7	18.5	18.9
West Virginia	15.2	17.8	22.9	23.9	22.8	24.6
Wisconsin	12.7	15.3	17.9	19.3	19.4	21.9
Wyoming	n/a	13.9	14.5	16.4	17.6	19.2

*Behavioral Risk Factor Surveillance System.

4   Currently, more than 44 million Americans are considered obese by BMI index; that is, have a Body Mass Index (Kg/m^2) greater than or equal to 30. This reflects an increase of 74 percent since 1991.

5   This table reflects the percentages of individuals who are obese within specific categories such as, gender, age, race, education, and smoking status.

Prevalence of Obesity Among U.S. Adults, by State

6   [There is an] obesity epidemic within the U.S. . . . [In] 1991, only 4 of 45 participating states had obesity prevalence rates of 15 to 19 percent and none had prevalence greater than 20 percent.

7   By the year 2000, all of the 50 states except Colorado had prevalences of 15 percent or greater, with 22 of the 50 states having obesity prevalence as high as 20 percent or greater.

8   In 2001, 20 states had obesity prevalence of 15–19 percent; 29 states had prevalences of 20–24 percent; and one state reported a prevalence more than 25 percent. The prevalence of obesity among U.S. adults increased to 20.9 percent in 2001, a 5.6 percent increase in 1 year and a 74 percent increase since 1991.

References

Mokdad AH, Serdula M, Dietz W, et al. The spread of the obesity epidemic in the United States, 1991–1998. *JAMA* 1999;282:1519–1522.

Mokdad AH, Serdula M, Dietz W, et al. The continuing obesity epidemic in the United States. *JAMA* 2000;284:1650–1651.

Mokdad AH, Bowman BA, Ford ES, et al. The continuing epidemics of obesity and diabetes in the United States. *JAMA* 2001;286(10):1195–1200.

Mokdad AH, Bowman BA, Ford ES, et al. Prevalence of obesity, diabetes, and obesity related health risk factors, 2001. *JAMA* 2003:289;76–79.

Review Questions

1. As you study the Characteristics table, what correlation do you find between race/ethnicity and obesity?

2. In the Characteristics table, what correlation do you find between level of education and incidence of obesity?

3. Review both CDC tables and summarize the general trend in incidence of obesity.

4. According to the "Obesity Prevalence . . . by State" table, which are the least obese and most obese areas of the country?

Discussion and Writing Suggestions

1. Select your age group, race/ethnicity, educational level, and smoking status in the Characteristics table. To what extent do the percentages reported reflect what you have observed about the prevalence of obesity?

2. Select your state in the "Obesity Prevalence . . . by State" table. Do the percentages reported reflect what you have observed about the prevalence of obesity?

3. Focus on the 1991 through 2001 percentages of obesity among people who have smoked and quit, never smoked, or presently smoke. What inferences can you draw between smoking status and obesity?

4. Speculate on possible explanations for the relationship between obesity and level of education.

5. To what extent are you surprised to find differences among states in levels of obesity? Identify one such difference and speculate on the causes of the difference.

6. Why might those older than 70 tend to be less obese than those aged 30–69?

7. Do you find any surprises in the CDC data? Discuss.

8. Write a paragraph summarizing what for you are the key findings in one of the two tables.

Too Much of a Good Thing
Greg Critser

In an op-ed essay for the Los Angeles Times *(22 July 2001), Greg Critser argues that, faced with a rising obesity epidemic, we should stigmatize overeating. Critser is careful to distinguish between stigmatizing the person and the act, but he makes no apologies for urging that we teach children that "[e]ating too much food is a bad thing." Critser has written a book on the obesity epidemic:* Fat Land *(Houghton Mifflin, 2003).*

1   Sometime over the next month or so, United Nations health and nutrition experts will convene in New York to begin discussing what many consider to be the pivotal medical issue of our day: obesity and its impact on children. For the U.N., traditionally concerned with starvation and malnutrition, it is a historic first, following up on an alarm it sounded about obese adults in 1999. "Obesity," the U.N. proclaimed, "is the dominant unmet global health issue, with Westernized countries topping the list."

2   Solid epidemiological data drives the effort. In Canada, Great Britain, Japan, Australia—even coastal China and Southeast Asia—the rate of childhood obesity has been soaring for more than a decade. Closer to home, at least 25% of all Americans under age nineteen are overweight or obese, a figure that has doubled over the last 30 years and a figure that moved the surgeon general to declare childhood obesity an epidemic. The cost in health care dollars to treat obesity's medical consequences—from diabetes to coronary heart disease to a variety of crippling bone conditions—will eventually make the battle against HIV/AIDS seem inexpensive. Yet in the U.S., the most important foot soldiers against obesity are increasingly paralyzed by years of media-induced food hysteria, over-generalized and outdated nutritional wisdom, and, truth be told, an unwillingness to set firm and sometimes unpopular food parameters. That infantry is the much-strained American family and its increasingly harried commandant, *Parentis americanus.* What it needs to promulgate is dietary restraint, something our ancestors knew simply as avoiding gluttony.

3   This is not to say that parents should be blamed for the nation's growing dietary permissiveness. They are wary of confronting their children's eating habits for a reason: For years, conventional wisdom held that food should never become a dinner table battleground. "Pressure causes tension," write Harvey and Marilyn Diamond, authors of the classic *Fit for Life,* which has sold more than 3 million copies. "Where food is concerned, tension is always to be avoided." The operative notion is that a child restrained from overeating will either rebel by secretly gorging when away from the table or, worse, will suffer such a loss of self-esteem that a lifetime of disastrous eating behavior will follow.

4   Of course, no one should be stigmatized for being overweight. But stigmatizing the unhealthful behaviors that cause obesity would conform with what we know about effective health messages. In both the campaign against unsafe sex and the campaign against smoking, stigmatizing such behaviors proved highly effective in reducing risk and harm. It's true, smokers—and homosexuals—may have experienced a modicum of stereotyping in the short run, but such is the price of every public health advance: short-term pain for long-term gain.

5   Another inhibition to imposing dietary restraint is the belief, promoted in handbook after handbook of parental advice, that "kids know when they are full." But perhaps not. In fact, new research suggests just the opposite: Kids don't know when they are full.

6   In a recent study, Pennsylvania State University nutritional scholar Barbara Rolls and her associates examined the eating habits of two groups of kids, one

of three-year-olds, another of five-year-olds. The children were presented with a series of plates of macaroni and cheese. The first plate was a normal serving built around baseline nutritional needs; the second was slightly larger; the third was what might be called "supersized."

7   What the researchers found is that the younger children consistently ate the same baseline amount, leaving more food on the plates with larger servings. The 5-year-olds, though, altered their eating behavior dramatically depending on the amount they were served, devouring whatever was on the plate. Something had happened. The mere presence of an oversized portion had induced exaggerated eating. The authors concluded that "these early years may provide a unique opportunity for interventions that reduce the risk of developing overweight." Those interventions "should include clear information on appropriate portion sizes for children."

8   Theorizing aside, our disinclination to restrain eating flies in the face of overwhelming evidence that, of all age groups, children seem to be the ones who respond most positively to dietary advice. In four randomized studies of obese 6- to 12-year-olds, those who were offered frequent, simple behavioral advice were substantially less overweight 10 years later than kids who did not get the advice. In fact, 30% of those studied were no longer obese at all.

9   The case for early intervention has been further buttressed by new studies on another age-old medical injunction: never put a kid on a diet. (The concern was that under-nutrition could lead to stunted growth.) But as the authors of a study of 1,062 kids under age three concluded in the journal *Pediatrics,* "a supervised, low-saturated-fat and low-cholesterol diet has no influence on growth during the first three years of life." Overweight kids who were put on such a diet ended up with better, more moderate eating habits.

10   Changing the eating habits of children, though, is antithetical to some notions many parents hold dear. And to some it seems a relic of an earlier, more religious era of moral certainties when gluttony was vilified as one of the seven deadly sins. Many boomer parents believe, as one parent and nutritionist said at a recent summit on childhood obesity, that "kids have the right to make bad nutrition decisions." That may be true. But ours is a world where at least a billion dollars a year is spent by just one fast-food chain to convince families to visit a crazy-looking clown with his own playground and purchase a thousand supersize calories for a mere $2.50. McDonald's official line today is that three meals a week at its restaurants are perfectly acceptable for an average kid. That's three meals a week of grease, refined flour, and a jumbo shot of sugar.

11   Given today's bounty of cheap and unhealthful food alternatives, and given the inconvenience that goes with making good nutritional choices, one might wonder if a campaign against over-consumption, a campaign advocating restraint, could work. On this point, we might take a cue from the French. In the early 20th century France, in response to its first experiences with widespread child obesity, launched the puericulture movement, which focused on excessive weight gain in early childhood and adolescence. Its prescription: All meals should be adult-supervised; all portions should be moderate, with "seconds" a rare treat. All but an occasional small snack were forbidden. As its historian Peter

N. Stearns writes in *Fat History,* puericulture's message was simple: Eating too much food is a bad thing.

12   Therein lies at least part of the explanation for the legendary leanness of the French: They were taught in childhood not to overeat. And it didn't seem to do much harm to their self-esteem.

Review Questions

1. With what particular problem is Crister concerned in this essay?

2. According to conventional wisdom, how should parents set limits with respect to their children's intake of food?

3. Notwithstanding conventional wisdom, what are the three arguments (two supported by research studies) that Crister makes for curtailing the food intake of children?

4. What objections does Crister anticipate to his proposals, and how does he rebut these objections?

Discussion and Writing Suggestions

1. Crister advocates that we teach children that "[e]ating too much food is a bad thing." Do you agree? In your view, what are a parent's responsibilities in teaching children about eating and overeating?

2. Some parents and nutritionists have objected to Crister's proposed instruction of children and they maintain that children "have the right to make bad nutrition decisions." Who is more persuasive on this point (discussed in paragraph 10), Crister or those who argue for a child's nutritional autonomy?

3. Reread paragraph 4, which Crister begins: "Of course, no one should be stigmatized for being overweight." In fact, is Crister advocating stigmatization? What is the difference between stigmatizing an act (that is, overeating) and stigmatizing an actor (the person who overeats)?

4. Notwithstanding Crister's assertion that "no one should be stigmatized for being overweight," to what extent do you find him to be morally intolerant in this essay? Of whom does he disapprove— children who overeat, their parents, the broader culture that fosters overeating? Or do you find that his objection is to overeating itself?

5. What assumptions does Crister make about the origins of overeating? In considering this question, you might think about the roles of individual willpower, genes, parental and institutional authority, and a child's autonomy.

NAAFA Policy on Dieting and the Diet Industry
National Association to Advance Fat Acceptance

The National Association to Advance Fat Acceptance (NAAFA) was founded in 1969 as a "non-profit human rights organization dedicated to improving the quality of life for fat people." NAAFA is both an advocacy group, publishing and advocating for positions on issues that affect fat people, like the following policy statement on dieting, and a support group that offers members "tools for self empowerment." You can visit the NAAFA Web site at http://www.naafa.org for a closer look at the organization's official documents, informational brochures, book service, and more. What you will find consistently is a content and a tone that promotes fat acceptance.

History/Existing Condition

1   The term "diet" within this policy refers exclusively to weight reduction diets. "Dieting" is defined as any attempt to achieve or maintain lower body weight by intentionally limiting or manipulating the amount or type of food intake. Weight reduction diets include medically supervised diets; self-administered diets; commercial diet organizations and centers; weight-loss support groups or behavior modification programs; "fad" diets; "sensible, well-balanced" diets; in-hospital fasts; very-low-calorie diets (VLCDs); prepackaged food plans; and diets supplemented by drugs or artificial food products or supplements.

2   "Dieting" does not refer to attempts to lower fat, sugar, salt, or cholesterol intake, increase fiber intake, exercise or pursue a medically mandated nutritional regimen prescribed for specific medical conditions. Weight-loss diets have long been promoted as a permanent cure for "obesity," although they rarely produce long-lasting or permanent results. According to existing medical research, fewer than five percent of all dieters succeed in losing a significant amount of weight and maintaining that weight loss over a five-year period. Ninety percent of all dieters regain some or all of the weight originally lost and at least one-third gain more. In recent years, an increasing body of research has substantiated this diet failure rate and acknowledged genetic and physiological factors in the determination of body size.

3   Although these statistics apply to all types of diets, even those considered "sensible," physicians continue to prescribe weight-loss diets as a viable treatment for fat patients; and researchers, the media, and the diet industry continue to urge fat people to resist their body's natural predisposition and struggle harder to lose weight. As diet failure rates become widely publicized, some "experts" pretend to abandon "dieting" and encourage their clients to "just eat less and exercise more."

4   Promoting diets and diet products is a major industry in the United States. According to Marketdata Enterprises, the annual revenue for the diet industry was over $30 billion dollars in 1990. This figure includes money spent on diet centers and programs, group and individual weight-loss, diet camps, prepackaged foods; over-the-counter and prescription diet drugs; weight-loss books and magazines; and physicians, nurses, nutritionists, and other health professionals specializing in weight-loss (total 1990 revenue—$8 billion); commercial and

residential exercise clubs with weight-loss programs (total 1990 revenue—$8 billion); and sugar-free, fat-free, and reduced calorie ("lite") food products, imitation fats and sugar substitutes (total 1990 revenue—$14 billion).

5   The diet industry's advertising and marketing strategy is based on the creation and perpetuation of fear, biases, and stereotypes. Fat people are portrayed as unhealthy, unattractive, asexual, weak-willed, lazy, and gluttonous. Weight loss or a thin figure are equated with virtue, health, and success. Failure to participate in dieting or lack of success in losing weight are blamed on a lack of willpower or determination and a lack of moral values. Fat people are taught to feel guilty and blame themselves for the failures of weight-loss programs, and to expect and accept rejection, mistreatment, and discrimination regarding their weight. This negative media campaign has a devastating impact on millions of fat people. These messages lower fat people's self-esteem and foster discontent, self-doubt, and self-hatred, especially during the weight regain state of the dieting "yo-yo" cycle.

6   Diet promoters also emphasize dieting's supposed health benefits and minimize risks related to dieting. People of all sizes are misled about the extent and severity of the health risks associated with being fat and are told that being thin is the only way to good health, and that dieting makes people thin. Many health problems traditionally attributed to "obesity," such as high blood pressure, heart problems, high cholesterol, and gallbladder problems, are often caused by the dieting process itself. Recent studies indicate that repeated "yo-yo" dieting may actually reduce one's life span rather than increase longevity.

7   Currently there are very few controls or regulations to inform and protect the dieting consumer. Weight loss "success" is only vaguely defined using short-term results, and weight loss "failure is always blamed on the consumer, and health risks are not disclosed. The few regulations that do exist are rarely, or at most, loosely enforced.

NAAFA's Official Position

8   Since reducing diets rarely achieve permanent weight loss and can result in negative health consequences, since laws and regulations protecting the consumer are nonexistent or remain unenforced, and since people undertaking diets are rarely given sufficient information to allow them to give true informed consent, the National Association to Advance Fat Acceptance strongly discourages participation in weight-reduction dieting. Further, NAAFA strongly condemns any diet marketing strategy based on guilt and fear. Such approaches cause untold suffering to fat people by ruining their self-esteem and by perpetuating negative stereotypes. NAAFA demands that local, state, and federal governments regulate the diet industry to protect the consumer from misleading claims regarding safety and long-term effectiveness.

NAAFA Advocates:

- That local, state, and federal legislatures introduce, pass, enact, and enforce legislation which protects consumers against dangerous or ineffective diets and misleading diet advertising.
- That state and federal regulatory agencies, such as the Food and Drug Administration (FDA) and the Federal Trade Commission (FTC), adopt

regulations based on NAAFA's "Guidelines for the Diet Industry" and closely monitor and control all aspects of the multi-billion-dollar diet industry.

- That all commercials for weight-loss diets and diet products be banned from radio and television because of lack of product success, negative health consequences, and the extreme negative impact of anti-fat propaganda on the self-esteem and quality of life of fat people.
- That federal regulations require all diets and weight-loss products to clearly display a health warning (similar to those found on cigarettes) regarding possible hazards and side effects.
- That regulations be adopted that require the diet industry to publish five-year (minimum) follow-up studies and "success" rates. All such statistics must be verifiable by objective outside researchers and clearly displayed on all diet products and advertising.
- That the Centers for Disease Control track morbidity and mortality caused by dieting and make the findings available to the public.
- That the National Institutes of Health (NIH) include input from consumer advocacy groups in establishing public health policy about dieting and obesity.
- That consumer protection agencies, such as Consumers Union, conduct biannual studies on the efficacy of diet products and programs.
- That institutions such as the military, hospitals, schools, mental institutions, or prisons provide adequate food and not force anyone to diet against their will.
- That employers, schools, and judges never use weight loss or dieting as a condition for employment, promotion, admission, or avoiding incarceration.
- That health care professionals and medical institutions never deny other medical treatment to patients who choose not to diet.
- That the diet industry refrain from creating or perpetuating negative stereotypes about fat people in its marketing strategies.
- That diet companies and diet industry trade organizations voluntarily comply with NAAFA's "Guidelines for the Diet Industry."
- That individuals considering dieting study available literature on long-term results and side effects and carefully weigh dieting's possible benefits and risks.
- That dieters refuse to feel guilty or blame themselves for presumed lack of willpower if a diet fails.
- That no one allow themselves to be coerced into dieting against their will.
- That no one make assumptions or judge another person on the basis of body size or dietary preferences.

NAAFA Resolves to:

- Educate the public, the media, and potential dieters as to the low long-term success rates and possible negative health consequences of weight reduction dieting.
- Discourage the diet industry from basing their product advertising on fear and guilt and from using and perpetuating negative stereotypes of fat people.
- Promote alternatives to weight-loss diets in a manner which is sensitive to the emotional and financial investment which many fat people have made in repeated weight-loss attempts.

- Provide advice and emotional support to individuals who have dieted unsuccessfully and blame themselves, rather than the product, for the diet's failure.
- Alert consumers to diets or weight-loss schemes which have been determined to be dangerous or fraudulent, have lawsuits pending against them, or are being investigated by government agencies.
- Assist plaintiffs and/or their attorneys engaged in litigation involving diet fraud and ill effects of dieting, by providing them with referrals to expert witnesses who might testify on their behalf.
- Advocate for the safety and emotional and physical well-being of consumers by attempting to influence public policy about dieting, obesity, and diet industry regulation.

Review Questions

1. How does NAAFA define "dieting"?
2. What percentage of dieters lose weight and keep it off five years after beginning their diet?
3. How much money was spent on the diet industry in 1990? (In 2004, the amount was $33 billion.)
4. What are the risks of dieting, according to NAAFA?
5. What is NAAFA's official position on dieting, and what action does it want taken regarding the dieting industry?

Discussion and Writing Suggestions

1. NAAFA states that "[t]he diet industry's advertising and marketing strategy is based on the creation and perpetuation of fear, biases, and stereotypes." Locate a print, television, or radio ad for a diet program and analyze its content for "fear, biases, and stereotypes." Discuss the ways in which NAAFA's assertion is or is not validated by your research.

2. How does NAAFA summarize the stereotypes of fat people? What stereotypes about fat people have you encountered in your experience? List these and compare your list with those of others in your class.

3. Do you believe that the regulation of weight-loss diets is feasible? How do you imagine this regulation would be accomplished?

4. Explore the NAAFA Web site at <http://www.naafa.org>. What are your reactions to the content on the Web site? How would you describe its tone? To what extent does NAAFA present itself as a well-run organization?

5. Review the positions that NAAFA advocates. Which strike you as most workable? Least workable? Why?

Fat and Happy: In Defense of Fat Acceptance
Mary Ray Worley

Mary Ray Worley is a member of NAAFA, the National Association to Advance Fat Acceptance. Hers is the only first-person account you will read in this chapter of the social and psychological pressures that fat people can experience. She does much to elucidate anti-fat stereotypes and, through her spirited writing, does much to dispel them. As you read, you might bear in mind the contrasts between Worley's position on obesity and that of Greg Crister, who argues that we should stigmatize the act of overeating.

1   If you've grown up in twentieth-century American society, you probably believe that being fat is a serious personal, social, and medical liability. Many Americans would rather die or cut off a limb than be fat, many believe that fatness is a serious health risk, and many are convinced that it is a simple matter to reduce one's body size and are so offended by body fat that they believe it is acceptable to shun fat people and make them the butt of cruel jokes. Those who are fat quickly learn to be deeply ashamed of their bodies and spend their lives trying to become what they are not and hide what cannot be hidden. Our society believes that thinness signals self-discipline and self-respect, whereas fatness signals self-contempt and lack of resolve. We're so accustomed to this way of thinking that many of us have never considered that there might be an alternative.

2   Nevertheless, a growing number of people believe it's possible to be happy with your body even if it happens to be fat. In August 2000 I attended the annual convention of the National Association to Advance Fat Acceptance (NAAFA) in San Diego, and it was like visiting another planet altogether. I hadn't realized how deeply my body shame affected my life until I spent a glorious week without it. I'll never be the same again.

3   The first time I had that "different planet" feeling was at the pool party on the first night of the convention. Here were all these fat people in stylish swimsuits and cover-ups, and whereas on my home planet a fat person was expected to feel apologetic and embarrassed about her body—especially in a swimsuit—here were a hundred or so fat people who were enjoying being in their bodies without a shred of self-consciousness. They were having so much fun it was infectious. I felt light-headed and giddy. I kept noticing how great everyone looked. They were confident and radiant and happy—and all sizes of fat. Definitely not my planet.

4   One of the features of NAAFA's conventions is that they invite vendors who sell stylish large-size clothing. So whereas on my home planet, you're lucky if you can find a swimsuit that fits at all, on this planet you have choices and can find a swimsuit that's made from beautiful fabric and looks absolutely smash-

ing on you. Where I come from, you're grateful if you can find clothes that you can actually get on, and forget finding clothes that really fit you. But on this planet there were play clothes, dress-up clothes, you name it. Choices galore. Beautiful fabrics with an elegant drape and a certain panache. I'd never before had so many choices. The clothes I tried on (and bought) not only fit me but looked terrific. As the week wore on and everyone had visited the vendors' booths, we all looked snazzier and snazzier, and the ones who had been to past conventions looked snazzy from the get-go.

5   The next night at the talent show those of us who didn't get a part in the high school musical because we were too fat had a chance to play the lead for five minutes. (I sang a snappy little number by Stephen Sondheim called "The Ladies Who Lunch," from *Company,* and hammed it up big time. I had a blast!) Top billing was given to a troupe of belly dancers called the Fatimas. Now, I had read about this attraction in the literature I received about the convention, and I have to admit that I thought it would be some kind of a spoof or a joke. I just couldn't conceive of a group of fat women doing serious belly dancing, but it was no joke. These women were indeed serious—and excellent—belly dancers. They wore the full belly-dancing regalia—that is, gauze and bangles and beads and not much else. When they first looped and bobbed their way out into the middle of the room, I think my chin must have dropped through the floor. They were exquisitely beautiful and voluptuous and graceful and serene. I thought that anyone, no matter how acculturated to my home planet, would have to be just about dead not to recognize how beautiful they were. And they were all so different from each other. We are accustomed to seeing mostly thin bodies that look more or less the same, but these bodies showed an amazing degree of delightful diversity. Body fat does not distribute itself on every fat person in the same way, so there's lots of variety. Plus they weren't all young. A couple of them had to have been past fifty, and they were so beautiful. And exotic, and mesmerizing. I had always assumed that as a fat woman I could never do that, and especially not as a fat woman past fifty. Wrong, wrong, wrong. I felt a jolt as my old assumptions were jettisoned out into space. Bag that old paradigm. This one is definitely a lot more fun.

6   One of the featured speakers at the convention was Dr. Diane Budd, who spoke about the medical and scientific communities' take on fatness. Although the data gathered for most current studies indicate that body size is primarily determined by one's genetic makeup, most researchers conclude—in spite of their own findings—that fat individuals should try to lose weight anyway. There are no data that indicate (a) that such efforts are likely to be effective (in fact, more than 90 percent of those who lose weight gain it back), (b) that a person's overall health would be improved by losing weight, or (c) that the effort to lose weight won't in fact turn out to have lasting harmful effects on one's appetite, metabolism, and self-esteem. Our assumptions about the desirability of thinness are so deeply ingrained that scientists find it next to impossible to align their recommendations with their findings; apparently they cannot bring themselves to say that since body size is largely a result of one's genetic makeup it's best to get on with the business of learning to live in the body you have, whatever its size.

7   Moreover, none of the studies take into account the physical implications of the social ostracism and body hate that are a regular part of most fat people's lives. Fat people are often taunted in public and are pressured by family members to lose weight. Complete strangers feel they are not out of line to criticize the contents of a fat person's grocery cart, and family members may evaluate everything a fat person puts on her plate. Fat people need to be active and strong enough to carry their body weight comfortably, but they may feel ill at ease exercising in public because of unkind stares and comments. They may feel that they can't wear shorts or sleeveless t-shirts or swimsuits for fear of offending the delicate sensibilities of others and inviting rude comments, and so they will be too hot and too embarrassed and will give up on regular exercise because they don't have the support they need to continue. Now *that* is a health risk.

8   Moreover, fat people are often reluctant to seek medical attention because health professionals are among the most prejudiced people around. Regardless of the ailment you are seeking treatment for, if you are fat, your doctor may put you on a diet before she treats your cough, and attribute whatever complaint you have to your weight. Pressures like these must certainly contribute to the shortening of many fat people's lives, quite apart from any physical risk resulting from a preponderance of body fat.

9   The upshot is that it's very likely that the health risks of being fat have been highly overestimated. In combination with other risk factors, being fat may occasionally contribute to compromised health, but not nearly to the degree that many people think. When a fat person goes to a weight-loss clinic, the goal is usually to lose weight as quickly as possible, as though to snatch the poor fat soul out of the jaws of imminent death. And often the harsh methods used to effect that weight loss are in and of themselves much more harmful than being fat is. In fact, it is my understanding that statistically a person is much less likely to regain weight that is lost very slowly. So what's the big rush? The big rush is that we hate fat and want to put as much distance between ourselves and it as quickly as possible. Quick and dramatic weight loss sells; slow and gradual weight loss does not. There's nothing compassionate, rational, or scientific about it. We just hate fat.

10   Many fat people have made numerous efforts and spent thousands of dollars throughout their lives to lose weight and each time regained the lost pounds plus a few more. Have this happen to you enough times and you will be apprehensive at the prospect of losing weight for fear of gaining back more than you lose. On my own account, there's no way I want to diet again, because it will just make me fatter in the long run. Help like that I don't need, and I sure as spitfire don't need to pay through the nose for it.

11   After years and years of dieting it slowly dawned on me that my body rebelled when I tried to restrict my food intake. All those years I figured that it was me who was failing, and then I began to realize that it was the method that was failing. I began to wonder whether the problem itself was being incorrectly defined. I began raising new questions just about the time that researchers were discovering that, rather than being a simple intake-outtake equation, body weight resulted from a complex interplay of set point (the body's tendency to stay within a certain narrow weight range), appetite and satiety cues, metabo-

lism, and genes. Moreover, our bodies are designed to protect us from starvation and have some powerful defenses against it. They react to dieting just as they do to starving. They don't know there is a McDonald's around every corner. For all they know, we're still living in the Ice Age, when the next meal may be hours or days or miles away. So when we decrease the amount of food we eat, our bodies slow the metabolic rate to fend off possible starvation. It's a great system, really. In my case I'm convinced that as determined as I have been to become thin, my body has always been more determined to save me from starvation. My body is more stubborn than I am. Amazing.

12   So I stopped dieting and began to make peace with food and with my body. I slowly stopped being afraid of food. In 1999 I became a vegetarian, and somehow that change—and the culture that seems to go with it—put food in a new light for me. Food was no longer the enemy; it was a gift and a source of joy. I began to slow down and relish my meals, to enjoy food and be grateful for all the ways that it nourishes me.

13   Over the last fifteen years or so I've made many attempts to become more active on a regular basis with varying degrees of success. I often would go swimming three or four times a week for two, three, or four months followed by a hiatus of several weeks or months. About two years ago, I realized that I always felt better when I was being active. So why the long hiatuses? Because I was exercising in hopes of losing weight. After months of dogged discipline with what I considered to be meager results at best, I would naturally become discouraged and stop. Within a few weeks I would stop feeling the surge of energy and well-being that comes with regular exercise.

14   So what would happen if I just exercised because I felt better when I did? How about moving just for the fun of it? So I gave up the notion of losing weight and consequently gave up feeling hopeless, and as a result the hiatuses have become fewer and shorter in duration. I began to vary my workouts more, so that I got less bored and enjoyed myself more. Who knew that moving, even in a large body, could be this much fun? I'd never allowed myself to have this kind of fun in my body before.

15   I discovered to my delight that the more physically competent I became, the better I felt about my body. My husband, Tom, and I go for long hikes in the woods, and some of those hikes have been challenging for me—not too challenging, but just enough. Two years ago we visited Yosemite National Park, and we hiked partway up to the top of Vernal Fall. It was a demanding hike, and pretty much everybody was huffing and puffing. We made it up to the bridge that's just shy of halfway to the top. It was good to know when to stop, but it rankled me that I didn't have the energy or stamina to make it all the way. So I decided that next time I will. Next spring we're planning another trip to Yosemite, and I'm going to make it to the top of Vernal Fall. I don't care how long it takes me or how much I have to huff and puff. My only stipulation is that I have to be strong enough to have fun doing it. I don't want it to be a torture session.

16   I've been training with that goal in mind for months now. Instead of avoiding stairs, I look for them. I'm no longer ashamed of huffing and puffing—I'm proud. I'm pushing myself just enough so that I'm becoming stronger and have more endurance all the time. This summer I discovered that I can hike all day long. What

a thrill! In July, Tom and I hiked in Copper Falls State Park from 12 noon until 8 P.M. (we stopped to rest three times). And in August I traipsed around the San Diego Wild Animal Park from 9 A.M. until 8 P.M. (again with three rests). How wonderful to have a body that will carry me through an entire day of fun! I never realized before what a miracle my body is, its glorious ability to build muscle and save me from starvation. I'm only beginning to discover what a marvelous gift it is.

17   After years of fighting our set points, our metabolism, our genes, and our hunger, after decades of being ashamed, hating our bodies, and trying to manipulate them into being something they're not, after spending mountains of money and energy trying to conform to someone else's ideal, it isn't surprising that some of us question whether this is the best way to for us to live. A few of us brave adventurers have found another way, and it involves much less agony, costs much less money, and is much more fun.

18   We're not giving up, and we're not letting ourselves go. Rather we're forging a new relationship with our bodies, one that doesn't involve self-loathing, one that appreciates the miraculous bodies we have, one that brings joy. There's plenty of room on this new planet, and here you needn't apologize for your size. You're entitled to the space you take up. You can find clothes that show off the gorgeous person you are, you can play and dance without self-consciousness, you can be proud of yourself and never dread unwanted attention, you can be a brave pioneer and a friend to those who have suffered on planets less kind and less joyous than this one.

Discussion and Writing Suggestions

1. How would you characterize Worley's point of view in this essay? Distilled to a single statement, what is she arguing? To what extent do you find yourself sympathetic to her point of view?

2. Worley writes: "Our society believes that thinness signals self-discipline and self-respect, whereas fatness signals self-contempt and lack of resolve" (paragraph 1). To what extent do you find this statement a fair and accurate representation of how our society views fat people? How do you define "society" in this case? Who (or what) are its agents?

3. What role has NAAFA played in helping Worley think and feel differently about herself?

4. Is Worley's self-acceptance the same thing as complacency about her obesity? Explain your answer.

5. Writing an editorial in the *Journal of the American Medical Association*, Koplan and Dietz claim that "[g]enes related to obesity are clearly not responsible for the epidemic of obesity" (page 474). To what extent does their claim negate the force of Worley's argument (paragraph 6) that "it's best to get on with the business of learning to live in the body you have, whatever its size"?

6. Reread paragraphs 7 and 8 on "the social ostracism and body hate that are a regular part of most fat people's lives." Even if one allows that, in light of new research, Worley is wrong about the causes and medical impact of being fat, to what extent do the points she makes about the social, psychological, and emotional costs of obesity still have force?

7. What are the differences between exercising to lose weight and exercising to feel better? (See paragraphs 13–16.) What lessons are embedded in this distinction?

8. Comment on the "old planet"/"new planet" distinction that Worley develops in paragraphs 2, 3, and 18.

Too "Close to the Bone": The Historical Context for Women's Obsession with Slenderness
Roberta Seid

Roberta Seid critiques our culture's "religion" of thinness and explains how Americans have come to be adherents of this religion, as well of the psychological and even spiritual costs of adherence. You will find in Seid's essay an excellent example of how scholarship—historical and cultural scholarship, in this case—can shine a light on complex problems, helping us to view them in entirely new ways. When she wrote this piece in 1994, Seid was a lecturer in the Program for the Study of Women and Men in Society at the University of Southern California, Los Angeles.

1   Why have Americans, particularly American women, become fatphobic? Why and how have they come to behave as though the shape of their lives depends on the shape of their bodies? Why have they clung to these beliefs despite the toll they take on private lives, and especially despite their most extreme and dangerous manifestation, eating disorders? This chapter addresses these questions by placing the phenomenon in a broad historical context, with particular focus on fashion and the unique and dangerous twist it has taken in our era.

2   Although current explanations for our thinness mania are valuable, they often leave many questions unanswered. Feminists have often blamed fashion for oppressing and subordinating women, but fashion has rarely had the destructive effects we see today. Moreover, the fashion for thinness, which has prevailed only for the past 40 years or so, requires explanation itself. The eating disorders literature, often focused on individual psychopathology, has found neither a consistent etiological profile nor a universally accepted explanation for why eating disorders have swelled into a social disease. Nor does it explain why millions of women without clinical eating disorders mimic the behavior and mind set of affected women. Finally, a much weaker body of literature attributes the phenomenon to the mass media's influence. Although the media's power to shape our perceptions cannot be underestimated, this explanation also begs the question. Why would the media necessarily promote slenderness?

3   A more comprehensive explanation emerges when we stand back and, employing a broad historical perspective, look at the underlying cultural beliefs that affect both genders. Our culture is swept up in a web of peculiar and distorted beliefs about beauty, health, virtue, eating, and appetite. We have elevated the pursuit of a lean, fat-free body into a new religion. It has a creed: "I eat right, watch my weight, and exercise." Indeed, anorexia nervosa could be called the paradigm of our age, for our creed encourages us all to adopt the behavior and attitudes of the anorexic. The difference is one of degree, not of kind. Like any religion worthy of the name, ours also has its damnation. Failure to follow the creed—and the corporeal stigmata of that failure, fatness and flabbiness—produce a hell on earth. The fat and flabby are damned to failure, regardless of professional and personal successes. Our religion also has its rewards, its salvation. In following the creed, one is guaranteed beauty, energy, health, and a long successful life. Followers are even promised self-transformation: The "thin person within," waiting to burst through the fat, is somehow a more exciting, sexy, competent, successful self. Virtue can be quantified by the numbers on the scale, the lean-to-fat ratio, clothing size, and body measurements. And, in a curious inversion of capitalist values, less is always better.

Body Ideals Before the 20th Century

4 The creed of thinness is composed of prejudices, and they have a history. A cursory review of Western civilization's aesthetic and health ideals indicates the novelty and arbitrariness of current beliefs. The female body has not altered for thousands of years; the range of body types in the past does not differ from the range we know today. What has changed is the body type (or types) regarded as ideal, as well as the effort put into meeting this ideal and the methods used to do so. Although styles of dress have tended to change at an ever-quickening tempo since the 12th century, body ideals have changed slowly. By looking at the visual evidence provided by paintings of dressed people and of the nude, we can see that never before have men or women desired a body so "close to the bone."

5   There have been, of course, other periods when slenderness was admired. During the 15th century, paintings of long-limbed ladies reverberated with the vaulting reaches of Gothic cathedrals. Sixteenth-century Mannerists in northern Europe painted elongated nudes, such as the nymphs in Cranach the Elder's *The Judgment of Paris.* More recently, the Romantic vogue for slenderness in the 1830s–1850s encouraged young ladies to strive for the tiny waist favored by fashion—an effort later immortalized in *Gone with the Wind* when Scarlett O'Hara's stays are tightened to achieve a 17-inch waist.[1]

6   Nonetheless, it would be misleading to assume that these eras resembled our own. Gothic and Mannerist nudes had not a bone or muscle showing; they

---

[1] For a fuller discussion of past body ideals, see Roberta P. Seid, *Never Too Thin: Why Women Are at War with Their Bodies* (New York: Prentice-Hall Press, 1989), 37–81. The best sources for a general overview are Francois Boucher, *20,000 Years of Fashion: The History of Costume and Personal Adornment,* expanded edition (New York: Harry N. Abrams, 1987) and Kenneth Clark, *The Nude: A Study in Ideal Form* (Princeton, NJ: Princeton University Press, 1956).

were sweetly and fully fleshed. Women of the Romantic period may have wanted tiny waists, but they also wanted their shoulders, arms, calves, and bosoms ample, indicating an "amorous plenitude."[2] Indeed, thinness was considered ugly, a woman's misfortune. The French epicure J. A. Brillat-Savarin defined thinness as those of his epoch typically did—as "the condition of the individual whose muscular flesh, not being filled with fat, reveals the forms and angles of the bony structure." Thinness in women was, he observed, "a terrible misfortune. . . . The most painstaking toilette, the sublimest costume, cannot hide certain absences, or disguise certain angles."[3] Nor did the Romantic lady equate slenderness with health and energy as we do today; health was not part of her aesthetic ideal. Rather, slenderness signified delicacy and fragility, the qualities she sought.

7   Just a century ago, body ideals and ideas were the reverse of our own, underscoring the fact that there was no folk wisdom about the value of slenderness that science has recently confirmed. Indeed, the female ideal was Junoesque: tall, full-busted, full-figured, mature. Dimpled flesh—what we today shudderingly call "cellulite"—was considered desirable. Sinewy, "close to the bone" women "no bigger than a whipping post" suffered disdain, not those with amply fleshed curves properly distributed and disciplined only by the corset.[4] The undergarment industry even came to the aid of the slighted thin woman with inflatable rubber garments (replete with dimples) for her back, calves, shoulders, and hips. They may have provided meager comfort, for they could deflate at unexpected moments.[5]

8   Fat was seen as a "silken layer" that graced the frames of elegant ladies. It was regarded as "stored-up force," equated with reserves of energy and strength. Plumpness was deemed a sign of emotional well-being; it was identified with a good temperament, with a clean conscience, with temperate and disciplined habits, and above all with good health. Today, of course, we have totally inverted these associations.[6]

9   In the mid-19th century, the prolific writer Catherine Beecher described healthy weight. If you felt heavy and got on the scale (a rare experience in the 19th century), and weighed either heavy or light, you were in bad health. But if you felt light and weighed heavy, then you were in excellent health; weighing heavy was good. More importantly, Beecher distinguished between feelings

[2] See the excellent discussion of this ideal in Valerie Steele, *Fashion and Eroticism: Ideals of Feminine Beauty from the Victorian Era to the Jazz Age* (New York: Oxford University Press, 1985), 108–110.

[3] Jean Anthelme Brillat-Savarin, *The Physiology of Taste or Meditations on Transcendental Gastronomy* (New York: Doubleday, 1926 [orig. 1826]), 172, 187.

[4] Steele, 1985, 218–223; Hillel Schwartz, *Never Satisfied: A Cultural History of Diets, Fantasies, and Fat* (New York: Free Press, 1986), Illustration 5 (1857 cartoon from *Harper's Weekly*).

[5] David Kunzle, "The Corset as Erotic Alchemy: From Rococo Galanterie to Montaut's Physiologies," in Thomas Hess and Linda Nochlin, eds., *Art News Annual*, vol. 38, *Woman as Sex Object: Erotic Art, 1730–1970* (1972); Steele, 1985, 128, 221.

[6] Seid, 1989, 70–80.

and actual weight—a distinction lost to many today, who determine how they feel by the numbers on the scale.[7]

Development of the Obsession with Thinness

10 The transformation of these values began at about the turn of the present century, when slenderness came into fashion. This occurred for a variety of reasons, among them the modernist aesthetic with its idealization of speed and motion, and its penchant for stripping things down to their essential forms. (Some called it the revenge of the thin who for so long had been slighted.) But "slim" is a relative term, and the women who boasted the new form would by contemporary standards be called overweight. In addition, in the first half of this century, the belief that plumpness signaled robust health remained strong.

11   The culture of slimming as we know it is really a post–World War II phenomenon.[8] Fashion continued to value a slender (if curving) form, and the health industry, finally convinced by insurance companies, launched massive campaigns to persuade Americans to lose weight. Key ideas that would take full force in subsequent decades began to emerge. Chief among these was "fatphobia," the conviction that animal fat of any kind—on the body, in the blood, on the plate—was dangerous. The perception developed that Americans were too fat and getting fatter; that they ate too much, ate the wrong foods, and were sedentary and therefore flabby. Americans' self-perception shifted to that of a diseased, unhealthy group, even though they enjoyed the best health and greatest longevity ever known in American society. These pronouncements did not abate, even though average life expectancy continued to improve. Most important was the growing fear that Americans were getting physically and *morally* soft. For at the heart of all the campaign literature was a moral concern about how Americans would react to postwar plenty and leisure—how they would handle modernization.

12   In subsequent decades, these ideas intensified. Weight loss techniques began to be seen as life-prolonging in and of themselves. The fitness ethic emerged from these beliefs and fueled obsession with exercise. But the new emphasis on fitness was just a variation on the theme of slenderness. The ideal remained a fat-free body. The "health food" craze played on the same dynamic, growing out of and then later helping to fuel and dignify diet obsessions. In addition, the standards of slenderness grew more extreme, both in charts of ideal weight and in fashion. The famous 1960s model Twiggy, at 5 feet 7 inches and 98 pounds, represented the boundary beyond which no ambulatory person could go; however, her image became one that women thereafter aspired to meet. Female beauty had come to be represented by a gawky, bare-boned adolescent. Simultaneously, definitions of "overweight" and "obesity" began to include normal-sized Americans.

---

[7] Beecher's standards are quoted by Harvey Green, *Fit for America: Health–Fitness–Sport and American Society* (New York: Pantheon Books, 1986), 64.

[8] For a fuller discussion with citations of sources, see Seid, 1989, Chapters 12 and 13.

13   More compelling, however, were the principles underlying fatphobia, which turned it into a national obsession. The health industry embraced the questionable concept of "ideal weight"—the idea that the weight associated with optimum health and longevity could be determined by height. It was then decreed that everyone of the same height and bone structure should meet this ideal. But this injunction assumed that body weight and the ratios of fat to lean tissue were direct functions of exercise and eating habits. The obvious corollary was that everybody should reduce to ideal weight and that everybody could easily do so—if they exerted enough willpower. In short, these decrees blamed the victim: if you were fat, it was your fault. This is the most powerful and pernicious aspect of fatphobia; indeed, in modern America, being fat is as shameful as being dirty. We seem to believe that slenderness is as attainable as cleanliness, and as crucial to respectable grooming. We can easily embrace these ideas because they fit so well with America's self-help-oriented, democratic ideology. We can all be body aristocrats, we believe, if we just try hard enough. This set of beliefs fuels prejudices against fat and has allowed the thinness mania to spiral into a religion.

14   More and more evidence is emerging that discredits this whole ideology and shows that its premises are empirically flawed. The thinner are not necessarily healthier, nor are they more fit. Our fundamental beliefs—that people of the same height should have the same weight, and that people can exercise absolute control over their body weights—are also flawed. Numerous studies demonstrate that the majority of the "fat" cannot slim down permanently. The problem is not their lack of willpower, but the unreasonable expectation placed on them to weigh a certain amount. Animal breeders have long known that nature did not intend everyone to be the same size, but modern science seems to have temporarily forgotten.

15   Sadly, efforts to squeeze into the ideal size are often useless and destructive—not only because they can exacerbate the problem they are designed to cure, but because they trigger psychological, physiological, and behavioral consequences, including binge eating, food obsessions, and, in susceptible individuals, eating disorders. Even worse, dieters pay a price in sense of well-being, in health, and in the ability to lead rich and productive lives. The contemporary and historical literature on famine describes ennui, tension, irritability, preoccupation with food, loss of libido, and lassitude created by diets equivalent to those advised for weight loss. The United Nations World Health Organization has established a daily intake of 1000 calories as the border of semistarvation; modern diets often recommend less. The famine literature attributes these symptoms to hunger and undernourishment; the literature on overweight attributes them to lack of willpower or to psychopathology.

16   Laboring under perverse notions about food and appetite, we believe that permanent dieting and chronic hunger are healthy and energy-giving; we are convinced that food does not nourish, but rather kills. If we find ourselves eating with unbridled appetite, we believe that there is either something wrong with us or with the food itself, which must be "addictive." In truth, the well-nourished, not the undernourished, grow strong, healthy, and productive. Poor appetite is a sign of the depressed and the ill; indeed, women are often grateful for an illness—it makes dieting easier.

17   It is hard to resist the parallel between Victorian attributes toward sex and modern attitudes toward food. In the 19th century, the control of sexual instincts was the acme of virtue; sexual behavior was the yardstick of goodness. Today, eating habits and body weights have become the yardsticks of virtue, and food rules have become as dour and inhibitory as the sex rules of the 19th century. Perhaps cultures require some kind of instinctual control to feel that they qualify as "civilized."

Why Women More Than Men?

18 Given that this belief system pervades our culture, why does it affect women so much more than men? Why do more women than men suffer from eating disorders, obesity, and distorted body image? Why are women, not men, at war with their bodies? There are many reasons, some more obvious than others.

19   One reason is biological. Standards for males simply are not as extreme or as inimical to normal masculine body builds as are women's standards. Indeed, our female ideal violates the anthropomorphic reality of the average female body. The ideal female weight, represented by actresses, models, and Miss Americas, has progressively decreased to that of the thinnest 5–10% of American women. Consequently, 90–95% of American women feel that they don't "measure up."[9] Societies have never been kind to deviants, but in America a statistical deviation has been normalized, leading millions of women to believe that they are abnormal.

20   In addition, the taut, lean, muscled body—the "fit" form so many strive to achieve—is more like the body of a male than of a female. The goal is to suppress female secondary sexual characteristics, from dimpled flesh to plumpness in thighs, behinds, hips, and bosom. Women consequently are pitted in a war against their own biologies to meet the standard.

21   It is not just biology that confounds women. They strive to meet this unreasonable standard because it has become a moral imperative in our society, and because, despite a quarter-century of feminism, the quest for physical beauty

---

[9] Although exact figures on this subject remain elusive, many sources confirm this general trend. This percentage was suggested by Rita Freedman, *Beauty Bound* (Lexington, Mass.: Lexington Books, 1986), 149, but it is corroborated by other sources. I studied statistics of Miss America contenders with data for the earlier periods from Frank Deford, *There She Is: The Life and Times of Miss America* (New York: Viking Press, 1971), 313–316, and from Miss America Pageant Yearbooks, 1972–1983, and found a dramatic slenderizing trend. For more details, see Seid, 1989, Chapter 10. For a study of a similar development in the *Playboy* centerfolds, whose average weights dropped from 11% below the national average in 1970 to 17% below it in 1978, see Paul E. Garfinkel and David M. Garner, *Anorexia Nervosa: A Multidimensional Perspective* (New York: Brunner/Mazel, 1982), 108–109, and D. M. Garner, P. E. Garfinkel, D. Schwartz, and M. Thompson, "Cultural Expectations of Thinness in Women," *Psychological Reports* 47 (1980): 483–491. On the rise of an emaciated ideal in the ballet subculture, see L. M. Vincent, *Competing with the Sylph* (New York: Andrews & McMeel, 1979). Jennifer Brenner, professor of psychology at Brandeis University, and Dr. Joseph Cunningham recently reported the results of their study comparing the weights of New York fashion models and Brandeis students. "Female models are 9 percent taller and 16 percent thinner than average women," Brenner reported in an article by Lena Williams, "Girl's Self-Image Is Mother of the Woman," *New York Times* (National Edition), February 6, 1992, A1, A12.

remains deeply powerful. On even a practical level, women's self-image, their social and economic success, and even their survival can still be determined largely by their beauty and by the men it allows them to attract, while for men these are based largely on how they act and what they accomplish. Looks simply are of secondary importance for male success.

22   But the impulse toward beauty runs much deeper than the desire for social acceptance and success. Beauty and fashion are intertwined, and women try to meet unreasonable weight standards also because fashion—our system of dress—requires them to do so. Though many have castigated fashion as a shallow and frivolous vanity, it is propelled by profound impulses, which it shares with all dress systems. Dress and adornment are basic to all human cultures. Even the most primitive tribes find ways to decorate the body. The overwhelming importance of dress is underscored by the fact that from the moment we slip out of the womb to the moment of our deaths, we alter our natural appearance. How we choose to dress is a complex cultural phenomenon. Clothing and adornment are simultaneously a material object, a social signal, a ritual, and a form of art. Every facet of a society—from its economic base to its social structure, from its values about human beings and their bodies to its loftiest spiritual and aesthetic ideals—influences the forms and rules of dress. Each culture sets up its own rules, and in following them, people defer to and perpetuate fundamental social values and norms.

23   In obeying fashion's dictates, we are bowing to powerful constraints about self-presentation and about how others should interpret our attitudes, behavior, and identity. The enormous time and energy women (and men) devote to it is simply another of civilization's many demands and, possibly, pleasures. For in dressing, in following fashion, we are engaged in a game, a plastic art, a process whereby we partially create ourselves. We are involved in social and private play of the profoundest type—trying to transcend our uncivilized, animal state, to make ourselves human. Friedrich Nietzsche, in *The Birth of Tragedy,* argued that "We derive such dignity as we possess from our status as art works." Fun, fantasy, humor, artistic creativity, and our deepest aspirations exist in the dress constraints of everyday life.[10]

24   Fashion, the dress system of the West, has, however, taken a rather peculiar twist in recent decades—one that helps explain our body obsessions. Fashionable beauty is no longer about the clothes covering the body, but about the naked body itself. This has not been true before in the history of fashion. Fashion is, as we have seen, a plastic art. Although it would be foolhardy to describe the past as Edenic, it nonetheless is true that fashion has traditionally been a handmaiden to beauty. It allowed people to approach the reigning ideal by manipulating cosmetics and clothing—that is, by manipulating what they put *on* themselves, not what they *were* underneath those clothes, stays, girdles, and so forth.

---

[10] Nietzsche's statement is quoted in Steele, 1985, 245. For a fuller theoretical discussion and bibliography on the role of dress and adornment in human culture, see Roberta P. Seid, *The Dissolution of Traditional Rural Culture in Nineteenth-Century France: A Study of the Bethmale Costume* (New York: Garland Press, 1987), 1–45.

25   By the late 20th century, however, women's bodies, which heretofore had never been exposed to the public eye, virtually became wholly exposed. With the introduction of the miniskirt and teeny tops, women's legs, thighs, and upper bodies were suddenly revealed, bereft of the aid of body-shaping undergarments. The fitness craze and the growing liberalization in censorship and in acceptable norms of nudity intensified the trend.

26   By the 1980s, even fashion magazines showed naked or leotarded bodies more than they showed clothing. The undressed body—the bare bones of being, celebrated as liberating and "natural"—had become the focus of fashion. No longer did a woman have the luxury of manipulating only what was outside her body, the "not me"; now she had to manipulate her self, the once private stretches of the body.

27   This new, "natural" look could not really be liberating, because fashion is antithetical (almost by definition) to nature, so stringent standards began being set for the now-exposed form. Suddenly, the average American woman became aware of flaws she never knew existed; pronouncements were made about how every private crevice of her anatomy was to look. Women consequently ran smack into a dilemma between the naked and the nude.

28   The art historian Sir Kenneth Clark argued that the nude is a form of art; the naked is merely the human body undressed, replete with all its flaws and blemishes. The naked becomes the nude through art, with the artist transforming that humble and flawed form into an ideal of beauty.[11] Yet today, bombarded by verbal and visual commercial images of the nude, women have been seduced into believing that they should—and could, with enough effort—have one of those perfect bodies. They expect the image reflected in their mirrors to look like the nude. It almost never does. And so they renew their battle against their recalcitrant bodies.

29   Changes in the structure of fashion contributed further to the battle: No authorities put brakes on the urge to meet the slender ideal. This, too, was new in fashion's history. Although there has always been considerable harmony among standards of feminine beauty, health, and the gestalt of an era, excesses of fashion were heretofore severely criticized by social authorities, including doctors, teachers, and clergy, parents, and, since the 19th century, feminists. The clergy and moralists, in particular, stressed that there were values more important than outward appearance; that the soul and one's deeds mattered, not fashion standards; that, in the words of the old adage, "Pretty is as pretty does." In the late 20th century—at least until alarm about eating disorders spread—all these authorities, especially physicians, seemed to agree that one could never be too thin. This unholy alliance between societal and fashion authorities allowed the vogue for thinness to go to extremes.

30   Even contemporary feminists have been slow to resist the slenderness fashion. They were initially seduced, perhaps, by its underlying message that biology is not destiny. Even more, the rhetoric of the slenderness ideal—that health

---

[11] Clark, 1956, 3–9.

is beauty and beauty health, and both are fit and thin—may have persuaded them. They applauded the fact that physical strength and health were now feminine ideals. It took a while for them to realize that what was sought, what had become ideal, was merely the *appearance* of health and vigor—and that dangerous means were being used to achieve it.

31   Despite the historical uniqueness of these developments, some rather cruel historical consistencies remain. More stringent bodily controls are still required of the female than of the male. Animal-like functions, such as belching, nose wiping, urinating, sweating, scratching, spitting, masturbating, farting, and even body odor, remain less permissible for women than for men. In the male subculture, unlike female subcultures, there is an acceptance of and a certain humor about these behaviors, which sometimes become the subject of good-natured contests. Men simply are permitted to be more comfortable about natural functions and to exhibit them to a greater extent in public. They do not compromise masculinity; rather, they often confirm it. Women, on the other hand, compromise their femininity if they do not control these behaviors. The same discrepancy applies to diet and body size: Women are expected to manage these even more stringently than men. Similarly, as long as control of appetite and body weight is regarded as virtuous, women must exercise this control more than men. Once again, women are expected to be the custodians and embodiments of virtue for the culture.

Thinness and Our Cultural and Spiritual Values

32 What remains puzzling about this unique fashion for bare-boned skinniness is what it suggests about our aesthetic ideals—and, even more importantly, about our values, our gestalt. If we step back a moment and look at our ideal of beauty from a more distant perspective (perhaps that of a future historian or anthropologist), we can perhaps see how peculiar it is that we celebrate the living version of Giacometti sculptures, anorexics with barbells.

33   Future historians might conjecture that Americans had fallen in love with death, or at least with mortification of the flesh. They might speculate that terror of nuclear destruction had made fashion play with cadavers and turn them into images of beauty. Or they might argue that we had been so influenced by modern art, Bauhaus aesthetics, and contemporary steel architecture that our ideal human body also had come to consist only of the scaffolding that held it up and of the machinery that made it move. Or they might suggest that we had come to see technology, not human beings, as the prime force in history, and so had chosen to resemble our conquerors.

34   Alternatively, they might argue that our fascination with the unconscious, and our new awareness that scientific reality was concealed from us—that the universe was made up of particles we could not see and governed by laws that defied the logic of our senses—led us to strip the outer body of any meaning or significance and of any possible beauty. Or, more simply, they might conjecture that in an era of population density, it was more practical and economical to have skinny people. Thin people would need less room, so more of them could be squeezed into the spaces on mass transit and into workplaces, and they

could live in smaller houses. It certainly also might be interpreted as democratic. No one had the right to take up more space than another or to command respect through the imposing grandeur of body size.

35   They might also conjecture that late 20th-century America had so confused its image of women that what looked female could no longer be considered beautiful. Even more, they might contend that we had dehumanized, not just masculinized, the human form. We had reduced it to its smallest, least imposing form. They might argue that we had come to idealize technology, and also (befitting our secular age) to distinguish humans from other animals and the civilized from the uncivilized not by the presence of consciousness, a soul, and a conscience, but by the suppression of animal fat. They might even suggest that we had become so terrified of what made us human—especially our passions and our vulnerability—that we didn't want our bodies to betray any softness, curves, or idiosyncracies. Or they might think that we had suppressed tender flesh because we no longer saw human beings as sources of comfort and nurture.

36   From a purely aesthetic perspective, our fat-free beauties might come out no better. Indeed, even unprejudiced present-day observers may be taken aback. Faces are gaunt and angular; necks are steeples of bones. Unfleshed arms and legs, full of sharp angles, look gangly and disproportionately long. Indeed, dieted women look as though the life and color have been sucked out of them. Nor, for all the paeans to strength, do these scrawny, narrow women look strong or stable, or as if they have a stature to be reckoned with. Indeed, the lean body looks as repressed and controlled as the spirit that must have gotten it that way.

37   It is odd, too, that we have developed an erotic ideal that suppresses flesh and minimizes sexual characteristics. There is little to linger over, to explore, to discover. When the body has been efficiently reduced to a flat surface, it offers no softness, no warmth, no tenderness, no mysteries—qualities once integral to images of sexuality. Our erotic ideal has become as hard and unyielding, perhaps, as the love relationships that dominate social life.

38   In criticizing our new religion, I am not suggesting that we gorge wantonly or that we ignore our health and our physical appearance. This would be a surrender to the treacherous polarities that dominate our thinking: Our choices seem to be thinness or fatness, gluttony or starvation, vigorous exercise or lethargy, ascetic rituals or self-indulgence, youthfulness or old age, beauty or ugliness. I am suggesting that we recultivate our tastes and find a saner middle ground where our bodies can round out with more life, flesh, and health; where we can relish the fruits of our prosperity without self-punishment; and where we understand that the nourishment that is one of life's greatest pleasures is also one of its most basic necessities.

39   It would be a tragedy, after 25 years of the women's movement, if women did not rebel against this "religion" that threatens to sabotage their hard-won victories. Is the "liberated woman," supposedly at ease in the boardroom, really consumed with self-loathing and obsessed with tallying calories, exercise, and the vital statistics of the body (weight, muscle-to-fat ratio, inches of breast, hip, and thigh)? Never measuring quite right, she may be as victimized by biology as her predecessors.

40   I am not suggesting, as many past and present feminists have, that we do away with beauty and fashion standards altogether. It would be a bleak world if we did not celebrate beauty and if we did not encourage the imagination and play involved in bedecking ourselves and molding our own images. The impulses toward adornment and self-beautification run deep in human culture and are connected to its noblest aspirations. Nor am I suggesting that fashion standards of the past were always benign. Each era has exacted its own price for beauty, though our era is unique in producing a standard based exclusively on the bare bones of being, which can be disastrous for human health, happiness, and productivity.

41   But I am urging that we dismantle this new religion, because it is misguided and destructive. It does not provide reasonable guidelines by which to live. Our bodies, our fitness, and our food should not be our paramount concerns. They have nothing to do with ethics, or relationships, or community responsibilities, or with the soul. They have nothing to say about the purpose of life, except that we should survive as well and as long and as beautifully as we can. They give us no purpose beyond ourselves. This is a religion appropriate only for a people whose ideals do not extend beyond their physical existence, and whose vision of the future and of the past is strangely empty. Surely Americans can produce a worthier creed.

42   In making the denial of hunger and its physical manifestations, thinness, into a primary virtue, our "religion" is unique among the major world religions. Although there is a long history of fasting for spiritual cleansing or purity, no religion has set it up as a virtue; indeed, most have condemned it. Buddha rejected fasting because he did not find it a way to enlightenment. Judaism prescribes only a few fast days a year. Otherwise, it proscribes such deprivation: According to the Talmud, people must be well nourished so they can do what is important in life—follow God's commandments and perform *mitzvot* (good deeds). The early fathers of the Christian Church, too, condemned fasting, and the Church exacted higher penances for the sin of not eating than it did for the sin of gluttony. The Muslims, even during their great fast of Ramadan, do not abstain from food. They are merely proscribed from eating during certain hours, and the other hours are given to feasting. In these religions, food has not been seen as a temptation put in humanity's path, but as vital for people to carry out their larger spiritual tasks.

43   It is one thing to follow a rigid dietary code and rituals of behavior in accordance with the laws of a God or gods we worship. The faithful are trying to fulfill God's or the gods' commandments, not only for their own salvation, but also to hasten the arrival of a more perfect world. It is quite another thing to follow rigid dietary and behavior codes only to improve our physical selves. Such actions are not part of a larger system of morals. They have no vision of a higher good or of a better future that their rituals might help create. This is a solipsistic religion in the narrowest and strictest sense, in that it is only about the bare bones of being. If avoiding fatness and possible disease is the main preoccupation of our lives, then what are we living for?

44   Our new religion bankrupts us. Historically unprecedented numbers of us are healthy—able to enjoy sex without fear of unwanted pregnancy, to go

through childbirth without the once omnipresent threat of death, to treat once-fatal infectious diseases easily, and to alleviate the minor aches and pains that caused discomfort to our forebears (from toothaches to earaches to headaches to skin eruptions to upset stomachs). Advances in technology, medicine, and food production, wrought by painstaking human efforts, have given us a well-being virtually unknown in previous centuries. We should be grateful, but instead we hate our bodies because they bulge here or are flabby there or fail to respond to our most rigorous diets. Surely this is the worst form of hubris—to despise our bodies because they are not perfect. Our new religion neither puts checks on this kind of vanity nor underscores how trivial is the accomplishment of weight loss and of physical perfection. Instead, it seduces us into believing that this quest is the worthiest of human goals.

45   We must abandon our new religion because it trivializes human life itself. We must restore a humanistic vision in which self-improvement means cultivating the mind and enlarging the soul; developing generosity, humor, dignity, and humility; living more graciously with biology, aging, and death; living with our limitations. We need a concept of self-improvement that reminds us to learn from the past, to build on it, and to bequeath wisdom to future generations. We stand poised between a past for which we have lost respect and a future we must now struggle to envision.

Review Questions

1. According to Seid, what is our "new religion," and what is its creed?

2. In what ways is the 20th- and 21st-century ideal of beauty arbitrary?

3. To what does "close to the bone" of Seid's title refer?

4. In what ways has the ideal of female beauty changed in the last 100 years?

5. Why did the current "fatphobia" take hold?

6. What, according to Seid, is the "most . . . pernicious aspect of fatphobia" (paragraph 13)?

7. In what ways is the blame-the-victim logic directed against fat people flawed, according to Seid?

8. In paragraph 18, Seid asks: "Why do more women than men suffer from eating disorders, obesity, and distorted body image?" What is her answer?

9. After launching her extended critique against the "religion" of dieting and the "close to the bone" ideal of beauty, what recommendation does Seid make?

Discussion and Writing Suggestions

1. In paragraph 3, Seid challenges the reader with a daring assertion: "[A]norexia nervosa could be called the paradigm of our age, for our creed encourages us all to adopt the behavior and attitudes of the anorexic. The difference is one of degree, not of kind." Two questions: First, if you have followed the logic of Seid's argument, does this assertion follow? Second, to what extent do you agree?

2. In paragraphs 13–14, Seid explains the logic by which Americans come to blame fat people for being fat. Summarize that logic—and then comment on it. For instance, have you ever encountered this type of blame-the-victim thinking? Is it reasonable, in your view, to regard fat people as victims?

3. In your experience, or in the experience of people you know, to what extent is it true that "dieters pay a price in sense of well-being, in health, and in the ability to lead rich and productive lives" (paragraph 15)?

4. In paragraph 15, Seid juxtaposes the "contemporary and historical literature on famine" with the messages implied in and stated directly by our dieting culture. What is your response?

5. How do you respond to Seid's assertion in paragraph 17 comparing our culture's preoccupation with weight to Victorian culture's preoccupation with sex?

6. Seid argues that in the twentieth century the world of fashion has focused not only on clothes but on the body, the result being that a woman who wants to dress fashionably must attend to the body beneath the clothes as well as to the clothes themselves (see paragraphs 24–27). How consciously aware are you of having to "manipulate" yourself—that is your body—in order to be fashionably correct? After you have answered this question, meet in a group of four or more classmates, with equal numbers of men and women. Compare answers.

7. In paragraph 29, Seid speaks of an "unholy alliance between societal and fashion authorities." What, in her view, is so unholy? Do you agree?

8. Seid writes in paragraph 41: "Our bodies, our fitness, and our food . . . have nothing to do with ethics, or relationships, or community responsibilities, or with the soul." In paragraph 43 she writes that severe dieting for the sake of thinness, alone, is a "solipsistic religion" and contributes nothing to the greater good of society. Seid makes a strong and cogent argument in this essay against the "religion" of thinness and the ways in which it "trivializes human life itself." Discuss her conclusions and recommendations. Do you

agree? Could you imagine yourself or others agreeing and *still* wanting to diet?

9. Notwithstanding Seid's arguments, statistical trends are clear (see the selections in this chapter from the *Journal of the American Medical Association* and the Centers for Disease Control) that the number of overweight and obese people is rising, which in turn is leading to increased levels of illness and death. In what ways do these scientific reports affect your reading of Seid?

Fat and Happy?
Hillel Schwartz

"Fat and Happy?" forms the final chapter of historian Hillel Schwartz's book-length study of dieting, Never Satisfied *(Free Press, 1986). Like Seid, who critiques what she terms a "religion" of thinness, Schwartz critiques what he calls a "despotism of slenderness." The selection has a satiric feel to it, but underlying all satire—this included—are points seriously made. Indeed, much of the logic presented here you will find shared by other writers, such as Seid and Worley. In the two sections of the chapter reproduced here, Schwartz presents a "Vindication of Fat" and an image of "The Fat Society: A Utopia."*

Recently there has been a growing protest against the despotism of slenderness, and a scientific debate over the dangers of a moderate fatness. Underlying the protest and the debate is a utopian vision of a Fat Society where neither overweight nor obesity stands in the way of social freedom or personal happiness.

The Vindication of Fat

1   Fatness is fine.

2   If fat people are unhappy people, blame not their fat but their fellow citizens who bill them as clowns, clodhoppers, cannibals, or criminals; who spread such commercial rumors as "To be fat is the end of life"; who sport bumper stickers on their vans, "No fat chicks"; who print posters which read, "It's in to be thin. It's out to be stout."[1] Blame the kindergarten teachers, the coaches, the friends and physicians who goad fat people into a maze of diets from which they may never return. Dieting makes everything worse, for the chances are high that fat people will fail. They will be saddened and frustrated by their failures, and they will come to agree with everyone else that they are failures in all of life. Because they have failed they are fat, and because they are fat they fail.

3   It is the taking off and the putting on of weight that endangers the body. Not the fat or the pounds but the dieting itself, the frustration, and the constant

---

"Fat and Happy?" from *Never Satisfied: A Cultural History of Diets, Fantasies and Fat* by Hillel Schwartz. Copyright © 1996 by Hillel Schwartz. Reprinted with the permission of The Free Press, a Division of Simon & Schuster, Inc.

[1] Marvin Grosswirth, *Fat Pride* (NY, 1971) 161, D-Zerta ad, and American Physical Fitness Research Institute poster, "Fit to Quote" (Santa Monica, Calif., 1969).

hunger. No one has been able to prove that fatness *per se* cuts life short. If left alone, 99 percent of human beings will reach a plateau weight, a set point at which their metabolisms will be satisfied and their bodies healthy. It is the dieting, the anxiety, and the perpetual scrimmaging with food that lead to illness. "What causes the most damage is not the actual weight itself, but the fear of weight." People who drive their weights down and up through a series of diets are those most likely to become fatter and unhappier than before, for they upset the natural equilibrium of their bodies. In self-defense, their bodies stock-pile fat whenever and wherever possible, hedging as they may against the next (self-imposed) privation. Meanwhile hearts suffer through cycles of feast and famine, strained at each new feast, shocked at each new famine. "To fat, to starve—/Perchance to die of it! Ah, there's the rub." Pokeberry, dinitrophenol, rainbow pills, liquid protein—there is no end to death by dieting.[2]

4   And still the dieting goes on, as fat people are compromised and persecuted. Like other minorities, fat people are treated like children, given silly nicknames, considered socially and sexually immature. The "Diet Conscience," an electronic guardian, sneers when the refrigerator door is opened, "Are you eating again? Shame on you! No wonder you look the way you do! Ha! Ha! Ha! You'll be sorry, fatty. Do yourself a favor; *shut the door!*"[3]

5   Like other minorities, fat people are seen as throwbacks to a more primitive time. Neanderthals in museum dioramas are squat and fat; cannibals stirring pots are fat; Oriental despots are fat; harems are full of slothful fat women and

---

[2] Louis I. Dublin believed that he had demonstrated that weight-reducing decreased mortality: "Overweight shortens life," *MLIC* 32 (Oct 1951) 1–4, and idem, "Relation of obesity to longevity," *NEJM* 248 (1953) 971–74. But see Public Health Service, *Obesity and Health* (Washington, D.C., 1966) 59; George V. Mann, "Obesity, the national spook," *AJPH* 61 (1971) 1491–98; idem, "Influence of obesity on health," *NEJM* 291 (1974) 178–85, 226–32; and William Bennett and Joel Gurin, *The Dieter's Dilemma* (NY, 1982) 134–35.

On the absence of a causal relationship between fatness or overweight and increased mortality, see Ancel Keys et al., "Coronary heart disease: overweight and obesity as risk factors," *AIM* 77 (1972) 15–27; Tavia Gordon and William B. Kannel, "Obesity and cardiovascular disease: the Framingham study," *Clinics in Endocrinology and Metabolism* 5 (1976) 367–75; Susan C. Wooley et al., "Obesity and women—I. A closer look at the facts," *Women's Studies Int Q* 2 (1979) 74; Reubin Andres, "Effect of obesity on total mortality," *IJO* 4 (1980) 381–86; Kelly D. Brownell, "Obesity," *J of Consulting and Clinical Psych* 50 (1982) 820; and Carol Sternhill, "We'll always be fat, but fat can be fit," *Ms.* (May 1985) 142. On the dangers of a weight-loss/weight-gain cycle, see Vinne Young, *It's Fun to Be Fat* (NY, 1953) 10, 26 and quote on 23; Nick Lyons, *Locked Jaws* (NY, 1979) 13 quote; and Sharon G. Patton, "Why dieting can make you fat," *New Woman* (Aug 1984) 34.

On deaths from dieting, see Roland C. Curtin, "The heart and its danger in the treatment of obesity," *J of Balneology and Climatology* 12 (1908) 223 on pokeberry; Chapter Seven on dinitrophenol and amphetamines; House of Representatives Subcommittee on Health and the Environment, *Hearing . . . on the Most Popular Diet in America Today, Liquid Protein, Dec 28, 1977* (Washington, D.C., 1978) 3–7; Centers for Disease Control, "Follow-up on deaths associated with liquid protein diets," *Morbidity and Mortality Weekly Report* 27 (1978) 223–24; Harold E. Sours et al., "Sudden death associated with very low calorie weight reduction regimens," *AJCN* 34 (1981) 453–61, and see also 1639–40, 2855–57.

[3] Ann M. Lingg, "A plump girl talks back," *Amer Mercury* 78 (March 1954) 30, an early reference to minority status; Lew Louderback, "More people should be fat," *SEP* 240 (Nov 4, 1967) 10; Grosswirth, *Fat Pride,* 40; and Mildred Klingman, *Secret Lives of Fat People* (Boston, 1981) 72 on Diet Conscience. See also Lisa Schoenfielder and Barb Wieser, eds., *Shadow on a Tightrope: Writings by Women on Fat Oppression* (Iowa City, Ia., 1983).

supervised by fat eunuchs. The modern world is passing them by. Fat people are stuck in the past, so much so that modern businessmen and scientists prefer an employee who has been in jail or in a mental ward to one who is fat. Criminality and insanity seem less intransigent, less rooted, than obesity.[4]

6   If fat people are not such atavisms, why do they do so poorly in school and in business? The same vicious circle surrounding other minorities surrounds fat people, who have more difficulty getting into the best colleges and who are not promoted as quickly as their leaner rivals. How they look is more important than how well they do their jobs. The New York City Traffic Department in 1965 dismissed six meter maids for being overweight; National Airlines fired a stewardess for being 4 lbs overweight. As of 1982 only Michigan had a law specifically banning discrimination on account of weight. In 1980 a *New Yorker* cartoon depicted a judge sentencing a defendant: "It is the Court's opinion that, although innocent, you are dangerously overweight." This comedy had already been played out in Miami, where a woman being sentenced for a misdemeanor assault explained that at 315 lbs she was too heavy to work. The judge gave her three years' probation on the condition that she lose 65 lbs at 3 lbs per week; if she went off her diet, she would go to prison.[5]

7   Physicians are equally unsympathetic. They find fat patients distasteful. Fat people seem more difficult to examine, less likely to cooperate. Fat people are waddling reminders of the failure of medicine to come up with a safe, workable program for long-term weight reduction, just as poor people and homeless people are stark reminders of the failure of the economic system. Like politicians, physicians blame the victims. It is not the doctor's fault if fat people are weak, dishonest, lazy, and childish. All one can do with such people is to threaten them with disease and death, play on their fears. "If, knowing these dangers—as you now do—you continue to overeat, it must be obvious that you are acting in a childish fashion. You are immature. This *alone* will prove to you that you are acting *like a child* if you continue to be fat. Now it is up to you. . . . Be childish and die, or grow up and live!"[6]

---

[4] Robert J. Homant and Daniel B. Kennedy, "Attitudes toward ex-offenders: a comparison of social stigmas," *J of Criminal Justice* 10 (1982) 383–91.

[5] Peter L. Benson et al., "Social costs of obesity," *Social Behavior and Personality* 8 (1980) 91–96 on colleges; Llewellyn Louderback, *Fat Power* (NY, 1970) 47, 52, 53, 55; Chris Chase, *The Great American Waistline* (NY, 1981) 196 on stewardesses; *New Yorker* (Sept 29, 1980) 49; and "Better than prison," *Time* 97 (June 7, 1971) 39. Concerning weight discrimination at law, see David H. Tucker for the Maryland Commission on Human Relations, *Report on the Study of Weight and Size Discrimination*, typescript (Baltimore, 1980); Jane O. Baker, "The Rehabilitation Act of 1973: protection for victims of weight discrimination?" *UCLA Law R* 29 (April 1982) 947–71; David Berreby, "Is being fat a handicap? Courts differ," *National Law J* 4 (Aug 30, 1982) 3:1; Lynne Reaves, "Fat folks' rights: weight bias issues emerging," *Amer Bar Assoc J* 69 (1983) 878; and Lauren R. Reskin, "Employers must give obese job applicants a fat chance," *Amer Bar Assoc J* 71 (Sept 1985) 104.

[6] George L. Maddox et al., "Overweight as a problem of medical management in a public outpatient clinic," *AJMS* 252 (Oct 1966) 394–402; Hilde Bruch, *The Importance of Overweight* (NY, 1957) 318–24; Howard D. Kurland, "Obesity: an unfashionable problem," *Psychiatric Opinion* 7,6 (1970) 20–24; and Alfred J. Cantor, *How to Lose Weight the Doctor's Way* (NY, 1959) quote on 40.

8   Yet nearly half of all dieters get their dieting information from such patron-
izing doctors, doctors who until recently have had no specific training in nutrition. In 1970, three-quarters of doctors surveyed found obesity and overweight
to be very frequent among their patients, yet few have pursued the study of
obesity (bariatrics) in order to improve their courses of treatment. Nor have
they been in particularly good shape themselves; the Scarsdale diet doctor
Herman Tarnower was 15 lbs overweight according to his own charts.
Physicians are no better than gamblers playing "statistical roulette with the lives
of fat people," prescribing diet pills that affect blood pressure and kidneys,
dictating diets that are subtle forms of sadism, calling for a "grim, dour self-
punishment. If we submit we become miserable, if not actually neurotic."[7]

9   And then? "Then you are told that your frustrations, your worries, your inhibi-
tions, and your insecurities turn into fat." Tranquilizers will not work; they make you
fatter. You need psychological help. A woman in the 1950s was given the name
of a psychiatrist because she was fat. She wrote to Dear Abby, "Now Abby, I am
not *crazy*, I am just a little overweight. Have you ever heard of anything so insulting?" Abby thought a psychiatrist might do her a world of good, but Abby had no
statistics to support such a claim, and there are none now. Psychiatrists are as
inept with fat people as they are, still, with the schizophrenics whom they often
use as a model for the obese. Perhaps because they are so inept, they demand
much more of their fat patients. "Goddammit!" cried one fat woman at her psychiatrist, "You call *me* insatiable; you're the one who's never satisfied."[8]

10   Society itself will not be satisfied until all fat people are gone. Aldebaran, a
member of the Los Angeles Fat Underground, wrote an open letter to a doctor
in 1977: "You see fat as suicide, I see weight-loss as murder—genocide, to be
precise—the systematic murder of a biological minority by organized medicine."
But not just by organized medicine. By society as a whole. In the United States,
a fat person's prior identification is with fatness; as a status, fatness comes
before religion, race, sexual preference, income, gender. Only in a society intent
on doing away with fat people could fatness become so distinct and so negative a stigma. George Nathan Blomberg, fat hero of the 1978 novel by Mark
Dintenfass, *The Case Against Org*, becomes defiant in the face of such genocide: "Listen, one must choose to be obese: it is an act of courage." Near the

---

[7] Ruth Adams, *Did You Ever See a Fat Squirrel?* (Emmaus, Pa., 1972) 197; Tillie Lewis Tasti Diet ad in
Supermarket News (March 29, 1976) on "Where Do Diet Food Customers Get Their Information?";
Louis Harris and Associates, *Harris Survey Yearbook* (NY, 1971) 203, 213; Diana Trilling, *Mrs. Harris:
The Death of the Scarsdale Diet Doctor* (NY, 1981) 85 and cf. Peter Wyden and Barbara Wyden, *How
the Doctors Diet* (NY, 1968); interview with Dr. Frederick J. Stare, Sept 27, 1984, concerning physi-
cian education in nutrition; and Martin Lederman, *The Slim Gourmet* (NY, 1955) quote on 8.

[8] Vinne Young, "Don't get ill getting thin," *Science Digest* 36 (Aug 1954) 1 (quote); Abigail van Buren
(= Pauline Phillips), *Dear Abby* (Englewood Cliffs, N.J., 1958) 121; Walter W. Hamburger, "Psychology
of dietary change," *AJPH* 48 (1958) 1342–48; Robert M. Lindner, *The Fifty-Minute Hour* (NY, 1955)
133 (quote); Albert J. Stunkard and A. J. Rush, "Dieting and depression reexamined," *AIM* 81 (1974)
526–33; and Colleen S. W. Rand, "Treatment of obese patients in psychoanalysis," *Psychiatric Clinics
of North Amer* 1 (1978) 661–72.

end he knows, "There is no skinny guy inside me struggling to get out. I am Org forever." And on the last page he imagines "I and the world and a chocolate cherry all melting together, becoming one and everything."[9]

The Fat Society: A Utopia

11 If the tables could be turned, if this were a fat society, a society that admired and rewarded fatness—a society that has never existed in this country for both sexes at the same time—things would be very much different and very much better. It would be like Servia, Indiana, in 1899, "A Town of Fat People," population 206, temperate, quiet, and affluent. Or like Roseto, Pennsylvania, in the 1960s, population 1,700, nearly all of the residents obese and hardly a heart murmur among them.[10]

12   In a fat society, dinners would be scrumptious, sociable, and warm. No Mixed Gelatinoids as hors d'oeuvres, no Strained Nitrogen Gumbo for the soup, no Grilled Proteids with Globulin Patties for the entrée, no Compôte of Assorted Vitamins for dessert. There would be 101 Things To Do With Cottage Cheese—use it as a facial, take it out on a leash for a walk, build a snowman—but no one would have to eat it.[11]

13   In a fat society, children would be fed and fed well when hungry. When they were fed, they would be satisfied, because there would be no snares laid around food. Feeding would be calm and loving, always sufficient, never forced. Children as they grew into adolescence would acquire no eating disorders, since fat people and thin people would be on equal terms and there would be none of that anxious dieting which so often starts off the career of an anorectic or bulimic. No one would be obsessed with food because all people would have the opportunity to be powerful and expressive beyond the dining table.[12]

14   In a fat society, fat people would dress expressively. Their fashions would no longer be called "oversize" or "halfsize," and they would have the same choice of fabrics and designs as everyone else. Not just pantyhose but all clothes would be "Just my Size." Full-size models would be featured in the salons of *haute couture;* full-size fiberglass mannequins would pose with others in the most elite shop-windows. Fat people would no longer need to buy their clothes at specialty shops like The Forgotten Woman and Catherine Stout, or discreetly through the mails from Lane Bryant, Roaman's, and King-Size. A fat woman

---

[9] Aldebaran, "Fat liberation—a luxury?" *State and Mind* 5 (June–July 1977) 34; Stuart Byron, "The unmaking of a fattie," *Village Voice* (Dec 17, 1970) 10; and Mark Dintenfass, *The Case Against Org* (Boston, 1978) 5, 189, 246, quoted with permission from Little, Brown & Co.

[10] *NYDT* (Sept 3, 1899) illus, supp. 20:3; Louderback, *Fat Power,* 167.

[11] Irvin S. Cobb, *At His Best* (Garden City, N.Y., 1929) 244 on gelatinoids, and Totie Fields, *I Think I'll Start on Monday: The Official 8 1/2 Oz Mashed Potato Diet* (NY, 1972) 32 on cottage cheese. On conviviality and its suppression by dieters, see James A. Pike and Howard A. Johnson, *Man in the Middle* (Greenwich, Conn., 1956) 53; Robert Waithman, "Plea to the joyless eaters," *NYT Mag* (Feb 12, 1956) 19, 62; and Jean Kerr, *Please Don't Eat the Daisies* (NY, 1957) 172.

[12] Cf. Margaret Atwood, *Lady Oracle* (NY, 1976) esp. 74, 321; Susan C. Wooley and Orland W. Wooley, "Should obesity be treated at all?" in *Eating and Its Disorders,* eds. A. J. Stunkard and E. Stellar (NY, 1984) 185–92.

could wear dramatic colors and horizontal stripes when the fancy struck; a fat man could indulge a secret desire to wear a large-checked light gray suit.[13]

15   A fat society would be forthright about the body beneath the clothes. It would be relaxed about bodily functions, assured about sensuality, confident with sexuality. Compulsive weighing would disappear; no longer would the scale (always described as a male) lord it over anyone's body. The prudery of weight-watching, the overzealous guardianship of the body, would vanish. Beauty and sexuality would be independent of pounds and of calipers. The fat person would be a "strikingly *unavoidable* creature," and neither the fat man nor the fat woman would be typed as nonsexual or sexually corrupt. "I am touchable," fat people would say to themselves, and they would think of their pounds as "voluptuous planes." Like Sarah Fay Cohen Campbell in the novel *Fat People* (1982), they would accept their bodies as loving instruments and learn to play them in an open tuning.[14]

16   Women in particular would wear their weight with new conviction. They would affirm their physiological gifts, their genetic and cultural tendencies to put on flesh, their extra layering of body fat. Fat women would not live in the future conditional, suspended between what they are and who they will be when they are finally thin. Fat women would not have to invent fantasy selves a quarter their bulk and four times as lovely. "I've earned my wrinkles and padding," women would say with Ruthanne Olds. "They represent a lot of rewarding life experience." So everyone would at last welcome back the Earth Mother, the Venus of Willendorf, the female colossus, the grand diva, "La Stupenda," and divinity would once more be nurturant rather than vindictive.[15]

17   A fat society would be a comforting society, less harried, more caring. It would favor the gourmet over the glutton, slow food over fast food, matriarchy and communal affection over patriarchy and self-hate, eroticism over pornography, philanthropy and art over greed and blind technology. It would mean

---

[13] Margaret Dana, *Behind the Label* (Boston, 1938) 117–20; Marya Mannes, "Juno in limbo: the trauma of size 16," *Harper's Mag* (July 1964) 37–40; Grosswirth, *Fat Pride,* 69; Susie Orbach, *Fat Is a Feminist Issue* (NY, 1979) 90–91; Jean DuCoffe and Sherry Suib Cohen, *Making It Big* (NY, 1980) 12, 22, 25–31; Evelyn Roaman and Dee Ratterree, *The Evelyn Roaman Book: An Expert Shows You How Heavy Can Be Happy* (NY, 1980); Dale Godey, *Your Guide to Dressing Thin* (NY, 1981) 12–27; Ann Harper and Glenn Lewis, *The Big Beauty Book* (NY, 1982) 104; and William Johnston, "The fun of being a fat man," *Amer Mag* 94 (July 1922) 54–55.

[14] Lila Austin, "I'm fat, and I like it!" *GH* III (Sept 1940) 48; Nora S. Kinzer, *Put Down and Ripped Off* (NY, 1977) 34, 49–50; Marcia Millman, *Such a Pretty Face: Being Fat in America* (NY, 1980) 106, 162–63; Harper and Lewis, *Big Beauty Book,* quote on 3; DuCoffe and Cohen, *Making It Big,* 258 (quote), 260–63; David Newman and Robert Benton, "Fat power," *Esquire* 66 (Dec 1966) 212–15 on visual grandeur of fat men; Carol S. Smith, *Fat People* (NY, 1978); and see "Fatso" film (20th-Century Fox, 1980).

[15] Charlotte C. Rowett, "Success, avoirdupois, and clothes," *Woman Beautiful* 4 (June 1910) 40–41; DuCoffe and Cohen, *Making It Big,* 334; Anne Scott Beller, *Fat and Thin* (NY, 1977) esp. ch. 7; Kim Chernin, *The Obsession: Reflections on the Tyranny of Slenderness* (NY, 1981) esp. 133, 139; Jean Stafford, "The echo and the nemesis," *Children Are Bored on Sunday* (NY, 1953) 10–39, a fantasy self; Ruthanne Olds, *Big and Beautiful: Overcoming Fat Phobia* (Washington, D.C., 1982) 13; Stella J. Reichman, *Great Big Beautiful Doll* (NY, 1977) 26–28; and Marion Woodman, *The Owl Was a Baker's Daughter* (Toronto, 1980) 10, 18.

therefore an end to narcotics and narcissism. In a fat society, there would be no "flight from feelings," no need to resort to a form of privacy that kills as it protects. No one would have such stingy personal boundaries that the self would seem always under siege. Mirrors would neither frighten nor enchant. There would be more to the person than a mercurial reflection from shopwindows. "Sizing up" a person would be a wonderfully complex experience; tape measures and scales would have nothing to do with it.[16]

18   A fat society would be less harshly competitive, less devouring. People could be assertive without seeming aggressive or threatening. There would be no cannibalism, no fear of swallowing or being swallowed up. Accepting one's own bulk, one need not consume others or gnaw at one's self. Dieting is cannibalism. Dieters eat off their own bodies: "You start to get thin when you begin to *live on your own fat.*" Dieters are encouraged to be cannibals: "If your body-republic doesn't get enough food to support all the citizens, some will die and be cannibalized to feed the others. . . . In this body-politic of cell-citizens, you can fool all of the people all of the time, and if you want to *get* thin and *stay* thin, that's what you must do." Dieters have no recourse but to be cannibals: "To reduce weight, an obese person must burn his own body fat. It's as simple as that. He must eat himself up! A bit cannibalistic? I'm afraid so. But it's the only way to lose weight." That legendary diet drug which was nothing but a live tapeworm was the folkloric representation of such cannibalism. In a fat society, no one would be eaten up from within and no one would be eaten alive. Fat people, weighted, solid, would not fear the desires of others or their own desires. If fat people now lie or steal or hide, that is because they are always trying to save face ("such a pretty face") and disguise their needs. They must act surreptitiously, with the night and the bathroom as their refuge. In a fat society, no one would be forced to such humiliating secrecy. All hunger would be honest hunger.[17]

Review Questions

1. What is the "vicious circle" that affects fat people and "other minorities," according to Schwartz?

2. Schwartz asserts that physicians play an important, and largely negative, role in the lives of fat people. What is this role?

---

[16] See Donald B. Meyer, *The Positive Thinkers* (Garden City, N.Y., 1965) 120 on the "flight from feelings"; Véronique Nahoum, "La belle femme ou le stade du miroir en histoire," *Communications* 31 (1979) 22–32 on mirrors; and Susan Griffin, *Pornography and Silence* (NY, 1981) esp. 60–62.

[17] Nina W. Putnam, *Tomorrow We Diet* (NY, 1922) 89; Phillip W. Haberman, Jr., "How to diet if you have no character at all," *Vogue* 135 (June 1960) 148; and Thyra S. Winslow, *Think Yourself Thin* (NY, 1951) 113. On tapeworms, Ronald L. Baker, *Hoosier Folk Legends* (Bloomington, Ind., 1982) 226, and Jane Fonda, *Workout Book* (NY, 1981) 10.

3. In the section titled "The Fat Society: A Utopia" (paragraphs 11–18), what attributes of our current culture does Schwartz link to slenderness?

4. List any three of Schwartz's especially strong assertions, what you would consider to be his "zingers"—his most highly charged, argumentative statements. Quote carefully, cite paragraph numbers, and explain in a sentence or two what makes each statement argumentative.

Discussion and Writing Suggestions

1. In his introduction to "Fat and Happy?"—the final chapter in his book *Never Satisfied*—Hillel Schwartz observes that "[r]ecently there has been a growing protest against the despotism of slenderness." In what sense can the culture of slenderness be said to be despotic?

2. To what extent does modern medical evidence contradict Schwartz's assertion that "[no] one has been able to prove that fatness *per se* cuts life short"? (See Gawande, the editorial in the *Journal of the American Medical Association*, and the Surgeon General's "Call to Action" at <http://www.surgeongeneral.gov/topics/obesity/default.htm>.) If medical evidence invalidates Schwartz's assertion about fatness and duration of life, does this same evidence also invalidate Schwartz's other points about being fat and happy?

3. In paragraph 10, Schwartz makes an extreme assertion, quoting a fat activist to suggest that weight-loss regimes are a species of "murder" by organized medicine and the larger society. Your response?

4. Schwartz observes that in "the United States, . . . fatness comes before religion, race, sexual preference, income, [and] gender" (paragraph 10). Is Schwartz's observation accurate? Do you find yourself ordering your initial impressions of people by weight first? How might you argue against Schwartz on this point?

5. To what extent does Schwartz's "fat utopia" appeal to you? Would it, in fact, be a more enjoyable world than our currently "despotic" world of slenderness? What problems can you anticipate in Schwartz's utopia?

6. Schwartz has carefully cited evidence for many of his claims, even the seemingly extreme ones. Locate one such footnoted claim (perhaps, "a fat man could indulge a secret desire to wear a large-checked light gray suit") and then locate and read some of the cited sources. Report to your class on what you find.

7. Schwartz wrote the book *Never Satisfied*, in which this selection appears, in 1986. In the two decades that have elapsed, how well

does his critique of slim culture and his imagined utopia of fat culture hold up for you?

The Ironic Politics of Obesity
Marion Nestle

In this editorial, which appeared in the journal Science *(7 February 2003), Marion Nestle identifies several ironies relating to the obesity epidemic, including the sources of a "leadership vacuum" that compromises our government's ability to fight the problem. A professor in the Department of Nutrition and Food Sciences at New York University, Nestle is the author of* The Food Pushers: How the Food Industry Influences Nutrition and Health *(University of California Press, 2002) and* Safe Food: Bacteria, Biotechnology, and Bioterrorism *(University of California Press, Berkeley, 2003). She has worked with the U.S. Surgeon General and the Food and Drug Administration on dietary issues and consults with the food industry.*

1   Here is a great irony of 21st-century global public health: While many hundreds of millions of people lack adequate food as a result of economic inequities, political corruption, or warfare, many hundreds of millions more are overweight to the point of increased risk for diet-related chronic diseases. Obesity is a worldwide phenomenon, affecting children as well as adults and forcing all but the poorest countries to divert scarce resources away from food security to take care of people with preventable heart disease and diabetes.

2   To reverse the obesity epidemic, we must address fundamental causes. Overweight comes from consuming more food energy than is expended in activity. The cause of this imbalance also is ironic: improved prosperity. People use extra income to eat more and be less active. Market economies encourage this. They turn people with expendable income into consumers of aggressively marketed foods that are high in energy but low in nutritional value, and of cars, television sets, and computers that promote sedentary behavior. Gaining weight is good for business. Food is particularly big business because everyone eats.

3   Moreover, food is so overproduced that many countries, especially the rich ones, have far more than they need—another irony. In the United States, to take an extreme example, most adults—of all ages, incomes, educational levels, and census categories—are overweight. The U.S. food supply provides 3800 kilocalories per person per day, nearly twice as much as required by many adults. Overabundant food forces companies to compete for sales through advertising, health claims, new products, larger portions, and campaigns directed toward children. Food marketing promotes weight gain. Indeed, it is difficult to think of any major industry that might benefit if people ate less food; certainly not the agriculture, food product, grocery, restaurant, diet, or drug industries. All flourish when people eat more, and all employ armies of lobbyists to discourage governments from doing anything to inhibit overeating.

4   Food companies are well aware of the economic implications of reversing the obesity epidemic, as are government agencies. Economists at the U.S.

Department of Agriculture (USDA) calculate that "large adjustments" would occur in the agriculture and processed food industries if people ate more healthfully. That threat is one reason why food producers contribute generously to congressional campaigns, and why federal agencies have failed to take the obvious first step: a national obesity-prevention campaign in response to the Surgeon General's 2001 *Call to Action.** Such a campaign would have to address dietary aspects and include messages to eat less as well as the far less controversial "be more active." No other federal health agency has stepped in to lead the nation on dietary issues, which explains why USDA is left in charge of national nutrition policy. USDA's primary mission is to promote U.S. agricultural products ("eat more"), but it also issues advice about diet and health (sometimes meaning "eat less"). This notorious conflict accounts for the ambiguity of federal dietary guidelines ("aim for a healthy weight," "choose beverages and foods to moderate your intake of sugars") and the confusing nature of USDA's food guide pyramid.

5   If campaigns to promote more healthful eating are not in the best interest of industry, and government agencies are caught in conflicts of interest, how can any society address its obesity epidemic? The leadership vacuum in the United States leaves much room for litigation against the obesity-promoting practices of food companies. Whatever their legal merits, the current lawsuits engage the food industry's rapt attention and encourage scrutiny of their current products and practices. The vacuum also creates an opportunity for scientists and public interest groups to advocate better policies. Existing food policies could be tweaked to improve the environment of food choice through small taxes on junk foods and soft drinks (to raise funds for anti-obesity campaigns); restrictions on food marketing to children, especially in schools and on television; calorie labels on fast foods; and changes in farm subsidies to promote the consumption of fruits and vegetables. The politics of obesity demand that we revisit campaign contribution laws and advocate for a government agency—independent of industry—with clear responsibility for matters pertaining to food, nutrition, and health.

Review Questions

1. What are some of the "ironies" Nestle calls your attention to in this editorial?

2. Why have federal agencies not responded with plans to combat obesity response to the Surgeon General's *Call to Action* (against unhealthy weight gain)?

3. The U.S. Department of Agriculture faces a conflict of interest, according to Nestle. What is it? Nestle believes that the current

---

* The *Surgeon General's Call to Action to Prevent and Decrease Overweight and Obesity* (2001) can be found at <http://www.surgeongeneral.gov/topics/obesity/>.

"leadership vacuum" in the United States with regard to fighting the obesity epidemic has created opportunities. What are they?

4. What solution does Nestle offer to resolve the ironies that she points to in this editorial?

Discussion and Writing Suggestions

1. Before reading this editorial, to what extent were you aware of the "politics" associated with obesity? What is especially political about the topic? What are the origins of the politics?

2. Do you think it a good idea for the government to create a new agency—and bureaucracy—to coordinate a response to the obesity epidemic? Explain your response.

3. Reflect on the amount of advertising in various media devoted to food. List the number and types of food-related ads you encounter during a typical day.

4. Dwell for a moment on the first irony to which Nestle points: the existence of obesity and obesity-related illnesses alongside malnutrition and its related illnesses. Devote five minutes to writing out your thoughts. Sometime after you've finished, return to what you've written and circle a line or two that you think might be developed into a paper.

The Man Who Couldn't Stop Eating
Atul Gawande

Atul Gawande tells the story of Vincent Caselli, who underwent a gastric bypass to lose weight by surgically reducing the size of his stomach, thus making him physically unable to eat and absorb the nutrients from more than an ounce of food at a sitting. The statistics on the gastric-bypass procedure, the last resort of people who cannot shed weight in other ways, confirm the sharp rise of obesity in this country. According to the American Society for Bariatric Surgery, in 1992 surgeons performed 16,200 of the procedures. In 2002, the number jumped to 63,100 and one year later to 103,200. Gawande, who assisted on the surgery, calls this "among the strangest operations surgeons perform" in that it "is intended to control a person's will—to manipulate his innards so that he does not overeat." Those who, like Caselli, are morbidly obese and whose weight profoundly reduces their quality of life are turning to the gastric bypass more frequently. Gawande, a surgical resident and also a staff writer for the New Yorker, *uses the story of Caselli to "contemplate the human appetite." As such, he provides a fitting and compelling end to the selections in this chapter on obesity. The essay appeared originally in the 9 July 2001 issue of the* New Yorker. *Gawande is the author of* Complications: A Surgeon's Notes on an Imperfect Science *(Picador, 2002).*

1   At 7:30 A.M. on September 13, 1999, an anesthesiologist and two orderlies rolled our patient, whom I will call Vincent Caselli, into the operating room,

where his attending surgeon and I awaited him. Caselli was a short man of middle age—five feet seven, fifty-four years old. The son of Italian immigrants, he had worked as a heavy-machine operator and road-construction contractor. (He and his men had paved a rotary in my own neighborhood.) He had been married for thirty-five years; he and his wife had three girls, all grown now. And he weighed four hundred and twenty-eight pounds. Housebound, his health failing, he no longer had anything resembling a normal life. And so, although he was afraid of surgery, he had come for a Roux-en-Y gastric-bypass operation. It is the most drastic treatment we have for obesity. It is also among the strangest operations surgeons perform. It removes no disease, repairs no defect or injury. It is an operation that is intended to control a person's will—to manipulate his innards so that he does not overeat—and it is soaring in popularity. Some forty-five thousand patients underwent obesity surgery in 1999, and the number is expected to double by 2003.

2   For the very obese, general anesthesia alone is a dangerous undertaking; major abdominal surgery can easily become a disaster. Obesity substantially increases the risk of respiratory failure, heart attacks, wound infections, hernias—almost every complication possible, including death. Nevertheless, Dr. Sheldon Randall, the attending surgeon, was relaxed, having done more than a thousand of these operations. I, the assisting resident, remained anxious. Watching Caselli struggle to shift himself from the stretcher onto the operating table and then stop halfway to catch his breath, I was afraid that he would fall in between. Once he was on the table, his haunches rolled off the sides, and I double-checked the padding that protected him from the table's sharp edges. He was naked except for his "universal"–size johnny, which covered him like a napkin, and a nurse put a blanket over his lower body for the sake of modesty. When we tried to lay him down, he lost his breath and started to turn blue, and the anesthesiologist had to put him to sleep sitting up. Only with the breathing tube and a mechanical ventilator in place were we able to lay him flat.

3   He was a mountain on the table. I am six feet two, but even with the table as low as it goes I had to stand on a step stool; Dr. Randall stood on two stools stacked together. He nodded to me, and I cut down the middle of our patient's belly, through skin and then dense inches of glistening yellow fat, and we opened the abdomen. Inside, his liver was streaked with fat, too, and his bowel was covered by a thick apron of it, but his stomach looked ordinary—a smooth, grayish-pink bag the size of two fists. We put metal retractors in place to hold the wound open and keep the liver and the slithering loops of bowel out of the way. Working elbow deep, we stapled his stomach down to the size of an ounce. Before the operation, it could accommodate a quart of food and drink; now it would hold no more than a shot glass. We then sewed the opening of this little pouch to a portion of bowel two feet past his duodenum—past the initial portion of the small bowel, where bile and pancreatic juices break food down. This was the bypass part of the operation, and it meant that what food the stomach could accommodate would be less readily absorbed.

4   The operation took us a little over two hours. Caselli was stable throughout, but his recovery was difficult. Patients are usually ready to go home three days after surgery; it was two days before Caselli even knew where he was. His kidneys failed for twenty-four hours, and fluid built up in his lungs. He became

delirious, seeing things on the walls, pulling off his oxygen mask, his chest leads for the monitors, even yanking out the I.V. We were worried, and his wife and daughters were terrified, but gradually he pulled through.

5   By the third day after surgery, he was well enough to take sips of clear liquids (water, apple juice, ginger ale), up to one ounce every four hours. On my afternoon rounds, I asked him how he'd done. "O.K.," he said. We began giving him four-ounce servings of Carnation Instant Breakfast for protein and modest calories. He could finish only half, and that took him an hour. It filled him up and, when it did, he felt a sharp, unpleasant pain. This was to be expected, Dr. Randall told him. It would be a few days before he was ready for solid food. But he was doing well. He no longer needed I. V. fluids. And, after he'd had a short stay in a rehabilitation facility, we sent him home.

6   A couple of weeks later, I asked Dr. Randall how Caselli was getting on. "Just fine," the surgeon said. Although I had done a few of these cases with him, I had not seen how the patients progressed afterward. Would he really lose all that weight? I asked. And how much could he eat? Randall suggested that I see Caselli for myself. So one day that October, I gave him a call, and he invited me to stop by.

7   Vincent Caselli and his wife live in an unassuming saltbox house not far outside Boston. To get there, I took Route 1, past four Dunkin' Donuts, four pizzerias, three steak houses, two McDonald's, two Ground Rounds, a Taco Bell, a Friendly's, and an International House of Pancakes. (A familiar roadside vista, but that day it seemed a sad tour of our self-destructiveness.) I rang the doorbell, and a long minute passed. I heard a slow footfall coming toward the door, and Caselli, visibly winded, opened it. But he smiled broadly when he saw me and gave my hand a warm squeeze. He led me—his hand on table, wall, doorjamb for support—to a seat at a breakfast table in his flowered-wallpaper kitchen.

8   I asked him how things were going. "Real good," he said. He had no more pain from the operation, the incision had healed, and, though it had been only three weeks, he'd already lost forty pounds. But, at three hundred and ninety, and still stretching his size-64 slacks and size-XXXXXXL T-shirts (the largest he could find at the local big-and-tall store), he did not yet feel different. Sitting, he had to keep his legs apart to let his abdomen sag between them, and the weight of his body on the wooden chair forced him to shift every minute or two because his buttocks would fall asleep. Sweat rimmed the folds of his forehead and made his thin salt-and-pepper hair stick to his pate. His brown eyes were rheumy, above dark bags. He breathed with a disconcerting wheeze.

9   We talked about his arrival home from the hospital. The first solid food he had tried was a spoonful of scrambled eggs. Just that much, he said, made him so full it hurt, "like something was ripping," and he threw it up. He was afraid that nothing solid would ever go down. But he gradually found that he could tolerate small amounts of soft foods—mashed potatoes, macaroni, even chicken if it was finely chopped and moist. Breads and dry meats, he found, got "stuck," and he'd have to put a finger down his throat and make himself vomit.

10   Caselli's battle with obesity, he explained, began in his late twenties. "I always had some weight on me," he said—he was two hundred pounds at nineteen,

when he married Teresa (as I'll call her), and a decade later he reached three hundred. He would diet and lose seventy-five pounds, then put a hundred back on. By 1985, he weighed four hundred pounds. On one diet, he got down to a hundred and ninety, but he gained it all back. "I must have gained and lost a thousand pounds," he told me. He developed high blood pressure, high cholesterol, and diabetes. His knees and his back ached all the time, and he had limited mobility. He used to get season tickets to Boston Bruins games, and go out regularly to the track at Seekonk every summer to see the auto racing. Years ago, he drove in races himself. Now he could barely walk to his pickup truck. He hadn't been on an airplane since 1983, and it had been two years since he had been to the second floor of his own house, because he couldn't negotiate the stairs. "Teresa bought a computer a year ago for her office upstairs, and I've never seen it," he told me. He had to move out of their bedroom, upstairs, to a small room off the kitchen. Unable to lie down, he had slept in a recliner ever since. Even so, he could doze only in snatches, because of sleep apnea, which is a common syndrome among the obese and is thought to be related to excessive fat in the tongue and in the soft tissues of the upper airway. Every thirty minutes, his breathing would stop, and he'd wake up asphyxiating. He was perpetually exhausted.

11   There were other troubles, too, the kind that few people speak about. Good hygiene, he said, was nearly impossible. He could no longer stand up to urinate, and after moving his bowels he often had to shower in order to get clean. Skin folds would become chafed and red, and sometimes develop boils and infections. And, he reported, "Sex life is nonexistent. I have real hopes for it." For him, though, the worst part was his diminishing ability to earn a livelihood.

12   Vincent Caselli's father had come to Boston from Italy in 1914 to work in construction, and he soon established his own firm. In 1979, Vincent went into business for himself. He was skilled at operating heavy equipment—his specialty was running a Gradall, a thirty-ton, three-hundred-thousand-dollar hydraulic excavator—and he employed a team of men year-round to build roads and sidewalks. Eventually, he owned his own Gradall, a ten-wheel Mack dump truck, a backhoe, and a fleet of pickup trucks. But in the past three years he had become too big to operate the Gradall or keep up with the daily maintenance of the equipment. He had to run the business from his house, and pay others to do the heavy work; he enlisted a nephew to help manage the men and the contracts. Expenses rose, and since he could no longer go around to city halls himself, he found contracts harder to get. If Teresa hadn't had a job—she is the business manager for an assisted-living facility in Boston—they would have gone bankrupt.

13   Teresa, a freckled redhead, had been pushing him for a long time to diet and exercise. He, too, wanted desperately to lose weight, but the task of controlling himself, day to day, meal to meal, seemed beyond him. "I'm a man of habits," he told me. "I'm very prone to habits." And eating, he said, was his worst habit. But, then, eating is everyone's habit. What was different about *his* habit? I asked. Well, the portions he took were too big, and he could never leave a crumb on his plate. If there was pasta left in the pot, he'd eat that, too. But why, I wanted to know. Was it that he just loved food? He pondered this question for

a moment. It wasn't love, he decided. "Eating felt good instantaneously," he said, "but it only felt good instantaneously." Was it excessive hunger that drove him? "I was never hungry," he said.

14   As far as I could tell, Caselli ate for the same reasons that everyone eats: because food tasted good, because it was seven o'clock and time for dinner, because a nice meal had been set out on the table. And he stopped eating for the same reason everyone stops: because he was full and eating was no longer pleasurable. The main difference seemed to be that it took an unusual quantity of food to make him full. (He could eat a large pizza as if it were a canapé.) To lose weight, he faced the same difficult task that every dieter faces—to stop eating before he felt full, while the food still tasted good, and to exercise. These were things that he could do for a little while, and, with some reminding and coaching, for perhaps a bit longer, but they were not, he had found, things that he could do for long. "I am not strong," he said.

15   In the spring of 1999, Caselli developed serious infections in both legs: as his weight increased, and varicosities appeared, the skin thinned and broke down, producing open, purulent ulcers. Despite fevers and searing pain, it was only after persistent coaxing from his wife that he finally agreed to see his doctor. The doctor diagnosed a serious case of cellulitis, and he spent a week in the hospital receiving intravenous antibiotics.

16   At the hospital, he was given an ultrasound scan to check whether blood clots had formed in the deep veins of his legs. A radiologist came to give him the results. Caselli recounted the conversation to me. "He says, 'You don't have blood clots, and I'm really surprised. A guy like you, in the situation you're in, the odds are you're gonna have blood clots. That tells me you're a pretty healthy guy'"—but only, he went on, if Caselli did something about his weight. A little later, the infectious-disease specialist came by to inspect his wounds. "I'm going to tell you something," Caselli recalls the man saying. "I've been reading your whole file— where you were, what you were, how you were. You take that weight off—and I'm not telling you this to bust your ass—you take that weight off and you're a very healthy guy. Your heart is good. Your lungs are good. You're strong."

17   "I took that seriously," Caselli said. "You know, there are two different doctors telling me this. They don't know me other than what they're reading from their records. They had no reason to tell me this. But they knew the weight was a problem. And if I could get it down somewhere near reality . . ."

18   When he got home, he remained sick in bed for another two weeks. Meanwhile, his business collapsed. Contracts stopped coming in entirely, and he knew that when his men finished the existing jobs he would have to let them go. Months before, his internist had suggested that he consider surgery and he had dismissed the notion. But he didn't now. He went to see Dr. Randall, who spoke with him frankly about the risks involved. There was a one-in-two-hundred chance of death and a one-in-ten chance of a significant complication, such as bleeding, infection, gastric ulceration, blood clots, or leakage into the abdomen. The doctor also told him that it would change how he ate forever. Unable to work, humiliated, ill, and in pain, Vincent Caselli decided that surgery was his only hope.

19   It is hard to contemplate the human appetite without wondering if we have any say over our lives at all. We believe in will—in the notion that we have a

choice over such simple matters as whether to sit still or stand up, to talk or not talk, to have a slice of pie or not. Yet very few people, whether heavy or slim, can voluntarily reduce their weight for long. The history of weight-loss treatment is one of nearly unremitting failure. Whatever the regimen—liquid diets, high-protein diets, or grapefruit diets, the Zone, Atkins, or Dean Ornish diet—people lose weight quite readily, but they do not keep it off. A 1993 National Institutes of Health expert panel reviewed decades of diet studies and found that between ninety and ninety-five per cent of people regained one-third to two-thirds of any weight lost within a year—and all of it within five years. Doctors have wired patients' jaws closed, inflated plastic balloons inside their stomachs, performed massive excisions of body fat, prescribed amphetamines and large amounts of thyroid hormone, even performed neurosurgery to destroy the hunger centers in the brain's hypothalamus—and still people do not keep the weight off. Jaw wiring, for example, can produce substantial weight loss, and patients who ask for the procedure are highly motivated; yet some still take in enough liquid calories through their closed jaws to gain weight, and the others regain it once the wires are removed. We are a species that has evolved to survive starvation, not to resist abundance.

20   Children are the surprising exception to this history of failure. Nobody would argue that children have more self-control than adults; yet in four randomized studies of obese children between the ages of six and twelve, those who received simple behavioral teaching (weekly lessons for eight to twelve weeks, followed by monthly meetings for up to a year) ended up markedly less overweight ten years later than those who didn't; thirty percent were no longer obese. Apparently, children's appetites are malleable. Those of adults are not.

21   There are at least two ways that humans can eat more than they ought to at a sitting. One is by eating slowly but steadily for far too long. This is what people with Prader-Willi syndrome do. Afflicted with a rare inherited dysfunction of the hypothalamus, they are incapable of experiencing satiety. And though they eat only half as quickly as most people, they do not stop. Unless their access to food is strictly controlled (some will eat garbage or pet food if they find nothing else), they become mortally obese.

22   The more common pattern, however, relies on rapid intake. Human beings are subject to what scientists call a "fat paradox." When food enters your stomach and duodenum (the upper portion of the small intestine), it triggers stretch receptors, protein receptors, and fat receptors that signal the hypothalamus to induce satiety. Nothing stimulates the reaction more quickly than fat. Even a small amount, once it reaches the duodenum, will cause a person to stop eating. Still we eat too much fat. How can this be? It turns out that foods can trigger receptors in the mouth which get the hypothalamus to *accelerate* our intake—and, again, the most potent stimulant is fat. A little bit on the tongue, and the receptors push us to eat fast, before the gut signals shut us down. The tastier the food, the faster we eat—a phenomenon called "the appetizer effect." (This is accomplished, in case you were wondering, not by chewing faster but by chewing less. French researchers have discovered that, in order to eat more and eat it faster, people shorten their "chewing time"—they take fewer "chews per standard food unit" before swallowing. In other words, we gulp.)

23   Apparently, how heavy one becomes is determined, in part, by how the hypothalamus and the brain stem adjudicate the conflicting signals from the mouth and the gut. Some people feel full quite early in a meal; others, like Vincent Caselli, experience the appetizer effect for much longer. In the past several years, much has been discovered about the mechanisms of this control. We now know, for instance, that hormones, like leptin and neuropeptide Y, rise and fall with fat levels and adjust the appetite accordingly. But our knowledge of these mechanisms is still crude at best.

24   Consider a 1998 report concerning two men, "BR" and "RH," who suffered from profound amnesia. Like the protagonist in the movie *Memento,* they could carry on a coherent conversation with you, but, once they had been distracted, they recalled nothing from as recently as a minute before, not even that they were talking to you. (BR had had a bout of viral encephalitis; RH had had a severe seizure disorder for twenty years.) Paul Rozin, a professor of psychology at the University of Pennsylvania, thought of using them in an experiment that would explore the relationship between memory and eating. On three consecutive days, he and his team brought each subject his typical lunch (BR got meat loaf, barley soup, tomatoes, potatoes, beans, bread, butter, peaches, and tea; RH got veal parmigiana with pasta, string beans, juice, and apple crumb cake). Each day, BR ate all his lunch, and RH could not quite finish. Their plates were then taken away. Ten to thirty minutes later, the researchers would reappear with the same meal. "Here's lunch," they would announce. The men ate just as much as before. Another ten to thirty minutes later, the researchers again appeared with the same meal. "Here's lunch," they would say, and again the men would eat. On a couple of occasions, the researchers even offered RH a fourth lunch. Only then did he decline, saying that his "stomach was a little tight." Stomach stretch receptors weren't completely ineffectual. Yet, in the absence of a memory of having eaten, social context alone—someone walking in with lunch—was enough to re-create appetite.

25   You can imagine forces in the brain vying to make you feel hungry or full. You have mouth receptors, smell receptors, visions of tiramisu pushing one way and gut receptors another. You have leptins and neuropeptides saying you have either too much fat stored or too little. And you have your own social and personal sense of whether eating more is a good idea. If one mechanism is thrown out of whack, there's trouble.

26   Given the complexity of appetite and our imperfect understanding of it, we shouldn't be surprised that appetite-altering drugs have had only meager success in making people eat less. (The drug combination of fenfluramine and phentermine, or "fen-phen," had the most success, but it was linked to heart-valve abnormalities and was withdrawn from the market.) University researchers and pharmaceutical companies are searching intensively for a drug that will effectively treat serious obesity. So far, no such drug exists. Nonetheless, one treatment has been found to be effective, and, oddly enough, it turns out to be an operation.

27   At my hospital, there is a recovery-room nurse who is forty-eight years old and just over five feet tall, with boyish sandy hair and an almost athletic physique. Over coffee one day at the hospital café, not long after my visit with

Vincent Caselli, she revealed that she once weighed more than two hundred and fifty pounds. Carla (as I'll call her) explained that she had had gastric-bypass surgery some fifteen years ago.

28   She had been obese since she was five years old. She started going on diets and taking diet pills—laxatives, diuretics, amphetamines—in junior high school. "It was never a problem losing weight," she said. "It was a problem keeping it off." She remembers how upset she was when, on a trip with friends to Disneyland, she found that she couldn't fit through the entrance turnstile. At the age of thirty-three, she reached two hundred and sixty-five pounds. One day, accompanying her partner, a physician, to a New Orleans medical convention, she found that she was too short of breath to walk down Bourbon Street. For the first time, she said, "I became fearful for my life—not just the quality of it but the longevity of it."

29   This was 1985. Doctors were experimenting with radical obesity surgery, but there was dwindling enthusiasm for it. Two operations had held considerable promise. One, known as jejunoileal bypass—in which nearly all the small intestine was bypassed, so that only a minimum amount of food could be absorbed—was killing people. The other, stomach stapling, was proving not to be very effective over time; people tended to adapt to the tiny stomach, eating densely caloric foods more and more frequently.

30   Working in the hospital, however, Carla heard encouraging reports about the gastric-bypass operation—stomach stapling plus a rerouting of the intestine so that food bypassed only the duodenum. She knew that the data about its success was still sketchy, that other operations had failed, but in May of 1986, after a year of thinking about it, she had the surgery.

31   "For the first time in my life, I experienced fullness," she told me. Six months after the operation, she was down to a hundred and eighty-five pounds. Six months after that, she weighed a hundred and thirty pounds. She lost so much weight that she had to have surgery to remove the aprons of skin that hung from her belly and thighs down to her knees. She was unrecognizable to anyone who had known her before, and even to herself. "I went to bars to see if I could get picked up—and I did," she said. "I always said no," she quickly added, laughing. "But I did it anyway."

32   The changes weren't just physical, though. She said she felt a profound and unfamiliar sense of will power. She no longer *had* to eat anything: "Whenever I eat, somewhere in the course of that time I end up asking myself, 'Is this good for you? Are you going to put on weight if you eat too much of this?' And I can just stop." She knew, intellectually, that the surgery was why she no longer ate as much as she used to. Yet she felt as if she were choosing not to do it.

33   Studies report this to be a typical experience of a successful gastric-bypass patient. "I do get hungry, but I tend to think about it more," another woman who had had the operation told me, and she described an internal dialogue very much like Carla's: "I ask myself, 'Do I really need this?' I watch myself." For many, this feeling of control extends beyond eating. They become more confident, even assertive—sometimes to the point of conflict. Divorce rates, for example, have been found to increase significantly after the surgery. Indeed, a few months after her operation, Carla and her partner broke up.

34   Carla's dramatic weight loss has proved to be no aberration. Published case series now show that most patients undergoing gastric bypass lose at least two-thirds of their excess weight (generally more than a hundred pounds) within a year. They keep it off, too: ten-year follow-up studies find an average regain of only ten to twenty pounds. And the health benefits are striking: patients are less likely to have heart failure, asthma, or arthritis; eighty percent of those with diabetes are completely cured of it.

35   I stopped in to see Vincent Caselli one morning in January of 2000, about four months after his operation. He didn't quite spring to the door, but he wasn't winded this time. The bags under his eyes had shrunk. His face was more defined. Although his midriff was vast, it seemed smaller, less of a sack.

36   He told me that he weighed three hundred and forty-eight pounds—still far too much for a man who was only five feet seven inches tall, but ninety pounds less than he weighed on the operating table. And it had already made a difference in his life. Back in October, he told me, he missed his youngest daughter's wedding because he couldn't manage the walking required to get to the church. But by December he had lost enough weight to resume going to his East Dedham garage every morning. "Yesterday, I unloaded three tires off the truck," he said. "For me to do that three months ago? There's no way." He had climbed the stairs of his house for the first time since 1997. "One day around Christmastime, I say to myself, 'Let me try this. I gotta try this.' I went very slow, one foot at a time." The second floor was nearly unrecognizable to him. The bathroom had been renovated since he last saw it, and Teresa had, naturally, taken over the bedroom, including the closets. He would move back up eventually, he said, though it might be a while. He still had to sleep sitting up in a recliner, but he was sleeping in four-hour stretches now—"Thank God," he said. His diabetes was gone. And although he was still unable to stand up longer than twenty minutes, his leg ulcers were gone, too. He lifted his pants legs to show me. I noticed that he was wearing regular Red Wing work boots—in the past, he had to cut slits along the sides of his shoes in order to fit into them.

37   "I've got to lose at least another hundred pounds," he said. He wanted to be able to work, pick up his grandchildren, buy clothes off the rack at Filenes, go places without having to ask himself, "Are there stairs? Will I fit in the seats? Will I run out of breath?" He was still eating like a bird. The previous day, he'd had nothing all morning, a morsel of chicken with some cooked carrots and a small roast potato for lunch, and for dinner one fried shrimp, one teriyaki chicken strip, and two forkfuls of chicken-and-vegetable lo mein from a Chinese restaurant. He was starting up the business again, and, he told me, he'd gone out for a business lunch one day recently. It was at a new restaurant in Hyde Park—"beautiful"—and he couldn't help ordering a giant burger and a plate of fries. Just two bites into the burger, though, he had to stop. "One of the fellas says to me, 'Is that all you're going to eat?' And I say, 'I can't eat any more.' 'Really?' I say, 'Yeah, I can't eat any more. That's the truth.'"

38   I noticed, however, that the way he spoke about eating was not the way Carla had spoken. He did not speak of stopping because he wanted to. He spoke of stopping because he had to. You want to eat more, he explained, but "you start to get that feeling in your insides that one more bite is going to

push you over the top." Still, he often took that bite. Overcome by waves of nausea, pain, and bloating—the so-called dumping syndrome—he'd have to vomit. If there were a way to eat more, he would. This scared him, he admitted. "It's not right," he said.

39   Three months later, in April, Caselli invited me and my son to stop by his garage in East Dedham. My son was four years old and, as Vince remembered my once saying, fascinated with all things mechanical. The garage was huge, cavernous, with a two-story rollup door and metal walls painted yellow. There, in the shadows, was Vince's beloved Gradall, a handsome tank of a machine, as wide as a county road, painted yield-sign yellow, with shiny black tires that came up to my chest and his company name emblazoned in curlicue script along its flanks. On the chassis, six feet off the ground, was a glass-enclosed control cab and a thirty-foot telescoping boom, mounted on a three-hundred-and-sixty-degree swivel. Vince and a friend of his, a fellow heavy-equipment contractor I'll call Danny, were sitting on metal folding chairs in a sliver of sunlight, puffing fat Honduran cigars, silently enjoying the day. They both rose to greet us. Vince introduced me as "one of the doctors who did my stomach operation."

40   I let my son go off to explore the equipment and asked Vince how his business was going. Not well, he said. Except for a few jobs in late winter plowing snow for the city in his pickup truck, he had brought in no income since the previous August. He'd had to sell two of his three pickup trucks, his Mack dump truck, and most of the small equipment for road building. Danny came to his defense. "Well, he's been out of action," he said. "And you see we're just coming into the summer season. It's a seasonal business." But we all knew that wasn't the issue.

41   Vince told me that he weighed about three hundred and twenty pounds. This was about thirty pounds less than when I had last seen him, and he was proud of that. "He don't eat," Danny said. "He eats half of what I eat." But Vince was still unable to climb up into the Gradall and operate it. And he was beginning to wonder whether that would ever change. The rate of weight loss was slowing down, and he noticed that he was able to eat more. Before, he could eat only a couple of bites of a burger, but now he could sometimes eat half of one. And he still found himself eating more than he could handle. "Last week, Danny and this other fellow, we had to do some business," he said. "We had Chinese food. Lots of days, I don't eat the right stuff—I try to do what I can do, but I ate a little bit too much. I had to bring Danny back to Boston College, and before I left the parking lot there I just couldn't take it anymore. I had to vomit.

42   "I'm finding that I'm getting back into that pattern where I've always got to eat," he went on. His gut still stopped him, but he was worried. What if one day it didn't? He had heard about people whose staples gave way, returning their stomach to its original size, or who managed to put the weight back on in some other way.

43   I tried to reassure him. I told him what I knew Dr. Randall had already told him during a recent appointment: that a small increase in the capacity of his stomach pouch was to be expected, and that what he was experiencing seemed normal. But could something worse happen? I didn't want to say.

44   Among the gastric-bypass patients I had talked with was a man whose story remains a warning and a mystery to me. He was forty-two years old, married, and had two daughters, both of whom were single mothers with babies and still lived at home, and he had been the senior computer-systems manager for a large local company. At the age of thirty-eight, he had had to retire and go on disability because his weight—which had been above three hundred pounds since high school—had increased to more than four hundred and fifty pounds and was causing unmanageable back pain. He was soon confined to his home. He could not walk half a block. He could stand for only brief periods. He went out, on average, once a week, usually for medical appointments. In December, 1998, he had a gastric bypass. By June of the following year, he had lost a hundred pounds.

45   Then, as he put it, "I started eating again." Pizzas. Boxes of sugar cookies. Packages of doughnuts. He found it hard to say how, exactly. His stomach was still tiny and admitted only a small amount of food at a time, and he experienced the severe nausea and pain that gastric-bypass patients get whenever they eat sweet or rich things. Yet his drive was stronger than ever. "I'd eat right through pain—even to the point of throwing up," he told me. "If I threw up, it was just room for more. I would eat straight through the day." He did not pass a waking hour without eating something. "I'd just shut the bedroom door. The kids would be screaming. The babes would be crying. My wife would be at work. And I would be eating." His weight returned to four hundred and fifty pounds, and then more. The surgery had failed. And his life had been shrunk to the needs of pure appetite.

46   He is among the five to twenty percent of patients—the published reports conflict on the exact number—who regain weight despite gastric-bypass surgery. (When we spoke, he had recently submitted to another, more radical gastric bypass, in the desperate hope that something would work.) In these failures, one begins to grasp the power that one is up against. An operation that makes overeating both extremely difficult and extremely unpleasant—which, for more than eighty percent of patients, is finally sufficient to cause appetite to surrender and be transformed—can sometimes be defeated after all. Studies have yet to uncover a single consistent risk factor for this outcome. It could, apparently, happen to anyone.

47   It was a long time before I saw Vince Caselli again. Earlier this year, I called him to ask about getting together, and he suggested that we go out to see a Boston Bruins game. A few days later, he picked me up at the hospital in his rumbling Dodge Ram. For the first time, he looked almost small in the outsized truck. He was down to about two hundred and fifty pounds. "I'm still no Gregory Peck," he said, but he was now one of the crowd—chubby, in an ordinary way. The rolls beneath his chin were gone. His face had a shape. His middle no longer rested between his legs. And, almost a year and a half after the surgery, he was still losing weight. At the FleetCenter, where the Bruins play, he walked up the escalator without getting winded. Our tickets were taken at the gate—the Bruins were playing the Pittsburgh Penguins—and we walked through the turnstiles. Suddenly, he stopped and said, "Look at that. I went right through, no problem. I never would have made it through there before." It was the first time he'd gone to an event like this in years.

48   We took our seats about two dozen rows up from the ice, and he laughed a little about how easily he fit. The seats were as tight as coach class, but he was quite comfortable. (I, with my long legs, was the one who had trouble finding room.) Vince was right at home here. He had been a hockey fan his whole life, and could supply me with all the details: the Penguins' goalie Garth Snow was a local boy from Wrentham and a friend of one of Vince's cousins; Joe Thornton and Jason Allison were the Bruins' best forwards, but neither could hold a candle to the Penguins' Mario Lemieux. There were nearly twenty thousand people at the game, but within ten minutes Vince had found a friend from his barbershop sitting just a few rows away.

49   The Bruins won, and we left cheered and buzzing. Afterward, we went out to dinner at a grill near the hospital. Vince told me that his business was finally up and running. He could operate the Gradall without difficulty, and he'd had full-time Gradall work for the past three months. He was even thinking of buying a new model. At home, he had moved back upstairs. He and Teresa had taken a vacation in the Adirondacks; they were going out evenings, and visiting their grandchildren.

50   I asked him what had changed since I saw him the previous spring. He could not say precisely, but he gave me an example. "I used to love Italian cookies, and I still do," he said. A year ago, he would have eaten to the point of nausea. "But now they're, I don't know, they're too sweet. I eat one now, and after one or two bites I just don't want it." It was the same with pasta, which had always been a problem for him. "Now I can have a bite and I'm satisfied."

51   Partly, it appeared that his taste in food had changed. He pointed to the nachos and buffalo wings and hamburgers on the menu, and said that, to his surprise, he no longer felt like eating any of them. "It seems like I lean toward protein and vegetables nowadays," he said, and he ordered a chicken Caesar salad. But he also no longer felt the need to stuff himself. "I used to be real reluctant to push food away," he told me. "Now it's just—it's different." But when did this happen? And how? He shook his head. "I wish I could pinpoint it for you," he said. He paused to consider. "As a human, you adjust to conditions. You don't think you are. But you are."

52   These days, it isn't the failure of obesity surgery that is prompting concerns but its success. Physicians have gone from scorning it to encouraging, sometimes imploring, their most severely overweight patients to undergo a gastric-bypass operation. That's not a small group. More than five million adult Americans meet the strict definition of morbid obesity. (Their "body mass index"—that is, their weight in kilograms divided by the square of their height in metres—is forty or more, which for an average man is roughly a hundred pounds or more overweight.) Ten million more weigh just under the mark but may nevertheless have obesity-related health problems that are serious enough to warrant the surgery. There are ten times as many candidates for obesity surgery right now as there are for heart-bypass surgery in a year. So many patients are seeking the procedure that established surgeons cannot keep up. The American Society of Bariatric Surgery has only five hundred members nationwide who perform gastric-bypass operations, and their waiting lists are typically months long. Hence the too familiar troubles associated with new and

lucrative surgical techniques (the fee can be as much as twenty thousand dollars): newcomers are stampeding to the field, including many who have proper training but have not yet mastered the procedure, and others who have no training at all. Complicating matters further, individual surgeons are promoting a slew of variations on the standard operation which haven't been fully researched—the "duodenal switch," the "long limb" bypass, the laparoscopic bypass. And a few surgeons are pursuing new populations, such as adolescents and people who are only moderately obese.

53   Perhaps what's most unsettling about the soaring popularity of gastric-bypass surgery, however, is simply the world that surrounds it. Ours is a culture in which fatness is seen as tantamount to failure, and get-thin-quick promises—whatever the risks—can have an irresistible allure. Doctors may recommend the operation out of concern for their patients' health, but the stigma of obesity is clearly what drives many patients to the operating room. "How can you let yourself look like that?" is society's sneering, unspoken question, and often its spoken one as well. Women suffer even more than men from the social sanction, and it's no accident that seven times as many women as men have had the operation. (Women are only an eighth more likely to be obese.)

54   Indeed, deciding *not* to undergo the surgery, if you qualify, is at risk of being considered the unreasonable thing to do. A three-hundred-and-fifty-pound woman who did not want the operation told me of doctors browbeating her for her choice. And I have learned of at least one patient with heart disease being refused treatment by a doctor unless she had a gastric bypass. If you don't have the surgery, you will die, some doctors tell their patients. But we actually do not know this. Despite the striking improvements in weight and health, studies have not yet proved a corresponding reduction in mortality.

55   There are legitimate grounds for being wary of the procedure. As Paul Ernsberger, an obesity researcher at Case Western Reserve University, pointed out to me, many patients undergoing gastric bypass are in their twenties and thirties. "But is this really going to be effective and worthwhile over a forty-year span?" he asked. "No one can say." He was concerned about the possible long-term effects of nutritional deficiencies (for which patients are instructed to take a daily multivitamin). And he was concerned about evidence from rats that raises the possibility of an increased risk of bowel cancer.

56   We want progress in medicine to be clear and unequivocal, but of course it rarely is. Every new treatment has gaping unknowns—for both patients and society—and it can be hard to decide what to do about them. Perhaps a simpler, less radical operation will prove effective for obesity. Perhaps the long-sought satiety pill will be found. Nevertheless, the gastric bypass is the one thing we have now that works. Not all the questions have been answered, but there are more than a decade of studies behind it. And so we forge ahead. Hospitals everywhere are constructing obesity-surgery centers, ordering reinforced operating tables, training surgeons and staff. At the same time, everyone expects that, one day, something new and better will be discovered that will make what we're now doing obsolete.

57   Across from me, in our booth at the grill, Vince Caselli pushed his chicken Caesar salad aside only half eaten. "No taste for it," he said, and he told me

he was grateful for that. The operation, he said, had given him his life back. But, after one more round of drinks, it was clear that he still felt uneasy.

58   "I had a serious problem and I had to take serious measures," he said. "I think I had the best technology that is available at this point. But I do get concerned: Is this going to last my whole life? Someday, am I going to be right back to square one—or worse?" He fell silent for a moment, gazing into his glass. "Well, that's the cards that God gave me. I can't worry about stuff I can't control."

Review Questions

1. "The Man Who Couldn't Stop Eating" is a long article, which the author has broken into unlabeled sections. Identify these sections—and label them.
2. What made Vince Caselli a candidate for stomach bypass surgery?
3. What does the research show on the success of weight loss among adults? Among children?
4. Identify some of the ways that people can overeat.
5. What are some of the conflicting body signals regarding appetite that make the scientific understanding of obesity so complex and difficult to understand?
6. What are the positive and negative effects of the surgery?
7. Why is the stomach-bypass surgery beginning to concern physicians?

Discussion and Writing Suggestions

1. How would you describe Gawande's attitude toward gastric-bypass surgery? Toward obesity itself?

2. What evidence can you find—for instance, in the tone of his writing, in the questions that he poses, or in his choice of subject matter—that Gawande is a physician?

3. In paragraph 7, Gawande writes that on his way to Vince Caselli's house he passes several fast food restaurants. What effect does this paragraph have on you? Why do you think he includes it in the essay?

4. Discuss Gawande's use of Vincent Caselli's story as a structural backbone to this essay. Citing examples, show how Gawande builds the essay by retelling, and playing off, Vince's story. (Note that the essay is not about Vince Caselli, per se, but about obesity, obesity surgery, and the place of obesity in the larger culture.)

5. In paragraph 19, Gawande writes: "It is hard to contemplate the human appetite without wondering if we have any say over our lives at all." What does Gawande mean by this? What is your reaction to the statement?

6. Given the increasing incidence of obesity in America, how reasonable a solution do you think gastric-bypass surgery is? As a society, how much emphasis should we be placing on treating obesity, as opposed to preventing it?

SYNTHESIS ACTIVITIES

1. In the opening of "Fat and Happy?" Schwartz remarks that fat people are unhappy largely due to the pressures that the larger culture places on them to go on diets that inevitably fail. Worley makes a similar point about the futility of dieting. And medical specialists (see Gawande and also Koplan and Dietz, the authors of the editorial in the *Journal of the American Medical Association*) observe that most dieters are doomed to regain the weight they lose. Given such overwhelming agreement on the prospects for successful dieting, what then is an overweight or obese person to do? Drawing on the selections in this chapter, write an argument synthesis structured in a problem-solution format. Use your sources to define the problem: the apparent fact that diets don't work, and that we're facing a marked increase in overweight and obese people who need to lose weight. Use the remainder of your essay to formulate a sensible response to this problem.

2. For cultural reasons (see Seid, Schwartz, and Worley), women and men may feel the need to lose weight. But the scientific reality is that many should lose weight to maintain good health (see the CDC tables, Gawande, Spake, and the *JAMA*). Compare and contrast the argument that being overweight or obese is a social problem with the argument that excess weight is a medical condition. Recall that your comparison and contrast should lead to a central claim. That claim, your thesis, will help you to organize the synthesis.

3. Drawing primarily on the selections by Seid, Schwartz, Worley, and Spake, write an explanatory synthesis that presents the ways in which fat people are made to feel inadequate by the culture at large.

4. If, as several of the authors in this chapter report, diets are ineffective for the great majority of dieters, then one could conclude that dieters themselves are not to blame for their failure to lose weight. If there is no one to blame, if we can't point an accusing finger to a dieter's lack of willpower, how should we think about the problems of being overweight and obese? What evidence do you see, if any, that we as a culture are prepared to approach problems *without* laying blame? In preparing an argument synthesis that responds to this question,

reread the selections by Spake (who addresses the question of whether or not obesity ought to be regarded as a disease), Worley, Crister, Seid (especially paragraph 13), and Schwartz. Focus your reading on discussions of blame-making—of who takes or should take responsibility for the problems of being overweight or obese. What patterns emerge that you can discuss in your synthesis?

5. Hillel Schwartz writes that our culture promotes a "despotism of slenderness." First, do you agree that the ideal body type in our culture is slender? Second, do you agree that this slender ideal is despotic? Despotism requires a despot, does it not? Who—or what—in this case is the despot? Drawing on the selections by Schwartz and others in this chapter, write a synthesis that argues for or against a cultural "despotism of slenderness." In making your case, you might refer to sources outside this chapter—for instance, to the worlds of advertising, fashion, weight-loss products, and fast food.

6. Write an explanatory synthesis on the mixed messages that consumers receive concerning body weight from the medical community, the food industry, the clothing industry, and the entertainment industry. Draw on any observations you have made about the topic, based on your experiences with mass media (ads, TV, movies, billboards, radio, etc.). Also draw on the selections by Seid, Nestle, *JAMA*, Schwartz, and Worley.

7. In a synthesis that draws upon your own experiences or those of someone you know, explain the challenges of trying to maintain your weight in a culture that does not readily forgive being overweight or obese. In your synthesis, refer to the selections in this chapter that discuss the cultural pressures of being fat—including Seid, Schwartz, Crister, and Worley.

8. Compare and contrast Crister's belief that bad eating behaviors should be stigmatized with Worley's realization that she should accept being fat and forge "a new relationship" with her body. Alternatively, compare and contrast Crister's position with that of experts cited by Spake, who believe that obesity has more to do with genetic makeup than with willpower.

9. How extreme do you find the gastric-bypass surgery described by Gawande? Do you understand why morbidly obese people would elect to undergo the operation? Do you understand why "moderately obese" people would do so? Write a synthesis in which you discuss the various cultural pressures to be thin (see Seid and Schwartz) and the various remedies available to achieve this goal—including dieting, exercise, and surgery (see Spake, Koplan and Dietz, and Gawande). If you have no strongly held views on the topic, write an explanatory synthesis. If you do, write an argument synthesis. Either way, your synthesis should be governed by a carefully constructed thesis.

10. Nestle observes that there is no independent federal agency, outside the U.S. Department of Agriculture, that is responsible for forming a coordinated, national response to the epidemic of overweight and obesity. If you agree with Nestle that the USDA is hopelessly compromised in this matter (see paragraphs 4 and 5), do you advocate the creation of a new agency (and a new bureaucracy)? Do you believe the problem warrants an effort of that magnitude? (In establishing the extent of the problem in your paper, draw on the *JAMA* article and the CDC tables. Also, see the introduction to this chapter for current dollar figures relating to obesity expenditures.)

11. Using Nestle's notion of "ironic politics," analyze the mixed messages people receive concerning the incidence of obesity and overweight in this country. Recall that your success with an analysis (see Chapter 6) turns on your ability to state an analytical principle clearly (Nestle's "irony") and to use that principle to illuminate some phenomenon in the world. What are the ironies you see in our culture's confused interactions with food, weight, self-image, and health?

12. Reread Seid's "Too 'Close to the Bone'" and critique it as an example of analysis. Explain why her article is an analysis and then, step by step, *how* she goes about conducting this analysis. What is (are) the analytical principle(s) she draws on? (See paragraph 3, especially.) To what phenomena does she apply them? How do her analytical principles help to illuminate her subject? What are her conclusions—and how do you imagine a *different* analytical principle might be used to draw other conclusions? Conclude your critique with an overall assessment of Seid's article.

RESEARCH ACTIVITIES

1. Research the debate surrounding the creation of the U.S. government's "Food Pyramid." You will readily be able to locate official government publications online that describe the pyramid. Locate articles in the library and online describing the disagreements and compromises involved in designing the pyramid. You may want to consult Walter C. Willett's *Eat, Drink, and Be Healthy* (Simon and Schuster, 2001) for a critique of the pyramid on nutritional grounds. See also Marion Nestle's editorial in this chapter, discussing the U.S. Department of Agriculture's conflicts of interest in creating the pyramid.

2. According to some experts, pharmaceutical research may hold out the best hope for addressing the problems of obesity. Research the history of and present state-of-the-art regarding diet pills. When were they introduced? To date, how effective have they been? You may want to reserve special attention for the recent "fen-phen" diet

pill scare, in which a potent combination of appetite suppressants was found to cause heart-valve problems.

3. Conduct research into Body Mass Index (BMI), which you can find on page 478, and is discussed in the editorial by Koplan and Dietz. In your report, answer these basic questions: Why and when was the index developed? By whom? What did it replace? What medical assumptions underlie the index? How has it been used, and how is it being used today?

4. Hillel Schwartz's article contains extensive footnotes. Review the entries in his list and select several to track down and read, according to your interests. Based on your findings, devise a research question and conduct additional research. Write a paper in which you present your results.

5. Roberta Seid observes that the modern conception of being overweight and obese came into being at an identifiable historical moment—her point being that ideal body types have changed over time and that we live in a time in which the ideal is "close to the bone." Write a research paper that presents an explanatory overview of the changing conceptions of the ideal body type, from ancient times through the present. Take Seid's article as your starting point. As a next step, you might move outward from her footnotes. You may want to consult Peter Stearns's *Fat History* (New York University Press, 1997).

6. Identify a commercially successful dieting program. Collect the company's literature and then conduct an inquiry, over the Internet and in the library, on the effectiveness of that program. Locate, if you can, any complaints—you can try the local Better Business Bureau—and prepare a final report in which you assess the program's credibility. (You might also wish to investigate the effectiveness of a diet program as presented in a book, such as *The South Beach Diet*.)

7. Research the prevalence of obesity in other countries or cultures. You might begin with the World Health Organization's Web site <http://www.who.int/en/> and the International Association for the Study of Obesity <http://www.iaso.org>. You will need to narrow your focus, given the broadness of the topic. You might research obesity among the French, whom Greg Crister says are known for their "legendary leanness." You might investigate the Pima Indians or inhabitants of Nauru. Consider beginning your research with an article that appeared in the Boston *Globe* on 26 February 2002: "Developing Nations Taking on West's Flabby Look," by Stephen Smith. (You can access the *Globe*'s archives at http://www.globe.com.) Following an observation made by Marion Nestle, you might look at countries whose populations suffer simultaneously from malnutrition *and* obesity.

8. Research the various elective surgical techniques for managing weight, including liposuction and the gastric-bypass described by Gawande. Where were these procedures developed? By whom? What is their rate of success? The dangers associated with them? What new weight reduction surgeries are being developed?

9. Research the social and psychological effects of being overweight or obese. You might start with "Social, Educational, and Psychological Correlates of Weight Status in Adolescents" by Nicole H. Falkner et al. in *Obesity Research* (v. 9: pp. 32–42, 2001, available online at http://www.obesityresearch.org/). The references section should be very helpful in steering you to related articles.

10. Research the topic of obesity-related bias and discrimination. You might begin with "Bias, Discrimination, and Obesity" by Rebecca Puhl and Kelly Brownell in *Obesity Research* (v. 9, pp. 788–805, 2001, available online at http://www.obesityresearch.org/). The references section should be helpful in steering you to related articles.

Fairy Tales: A Closer Look at Cinderella

12

In August 2001, when the crown prince of Norway married a single mother and former waitress, hundreds of thousands of Norwegians cheered, along with an estimated 300 million television viewers worldwide. Observers called it a "Cinderella" tale—and everyone everywhere understood the reference. Mette-Marit Tjessem Hoiby had become a Cinderella figure. But why had the bride's humble beginnings so endeared her to a nation? We can begin to offer answers by examining an ancient and universally known tale in which a young girl—heartsick at the death of her mother, deprived of her father's love, and scorned by her new family—is nonetheless recognized for her inner worth.

"Once upon a time. . . ." Millions of children around the world have listened to these (or similar) words. And, once upon a time, such words were magic archways into a world of entertainment and fantasy for children and their parents. But in our own century, fairy tales have come under the scrutiny of anthropologists, linguists, educators, psychologists, and psychiatrists, as well as literary critics, who have come to see them as a kind of social genetic code—a means by which cultural values are transmitted from one generation to the next. Some people, of course, may scoff at the idea that charming tales like "Cinderella" or "Snow White" are anything other than charming tales, at the idea that fairy tales may really be ways of inculcating young and impressionable children with culturally approved values. But even if they are not aware of it, adults and children use fairy tales in complex and subtle ways. We can, perhaps, best illustrate this by examining variants of "Cinderella."

"Cinderella" appears to be the best-known fairy tale in the world. In 1892, Marian Roalfe Cox published 345 variants of the story, the first systematic study of a single folktale. In her collection, Cox gathered stories from throughout Europe in which elements or motifs of "Cinderella" appeared, often mixed with motifs of other tales. All told, more than 700 variants exist throughout the world—in Europe, Africa, Asia, and North and South America. Scholars debate the extent to which such a wide distribution is explained by population migrations or by some universal quality of imagination that would allow people at different times and places to create essentially the same story. But for whatever reason, folklorists agree that "Cinderella" has appealed to storytellers and listeners everywhere.

The great body of folk literature, including fairy tales, comes to us from an oral tradition. Written literature, produced by a particular author, is preserved through the generations just as the author recorded it. By contrast, oral literature changes with every telling: The childhood game comes to mind in which one child whispers a sentence into the ear of another; by the time the second child repeats the sentence to a third, and the third to a fourth (and so on), the sentence has changed considerably. And so it is with oral literature, with the qualification that these stories are also changed quite consciously when a teller wishes to add or delete material.

Modern students of folk literature find themselves in the position of *reading* as opposed to hearing a tale. The texts we read tend to be of two types, which are at times difficult to distinguish. We might read a faithful transcription of an oral tale or a tale of *literary* origin—a tale that was originally written (as a short story would be), not spoken, but that nonetheless may contain elements of an oral account. In this chapter, we include tales of both oral and literary origin. Jakob and Wilhelm Grimm published their transcription of "Cinderella" in 1812. The version by Charles Perrault (1697) is difficult to classify as the transcription of an oral source, since he may have heard the story originally but appears (according to Bruno Bettelheim) to have "freed it of all content he considered vulgar, and refined its other features to make the product suitable to be told at court." Of unquestionable literary origin are the Walt Disney version of the story, based on Perrault's text; Anne Sexton's poem; Tanith Lee's "When the Clock Strikes," a version in which the Cinderella figure is a witch bent on avenging the murder of her royal family; and John Gardner's "Gudgekin the Thistle Girl."

Preceding these variants of "Cinderella," we present two selections that will orient you, we hope, to the experience of reading fairy tales as "literature": the first, a general introduction to the topic by renowned folklorist Stith Thompson; the second, an analysis by Catherine Orenstein of the links between fairy tales and romance-based reality television shows such as *Joe Millionaire*. Following the variants are four selections that respond directly to the tale. We hear from Bruno Bettelheim, who, employing psychoanalytic theory, finds in "Cinderella" a story of "Sibling Rivalry and Oedipal Conflicts." On a lighter note, in "I Am Cinderella's Stepmother and I Know My Rights," Judith Rossner sets the record straight on "Cinderella" from a point of view not typically represented in variants of the tale. Next, Jungian analyst Jacqueline M. Schectman examines "Cinderella" to find a sympathetic stepmother in "'Cinderella' and the Loss of Father-Love." The chapter concludes with "'Cinderella': *Not* So Morally Superior," Elisabeth Panttaja's surprising analysis that our heroine succeeds not because she is patient or virtuous (the standard moral to the story) but because "she disobeys the stepmother, enlists forbidden helpers, uses magic powers, lies, hides, dissembles, disguises herself, and evades pursuit."

A note on terminology: "Cinderella," "Jack and the Beanstalk," "Little Red Riding Hood," and the like are commonly referred to as fairy tales, although, strictly speaking, they are not. True fairy tales concern a "class of supernatural beings of diminutive size, who in popular belief are said to possess magical powers and to have great influence for good or evil over the affairs of humans" (*Oxford English Dictionary*). "Cinderella" and the others just mentioned concern no beings of diminutive size, although extraordinary, magical events do occur in the stories. Folklorists would be more apt to call these stories "wonder tales."

We retain the traditional "fairy tale," with the proviso that in popular usage the term is misapplied. You may notice that the authors in this chapter use the terms "folktale" and "fairy tale" interchangeably. The expression "folktale" refers to *any* story conceived orally and passed on in an oral tradition. Thus, "folktale" is a generic term that incorporates both fairy tales and wonder tales.

Universality of the Folktale
Stith Thompson

Folklorists travel around the world, to cities and rural areas alike, recording the facts, traditions, and beliefs that characterize ethnic groups. Some folklorists record and compile jokes; others do the same with insults or songs. Still others, like Stith Thompson, devote their professional careers to studying tales. And, as it turns out, many aspects of stories and story-telling are worth examining. Among them: the art of narrative—how tellers captivate their audiences; the social and religious significance of tale telling; the many types of tales that are told; the many variants, worldwide, of single tales (such as "Cinderella"). In a preface to one of his own books, Thompson raises the broad questions and the underlying assumptions that govern the folklorist's study of tales. We begin this chapter with Thompson's overview to set a context for the variants of "Cinderella" that you will read.

Note the ways that Thompson's approach to fairy tales differs from yours. Whether or not you're conscious of having an approach, you do have one: Perhaps you regard stories such as "Cinderella" as entertainment. Fine—this is a legitimate point of view, but it's only one of several ways of regarding folktales. Stith Thompson claims that there's much to learn in studying tales. He assumes, as you might not, that tales should be objects of study as well as entertainment.

Stith Thompson (1885–1976) led a distinguished life as an American educator, folklorist, editor, and author. Between 1921 and 1955, he was a professor of folklore and English, and later dean of the Graduate School and Distinguished Service Professor at Indiana University, Bloomington. Five institutions have awarded Thompson honorary doctorates for his work in folklore studies. He published numerous books on the subject, including European Tales Among North American Indians *(1919),* The Types of the Folktales *(1928), and* Tales of the North American Indian *(1929). He is best known for his six-volume* Motif Index of Folk Literature *(1932–1937; 1955–1958, 2nd ed.).*

1   The teller of stories has everywhere and always found eager listeners. Whether his tale is the mere report of a recent happening, a legend of long ago, or an elaborately contrived fiction, men and women have hung upon his words and satisfied their yearnings for information or amusement, for incitement to heroic deeds, for religious edification, or for release from the overpowering monotony of their lives. In villages of central Africa, in outrigger boats on the Pacific, in the Australian bush, and within the shadow of Hawaiian volcanoes, tales of the present and of the mysterious past, of animals and gods and heroes, and of men and women like themselves, hold listeners in their spell or enrich the conversation of daily life. So it is also in Eskimo igloos under the light of seal-oil lamps,

in the tropical jungles of Brazil, and by the totem poles of the British Columbian coast. In Japan too, and China and India, the priest and the scholar, the peasant and the artisan all join in their love of a good story and their honor for the man who tells it well.

2   When we confine our view to our own occidental world, we see that for at least three or four thousand years, and doubtless for ages before, the art of the story-teller has been cultivated in every rank of society. Odysseus entertains the court of Alcinous with the marvels of his adventures. Centuries later we find the long-haired page reading nightly from interminable chivalric romances to entertain his lady while her lord is absent on his crusade. Medieval priests illustrate sermons by anecdotes old and new, and only sometimes edifying. The old peasant, now as always, whiles away the winter evening with tales of wonder and adventure and the marvelous workings of fate. Nurses tell children of Goldilocks or the House that Jack Built. Poets write epics and novelists novels. Even now the cinemas and theaters bring their stories directly to the ear and eye through the voices and gestures of actors. And in the smoking-rooms of sleeping cars and steamships and at the banquet table the oral anecdote flourishes in a new age.

3   In the present work we are confining our interest to a relatively narrow scope, the traditional prose tale—the story which has been handed down from generation to generation either in writing or by word of mouth. Such tales are, of course, only one of the many kinds of story material, for, in addition to them, narrative comes to us in verse as ballads and epics, and in prose as histories, novels, dramas, and short stories. We shall have little to do with the songs of bards, with the ballads of the people, or with poetic narrative in general, though stories themselves refuse to be confined exclusively to either prose or verse forms. But even with verse and all other forms of prose narrative put aside, we shall find that in treating the traditional prose tale—the folktale—our quest will be ambitious enough and will take us to all parts of the earth and to the very beginnings of history.

4   Although the term "folktale" is often used in English to refer to the "household tale" or "fairy tale" (the German *Märchen*), such as "Cinderella" or "Snow White," it is also legitimately employed in a much broader sense to include all forms of prose narrative, written or oral, which have come to be handed down through the years. In this usage the important fact is the traditional nature of the material. In contrast to the modern story writer's striving after originality of plot and treatment, the teller of a folktale is proud of his ability to hand on that which he has received. He usually desires to impress his readers or hearers with the fact that he is bringing them something that has the stamp of good authority, that the tale was heard from some great story-teller or from some aged person who remembered it from old days.

5   So it was until at least the end of the Middle Ages with writers like Chaucer, who carefully quoted authorities for their plots—and sometimes even invented originals so as to dispel the suspicion that some new and unwarranted story was being foisted on the public. Though the individual genius of such writers appears clearly enough, they always depended on authority, not only for their basic theological opinions but also for the plots of their stories. A study of the

sources of Chaucer or Boccaccio takes one directly into the stream of tradition-al narrative.

6   The great written collections of stories characteristic of India, the Near East, the classical world, and Medieval Europe are almost entirely traditional. They copy and recopy. A tale which gains favor in one collection is taken over into others, sometimes intact and sometimes with changes of plot or characteriza-tion. The history of such a story, passing it may be from India to Persia and Arabia and Italy and France and finally to England, copied and changed from manuscript to manuscript, is often exceedingly complex. For it goes through the hands of both skilled and bungling narrators and improves or deteriorates at nearly every retelling. However well or poorly such a story may be written down, it always attempts to preserve a tradition, an old tale with the authority of antiq-uity to give it interest and importance.

7   If use of the term "folktale" to include such literary narratives seems some-what broad, it can be justified on practical grounds if on no other, for it is impos-sible to make a complete separation of the written and the oral traditions. Often, indeed, their interrelation is so close and so inextricable as to present one of the most baffling problems the folklore scholar encounters. They differ somewhat in their behavior, it is true, but they are alike in their disregard of originality of plot and of pride of authorship.

8   Nor is complete separation of these two kinds of narrative tradition by any means necessary for their understanding. The study of the oral tale . . . will be valid so long as we realize that stories have frequently been taken down from the lips of unlettered taletellers and have entered the great literary collections. In contrary fashion, fables of Aesop, anecdotes from Homer, and saints' legends, not to speak of fairy tales read from Perrault or Grimm, have entered the oral stream and all their association with the written or printed page has been for-gotten. Frequently a story is taken from the people, recorded in a literary doc-ument, carried across continents or preserved through centuries, and then retold to a humble entertainer who adds it to his repertory.

9   It is clear then that the oral story need not always have been oral. But when it once habituates itself to being passed on by word of mouth it undergoes the same treatment as all other tales at the command of the raconteur. It becomes something to tell to an audience, or at least to a listener, not some-thing to read. Its effects are no longer produced indirectly by association with words written or printed on a page, but directly through facial expression and gesture and repetition and recurrent patterns that generations have tested and found effective.

10   This oral art of taletelling is far older than history, and it is not bounded by one continent or one civilization. Stories may differ in subject from place to place, the conditions and purposes of taletelling may change as we move from land to land or from century to century, and yet everywhere it ministers to the same basic social and individual needs. The call for entertainment to fill in the hours of leisure has found most peoples very limited in their resources, and except where modern urban civilization has penetrated deeply they have found the telling of stories one of the most satisfying of pastimes. Curiosity about the past has always brought eager listeners to tales of the long ago which supply the simple man with all he

knows of the history of his folk. Legends grow with the telling, and often a great heroic past evolves to gratify vanity and tribal pride. Religion also has played a mighty role everywhere in the encouragement of the narrative art, for the religious mind has tried to understand beginnings and for ages has told stories of ancient days and sacred beings. Often whole cosmologies have unfolded themselves in these legends, and hierarchies of gods and heroes.

11   Worldwide also are many of the structural forms which oral narrative has assumed. The hero tale, the explanatory legend, the animal anecdote—certainly these at least are present everywhere. Other fictional patterns are limited to particular areas of culture and act by their presence or absence as an effective index of the limits of the area concerned. The study of such limitations has not proceeded far, but it constitutes an interesting problem for the student of these oral narrative forms.

12   Even more tangible evidence of the ubiquity and antiquity of the folktale is the great similarity in the content of stories of the most varied peoples. The same tale types and narrative motifs are found scattered over the world in most puzzling fashion. A recognition of these resemblances and an attempt to account for them brings the scholar closer to an understanding of the nature of human culture. He must continually ask himself, "Why do some peoples borrow tales and some lend? How does the tale serve the needs of the social group?" When he adds to his task an appreciation of the aesthetic and practical urge toward storytelling, and some knowledge of the forms and devices, stylistic and histrionic, that belong to this ancient and widely practiced art, he finds that he must bring to his work more talents than one man can easily possess. Literary critics, anthropologists, historians, psychologists, and aestheticians are all needed if we are to hope to know why folktales are made, how they are invented, what art is used in their telling, how they grow and change and occasionally die.

Review Questions

1. According to Thompson, why do people venerate a good storyteller?

2. For Thompson, what features distinguish a "folktale" from modern types of fiction?

3. How does religion help encourage the existence of folktale art?

4. What is a strong piece of evidence for the great antiquity and universality of folktales?

Discussion and Writing Suggestions

1. Based on Thompson's explanation of the qualities of oral folktales, what do you feel is gained by the increasing replacement of this form of art and entertainment by TV?

2. What do you suppose underlies the apparent human need to tell stories, given that storytelling is practiced in every culture known?

3. Interview older members of your family, asking them about stories they were told as children. As best you can, record a story. Then examine your work. How does it differ from the version you heard? Write an account of your impressions on the differences between an oral and a written rendering of a story. Alternatively, you might record a story and then speculate on what the story might mean in the experiences of the family member who told it to you.

Fairy Tales and a Dose of Reality
Catherine Orenstein

With shows like Joe Millionaire, The Bachelorette, *and* Married in America, *producers of romance-based reality television have reflected (or helped to create, depending on your point of view) our fascination with fairy tales. Which suitor will Trista choose? The nation intently watches the (melo)drama because we have an emotional stake in the right guy marrying the right girl. We love storybook romance, says Catherine Orenstein, partly because we love fairy tales and the promise of happily-ever-after. But is our understanding of these tales accurate? Take a closer look and we find "cruelty, deceit, greed, murder and nasty in-laws." Maybe this is the stuff that draws us to reality TV. Catherine Orenstein is the author of* Little Red Riding Hood Uncloaked: Sex, Morality, and the Evolution of the Fairy Tale *(2002). This article first appeared in the* New York Times *on 3 March 2003.*

1   The most recent crop of reality television shows taps the fantasies we first learned from fairy tales: castles and fortunes, true love and romantic destiny, and above all that most perfect storybook union, the "fairy tale wedding." On the rose-strewn finale of "The Bachelorette," Trista chose the shy fireman Ryan, who promptly got down on one knee and held out a diamond. "I don't think that I could have imagined a better ending to this fairy tale story," she sighed. Meanwhile, on "Joe Millionaire," 20 would-be Cinderellas competed for the hand of a modern-day Prince Charming.

2   Of course, in addition to pandering to our storybook fantasies, reality television plays to far crasser conceits—lies and manipulation, an ample display of female flesh and a sadistic interest in the rejected suitors' humiliation. Fox's new show "Married by America," which premieres tonight, will take love out of the equation entirely, with viewers picking who gets paired off. In NBC's coming "Race to the Altar," a sort of hybrid of "The Great Race" and "The Bachelor," couples will compete for a fantasy prime-time wedding.

"Fairy Tales and a Dose of Reality" by Catherine Orenstein, *New York Times,* March 3, 2003.

3   Sounds like fairy tales run amok. In fact, though, this reality comes closer to the true storybook than one might imagine. Those who wish for a real-life fairy tale romance might want to read their fairy tales again. The first published *contes de fees,* as they were called by the Parisian aristocracy at the end of the 17th century, did indeed revolve around courtship and weddings, but they told of unions that were anything but sweet and loving. Charles Perrault's 1697 collection, "Tales of Times Past with Morals," better known today as the "Mother Goose Tales," featured cruelty, deceit, greed, murder and nasty in-laws.

4   His pre-Disney Sleeping Beauty is not chastely awakened by a kiss, but rather impregnated by a passing prince and hidden in the woods. Years later the prince's mother tries to eat her. The young bride in Perrault's "Bluebeard" appears to have made a better match by marrying a wealthy widower. Alas, it turns out her groom is a serial killer. One day she discovers the corpses of his former wives hanging in a secret chamber.

5   As for Cinderella, Hollywood's various versions may preach about true love transcending class, but in Perrault's original story Prince Charming falls for Cinderella's gown and slippers but fails to recognize her face. He mistakes her for her stepsisters, and has to rely on shoe size to be sure he gets the right bride.

6   These early fairy tales suggest how much our expectations of love and marriage have changed in three centuries. Perrault's "fairy tale wedding" was not entirely make-believe. It was based on the prevailing aristocratic marriage of the 17th century, the *mariage de raison,* where newlyweds were often strangers, money was more important than romance and love was not the key but rather an impediment to a successful marriage.

7   Orchestrated by parents, marriage was a business affair. Take, for example, the noble but indebted Grignan family, who sold their son to the daughter of a wealthy tax collector for the sum of 400,000 livres. "Console yourselves for a mesalliance,"* urged a cousin of the groom's mother in a 1694 letter, "by the relief you will feel at no longer being harassed by creditors when you sojourn in your large, beautiful, magnificent chateau."

8   The modern romantic understanding of the fairy tale, and especially the romantic ideal of a "fairy tale wedding," owes most to the 20th century, when Americans began to glorify marriage and domesticity. In 1937, Walt Disney's first full-length animated feature, "Snow White and the Seven Dwarfs," showed the cartoon heroine whistling and singing with rabbits and deer while she cooks, darns and scrubs the dwarfs' bachelor pad. Similarly in 1950, the heroine of Disney's "Cinderella" sings and dances with mice and birds while she cleans house and stitches her ball gown, chores that anticipate her future life as happy housewife to Prince Charming.

9   Those films transformed the message of the fairy tale, just as today we continue to spin our own romantic wives' tales, recasting Prince Charming and Cinderella as prime-time bachelors and bachelorettes who court, propose and even wed for cash, beauty and network profits—not to mention America's enter-

---

* A *mesalliance* is a "marriage with a person of inferior social position." [*American Heritage Dictionary*]

tainment. The fantasy is not that reality television is delivering a fairy tale romance, but that there ever was one at all.

Review Questions

1. Orenstein claims that reality television appeals not only to our romantic fantasies concerning fairy tales but also to certain darker elements in the tales. How so?

2. From where, and when, do our modern romantic interpretations of fairy tales derive?

3. How do fairy tales reveal the extent to which "our expectations of love and marriage have changed"?

4. Explain Orenstein's final line: "The fantasy is not that reality television is delivering a fairy tale romance, but that there ever was one at all."

Discussion and Writing Suggestions

1. Have you watched any romance-based reality television? What are your impressions of it? In what ways do the shows resemble a fairy tale? In what ways, not?

2. Prior to reading the variants of "Cinderella" in this chapter, consider the associations you have had with the tale. To what extent, when recalling it, do you conjure images of "true love" and "happily ever after"? Examine your images in light of Orenstein's statement that reality-based television, with its displays of sadism and humiliation, "comes closer to the true storybook [version of fairy tales like 'Cinderella'] than one might imagine." Do you find sadism and humiliation on display in "Cinderella"?

3. Some cultures regard marriage more as a business arrangement between families than as a love interest between individuals. Why is this notion so difficult for many people to accept? If you have difficulty with it, can your difficulty be traced in any way, even partially, to fairy-tale literature? Explain.

4. Brainstorm with some classmates to create the concept for a new romance-based reality television program—one that would meet with Catherine Orenstein's approval. First, you'll need to clarify the ways in which Orenstein finds our current responses to these shows to be based on a *mis*-reading of fairy tale literature. Then, given what you take to be Orenstein's understanding of fairy tale literature, one acknowledging its "cruelty, deceit, [and] greed," create the outlines of a new show.

Nine Variants of "Cinderella"

The existence of Chinese, French, German, African, and Native American versions of the popular Cinderella tale, along with 700 other versions worldwide, comes as a surprise to many. Which is the real "Cinderella"? The question is misleading in that each version is "real" for a particular group of people in a particular place and time. Certainly, you can judge among versions and select the most appealing. You can also draw comparisons and contrasts. Indeed, the grouping of the stories that we present here invites comparisons. You might wish to consider a few of the following categories as you read:

- Cinderella's innocence or guilt, concerning the treatment she receives at the hands of her stepsisters

- Cinderella's passive (or active) nature

- Sibling rivalry—the relationship of Cinderella with her sisters

- The father's role

- The rule that Cinderella must return from the ball by midnight

- The levels of violence

- The presence or absence of the fairy godmother

- Cinderella's relationship with the prince

- The characterization of the prince

- The presence of Cinderella's dead mother

- The function of magic

- The ending

Cinderella
Charles Perrault

Charles Perrault (1628–1703) was born in Paris of a prosperous family. He practiced law for a short time and then devoted his attentions to a job in government, in which capacity he was instrumental in promoting the advancement of the arts and sciences and in securing pensions for writers, both French and foreign. Perrault is best known as a writer for his Contes de ma mère l'oye (Mother Goose Tales), a collection of fairy tales taken from popular folklore. He is widely suspected of having changed these stories in an effort to make them more acceptable to his audience—members of the French court.

1   Once there was a nobleman who took as his second wife the proudest and haughtiest woman imaginable. She had two daughters of the same character, who took after their mother in everything. On his side, the husband had a daughter who was sweetness itself; she inherited this from her mother, who had been the most kindly of women.

2   No sooner was the wedding over than the stepmother showed her ill-nature. She could not bear the good qualities of the young girl, for they made her own daughters seem even less likable. She gave her the roughest work of the house to do. It was she who washed the dishes and the stairs, who cleaned out Madam's room and the rooms of the two Misses. She slept right at the top of the house, in an attic, on a lumpy mattress, while her sisters slept in panelled rooms where they had the most modern beds and mirrors in which they could see themselves from top to toe. The poor girl bore everything in patience and did not dare to complain to her father. He would only have scolded her, for he was entirely under his wife's thumb.

3   When she had finished her work, she used to go into the chimney-corner and sit down among the cinders, for which reason she was usually known in the house as Cinderbottom. Her younger stepsister, who was not so rude as the other, called her Cinderella. However, Cinderella, in spite of her ragged clothes, was still fifty times as beautiful as her sisters, superbly dressed though they were.

4   One day the King's son gave a ball, to which everyone of good family was invited. Our two young ladies received invitations, for they cut quite a figure in the country. So there they were, both feeling very pleased and very busy choosing the clothes and the hair-styles which would suit them best. More work for Cinderella, for it was she who ironed her sisters' underwear and goffered their linen cuffs. Their only talk was of what they would wear.

5   "I," said the elder, "shall wear my red velvet dress and my collar of English lace."

6   "I," said the younger, "shall wear just my ordinary skirt; but, to make up, I shall put on my gold-embroidered cape and my diamond clasp, which is quite out of the common."

7   The right hairdresser was sent for to supply double-frilled coifs, and patches were bought from the right patch-maker. They called Cinderella to ask her opinion, for she had excellent taste. She made useful suggestions and even offered to do their hair for them. They accepted willingly.

8   While she was doing it, they said to her:

9   "Cinderella, how would you like to go to the ball?"

10   "Oh dear, you are making fun of me. It wouldn't do for me."

11   "You are quite right. It would be a joke. People would laugh if they saw a Cinderbottom at the ball."

12   Anyone else would have done their hair in knots for them, but she had a sweet nature, and she finished it perfectly. For two days they were so excited that they ate almost nothing. They broke a good dozen laces trying to tighten their stays to make their waists slimmer, and they were never away from their mirrors.

13   At last the great day arrived. They set off, and Cinderella watched them until they were out of sight. When she could no longer see them, she began to cry. Her godmother, seeing her all in tears, asked what was the matter.

14   "If only I could . . . If only I could . . . " She was weeping so much that she could not go on.

15   Her godmother, who was a fairy, said to her: "If only you could go to the ball, is that it?"

16   "Alas, yes," Said Cinderella with a sigh.

17   "Well," said the godmother, "be a good girl and I'll get you there."

18   She took her into her room and said: "Go into the garden and get me a pumpkin."

19   Cinderella hurried out and cut the best she could find and took it to her godmother, but she could not understand how this pumpkin would get her to the ball. Her godmother hollowed it out, leaving only the rind, and then tapped it with her wand and immediately it turned into a magnificent gilded coach.

20   Then she went to look in her mouse-trap and found six mice all alive in it. She told Cinderella to raise the door of the trap a little, and as each mouse came out she gave it a tap with her wand and immediately it turned into a fine horse. That made a team of six horses, each of fine mouse-coloured grey.

21   While she was wondering how she would make a coachman, Cinderella said to her:

22   "I will go and see whether there is a rat in the rat-trap, we could make a coachman of him."

23   "You are right," said the godmother. "Run and see."

24   Cinderella brought her the rat-trap, in which there were three big rats. The fairy picked out one of them because of his splendid whiskers and, when she had touched him, he turned into a fat coachman, with the finest moustaches in the district.

25   Then she said: "Go into the garden and you will find six lizards behind the watering-can. Bring them to me."

26   As soon as Cinderella had brought them, her godmother changed them into six footmen, who got up behind the coach with their striped liveries, and stood in position there as though they had been doing it all their lives.

27   Then the fairy said to Cinderella:

28   "Well, that's to go to the ball in. Aren't you pleased?"

29   "Yes. But am I to go like this, with my ugly clothes?"

30   Her godmother simply touched her with her wand and her clothes were changed in an instant into a dress of gold and silver cloth, all sparkling with precious stones. Then she gave her a pair of glass slippers, most beautifully made.

31   So equipped, Cinderella got into the coach: but her godmother warned her above all not to be out after midnight, telling her that, if she stayed at the ball a moment later, her coach would turn back into a pumpkin, her horses into mice, her footmen into lizards, and her fine clothes would become rags again.

32   She promised her godmother that she would leave the ball before midnight without fail, and she set out, beside herself with joy.

33   The King's son, on being told that a great princess whom no one knew had arrived, ran out to welcome her. He handed her down from the coach and led her into the hall where his guests were. A sudden silence fell; the dancing stopped, the violins ceased to play, the whole company stood fascinated by the beauty of the unknown princess. Only a low murmur was heard: "Ah, how lovely she is!" The King himself, old as he was, could not take his eyes off her and kept whispering to the Queen that it was a long time since he had seen such a beautiful and charming person. All the ladies were absorbed in noting her clothes and the way her hair was dressed, so as to order the same things for them-

selves the next morning, provided that fine enough materials could be found, and skillful enough craftsmen.

34 The King's son placed her in the seat of honour, and later led her out to dance. She danced with such grace that she won still more admiration. An excellent supper was served, but the young Prince was too much occupied in gazing at her to eat anything. She went and sat next to her sisters and treated them with great courtesy, offering them oranges and lemons which the Prince had given her. They were astonished, for they did not recognize her.

35 While they were chatting together, Cinderella heard the clock strike a quarter to twelve. She curtsied low to the company and left as quickly as she could.

36 As soon as she reached home, she went to her godmother and, having thanked her, said that she would very much like to go again to the ball on the next night—for the Prince had begged her to come back. She was in the middle of telling her godmother about all the things that had happened, when the two sisters came knocking at the door. Cinderella went to open it.

37 "How late you are!" she said, rubbing her eyes and yawning and stretching as though she had just woken up (though since they had last seen each other she had felt very far from sleepy).

38 "If you had been at the ball," said one of the sisters, "you would not have felt like yawning. There was a beautiful princess there, really ravishingly beautiful. She was most attentive to us. She gave us oranges and lemons."

39 Cinderella could have hugged herself. She asked them the name of the princess, but they replied that no one knew her, that the King's son was much troubled about it, and that he would give anything in the world to know who she was. Cinderella smiled and said to them:

40 "So she was very beautiful? Well, well, how lucky you are! Couldn't I see her? Please, Miss Javotte, do lend me that yellow dress which you wear about the house."

41 "Really," said Miss Javotte, "what an idea! Lend one's dress like that to a filthy Cinderbottom! I should have to be out of my mind."

42 Cinderella was expecting this refusal and she was very glad when it came, for she would have been in an awkward position if her sister really had lent her her frock.

43 On the next day the two sisters went to the ball, and Cinderella too, but even more splendidly dressed than the first time. The King's son was constantly at her side and wooed her the whole evening. The young girl was enjoying herself so much that she forgot her godmother's warning. She heard the clock striking the first stroke of midnight when she thought that it was still hardly eleven. She rose and slipped away as lightly as a roe-deer. The Prince followed her, but he could not catch her up. One of her glass slippers fell off, and the Prince picked it up with great care.

44 Cinderella reached home quite out of breath, with no coach, no footmen, and wearing her old clothes. Nothing remained of all her finery, except one of her little slippers, the fellow to the one which she had dropped. The guards at the palace gate were asked if they had not seen a princess go out. They answered that they had seen no one go out except a very poorly dressed girl, who looked more like a peasant than a young lady.

45   When the two sisters returned from the ball, Cinderella asked them if they had enjoyed themselves again, and if the beautiful lady had been there. They said that she had, but that she had run away when it struck midnight, and so swiftly that she had lost one of her glass slippers, a lovely little thing. The Prince had picked it up and had done nothing but gaze at it for the rest of the ball, and undoubtedly he was very much in love with the beautiful person to whom it belonged.

46   They were right, for a few days later the King's son had it proclaimed to the sound of trumpets that he would marry the girl whose foot exactly fitted the slipper. They began by trying it on the various princesses, then on the duchesses and on all the ladies of the Court, but with no success. It was brought to the two sisters, who did everything possible to force their feet into the slipper, but they could not manage it. Cinderella, who was looking on, recognized her own slipper, and said laughing:

47   "Let me see if it would fit me!"

48   Her sisters began to laugh and mock at her. But the gentleman who was trying on the slipper looked closely at Cinderella and, seeing that she was very beautiful, said that her request was perfectly reasonable and that he had instructions to try it on every girl. He made Cinderella sit down and, raising the slipper to her foot, he found that it slid on without difficulty and fitted like a glove.

49   Great was the amazement of the two sisters, but it became greater still when Cinderella drew from her pocket the second little slipper and put it on her other foot. Thereupon the fairy godmother came in and, touching Cinderella's clothes with her wand, made them even more magnificent than on the previous days.

50   Then the two sisters recognized her as the lovely princess whom they had met at the ball. They flung themselves at her feet and begged her forgiveness for all the unkind things which they had done to her. Cinderella raised them up and kissed them, saying that she forgave them with all her heart and asking them to love her always. She was taken to the young Prince in the fine clothes which she was wearing. He thought her more beautiful than ever and a few days later he married her. Cinderella, who was as kind as she was beautiful, invited her two sisters to live in the palace and married them, on the same day, to two great noblemen of the Court.

Ashputtle
Jakob and Wilhelm Grimm

Jakob Grimm (1785–1863) and Wilhelm Grimm (1786–1859) are best known today for the 200 folktales they collected from oral sources and reworked in Kinder- und Hausmärchen *(popularly known as* Grimm's Fairy Tales*), which has been translated into seventy languages. The techniques Jakob and Wilhelm Grimm used to collect and comment on these tales became a model for other collectors, providing a basis for the science of folklore. Although the Grimm brothers argued for preserving the tales exactly as heard from oral sources, schol-*

ars have determined that they sought to "improve" the tales by making them more read-
able. The result, highly pleasing to lay audiences the world over, nonetheless represents a
literary reworking of the original oral sources.

1   A rich man's wife fell sick and, feeling that her end was near, she called her only daughter to her bedside and said: "Dear child, be good and say your prayers; God will help you, and I shall look down on you from heaven and always be with you." With that she closed her eyes and died. Every day the little girl went out to her mother's grave and wept, and she went on being good and saying her prayers. When winter came, the snow spread a white cloth over the grave, and when spring took it off, the man remarried.

2   His new wife brought two daughters into the house. Their faces were beautiful and lily-white, but their hearts were ugly and black. That was the beginning of a bad time for the poor stepchild. "Why should this silly goose sit in the parlor with us?" they said. "People who want to eat bread must earn it. Get into the kitchen where you belong!" They took away her fine clothes and gave her an old gray dress and wooden shoes to wear. "Look at the haughty princess in her finery!" they cried and, laughing, led her to the kitchen. From then on she had to do all the work, getting up before daybreak, carrying water, lighting fires, cooking and washing. In addition the sisters did everything they could to plague her. They jeered at her and poured peas and lentils into the ashes, so that she had to sit there picking them out. At night, when she was tired out with work, she had no bed to sleep in but had to lie in the ashes by the hearth. And they took to calling her Ashputtle because she always looked dusty and dirty.

3   One day when her father was going to the fair, he asked his two step-daughters what he should bring them. "Beautiful dresses," said one. "Diamonds and pearls," said the other. "And you, Ashputtle. What would you like?" "Father," she said, "break off the first branch that brushes against your hat on your way home, and bring it to me." So he brought beautiful dresses, diamonds, and pearls for his two stepdaughters, and on the way home, as he was riding through a copse, a hazel branch brushed against him and knocked off his hat. So he broke off the branch and took it home with him. When he got home, he gave the stepdaughters what they had asked for, and gave Ashputtle the branch. After thanking him, she went to her mother's grave and planted the hazel sprig over it and cried so hard that her tears fell on the sprig and watered it. It grew and became a beautiful tree. Three times a day Ashputtle went and sat under it and wept and prayed. Each time a little white bird came and perched on the tree, and when Ashputtle made a wish the little bird threw down what she had wished for.

4   Now it so happened that the king arranged for a celebration. It was to go on for three days and all the beautiful girls in the kingdom were invited, in order that his son might choose a bride. When the two stepsisters heard they had been asked, they were delighted. They called Ashputtle and said: "Comb our hair, brush our shoes, and fasten our buckles. We're going to the wedding at the king's palace." Ashputtle obeyed, but she wept, for she too would have liked to go dancing, and she begged her stepmother to let her go. "You little sloven!" said the stepmother. "How can you go to a wedding when you're all dusty and dirty? How can

you go dancing when you have neither dress nor shoes?" But when Ashputtle begged and begged, the stepmother finally said: "Here, I've dumped a bowlful of lentils in the ashes. If you can pick them out in two hours, you may go." The girl went out the back door to the garden and cried out: "O tame little doves, O turtledoves, and all the birds under heaven, come and help me put

> *the good ones in the pot,*
> *the bad ones in your crop."*

Two little white doves came flying through the kitchen window, and then came the turtledoves, and finally all the birds under heaven came flapping and fluttering and settled down by the ashes. The doves nodded their little heads and started in, peck peck peck peck, and all the others started in, peck peck peck peck, and they sorted out all the good lentils and put them in the bowl. Hardly an hour had passed before they finished and flew away. Then the girl brought the bowl to her stepmother, and she was happy, for she thought she'd be allowed to go to the wedding. But the stepmother said: "No, Ashputtle. You have nothing to wear and you don't know how to dance; the people would only laugh at you." When Ashputtle began to cry, the stepmother said: "If you can pick two bowlfuls of lentils out of the ashes in an hour, you may come." And she thought: "She'll never be able to do it." When she had dumped the two bowlfuls of lentils in the ashes, Ashputtle went out the back door to the garden and cried out: "O tame little doves, O turtledoves, and all the birds under heaven, come and help me put

> *the good ones in the pot,*
> *the bad ones in your crop."*

Two little white doves came flying through the kitchen window, and then came the turtledoves, and finally all the birds under heaven came flapping and fluttering and settled down by the ashes. The doves nodded their little heads and started in, peck peck peck peck, and all the others started in, peck peck peck peck, and they sorted out all the good lentils and put them in the bowls. Before half an hour had passed, they had finished and they all flew away. Then the girl brought the bowls to her stepmother, and she was happy, for she thought she'd be allowed to go to the wedding. But her stepmother said: "It's no use. You can't come, because you have nothing to wear and you don't know how to dance. We'd only be ashamed of you." Then she turned her back and hurried away with her two proud daughters.

5   When they had all gone out, Ashputtle went to her mother's grave. She stood under the hazel tree and cried:

> *"Shake your branches, little tree,*
> *Throw gold and silver down on me."*

Whereupon the bird tossed down a gold and silver dress and slippers embroidered with silk and silver. Ashputtle slipped into the dress as fast as she could and went to the wedding. Her sisters and stepmother didn't recognize her. She was so beautiful in her golden dress that they thought she must be the daughter of some foreign king. They never dreamed it could be Ashputtle, for they thought she was sitting at home in her filthy rags, picking lentils out of the ashes. The king's son came up to her, took her by the hand and danced with her. He wouldn't dance with anyone else and he never let go her hand. When someone else asked for a dance, he said: "She is my partner."

6   She danced until evening, and then she wanted to go home. The king's son said: "I'll go with you, I'll see you home," for he wanted to find out whom the beautiful girl belonged to. But she got away from him and slipped into the dovecote. The king's son waited until her father arrived, and told him the strange girl had slipped into the dovecote. The old man thought: "Could it be Ashputtle?" and he sent for an ax and a pick and broke into the dovecote, but there was no one inside. When they went indoors, Ashputtle was lying in the ashes in her filthy clothes and a dim oil lamp was burning on the chimney piece, for Ashputtle had slipped out the back end of the dovecote and run to the hazel tree. There she had taken off her fine clothes and put them on the grave, and the bird had taken them away. Then she had put her gray dress on again, crept into the kitchen and lain down in the ashes.

7   Next day when the festivities started in again and her parents and stepsisters had gone, Ashputtle went to the hazel tree and said:

> "Shake your branches, little tree,
> Throw gold and silver down on me."

Whereupon the bird threw down a dress that was even more dazzling than the first one. And when she appeared at the wedding, everyone marveled at her beauty. The king's son was waiting for her. He took her by the hand and danced with no one but her. When others came and asked her for a dance, he said: "She is my partner." When evening came, she said she was going home. The king's son followed her, wishing to see which house she went into, but she ran away and disappeared into the garden behind the house, where there was a big beautiful tree with the most wonderful pears growing on it. She climbed among the branches as nimbly as a squirrel and the king's son didn't know what had become of her. He waited until her father arrived and said to him: "The strange girl has got away from me and I think she has climbed up in the pear tree." Her father thought: "Could it be Ashputtle?" He sent for an ax and chopped the tree down, but there was no one in it. When they went into the kitchen, Ashputtle was lying there in the ashes as usual, for she had jumped down on the other side of the tree, brought her fine clothes back to the bird in the hazel tree, and put on her filthy gray dress.

8   On the third day, after her parents and sisters had gone, Ashputtle went back to her mother's grave and said to the tree:

> "Shake your branches, little tree,
> Throw gold and silver down on me."

Whereupon the bird threw down a dress that was more radiant than either of the others, and the slippers were all gold. When she appeared at the wedding, the people were too amazed to speak. The king's son danced with no one but her, and when someone else asked her for a dance, he said: "She is my partner."

9   When the evening came, Ashputtle wanted to go home, and the king's son said he'd go with her, but she slipped away so quickly that he couldn't follow. But he had thought up a trick. He had arranged to have the whole staircase brushed with pitch, and as she was running down it the pitch pulled her left slipper off. The king's son picked it up, and it was tiny and delicate and all gold. Next morning he went to the father and said: "No girl shall be my wife but the one this golden shoe fits." The sisters were overjoyed, for they had beautiful feet. The eldest took the shoe to her room to try it on and her mother went with her. But the shoe was too small and she couldn't get her big toe in. So her mother handed her a knife and said: "Cut your toe off. Once you're queen you won't have to walk any more." The girl cut her toe off, forced her foot into the shoe, gritted her teeth against the pain, and went out to the king's son. He accepted her as his bride-to-be, lifted her up on his horse, and rode away with her. But they had to pass the grave. The two doves were sitting in the hazel tree and they cried out:

> "Roocoo, roocoo,
> There's blood in the shoe.
> The foot's too long, the foot's too wide,
> That's not the proper bride."

He looked down at her foot and saw the blood spurting. At that he turned his horse around and took the false bride home again. "No," he said, "this isn't the right girl; let her sister try the shoe on." The sister went to her room and managed to get her toes into the shoe, but her heel was too big. So her mother handed her a knife and said: "Cut off a chunk of your heel. Once you're queen you won't have to walk any more." The girl cut off a chunk of her heel, forced her foot into the shoe, gritted her teeth against the pain, and went out to the king's son. He accepted her as his bride-to-be, lifted her up on his horse, and rode away with her. As they passed the hazel tree, the two doves were sitting there, and they cried out:

> "Roocoo, roocoo,
> There's blood in the shoe.
> The foot's too long, the foot's too wide,
> That's not the proper bride."

He looked down at her foot and saw that blood was spurting from her shoe and staining her white stocking all red. He turned his horse around and took the false bride home again. "This isn't the right girl, either," he said. "Haven't you got another daughter?" "No," said the man, "there's only a puny little kitchen drudge that my dead wife left me. She couldn't possibly be the bride." "Send her up," said the king's son, but the mother said: "Oh, no, she's much too dirty to be seen." But he insisted and they had to call her. First she washed her face and hands, and when they were clean, she went upstairs and curtseyed to the king's son. He handed her the golden slipper and sat down on a footstool, took her foot out of her heavy wooden shoe, and put it into the slipper. It fitted perfectly. And when she stood up and the king's son looked into her face, he recognized the beautiful girl he had danced with and cried out: "This is my true bride!" The stepmother and the two sisters went pale with fear and rage. But he lifted Ashputtle up on his horse and rode away with her. As they passed the hazel tree, the two white doves called out:

> *"Roocoo, roocoo,*
> *No blood in the shoe.*
> *Her foot is neither long nor wide,*
> *This one is the proper bride."*

Then they flew down and alighted on Ashputtle's shoulders, one on the right and one on the left, and there they sat.

10   On the day of Ashputtle's wedding, the two stepsisters came and tried to ingratiate themselves and share in her happiness. On the way to church the elder was on the right side of the bridal couple and the younger on the left. The doves came along and pecked out one of the elder sister's eyes and one of the younger sister's eyes. Afterward, on the way out, the elder was on the left side and younger on the right, and the doves pecked out both the remaining eyes. So both sisters were punished with blindness to the end of their days for being so wicked and false.

When the Clock Strikes
Tanith Lee

Tanith Lee has written what might be called an inversion of "Cinderella" wherein the heroine is a witch. You will find all elements of the traditional tale here, and Lee's rendering is unmistakably "Cinderella." But with devious consistency, Lee turns both the magic and the unrighted wrong that lie at the heart of the tale to a dark purpose: revenge. Tanith Lee is a prolific writer of stories for young adults and of adult fantasy and science fiction. Born in 1947 in London, Lee had her first story published when she was twenty-four and has written more than two dozen stories and plays since.

1   Yes, the great ballroom is filled only with dust now. The slender columns of white marble and the slender columns of rose-red marble are woven together by cobwebs. The vivid frescoes, on which the Duke's treasury spent so much, are dimmed by the dust; the faces of the painted goddesses look grey. And the velvet curtains—touch them and they will crumble. Two hundred years now, since anyone danced in this place on the sea-green floor in the candle-gleam. Two hundred years since the wonderful clock struck for the very first time.

2   I thought you might care to examine the clock. It was considered exceptional in its day. The pedestal is ebony and the face fine porcelain. And these figures, which are of silver, would pass slowly about the circlet of the face. Each figure

represents, you understand, an hour. And as the appropriate hours came level with this golden bell, they would strike it the correct number of times. All the figures are unique, as you see. Beginning at the first hour, they are, in this order, a girl-child, a dwarf, a maiden, a youth, a lady, and a knight. And here, notice, the figures grow older as the day declines: a queen and king for the seventh and eighth hours, and after these, an abbess and a magician and next to last, a hag. But the very last is strangest of all. The twelfth figure; do you recognize him? It is Death. Yes, a most curious clock. It was reckoned a marvelous thing then. But it has not struck for two hundred years. Possibly you have been told the story? No? Oh, but I am certain that you have heard it, in another form, perhaps.

3   However, as you have some while to wait for your carriage, I will recount the tale, if you wish.

4   I will start with what was said of the clock. In those years, this city was prosperous, a stronghold—not as you see it today. Much was made in the city that was ornamental and unusual. But the clock, on which the twelfth hour was Death, caused something of a stir. It was thought unlucky, foolhardy, to have such a clock. It began to be murmured, jokingly by some, by others in earnest, that one night when the clock struck the twelfth hour, Death would truly strike with it.

5   Now life has always been a chancy business, and it was more so then. The Great Plague had come but twenty years before and was not yet forgotten. Besides, in the Duke's court there was much intrigue, while enemies might be supposed to plot beyond the city walls, as happens even in our present age. But there was another thing.

6   It was rumored that the Duke had obtained both his title and the city treacherously. Rumor declared that he had systematically destroyed those who had stood in line before him, the members of the princely house that formerly ruled here. He had accomplished the task slyly, hiring assassins talented with poisons and daggers. But rumor also declared that the Duke had not been sufficiently thorough. For though he had meant to rid himself of all that rival house, a single descendant remained, so obscure he had not traced her—for it was a woman.

7   Of course, such matters were not spoken of openly. Like the prophecy of the clock, it was a subject for the dark.

8   Nevertheless, I will tell you at once, there was such a descendant he had missed in his bloody work. And she was a woman. Royal and proud she was, and seething with bitter spite and a hunger for vengeance, and as bloody as the Duke, had he known it, in her own way.

9   For her safety and disguise, she had long ago wed a wealthy merchant in the city, and presently bore the man a daughter. The merchant, a dealer in silks, was respected, a good fellow but not wise. He rejoiced in his handsome and aristocratic wife. He never dreamed what she might be about when he was not with her. In fact, she had sworn allegiance to Satanas. In the dead of night she would go up into an old tower adjoining the merchant's house, and there she would say portions of the Black Mass, offer sacrifice, and thereafter practise witchcraft against the Duke. This witchery took a common form, the creation of a wax image and the maiming of the image that, by sympathy, the injuries inflicted on the wax be passed on to the living body of the victim. The woman was capable in what she did. The Duke fell sick. He lost the use of his limbs and

was racked by excruciating pains from which he could get no relief. Thinking himself on the brink of death, the Duke named his sixteen-year-old son his heir. This son was dear to the Duke, as everyone knew, and be sure the woman knew it too. She intended sorcerously to murder the young man in his turn, preferably in his father's sight. Thus, she let the Duke linger in his agony, and commenced planning the fate of the prince.

10   Now all this while she had not been toiling alone. She had one helper. It was her own daughter, a maid of fourteen, that she had recruited to her service nearly as soon as the infant could walk. At six or seven, the child had been lisping the satanic rite along with her mother. At fourteen, you may imagine, the girl was well versed in the Black Arts, though she did not have her mother's natural genius for them.

11   Perhaps you would like me to describe the daughter at this point. It has a bearing on the story, for the girl was astonishingly beautiful. Her hair was the rich dark red of antique burnished copper, her eyes were the hue of the reddish-golden amber that traders bring from the East. When she walked, you would say she was dancing. But when she danced, a gate seemed to open in the world, and bright fire spangled inside it, but she was the fire.

12   The girl and her mother were close as gloves in a box. Their games in the old tower bound them closer. No doubt the woman believed herself clever to have got such a helpmate, but it proved her undoing.

13   It was in this manner. The silk merchant, who had never suspected his wife for an instant of anything, began to mistrust the daughter. She was not like other girls. Despite her great beauty, she professed no interest in marriage, and none in clothes or jewels. She preferred to read in the garden at the foot of the tower. Her mother had taught the girl her letters, though the merchant himself could read but poorly. And often the father peered at the books his daughter read, unable to make head or tail of them, yet somehow not liking them. One night very late, the silk merchant came home from a guild dinner in the city, and he saw a slim pale shadow gliding up the steps of the old tower, and he knew it for his child. On impulse, he followed her, but quietly. He had not considered any evil so far, and did not want to alarm her. At an angle of the stair, the lighted room above, he paused to spy and listen. He had something of a shock when he heard his wife's voice rise up in glad welcome. But what came next drained the blood from his heart. He crept away and went to his cellar for wine to stay himself. After the third glass he ran for neighbours and for the watch.

14   The woman and her daughter heard the shouts below and saw the torches in the garden. It was no use dissembling. The tower was littered with evidence of vile deeds, besides what the woman kept in a chest beneath her unknowing husband's bed. She understood it was all up with her, and she understood too how witchcraft was punished hereabouts. She snatched a knife from the altar.

15   The girl shrieked when she realized what her mother was at. The woman caught the girl by her red hair and shook her.

16   "Listen to me, my daughter," she cried, "and listen carefully, for the minutes are short. If you do as I tell you, you can escape their wrath and only I need die. And if you live I am satisfied, for you can carry on my labor after me. My vengeance I shall leave you, and my witchcraft to exact it by. Indeed, I promise

you stronger powers than mine. I will beg my lord Satanas for it and he will not deny me, for he is just, in his fashion, and I have served him well. Now, will you attend?"

17   "I will," said the girl.

18   So the woman advised her, and swore her to the fellowship of Hell. And then the woman forced the knife into her own heart and dropped dead on the floor of the tower.

19   When the men burst in with their swords and staves and their torches and their madness, the girl was ready for them.

20   She stood blank-faced, blank-eyed, with her arms hanging at her sides. When one touched her, she dropped down at his feet.

21   "Surely she is innocent," this man said. She was lovely enough that it was hard to accuse her. Then her father went to her and took her hand and lifted her. At that the girl opened her eyes and she said, as if terrified: "How did I come here? I was in my chamber and sleeping—"

22   "The woman has bewitched her," her father said.

23   He desired very much that this be so. And when the girl clung to his hand and wept, he was certain of it. They showed her the body with the knife in it. The girl screamed and seemed to lose her senses totally.

24   She was put to bed. In the morning, a priest came and questioned her. She answered steadfastly. She remembered nothing, not even of the great books she had been observed reading. When they told her what was in them, she screamed again and apparently would have thrown herself from the narrow window, only the priest stopped her.

25   Finally, they brought her the holy cross in order that she might kiss it and prove herself blameless.

26   Then she knelt, and whispered softly, that nobody should hear but one—"Lord Satanas, protect thy handmaid." And either that gentleman has more power than he is credited with or else the symbols of God are only as holy as the men who deal in them, for she embraced the cross and it left her unscathed.

27   At that, the whole household thanked God. The whole household saving, of course, the woman's daughter. She had another to thank.

28   The woman's body was burnt, and the ashes put into unconsecrated ground beyond the city gates. Though they had discovered her to be a witch, they had not discovered the direction her witchcraft had selected. Nor did they find the wax image with its limbs all twisted and stuck through with needles. The girl had taken that up and concealed it. The Duke continued in his distress, but he did not die. Sometimes, in the dead of night, the girl would unearth the image from under a loose brick by the hearth, and gloat over it, but she did nothing else. Not yet. She was fourteen and the cloud of her mother's acts still hovered over her. She knew what she must do next.

29   The period of mourning ended.

30   "Daughter," said the silk merchant to her, "why do you not remove your black? The woman was malign and led you into wickedness. How long will you mourn her, who deserves no mourning?"

31   "Oh my father," she said, "never think I regret my wretched mother. It is my own unwitting sin I mourn." And she grasped his hand and spilled her tears on it. "I would rather live in a convent," said she, "than mingle with proper folk. And I would seek a convent too, if it were not that I cannot bear to be parted from you."

32   Do you suppose she smiled secretly as she said this? One might suppose it. Presently she donned a robe of sackcloth and poured ashes over her red-copper hair. "It is my penance," she said, "I am glad to atone for my sins."

33   People forgot her beauty. She was at pains to obscure it. She slunk about like an aged woman, a rag pulled over her head, dirt smeared on her cheeks and brow. She elected to sleep in a cold cramped attic and sat all day by a smoky hearth in the kitchens. When someone came to her and begged her to wash her face and put on suitable clothes and sit in the rooms of the house, she smiled modestly, drawing the rag or a piece of hair over her face. "I swear," she said, "I am glad to be humble before God and men."

34   They reckoned her pious and they reckoned her simple. Two years passed. They mislaid her beauty altogether, and reckoned her ugly. They found it hard to call to mind who she was exactly, as she sat in the ashes, or shuffled unattended about the streets like a crone.

35   At the end of the second year, the silk merchant married again. It was inevitable, for he was not a man who liked to live alone.

36   On this occasion, his choice was a harmless widow. She already had two daughters, pretty in an unremarkable style. Perhaps the merchant hoped they would comfort him for what had gone before, this normal cheery wife and the two sweet, rather silly daughters, whose chief interests were clothes and weddings. Perhaps he hoped also that his deranged daughter might be drawn out by company. But that hope foundered. Not that the new mother did not try to be pleasant to the girl. And the new sisters, their hearts grieved by her condition, went to great lengths to enlist her friendship. They begged her to come from the kitchens or the attic. Failing in that, they sometimes ventured to join her, their fine silk dresses trailing on the greasy floor. They combed her hair, exclaiming, when some of the ash and dirt were removed, on its color. But no sooner had they turned away, than the girl gathered up handfuls of soot and ash and rubbed them into her hair again. Now and then, the sisters attempted to interest their bizarre relative in a bracelet or a gown or a current song. They spoke to her of the young men they had seen at the suppers or the balls which were then given regularly by the rich families of the city. The girl ignored it all. If she ever said anything it was to do with penance and humility. At last, as must happen, the sisters wearied of her, and left her alone. They had no cares and did not want to share in hers. They came to resent her moping greyness, as indeed the merchant's second wife had already done.

37   "Can you do nothing with the girl?" she demanded of her husband. "People will say that I and my daughters are responsible for her condition and that I ill-treat the maid from jealousy of her dead mother."

38   "Now how could anyone say that?" protested the merchant, "when you are famous as the epitome of generosity and kindness."

39   Another year passed, and saw no huge difference in the household.

40   A difference there was, but not visible.

41   The girl who slouched in the corner of the hearth was seventeen. Under the filth and grime she was, impossibly, more beautiful, although no one could see it.

42   And there was one other invisible item—her power (which all this time she had nurtured, saying her prayers to Satanas in the black of midnight), her power was rising like a dark moon in her soul.

43   Three days after her seventeenth birthday, the girl straggled about the streets as she frequently did. A few noted her and muttered it was the merchant's ugly simple daughter and paid no more attention. Most did not know her at all. She had made herself appear one with the scores of impoverished flotsam which constantly roamed the city, beggars and starvelings. Just outside the city gates, these persons congregated in large numbers, slumped around fires of burning refuse or else wandering to and fro in search of edible seeds, scraps, the miracle of a dropped coin. Here the girl now came, and began to wander about as they did. Dusk gathered and the shadows thickened. The girl sank to her knees in a patch of earth as if she had found something. Two or three of the beggars sneaked over to see if it were worth snatching from her—but the girl was only scrabbling in the empty soil. The beggars, making signs to each other that she was touched by God—mad—left her alone. But, very far from mad, the girl presently dug up a stoppered clay urn. In this urn were the ashes and charred bones of her mother. She had got a clue as to the location of the urn by devious questioning here and there. Her occult power had helped her to be sure of it.

44   In the twilight, padding along through the narrow streets and alleys of the city, the girl brought the urn homewards. In the garden at the foot of the old tower, gloom-wrapped, unwitnessed, she unstoppered the urn and buried the ashes freshly. She muttered certain unholy magics over the grave. Then she snapped off the sprig of a young hazel tree, and planted it in the newly turned ground.

45   I hazard you have begun to recognize the story by now. I see you suppose I tell it wrongly. Believe me, this is the truth of the matter. But if you would rather I left off the tale. . . No doubt your carriage will soon be here—No? Very well. I shall continue.

46   I think I should speak of the Duke's son at this juncture. The prince was nineteen, able, intelligent, and of noble bearing. He was of that rather swarthy type of looks one finds here in the north, but tall and slim and clear-eyed. There is an ancient square where you may see a statue of him, but much eroded by two centuries, and the elements. After the city was sacked, no care was lavished on it.

47   The Duke treasured his son. He had constant delight in the sight of the young man and what he said and did. It was the only happiness the invalid had.

48   Then, one night, the Duke screamed out in his bed. Servants came running with candles. The Duke moaned that a sword was transfixing his heart, an inch at a time. The prince hurried into the chamber, but in that instant the Duke spasmed horribly and died. No mark was on his body. There had never been a mark to show what ailed him.

49   The prince wept. They were genuine tears. He had nothing to reproach his father with, everything to thank him for. Nevertheless, they brought the young man the seal ring of the city, and he put it on.

50   It was winter, a cold blue-white weather with snow in the streets and countryside and a hard wizened sun that drove thin sharp blades of light through the
sky, but gave no warmth. The Duke's funeral cortege passed slowly across the
snow, the broad open chariots draped with black and silver, the black-plumed
horses, the chanting priests with their glittering robes, their jeweled crucifixes
and golden censers. Crowds lined the roadways to watch the spectacle. Among
the beggar women stood a girl. No one noticed her. They did not glimpse the
expression she veiled in her ragged scarf. She gazed at the bier pitilessly. As the
young prince rode by in his sables, the seal ring on his hand, the eyes of the girl
burned through her ashy hair, like a red fox through grasses.

51   The Duke was buried in the mausoleum you can visit to this day, on the east
side of the city. Several months elapsed. The prince put his grief from him, and
took up the business of the city competently. Wise and courteous he was, but
he rarely smiled. At nineteen his spirit seemed worn. You might think he
guessed the destiny that hung over him.

52   The winter was a hard one, too. The snow had come, and having come was
loath to withdraw. When at last the spring returned, flushing the hills with color,
it was no longer sensible to be sad.

53   The prince's name day fell about this time. A great banquet was planned, a
ball. There had been neither in the palace for nigh on three years, not since the
Duke's fatal illness first claimed him. Now the royal doors were to be thrown
open to all men of influence and their families. The prince was liberal, charming, and clever even in this. Aristocrat and rich trader were to mingle in the
beautiful dining room, and in this very chamber, among the frescoes, the mar-
bles and the candelabra. Even a merchant's daughter, if the merchant were
notable in the city, would get to dance on the sea-green floor, under the white
eye of the fearful clock.

54   The clock. There was some renewed controversy about the clock. They did not
dare speak to the young prince. He was a skeptic, as his father had been. But had
not a death already occurred? Was the clock not a flying in the jaws of fate? For
those disturbed by it, there was a dim writing in their minds, in the dust of the
street or the pattern of blossoms. *When the clock strikes*—But people do not positively heed these warnings. Man is afraid of his fears. He ignores the shadow of
the wolf thrown on the paving before him, saying: It is only a shadow.

55   The silk merchant received his invitation to the palace, and to be sure, thought
nothing of the clock. His house had been thrown into uproar. The most luscious
silks of his workshop were carried into the house and laid before the wife and her
two daughters, who chirruped and squealed with excitement. The merchant stood
smugly by, above it all yet pleased at being appreciated. "Oh, father!" cried the
two sisters, "may I have this one with the gold piping?" "Oh, father, this one with
the design of pineapples?" Later, a jeweler arrived and set out his trays. The merchant was generous. He wanted his women to look their best. It might be the
night of their lives. Yet all the while, at the back of his mind, a little dark spot, itch-
ing, aching. He tried to ignore the spot, not scratch at it. His true daughter, the mad
one. Nobody bothered to tell her about the invitation to the palace. They knew
how she would react, mumbling in her hair about her sin and her penance, pad-
dling her hands in the greasy ash to smear her face. Even the servants avoided

her, as if she were just the cat seated by the fire. Less than the cat, for the cat saw to the mice—Just a block of stone. And yet, how fair she might have looked, decked in the pick of the merchant's wares, jewels at her throat. The prince himself could not have been unaware of her. And though marriage was impossible, other less holy, though equally honorable contracts, might have been arranged to the benefit of all concerned. The merchant sighed. He had scratched the darkness after all. He attempted to comfort himself by watching the two sisters exult over their apparel. He refused to admit that the finery would somehow make them seem but more ordinary than they were by contrast.

56   The evening of the banquet arrived. The family set off. Most of the servants sidled after. The prince had distributed largesse in the city; oxen roasted in the squares and the wine was free by royal order.

57   The house grew somber. In the deserted kitchen the fire went out.

58   By the hearth, a segment of gloom rose up.

59   The girl glanced around her, and she laughed softly and shook out her filthy hair. Of course, she knew as much as anyone, and more than most. This was to be her night, too.

60   A few minutes later she was in the garden beneath the old tower, standing over the young hazel tree which thrust up from the earth. It had become strong, the tree, despite the harsh winter. Now the girl nodded to it. She chanted under her breath. At length a pale light began to glow, far down near where the roots of the tree held to the ground. Out of the pale glow flew a thin black bird, which perched on the girl's shoulder. Together, the girl and the bird passed into the old tower. High up, a fire blazed that no one had lit. A tub steamed with scented water that no one had drawn. Shapes that were not real and barely seen flitted about. Rare perfumes, the rustle of garments, the glint of gems as yet invisible filled and did not fill the restless air.

61   Need I describe further? No. You will have seen paintings which depict the attendance upon a witch of her familiar demons. Now one bathes her, another anoints her, another brings clothes and ornaments. Perhaps you do not credit such things in any case. Never mind that. I will tell you what happened in the courtyard before the palace.

62   Many carriages and chariots had driven through the square, avoiding the roasting oxen, the barrels of wine, the cheering drunken citizens, and so through the gates into the courtyard. Just before ten o'clock (the hour, if you recall the clock, of the magician) a solitary carriage drove through the square and into the court. The people in the square gawked at the carriage and pressed forward to see who would step out of it, this latecomer. It was a remarkable vehicle that looked to be fashioned of solid gold, all but the domed roof that was transparent flashing crystal. Six black horses drew it. The coachman and postillions were clad in crimson, and strangely masked as curious beasts and reptiles. One of these beast-men now hopped down and opened the door of the carriage. Out came a woman's figure in a cloak of white fur, and glided up the palace stair and in at the doors.

63   There was dancing in the ballroom. The whole chamber was bright and clamorous with music and the voices of men and women. There, between

those two pillars, the prince sat in his chair, dark, courteous, seldom smiling. Here the musicians played, the deep-throated viol, the lively mandolin. And there the dancers moved up and down on the sea-green floor. But the music and the dancers had just paused. The figures on the clock were themselves in motion. The hour of the magician was about to strike.

64   As it struck, through the doorway came the figure in the fur cloak. And, as if they must, every eye turned to her.

65   For an instant she stood there, all white, as though she had brought the winter snow back with her. And then she loosed the cloak from her shoulders, it slipped away, and she was all fire.

66   She wore a gown of apricot brocade embroidered thickly with gold. Her sleeves and the bodice of her gown were slashed over ivory satin sewn with large rosy pearls. Pearls, too, were wound in her hair that was the shade of antique burnished copper. She was so beautiful that when the clock was still, nobody spoke. She was so beautiful it was hard to look at her for very long.

67   The prince got up from his chair. He did not know he had. Now he started out across the floor, between the dancers, who parted silently to let him through. He went toward the girl in the doorway as if she drew him by a chain.

68   The prince had hardly ever acted without considering first what he did. Now he did not consider. He bowed to the girl.

69   "Madam," he said. "You are welcome. Madam," he said. "Tell me who you are."

70   She smiled.

71   "My rank," she said. "Would you know that, my lord? It is similar to yours, or would be were I now mistress in my dead mother's palace. But, unfortunately, an unscrupulous man caused the downfall of our house."

72   "Misfortune indeed," said the prince. "Tell me your name. Let me right the wrong done you."

73   "You shall," said the girl. "Trust me, you shall. For my name, I would rather keep it secret for the present. But you may call me, if you will, a pet name I have given myself—Ashella."

74   "Ashella. . . . But I see no ash about you," said the prince, dazzled by her gleam, laughing a little, stiffly, for laughter was not his habit.

75   "Ash and cinders from a cold and bitter hearth," said she. But she smiled again. "Now everyone is staring at us, my lord, and the musicians are impatient to begin again. Out of all these ladies, can it be you will lead me in the dance?"

76   "As long as you will dance," he said. "You shall dance with me."

77   And that is how it was.

78   There were many dances, slow and fast, whirling measures and gentle ones. And here and there, the prince and the maiden were parted. Always then he looked eagerly after her, sparing no regard for the other girls whose hands lay in his. It was not like him, he was usually so careful. But the other young men who danced on that floor, who clasped her fingers or her narrow waist in the dance, also gazed after her when she was gone. She danced, as she appeared, like fire. Though if you had asked those young men whether they would rather tie her to themselves, as the prince did, they would have been at a loss. For it is not easy to keep pace with fire.

79   The hour of the hag struck on the clock.

80   The prince grew weary of dancing with the girl and losing her in the dance to others and refinding her and losing her again.

81   Behind the curtains there is a tall window in the east wall that opens on the terrace above the garden. He drew her out there, into the spring night. He gave an order, and small tables were brought with delicacies and sweets and wine. He sat by her, watching every gesture she made, as if he would paint her portrait afterward.

82   In the ballroom, here, under the clock, the people murmured. But it was not quite the murmur you would expect, the scandalous murmur about a woman come from nowhere that the prince had made so much of. At the periphery of the ballroom, the silk merchant sat, pale as a ghost, thinking of a ghost, the living ghost of his true daughter. No one else recognized her. Only he. Some trick of the heart had enabled him to know her. He said nothing of it. As the step-sisters and wife gossiped with other wives and sisters, an awful foreboding weighed him down, sent him cold and dumb.

83   And now it is almost midnight, the moment when the page of the night turns over into day. Almost midnight, the hour when the figure of Death strikes the golden bell of the clock. And what will happen when the clock strikes? Your face announces that you know. Be patient; let us see if you do.

84   "I am being foolish," said the prince to Ashella on the terrace. "But perhaps I am entitled to be foolish, just once in my life. What are you saying?" For the girl was speaking low beside him, and he could not catch her words.

85   "I am saying a spell to bind you to me," she said.

86   "But I am already bound."

87   "Be bound then. Never go free."

88   "I do not wish it," he said. He kissed her hands and he said, "I do not know you, but I will wed you. Is that proof your spell has worked? I will wed you, and get back for you the rights you have lost."

89   "If it were only so simple," said Ashella, smiling, smiling. "But the debt is too cruel. Justice requires a harsher payment."

90   And then, in the ballroom, Death struck the first note on the golden bell.

91   The girl smiled and she said,

92   "I curse you in my mother's name."

93   The second stroke.

94   "I curse you in my own name."

95   The third stroke.

96   "And in the name of those that your father slew."

97   The fourth stroke.

98   "And in the name of my Master, who rules the world."

99   As the fifth, the sixth, the seventh strokes pealed out, the prince stood nonplussed. At the eighth and ninth strokes, the strength of the malediction seemed to curdle his blood. He shivered and his brain writhed. At the tenth stroke, he saw a change in the loveliness before him. She grew thinner, taller. At the eleventh stroke, he beheld a thing in a ragged black cowl and robe. It grinned at him. It was all grin below a triangle of sockets of nose and eyes. At the twelfth stroke, the prince saw Death and knew him.

100   In the ballroom, a hideous grinding noise, as the gears of the clock failed. Followed by a hollow booming, as the mechanism stopped entirely.

101   The conjuration of Death vanished from the terrace.

102   Only one thing was left behind. A woman's shoe. A shoe no woman could ever have danced in. It was made of glass.

103   Did you intend to protest about the shoe? Shall I finish the story, or would you rather I did not? It is not the ending you are familiar with. Yes, I perceive you understand that, now.

104   I will go quickly, then, for your carriage must soon be here. And there is not a great deal more to relate.

105   The prince lost his mind. Partly from what he had seen, partly from the spells the young witch had netted him in. He could think of nothing but the girl who had named herself Ashella. He raved that Death had borne her away but he would recover her from Death. She had left the glass shoe as token of her love. He must discover her with the aid of the shoe. Whomsoever the shoe fitted would be Ashella. For there was this added complication, that Death might hide her actual appearance. None had seen the girl before. She had disappeared like smoke. The one infallible test was the shoe. That was why she had left it for him.

106   His ministers would have reasoned with the prince, but he was past reason. His intellect had collapsed as totally as only a profound intellect can. A lunatic, he rode about the city. He struck out at those who argued with him. On a particular occasion, drawing a dagger, he killed, not apparently noticing what he did. His demand was explicit. Every woman, young or old, maid or married, must come forth from her home, must put her foot into the shoe of glass. They came. They had no choice. Some approached in terror, some weeping. Even the aged beggar women obliged, and they cackled, enjoying the sight of royalty gone mad. One alone did not come.

107   Now it is not illogical that out of the hundreds of women whose feet were put into the shoe, a single woman might have been found that the shoe fitted. But this did not happen. Nor did the situation alter, despite a lurid fable that some, tickled by the idea of wedding the prince, cut off their toes that the shoe might fit them. And if they did, it was to no avail, for still the shoe did not.

108   Is it really surprising? The shoe was sorcerous. It constantly changed itself, its shape, its size, in order that no foot, save one, could ever be got into it.

109   Summer spread across the land. The city took on its golden summer glaze, its fetid summer smell.

110   What had been a whisper of intrigue, swelled into a steady distant thunder. Plots were being hatched.

111   One day, the silk merchant was brought, trembling and grey of face, to the prince. The merchant's dumbness had broken. He had unburdened himself of his fear at confession, but the priest had not proved honest. In the dawn, men had knocked on the door of the merchant's house. Now he stumbled to the chair of the prince.

112   Both looked twice their years, but, if anything, the prince looked the elder. He did not lift his eyes. Over and over in his hands he turned the glass shoe.

113   The merchant, stumbling too in his speech, told the tale of his first wife and his daughter. He told everything, leaving out no detail. He did not even omit the

end: that since the night of the banquet the girl had been absent from his house, taking nothing with her—save a young hazel from the garden beneath the tower.

114   The prince leapt from his chair.

115   His clothes were filthy and unkempt. His face was smeared with sweat and dust . . . it resembled, momentarily, another face.

116   Without guard or attendant, the prince ran through the city toward the merchant's house, and on the road, the intriguers waylaid and slew him. As he fell, the glass shoe dropped from his hands, and shattered in a thousand fragments.

117   There is little else worth mentioning.

118   Those who usurped the city were villains and not merely that, but fools. Within a year, external enemies were at the gates. A year more, and the city had been sacked, half burnt out, ruined. The manner in which you find it now, is somewhat better than it was then. And it is not now anything for a man to be proud of. As you were quick to note, many here earn a miserable existence by conducting visitors about the streets, the palace, showing them the dregs of the city's past.

119   Which was not a request, in fact, for you to give me money. Throw some from your carriage window if your conscience bothers you. My own wants are few.

120   No, I have no further news of the girl, Ashella, the witch. A devotee of Satanas, she has doubtless worked plentiful woe in the world. And a witch is long-lived. Even so, she will die eventually. None escapes Death. Then you may pity her, if you like. Those who serve the gentleman below—who can guess what their final lot will be? But I am very sorry the story did not please you. It is not, maybe, a happy choice before a journey.

121   And there is your carriage at last.

122   What? Ah, no, I shall stay here in the ballroom where you came on me. I have often paused here through the years. It is the clock. It has a certain—what shall I call it—power, to draw me back.

123   I am not trying to unnerve you. Why should you suppose that? Because of my knowledge of the city, of the story? You think that I am implying that I myself am Death? Now you laugh. Yes, it is absurd. Observe the twelfth figure on the clock. Is he not as you have always heard Death described? And am I in the least like that twelfth figure?

124   Although, of course, the story was not as you have heard it, either.

A Chinese "Cinderella"
Tuan Ch'êng-shih

"The earliest datable version of the Cinderella story anywhere in the world occurs in a Chinese book written about 850–860 A.D." Thus begins Arthur Waley's essay on the Chinese "Cinderella" in the March 1947 edition of Folk-Lore. *The recorder of the tale is a*

man named Tuan Ch'êng-shih, whose father was an important official in Szechwan and
who himself held a high post in the office arranging the ceremonies associated with impe-
rial ancestor worship.

1 Among the people of the south there is a tradition that before the Ch'in and
Han dynasties there was a cave-master called Wu. The aborigines called the
place the Wu cave. He married two wives. One wife died. She had a daughter
called Yeh-hsien, who from childhood was intelligent and good at making pot-
tery on the wheel. Her father loved her. After some years the father died, and
she was ill-treated by her step-mother, who always made her collect firewood
in dangerous places and draw water from deep pools. She once got a fish about
two inches long, with red fins and golden eyes. She put it into a bowl of water.
It grew bigger every day, and after she had changed the bowl several times she
could find no bowl big enough for it, so she threw it into the back pond.
Whatever food was left over from meals she put into the water to feed it. When
she came to the pond, the fish always exposed its head and pillowed it on the
bank; but when anyone else came, it did not come out. The step-mother knew
about this, but when she watched for it, it did not once appear. So she tricked
the girl, saying, "Haven't you worked hard! I am going to give you a new dress."
She then made the girl change out of her tattered clothing. Afterwards she sent
her to get water from another spring and reckoning that it was several hundred
leagues, the step-mother at her leisure put on her daughter's clothes, hid a
sharp blade up her sleeve, and went to the pond. She called to the fish. The fish
at once put its head out, and she chopped it off and killed it. The fish was now
more than ten feet long. She served it up and it tasted twice as good as an ordinary fish. She hid the bones under the dung-hill. Next day, when the girl came
to the pond, no fish appeared. She howled with grief in the open countryside,
and suddenly there appeared a man with his hair loose over his shoulders and
coarse clothes. He came down from the sky. He consoled her, saying, "Don't
howl! Your step-mother has killed the fish and its bones are under the dung.
You go back, take the fish's bones and hide them in your room. Whatever you
want, you have only to pray to them for it. It is bound to be granted." The girl
followed his advice, and was able to provide herself with gold, pearls, dresses,
and food whenever she wanted them.

2 When the time came for the cave-festival, the step-mother went, leaving the
girl to keep watch over the fruit-trees in the garden. She waited till the stepmother was some way off, and then went herself, wearing a cloak of stuff spun
from kingfisher feathers and shoes of gold. Her step-sister recognized her and
said to the step-mother, "That's very like my sister." The step-mother suspected the same thing. The girl was aware of this and went away in such a hurry
that she lost one shoe. It was picked up by one of the people of the cave. When
the step-mother got home, she found the girl asleep, with her arms around one
of the trees in the garden, and thought no more about it.

3 This cave was near to an island in the sea. On this island was a kingdom
called T'o-han. Its soldiers had subdued twenty or thirty other islands and it had
a coast-line of several thousand leagues. The cave-man sold the shoe in T'o-
han, and the ruler of T'o-han got it. He told those about him to put it on; but it

was an inch too small even for the one among them that had the smallest foot. He ordered all the women in his kingdom to try it on, but there was not one that it fitted. It was light as down and made no noise even when treading on stone. The king of T'o-han thought the cave-man had got it unlawfully. He put him in prison and tortured him, but did not end by finding out where it had come from. So he threw it down at the wayside. Then they went everywhere* through all the people's houses and arrested them. If there was a woman's shoe, they arrested them and told the king of T'o-han. He thought it strange, searched the inner-rooms and found Yeh-hsien. He made her put on the shoe, and it was true.

4   Yeh-hsien then came forward, wearing her cloak spun from halcyon feathers and her shoes. She was as beautiful as a heavenly being. She now began to render service to the king, and he took the fish-bones and Yeh-hsien, and brought them back to his country.

5   The step-mother and step-sister were shortly afterwards struck by flying stones, and died. The cave people were sorry for them and buried them in a stone-pit, which was called the Tomb of the Distressed Women. The men of the cave made mating-offerings there; any girl they prayed for there, they got. The king of T'o-han, when he got back to his kingdom, made Yeh-hsien his chief wife. The first year the king was very greedy and by his prayers to the fish-bones got treasures and jade without limit. Next year, there was no response, so the king buried the fish-bones on the seashore. He covered them with a hundred bushels of pearls and bordered them with gold. Later there was a mutiny of some soldiers who had been conscripted and their general opened (the hiding-place) in order to make better provision for his army. One night they (the bones) were washed away by the tide.

6   This story was told me by Li Shih-yuan, who has been in the service of my family a long while. He was himself originally a man from the caves of Yung-chou and remembers many strange things of the South.

The Maiden, the Frog, and the Chief's Son (An African "Cinderella")

The version of the Cinderella tale that follows was recorded in the Hausa (West African) language and published, originally, in 1911 by Frank Edgar. The tale remained unavailable to non-speakers of Hausa until 1965, when Neil Skinner (of UCLA) completed an English translation.

1   There was once a man had two wives, and they each had a daughter. And the one wife, together with her daughter, he couldn't abide; but the other, with her daughter, he dearly loved.

---

* Something here seems to have gone slightly wrong with the text. [Waley]

2   Well, the day came when the wife that he disliked fell ill, and it so happened that her illness proved fatal, and she died. And her daughter was taken over by the other wife, the one he loved; and she moved into that wife's hut. And there she dwelt, having no mother of her own, just her father. And every day the woman would push her out, to go off to the bush to gather wood. When she returned, she had to pound up the *fura.* Then she had the *tuwo* to pound, and, after that, to stir. And then they wouldn't even let her eat the *tuwo.* All they gave her to eat were the burnt bits at the bottom of the pot. And day after day she continued thus.

3   Now she had an elder brother, and he invited her to come and eat regularly at his home—to which she agreed. But still when she had been to the bush, and returned home, and wanted a drink of water, they wouldn't let her have one. Nor would they give her proper food—only the coarsest of the grindings and the scrapings from the pot. These she would take, and going with them to a borrow-pit, throw them in. And the frogs would come out and start eating the scrapings. Then, having eaten them up, they would go back into the water; and she too would return home.

4   And so things went on day after day, until the day of the Festival arrived. And on this day, when she went along with the scrapings and coarse grindings, she found a frog squatting here; and realized that he was waiting for her! She got there and threw in the bits of food. Whereupon the frog said, "Maiden, you've always been very kind to us, and now we—but just you come along tomorrow morning. That's the morning of the Festival. Come along then, and we'll be kind to you, in our turn." "Fine," she said, and went off home.

5   Next morning was the Festival, and she was going off to the borrow-pit, just as the frog had told her. But as she was going, her half-sister's mother said to her, "Hey—come here, you good-for-nothing girl! You haven't stirred the *tuwo,* or pounded the *fura,* or fetched the wood or the water." So the girl returned. And the frog spent the whole day waiting for her. But she, having returned to the compound, set off to fetch wood. Then she fetched water, and set about pounding the *tuwo,* and stirred it till it was done and then took it off the fire. And presently she was told to take the scrapings. She did so and went off to the borrow-pit, where she found the frog. "Tut tut, girl!" said he, "I've been waiting for you here since morning, and you never came." "Old fellow," she said, "You see, I'm a slave." "How come?" he asked. "Simple," she said, "My mother died— died leaving me her only daughter. I have an elder brother, but he is married and has a compound of his own. And my father put me in the care of his other wife. And indeed he had never loved my mother. So I was moved into the hut of his other wife. And, as I told you, slavery is my lot. Every morning I have to go off to the bush to get wood. When I get back from that I have to pound the *fura,* and then I pound the *tuwo,* and then start stirring it. And even when I have finished stirring the *tuwo,* I'm not given it to eat—just the scrapings." Says the frog, "Girl, give us your hand." And she held it out to him, and they both leaped into the water.

6   Then he went and picked her up and swallowed her. (And he vomited her up.) "Good people," said he, "Look and tell me, is she straight or crooked?" And they looked and answered, "She is bent to the left." So he picked her up and

swallowed her again and then brought her up, and again asked them the same question. "She's quite straight now," they said. "Good," said he.

7 Next he vomited up cloths for her, and bangles, and rings, and a pair of shoes, one of silver, one of gold. "And now," said he, "Off you go to the dancing." So all these things were given to her, and he said to her, "When you get there, and when the dancing is nearly over and the dancers dispersing, you're to leave your golden shoe, the right one, there." And the girl replied to the frog, "Very well, old fellow, I understand," and off she went.

8 Meanwhile the chief's son had caused the young men and girls to dance for his pleasure, and when she reached the space where they were dancing he saw her. "Well!" said the chief's son, "*There's* a maiden for you, if you like. Don't you let her go and join in the dancing—I don't care whose home she comes from. Bring her here!" So the servants of the chief's son went over and came back with her to where he was. He told her to sit down on the couch, and she took her seat there accordingly.

9 They chatted together for some time, till the dancers began to disperse. Then she said to the chief's son, "I must be going home." "Oh, are you off?" said he. "Yes," said she and rose to her feet. "I'll accompany you on your way for a little," said the chief's son, and he did so. But she had left her right shoe behind. Presently she said, "Chief's son, you must go back now," and he did so. And afterwards she too turned and made her way back.

10 And there she found the frog by the edge of the water waiting for her. He took her hand and the two of them jumped into the water. Then he picked her up and swallowed her, and again vomited her up; and there she was just as she had been before, a sorry sight. And taking her ragged things she went off home.

11 When she got there, she said, "Fellow-wife of my mother, I'm not feeling very well." And the other said, "Rascally slut! You have been up to no good—refusing to come home, refusing to fetch water or wood, refusing to pound the *fura* or make the *tuwo*. Very well then! No food for you today!" And so the girl set off to her elder brother's compound, and there ate her food, and so returned home again.

12 But meanwhile, the chief's son had picked up the shoe and said to his father, "Dad, I have seen a girl who wears a pair of shoes, one of gold, one of silver. Look, here's the golden one—she forgot it and left it behind. She's the girl I want to marry. So let all the girls of this town, young and old, be gathered together, and let this shoe be given to them to put on." "Very well," said the chief.

13 And so it was proclaimed, and all the girls, young and old, were collected and gathered together. And the chief's son went and sat there beside the shoe. Each girl came, and each tried on the shoe, but it fitted none of them, none of the girls of the town; until only the girl who had left it was left. Then someone said "Just a minute! There's that girl in so-and-so's compound, whose mother died." "Yes, that's right," said another, "Someone go and fetch her." And someone went and fetched her.

14 But the minute she arrived to try it on, the shoe itself of its own accord, ran across and made her foot get into it. Then said the chief's son, "Right, here's my wife."

15 At this, the other woman—the girl's father's other wife—said, "But the shoe belongs to my daughter; it was she who forgot it at the place of the dancing, not this good-for-nothing slut." But the chief's son insisted that, since he had seen the shoe fit the other girl, as far as he was concerned, she was the one to be taken to his compound in marriage. And so they took her there, and there she spent one night.

16 Next morning she went out of her hut and round behind it, and there saw the frog. She knelt respectfully and said, "Welcome, old fellow, welcome," and greeted him. Says he, "Tonight we shall be along to bring some things for you." "Thank you" said she, and he departed.

17 Well, that night, the frog rallied all the other frogs, and all his friends, both great and small came along. And he, their leader, said to them, "See here—my daughter is being married. So I want every one of you to make a contribution." And each of them went and fetched what he could afford, whereupon their leader thanked them all, and then vomited up a silver bed, a brass bed, a copper bed, and an iron bed, and went on vomiting up things for her—such as woollen blankets, and rugs, and satins, and velvets.

18 "Now," said he to the girl, "If your heart is ever troubled, just lie down on this brass bed," and he went on, "And when the chief's son's other wives come to greet you, give them two calabashes of cola-nuts and ten thousand cowrie shells; then, when his concubines come to greet you, give them one calabash of cola-nuts and five thousand cowries." "Very well," said she. Then he said, "And when the concubines come to receive corn for making *tuwo,* say to them, 'There's a hide-bag full, help yourselves.'" "Very well," she said. "And," he went on, "If your father's wife comes along with her daughter and asks you what it is like living in the chief's compound, say 'Living in the chief's compound is a wearisome business—for they measure out corn there with the shell of a Bambara groundnut.'"

19 So there she dwelt, until one day her father's favorite wife brought her daughter along at night, took her into the chief's compound, and brought the other girl out and took her to her own compound. There she said, "Oh! I forgot to get you to tell her all about married life in the chief's compound." "Oh, it's a wearisome business," answered our girl. "How so?" asked the older woman, surprised. "Well, they use the shell of a Bambara groundnut for measuring out corn. Then, if the chief's other wives come to greet you, you answer them with the 'Pf' of contempt. If the concubines come to greet you, you clear your throat, hawk, and spit. And if your husband comes into your hut, you yell at him." "I see," said the other—and her daughter stayed behind the chief's son's compound.

20 Next morning when it was light, the wives came to greet her—and she said "Pf" to them. The concubines came to greet her, and she spat at them. Then when night fell, the chief's son made his way to her hut, and she yelled at him. And he was amazed and went aside, and for two days pondered the matter.

21 Then he had his wives and concubines collected and said to them, "Look, now—I've called you to ask you. They haven't brought me the same girl. How did that one treat all of you?" "Hm—how indeed!" they all exclaimed. "Each

morning, when we wives went to greet her, she would give us cola-nuts, two calabashes full, and cowries, ten thousand of them to buy tobacco flowers. And when the concubines went to greet her, she would give them a calabash of cola-nuts, and five thousand cowries to buy tobacco flowers with; and in the evening, for corn for *tuwo,* it would be a whole hide-bag full." "You see?" said he, "As for me, whenever I came to enter her hut, I found her respectfully kneeling. And she wouldn't get up from there, until I had entered and sat down on the bed."

22   "Hey," he called out, "Boys, come over here!" And when they came, he went into her hut and took a sword, and chopped her up into little pieces, and had them collect them and wrap them up in clothing; and then taken back to her home.

23   And when they got there, they found his true wife lying in the fireplace, and picking her up they took her back to her husband.

24   And next morning when it was light, she picked up a little gourd water-bottle and going around behind her hut, there saw the frog. "Welcome, welcome, old fellow," said she, and went on. "Old fellow, what I should like is to have a well built; and then you, all of you, can come and live in it and be close to me." "All right," said the frog, "You tell your husband." And she did so.

25   And he had a well dug for her, close to her hut. And the frogs came and entered the well and there they lived. That's all. *Kungurus kan kusu.*

Oochigeaskw—The Rough-Faced Girl (A Native American "Cinderella")

The following version of the Cinderella tale was told, originally, in the Algonquin language. Native Americans who spoke Algonquian lived in the Eastern Woodlands of what is now the United States and in the northern, semiarctic areas of present-day Canada.

1   There was once a large village of the MicMac Indians of the Eastern Algonquins, built beside a lake. At the far end of the settlement stood a lodge, and in it lived a being who was always invisible. He had a sister who looked after him, and everyone knew that any girl who could see him might marry him. For that reason there were very few girls who did not try, but it was very long before anyone succeeded.

2   This is the way in which the test of sight was carried out: at evening-time, when the Invisible One was due to be returning home, his sister would walk with any girl who might come down to the lakeshore. She, of course, could see her brother, since he was always visible to her. As soon as she saw him, she would say to the girls:

3   "Do you see my brother?"

4   "Yes," they would generally reply—though some of them did say "No."

5   To those who said that they could indeed see him, the sister would say:

6   "Of what is his shoulder strap made?" Some people say that she would enquire:

7   "What is his moose-runner's haul?" or "With what does he draw his sled?"

8   And they would answer:

9   "A strip of rawhide" or "a green flexible branch," or something of that kind.

10   Then she, knowing that they had not told the truth, would say:

11   "Very well, let us return to the wigwam!"

12   When they had gone in, she would tell them not to sit in a certain place, because it belonged to the Invisible One. Then, after they had helped to cook the supper, they would wait with great curiosity to see him eat. They could be sure he was a real person, for when he took off his moccasins they became visible, and his sister hung them up. But beyond this they saw nothing of him, not even when they stayed in the place all the night, as many of them did.

13   Now there lived in the village an old man who was a widower, and his three daughters. The youngest girl was very small, weak, and often ill: and yet her sisters, especially the elder, treated her cruelly. The second daughter was kinder, and sometimes took her side: but the wicked sister would burn her hands and feet with hot cinders, and she was covered with scars from this treatment. She was so marked that people called her *Oochigeaskw,* the Rough-Faced Girl.

14   When her father came home and asked why she had such burns, the bad sister would at once say that it was her own fault, for she had disobeyed orders and gone near the fire and fallen into it.

15   These two elder sisters decided one day to try their luck at seeing the Invisible One. So they dressed themselves in their finest clothes, and tried to look their prettiest. They found the Invisible One's sister and took the usual walk by the water.

16   When he came, and when they were asked if they could see him, they answered: "Of course." And when asked about the shoulder strap or sled cord, they answered: "A piece of rawhide."

17   But of course they were lying like the others, and they got nothing for their pains.

18   The next afternoon, when the father returned home, he brought with him many of the pretty little shells from which wampum was made, and they set to work to string them.

19   That day, poor Little Oochigeaskw, who had always gone barefoot, got a pair of her father's moccasins, old ones, and put them into water to soften them so that she could wear them. Then she begged her sisters for a few wampum shells. The elder called her a "little pest," but the younger one gave her some. Now, with no other clothes than her usual rags, the poor little thing went into the woods and got herself some sheets of birch bark, from which she made a dress, and put marks on it for decoration, in the style of long ago. She made a petticoat and a loose gown, a cap, leggings, and a handkerchief. She put on her father's large old moccasins, which were far too big for her, and went forth to try her luck. She would try, she thought, to discover whether she could see the Invisible One.

20   She did not begin very well. As she set off, her sisters shouted and hooted, hissed and yelled, and tried to make her stay. And the loafers around the village, seeing the strange little creature, called out "Shame!"

21   The poor little girl in her strange clothes, with her face all scarred, was an awful sight, but she was kindly received by the sister of the Invisible One. And this was, of course, because this noble lady understood far more about things than simply the mere outside which all the rest of the world knows. As the brown of the evening sky turned to black, the lady took her down to the lake.

22   "Do you see him?" the Invisible One's sister asked.

23   "I do indeed—and he is wonderful!" said Oochigeaskw.

24   The sister asked:

25   "And what is his sled-string?"

26   The little girl said:

27   "It is the Rainbow."

28   "And, my sister, what is his bow-string?"

29   "It is The Spirit's Road—the Milky Way."

30   "So you *have* seen him," said his sister. She took the girl home with her and bathed her. As she did so, all the scars disappeared from her body. Her hair grew again, as it was combed, long, like a blackbird's wing. Her eyes were now like stars: in all the world there was no other such beauty. Then, from her treasures, the lady gave her a wedding garment, and adorned her.

31   Then she told Oochigeaskw to take the *wife's* seat in the wigwam: the one next to where the Invisible One sat, beside the entrance. And when he came in, terrible and beautiful, he smiled and said:

32   "So we are found out!"

33   "Yes," said his sister. And so Oochigeaskw became his wife.

Walt Disney's "Cinderella"
Adapted by Campbell Grant

Walter Elias Disney (1901–1966), winner of thirty-two Academy Awards, is famous throughout the world for his cartoon animations. After achieving recognition with cartoon shorts populated by such immortals as Mickey Mouse and Donald Duck, he produced the full-length animated film version of Snow White and the Seven Dwarfs *in 1937. He followed with other animations, including* Cinderella *(1950), which he adapted from Perrault's version of the tale. A Little Golden Book,* the text of which appears here, *was then adapted by Campbell Grant from the film.*

1   Once upon a time in a far-away land lived a sweet and pretty girl named Cinderella. She made her home with her mean old stepmother and her two stepsisters, and they made her do all the work in the house.

2   Cinderella cooked and baked. She cleaned and scrubbed. She had no time left for parties and fun.

3   But one day an invitation came from the palace of the king.

4   A great ball was to be given for the prince of the land. And every young girl in the kingdom was invited.

5   "How nice!" thought Cinderella. "I am invited, too."

6   But her mean stepsisters never thought of her. They thought only of themselves, of course. They had all sorts of jobs for Cinderella to do.

7   "Wash this slip. Press this dress. Curl my hair. Find my fan."

8   They both kept shouting, as fast as they could speak.

9   "But I must get ready myself. I'm going, too," said Cinderella.

10   "You!" they hooted. "The Prince's ball for you?"

11   And they kept her busy all day long. She worked in the morning, while her stepsisters slept. She worked all afternoon, while they bathed and dressed. And in the evening she had to help them put on the finishing touches for the ball. She had not one minute to think of herself.

12   Soon the coach was ready at the door. The ugly stepsisters were powdered, pressed, and curled. But there stood Cinderella in her workaday rags.

13   "Why, Cinderella!" said the stepsisters. "You're not dressed for the ball."

14   "No," said Cinderella. "I guess I cannot go."

15   Poor Cinderella sat weeping in the garden.

16   Suddenly a little old woman with a sweet, kind face stood before her. It was her fairy godmother.

17   "Hurry, child!" she said. "You are going to the ball!"

18   Cinderella could hardly believe her eyes! The fairy godmother turned a fat pumpkin into a splendid coach.

19   Next her pet mice became horses, and her dog a fine footman. The barn horse was turned into a coachman.

20   "There, my dear," said the fairy godmother. "Now into the coach with you, and off to the ball you go."

21   "But my dress—" said Cinderella.

22   "Lovely, my dear," the fairy godmother began. Then she really looked at Cinderella's rags.

23   "Oh, good heavens," she said. "You can never go in that." She waved her magic wand.

"Salaga doola,
Menchicka boola,
Bibbidi bobbidi boo!" she said.

24   There stood Cinderella in the loveliest ball dress that ever was. And on her feet were tiny glass slippers!

25   "Oh," cried Cinderella. "How can I ever thank you?"

26   "Just have a wonderful time at the ball, my dear," said her fairy godmother. "But remember, this magic lasts only until midnight. At the stroke of midnight, the spell will be broken. And everything will be as it was before."

27   "I will remember," said Cinderella. "It is more than I ever dreamed of."

28   Then into the magic coach she stepped, and was whirled away to the ball.

29   And such a ball! The king's palace was ablaze with lights. There was music and laughter. And every lady in the land was dressed in her beautiful best.

30   But Cinderella was the loveliest of them all. The prince never left her side, all evening long. They danced every dance. They had supper side by side. And they happily smiled into each other's eyes.

31   But all at once the clock began to strike midnight, Bong Bong Bong—

32   "Oh!" cried Cinderella. "I almost forgot!"

33   And without a word, away she ran, out of the ballroom and down the palace stairs. She lost one glass slipper. But she could not stop.

34   Into her magic coach she stepped, and away it rolled. But as the clock stopped striking, the coach disappeared. And no one knew where she had gone.

35   Next morning all the kingdom was filled with the news. The Grand Duke was going from house to house, with a small glass slipper in his hand. For the prince had said he would marry no one but the girl who could wear that tiny shoe.

36   Every girl in the land tried hard to put it on. The ugly stepsisters tried hardest of all. But not a one could wear the glass shoe.

37   And where was Cinderella? Locked in her room. For the mean old stepmother was taking no chances of letting her try on the slipper. Poor Cinderella! It looked as if the Grand Duke would surely pass her by.

38   But her little friends the mice got the stepmother's key. And they pushed it under Cinderella's door. So down the long stairs she came, as the Duke was just about to leave.

39   "Please!" cried Cinderella. "Please let me try."

40   And of course the slipper fitted, since it was her very own.

41   That was all the Duke needed. Now his long search was done. And so Cinderella became the prince's bride, and lived happily ever after—and the little pet mice lived in the palace and were happy ever after, too.

Cinderella
Anne Sexton

Anne Sexton (1928–1974) has been acclaimed as one of America's outstanding contemporary poets. In 1967, she won the Pulitzer Prize for poetry for Live or Die. *She published four other collections of her work, including* Transformations, *in which she recast, with a modern twist, popular European fairy tales such as "Cinderella." Sexton's poetry has appeared in the* New Yorker, Harper's, *the* Atlantic, *and* Saturday Review. *She received a Robert Frost Fellowship (1959), a scholarship from Radcliffe College's New Institute for Independent Study (1961–1963), a grant from the Ford Foundation (1964), and a Guggenheim Award (1969). In her book* All My Pretty Ones, *Sexton quoted Franz Kafka: "The books we need are the kind that act upon us like a misfortune, that make us suffer like the death of someone we love more than ourselves. A book should serve as the axe for the frozen sea within us." Asked in an interview (by Patricia Marz) about this quotation, Sexton responded: "I think [poetry] should be a shock to the senses. It should almost hurt."*

You always read about it;
the plumber with twelve children
who wins the Irish Sweepstakes.
From toilets to riches.

5   That story.

Or the nursemaid,
some luscious sweet from Denmark
who captures the oldest son's heart,
From diapers to Dior.
10   That story.

Or a milkman who serves the wealthy,
eggs, cream, butter, yogurt, milk,
the white truck like an ambulance
who goes into real estate
15   and makes a pile.
From homogenized to martinis at lunch.

Or the charwoman
who is on the bus when it cracks up
and collects enough from the insurance.
20   From mops to Bonwit Teller.
That story.

Once
the wife of a rich man was on her deathbed
and she said to her daughter Cinderella:
25   Be devout. Be good, Then I will smile
down from heaven in the seam of a cloud.
The man took another wife who had
two daughters, pretty enough
but with hearts like blackjacks.
30   Cinderella was their maid.
She slept on the sooty hearth each night
and walked around looking like Al Jolson.
Her father brought presents home from town,
jewels and gowns for the other women
35   but the twig of a tree for Cinderella.
She planted that twig on her mother's grave
and it grew to a tree where a white dove sat.
Whenever she wished for anything the dove
would drop it like an egg upon the ground.
40   The bird is important, my dears, so heed him.
Next came the ball, as you all know.
It was a marriage market.
The prince was looking for a wife.
All but Cinderella were preparing
45   and gussying up for the big event.
Cinderella begged to go too.
Her stepmother threw a dish of lentils
into the cinders and said: Pick them
up in an hour and you shall go.
50   The white dove brought all his friends;
all the warm wings of the fatherland came,
and picked up the lentils in a jiffy.
No, Cinderella, said the stepmother,

you have no clothes and cannot dance.
55   That's the way with stepmothers.

Cinderella went to the tree at the grave
and cried forth like a gospel singer:
Mama! Mama! My turtledove,
send me to the prince's ball!
60   The bird dropped down a golden dress
and delicate little gold slippers.
Rather a large package for a simple bird.
So she went. Which is no surprise.

Her stepmother and sisters didn't
65   recognize her without her cinder face
and the prince took her hand on the spot
and danced with no other the whole day.

As nightfall came she thought she'd better
get home. The prince walked her home
70   and she disappeared into the pigeon house
and although the prince took an axe and broke
it open she was gone. Back to her cinders.
These events repeated themselves for three days.
However on the third day the prince
75   covered the palace steps with cobbler's wax
and Cinderella's gold shoe stuck upon it.
Now he would find whom the shoe fit
and find his strange dancing girl for keeps.
He went to their house and the two sisters
80   were delighted because they had lovely feet.
The eldest went into a room to try the slipper on
but her big toe got in the way so she simply
sliced it off and put on the slipper.
The prince rode away with her until the white dove
85   told him to look at the blood pouring forth.
That is the way with amputations.
They don't just heal up like a wish.
The other sister cut off her heel
but the blood told as blood will.
90   The prince was getting tired.
He began to feel like a shoe salesman.
But he gave it one last try.
This time Cinderella fit into the shoe
like a love letter into its envelope.

95   At the wedding ceremony
the two sisters came to curry favor
and the white dove pecked their eyes out.
Two hollow spots were left
like soup spoons.

100   Cinderella and the prince
      lived, they say, happily ever after,
      like two dolls in a museum case
      never bothered by diapers or dust,
      never arguing over the timing of an egg,
105   never telling the same story twice,
      never getting a middle-aged spread,
      their darling smiles pasted on for eternity.

      Regular Bobbsey Twins.
      That story.

Gudgekin the Thistle Girl
John Gardner

John Gardner (1933–1982), accomplished novelist, critic, and much-loved teacher of writing at the State University of New York, Binghamton, received the National Book Critics Award for his novel October Light *in 1976. His other works include* Grendel *(1971),* The Sunlight Dialogues *(1972),* Nickel Mountain *(1973), and numerous short stories and critical pieces for magazines such as* Esquire *and the* Hudson Review. *Folktale literature fascinated Gardner, and he wrote three collections of tales himself:* The King's Indian and Other Fireside Tales *(1974),* Dragon, Dragon and Other Tales *(1975), and* Gudgekin the Thistle Girl and Other Tales *(1976). Gardner died at the age of 49 in a motorcycle accident.*

1   In a certain kingdom there lived a poor little thistle girl. What thistle girls did for a living—that is, what people did with thistles—is no longer known, but whatever the reason that people gathered thistles, she was one of those who did it. All day long, from well before sunrise until long after sunset, she wandered the countryside gathering thistles, pricking her fingers to the bone, piling the thistles into her enormous thistle sack and carrying them back to her stepmother. It was a bitter life, but she always made the best of it and never felt the least bit sorry for herself, only for the miseries of others. The girl's name was Gudgekin.

2   Alas! The stepmother was never satisfied. She was arrogant and fiercely competitive, and when she laid out her thistles in her market stall, she would rather be dead than suffer the humiliation of seeing that some other stall had more thistles than she had. No one ever did, but the fear preyed on her, and no matter how many sacks of thistles poor Gudgekin gathered, there were never enough to give the stepmother comfort. "You don't earn your keep," the stepmother would say, crossing her arms and closing them together like scissors. "If you don't bring more thistles tomorrow, it's away you must go to the Children's Home and good riddance!"

3   Poor Gudgekin. Every day she brought more than yesterday, but every night the same. "If you don't bring more thistles tomorrow, it's away to the Home with you." She worked feverishly, frantically, smiling through her tears, seizing the thistles by whichever end came first, but never to her stepmother's satisfaction. Thus she lived out her miserable childhood, blinded by burning tears and pink with thistle pricks, but viewing her existence in the best light possible. As she grew older she grew more and more beautiful, partly because she was always smiling and refused to pout, whatever the provocation; and soon she was as lovely as any princess.

4   One day her bad luck changed to good. As she was jerking a thistle from between two rocks, a small voice cried, "Stop! You're murdering my children!"

5   "I beg your pardon?" said the thistle girl. When she bent down she saw a beautiful little fairy in a long white and silver dress, hastily removing her children from their cradle, which was resting in the very thistle that Gudgekin had been pulling.

6   "Oh," said Gudgekin in great distress.

7   The fairy said nothing at first, hurrying back and forth, carrying her children to the safety of the nearest rock. But then at last the fairy looked up and saw that Gudgekin was crying. "Well," she said. "What's this?"

8   "I'm sorry," said Gudgekin. "I always cry. It's because of the misery of others, primarily. I'm used to it."

9   "Primarily?" said the fairy and put her hands on her hips.

10   "Well," sniffled Gudgekin, "to tell the truth, I do sometimes imagine I'm not as happy as I might be. It's shameful, I know. Everyone's miserable, and it's wrong of me to whimper."

11   "Everyone?" said the fairy, "—miserable? Sooner or later an opinion like that will make a fool of you!"

12   "Well, I really don't know," said Gudgekin, somewhat confused. "I've seen very little of the world, I'm afraid."

13   "I see," said the fairy thoughtfully, lips pursed. "Well, that's a pity, but it's easily fixed. Since you've spared my children and taken pity on my lot, I think I should do you a good turn."

14   She struck the rock three times with a tiny golden straw, and instantly all the thistles for miles around began moving as if by their own volition toward the thistle girl's sack. It was the kingdom of fairies, and the beautiful fairy with whom Gudgekin had made friends was none other than the fairies' queen. Soon the fairies had gathered all the thistles for a mile around, and had filled the sack that Gudgekin had brought, and had also filled forty-three more, which they'd fashioned on the spot out of gossamer.

15   "Now," said the queen, "it's time that you saw the world."

16   Immediately the fairies set to work all together and built a beautiful chariot as light as the wind, all transparent gossamer woven like fine thread. The chariot was so light that it needed no horses but flew along over the ground by itself, except when it was anchored with a stone. Next they made the thistle girl a gown of woven gossamer so lovely that not even the queen of the kingdom had anything to rival it; indeed, no one anywhere in the world had such a gown or has ever had, even to this day. For Gudgekin's head the fairies fashioned a flowing veil as

light and silvery as the lightest, most silvery of clouds, and they sprinkled both the veil and the gown with dew so they glittered as if with costly jewels.

17   Then, to a tinny little trumpeting noise, the queen of the fairies stepped into the chariot and graciously held out her tiny hand to the thistle girl.

18   No sooner was Gudgekin seated beside the queen than the chariot lifted into the air lightly, like a swift little boat, and skimmed the tops of the fields and flew away to the capital.

19   When they came to the city, little Gudgekin could scarcely believe her eyes. But there was no time to look at the curious shops or watch the happy promenading of the wealthy. They were going to the palace, the fairy queen said, and soon the chariot had arrived there.

20   It was the day of the kingdom's royal ball, and the chariot was just in time. "I'll wait here," said the kindly queen of the fairies. "You run along and enjoy yourself, my dear."

21   Happy Gudgekin! Everyone was awed by her lovely gown and veil; and even the fact that the fairies had neglected to make shoes for her feet, since they themselves wore none, turned out to be to Gudgekin's advantage. Barefoot dancing immediately became all the rage at court, and people who'd been wearing fine shoes for years slipped over to the window and slyly tossed them out, not to be outdone by a stranger. The thistle girl danced with the prince himself, and he was charmed more than words can tell. His smile seemed all openness and innocence, yet Gudgekin had a feeling he was watching her like a hawk. He had a reputation throughout the nine kingdoms for subtlety and shrewdness.

22   When it was time to take the thistle sacks back to her cruel stepmother, Gudgekin slipped out, unnoticed by anyone, and away she rode in the chariot.

23   "Well, how was it?" asked the queen of the fairies happily.

24   "Wonderful! Wonderful!" Gudgekin replied. "Except I couldn't help but notice how gloomy people were, despite their merry chatter. How sadly they frown when they look into their mirrors, fixing their make-up. Some of them frown because their feet hurt, I suppose; some of them perhaps because they're jealous of someone; and some of them perhaps because they've lost their youthful beauty. I could have wept for them!"

25   The queen of the fairies frowned pensively. "You're a good-hearted child, that's clear," she said, and fell silent.

26   They reached the field, and the thistle girl, assisted by a thousand fairies, carried her forty-four sacks to her wicked stepmother. The stepmother was amazed to see so many thistle sacks, especially since some of them seemed to be coming to the door all by themselves. Nevertheless, she said—for her fear of humiliation so drove her that she was never satisfied—"A paltry forty-four, Gudgekin! If you don't bring more thistles tomorrow, it's away to the Home with you!"

27   Little Gudgekin bowed humbly, sighed with resignation, forced to her lips a happy smile, ate her bread crusts, and climbed up the ladder to her bed of straw.

28   The next morning when she got to the field, she found eighty-eight thistle sacks stuffed full and waiting. The gossamer chariot was standing at anchor, and the gossamer gown and veil were laid out on a rock, gleaming in the sun.

29   "Today," said the queen of the fairies, "we're going on a hunt."

30   They stepped into the chariot and flew off light as moonbeams to the royal park, and there, sure enough, were huntsmen waiting, and huntswomen beside them, all dressed in black riding-pants and riding-skirts and bright red jackets. The fairies made the thistle girl a gossamer horse that would sail wherever the wind might blow, and the people all said she was the most beautiful maiden in the kingdom, possibly an elf queen. Then the French horns and bugles blew, and the huntsmen were off. Light as a feather went the thistle girl, and the prince was so entranced he was beside himself, though he watched her, for all that, with what seemed to her a crafty smile. All too soon came the time to carry the thistle sacks home, and the thistle girl slipped from the crowd, unnoticed, and rode her light horse beside the chariot where the queen of the fairies sat beaming like a mother.

31   "Well," called the queen of the fairies, "how was it?"

32   "Wonderful!" cried Gudgekin, "it was truly wonderful! I noticed one thing, though. It's terrible for the fox!"

33   The queen of the fairies thought about it. "Blood sports," she said thoughtfully, and nodded. After that, all the rest of the way home, she spoke not a word.

34   When the thistle girl arrived at her stepmother's house, her stepmother threw up her arms in amazement at sight of those eighty-eight thistle-filled sacks. Nonetheless, she said as sternly as possible, "Eighty-eight! Why not a hundred? If you don't bring in more sacks tomorrow, it's the Home for you for sure!"

35   Gudgekin sighed, ate her dry crusts, forced a smile to her lips, and climbed the ladder.

36   The next day was a Sunday, but Gudgekin the thistle girl had to work just the same, for her stepmother's evil disposition knew no bounds. When she got to the field, there stood two times eighty-eight thistle sacks, stuffed to the tops and waiting. "*That* ought to fix her," said the queen of the fairies merrily. "Jump into your dress."

37   "Where are we going?" asked Gudgekin, as happy as could be.

38   "Why, to church, of course!" said the queen of the fairies. "After church we go to the royal picnic, and then we dance on the bank of the river until twilight."

39   "Wonderful!" said the thistle girl, and away they flew.

40   The singing in church was thrilling, and the sermon filled her heart with such kindly feelings toward her friends and neighbors that she felt close to dissolving in tears. The picnic was the sunniest in the history of the kingdom, and the dancing beside the river was delightful beyond words. Throughout it all the prince was beside himself with pleasure, never removing his eyes from Gudgekin, for he thought her the loveliest maiden he'd met in his life. For all his shrewdness, for all his aloofness and princely self-respect, when he danced with Gudgekin in her bejeweled gown of gossamer, it was all he could do to keep himself from asking her to marry him on the spot. He asked instead, "Beautiful stranger, permit me to ask you your name."

41   "It's Gudgekin," she said, smiling shyly and glancing at his eyes.

42   He didn't believe her.

43   "Really," she said, "it's Gudgekin." Only now did it strike her that the name was rather odd.

44   "Listen," said the prince with a laugh, "I'm *serious*. What is it really?"

45   "I'm serious too," said Gudgekin bridling. "It's Gudgekin the Thistle Girl. With the help of the fairies I've been known to collect two times eighty-eight sacks of thistles in a single day."

46   The prince laughed more merrily than ever at that. "Please," he said, "don't tease me, dear friend! A beautiful maiden like you must have a name like bells on Easter morning, or like songbirds in the meadow, or children's laughing voices on the playground! Tell me now. Tell me the truth. What's your name?"

47   "Puddin Tane," she said angrily, and ran away weeping to the chariot.

48   "Well," said the queen of the fairies, "how was it?"

49   "Horrible," snapped Gudgekin.

50   "Ah!" said the queen. "Now we're getting there!"

51   She was gone before the prince was aware that she was leaving, and even if he'd tried to follow her, the gossamer chariot was too fast, for it skimmed along like wind. Nevertheless, he was resolved to find and marry Gudgekin—he'd realized by now that Gudgekin must indeed be her name. He could easily understand the thistle girl's anger. He'd have felt the same himself, for he was a prince and knew better than anyone what pride was, and the shame of being made to seem a fool. He advertised far and wide for information on Gudgekin the Thistle Girl, and soon the news of the prince's search reached Gudgekin's cruel stepmother in her cottage. She was at once so furious she could hardly see, for she always wished evil for others and happiness for herself.

52   "I'll never in this world let him find her," thought the wicked stepmother, and she called in Gudgekin and put a spell on her, for the stepmother was a witch. She made Gudgekin believe that her name was Rosemarie and sent the poor baffled child off to the Children's Home. Then the cruel stepmother changed herself, by salves and charms, into a beautiful young maiden who looked exactly like Gudgekin, and she set off for the palace to meet the prince.

53   "Gudgekin!" cried the prince and leaped forward and embraced her. "I've been looking for you everywhere to implore you to forgive me and be my bride!"

54   "Dearest prince," said the stepmother disguised as Gudgekin, "I'll do so gladly!"

55   "Then you've forgiven me already, my love?" said the prince. He was surprised, in fact, for it had seemed to him that Gudgekin was a touch more sensitive than that and had more personal pride. He'd thought, in fact, he'd have a devil of a time, considering how he'd hurt her and made a joke of her name. "Then you really forgive me?" asked the prince.

56   The stepmother looked slightly confused for an instant but quickly smiled as Gudgekin might have smiled and said, "Prince, I forgive you everything!" And so, though the prince felt queer about it, the day of the wedding was set.

57   A week before the wedding, the prince asked thoughtfully, "Is it true that you can gather, with the help of the fairies, two times eighty-eight thistle sacks all in one day?"

58   "Haven't I told you so?" asked the stepmother disguised as Gudgekin and gave a little laugh. She had a feeling she was in for it.

59   "You did say that, yes," the prince said, pulling with two fingers at his beard. "I'd surely like to see it!"

60   "Well," said the stepmother, and curtsied, "I'll come to you tomorrow and you shall see what you shall see."

61   The next morning she dragged out two times eighty-eight thistle sacks, thinking she could gather in the thistles by black magic. But the magic of the fairies was stronger than any witch's, and since they lived in the thistles, they resisted all her fiercest efforts. When it was late afternoon the stepmother realized she had only one hope: she must get the real Gudgekin from the Children's Home and make her help.

62   Alas for the wicked stepmother, Gudgekin was no longer an innocent simpleton! As soon as she was changed back from simple Rosemarie, she remembered everything and wouldn't touch a thistle with an iron glove. Neither would she help her stepmother now, on account of all the woman's cruelty before, nor would she do anything under heaven that might be pleasing to the prince, for she considered him cold-hearted and inconsiderate. The stepmother went back to the palace empty-handed, weeping and moaning and making a hundred excuses, but the scales had now fallen from the prince's eyes—his reputation for shrewdness was in fact well founded—and after talking with his friends and advisers, he threw her in the dungeon. In less than a week her life in the dungeon was so miserable it made her repent and become a good woman, and the prince released her. "Hold your head high," he said, brushing a tear from his eye, for she made him think of Gudgekin. "People may speak of you as someone who's been in prison, but you're a better person now than before." She blessed him and thanked him and went her way.

63   Then once more he advertised far and wide through the kingdom, begging the real Gudgekin to forgive him and come to the palace.

64   "Never!" thought Gudgekin bitterly, for the fairy queen had taught her the importance of self-respect, and the prince's offense still rankled.

65   The prince mused and waited, and he began to feel a little hurt himself. He was a prince, after all, handsome and famous for his subtlety and shrewdness, and she was a mere thistle girl. Yet for all his beloved Gudgekin cared, he might as well have been born in some filthy cattle shed! At last he understood how things were, and the truth amazed him.

66   Now word went far and wide through the kingdom that the handsome prince had fallen ill for sorrow and was lying in his bed, near death's door. When the queen of the fairies heard the dreadful news, she was dismayed and wept tears of remorse, for it was all, she imagined, her fault. She threw herself down on the ground and began wailing, and all the fairies everywhere began at once to wail with her, rolling on the ground, for it seemed that she would die. And one of them, it happened, was living among the flowerpots in the bedroom of cruel little Gudgekin.

67   When Gudgekin heard the tiny forlorn voice wailing, she hunted through the flowers and found the fairy and said, "What in heaven's name is the matter, little friend?"

68   "Ah, dear Gudgekin," wailed the fairy, "our queen is dying, and if she dies we will all die of sympathy, and that will be that."

69 "Oh, you mustn't!" cried Gudgekin, and tears filled her eyes. "Take me to the queen at once, little friend, for she did a favor for me and I see I must return it if I possibly can!"

70 When they came to the queen of the fairies, the queen said, "Nothing will save me except possibly this, my dear: ride with me one last time in the gossamer chariot for a visit to the prince."

71 "Never!" said Gudgekin, but seeing the heartbroken looks of the fairies, she instantly relented.

72 The chariot was brought out from its secret place, and the gossamer horse was hitched to it to give it more dignity, and along they went skimming like wind until they had arrived at the dim and gloomy sickroom. The prince lay on his bed so pale of cheek and so horribly disheveled that Gudgekin didn't know him. If he seemed to her a stranger it was hardly surprising; he'd lost all signs of his princeliness and lay there with his nightcap on sideways and he even had his shoes on.

73 "What's this?" whispered Gudgekin. "What's happened to the music and dancing and the smiling courtiers? And where is the prince?"

74 "Woe is me," said the ghastly white figure on the bed. "I was once that proud, shrewd prince you know, and this is what's become of me. For I hurt the feelings of the beautiful Gudgekin, whom I've given my heart and who refuses to forgive me for my insult, such is her pride and uncommon self-respect."

75 "My poor beloved prince!" cried Gudgekin when she heard this, and burst into a shower of tears. "You have given your heart to a fool, I see now, for I am your Gudgekin, simple-minded as a bird! First I had pity for everyone but myself, and then I had pity for no one but myself, and now I pity all of us in this miserable world, but I see by the whiteness of your cheeks that I've learned too late!" And she fell upon his bosom and wept.

76 "You give me your love and forgiveness forever and will never take them back?" asked the poor prince feebly, and coughed.

77 "I do," sobbed Gudgekin, pressing his frail, limp hand in both of hers.

78 "Cross your heart?" he said.

79 "Oh, I do, I *do!*"

80 The prince jumped out of bed with all his wrinkled clothes on and wiped the thick layer of white powder off his face and seized his dearest Gudgekin by the waist and danced around the room with her. The queen of the fairies laughed like silver bells and immediately felt improved. "Why you fox!" she told the prince. All the happy fairies began dancing with the prince and Gudgekin, who waltzed with her mouth open. When she closed it at last it was to pout, profoundly offended.

81 "Tr-tr-*tricked!*" she spluttered.

82 "Silly goose," said the prince, and kissed away the pout. "It's true, I've tricked you, I'm not miserable at all. But you've promised to love me and never take it back. My advice to you is, make the best of it!" He snatched a glass of wine from the dresser as he merrily waltzed her past, and cried out gaily, "As for myself, though, I make no bones about it: I intend to watch out for witches and live happily ever after. You must too, my Gudgekin! Cross your heart!"

83 "Oh, very well," she said finally, and let a little smile out. "It's no worse than the thistles."

84 And so they did.

"Cinderella": A Story of Sibling Rivalry and Oedipal Conflicts
Bruno Bettelheim

Having read several variants of "Cinderella," you may have wondered what it is about this story that's prompted people in different parts of the world, at different times, to show interest in a child who's been debased but then rises above her misfortune. Why are people so fascinated with "Cinderella"?

Depending on the people you ask and their perspectives, you'll find this question answered in various ways. As a Freudian psychologist, Bruno Bettelheim believes that the mind is a repository of both conscious and unconscious elements. By definition, we aren't aware of what goes on in our unconscious; nonetheless, what happens there exerts a powerful influence on what we believe and on how we act. This division of the mind into conscious and unconscious parts is true for children no less than for adults. Based on these beliefs about the mind, Bettelheim analyzes "Cinderella" first by pointing to what he calls the story's essential theme: sibling rivalry, or Cinderella's mistreatment at the hands of her stepsisters. Competition among brothers and sisters presents a profound and largely unconscious problem to children, says Bettelheim. By hearing "Cinderella," a story that speaks directly to their unconscious, children are given tools that can help them resolve conflicts. Cinderella resolves her difficulties; children hearing the story can resolve theirs as well: This is the unconscious message of the tale.

To accept this argument, you'd have to agree with the author's reading of "Cinderella" and its hidden meanings; and you'd have to agree with his assumptions concerning the conscious and unconscious mind and the ways in which the unconscious will seize upon the content of a story in order to resolve conflicts. Even if you don't accept Bettelheim's analysis, his essay makes fascinating reading. First, it is internally consistent—that is, he begins with a set of principles and then builds logically upon them, as any good writer will. Second, his analysis demonstrates how a scholarly point of view—a coherent set of assumptions about the way the world (in this case, the mind) works—creates boundaries for a discussion. Change the assumptions and you'll change the analyses that follow from them.

Bettelheim's essay is long and somewhat difficult. While he uses no subheadings, he has divided his work into four sections: paragraphs 2–10 are devoted to sibling rivalry; paragraphs 11–19, to an analysis of "Cinderella's" hidden meanings; paragraphs 20–24, to the psychological makeup of children at the end of their Oedipal period; and paragraphs 25–27, to the reasons "Cinderella," in particular, appeals to children in the Oedipal period.

Bruno Bettelheim, a distinguished psychologist and educator, was born in 1903 in Vienna. He was naturalized as an American citizen in 1939 and served as a professor of psychology at Rockford College and the University of Chicago. Awarded the honor of fellow by several prestigious professional associations, Bettelheim was a prolific writer and contributed articles to numerous popular and professional publications. His list of books includes Love Is Not Enough: The Treatment of Emotionally Disturbed Children *(1950),* The Informed Heart *(1960), and* The Uses of Enchantment *(1975), from which this selection has been excerpted. Bettelheim died in 1990.*

1   By all accounts, "Cinderella" is the best-known fairy tale, and probably also the best-liked. It is quite an old story; when first written down in China during the ninth century A.D., it already had a history. The unrivaled tiny foot size as a mark of extraordinary virtue, distinction, and beauty, and the slipper made of precious material are facets which point to an Eastern, if not necessarily Chinese, origin.* The modern hearer does not connect sexual attractiveness and beauty in general with extreme smallness of the foot, as the ancient Chinese did, in accordance with their practice of binding women's feet.

2   "Cinderella," as we know it, is experienced as a story about the agonies and hopes which form the essential content of sibling rivalry; and about the degraded heroine winning out over her siblings who abused her. Long before Perrault gave "Cinderella" the form in which it is now widely known, "having to live among the ashes" was a symbol of being debased in comparison to one's siblings, irrespective of sex. In Germany, for example, there were stories in which such an ashboy later becomes king, which parallels Cinderella's fate. "Aschenputtel" is the title of the Brothers Grimm's version of the tale. The term originally designated a lowly, dirty kitchenmaid who must tend to the fireplace ashes.

3   There are many examples in the German language of how being forced to dwell among the ashes was a symbol not just of degradation, but also of sibling rivalry, and of the sibling who finally surpasses the brother or brothers who have debased him. Martin Luther in his *Table Talks* speaks about Cain as the God-forsaken evildoer who is powerful, while pious Abel is forced to be his ash-brother (*Asche-brüdel*), a mere nothing, subject to Cain; in one of Luther's sermons he says that Esau was forced into the role of Jacob's ash-brother. Cain and Able, Jacob and Esau are Biblical examples of one brother being suppressed or destroyed by the other.

4   The fairy tale replaces sibling relations with relations between step-siblings—perhaps a device to explain and make acceptable an animosity which one wishes would not exist among true siblings. Although sibling rivalry is universal and "natural" in the sense that it is the negative consequence of being a sibling, this same relation also generates equally as much positive feeling between siblings, highlighted in fairy tales such as "Brother and Sister."

5   No other fairy tale renders so well as the "Cinderella" stories the inner experiences of the young child in the throes of sibling rivalry, when he feels hopelessly outclassed by his brothers and sisters. Cinderella is pushed down and degraded by her stepsisters; her interests are sacrificed to theirs by her (step)mother; she is expected to do the dirtiest work and although she performs it well, she receives no credit for it; only more is demanded of her. This is how the child feels when devastated by the miseries of sibling rivalry. Exaggerated though Cinderella's tribulations and degradations may seem to the adult, the child carried away by sibling rivalry feels, "That's me; that's how they

---

* Artistically made slippers of precious material were reported in Egypt from the third century on. The Roman emperor Diocletian in a decree of A.D. 301 set maximum prices for different kinds of footwear, including slippers made of fine Babylonian leather, dyed purple or scarlet, and gilded slippers for women. [Bettelheim]

mistreat me, or would want to; that's how little they think of me." And there are moments—often long time periods—when for inner reasons a child feels this way even when his position among his siblings may seem to give him no cause for it.

6   When a story corresponds to how the child feels deep down—as no realistic narrative is likely to do—it attains an emotional quality of "truth" for the child. The events of "Cinderella" offer him vivid images that give body to his overwhelming but nevertheless often vague and nondescript emotions; so these episodes seem more convincing to him than his life experiences.

7   The term "sibling rivalry" refers to a most complex constellation of feelings and their causes. With extremely rare exceptions, the emotions aroused in the person subject to sibling rivalry are far out of proportion to what his real situation with his sisters and brothers would justify, seen objectively. While all children at times suffer greatly from sibling rivalry, parents seldom sacrifice one of their children to the others, nor do they condone the other children's persecuting one of them. Difficult as objective judgments are for the young child—nearly impossible when his emotions are aroused—even he in his more rational moments "knows" that he is not treated as badly as Cinderella. But the child often feels mistreated, despite all his "knowledge" to the contrary. That is why he believes in the inherent truth of "Cinderella," and then he also comes to believe in her eventual deliverance and victory. From her triumph he gains the exaggerated hopes for his future which he needs to counteract the extreme misery he experiences when ravaged by sibling rivalry.

8   Despite the name "sibling rivalry," this miserable passion has only incidentally to do with a child's actual brothers and sisters. The real source of it is the child's feelings about his parents. When a child's older brother or sister is more competent than he, this arouses only temporary feelings of jealousy. Another child being given special attention becomes an insult only if the child fears that, in contrast, he is thought little of by his parents, or feels rejected by them. It is because of such an anxiety that one or all of a child's sisters or brothers may become a thorn in his flesh. Fearing that in comparison to them he cannot win his parents' love and esteem is what inflames sibling rivalry. This is indicated in stories by the fact that it matters little whether the siblings actually possess greater competence. The Biblical story of Joseph tells that it is jealousy of parental affection lavished on him which accounts for the destructive behavior of his brothers. Unlike Cinderella's, Joseph's parent does not participate in degrading him, and, on the contrary, refers him to his other children. But Joseph, like Cinderella, is turned into a slave, and, like her, he miraculously escapes and ends by surpassing his siblings.

9   Telling a child who is devastated by sibling rivalry that he will grow up to do as well as his brothers and sisters offers little relief from his present feelings of dejection. Much as he would like to trust our assurances, most of the time he cannot. A child can see things only with subjective eyes, and comparing himself on this basis to his siblings, he has no confidence that he, on his own, will someday be able to fare as well as they. If he could believe more in himself, he would not feel destroyed by his siblings no matter what they might do to him,

since then he could trust that time would bring about a desired reversal of fortune. But since the child cannot, on his own, look forward with confidence to
some future day when things will turn out all right for him, he can gain relief
only through fantasies of glory—a domination over his siblings—which he hopes
will become reality through some fortunate event.

10   Whatever our position within the family, at certain times in our lives we are
beset by sibling rivalry in some form or other. Even an only child feels that
other children have some great advantages over him, and this makes him
intensely jealous. Further, he may suffer from the anxious thought that if he did
have a sibling, his parents would prefer this other child to him. "Cinderella" is
a fairy tale which makes nearly as strong an appeal to boys as to girls, since
children of both sexes suffer equally from sibling rivalry, and have the same
desire to be rescued from their lowly position and surpass those who seem
superior to them.

11   On the surface, "Cinderella" is as deceptively simple as the story of Little Red
Riding Hood, with which it shares greatest popularity. "Cinderella" tells about the
agonies of sibling rivalry, of wishes coming true, of the humble being elevated,
of true merit being recognized even when hidden under rags, of virtue rewarded and evil punished—a straightforward story. But under this overt content is
concealed a welter of complex and largely unconscious material, which details
of the story allude to just enough to set our unconscious associations going. This
makes a contrast between surface simplicity and underlying complexity which
arouses deep interest in the story and explains its appeal to the millions over
centuries. To begin gaining an understanding of these hidden meanings, we
have to penetrate behind the obvious sources of sibling rivalry discussed so far.

12   As mentioned before, if the child could only believe that it is the infirmities
of his age which account for his lowly position, he would not have to suffer so
wretchedly from sibling rivalry, because he could trust the future to right matters. When he thinks that his degradation is deserved, he feels his plight is utterly hopeless. Djuna Barnes's perceptive statement about fairy tales—that the child
knows something about them which he cannot tell (such as that he likes the
idea of Little Red Riding Hood and the wolf being in bed together)—could be
extended by dividing fairy tales into two groups: one group where the child
responds only unconsciously to the inherent truth of the story and thus cannot
tell about it; and another large number of tales where the child preconsciously
or even consciously knows what the "truth" of the story consists of and thus
could tell about it, but does not want to let on that he knows. Some aspects
of "Cinderella" fall into the latter category. Many children believe that Cinderella
probably deserves her fate at the beginning of the story, as they feel they would,
too; but they don't want anyone to know it. Despite this, she is worthy at the
end to be exalted, as the child hopes he will be too, irrespective of his earlier
shortcomings.

13   Every child believes at some period of his life—and this is not only at rare
moments—that because of his secret wishes, if not also his clandestine actions,
he deserves to be degraded, banned from the presence of others, relegated to
a netherworld of smut. He fears this may be so, irrespective of how fortunate

his situation may be in reality. He hates and fears those others—such as his siblings—whom he believes to be entirely free of similar evilness, and he fears that they or his parents will discover what he is really like, and then demean him as Cinderella was by her family. Because he wants others—most of all, his parents—to believe in his innocence, he is delighted that "everybody" believes in Cinderella's. This is one of the great attractions of this fairy tale. Since people give credence to Cinderella's goodness, they will also believe in his, so the child hopes. And "Cinderella" nourishes this hope, which is one reason it is such a delightful story.

14   Another aspect which holds large appeal for the child is the vileness of the stepmother and stepsisters. Whatever the shortcomings of a child may be in his own eyes, these pale into insignificance when compared to the stepsisters' and stepmother's falsehood and nastiness. Further, what these stepsisters do to Cinderella justifies whatever nasty thoughts one may have about one's siblings: they are so vile that anything one may wish would happen to them is more than justified. Compared to their behavior, Cinderella is indeed innocent. So the child, on hearing her story, feels he need not feel guilty about his angry thoughts.

15   On a very different level—and reality considerations coexist easily with fantastic exaggerations in the child's mind—as badly as one's parents or siblings seem to treat one, and much as one thinks one suffers because of it, all this is nothing compared to Cinderella's fate. Her story reminds the child at the same time how lucky he is, and how much worse things could be. (Any anxiety about the latter possibility is relieved, as always in fairy tales, by the happy ending.)

16   The behavior of a five-and-a-half-year-old girl, as reported by her father, may illustrate how easily a child may feel that she is a "Cinderella." This little girl had a younger sister of whom she was very jealous. The girl was very fond of "Cinderella," since the story offered her material with which to act out her feelings, and because without the story's imagery she would have been hard pressed to comprehend and express them. This little girl had used to dress very neatly and liked pretty clothes, but she became unkempt and dirty. One day when she was asked to fetch some salt, she said as she was doing so, "Why do you treat me like Cinderella?"

17   Almost speechless, her mother asked her, "Why do you think I treat you like Cinderella?"

18   "Because you make me do all the hardest work in the house!" was the little girl's answer. Having thus drawn her parents into her fantasies, she acted them out more openly, pretending to sweep up all the dirt, etc. She went even further, playing that she prepared her little sister for the ball. But she went the "Cinderella" story one better, based on her unconscious understanding of the contradictory emotions fused into the "Cinderella" role, because at another moment she told her mother and sister, "You shouldn't be jealous of me just because I am the most beautiful in the family."

19   This shows that behind the surface humility of Cinderella lies the conviction of her superiority to mother and sisters, as if she would think: "You can make me do all the dirty work, and I pretend that I am dirty, but within me I know that you treat me this way because you are jealous of me because I am

so much better than you." This conviction is supported by the story's ending, which assures every "Cinderella" that eventually she will be discovered by her prince.

20   Why does the child believe deep within himself that Cinderella deserves her dejected state? This question takes us back to the child's state of mind at the end of the oedipal period.* Before he is caught in oedipal entanglements, the child is convinced that he is lovable, and loved, if all is well within his family relationships. Psychoanalysis describes this stage of complete satisfaction with oneself as "primary narcissism." During this period the child feels certain that he is the center of the universe, so there is no reason to be jealous of anybody.

21   The oedipal disappointments which come at the end of this developmental stage cast deep shadows of doubt on the child's sense of his worthiness. He feels that if he were really as deserving of love as he had thought, then his parents would never be critical of him or disappoint him. The only explanation for parental criticism the child can think of is that there must be some serious flaw in him which accounts for what he experiences as rejection. If his desires remain unsatisfied and his parents disappoint him, there must be something wrong with him or his desires, or both. He cannot yet accept that reasons other than those residing within him could have an impact on his fate. In this oedipal jealousy, wanting to get rid of the parent of the same sex had seemed the most natural thing in the world, but now the child realizes that he cannot have his own way, and that maybe this is so because the desire was wrong. He is no longer so sure that he is preferred to his siblings, and he begins to suspect that this may be due to the fact that *they* are free of any bad thoughts or wrongdoing such as his.

22   All this happens as the child is gradually subjected to ever more critical attitudes as he is being socialized. He is asked to behave in ways which run counter to his natural desires, and he resents this. Still he must obey, which makes him very angry. This anger is directed against those who make demands, most likely his parents; and this is another reason to wish to get rid of them, and still another reason to feel guilty about such wishes. This is why the child also feels that he deserves to be chastised for his feelings, a punishment he believes he can escape only if nobody learns what he is thinking when he is angry. The feeling of being unworthy to be loved by his parents at a time when his desire for their love is very strong leads to the fear of rejection, even when in reality there is none. This rejection fear compounds the anxiety that others are preferred and also maybe preferable—the root of sibling rivalry.

23   Some of the child's pervasive feelings of worthlessness have their origin in his experiences during and around toilet training and all other aspects of his education to become clean, neat, and orderly. Much has been said about how children are made to feel dirty and bad because they are not as clean as their parents want or require them to be. As clean as a child may learn to be, he

---

* *Oedipal:* Freud's theory of the Oedipus complex held that at an early stage of development a child wishes to replace the parent of the same sex in order to achieve the exclusive love of the parent of the opposite sex.

knows that he would much prefer to give free rein to his tendency to be messy, disorderly, and dirty.

24   At the end of the oedipal period, guilt about desires to be dirty and disorderly becomes compounded by oedipal guilt, because of the child's desire to replace the parent of the same sex in the love of the other parent. The wish to be the love, if not also the sexual partner, of the parent of the other sex, which at the beginning of the oedipal development seemed natural and "innocent," at the end of the period is repressed as bad. But while this wish as such is repressed, guilt about it and about sexual feelings in general is not, and this makes the child feel dirty and worthless.

25   Here again, lack of objective knowledge leads the child to think that he is the only bad one in all these respects—the only child who has such desires. It makes every child identify with Cinderella, who is relegated to sit among the cinders. Since the child has such "dirty" wishes, that is where he also belongs, and where he would end up if his parents knew of his desires. This is why every child needs to believe that even if he were thus degraded, eventually he would be rescued from such degradation and experience the most wonderful exaltation—as Cinderella does.

26   For the child to deal with his feelings of dejection and worthlessness aroused during this time, he desperately needs to gain some grasp on what these feelings of guilt and anxiety are all about. Further, he needs assurance on a conscious and an unconscious level that he will be able to extricate himself from these predicaments. One of the greatest merits of "Cinderella" is that, irrespective of the magic help Cinderella receives, the child understands that essentially it is through her own efforts, and because of the person she is, that Cinderella is able to transcend magnificently her degraded state, despite what appear as insurmountable obstacles. It gives the child confidence that the same will be true for him, because the story relates so well to what has caused both his conscious and his unconscious guilt.

27   Overtly "Cinderella" tells about sibling rivalry in its most extreme form: the jealousy and enmity of the stepsisters, and Cinderella's sufferings because of it. The many other psychological issues touched upon in the story are so covertly alluded to that the child does not become consciously aware of them. In his unconscious, however, the child responds to these significant details which refer to matters and experiences from which he consciously has separated himself, but which nevertheless continue to create vast problems for him.

Review Questions

1. What does living among ashes symbolize, according to Bettelheim?
2. What explanation does Bettelheim give for Cinderella's having stepsisters, not sisters?
3. In what ways are a child's emotions aroused by sibling rivalry?

4. To a child, what is the meaning of Cinderella's triumph?

5. Why is the fantasy solution to sibling rivalry offered by "Cinderella" appropriate for children?

6. Why is Cinderella's goodness important?

7. Why are the stepsisters and stepmother so vile, according to Bettelheim?

8. In paragraphs 20–26, Bettelheim offers a complex explanation of oedipal conflicts and their relation to sibling rivalry and the child's need to be debased, even while feeling superior. Summarize these seven paragraphs, and compare your summary with those of your classmates. Have you agreed on the essential information in this passage?

Discussion and Writing Suggestions

1. One identifying feature of psychoanalysis is the assumption of complex unconscious and subconscious mechanisms in human personality that explain behavior. In this essay, Bettelheim discusses the interior world of a child in ways that the child could never articulate. The features of this world include the following:

All children experience sibling rivalry.

The real source of sibling rivalry is the child's parents.

Sibling rivalry is a miserable passion and a devastating experience.

Children have a desire to be rescued from sibling rivalry (as opposed to rescuing themselves, perhaps).

Children experience an Oedipal stage, in which they wish to do away with the parent of the same sex and be intimate with the parent of the opposite sex.

"Every child believes at some point in his life . . . that because of his secret wishes, if not also his clandestine actions, he deserves to be degraded, banned from the presence of others, relegated to a netherworld of smut."

To what extent do you agree with these statements? Take one of the statements and respond to it in a four- or five-paragraph essay.

2. A critic of Bettelheim's position, Jack Zipes, argues that Bettelheim distorts fairy-tale literature by insisting that the tales have therapeutic value and speak to children almost as a psychoanalyst might. Ultimately, claims Zipes, Bettelheim's analysis corrupts the story of "Cinderella" and closes down possibilities for interpretation. What is your view of Bettelheim's psychoanalytic approach to fairy tales?

I Am Cinderella's Stepmother and I Know My Rights
Judith Rossner

In another selection in this chapter, Jungian analyst Jacqueline M. Schectman gives us several reasons to find the stepmother in "Cinderella" sympathetic: she, too, has suffered a grievous loss (her husband); she has had to raise two girls on her own; she is searching for emotional comfort in her life like everyone else. In the humorous piece that follows, Judith Rossner lets Cinderella's stepmother speak for herself, and we learn that she has successfully sued the Disney corporation for bringing out a movie that unfairly characterizes her and her daughters and misrepresents Cinderella as "a saint incapable of thoughts of revenge." Judith Rossner has written many novels, the most well-known being Looking for Mr. Goodbar *(1975). One of her continuing interests, expressed most notably in* Olivia *(1994) and* Perfidia *(1997), has been the psychological entanglements of complex mother-daughter relationships. The following selection appeared originally in the* New York Times *on 19 April 1987. The piece begins with the following disclaimer:*

> I have been asked to verify for those to whom it is not immediately apparent that since the following is a work of fiction . . . "written by" a person who never existed, the events referred to in it could not have taken place.

1   I've been often asked to explain why I never sued the Brothers Grimm or took public exception to the ugly little tale people think is about me and my daughters, yet have chosen to sue Mr. Disney over his loathsome movie. It's fair to guess that if I hadn't won the lawsuit, no one would care a bit about us or about the damages we've sustained. Having succeeded in getting the movie out of circulation, and in discouraging new editions of the story as well, I am besieged by hostile queries and comments, usually masquerading as concern for the storyteller's freedom.

2   First, it's essential to say I didn't look forward to pressing the suit and had hoped the whole matter would simply go away. If the picture the Grimms painted was distorted beyond belief, at least the name Cinderella—a name not bequeathed to my daughter by her parents or used by anyone who ever knew her—seemed to afford us some protection. Between scholars explicating the text and psychiatrists relating it to the events of our lives, not to speak of reporters investigating us for some gossip magazine, the story has not blown over. In fact, I have felt hostile eyes upon me all the time.

3   One of the defense attorneys claimed it wasn't the restoration of my good name I was after, but only attention. I was jealous, he said, of the unending spotlight on my stepdaughter Cinderella. I can only wish that he be locked in a room with the Grimms for eternity. He deserves the company of two men who constantly rewrite reality to make it bearable to themselves, no matter what havoc they create for those around them.

"I Am Cinderella's Stepmother and I Know My Rights" by Judith Rossner, *New York Times,* 19 April 1987.

4   I have never claimed my girls were easy. Their father, my first husband, a remote and undemonstrative man, tended to show affection by lavishing gifts of clothing and jewelry upon them. When he died suddenly, leaving a legacy of debt and an estate in disorder, the girls were denied, not only the token protection of his presence, but also those material compensations he had provided. They became anxious and moody and worried that their prospects for decent marriages had been ruined.

5   At that time, Cinderella—as I shall call her to avoid confusion—was 14. Her father was a man of no particular ability or ambition who had made a good deal of money on a stock-market fluke. When he began to court me he was floundering, incapable of mobilizing himself or controlling his strong-willed daughter. She would not go to school. She had a foul mouth. She would not dress decently for any occasion. And she was filthy.

6   The notion of anyone's being forced to sweep the cinders in a household that can afford help is ludicrous except in certain circumstances. Cinderella spent her waking time at home, sitting at the fire, poking at the cinders and getting covered with ash, which she did not mind in the least! Since she neither kept her own room neat or helped in other household tasks, tending the fireplace seemed a perfect job for her. Nor did she appear to mind! That is one of the ironies of the charming little tale she later told people who relayed it to the people who told the Grimms. She would starve before she'd cook a meal and let her clothing get stiff with dirt before she'd wash it, but tending the fireplace was a task she appeared to enjoy!

7   Allow me to move to the tale of her father's bringing home from town (as requested by them respectively) fine clothing and jewelry for my daughters, the branch of a hazelnut tree for Cinderella. As the Grimms told it, Cinderella planted the branch in memory of her mother and proceeded to weep over it such copious tears as to cause it to sprout into a tree.

8   I promise you that her mother would not have done the same for Cinderella, who, she'd often said, would be the death of her. And her father, if he let her come close, was usually rewarded by a slap in the face. What I am saying is that those tears that watered the hazelnut tree were tears not of mourning but of jealously and guilt. The girl had ample reason for both. One of the qualities that made the Grimms' tale less objectionable to us than Mr. Disney's was that in their own way, the Grimms showed the suffering my girls endured. Those birds that pecked the beans from the fireplace and brought Cinderella the gown, and were thus clearly seen to be in her service, also pecked out my daughters' eyes. Mr. Disney, of course, gives us a saint incapable of thoughts of revenge, a portrait which, in its deep untruth, is much more unsettling to us.

9   Let us pass on to the matter of the Prince, who and what he was (a Prince, of course), and who he most distinctly was not (a responsible young man). Even if the rumors of drink and seductions and shoplifting were true, time might have turned him into a responsible adult. On the other hand, such escapades would worry any parent and were strikingly similar to our experiences with Cinderella. I've always found it peculiar that people failed to wonder why the

Prince should have wanted this one pretty young girl of all the pretty young girls, including my two daughters, who lived in his kingdom.

10   To make a long story short, they were two of a kind. Those same stores in the village that locked the doors when they saw Cinderella approaching (do we need to deal, at all, with the nonsense of fairy godmothers and/or mice who provide her with clothes?) had, obviously, a much greater problem in dealing with our little Prince, who could buy whatever he wanted but chose to rip it off instead. If Cinderella didn't drink it was only because she liked to be in full control of everyone around her; if she was not promiscuous, it was because her filth discouraged advances (though it has always amused me that people swallowed whole the notion of a girl's being unrecognizable because she took a bath, combed her hair and put on a new dress).

11   In any event, my daughters were as eager as all the other young girls in the kingdom to be chosen by the Prince. Even in the modern era, when television has given an idea of the boredom of royalty's daily life, many girls might say they would give an arm or a leg to be a princess. Surely the Grimms knew the difference between using such an expression and actually cutting off one's big toe so one's foot will fit a glass slipper! Just as surely, any sane girl who thought of performing such a lunatic act would have been afraid of losing the Prince upon his discovery that she had a stump where her big toe had been! This is one of the few places where Mr. Disney's story is less objectionable than the Grimms'.

12   Which returns us to the matter of my motive in bringing this suit. Simply put, I owed it to my daughters. As you have seen, I have never claimed they were perfect. But beautiful they were. We knew it, everyone in town knew it, the Grimms knew it! It is the only quality allowed them in a tale that is otherwise a nightmare of caricature. Yet Mr. Disney chose to send them into history via the movies— which are seen in one theatrical showing by more people than read the Grimms' tales in the decade after they were written—as not only unhappy, but hideously ugly! Still, I was reluctant to sue. If I dreaded each release of the movie, I dreaded more the revelation and recrimination trying to stop it would entail.

13   Then video stores began to open near my home. I couldn't pass them without wondering if they stocked The Movie. I'd feel a change in some neighbor and sense she'd seen it and connected me and my girls to the story for the first time. Nightmares made sleep increasingly difficult. I entered therapy with a man I thought was being kind because he felt sorry for me. Finally, I talked to a lawyer who urged that I bring suit, with the results that you know. I FEEL vindicated by the court's decision, almost as pleased that certain bookstores have ceased to carry the Grimms. I think my life would now be pleasant and "normal" were I not being subjected to all sorts of pressures from disturbed children and misguided parents who are angry when they can't find "Cinderella" at their book or video stores.

14   I'm sick of the argument that a child's imagination conjures stories more frightening than anything in Grimm, and that the stories offer deep consolation for the difficulties of the real world. It is my own feeling that children will be better rather than worse off if confined to a diet of after-school specials and quiz

shows. I wish that both had been available when I was raising my girls. They have a variety of problems that might never have arisen had they not been exposed, too young, to the ugly fantasies of the Brothers Grimm.

15   The other day a little girl and her mother got on the elevator in my building and the little girl shrieked "Mommy, is that the witch who killed 'Cinderella'?" Nobody can tell me that this idea came from a child's mind, and when I find out where she got that one, I'll sue him, her or them, too.

Discussion and Writing Suggestions

1. Discuss the ways in which this selection is both a parody and a critique of two versions of "Cinderella." How does Rossner achieve her humor? How does she embed a critique within her humor? Base your answers on a particular passages from the selection.

2. The stepmother objects less to the portrait of her family as painted by the brothers Grimm than she does to the one offered by the makers of the Disney animation. Why? (Why did she sue Disney, not Jakob and Wilhelm Grimm?) If you have not done so, read the Disney version of the story (pages 576–78), which parallels the movie, and the version by the brothers Grimm (pages 552–57). What, exactly, is the stepmother's complaint against Disney? Why has the Disney version offended her while the Grimm version has not?

3. What was the "truth" about Cinderella, according to the stepmother? What kind of girl was she when the stepmother first met her? What was she like later, when the prince entered the picture? In what ways were they "two of a kind"?

4. In paragraph 14, Cinderella's stepmother rejects the claims of analysts like Bettelheim and Schectman who assert that in themes, plot lines, and tensions fairy-tale literature expresses the complex inner lives of children. On reading or listening to fairy tales, goes the argument, children find a tool that helps them understand their inner turmoil. The stepmother disagrees, saying that as far as her daughters are concerned the "ugly fantasies of the Brothers Grimm" may well have *caused* inner turmoil, not helped to resolve it. Do you have an opinion on this important point? Insofar as you can tell, to what extent were fairy tales a psychological boon to you—or a problem?

5. Rossner relates the "Cinderella" story from an unexpected point of view. To what extent do you find the stepmother to be sympathetic in Rossner's telling? Is she any less "wicked" to you in this version?

"Cinderella" and the Loss of Father-Love
Jacqueline M. Schectman

Jacqueline M. Schectman, director of training for the Jung Institute of Boston, is a therapist who draws on the theories of Carl Jung (1875–1961) to help clients understand and address the root causes of their unhappiness. Jung was the founder of analytical psychology. A one-time associate of Sigmund Freud, he developed the theory of the collective unconscious: a set of unconscious patterns in the psyche by which we order our world. These patterns emerge from the unconscious as "archetypes" in stories, myths, and religions—as elements we seem to recognize instantly (perhaps without knowing why) and find deeply resonant, whichever culture we call our own. In "Cinderella," at least four archetypes—Father, Mother, wicked Stepmother, and the Shadow—figure prominently.

In her preface to The Stepmother in Fairy Tales: Bereavement and the Feminine Shadow *(1993), the book in which "'Cinderella' and the Loss of Father-Love" appears, Schectman writes: "My approach to fairy tales is a reflection of my work with families and young children in that I tend to read the tales as bridges between inner and outer life, as stories of the struggle to find and define one's place in the world." For Schectman, the archetypal Stepmother is an important—and sympathetic—force both in the tale and in our lives, for "[s]he is a force against which the child can test his growing strength and maturity."*

Throughout her essay, Schectman interweaves her analyst's notes on various clients with her analysis of "Cinderella." It is fascinating to watch how her understanding of her clients' inner lives informs her understanding of "Cinderella," and vice versa.

1   In my work with young children I have always been moved by the child's miraculous ability to find and use just those materials—games, stories, images, even pieces of furniture—best suited for the healing of his or her wounds. So it was with Ginny, the quick and independent sister of a chronically ill child. Given her sister's special needs, Ginny was always second in her parents' hearts and minds; her frequent misbehavior was her only means of briefly holding center stage. In therapy she learned to use her hours in most expressive ways, directing me to play the role of rescuer/protector/friend, Godmother, Good Fairy or the Prince. At not quite four years of age, "Cinderella" was her chosen tale.

> Ginny's favorite made-up game was to run into the waiting room and hide in a space behind her mother's chair. In my part as Prince, I was to enter with an object, meant to be a shoe, in hand. I'd make a show of searching for the proper foot to fit the shoe, then discover Ginny in her niche. Thus found, she'd emerge in triumph from behind the chair, try on the "shoe," and prance around the room, a tiny Cinderella ready to be seen and loved.

2   "Cinderella" is a story for the Stepchild in us all, for the lonely one waiting for her Prince, for the one who feels unseen by those she loves. We weep with Cinderella when we feel harried and abused, when a Stepmother within warns

against our dreams. Joy, she seems to say, is gold that will surely turn to lead at the stroke of twelve. Cinderella's triumph at the ball is a victory for all who'd prove Stepmother wrong, who would naysay her mocking, deprecating voice. When Cinderella dances with The Prince she dances for all who dare to wish for love, for recognition, for better days to come.[*]

3   When we recall the Cinderellas of our youth we probably remember Disney's lovely, laughing film, or the genteel stories of Perrault, in which a graciously forgiving Cinderella brings her sisters to her royal court.[†] The Grimms' Germanic version that we'll look at here is a darker tale, bloody and vengeful and full of mutilating loss.[‡] Like most Stepmother tales, this "Cinderella" is a tale of grief. It begins, fittingly, with Mother's death-bed scene:

> The wife of a wealthy man fell ill, and was close to death. As her end drew near, she called her beloved daughter to her side, and said: "My dear and only child, remember to be pious and be good. God, then, will protect you, and I shall watch from heaven and be ever near." With that she died. The young girl visited her mother's grave each day and wept . . .

4   In this bereavement tale, every member of the family responds to loss. Cinderella weeps and pines in her attachment to her grief; Stepmother and her daughters carry coldness and envy in their hearts, while father meets their cruel, unconscious power with an equally unconscious weakness and withdrawal. Cinderella is not the only orphan in this tale; her stepsisters have suffered loss and will suffer more throughout this tale, as cruelty turns upon itself in a mockery of Mother Love. The story begins with the Good Mother's death, ends with her punishing revenge and is taken up throughout with a desperate search for masculine security and love. When Mother dies, Father's love is lost as well, buried in the coldness of his grief.

> Winter came and went, and with the Spring the man had found another wife. The woman had two daughters of her own, beautiful like she, but vile in temperament and black of heart.

5   Cinderella's father takes a wife to ease his family's pain. Instead, he brings home grief equal to his own; each family amplifies the others' need. This "proud

---

[*] A . . . version of this tale, the movie *Pretty Woman,* takes great pleasure in proving the disapproving wrong. The heroine, dressed in her newly purchased clothes, returns to the store where she'd been insulted and ignored the day before. The look of shocked recognition on the saleswomen's faces sends a cheer up in the audience every time the film is shown.

[†] C. F. Neil Philip, ed., *The Cinderella Story: The Origins and Variations of the Story Known as "Cinderella,"* for the history and evolution of this tale. In 1892, M. R. Cox compiled 345 variants of "Cinderella" in a collection reissued by Kraus Reprinted Limited in 1967.

[‡] Children take great pleasure in the gory details of this tale, in which they find their fantasies of vengeance played out to the full. Adults, on the other hand, are shocked and prefer the prettied versions they recall.

and haughty" Stepmother* has no softness for her husband's child; her widowhood has left her hard and dry. Her husband and the father of her family has gone, and she's raised two daughters as lonely and unhappy as herself. "Beautiful and fair of face" they may well be, but they seem to lack a lens through which to view the beauty that is theirs. It brings them little joy.

6   The bereavement that binds all the women in this tale—Stepmother, her daughters, surely the heroine herself—is that of father-loss. Each plays out an aspect of this loss, Cinderella in her flights from love, her sisters in their wish to win the Prince, Stepmother in her desperate need to see her daughters wed. She has had to raise her family alone, and her pride and haughtiness may well be her defense against the helplessness she has felt along the way. She's determined that her daughters have a better life than she, a life safely in a husband's care. Her stepchild is a mere distraction from her overall campaign, another burden in her overburdened life.

7   Fathers have played minor, seemingly unimportant, roles in the other tales we've looked at here. In "The Laidly Worm . . . ," and in "Snow White," the widowed fathers seek and find their second wives, and then all but disappear, seemingly enchanted by the witches in their homes. "Hansel and Gretel"'s Woodsman-Father can do little more throughout the tale than wring his hands. In each of these tales, a son or brother or some passing foreign prince has appeared to defeat the Witch, rescue the princess and bring balance and completion to the tale. These young heroes are stepping into Father's shoes, for once-upon-a-time the Old King was a hero too, with a vitally important role in family life.

8   Neumann (1973:198) sees Father as the bearer of "tradition, culture and the development of consciousness," without whom the child might be lost in a maternal uroboric state. In familial terms, one might understand Father as a necessary third to the perfect twoness of the mother-child bond. His presence moves the child from the paradise of mother's arms into an awareness of others in the world, and thus into awareness of himself as separate being. This archetypal Father carries conflict, therefore consciousness, into the child's life.

9   In Freudian terms, the Oedipal father stands between a mother and her son, challenging the child to take him on or to forego instinctual desire. A daughter, too, must give up her desire for her father, but not before experiencing, at a feeling level, the mutuality of that desire. Father's love, returned, is an acknowledgement of her as a sexual being. Samuels (1986) speaks to the importance of this relationship in feminine development:

> [The] erotic element guarantees the significance of the relationship. . . . The father could not be more different from his daughter; he is male and from another generation. This is what gives him his potential to stimulate an expansion and deepening of her personality. But he is also part of the same

---

* So she is described in Perrault's French version of the tale, in which Stepmother is also called "the most disagreeable lady in the whole country" (Philip, 1989), and (Howell, 1985).

family as his daughter; that should make him "safe" as regards physical expression of this necessary sexuality and also provides a reason for his own emotional investment.

10   Aside from his role in his children's development, father's greatest contribution to a family's life may be in his support of mother in her nurturing and containing role. Ideally, he provides her with a place of rest, with a means of regathering her strength and her stores of loving care. A year ago I joined family and friends in the huge public picnic that marks Boston's celebration of the Fourth of July. A young woman sat among us and nursed her infant child, while her husband knelt beside her, feeding her while she fed their son. The small circle they created for themselves was so protective and complete that neither the surrounding crowd nor the fireworks could disturb their peace. In the absence of Father, this loving and protective third to the mother-child pair, the demands of mothering may make Stepmothers of us all. A depleted, isolated mother has less and less to give her child, and raising one's family alone may well evoke the Witch:

> Janet's husband, a submariner in the nuclear fleet, spent half his year at sea, three months on shore, three months on the sub. The first month of his sea-time went relatively well; Janet, warmed by the last weeks of his time with her, felt cared-for and relaxed, and while she missed him she could feel his presence in their home. Her children felt this too, and joined her in her efforts toward a structured family life. By the second month they'd begin to test her limits and her will, and her unsupported weariness would begin to show: the grass would go unmowed, dishes go unwashed, and she'd lose her patience earlier each day. By the time the petty officer returned he'd find his children wild, his home a mess and his wife a screaming hag. They'd repair the damage over several weeks, but by then it was nearly time for him to leave again.

11   Father's absence need not be so stark to bring Stepmother to the scene. His partial withdrawal, born of helplessness and fear, and played out in rigidity of roles, can be just as keenly felt and not so easily addressed:

> Anne was five, her brother seven, when her parents were divorced. Her father, at a loss for how to spend his weekend visit time with her, left her with his new young bride while he and brother washed the car, mowed the lawn and made household repairs. The four would meet only around meals. No one openly complained; father, after all, was a conscientious man trying hard to do his best. As one might guess, his wife and daughter blamed one another for their loneliness and loss, and their shared resentment grew into week-end dread. The stepmother acted out her archetypal role and Anne responded as a weepy, angry stepchild in her father's home.

12   "Cinderella" brings the theme of father-loss into sharp relief. In no other tale is his distance quite so darkly felt, his grief-borne blindness to the women's

needs so stark. He takes no protective role in any version of the tale, and in some he is altogether gone. A Spanish "Cinderella"* has it thus:

> All were very happy for some months, until the father had to take a long trip, from which he never returned. With the absence of [Cinderella's] father, things began to change . . .

13   We can imagine the rage and disappointment in Cinderella's home. A widow remarries, seeking that second chance at life: comfort, warmth, an end to loneliness; a partner in parenting her difficult, demanding girls. Instead, she finds herself in sole charge of a grieving child, a child so attached to mourning that ashes seem her natural milieu. The widow, having been betrayed into a caretaker's role, is clearly having none of it; she has no comfort left to give. The child becomes the target of her wrath and her daughters join her in her outraged sense of loss. They've made do with very little loving parent-care, and scarcity has fed their greed. They are not about to share the little that they have.

> . . . the sisters plagued her with their insults and their ugly ways. They took her pretty clothes and bade her dress in rags and wooden shoes. "Where is the proud princess now?" they laughed, and had her work from dawn to dusk . . .

14   What deprivation lies behind the sisters' mocking cries, their need to taunt the grieving girl? Do they sense in her her mother's parting gift, the ever present nearness of the love they have never known? Like Psyche's sisters, they must destroy this stranger Eros in their midst, that which never has been, never can be, theirs. Love, beginning with a love of self, is an alien invader in their home, always longed for, always pushed away.

15   How does one empathize with ugliness, with the heartless lack of empathy played out by the sisters in this tale? Sitting with such darkness in an analytic hour is the most difficult of therapeutic tasks, for it constellates one's hateful sister when an understanding soulmate is the patient's desperate need:

> Beth, the fourth of seven girls, spent her childhood vying for her mother's ear, her father's eye. She feels today that she was never truly seen or heard. At thirty-five she is talented, quite beautiful, and by her own sad doing, utterly alone. At family gatherings she provokes her sisters and their mates until they turn their backs on her and leave. She undermines her colleagues, challenges her boss, and throws away her lovers whenever they want loving in return. I am often flooded with revulsion as she tells her tales; she seems so totally devoid of the capacity for empathy and love. Finally, at the nadir of my own disgust, I find that I am with her after all. The rage, and the separateness from her I feel are what she suffers through every hour of her life. I have a glimpse into the depth of her misery and pain.

---

* Tardy, William T., *Treasury of Children's Classics in Spanish and English,* Lincolnwood, National Textbook Company, 1987.

16   The suffering of the "vile and black of heart" can be profound—a hopeless, lonely journey that would seem to have no end. In a gathering following one of my "Stepmother" talks, a young woman handed me this poem, then slipped away:

The Ugly Stepsister

I am an ugly stepsister.
Never have I lovingly done work.
Only cried and wanted to be rescued
By the Prince divinely dancing.
But my feet
They're too big.
Size nine.
Some seem to think
I could have been
     Cinderella if I'd only tried.
She who was born from love
And knew her true worth.
What did I have to sing about?
                    —D.M., Vancouver

17   What to sing about, indeed? A young woman growing up needs a mother, well-grounded in her own femininity, with whom she can identify if she's to value the woman in herself. Cinderella's mother, close to her child even in the moment of her death, provides the girl with that sense of self that shines through all her ashes and her tattered clothes. This centeredness provokes the envy that her sisters feel. The sisters, it would seem, lack that model in their lives; they've only known their mother in her darkness, in the incompleteness of her widow's grief. Worse, they've missed the sparkle in their father's eye, the admiring glance that can take a daughter's beauty in and return it to her with delight and love. Without that loving and reflective eye, what can these sisters know of their true worth? Samuels continues:

> Many fathers and daughters fail to achieve this [erotic] link. This is because men tend to be extremely cautious about becoming erotically involved with their daughters (even in fantasy). . . . The father's failure to participate in a mutual attraction and mutual, painful renunciation of erotic fulfillment with his daughter deprives her of psychological enhancement. This can take many forms: mockery of her sexuality, over-strictness, indifference—and, if the symbolic dimension is savagely repressed, actual incest. In the absence of eros or its excess the daughter loses sight of herself as a sexually viable adult, with disastrous consequences. (Samuels, 1986)

18   All that the sisters in this tale know about father is his absence in their lives. Their loss is so profoundly felt it can only be expressed in surface greed, in a need for all the glitter that the world provides:

> One day, when [Cinderella's] father was about to travel to the nearest town, he asked his step-daughters what he might bring them from the

fair. "Pretty dresses," said the one, while her sister asked for emeralds and pearls.

19   Their wish, in its essence, is to be remembered while father journeys to and from the fair. The child (of any age) who assaults the returning traveler with cries of "What did you bring for me?" wants to know that he was missed along the way. Cinderella has what seems, at first, to be a different sort of wish, but she, too, needs to be carried in her father's mind; good mothering is never quite enough:

> "Father, bring me the first branch to touch your hat as you ride toward home."

Nature herself seems to tap father on the head. He returns with a hazel twig, a symbol of hidden wisdom, divine inspiration and the Earth Goddess's chthonic powers (Cooper, 80). A grateful Cinderella plants the twig on her mother's grave:

> The Hazel twig, watered by Cinderella's many tears, grew to be a handsome tree, and a small white bird nestled in the tree and granted Cinderella's every wish.

20   This bird—the departed mother's spirit, always near—brings Cinderella everything but her father's loving eye. He seems to be oblivious to the abuse she suffers at her sisters' hands, nor does he see the envy eating at his stepdaughters' hearts. Could this father be determined not to see the younger women in his home, in an effort to deny the erotic energy he feels? In "Thousandfurs" (Grimm, #65), a variant on the Cinderella theme, a King is enjoined to incest by his dying wife; he promises to marry no one not as beautiful as she. As his daughter grows to be the beauty that her mother was, she becomes the object of the King's desire, and must protect herself by running off, hidden in a cloak of many furs. In family life, fathers may protect their daughters and themselves from their desires by turning a blind eye, by not seeing the young beauties growing up before their eyes. While father-daughter incest, acted out, may be the worst sort of sexual abuse, this denial of incestuous desire abuses sexuality in its most delicate and nascent state (cf. Samuels, above). When father turns away in fear, the admiring glances of a passing Prince may take on great importance for a Princess coming into bloom:

> Kate remembers the party for her "Sweet Sixteen," one of her first dates with the boy she'd eloped with at eighteen: "I'd had my hair cut short that day in a becoming style and I wore a dance dress I'd picked out for myself. When my father saw me he was furious, and told me I looked ugly, like some sort of tramp. Even I could see that wasn't so, but he had me close to tears. J. arrived just then and he was so impressed he could barely speak; I was a different girl than the one he'd seen that afternoon in school! The look on his face meant everything to me."

21   The longed for Prince may arrive in more pernicious forms. In Chapter One we looked at brother-sister incest as a saving grace. When kept at the level of

desire, this intensity of sibling love serves as container for familial eros, for love that has no other place to go. Sadly, separating action from desire is at times too great a task for a child prince to bear. Brother-sister incest, acted out and then repressed, becomes a hidden source of shame in adult life, a shadow on one's erotic life.

> Gwen and her brother Josh grew up with a father who'd learned to keep his feelings under wraps. He viewed his wife and children from an icy distance that left all in a state of aching need. At some time early in their lives Gwen and Josh discovered comfort in one another's sexual touch. Gwen cannot yet say when this activity began, nor when it ceased to be. She only knows that pleasure, now, is inextricably bound with shame; her body's needs evoke her greatest fears.

22   In our tale, as in the memory above, father's distance keeps everyone in a state of need. As we might expect, the announcement of the Prince's Ball stirs a flurry of excitement in Cinderella's home:

> The king in those days had a son, and the son was looking for a bride. Accordingly, the King ordered that a feast be held to last three days, to which all the beautiful young maidens in the country were to come. When the sisters learned that they would go they began ordering their stepsister about . . . "We will soon be dancing with the King!" Cinderella did as she was told, but longed to go herself . . .

23   Here, indeed, is the answer to all the women's prayers: A young man with eyes for the beauties in his realm, with a heart ready to be won, with a throne to give his bride. The sisters primp and preen and prepare to meet their Prince; Cinderella weeps, and begs her Stepmother for leave to go along. The woman is aghast:

> "You go to the Feast? How can it be? You have no clothes and shoes, but you would dance? Nonsense!"

24   Three times Cinderella cries and pleads, and twice Stepmother sends her off to pick the lentils from the ashes in the hearth. Like Psyche, enjoined by Aphrodite to separate a pile of grain, Cinderella too—with the help of all the creatures of the air—must sort things out before she can hope to meet her Eros in the Prince. This sifting through the ashes of one's life, "The good for the pot, the bad for the crop," is the torturous inner task that must precede true marriages of heart and mind. Note that nothing here is thrown away; the "bad" is recognized, and taken in. This is the work on Shadow, a task so painful only a Stepmother would demand that it be done.

> Paul spent his hour in recital of his lover's faults. They'd had one of their frequent fights and he wanted sympathy from me, support for his anger and his sense of being wronged. Instead, I asked him to examine his part in what transpired. How had he provoked her wrath, what might he have done to bring things to a different end? Such reflections were the last things

on his mind and he snarled his disgust with me. What good was I if I could-
n't take his side?

25   Cinderella never questions the rightness of her task. Always the good and
pious child, she does as she is told, only to be turned away again:

> Cinderella thought: "Now I can go to the feast!" But her stepmother said
> again: "No Cinderella, you may not go. You have no gown and you cannot
> dance. The King would only laugh!"

26   Stepmother, in all her harshness, tells Cinderella one more necessary truth:
the sackcloth and ashes of her grief are hardly proper dress for a royal ball, nor
has she learned to dance while weeping on her mother's grave. If she's to meet
The Prince she must put her mournful piety away.

> In the years in which I led discussion groups for single and divorced adults,
> I watched participants arrive in every stage of need, some still in mourning
> for the lover (husband, wife) they'd lost, or indeed had never had. Others
> were more ready to explore their newly "liberated" lives. The former fre-
> quently found sympathy and kindly nods of understanding in the group.
> Just as frequently they left the social hour alone. Something in their bear-
> ing said, "Not Yet," in words that all could understand.

27   Cinderella, having served her mourning time, is more ready than anyone can
know. She calls upon her source of strength, and wastes no time in dressing for
the ball:

> When all had gone, Cinderella repaired to her mother's grave, where she
> wept and wished beneath the tree:
>
> > *"Tremble, tremble little tree,*
> > *Gold and silver rain on me."*
>
> And the bird let fall a ballgown made of silver and of gold, and dancing
> shoes embroidered with the finest silk. Quickly Cinderella dressed, and just
> as quickly made her way to the palace of the King. There no one knew her
> in her golden gown . . .

28   We can imagine the fury and dismay of the sisters here, as they watch this
lovely stranger dancing with the Prince. Why can't they catch his eye? They too
have done just as mother said, but her motherly advice to them has been very
different than she offered to the stepchild in their home. All of their energies
and hopes have gone into selection of their clothes and jewels; into polishing
their courtly manners and their nails. Their every hair is perfectly in place, but
they've not been asked to do the inner work demanded of this "foreign
princess" clothed in gold. How are they to understand the apparent ease with
which she's captured the young man's heart? Neither Stepmother nor her
daughters can recognize the hard-working maiden within the golden dress; they
see only that she has what they have not.

After years of agonizing work, Gloria is in reunion with her gifted inner Prince. She plays piano with a local band, sings through her days and steals the time to write the poetry she loves. Her husband, however, feels great envy when he sees her living out her gifts; he is tied to work that brings him little joy. While he rationally connects her blossoming with her therapeutic work he is nonetheless enraged; how dare she find the inner fire that still eludes his life?

29   Cinderella's sisters need not have envied her so much; for all her work, she is unprepared for the suddenness of her success, and flies away in fear:

> Cinderella danced until evening fell. But then she begged her leave. The Prince wished to see her home but Cinderella fled from him . . .

30   How can Cinderella trust the love and admiration of the Prince when her own father seems to see her not at all? Like his wife and stepdaughters, he's failed to recognize the beautiful young woman dancing at the ball.

> Bridget's father died when she was just thirteen, too soon to see his "little nurse" become the sprightly beauty she would grow to be. Today she is indeed a nurse, and she has married well, to a man who loves her more than she can quite believe. When they meet with friends she compares herself to all the other women in the room, and imagines that her husband finds her wanting in some way; they must be more desirable than she. She cannot find that father-voice within herself to say: You are the fairest in *this* land!

31   How is Cinderella's Prince to capture the mysterious, elusive girl? He asks the man who ought to know her best:

> The Prince waited until Cinderella's father came, and told him of the unknown princess hidden in the pigeon-house. Her father thought: "Could it be Cinderella?" At that the old man took an axe and chopped the pigeon-house to bits, but no one was inside.

32   "Can it be Cinderella?" We can hear the shock and wonder in the old man's voice. As the veil of his denial slowly lifts, he must contemplate his daughter in all of her nubility and charm. Can this lovely woman be his little girl? When he attacks the pigeon-house, and then the pear tree into which the Prince has seen the maiden flee, it's as if the very nature of her feminine allure must be destroyed before she leaves him for a younger man! When we ask, "Who gives this bride to wed?" we are asking father no small thing. His sense of loss at such a time may well evoke an angry, vengeful "Stepfather," not unlike the "Stepmother" who is forced to see her sons off into the world.

33   The father Kate recalls could not bear to see her sexuality emerge. When she eloped with the man who'd caught her eye, father's pain and grief made for an encounter he'd regret throughout his life.

> When Kate eloped, her father, furious, summoned her, her husband and his parents to a meeting at his home. He told her husband that he'd made a

terrible mistake: his bride was lazy, disobedient, dishonest and a tramp. "She will be a rope around your neck for life!" The bridegroom was not inclined to "give her back," but the father-daughter rift took many years to heal.

34   Three times Cinderella ventures out to dance, and three times runs away, to hide once more among the ashes by the hearth. This retreat until the time is right, until the world feels safe enough for love, is part of the connection to the earth Cinderella demonstrates throughout this tale. There is safety in her dirty rags, and she'll hide in them until her doubts and fears release her into life.

> Anne's first forays into sexuality were frightening and harsh; she needed time then to withdraw into herself, to feel into her fear and rage, to learn to be more conscious of the woman she'd become. Accordingly, she made herself as unattractive as her natural beauty would allow: cropped her hair, gained thirty pounds, dressed in shapeless, faded clothes. She remained thus, to her family's dismay, for several years. When a gentle Prince appeared, with the capacity to see the woman hidden in the rags, she allowed herself to venture forth, to see and to be seen. The Prince has come and gone, but Anne has thrown her rags away.

35   Cinderella's Prince has made his choice, and as the festival comes to an end he determines not to let his disappearing partner go again:

> [The Prince] . . . had seen that the palace steps were smeared with tar and pitch, and when she fled one of her golden slippers remained, caught in the sticky tar. The Prince held the slipper in his hand, and felt he would surely find the maiden now.
> When morning came, he took the golden slipper to Cinderella's house, and showed it to her father, saying: "I will only wed the maid who fits this shoe." Then the sisters had some hope, for they had dainty feet.

36   Now begins the darkest portion of this tale, for while Cinderella hides herself and waits, her sisters try to fit themselves into her tiny shoe. As they try the slipper on their soft, uncalloused feet we hear that most dangerous of sounds, the well-intentioned voice of an ambitious mother-who-knows-best:

> The elder of the two took the shoe into another room to try it on, her mother at her side. Alas, the slipper would not fit. But her mother handed her a knife and said: "Cut off your toe; you'll have no need to walk when you are Queen." This the maiden did, and despite her pain, forced her foot into the tiny shoe. The King's son, seeing her thus shod, carried her away to be his bride.

37   With the advent of an eligible Prince, mothers may see a life of ease ahead for their daughters—better lives, indeed, than they have had! They beseech their daughters to conform, to fit themselves into some pre-formed, perfect mold. There is freedom in security, they say, and time enough ahead for all your little quirks and dreams, for all the imperfections that make you who you are. There

will be a time to take a stand, to run that race or write that book, time enough for wholeness when you are safely married to The Prince.

38   Perhaps modern women should know better, should know that a woman must accept herself—stand on her own two feet—if she hopes to find a Prince. But for all of that, one can't quite shut out the loud, collective voice that joins the desperate-mother voice within. "Reshape your nose," one hears. "File down your teeth and suck the fat out of your thighs; don't you know the competition's terrible out there?" When one's sense of self depends upon a Prince out in the world, no sacrifice of flesh, no loss of spirit feels too great.

39   What is tragic for the sisters in this tale is that their sacrifices are in vain. The Prince carries each of the pain-wracked maidens off in turn, only to be cautioned by the pigeons perched in Cinderella's magic tree: his bloodied bride is false. Now the younger of the sisters has her turn:

> Then the second sister took the shoe into another room, where her mother waited with a knife. Again, the shoe was just too small, and the mother said, "Cut a bit off your heel . . ."[*]

and once more, the Prince is warned as he carries the false sister by the hazel tree. Both young women offer up their mutilated feet, but the Prince has no desire for a bloodied, martyred bride.

> Linda recalls her mother when her family was young: "She had a joyful, playful side to her that she completely put away whenever my father was at home. None of us ever saw him laugh, and she assumed, I think, that laughter was not permitted in our house. I know she loved to swim and run and play out in the woods—other people told me this—but she simply let this go in an effort to 'grow up.' Eventually my father found his pleasure far from home; he told my mother that she'd ceased to move him long ago."

40   We must admire the determination of the Prince. He returns each of the injured sisters to her home, and asks Cinderella's father, one more time, for assistance in finding his true bride. Father must finally release his only child, his last reminder of the wife and happy home he'd once enjoyed. His answer is so cruel and final in its disavowal that it serves to free Cinderella from his grasp. If she'd ever hoped to catch her father's eye, to win his love, that hope is surely gone with his reply:

---

[*] "Cinderella" has its source in seventh-century China, and this version of the tale may be a commentary on the practice of binding female feet. In China, highborn female children had their feet bound into tiny, lotus shapes. "The four smaller toes were folded under the sole, the whole foot was folded so the underside of the heel and toes were brought together." Women with bound feet were the essence of beauty and nobility. "Chinese men were conditioned to intense fetishistic passion for deformed female feet. Chinese poets sang ecstatic praises of the lotus feet that aroused their desire to fever pitch. The crippled woman was considered immeasurably charming by reason of her vulnerability, her suffering and her helplessness—she couldn't even escape an attacker by running away (Walker 319).

"These maids have proved themselves untrue. Have you none other here beneath your roof?" "No," said the man; "only a scrawny servant-girl, here before my late wife died. She could not be your bride, I know." But when the Prince persisted, they called Cinderella in.

41 For Cinderella and her Prince, what follows is the moment of surrender, recognition, and a sense that all is as it's meant to be. Cinderella, her face washed clean of ashes and of grief, tries on the golden shoe that fits her perfectly:

When Cinderella stood to face her dancing partner once again, the King's son knew her then, and cried out in great joy, "That is my true bride!"

42 Such moments are the stuff of which romantic literature and art are made.[*] Our beloved—the one we've dreamed of all our lives and have always known within ourselves—suddenly appears, fantasy made flesh. All of our ambivalence is gone, there is nothing left to do but bow to love, and pray that it will last.

43 As the Prince carries Cinderella off, we're told that Stepmother and her daughters become "pale with rage"—and pale, perhaps, with the sisters' loss of blood. One would think the tale could end right there: justice has been done, Cinderella has her man, her vain and selfish sisters have their mutilated feet and empty beds. But the worst is yet to come for the unhappy sisters in this tale:

On the wedding day, the false sisters came to join the royal train, hoping to find favor in their sister's eyes. On the way to the church they walked at Cinderella's side, the elder on the left, the younger on the right. The birds pecked out one eye of each. On their return from church, each walked on Cinderella's other side, and the doves pecked out their remaining eyes. Thus the sisters were struck blind, and were punished for their falseness all their days.

44 Blindness has been a theme throughout this tale: Father, blind with hope, seeks a second wife, then shuts his eyes to the redoubled family grief within his home, to his daughters' needs and the abuse being perpetrated out of unmet needs. His blindness in the dark further darkens every facet of his family's life. The stepsisters, blinded by their envy of Cinderella's glowing inner light, attempt to douse it with their cruel and mocking taunts. And Stepmother, who can see very well what *Cinderella* needs to bring her into life, cannot provide her daughters with the guidance they require. She is too close to them to see them as they are, too attached to their "well being" to offer them an honestly reflective eye. As a "good" mother she has indeed been blind, closed against the wisdom that the harsh, truth-telling Stepmother can, and does, provide.

45 The pigeons in this tale, embodiments of mother-nurturance throughout, provide the sisters with the sort of cursed gift a Stepmother might give. What might blindness to the outer world mean to the "vile, black-hearted" daugh-

---

* Cf. Haule, John, *Divine Madness: Archetypes of Romantic Love,* Boston, Shambhala Press, 1990.

ters we have come to know? Their focus has always been "out there," on all the pretty things that shine and glow in the material world, on all the treasures others might possess. They've had no insight, for to peer inside themselves would have revealed an emptiness too terrible to bear. Their sunlight gone, perhaps their helpless groping in the dark will provide the inward shift of vision that their souls require, the clear reflective eye always absent from their lives.

46   Cinderella's tale begins with her loving mother's death; her time in rags and ashes prepares her for her life ahead. Her sisters face another sort of death. They can never be the prancing, carefree careless girls they were; their hopes of dancing at another ball are gone. What their lives will be we cannot know, but the necessary darkness that precedes all inner work has come. It is in this darkness that the sisters' tale begins.

Bibliography

Cooper, J.C., *An Illustrated Encyclopedia of Traditional Symbols*. London: Thames and Hudson, Ltd., 1979.

Neumann, Erich, *The Child*. Ralph Manheim, Translator; New York: Harper & Row, 1973.

———. *The Great Mother*, Ralph Manheim, Translator; Princeton: Princeton University Press, 1963.

Walker, Barbara G., *The Woman's Encyclopedia of Myths and Secrets*. San Francisco: Harper & Row, 1983.

Review Questions

1. Schectman explains that "Cinderella" is a "bereavement tale [in which] every member of the family responds to loss." What does she mean? More particularly, what role does "father-loss" play in this bereavement? Why is father-loss so significant in this story?

2. In which ways, according to Schectman, can the stepmother and the stepsisters be seen in a sympathetic light?

3. In paragraph 10, Schectman writes that "the demands of mothering may make Stepmothers of us all." How so? What is the father's role in a mother's becoming a "wicked" stepmother?

4. In the tale, the stepmother orders Cinderella to separate lentils from ashes in the hearth. What is the Jungian explanation of this cruel task, and why is it the stepmother's job to inflict this cruelty?

5. What is the significance of Cinderella's three visits to the ball?

6. What is the significance of the sisters' cutting off parts of their feet to fit the slipper, according to Schectman? Psychologically, why does Cinderella not need to cut off parts of her feet?

7. According to Schectman, what is the significance of the birds pecking out the eyes of the stepsisters?

Discussion and Writing Suggestions

1. Schectman has presented the stepmother and stepsisters of "Cinderella" sympathetically, making it possible for us to empathize with them. Given your reading of this essay, are you convinced? Do you now see the stepmother and stepsisters in a new light?

2. Comment on Schectman's use of notes made about her clients to inform her reading of "Cinderella"—and, conversely, of her use of the fairy tale to better understand issues in the lives of her clients. Make a few general observations about this use of an analyst's notes, and then discuss one particular example in depth.

3. In paragraph 8, Schectman writes that the father's "presence moves the child from the paradise of mother's arms into an awareness of others in the world, and thus into awareness of himself as separate being. This archetypal Father carries conflict, therefore conscious-ness, into the child's life." Schectman is claiming a necessary rela-tionship between conflict and consciousness. How can conflict lead to consciousness?

4. What is the process by which a good mother can turn into a wicked stepmother? (See paragraph 10—especially Schectman's own notes as an analyst—for a starting point.) How can good mother and wicked stepmother coexist in one person?

5. Identify one of Schectman's insights into "Cinderella" that seems especially new and powerful. How has Schectman used principles of Jungian analysis to arrive at this insight?

6. Are there any instances in which Schectman's use of Jungian analy-sis leads to a strained or unconvincing insight into "Cinderella," in your view? Discuss.

7. Reread "The Ugly Stepsister," the poem that Schectman quotes in paragraph 16. Your comments? (If you're temporarily stumped for reactions, consider: What assumption does the author of the poem make about the relationship between readers of "Cinderella" and the tale itself? Do you share this assumption? Have you ever identi-fied with a character in a fairy tale?)

Cinderella: *Not* So Morally Superior
Elisabeth Panttaja

In this brief analysis of "Cinderella," Elisabeth Panttaja offers what for some will be an unset-tling claim: that Cinderella succeeds not because she is more patient or virtuous than her stepsisters or stepmother (the typical moral of the story) but because she is craftier, willing

to employ powerful magic to defeat the forces arrayed against her. Nor can it be said from
the evidence of the story, according to Panttaja, that the prince or Cinderella love each other.
Is this the same "Cinderella" that you grew up with? The article from which this selection was
excerpted appeared originally in Western Folklore *in January 1993. Elisabeth Panttaja taught*
at Tufts University when the article was written.

1   It is not surprising . . . that modern criticism of "Cinderella" . . . has been so strangely indifferent to the role that Cinderella's mother plays in the story. In our post-Freudian world, Cinderella's mother is imagined as absent despite the fact that she plays a central part in the unfolding of Cinderella's destiny. Indeed, Cinderella's mother's role is far from marginal: the words and actions of Cinderella's mother are of vital importance in narrative sequencing and the over-all "moral" of the story. The Grimms' version of "Cinderella" opens significantly with the dying mother's injunction to the soon-to-be-orphaned girl. On her deathbed, the mother gives Cinderella the following advice: "Dear child, be good and pious. Then the dear Lord shall always assist you, and I shall look down from heaven and take care of you." In fairy tales, the opening scene is always of particular importance, since it is here that the tale sets forth the prob-lem which it will then go on to solve. Cinderella's problem is precisely the fact that her mother has died. It is this "lack," the lack of the mother, which Cinderella must overcome in the course of the story. The narrative instantly complicates her task by staging the arrival of a powerful mother and her two daughters, who, in the strength of their unity, hope to vanquish the mother-less girl. Thus the story quickly amplifies the mother/daughter theme, rubbing salt, if you will, in Cinderella's wound. For just as Cinderella's powerlessness is a result of her mother's death, so the stepsisters' power is associated with their strong, scheming mother. In short order, then, Cinderella finds herself in need of her mother's good advice, and it is through keeping her mother's advice that she manages to overcome her own social isolation and the plots of her ene-mies. In the end, Cinderella rises to a position of power and influence, and she accomplishes this, apparently, despite her motherless status.

2   But is she really motherless? Not really, since the twig that she plants on her mother's grave grows into a tree that takes care of her, just as her mother promised to do. The mother, then, is figured in the hazel tree and in the birds that live in its branches. Early in the story, the tree offers solace to the grieving girl; later, it gives her the dresses she needs to attend the ball. Likewise, the two pigeons who live in the tree expose the false brides as they ride away, with bleeding feet, on the prince's horse, and they lead the flock of birds who help Cinderella sort the lentils that the stepmother throws on the hearth. In addition, the fleeing Cinderella is said to find safety in a dovecote and a pear tree ("a beautiful tall tree covered with the most wonderful pears"). Since these places of refuge continue the bird/tree symbolism, it is quite possible that we are meant to see the mother's influence also at work in the rather mysterious way that Cinderella manages to avoid too-early detection. Thus, at every turn in the narrative, the magical power of the mother vies with the forces arrayed against Cinderella, whether they be the selfish designs of the stepmother and stepsis-ters or the futile attempts of the father and prince to capture and identify her. In the end, the mother, despite death, reigns supreme. Not only does she take

her revenge on her daughter's enemies by plucking out the eyes of the step-sisters, but, more importantly, she succeeds in bringing about her daughter's advantageous marriage. The happy ending proves that it is the mother, after all, who has been the power of the story. Cinderella's success resides in the fact that, while apparently motherless, she is in fact well-mothered. In spite of death, the mother/daughter dyad has kept its bonds intact. At its most basic level, the story is about this mother/daughter relationship. It is about the daughter's loyalty to the (good) mother's words and the mother's continuing, magical influence in the (good) daughter's life.

3   Unlike the narratives favored by psychoanalysis, which are about mater-nal absence and disempowerment, this tale tells a story about a strong mother/daughter relationship that actively shapes events. Cinderella's mother performs a specific social function vis-à-vis her daughter—she assists in her coming out. Her gifts are directed toward a specific goal—to help Cinderella into an advantageous marriage. From this perspective, what is most interest-ing about Cinderella's mother is her similarity to the stepmother. These two women share the same devotion to their daughters and the same long-term goals: each mother wants to ensure a future of power and prestige for her daughter, and each is willing to resort to extreme measures to achieve her aim. Thus, Cinderella's mother is a paradoxical figure: while her power is asso-ciated at the outset with the power of the Christian god and while she seems to instruct Cinderella in the value of long-suffering self-sacrifice, she is also a wily competitor. She plots and schemes, and she wins. She beats the step-mother at the game of marrying off daughters. She does for Cinderella exact-ly what the wicked stepmother wishes to do for her own daughters—she gets her married to the "right" man.

4   Considering the similarities in their goals and strategies, the idea that Cinderella and her mother are morally superior to the stepsisters and their mother is shot through with contradictions. Throughout the tale, there exists a structural tension between the character that is drawn thematically (the pious Cinderella) and the character that acts in the narrative (the shrewd, competitive Cinderella). The superficial moral of the story would have us believe that Cinderella's triumph at the ball is a reward for her long-suffering patience. But while Cinderella's piety does play an important role in the forging of her super-natural alliance, it plays almost no role in the important practical business of seducing the prince. Indeed, the battle for the prince's attention is not waged at the level of character at all but at the level of clothes. Cinderella wins the battle because her mother is able, through magic, to provide raiment so stunning that no ordinary dress can compete. Cinderella's triumph at the ball has less to do with her innate goodness and more to do with her loyalty to the dead mother and a string of subversive acts: she disobeys the stepmother, enlists forbidden helpers, uses magic powers, lies, hides, dissembles, disguises herself, and evades pursuit. The brutal ending of the tale, in which Cinderella allows the mother (in the form of two pigeons) to peck out the eyes of the stepsisters, fur-ther complicates the story's moral thematics.

5   Just as there is a structural tension between the tale's thematization of Cinderella's goodness and the actual plot, so there is a tension between plot

and the alleged theme of romantic love. I say "alleged" here because although modern readers and critics have sought to enshrine romantic love as a central value of the tale, there is actually nothing in the text itself to suggest either that Cinderella loves the prince or that the prince loves her. The prince marries Cinderella because he is enchanted (literally) by the sight of her in her magical clothes. What is interesting about these clothes, at least in the Grimms' version, is that, far from simply enhancing a natural but hidden beauty, they actually create it. In the Grimms' version, Cinderella is described as "deformed," while the sisters are described as "fair," so we can only conclude that the power of Cinderella's clothes is indeed miraculous, since they turn a deformed girl into a woman whose beauty surpasses that of the already fair. Thus, the prince's choice of Cinderella can be explained neither by her piety, which he has never experienced, nor by her own beauty, which does not exist. It is the mother's magic which brings about the desired outcome, an outcome in which the prince has actually very little choice. The prince's oft-repeated statement, "She's my partner," as well as his obsessive tracking down of the true bride, suggests that he is operating under a charm rather than as an autonomous character, and the fact that both these motifs are repeated three times is further evidence that magic, not free choice, is at work here.

6   This is not surprising: the enchantment of a potential marriage partner is one of the most common motifs in fairy tales and mythology. The motif of an enchanted or somehow disguised bride or bridegroom usually appears in tales that depict some kind of unusual marriage, either the marriage of a god or demon to a human (Cupid and Psyche) or the marriage of a poor or ordinary mortal to a member of the deity or the nobility (Beauty and the Beast). The idea, of course, is that one member, by being disguised or by disguising another, can enter into a marriage that he or she would not normally enter into, usually one that crosses class lines. Thus, the enchantment of a prospective bride or bridegroom has more to do with power and manipulation than it does with romance or affection. Rather than talking about Cinderella's love for the prince, then, it is more accurate to say that Cinderella, in alliance with her mother, bewitches the prince in order to gain the power and prestige that will accrue to her upon her marriage to a member of the nobility.

Review Questions

1. Generally, why is the opening scene of a fairy tale so important? Why is it of particular importance in "Cinderella"?

2. Panttaja claims that, despite death, Cinderella's mother remains very much present in the story. How so?

3. How is Cinderella's mother similar to the stepmother?

4. The claim that Cinderella and her mother are morally superior to the sisters and their mother is "shot through with contradictions." What are these contradictions?

5. Why is romantic love *not* central to winning the prince, according to Panttaja? What (and whose) personal qualities *are* essential?

6. What is often the purpose of a disguise or enchantment in fairy tales?

Discussion and Writing Suggestions

1. Does Panttaja's claim that Cinderella's mother is not absent surprise you? Convince you? Explain.

2. What is your response to the claim that Cinderella is not morally superior to the wicked stepsisters or stepmother? Do you find Panttaja's argument compelling? Do you find yourself resisting it at all?

3. Number the sentences of paragraph 2, and then reread the paragraph and respond to these questions: What is the main point (the topic sentence) and where is it located? How does each sentence advance the main idea of the paragraph? Finally, examine the sequence of sentences. Why does Panttaja place sentences where she does? Having completed the analysis, what is your assessment of the paragraph? How successful is it?

4. If Panttaja is correct in her analysis of "Cinderella," what is the moral of the story? How does this moral compare with the one(s) you more typically associate with the story? Do you prefer one moral to another? Why?

5. Read the Grimm brothers' version of "Cinderella" and compare your reading with Panttaja's. Do you find her use of evidence in support of her main points persuasive? Have you, reading the same story, reached different conclusions? Explain, if you can, how two people reading one story can reach different conclusions. What does this say about the story? About the people reading it?

SYNTHESIS ACTIVITIES

1. In 1910, Antti Aarne published one of the early classifications of folktale types as an aid to scholars who were collecting tales and needed an efficient means for telling where, and with what changes, similar tales had appeared. In 1927, folklorist Stith Thompson, translating and enlarging Aarne's study, produced a work that is now a standard reference for folklorists the world over. We present the authors' description of type 510 and its two forms, 510A ("Cinderella") and 510B. Use this description as a basis on which to analyze any two versions of "Cinderella," in this chapter, determining the extent to which they conform to the stated pattern.

Compare and contrast the versions and decide which, in your view, is more authentic.

510.   *Cinderella and Cap o' Rushes.*

   I.   *The Persecuted Heroine.* (a) The heroine is abused by her stepmother and stepsisters, or (b) flees in disguise from her father who wants to marry her, or (c) is cast out by him because she has said that she loved him like salt, or (d) is to be killed by a servant.

   II.   *Magic Help.* While she is acting as servant (at home or among strangers) she is advised, provided for, and fed (a) by her dead mother, (b) by a tree on the mother's grave, or (c) by a supernatural being, or (d) by birds, or (e) by a goat, a sheep, or a cow. When the goat is killed, there springs up from her remains a magic tree.

   III.   *Meeting with Prince.* (a) She dances in beautiful clothing several times with a prince who seeks in vain to keep her, or she is seen by him in church. (b) She gives hints of the abuse she has endured, as servant girl, or (c) she is seen in her beautiful clothing in her room or in the church.

   IV.   *Proof of Identity.* (a) She is discovered through the slipper-test, or (b) through a ring which she throws into the prince's drink or bakes in his bread. (c) She alone is able to pluck the gold apple desired by the knight.

   V.   *Marriage with the Prince.*

   VI.   *Value of Salt.* Her father is served unsalted food and thus learns the meaning of her earlier answer.

   Two forms of the type follow.

   A.   *Cinderella.* The two stepsisters. The stepdaughter at the grave of her own mother, who helps her (milks the cow, shakes the apple tree, helps the old man). Threefold visit to church (dance). Slipper-test.

   B.   *The Dress of Gold, of Silver, and of Stars. (Cap o' Rushes).* Present of the father who wants to marry his own daughter. The maiden as servant of the prince, who throws various objects at her. The threefold visit to the church and the forgotten shoe. Marriage.

2. Speculate on the reasons folktales are made and told. As you develop a theory, rely first on your own hunches regarding the origins and functions of folktale literature. You might want to recall your experiences as a child listening to tales so that you can discuss their effects on you. Rely as well on the variants of "Cinderella," which you should regard as primary sources (just as scholars do). And make use of the critical pieces you've read—Thompson, Bettelheim, Schectman, and Panttaja—selecting pertinent points from each that

will help clarify your points. *Remember:* Your own speculation should dominate the paper. Use sources to help you make *your* points.

3. At the conclusion of his article, Stith Thompson writes:

> Literary critics, anthropologists, historians, psychologists, and aestheticians are all needed if we are to hope to know why folktales are made, how they are invented, what art is used in their telling, how they grow and change and occasionally die.

What is your opinion of the critical work you've read on "Cinderella"? Writing from various perspectives, authors in this chapter have analyzed the tale. To what extent have the analyses illuminated "Cinderella" for you? (Have the analyses in any way "ruined" your ability to enjoy "Cinderella"?) To what extent do you find the analyses off the mark? Are the attempts at analysis inappropriate for a children's story? In your view, what place do literary critics, anthropologists, historians, and psychologists have in discussing folktales?

In developing a response to these questions, you might begin with Thompson's quotation and then follow directly with a statement of your thesis. In one part of your paper, critique the work of Bettelheim, Schectman, and/or Panttaja as a way of demonstrating which analyses of folktales (if any) seem worthwhile to you. In another section of the paper (or, perhaps, woven into the critiques), refer directly to the variants of "Cinderella." For the sake of convenience, you might refer to a single variant. If so, state as much to the reader and explain your choice of variant.

4. Review the variants of "Cinderella" and select two you would read to a favorite child. In an essay, justify your decision. Which of the older European variants do you prefer—Grimm or Perrault? How do the recent versions by Sexton, Lee, Disney, and Gardner affect you? And what of the Chinese, African, and Algonquin versions—are they recognizably "Cinderella"?

You might justify the variants you've selected by defining your criteria for selection and then analyzing the stories separately. (Perhaps you will use Aarne and Thompson's classification—see Synthesis Activity 1.) You might justify your choices negatively—that is, by defining your criteria and then *eliminating* certain variants because they don't meet the criteria. In concluding the paper, you might explain how the variants you've selected work as a pair. How do they complement each other? (Or, perhaps, they *don't* complement each other and this is why you've selected them.)

5. Try writing a version of "Cinderella" and setting it on a college campus. For your version of the story to be an authentic variant, you'll need to retain certain defining features, or motifs. See Aarne and Thompson—Synthesis Activity 1. As you consider the possibilities for your story, recall Thompson's point that the teller of a folk-

tale borrows heavily on earlier versions; the virtue of telling is not in rendering a new story but in retelling an old one and *adapting* it to local conditions and needs. Unless you plan to write a commentary "Cinderella," as Sexton does, you should retain the basic motifs of the old story and add details that will appeal to your particular audience: your classmates. An option: following Catherine Orenstein, create a reality television show based on elements of "Cinderella."

6. In her 1981 book *The Cinderella Complex*, Colette Dowling wrote:

> It is the thesis of this book that personal, psychological dependency—the deep wish to be taken care of by others—is the chief force holding women down today. I call this "The Cinderella Complex"—a network of largely repressed attitudes and fears that keep women in a kind of half-light, retreating from the full use of their minds and creativity. Like Cinderella, women today are still waiting for something external to transform their lives.

In an essay, respond to Dowling's thesis. First, in an analysis, test her thesis by applying it to a few of the variants of "Cinderella." Does the thesis hold in each case? Next, respond to her view that "the chief force holding women down today" is psychological dependency, or the need for "something external" (i.e., a Prince) to transform their lives. In your experience, have you observed a Cinderella complex at work?

7. Explain the process by which Cinderella falls in love in these tales. The paper that you write will be an extended comparison and contrast in which you observe this process at work in the variants and then discuss similarities and differences. (In structuring your paper, you'll need to make some choices: Which variants will you discuss and in what order?) At the conclusion of your extended comparison and contrast, try to answer the "so what" question. That is, pull your observations together and make a statement about Cinderella's falling in love. What is the significance of what you've learned? Share this significance with your readers. At some point, you should raise and respond to Elisabeth Panttaja's assertion that Cinderella does *not*, in fact, fall in love in this tale.

8. Based on your own reading of the tale and on your response to the selections by Schectman and Rossner, develop a point of view about Cinderella's stepmother. Is she truly wicked? Is she misunderstood? Is she worthy of our sympathy? Develop your response into an argument. Be sure to point generously to the story itself.

9. Compare and contrast Bettelheim's Freudian analysis of "Cinderella" with Schectman's Jungian analysis. Which seems the more illuminating? Realize that you are not comparing the work of Freud and Jung (a daunting task!). Rather (and more modestly), concentrate on the limited material at hand. Two analysts, working

in different traditions, apply the principles of their traditions in order to better understand a fairy tale—and ourselves. What are the relative strengths and weaknesses of these two efforts?

10. Many people read the tale as an ideal expression of courtship. Is this your view? What are the romantic legacies of stories like "Cinderella" for relationships today? In developing your answer, how will you account for Catherine Orenstein's position that marriage in fairy tales is usually more about business than it is about love? And how will you account for Elisabeth's Panttaja's claim that romantic love has nothing to do with the eventual union of Cinderella and her prince? Develop your response into an argument.

RESEARCH ACTIVITIES

1. Research the fairy-tale literature of your ancestors, both the tales and any critical commentary that you can find on them. Once you have read the material, talk with older members of your family to hear any tales they have to tell. (Seek, especially, oral versions of stories you have already read.) In a paper, discuss the role that fairy-tale literature has played, and continues to play, in your family.

2. Locate the book *Morphology of the Folktale* (1958) by Russian folklorist Vladimir Propp. Use the information you find there to analyze the elements of any three fairy tales of your choosing. In a paper, report on your analysis and evaluate the usefulness of Propp's system of classifying the key elements of fairy-tale literature.

3. Bruno Bettelheim's *Uses of Enchantment* (1975) generated a great deal of reaction on its publication. Read Bettelheim and locate as many reviews of his work as possible. Based on your own reactions and on your reading of the reviews, write an evaluation in which you address Bettelheim's key assumption that fairy-tale literature provides important insights into the psychological life of children.

4. Locate and study multiple versions of any fairy tale other than "Cinderella." Having read the versions, identify—and write your paper on—what you feel are the defining elements that make the tales variants of a single story. See if you can find the tale listed as a "type" in Aarne and Thompson, *The Types of Folk-Tales*. If you wish, argue that one version of the tale is preferable to others.

5. Jack Zipes, author of *Breaking the Magic Spell* (1979), takes the approach that fairy tales are far from innocuous children's stories; rather, they inculcate the unsuspecting with the value systems of the dominant culture. In a research paper, explicitly address the assumption that fairy tales are not morally or politically neutral but, rather, imply a distinct set of values.

6. In anticipation of writing a children's story, decide on an age group that you will address, and then go to a local public library and find several books directed to the same audience. (1) Analyze these books and write a brief paper in which you identify the story elements that seem especially important for your intended audience. (2) Then attempt your own story. (3) When you have finished, answer two questions: What values are implicit in your story? What will children who read or hear the story learn about themselves and their world? Plan to submit your brief analytical paper, your story, and your final comment.

7. Videotape, and then study, several hours of Saturday morning cartoons. Then locate and read a collection of Grimm's fairy tales. In a comparative analysis, examine the cartoons and the fairy tales along any four or five dimensions that you think are important. The point of your comparisons and contrasts will be to determine how well the two types of presentations stack up against each other. Which do you find more entertaining? Illuminating? Ambitious? Useful? (These criteria are suggestions only. You should generate your own criteria as part of your research.)

8. Arrange to read to your favorite young person a series of fairy tales. Based on your understanding of the selections in this chapter, develop a list of questions concerning the importance or usefulness of fairy-tale literature to children. Read to your young friend on several occasions and, if possible, talk about the stories after you read them (or while you are reading). Then write a paper on your experience, answering as many of your initial questions as possible. (Be sure in your paper to provide a profile of the child with whom you worked; to review your selection of stories; and to list the questions you wanted to explore.)

13 New and Improved: Six Decades of Advertising

Possibly the most memorable ad campaign of the twentieth century (dating from the late 1920s) takes the form of a comic strip. A bully kicks sand into the face of a skinny man relaxing on the beach with his girlfriend. Humiliated, the skinny man vows to get even. "Don't bother, little boy!" huffs the scornful girlfriend, who promptly dumps him. At home, the skinny man kicks a chair in frustration, declares that he's sick of being a scarecrow, and says that if Charles Atlas (once a "97-lb. weakling" himself) can give him a "real body," he'll send for his FREE book. In the next frame, the once-skinny man, now transformed into a hunk, thanks to Atlas's "Dynamic Tension" fitness program, admires himself in front of the mirror: "Boy, it didn't take Atlas long to do this for me. Look, how those muscles bulge! . . . That big stiff won't dare insult me now!" Back on the beach, the bully is decked by the once-skinny man, as his adoring girlfriend looks on: "Oh Mac! You are a real man after all!"

Crude? Undoubtedly. But variations of this ad, which made Atlas a multimillionaire, ran for decades (his company is still in business). Like other successful ads, it draws its power from skillful appeals to almost primitive urges—in this particular case, the urge to gain dominance over a rival for the attention of the opposite sex. Of course, effective ads don't always work on such a primal level. Another famous ad of the 1920s appeals to our need to gain respect from others for higher accomplishments than punching out opponents. Headlined "They Laughed When I Sat Down at the Piano—But When I Started to Play. . . !" the text offers a first-person account of a man who sits down to play the piano at a party. As he does so, the guests make good-natured fun of him; but once he began to play, "a tense silence fell on the guests. The laughter died on their lips as if by magic. I played through the first bars of Liszt's immortal 'Liebenstraum.' I heard gasps of amazement. My friends sat breathless—spellbound." For sixteen additional paragraphs, the writer goes on to detail the effect of his playing upon the guests and to explain how "You, too, can now *teach yourself* to be an accomplished musician—right at home," by purchasing the program of the U.S. School of Music. Again, the reader is encouraged to send for the free booklet. And by the way, "Forget the old-fashioned idea that you need 'special talent'" to play an instrument.

The ubiquity of advertising is a fact of modern life. In fact, advertising can be traced as far back as ancient Roman times when pictures were inscribed on walls to

624

promote gladiatorial contests. In those days, however, the illiteracy of most of the population and the fact that goods were made by hand and could not be mass produced limited the need for more widespread advertising. One of the first American advertisers was Benjamin Franklin, who pioneered the use of large headlines and made strategic use of white space. But advertising as the mass phenomenon we know is a product of the twentieth century, when the United States became an industrial nation—and particularly of the post–World War II period, when a prosperous economy created our modern consumer society, marked by the middle-class acquisition of goods, the symbols of status, success, style, and social acceptance. Today, we are surrounded not only by a familiar array of billboards, print ads, and broadcast ads, but also by the Internet, which has given us "spam," the generic name for an entire category of digital pitches for debt reduction, low mortgage rates, and enhanced body parts—compared to which the average Buick ad in a glossy magazine reads like great literature.

Advertisements are more than just appeals to buy; they are windows into our psyches and our culture. They reveal our values, our (not-so-hidden) desires, our yearnings for a different lifestyle. For example, the Marlboro man, that quintessence of taciturn cowboy masculinity, at home only in the wide open spaces of Marlboro Country, is a mid-twentieth-century American tribute to (what is perceived as) nineteenth-century American values, popularized in hundreds of westerns. According to James Twitchell, a professor of English and advertising at the University of Florida, "He is what we have for royalty, distilled manhood. . . . The Marlboro Man needs to tell you nothing. He carries no scepter, no gun. He never even speaks. Doesn't need to." He is also the product of a bolt of advertising inspiration: previously, Marlboro had been marketed—unsuccessfully—as a woman's cigarette. Another example of how ads reveal culture is the memorable campaign for the Volkswagen Beetle in the 1960s. That campaign spoke to the counterculture mentality of the day: instead of appealing to the traditional automobile customer's desire for luxury, beauty, size, power, and comfort, Volkswagen emphasized how small, funny-looking, bare bones—but economical and sensible—their cars were. On the other hand, snob appeal—at an affordable price, of course—has generally been a winning strategy. In the 1980s and 1990s Grey Poupon mustard ran a successful campaign of TV commercials featuring one Rolls-Royce pulling up alongside another. A voice from one vehicle asks, "Pardon me; do you have any Grey Poupon?" "But of course!" replies a voice in the other car; and a hand with a jar of mustard reaches out from the window of the second car to pass to the unseen occupant of the first car. This campaign is a perfect illustration of what University of California at Davis history professor Roland Marchand calls the appeal of the democracy of goods: "the wonders of modern mass production and distribution enable . . . everyone to enjoy society's most desirable pleasures, conveniences, or benefits."

So pervasive and influential has advertising become that it has created a significant backlash among social critics. Among the most familiar charges against advertising: it fosters materialism, it psychologically manipulates people to buy things they don't need, it perpetuates gender and racial stereotypes (particularly in its illustrations), it is deceptive, it is offensive, it debases the language, and it is omnipresent—we cannot escape it. Although arguing the truth or falsity of these assertions (more fully covered in the selection by Bovée and Arens, pages 655–60) makes for lively debate, our focus in this chapter is not on the ethics of advertising, but rather on how it works. What makes for successful advertising? How do advertisers—and by advertisers we mean not only manufacturers but also the agencies they hire to produce their advertisements—pull our psychological levers to influence us to buy (or think favorably of) their products? What are the textual and graphic components of an effective advertisement—of an effective advertising campaign? How—if at all—has advertising evolved over the past several decades?

Advertising has seen significant changes in the six decades since the end of World War II. It is unlikely that the comic-strip Charles Atlas ad or the verbose "They Laughed When I Sat Down at the Piano" ad would succeed today. Both seem extremely dated. More representative of today's advertising style is the successful milk campaign; each ad features a celebrity such as Bernie Mac or Lauren Bacall with a milk mustache, a headline that says simply "got milk?", and a few short words of text supposedly spoken by the pictured celebrity. But the changes in advertising during the six decades covered in this chapter are more of style than of substance. On the whole, the similarities between an ad produced in the 1950s and one produced today are more significant than the differences. Of course, hair and clothing styles change with the times, message length recedes, and both text and graphics assume a lesser degree of apple-pie social consensus on values. But on the whole, the same psychological appeals, the same principles of headline and graphic design that worked sixty years ago, continue to work today. We choose one automobile over another, for instance, less because our vehicle of choice gets us from point A to point B, than because we invest it—or the advertiser does—with rich psychological and cultural values. In 1957 the French anthropologist and philosopher Roland Barthes wrote (in a review of a French automobile, the Citroën DS), "I think that cars today are almost the exact equivalent of the great Gothic cathedrals: I mean the supreme creation of an era, conceived with passion by unknown artists, and consumed in image if not in usage by a whole population which appropriates them as a purely magical object." It's not known whether Barthes ever considered a career as an advertising copywriter; but he probably would have been a good one.

How advertising works, then, is the subject of the present chapter. By applying a variety of theoretical and practical perspectives to a gallery of six decades of advertisements (and to other ads of your own choosing), you'll be able to practice your analytical skills upon one of the more fascinating areas of American mass culture. The main subjects of your analyses are represented later in this chapter by a portfolio of forty-two advertisements that originally appeared in such magazines as *Time, Newsweek, U.S. News and World Report,* and *Sunset.* For ease of comparison and contrast, most of the ads can be classified into a relatively few categories: cigarettes, alcohol, automobiles, and food, with a number of other ads in the "miscellaneous" category. These ads have been selected for their inherent interest, as well as for the variety of tools that have been employed to communicate the message, what some advertisers call the USP—the Unique Selling Proposition.

The first part of the chapter, however, consists of a number of articles or passages from books, each representing an analytical tool, a particular perspective from which one can view individual advertisements. In the first selection, "Advertising's Fifteen Basic Appeals," Jib Fowles offers a psychological perspective. Fowles identifies and discusses the most common needs to which advertisers attempt to appeal. Among these are the need for sex, the need for affiliation with other people, the need for dominance, and the need for autonomy. In "Making the Pitch in Print Advertising," Courtland L. Bovée et al. outline the key elements of the textual component of advertising—including headlines, subheadlines, and body text. In "Elements of Effective Layout," Dorothy Cohen discusses the key components of advertising graphics: balance, proportion, movement, unity, clarity and simplicity, and emphasis. In "The Indictments Against Advertising" Courtland L. Bovée and William F. Arens consider and respond to some of the most frequent charges leveled against Madison Avenue.

Finally, as indicated above, the chapter continues and concludes with "A Portfolio of Advertisements: 1945–2003," a collection of forty-two ads for various products published in popular magazines in the United States and Great Britain during the last sixty years.

Charles O'Neill, an independent marketing consultant, has written, "Perhaps, by learning how advertising works, we can become better equipped to sort out content from hype, product values from emotions, and salesmanship from propaganda." We hope that the selections in this chapter will allow you to do just that, as well as to develop a greater understanding of one of the most pervasive components of American mass culture.

Advertising's Fifteen Basic Appeals
Jib Fowles

Our first selection provides what you will likely find the single most useful analytical tool for studying advertisements. Drawing upon studies of numerous ads and upon interviews with subjects conducted by Harvard psychologist Henry A. Murray, Fowles developed a set of fifteen basic appeals he believes to be at the heart of American advertising. These appeals, according to Fowles and to Murray, are directed primarily to the "lower brain," to those "unfulfilled urges and motives swirling in the bottom half of [our] minds," rather than to the part of the brain that processes our more rational thoughts and impulses. As you read Fowles's article and his descriptions of the individual appeals, other examples from contemporary print and broadcast ads may occur to you. You may find it useful to jot down these examples for later incorporation into your responses to the discussion and synthesis questions that follow.

Jib Fowles has written numerous articles and books on the popular media, including Mass Advertising as Social Forecast: A Method for Futures Research *(1976),* Why Viewers Watch: A Reappraisal of Television's Effects *(1992),* Advertising and Popular Culture *(1996), and* The Case for Television Violence *(1999). This selection first appeared in* Etc. *39:3 (1982) and was reprinted in* Advertising and Popular Culture.

Emotional Appeals

1 The nature of effective advertisements was recognized full well by the late media philosopher Marshall McLuhan. In his *Understanding Media,* the first sentence of the section on advertising reads, "The continuous pressure is to create ads more and more in the image of audience motives and desires."

2   By giving form to people's deep-lying desires, and picturing states of being that individuals privately yearn for, advertisers have the best chance of arresting attention and affecting communication. And that is the immediate goal of advertising: to tug at our psychological shirtsleeves and slow us down long enough for a word or two about whatever is being sold. We glance at a picture of a solitary rancher at work, and "Marlboro" slips into our minds.

3   Advertisers (I'm using the term as a shorthand for both the products' manufacturers, who bring the ambition and money to the process, and the advertising agencies, who supply the know-how) are ever more compelled to invoke consumers' drives and longings; this is the "continuous pressure" McLuhan refers to. Over the past century, the American marketplace has grown increasingly congested as more and more products have entered into the frenzied competition after the public's dollars. The economies of other nations are quieter than ours since the volume of goods being hawked does not so greatly exceed demand. In some economies, consumer wares are scarce enough that no advertising at all is necessary. But in the United States, we go to the other extreme. In order to stay in business, an advertiser must strive to cut through the considerable commercial hub-bub by any means available—including the emotional appeals that some observers have held to be abhorrent and underhanded.

4   The use of subconscious appeals is a comment not only on conditions among sellers. As time has gone by, buyers have become stoutly resistant to advertisements. We live in a blizzard of these messages and have learned to turn up our collars and ward off most of them. A study done a few years ago at Harvard University's Graduate School of Business Administration ventured that the average American is exposed to some 500 ads daily from television, newspapers, magazines, radio, billboards, direct mail, and so on. If for no other reason than to preserve one's sanity, a filter must be developed in every mind to lower the number of ads a person is actually aware of—a number this particular study estimated at about seventy-five ads per day. (Of these, only twelve typically produced a reaction—nine positive and three negative, on the average.) To be among the few messages that do manage to gain access to minds, advertisers must be strategic, perhaps even a little underhanded at times.

5   There are assumptions about personality underlying advertisers' efforts to communicate via emotional appeals, and while these assumptions have stood the test of time, they still deserve to be aired. Human beings, it is presumed, walk around with a variety of unfulfilled urges and motives swirling in the

bottom half of their minds. Lusts, ambitions, tendernesses, vulnerabilities—they are constantly bubbling up, seeking resolution. These mental forces energize people, but they are too crude and irregular to be given excessive play in the real world. They must be capped with the competent, sensible behavior that permits individuals to get along well in society. However, this upper layer of mental activity, shot through with caution and rationality, is not receptive to advertising's pitches. Advertisers want to circumvent this shell of consciousness if they can, and latch on to one of the lurching, subconscious drives.

6   In effect, advertisers over the years have blindly felt their way around the underside of the American psyche, and by trial and error have discovered the softest points of entree, the places where their messages have the greatest likelihood of getting by consumers' defenses. As McLuhan says elsewhere, "Gouging away at the surface of public sales resistance, the ad men are constantly breaking through into the *Alice in Wonderland* territory behind the looking glass, which is the world of subrational impulses and appetites."

7   An advertisement communicates by making use of a specially selected image (of a supine female, say, or a curly-haired child, or a celebrity) which is designed to stimulate "subrational impulses and desires" even when they are at ebb, even if they are unacknowledged by their possessor. Some few ads have their emotional appeal in the text, but for the greater number by far the appeal is contained in the artwork. This makes sense, since visual communication better suits more primal levels of the brain. If the viewer of an advertisement actually has the importuned motive, and if the appeal is sufficiently well fashioned to call it up, then the person can be hooked. The product in the ad may then appear to take on the semblance of gratification for the summoned motive. Many ads seem to be saying, "If you have this need, then this product will help satisfy it." It is a primitive equation, but not an ineffective one for selling.

8   Thus, most advertisements appearing in national media can be understood as having two orders of content. The first is the appeal to deep-running drives in the minds of consumers. The second is information regarding the good[s] or service being sold: its name, its manufacturer, its picture, its packaging, its objective attributes, its functions. For example, the reader of a brassiere advertisement sees a partially undraped but blandly unperturbed woman standing in an otherwise commonplace public setting, and may experience certain sensations; the reader also sees the name "Maidenform," a particular brassiere style, and, in tiny print, words about the material, colors, price. Or, the viewer of a television commercial sees a demonstration with four small boxes labeled 650, 650, 650, and 800; something in the viewer's mind catches hold of this, as trivial as thoughtful consideration might reveal it to be. The viewer is also exposed to the name "Anacin," its bottle, and its purpose.

9   Sometimes there is an apparently logical link between an ad's emotional appeal and its product information. It does not violate common sense that Cadillac automobiles be photographed at country clubs, or that Japan Air Lines be associated with Orientalia. But there is no real need for the linkage to have a bit of reason behind it. Is there anything inherent to the connection between Salem cigarettes and mountains, Coke and a smile, Miller Beer and comradeship? The link being forged in minds between product and appeal is a pre-logical one.

10   People involved in the advertising industry do not necessarily talk in the terms being used here. They are stationed at the sending end of this communications channel, and may think they are up to any number of things—Unique Selling Propositions, explosive copywriting, the optimal use of demographics or psychographics, ideal media buys, high recall ratings, or whatever. But when attention shifts to the receiving end of the channel, and focuses on the instant of reception, then commentary becomes much more elemental: an advertising message contains something primary and primitive, an emotional appeal, that in effect is the thin end of the wedge, trying to find its way into a mind. Should this occur, the product information comes along behind.

11   When enough advertisements are examined in this light, it becomes clear that the emotional appeals fall into several distinguishable categories, and that every ad is a variation on one of a limited number of basic appeals. While there may be several ways of classifying these appeals, one particular list of fifteen has proven to be especially valuable.

Advertisements can appeal to:

1. The need for sex
2. The need for affiliation
3. The need to nurture
4. The need for guidance
5. The need to aggress
6. The need to achieve
7. The need to dominate
8. The need for prominence
9. The need for attention
10. The need for autonomy
11. The need to escape
12. The need to feel safe
13. The need for aesthetic sensations
14. The need to satisfy curiosity
15. Physiological needs: food, drink, sleep, etc.

Murray's List

12 Where does this list of advertising's fifteen basic appeals come from? Several years ago, I was involved in a research project which was to have as one segment an objective analysis of the changing appeals made in post-World War II American advertising. A sample of magazine ads would have their appeals coded into the categories of psychological needs they seemed aimed at. For this content analysis to happen, a complete roster of human motives would have to be found.

13   The first thing that came to mind was Abraham Maslow's famous four-part hierarchy of needs. But the briefest look at the range of appeals made in advertising was enough to reveal that they are more varied, and more profane, than Maslow had cared to account for. The search led on to the work of psychologist Henry A. Murray, who together with his colleagues at the Harvard Psychological Clinic has constructed a full taxonomy of needs. As described in *Explorations in Personality,* Murray's team had conducted a lengthy series of in-depth inter-

views with a number of subjects in order to derive from scratch what they felt to be the essential variables of personality. Forty-four variables were distinguished by the Harvard group, of which twenty were motives. The need for achievement ("to overcome obstacles and obtain a high standard") was one, for instance; the need to defer was another; the need to aggress was a third; and so forth.

14   Murray's list had served as the groundwork for a number of subsequent projects. Perhaps the best-known of these was David C. McClelland's extensive study of the need for achievement, reported in his *The Achieving Society*. In the process of demonstrating that a people's high need for achievement is predictive of later economic growth, McClelland coded achievement imagery and references out of a nation's folklore, songs, legends, and children's tales.

15   Following McClelland, I too wanted to cull the motivational appeals from a culture's imaginative product—in this case, advertising. To develop categories expressly for this purpose, I took Murray's twenty motives and added to them others he had mentioned in passing in *Explorations in Personality* but not included on the final list. The extended list was tried out on a sample of advertisements, and motives which never seemed to be invoked were dropped. I ended up with eighteen of Murrays' motives, into which 770 print ads were coded. The resulting distribution is included in the 1976 book *Mass Advertising as Social Forecast*.

16   Since that time, the list of appeals has undergone refinements as a result of using it to analyze television commercials. A few more adjustments stemmed from the efforts of students in my advertising classes to decode appeals; tens of term papers surveying thousands of advertisements have caused some inconsistencies in the list to be hammered out. Fundamentally, though, the list remains the creation of Henry Murray. In developing a comprehensive, parsimonious inventory of human motives, he pinpointed the subsurface mental forces that are the least quiescent and most susceptible to advertising's entreaties.

Fifteen Appeals

17   **1. Need for Sex.**   Let's start with sex, because this is the appeal which seems to pop up first whenever the topic of advertising is raised. Whole books have been written about this one alone, to find a large audience of mildly titillated readers. Lately, due to campaigns to sell blue jeans, concern with sex in ads has redoubled.

18   The fascinating thing is not how much sex there is in advertising, but how little. Contrary to impressions, unambiguous sex is rare in these messages. Some of this surprising observation may be a matter of definition: the Jordache ads with the lithe, blouse-less female astride a similarly clad male is clearly an appeal to the audience's sexual drives, but the same cannot be said about Brooke Shields* in the Calvin Klein commercials. Directed at young women and their credit-card carrying mothers, the image of Miss Shields instead invokes the

---

* *Brooke Shields* (b. 1965) is a model (at age 3 she was the Ivory Snow baby), as well as a stage (*Grease*), TV, and film actress; her most well known films are *Pretty Baby* (1978) and *Blue Lagoon* (1980).

need to be looked at. Buy Calvins and you'll be the center of much attention, just as Brooke is, the ads imply; they do not primarily inveigle their target audience's need for sexual intercourse.

19   In the content analysis reported in *Mass Advertising as Social Forecast* only two percent of ads were found to pander to this motive. Even *Playboy* ads shy away from sexual appeals: a recent issue contained eighty-three full-page ads, and just four of them (or less than five percent) could be said to have sex on their minds.

20   The reason this appeal is so little used is that it is too blaring and tends to obliterate the product information. Nudity in advertising has the effect of reducing brand recall. The people who do remember the product may do so because they have been made indignant by the ad; this is not the response most advertisers seek.

21   To the extent that sexual imagery is used, it conventionally works better on men than women; typically a female figure is offered up to the male reader. A Black Velvet liquor advertisement displays an attractive woman wearing a tight black outfit, recumbent under the legend, "Feel the Velvet." The figure does not have to be horizontal, however, for the appeal to be present as National Airlines revealed in its "Fly me" campaign. Indeed, there does not even have to be a female in the ad; "Flick my Bic"* was sufficient to convey the idea to many.

22   As a rule, though, advertisers have found sex to be a tricky appeal, to be used sparingly. Less controversial and equally fetching are the appeals to our need for affectionate human contact.

23   **2. Need for Affiliation.**   American mythology upholds autonomous individuals, and social statistics suggest that people are ever more going it alone in their lives, yet the high frequency of affiliative appeals in ads belies this. Or maybe it does not: maybe all the images of companionship are compensation for what Americans privately lack. In any case, the need to associate with others is widely invoked in advertising and is probably the most prevalent appeal. All sorts of goods and services are sold by linking them to our unfulfilled desires to be in good company.

24   According to Henry Murray, the need for affiliation consists of desires "to draw near and enjoyably cooperate or reciprocate with another; to please and win affection of another; to adhere and remain loyal to a friend." The manifestations of this motive can be segmented into several different types of affiliation, beginning with romance.

25   Courtship may be swifter nowadays, but the desire for pair-bonding is far from satiated. Ads reaching for this need commonly depict a youngish male and female engrossed in each other. The head of the male is usually higher than the female's, even at this late date; she may be sitting or leaning while he is standing. They are not touching in the Smirnoff vodka ads, but obviously there is an intimacy, sometimes frolicsome, between them. The couple does touch

---

* *"Flick my Bic"* became a famous and successful slogan in advertisements for Bic cigarette lighters during the late 1970s and 1980s. Fowles hints at the not-too-subtle sexual implications of the line.

for Martell Cognac when "The moment was Martell." For Wind Song perfume they have touched, and "Your Wind Song stays on his mind."

26   Depending on the audience, the pair does not absolutely have to be young—just together. He gives her a DeBeers diamond, and there is a tear in her laugh lines. She takes Geritol* and preserves herself for him. And numbers of consumers, wanting affection too, follow suit.

27   Warm family feelings are fanned in ads when another generation is added to the pair. Hallmark Cards brings grandparents into the picture, and Johnson and Johnson Baby Powder has Dad, Mom, and baby, all fresh from the bath, encircled in arms and emblazoned with "Share the Feeling." A talc has been fused to familial love.

28   Friendship is yet another form of affiliation pursued by advertisers. Two women confide and drink Maxwell House coffee together; two men walk through the woods smoking Salem cigarettes. Miller Beer promises that afternoon "Miller Time" will be staffed with three or four good buddies. Drink Dr. Pepper, as Mickey Rooney is coaxed to do, and join in with all the other Peppers. Coca-Cola does not even need to portray the friendliness; it has reduced this appeal to "a Coke and a smile."

29   The warmth can be toned down and disguised, but it is the same affiliative need that is being fished for. The blonde has a direct gaze and her friends are firm businessmen in appearance, but with a glass of Old Bushmill you can sit down and fit right in. Or, for something more upbeat, sing along with the Pontiac choirboys.

30   As well as presenting positive images, advertisers can play to the need for affiliation in negative ways, by invoking the fear of rejection. If we don't use Scope, we'll have the "Ugh! Morning Breath" that causes the male and female models to avert their faces. Unless we apply Ultra Brite or Close-Up to our teeth, it's good-bye romance. Our family will be cursed with "House-a-tosis" if we don't take care. Without Dr. Scholl's antiperspirant foot spray, the bowling team will keel over. There go all the guests when the supply of Dorito's nacho cheese chips is exhausted. Still more rejection if our shirts have ring-around-the-collar, if our car needs to be Midasized. But make a few purchases, and we are back in the bosom of human contact.

31   As self-directed as Americans pretend to be, in the last analysis we remain social animals, hungering for the positive, endorsing feelings that only those around us can supply. Advertisers respond, urging us to "Reach out and touch someone," in the hopes our monthly [phone] bills will rise.

32   **3. Need to Nurture.**   Akin to affiliative needs is the need to take care of small, defenseless creatures—children and pets, largely. Reciprocity is of less consequence here, though; it is the giving that counts. Murray uses synonyms like "to feed, help, support, console, protect, comfort, nurse, heal." A strong need

---

* The original *Geritol* (a combination of the words "geriatric" and "tolerance") was an iron tonic and vitamin supplement marketed to people over forty between 1950 and 1979 with the slogan, "Do you have iron poor, tired blood?" Though today Geritol is the label on a group of health-related products, the name became famous—and, to some extent, funny—as a means of restoring energy and youthful vigor to middle-aged and elderly people.

it is, woven deep into our genetic fabric, for if it did not exist we could not successfully raise up our replacements. When advertisers put forth the image of something diminutive and furry, something that elicits the word "cute" or "precious," then they are trying to trigger this motive. We listen to the childish voice singing the Oscar Mayer weiner song, and our next hot-dog purchase is prescribed. Aren't those darling kittens something, and how did this Meow Mix get into our shopping cart?

33   This pitch is often directed at women, as Mother Nature's chief nurturers. "Make me some Kraft macaroni and cheese, please," says the elfin preschooler just in from the snowstorm, and mothers' hearts go out, and Kraft's sales go up. "We're cold, wet, and hungry," whine the husband and kids, and the little woman gets the Manwiches ready. A facsimile of this need can be hit without children or pets: the husband is ill and sleepless in the television commercial, and the wife grudgingly fetches the NyQuil.

34   But it is not women alone who can be touched by this appeal. The father nurses his son Eddie through adolescence while the John Deere lawn tractor survives the years. Another father counts pennies with his young son as the subject of New York Life Insurance comes up. And all over America are businessmen who don't know why they dial Qantas Airlines* when they have to take a trans-Pacific trip; the koala bear knows.

35   **4. Need for Guidance.**   The opposite of the need to nurture is the need to be nurtured: to be protected, shielded, guided. We may be loath to admit it, but the child lingers on inside every adult—and a good thing it does, or we would not be instructable in our advancing years. Who wants a nation of nothing but flinty personalities?

36   Parent-like figures can successfully call up this need. Robert Young† recommends Sanka coffee, and since we have experienced him for twenty-five years as television father and doctor, we take his word for it. Florence Henderson‡ as the expert mom knows a lot about the advantages of Wesson oil.

37   The parent-ness of the spokesperson need not be so salient; sometimes pure authoritativeness is better. When Orson Welles§ scowls and intones, "Paul Masson will sell no wine before its time," we may not know exactly what he means, but we still take direction from him. There is little maternal about

---

* *Qantas Airlines* is an Australian airline whose ads during the 1980s and 1990s featured a cuddly koala bear standing in for both the airline and the exotic delights of Australia.

† *Robert Young* (1907–1988) acted in movies (including Alfred Hitchcock's *Secret Agent* (1936) and *Crossfire* (1947) and TV (starring in the long-running 1950s series *Father Knows Best* and the 1960s series *Marcus Welby, M.D.*). A classic father figure, in his later career he appeared in ads for Sanka coffee.

‡ *Florence Henderson* (b. 1934), acted on Broadway and TV (primarily, in musical and comedy roles). Her most famous TV show was *The Brady Bunch* (1968–1974), where she played a mother of three daughters who married a man with three sons.

§ *Orson Welles* (1915–1985) was a major American filmmaker and actor whose films include *Citizen Kane* (1941—generally considered the greatest American film of all time), *The Magnificent Ambersons* (1942), *The Lady from Shanghai* (1947), *Macbeth* (1948), and *Touch of Evil* (1958). Toward the end of his life—to the dismay of many who revered him—the magisterial but financially depleted Welles became a spokesman for Paul Masson wines.

Brenda Vaccaro* when she speaks up for Tampax, but there is a certainty to her that many accept.

38   A celebrity is not a necessity in making a pitch to the need for guidance, since a fantasy figure can serve just as well. People accede to the Green Giant, or Betty Crocker, or Mr. Goodwrench.† Some advertisers can get by with no figure at all: "When E. F. Hutton‡ talks, people listen."

39   Often it is tradition or custom that advertisers point to and consumers take guidance from. Bits and pieces of American history are used to sell whiskeys like Old Crow, Southern Comfort, Jack Daniel's. We conform to traditional male/female roles and age-old social norms when we purchase Barclay cigarettes, which informs us "The pleasure is back."

40   The product itself, if it has been around for a long time, can constitute a tradition. All those old labels in the ad for Morton salt convince us that we should continue to buy it. Kool-Aid says "You loved it as a kid. You trust it as a mother," hoping to get yet more consumers to go along.

41   Even when the product has no history at all, our need to conform to tradition and to be guided are strong enough that they can be invoked through bogus nostalgia and older actors. Country-Time lemonade sells because consumers want to believe it has a past they can defer to.

42   So far the needs and the ways they can be invoked which have been looked at are largely warm and affiliative; they stand in contrast to the next set of needs, which are much more egoistic and assertive.

43   **5. Need to Aggress.**   The pressures of the real world create strong retaliatory feelings in every functioning human being. Since these impulses can come forth as bursts of anger and violence, their display is normally tabooed. Existing as harbored energy, aggressive drives present a large, tempting target for advertisers. It is not a target to be aimed at thoughtlessly, though, for few manufacturers want their products associated with destructive motives. There is always the danger that, as in the case of sex, if the appeal is too blatant, public opinion will turn against what is being sold.

44   Jack-in-the-Box sought to abruptly alter its marketing by going after older customers and forgetting the younger ones. Their television commercials had a seventy-ish lady command, "Waste him," and the Jack-in-the-Box clown exploded before our eyes. So did public reaction until the commercials were toned down. Print ads for Club cocktails carried the faces of octogenarians under the headline, "Hit me with a Club"; response was contrary enough to bring the campaign to a stop.

---

* *Brenda Vaccaro* (b. 1939) is a stage, TV, and film actress; her films include *Midnight Cowboy* (1969), *Airport '77* (1977), *Supergirl* (1984), and *The Mirror Has Two Faces* (1996).

† *Mr. Goodwrench* (and the slogan "Looking for Mr. Goodwrench"), personified as an engaging and highly capable auto mechanic, is a product of the General Motors marketing department.

‡ *E. F. Hutton* (named after its founder Edward Francis Hutton) was a major brokerage firm that was brought down in the 1980s by corporate misconduct. Its most famous TV ad portrayed, typically, two well-dressed businesspeople in conversation in a crowded dining room or club room. The first man says to the other, "My broker says. . . . " The second man listens politely and responds, "Well, my broker is E. F. Hutton, and *he* says . . . ," and everyone else in the room strains to overhear the conversation. The tag line: "When E. F. Hutton talks, people listen."

45   Better disguised aggressive appeals are less likely to backfire: Triumph cigarettes has models making a lewd gesture with their uplifted cigarettes, but the individuals are often laughing and usually in close company of others. When Exxon said, "There's a Tiger in your tank," the implausibility of it concealed the invocation of aggressive feelings.

46   Depicted arguments are a common way for advertisers to tap the audience's needs to aggress. Don Rickles* and Lynda Carter† trade gibes, and consumers take sides as the name of Seven-Up is stitched on minds. The Parkay [margarine] tub has a difference of opinion with the user; who can forget it, or who (or what) got the last word in?

47   **6. Need to Achieve.**   This is the drive that energizes people, causing them to strive in their lives and careers. According to Murray, the need for achievement is signalled by the desires "to accomplish something difficult. To overcome obstacles and attain a high standard. To excel one's self. To rival and surpass others." A prominent American trait, it is one that advertisers like to hook on to because it identifies their product with winning and success.

48   The Cutty Sark ad does not disclose that Ted Turner failed at his latest attempt at yachting's America Cup; here he is represented as a champion on the water as well as off in his television enterprises. If we drink this whiskey, we will be victorious alongside Turner. We can also succeed with O. J. Simpson‡ by renting Hertz cars, or with Reggie Jackson§ by bringing home some Panasonic equipment. Cathy Rigby‖ and Stayfree maxipads will put people out front.

49   Sports heroes are the most convenient means to snare consumers' needs to achieve, but they are not the only one. Role models can be established, ones which invite emulation, as with the profiles put forth by Dewar's scotch. Successful, tweedy individuals relate they have "graduated to the flavor of Myer's rum." Or the advertiser can establish a prize: two neighbors play one-on-one

---

* *Don Rickles* (b. 1926) is a night-club comedian (who has also appeared in TV and films) famous for his caustic wit and for humorously insulting people in the audience.

† *Lynda Carter* (b. 1951) is an actress, whose most famous role was the heroine of the 1976 TV series *Wonder Woman*.

‡ *O. J. Simpson* (b. 1957) is a famous football player–turned film actor (*The Naked Gun*) and defendant in a notorious murder trial in the 1990s. In a highly controversial decision, Simpson was acquitted of killing his ex-wife Nicole Simpson and her friend Ron Goldman; but in a subsequent civil trial he was found liable for the two deaths. Before the trial, Simpson was well known for his TV commercials for Hertz rental cars, featuring him sprinting through airports to get to the gate to demonstrate what you *wouldn't* have to do if you rented a car through Hertz.

§ *Reggie Jackson* (b. 1946), a member of the Baseball Hall of fame, played as an outfielder between 1967 and 1987. Known as "Mr. October" for his dramatic game-winning at-bats during post-season play, he had more strikeouts (2,597) than any other player. He was the first baseball player to have a candy bar (the "Reggie Bar") named after him, and toward the end of his career was a pitchman for Panasonic televisions.

‖ *Cathy Rigby*, an Olympian, was the first American gymnast to win a medal (in 1970) at the World Championships. She went on to star in a Broadway revival of the musical *Peter Pan* (surpassing Mary Martin for the greatest number of performances). Subsequently, she became a sportscaster for ABC Sports.

basketball for a Michelob beer in a television commercial, while in a print ad a bottle of Johnnie Walker Black Label has been gilded like a trophy.

50   Any product that advertises itself in superlatives—the best, the first, the finest—is trying to make contact with our needs to succeed. For many consumers, sales and bargains belong in this category of appeals, too; the person who manages to buy something at fifty percent off is seizing an opportunity and coming out ahead of others.

51   **7. Need to Dominate.**   This fundamental need is the craving to be powerful—perhaps omnipotent, as in the Xerox ad where Brother Dominic exhibits heavenly powers and creates miraculous copies. Most of us will settle for being just a regular potentate, though. We drink Budweiser because it is the King of Beers, and here comes the powerful Clydesdales to prove it. A taste of Wolfschmidt vodka and "The spirit of the Czar lives on."

52   The need to dominate and control one's environment is often thought of as being masculine, but as close students of human nature advertisers know, it is not so circumscribed. Women's aspirations for control are suggested in the campaign theme, "I like my men in English Leather, or nothing at all." The females in the Chanel No. 19 ads are "outspoken" and wrestle their men around.

53   Male and female, what we long for is clout; what we get in its place is Mastercard.

54   **8. Need for Prominence.**   Here comes the need to be admired and respected, to enjoy prestige and high social status. These times, it appears, are not so egalitarian after all. Many ads picture the trappings of high position; the Oldsmobile stands before a manorial doorway, the Volvo is parked beside a steeplechase. A book-lined study is the setting for Dewar's 12, and Lenox China is displayed in a dining room chock full of antiques.

55   Beefeater gin represents itself as "The Crown Jewel of England" and uses no illustrations of jewels or things British, for the words are sufficient indicators of distinction. Buy that gin and you will rise up the prestige hierarchy, or achieve the same effect on yourself with Seagram's 7 Crown, which ambiguously describes itself as "classy."

56   Being respected does not have to entail the usual accoutrements of wealth: "Do you know who I am?" the commercials ask, and we learn that the prominent person is not so prominent without his American Express card.

57   **9. Need for Attention.**   The previous need involved being *looked up to,* while this is the need to be *looked at.* The desire to exhibit ourselves in such a way as to make others look at us is a primitive, insuppressible instinct. The clothing and cosmetic industries exist just to serve this need, and this is the way they pitch their wares. Some of this effort is aimed at males, as the ads for Hathaway shirts and Jockey underclothes. But the greater bulk of such appeals is targeted singlemindedly at women.

58   To come back to Brooke Shields: this is where she fits into American marketing. If I buy Calvin Klein jeans, consumers infer, I'll be the object of fascination. The desire for exhibition has been most strikingly played to in a print campaign of many years' duration, that of Maidenform lingerie. The woman exposes herself, and sales surge. "Gentlemen prefer Hanes" the ads dissemble,

and women who want eyes upon them know what they should do. Peggy Fleming* flutters her legs for L'eggs, encouraging females who want to be the star in their own lives to purchase this product.

59   The same appeal works for cosmetics and lotions. For years, the little girl with the exposed backside sold gobs of Coppertone, but now the company has picked up the pace a little: as a female, you are supposed to "Flash 'em a Coppertone tan." Food can be sold the same way, especially to the diet-conscious; Angie Dickinson poses for California avocados and says, "Would this body lie to you?" Our eyes are too fixed on her for us to think to ask if she got that way by eating mounds of guacomole.

60   **10. Need for Autonomy.**   There are several ways to sell credit card services, as has been noted: Mastercard appeals to the need to dominate, and American Express to the need for prominence. When Visa claims, "You can have it the way you want it," yet another primary motive is being beckoned forward—the need to endorse the self. The focus here is upon the independence and integrity of the individual; this need is the antithesis of the need for guidance and is unlike any of the social needs. "If running with the herd isn't your style, try ours," says Rotan-Mosle, and many Americans feel they have finally found the right brokerage firm.

61   The photo is of a red-coated Mountie on his horse, posed on a snow-covered ledge; the copy reads, "Windsor—One Canadian stands alone." This epitome of the solitary and proud individual may work best with male customers, as may Winston's man in the red cap. But one-figure advertisements also strike the strong need for autonomy among American women. As Shelly Hack[†] strides for Charlie perfume, females respond to her obvious pride and flair; she is her own person. The Virginia Slims tale is of people who have come a long way from subservience to independence. Cachet perfume feels it does not need a solo figure to work this appeal, and uses three different faces in its ads; it insists, though, "It's different on every woman who wears it."

62   Like many psychological needs, this one can also be appealed to in a negative fashion, by invoking the loss of independence or self-regard. Guilt and regrets can be stimulated: "Gee, I could have had a V-8." Next time, get one and be good to yourself.

63   **11. Need to Escape.**   An appeal to the need for autonomy often co-occurs with one for the need to escape, since the desire to duck out of our social obligations, to seek rest or adventure, frequently takes the form of one-person flight. The dashing image of a pilot, in fact, is a standard way of quickening this need to get away from it all.

64   Freedom is the pitch here, the freedom that every individual yearns for whenever life becomes too oppressive. Many advertisers like appealing to the need for escape because the sensation of pleasure often accompanies escape, and what nicer emotional nimbus could there be for a product? "You deserve a break today," says McDonald's, and Stouffer's frozen foods chime in, "Set yourself free."

---

* *Peggy Fleming* (b. 1948), an Olympic figure skater, and Gold Medal winner (1968), later became a TV sports commentator and a representative for UNICEF (the United Nations Children's Emergency Fund).

† *Shelly Hack* (b. 1952) portrayed Tiffany Welles in the 1970s TV show "Charlie's Angels."

65   For decades men have imaginatively bonded themselves to the Marlboro cowboy who dwells untarnished and unencumbered in Marlboro Country some distance from modern life; smokers' aching needs for autonomy and escape are personified by that cowpoke. Many women can identify with the lady ambling through the woods behind the words, "Benson and Hedges and mornings and me."

66   But escape does not have to be solitary. Other Benson and Hedges ads, part of the same campaign, contain two strolling figures. In Salem cigarette advertisements, it can be several people who escape together into the mountaintops. A commercial for Levi's pictured a cloudbank above a city through which ran a whole chain of young people.

67   There are varieties of escape, some wistful like the Boeing "Someday" campaign of dream vacations, some kinetic like the play and parties in soft drink ads. But in every instance, the consumer exposed to the advertisement is invited to momentarily depart his everyday life for a more carefree experience, preferably with the product in hand.

68   **12. Need to Feel Safe.**   Nobody in their right mind wants to be intimidated, menaced, battered, poisoned. We naturally want to do whatever it takes to stave off threats to our well-being, and to our families'. It is the instinct of self-preservation that makes us responsive to the ad of the St. Bernard with the keg of Chivas Regal. We pay attention to the stern talk of Karl Malden* and the plight of the vacationing couples who have lost all their funds in the American Express travelers cheques commercials. We want the omnipresent stag from Hartford Insurance to watch over us too.

69   In the interest of keeping failure and calamity from our lives, we like to see the durability of products demonstrated. Can we ever forget that Timex takes a licking and keeps on ticking? When the American Tourister suitcase bounces all over the highway and the egg inside doesn't break, the need to feel safe has been adroitly plucked.

70   We take precautions to diminish future threats. We buy Volkswagen Rabbits for the extraordinary mileage, and MONY insurance policies to avoid the tragedies depicted in their black-and-white ads of widows and orphans.

71   We are careful about our health. We consume Mazola margarine because it has "corn goodness" backed by the natural food traditions of the American Indians. In the medicine cabinet is Alka-Seltzer, the "home remedy"; having it, we are snug in our little cottage.

72   We want to be safe and secure; buy these products, advertisers are saying, and you'll be safer than you are without them.

73   **13. Need for Aesthetic Sensations.**   There is an undeniable aesthetic component to virtually every ad run in the national media: the photography or filming

---

* *Karl Malden* (b. 1912) with his familiar craggy face and outsized nose, was a stage and later a film actor. He was the original Mitch in the Broadway production of Tennessee Williams's *Streetcar Named Desire*, a role he reprised in the 1951 movie version. His films include *On the Waterfront* (1954), *Cheyenne Autumn* (1964), and *Patton* (1970), and he starred in the 1972 TV series *Streets of San Francisco*. Malden became famous to a later generation of viewers as a pitchman for the American Express card, with the slogan, "Don't leave home without it!"

or drawing is near-perfect, the type style is well chosen, the layout could scarcely be improved upon. Advertisers know there is little chance of good communication occurring if an ad is not visually pleasing. Consumers may not be aware of the extent of their own sensitivity to artwork, but it is undeniably large.

74   Sometimes the aesthetic element is expanded and made into an ad's primary appeal. Charles Jordan shoes may or may not appear in the accompanying avant-grade photographs; Kohler plumbing fixtures catch attention through the high style of their desert settings. Beneath the slightly out of focus photograph, languid and sensuous in tone, General Electric feels called upon to explain, "This is an ad for the hair dryer."

75   This appeal is not limited to female consumers: J&B scotch says "It whispers" and shows a bucolic scene of lake and castle.

76   **14. Need to Satisfy Curiosity.**   It may seem odd to list a need for information among basic motives, but this need can be as primal and compelling as any of the others. Human beings are curious by nature, interested in the world around them, and intrigued by tidbits of knowledge and new developments. Trivia, percentages, observations counter to conventional wisdom—these items all help sell products. Any advertisement in a question-and-answer format is strumming this need.

77   A dog groomer has a question about long distance rates, and Bell Telephone has a chart with all the figures. An ad for Porsche 911 is replete with diagrams and schematics, numbers and arrows. Lo and behold, Anacin pills have 150 more milligrams than its competitors; should we wonder if this is better or worse for us?

78   **15. Physiological Needs.**   To the extent that sex is solely a biological need, we are now coming around full circle, back toward the start of the list. In this final category are clustered appeals to sleeping, eating, drinking. The art of photographing food and drink is so advanced, sometimes these temptations are wondrously caught in the camera's lens: the crab meat in the Red Lobster restaurant ads can start us salivating, the Quarterpounder can almost be smelled, the liquor in the glass glows invitingly. Imbibe, these ads scream.

Styles

79 Some common ingredients of advertisements were not singled out for separate mention in the list of fifteen because they are not appeals in and of themselves. They are stylistic features, influencing the way a basic appeal is presented. The use of humor is one, and the use of celebrities is another. A third is time imagery, past and future, which goes to several purposes.

80   For all of its employment in advertising, humor can be treacherous, because it can get out of hand and smother the product information. Supposedly, this is what Alka-Seltzer discovered with its comic commercials of the late sixties; "I can't believe I ate the whole thing," the sad-faced husband lamented, and the audience cackled so much it forgot the antacid. Or, did not take it seriously.

81   But used carefully, humor can punctuate some of the softer appeals and soften some of the harsher ones. When Emma says to the Fruit-of-the-Loom fruits, "Hi, cuties. Whatcha doing in my laundry basket?" we smile as our curios-

ity is assuaged along with hers. Bill Cosby gets consumers tickled about the children in his Jell-O commercials, and strokes the need to nurture.

82   An insurance company wants to invoke the need to feel safe, but does not want to leave readers with an unpleasant aftertaste; cartoonist Rowland Wilson creates an avalanche about to crush a gentleman who is saying to another, "My insurance company? New England Life, of course. Why?" The same tactic of humor undercutting threat is used in the cartoon commercials for Safeco when the Pink Panther wanders from one disaster to another. Often humor masks aggression: comedian Bob Hope in the outfit of a boxer promises to knock out the knock-knocks with Texaco; Rodney Dangerfield, who "can't get no respect," invites aggression as the comic relief in Miller Lite commercials.

83   Roughly fifteen percent of all advertisements incorporate a celebrity, almost always from the fields of entertainment or sports. The approach can also prove troublesome for advertisers, for celebrities are human beings too, and fully capable of the most remarkable behavior. If anything distasteful about them emerges, it is likely to reflect on the product. The advertisers making use of Anita Bryant* and Billy Jean King[†] suffered several anxious moments. An untimely death can also react poorly on a product. But advertisers are willing to take risks because celebrities can be such a good link between producers and consumers, performing the social role of introducer.

84   There are several psychological needs these middlemen can play upon. Let's take the product class of cameras and see how different celebrities can hit different needs. The need for guidance can be invoked by Michael Landon, who plays such a wonderful dad on "Little House on the Prairie"; when he says to buy Kodak equipment, many people listen. James Garner for Polaroid cameras is put in a similar authoritative role, so defined by a mocking spouse. The need to achieve is summoned up by Tracy Austin and other tennis stars for Canon AE-1; the advertiser first makes sure we see these athletes playing to win. When Cheryl Tiegs[‡] speaks up for Olympus cameras, it is the need for attention that is being targeted.

85   The past and future, being outside our grasp, are exploited by advertisers as locales for the projection of needs. History can offer up heroes (and call up the need to achieve) or traditions (need for guidance) as well as art objects

---

* *Anita Bryant* (b. 1940), a singer and entertainer (and as Miss Oklahoma, runner-up in the 1958 Miss America competition), became controversial during the late 1970s with her campaigns against homosexuality and AIDS. At the time, she was making ads and TV commercials for Florida orange juice, but was dropped by the sponsor after boycotts by activists.

† *Billy Jean King* (b. 1943) was a championship tennis player in the late 1960s and 1970s. In 1973 she was named *Sports Illustrated*'s "Sportsperson of the Year," the first woman to win this honor. She won four U.S. championships and six Wimbledon's single championships. In 1973, in a much publicized "Battle of the Sexes" match, King won all three sets against the 55-year-old Bobby Riggs (once ranked as the best tennis player in the world), who had claimed that "any half-decent male player could defeat even the best female players."

‡ *Cheryl Tiegs* (b. 1947) is a supermodel perhaps best known for her affiliation with the *Sports Illustrated Annual Swimsuit Issue*. A 1978 poster of Tiegs in a pink swimsuit became a cultural icon. Recently, she has entered the business world with an accessory and wig line for Revlon.

(need for aesthetic sensations). Nostalgia is a kindly version of personal history and is deployed by advertisers to rouse needs for affiliation and for guidance; the need to escape can come in here, too. The same need to escape is sometimes the point of futuristic appeals but picturing the avant-garde can also be a way to get at the need to achieve.

Analyzing Advertisements

86 When analyzing ads yourself for their emotional appeals, it takes a bit of practice to learn to ignore the product information (as well as one's own experience and feelings about the product). But that skill comes soon enough, as does the ability to quickly sort out from all the non-product aspects of an ad the chief element which is the most striking, the most likely to snag attention first and penetrate brains farthest. The key to the appeal, this element usually presents itself centrally and forwardly to the reader or viewer.

87   Another clue: the viewing angle which the audience has on the ad's subjects is informative. If the subjects are photographed or filmed from below and thus are looking down at you much as the Green Giant does, then the need to be guided is a good candidate for the ad's emotional appeal. If, on the other hand, the subjects are shot from above and appear deferential, as is often the case with children or female models, then other needs are being appealed to.

88   To figure out an ad's emotional appeal, it is wise to know (or have a good hunch about) who the targeted consumers are; this can often be inferred from the magazine or television show it appears in. This piece of information is a great help in determining the appeal and in deciding between two different interpretations. For example, if an ad features a partially undressed female, this would typically signal one appeal for readers of *Penthouse* (need for sex) and another for readers of *Cosmopolitan* (need for attention).

89   It would be convenient if every ad made just one appeal, were aimed at just one need. Unfortunately, things are often not that simple. A cigarette ad with a couple at the edge of a polo field is trying to hit both the need for affiliation and the need for prominence; depending on the attitude of the male, dominance could also be an ingredient in this. An ad for Chimere perfume incorporates two photos: in the top one the lady is being commanding at a business luncheon (need to dominate), but in the lower one she is being bussed (need for affiliation). Better ads, however, seem to avoid being too diffused; in the study of post-World War II advertising described earlier, appeals grew more focused as the decades passed. As a rule of thumb, about sixty percent have two conspicuous appeals; the last twenty percent have three or more. Rather than looking for the greatest number of appeals, decoding ads is most productive when the loudest one or two appeals are discerned, since those are the appeals with the best chance of grabbing people's attention.

90   Finally, analyzing ads does not have to be a solo activity and probably should not be. The greater number of people there are involved, the better chance there is of transcending individual biases and discerning the essential emotional lure built into an advertisement.

Do They or Don't They?

91 Do the emotional appeals made in advertisements add up to the sinister manipulation of consumers?

92   It is clear that these ads work. Attention is caught, communication occurs between producers and consumers, and sales result. It turns out to be difficult to detail the exact relationship between a specific ad and a specific purchase, or even between a campaign and subsequent sales figures, because advertising is only one of a host of influences upon consumption. Yet no one is fooled by this lack of perfect proof; everyone knows that advertising sells. If this were not the case, then tight-fisted American businesses would not spend a total of fifty billion dollars annually on these messages.

93   But before anyone despairs that advertisers have our number to the extent that they can marshal us at will and march us like automatons to the check-out counters, we should recall the resiliency and obduracy of the American consumer. Advertisers may have uncovered the softest spots in minds, but that does not mean they have found truly gaping apertures. There is no evidence that advertising can get people to do things contrary to their self-interests. Despite all the finesse of advertisements, and all the subtle emotional tugs, the public resists the vast majority of the petitions. According to the marketing division of the A. C. Nielsen Company, a whopping seventy-five percent of all new products die within a year in the marketplace, the victims of consumer disinterest which no amount of advertising could overcome. The appeals in advertising may be the most captivating there are to be had, but they are not enough to entrap the wily consumer.

94   The key to understanding the discrepancy between, on the one hand, the fact that advertising truly works, and, on the other, the fact that it hardly works, is to take into account the enormous numbers of people exposed to an ad. Modern-day communications permit an ad to be displayed to millions upon millions of individuals; if the smallest fraction of that audience can be moved to buy the product, then the ad has been successful. When one percent of the people exposed to a television advertising campaign reach for their wallets, that could be one million sales, which may be enough to keep the product in production and the advertisements coming.

95   In arriving at an evenhanded judgment about advertisements and their emotional appeals, it is good to keep in mind that many of the purchases which might be credited to these ads are experienced as genuinely gratifying to the consumer. We sincerely like the goods or service we have bought, and we may even like some of the emotional drapery that an ad suggests comes with it. It has sometimes been noted that the most avid students of advertisements are the people who have just bought the product; they want to steep themselves in the associated imagery. This may be the reason that Americans, when polled, are not negative about advertising and do not disclose any sense of being misused. The volume of advertising may be an irritant, but the product information as well as the imaginative material in ads are partial compensation.

96   A productive understanding is that advertising messages involve costs and benefits at both ends of the communications channel. For those few ads which

do make contact, the consumer surrenders a moment of time, has the lower brain curried, and receives notice of a product; the advertiser has given up money and has increased the chance of sales. In this sort of communications activity, neither party can be said to be the loser.

Review Questions

1. Why is advertising more common in highly industrialized countries like the United States than in countries with "quieter" economies?

2. How are advertisers' attempts to communicate their messages, and to break through customer resistance, keyed to their conception of human psychology, according to Fowles?

3. What are the "two orders of content" of most advertisements, according to Fowles?

4. How is Fowles indebted to Henry Murray?

5. Why must appeals to our need for sex and our need to aggress be handled carefully, according to Fowles?

6. How does the use of humor or the use of celebrities fit into Fowles's scheme?

Discussion and Writing Suggestions

1. In paragraph 4 Fowles cites a study indicating that only a fraction of the advertisements bombarding consumers every day are even noticed, much less acted upon. How do the results of this study square with your own experience? About how many of the commercial messages that you view and hear every day do you actually pay attention to? What kinds of messages draw your attention? What elicits positive reactions? Negative reactions? What kinds of appeals are most successful in making you want to actually purchase the advertised product?

2. What do you think of Fowles's analysis of "advertising's fifteen basic appeals"? Does this classification seem an accurate and useful way of accounting for how most advertising works upon us? Would you drop any of his categories, or perhaps incorporate one set into another set? Has Fowles neglected to consider other appeals that you believe to be equally important? If so, can you think of one or more advertisements that employ such appeals omitted by Fowles?

3. Categorize several of the ads in the ad portfolio later in the chapter (pages 663–707) using Fowles's schema. Explain how the headlines, body text, and graphics support your categorization choices.

4. Fowles asserts that "[c]ontrary to impressions, unambiguous sex is rare in [advertising] messages." This article first appeared in 1982. Does Fowles's statement still seem true today? To what extent do you believe that advertisers in recent years have increased their reliance on overt sexual appeals? Cite examples.

5. Fowles believes that "the need to associate with others [affiliation]. . . is probably the most prevalent appeal" in advertising. To what extent do you agree with this statement? Locate or cite print or broadcast ads that rely on the need for affiliation. How do the graphics and text of these ads work on what Fowles calls "the deep running drives" of our psyches or "the lower brain"?

6. Locate ads that rely upon the converse appeals to nurture and to guidance. Explain how the graphics and text in these ads work upon our human motivations. If possible further categorize the appeal: for example, are we provided with guidance from a parent-figure, some other authority figure, or from the force of tradition?

7. Conduct (perhaps with one or more teammates) your own analysis of a set of contemporary advertisements. Select a single issue of a particular magazine, such as *Time* or the *New Yorker*. Review all of the full-page ads, classifying each according to Fowles's categories. An ad may make more than one appeal (as Fowles points out in paragraph 89), but generally one will be primary. What do your findings show? Which appeals are the most frequent? The least frequent? Which are most effective? Why? You may find it interesting to compare the appeals of advertising in different magazines aimed at different audiences—for example, a general interest magazine, such as *Newsweek*, compared with a more specialized magazine, such as the *New Republic*, or *People*, or *Glamour*, or *Guns and Ammo*. To what extent do the types of appeals shift with the gender or interests of the target audience?

Making the Pitch in Print Advertising
Courtland L. Bovée, John V. Thill, George P. Dovel, Marian Burk Wood

No two ads are identical, but the vast majority employ a common set of textual features: headlines, body copy, and slogans. In the following selection, the authors discuss each of these features in turn, explaining their importance in attracting the potential customer's attention and selling the virtues of the product or service offered. You will find this discussion useful in making your own analyses of advertisements.

Courtland L. Bovée is the C. Allen Paul Distinguished Chair at Grossmont College. John V. Thill is CEO of Communication Specialists of America. George P. Dovel is president of the Dovel Group. Marian Burk Wood is president of Wood and Wood Advertising. This passage originally appeared in the authors' textbook Advertising Excellence, McGraw-Hill (1995).

Copywriters and Copywriting

1 Given the importance of copy, it comes as no surprise that copywriters are key players in the advertising process. In fact, many of the most notable leaders and voices in the industry began their careers as copywriters, including Jane Maas, David Ogilvy, Rosser Reeves, Leo Burnett, and William Bernbach. As a profession, copywriting is somewhat unusual because so many of its top practitioners have been in their jobs for years, even decades (rather than moving up the management ranks as is usual in many professions). Copywriters can either work for agencies or set themselves up as free-lancers, selling their services to agencies and advertisers. Because it presents endless opportunities to be creative, copywriting is one of those rare jobs that can be fresh and challenging year after year.

2 Although successful copywriters share a love of language with novelists, poets, and other writers, copywriting is first and foremost a business function, not an artistic endeavor. The challenge isn't to create works of literary merit, but to meet advertising objectives. This doesn't mean that copywriting isn't an art, however; it's simply art in pursuit of a business goal. Nor is it easy. Such noted literary writers as Stephen Vincent Benét, George Bernard Shaw, and Ernest Hemingway tried to write ad copy and found themselves unable to do it effectively. It's the combined requirements of language skills, business acumen, and an ability to create under the pressure of tight deadlines and format restrictions (such as the limited number of words you have to work with) that make copywriting so challenging—and so endlessly rewarding.

3 Copywriters have many styles and approaches to writing, but most agree on one thing: copywriting is hard work. It can involve a great deal of planning and coordinating with clients, legal staffers, account executives, researchers, and art directors. In addition, it usually entails hammering away at your copy until it's as good as it can be. David Ogilvy talked about doing 19 drafts of a single piece of copy and writing 37 headlines for a Sears ad in order to get 3 possibilities to show to the client. Actually, the chance to write and rewrite that many times is a luxury that most copywriters don't have; they often must produce copy on tight schedules with unforgiving deadlines (such as magazine publication deadlines).

4 The task of copywriting is most often associated with the headlines and copy you see in an ad, but copywriters actually develop a wide variety of other materials, from posters to catalogs to press releases, as well as the words you hear in radio and television commercials.

Print Copy

5 Copywriters are responsible for every word you see in print ads, whether the words are in a catchy headline or in the fine print at the bottom of the page. The three major categories of copy are headlines, body copy, and slogans.

Headlines

6 The *headline*, also called a *heading* or a *head*, constitutes the dominant line or lines of copy in an ad. Headlines are typically set in larger type and appear at the top of the ad, although there are no hard-and-fast rules on headline layout. *Subheads* are secondary headlines, often written to move the reader from the main headline to the body copy. Even if there is a pageful of body copy and only a few words in the headline, the headline is the most important piece of copy for two reasons: First, it serves as the "come-on" to get people to stop turning the page and check out your ad. Second, as much as 80 percent of your audience may not bother to read the body copy, so whatever message these nonreaders carry away from the ad will have to come from the headline.

7 Copywriters can choose from a variety of headline types, each of which performs a particular function.

- *News headlines.* News headlines present information that's new to the audience, such as announcing a new store location, a new product, or lower prices. This approach is common because potential customers are often looking for new solutions, lower prices, and other relevant changes in the marketplace. For example, a newspaper ad from the Silo home electronics chain announced a recent sale using a news headline: "Everything on Sale! 4 Days Only! 5–20% Off Everything!" Headlines like this are typical in local newspaper advertising.

- *Emotional headlines.* The emotional appeal described earlier in the chapter is represented by emotional headlines. The quotation headline "I'm sick of her ruining our lives" was used in an ad for the American Mental Health Fund to echo the frustration some parents feel when they can't understand their teenagers' behavior. Combined with a photo of a sad and withdrawn teenage girl, the headline grabs any parent who has felt such frustration, and the body copy goes on to explain that families shouldn't get mad at people with mental illnesses but should help them get treatment for their conditions.

- *Benefit headlines.* The benefit headline is a statement of the key customer benefit. An ad for Quicken personal finance software used the question-form headline: "How do you know exactly where your money goes and how much you have?" followed by "It's this simple" above a photograph of the product package. The customer benefit is keeping better track of your money, and Quicken is the solution offered.

- *Directive headlines.* Headlines that direct the reader to do something, or at least suggest the reader do something, can motivate consumer action. Such headlines can be a hard sell, such as "Come in now and save," or they can be something more subtle, such as "Just feel the color in these black and whites," the headline in an ad for Ensoniq keyboards.

- *Offbeat and curiosity headlines.* Humor, wordplay, and mystery can be effective ways to draw readers into an ad. An ad promoting vacation travel to Spain used the headline "Si in the dark," with a photo of a lively nighttime scene. The word *Si* is catchy because it first looks like an error, until the reader reads the body copy to learn that the ad is talking about Spain (*si* is Spanish for "yes").

- *Hornblowing headlines.* The hornblowing headline, called "Brag and Boast" heads by the Gallup & Robinson research organization, should be used with care. Customers have seen it all and heard it all, and "We're the greatest" headlines tend to sound arrogant and self-centered. This isn't to say that you can't stress superiority; you just need to do it in a way that takes the customer's needs into account, and the headline must be honest. The headline "Neuberger & Berman Guardian Fund" followed by the subhead "#1 Performing Growth and Income Fund" blows the company's own horn but also conveys an important product benefit. Since investors look for top-performing mutual funds, the information about being number one is relevant.
- *Slogan, label, or logo headlines.* Some headlines show a company's slogan, a product label, or the organization's logo. Powerful slogans like Hallmark's "When you care enough to send the very best" can make great headlines because they click with the reader's emotions. Label and logo headlines can build product and company awareness, but they must be used with care. If the label or logo doesn't make some emotional or logical connection with the reader, the ad probably won't succeed.

8 Headlines often have maximum impact when coupled with a well-chosen graphic element, rather than trying to carry the message with words alone. In fact, the careful combination of the two can increase the audience's involvement with the ad, especially if one of the two says something ironic or unexpected that has to be resolved by considering the other element. A magazine ad for Easter Seals had the headline "After all we did for Pete, he walked out on us." At first, you think the birth-defects organization is complaining. Then you see

---

CHECKLIST FOR PRODUCING EXCELLENT COPY

❑ A. Avoid clichés.
- Create fresh, original phrases that vividly convey your message.
- Remember that clever wordplay based on clichés can be quite effective.

❑ B. Watch out for borrowed interest.
- Make sure you don't use inappropriate copy or graphics since they can steal the show from your basic sales message.
- Be sure nothing draws attention from the message.

❑ C. Don't boast.
- Be sure the ad's purpose isn't merely to pat the advertiser on the back.
- Tout success when you must convince nonbuyers that lots of people just like them have purchased your product; this isn't the same as shouting "We're the best!"

a photo of Pete with new artificial legs, walking away from a medical facility. It's a powerful combination that makes the reader feel good about the things Easter Seals can do for people.

Body Copy

9 The second major category of copy is the *body copy,* which constitutes the words in the main body of the ad, apart from headlines, photo captions, and other blocks of text. The importance of body copy varies from ad to ad, and some ads have little or no body copy. Ads for easy-to-understand products, for instance, often rely on the headline and a visual such as a photograph to get their point across. In contrast, when the selling message needs a lot of supporting detail to be convincing, an ad can be packed full of body copy. Some advertisers have the impression that long body copy should be avoided, but that isn't always the case. The rule to apply here is to use the "right" number of words. You might not need many words in a perfume ad, but you might need a page or two to cover a complex industrial product.

10 As with headlines, body copy can be built around several different formats. *Straight-line copy* is copy that takes off from the headline and develops the selling points for the product. *Narrative copy,* in contrast, tells a story as it persuades; the same selling points may be covered, but in a different context. *Dialog/monolog copy* lets one or two characters in the ad do the selling through what they are saying. *Picture-and-caption copy* relies on photographs or illustrations to tell the story, with support from their accompanying captions.

❏ D. Make it personal, informal, and relevant.
- Connect with the audience in a way that is personal and comfortable. Pompous, stiff, and overly "businesslike" tends to turn people away.
- Avoid copy that sounds like it belongs in an ad, with too many overblown adjectives and unsupported claims of superiority.

❏ E. Keep it simple, specific, and concise.
- Make your case quickly and stick to the point. This will help you get past all the barriers and filters that people put up to help them select which things they'll pay attention to and which they'll ignore.
- Avoid copy that's confusing, meandering, too long, or too detailed.

❏ F. Give the audience a reason to read, listen, or watch.
- Offer a solution to your audience's problems.
- Entertain your audience.
- Consider any means possible to get your audience to pay attention long enough to get your sales message across.

Slogans

11 The third major category of copy includes *slogans,* or *tag lines,* memorable say-
ings that convey a selling message. Over the years, Coca-Cola has used such slogans as "Coke is it," "It's the real thing," and "Always Coca-Cola." Slogans are
sometimes used as headlines, but not always. Their importance lies in the fact they
often become the most memorable result of an advertising campaign. You've
probably got a few slogans stuck in your head. Ever heard of "Quality is job number
1," "Don't leave home without it," or "Melts in your mouth, not in your hand"?

12   The Korean automaker Hyundai recently switched back to the slogan "Cars that
make sense," which is a great way of expressing its desired positioning as a lower-
cost but still reliable alternative to Japanese and U.S. cars. For several years, the
company had used "Hyundai. Yes, Hyundai," but "Cars that make sense" has
proved to be a much more effective way to define the value it offers consumers.

Review Questions

1. What are the particular challenges of copywriting , as opposed to
   other types of writing?

2. How do the authors classify the main types of ad headlines?

3. What are the main types of body copy styles, according to the
   authors?

Discussion and Writing Suggestions

1. Apply the authors' criteria for effective headlines to three or four of
   the ads in the portfolio (pages 663–707)—or to three or four ads of
   your own choosing. To what extent do these headlines succeed in
   attracting attention, engaging the audience, and fulfilling the other
   requirements of effective headlines?

2. Imagine that you are a copywriter who has been assigned the
   account for a particular product (your choice). Develop three possible headlines for an advertisement for this product. Incorporate as
   many as possible of the criteria for effective headlines discussed by
   the authors (paragraphs 6–8).

3. Classify the *types* of headlines in a given product category in the ad
   portfolio (pages 663–707). Or classify the types of headlines in full-
   page ads in a single current magazine. Which type of headline
   appears to be the most common? Which type appears to be the
   most effective in gaining your attention and making you want to
   read the body copy?

4. Classify the *types* of body copy styles in a given product category in
   the ad portfolio. Or classify the types of body copy styles in full-
   page ads in a single current magazine. How effective is the copy in

selling the virtues of the product or the institution or organization behind the product?

5. Assess the effectiveness of a given ad either in the ad portfolio or in a recent magazine or newspaper. Apply the criteria discussed by the authors in the box labeled "Checklist for Producing Excellent Copy." For example, to what extent is the copy fresh and original? To what extent does the copy make the message "personal, informal, and relevant" to the target audience? To what extent is the message "simple, specific, and concise"?

6. Write your own ad for a product that you like and use frequently. In composing the ad, apply the principles of effective headlines, subheads, body copy, and slogans discussed by the authors. Apply also the principles of "Checklist for Producing Excellent Copy." You will also need to think of (though not necessarily create) an effective graphic for the ad.

Elements of Effective Layout
Dorothy Cohen

In the previous selection, Courtland L. Bovée et al. discusses the chief textual features of print advertising. In the following passage Dorothy Cohen reviews the equally important (and perhaps more important, in terms of seizing the reader's attention) graphic components. Chief among these are balance, proportion, movement, unity, clarity and simplicity, and emphasis. After reading Cohen, you should be well equipped to work on the analysis assignments in this chapter and, more generally, to assess the graphic quality of the ads you regularly encounter in magazines and newspapers.

This selection originally appeared in Dorothy Cohen's textbook Advertising *(1988).*

1   Fundamentally a good layout should attract attention and interest and should provide some control over the manner in which the advertisement is read. The message to be communicated may be sincere, relevant, and important to the consumer, but because of the competitive "noise" in the communication channel, the opportunity to be heard may depend on the effectiveness of the layout. In addition to attracting attention, the most important requisites for an effective layout are balance, proportion, movement, unity, clarity and simplicity, and emphasis.

Balance

2   Balance is a fundamental law in nature and its application to layout design formulates one of the basic principles of this process. Balance is a matter of weight distribution; in layout it is keyed to the *optical center* of an advertisement, the point which the reader's eye designates as the center of an area. In an advertisement a vertical line which divides the area into right and left

halves contains the center; however the optical center is between one-tenth and one-third the distance above the mathematical horizontal center line. . . .

3   In order to provide good artistic composition, the elements in the layout must be in equilibrium. Equilibrium can be achieved through balance, and this process may be likened to the balancing of a seesaw. The optical center of the advertisement serves as the fulcrum or balancing point, and the elements may be balanced on both sides of this fulcrum through considerations of their size and tonal quality.

4   The simplest way to ensure *formal balance* between the elements to the right and left of the vertical line is to have all masses in the left duplicated on the right in size, weight, and distance from the center. . . . Formal balance imparts feelings of dignity, solidity, refinement, and reserve. It has been used for institutional advertising and suggests conservatism on the part of the advertiser. Its major deficiency is that it may present a static and somewhat unexciting appearance; however, formal balance presents material in an easy-to-follow order and works well for many ads.

5   To understand *informal balance,* think of children of unequal weight balanced on a seesaw; to ensure equilibrium it is necessary to place the smaller child far from the center and the larger child closer to the fulcrum. In informal balance the elements are balanced, but not evenly, because of different sizes and color contrast. This type of a symmetric balance requires care so that the various elements do not create a lopsided or top-heavy appearance. A knowledge or a sense of the composition can help create the feeling of symmetry in what is essentially asymmetric balance.

6   Informal balance presents a fresh, untraditional approach. It creates excitement, a sense of originality, forcefulness, and, to some extent, the element of surprise. Whereas formal balance may depend on the high interest value of the illustration to attract the reader, informal balance may attract attention through the design of the layout. . . .

Proportion

7   Proportion helps develop order and creates a pleasing impression. It is related to balance but is concerned primarily with the division of the space and the emphasis to be accorded each element. Proportion, to the advertising designer, is the relationship between the size of one element in the ad to another, the amount of space between elements, as well as the width of the total ad to its depth. Proportion also involves the tone of the ad: the amount of light area in relation to dark area and the amount of color and noncolor.

8   As a general rule unequal dimensions and distances make the most lively design in advertising. The designer also places the elements on the page so that each element is given space and position in proportion to its importance in the total advertisement and does not look like it stands alone.

Movement

9   If an advertisement is to appear dynamic rather than static, it must contain some movement. *Movement* (also called *sequence*) provides the directional flow for

the advertisement, gives it its follow-through, and provides coherence. It guides the reader's eye from one element to another and makes sure he or she does not miss anything.

10   Motion in layout is generally from left to right and from top to bottom—the direction established through the reading habits of speakers of Western language. The directional impetus should not disturb the natural visual flow but should favor the elements to be stressed, while care should be taken not to direct the reader's eye out of the advertisement. This can be done by the following:

- *Gaze motion* directs the reader's attention by directing the looks of the people or animals in an ad. If a subject is gazing at a unit in the layout, the natural tendency is for the reader to follow the direction of that gaze; if someone is looking directly out of the advertisement, the reader may stop to see who's staring.
- *Structural motion* incorporates the lines of direction and patterns of movement by mechanical means. An obvious way is to use an arrow or a pointed finger. . . .

Unity

11 Another important design principle is the unification of the layout. Although an advertisement is made up of many elements, all of these should be welded into a compact composition. Unity is achieved when the elements tie into one another by using the same basic shapes, sizes, textures, colors, and mood. In addition, the type should have the same character as the art.

12   A *border* surrounding an ad provides a method of achieving unity. Sets of borders may occur within an ad, and, when they are similar in thickness and tone, they provide a sense of unity.

13   Effective use of white space can help to establish unity. . . . *White space* is defined as that part of the advertising space which is not occupied by any other elements; in this definition, white space is not always white in color. White space may be used to feature an important element by setting it off, or to imply luxury and prestige by preventing a crowded appearance. It may be used to direct and control the reader's attention by tying elements together. If white space is used incorrectly, it may cause separation of the elements and create difficulty in viewing the advertisement as a whole.

Clarity and Simplicity

14 The good art director does not permit a layout to become too complicated or tricky. An advertisement should retain its clarity and be easy to read and easy to understand. The reader tends to see the total image of an advertisement; thus it should not appear fussy, contrived, or confusing. Color contrasts, including tones of gray, should be strong enough to be easily deciphered, and the various units should be clear and easy to understand. Type size and design should be selected for ease of reading, and lines of type should be a comfortable reading length. Too many units in an advertisement are distracting; therefore, any elements that can be eliminated without destroying the message should be. One way in which clarity can be achieved is by combining the logo, trademark, tag line, and company name into one compact group.

Emphasis

15 Although varying degrees of emphasis may be given to different elements, one unit should dominate. It is the designer's responsibility to determine how much emphasis is necessary, as well as how it is to be achieved. The important element may be placed in the optical center or removed from the clutter of other elements. Emphasis may also be achieved by contrasts in size, shape, and color, or the use of white space.

Review Questions

1. How does balance in an ad differ from proportion?
2. What two possible types of movement can be incorporated into an advertisement?
3. Cite some of the chief ways of achieving unity in an ad.

Discussion and Writing Suggestions

1. Select an advertisement either in the ad portfolio (pages 663–707) or in a current magazine or newspaper. Analyze the ad in terms of Cohen's discussion of effective layout. How well does the ad employ *balance, proportion, movement, unity, clarity and simplicity,* and *emphasis* to sell the product or communicate the main idea? Which of these elements are most important in accomplishing the task?

2. Cohen writes that "balance is a fundamental law in nature." What do you think she means by this? What natural examples of balance occur to you?

3. Select two ads, one demonstrating what Cohen calls "formal balance," one demonstrating "informal balance." Cohen writes that formal balance "imparts feelings of dignity, solidity, refinement, and reserve" and that it suggests "conservatism on the part of the advertiser." Informal balance, on the other hand, "presents a fresh, untraditional approach" and "creates a sense of originality, forcefulness, and, to some extent, the element of surprise." To what degree do the ads you have selected demonstrate the truth of Cohen's assertions?

4. Find an ad demonstrating unusual use of proportion among its graphic elements. How does the distinctive proportionality help communicate the advertiser's message?

5. Find an ad demonstrating striking use of movement, clarity and simplicity, or emphasis. How does the element you have chosen work to help communicate the ad's message?

6. Find an ad that violates one or more of the graphic principles that Cohen discusses. To what extent do such violations hurt (or even destroy) the ad's effectiveness? How would you fix the problem?

The Indictments Against Advertising
Courtland L. Bovée and William F. Arens

If we were completely rational beings, then advertisements would simply inform us that a particular product or service was available and explain its benefits—if not also its drawbacks. (Some ads still do this: If we wanted to sell a CD, for example, we might just post a "For Sale" notice on a bulletin board, giving the name of the CD and its price.) Since—for better or for worse—we're not completely rational beings, but subject to the sway of powerful emotional appeals (as Jib Fowles explains, in the first selection of this chapter), and since modern advertising is a multibillion-dollar enterprise involving market research, customer psychology, skillful copywriting, and sophisticated graphic arts, the typical magazine or broadcast ad aims to do much more than simply inform us of the availability of consumer products. In addition, the pervasiveness of contemporary advertising means that almost everywhere we turn, we are bombarded with appeals to buy—mostly under the guise of persuading us that buying will somehow improve our lives. The ubiquity and apparent power of advertising (it does work, to some degree, or why would companies continue to advertise?) have inevitably caused a backlash, not only among the general public, but also among social critics, who see advertising—the original spam—as more than just an annoyance, but also as a pernicious influence in contemporary society.

The following selection sums up the chief arguments against advertising and also attempts to respond to these arguments. As you read this passage, think of current ads, either print or broadcast, that may illustrate the points made by the authors.

Courtland L. Bovée is the author or coauthor of several textbooks on business and advertising, including Techniques of Writing Business Letters, Memos, and Reports *(1974),* Advertising Excellence *(1995), and* Contemporary Advertising *(1986), where the following selection first appeared. William F. Arens is coauthor of* Contemporary Advertising.

Social Criticism of Advertising

1   Advertising is the most visible activity of business. What a company may have been doing privately for many years suddenly becomes public the moment it starts to advertise. By publicly inviting people to try their products, companies invite public criticism and attack if their products do not live up to the promised benefits. Defenders of advertising say it is therefore safer to buy advertised than unadvertised products. By putting their names behind the goods, the makers of advertised articles stick their necks out and will try harder to fulfill their promises.

2   Because advertising is so public, it is widely criticized, not only for the role it plays in selling products but also for the way it influences our society. As a selling tool, advertising is attacked for its excesses. Some critics charge that, at its worst, advertising is downright untruthful and, at best, it presents only positive information about products. Others charge that advertising manipulates people psychologically to buy things they can't afford by promising greater sex appeal, improved social status, or other unrealistic expectations. Still others attack advertising for being offensive or in bad taste. Many argue that there is just too much

advertising and that this overwhelming quantity is one reason it has such an impact on our society.

3   As a social influence, advertising is often charged, on the one hand, with contributing to crime and violence and, on the other hand, with making people conform. Critics attack advertising for perpetuating stereotypes of people, for making people want things they don't need and can't afford, and for creating insecurity in order to sell goods. Advertising, they say, debases our language, takes unfair advantage of our children, makes us too materialistic, and encourages wastefulness. Finally, by influencing the media, critics charge, advertising interferes with freedom of the press. . . .

4   Let's examine some of the more common criticisms as they are usually expressed. . . .

Advertising Makes Us Too Materialistic

5 Critics claim that advertising adversely affects our value system because it suggests that the means to a happier life is the acquisition of more things instead of spiritual or intellectual enlightenment. Advertising, they say, encourages people to buy more automobiles, more clothing, and more appliances than they need, all with the promise of greater status, greater social acceptance, and greater sex appeal. For example, they point to the fact that millions of Americans own 20 or more pairs of shoes, several TV sets, and often more than one vehicle.

6   There is no doubt that we are the most materialistic society in the world. So the basic question concerning materialism is this: Is there a relationship between happiness and materialism? Does the acquisition of more goods and services contribute to contentment and the joy of living.

7   Philosophers and social scientists have debated the relationship between affluence and happiness for centuries, but they have reached no concrete conclusions. Defenders of advertising maintain that material comfort is necessary before a person can devote time to higher cultural and spiritual values. Therefore, they say, the stress on material things doesn't rule out spiritual and cultural values. In fact, they believe it may create a greater opportunity for it since the satisfaction of a person's higher desires is more likely when that person's lower, more basic desires have been met. They also like to point out that, through its support of the media, advertising has brought literature, opera, drama, and symphonies to millions who would never have seen them otherwise.

8   In reality, the first responsibility of advertising is to aid its sponsor by informing, persuading, and reminding the sponsor's customers and prospects. Most sponsors are frankly more interested in selling goods and making profits than in bringing about cultural changes or improvements. Sponsors find that advertising is most effective when it accurately reflects the society and the market to which it is targeted. Therefore, when culturally uplifting advertising copy sells goods, advertisers will use it. And some of them do. Likewise, if people want a more cultural approach to advertisements and respond to them, advertisers will probably be delighted to comply because it will be in their own best interest. Ultimately, the bottom line will prevail. The profit and loss in dollars and cents determine the advertising approach.

Advertising Manipulates People Psychologically to Buy Things They Don't Need

9 Advertising is often criticized for its power to make people do irrational things. The following are some suggestions based on variations of this criticism:

1. Advertising should be informative but not persuasive.
2. Advertising should report only factual, functional information.
3. Advertising shouldn't play on people's desires, emotions, fears, or anxieties.
4. Advertising should deal only with people's functional needs for products not their psychological needs for status, appeal, security, sexual attractiveness, or health.

10 Underlying all these criticisms is (1) a belief in the power of advertising to control customers against their will, or (2) an attitude that consumers simply have no freedom of choice when confronted with advertising persuasion.

11 Apologists for advertising point out that persuasion is a fact of life and so is our need to confront persuasion on a daily basis. We see it in every avenue of our existence, not just in advertising. Teachers try to persuade students to study. Students try to persuade teachers to give them better grades. Girlfriends persuade boyfriends; preachers persuade congregations; charities persuade donors; borrowers persuade lenders; stockbrokers persuade investors; kids persuade parents; and advertising persuades people. In short, we are all busy persuading or being persuaded in one way or another.

12 Second, they point out that when we persuade, we usually use a variety of tactics depending on the subject matter and the response of the listener. Sometimes the simple facts of our case are overwhelmingly persuasive. Other times we appeal to some other need or motive of our listener because the facts alone aren't persuasive enough. Should we use emotional appeals in persuasion? If not, say the defenders, then we are all guilty because we all do it.

13 Frankly, all of us have needs and desires beyond the basics of food, clothing, and shelter. One benefit of a free society is that we can choose to what degree we wish to indulge our desires, needs, and fantasies. Some people prefer a simple life without mortgage payments, fancy cars, and trips abroad. Others enjoy the material pleasures of a modern, technological society. There are advertising sponsors at both ends of that spectrum. Food companies offer natural products as well as convenience packaged goods. Shoe companies offer simple sandals as well as formal footwear.

14 Perhaps, if we recognize that advertising is persuasive by definition, then we can become better consumers and critics of advertising. All companies attempt to persuade consumers to try their products. Not all are successful, though. In spite of the fact that advertising techniques have become far more effective and efficient in recent years, there is still no black magic. The final reality is that many more products fail than succeed in the marketplace. . . .

Advertising Is Offensive or in Bad Taste

15 Many people find advertising offensive to their religious convictions, morality, or political perspective. Others find the use of advertising techniques that

emphasize sex, violence, or body functions to be in bad taste. Certainly this is one of the most controversial issues.

16   Taste is highly subjective. Apologists point out that what is good taste to some is bad taste to others. And tastes change. What is considered offensive today may not be offensive in the future. People were outraged when the first advertisement for underarm deodorant was published in the *Ladies Home Journal,* but today no one questions such an advertisement. Some people find liquor ads offensive, while others find them simply informative. There has been some experimentation with advertising birth control products on television. Some feel this advertising supplies badly needed consumer information. Others feel that birth control is not a proper subject for a mass medium.

17   In the not-so-distant past, nudity was rarely seen in print advertisements. Today it is often featured in ads for grooming and personal hygiene products. Where nudity is relevant to the product being advertised, people are less likely to regard it as obscene or offensive.

18   Often the products themselves are not offensive, but the way they are advertised may be open to criticism. Advertising frequently emphasizes the sensational aspects of a product, particularly a book or motion picture. Shock value may be used to gain attention, particularly by inexperienced copywriters. However, this sensationalism is often a reflection of the tastes and interests of the American people. If the advertisements don't attract the people they seek, the advertising campaign will falter and die. The audience, therefore, has the ultimate veto authority by ignoring offensive material.

19   It is unrealistic to assume that advertising, particularly mass advertising, will ever be free of this criticism. But reputable advertisers try to be aware of what the public considers to be tasteful advertising.

Advertising Perpetuates Stereotypes

20 Groups such as the National Organization for Women (NOW) protest that many of today's advertisements do not acknowledge the changing role of women in our society. One feminist says:

> Advertising is an insidious propaganda machine for a male supremacist society. It spews out images of women as sex mates, housekeepers, mothers, and menial workers—images that perhaps reflect the true status of women in society, but which also make it increasingly difficult for women to break out of the sexist stereotypes that imprison them.

21   Consumer charges of ethnic and racial bias and of animal abuse in advertising were made to federal and business regulatory agencies for some time. The targets of these complaints included ads that showed a Japanese gardener at work and floor wax commercials that featured a black scrubwoman. Charges of animal abuse were made against beer commercials in which a dray horse was seen hauling a huge, old-fashioned brewery wagon. While none of these advertisements were illegal, all were objects of consumer efforts to halt their use, even to penalizing the advertisers.

22   Unfortunately, despite the efforts of many, there is still too much bias and sexism in advertising. The proper portrayal of women and minorities is still open to debate, however, and changes with the times.

23   Today it is especially important to portray women realistically, since they make so many important purchasing decisions. An area of vast change is the representation of minorities. Blacks, Hispanics, Italians, Chinese, American Indians, and others are now shown in favorable environments as a result of their upward mobility as well as organized pressure and threats of boycotts. New advertising agencies staffed with minority personnel are succeeding in reaching minority markets. Likewise, advertisers are taking special care to create advertisements that will neither offend nor alienate minority groups.

Advertising Is Deceptive

24 Perhaps the greatest attack on advertising has been and continues to be against the deceptive practices of some advertisers. This area has also received the greatest regulatory scrutiny . . .

25   Critics define deceptiveness not only as false and misleading statements but also as any false impression conveyed, whether intentional or unintentional. Advertising deception can take a number of forms, and many of these are highly controversial with no hard and fast rules. . . .

26   Advertising must have the confidence of consumers if it is to be effective. Continued deception is self-defeating because, in time, it causes consumers to turn against a product.

27   Advertising puts the advertiser on record for all who care to look. Because of greater scrutiny by consumers and the government, it is in the advertisers' own interest to avoid trouble by being honest. The company that wants to stay in business over the long term knows it can do so only with a reputation for honest dealing.

Defense of Advertising

28 Advertising professionals admit that advertising has often been used irresponsibly over the years. But they like to use the analogy of a high-powered automobile: if a drunk is at the wheel, there's going to be a lot of damage. The problem, though, is the drunk at the wheel, not the car.

29   In other words, they admit that advertising has been and sometimes still is misused. But they believe the abuse that has been heaped on advertising as a marketing tool and as a social influencer is no longer justified and is so excessive as to make all advertising appear bad. In support, they point out that of all the advertising reviewed by the Federal Trade Commission in a typical year, 97 percent is found to be satisfactory. Moreover, they say, the very critics who attack advertising's excesses use advertising techniques themselves to sell their books and further their points of view.

30   Frankly, the sins of the past still haunt advertising today. What was once an unchecked, free-swinging business activity is now a closely scrutinized and heavily regulated profession. The excesses with which advertising has been

rightfully or wrongfully charged have created layer upon layer of laws, regulations, and regulatory bodies. These are used by consumer groups, government,
special-interest groups, and even other advertisers to review, check, control, and
change advertising.

Review Questions

1. How do defenders of advertising respond to the charge that advertising makes us too materialistic?

2. According to the authors, what are the main rebuttals to the charge
   that advertising manipulates us to buy things that we don't need?

3. What evidence is cited by those who charge that advertising perpetuates stereotypes?

4. What do the authors see as effective checks on deception in
   advertising?

Discussion and Writing Suggestions

1. Find an ad, either in the ad portfolio (pages 663–707), or in a newspaper or magazine, that might be charged with debasing our language. What specifically in this ad might provoke such a charge? To
   what extent could you defend the ad from the charge in the terms
   described by Bovée and Arens?

2. That advertising makes us more materialistic than we otherwise
   would be is one of the most common charges leveled against advertising. Find ads, either in the ad portfolio or in magazines or newspapers, that would lend credence to such a charge, and explain your
   conclusions with specific references to the text and graphics of the ad.

3. In general, to what extent do you think it is a good thing to encourage materialism—that is, to encourage people not only to buy products and services but also to encourage them to *want* to buy? What
   specific evidence do you find in contemporary American society of
   the benefits and problems of materialism?

4. Recall an advertising campaign—either print or broadcast—that
   seems to support the charge that "advertising manipulates people
   psychologically to buy things they don't need." What particular
   features of this advertising campaign are manipulative? To what
   extent do you believe that the rebuttals to such charges by the
   "[a]pologists" for the advertisers (paragraph 16) effectively refute
   this charge? You might consider other social forces, besides advertising, that manipulate people to buy what they don't need.

5. Cite one or more examples of advertisements or advertising campaigns that you believe are in bad taste. What particular features of these ads are distasteful, and why? What evidence do you see that the distasteful campaign has either failed or been successful?

6. Select an ad, either in the ad portfolio or in a newspaper or magazine, that you believe perpetuates racial, gender, or other stereotypes. What features of the text and graphics in the ad encourage and perpetuate such stereotypes? How do you believe that such stereotyping might be considered, and perhaps even intended, by the sponsor of the ad as being necessary or desirable to help sell the product or service?

7. To what extent does the ad portfolio provide evidence of changing attitudes toward racial, gender, sexual, or other stereotyping from 1945 to the present? Discuss particular ads in developing your response.

8. Find an ad—either in the ad portfolio or in a newspaper or magazine, or on TV—that you believe to be deceptive, and explain the nature of the deception. Refer to particular features of the ad's language and/or graphics.

A Portfolio of Advertisements: 1945–2003

The following portfolio offers for your consideration and analysis a selection of forty-two full-page advertisements that appeared in American and British magazines between 1945 (shortly after the end of World War II) and 2003. In terms of products represented, the ads fall into several categories—cigarettes, alcohol (beer and liquor), automobiles, food and drink, household cleaners, lotions, and perfumes. The portfolio also includes a few miscellaneous ads for such diverse products as men's hats, telephones, and airlines. These ads originally appeared in such magazines as Time, Newsweek, U.S. News and World Report, Sports Illustrated, Ladies Home Journal, Ebony, *and* Ms. *A number of the ads were researched in the Advertising Archive, an online (and subscription) collection maintained by The Picture Desk <www.picture-desk.com>.*

The advertisements in this portfolio are not representative of all ads that appeared during the last sixty years. We made our selection largely on the basis of how interesting, striking, provocative, and unusual these particular ads appeared to us. Admittedly, the selection process was biased. That said, the ads in this portfolio offer rich possibilities for analysis. With practice, and by applying principles for analysis that you will find in the earlier selections in this chapter, you will be able to "read" into these ads numerous messages about cultural attitudes toward gender relations, romance, smoking, and automobiles. The ads will prompt you to consider why we buy products that we may not need or why we prefer one product over another when the two products are essentially identical. Each advertisement is a window into the culture. Through careful analysis, you will gain insights not only into the era in which the ads were produced but also into shifting cultural attitudes over the last sixty years.

Note: As some of the body text in the following ads (reduced in size from their originals) may not be easily legible, we have reprinted potentially problematic passages at the end of the chapter, following the Research Activities (pages 721–32). References at the bottom of the ads indicate where more readable text may be found.

Following the portfolio, we provide two or three specific questions for each ad (pages 708–17), questions designed to stimulate your thinking about the particular ways that the graphics and text are intended to work. As you review the ads, however, you may want to think about the more general questions about advertisements raised by the readings in this chapter:

1. *What appears to be the target audience for the ad? If this ad was produced more than two decades ago, does its same target audience exist today? If so, how would this audience likely react today to the ad?*
2. *What is the primary appeal made by the ad, in terms of Fowles's categories? What, if any, are the secondary appeals?*
3. *What assumptions do the ad's sponsors make about such matters as (1) commonly accepted roles of women and men; (2) the relationship between the sexes; (3) the priorities of men and women?*
4. *What is the chief attention-getting device in the ad?*
5. *How does the headline and body text communicate the ad's essential appeals?*
6. *How do the ad's graphics communicate the ad's essential appeals?*
7. *How do the expressions, clothing, and postures of the models, as well as the physical objects in the illustration, help communicate the ad's message?*
8. *How do the graphic qualities of balance, proportion, movement, unity, clarity and simplicity, and emphasis help communicate the ad's message?*

Camels, 1947: For legible body text of this ad, see pp. 721–22.

The Christmas Gift
for Important Men

• Websters are being specially boxed and Christmas wrapped this year. Boxes of 25, as low as $3.75. Give Websters by the box. A luxurious gift to yourself and to men who are used to the best.

• There are five different sizes of Websters. Each is made of 100% long Havana, bound in top-quality Broadleaf and wrapped in finest Connecticut Shadegrown. Boxes of 25 and 50 in all sizes. Wherever fine cigars are smoked.

WEBSTER CIGARS
EXECUTIVE AMERICA'S TOP CIGAR

| Golden Wedding, 15c | Chico, 15c | Queens, 18c | Fancy Tales, 25c | Directors, 35c |
| Box of 25—$3.75 | Box of 25—$3.75 | Box of 25—$4.50 | Box of 25—$6.25 | Box of 25—$8.75 |

A PRODUCT OF THE WEBSTER TOBACCO COMPANY, INC., NEW YORK

Webster Cigars, 1945: For legible body text of this ad, see p. 722.

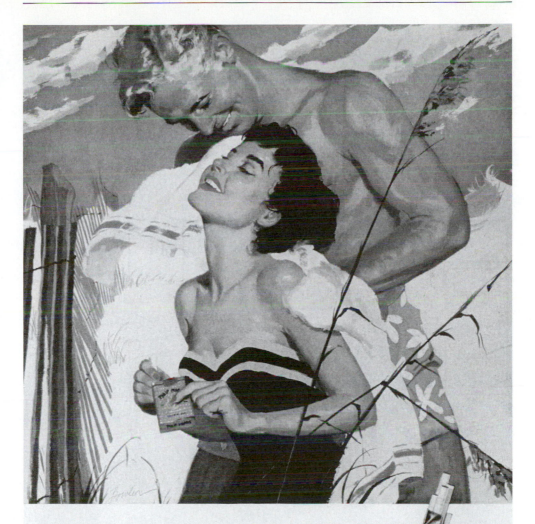

Gently Does It

Gentleness makes good friends in fun-making . . . and in a cigarette, where gentleness is one of the greatest requirements of modern taste. That's why today's Philip Morris, born gentle, refined to special gentleness in the making, makes so many friends among our young smokers. Enjoy the gentle pleasure, the fresh unfiltered flavor, of today's Philip Morris. In the convenient snap-open pack, regular or smart king-size.

Philip Morris

. . . gentle for modern taste

Philip Morris, 1950s: For legible body text of this ad, see p. 722.

Marlboro, 1970s

Camels, 1979

Can you spot the Camel Filters smoker?

©1972 R. J. Reynolds Tobacco Company, Winston-Salem, N. C.

In this picture everybody has a gimmick... almost everybody. Try picking the one who doesn't go along.

1. Nope. He's Lance Boyle. Gimmick: brags about wars he was never in. Yells "bombs away" as he flicks his French cigarette. **2.** Sorry. He's Harvey Dibble. His restaurant specializes in dried prunes. Gimmick: smokes wheat germ cigarettes. **3.** Eunice Trace, Starlet. Gimmick: restoring wholesomeness to movies. (Last film review: "At last, a movie the entire family can walk out on.") **4.** Smokey Stanhope, accountant. Gimmick: a guitar. Unfortunately makes the mistake of playing it. **5.** Right. He's just himself. And he sees through all the gimmicks. That's why he wants an honest, no-nonsense cigarette. Camel Filters. Easy and good tasting. Made from fine tobacco. **6.** Calls himself "Killer." Gimmick: thinks soccer uniform enhances his image. When he puffs out his chest, his pants fall down.

Camel Filters.
They're not for everybody
(but they could be for you).

CAMEL
FILTER CIGARETTES

Famous Camel Quality!

20 mg. "tar," 1.4 mg. nicotine av. per cigarette, FTC Report AUG. '72.

Camel Filters, 1972

More, 1980s

Camel Lights, 1992

Camels, 2000s

Pabst Blue Ribbon, 1940s: For legible body text of this ad, see pp. 722–23.

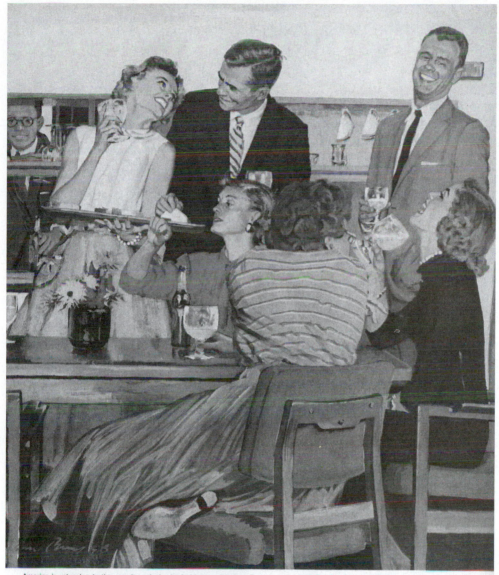

America is returning to the genuine — in foods, fashions and tastes. Today's trend to Ballantine light Ale fits right into this modern picture. In all the world, no other beverage brewed has such extra excellence brewed into it. And "Brewer's Gold" is one big reason for Ballantine Ale's deep, rich, genuine flavor.

They all ask for ale Ballantine LIGHT Ale !

Ballantine Ale, 1950s: For legible body text of this ad, see p. 723.

ERNEST HEMINGWAY, who has been called the greatest living American writer, is also internationally famous as a deep-sea fisherman. Since publication of *The Sun Also Rises* in 1926, his novels and short stories have enriched the literature of the English language consistently, year after year. His newest book is *The Old Man and the Sea*.

Ballantine Ale, 1953: For legible body text of this ad, see p. 723.

HOW WOULD YOU put a glass of Ballantine Ale into words?

Here—Ernest Hemingway turns his famous hand to it...

Ernest Hemingway

FINCA VIGIA, SAN FRANCISCO DE PAULA, CUBA

Bob Benchley first introduced me to Ballantine Ale. It has been a good companion ever since.

You have to work hard to deserve to drink it. But I would rather have a bottle of Ballantine Ale than any other drink after fighting a really big fish.

We keep it iced in the bait box with chunks of ice packed around it. And you ought to taste it on a hot day when you have worked a big marlin fast because there were sharks after him.

You are tired all the way through. The fish is landed untouched by sharks and you have a bottle of Ballantine cold in your hand and drink it cool, light, and full-bodied, so it tastes good long after you have swallowed it. That's the test of an ale with me: whether it tastes as good afterwards as when it's going down. Ballantine does.

Ernest Hemingway

More people like it... More people buy it... than any other ale... ...by Four to One!

BALLANTINE ALE

PURITY BODY FLAVOR

Since 1840

P. Ballantine & Sons, Newark, N.J.

BACARDI. rum is so "mixable"... It's a one-brand bar.

Big, bold highballs, sassy Daiquiris, cool tonics and colas—Bacardi rum is enjoyable always and *all* ways. Extra Special: our man Fernando is pouring very rare Bacardi Añejo rum (Ahn-YAY-ho), one of the fine rums from Bacardi. So incredibly smooth he enjoys it even in a snifter. Try it, too!

°BACARDI IMPORTS, INC., MIAMI, FLA. RUM, 80 PROOF.

Bacardi Rum, 1960s: For legible body text of this ad, see p. 723.

AT THE PULITZER FOUNTAIN, N.Y.C.

In Fine Whiskey...

FLEISCHMANN'S
is the <u>BIG</u> buy!

The First Taste will tell you why!

BLENDED WHISKEY • 86 AND 90 PROOF • 65% GRAIN NEUTRAL SPIRITS
THE FLEISCHMANN DISTILLING CORPORATION, NEW YORK CITY

661 Whiskey, 1964

"I'll have a Hennessy Very Superior Old Pale Reserve Cognac, thank you."

The Taste of Success

Every drop of Hennessy V.S.O.P. Reserve is Grande Fine Champagne Cognac.
It's made solely from grapes grown in La Grande Champagne—the small district in
the Cognac region which is the source of the very greatest Cognac.
What's more, Hennessy is selected from the largest reserves of aged Cognacs in existence.
Enjoy a taste of success today…

Hennessy V.S.O.P. Reserve Cognac

Hennessy V.S.O.P. Grande Fine Champagne Cognac. 80 Proof. ©Schieffelin & Co., N.Y.

Hennessy Cognac, 1968: For legible body text of this ad, see pp. 723–24.

Smirnoff Vodka, 1970s

Cossack Vodka, 1970s

Now comes Miller time.
Time to head for the best-tasting beer
you can find. Miller High Life.
America's quality beer since 1855.

© 1979 Miller Brewing Co., Milwaukee, Wis.

Miller Beer, 1979

Bring out your best.

All they needed was an inch.

You had to stop them. So you built a wall. A determined wall made of you and the rest of the line.

And when the play unfolded, when they came at you with their cunning, they ran into your wall of strength.

They just couldn't move you an inch.

Standing your ground takes more than raw strength. It takes fierce determination. A strong sense of pride. And the very best a man has to give. At Anheuser-Busch we understand that. Which is why we brew a light beer with a clean, distinctive taste. Budweiser Light.

We know the best never comes easy. That's why there's nothing else like it.

Budweiser Beer, 1990s: For legible body text of this ad, see p. 724.

Pay-off for Pearl Harbor!

Three years ago, the sneak attack on Pearl Harbor found America unprepared to defend its rights. Yet, even at that early date, Cadillac was in its third year of building aircraft engine parts for military use. Today are look hopefully forward to the time when this important contribution to America's air power will pay off in such a scene as that illustrated above.

For more than five years we have been working toward that end. Back in 1939, we started building precision parts for Allison—America's famous liquid-cooled aircraft engine—used to power such potent fighters as the Lightning, the Warhawk, the Mustang, the Airacobra and the new Kingcobra.

In addition to our work for Allison, which has included more than 57,000,000 man-hours of precision production—we assisted Army Ordnance Engineers in designing the M-5 Light Tank and the M-8 Howitzer motor carriage, and have produced them in quan-

tities. Both are powered by Cadillac engin equipped with Hydra-Matic transmission

We are now building other weapons whi utilize some of our Cadillac peacetime pr ucts. We can't talk about all of them yet—k we are confident they will prove signific additions to Allied armor.

Every Sunday Afternoon . . . GENERAL MOTORS SYMPHONY OF THE AIR—NBC Network

CADILLAC MOTOR CAR DIVISION  GENERAL MOTORS CORPORATION

LET'S ALL
BACK THE ATTACK
BUY WAR BONDS

Cadillac, 1945: For legible body text of this ad, see p. 724.

Of all the De Soto cars ever built, 7 out of 10 are still running

8 out of 10 owners say, "De Soto is the most satisfactory car I ever owned"*

‡FROM A MAIL SURVEY AMONG THOUSANDS OF OWNERS
OF 1941 AND 1942 DE SOTO CARS

DE SOTO DIVISION OF CHRYSLER CORPORATION

DeSoto

DESIGNED TO ENDURE

De Soto, 1947: For legible body text of this ad, see p. 724.

"Ford's out Front from a Woman's Angle"

1. "I don't know synthetic enamel from a box of my children's paints... but if synthetic enamel is what it takes to make that beautiful, shiny Ford finish, I'm all for it!

2. "My husband says the brakes are self-centering and hydraulic—whatever that means! All I know is they're so easy that I can taxi the children all day without tiring out!

3. "Peter, he's my teen-age son, tells me that 'Ford is the only car in its price class with a choice of a 100-horsepower V-8 engine or a brilliant new Six.' He says no matter which engine people pick, they're out front with Ford!

6. "Now here's another thing women like and that's a blissfully comfortable ride—one that isn't bumpity-bump even on some of our completely forgotten roads."

Listen to the Ford Show starring Dinah Shore on Columbia Network Stations Wednesday Evenings.

There's a *Ford* in your future

4. "The interior of our Ford is strictly my department! It's tailored with the dreamiest broadcloth. Such a perfect fit! Mary Jane says women help design Ford interiors. There's certainly a woman's touch there!

5. "Do you like lovely silver, beautifully simple and chaste looking? That's what I always think of when I touch those smart Ford door handles and window openers.

Ford, 1947: For legible body text of this ad, see p. 725.

Worth Its Price

If a motorist wanted to make the move to Cadillac solely for the car's prestige—he would most certainly be justified in doing so. For the Cadillac car has never stood so high in public esteem as it does today—and the rewards which grow out of this unprecedented acceptance comprise the rarest and greatest satisfactions in all motordom.

There is, for instance, *the inescapable feeling of pride* that comes with ownership of so distinguished and beloved a possession . . . the wonderful *sense of well-being* that comes from having reached a point of achievement where you can enjoy one of the world's most sought-after manufactured products . . . and the *marvelous feeling of confidence and self-esteem* that is found

CADILLAC MOTOR CAR DIVISION

Cadillac, 1954: For legible body text of this ad, see p. 725–26.

in PRESTIGE !

in the respect and admiration universally accorded the owner of a Cadillac car. Those who presently enjoy these unique Cadillac virtues will tell you that they are, in themselves, worth the car's whole purchase price.

Of course, most motorists would hesitate to take such a step purely for their personal edification. But in Cadillac's case, this wonderful prestige is actually a "bonus", so to speak—an extra dividend that comes with every Cadillac car, in addition to its breath-taking styling, its magnificent performance, its superlative luxury and its remarkable economy.

Have you seen and driven the 1954 Cadillac? If you haven't, then you've a truly wonderful adventure awaiting you—and one that you should postpone no longer.

GENERAL MOTORS CORPORATION

This is your reward for the great Dodge advance—the daring new, dramatic new '56 Dodge.

The Magic Touch of Tomorrow!

The *look* of success! The *feel* of success! The *power* of success!
They come to you in a dramatically beautiful, dynamically powered
new Dodge that introduces the ease and safety of push-button driving
–the Magic Touch of Tomorrow! It is a truly great value.

New '56 DODGE

Dodge, 1955: For legible body text of this ad, see p. 726.

Drive a Riviera home tonight. Who cares if people
think you're younger, richer and more romantic than you really are?

A Riviera has a strange effect on people. Simply looking at one makes your mouth water, your eyes
open wider and your heart beat faster. You grin admiringly when you notice the headlights, tucked
behind shields that open with the touch of the headlight switch. You breathe harder when you
turn loose some of those 325 horsepower. And that's just what happens to the driver. Wait till you see the
awe a Riviera inspires in passersby! Amazing. Also attainable, for considerably less than
you might suspect. (Before you fall headlong for a Riviera, ask yourself if a firmer suspension and
assorted other sporting touches give you a twinge of anticipation. Yes? Ask your dealer about
our new Riviera Gran Sport. The name alone is a hint of what's in it for you.) Check with your Buick dealer
soon. He may convince you you're younger, richer and more romantic than you thought you were.

Wouldn't you really rather have a Buick?

Buick, 1965: For legible body text of this ad, see p. 726.

Corvette Sting Ray Sport Coupe with eight standard safety features, including outside rearview mirror. Use it always before passing.

The day she flew the coupe

What manner of woman is this, you ask, who stands in the midst of a mountain stream eating a peach?

Actually she's a normal everyday girl except that she and her husband own the Corvette Coupe in the background. (He's at work right now, wondering where he misplaced his car keys.)

The temptation, you see, was over-

powering. They'd had the car a whole week now, and not once had he offered to let her drive. His excuse was that this, uh, was a big hairy sports car. Too much for a woman to handle: the trigger-quick steering, the independent rear suspension, the disc brakes—plus the 4-speed transmission and that 425-hp engine they had ordered—egad! He would

teach her to drive it some weekend. So he said.

That's why she hid the keys, forcing him to seek public transportation. Sure of his departure, she went to the garage, started the Corvette, and was off for the hills, soon upshifting and downshifting as smoothly as he. His car. Hard to drive. What propaganda!

'66 CORVETTE BY CHEVROLET
Chevrolet Division of General Motors, Detroit, Michigan

Corvette, 1966: For legible body text of this ad, see pp. 726–27.

Jeep vehicle, 2003

The Turbo engine with the Family Pack.

The Diesel engine with

VOLVO GIVE THEIR BLESSING

When it comes to marriages Volvo like to put on a big spread.

That's why, with the 400 series, we're giving you a wider choice than any other manufacturer. You can pick a bigger engine with standard specification or a smaller engine with the luxury package.

In fact, with a total of five different engine sizes and six different interior packages on offer, you can mix and match as much as you like.

You could for instance, unite the 1.6 engine with the Luxury Pack, which features air-conditioning and leather upholstery.

With other manufacturers however, you don't get such a happy coupling. You'll find that the luxury package for example, only comes with the larger engine.

Volvo, 1990s: For legible body text of this ad, see p. 727.

the Business Pack.   The 1.6 engine with the Leather Interior.

TO ALL SORTS OF MARRIAGES.

Volvo's approach (which applies to the 440 hatchback and 460 saloon) means you not only get the car that suits your exact needs, but you decide exactly where your money goes.

And you don't have to wait any longer for

delivery of your specially built car. For information pack call 0800 400 430.

The Volvo 400 series. From $11,175 (w ribbons not included).

THE VOLVO 400 SERIES. A CAR YOU CAN BELIEV

Good School Day Lunches

make healthier, brighter youngsters

Many children do not get adequate lunches! And yet upon proper food depends not only their future health, but today's well-being, cheerfulness—and even report cards!

Lunch should include a hot dish, and be substantial but easy to digest. Good nourishing soup is a big help—and Campbell's Vegetable Soup is just right! Children love it, and it brings them all the sturdy goodness of 15 different garden vegetables combined with a rich, invigorating beef stock. No wonder mothers everywhere agree "It's almost a meal in itself!"

Campbell's VEGETABLE SOUP

LOOK FOR THE RED-AND-WHITE LABEL

A WEEK'S SCHOOL LUNCHES

MONDAY
Campbell's Vegetable Soup
Peanut Butter Sandwich
Baked Custard   Celery
Orange   Graham Crackers

TUESDAY
Campbell's Tomato Soup
Cottage Cheese and Orange Marmalade Sandwich
Banana   Carrot Sticks
Molasses Cookies

WEDNESDAY
Campbell's Scotch Broth
Lettuce and Hard-Cooked Egg Salad
Toasted Raisin Bread
Fresh Pear   Cocoa

THURSDAY
Campbell's Vegetable Soup
Cold Roast Veal Sandwich
Baked Apple   Celery
Milk

FRIDAY
Campbell's Cream of Spinach Soup
Toasted Tuna Fish Salad Sandwich
Sliced Tomatoes
Stewed Peaches   Chocolate Milk

Campbell's, 1945: For legible body text of this ad, see p. 727.

Coca-Cola, 1945: For legible body text of this ad, see p. 728.

What's for dinner, Duchess?

Prediction: The new wives of 1947 are going to have more fun in the kitchen.

Previous cooking experience is desirable, perhaps, but not essential. There are so many new easy-to-use foods, so many new ways to prepare foods, so many interesting ways to serve foods, cooking will be a novel and exciting adventure.

Further prediction: Cheese dishes will be featured more often on their menus. They'll know that cheese gives tastiness and variety to meals. And cheese, like milk (nature's most nearly perfect food), is rich in protein, calcium, phosphorus, in vitamins A and G.

Yes, we have a personal interest in cheese. For Kraft, pioneer in cheese, is a unit of National Dairy. And what we've said about housewives using more cheese is entirely true.

It's also true that they're learning more about the whys and wherefores of food each year — just as the scientists in our laboratories are learning more about better ways to process, improve and supply it.

These men are backed by the resources of a great organization. They explore every field of dairy products, discover new ones. And the health of America benefits constantly by this National Dairy research.

Dedicated to the wider use and better understanding of dairy products as human food . . . as a base for the development of new products and materials . . . as a source of health and enduring progress on the farms and in the towns and cities of America.

NATIONAL DAIRY
PRODUCTS CORPORATION
AND AFFILIATED COMPANIES

National Dairy Products Corporation, 1947: For legible body text of this ad, see p. 728.

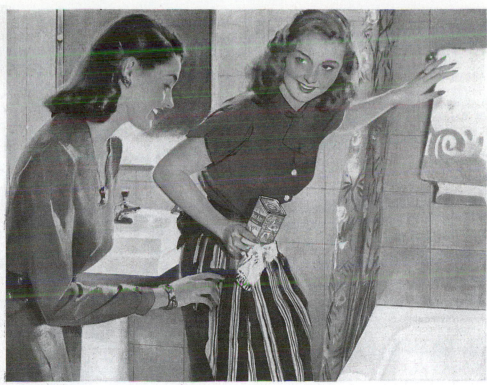

MAY: # Heavens, Ann — wish I could clean up quick as that!

ANN: You could, hon! Just use a cleanser that doesn't leave dirt-catching scratches.

MAY: Goodness! What in the world do scratches have to do with it?

ANN: A lot, silly! Those tiny scratches you get from gritty cleansers hold onto dirt and double your cleaning time.

MAY: Well, you old smartie! I'd never thought of *that* before.

ANN: I hadn't thought of it either—till I discovered Bon Ami! See how fine-textured and white it is. It just *slides* di.t off—and when you rinse it away, it doesn't leave any of that horrid grit in the tub.

MAY: Say no more, darling! From now on there's going to be a new cleaning team in our house —me and Bon Ami!

Bon Ami

THE SPEEDY CLEANSER *that* *"hasn't scratched yet!"*

EASY ON YOUR HANDS, Bon Ami *Powder* is the ideal cleanser for kitchen sinks, as well as bathtubs. Also try Bon Ami *Cake* for cleaner windows, mirrors and windshields.

Bon Ami, 1947: For legible body text of this ad, see pp. 728–29.

This is the story of Annie...

NOW ANNIE WAS...

AS BEAUTIFUL A GIRL...

AS EVER WAS PUT TOGETHER!

WHY, WHEN ANNIE WALKED DOWN THE STREET... WOW!

YET ANNIE HAD HER BAD MOMENTS...LIKE ANY OTHER GAL.

AND YOU WANT TO KNOW WHY? ANNIE'S HANDS WERE A MESS, ALWAYS ROUGH AND DRY, LIKE SANDPAPER.

AND WHEN A MAN WANTS TO HOLD A GIRL'S HANDS... EVEN A GIRL LIKE ANNIE ...HE DOESN'T WANT TO WEAR GLOVES...

THEN, LUCKILY, FANNIE TOLD ANNIE ABOUT AN ENTIRELY NEW AND DIFFERENT HAND LOTION! THE **BEFOREHAND** LOTION...**TRUSHAY!**

SO ANNIE SMOOTHED CREAMY, FRAGRANT **TRUSHAY** ON HER HANDS BEFORE SHE DID DISHES...BECAUSE **TRUSHAY** GUARDS HANDS EVEN IN HOT, SOAPY WATER!

AND ANNIE PUT **TRUSHAY** ON HER HANDS BEFORE SHE TUBBED HER UNDIES...SO **TRUSHAY'S** SPECIAL "OIL-RICHNESS" COULD HELP PREVENT DRYNESS AND ROUGHNESS.

SO NOW ANNIE IS ABLE TO KEEP HER HANDS SOFT AND SMOOTH AND HOLDABLE... THANKS TO **TRUSHAY'S** WONDERFUL SOFTENING HELP.

TRUSHAY

The "Beforehand" Lotion

PRODUCT OF BRISTOL-MYERS

P. S. Trushay's grand for softening hands at *any* time. Wonderful, too, for rough, dry elbows and heels...as a powder base...before and after exposure to weather. Trushay contains no alcohol, is not sticky. Begin today to use Trushay.

Trushay, 1947: For legible body text of this ad, see p. 729.

Mrs. Dorian Mehle of Morrisville, Pa., is all three: a housewife, a mother, and a very lovely lady.

"I wash 22,000 dishes a year... but I'm proud of my pretty hands!"

You and Dorian Mehle have something in common. Every year, you wash a stack of dishes a quarter-mile high!

Detergents make your job so much easier. They cut right into grease and grime. They get you through dishwashing in much less time, but while they dissolve grease, they also take away the natural oils and youthful softness of your hands!

Although Dorian hasn't given up detergents her hands are as soft, as smooth, as young-looking as a teenager's. Her secret is no secret at all. It's the world's best-known beauty routine. It's pure, white Jergens Lotion, after every chore.

When you smooth on Jergens Lotion, this liquid formula doesn't just "coat" your hands. It penetrates right away, to help *replace* that softening moisture your skin needs.

Jergens Lotion has two ingredients doctors recommend for softening. Women must be recommending it, too, for more women use it than any other hand care in the world. Dorian's husband is the best testimonial to Jergens Lotion care. Even after years of married life, he still loves to hold her pretty hands!

Use Jergens Lotion like a prescription: three times a day, after every meal!

Use JERGENS LOTION – avoid detergent hands

Now—lotion dispenser FREE of extra cost with $1.00 size. Supply limited.

Jergens Lotion, 1954: For legible body text of this ad, see p. 730.

President Lee A. Potter Jr., *of the Young Presidents Organization Inc. and Forman, Ford & Co. "To be successful, look the part. That certain look of success attracts the confidence of important men."*

A man's hat speaks eloquently of his personal measure of authority. That's why Disney hats are so often considered part of a businessman's equipment. The rare skill of their handcraftsmanship, the executive character of their styling reflect the critical judgment and taste of the wearer.* Disney's uniquely impressive effect has made these hats the choice of prominent men for 65 years.

*Case in point, THE DISNEY CAPELLO. This marvelously light hat, styled with flattering tapered crown and narrow brim, is fashion at its finest. At fine stores, $20. Many other Disney hats from $10 to $40.
Free! Handsome booklet containing helpful hints by American business leaders. Ask your Disney dealer for "Guide Quotes to Success."

The Hat of Presidents

Disney Hats, 1954: For legible body text of this ad, see p. 730.

Madam! Suppose you traded jobs with your husband?

You can just bet the first thing he'd ask for would be a telephone in the kitchen.

You wouldn't catch him dashing to another room every time the telephone rang, or he had to make a call.

He doesn't have to do it in his office in town. It would be mighty helpful if you didn't have to do it in your "office" at home.

That's in the kitchen where you do so much of your work. And it's right there that an additional telephone comes in so handy for so many things.

Along with a lot of convenience is that nice feeling of pride in having the best of everything—especially if it is one of those attractive new telephones in color.

P.S. *Additional telephones in kitchen, bedroom and other convenient places around the house cost little. The service charge is just pennies a day.*

Bell Telephone System

Bell Telephone, 1956: For legible body text of this ad, see pp. 730–31.

The phone company wants more installers like Alana MacFarlane.

Alana MacFarlane is a 20-year-old from San Rafael, California. She's one of our first women telephone installers. She won't be the last.

We also have several hundred male telephone operators. And a policy that there are no all-male or all-female jobs at the phone company.

We want the men and women of the telephone company to do what they want to do, and do best.

For example, Alana likes working outdoors. "I don't go for office routine," she said. "But as an installer, I get plenty of variety and a chance to move around."

Some people like to work with their hands, or, like Alana, get a kick out of working 20 feet up in the air.

Others like to drive trucks. Some we're helping to develop into good managers.

Today, when openings exist, local Bell Companies are offering applicants and present employees some jobs they may never have thought about before. We want to help all advance to the best of their abilities.

AT&T and your local Bell Company are equal opportunity employers.

Bell Telephone, 1974: For legible body text of this ad, see p. 731.

Think of her as your mother.

She only wants what's best for you.
A cool drink. A good dinner. A soft pillow and a warm blanket.
This is not just maternal instinct. It's the result of the longest
Stewardess training in the industry.
Training in service, not just a beauty course.
Service, after all, is what makes professional travelers prefer American.
And makes new travelers want to keep on flying with us.
So we see that every passenger gets the same professional treatment.
That's the American Way.

Fly the American Way
American Airlines.

American Airlines, 1968: For legible body text of this ad, see p. 731.

Charlie, 1988

Shineaway 17 Lotion, 1980s: For legible body text of this ad, see p. 732.

A hard man is good to find.

Ken Norton Pugilist/Thespian

To unlock your body's potential, we proudly offer Soloflex.
Twenty-four old-fashioned iron pumping exercises, each correct in form
and balance. All on a simple machine that fits in a corner of your home.
For a free Soloflex brochure, call anytime **1-800-453-9000.**
In Canada, **1-800-543-1005.**

SOLOFLEX®
Weightlifting, Pure and Simple.
VHS Video Brochure™ available upon request.   © 1985, Soloflex, Inc. Hillsboro, Oregon 97124

Soloflex, 1985

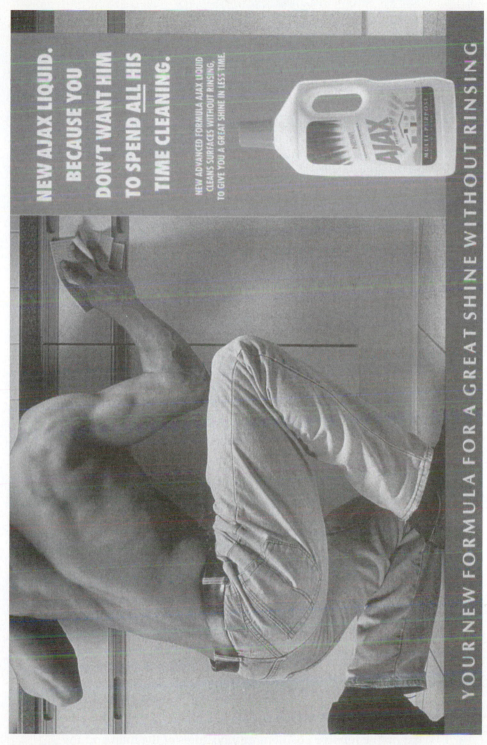

Ajax, 1990s

Discussion and Writing Suggestions

TOBACCO

Camels, 1947 (p. 663)

1. How does the intended appeal of this ad differ most dramatically from a comparable ad today?

2. What kind of psychological appeals are made by the picture in the top half of this ad and the text accompanying it? How does the image of a doctor out on a night call tie in, for selling purposes, with the ad's headline?

Webster Cigars, 1945 (p. 664)

1. How does the dress and general appearance of the people in the ad, as well as the setting depicted, communicate meaning, particularly as it applies to the appeal of the product?

2. To whom is this advertisement addressed? Cite headline and body text, as well as graphics, that support your response. What kind of ads today are addressed to a similar audience?

Philip Morris, 1950s (p. 665)

1. How do the placement, posture, and dress of the models in the ad help create its essential psychological appeal? Why do you suppose (in relation to the selling of cigarettes) the models' eyes are closed?

2. Discuss some of the messages communicated both by the graphic and the text of this ad. Focus in particular on the quality of "gentleness" emphasized in the ad.

Marlboro, 1970s (p. 666)

1. The Marlboro Man has become one of the most famous—and successful—icons of American advertising. What elements of the Marlboro Man (and his setting, Marlboro Country) do you notice, and what role do these elements play in the appeal being made by this ad?

2. This ad appeared during the 1970s. (The popularity of the Marlboro Man extended into the 1980s, however.) To what extent do you think it would have the same appeal today?

3. Comment on the elements of graphic design (balance, proportion, movement, unity, clarity and simplicity, emphasis) that help make this ad effective. Focus particularly on the element of movement.

Camels, 1979 (p. 667)

1. What do the relative positions and postures of the man and the woman in the ad indicate about the ad's basic appeal?

2. What roles do the props—particularly, the motorcycle and the models' outfits—and the setting play in helping to sell the product?

3. How do the design elements in the ad emphasize the product?

4. Compare the graphic elements of this ad to those of the Fleischmann's Whiskey ad (page 677).

Virginia Slims, 1985 (p. 668)

1. How do the thematic and graphic contrasts between elements in the two separate illustrations support the ad's essential appeal?

2. Comment on the placement and postures of the figures in the ad and how they contribute to the ad's meaning.

More, 1980s (p. 669)

1. What qualities are conveyed by the couple depicted in the ad? Focus on their dress, posture, and facial expressions. How do these qualities contribute to the appeal of the product?

2. Compare and contrast the effect of this ad with earlier ads depicted for this product (Webster Cigars, Philip Morris) that also show two or more people enjoying tobacco products.

3. Comment on the effectiveness of the graphic elements of this advertisement.

Camel Filters, 1972 (p. 670)

1. How do the contrasts in appearance (including posture and facial expressions) between the Camel Filters smoker and the others in the graphic support the essential appeal made by this ad?

2. How does the body text—particularly the thumbnail descriptions of each of the five candidates for Camels Filters smoker—reinforce the ad's intended meaning?

Camels, 2000s (p. 671)

1. This is an example of retro appeal. What elements make it so? What elements mark the ad, on the other hand, as a contemporary one? How does the combination of retro and contemporary elements (including, for example, the posture and attitude of the model) contribute to create a particular type of appeal?

2. Compare and contrast the three Camels ads presented in this section of the portfolio. Focus on the psychological appeals, the cultural values implied in the ads, and the graphic and textual means used to persuade the buyer to smoke Camels.

BEER AND LIQUOR

Pabst Blue Ribbon, 1940s (p. 672)

1. Ads in the 1940s often took comic-book form. (See also the 1947 Trushay ad later in this portfolio, page 698.) To what kind of audience is this format most likely to appeal? What are some of the advantages and disadvantages of the comic-book format?

2. The problem/solution structure of the narrative in this ad is one of the oldest and still most frequently employed (particularly in TV commercials) in marketing. To what extent does it seem appropriate for the selling of beer? To what extent is it appropriate for other products and services? (Cite examples from contemporary or recent ads.)

3. To what extent do you find examples of outdated social attitudes in this ad?

Ballantine Ale, 1950s (p. 673)

1. This illustration, reminiscent of some of Norman Rockwell's paintings, is typical of many beer and ale ads in the 1950s, which depict a group of well-dressed young adults enjoying their brew at a social event. Comment on the distinctive graphic elements in this ad and speculate as to why these elements are seldom employed in contemporary advertisements for beer and ale. Why, in other words, does this ad seem old-fashioned?

2. Contrast the appeal and graphics of this ad with the ads for Miller and Budweiser later in this portfolio.Contrast the appeal and graphics of this ad with the ads for Miller and Budweiser later in this portfolio.

3. Identify the adjectives in the body text and attempt to correlate them to the graphic in helping to construct the message of the ad.

Ballantine Ale, 1953 (pp. 674–75)

1. You may be surprised to find Ernest Hemingway selling ale. To what extent do you find celebrity endorsements an effective method of marketing? Why do you think that the creators of this ad might have believed that Hemingway (as opposed, say, to a professional athlete) might be an effective promoter of (or is qualified to address the need for guidance on) Ballantine Ale?

2. Comment on the apparent strategy behind the graphic and textual elements in this ad—particularly, the setting, Hemingway's posture, and his letter.

3. If you are familiar with any of Hemingway's stories or novels, do you notice any similarity of style or subject matter between what

you have previously read and Hemingway's testimonial letter to
Ballantine Ale?

Bacardi Rum, 1960s (p. 676)

1. What meaning is conveyed by the placement, posture, and expressions of the four models in this ad? How do you think this meaning
   is intended to help sell the product? (Does the picture remind you
   of a particular movie hero?)
2. Comment on the significance of the props in the photo.
3. How does the text ("Big, bold highballs, sassy Daiquiris, cool
   tonics . . . ") help reinforce the meaning created by the picture?

661 Whiskey, 1964 (p. 677)

1. Comment on (1) the significance of the extra-large bottle of
   whiskey; (2) the stances of the two models in the ad; (3) the way
   the headline contributes to the ad's meaning.
2. Compare and contrast the graphic in this ad with that of the
   1979 Camels ad earlier in this portfolio (the man on the motorcycle).

Hennessy Cognac, 1968 (p. 678)

1. What is the primary appeal of this ad? How do the woman,
   the horse, and the headline work to create and reinforce this
   appeal?
2. Compare and contrast this ad to the Webster Cigar ad in terms of
   their appeal and their graphics.

Smirnoff Vodka, 1970s (p. 679)

1. What meaning is conveyed by the two figures in this ad?
   How do the models' postures and the props help reinforce this
   meaning?
2. How do you interpret the headline? How does the headline—and
   the sub-headline ("You drink it for what it is")—tie in to the meaning created by the photo?

Cossack Vodka, 1970s (p. 680)

1. What is the essential appeal behind this ad?
2. The comic-book style of the drawing is reminiscent of the work of
   Roy Lichtenstein (1923–1997), an American painter who drew inspiration from advertisements and romance magazines, as well as
   comic books, to depict and parody artifacts of pop culture. What is

the effect of this particular style on creating—and perhaps commenting upon—the message in the text balloon and in the ad in which it appears?

3. How does the text at the bottom of the idea reinforce the message created by the graphic? In particular, how is this message intended to sell the product?

Miller Beer, 1979 (p. 681)

1. To what extent does this 1979 ad embody marketing techniques for beer that are still employed today?

2. Comment on the posture and expressions of the three models depicted in the ad. How do these elements help create the ad's essential appeal?

3. Compare and contrast this ad with the 1950s Ballantine Ale ad earlier in this portfolio (page 673).

Budweiser Beer, 1990s (p. 682)

1. To what extent is this ad based on a similar appeal as the preceding Miller ad? To what extent is it based on other appeals?

2. What's the advantage (in terms of effectiveness of appeal) of using the second person—"you"—in the body text? How does the text attempt to make the connection between the product advertised and the activities of the football players? To what extent do you think that this is an effective ad?

3. Comment on the workings and effectiveness of the graphic design elements in this ad.

AUTOMOBILES

Cadillac, 1945 (p. 683)

1. What is the essential strategy behind portraying a group of military aircraft on a bombing raid in an automobile ad? What, exactly, is this ad selling?

2. Explain how the graphic elements of this ad—and the interplay between the elements of the graphic and the text (headline and body text)—reinforce the ad's basic appeal.

De Soto, 1947 (p. 684)

1. How does the scene portrayed in the illustration help create the basic appeal of this ad? Focus on as many significant individual elements of the illustration as you can.

2. To what extent does the caption (in the illustration) and the headline support the message communicated by the graphic?

3. Explain why both this ad and the preceding Cadillac ad are products of their particular times.

Ford, 1947 (p. 685)

1. Cite and discuss those textual elements in the ad that reflect a traditional conception of the American woman.

2. How do the visual elements of the ad reinforce the assumptions about traditional gender roles reflected in the ad?

Cadillac, 1954 (pp. 686–87)

1. What is the particular marketing strategy behind this ad? Based on the ad's text, compose a memo from the head of marketing to the chief copywriter proposing this particular ad and focusing on the strategy. The memo doesn't have to be cynical or to insult the prospective Cadillac buyers; it should just be straightforward and direct.

2. How do the ad's graphics reinforce the message in the text?

Dodge, 1955 (p. 688)

1. Discuss the multiple appeals of this ad. How are these appeals reflected in the ad's text and graphics? For instance, discuss the angle from which the automobile is photographed.

2. Both this ad and the 1947 Ford ad (page 685) feature one or more women in the graphic. Compare and contrast the use of women in the two ads.

Buick, 1965 (p. 689)

1. Compare and contrast the appeal made in this ad to the appeal made in either the 1947 Ford ad (page 685) or the 1954 Cadillac ad (pages 686–87). Cite particular aspects of the text and graphics to support your comparison.

2. The text of the ad discusses two categories of the "people" mentioned in the first sentence. Discuss how the ad makes different, if related, appeals to these two categories of "people."

3. Discuss, in terms of their overall effect, the placement of the automobile and the woman in the ad, as well as the perspective from which both are viewed.

Corvette, 1966 (p. 690)

1. How do the graphic elements reinforce the message developed in the text of this ad?

2. Comment on the dress and the posture of the model, as these relate to the ad's essential appeal. What's the significance of the woman eating a peach in a mountain stream?

3. The body text in this ad tells a story. What kind of husband-wife dynamic is implied by this story? To what extent do you find similarities between the implied gender roles in this ad and those in the 1947 Ford ad ("Ford's out Front from a Woman's Angle," page 685)? To what extent do you find differences, ones that may be attributable to the twenty years between the two ads?

Jeep vehicle, 2003 (p. 691)

1. Explain the meaning of the ad's headline.
2. Discuss the graphic, in terms of the ad's headline. Consider the significance of the viewing angle.

Volvo, 1990s (pp. 692–93)

1. What cultural phenomenon is being addressed in the graphic and the headline of this ad? To what extent do you believe that associating Volvo with this phenomenon is an effective way to market this particular automobile?
2. What is the connection between the three apparently ill-matched couples in the illustration and the ad's basic message and appeal?
3. How is humor used to enhance the ad's (and the message's) appeal? That is, how are the couples in the illustration presented as incongruous (if happy)?

FOOD, CLEANSERS, BEAUTY PRODUCTS, AND OTHER

Campbell's, 1945 (p. 694)

1. What kind of appeal is being made in the first two sentences of the body text? How does the graphic in the top half of the ad support this appeal?
2. What kind of marketing strategy is behind the menu in the lower right portion of the ad?

Coca-Cola, 1945 (p. 695)

1. This ad appeared shortly after the conclusion of World War II. How do the text and the graphics of the ad take advantage of the international mood at the time? Comment on the appearance and arrangement of the men portrayed in the ad.
2. Compare the strategy of this Coca-Cola ad (text and graphics) with that of the 1950s Ballantine ad (page 673).

National Dairy Products Corporation, 1947 (p. 696)

1. How does the couple pictured in the ad illustrate gender expectations of the period? Comment on the dress, postures, and expressions of the models.

2. What, exactly is this ad *selling?* (It is presented more as a news-magazine article than as a conventional advertisement.) How is the appeal tied to contemporary developments by "scientists" and their "research," particularly as these relate to "the new wives of 1947"?

3. What does the text of this ad imply about the situation of young married couples in postwar households?

Bon Ami, 1947 (p. 697)

1. How do the text and graphics of this ad illustrate a bygone cultural attitude toward gender roles? Notice, in particular, the dress, postures, and expressions of the women pictured, as well as the style of the illustration. Focus also on the wording of the text.

2. In terms of Jib Fowles's categories, what kind of appeal is being made by the Bon Ami ad?

Trushay, 1947 (p. 698)

1. Retell the "story of Annie" in narrative form, in a paragraph. What does Annie's story tell us about gender relations in the 1940s? To what extent have gender relations changed on the particular issue covered by Annie's story?

2. Ads that resembled comic strips were not uncommon sixty years ago. Based on the impact made by this ad today, why do you think the comic strip format might have gone out of fashion?

3. Suppose you were a contemporary copywriter for a hand lotion product. Develop some ideas for an ad or a campaign that might be effective for today's potential customers.

Jergens Lotion, 1954 (p. 699)

1. Compare and contrast the appeals and the strategies of this Jergens Lotion ad and the Trushay ad preceding it. Are the ads intended to appeal to the same target audiences? To what extent are the psychological appeals of the two ads similar? Compare the illustrations of the two ads. How do they differ in basic strategy?

2. The model in the Jergens Lotion ad is immaculately dressed and groomed, and she is sitting among stacks of fine china (as opposed to everyday dishware). What do you think is the marketing strategy behind these graphic choices?

Disney Hats, 1954 (p. 700)

1. Point out specific language in the headline and body that helps create the basic appeal of this ad for Disney hats. How does the illustration—both the man in the hat and the background against which he is posed—reinforce this appeal?

2. Comment on how the connotations and significance of men's head-wear have changed—and not changed—over the years or how they help support the appeal of the product advertised. (Notice, for example, the hat-wearing models in the 1947 Camels ad, the 1954 Cadillac ad, the 1983 Marlboro ad, and the 1990s Camels ad.

Bell Telephone, 1956 (p. 701)

1. Discuss the attitude toward gender roles implicit in the 1956 Bell ad. How do the graphics, the headline, and the body text, reinforce this attitude? What is the significance of the quotation marks around "office" in the final sentence of the third paragraph?

2. Notice that the woman at the desk seems a lot more comfortable and at ease than the man holding the crying baby and the dishes. What does this fact tell us about the attitudes toward gender roles of those who created this ad?

Bell Telephone, 1974 (p. 702)

1. Compare and contrast the 1956 Bell ad with the 1974 Bell ad, in terms of their attitudes toward gender roles. How do the text and graphics reinforce the essential differences?

2. The 1956 Bell ad pictures a woman at a desk (a white-collar job); the 1974 ad pictures a woman working at a telephone pole (a blue-collar job). Would the 1974 ad have the same impact if "Alana MacFarlane" had, like her 1956 counterpart, been pictured at a desk?

3. Like the 1945 Cadillac ad (page 686–87) the 1974 Bell ad seems more of a public service announcement than a conventional adver-tisement. Compare and contrast these ads in terms of their mes-sages to readers.

American Airlines, 1968 (p. 703)

1. Discuss the mixed messages (in terms of appeal) being transmitted by the American Airlines ad. To what extent do you think the apparently conflicting appeals make for an effective ad?

2. Comment on the dress, pose, and expression of the model in the ad, which appeared in *Ebony* magazine. How do these create a different impact than would an illustration, say, of a flight attendant serving a drink or giving a pillow to an airline passenger?

Charlie, 1988 (p. 704)

1. Notice the woman's outfit, as well as her briefcase, in the Charlie ad. How is appearance of this woman as significant as the appear-ance of the woman in the Smirnoff Vodka ad (page 679) for the ad's basic message?

2. The Charlie ad and the Bell 1974 ad (page 702) are as different as can be imagined from the Trushay ad. Yet, the Bell and the Charlie ads make quite different appeals. Explain. Consider, for example, how a woman—or a man—of the late 1940s might respond to the Bell ad, on the one hand, and the Charlie ad, on the other.

Shineaway 17 Lotion, 1980s (p. 705)

1. Account for the postures of the man and the woman, in terms of the essential message and appeal of this ad.

2. Both this and the preceding Charlie ad rely to some extent on sex appeal. Compare and contrast other aspects of these two ads.

Soloflex, 1985 (p. 706)

1. How does the illustration in this ad reinforce the basic appeal of the headline?

2. Ads are frequently criticized for the incongruity between illustration and product being advertised—for example, a scantily clad woman posed provocatively in front of a pickup truck. To what extent does the Soloflex ad present an appropriate fit between graphic and product advertised?

Ajax, 1990s (p. 707)

1. Why do you suppose the model's head is not pictured?

2. How does this ad play off shifting cultural attitudes toward gender roles? Would the ad be more objectionable if it pictured a female in a comparable state of undress?

3. Compare and contrast this ad to earlier ads for cleaners and cleansing lotions, such as Bon Ami and Jergens Lotion.

SYNTHESIS ACTIVITIES

1. Select one *category* of advertisements (cigarettes, alcohol, etc.) represented in the ad portfolio. Compare and contrast the types of appeals underlying these ads, as discussed by Fowles. To what extent do you notice significant shifts of appeal from the 1940s to the present? Which types of appeal seem to you most effective with particular product categories? Is it more likely, for example, that people will buy cigarettes because they want to feel autonomous or because the cigarettes will make them more attractive to the opposite sex?

2. Select a series of ads in different product categories that all appear to rely on the same primary appeal—perhaps the appeal to sex or the appeal to affiliation. Compare and contrast the overall strategies of these ads. Draw upon Fowles and other authors represented in

this chapter to develop your ideas. To what extent do your analyses support arguments often made by social critics (and advertising people) that what people are really buying is the image, rather than the product?

3. Discuss how a selection of ads reveals shifting cultural attitudes over the past six decades toward either (a) gender relations; (b) romance between men and women; (c) smoking; (d) automobiles. In the case of (a) or (b) above, the ads don't have to be for the same category of product. In terms of their underlying appeal, in terms of the implicit or explicit messages embodied both in the text and the graphics, how and to what extent do the ads reveal that attitudes of the target audiences have changed over the years?

4. Select a TV commercial or a TV ad campaign (for example, for Sprint phone service) and analyze the commercial(s) in terms of Fowles's categories, as well as the discussions of some of the authors in this chapter. To what extent do the principles discussed by these authors apply to broadcast, as well as to print ads? What are the special requirements of TV advertising?

5. Find a small group of ads that rely upon little or no body copy—just a graphic, perhaps a headline, and the product name. What common features underlie the marketing strategies of such ads? What kinds of appeal do they make? How do their graphic aspects compare? What makes the need for text superfluous?

6. As indicated in the introduction to this chapter, social critics have charged advertising with numerous offenses: "it fosters materialism, it psychologically manipulates people to buy things they don't need, it perpetuates gender and racial stereotypes (particularly in its illustrations), it is deceptive, it is offensive, it debases the language." To what extent do some of the advertisements presented in the ad portfolio (and perhaps others of your own choosing) demonstrate the truth of one or more of these charges? In developing your response, draw upon Bovée and Arens as well as some of the ads in the portfolio (or elsewhere).

7. Read the textual content (headlines and body text) of several ads *without* paying attention (if possible) to the graphics. Compare the effectiveness of the headline and body text by themselves with the effectiveness of the ads, *including* the graphic elements. Focusing on a group of related ads (related by product category, by appeal, by decade, etc.), devise an explanation of how graphics work to effectively communicate the appeal and meaning of the products advertised.

8. Many ads employ humor—in the graphics, in the body copy, or both—to sell a product. Examine a group of advertisements that rely on humor to make their appeal and explain how they work. For example, do they play off an incongruity between one element of the ad and another (such as between the headline and the

graphic), or between one element of the ad (or the basic message of the ad) and what we know or assume to be the case in the "real world"? Do they employ wordplay or irony? Do they picture people doing funny things (funny because inappropriate or unrealistic)? What appeal underlines the humor? Aggression? Sex? Nurture? Based on your examination and analyses, what appear to be some of the more effective ways of employing humor?

9. Think of a new product that you have just invented. This product, in your opinion, will revolutionize the world of [fill in the blank]. Devise an advertisement to announce this product to the world. Consider (or reject) using a celebrity to help sell your product. Select the basic appeal of your product (see Fowles). Then, applying concepts and principles discussed by other authors in this chapter, write the headline, subhead, and body copy for the product. Sketch out (or at least describe) the graphic that will accompany the text. Show your proposed ad to one or more of your classmates, get reactions, and then revise the ad, taking into account your market feedback.

10. Imagine that you own a small business—perhaps an independent coffee shop (not Starbucks, Peet's, or Coffee Bean), a videogame company, or a pedicab service that conveys tourists around a chic beach town. Devise an ad that announces your services and extols its benefits. Apply the principles discussed by Fowles and other writers in this chapter.

11. Write a parody ad—one that would never ordinarily be written— applying the selling principles discussed by Fowles and other authors in this unit. For example, imagine you are the manager of the Globe Theatre in Elizabethan England and want to sell season tickets to this season's plays, including a couple of new tragedies by your playwright in residence, Will Shakespeare. Or imagine that you are trying to sell Remington typewriters in the age of computers (no software glitches!). Or—as long as people are selling bottled water—you have found a way to package and sell air. Advertisers can reportedly sell anything with the right message. Give it your best shot.

12. Based on the reading you have done in this chapter, discuss the extent to which you believe advertisements create needs in consumers, reflect existing needs, or some combination of both. In developing your paper, draw on both particular advertisements and on the more theoretical overviews of advertising developed in the chapter.

13. Select one advertisement and conduct two analyses of it, using two different analytical principles: perhaps one from Fowles's list of fifteen emotional appeals and one from Cohen's principles of effective layout. Having conducted your analyses and developed your insights, compare and contrast the strengths and weaknesses of the

analytical principles you've employed. Conclude more broadly with a discussion of how a single analytical principle can close down, as well as open up, understanding of an object under study.

14. As you have seen, advertisements change over time, both across product categories and within categories. And yet the advertisements remain a constant, their presence built on the assumption that consumers can be swayed both overtly and covertly in making purchasing decisions. In a paper drawing on the selections in this chapter, develop a theory on why ads change over time. Is it because people's needs have changed and, therefore, new ads are required? (Do the older ads appeal to the same needs as newer ads?) In developing your discussion, you might track the changes over time in one product category.

RESEARCH ACTIVITIES

1. Drawing upon contemporary magazines (or magazines from a given period), select a set of advertisements in a particular product category. Analyze these advertisements according to Fowles's categories, and assess their effectiveness in terms of the discussions of other authors in this chapter.

2. Select a particular product that has been selling for at least 25 years (e.g., Bayer aspirin, Tide detergent, IBM computers, Oldsmobile—as in "This is not your father's Oldsmobile") and trace the history of print advertising for this product over the years. To what extent has the advertising changed over the years? To what extent has the essential sales appeal remained the same? In addition to examining the ads themselves, you may want to research the company and its marketing practices. You will find two business databases particularly useful: ABI/INFORM and the academic version of LexisNexis.

3. One of the landmark campaigns in American advertising was Doyle, Dane, Bernbach's series of ads for the Volkswagen Beetle in the 1960s. In effect a rebellion against standard auto advertising, the VW ads' Unique Selling Proposition was that ugly is beautiful—an appeal that was overwhelmingly successful. Research the VW ad campaign for this period, setting it in the context of the agency's overall marketing strategy.

4. Among the great marketing debacles of recent decades was Coca-Cola's development in 1985 of a new formula for its soft drink which (at least temporarily) replaced the much beloved old formula. Research this major development in soft drink history, focusing on the marketing of New Coke and the attempt of the Atlanta-based Coca-Coca company to deal with the public reception of its new product.

5. Advertising agencies are hired not only by manufacturers and by service industries; they are also hired by political candidates. In fact, one of the common complaints about American politics is that candidates for public office are marketed just as if they were bars of soap. Select a particular presidential or gubernatorial election and research the print and broadcast advertising used by the rival candidates. You may want to examine the ads not only of the candidates of the major parties but also the candidates of the smaller parties, such as the Green and the Libertarian parties. How do the appeals and strategies used by product ads compare and contrast with those used in ads for political candidates?

6. Public service ads comprise another major category of advertising (in addition to product and service advertising and political advertising). Such ads have been used to recruit people to military service, to get citizens to buy war bonds, to contribute to charitable causes, to get people to support or oppose strikes, to persuade people to stop using (or not to start using) drugs, to prevent drunk driving, etc. Locate a group of public service ads, describe them, and assess their effectiveness. Draw upon Fowles, Bovée, *et al.*, and Cohen in developing your conclusions.

7. Research advertising in American magazines and newspapers before World War II. Focus on a limited number of product lines— for example, soft drinks, soap and beauty products, health-related products. What kind of differences do you see between ads in the first part of the twentieth century and more recent or contemporary advertising for the same types of products? In general, how have the predominant types of appeal used to sell products in the past changed (if they have) with the times? How are the graphics of early ads different from preferred graphics today? How has the body copy changed? (Hint: you may want to be on the alert for ads that make primarily negative appeals—i.e., what may happen to you if you don't use the product advertised.)

Body Text from Selected Portfolio Ads

Camels, 1947 (p. 663)

[Box in illustration] You remember how it starts—that beloved old Christmas poem:

'Twas the night before Christmas,
when all through the house,
Not a creature was stirring,
—not even a mouse.

Well, that isn't always true for the doctor. Sometimes there's just no rest at all for him—even on Christmas Eve.

Blizzard or heat wave . . . December or July . . . night or day . . . near or far . . . early or late . . . no matter when you call, he comes!

[Below headline] Not a single branch of medicine was overlooked in the nationwide survey made by three leading independent research organizations. To 113,597 doctors from Canada to Mexico, from the Atlantic to the Pacific went the query—*What cigarette do you smoke, Doctor?*

The brand named most was Camel.

Like anyone else, a doctor smokes for pleasure. He appreciates rich, full flavor and cool mildness just as any other smoker. If you don't happen to be a Camel smoker now, try Camels. Let your "T-Zone" give you the answer.

Webster Cigars, 1945 (p. 664)

- Websters are being specially boxed and Christmas wrapped this year. Boxes of 25, as low as $3.75. Give Websters by the box. A luxurious gift to yourself and to men who are used to the best.
- There are five different sizes of Websters. Each is made of 100% long Havana, bound in top-quality Broadleaf and wrapped in finest Connecticut Shadegrown. Boxes of 25 and 50 in all sizes. Wherever fine cigars are smoked.

Philip Morris, 1950s (p. 665)

[Below headline] Gentleness makes good friends in fun-making . . . and in a cigarette, where gentleness is one of the greatest requirements of modern taste. That's why today's Philip Morris, born gentle, refined to special gentleness in the making, makes so many friends among our young smokers. Enjoy the gentle pleasure, the fresh unfiltered flavor, of today's Philip Morris. In the convenient snap-open pack, regular or smart king-size.

Pabst Blue Ribbon, 1940s (p. 672)

[Following first panel] **Tom:** Good grief! I promised Mabel I'd be home at 6—It's 10 to 7 now!

Ed: Relax, Tom! We'll take care of you . . . and Mabel, too, "33 to 1"!

Tom: Stop joking, Ed. She'll never let me go to another ball game.

Ed: No jokes . . . I'm serious! Here!—let's have our 33 to 1 right now.

Tom: Oh—Pabst Blue Ribbon! S-a-y, this *is* a treat! But 33 to 1 . . . I'm afraid I don't get the connection.

Ed: That's easy. It's 33 fine brews blended into one great beer. Blending's what gives it that swell flavor.

Flavor! Mild, mellow, distinctive . . . because it's a blend of not two, or five, or twelve . . . but 33 separate brews—specially blended like finest champagnes.

Later in Tom's Home

Mabel: W-e-l-l!! . . . Well, what's this—Pabst Blue Ribbon. Why Tom, you *are* an old smoothie!

Tom: Just a blue ribbon gift for a prize-winning wife—heh heh. *[thinking] Ed was right. 33 to 1 does make a "home run" smoother!*

Text: Why is Pabst Blue Ribbon the most popular beer in the homes of America? Your first delicious sip provides the answer. For here is a beer that's blended like finest champagnes . . . each sparkling drop a winning blend of 33 fine brews. Enjoy it in the handsome regular and new quart size bottles—or on draft at better places everywhere.

Ballantine Ale, 1950s (p. 673)

[Below picture] America is returning to the genuine—in foods, fashions and tastes. Today's trend to Ballantine light Ale fits right into this modern picture. In all the world, no other beverage brewed has such extra excellence brewed into it. And "Brewer's Gold" is one big reason for Ballantine Ale's deep, rich, genuine flavor.

Ballantine Ale, 1953 (pp. 674–75)

[Lower left] ERNEST HEMINGWAY, who has been called the greatest living American writer, is also internationally famous as a deep-sea fisherman. Since publication of *The Sun Also Rises* in 1926, his novels and stories have enriched the literature of the English language consistently, year after year. His newest book is *The Old Man and the Sea.*

Bacardi Rum, 1960s (p. 676)

[Below headline] Big, bold highballs, sassy Daiquiris, cool tonics, and colas—Bacardi rum is enjoyable always and *all* ways. Extra Special: our man Fernando is pouring very rare Bacardi Anejo rum (Ahn-YAY-ho), one of the fine rums from Bacardi. So incredibly smooth he enjoys it even in a snifter. Try it, too!

Hennessy Cognac, 1968 (p. 678)

[Below headline] Every drop of Hennessy V.S.O.P. Reserve is Grande Fine Champagne Cognac. It's made solely from grapes grown in La Grande Champagne—the small district in the Cognac region which is the source of the very greatest Cognac.

What's more, Hennessy is selected from the largest reserves of aged Cognacs in existence. Enjoy a taste of success today . . .

Budweiser Beer, 1990s (p. 682)

[Body text]

All they needed was an inch.

You had to stop them. So you built a wall. A determined wall made of you and the rest of the line.

And when the play unfolded, when they came at you with their cunning, they ran into your wall of strength.

They just couldn't move you an inch.

Standing your ground takes more than raw strength. It takes fierce determination. A strong sense of pride. And the very best a man has to give. At Anheuser-Busch we understand that. Which is why we brew a light beer with a clean, distinctive taste. Budweiser® Light.

We know the best never comes easy. That's why there's nothing else like it.

Cadillac, 1945 (p. 683)

[Below headline] Three years ago, the sneak attack on Pearl Harbor found America unprepared to defend its rights. Yet, even at that early date, Cadillac was in its third year of building aircraft engine parts for military use. Today we are look[ing] hopefully forward to the time when this important contribution to America's air power will pay off in such a scene as that illustrated above.

For more than five years we have been working toward that end. Back in 1939, we started building precision parts for Allison— America's famous liquid-cooled aircraft engines—used to power such potent fighters as the Lightning, the Warhawk, the Mustang, the Airacobra and the new Kingcobra.

In addition to our work for Allison, which has included more than 57,000,000 man-hours of precision production—we assisted Army Ordnance Engineers in designing the M-5 Light Tank and the M-8 Howeitzer motor carriage, and have produced them in quantities. Both are powered by Cadillac engines equipped with Hydra-Matic transmissions.

We are now building other weapons which utilize some of our Cadillac peacetime products. We can't talk about all of them yet— but we are confident they will prove significant additions to Allied armor.

De Soto, 1947 (p. 684)

[Below headline] *From a mail survey among thousands of owners of 1941 and 1942 De Soto cars.

Ford, 1947 (p. 685)

1. **"I don't know** synthetic enamel from a box of my children's paints . . . but if synthetic enamel is what it takes to make that beautiful, shiny Ford finish, I'm all for it!

2. **"My husband says** the brakes are self-centering and hydraulic—whatever that means! All I know is they're so easy that I can taxi the children all day without tiring out!

3. **"Peter, he's my teen-age son,** tells me that 'Ford is the only car in its price class with a choice of 100-horsepower V-8 engine or a brilliant new Six.' He says no matter which engine people pick, they're out front with Ford!

4. **"The interior** of our Ford is strictly my department! It's tailored with the dreamiest broadcloth. Such a perfect fit! Mary Jane says women help design Ford interiors. There's certainly a woman's touch there!

5. **"Do you like** lovely silver, beautifully simple and chaste looking? That's what I always think of when I touch those smart Ford door handles and window openers.

6. **"Now here's another thing** women like and that's a blissfully comfortable ride—one that isn't bumpity-bump even on some of our completely forgotten roads.

Listen to the Ford Show starring Dinah Shore on Columbia Network Stations Wednesday evenings.

Cadillac, 1954 (p. 686–87)

[Below headline] If a motorist wanted to make the move to Cadillac solely for the car's prestige—he would most certainly be justified in doing so. For the Cadillac car has never stood so high in public esteem as it does today—and the rewards which grow out of this unprecedented acceptance comprise the rarest and greatest satisfactions in all motordom.

There is, for instance, *the inescapable feeling of pride* that comes with ownership of so distinguished and beloved a possession . . . the wonderful *sense of well-being* that comes from having reached a point of achievement where you can enjoy one of the world's most sought-after manufactured products . . . and the *marvelous feeling of confidence and self-esteem* that is found in the respect and admiration universally accorded the owner of a Cadillac car. Those who presently enjoy these unique Cadillac virtues will tell you that they are, in themselves, worth the car's whole purchase price.

Of course, most motorists would hesitate to take such a step purely for their personal edification. But in Cadillac's case, this wonderful prestige is actually a "bonus", so to speak—an extra dividend that comes with every Cadillac car, in addition to its breath-taking styling, its magnificent performance, its superlative luxury and its remarkable economy.

Have you seen and driven the 1954 Cadillac? If you haven't, then you've a truly wonderful adventure awaiting you—and one that you should postpone no longer.

Dodge, 1955 (p. 688)

[Below headline] The *look* of success! The *feel* of success! The *power* of success!

They come to you in a dramatically beautiful, dynamically powered new Dodge that introduces the ease and safety of push-button driving—and Magic Touch of Tomorrow! It is a truly great value.

Buick, 1965 (p. 689)

[Headline] **Drive a Rivera home tonight. Who cares if people think you're younger, richer and more romantic than you really are?**

[Body text] A Riviera has a strange effect on people. Simply looking at one makes your mouth water, your eyes open wider and your heart beat faster. You grin admiringly when you notice the headlights, tucked behind shields that open with the touch of the headlight switch. You breathe harder when you turn loose some of those 325 horsepower. And that's just what happens to the driver. Wait till you see the awe a Riviera inspires in passersby! Amazing. Also attainable, for considerably less than you might suspect. (Before you fall headlong for a Riviera, ask yourself if a firmer suspension and assorted other sporting touches give you a twinge of anticipation. Yes? Ask your dealer about our new Riviera Gran Sport. The name alone is a hint of what's in it for you.) Check with your Buick dealer soon. He may convince you you're younger, richer and more romantic than you thought you were.

Wouldn't you really rather have a Buick?

Corvette, 1966 (p. 690)

[Below headline] What manner of woman is this, you ask, who stands in the middle of a mountain stream eating a peach?

Actually, she's a normal everyday girl except that she and her husband own the Corvette Coupe in the background. (He's at work right now, wondering where he misplaced his car keys.)

The temptation, you see, was overpowering. They'd had the car a whole week now, and not once had he offered to let her drive. His excuse was that this, uh, was a big hairy sports car. Too much for a woman to handle: the trigger-quick steering, the independent rear suspension, the disc brakes—plus the 4-speed transmission and that 425-hp engine they had ordered—egad! He would teach her to drive it some weekend. So he said.

That's why she hid the keys, forcing him to seek public transportation. Sure of his departure, she went to the garage, started the Corvette, and was off for the hills, soon upshifting and downshifting as smoothly as he. His car. Hard to drive. What propaganda!

Volvo, 1990s (pp. 692–93)

[Below headline] When it comes to marriages, Volvo like[s] to put on a big spread.

That's why, with the 400 series, we're giving you a wider choice than any other manufacturer. You can pick a bigger engine with standard specification or a smaller engine with the luxury package.

In fact, with a total of five different engine sizes and six different interior packages on offer, you can mix and match as much as you like.

You could, for instance, unite the 1.6 engine with the Luxury Pack, which features air-conditioning and leather upholstery.

With other manufacturers, however, you don't get such a happy coupling. You'll find that the luxury package, for example, only comes with the larger engine.

Volvo's approach (which applies to the 440 hatchback and 460 saloon) means you not only get the car that suits your exact needs, but you decide exactly where your money goes.

And you don't have to wait any longer for delivery of your specially built car. . . .

Campbell's, 1945 (p. 694)

[Below headline] Many children do not get adequate lunches! And yet upon proper food depends not only their future health, but today's well-being, cheerfulness—and even report cards!

Lunch should include a hot dish, and be substantial but easy to digest. Good nourishing soup is a big help—and Campbell's Vegetable Soup is just right! Children love it, and it brings them all the sturdy goodness of 15 different garden vegetables combined with a rich, invigorating beef stock. No wonder mothers everywhere agree "It's almost a meal in itself!"

Coca-Cola, 1945 (p. 695)

[Below box on left] It's natural for popular names to acquire friendly abbreviations. That's why you hear Coca-Cola called Coke. Coca-Cola and Coke mean the same thing . . . *"the real thing . . ."* a single thing coming from a single source, and well known to the community."

[Below illustration on right] Ice-cold Coca-Cola gets a hearty welcome. It's the answer to thirst that adds refreshment. Coca-Cola has *that extra something* to do the job of complete refreshment. It has a taste that's uniquely satisfying—a quality that's unmistakable. That's why the only thing like Coca-Cola is Coca-Cola itself. Thirst asks nothing more.

National Dairy Products Corporation, 1947 (p. 696)

[Below headline] Prediction: The new wives of 1947 are going to have more fun in the kitchen.

Previous cooking experience is desirable, perhaps, but not essential. There are so many new easy-to-use foods, so many new ways to prepare foods, so many interesting ways to serve foods, cooking will be a novel and exciting adventure.

Further prediction: Cheese dishes will be featured more often on their menus. They'll know that cheese gives tastiness and variety to meals. And cheese, like milk (nature's most nearly perfect food), is rich in protein, calcium, phosphorus, in vitamins A and G.

Yes, we have a personal interest in cheese. For Kraft, pioneer in cheese, is a unit of National Dairy. And what we've said about housewives using more cheese is entirely true.

It's also true that they're learning more about the whys and wherefores of food each year—just as the scientists in our laboratories are learning more about better ways to process, improve and supply it.

These men are backed by the resources of a great organization. They explore every field of dairy products, discover new ones. And the health of America benefits constantly by this National Dairy research.

Dedicated to the wider use and better understanding of diary products as human food . . . as a base for the development of new products and materials . . . as a source of health and enduring progress on the farms and in the towns and cities of America.

Bon Ami, 1947 (p. 697)

[Below headline]

Ann: You could, hon! Just use a cleanser that doesn't leave scratches.

May: Goodness! What in the world do scratches have to do with it?

Ann: A lot, silly! Those tiny scratches you get from gritty cleaners hold onto dirt and double your cleaning time.

May: Well, you old smartie! I'd never thought of *that* before!

Ann: I hadn't thought of it either—till I discovered Bon Ami! See how fine-textured and white it is. It just *slides* dirt off—and when you rinse it away, it doesn't leave any of that horrid grit in the tub.

May: Say no more, darling! From now on there's going to be a new cleaning team in our house—*me* and Bon Ami!

Trushay, 1947 (p. 698)

[Row 1, frame 1] Now Annie was . . .

[Row 1, frame 2] as beautiful a girl . . .

[Row 1, frame 3] as ever was put together!

[Row 1, frame 4] Why, when Annie walked down the street . . . **Wow!**

[Row 2, frame 1] Yet Annie had her bad moments . . . like any other gal.

[Row 2, frame 2] And you want to know why? Annie's hands were a mess, always rough and dry, like sandpaper.

[Row 2, frame 3] And when a man wants to hold a girl's hands . . . even a girl like Annie . . . he doesn't want to wear gloves . . .

[Row 2, frame 4] Then, luckily, Fannie told Annie about an entirely new and different hand lotion! The **beforehand** lotion . . . **Trushay!**

[Row 3, frame 1] So Annie smoothed creamy, fragrant **Trushay** on her hands <u>before</u> she did dishes . . . because **Trushay** guards hands <u>even</u> in hot, soapy water!

[Row 3, frame 2] And Annie put **Trushay** on her hands <u>before</u> she tubbed her undies . . . so **Trushay**'s special "oil-richness" could help prevent dryness and roughness.

[Row 3, frame 3] So now Annie is able to keep her hands soft and holdable . . . thanks to **Trushay**'s wonderful softening help.

P.S. Trushay's grand for softening hands at any time. Wonderful, too, for rough, dry elbows and heels . . . as a powder base . . . before and after exposure to weather. Trushay contains no alcohol, is not sticky. Begin today to use Trushay.

Jergens Lotion, 1954 (p. 699)

[Below headline] You and Dorian Mehle have something in common. Every year, you wash a stack of dishes a quarter-mile high!

Detergents make your job so much easier. They cut right into grease and grime. They get you through dishwashing in much less time, but while they dissolve grease, they also take away the natural oils and youthful softness of your hands!

Although Dorian hasn't given up detergents her hands are as soft, as smooth, as young-looking as a teenager's. Her secret is no secret at all. It's the world's best-known beauty routine. It's pure, white Jergens Lotion, after every chore.

When you smooth on Jergens Lotion, this liquid formula doesn't just "coat" your hands. It penetrates right away, to help *replace* that softening moisture your skin needs.

Jergens Lotion has two ingredients doctors recommend for softening. Women must be recommending it, too, for more women use it than any other hand care in the world. Dorian's husband is the best testimonial to Jergens Lotion care. Even after years of married life, he still loves to hold her pretty hands!

Use Jergens Lotion like a prescription: three times a day, after every meal!

Disney Hats, 1954 (p. 700)

[Below illustration] President Lee A. Potter Jr., of the Young Presidents Organization Inc. and Forman, Ford & Co. "To be successful, look the part. That certain look of success attracts the confidence of important men."

A man's hat speaks eloquently of his personal measure of authority. That's why Disney hats are so often considered part of a businessman's equipment. The rare skill of their handcraftsmanship, the executive character of their styling reflect the critical judgment and taste of the wearer. Disney's uniquely impressive effect has made these hats the choice of prominent men for 65 years.

Bell, 1956 (p. 701)

[Below illustration] You can just bet the first thing he'd ask for would be a telephone in the kitchen.

You wouldn't catch him dashing to another room every time the telephone rang or he had to make a call.

He doesn't have to do it in his office in town. It would be mighty helpful if you didn't have to do it in your "office" at home.

That's in the kitchen where you do so much of your work. And it's right there that an additional telephone comes in so handy for so many things.

Along with a lot of convenience is that nice feeling of pride in having the best of everything especially if it is one of those attractive new telephones in color.

P.S. Additional telephones in kitchen, bedroom, and other convenient places around the house cost little. The service charge is just pennies a day.

Bell, 1974 (p. 702)

[Below headline] Alana MacFarlane is a 20-year-old from San Rafael, California. She's one of our first women telephone installers. She won't be the last.

We also have several hundred male telephone operators. And a policy that there are no all-male or all-female jobs at the phone company.

We want men and women of the telephone company do to what they want to do, and do best.

For example, Alana likes working outdoors. "I don't go for office routine," she said. "But as an installer, I get plenty of variety and a chance to move around."

Some people like to work with their hands, or, like Alana, get a kick out of working 20 feet up in the air.

Others like to drive trucks. Some we're helping to develop into good managers.

Today, when openings exist, local Bell Companies are offering applicants and present employees some jobs they may never have thought about before. We want to help all advance to the best of their abilities.

AT&T and your local Bell Company are equal opportunity employers.

American Airlines, 1968 (p. 731)

[Below headline] She only wants what's best for you.

A cool drink. A good dinner. A soft pillow and a warm blanket.

This is not just maternal instinct. It's the result of the longest Stewardess training in the industry.

Training in service, not just a beauty course.

Service, after all, is what makes professional travelers prefer American.

And makes new travelers want to keep on flying with us.

So we see that every passenger gets the same professional treatment.

That's the American way.

Shineaway 17 Lotion, 1980s (p. 705)

[Below headline] For skin that looks flawless even when it isn't, get the new Shineaway range from 17. Prices from £1.69 to £2.50. Exclusive to Boots. Dermatologically tested and fragrance-free. 17 Products are not tested on animals.

You, the Jury

WILLIAM ROPER: So now you'd give the Devil benefit of law!

MORE: Yes. What would you do? Cut a great road through the law to get after the Devil?

ROPER: I'd cut down every law in England to do that!

MORE: Oh? And when the last law was down, and the Devil turned round on you—where would you hide, Roper, the laws all being flat? This country's planted thick with laws from coast to coast—man's laws, not God's—and if you cut them down—and you're just the man to do it—d'you really think you could stand upright in the winds that would blow then? [*Quietly.*] Yes, I'd give the Devil benefit of law, for my own safety's sake.

—Robert Bolt, *A Man for All Seasons*

The lines above indicate one way of looking at the law, but clearly, many people take a different view of the legal profession. One of Shakespeare's characters declares, "The first thing we do, let's kill all the lawyers" (*Henry VI*, Pt II). Never mind that while playing off the public's perennial resentment of lawyers, Shakespeare intended this line as a sardonic commentary on mob mentality. Still, everyone loves a good lawyer joke. ("Why didn't the shark eat the lawyer who fell out of his boat? Professional courtesy.") Of course, in these litigious times, the same people who tell lawyer jokes hurry to get their own after they slip on the ice in their neighbor's driveway or when they're arrested on a drunk driving charge.

In Robert Bolt's play, Thomas More views the law as civilized society's first line of defense against chaos and anarchy. Without the law, he argues, we would have no protection against "the winds that would blow" in a lawless society. But even if we don't accept this exalted view of the law, it's certainly true that all of us, at some points in our lives, will have dealings with the law (not necessarily as a defendant, we hasten to add), and that as citizens of society, most of us rely upon the law to protect us against those who would violate our rights and to impose damages upon those who have injured us. (Those who don't rely on the law often rely instead on their own private arsenals to repel invaders and predators.)

If the average citizen is not the plaintiff or the defendant in a court case, then her or his most common direct experience with the law may be as a juror. Chosen at random from a cross section of the population, jurors may be called upon to render a verdict in a civil case (a case of product liability, for example, or negligence, or libel) or in a criminal case (such as robbery or murder). After the lawyers on both sides have presented their witnesses and their evidence, after they have made their arguments and rebutted their opponents, and after the judge has explained the law to the jury in language they can understand, it falls to the jury to apply the law to the facts of the particular case. They must decide whether or not a rule has been violated, and if it has, the price the defendant must pay—perhaps a fine, perhaps a jail term, perhaps even the forfeiture of his or her life.

Underlying this chapter is the assumption that you are a jury member (or perhaps a judge) in a particular case. You will be presented with the facts of the case. You will also be presented with the relevant law. It will be your task to consider the facts, to study the issues, to render a verdict either for the plaintiff or for the defendant, and—most importantly, for our purposes—to explain your reasoning. Don't worry about becoming tangled in the thickets of the law (and some of these thickets are very dense indeed). We will assume no previous legal knowledge, and for each case we will present enough facts and enough statements about the law to enable you to make an educated judgment, just as if you were a member of a jury.

Don't worry, either, about making the "right" choice. The most important thing is not that you come out on the correct side or even the side that actually prevailed in the end. (Keep in mind that through the appeals process, a higher court can reverse the ruling of a lower court—saying, in effect, that the lower court was wrong.) What is important is that you carefully analyze the case, that you go through the reasoning process systematically and logically, in a manner consistent with the facts. This material will therefore provide you with additional opportunities to practice the analysis skills you learned in Chapter 6.

In one sense, this chapter previews a particular situation in which you might one day find yourself—fulfilling your civic duty as a juror in an actual case. More generally, it will provide you with some interesting cases through which you can practice a very fundamental intellectual task in the academic and professional worlds: the task of applying a general rule or principle to a particular case or circumstance. Obviously, this is a process that doesn't happen only in law. As a student in a sociology course, for example, you might show how some principles relating to the ways that individuals obey authority apply in particular cases (for example, the suicides in the Heaven's Gate cult) and even allow you to make certain broad predictions about behavior. As a film student, you might show how the general features of the typical *film noir* operate in particular films, such as *The Big Sleep* or *A Touch of Evil.*

Besides exercising your intellectual faculties, you'll see that it's often fascinating to plunge into legal battles. After all, legal cases are, at heart, conflicts, and conflicts are inherently interesting. That's why we like to read books or watch TV shows or movies that are set in the courtroom.

We begin our chapter with a number of civil cases (that is, cases of private wrongs), starting with "The Maiden and the Pot of Gold: A Case of Emotional

Distress," in which a woman sues some men who tricked her into believing that she had recovered a pot of gold from a field. Two selections that will help orient you to the legal system and legal reasoning follow. In "The American Legal System," attorney David Hricik explains where the law comes from and describes the process of the typical lawsuit. In "IRAC: How to Write About Legal Cases," Leonard Tourney and Gina Genova describe legal thinking and legal writing, focusing in particular on the important IRAC (issue, rule, application, conclusion) technique as applied to "Incident at the Airport," a hypothetical case involving a lawsuit for battery.

"The Ridiculed Employee" and "The Overweight Nursing Student" deal with two additional cases of emotional distress upon which you, as a jury member, can deliberate. (Can a man collect damages from a supervisor who repeatedly makes fun of his stuttering? Can a former student collect damages from the college that forced her to withdraw because she was overweight?) These selections are followed by "Assault and Battery on the Gridiron: A Case of Reckless Disregard of Safety," an unusual case in which one football player sues another for injuries sustained on the playing field. In "Who Gets the Kids? Some Cases of Child Custody," you will get a chance to consider some of the bitterest lawsuits that pass through the civil courts. Next, in "Hot Coffee Spills," we offer some coffee cases that both precede and follow the famous McDonald's case involving a woman who was awarded almost three million dollars (later reduced to half a million) when a cup of hot coffee she had purchased at the fast food restaurant spilled as she was driving away, severely burning her.

The next part of the chapter deals with criminal cases. In "The Felled Stop Signs," you will decide the legal responsibility of some teenagers who pulled down highway signs, including a stop sign—a piece of "fun" that resulted in a fatal accident. In "Drag Racing and Death: Some Cases of Manslaughter," you will consider the question of how seriously the law should deal with someone who participates in a fatal drag race, even though he may not have driven the car actually involved in the accident. Next, as a guide to the entire chapter, we offer a "Legal Glossary" to help you understand the unfamiliar legal language you will encounter while working with these cases. Finally, an expanded section on research activities shows how to conduct respectable legal research without actually being enrolled in law school.

Each selection dealing with a particular case consists of two elements. The first element presents the "Facts of the Case," as written by the panel of appeals court judges who ruled upon the case. All of the cases you will read in this chapter are cases that have been appealed by either the plaintiff or the defendant to an appeals court after the original jury verdict. The second element presents the "Statements of the Law," statements that you will apply to the facts of the case, just as if you were following the judge's instructions. In some selections, these statements do consist of the kind of instructions that a judge would give to a jury in such cases. In others, they will be the actual statutes that may or may not have been violated. You may also read excerpts from case law—judicial opinions from previous cases dealing with similar issues that may have bearing upon the case you are currently considering.

What you will not find, however, as you consider these cases, is the ultimate outcome. If you know the outcome in advance, you are likely to be unduly swayed in your reasoning, attempting to bring it in line with the arguments of the side that prevailed. As we suggested earlier, which side won is less important for our purposes than the process of logically applying general principles to specific cases. Nevertheless, if you have to know which side won, ask your instructor to consult the *Instructor's Manual* for this book.

Occasionally, however, it will be difficult or even impossible to find out which side ultimately won. That's because some cases are sent back by the appeals court to the trial court, and most trial court cases are not published—though photocopied transcripts are available (for a hefty fee) from the clerk of the court—and the more newsworthy cases are covered by reporters. Also, a good many civil cases, after going up and down through the appeals process, are ultimately settled out of court—and frequently, the terms of the settlement are not publicly available.

This chapter offers considerable opportunities for group work. After all, work on a jury is a collective enterprise, and before a jury arrives at a verdict, unanimous or otherwise, its individual members must engage in a good deal of discussion, perhaps even argument. In some cases, your papers may be written collectively by the group; but even when individually written, they could reflect the views of more than one viewpoint. In fact, as you will see in Tourney and Genova's selection, the IRAC format, used widely in legal writing, should include a consideration and a rebuttal of opposing arguments.

A NOTE ON SYNTHESIS ACTIVITIES

Because of the special nature of legal reasoning, we include synthesis activities, where appropriate, as part of the Discussion and Writing Suggestions following some of the grouped case selections, rather than at the end of the chapter.

Lawyers synthesize cases as a matter of course, but only when they are closely related, in order to point out legal precedents. We do include a few closely related cases in this chapter (for example, *Nickerson v. Hodges* and *Harris v. Jones,* both in the "emotional distress" section as well as in the "drag racing" and "stop sign" cases); but for the most part, the cases we have selected are too different in facts and legal issues to be usefully synthesized.

> ### The Maiden and the Pot of Gold:
> ### A Case of Emotional Distress
> #### *(Nickerson v. Hodges)*

You may have heard the phrase "emotional distress" in connection with a lawsuit and wondered how such a vague term could possibly have legal meaning. After all, people are always doing things that distress other people. Bosses inflict distress on their employees, teachers distress students, lovers distress each other. Undoubtedly, your parents drive you to emotional distress (and vice versa), yet few children sue their parents—though that has happened.

Still, there's emotional distress and there's emotional distress; some people seem to go out of their way to maliciously and outrageously distress others, and the distress they occasion sometimes is particularly severe. In these cases, we feel that the perpetrators should be legally liable—meaning that they should be forced to pay financial damages to their victims. But plaintiffs must do more than claim that they have suffered emotional distress at the hands of the defendants. They must prove such a claim, by showing how the legal defini-tion of emotional distress applies to their particular case, or by showing how their particu-lar case is similar, if not identical, to one or more previous cases of proven emotional distress.

The following selection presents one such case: It is part of an opinion by the Supreme Court of Louisiana in 1920. First, we present the Facts of the Case as summarized by the panel of judges who wrote the opinion. (Their ruling itself and the reasoning behind it are not presented here; these are for you to decide. Your instructor, however, will be able to consult the Instructor's Manual and tell you how the case turned out.) Following the facts of the case, we offer a set of instructions that the judge might give to the jury before they begin deliberating in a case involving emotional distress. Strictly speaking, these instructions are anachronistic, since they were written decades after the Nickerson case (and are intended for California juries). Nonetheless, they embody the same essential assumptions about liability for emotional dis-tress that were considered by the judges who decided the case of Nickerson v. Hodges.

Note: In civil (as opposed to criminal) cases, such as this one, a jury will render a verdict of either "liable" or "not liable" (as opposed to "guilty" or "not guilty").

Carrie E. Nickerson et al.

v.

A. J. Hodges et al.
Supreme Court of Louisiana
Feb. 2, 1920

The Facts of the Case*

1   Miss Carrie E. Nickerson brought this suit against H. R. Hayes, William or "Bud" Baker, John W. Smith, Mrs. Fannie Smith, Miss Minnie Smith, A. J. Hodges, G. G. Gatling, R. M. Coyle, Sam P. D. Coyle, and Dr. Charles Coyle, claiming $15,000 as damages, alleged to have been caused in the form of financial outlay, loss in business, mental and physical suffering, humiliation, and injury to reputation and social standing, all growing out of an alleged malicious deception and conspir-acy with respect to the finding of a supposed pot of gold. Subsequent to the filing of the petition, and before the trial, the said Miss Nickerson died, and her legal heirs, some 10 in number, were made parties plaintiff, and now prosecute this suit.

2   Miss Nickerson was a kinswoman of Burton and Lawson Deck, the exact degree of relationship not being fully shown by the record, and there had been, in the family, a tradition that these two gentlemen, who died many years ago, had, prior to their deaths, buried a large amount of gold coin on the place now owned by the defendant John W. Smith, or on another near by. She was employed by the California Perfume Company to solicit orders for their wares

---

* *Nickerson v. Hodges.* 84 So. 37 (1920).

in the towns, villages, etc., in Webster and other parishes, and on the occasion of a visit to the city of Shreveport seems to have interviewed a fortune teller, who told her that her said relatives had buried the gold, and gave her what purported to be a map or plat showing its location on the property of Smith.

3   Thereafter, with the help of some three or four other persons, principally relatives, and one Bushong, she spent several months digging, at intervals, around the house and on the premises of Smith, who seems to have extended them a cordial welcome, and to have permitted them to dig almost without limit as to time and place, and in addition boarded the fortune hunters, while so engaged, without charge. We assume that this was due, perhaps, to the fact that he, too, had a slight hope that they might find something, and he was to receive a part thereof for his concessions. At any rate, the diggers pursued their course with such persistence and at such lengths, digging around the roots of shade trees, the pillars of his house, etc., until finally, his daughter, the said Minnie Smith, William or "Bud" Baker, and H. R. Hayes conceived the idea of themselves providing a "pot of gold" for the explorers to find.

4   Accordingly they obtained an old copper kettle or bucket, filled it with rocks and wet dirt, and buried it in an old chimney seat on the adjoining place, where the searchers had been or were intending to also prospect for the supposed treasure. Two lids or tops were placed on the pot, the first being fastened down with hay wire; then a note was written by Hayes, dated, according to some July 1, 1884, and, as to others, 1784, directing whoever should find the pot not to open it for three days, and to notify all the heirs. This note was wrapped in tin, placed between the first and second lids, and the latter was also securely fastened down with hay wire. This took place some time toward the latter part of March, and, according to these three defendants, was to have been an April fool; but plans miscarried somewhat, and the proper opportunity for the "find" did not present itself until April 14th.

5   On that day Miss Nickerson and her associates were searching and digging near the point where the pot had been buried, when Grady Hayes, a brother of H. R. Hayes, following directions from the latter, and apparently helping the explorers to hunt for the gold, dug up the pot and gave the alarm. All of those in the vicinity, of course, rushed to the spot, those who were "in" on the secret being apparently as much excited as the rest, and, after some discussion, it was decided to remove the lid. When this was done, the note was discovered, and H. R. Hayes advised Miss Nickerson that he thought it proper that its directions should be carried out, and that the bank at Cotton Valley, a few miles distant, was the best place to deposit the "gold" for safe-keeping, until the delays could run and the heirs be notified, as requested. Following this suggestion, the pot was placed in a gunny sack, tied up, and taken to the bank for deposit. Defendant Gatling was the cashier of the bank, but refused to give a receipt for the deposit as a "pot of gold," because, as he insisted, he did not know what it contained.

6   As might have been supposed, it did not take long for the news to spread that Miss Nickerson and her associates in the search for fortune, had found a pot of gold, and the discussion and interest in the matter became so general that defendant A. J. Hodges, vice president of the bank, went over from his place of business in Cotton Valley to the bank, and he and Gatling, after talking the matter over,

decided to examine the pot, so that, in event it did contain gold, proper precautions to guard the bank might be taken, pending the return of Miss Nickerson and the appearance of those who might claim the fortune. These two undid the wire sufficiently to peep into the pot, and discovered that it apparently contained only dirt. They then replaced the lid and held their tongues until the reappearance of Miss Nickerson. However, the secret leaked out from other sources, that the whole matter was a joke, and this information too, became pretty well distributed.

7   After depositing the pot in the bank, Miss Nickerson went to Minden, La., and induced Judge R. C. Drew to agree to accompany her to Cotton Valley on the following Monday (the deposit at the bank having been made on Saturday) for the purpose of seeing that the ceremonies surrounding the opening of the treasure were properly conducted. Judge Drew swears that he had heard in some way that the matter was a joke, and so informed Miss Nickerson, warning her not to place too much faith in the idea that she was about to come into a fortune, but that finally, because of his friendly relations with and kindly feeling toward her, he consented and did go, mainly to gratify her wishes in the premises. Some half a dozen other relatives of Burton and Lawson Deck were notified, and either accompanied or preceded Miss Nickerson to Cotton Valley.

8   With the stage thus set, the parties all appeared at the bank on Monday morning at about 11 o'clock, and among the number were H. R. Hayes, one of the defendants, who seems to have been one of the guiding spirits in the scheme, and one Bushong, the latter, we infer, from intimations thrown out by witnesses in the record, being at the time either an avowed or supposed suitor of Miss Nickerson's. Judge Drew, as the spokesman for the party, approached Gatling and informed him that it was desired that the pot be produced for the purpose of opening and examining the contents for the benefit of those thus assembled. The testimony of the witnesses varies a little as to just when the storm began; some say, as soon as the sack was brought out. Miss Nickerson discovered that the string was tied near the top, instead of down low around the pot, and immediately commenced to shout that she had been robbed; others insist that she was calm until the package was opened and the mocking earth and stones met her view. Be that as it may, she flew into a rage, threw the lid of the pot at Gatling, and for some reason, not clearly explained, turned the force of her wrath upon Hayes to such an extent that he appealed for protection, and Bushong, with another, held her arms to prevent further violence.

9   Miss Nickerson was a maiden, nearing the age of 45 years, and some 20 years before had been an inmate of an insane asylum, to the knowledge of those who had thus deceived her. She was energetic and self-supporting in her chosen line of employment, as a soap drummer, until she met the fortune teller who gave her the "information" which she evidently firmly believed would ultimately enable her to find the fortune which the family tradition told her had been left hidden by her deceased relatives. The conspirators, no doubt, merely intended what they did as a practical joke, and had no willful intention of doing the lady any injury. However, the results were quite serious indeed, and the mental suffering and humiliation must have been quite unbearable, to say nothing of the disappointment and conviction, which she carried to her grave some two years later, that she had been robbed.

Judge's Instructions to the Jury*

1   Ladies and Gentlemen of the Jury:

2   It is now my duty to instruct you on the law that applies to this case. It is your duty to follow the law.

3   As jurors it is your duty to determine the effect and value of the evidence and to decide all questions of fact.

4   You must not be influenced by sympathy, prejudice, or passion.

5   The plaintiff *Carrie E. Nickerson* seeks to recover damages based upon on a claim of intentional infliction of emotional distress.

6   The essential elements of such a claim are:

1. The defendant engaged in outrageous, [unprivileged] conduct;
2. [a. The] defendant intended to cause plaintiff to suffer emotional distress; [or [b.] [(1) The defendant engaged in the conduct with reckless disregard of the probability of causing plaintiff to suffer emotional distress;
    (2) The plaintiff was present at the time the outrageous conduct occurred; and
    (3) The defendant knew that the plaintiff was present;]
3. The plaintiff suffered severe emotional distress; and
4. Such outrageous conduct of the defendant was a cause of the emotional distress suffered by the plaintiff.

7   The term "emotional distress" means mental distress, mental suffering, or mental anguish. It includes all highly unpleasant mental reactions, such as fright, nervousness, grief, anxiety, worry, mortification, shock, humiliation, and indignity, as well as physical pain.

8   The word "severe," in the phrase "severe emotional distress," means substantial or enduring as distinguished from trivial or transitory. Severe emotional distress is emotional distress of such substantial quantity or enduring quality that no reasonable person in a civilized society should be expected to endure it.

9   In determining the severity of emotional distress you should consider its intensity and duration.

10   Extreme and outrageous conduct is conduct which goes beyond all possible bounds of decency so as to be regarded as atrocious and utterly intolerable in a civilized community.

11   Extreme and outrageous conduct is not mere insults, indignities, threats, annoyances, petty oppressions or other trivialities. All persons must necessarily be expected and required to be hardened to a certain amount of rough language and to occasional acts that are definitely inconsiderate and unkind.

12   Extreme and outrageous conduct, however, is conduct which would cause an average member of the community to immediately react in outrage.

13   The extreme and outrageous character of a defendant's conduct may arise from defendant's knowledge that a plaintiff is peculiarly susceptible to emotional

---

* *California Jury Instructions, Civil: Book of Approved Jury Instructions (BAJI).* 8th ed. Prepared by The Committee on Standard Jury Instruction Civil, of the Superior Court of Los Angeles County, California. Hon. Stephen M. Lachs, Judge of the Superior Court, Chairman. Compiled and edited by Paul G. Breckenridge, Jr. St. Paul, MN: West Publishing Co., 1994.

distress by reason of some physical or mental condition or peculiarity. Conduct may become extreme and outrageous when a defendant proceeds in the face of such knowledge, where it would not be so if defendant did not know.

14   If you find that plaintiff is entitled to a verdict against defendant, you must then award plaintiff damages in an amount that will reasonably compensate plaintiff for all loss or harm, provided that you find it was [or will be] suffered by plaintiff and was caused by the defendant's conduct. The amount of such award shall include:

15   Reasonable compensation for any fears, anxiety and other emotional distress suffered by the plaintiff.

16   No definite standard [or method of calculation] is prescribed by law by which to fix reasonable compensation for emotional distress. Nor is the opinion of any witness required as to the amount of such reasonable compensation. [Furthermore, the argument of counsel as to the amount of damages is not evidence of reasonable compensation.] In making an award for emotional distress you shall exercise your authority with calm and reasonable judgment and the damages you fix shall be just and reasonable in the light of the evidence.

Discussion and Writing Suggestions

1. If you were a member of the jury in the case of *Nickerson v. Hodges*, would you vote for a verdict of "liable for intentional infliction of emotional distress" against the defendants? Explain your vote, applying the "Judge's Instructions to the Jury"—and in particular, the definitions concerning "emotional distress"—to the particular facts of this case.

2. If you vote "liable," what damages would you award the plaintiffs? Keep in mind that Miss Nickerson herself has died and the plaintiffs are now her heirs.

3. Notice that the instructions to the jury include the admonition that "All persons must necessarily be expected and required to be hardened . . . to occasional acts that are definitely inconsiderate and unkind." This is distinguished from conduct that is "[e]xtreme and outrageous." Define the conduct at issue according to one set of terms or the other, explaining your reasoning.

4. How do the particular circumstances of the plaintiff, Miss Nickerson, affect your vote on the verdict? For example, if Miss Nickerson were a different kind of person, or if the "practical joke" had been differently handled, how (if at all) would this have changed your view of the case and your view of whether the plaintiff had suffered emotional distress and was due financial damages?

5. Of the ten defendants charged, only three (Minnie Smith, William or "Bud" Baker, and H. R. Hayes) admitted to being in on the phony pot of gold scheme, but they denied "any malicious or unlawful intent." As a juror, how would you respond to this defense? How do

you assess the moral and legal responsibility of some of the other figures in the case—such as the bank cashier G. G. Gatling and bank
vice president A. H. Hodges?

The American Legal System
David Hricik

*Where does the law come from? What is a plaintiff? Why does this country need so many
different kinds of law courts? How does a case get to the Supreme Court? These basic questions about American law are addressed by David Hricik in the following selection from his
book* Law School Basics: A Preview of Law School and Legal Reasoning *(2000). Hricik's explanations—intended for prospective law students as an introduction to law school—will provide
an important foundation for your understanding of the cases you read and write about in
this chapter.*

*A graduate of Northwestern University School of Law, Professor Hricik teaches at Mercer
University School of Law, and he has published articles and given lectures on topics ranging
from legal ethics, to patent litigation, to judicial reform.*

1   Here are some basic questions: What is the "law"? Where does "law" come
from? What is the purpose of law?

2   The last question first: What is the purpose of law?

A. What Is the Purpose of Law?

3   For our purposes, it is easier to begin by saying what the purpose of law is not,
rather than what it is. Laws are not the same as personal or individual morality.
This is easy to prove: some things are legal, yet are considered immoral by
some people. *See, e.g., Roe v. Wade,* 410 U.S. 113, 119 (1973) (abortion is
protected by the United States Constitution). . . .*

4   Some things which are moral to some people are nonetheless always illegal.
See, e.g., Reynolds v. United States, 98 U.S. 145, 167 (1878) (polygamy is ille-
gal). Some laws even require people to do things which they find utterly immoral.
For example, Christian Scientists may be forced to accept blood transfusions, even

---

* You have just seen a case cited . . . as a lawyer would do in a brief or memorandum. A few words
about case *citations* are in order here. Look at the cite for *Roe.* The words *"See, e.g. . . .,"* mean "See,
for example." *"Roe v. Wade"* means that someone named Roe is involved in a suit with someone
named Wade. (You can't tell who sued whom, though, not just from the *style* of the case.) "410 U.S.
113, 119" means that the Roe versus Wade case is "reported" (*i.e.,* printed) at volume 410 of the
United States Reporters, beginning at page 113, and that the specific words from the case to which I'm
referring are on page 119 of that Reporter. The fact that it is in the United States Reporters means it
was decided by the United States Supreme Court, as that particular Reporter publishes only its decisions. The date in the parentheses is when the case was decided. The parenthetical explanation of
"abortion is protected by the United States Constitution" is what *I* say that the court said. It is one way
to let the reader know what a case says.

though they believe it damns them to eternal hell. Laws are not morals—at least not an individual's or a particular group's morals. That much is clear.

5   There are many theories about why we have laws, about what purpose is served by our explicit, institutionalized and complex legal system. Some view law as merely a tool to oppress people; others argue that laws express reason and order. Many view law as a system of rules which, when applied to facts by judges and juries, should result in rational and reasonable results to particular cases—to particular facts. We will not decide who is right. As with most things, the truth no doubt lies somewhere in between.

6   For our purpose, we do not care too much about what the purpose of law is, at least not on this fundamental level. For lawyers and law students, the law is a set of "rules" which create "duties," the breaking of which may result in "liability," usually in the form of money damages. Put at its simplest, "the law" is an expression of the social policy that people have a duty to follow the rules, and those who don't will incur liability for any harm they cause.

7   The "rule" is very often something so vague as having a duty to "act reasonably under the circumstances." Or, the rule can be very specific: having to stop at a stop sign, having to drive no more than 30 miles per hour, having to do what you have agreed in a contract to do.

8   "Liability" for breaking a rule often comes in the form of a "judgment" for money damages, which is a court's order for one person to pay money to another person. It can also take the form of an "injunction," which is a court order prohibiting someone from doing something. For example, a court could enjoin a party from selling dangerous products. (In criminal cases, "liability" can take the form of a jail or prison sentence or a fine—which is a court's order that a person pay money to the government.)

9   So the "purpose" of law is to have rules which create duties which, when broken, result in some sort of liability to the injured party. Obviously that is an oversimplification: for example, some of the law comprises those rules that define *how much* someone who breaks a "rule" must pay the injured party. But, as a general concept, law is meant to define the duties which people owe one another.

B. Where Does "Law" Come From?

10 As to where this "law" comes from, it is again probably easiest to first say what the law is *not*. The western world's legal systems are of two primary kinds: common law and civil law. For our purposes, the "common law" system, which we have in the United States, can be described by contrasting it to civil law systems. By illuminating the differences, we can better see the common law methods. Understanding how the common law system works will help you understand why you spend so much of law school reading cases.

11   Civil law jurisdictions* place their primary emphasis on legislation—statutes or codes enacted by a parliament or similar legislative body. The governing legislatures of civil law countries try to enact comprehensive codes on every

---

* An example of a civil law jurisdiction is France.

subject. These statutes or codes provide the main source of the legal rules. In theory, everything necessary for the legal operation of society is covered in a code or statute. Consequently, in civil law countries, decisions by courts are not as important as those codes. The courts play a role, to be sure, but it is comparatively less than in common law countries.

12   In contrast, under the common law system, like we have in the United States, the society places less overall emphasis on statutes and codes. The "common" law plays a much greater role because there are *no* statutes or codes governing *most* legal issues. Instead, most of the "rules" are in the form of previously decided judicial opinions, not statutes or codes. Unlike civil law systems, in common law countries, *judicially* developed "rules"—that have never been approved by any voters or elected legislative body, such as a Congress, a state legislature, or even a city council—provide much of the governing legal framework.

13   The common law method means building up the law by court opinions, case-by-case, as opposed to creating the law by legislative enactment. The facts surrounding origins of the English system are illuminating:

> England had laws just as Continental countries did, even though these laws were not "written" in the Romanist sense of being declared in authoritative texts. The rules established by general custom were declared not by a single judge alone but by the whole court of the king, which represented the magnates of the kingdom; *but there was no authorized version of these rules.**

14   Under our common law system, most law comes in the form of these judicial opinions: there is no big encyclopedia of "rules" setting out what can, must, or should be done under any set of facts or circumstances. You will seldom go to a "rule book" to find an "outline" of legal rules on the issue you are researching. As will become more clear later, the common law is really a series of *cases*—not rules—which can be applied to later fact patterns.

15   The point is so important that it bears repeating: most "law" in common law systems is case law, decided by judges and memorialized only in written "opinions"—not statutes, codes, or other "rule books." For instance, the "elements" which must be alleged to effectively claim that a party was negligent in injuring another person were essentially created by the courts of England in the sixteenth century, and were adopted by America's state courts throughout the nineteenth century. Likewise, most contract law is primarily found only in cases decided over hundreds of years by judges. Similarly, the rules governing real property come from cases which were written by judges in England long, long ago involving fee tails, fee simples, and other legal concepts whose importance has left us, but whose labels have not.

16   Of course, there are specialized statutes in common law jurisdictions such as the United States. Statutes provide a very comprehensive set of legal rules for some issues. For instance, significant federal legislation, called ERISA, governs employee benefit plans. ERISA is a complex statute, and the government has

---

* *Dictionary of the History of Ideas* 694 (emphasis added).

promulgated hundreds of pages of rules and regulations which further clarify and add to the statute. The patent statutes are comprehensive, as are some of the federal environmental statutes. Similarly, many state legislatures have enacted very detailed state statutes on various subjects. For example, the Texas Deceptive Trade Practices Act (often called the "DTPA"), provides a fairly complex codification of law designed to protect consumers. There are also a *lot* of federal and state regulations which are relatively comprehensive.

17   Nonetheless, with certain exceptions, statutes play a comparatively insignificant role in the common law system. For example, even though the DTPA is probably one of the longer Texas statutes, the legislature left many issues for the courts to decide by applying the statute to various facts. Those judicial interpretations are as important—if not more so—than the words of the DTPA statute itself.

18   The main supposed benefit of the common law system is its flexibility: a judge can decide that the facts before him or her are different enough under the rules so that a different *result* from an earlier case should be reached. Courts can also create a different, new rule when needed to apply to new problems or social changes. The common law has an additional benefit: judges decide cases based on actual, concrete disputes, not hypotheticals. A statute cannot be written which will govern every possible fact pattern, but a court can decide what rule should apply to specific facts, and a jury can decide what result is just under all kinds of different and unforeseeable fact patterns. The common law system allows for a lot of discretion in order to achieve justice in each dispute.

19   Most people are surprised to learn that many, if not most, of the laws that lawyers rely on in their day-to-day practice were never passed by a legislature or by Congress, but instead evolved over hundreds of years as courts developed and applied judge-made rules to the facts presented in each new dispute brought before them. That arguably makes judges very powerful. That power, in turn, means that *your* ability to effectively argue the law can shape the outcome of your client's cases. Knowing how to find the law and how to write about it will make you a more effective, and therefore a more powerful, lawyer.

20   To sum up, the "purpose" of law is to create duties which, if broken, mean that the wrong-doer must compensate the injured party. This "set of rules," however, exists only in the form of case law; there is no "rule book," as there is in civil law countries.

C. Why Do We Have "Cases" Anyway?

21 Lawyers use the word "case" to refer to many very different things. "Case" means a dispute: your client has been sued by IBM. That is a case. "Case" also refers to the published opinions which judges have written when they decided earlier disputes. Thus, if IBM's case against your client went to trial and the judge wrote an opinion explaining the case, that opinion is also a "case." I will refer to the latter kinds of "cases" as "opinions" whenever I think the context is confusing.

22   How are opinions created? As next shown a court may, when it decides a case, write an opinion that will be published in a reporter. Those published opinions then become *precedent*—the law—for other courts to use when deciding later cases. To understand why opinions get written, you need to understand

how lawsuits are resolved. To illustrate, I will give you something you will not get in law school: a brief and over-simplified synopsis of a lawsuit.

23   The *plaintiff* is the party which sues. The plaintiff files a "complaint." The complaint lays out the allegations which, plaintiff claims to show, why the defendant (the party being sued) owes the plaintiff money. Put in terms of the "purpose" of law: the plaintiff alleges facts which show that the defendant owed a duty to the plaintiff, breached that duty, and injured the plaintiff. For example, in a case you will read as a 1-L,* the plaintiff claims that the defendant had agreed to deliver a load of coal to the plaintiff's lumber mill; because the defendant failed to deliver the coal on time and as promised, the mill had to shut down, causing the plaintiff to lose business; because he had no coal, he could not run the mill, and so could not cut wood to sell to his customers.

24   After being served with the plaintiff's complaint, a defendant must file an "answer." The defendant will "deny" those allegations in the plaintiff's complaint which, the defendant contends, are not true, and will assert any "affirmative defenses" he might have. Again, for example, the defendant will deny that there was a contract to deliver coal; if there was a contract, it is legally unenforceable because it was not in writing; even if there were an enforceable contract, the damages were caused or at least exacerbated by plaintiff's failure to order coal from some other supplier.

25   The judge will then issue a "scheduling order." Scheduling orders typically set the case for trial in a year or so, and establish certain deadlines along the way, the most important of which is a "discovery cut-off" deadline. The parties will have up to that date to take "discovery" of each other. Discovery consists of asking each other written questions (called "interrogatories"); asking each other to produce documents which are relevant to the suit (called "requests for production"); and taking each other's sworn answers to oral questions (called "depositions").[. . .]

26   Typically, at some point near the end of the discovery period, one side or the other will file a "motion for summary judgment." This motion says that the moving party is entitled to "win as a matter of law": the *movant* will argue that given the undisputed facts and under the controlling case law, it is entitled to have the court enter judgment in its favor. For example, the defendant coal supplier could file a motion for summary judgment contending that there had been no enforceable written contract, and so a judgment should be entered in the defendant's favor ordering that the plaintiff "take nothing" for the lawsuit. The other side will oppose this motion by filing a response in which it argues either that a jury must be allowed to decide the case because there are disputed facts, or, for various legal reasons, that the controlling opinions do not mean that the movant should win as a matter of law. So, the plaintiff in our coal case might contend that there really was a written contract and that a jury needs to decide whether to believe the plaintiff's story that his dog had eaten it.

27   When the trial court judge grants or denies the motion for summary judgment, he may write an opinion which explains the facts of the case and the con-

---

* 1-L—a first-year law student.

trolling legal principles, and then *applies* those legal principles to the facts of that particular lawsuit to explain why the court reached the result it did. Judges write opinions so that the parties understand why he ruled as he did; so that the appellate court can review whether his decision was correct (if there is a later appeal); and, in a larger sense, so that in the future other parties can conduct themselves in accordance with the law. This is one way the published opinions are created: district court judges sometimes write and publish opinions when deciding cases.

28   If the trial judge determines that the movant is entitled to win the case as a matter of law, the losing side can appeal after he writes the opinion. If the judge denies the motion, then there must be a jury trial, after which the losing side can still appeal. Judges sometimes write an opinion even after a jury trial, when denying the losing party's motion for new trial or motion for judgment as a matter of law. This is another way published opinions are created: by district judges when explaining why the result reached after a trial by jury was correct and fair.

29   Any appeal will be decided by an intermediate appellate court (the exact name of which depends on whether the suit is in state or federal court). The party that *lost* in the lower court will appeal, and will be called the "appellant." The party that won will be called the "appellee." The parties will file their *briefs* in the appellate court. After reading the briefs and perhaps allowing a short oral argument, the appellate court will write an opinion that either *affirms* the trial court's judgment as correct, or *reverses* the trial court because it committed some reversible error. Any appellate court opinion which is published becomes part of the common law that can be applied by later courts. This is another way the published opinions are created.

30   The loser in the court of appeals can then try to appeal to the highest appellate court (usually called a supreme court). As with appellate court decisions, the published opinions of the supreme court join the common law decision.

31   Thus, we have opinions because of the way by which we resolve lawsuits in the common law system. The parties need to know *why* one side won. The reviewing appellate court needs to be able to check whether the lower court got it right. Society needs to know what the legal rules are so that in the future, people can avoid breaking the rules. That's why we have all these opinions.

D. The State and Federal Court Systems

32 The next piece of the puzzle which no one will ever *explain* to you in law school is how the courts are structured. You are just supposed to already know it, or you are supposed to figure it out from reading opinions for class.

33   There are at least two reasons why you need to understand the court systems. (Systems, not system.) First, it will help you understand cases better when you are preparing for class. When you read the case, and it says that the plaintiff lost in the trial court, but won a reversal in the appellate court, you will know that the plaintiff will be the appellee in the decision in the supreme court. Second, the fundamental principle of legal reasoning is the doctrine of precedent. You have to know which earlier cases are *controlling* precedent over the particular court your case is in. In order to know which cases are *binding* on

your court, you have to understand how the state and federal judicial systems in the United States are structured. (You'll see why in a moment.) The doctrine of precedent is crucial in the practice of law and in the United States legal systems.

34   The fact that the United States has the federal judiciary, along with fifty independent state court systems, as well as countless administrative and quasi-judicial bodies, makes it probably the most complex judicial system in the world. Welcome to it!

1. The Structure of the Federal Court System

35 The federal court system has a pyramid structure. The federal district courts, of which there are about ninety, are at the base. Twelve federal appellate (or "circuit") courts make up the middle. At the top of the judicial pyramid sits the United States Supreme Court.

36   We'll study the federal judicial pyramid from the bottom up.

37   *A. United States District Courts*   As mentioned, there are about ninety federal district courts. Each state has at least one, and most states are divided into several districts.

38   Lawsuits must originally be filed in district courts. All federal trials take place in the district courts. Witnesses testify, evidence is received, and juries reach their decisions *only* in these district courts. District courts are the only courts which *find facts;* appellate courts cannot do so, but instead merely apply the law to the facts as found by the district court, or determine whether there is evidence to support the district court's fact-findings. Appellate courts merely review the written "record" of testimony and exhibits taken in by the trial court and apply the law to double-check whether the trial court was correct. . . .

39   *B. United States Courts of Appeal—The Circuit Courts*   Appeals from district courts, with few exceptions, are heard by federal appellate courts, called "circuit courts." The United States is divided into twelve regional circuits—the first through eleventh, plus the Court of Appeals for the District of Columbia. (There is also the "Federal Circuit," which takes appeals from all over the country, but only on certain issues, like patent cases.)

40   An appeal from a district court must go to the circuit court for that particular region. For example, Texas is within the Fifth Circuit. California is within the Ninth. New York is in the Second. Illinois is in the Seventh. The District of Columbia has its own circuit. If you look in the front of any volume of the "F.2d's" (the Federal Second) Reporters, you'll see a map of which states are in each circuit. So, if you lose a case in a federal district court in Texas, you file your appeal with the Fifth Circuit. If you lose one in a California federal district court, you appeal to the Ninth Circuit.

41   Whoever lost in the district court may appeal. The loser—called in the appellate court the "appellant"—will file an opening brief in the circuit court which explains why the district court's decision was wrong. Typically, the circuit courts limit appellants' briefs to fifty pages. Whoever won below will file

an appellee's brief, which is also typically fifty pages. The appellant then usually gets a 25-page reply brief.

42   The appeal will be assigned to a "panel" from among the judges in that particular circuit. A panel usually has three judges. These three judges then read
the briefs and sometimes permit a 30-minute (15 minutes per side) oral argument. (Oral argument is becoming rare, which—you guessed it—is [one] reason
why legal writing is so important.) Some time after oral argument, the court will
issue a written opinion explaining why the district court was right or wrong, and
so whether it is affirming or reversing the decision of the district court.

43   Lawsuits may not originally be filed in the appellate courts—each appellate
court only *reviews* the decisions of the district courts in its circuit. As Justice
Thurgood Marshall was quoted by *The Wall Street Journal,* "such appeals
should await the outcome of the trial." It is hard to argue with that.

44   *C. The United States Supreme Court*   If the loser in the court of appeals
wants to try, it can ask the United States Supreme Court to review the case.
Again, the United States Supreme Court sits alone at the top of the federal judicial pyramid.

45   The principal way by which cases reach the Supreme Court is through the
writ of *certiorari.* Whoever lost in the appellate court will write a "petition for a
writ of *certiorari,*" which argues why the Court should issue an order (a "writ
of *certiorari*") directing the lower court to send up records of the case so that
the Supreme Court can consider the issues which it is interested in, to see if the
result reached in the case was correct. The loser is called a "petitioner" in the
Supreme Court because that's what it's doing; it is petitioning the Court for a
writ of *certiorari.* The winner in the circuit court will write a brief opposing *cert*
(pronounced like the candy), arguing that either the circuit court decided the
issues correctly, or that essentially the issues are just not important enough to
warrant the Supreme Court's time, or both. The winner below is called a
"respondent" in the Supreme Court because that is what it is doing: it is
responding to a petition for a writ.

46   Nine justices (not, mind you, "judges") sit on the United States Supreme
Court. Like all federal judges, they are appointed by the President, subject to
approval by the Senate, and serve for life unless impeached. One of the nine is
appointed Chief Justice, also subject to Senate approval. He (there has never
been a female Chief Justice) presides over the Court's sessions and determines
which justice will write each opinion.

47   If the Court grants *cert,* then the parties write briefs, much as they did in
the circuit court. The Supreme Court then holds an oral argument and will later
issue an opinion deciding the case. . . .

48   The Supreme Court is the ultimate judicial tribunal: if you lose there, it's
"game over."

2. The Structures of the State Court Systems

49 The vast majority of cases are handled by state courts. Why? There are far more
state courts than federal district courts, there are far more disputes which can

be heard only in state court, there are more state laws than federal laws, and there is virtually no federal common law—only federal statutory law. Federal courts are courts of *limited jurisdiction.* Only suits which are expressly recognized by federal law may be filed in federal court. Everything else must go to state court.* There is very, very little federal law governing divorce, car wrecks, breach of contract, products liability, and most common disputes. Thus, most cases must go where most of the governing law subsists: in state court.

50   The structure of each state court system varies by state. Each state has between two and four levels of courts. Generally, most states have lower courts of limited jurisdiction. Examples of this kind of court include county courts, family courts, municipal courts, JP (justice of the peace) courts, or small claims courts. The next higher level are the district or superior courts, which also act as appellate courts for cases decided by the courts of limited jurisdiction. Next up are the "true" appellate courts often thought of as intermediate appellate courts. Finally, at the top, sits a court of last resort, usually, but not always, called the state's "supreme court."

51   *A. Courts of Limited Jurisdiction*   At the bottom of each state court "pyramid" are its courts of limited jurisdiction. These can include municipal courts, JP courts, small claim courts, family courts, and the like. These courts have limited jurisdiction. This means that they have jurisdiction to handle cases involving only smaller amounts of money, or only certain kinds of cases (for example, landlord-tenant disputes).

52   Generally, these courts are informal. Parties often file suits without a lawyer; the rules of evidence may not apply; and the judges probably never write opinions that will be published in the Reporters. These courts are critically important to solving the problems that confront people every day, but they generally do not add much to the common law, because they do not write opinions that are published in the reporters.

53   *B. District or Superior Courts*   Just above the courts of limited jurisdiction are the district courts. In some states, they are called superior courts. District courts handle the bulk of the state court caseload. They also handle appeals from the courts of limited jurisdiction: the loser in a lawsuit filed in a court of limited jurisdiction can "appeal" up to the district or superior court, although usually the "appeal" takes the form of a completely new trial—"*de novo* review"— rather than the review only by written briefs which takes place in the typical appeal.

54   Practice before a state district court is, in broad view, much the same as in a federal district court (discussed above). The procedural rules can be quite different, however, and so the actual daily practice may be very different. For our

---

* There is something called "diversity jurisdiction," which allows people to file a lawsuit in federal court only because the defendant resides in a different state than the state in which suit is brought. Even in such suits, however, state law is applied to the merits of the dispute.

purposes, however, they are quite similar: the written practice consists of pleadings and motions supported by briefs. . . .

55   *C. Intermediate Appellate Courts*   Intermediate appellate courts exist in many states, and are much like the federal circuit courts. In most states, as a matter of right the loser in a district court can appeal and have a state court of appeals review the district court's decision for error.

56   The briefing practice in state appellate courts is much as it is in the federal circuit courts: main brief, response; reply, followed (perhaps) by oral argument. . . .

57   *D. Courts of Last Resort: State Supreme Courts*   At the top of state court systems is a court of ultimate review. In a deliberate scheme to confuse you, New York calls its supreme court the "court of appeals," and Texas has *two* supreme courts—one for criminal matters and the other for civil suits. Most states, thankfully, have only one highest court, and they call it the supreme court.

58   Most state supreme courts act like the United States Supreme Court, taking only those cases in which they are interested and ignoring the others. They will decide whether to take your case based only on the written briefs. This means that only your *writing* can persuade the court to review your case. (Which, you guessed it, is yet another reason writing is so important.)

Review Questions

1. How does Hricik define the law?
2. What is the difference between civil law and common law?

Discussion and Writing Suggestions

1. Does the law as Hricik describes it—a set of rules that create duties—seem different from the way you have previously thought of the law? If so, what were your previous impressions?

2. Based on how Hricik describes the difference between statutory law and case law, what advantages and disadvantages do you see with a legal system based largely on case law, like the one that operates in the United States?

3. If you or someone you know has ever had experience with the legal system—particularly in terms of the way that Hricik describes the process of the typical lawsuit—describe what happened. Based on this experience, what advantages and problems did you find with the system?

IRAC: How to Write About Legal Cases
Leonard Tourney
Gina Genova

What differentiates legal writing—good legal writing—from writing on other subjects is not such legalistic phrases as "aforesaid," "wherein," "prima facie," or "cease and desist." It is, rather, the systematic application of general rules to specific facts for the purpose of arriving at reasonable, persuasive conclusions. An attorney writing a legal memorandum to her colleagues, or a motion to a judge, or presenting a closing argument to a jury is applying the law to the particular set of circumstances constituting the case at hand. She or he may have an opinion as to the guilt or innocence of the defendant (if the case at hand is a criminal one). But these opinions must be subordinate to the logical conclusions that follow from the careful application of rules to facts.

The selections that follow demonstrate this process of application of rule to fact. We present a hypothetical case—a particular set of facts, only some of which are legally relevant. We then offer a systematic analysis, in outline form, of these facts, based on the applicable laws. Next, we present a legal essay on the case based on our analysis. This example should serve as a useful model for much of your own writing in the subsequent cases presented in this chapter.

Before presenting our case, we should introduce IRAC, a method of presenting arguments on legal cases that has been successfully used by generations of law students. IRAC is an acronym created from the following words:

Issue
Rule
Analysis (or **A**pplication)
Conclusion

Let's define each of these terms:

The **Issue** is the central question around which the case turns. It is generally couched in the following form: "Is a defendant who [indicate specifically what the defendant did] guilty of (in a criminal case) or liable for (in a civil case, or lawsuit) [the specific crime/legal wrongdoing (tort) charged]?" For example, "Is the defendant, who was recorded by a police officer as traveling 80 mph in a 55 mph zone, guilty of speeding?" This section is generally one sentence long. (See "A Short Guide to Writing Effective Issue Statements," pages 758–59.)

The **Rule** is the primary law (or set of laws) that apply in this case. It is quoted verbatim (and placed within quotation marks) because the letter of the law is crucial. This rule may be a statutory law (such as a section of the criminal code, like arson) or it may be an accepted legal principle based on precedent. This section is frequently one sentence long. Note: secondary rules—those that define or clarify certain elements or terms of the primary rule (such as "privileged" or "intent")—may also apply to the case. These secondary rules are introduced in the appropriate places in the next section, the analysis.

The **Analysis,** the longest section of the essay, is a systematic application of components—or elements of the primary and secondary rules—to those facts of the case that are legally relevant. For example, robbery is defined in the California Penal Code (section 211) as "the <u>felonious taking</u> of <u>personal property in the possession of another</u>, <u>from his person or immediate presence</u>, and <u>against his will</u>, and <u>accomplished by means of force or fear</u>." The separately underlined phrases are individual elements of robbery, and each element must be satisfied for the defendant to be found guilty of robbery. In the case of phrases joined by "or" (as in "force or fear"), only one of the two elements need be satisfied.

In the analysis, it is frequently necessary to bring in additional legal principles that provide definitions or clarifications of key terms in the primary rule. These secondary rules should *also be quoted verbatim. For example, the self-defense privilege is a secondary rule that clarifies the conditions under which an attack against another may be legally justified, or "privileged." By "facts of the case that are legally relevant" (in the paragraph above) we mean those facts that can be associated with one or more elements of the rule. For example, the fact that the defendant used a gun to inspire fear would be legally relevant. The fact that the defendant was in a bad mood because he had just been fired from his job is legally irrelevant. In general, it is a good idea to use climactic order in developing your analysis. That is, first dispose of those elements about which there is likely to be little dispute or about which there is little question as to whether they have been satisfied. Then, move on to the elements that require more extended discussion.*

It is a good idea to conclude each section of the analysis by indicating in some manner that a particular element of the rule has or has not been satisfied. However, defer the overall conclusion (the guilt or innocence or liability or nonliability of the defendant) for the very end of the essay. Do not conclude guilt or liability prematurely, before you have analyzed all the applicable facts.

Also, do not merely summarize facts in this section, as if they speak for themselves. Analyze them by applying rule to fact.

The **Conclusion** *is the answer to the question that is posed in the issue statement. It is generally no more than a few sentences (and sometimes just one sentence) long.*

To see how this process works, read the selections that follow. First we present a hypothetical case, "Incident at the Airport," written by Leonard Tourney, who teaches legal writing at the University of California at Santa Barbara. Next we present an analysis of this case in outline format, with a systematic application of each element of the rule (in this case, the rule for battery) to the relevant facts of the case. The analysis was written by Gina Genova, who also teaches legal writing at U.C., Santa Barbara, and who practices law in that city. Next, we present a model legal essay based on Genova's analysis, written by Leonard Tourney. Tourney's essay is followed by his "Short Guide to Writing Effective Issue Statements." Finally, we present three problematic model essays (written by Tourney) based on the "Incident at the Airport" scenario. You are invited to discover and discuss the problems.

Incident at the Airport
Leonard Tourney

1 Lisa St. John arrived at Los Angeles International Airport late in the afternoon after a grueling flight from London via New York and Chicago. She was exhausted and irritable, ready to chuck her job as a computer consultant for international corporations. Her mood did not improve when she found that Frank Mason, her fiancé, was not waiting to pick her us as he had promised. She had long suspected Frank of being a closet flake just waiting to reveal himself to her after he and Lisa were married and only an expensive divorce would undo the damage. The upside of his failure to show was that it gave Lisa cause to break things off. While she waited, she steamed and rehearsed just how she would tell him to marry someone else.

2 The plane had arrived at 4. Frank didn't appear until nearly 7. Lisa had avoided eating so that her blood sugar level would drop. She wanted to feel awful, look awful. Frank deserved what he got: a whining, inconsolable wreck. Then she saw him, and her cup of wrath overflowed. Frank was smiling, carrying a

dozen roses and a box that looked very much like Lisa's favorite chocolates. He threw his arms open wide to greet her and in so doing hit Eben Sommers, a 90 year old man waiting to get a plane to Detroit. The blow broke Mr. Sommers' glasses and his nose.

3   "You moron, why don't you watch what you're doing?" Lisa cried, as Frank struggled with the roses, candy, and Mr. Sommers, whom he was trying to help up off the floor. The old man had reminded her of her grandfather who had died a month earlier. Enraged, Lisa kicked at Frank but missed, hitting Mr. Sommers in the leg, breaking his tibia. Mr. Sommers cried out in agony. His cries brought Albert Fenstermocker, a German tourist, to his aid. Fenstermocker, thinking Lisa and Frank were assaulting the old man, began to beat Frank over the head with his cane. Seeing her fiancé assaulted by a perfect stranger, Lisa's feelings changed. She threw herself at Fenstermocker, knocking him to the ground.

4   *Write an analysis of the case above, focusing your attention of Lisa St. John's liability for battery to Eben Sommers. Use the following rules:*

1. **Battery.** Battery is a harmful or offensive touching of another that is intentional, unconsented, and unprivileged. [primary rule]
2. **Transfer of Intent.** In tort law [the law covering the wrongs committed by individuals against one another], if A, intending to strike B, misses B and hits C instead, the intent to strike B is transferred and supplies the necessary intent for the tort against C. [secondary rule]
3. **Self-Defense Privilege.** The right to protect oneself or another from unlawful attack, the law of self-defense justifies an act done in reasonable belief of immediate danger, with use of reasonable force in the absence of more peaceful alternatives. [secondary rule]

Pre-Writing Analysis of "Incident at the Airport"
Gina Genova

Issue: Does defendant who inadvertently kicked plaintiff while intending to kick a third party who had accidentally struck the plaintiff commit a battery?

  A. Did Lisa batter Mr. Sommers?
1. **Battery** is a <u>harmful OR offensive touching of another</u> that is <u>intentional, unconsented</u> and <u>unprivileged</u>.
    a. *Harmful or offensive*—Lisa kicked Mr. Sommers so hard it broke his tibia and caused him to fall to the ground, his cries of pain so loud they brought Albert Fenstermocker to the scene. Thus, the blow was harmful to another, Mr. S. Because this element can be either harmful OR offensive and we have proven harm, no discussion of offense needs to be made. However, his age makes this act offensive to our cultural sensibilities as well as to Mr. S personally.
    b. *Touching*—Lisa's foot touched Mr. S's tibia, satisfying this element.

   c. *Intentional*—After a grueling flight that left her exhausted and irritable, Lisa intentionally missed a meal and "steamed" herself into an
"inconsolable wreck" because Frank was late. She let herself get
more angered by Frank's flowers and chocolate, and his mishap
with Mr. S who reminded her of her recently deceased grandfather.
Lisa could have stopped her mounting ire at any of these points or
even at her verbal abuse but she went further. Showing a clear
intent to welcome her aggravated mental state, unwilling or unable
to restrain her rage, she used it to aim a kick at the object of her
wrath, Frank. Unfortunately for Mr. S's tibia, her aim was off and
her foot found it instead. By all factual accounts, Lisa did not
intend to hit Mr. S. This element has not been met.

   Is there a rule that allows for this element to be circumvented? Yes.
Transfer of Intent. In tort law, if <u>A, intending to strike B, misses</u> B
and <u>strikes C instead</u>, the <u>intent to strike B is transferred</u> and supplies the <u>requisite intent for the tort against C.</u>

    1. For this rule to apply, we must decide whether Lisa <u>intended</u> to
harm another when she inadvertently struck Mr. S.

    2. As analyzed above, Lisa intended to hit Frank when she
missed and struck Mr. S instead. She purposely worked herself
into a fit and was so "enraged" by Frank that she aimed to kick
him. At any time before the kick she could have stopped herself. Frank did arrive with flowers and candy, and a reasonable
person might assume he got the pickup time wrong. He also
held his arms out to hug her and accidentally hit Mr. S in the
nose. She acknowledges this accident with her statement "You
moron, why don't you watch what you're doing," implying
clumsiness not malice. Instead, she chose to disregard these
facts, manifesting clear intent to harm Frank.

    3. Because Lisa intended to harm Frank, that intent is transferred
to Mr. S, the actual but unintended victim.

 d. *Unconsented*—There is no evidence that Mr. S, a total stranger to Lisa
and only in the airport to board a flight, asked or allowed Lisa to strike
him.

 e. *Unprivileged*—There is no evidence that a relational privilege exits
between the two strangers: Mr. S, an innocent bystander embarking
on a plane, and Lisa arriving on one. Mr. S had nothing to do with the
argument between Lisa and Frank nor had he any apparent relationship or contact with either of them prior to this incident to create a
privilege. There is, however, the possible applicability of the self-
defense privilege—the right to <u>protect oneself or another</u> from
<u>unlawful attack</u> and justifies an act done in <u>reasonable belief of imme-
diate danger</u>, with the use of <u>reasonable force</u> in the <u>absence of more
peaceful alternatives</u>.

    1. *Protect oneself or another*—Lisa was not under attack but she
could argue she was protecting another, Mr. S, from Frank.

    2. *Unlawful attack*—Since battery is a crime, if Frank battered Mr.
S, his actions would constitute an unlawful attack. Thus, we

need to work through a quick battery IRAC: Frank hit Mr. S so hard it broke Mr. S's nose and glasses = offensive and harmful; the two were strangers with no apparent consent and no relationship to form a privilege = unconsented; Frank; however, threw his arms wide open to greet Lisa, not to hit Mr. S. The element of intent is missing and nothing in the facts invokes the transfer of intent rule to create liability for battery. We may argue then that this blow was pure accident and did not rise to the level of "unlawful" or an "attack."

3. *Belief of immediate danger*—Lisa's cry "you moron," etc. indicates that she knew Frank's actions were not intentional and she knew that she was not in any danger. It is also unreasonable for her to fear attack from her fiancé since there is no indication that Frank had been abusive to her in the past. Frank also had flowers and candy in his hands, making it difficult for him to attack anything. Finally, Frank, fully loaded with his gifts, "struggled" to help Mr. S up—clearly contradictory to the behavior of an aggressor. Based on all the above, Lisa could not have held any reasonable belief of immediate danger from Frank.

4. *Reasonable force*—Even if Lisa argues her belief of immediate danger, was the force she used commensurate with the threat posed? Frank's blow did break Mr. S's glasses and his nose. She responded with a kick so forceful that it broke Mr. S's tibia, a traditionally strong bone. But the elderly are known to break bones more easily than the rest of the population so, perhaps, her kick was less forceful than Frank's backhand. Also, since she was kicking at Frank and missed, perhaps some of the action's momentum and force was lost. One more thing—she is a female and although we don't know her stature, maybe Frank is a much larger person and thus a bigger threat to her and a feeble 90-year-old, warranting greater force. However, it is more likely that her force was unreasonable given any slight threat she felt from Frank's accidental blow to Mr. S.

5. *Absence of alternatives*—Lisa could easily have stopped at her verbal abuse of Frank. Or she could have merely grabbed his arms or pushed him back down. These alternatives were far more peaceful and readily available to her at the time since Frank was busy picking Mr. S up off the ground with his hands full of gifts for her.

6. Thus, Lisa cannot invoke the privilege of self-defense to avoid liability.

B. *Conclusion:* Lisa committed an unprivileged battery upon Mr. S. Mr. S suffered damages as a result: bodily harm of a broken leg and emotional distress. Mr. S is entitled to compensation for these damages, which are a direct result of the battery. Lisa is therefore civilly liable to Mr. S for the above damages in an amount to be proven at trial.

Model Student Analysis and Commentary:
"Incident at the Airport"
Leonard Tourney

ESSAY	DISCUSSION OF ESSAY
Does defendant who inadvertently kicked plaintiff while intending to kick a third party who had accidentally struck the plaintiff commit a battery?	*The issue statement, in one sentence meets the guidelines in the "Short Guide to Writing Issue Statements" below.*
According to the law, "battery is the harmful or offensive touching of another that is intentional, unconsented, and unprivileged."	*The primary rule is quoted verbatim.*
At LAX, Lisa St. John, defendant, kicked Eben Sommers, plaintiff, breaking his tibia. This constitutes harmful and, surely, offensive touching to which Sommers, a total stranger, did not consent. Sommers was aiming at a third party, her fiancé, Frank Mason, who had accidentally struck Sommers moments before, breaking his nose and glasses. Nevertheless, according to the rule of transfer of intent, "in tort law, if A, intending the strike B, misses B and hits C instead, the intent to strike B is transferred and supplies the necessary intent for the tort against C." Therefore, Ms. St. John's intent to kick Mason is transferred to the actual victim, Sommers.	*Only the undisputed relevant facts relating to primary rule are summarized at the outset of the analysis: those dealing with "harmful" or "offensive touching" that is "unconsented."* *Having disposed of the "easy calls," the writer takes up the matter of intent, an element about which there is some question since Lisa did not intend to hit Mr. S. The secondary rule of transfer of intent is quoted and then applied to the facts. Having applied this secondary rule, the writer can now conclude that the element of intent in the primary rule has been satisfied.*
But can Ms. St. John invoke the self-defense privilege to shield her from liability? "The right to protect oneself from another from unlawful attack, the law of self-defense justifies an act done in reasonable belief of immediate danger, with use of reasonable force in the absence of more peaceful alternatives."	*All that remains to discuss of the primary rule is whether the element of "unprivileged" has been met. To deal with this question, the writer brings in the secondary rule for the only applicable privilege in this case, the self-defense privilege.*

Ms. St. John might argue that she kicked Mason to protect Sommers from further harm. But since her statement to Mason asking him to "watch what he was doing" suggests she knew that Mason's striking of Sommers was accidental and therefore not likely to be repeated since he was immediately aware of what he had done, she cannot be said to have acted to protect Sommers from further immediate danger as the law requires. Nor was the force she exerted reasonable. If she had really believed that Mason intended another blow against Sommers, she could have seized Mason's arms or flung herself at him, as she did later when she threw herself at a German tourist assaulting Mason. The kick was excessive force, reckless, given the proximity of bystanders, and more likely motivated by anger against Mason for his tardiness than a desire to protect Sommers.

The writer begins the discussion of privilege by offering a counter-argument that might be offered by the plaintiff: she did act in self-defense to protect plaintiff from harm. The writer then draws upon the facts to rebut this defense.

Having disposed of the question of whether Lisa acted to prevent Mr. Sommers from harm (and thus acted to "protect another"), the writer next turns to another element of the self-defense privilege: whether the force Lisa used was "reasonable." Facts are cited to support the argument that the force was not reasonable, but rather excessive.

Given the evidence, it seems likely that Lisa St. John will be liable to Sommers for battery.

Having addressed all of the elements of the primary and secondary rules, the writer can now conclude that the defendant will likely be held for battery. The conclusion as to <u>Lisa's liability for battery has been delayed until the end, until all analysis has been completed</u>.

A Short Guide to Writing Effective Issue Statements
Leonard Tourney

An issue statement is a single sentence defining exactly and correctly the legal question to be addressed. It must define the point on which the case turns—the question that when answered really makes a difference. Here are some basic rules for formulating such a sentence:

1. Do *not* use personal names in issue statements; instead, refer to parties in the case by legal status (defendant, plaintiff) or by relevant occupational categories (employer, employee, contractor, minor, etc.). An issue statement, while originating in a specific factual situation, is a hypothetical extrapolation. The particular names of the individuals, businesses, or institutions involved are usually immaterial.
2. The issue statement *must* name the specific cause of legal action (i.e., the grounds of the suit or prosecution). Vague references to defendant's wrongdoing, liability, or criminal conduct are not enough.
3. The issue statement *should* provide specific details of the case, especially those relevant to the key elements of the rule. ("Did the defendant commit robbery" is insufficient.) Your issue statement should enable the reader to distinguish your case from other cases involving the same crime or tort.
4. The issue statement should be grammatically correct. This means that the sentence must be grammatically complete: verbs should agree with their subjects, and modifiers such as relative clauses and descriptive phrases should be clearly and correctly linked to the words they modify. An issue statement can be expressed as a question (e.g., one beginning with "Is . . ." or "Does"), or it may be presented as a "Whether" statement ("Whether defendant, who [specific actions] commits (or is guilty of/liable for) [specific offense charged].
5. An effective issue statement is concise: it does not use unnecessary words, flowery language, or redundant phrases. Good sentences are fat free.
6. Spell and punctuate your issue statement correctly. Avoid unnecessary commas.
7. Use legal terminology correctly. Check your usage with a good legal dictionary. (See the Legal Glossary on pages 825–31.)
8. Revise your issue statement carefully. A good issue statement reflects the quality of your thinking about the case and increases the likelihood that the discussion that follows will have the same qualities.

Problematic Student Responses: "Incident at the Airport"

Here are three additional student responses to the "Incident at the Airport" case. All are problematic. Explain why.

Response B

Here the issue in this case is whether Lisa St. John is liable for battery against Eben Sommers, a 90 year old man, injured at LAX when Lisa returned from a business trip. Battery is the harmful or offensive touching of another that is intentional, unconsented, and unprivileged. Lisa St. John is definitely liable for battery. While she meant to kick her fiancé, she kicked Mr. Sommers instead, causing him harm and offense. Furthermore, he didn't consent to being kicked. The big problem here is transfer of intent. According to that rule, if A, intending the strike B, misses B and hits C instead, the intent to strike B is transferred and supplies the necessary intent for the tort against C. This means that her intent to strike Frank is transferred to Mr. Sommers. Thus, she committed a battery against Eben Sommers.

Response C

Lisa St. John arrived at LAX late in the afternoon. She was mad at her fiancé for being late, so when he greeted her she kicked at him, missing and hitting Eben Sommers, who was this old guy. She broke his tibia in doing so, which was a harmful or offensive touching. It was also unconsented and unprivileged. But was it intended? According to the transfer of intent rule, it was.

The facts speak for themselves. Lisa is guilty of battery.

Response D

Sometimes we aim at one thing and do another, hurting another person in the process. That's basically what happened in this case, the issue of which is if Lisa St. John committed a crime or tort against Eben Sommers.

Lisa St. John committed a battery. She kicked Eben Sommers even though she did not mean to do it, because the transfer of intent rule applies. Thus, she meets all the elements of the following two rules. . . .

The Ridiculed Employee, The Overweight Nursing Student: Two Additional Cases of Emotional Distress
(Harris v. Jones)
(Russell v. Salve Regina College)

The first selection in this chapter, "The Maiden and the Pot of Gold," presented a case of emotional distress. Now that you have had an opportunity, through the two subsequent selections, to learn more about how the law operates and how legal writing is used to formulate arguments, you are in a position to develop more knowledgeable, systematic responses to two other cases of intentional infliction of emotional distress.

In Harris v. Jones *("The Ridiculed Employee"), a man sues his supervisor for repeatedly ridiculing and mimicking him. In* Russell v. Salve Regina *("The Overweight Nursing Student"), a student sues the nursing school she attended for forcing her to withdraw because of her overweight. (See Chapter 11 for additional readings on the controversy concerning overweight and obesity.) Following the facts of these cases, as presented in the ruling of the appellate court, we present a number of statements on the law, which help to establish the legal basis of claims for emotional distress. (Refer also to the judge's instructions to the jury in the Nickerson case, pages 737–41.)*

William R. Harris

v.

H. Robert Jones et al.
Court of Appeals of Maryland
Dec. 9, 1977

Facts of the Case*

1   The plaintiff, William R. Harris, a 26-year-old, 8-year employee of General Motors Corporation (GM), sued GM and one if its supervisory employees, H. Robert Jones, in the Superior Court of Baltimore City. The declaration alleged that Jones, aware that Harris suffered from a speech impediment which caused him to stutter, and also aware of Harris' sensitivity to this disability, and his insecurity because of it, nevertheless "maliciously and cruelly ridiculed . . . [him] thus causing tremendous nervousness, increasing the physical defect itself and further injuring the mental attitude fostered by the Plaintiff toward his problem and otherwise intentionally inflicting emotional distress." It was also alleged in the declaration that Jones' actions occurred within the course of his employment with GM and that GM ratified Jones' conduct.

2   The evidence at trial showed that Harris stuttered throughout his entire life. While he had little trouble with one-syllable words, he had great difficulty with longer words or sentences, causing him at times to shake his head up and down when attempting to speak.

3   During part of 1975, Harris worked under Jones' supervision at a GM automobile assembly plant. Over a five-month period, between March and August of 1975, Jones approached Harris over 30 times at work and verbally and physically mimicked his stuttering disability. In addition, two or three times a week during this period, Jones approached Harris and told him, in a "smart manner," not to get nervous. As a result of Jones' conduct, Harris was "shaken up" and felt "like going into a hole and hide."

4   On June 2, 1975, Harris asked Jones for a transfer to another department; Jones refused, called Harris a "troublemaker" and chastised him for repeatedly seeking the assistance of his committeeman, a representative who handles employee grievances. On this occasion, Jones, "Shaking his head up and down" to imitate Harris, mimicked his pronunciation of the word "committeeman" which Harris pronounced "mmitteeman." As a result of this incident, Harris filed an employee grievance against Jones, requesting that GM instruct Jones to properly conduct himself in the future; the grievance was marked as satisfactorily settled after GM so instructed Jones. On another occasion during the five-month period, Harris filed a similar grievance against Jones; it too was marked as satisfactorily settled after GM again instructed Jones to properly conduct himself.

5   Harris had been under the care of a physician for a nervous condition for six years prior to the commencement of Jones' harassment. He admitted that many things made him nervous, including "bosses." Harris testified that Jones'

---

* *Harris v. Jones.* 380 A.2d 611 (1977).

conduct heightened his nervousness and his speech impediment worsened. He saw his physician on one occasion during the five-month period that Jones was mistreating him; the physician prescribed pills for his nerves.

6   Harris admitted that other employees at work mimicked his stuttering. Approximately 3,000 persons were employed on each of two shifts, and Harris acknowledged the presence at the plant of a lot of "tough guys," as well as profanity, name-calling and roughhousing among the employees. He said that a bad day at work caused him to become more nervous than usual. He admitted that he had problems with supervisors other than Jones, that he had been suspended or relieved from work 10 or 12 times, and that after one such dispute, he followed a supervisor home on his motorcycle, for which he was later disciplined.

7   Harris' wife testified that her husband was "in a shell" at the time they were married, approximately seven years prior to the trial. She said that it took her about a year to get him to associate with family and friends and that while he still had a difficult time talking, he thereafter became "calmer." Mrs. Harris testified that beginning in November of 1974, her husband became ill-tempered at home and said that he had problems at work. She said that he was drinking too much at that time, that on one occasion he threw a meat platter at her, that she was afraid of him, and that they separated for a two-week period in November of 1974. Mrs. Harris indicated that her husband's nervous condition got worse in June of 1975. She said that at a christening party held during that month Harris "got to drinking" and they argued.

8   On this evidence, the case was submitted to the jury after the trial court denied the defendants' motions for directed verdicts; the jury awarded Harris $3,500 compensatory damages and $15,000 punitive damages against both Jones and GM. [The verdict was then appealed by the defendant.]

Sharon L. RUSSELL, Plaintiff,

v.

SALVE REGINA COLLEGE
United States District Court for the District of Rhode Island
649 F. Supp. 391; 1986 U.S. Dist. LEXIS 17641 November 17, 1986
United States Court of Appeals for the First Circuit
890 F.2d 484; 1989 U.S. App. LEXIS 17412 November 20, 1989

Facts of the Case

[Note: The following is a composite text based on separate descriptions of the facts of this case by the U.S. District Court for the District of Rhode Island (1986) and the United States Court of Appeals for the First Circuit (1989).]

1   Salve [Regina] is a religiously affiliated college located in Newport, Rhode Island, administered by the Sisters of Mercy of the Roman Catholic Church. Sharon Russell was admitted to the College by early decision in the winter of 1981–82.

By all accounts, Russell was an extremely overweight young woman. In her application for admission to Salve Regina, Russell stated her weight as 280 pounds. The College apparently did not consider her condition a problem at that time, as it accepted her under an early admissions plan.

2   She began her studies in September 1982. Russell's interest in a nursing career antedated her matriculation: she had applied only to colleges with nursing programs and had expressed her intention to pursue such a course of study both in her original application to Salve and in her admissions interview. She commenced her academic endeavors at the College with the avowed intention of gaining admittance to Salve's program of nursing education. . . .

3   During her inaugural year at the College, there is rather fragile evidence that Russell sought some treatment for obesity. At various times during that school year, her 5' 6" frame recorded weights between 306 and 315 pounds according to data on file at the College's health services unit. It is plain that, although she achieved no meaningful weight loss during her freshman year, Russell was considerably more successful as a student. Her work in liberal arts courses was adequate and her grades were respectable. Consequently, Russell was admitted to the nursing program, effective at the start of her sophomore year. She was given a copy of the "Nursing Handbook" issued by the College, and clearly understood that the Handbook set out the requirements for successful completion of the degree in nursing.

4   The fabric of Russell's aspirations began to unravel in the fall of 1983, when she entered her sophomore year (her first as a nursing student per se). The parties have presented an intricate (and sometimes conflicting) history of the interaction between the plaintiff and her sundry academic supervisors. . . . The year began on a sour note when a school administrator told Russell in public that they would have trouble finding a nurse's uniform to fit her. Later, during a class on how to make beds occupied by patients, the instructor had Russell serve as the patient, reasoning aloud that if the students could make a bed occupied by Russell, who weighed over 300 pounds, they would have no problem with real patients. The same instructor used Russell in similar fashion for demonstrations on injections and the taking of blood pressure. [There were also] prolonged lectures and discussions about the desirability of weight loss. . . . Indeed, the record reveals a veritable smorgasbord of verbal exchanges characterized by [Russell] as "torment" or "humiliation" and by [the College] as "expressions of concern" or "forthright statements of school policy."

5   The court recognizes, of course, that sadism and benevolence—like beauty—often reside principally in the eye of the beholder. . . . For the purposes at hand, it is enough to acknowledge that an array of such incidents occurred and that, by the end of her sophomore year, Russell's size had become a matter of concern for all of the parties.

6   The start of Russell's junior year, 1984–85, coincides with the time school officials began to pressure her directly to lose weight. In the first semester, they tried to get Russell to sign a "contract" stating that she would attend Weight Watchers and to prove it by submitting an attendance record. Russell offered to try to attend weekly, but refused to sign a written promise.

Apparently, she did go to Weight Watchers regularly, but did not lose significant weight. One of Russell's clinical instructors gave her a failing grade in the
first semester for reasons which, the jury found, were related to her weight
rather than her performance.

7   According to the rules of the Nursing Department, failure in a clinical course
generally entailed expulsion from the program. But school officials offered Russell
a deal, whereby she would sign a "contract"* similar to the one she rejected earlier, with the additional provision that she needed to lose at least two pounds per
week to remain in good standing. The "contract" provided that the penalty for failure would be immediate withdrawal from the program. Confronting the choice of
signing the agreement or being expelled, Russell signed.

8   Russell apparently lived up to the terms of the "contract" during the second
semester by attending Weight Watchers weekly and submitting proof of attendance, but she failed to lose two pounds per week steadily. She was nevertheless allowed to complete her junior year. During the following summer,
however, Russell did not maintain satisfactory contact with College officials
regarding her efforts, nor did she lose any additional weight. She was asked to
withdraw from the nursing program voluntarily and she did so. She transferred
to a program at another school.† Since that program had a two year residency
requirement, Russell had to repeat her junior year, causing her nursing education to run five years rather than the usual four. Russell completed her education successfully in 1987 and is now a registered nurse.

9   Soon after her departure from Salve Regina, she commenced the instant
action which led to this appeal. . . . Russell has alleged nausea, vomiting,
headaches, etc., resulting from the College's conduct.

---

* CONTRACT

I, Sharon Russell, agree to the following conditions for continuing in Nursing 312 during the Spring
1985 Semester. I understand that failure to meet any and all of these conditions will result in my voluntary and immediate withdrawal from the Nursing Program at Salve Regina College thus making me
ineligible for Nursing 411.

1. Maintain a minimum weight loss of 2 pounds per week effective immediately.
2. Report to Mrs. Chapdelaine or Faculty Secretary weekly (every Friday morning) with evidence of
    progress in weight loss program. This will commence January 25th, 1985.
    NB - Report January 22nd for first accounting after the holiday.
3. Maintain academic standing as required.

Additionally, I will be aware of all requirements listed in the Nursing Department Handbook, 1983–85
Edition.

Sharon Russell

†Although the record is unclear, it appears that the College told Russell that she would not be eligible
to register for her senior year, but could apply for a change of status if she met the College's conditions.
Russell instead chose to transfer. At any rate Salve Regina does not dispute that Russell's departure was
not truly "voluntary."

Statements on the Law*

Restatement of Torts, Second

[Section] 46. OUTRAGEOUS CONDUCT CAUSING SEVERE EMOTIONAL DISTRESS

1. One who by extreme and outrageous conduct intentionally or recklessly causes severe emotional distress to another is subject to liability for such emotional distress, and if bodily harm to the other results from it, for such bodily harm.
2. Where such conduct is directed at a third person, the actor is subject to liability if he intentionally or recklessly causes severe emotional distress
   (a) to a member of such person's immediate family who is present at the time, whether or not such distress results in bodily harm, or
   (b) to any other person who is present at the time, if such distress results in bodily harm.

[Comment]

1   *d. Extreme and outrageous conduct.* The cases thus far decided have found liability only where the defendant's conduct has been extreme and outrageous. It has not been enough that the defendant has acted with an intent which is tortious or even criminal, or that he has intended to inflict emotional distress, or even that his conduct has been characterized by "malice," or a degree of aggravation which would entitle the plaintiff to punitive damages for another tort. Liability has been found only where the conduct has been so outrageous in character, and so extreme in degree, as to go beyond all possible bounds of decency, and to be regarded as atrocious, and utterly intolerable in a civilized community. Generally, the case is one in which the recitation of the facts to an average member of the community would arouse his resentment against the actor, and lead him to exclaim, "Outrageous!"

2   The liability clearly does not extend to mere insults, indignities, threats, annoyances, petty oppressions, or other trivialities. The rough edges of our society are still in need of a good deal of filing down, and in the meantime plaintiffs must necessarily be expected and required to be hardened to a certain amount of rough language, and to occasional acts that are definitely inconsiderate and unkind. There is no occasion for the law to intervene in every case where someone's feelings are hurt. There must still be freedom to express an unflattering opinion, and some safety valve must be left through which irascible tempers may blow off relatively harmless steam.

    Illustrations [liable]:

3   1. As a practical joke, A falsely tells B that her husband has been badly injured in an accident, and is in the hospital with both legs broken. B suffers severe emo-

---

* *Restatement of The Law, Second: Torts 2nd.* As Adapted and Promulgated by The American Law Institute at Washington, D.C. May 25, 1963 and May 22, 1964. St. Paul, MN: West Publishing Co., 1965.

tional distress. A is subject to liability to B for her emotional distress. If it causes nervous shock and resulting illness, A is subject to liability to B for her illness.

4   2. A, the president of an association of rubbish collectors, summons B to a meeting of the association, and in the presence of an intimidating group of associates tells B that B has been collecting rubbish in territory which the association regards as exclusively allocated to one of its members. A demands that B pay over the proceeds of his rubbish collection, and tells B that if he does not do so the association will beat him up, destroy his truck, and put him out of business. B is badly frightened, and suffers severe emotional distress. A is subject to liability to B for his emotional distress, and if it results in illness, A is also subject to liability to B for his illness.

5   3. A is invited to a swimming party at an exclusive resort. B gives her a bathing suit which he knows will dissolve in water. It does dissolve while she is swimming, leaving her naked in the presence of men and women whom she has just met. A suffers extreme embarrassment, shame, and humiliation. B is subject to liability to A for her emotional distress. . . .

Illustrations [not liable]:

6 8. A, a creditor, seeking to collect a debt, calls on B and demands payment in a rude and insolent manner. When B says that he cannot pay, A calls B a deadbeat, and says that he will never trust B again. A's conduct, although insulting, is not so extreme or outrageous as to make A liable to B. . . .

7   17. The same facts as Illustration 1 [above], except that B does not believe A's statement, and is only sufficiently disturbed to telephone to the hospital to find out whether it could possibly be true. A is not liable to B.

[Comment on Illustrations]

8 *Severe emotional distress.* The rule stated in this Section applies only where the emotional distress has in fact resulted, and where it is severe. Emotional distress passes under various names, such as mental suffering, mental anguish, mental or nervous shock, or the like. It includes all highly unpleasant mental reactions, such as fright, horror, grief, shame, humiliation, embarrassment, anger, chagrin, disappointment, worry, and nausea. It is only where it is extreme that the liability arises. Complete emotional tranquility is seldom attainable in this world, and some degree of transient and trivial emotional distress is a part of the price of living among people. The law intervenes only where the distress inflicted is so severe that no reasonable man could be expected to endure it. The intensity and the duration of the distress are factors to be considered in determining its severity. Severe distress must be proved; but in many cases the extreme and outrageous character of the defendant's conduct is in itself important evidence that the distress has existed. For example, the mere recital of the facts in Illustration 1 above goes far to prove that the claim is not fictitious.

9   The distress must be reasonable and justified under the circumstances, and there is no liability where the plaintiff has suffered exaggerated and unreasonable emotional distress, unless it results from a peculiar susceptibility to such distress of which the actor has knowledge.

10   It is for the court to determine whether on the evidence severe emotional distress can be found; it is for the jury to determine whether, on the evidence, it has in fact existed.

From Harris *ruling:**
11 In his now classic article, *Mental and Emotional Disturbance in the Law of Torts,* 49 Harv.L.Rev. 1033 (1936), Professor Calvert Magruder warned against imposing liability for conduct which is not outrageous and extreme; he observed at 1035 that "Against a large part of the frictions and irritations and clashing of temperments incident to participation in a community life, a certain toughening of the mental hide is a better protection than the law could ever be," and at 1053, he said:

> there is danger of getting into the realm of the trivial in this matter of insulting language. No pressing social need requires that every abusive outburst be converted into a tort; upon the contrary, it would be unfortunate if the law closed all the safety valves through which irascible tempers might legally blow off steam.

From Harris *ruling:*†
12 In *Samms* [*v. Eccles,* 11 Utah 2d 289, 358 P.2d 344 (1961)], the Supreme Court of Utah aptly stated:

> . . . [T]he best considered view recognizes an action for severe emotional distress, though not accompanied by bodily impact or physical injury, where the defendant intentionally engaged in some conduct toward the plaintiff, (a) with the purpose of inflicting emotional distress, *or,* (b) where any reasonable person would have known that such would result; and his actions are of such a nature as to be considered outrageous and intolerable in that they offend against the generally accepted standards of decency and morality. 210 S.E.2d at 147–148.

From Harris *ruling:*‡
13 The "severe emotional distress" required to support a cause of action for intentional infliction of emotional distress was discussed by the Supreme Court of Illinois in *Knierim v. Izzo,* 22 Ill.2d 73, 174 N.E.2d 157 (1961):

> . . . not . . . every emotional upset should constitute the basis of an action. Indiscriminate allowance of actions for mental anguish would encourage neurotic overreactions to trivial hurts, and the law should aim to toughen the pysche of the citizen rather than pamper it. But a line can be drawn between the slight hurts which are the price of a complex society and the

---

* [380 A.2d at 615].

† [380 A.2d at 614].

‡ [380 A.2d at 617].

severe mental disturbances inflicted by intentional actions wholly lacking in social utility. 174 N.E.2d at 164.

Caselaw: Womack v. Eldridge*

14 We adopt the view that a cause of action will lie for emotional distress, unaccompanied by physical injury, provided four elements are shown: One, the wrongdoer's conduct was intentional or reckless. This element is satisfied where the wrongdoer had the specific purpose of inflicting emotional distress or where he intended his specific conduct and knew or should have known that emotional distress would likely result. Two, the conduct was outrageous and intolerable in that it offends against the generally accepted standards of decency and morality. This requirement is aimed at limiting frivolous suits and avoiding litigation in situations where only bad manners and mere hurt feelings are involved. Three, there was a causal connection between the wrongdoer's conduct and the emotional distress. Four, the emotional distress was severe.

Discussion and Writing Suggestions

1. Select either *Harris v. Jones* or *Russell v. Salve Regina*. Assume that you have heard the evidence, as summarized in the facts of the case. Assume also that you have heard the same jury instructions as were given in the Nickerson case (pages 737–41). Finally, assume that in asking for clarification of "emotional distress," the jury has received additional information in the form of the Statements on the Law presented after the Facts of the Case.

   If you were a member of the jury deliberating on a verdict, how would you vote? Explain your reasoning, specifically referring to the particular facts of the case and to the definitions or explanations of "emotional distress." How do these definitions and explanations either support or fail to support the plaintiff's claim for damages? Emphasize those elements of the case that seemed crucial to you in reaching a determination.

2. Select either *Harris v. Jones* or *Russell v. Salve Regina*. Assume that you are an attorney *either* for the plaintiff (Harris *or* Russell) *or* for the defendant (Jones *or* Salve Regina). Assume also that you have researched the case and discovered a precedent, *Nickerson v. Hodges*. You believe that this precedent can support your position, owing to either its similarities to or differences from the *Harris* case or the *Russell* case. Write a brief argument to the appellate court in IRAC format explaining how the facts in *Nickerson* are similar to or different from those in *Harris* or *Russell*. (Ask your instructor for the appellate court ruling on *Nickerson*; it is included in the *Instructor's Manual*.) In

---

* [210 S.E.2d at 148].

developing your argument, draw upon relevant statements on the law following the facts of the case. As an IRAC model, see the "Model Student Analysis" for "Incident at the Airport" (pages 757–58).

3. Have you (or has someone you know) ever suffered emotional distress of the type that would fit the legal definition of this term? If so, lay out the facts of the case in a manner similar to the narratives in this section. Then, using IRAC format, apply the legal standards for a judgment of emotional distress to the event or events you have described.

4. As an alternate assignment to the previous question, select a character in a story, novel, film, or TV show who has suffered emotional distress. Using IRAC format, write a brief either for the plaintiff or the defendant. For example, could Othello charge Iago with intentional infliction of emotional distress? Could "Piggy" in *Lord of the Flies* charge Jack and others?

5. *Group Assignment:* Form a jury, a group consisting of several other members of the class. (It doesn't have to have 12 members.) Choose a foreperson, someone to moderate, though not dominate, the discussion—someone who will keep the deliberations on track and keep the main issues in the forefront. Appoint someone to take notes. You may wish to tape-record the discussion.

   Deliberate on the case before you: study the facts of the case; study the applicable law; apply the law to the facts of the case. Before or while you are developing your own conclusions, take into account other people's arguments. Weigh the merits of these arguments before deciding upon your vote. At the conclusion of discussion, the group will vote on a verdict. (Criminal cases require a unanimous vote; civil cases require a three-quarters majority.) If the jury is badly split, deliberate more in order to reach greater consensus.

   After you arrive at a verdict, work with the foreperson as she or he prepares a report, written in IRAC format, that presents your verdict (as a conclusion), and that explains the issue and the rule, and also summarizes the main points of the discussion in the "counterargument" and "response" sections.

Assault and Battery on the Gridiron: A Case of Reckless Disregard of Safety
(Hackbart v. Cincinnati Bengals)

Should a professional football player be entitled to collect damages from another player who has injured him in the course of a game? At first, the question seems laughable: after all, if pro football is about anything, it's about organized (sometimes disorganized) violence, and players who aren't willing to run the risk of being injured, it might be argued, have no business playing the game.

Still, there must be some limits to violence, even in football. The game has rules, and one of those rules provides that "All players are prohibited from striking on the head, face or neck with the heel, back or side of the hand, wrist, forearm, elbow, or clasped hands."* Admittedly, most violations of the rules are penalized by a loss of yardage: But are there particularly extreme cases in which recourse to the law is appropriate?

In June 1997, millions of people were outraged when Mike Tyson bit off part of Evander Holyfield's ear during a heavyweight title bout in Las Vegas. Tyson was fined $3 million and suspended indefinitely from professional boxing; some commentators noted that Holyfield could have filed a lawsuit against the offender. Even boxing, which is conflict at its most primal, has its rules of fair play, and Tyson clearly and egregiously violated those rules.

In February 2000, Marty McSorley, a player for the Boston Bruins hockey team, was convicted of assault with a weapon for hitting Donald Brashear, a Vancouver Cougar player with his stick. More recently (March 2004), another hockey player, Todd Bertuzzi of the Canucks, was suspended indefinitely, pending a hearing before the NHL, for punching Colorado Avalanche player Steve Moore, breaking his neck, while both were on the ice. (Bertuzzi's action was widely considered payback for an injury Moore had inflicted the previous month on a Canucks player.)

The case that follows deals with an incident that occurred during an NFL game played in Denver in September 1973 between the Denver Broncos and the Cincinnati Bengals. After the initial trial, the case was appealed, first to the U.S. District Court in Colorado (1977), and then to the U.S. Court of Appeals, Tenth Circuit (1979).

Following the Facts of the Case, we present Statements on the Law: Section 500 of the Restatement of Torts, 2d., which, the plaintiff argued, applied to the defendant's action.

Dale HACKBART, Plaintiff

v.

Cincinnati Bengals, Inc.

and Charles "Booby" CLARK, Defendants
United States District Court
D. Colorado

Facts of the Case[†]

The Parties

1   The Plaintiff, Dale Hackbart, is a citizen of Colorado who was a 35-year-old contract player for the Denver Broncos Football Club in the National Football League at the time of the incident. He was then 6 feet 3 inches tall and weighed 210 pounds. Mr. Hackbart had 13 years' experience as a professional football player

---

* NFL Rules of Football: Article 1, Item 1, Subsection C.

† *Hackbart v. Cincinnati Bengals.* 601 F.2d 516 (1979).

after competing in college and high school football, making a total of 21 years of experience in organized football.

2   The Denver game was the first regular season professional football game for the defendant, Charles Clark, who was then 23 years old with a weight of 240 pounds and a height of 6 feet 1 3/4 inches. Mr. Clark was a contract player for the Cincinnati Bengals Football Club, Inc., defendant herein, which was also a member of the National Football League. Both defendants are citizens of states other than Colorado.

The Incident

3   The incident which gave rise to this lawsuit occurred near the end of the first half of the game at a time when the Denver team was leading by a score of 21 to 3. Dale Hackbart was playing a free safety position on the Broncos' defensive team and Charles Clark was playing fullback on the Bengals' offensive team. The Cincinnati team attempted a forward pass play during which Charles Clark ran into a corner of the north end zone as a prospective receiver. That took him into an area which was the defensive responsibility of Mr. Hackbart. The thrown pass was intercepted near the goal line by a Denver linebacker who then began to run the ball upfield. The interception reversed the offensive and defensive roles of the two teams. As a result of an attempt to block Charles Clark in the end zone, Dale Hackbart fell to the ground. He then turned and, with one knee on the ground and the other leg extended, watched the play continue upfield. Acting out of anger and frustration, but without a specific intent to injury, Charles Clark stepped forward and struck a blow with his right forearm to the back of the kneeling plaintiff's head with sufficient force to cause both players to fall forward to the ground. Both players arose and, without comment, went to their respective teams along the sidelines. They both returned to play during the second half of the game.

4   Because no official observed it, no foul was called on the disputed play and Dale Hackbart made no report of this incident to his coaches or to anyone else during the game. However, the game film showed very clearly what had occurred. Mr. Hackbart experienced pain and soreness to the extent that he was unable to play golf as he had planned on the day after the game, he did not seek any medical attention and, although he continued to feel pain, he played on specialty team assignments for the Denver Broncos in games against the Chicago Bears and the San Francisco Forty-Niners on successive Sundays. The Denver Broncos then released Mr. Hackbart on waivers and he was not claimed by any other team. After losing his employment, Mr. Hackbart sought medical assistance, at which time it was discovered that he had a neck injury. When that information was given to the Denver Broncos Football Club, Mr. Hackbart received his full payment for the 1973 season pursuant to an injury clause in his contract.

The Professional Football Industry

5   The claim of the plaintiff in this case must be considered in the context of football as a commercial enterprise. The National Football League (NFL) is an organization formed for the purpose of promoting and fostering the business of its members, the owners of professional football "clubs" with franchises to operate in designated cities. . . .

6   Football is a recognized game which is widely played as a sport. Commonly teams are organized by high schools and colleges and games are played according to rules provided by associations of such schools.

7   The basic design of the game is the same at the high school, college and professional levels. The differences are largely reflective of the fact that at each level the players have increased physical abilities, improved skills and differing motivations.

8   Football is a contest for territory. The objective of the offensive team is to move the ball through the defending team's area and across the vertical plane of the goal line. The defensive players seek to prevent that movement with their bodies. Each attempted movement involved collisions between the bodies of offensive and defensive players with considerable force and with differing areas of contact. The most obvious characteristic of the game is that all of the players engage in violent physical behavior.

9   The rules of play which govern the methods and style by which the NFL teams compete include limitations on the manner in which players may strike or otherwise physically contact opposing players. During 1973, the rules were enforced by six officials on the playing field. The primary sanction for a violation was territorial with the amounts of yardage lost being dependent upon the particular infraction. Players were also subject to expulsion from the game and to monetary penalties imposed by the league commissioner.

10   The written rules are difficult to understand and, because of the speed and violence of the game, their application is often a matter of subjective evaluation of the circumstances. Officials differ with each other in their rulings. The players are not specifically instructed in the interpretation of the rules, and they acquire their working knowledge of them only from the actual experience of enforcement by the game officials during contests.

11   Many violations of the rules do occur during each game. Ordinarily each team receives several yardage penalties, but many fouls go undetected or undeclared by the officials.

12   Disabling injuries are also common occurrences in each contest. Hospitalization and surgery are frequently required for repairs. Protective clothing is worn by all players, but it is often inadequate to prevent bodily damage. Professional football players are conditioned to "play with pain" and they are expected to perform even though they are hurt. The standard player contract imposes an obligation to play when the club physician determines that an injured player has the requisite physical ability.

13   The violence of professional football is carefully orchestrated. Both offensive and defensive players must be extremely aggressive in their actions and they must play with a reckless abandonment of self-protective instincts. The coaches make studied and deliberate efforts to build the emotional levels of their players to what some call a "controlled rage."

14   John Ralston, the 1973 Broncos coach, testified that the pre-game psychological preparation should be designed to generate an emotion equivalent to that which would be experienced by a father whose family had been endangered by another driver who had attempted to force the family car off the edge of a mountain road. The precise pitch of motivation for the players at the beginning of the game should be the feeling of that father when, after overtaking and

stopping the offending vehicle, he is about to open the door to take revenge upon the person of the other driver.

15   The large and noisy crowds in attendance at the games contribute to the emotional levels of the players. Quick changes in the fortunes of the teams, the shock of violent collisions and the intensity of the competition make behavioral control extremely difficult, and it is not uncommon for players to "flare up" and begin fighting. The record made at this trial indicates that such incidents as that which gave rise to this action are not so unusual as to be unexpected in any NFL game.

16   The end product of all of the organization and effort involved in the professional football industry is an exhibition of highly developed individual skills in coordinated team competition for the benefit of large numbers of paying spectators, together with radio and television audiences. It is appropriate to infer that while some of those persons are attracted by the individual skills and precision performances of the teams, the appeal to others is the spectacle of savagery.

Plaintiff's Theories of Liability

17 This case is controlled by the law of Colorado. While a theory of intentional misconduct is barred by the applicable statute of limitations, the plaintiff contends that Charles Clark's foul was so far outside of the rules of play and accepted practices of professional football that it should be characterized as reckless misconduct within the principles of Section 500 of the *Restatement of Torts, 2d.* . . .

18   Alternatively, the plaintiff claims that his injury was at least the result of a negligent act by the defendant. The difference in these contentions is but a difference in degree. Both theories are dependent upon a definition of a duty to the plaintiff and an objective standard of conduct based upon the hypothetical reasonably prudent person. Thus, the question is what would a reasonably prudent professional football player be expected to do under the circumstances confronting Charles Clark in this incident?

19   Two coaches testified at the trial of this case. Paul Brown had had 40 years of experience at all levels of organized football, with 20 years of coaching professional football. Both Mr. Brown and Mr. Ralston emphasized that the coaching and instructing of professional football players did not include any training with respect to a responsibility or even any regard for the safety of opposing players. They both said that aggressiveness was the primary attribute which they sought in the selection of players. Both emphasized the importance of emotional preparation of the teams. Mr. Brown said that flare-up fighting often occurred, even in practice sessions of his teams.

Statements on the Law*

Restatement of Torts, Second

[SECTION] 500. RECKLESS DISREGARD OF SAFETY DEFINED

> The actor's conduct is in reckless disregard of the safety of another if he
> does an act or intentionally fails to do an act which it is his duty to the other

---

* *Restatement of the Law, Second: Torts 2nd.* As Adapted and Promulgated by The American Law Institute at Washington, D.C. May 25, 1963 and May 22, 1964. St. Paul, MN: West Publishing Co., 1965.

to do, knowing or having reason to know of facts which would lead a reasonable man to realize, not only that his conduct creates an unreasonable
risk of physical harm to another, but also that such risk is substantially
greater than that which is necessary to make his conduct negligent.

1   *Special Note:* The conduct described in this Section is often called "wanton or
wilful misconduct" both in statutes and judicial opinions. On the other hand, this
phrase is sometimes used by courts to refer to conduct intended to cause harm
to another.

[Comment]

2   *a. Types of reckless conduct.* Recklessness may consist of either of two different
types of conduct. In one the actor knows, or has reason to know . . . of facts which
create a high degree of risk of physical harm to another, and deliberately proceeds
to act, or to fail to act, in conscious disregard of, or indifference to, that risk. In
the other the actor has such knowledge, or reason to know, of the facts, but does
not realize or appreciate the high degree of risk involved, although a reasonable
man in his position would do so. An objective standard is applied to him, and
he is held to the realization of the aggravated risk which a reasonable man in his
place would have, although he does not himself have it.

3   For either type of reckless conduct, the actor must know, or have reason to
know, the facts which create the risk. For either, the risk must itself be an unreasonable one under the circumstances. There may be exceptional circumstances
which make it reasonable to adopt a course of conduct which involves a high
degree of risk of serious harm to others. While under ordinary circumstances it
would be reckless to drive through heavy traffic at a high rate of speed, it may
not even be negligent to do so if the driver is escaping from a bandit or carrying a desperately wounded man to the hospital for immediately necessary treatment, or if his car has been commandeered by the police for the pursuit of a
fleeing felon. So too, there may be occasions in which action which would ordinarily involve so high a degree of danger as to be reckless may be better than
no action at all, and therefore both reasonable and permissible. Thus one who
finds another in a lonely place, and very seriously hurt, may well be justified in
giving him such imperfect surgical aid as a layman can be expected to give,
although it would be utterly reckless for him to meddle in the matter if professional assistance were available.

4   For either type of conduct, to be reckless it must be unreasonable; but to
be reckless, it must be something more than negligent. It must not only be
unreasonable, but it must involve a risk of harm to others substantially in
excess of that necessary to make the conduct negligent. It must involve an
easily perceptible danger of death or substantial physical harm, and the probability that it will so result must be substantially greater than is required for
ordinary negligence.

5   *b. Perception of risk.* Conduct cannot be in reckless disregard of the safety of
others unless the act or omission is itself intended, notwithstanding that the
actor knows of facts which would lead any reasonable man to realize the
extreme risk to which it subjects the safety of others. It is reckless for a driver of
an automobile intentionally to cross a through highway in defiance of a stop

sign if a stream of vehicles is seen to be closely approaching in both directions, but if his failure to stop is due to the fact that he has permitted his attention to be diverted so that he does not know that he is approaching the crossing, he may be merely negligent and not reckless. So too, if his failure to stop is due to the fact that his brakes fail to act, he may be negligent if the bad condition of the brakes could have been discovered by such an inspection as it is his duty to make, but his conduct is not reckless.

6   *c. Appreciation of extent and gravity of risk.* In order that the actor's conduct may be reckless, it is not necessary that he himself recognize it as being extremely dangerous. His inability to realize the danger may be due to his own reckless temperament, or to the abnormally favorable results of previous conduct of the same sort. It is enough that he knows or has reason to know of circumstances which would bring home to the realization of the ordinary, reasonable man the highly dangerous character of his conduct . . . .

7   *f. Intentional misconduct and recklessness contrasted.* Reckless misconduct differs from intentional wrongdoing in a very important particular. While an act to be reckless must be intended by the actor, the actor does not intend to cause the harm which results from it. It is enough that he realizes or, from facts which he knows, should realize that there is a strong probability that harm may result, even though he hopes or even expects that his conduct will prove harmless. However, a strong probability is a different thing from the substantial certainty without which he cannot be said to intend the harm in which his act results.

8   *g. Negligence and recklessness contrasted.* Reckless misconduct differs from negligence in several important particulars. It differs from that form of negligence which consists in mere inadvertence, incompetence, unskillfulness, or a failure to take precautions to enable the actor adequately to cope with a possible or probable future emergency, in that reckless misconduct requires a conscious choice of a course of action, either with knowledge of the serious danger to others involved in it or with knowledge of facts which would disclose this danger to any reasonable man. It differs not only from the above-mentioned form of negligence, but also from that negligence which consists in intentionally doing an act with knowledge that it contains a risk of harm to others, in that the actor to be reckless must recognize that his conduct involves a risk substantially greater in amount than that which is necessary to make his conduct negligent. The difference between reckless misconduct and conduct involving only such a quantum of risk as is necessary to make it negligent is a difference in the degree of the risk, but this difference of degree is so marked as to amount substantially to a difference in kind.

Instructions to the Jury*

1   The plaintiff *Dale Hackbart* [also] seeks to recover damages based upon a claim of reckless misconduct by a co-participant in an active sporting event.

2   The essential elements of such a claim are:

---

* *California Jury Instructions, Civil: Book of Approved Jury Instructions [BAJI].* 8th ed. Prepared by The Committee on Standard Jury Instruction Civil, of the Superior Court of Los Angeles County, California. Hon. Stephen M. Lachs, Judge of the Superior Court, Chairman. Compiled and Edited by Paul G. Breckenridge, Jr. St. Paul, MN: West Publishing Co., 1994.

1. Plaintiff and Defendant were co-participants in an active sporting event;
2. Defendant'[s] physical conduct caused plaintiff to suffer injury;
3. The defendant intended to injure plaintiff, or was so reckless as to be totally outside the range of the ordinary activity involved in the sport.

3   [A defendant intended to inflict injury if it is established that [he] [she] desired to cause such injury or knew that such an injury was substantially certain to result from [his] [her] conduct.]

4   [A co-participant in an active sport is not subject to liability for an injury resulting from conduct in the course of the sport that is merely accidental, careless, or negligent.]

Discussion and Writing Suggestions

1. If you were a member of the jury deliberating on a verdict, how would you vote? Explain your reasoning, specifically referring to the particular facts of the case and to the definitions or explanations of "reckless disregard of safety" in the Restatement of Torts. How do these definitions and explanations either support or fail to support the plaintiff's claim for damages? Emphasize those elements of the case that seemed crucial to you in reaching a determination.

2. Based on the explanations in the Restatement of Torts, would you characterize Charles Clark's actions as "negligent" or "reckless"— or neither? Explain.

3. One judge reviewing this case (whose opinion did not necessarily prevail), wrote this:

   > It is wholly incongruous to talk about a professional football player's duty of care for the safety of opposing players when he has been trained and motivated to be heedless of injury to himself. The character of NFL competition negates any notion that the playing conduct can be circumscribed by any standard of reasonableness. [452 F.Supp. at 356]

   Another judge reviewing the case (again, whose opinion did not necessarily prevail) wrote this:

   > . . . it is highly questionable whether a professional football player consents or submits to injuries caused by conduct not within the rules, and there is no evidence which we have seen which shows this. [602 F.2nd. at 520]

   Considering the facts of the case, which of these opinions do you find more persuasive? Explain.

4. One judge reviewing this case noted:

   > The NFL rules of play are so . . . difficult of application because of the speed and violence of the play that the differences between vio-

lations which could fairly be called deliberate, reckless or outrageous and those which are "fair play" would be so small and subjective as to be incapable of articulation. The question of causation
would be extremely difficult in view of the frequency of forceful
collisions. [435 F.Supp. at 358]

Essentially, the judge appears to be saying that given the nature of
professional football, there is no way to tell whether a violent act by
one player against another is fair or not. Looking at the particular
facts of this case, to what extent to you agree?

5. Have you (or has someone you know) ever been a victim of reckless disregard of safety that would fit the legal definition of this
   term? If so, lay out the facts of the case in a manner similar to the
   narratives in this section. Then, using IRAC format, apply the legal
   standards for a judgment of reckless disregard of safety to the event
   or events you have described.

6. *Group Assignment:* See Discussion and Writing Suggestion 5 for the
   Harris and *Russell* cases (page 769) and apply that assignment to
   this case.

Who Gets the Kids? Some Cases of Child Custody
(Ashwell v. Ashwell, Wood v. Wood, Fingert v. Fingert, In re B.G., B.A.S. v. G.R.S.)

*Custody battles are among the most bitter conflicts fought in the nation's courts—ironic,
considering that the adversaries generally began their relationship in an atmosphere of
love and trust. In many cases, the divorcing couple is able to resolve the issue of child custody through private negotiation, sometimes with the aid of a mediator. But in cases where
they cannot agree on which parent gets which kids, one will generally sue the other, and
a judge in a family court must resolve the matter. What usually needs to be decided is
which parent gets physical custody—that is, with which parent do the children live most
of the time?—as well as what kind of visitation rights are awarded to the other parent, and
what kind of child support must be paid by the noncustodial parent. In many cases, a court
will rule that a child or children live with one parent part of the week, or the year, and with
the other parent the rest of the time. Such arrangements are only made, of course, if both
adversaries are ruled fit parents.*

*During the first half of the last century, courts almost automatically awarded custody to the
mother. This preference arose from the assumption that the mother did not work and was
available at home to serve as a full-time caregiver for her children. With more women joining the workforce in the second half of the twentieth century, and with a general movement
toward equality of the sexes, awarding custody to the mother no longer became automat-
ic. Judges had to decide whether it would be in the best interest of the child to live with the
mother or the father. This "best interest of the child" standard has become the main criterion that determines who gets physical custody.*

What factors go into determining the best interest of the child? The courts look for a stable home environment, where a loving parent takes care of the children's physical and emotional needs: makes sure that they are well fed and housed, sees that they get adequate medical care, ensures that they regularly go to school. The custodial parent has to be financially able to take care of the child (which means, generally, that the parent must be gainfully employed), but otherwise the relative financial conditions of the two parents is not a factor in awarding custody. The parent with custody must also be considered morally fit by the court; this often precludes the awarding of custody to parents involved in criminal activities, who take illegal drugs, who drink to excess, or who have serious emotional problems. Sexual behavior or promiscuity (or sexual inclination) in itself does not necessarily bar a parent from being awarded custody unless the other parent or the state can show that such behavior has led to the parent neglecting the children's needs. The courts will also consider the age and sex of each child; judges will often award female children to the mother and male children to the father. Finally, courts may also take into account the children's wishes, but those wishes must be based on sound reasons (the child wants to continue going to the same school, for instance, not that the parent doesn't buy the child enough presents).

A significant change in any of the conditions that determined the original settlement (such as a planned out-of-state move by one parent) will often bring the parties back to court, with one arguing that the changed conditions justify a change in custody. And—as is the case in all of the following disputes—a losing party who disagrees with the trial court's judgment may appeal to a higher court for a reversal of the original ruling.

Norma Jeanne ASHWELL, Plaintiff-Appellant

v.

Curtis Lee ASHWELL, Defendant-Respondent
Court of Appeal of California, Third Appellate District
Division 6
August 24, 1955*

1   On August 17, 1953, an interlocutory [temporary] decree of divorce was entered in an action brought by Norma Jeanne Ashwell, appellant herein, against Curtis Lee Ashwell, respondent herein. The decree was granted to Norma upon the ground of extreme cruelty and upon default of Curtis. Custody of the four children of the marriage was given to Norma. The oldest of the children was 6 and the youngest less than 2. During the interlocutory period and on January 19, 1954, Curtis filed a notice of motion to modify the interlocutory decree by taking the custody of the children from Norma and awarding that custody to Curtis. The notice of motion stated that the modification sought would be to the effect that Norma was not a fit and proper person to have custody. . . .

2   Norma gave birth to a fifth child on February 14, 1954 (conceived prior to the interlocutory decree). The father of the child was one Barney Cassella. Norma, the five children and Cassella were living in the same house when the motion to modify the decree was heard. Curtis was a master sergeant in the

---

* *Ashwell v. Ashwell.* 286 P.2d 983 (1995).

United States Army, stationed in Sacramento [California]. That county had also been the situs of the domicile of the parties when the decree of divorce was granted. Curtis testified he had visited the children about once a week and a number of times had found them in the charge of a 12-year-old girl. He said they were generally raggedly dressed in dirty clothes and appeared to need a bath; that whenever he visited Barney Cassella was always present; that Norma and the children had, after the decree, moved from a residence in Sacramento and were living in West Sacramento, across the river in Yolo County; that on December 23, 1953, at about 10 P.M. he visited there and Cassella answered the door and was improperly dressed (he did not specify in what the impropriety consisted); that Norma then told him she was pregnant, but denied that Cassella was responsible. Curtis stated to the court that if he obtained custody of the children he intended to get a discharge from the Army and take the children back to Virginia to live with his parents who were living on a farm three miles out of Huddleston; that the home was an average home, with access to schools and churches; that his parents were Mormons; that his mother was 45 years of age and his father 54 years old; that he, Curtis, is a mechanic by trade and had been offered a job in Huddleston and expected to support his children from his earnings. He said he had never seen any improprieties between Norma and Cassella.

3   Barney Cassella testified he was a taxi driver employed in Sacramento and since November 1953 had been living in the same house with Norma and the children; that he rented the house; that before that time he rented an apartment from Mrs. Ashwell in Sacramento; that he had had sexual intercourse with her several times, but not since June of 1953; that he was the father of the child she bore February 14, 1954; that when he moved to West Sacramento it was to a house which he rented which had three bedrooms, one of which was occupied by him and his adult nephew, one by Norma with the new baby and the youngest Ashwell child, and the other by the three older children; that he loved Norma and intended to marry her as soon as her divorce became final. Norma testified that Cassella was the father of her last born child; that she and Cassella had had no sexual relations since she became pregnant in June of 1953; that she had not told Curtis at any time that Cassella was not the father of her last born child. In explanation of her conduct she testified that she had been compelled, while living in Sacramento and after her separation from Curtis, to rent an apartment to Cassella, and that the compulsion was from economic necessity; that she was compelled to leave her Sacramento home because Curtis came there at unreasonable hours and abused and insulted her beyond endurance; that she had moved into a house which Cassella rented because she could not afford a place of her own; that she loved Cassella and intended to marry him as soon as her divorce became final; that she had always properly cared for the children; that she loved them and devoted her full time to their care; that they were healthy and happy. She said: "I am living with Mr. Cassella now because of economic necessity. I receive $100.00 a month from him to apply toward the support of myself and my children. I cannot afford to live separate and apart from him at the present time. If my children were taken back to Virginia, I could not afford to go there to visit, and I would probably

never see them again." Two women, neighbors to Norma, testified that Norma was a good mother, cared for her children well and that they appeared to be healthy, happy, normal children; that she was conscientious and never neglected or abused her children in any way.

In re the Marriage of Patricia C. and Frank Howard WOOD,
Patricia L. WOOD, Appellant
v.
Frank Howard WOOD, Respondent
Court of Appeals of California, Fifth Appellate District
April 5, 1983*

1 This is an appeal by a mother who has lost physical custody of her two minor children to their father who successfully convinced the trial judge that the mother had engaged in a longstanding effort to interfere with his visitation rights. . . .

Father's Version

2 Father was, at the time of combined hearings, a 30-year-old painting contractor who lived in Bakersfield with his then present wife (a data support operator) and her son by a previous marriage. A school where the minor children of the parties would attend classes was nearby. When the children were with their father they got along well with his new family.

3   Mother moved to Oakland, California, with the children. Thereafter, Father attempted to exercise his visitation rights on alternate weekends, but by the time of the hearing had missed 16 weekends and 6 holidays, allegedly due to actions of Mother. When she moved, Mother refused to give Father her address, telephone number or the name of the school attended by the children. On three occasions, Father notified Mother that he was making the 700-mile round trip from Bakersfield to Oakland to exercise his visitation rights, but when he arrived at her house (the location of which he had learned from the children), no one was home. On some occasions when he telephoned the children, Mother refused to let them speak to him. When he wrote to the children, she would not let them reply unless he enclosed a self-addressed, stamped envelope. He asked her to share in the financial burden of transporting the children between Bakersfield and Oakland, but she refused, and when he once attempted to require her to obey the then existing court order by insisting that she pick up the children at his home in Bakersfield, she told him that he would never see the children again.

4   On three occasions when Father was scheduled to drive to Oakland to pick up the children for visitation, he was told by Mother that she had arranged to take them to a baseball game and he would have to delay his visitation. On one

---

* *Wood v. Wood.* 190 Cal. Rptr. 469 (1983).

occasion he arranged to have a relative pick up the children at her house in Oakland to attend a birthday party in the Bay Area; she refused, stating that he was required to personally exercise his visitation rights. She later agreed to let the relative pick up the children, but when the relative arrived at her home, no one was there. A $5 bill that Father had mailed to the children to buy a present for the party was returned to him, torn in quarters, in one of the self-addressed, stamped envelopes he was forced to provide. Father believed that Mother was attempting to sever his relationship with his children.

5   Father and his present wife reported earnings for tax purposes of $16,201 in 1978, $23,574 in 1979 and $20,988 in 1980. He felt that $75 per month child support per child was adequate and was unable to pay more at that time.

Mother's Version

6 Mother had primary care of the two minor children of the marriage since their birth and custody of them during the five years since the parties separated. Having become a licensed registered nurse since her divorce, she moved to Oakland to work at a hospital there and to be near her relatives. She owned a home, which she and the children shared with Raul Martinez, a student from Argentina who attended a local college and who babysat the children at night while she worked. She had not remarried.

7   Mother testified that she made the children available for Father's visitation on every appropriate weekend, but he frequently did not come to Oakland—he only came once a month. In the past he had become belligerent in dealing with her, used swear words, and harassed her, such as by calling the hospital where she worked. Someone did tear up a $5 bill he had sent to the children and mailed it back to him.

8   Her gross monthly income excluding child support was at the time of the hearing $1,745.12 and her net monthly income, $1,327.60. She could not afford to transport the children from Bakersfield to Oakland, and $75 per month child support per child was inadequate; she requested $150 per child.

Children's "Testimony"

9 Bryan, a first-grader, and David, a fourth-grader, initially expressed a preference to continue living with their mother and visiting their father. There had been times when their father was supposed to pick them up but their mother wouldn't let them go with him. Bryan thought they had moved from Bakersfield so that their father wouldn't make any problems. In response to questions by the court the children indicated that they would be willing to live with their father and have visits with their mother.

10   In the course of argument, Mother's counsel, after learning that the trial court proposed to place the children in the custody of Father, suggested to the court that joint physical custody be ordered. The trial court found both parents fit and ordered joint legal custody but expressed a desire that the maximum relationship be maintained by the children with both parents.

11   The court found that for the welfare of the children and to have the maximum beneficial relationship with each parent, greater exposure to the father

was desirable, and therefore granted the physical custody of the children to Father, with the visitation rights formerly ordered for him granted to Mother. She was ordered to pick up the children for visitation and Father to pick them up when visitation had concluded. Mother was ordered to pay $75 per child per month child support to Father.

In re the Marriage of Pamela M. and Michael J. FINGERT

Michael J. FINGERT, Respondent

v.

Pamela M. FINGERT, Appellant
California Court of Appeal, Second District
Division 6
July 13, 1990*

1   Pamela Fingert (Pamela) and Michael Fingert (Michael) were married on November 13, 1980, and lived in Ventura County [California]. They separated approximately nine months later when Pamela was pregnant. Michael filed a petition for dissolution of the marriage on December 28, 1981. Their son Joshua was born on February 1, 1982. In January 1983 Pamela and Michael executed a marital settlement agreement in which they agreed to joint legal custody, with actual physical custody to Pamela, and reasonable visitation rights to Michael. The interlocutory decree was entered making orders in accordance with the agreement.

2   During Joshua's first year of life, he and Pamela lived in Ventura. She decided to relocate to Chicago, Illinois, where her family resided. Michael sought and obtained an ex parte restraining order temporarily enjoining Pamela from moving. Pamela changed her plans and relocated to San Diego. The custody order was modified to provide that Pamela was to have physical custody of Joshua except for alternate weekends and certain summer and holiday periods, when the child was to be with Michael. Pamela obtained employment in San Diego in the computer industry and lived there for approximately 18 months. During that period, both Pamela and Michael would drive approximately 100 miles to a half-way point between Ventura and San Diego to exchange Joshua to implement the custody agreement.

3   Pamela accepted a better job which required her to move to San Mateo County. Pamela and Michael, through their attorneys, agreed to an informal modification of the visitation schedule. Michael had Joshua approximately one week per month. Joshua was met by one of his parents at both ends of his flights between the San Francisco and Los Angeles areas.

4   Pamela's father was ailing and wanted to retire from his small publishing business located in Chicago. He asked Pamela to take over the business. Pamela petitioned the court for permission to move to Chicago to take over this

---

* *Fingert v. Fingert.* 271 Cal Rptr. 389 (1990).

business. This request was denied but the court confirmed the informal arrangement agreed upon by the parents by ordering that Michael would have visitation from the second Friday to the third Saturday of each month and during certain summer and holiday periods. Joshua was now in kindergarten, and the arrangement meant he would attend one school for three weeks and another for one week each month.

5   Pamela became concerned about how this arrangement was affecting Joshua and how it would affect him when he started first grade. In April 1988 she filed a motion to modify the custody order to provide for visitation to Michael consistent with Joshua's school schedule. Pamela's suggestion was that Michael have Joshua on weekends, holidays, and during the summer. The parties were ordered to and did meet with a court mediator and a hearing was eventually set for September 12, 1988, by which time Joshua had already begun first grade in San Mateo County.

6   Michael filed a responsive declaration to Pamela's motion in which he suggested that "the optimum living arrangement for my six-year-old boy is for he and his mother to move back into the County of Ventura, allowing Joshua 50 percent time in each home while being a student at only one school." In the alternative, Michael suggested that Joshua live with him for one year and with Pamela the next.

7   In response Pamela argued that requiring Joshua to move to Ventura would not be in his best interests, that he attended the same school in San Mateo County for three years, he was enrolled in his second year in a Sunday school and had participated on the same soccer team for years and has had the same set of playmates ever since he was three years old. She contended that Joshua's "roots" were in San Mateo County.

8   On September 12, 1988, the court heard testimony from Pamela, Michael and Robert L. Beilin, Ph.D., the director and senior mediator of the family relations department on the Ventura County Superior Court.

9   The court mediator testified that he had met with Pamela and Michael, alone and together, and had spent some time with Joshua. He recommended that because of "the significance of the father and son relationship," Michael should be allowed to continue to see Joshua on a regular basis and that "neither a weekend father arrangement, nor paternal visitation during holidays and vacations was the best situation." He felt that "it would be best if Joshua and [Pamela] moved to Ventura in order to make it easier for [Michael] and Joshua to continue to spend time together regularly." He recommended that the court order Pamela to move back to west Ventura County.

10   Michael testified that he and his son needed to be together because they are father and son and that he and Joshua are very close and their time together is extremely important to them both. Pamela's testimony centered on the ties they had in San Mateo County. She objected to the dislocation in her own life if she and Joshua were ordered to move to Ventura County as recommended by the mediator.

11   The mediator testified that in considering whether Pamela should move instead of Michael, he was "swayed by the fact [Michael] owned a home and 10 year old business in Ventura and offered to help [Pamela] move to Ventura County whereas [Pamela] had only launched [her business] in the San Francisco

bay area in the last year, did not have substantial financial ties there, and was not financially in a position where she could meet [Michael's] offer and assist him in relocating."

12   The trial judge stated that he felt there were ". . . strong equities both ways" and that he considered granting summer custody to Michael and ordering Joshua to continue to spend the school year with Pamela in Northern California. However, the judge explained that he had faith in the court mediator and would follow his recommendations. He ordered that "[t]he minor's residence shall be in Ventura County and shall not be changed from said county without order of this court or written agreement signed by both parties . . . " and that Michael "financially assist [Pamela] in moving back to West Ventura County at a cost not to exceed $1,000.00 in connection with moving expenses."

13   The court acknowledged that its order would "force [Pamela] to Ventura County or else give up custody of her child." He stated it would not make sense to have Michael move because of Michael's "long-standing roots in business in Ventura and his greater ability financially to help [Pamela] relocate."

In re B. G.

Vlasta Z., Plaintiff and Appellant

v.

SAN BERNADINO COUNTY WELFARE DEPARTMENT,

Defendants and Respondents
Supreme Court of California
June 20, 1974*

1 V. G. and B. G. (hereinafter referred to as the children) were born in Czechoslovakia in 1963 and 1964, respectively, the children of the marriage of Bedrich and Vlasta Z. In August 1968, shortly after Soviet troops occupied Czechoslovakia, Bedrich, their father, fled the country with his two children. Vlasta, their mother, did not consent to the children's departure nor did she know about it until she arrived home from work. The father took the children to Munich, West Germany.

2   The father remained in Munich for about six months. During this period he attempted to persuade his wife to join him; she, in turn, sought to convince him to return to Czechoslovakia with the children.† In March 1969, the father's mother and stepfather (hereinafter referred to as grandparents, grandfather, or grandmother), residents of Yucaipa, California, sent the father funds to enable him to come to the United States. The father and children flew to California and entered the United States as political refugees. They went to live with the

---

* *In Re B.G.* 523 P.2d 244 (1974).

† In October 1968, without notice to her husband, Vlasta obtained a Czech divorce decree which awarded her custody of the children. She testified that she undertook these proceedings because she was advised by counsel that a custody decree would facilitate the return of the children to her own country.

grandparents; the father found employment and arranged for day care for the children with neighbors, Roy and Madeline Smith. Three weeks after his arrival in California the father collapsed; a medical examination revealed terminal cancer. In June 1969, the father, who was then too weak to write, dictated a "will" to an interpreter in which he stated that the children should remain in the United States.* The father died on July 8, 1969.

3   The mother, who was injured in an automobile accident in November 1968, was still recuperating in May 1969, when she first learned that the children's father was seriously ill. The grandparents sent her an airplane ticket but apparently failed to supply the necessary documents to secure a visa.†

4   The probation department, informed that the father had died and that the children were staying with the Smiths, who had applied for a foster home license, scheduled a dependency hearing. The department did not orally contact the grandparents, who could not be reached because of their work schedules, but sent them notice of the dependency hearing by mail. It did not notify the mother or any agency, such as the embassy, that might reasonably be expected to forward notice to the mother.‡

5   On August 29, 1969, the minors appeared in juvenile court in response to petitions filed by the social worker. The petitions stated that: (1) the father had died in California; (2) the "mother's exact whereabouts is unknown; she is presumed living in Czechoslovakia"; and (3) the children are Czechoslovakian nationals. The court found the allegations true, adjudged the minors dependent children of the juvenile court, and placed them in the custody of the welfare department to be maintained in the home of the Smiths as their foster parents.§

6   During the next two years the children resided with the foster parents. The matter came before the court for annual review in August 1970, but the mother received no notice of this proceeding; the court confirmed the disposition established by the August 1969 order. During this period the mother and grandmother continued to exchange correspondence, but the mother was never informed that the children were living with foster parents or that they were subject to court supervision. On September 27, 1970, the mother remarried. She continued her efforts to secure help from the Czechoslovakian Red Cross, the

---

* This "will" reads as follows: "Request: I, [father], undersigned—born in 1934—hereby request that my children [daughter], age 6—and [son], age 5—should remain in the United States of America. I do not want them to be sent back to Czechoslovakia. My first wish is that my mother should have the children. If she is not able to have them or care for them, I would like [the foster parents] to care for them."

† The grandparents later sent another airplane ticket accompanied by the required documentation, but the mother denies receiving this second ticket.

‡ The department file includes a dictated notation of July 7, 1969, suggesting that the department was aware of the mother's attempts to secure the return of the children through the auspices of the Red Cross and the Czechoslovakian Embassy; the notation indicates that the department had the mother's address or, at the very least, knew that it could be secured from the grandparents.

§ After the hearing, the welfare department received a letter from the International Social Service, dated September 8, 1969, acknowledging receipt of the department's letter which had requested help in locating the mother. The service stressed the difficulty of the task but requested more detailed information about the mother's whereabouts. This letter was never answered by the department nor were any further contacts made with the grandparents for over a year.

Brno Office for the Protection of Children, the Ministry of Foreign Affairs and the Czechoslovakian Embassy in Washington, D.C.

7   In December of 1970, the grandparents visited the welfare department and informed the department that they had received letters from the Czech Embassy indicating that the embassy thought the children were living with the grandparents and had engaged an attorney to institute proceedings to return the children to their mother. In re-examining the file, the social worker discovered an envelope with the mother's address on it, which apparently had been received some time earlier.

8   The matter again came before the court for annual review in August 1971. The court, now aware of the mother's desire to regain custody of her children, continued the case for 30 days. After further continuances, the mother appeared by counsel on November 4, 1971, acknowledged the personal and subject matter jurisdiction of the court, and requested the court to exercise that jurisdiction by transferring custody of the children to her. The court ordered that the children would be continued as dependent children of the court, in the custody of the probation officer, but to be maintained in the home of the mother.

9   The Czech Embassy arranged for the children to fly to Czechoslovakia on November 18, and the parties agreed that a welfare worker, the grandparents, and the foster parents would bring the children to the airport. On November 18, however, the children disappeared. The grandparents told the welfare worker "if you want to know where the kids are, watch T.V." The children and the foster parents appeared on the evening television news; the foster parents announced that they and the minors were going into hiding.

10   The next morning an attorney representing the foster parents filed a petition for writ of prohibition with the Court of Appeal.* That court denied the petition on condition that the juvenile court vacate its order of November 4, and reopen the proceedings "for the purpose of conducting the Dispositional Hearing."

11   When that hearing began on February 28, 1972, the foster parents asserted that the juvenile court lacked jurisdiction because of its failure to notify the mother of the August 1969 jurisdictional hearing. The mother's counsel stipulated to the court's jurisdiction over the mother as of the 1969 hearing. The court then denied the foster parents' motion to dismiss. The foster parents petitioned for habeas corpus in the Court of Appeal, again asserting that the juvenile court lacked jurisdiction over the minors, but the Court of Appeal denied the petition.

12   On March 15, 1972, at the end of the dispositional hearing, the juvenile court stated orally its findings and reasoning. The court first noted that everyone involved—the mother, the foster parents, and the grandparents—were "fine people," and that the children had received proper and loving care from the grandparents and foster parents.† He then expressly found that the mother was

---

* On November 23, 1971, the foster parents petitioned for appointment as guardian for the children. The guardianship petition has not been heard because of the pendency of the present proceeding under the Juvenile Court Law.

† The trial judge interviewed the children, who said they preferred to stay with the foster parents. The court observed, however, that the only reasons given by the children for their preference were "childish," and that he gave them no weight in reaching his decision.

a fit parent for the children.* The court, however, expressed its concern that the mother had encountered difficulties in relating to both her present and her former husband, that she displayed little warmth toward the children, and that the children had adapted to living in America and largely forgotten the Czech language.†

13   The court concluded that "We have to weigh and balance the good and the bad in both directions and then choose that which, all in all, will be in the best interests of the children. . . . At any rate, it is the considered decision of the Court and one, I might say, that I arrived only at the tag end of the trial, that the welfare and best interests of the children require that they be continued as

---

* "We come to the question of whether [the mother] is a fit or an unfit parent. There has been no evidence presented to this court whatsoever that would indicate that [the mother] is a bad person or an evil person, or that she has ever done anything other than provide adequate food, clothing, shelter, attention for her children while she had them and the child she has now. It is obvious to the court that she is an intelligent woman; she is neat, clean and dresses well. According to the testimony, she has a good job. She owns and maintains an adequate home. . . . Her personal morals appear to be adequate by modern standards. . . ."

† "I can't help but conclude from the testimony that [the mother] has not coped well with the problems of marriage and home and motherhood. I don't know whether this is due to her personal personality or psychological problems, or whether it is due to the culture in which she lives. Maybe, to some extent, it is due to the modern liberation of women movement. She apparently does a good job at her employment, but you can't help but note that both of her marriages were impelled by unwanted pregnancies, that the second child of the first marriage was unwanted.

"I can't help but observe from the testimony, particularly from reading the letters written to her by her first husband, [the father] and saved by her, that there were serious problems between her and [the father]. . . .

"There has been much talk in the evidence about [the mother's] inability to express her warmth, her love for the children.

". . . Apparently that has been a problem from the beginning.

"The little evidence we have of her second marriage seems to indicate bad omens for the future.

"I find it difficult to conceive how a woman marrying a younger man and requiring him to sleep in the living room, while she sleeps in the bedroom with the child, can expect a long and happy married life.

"These things, none of them are determinative. They are all just things which are apparently so and which I have to consider. . . .

"I have been extremely empathetic with [the mother], her situation in coming to a strange country, thinking she was just going to come pick up her children and go home apparently very quickly, and finding out that it's going to be a long, drawn-out court battle. . . .

"The evidence makes it quite clear that [the mother] was unable to cope with that situation, and I think just had to hope that upon getting the children back home and learning the language that these things would all work out; but there appeared to be no real effort on her part to start working them out now.

"I have been impressed by all of the evidence that [the mother], . . . perhaps being a bright woman, being a handsome woman, being a success in her occupation has grown much more accustomed to getting than to giving."

The trial court also relied upon the testimony of Dr. Beukema, a psychiatrist, that the children would suffer emotional damage at being separated from the foster parents and might have difficulty reestablishing a close relationship with their mother.

dependent children of the Court to be maintained at a home to be selected by the Court; in the meantime to be detained at the home of [the grandparents]." The court rendered no finding whether an award of custody to the mother would be detrimental to the children.* After concluding its statement, the court entered a minute order continuing the children in the custody of the probation officer, to be maintained at the grandparents' home pending a probation study. Shortly thereafter, the court returned the children to the foster parents.

14   The mother appeals from the juvenile court's minute order continuing the court's jurisdiction over the children, and denying her legal and physical custody.

In re the Marriage of B.A.S., Petitioner-Appellant [Mother]

v.

G.R.S., Respondent [Father]
Missouri Court of Appeals
St. Louis District
Division Three
Sept. 21, 1976[†]

1   The parties, married in 1961, have three children, a daughter C, 12, and two sons, B , 11, and E, 8. We find no indication of marital strife prior to 1970 when they purchased a home in St. Peters, Missouri. Personal discord soon surfaced, followed by marriage counseling, reconciliation efforts and finally a March 1973 agreement to separate in June at the end of the school term.

2   Appellant-mother, by prearrangement, moved the children and some furniture to St. Charles. Some quarreling occurred concerning temporary custodial arrangements; but the children, living principally with their mother through the summer of 1973, stayed five nights and two days each week with their father, under a plan designed to accommodate the parents' working hours. After September the children remained in the general custody of their mother, staying Tuesday through Thursday nights with her and three weekends per month with the father until the divorce in May 1975.

3   For eight months following the separation the husband, though requested, provided little or no support for appellant-mother or the children, while with her stating: "He didn't see any reason why he should." In April 1974 he was ordered to pay child support of $60 per week but from time to time arbitrarily deducted amounts from the weekly payments for items such as car insurance premiums for the automobile in appellant-mother's possession and the cost of shoes or similar purchases for the children.

4   In February of 1974 appellant-mother moved to a more suitable apartment less than one-half mile from her place of employment.

---

*The juvenile court admitted evidence on political conditions in Czechoslovakia to determine whether the children would encounter any disabilities by reason of their father's defection. The evidence on this point, however, was inconclusive, and the trial judge, in his oral presentation, stated that his decision was not based on political considerations.

[†] *In Re the Marriage of B.A.S.* 541 S.W.2d 762 (1976).

5   While at work, appellant-mother could conveniently communicate with the children by phone and sometime before the divorce changed her hours to 6:30 A.M. through 2:30 P.M. permitting her to be with the children on return from school. The respondent-husband points out she could not be with the children at breakfast but the evidence shows breakfast for the children was arranged each morning before she left, the children's clothes laid out, and plans made for the day. Further, as the mother explained, the money she received was insufficient to adequately care for the children and she needed to work. It seems unbecoming to fault appellant-mother for this effort; and if the father feels strongly she should not work, which requires her to be away during the children's breakfast time, this could be readily remedied by increased support payments. As the husband also works, neither can legitimately argue the other's disqualification as custodian because of their respective employment.

6   The living accommodations of each are suitable for the children; and while the jointly-owned home in St. Peters occupied by the husband is more commodious than appellant-mother's apartment, the court has ordered the home "divided equally between the parties," presenting a problem for his custodial claim.

7   Appellant-mother permits the children to have friends in the home for meals and overnight stays. Appellant-mother entered both sons in little league baseball and attended most if not all of their games. She also enrolled the younger son in cub scouts, bought his uniform and furnished the monthly dues.

8   The children keep numerous animals and the only difficulty in this area developed when, without consulting the mother, the father delivered a rabbit that was unsuitable as a pet. A more serious problem occurred when the father, aware of the children's love for their pets, attempted to poison their minds against their mother, saying if the children lived with her they would not be permitted to have animals and she will marry somebody who is "real bad."

9   Witnesses for appellant-mother included the fifth-grade teachers who testified that B was punctual, as clean and neat as other children, participated well in activities, was well-disciplined, courteous, and respectful and although at the beginning was not working up to his grade level, improved after appellant-mother's conference with the teachers. Neither of these teachers had ever seen the child's father.

10   E's third-grade teacher described his manner of dress and personal appearance as much like other children in the class, and though he had been below his grade level in some areas, several months after the conference with his mother E also improved academically. Further, he was not a discipline problem, treated the teachers with respect, and was apparently a very normal child.

11   An employee of the Howard Johnson Restaurant had seen the children on numerous occasions and stated they appeared normal, clean, and neat. Having observed the children with their mother, the witness testified: "She disciplined them but never mistreated" them.

12   The minister of the Calvary Evangelical Methodist Church of St. Charles where appellant-mother had attended for a year confirmed that the children attended Sunday school and church regularly when with the mother and she attended regularly at other times. He also testified the mother and the three children were clean and neat in their appearance. This testimony concerning the children's appearance and conditions in appellant-mother's home were

generally corroborated by the father's witness, Mr. Darrill Beebe, a social worker for the St. Charles County Family Services.

13   Though the husband charged the children were dirty and their clothes torn when they came to him on weekends, this evidence came exclusively from him and his mother who admitted attempts to persuade the children to choose her son, the respondent-husband as custodian. Respondent and his mother produced a number of articles of dirty and torn clothing claiming they were those of the children but appellant-mother stated she had not seen most of the items and the clothing she provided the children was usually kept at her home and that provided by the father at his.

14   During the trial, in March 1975, the parties agreed the court should examine the 12-year-old daughter and the 11-year-old son. The 8-year-old child did not appear in the chambers. The testimony of that examination is most revealing and important to our decision.

Trial Court's Interview of the Children

15 The 12-year-old daughter explained she was doing better in school as time went on and described living conditions at the home. She stated a part of her job was to take the clothes to the laundromat, fold them, and bring them home where her mother usually ironed them.

16   She testified her brothers played outside a good deal and would get dirty and this was true whether at her mother's or father's home. The clothes the children wore at the mother's or father's house were the same or similar.

17   She also described matters of grave concern to this court. The father-respondent has repeatedly attempted to poison the minds of the children against the mother. The following responses to the court's nonleading questions tell us much about the parties:

Q. "Has anyone tried to influence you as to whose custody you should be in?"

A. "Yes."

Q. "Who has done that?"

A. "My father."

Q. "What has he done in that respect?"

A. "He tells us that *my mom is no good and if we live with her I won't have any animals and she will marry somebody real bad and they will beat us and everything and stuff like that.*"

Q. "How often does he do this?"

A. "Mostly every weekend when we come out there."

Q. "What are your feelings toward your father and your mother?"

A. "Well, I like them both and everything. It's just *I get sick of hearing my dad talk about my mom, criticizing her and stuff and I don't like it.*"

Q. "Does your mother or anyone in the household other than your mother say anything critical of your father?"

A. *"Never.* Sometimes, you know, say something like tell her that he called her a name or something and she will say, 'I don't want you talking about your father like that.' She won't let me talk about it." [Emphasis ours.]

18   The child stated that she would prefer to stay with her mother and felt that spending three weekends a month with the father was too much as she would prefer to spend more free time with the mother.

19   The court then asked her if she had seen anything improper at the mother's or father's home to which she answered that at the father's home the grand-mother "has taken over the place of a mother and I don't think she should," and further that:

"And every time I ask if I can go somewhere I always . . . my dad always goes, 'Ask your grandmother,' and I don't think it's right because if we have to live with him, all she should be used for is a grandmother not a mother."

20   The court then asked concerning matters she might consider improper in the mother's home and she answered that she gets tired of having chicken all the time stating: "My mom gets chicken all the time and I go over to my dad's house and we have chicken and I'm tired of chicken but I like it still." Pressing this inquiry, the court asked concerning improper associations of either parent with other men or women. The child answered: "My dad never goes out or any-thing and my mother goes out about once a week and I don't think it's very bad," going on to explain that during the first months of the separation her mother went out only occasionally, returning usually about 11 o'clock and a baby sitter was always employed. The court then asked:

Q. "All right, do you know anything about your mother having . . . whether she did or did not associate with other men during the time your mother and father were living together. Did you know anything along that line?"

A. "No."

Q. "You did not?"

A. *"My dad tells me that she did but I don't know.* I don't think she did." [Emphasis supplied.]

21   He then directed attention to the matter of morals asking if she had observed anything immoral in the conduct of either the mother or the father to which she answered that her mother and father "don't get along together."

22   The daughter related that on one occasion her father pushed her mother against the bookcase and she started crying and when her mother got up he started pushing her again.

23   On the subject of cleanliness she explained that they had to take baths at her father's house and at her mother's house she took "showers and wash my hair." As far as the children getting dirty and playing she said "we don't have to change clothes unless we go to somebody's house because they are always dirty from playing."

Q. "Is this the same whether you are at your father's or mother's?"

A. "Yes."

24   When asked her personal preference she expressed a desire to live with her mother.

25   The court then examined the 11-year-old son who stated he was making fairly good grades in school, that he was being well-taken care of in both homes, but at his dad's house "we got to get dressed up and everything to go places and stuff and over here we don't just have to get all dressed up and everything." He also stated his father tried to influence him as to which home he should prefer:

Q. "And what has your father done or said to try to influence you?"

A. "He says my mom doesn't take near as much care as my dad and he says he keeps—he watches over us and stuff and my mom doesn't hardly do that."

26   Then he stated that his father does "keep an eye on us more" than his mother does. He said his mother tried to influence him by "getting me stuff and—and taking us some places." . . .

27   Darrill Beebe, who at the court's instance conducted an investigation and home study, testified as to child-parent relationship, living arrangements, financial and general fitness of each parent as custodian. . . . As Mr. Beebe described it, Mr. S was an "over firm person. Very strict. Perhaps more strict than desirable." Appellant aptly stated: "You can't raise children on bitterness and hate." Respondent-father admitted some of these things but stated they were done in a very limited way. Appellant-mother had stated her children's well-being is more important to her than anything else in the world and Beebe's report shows "she feels that they are happier with her since they are close to many friends in the neighborhood and school." In his opinion "[appellant-mother] seems to possess a deep understanding and insight into the respective needs of the children." His comment concerning the father was:

> [He] tends to lack insight into the needs and feelings of his children. . . . He does not appear to have understanding of their individual motivation. . . .

28   His behavior in the past has shown a limited ability to understand the children's respective personalities and motivate them in ways other than harsh discipline. The children have expressed a desire to be with their mother, and the worker feels this is quite significant. Since the children have shown no major disruption in their lives other than poor appearance and some rowdiness due to lack of discipline, it is felt that the present arrangement with their mother should be continued.

[Mr. Beebe's] decision was based "upon observations of her insight into the children's needs and her ability to provide a happy, stable home in which the children appear to be very secure."

29   The father, challenging the mother's suitability, points to the fact she admitted extramarital affairs with seven men during the period 1973 through 1975, though none occurred at the home and the children were unaware of any of the intimacies. The appellant-mother admitted the affairs to Mr. Beebe and again at trial, stating they occurred while the parties were married and at least on two occasions before the separation. During her cross-examination there

was some confusion as to statements made in deposition but at trial the witness frankly admitted her intimacies and the record belies respondent's contention these include other men whose names she could not remember.

30   Respondent admitted his daughter preferred to stay with appellant but charges the children were neither clean nor properly clad by her. This contrasted sharply with testimony of independent witnesses, i.e. the teachers, the minister, and the restaurant employee. Though the father and maternal grandmother insist the children bathe more often and are better clothed when with the father, it seems apparent both parties provide adequate clothing, hygienic conditions, and suitable homes.* Interestingly, after the separation the mother on three occasions went to the father's home and gave it sorely needed cleanings.

31   The father's conduct was not above reproach as he admitted calling his wife a "whore and a bitch" and in one instance grabbed her and threw her in the bookcase only leaving when she threatened to call the police. These episodes seemed to spring from jealousy or temporary rage, provoked by her dating other men. On the other hand appellant-mother complained that he showed very little affection during the years of their marriage. Appellant-mother admitted her intimacies with other men but believed her dating during the separation of almost two years did not adversely affect the children. She conceded that from time to time her "dates" called to see her at the home and one of them occasionally had meals there. No acts of adultery were committed in the home or in the presence of the children.

Statements on the Law

Uniform Marriage and Divorce Act, §402

The court shall determine custody in accordance with the best interest of the child. The court shall consider all relevant factors including:

(1) The wishes of the child's parent or parents as to his custody;
(2) The wishes of the child as to his custodian;
(3) The interaction and interrelationship of the child with his parent or parents, his siblings, and any other person who may significantly affect the child's best interest;
(4) The child's adjustment to his home, school and community; and
(5) The mental and physical health of all individuals involved.

The court shall not consider conduct of a proposed custodian that does not affect his relationship to the child.

California Civil Code §4600 (a)

The Legislature finds and declares that it is the public policy of this state to assure minor children of frequent and continuing contact with both parents

---

* The husband testified the younger son became ill, called him at work, and he took the child to the hospital. Learning this, the mother went to the hospital complaining she should have been notified. It eventuated the child was neither hospitalized nor seriously ill and the occurrence has no strong bearing on the case.

after the parents have separated or dissolved their marriage, and to encourage parents to share the rights and responsibilities of child rearing in order to effect this policy. In any proceeding where there is at issue the custody of a minor child, the court may, during the pendency of the proceeding or at any time thereafter, make such order for the custody of the child during minority as may seem necessary or proper. If a child is of sufficient age and capacity to reason so as to form an intelligent preference as to custody, the court shall consider and give due weight to the wishes of the child in making an award of custody or modification thereof. In determining the person or persons to whom custody shall be awarded under paragraph (2) or (3) of subdivision (b), the court shall consider and give due weight under Article 1 (commencing with Section 1500) of Chapter 1 of Part 2 of Division 4 of the Probate Code.

California Family Code §3011 (2001): Factors Considered in Determining Best Interest of Child

1   In making a determination of the best interest of the child in a proceeding described in Section 3021, the court shall, among any other factors it finds relevant, consider all of the following:

(a) The health, safety, and welfare of the child.
(b) Any history of abuse by one parent or any other person seeking custody against any of the following:
   (1) Any child to whom he or she is related by blood or affinity or with whom he or she has had a caretaking relationship, no matter how temporary.
   (2) The other parent.
   (3) A parent, current spouse, or cohabitant, of the parent or person seeking custody, or a person with whom the parent or person seeking custody has a dating or engagement relationship.

2   As a prerequisite to the consideration of allegations of abuse, the court may require substantial independent corroboration, including, but not limited to, written reports by law enforcement agencies, child protective services or other social welfare agencies, courts, medical facilities, or other public agencies or private nonprofit organizations providing services to victims of sexual assault or domestic violence. As used in this subdivision, "abuse against a child" means "child abuse" as defined in Section 11165.6 of the Penal Code and abuse against any of the other persons described in paragraph (2) or (3) means "abuse" as defined in Section 6203 of this code.
(c) The nature and amount of contact with both parents, except as provided in Section 3046.
(d) The habitual or continual illegal use of controlled substances or habitual or continual abuse of alcohol by either parent. Before considering these allegations, the court may first require independent corroboration, including, but not limited to, written reports from law enforcement agencies, courts, probation departments, social welfare agencies, medical facilities, rehabili-

tation facilities, or other public agencies or nonprofit organizations providing drug and alcohol abuse services. As used in this subdivision, "controlled substances" has the same meaning as defined in the California Uniform Controlled Substances Act, Division 10 (commencing with Section 11000) of the Health and Safety Code.

(e) (1) Where allegations about a parent pursuant to subdivision (b) or (d) have been brought to the attention of the court in the current proceeding, and the court makes an order for sole or joint custody to that parent, the court shall state its reasons in writing or on the record. In these circumstances, the court shall ensure that any order regarding custody or visitation is specific as to time, day, place, and manner of transfer of the child as set forth in subdivision (b) of Section 6323.

(2) The provisions of this subdivision shall not apply if the parties stipulate in writing or on the record regarding custody or visitation.

California Family Code §3020 (2001): Legislative Intent on Child Custody

(a) The Legislature finds and declares that it is the public policy of this state to assure that the health, safety, and welfare of children shall be the court's primary concern in determining the best interest of children when making any orders regarding the physical or legal custody or visitation of children. The Legislature further finds and declares that the perpetration of child abuse or domestic violence in a household where a child resides is detrimental to the child.

(b) The Legislature finds and declares that it is the public policy of this state to assure that children have frequent and continuing contact with both parents after the parents have separated or dissolved their marriage, or ended their relationship, and to encourage parents to share the rights and responsibilities of child rearing in order to effect this policy, except where the contact would not be in the best interest of the child, as provided in Section 3011.

(c) Where the policies set forth in subdivisions (a) and (b) of this section are in conflict, any court's order regarding physical or legal custody or visitation shall be made in a manner that ensures the health, safety, and welfare of the child and the safety of all family members.

California Family Code §3040 (2001): Order of Preference in Granting Custody

(a) Custody should be granted in the following order of preference according to the best interest of the child as provided in Sections 3011 and 3020:

(1) To both parents jointly pursuant to Chapter 4 (commencing with Section 3080) or to either parent. In making an order granting custody to either parent, the court shall consider, among other factors, which parent is more likely to allow the child frequent and continuing contact with the noncustodial parent, consistent with Section 3011 and 3020, and shall not prefer a parent as custodian because of that parent's sex. The court, in its discretion, may require the parents to

submit to the court a plan for the implementation of the custody order.

(2) If to neither parent, to the person or persons in whose home the child has been living in a wholesome and stable environment.

(3) To any other person or persons deemed by the court to be suitable and able to provide adequate and proper care and guidance for the child.

(b) This section establishes neither a preference nor a presumption for or against joint legal custody, joint physical custody, or sole custody, but allows the court and the family the widest discretion to choose a parenting plan that is in the best interest of the child.

California Family Code §3041 (2001): Custody Granted to Non-Parent

Before making an order granting custody to a person or persons other than a parent, without the consent of the parents, the court shall make a finding that granting custody to a parent would be detrimental to the child and that granting custody to the nonparent is required to serve the best interest of the child. Allegations that parental custody would be detrimental to the child, other than a statement of that ultimate fact, shall not appear in the pleadings. The court may, in its discretion, exclude the public from the hearing on this issue.

Discussion and Writing Suggestions

1. In *Ashwell v. Ashwell*, should Curtis Lee Ashwell be awarded custody of the four children he had with Norma Jeanne Ashwell? Apply relevant elements of child custody law to this case. To what extent should the following factors be significant in determining who gets custody: (1) Norma's sexual relationship and living arrangements with Cassella before her divorce became final; (2) Curtis's planned move across the country to Virginia; (3) Curtis's Army status; (4) Curtis's testimony about the children being frequently raggedly dressed and dirty when he visited and their being cared for by a 12-year-old babysitter. Take into primary account the best interest of the children.

2. In *Wood v. Wood*, should custody of the children remain, as the trial court judge ruled, with the father? Base your conclusion upon the best interest of the children. Reviewing the three "versions" of the situation—by father, mother, and children—what do you conclude about the actual facts of this case and about which parent was most/least blameworthy in terms of the father's visitations? To what extent should the trial court judge's rulings on custody, child support payments, and visitation arrangements, be upheld; to what extent, reversed? Apply the relevant laws on child custody to the facts of this case.

3. To what extent do you agree with the trial court judge's decision in *Fingert?* Should Pamela be required by the appellate court to either relocate to Ventura or give up custody of Joshua? Discuss the mediator's recommendation (one with which the judge agreed) that the father had a home and an established business in Ventura, whereas the mother "had only launched [her business] in the San Francisco bay area in the last year, did not have substantial ties there, and was not financially in a position where she could meet [Michael's] offer and assist him in relocating." In light of the relevant laws on child custody, consider whether or not the best interests of the child would be served by awarding the father custody.

4. How should the appellate court deal with the custody issue in *B.G.?* Should the children remain in the custody of their foster parents, or their paternal grandparents, or should they be placed in the custody of their natural mother? Among the factors you might consider: (1) the father's dying wishes; (2) the fact that the children were taken by the father without the mother's knowledge and consent; (3) the American grandparents' wishes; (4) the failure of the Welfare Department to contact the mother for a long time; (5) the children's wishes. Consider and discuss also the trial judge's finding that "the mother had encountered difficulties in relating to both her present and her former husband, that she displayed little warmth toward the children, and that the children had adapted to living in America and largely forgotten the Czech language." Apply the relevant laws on child custody to the facts of this case.

5. Applying the relevant laws on child custody to the facts of *B.A.S.*, do you think the interests of the children would best be served if they stayed with the mother or the father? In developing your conclusion, take into account some of the following factors: (1) one parent attempting to prejudice the children's minds against the other parent; (2) each parent's approach to raising his or her children; (3) the mother's extramarital affairs; (4) the expressed wishes of one or more of the children. To what extent does the testimony of the children influence your conclusions? To what extent do you think the court's questions were fair and impartial (that is, not trying to lead the children to respond with particular answers)?

6. If you have had direct experience with or knowledge of the effects of a child custody battle, you may want to comment on the adequacy of the laws governing child custody and of the legal system's ability to deal with custody fights. Given the often intractable conflicts between the parents, in what ways could the law and the court system better deal with child custody issues to minimize the adverse effects on all parties concerned, but particularly on the kids?

Hot Coffee Spills

Probably the most popular legal horror story of recent years is the notorious McDonald's coffee case—you know, the one about the woman who ordered hot coffee at a McDonald's drive-through, spilled it on herself while driving out, sued McDonald's, collected a cool $2.7 million from the deep pockets of the fast-food corporate empire, and laughed all the way to the bank. Of course, this description is mostly fantasy. In actual fact, the seventy-nine-year-old woman was not driving when the spill occurred, sustained third-degree burns over 6 percent of her body, required eight days of hospitalization and painful skin grafts, and eventually saw her judgment reduced to $480,000. McDonald's, which had been warned for years by previous plaintiffs and their lawyers about the abnormally high temperature of its coffee (180–90 degrees Fahrenheit), had initially refused to settle for $20,000.

The McDonald's case is an example of a product liability lawsuit—one in which the plaintiff sues because of injuries suffered owing to a defective or dangerous product. Other high-profile product liability cases in recent years involve cigarettes, asbestos, automobiles, and silicon breast implants. There were coffee cases before the McDonald's case, and there have been coffee cases afterward. In a 1941 Louisiana case, Miller v. Holsum Cafeteria, a woman sued a restaurant after the waiter accidentally spilled coffee down her neck and back, splashing her eye in the process. She itemized her damages as humiliation ($150), first-degree burns ($350), nervous collapse and confinement to her bed and residence ($1,000), and injuries to her eyes, pain and suffering and for the infection of her tonsils ($6,000). She collected, but the judge reduced her damage award to $1,450. Three years after the McDonald's case, another woman, who spilled coffee on herself while driving over a dip at a Hardee's restaurant in Virginia (she claimed that the lid was improperly attached), didn't collect anything, having failed to prove that the product she had purchased was defective.

The following selections give you an opportunity to decide damages in some other hot coffee cases: Harris v. Black, Pasela v. Brown Derby, Inc., Rudees v. Delta Airlines, and Nadel v. Burger King. Also provided is the Ohio Product Liability Law (which is fairly typical of its type) and a set of jury instructions for determining comparative fault (relative degrees of fault of the defendant and the plaintiff) in product liability cases.

Harris v. Black*

130 Ga.App. 807

HARRIS, INC.

v.

Randy G. BLACK.

No. 48842
Court of Appeals of Georgia,
Division No. 2
Feb. 12, 1974

1   The evidence as to how the plaintiff's injuries occurred is in conflict. The defendant's sole witness, the employee allegedly causing the injuries, testified that the

---

* *Harris v. Black.* 204 S.E.2d 779 (1974).

plaintiff and his friends had come into the restaurant at approximately 2:30 A.M. from a party at which alcoholic beverages were consumed, and that the plaintiff, upon being refused service because of unruly behavior and profane language; twisted the witness' arm, causing her to spill the coffee on him. The plaintiff's witnesses, all participants in the party with him, testified that their group was not noisy or rowdy, but that they were unable to obtain service; that the plaintiff used profanity to describe what the restaurant was not worth, whereupon the employee picked up a pot of coffee and threw it on the plaintiff. The jury had the opportunity to give more credibility to the defendant's sole witness than to those of the plaintiff, but declined to do so, even though the plaintiff's witnesses who were all teenagers, according to his own testimony, held their party in a motel rather than in a private home because they could not be trusted not to steal things.

Pasela v. Brown Derby, Inc.*

71 Ohio App.3d 636

PASELA et al., Appellants

v.

BROWN DERBY, INC. et al., Appellees[1]

No. 58247
Court of Appeals of Ohio
Cuyahoga County
Decided April 1, 1991

1   In the early afternoon of July 27, 1983, appellant Christine Pasela, then just under one year old, was taken to a Brown Derby Restaurant for lunch by her mother, Karen Pasela, and grandmother, Margaret Sinko. An older sister, Nicole, was also present. The party was seated at a table by the restaurant's hostess and cashier, Joann Sclimenti. Defendant-appellee Sclimenti brought a high chair for Christine to sit in and appellant Karen Pasela then placed her daughter in the chair. Karen Pasela notified Sclimenti that the high chair did not fasten properly and that there were no straps on the seat to secure Christine. Sclimenti never replaced the chair. Karen Pasela moved the high chair so that Christine was seated to her immediate left. Both Karen Pasela and Margaret Sinko were given large menus and were then asked by defendant-appellee, waitress Nancy Filler, if they would like coffee. They responded affirmatively. While Karen and Margaret were reviewing the menus, appellee, waitress Susan Heffner, brought two pots of coffee to the table where the party was seated without alerting the women that she had done so. One pot was placed on Karen Pasela's left side,

* *Pasela v. Brown Derby, Inc.* 594 N.E.2d 1112 (1991).

Footnote 1 text reference changed from original.
[1] The plaintiffs-appellants in the instant action are Christine Pasela, a minor, by and through her parents and next friends, Karen Pasela (mother) and Edward Pasela (father), and Edward Pasela and Karen Pasela. The defendants-appellees in the action are Brown Derby, Inc., Susan Heffner, Joann Sclimenti and Nancy Filler.

near the high chair where Christine was seated. Filler, who was in charge of training Heffner, saw the placement of the coffee pots on the table.

2   Karen Pasela indicated that while waiting for the coffee, she was reviewing the menu, trying to appease Nicole, who was hungry and cranky, and reaching into a diaper bag on the floor to retrieve some baby food. Karen testified that while she was reaching into the diaper bag, she heard Christine cry and turned towards her to find that a pot of coffee had spilled on Christine's high chair and on the front of Christine's clothing, causing severe burns to Christine's arms, chest, abdomen and right leg. Karen stated that she had only looked away from Christine for fifteen to twenty seconds. Margaret Sinko claimed that she glanced at Christine every ten seconds but had not witnessed the accident. Karen and Margaret both testified that they never saw a waitress bring two pots of coffee to their table, nor did they have any idea how the coffee pots had gotten on the table or how the accident had happened.

3   Christine was taken by ambulance to Cleveland Metro General Hospital, where she was treated for her burns by Dr. Robert Gerding. Christine's burns began to heal after several months, but the record reflects that she has suffered permanent scarring.

Rudees v. Delta Airlines*

Marvin RUDEES, Appellant

v.

DELTA AIRLINES, INC., Appellee

Court of Appeals of Tennessee,

Western Section

April 26, 1977
Certiorari Denied by Supreme Court
July 5, 1977

1 The plaintiff boarded the defendant's DC-9 airplane at Memphis for a flight to Atlanta, Georgia. The passengers were asked to keep their seat belts fastened due to the possibility that the plane might encounter air turbulence. At a point approximately 100 miles from Atlanta, a stewardess came down the aisle of the airplane carrying at waist level an open tray which contained several cups of scalding coffee. The plaintiff was seated on an aisle seat with his seat belt fastened; he had not ordered coffee. The airplane apparently hit some clear air turbulence which made the stewardess sway in the aisle and spill the contents of the cups on the plaintiff's lap. This resulted in rather severe burns to the plaintiff's thighs and groin area.

2   The defendant, on motion for directed verdict, argued that the plaintiff had not proved any negligence on its part. Counsel for the defendant argued, and

---

* *Rudees v. Delta Airlines.* 553 S.W.2d 85 (1977).

the trial judge apparently agreed, that the plaintiff could not recover because he failed to prove that the pilot was negligent or that the defendant knew or should have known about the air turbulence.

3   The foregoing argument overlooks the basis of the lawsuit. The plaintiff alleged that the stewardess was negligent: (1) in spilling the coffee; (2) in her manner of carrying scalding coffee down the aisle of the plane; (3) in carrying the coffee in uncovered containers; and (4) in attempting to serve scalding coffee during flight. The issue is the negligence of the stewardess; therein lies the lawsuit.

Nadel v. Burger King[*]

119 Ohio App.3d 578

NADEL et al., Appellants

v.

BURGER KING CORPORATION

et al., Appellees

No. C-960489
Court of Appeals of Ohio,
First District, Hamilton County
Decided May 21, 1997

1   On a morning in early December 1993, plaintiff-appellant Paul Nadel was driving his son, plaintiff-appellant Christopher, and two younger daughters, Ashley and Brittany, to school. Paul's mother, plaintiff-appellant Evelyn Nadel, was seated next to the passenger window. Christopher was seated in the front seat between Evelyn and Paul, with one foot on the transmission hump and one foot on the passenger side of the hump. Brittany and Ashley were in the back seat. On the way, they ordered breakfast from the drive-through window of a Burger King restaurant owned and operated by defendant-appellee Emil, Inc. ("Emil") under a franchise agreement with defendant-appellee Burger King Corporation ("BK"). Paul's order included several breakfast sandwiches and drinks and two cups of coffee. The cups of coffee were fitted with lids and served in a cardboard container designed to hold four cups, with the two cups placed on opposite diagonal corners. Emil's employee served the coffee through the car window to Paul, who passed it to Christopher, who handed it to Evelyn.

2   Evelyn testified that she tasted the coffee in the cup on the right side of the container, by raising the flap on its lid, and found it too hot to drink. She also testified that the lid of the coffee "jiggled off" and burned her on her right leg after she lifted the flap. After bending the flap of the lid so that it was closed, Evelyn returned the cup, covered by the lid, to the container. She then either started to place the container of coffees on the floor next to Christopher's foot

---

* *Nadel v. Burger King.* 695 N.E.2d 1185 (1997).
Footnotes deleted from original.

or placed the container on the dashboard, or she had already placed the container on the floor next to Christopher's foot, when Paul drove away from the restaurant, making a left turn onto a street. At that point Christopher began screaming that his foot was burned. Christopher, Paul, and Evelyn discovered that one or both of the cups had tipped, and that hot coffee had spilled on Christopher's right foot. Neither the cups, the lids, nor the container are in the record. Christopher was treated for second-degree burns on his right foot.

3   In their complaint, the Nadels (Brenda Nadel is the mother of Christopher Nadel) raised several claims, including (1) breach of a warranty of merchantability and breach of a warranty of fitness for a particular purpose, both based on the allegation that the coffee was too hot to consume, (2) products liability for a defective product and a failure to warn of the dangers of handling liquid served as hot as appellees' coffee, and (3) negligence both for failing to instruct employees how to properly serve hot coffee and for failing to warn business invitees of the danger of handling coffee at the temperature Emil's coffee was served.

4   . . . In support of its claim for summary judgment, Emil cited the deposition of Paul, in which he testified that he knew that coffee is served hot, that he expected coffee to be served hot, that he knew Emil's coffee was served hot, that coffee would burn someone if it was spilled on him or her, and that whoever was handling hot coffee needed to be careful not to spill it. Evelyn testified that she knew the coffee that was spilled was hot, and that it had burned her. Emil's owner's affidavit averred that BK's operating manual required coffee to be served at approximately one hundred seventy-five degrees, that the coffee machine thermostats were set at that temperature, and that Emil was unaware of any problems resulting from coffee being served at that temperature.

5   BK also moved for summary judgment and pointed to evidence in the depositions that appellants knew that the coffee was hot and that coffee was purchased and served as a hot beverage. It also contended that under the circumstances, Evelyn's and Paul's actions were intervening, superseding causes precluding any actionable negligence on its part.

6   In opposition to the motions for summary judgment, the Nadels argued that Emil and BK knew or should have known that second-degree burns could occur as a result of coffee served at one hundred seventy-five degrees, because "the whole industry has long been aware of the danger of liquid this hot," and they cited several journal articles in their supporting memorandum. The Nadels also attached the affidavit of their attorney with Christopher's medical records affixed, which averred that the medical records were true copies of what was received through discovery.

Statutory Law

1   "A manufacturer is subject to liability for compensatory damages based on a product liability claim *only* if the claimant establishes, by a preponderance of the evidence, *all* of the following:

"(1)   [T]he product was defective in manufacture or construction, . . . was defective in design or formulation, . . . was defective due to inadequate warning or instruction, . . . or was defective because it did not conform to a representation made by the manufacturer. . . .

"*[AND]*

"(2)   [A] defective aspect of the product . . . was a proximate cause of harm for which the claimant seeks to recover compensatory damages.

"*[AND]*

"(3)   The manufacturer designed, formulated, produced, created, made, constructed, assembled, or rebuilt the product."

2   [This statute] defines a product liability claim as a claim "asserted in a civil action and that seeks to recover compensatory damages from a manufacturer or supplier for death, physical injury to person, emotional distress, or physical damage to property other than the product involved, that allegedly arise from any of the following:

"(1)   The design, formulation, production, construction, creation, assembly, rebuilding, testing, or marketing of that product;

"(2)   Any warning or instruction, or lack of warning or instruction, associated with that product;

"(3)   Any failure of that product to conform to any relevant representation or warranty."

Jury Instructions on Negligence*

1   The plaintiff *Paul Nadel* seeks to recover damages based upon a claim of negligence.

2   The essential elements of such a claim are:

1.   The defendant was negligent;

2.   Defendant's negligence was a cause of injury, damage, loss or harm to plaintiff.

3   Negligence is the doing of something which a reasonably prudent person would not do, or the failure to do something which a reasonably prudent person would do, under circumstances similar to those shown by the evidence.

4   It is the failure to use ordinary or reasonable care.

5   Ordinary or reasonable care is that care which persons of ordinary prudence would use in order to avoid injury to themselves or others under circumstances similar to those shown by the evidence.

6   You will note that the person whose conduct we set up as a standard is not the extraordinarily cautious individual, nor the exceptionally skillful one, but a person of reasonable and ordinary prudence.

7   One test that is helpful in determining whether or not a person was negligent is to ask and answer the question whether or not, if a person of ordinary

* *California Jury Instructions, Civil: Book of Approved Jury Instructions*. 8th ed. Prepared by the Committee on Standard Jury Instruction Civil, of the Superior Court of Los Angeles County, California, Hon. Stephen M. Lachs, Judge of the Superior Court, Chairman. Compiled and edited by Paul G. Breckenridge, Jr. St Paul, MN: West Publishing, 1994.

prudence had been in the same situation and possessed of the same knowledge, [he][or][she] would have foreseen or anticipated that someone might have been injured by or as a result of [his][or][her] action or inaction. If the answer to that question is "yes," and if the action or inaction reasonably could have been avoided, then not to avoid it would be negligence.

8   Contributory negligence is negligence on the part of a plaintiff which, combining with the negligence of a defendant, contributes as a cause in bringing about the injury.

9   Contributory negligence, if any, on the part of the plaintiff does not bar a recovery by the plaintiff against the defendant but the total amount of damages to which the plaintiff would otherwise be entitled shall be reduced in proportion to the amount of negligence attributable to the plaintiff.

10   Comparative fault is negligence on the part of a plaintiff which combining [with the negligence of a defendant][or][with a defect in a product][or][with negligent or wrongful conduct of others] contributes as a cause in bringing about the injury.

11   Comparative fault, if any, on the part of plaintiff does not bar recovery by the plaintiff against the defendant but the total amount of damages to which plaintiff would otherwise be entitled shall be reduced by the percentage that plaintiff's comparative fault contributed as a cause to plaintiff's injury.

12   If you find that a cause of plaintiff's injury was [a defendant's negligence] [or][a defect in the product] and that the comparative fault of the plaintiff was also a cause of said injury, you will determine the amount of damages to be awarded by you as follows:

13   First: You will determine the total amount of damages to which the plaintiff would be entitled under the court's instructions if plaintiff had not been comparatively at fault.

14   Second: You will determine what percentage of the combined causes of plaintiff's injury is attributable to plaintiff's comparative fault and what percentage of such combined causes is attributable to the [defective product][and][or][a defendant's negligence].

15   Third: You will then reduce the total amount of plaintiff's damages by the percentage that plaintiff's comparative fault contributed as a cause to plaintiff's injury.

16   Fourth: The resulting amount, after making such reduction, will be the amount of your verdict.

For Deliberation and Argument

1. Assume that you are either an attorney for the plaintiff *or* an attorney for the defendant. Which of these coffee cases do you think would be easiest to win for your client? Which would be most difficult? Consider the rules relating to product liability and negligence following the cases and apply them to the facts of the case you have selected as the most difficult.

2. For any one of these cases, what additional information would you need as a jury member to cast your vote for the plaintiff or the defendant? Explain.

3. Select one of these cases and write an essay in which you argue your conclusion in IRAC format.

The Felled Stop Signs: Some Cases of Homicide
(State of Florida v. Miller, State of Utah v. Hallett)

The following selections deal with two remarkably similar cases, almost 20 years apart. In both cases—the earlier one in Utah, the later one in Florida—teenagers looking for an evening of fun pulled out or pulled down stop signs at intersections. In both cases, their actions resulted in one or more persons killed in automobile crashes. The teens were blameworthy: no one disputed that. But how blameworthy, from a legal standpoint? With what crime should they be charged? To what extent were they directly responsible for the fatalities that occurred? You'll explore these and other issues by reading accounts of the two cases: first, the more recent case, described in an article in the Los Angeles Times *(as of publication, no appeals ruling had been issued on this case); second, the Facts of the Case section of the earlier case, as described in the ruling of the Utah appellate court. Following these accounts are two statements on the law that will provide guidelines for your deliberations: the first offers excerpts from the "Homicide" section of the Utah Criminal Code, along with definitions of some key terms. The second is a brief distinction (contained in a later legal opinion from an Arizona appellate court) between "negligent homicide" and "manslaughter."*

For Fallen Stop Sign, Vandals Face Life
Mike Clary

1 Tampa, Fla.—It was a clear, dark February night when the fates collided in front of Tim's Cafe at a rural intersection where a stop sign lay face-down by the side of the road.

2 One of the vehicles involved was an eight-ton Mack truck loaded with phosphate. The other was a white Camaro carrying three 18-year-old friends on a one-way ride to eternity. Chances are, police said, they never knew what hit them.

3 Tow trucks and sheriff's deputies were still on the scene a few hours later when a fourth young man named Thomas Miller pulled up. He and a friend had just finished working the graveyard shift at a welding shop and were heading to Tim's for breakfast.

4 Miller got out of his car to see the wreckage better and, he recalled later, he stood right next to the fallen stop sign.

5 Now, 16 months after that fatal crash, Miller and two friends stand convicted on three counts of manslaughter, guilty of causing three deaths by pulling that stop sign out of the ground days earlier.

6 Although Miller, 20, and his housemates, Nissa Baillie, 21, and her boyfriend, Christopher Cole, 20, admitted taking about 20 road signs during a late-night

Mike Clary, "For Fallen Stop Sign, Vandals Face Life," *Los Angeles Times,* 11 June 1997.

spree sometime before the fatal crash, they denied tampering with the stop sign in front of Tim's Cafe.

7   But a jury did not believe them.

8   On June 19 Miller, Baillie, and Cole could be sentenced to life in prison in what is believed to be the first case in the United States in which the vandalism of a traffic sign has led to a multiple manslaughter conviction.

9   What has become known as the "stop sign case" has had a wrenching effect on the families of the six young people involved, while sparking a passionate community debate on the nexus of crime and punishment.

10   On one side is Assistant State Atty. Leland Baldwin, who prosecuted the three young people. "I have heard people ask: 'How dare you charge them with manslaughter? This was a prank. It was an unintentional crime,'" she said. "But this was not a prank. These were not young kids. These were young adults. So give me a break."

11   On the other side is Joseph Registrato, chief assistant to the Hillsborough County public defender, which represented Cole and Baillie.

12   "It's one thing to take a car when you're drunk and recklessly kill somebody," Registrato said. "That law is well-understood. But in this case, they may have committed criminal mischief and then later three people died. But others had gone through that intersection and didn't die. So there is a serious question about whether the [fallen] stop sign caused the deaths.

13   "From that they could get life in prison? It's hard to follow the ball here."

Road Sign Theft Called a Commonplace Prank

14 About this there is no debate: The chain of events that led up to that horrific crash in front of Tim's Cafe makes up a cautionary tale of sobering complexity.

15   Joe Episcopo figures at least half the population of America at one time or another has stolen a road sign to hang on a bedroom wall, to win a scavenger hunt or just for kicks.

16   In fact, says Episcopo, a lawyer who represents Miller, road sign theft is so common that, when potential jurors in the case against his client were asked if they had ever taken a sign, half the pool raised a hand and three of those who answered yes ended up being seated on the six-member panel. "Everybody has somebody in their family who takes signs," he said.

17   Indeed, vandalism and theft of road signs is a problem all across the country. After the trial here in the Hillsborough County courthouse was broadcast by Court TV, public officials from as far away as Washington state have been speaking out about the expense and danger resulting from defaced or stolen road signs.

18   In Iowa, a county engineer has announced plans to use the Tampa case as a springboard for a national education campaign on the issue.

19   Dave Krug, Hillsborough County public works department engineer, estimated that 25% of all road signs ever put up in the Tampa area are damaged by vandals, knocked down or stolen. Most road sign vandalism, however, does not result in triple fatalities, attract media attention and provoke heart-wrenching community anguish over wasted lives.

20   Moreover, most sign vandalism does not give rise to the sea of regrets among thousands of people—including at least 11 people who testified in the trial here—who noticed the downed stop sign during the 24 hours preceding the crash and failed to report it.

21   "Well, what did you do?" Baldwin asked of one witness who noticed that the stop sign was down.

22   "We just went back to work, got busy," the witness replied.

Three Target Signs "for a Rush"

23 Miller, Baillie, and Cole lived together in a rented $300-a-month mobile home on a country road less than three miles from the intersection of Keysville and Lithia-Pinecrest roads in eastern Hillsborough County where the fatal crash occurred just before midnight on Feb. 7, 1996.

24   According to interviews they gave to a local television station and Cole's testimony at trial, the three had been shopping at a nearby Wal-Mart, had drunk a couple of beers and were headed home when one of the three suggested that they take a few railroad signs. Cole told a television reporter that they began taking signs "for a rush."

25   Over a period of a couple of hours and a distance of about five miles, they unbolted and pulled up railroad signs, street name signs, a "Dead End" sign, a "Do Not Enter" sign and—from neighboring Polk County—at least one stop sign, tossing all of them in the back of their pickup truck.

26   Was it fun? Cole was asked. "I suppose so, yeah," he replied. "Yeah, it was fun at the time."

Night of Bowling Ends in Collision

27 Kevin Farr, who worked in his family's data processing business, had been bowling with his father, Les, and his two older brothers on the evening of his death. He rolled a 218 in his final league game and, as he left the bowling alley, he shouted at one of his brothers: "Tell Mom I'll be home between 11 o'clock and 12. I don't want her to worry."

28   From the bowling alley Farr drove to the house of Brian Hernandez, his best and oldest friend, and the pair then picked up Randall White. No one seems to know where they were going.

29   June Farr said that the death of the youngest of her four children has condemned her to live day by day. "And day by day takes on a whole new meaning after something like this," she said. "Sometimes it's more like a few minutes at a time."

30   The case against Miller, Cole and Baillie was circumstantial. There were no fingerprints on the stop sign and no eyewitnesses who put them at the scene. But the fallen stop sign was well within the general area of the thefts to which the three had confessed and prosecutors presented expert testimony that the stop sign appeared to have been pulled from the ground, not run over by a vehicle.

31   The defense also had its own expert witness, a mechanical engineer who testified that the stop sign had been struck by a "lateral force."

Defendants Say They Panicked Next Day

32 Perhaps the most damning evidence against Cole, Miller, and Baillie came from their own statements to police. Ron Bradish, a Sheriff's Department traffic homicide investigator, testified that Cole and Miller admitted that—during their stealing spree—they sometimes would pull signs from the ground and, if a car came by, leave them to pick up later.

33 The day after the fatal crash, the three defendants admitted to police, they panicked. They gathered up most of the stolen signs from inside and outside their mobile home and tossed them off a bridge into nearby Alafia Creek. According to Bradish, Cole said that they got rid of the signs "so no one would think they took the stop sign down at the crash."

34 Held without bail, Cole, Miller, and Baillie are to be sentenced next week after the judge hears from lawyers on both sides, as well as from relatives of the convicted and those who died.

35 While she will not lobby for life sentences, Baldwin says, she will insist on long terms. "I hope this case will be a deterrent, or, at least, somewhat thought-provoking," she said. "Perhaps this is one of the types of cases that have to be tried every generation to remind high school kids and others that vandalism has consequences. And this does have an effect. Just days ago some kids in Leon County [Tallahassee] had a stop sign in a scavenger hunt and the media [publicly] stopped them."

36 Again, Registrato demurs. "This case is useless as a deterrent," he said. "Send these three children to prison for life and the kids in Hillsborough County where it happened won't have a clue about it the next day."

37 Episcopo and Registrato said they have prepared their clients for the worst. Sentencing guidelines call for 28 years to life and Judge Bob Anderson Mitcham has been known to use the suggested maximum as a starting point. Last year he put a man convicted of wounding two Tampa police officers in prison for seven consecutive life terms, ignoring guidelines that called for 14 to 24 years.

38 For June Farr, the sentencing decision seems straightforward. "My child got the maximum penalty and he had no choice in the matter," she said. "They knew exactly what was going to happen. They just didn't know who the victims would be. This was not a prank. Pranks don't kill."

39 To those who would find life in prison too harsh a price to pay for yanking out a stop sign, Farr responds: "They didn't have to go pick out a coffin."

40 Registrato said he would argue that Miller, Cole and Baillie could better atone for their sins and better service society by doing "a couple of years hard time in Florida State Prison and then be required for the next 18 years to go to high schools twice a month and tell about the consequences of criminal mischief."

41 But Miller, Thomas Miller's father, clings to hope that his son will win a retrial and be found not guilty. He acknowledged that his son, who has a juvenile record for theft, has lied to him before. But this time, Miller said, "Tommy says he didn't take that sign and I believe it with all my heart. We know when he's lying."

42 Whatever the outcome, said Miller, 69, a retired postal worker, he knows that the lives of his family, as well as the other five families involved, are forever changed.

43   "I was in court every day," he said, "sitting in the front row on one side, across from the families of the dead boys. We didn't speak but I felt for them. . . . They lost their children. I understand.

44   "Now they have to understand that I've lost mine. Win or lose, this is a tragedy for both sides."

STATE of Utah, Plaintiff and Respondent

v.

Kelly K. HALLETT and Richard James FELSCH,

Defendants and Appellants
No. 15765
Supreme Court of Utah
Oct. 20, 1980

Facts of the Case*

1 On the evening of September 24, 1977, a number of young people gathered at the defendant's home in Kearns. During the evening, some of them engaged in drinking alcoholic beverages. At about 10:30 P.M., they left the home, apparently bent on revelry and mischief. When they got to the intersection of 5215 South and 4620 West, defendant and the codefendant Richard Felsch (not a party to this appeal) bent over a stop sign, which faced northbound traffic on 4620 West, until it was in a position parallel to the ground. The group then proceeded north from the intersection, uprooted another stop sign and placed it in the backyard of a Mr. Arlund Pope, one of the state's witnesses. Traveling further on, defendant and his friends bent a bus stop sign over in a similar manner.

2 The following morning, Sunday, September 25, 1977, at approximately 9:00 A.M., one Krista Limacher was driving east on 5215 South with her husband and children, en route to church. As she reached the intersection of 4620 West, the deceased, Betty Jean Carley, drove to the intersection from the south. The stop sign was not visible, since the defendant had bent it over, and Ms. Carley continued into the intersection. The result was that Mrs. Limacher's vehicle struck the deceased's car broadside causing her massive injuries which resulted in her death in the hospital a few hours later.

Statements on the Law
Utah Criminal Code[†]
Criminal Homicide
Criminal homicide—elements—designations of offenses

(1) (a) A person commits criminal homicide if he intentionally, knowingly, recklessly, with criminal negligence, or acting with a mental state otherwise

---

* *State of Utah v. Hallett.* 619 P.2d 337 (1980).

† *Utah Code Unannotated,* 1996. Vol. 4. Charlottesville, VA: Michie Law Publishers, 1988–96.

specified in the statute defining the offense, causes the death of another human being, including an unborn child.

Murder

(1) Criminal homicide constitutes murder if the actor:
    (a) intentionally or knowingly causes the death of another;
    (b) intending to cause serious bodily injury to another commits an act clearly dangerous to human life that causes the death of another;
    (c) acting under circumstances evidencing a depraved indifference to human life engages in conduct which creates a grave risk of death to another and thereby causes the death of another;
    (d) while in the commission, attempted commission, or immediate flight from the commission or attempted commission of aggravated robbery, robbery, rape, object rape, forcible sodomy, or aggravated sexual assault, aggravated arson, arson, aggravated burglary, burglary, aggravated kidnapping, kidnapping, child kidnapping, rape of a child, object rape of a child, sodomy of a child, forcible sexual abuse, sexual abuse of a child, aggravated sexual abuse of a child, or child abuse . . . , when the victim is younger than 14 years of age, causes the death of another person . . . ; or
    (e) recklessly causes the death of a peace officer while in the commission or attempted commission of:
        (i) an assault against a peace officer; or
        (ii) interference with a peace officer if the actor uses force against a peace officer.
(2) Murder is a first degree felony.

Manslaughter

(1) Criminal homicide constitutes manslaughter if the actor:
    (a) recklessly causes the death of another; or
    (b) causes the death of another under the influence of extreme emotional disturbance for which there is a reasonable explanation or excuse; or
    (c) causes the death of another under circumstances where the actor reasonably believes the circumstances provide a legal justification or excuse for his conduct although the conduct is not legally justifiable or excusable under the existing circumstances.
(2) Under Subsection (1)(b), emotional disturbance does not include a condition resulting from mental illness.
(3) The reasonableness of an explanation or excuse under Subsection (1)(b), or the reasonable belief of the actor under Subsection (1)(c), shall be determined from the viewpoint of a reasonable person under the then existing circumstances.
(4) Manslaughter is a felony of the second degree.

Negligent homicide

(1) Criminal homicide constitutes negligent homicide if the actor, acting with criminal negligence, causes the death of another.
(2) Negligent homicide is a class A misdemeanor.

Definitions

Requirements of criminal conduct and criminal responsibility

No person is guilty of an offense unless his conduct is prohibited by law and:

(1) He acts intentionally, knowingly, recklessly, with criminal negligence, or with a mental state otherwise specified in the statute defining the offense, as the definition of the offense requires; or
(2) His acts constitute an offense involving strict liability.

Definitions of "intentionally, or with intent or willfully"; "knowingly, or with knowledge"; "recklessly, or maliciously"; and "criminal negligence or criminally negligent"

A person engages in conduct:

(1) Intentionally, or with intent or willfully with respect to the nature of his conduct or to a result of his conduct, when it is his conscious objective or desire to engage in the conduct or cause the result.
(2) Knowingly, or with knowledge, with respect to his conduct or to circumstances surrounding his conduct when he is aware of the nature of his conduct or the existing circumstances. A person acts knowingly, or with knowledge, with respect to a result of his conduct when he is aware that his conduct is reasonably certain to cause the result.
(3) Recklessly, or maliciously, with respect to circumstances surrounding his conduct or the result of his conduct when he is aware of but consciously disregards a substantial and unjustifiable risk that the circumstances exist or the result will occur. The risk must be of such a nature and degree that its disregard constitutes a gross deviation from the standard of care that an ordinary person would exercise under all the circumstances as viewed from the actor's standpoint.
(4) With criminal negligence or is criminally negligent with respect to circumstances surrounding his conduct or the result of his conduct when he ought to be aware of a substantial and unjustifiable risk that the circumstances exist or the result will occur. The risk must be of such a nature and degree that the failure to perceive it constitutes a gross deviation from the standard of care that an ordinary person would exercise in all the circumstances as viewed from the actor's standpoint.

State v. Fisher*

Negligent homicide and manslaughter. The general rule is that negligent homicide is a lesser included offense of manslaughter. In *State v. Parker,* 128 Ariz.

---

* *State v. Fisher.* 686 P.2nd 750 (1984).

107, 624 P.2d 304 (App. 1980) . . . the Court of Appeals determined that the only difference between manslaughter and negligent homicide is an accused's mental state at the time of the incident. *See also State v. Montoya,* Ariz. 155, 608 P.2d 92 (App. 1980). Manslaughter is established where a person, aware of a substantial and unjustifiable risk that his or her conduct will cause the death of another, consciously disregards that risk. Negligent homicide is established where a person fails to perceive the substantial and unjustifiable risk that his or her conduct will cause the death of another. The element of the greater not found in the lesser is awareness of the risk.

Discussion and Writing Suggestions

1. You are either (1) a prosecuting attorney or (2) a defense attorney involved with the Miller case. In researching precedents, you find *State of Utah v. Hallett.* For purposes of preparing either your prose-cution or your defense, compare and contrast the circumstances of the *Miller* and *Hallett* cases. Consider (a) the activities of the respec-tive defendants prior to the action being prosecuted; (b) their moti-vations; (c) the relationship between the defendants' actions and the automobile accidents that subsequently occurred; (d) the rela-tive blameworthiness of the defendants; (e) with what crime, if any, the defendants should be charged; (f) any other factors you find rel-evant. Prepare your findings in the form of a memorandum to the district attorney (if you are prosecuting) or the partners in your law firm (if you are defending).

2. Read the Utah Criminal Code on homicide, focusing on the distinc-tions drawn between murder, or manslaughter, or negligent homi-cide. Should Hallett and Felsch be charged with murder, or manslaughter, or negligent homicide? In a memo to the District Attorney, justify your decision. To help you with your thinking on this subject, review the definitions provided by the Utah Code of various key phrases ("intentionally, or with intent or willfully," "recklessly, or maliciously," etc.) in the Code. Review also the dis-tinction drawn between "negligent homicide" and "manslaughter" in the opinion, *State [of Arizona] v. Fisher* (1984).

3. Hallett argued that the pulling down of a stop sign did not show the required *intent* to constitute negligent homicide. The Utah statute provides that a person is guilty of negligent homicide if he causes the death of another person

> with criminal negligence or is criminally negligent with respect to
> circumstances surrounding his conduct or the result of his conduct
> when he ought to be aware of a substantial and unjustifiable risk
> that the circumstances exist or the result will occur. The risk must

be of such a nature and degree that the failure to perceive it constitutes a gross deviation from the standard of care that an ordinary
person would exercise in all the circumstances as viewed from the
actor's standpoint.

Based on the evidence before you and the inferences you draw
from this evidence, do you believe, beyond a reasonable doubt, that
the defendant's conduct met the elements of the above statute?
Explain, in terms of the defendant's actions, viewed from his
standpoint.

4. Hallett argued that the evidence did not support the conclusion
   that his acts were the *proximate cause* of Ms. Carley's death. To quote
   from the court's "Opinion," summarizing this argument,

   > [Defendant] starts with a uniformly recognized definition: that
   > proximate cause is the cause which through its natural and foresee-
   > able consequence, unbroken by any sufficient intervening cause,
   > produces the injury which would not have occurred but for that
   > cause. His [argument] here is that there was evidence that as the
   > deceased approached from the south, she was exceeding the speed
   > limit of 25 mph; and that this was subsequent intervening and
   > proximate cause of her own death. This is based upon the fact that
   > a motorist, who was also coming from the south, testified that he
   > was going 25 mph and that Ms. Carley passed him some distance to
   > the south as she approached the intersection.

   Considering this argument, do you believe that the defendant's
   action in pulling down the stop sign was the *proximate cause* of the
   fatal accident? Explain your reasoning.

5. In separate opinions, two judges of the appellate court hearing
   Hallett made the following arguments concerning the defendant's
   degree of responsibility for the fatality:

   Maughan's Opinion

   > [W]here a party by his wrongful conduct creates a condition of peril,
   > his action can properly be found to be the proximate cause of a
   > resulting injury, even though later events which combined to cause
   > the injury may also be classified as negligent, so long as the later act
   > is something which can reasonably be expected to follow in the nat-
   > ural sequence of events. Moreover, when reasonable minds might
   > differ as to whether it was the creation of the dangerous condition
   > (defendant's conduct) which was the proximate cause, or whether it
   > was some subsequent act (such as Ms. Carley's driving), the question
   > is for the trier of the fact [the jury] to determine.
   >
   > Reflecting upon what has been said above, we [believe] that
   > whether the defendant's act of removing the stop sign was done in
   > merely callous and thoughtless disregard of the safety of others, or

with malicious intent, the result, which he should have foreseen, was the same: that it created a situation of peril; and that nothing that transpired thereafter should afford him relief from responsibility for the tragic consequences that did occur.

Hall's Opinion

The evidence produced at trial does not discount beyond a reasonable doubt the possibility that the actions of the decedent on the morning of September 25, 1977, constituted an independent, unforeseeable intervening cause. In this regard, it is to be noted that the evidence produced at trial clearly established that the accident occurred in broad daylight and that the stop sign in question had not been removed from the intersection, but merely bent over into a position where it was still marginally visible. Moreover, the word "Stop" was clearly printed in large block letters on the pavement leading into the intersection. Even if we were to assume, however, that defendant's action in bending the stop sign over erased all indication that vehicles proceeding north on 4620 West were obliged to yield right-of-way, such would render the location of the accident an unmarked intersection. The law requires due care in approaching such intersections, with such reasonable precautions as may be necessary under the circumstances.

Evidence also appearing in the record indicates that decedent was moving at an imprudent speed when she entered the intersection. Although the exact rate of speed is disputed, it is unchallenged that she had, less than a block behind, passed a truck which, itself, was doing the legal speed limit. All parties testified that she made no attempt to slow or brake upon entering the intersection. Under such circumstances, reasonable minds must entertain a reasonable doubt that the defendant's conduct was the sole efficient legal cause of her death. . . .

I would dismiss the charge of negligent homicide.

Which argument do you find more persuasive? Explain your reasoning.

6. Try to enter into the minds of the teenagers in the Florida case. One of these teens told a TV reporter that they pulled out the traffic signs "for a rush." What do you think he meant? Attempt to explain, from his point of view (to bewildered adults) why "it was fun at the time" to pull out traffic signs. What factors do you think contribute to some teenagers finding fun in such antisocial outlets? Suppose, for the sake of argument, that the teens were guilty of negligent homicide. Why would they fail to perceive the "substantial and unjustifiable risk that his or her conduct will cause the death of another"?

7. Almost certainly, you have not been involved in activities with such horrific consequences as those of the defendants in the Florida and Utah cases. Almost certainly, however, all of us have been involved in actions, which, under certain circumstances, could have resulted in very serious outcomes. And we must be prepared to deal with those outcomes. To quote a widespread slogan these days: "Actions have consequences." How do we go about determining—and dealing with—our responsibility for the consequences of our actions? To what extent are our conscious intentions a factor in our personal responsibility? Discuss these issues, drawing upon one or two specific incidents in your own life—or the life of someone you know.

8. *Group Assignment:* See Discussion and Writing Suggestion 5 on page 769 and apply that assignment to one of the cases in this group.

Drag Racing and Death: Some Cases of Manslaughter
(Commonwealth of Pennsylvania v. Levin, Commonwealth of Pennsylvania v. Root, Jacobs v. State of Florida)

Negligence, one of the most common charges in legal cases, is defined (in Black's Law Dictionary) as "the failure to exercise the standard of care that a reasonably prudent person would have exercised in the same situation." Such negligence is a tort (i.e., a private wrong), rather than a crime. But of course, there are degrees of negligence, depending upon the level of recklessness of the individual involved and the seriousness of the consequences. Another kind of legal negligence is "gross negligence": "a conscious, voluntary act or omission in reckless disregard of a legal duty and of the consequences to another party." Beyond that lies "criminal negligence," that is, "gross negligence so extreme that it is punishable as a crime ... for example, involuntary manslaughter or other negligent homicide." As we've seen in the felled stop sign cases, acts that might otherwise be chargeable as lesser offenses (such as vandalism) may be chargeable as manslaughter if they result in the death of a human being.

Of course, a jury may choose not to convict on such a charge, if it concludes that the defendant's actions do not justify a guilty verdict, or if it sees mitigating circumstances. By the same token, appeals court judges may overturn a trial court verdict if they believe that the jury's decision to convict is unsupported by the facts.

The following three cases involve drag racing. In all three cases, the races resulted in one or more fatalities. In all three cases, the defendants were convicted of involuntary manslaughter. In all three cases, the defendants appealed. As in other cases in this chapter, you will read the facts of each case, and you will read jury instructions relevant to the charge. You will also find that in two of the cases, individual judges on the appeal panel disagreed as to whether the conviction should be upheld or reversed. Once again, you are left to make your own judgment, applying the rules to the facts of the cases.

Commonwealth

v.

Ronald LEVIN
Superior Court of Pennsylvania
Nov. 12, 1957

Facts of the Case*

1 Between five and six o'clock in the morning of May 14, 1955, appellant and four other young men were together in a diner at Sixty-third and Lancaster Avenue in the City of Philadelphia. They departed in a car owned and operated by one of them, Robinson. At 5151 Dakota Street appellant transferred to his own car, and drove down Dakota Street. Robinson, with his three passengers, drove down the adjoining street. Both drivers turned right on Fifty-first Street, appellant's car being to the rear. They then turned into Wynnefield Avenue, going west. At Fifty-fourth and Wynnefield Avenue, appellant attempted to pass the Robinson car. Realizing that appellant was trying to pass, Robinson accelerated his speed. The drivers kept going faster, appellant's car being along the side of Robinson car to the left, in such proximity that it could have been touched by the passengers in the Robinson car. When the two cars arrived at Woodbine Avenue, they again bore left. As they approached the 5700 block of Woodbine Avenue, the cars were going approximately 80 miles per hour. One of the passengers, who was seated left rear in the Robinson car, opened his window, and shouted to appellant to get away. Appellant persisted in maintaining his position. The passengers called to their driver, Robinson, to slow down, and he replied: "Well, stop being chicken." The speed finally attained 85 to 95 miles per hour. As the cars reached Fifty-seventh Street appellant turned sharply to the right in front of Robinson, who thereupon lost control of his car, and hit a tree. One of the passengers, Klinghoffer, was thrown to the road and fatally injured.

Statements on the Law†

Instructions to the Jury

Involuntary Manslaughter—Defined

1 Defendant is accused of having committed the crime of involuntary manslaughter in violation of section 192, subdivision (b) of the Penal Code.

2 Every person who unlawfully kills a human being, without malice aforethought and without an intent to kill, is guilty of the crime of involuntary manslaughter in violation of Penal Code section 192, subdivision (b).

3 A killing is unlawful within the meaning of this instruction if it occurred:

1. During the commission of an unlawful act [not amounting to a felony] which is dangerous to human life under the circumstances of its commission; or

---

* *Commonwealth of Pennsylvania v. Levin.* 135 A.2d 764 (1957).

† *California Jury Instructions, Criminal: Book of Approved Jury Instructions [CALJIC].* 6th ed. Prepared by The Committee on Standard Jury Instruction Criminal, of the Superior Court of Los Angeles County, California. St. Paul, MN: West Publishing Co., 1996.

2. In the commission of an act, ordinarily lawful, which involves a high degree of risk of death or great bodily harm, without due caution and circumspection.

4 The commission of an unlawful act, without due caution and circumspection, would necessarily be an act that was dangerous to human life in its commission.

5 In order to prove this crime, each of the following elements must be proved:

1. A human being was killed; and
2. The killing was unlawful.

Due Caution and Circumspection—Defined

6 The term "without due caution and circumspection" refers to [a] negligent act[s] which [is] [are] aggravated, reckless and flagrant and which [is] [are] such a departure from what would be the conduct of an ordinarily prudent, careful person under the same circumstances as to be contrary to a proper regard for [human life] [danger to human life] or to constitute indifference to the consequences of such act[s]. The facts must be such that the consequences of the negligent act[s] could reasonably have been foreseen. It must also appear that the [death] [danger to human life] was not the result of inattention, mistaken judgment or misadventure, but the natural and probable result of an aggravated, reckless or grossly negligent act.

7 *Opinion in* Levin: In brief, a person is not guilty of involuntary manslaughter unless his unlawful and reckless conduct was the legal cause of the injury and death, and legal cause means conduct which is a substantial factor in bringing about the harm.

8 *Precedent cited in* Levin: In *Stark v. Rowley*, 323 Pa. 522, 187 A. 509, cars A and B were racing side by side. Car A finally dropped back but, in attempting to turn behind car B, skidded across the road and collided with car C. It was held that the driver of car B was jointly responsible with the driver of car A for the resultant injury to the driver of car C, even though there was no contact between car B and car C.

COMMONWEALTH of Pennsylvania

v.

Leroy W. ROOT, Appellant
Supreme Court of Pennsylvania
May 2, 1961

Facts of the Case*

1 The testimony, which is uncontradicted in material part, discloses that, on the night of the fatal accident, the defendant accepted the deceased's challenge to engage in an automobile race; that the racing took place on a rural 3-lane

---

* *Commonwealth of Pennsylvania v. Root.* 170 A.2d 310 (1961).

highway; that the night was clear and dry . . . ; that the speed limit on the highway was 50 miles per hour; that, immediately prior to the accident, the two
automobiles were being operated at varying speeds of from 70 to 90 miles
per hour; that the accident occurred in a no-passing zone on the approach to
a bridge where the highway narrowed to two directionally-opposite lanes; that,
at the time of the accident, the defendant was in the lead and was proceeding in his right hand lane of travel; that the deceased, in an attempt to pass
the defendant's automobile, when a truck was closely approaching from the
opposite direction, swerved his car to the left, crossed the highway's white
dividing line and drove his automobile on the wrong side of the highway
head-on into the oncoming truck with resultant fatal effect to himself.

Statements on the Law

1 *Justice Jones in* Root: This evidence would of course amply support a conviction
of the defendant for speeding, reckless driving and, perhaps, other violations of
The Vehicle Code of May 1, 1929, P.L. 905, as amended. In fact, it may be noted,
in passing, that the Act of January 8, 1960, P.L. (1959) 2118, Sec. 3, 75 P.S. 1041
. . . makes automobile racing on a highway an independent crime punishable by
fine or imprisonment or both up to $500 and three years in jail. As the highway
racing in the instant [present] case occurred prior to the enactment of the Act of
1960, that statute is, of course, not presently applicable.

2 In the case now before us, the deceased was aware of the dangerous condition created by the defendant's reckless conduct in driving his automobile at
an excessive rate of speed along the highway but, despite such knowledge, he
recklessly chose to swerve his car to the left and into the path of an oncoming
truck, thereby bringing about the head-on collision which caused his own death.

3 *Justice Bell in* Root: What is involuntary manslaughter? Involuntary
manslaughter is a misdemeanor and is very different from murder and from voluntary manslaughter. The prime difference between murder, voluntary
manslaughter, and involuntary manslaughter may be thus summarized: Murder
is an unlawful killing of another person with malice aforethought, expressed or
implied. . . .

4 Voluntary manslaughter is the intentional killing of another person which is
committed under the influence of passion. . . .

5 Involuntary manslaughter is an unintentional and nonfelonious killing of
another person without malice or passion, which results from conduct by defendant which is so unlawful as to be outrageous, provided such conduct is a direct
cause of the killing.

6 The unlawful racing by this defendant was not only unlawful, it was outrageous, but it was not a direct cause, i.e., one of the direct causes, of the killing.

7 *Justice Eagen in* Root: The opinion of the learned Chief Justice admits, under
the uncontradicted facts, that the defendant, at the time of the fatal accident
involved, was engaged in an unlawful and reckless course of conduct. Racing
an automobile at 90 miles per hour, trying to prevent another automobile going
in the same direction from passing him, in a no-passing zone on a two-lane

public highway, is certainly all of that. Admittedly also, there can be more than one direct cause of an unlawful death. To me, this is self-evident. But [say some of my fellow justices,] the defendant's recklessness was not a direct cause of the death. With this, I cannot agree.

8   If the defendant did not engage in the unlawful race and so operate his automobile in such a reckless manner, this accident would never have occurred. He helped create the dangerous event. He was a vital part of it. The victim's acts were a natural reaction to the stimulus of the situation. The race, the attempt to pass the other car and forge ahead, the reckless speed, all of these factors the defendant himself helped create. He was part and parcel of them. That the victim's response was normal under the circumstances, that his reaction should have been expected and was clearly foreseeable, is to me beyond argument. That the defendant's recklessness was a substantial factor is obvious. All of this, in my opinion, makes his unlawful conduct a direct cause of the resulting collision.

9   The act of passing was not an "extraordinarily negligent" act, but rather a "normal response" to the act of "racing." Furthermore, as Hall pulled out to pass, Root "dropped off" his speed to 90 miles an hour. Such a move probably prevented Hall from getting back into the right-hand lane since he was alongside of Root at the time and to brake the car at that speed would have been fatal to both himself and Root. Moreover, the dangerous condition of which the deceased had to become aware of before the defendant was relieved of his direct causal connection with the ensuing accident, was not the fact that the defendant was driving at an excessive rate of speed along the highway. He knew that when the race began many miles and minutes earlier. *The dangerous condition necessary was an awareness of the oncoming truck and the fact that at the rate of speed Root was traveling he couldn't safely pass him.*

10   *Case-law cited by Justice Eagen in* Root: Wharton, *Criminal Law and Procedure* [section] 68 (1957), speaking of causal connection, says: "A person is only criminally liable for what he has caused, that is, there must be a causal relationship between his act and harm sustained for which he is prosecuted. It is not essential to the existence of a causal relationship that the ultimate harm which has resulted was foreseen or intended by the actor. It is sufficient that the ultimate harm is one which a reasonable man would foresee as being reasonably related to the acts of the defendant." Section 295, in speaking about manslaughter, says: "When homicide is predicated upon the negligence of the defendant, it must be shown that his negligence was the proximate cause or a contributing cause of the victim's death. It must appear that the death was not the result of misadventure, but the natural and probable result of a reckless or culpably negligent act. To render a person criminally liable for negligent homicide, the duty omitted or improperly performed must have been his personal duty, and the negligent act from which death resulted must have been his personal act, and not the act of another. But he is not excused because the negligence of someone else contributed to the result, when his act was the primary or proximate cause and the negligence of the other did not intervene between his act and the result."

M. T. Connell JACOBS, Appellant

v.

STATE of Florida, Appellee
No. G-356
District Court of Appeal of Florida
First District
April 5, 1966

Facts of the Case*

1   The facts are not in dispute. On the critical date appellant, together with several others, engaged in a discussion regarding the relative speed of the automobiles owned by some of them. It was agreed that the Buick owned by Kinchen, one of the participants, was the fastest of the group, but a race would be necessary in order to determine whether the Ford owned by one Carter was faster than the Chevrolet owned by appellant. The group proceeded to an agreed starting point on State Road 40, a two-lane highway west of Ocala. Appellant's Chevrolet had a broken piston and Carter's Ford had a defective low gear. Because of the condition of Carter's Ford, he was given a head start in the race. Kinchen with the faster car was to go ahead of the other two and judge the winner, but at the last minute changed his mind and started last. Appellant, who left the starting line behind Carter, overtook the latter while traveling at a medium speed of about fifty-five miles an hour. All three vehicles proceeded in a westerly direction along the highway. A witness, Sands, driving along the highway in an easterly direction arrived at the crest of the hill and observed all three vehicles approaching in their correct right lane and traveling at an excessive speed. Sands saw Kinchen's Buick pull out into his left lane in order to pass the middle vehicle, and when he did Sands drove his car off the highway on to the right shoulder of the road. Another witness standing alongside the highway saw appellant's car proceeding westerly at an estimated speed of between fifty and seventy miles an hour. At the same time he observed a vehicle driven by one Buck traveling in an easterly direction at a speed of approximately twenty-five to forty miles an hour. As the Buick vehicle reached the crest of the hill, he met the two vehicles driven by Kinchen and Carter approaching him side by side traveling at an estimated speed of ninety miles and hour. The vehicle driven by Buck proceeding easterly in the south traffic lane met head-on the vehicle driven by Kinchen in a westerly direction which was also in the south traffic lane, resulting in the death of both drivers. At the time of the collision appellant was a quarter of a mile down the road ahead of the vehicles which were following him.

2   Under the foregoing factual situation appellant contends that the State failed to prove by any competent evidence that, as alleged in the information, he operated his vehicle in such a culpably negligent manner as to cause the collision which occurred between the vehicles operated by Kinchen and Buck.

---

* *Jacobs v. State of Florida.* 184 So.2d 710 (1966).

Appellant urges that the sole proximate cause of the collision was the culpable negligence of Kinchen over which appellant had no control, and for which he was not responsible. Appellant therefore concludes that the probata fails to conform to the allegata, and the court erred when it refused to direct a verdict in his favor.

Statements on the Law*

[Section] 776.011, Florida Statutes Annotated

1   *Principal in first degree*
     Whoever commits any criminal offense against the state, whether felony or misdemeanor, or aids, abets, counsels, hires, or otherwise procures such offense to be committed, is a principal in the first degree and may be charged, convicted and punished as such, whether he is or is not actually or constructively present at the commission of such offense.

2   *Judge Wigginton in* Jacobs: The evidence clearly shows that appellant, together with others, was engaged in what is commonly known as a "drag race" of motor vehicles on a two-lane public highway in Marion County. The race entailed the operation of three motor vehicles traveling in the same direction at excessive and unlawful rates of speed contrary to the laws of this state. While engaged in such unlawful activity one of the three vehicles actively participating in the race was negligently operated in such a manner as to cause the death of the person who drove that vehicle, as well as another innocent party who had no connection with the race. The deaths which proximately resulted from the activities of the three persons engaged in the unlawful activity of drag racing made each of the active participants equally guilty of the criminal act which caused the death of the innocent party. The fact that it was the vehicle driven by the person appointed to judge the outcome of the race which caused the death of the innocent party does not relieve appellant from his responsibility as an active participant in the unlawful event out of which the death arose.

3   In Wharton it is said:

     . . . If each of two persons jointly engage in the commission of acts which amount to criminal negligence, and as a result of which a third person is killed, each may be found guilty of manslaughter even though it may be impossible to say whose act actually caused the death.

4   The Supreme Court of Oregon, in the case of *State v. Newberg,* quoted with approval from Clark & Marshall as follows:

     There may be principals in the second degree and accessories before the fact to involuntary manslaughter. Thus, if two men drive separate vehicles at a furious and dangerous speed along the highway, each inciting and abetting the other, and one of them drives over and kills a person, the one

---

* *West's Florida Statutes, Annotated.* St. Paul, MN: West Publishing Co., 1992.

thus causing the death is guilty of manslaughter as principal in the first degree, and the other is guilty as principal in the second degree. . . .

5   *Judge Carroll in* Jacobs: I do not see how a reasonable man could lawfully conclude from the evidence adduced at the trial that, beyond a reasonable doubt, the appellant was guilty either of manslaughter or of aiding and abetting the commission of manslaughter. The culpable negligence of Willie Kinchen, as shown by the evidence, was his attempt to pass the two racing cars in the face of oncoming traffic. There is not a scintilla of evidence indicating that the appellant was aware of Kinchen's intention so to pass, and hence I do not think it reasonable to hold that the appellant aided and abetted the said culpable negligence. As I view the evidence, there was no causal relationship between the appellant's conduct in engaging in the drag race and Kinchen's culpable negligence. The only such relationship would have to be the discredited "if it hadn't been for" reasoning (if it hadn't been for the race, the collision would not have occurred), but that reasoning has long been discarded by the courts as insufficient to show proximate cause in civil cases or to show liability in criminal cases.

6   If the appellant is to be held criminally liable for manslaughter because he participated in a race during which an act of manslaughter occurred during the race, I would think that by the extension of such reasoning the spectators lined up along the road to watch the race might be legally tried and convicted as aiders and abettors to the manslaughter, simply because the collision might not have occurred if they had not congregated and encouraged the racing. By like reasoning, also, I would think that, if the starter in a foot race at a track meet had with culpable negligence loaded his pistol with live cartridges instead of the usual blanks and shot and killed someone in the grandstand, the sprinters might be held criminally liable as aiders and abettors. Such a result, of course, would be absurd. While I recognize that these two extreme illustrations differ from the facts of the case at bar in that the appellant and the other participants may have been violating the law by engaging in a drag race, I do not think that the fact of such violation can fairly be held to overcome the fatal deficiency in the evidence—that there was no proof of a causal connection between the acts of the appellant and the culpable negligence of Willie Kinchen that caused the death in question.

7   I have examined the entire transcript of trial proceedings, and, despite much conflicting and confusing testimony, the following facts appear to me to be established by the testimony concerning the automobile race in question: that the defendant was to race his 1950 Chevrolet against one Charles Carter, driving his Ford, for a quarter-mile distance from Geneva's Restaurant westerly to certain railroad tracks, over a highway (one lane for westbound traffic and one for eastbound); that Willie Kinchen, owner of a 1950 Buick, was to serve as the judge to determine the winner of the race; that Carter was permitted to take off first, because his car had a defective gear; that some seconds later the defendant took off and soon passed Carter's car; that shortly after the defendant had left the starting point, Kinchen jumped into his Buick and soon arrived just behind Carter's car; that in the process of passing Carter's car Kinchen drove his Buick into the eastbound lane and crashed head-on into an oncoming

Chevrolet being driven by one Buck who, along with Kinchen, was killed in the collision. There is, in my opinion, not a word of testimony in the transcript from which reasonable men could conclude that the defendant knew that Kinchen was planning to try to pass the racing cars, nor knew that Kinchen had even left the starting point for this or any other purpose, and certainly not a word that the defendant knew or had the slightest notion that Kinchen would be so reckless as to try to pass Carter's car by turning into the east lane in the face of oncoming traffic.

8   In view of this state of the evidence, I do not see how we can hold that the evidence supported the jury's finding that the defendant was guilty of the crime of manslaughter in the killing of Buck, or that he aided and abetted in the commission of that crime.

9   What perturbs me particularly about this case is that I do not think that the above evidence would be sufficient to hold the defendant even civilly responsible for the death of Buck, because, even if the defendant were negligent in engaging in the race, such negligence could not be properly held to have proximately caused Buck's death. As mentioned above, the reasoning is not permissible in civil cases that "if it hadn't been for" a certain act the accident would not or might not have happened and hence the doer of such act is liable for the accident. Certainly such reasoning, *a fortiori,* should not be used to convict a person of the crime of manslaughter, and yet that's the only kind of reasoning that links up the defendant's conduct to Kinchen's act that resulted in the collision.

Discussion and Writing Suggestions

1. In the Levin case, the defendant argued that he was not guilty of manslaughter because "his car did not come into contact with the victim or some instrumentality which contacted the victim." Do you agree? Explain. If you were on the jury, would you vote to convict Levin of involuntary manslaughter, taking into account the jury instructions on the definition of manslaughter and the opinion in the case itself concerning the requirements for a manslaughter conviction?

2. The appeals court panel in Levin offered a precedent for a verdict in this case. Does the precedent, *Stark v. Rowley,* support a manslaughter conviction? What are the essential similarities and differences (if any) between *Stark v. Rowley* and *Commonwealth v. Levin,* as presented here?

3. What are the key similarities and differences between *Levin* and *Root?* Specifically, how comparable are the actions of Levin and Root in directly causing the fatal accidents? How would you judge their relative degrees of responsibility? Should Root be convicted of involuntary manslaughter? Explain, using the IRAC format.

4. Justices Jones and Bell in *Root* appear to absolve the defendant of responsibility for involuntary manslaughter (though not of reckless and unlawful driving), maintaining that Root's actions were not a *direct cause* of the fatal accident. Rather, it was the deceased, they maintain, who directly caused his own death when he recklessly pulled out into the path of an oncoming truck. Justice Eagen, however, disagrees with this reasoning, claiming that *Root* was "part and parcel" of the sequence of events that resulted in the fatality. He also cites a well-known criminal law text that supports his idea that a defendant's negligence is not excused simply because someone else's negligence "contributed to the result." With whose arguments do you most agree? Explain.

5. In *Jacobs*, the defendant contended that he was not guilty of involuntary manslaughter because his vehicle was not directly involved in the fatal accident. Do you agree? Explain your verdict, using the IRAC format.

6. *Jacobs* is similar to *Root* in that both involve fatal accidents resulting from one car unsuccessfully attempting to overtake another with which it was racing and then crashing directly into a third vehicle. In both cases, also, the defendant was not directly involved in the crash. To what extent do you see significant differences in the two cases? How do these differences affect your judgment of the two defendants' relative degrees of criminal responsibility?

7. In *Jacobs*, Judge Wigginton appears to take a similar position to Justice Eagen in *Root*, maintaining that a defendant who willingly participates in a drag race cannot escape responsibility for a resulting fatality simply because he was not driving the vehicle directly involved in the crash that killed an "innocent party." Judge Carroll, on the other hand, argues that Jacobs should not be held responsible for Kinchen's recklessness and "culpable negligence." In particular, Judge Carroll relies on the important legal concept of *proximate cause*, defined (in *Black's Law Dictionary*) as "a cause that directly produces an event and without which the event would not have occurred." In Carroll's view, since Jacobs's actions were not the proximate cause of Buck's death, he cannot be held legally responsible for it. Assess Judge Wigginton's and Judge Carroll's positions, referring specifically to *Jacobs*, and, if you choose, also to *Levin* and *Root*.

8. *Group Assignment:* See Discussion and Writing Suggestion 5 on page 769 and apply that assignment to one of the cases in this group.

Legal Glossary

Like every other profession (and perhaps more than most), the law has its own special language—a language often so complicated and obscure that even lawyers have difficulty understanding it. Here is a glossary of legal terms that you will encounter while reading this chapter. The definitions, for the most part, are from The Plain Language Law Dictionary, *edited by Robert E. Rothenberg. In some cases (indicated by "[Black's]" after the definition), they are taken from* Black's Law Dictionary, 2nd Edition, (2001), *edited by Bryan A. Garner. In a very few other cases, we have provided in brackets definitions that do not appear in the dictionaries. Not included here are terms that are defined in the text itself—for example, when a statute or judicial instruction defines what is meant by "public nuisance" or "defective condition" or explains the meaning of "involuntary manslaughter."*

a fortiori   More effective; with greater reason (Latin).

abettor   One who promotes or instigates the performance of a criminal act.

affidavit   A written statement of facts, sworn to and signed by a deponent before a notary public or some other authority having the power to witness an oath.

allegata   [Statements that have been declared to be true in a legal proceeding, without yet having been proven.]

alleged   Claimed; charged.

amend   To correct; to change; to alter; so as to correct defects in a document.

appeal   The request for a review by a higher court of a verdict or decision made by a lower court.

appellant   The party who appeals a case from a lower to a higher court.

appellate court   A court with the authority to review the handling and decision of a case tried in a lower court.

appellee   The respondent; the party against whom an appeal is taken.

breach   A violation.

case   A contested issue in a court of law; a controversy presented according to the rules of judicial proceedings.

civil   Of or relating to private rights and remedies that are sought by action or suit, as distinct from criminal [Black's] proceedings.

civil law   Law dealing with civil [private], rather than criminal matters.

codify   A code is a collection of laws; the published statutes governing a certain area, arranged in a systematic manner [thus, to "codify" is to render into law].

common law   1. Law declared by judges in area not controlled by government regulation, ordinances, or statutes. 2. Law originating from usage and custom, rather than from written statutes. [Common law is the basis of the American and British legal systems.]

comparative negligence   A term that is used in a suit to recover damages, in which the negligence of the defendant is compared to that of the plaintiff.

In other words, if the plaintiff was slightly negligent but the defendant was grossly negligent, the plaintiff may be awarded damages. Or, if the plaintiff was grossly negligent and the defendant only slightly negligent, no award may be granted.

compensatory damages   The precise loss suffered by a plaintiff, as distinguished from punitive damages, which are over and above the actual losses sustained.

continue   To postpone or adjourn a case pending in court to some future date.

contributory negligence   Negligence in which there has been a failure on the part of the plaintiff to exercise ordinary, proper care, thus contributing toward an accident. Such contributory negligence on the part of the plaintiff in a damage suit often constitutes a defense for the defendant.

counsel   A lawyer, an attorney, a counsellor. To counsel means to advise.

court   A place where justice is administered.

criminal law   The branch of the law dealing with crimes and their punishment. In other words, this type of law concerns itself with public wrongs, such as robbery, burglary, forgery, and homicide.

culpable   At fault; indifferent to others' rights; blamable; worthy of censure.

decedent   A person who has died.

decision   A judgment or decree issued by a judge or jury; the deciding of a lawsuit; findings of a court.

declaration   [A statement, usually written.]

defendant   A person sued in a civil proceeding or accused in a criminal proceeding [Black's] .

deposition   The written testimony of a witness, given under oath. Such a statement may be presented in a trial, before a trial, at a hearing, or in response to written questions put to a witness. A deposition is also called an *affidavit* or a *statement under oath. Deponent:* One who gives a deposition.

directed verdict   A situation in which a judge tells the jury what its verdict must be [because the evidence is so compelling that only one decision can reasonably follow] [Black's].

discovery   Compulsory disclosure by a party to an action, at another party's request, of facts or documents relevant to the action; the primary discovery devices are interrogatories, depositions, requests for admissions, and requests for production [Black's].

diversity jurisdiction   The exercise of federal court authority over cases involving parties from different states and amounts in controversy greater than $50,000 [Black's].

duty   A legal obligation.

enjoin   To forbid; to issue an injunction, thus restraining someone from carrying out a specific act; a court order demanding that someone not do, or do, something.

evidence   Anything that is brought into court in a trial in an attempt to prove or disprove alleged facts. Evidence includes the introduction of exhibits, records, documents, objects, etc., plus the testimony of witnesses, for the purpose of proving one's case. The jury or judge considers the evidence and decides in favor of one party or the other.

ex parte   For the benefit of one party (Latin). An *ex parte* procedure is one carried out in court for the benefit of one party only, without a challenge from an opposing party.

fact   Something that took place; an act; something actual and real; an incident that occurred; an event.

felony   A major crime, as distinguished from a minor one, or misdemeanor. Felonies include robberies, burglaries, felonious assault, murder, etc.

finding of fact   A conclusion reached by a court after due consideration; a determination of the truth after consideration of statements made by the opposing parties in a suit.

findings   The result of the deliberations of a court or jury; the decisions expressed by a judicial authority after consideration of all the facts.

forms of action   Various kinds of suits brought in the common law.

fungible   A thing that can be replaced readily by another similar thing. For example, a sack of potatoes can easily be replaced by another sack of potatoes.

grand jury   A group of citizens whose duties include inquiring into crimes in their area for the purpose of determining the probability of guilt of a party or parties. Should a grand jury conclude that there is a good probability of guilt, it will recommend an indictment of the suspects.

highest court   A court of last resort; a court whose decision is final and cannot be appealed because there is no higher court to consider the matter.

impanel   To make a list of those selected for jury duty.

indictment   An accusation by a grand jury, made after thorough investigation, that someone should be tried for a crime. When an indictment is handed down, the accused must stand trial for the alleged offense, but the indictment in itself does not necessarily mean that the accused will be found guilty.

injunction   A restraining order issued by a judge that a person or persons can or cannot do a particular thing. . . . Injunctions may be temporary or permanent.

in re   "in the matter of" . . . not formally including adverse parties, but rather concerning something (such as an estate).

interlocutory Temporary; not final or conclusive, as an interlocutory decree of divorce or an interlocutory judgment.

interrogatories A set of written questions presented to a witness in order to obtain his written testimony (deposition) while he is under oath to tell the truth. Interrogatories are part of the right of discovery that a party in a suit has of obtaining facts from his adversary. They often take place prior to the commencement of the trial.

judge A public official, appointed or elected, authorized to hear and often to decide cases brought before a court of law.

judicial Anything related to the administration of justice; anything that has to do with a court of justice.

jurisdiction The power and right to administer justice; the geographic area in which a judge or a court has the right to try and decide a case.

jury A specified number of men and/or women who are chosen and sworn to look into matters of fact and, therefore, to determine and render a decision upon the evidence presented to them.

justice The attempt by judicial means to be fair and to give each party his due, under the law.

law The rules, regulations, ordinances, and statutes, created by the legislative bodies of government, under which people are expected to live.

lawsuit A dispute between two or more parties brought into court for a solution; a suit; a cause; an action.

liability Legal responsibility; the obligation to do or not do something; an obligation to pay a debt; the responsibility to behave in a certain manner.

litigation A lawsuit, a legal action; a suit.

lower court A trial court, or one from which an appeal may be taken, as distinguished from a court from which no appeal can be taken.

malice Hatred; ill will; the intentional carrying out of a hurtful act without cause; hostility of one individual toward another.

matter The subject of a legal dispute or lawsuit; the substance of the issues being litigated; the facts that go into the prosecution or defense of a claim.

negligence Failure to do what a reasonable, careful, conscientious person is expected to do; doing something that a reasonable, careful, conscientious person would not do. *Contributory negligence:* Negligence in which there has been a failure on the part of the plaintiff to exercise ordinary, proper care, thus contributing toward an accident. *Criminal negligence:* Negligence of such a nature that it is punishable as a crime. *Gross negligence:* Conscious disregard of one's duties, resulting in injury or damage to another. Gross negligence exists when an individual, by exercising ordinary good conduct, could have prevented injury or damage. *Ordinary negligence:* Negligence that could have been avoided if only one had exercised ordinary, reasonable, proper care. Ordinary negligence is not wishful or purposeful, but rather "unthinking." *Willful negligence:* Conscious, knowing neglect of duty, with knowledge that such conduct will result in injury or damage to another.

oath   A pledge to tell the truth; a sworn promise to perform a duty; a calling on God to witness a statement.

obligation   Something a person is bound to do or bound not to do; a moral or legal duty. Penalties may be imposed upon people who fail in their obligations.

ordinance   A local law; a law passed by a legislative body of a city or township or other local government; a statute; a rule.

party   1. A person engaged in a lawsuit, either a plaintiff or a defendant. 2. A person who has taken part in a transaction, such as a party to an agreement or contract.

petitioner   One who presents a petition [a written formal request for a particular thing to be done or a certain act to be carried out] to a court seeking relief in a controversial matter. The person against whom the petition is leveled is called a *respondent.*

plaintiff   The party who is bringing a lawsuit against a defendant; the person or persons who are suing.

prejudice, with   Indicates a matter has been settled without possibility of appeal.

probata (probatum)   Something proved or conclusively established; proof (Latin) [Black's].

proximate cause   The immediate cause of an injury or accident; the legal cause; the real cause; a direct cause. [A cause that directly produces an event and without which the event would not have occurred (Black's)].

punitive damages   An award to a plaintiff beyond actual possible loss. Such damages are by way of punishing the defendant for his act.

question of fact   The question of truth, such question to be decided after hearing evidence from both sides in a case. It is the judge's or jury's function to decide questions of fact.

question of law   A matter for the courts to decide, based on interpretation of existing laws pertaining to the matter at hand.

reasonable man   Someone who acts with common sense and has the mental capacity of the average, normal sensible human being, as distinguished from an emotionally unstable, erratic, compulsive individual. In determining whether negligence exists, the court will attempt to decide whether the defendant was a reasonable person.

rebuttal   The presentation of facts to a court demonstrating that testimony given by witnesses is not true.

reckless   Careless; indifferent to the outcome of one's actions; heedless; negligent; acting without due caution.

recovery The award of money given by a court to the person or persons who win the lawsuit.

redress The receiving of satisfaction for an injury one has sustained.

requisite [Required; necessary.]

respondent A person against whom an appeal is brought.

Restatement of Torts [A codification of the common law relating to torts (private wrongs) compiled by legal practitioners and scholars; most jurisdictions accept the Restatement as the equivalent of law, even though states have often passed their own laws on matters covered by the Restatements. The first series of Restatements (Restatement First) was begun in 1923; the second (Restatement Second) was begun in 1953. Restatements have been written in many other areas of civil law, such as contracts, property, and trusts.]

restraining order An order issued by the court without notice to the opposing party, usually granted temporarily to restrain him until the court decides whether an injunction should be ordered. In actuality, a restraining order is a form of an injunction.

reversal The annulment or voiding of a court's judgment or decision. Such reversal usually results from a higher court overruling a lower court's action or decision.

review 1. To re-examine, consider. 2. The consideration by a higher (appellate) court of a decision made by a lower (inferior) court.

ruling The outcome of a court's decision either on some point of law or on the case as a whole [Black's].

statute A law passed by the legislative branch of a government.

stipulation An agreement between the opposing parties in a lawsuit in respect to some matter or matters that are connected to the suit. Such stipulations are made in order to avoid delays in the conducting of the trial. Many stipulations consist of the admission of facts to which both parties agree.

strict liability Liability that does not depend on actual negligence or intent to harm, but is based on the breach of an absolute duty to make something safe.

summary judgment A means of obtaining the court's decision without resorting to a formal trial by jury. Such judgments are sought when the opposing parties are in agreement on the facts in the dispute but wish to obtain a ruling as to the question of law that is involved.

testimony Evidence given under oath by a witness, as distinguished from evidence derived from written documents.

tort A wrong committed by one person against another; a civil, not a criminal wrong; a wrong not arising out of a contract; a violation of a legal duty that one person has toward another. Every tort is composed of a legal obligation, a breach of that obligation, and damage as a result of the breach of the obligation. *Tort-feasor:* a wrongdoer.

tortious   Hurtful; harmful; wrongful; injurious; in the nature of a tort.

vacate   To cancel; to annul; to set aside.

verdict   The finding or decision of a jury, duly sworn and impaneled, after careful consideration, reported to and accepted by the court.

witness   1. An individual who testifies under oath at a trial, a hearing, or before a legislative body. 2. To see or hear something take place. 3. To be present, and often to sign, a legal document, such as a will or deed.

writ   A formal order of a court, ordering someone who is out of court to do something.

RESEARCH ACTIVITIES

LEGAL RESEARCH

Unless the institution you are attending has a law school, it will likely not have the resources you need to do genuine legal research, except at the secondary source level—i.e., general books and periodical articles dealing with legal matters. If you do not have access to a law school library but are in or near a city that serves as the county seat, you may be able to use the law library at the county courthouse. The public does have access to these libraries, which should contain the basic tools you need to conduct research—legal encyclopedias and dictionaries, legal periodicals and indexes, style manuals, and a set of state, regional, and federal case reporters, and state and federal statutes and codes.

Many college libraries will have a set of Supreme Court decisions (in *United States Reports*), even if they do not have collections of state-level cases in regional or state case reporters, such as the *Pacific Reporter* or the *California Reports*. Supreme Court cases are also available on the Web; see below. Thus, you should be able to conduct research on cases, such as *Roe v. Wade*, 410 U.S. 113 (1973), that reached the Supreme Court. (This citation means volume 410 of *United States Reports*, beginning on p. 113. To refer to a statement on a particular page, insert "at" before the page number; thus 410 U.S. at 125.)

Legal research has been transformed by the computer revolution, and vast legal databases are now available both online and on CD-ROM, through LexisNexis and Westlaw. If you do not have special access to online sources, however, legal research on the Internet is hit or miss. America Online, for example, does have a good site on the law, though it is not comprehensive enough to allow you to conduct systematic research on cases. You will find resources, however, on various federal, state, and local statutes, as well as a number of specialized sites on such issues as constitutional law and poverty/legal assistance. Some states have placed their statutes online: for example, you may find complete state penal and civil codes on the World Wide Web at

<http://www.findlaw.com/casecode/state/html>.

To find other legal information, try going to the home Web page of a law school library and following the links. For example, the Cornell University Law School Library site (with a link to its Legal Information Institute) is at

<http://www.lawschool.cornell.edu/>

The Law section of the World Wide Web Virtual Library, maintained by the Indiana University Law School, is at

<http://www.law.indiana.edu/v-lib/>

The Emory University Law Library Electronic Reference Desk is at

<http://www.law.emory.edu/LAW/refdesk/toc.html>

The Chicago-Kent College of Law (Illinois Institute of Technology) site is at

<http://www.kentlaw.edu/>

The Harvard University Law School Library is at

<http://www.law.harvard.edu/Library>

The University of California at Berkeley's Law School Library is at

<http://www.law.berkeley.edu/library/>

The UCLA Law School's site is at

<http://www1.law.ucla.edu/~library/>

There are several other useful Web sites for law:

Law on the Web (Saint Louis University School of Law):
     <http://lawlib.slu.edu/>
Meta-Index for U.S. Legal Research (Georgia State University College of Law):
     <http://gsulaw.gsu.edu/metaindex>
Washburn University School of Law:
     <http://www.washlaw.edu/>
RefLaw, the Virtual Law Library Reference Desk:
     <http://washlaw.edu/reflaw/reflaw.html>
FindLaw:
     <http://www.findlaw.com>

Note: The FindLaw site offers a searchable database of all Supreme Court opinions since 1893. Go to: <http://www.findlaw.com/casecode/supreme.html>

FindLaw also offers access to Federal Circuit Court cases and state codes and cases, though only for recent years. Searchability for these cases varies from state to state.

Federal Circuit Court cases:
     <http://www.findlaw.com/casecode/courts/index.html>
State codes and cases:
     <http://www.findlaw.com/casecode/state.html>

Using an electronic legal database such as LexisNexis or Westlaw is similar to using any other database; you conduct a systematic search, using key terms. If you wanted to conduct research on tobacco cases, and particularly on the issue of the liability of tobacco manufacturers for deaths resulting from their products, your search terms would include the words "tobacco" and "manufacturer" and "death" and "liability" and the appropriate connectors ("and," "or," etc.). Following the search, the Westlaw system would provide citations to all cases, within the time and regional boundaries you specify, that include these terms. (You can find the same citations, of course, by using printed indexes, such as *West's California Digest*. Such searches will take more time because printed indexes are less flexible than electronic ones that search by combinations of individual terms, and because you have to search the various printed supplements, as well as the basic indexes, to make sure your research is up-to-date.) Be forewarned that you may be charged a fee to use electronic search services.

Although a comprehensive guide to legal research is beyond the scope of this book, the list below includes some of the most useful sources you will need:

LEGAL ENCYCLOPEDIAS

Corpus Juris Secundum (includes case annotations)

American Jurisprudence 2d (includes case annotations)

The Guide to American Law

DICTIONARIES

Words and Phrases (includes definitions and case annotations)

Black's Law Dictionary

Ballentine's Law Dictionary

ANNOTATED DECISIONS INDEXED BY LEGAL TOPIC

ALR (American Law Review) Digest of Decisions and Annotations (extensive annotated cases on selected legal issues)

West's [State] Digest (index to legal issues with case annotations)

PERIODICAL INDEXES

Index to Legal Periodicals and Books

Current Law Index

Current Index to Legal Periodicals (also in microfilm, online, and on CD-ROM)

ELECTRONIC LEGAL PERIODICAL INDEXES

LexisNexis (includes Index to Legal Periodicals and Books and Legal Resource Index)

LegalTrac (CD-ROM) (part of the InfoTrac library)

MODEL CODES AND STATUTES

Restatement of the Law, 2d (covers areas of civil law, such as torts and contracts)

Model Penal Code

FEDERAL CASE REPORTERS (Collections of Case Opinions, in Chronological Order of Decision)

United States Reports (Supreme Court)

Supreme Court Reports, Lawyer's Edition

Federal Supplement (decisions of Federal District Courts)

Federal Reporter (decisions of Federal Circuit courts)

West's Supreme Court Reporter

REGIONAL AND STATE REPORTERS

Pacific Reporter (covers Alaska, Arizona, California, Colorado, Hawaii, Idaho, Kansas, Montana, Nevada, New Mexico, Oklahoma, Oregon, Utah, Washington, Wyoming)

North Eastern Reporter (Illinois, Indiana, Massachusetts, New York, Ohio)

North Western Reporter (Iowa, Michigan, Minnesota, Nebraska, North Dakota, South Dakota, Wisconsin)

Atlantic Reporter (Connecticut, Delaware, Maine, Maryland, New Hampshire, New Jersey, Pennsylvania, Rhode Island, Vermont)

South Western Reporter (Arkansas, Kentucky, Missouri, Tennessee, Texas)

South Eastern Reporter (Georgia, North Carolina, South Carolina, Virginia, West Virginia)

Southern (Alabama, Florida, Louisiana, Mississippi)

(State reporters)

STATUTES, CONSTITUTIONS, CODES

United States Code (U.S.C.)

United States Codes Annotated (U.C.S.A.)

United States Code Service (U.S.C.S.)

(State and local statutes and codes)

COMPUTER-ASSISTED LEGAL RESEARCH

LexisNexis

Westlaw

CITATORS (CITATION GUIDES)

Shepard's Citations (indicates if the case, statute, article, etc., you want to cite as authority has been cited in other cases, statutes, articles, etc. The process of conducting such searches is known as "Shepardizing.")

The example below is from West Publishing Company's *Words and Phrases.* It will give you an idea of how you can find particular cases on particular legal issues. Suppose you want to see how the concept of "malice" has been used in libel cases. The entry on "malice" begins with a series of cross references to related topics, then presents a long series of legal statements on malice that have appeared in legal opinions. Following the "general" category that begins most entries, you can look for the particular area in which you are interested—in this case, libel and slander.

MALICE
  See, also,
  Civil Action When Malice is not Gist of Action.
  Common-Law Malice.
  Constructive or Implied Malice.
  Deliberate Malice.
  Doctrine of Universal Malice.
  Fraud or Malice.
  Implied Malice.
  Inferred Malice.
  New York Times Malice.
  Presumed Malice.
  Secrecy and Malice.
  Times Malice.
  Willfulness and Malice.
  With Malice.
  With Malice and Unjustified in Law.

IN GENERAL

In the context of intentional torts, "malice" is defined under Massachusetts law as arising from improper motive or means, including age discrimination. *Galdauckas v. Interstate Hotels Corp.* No. 16, D.Mass., 901 F.Supp. 454, 465.

  "Malice," in context of peer review, means recklessness of consequences and mind regardless of social duty. *Cooper v. Delaware Valley Medical Center,* 654, A.2d 547, 553, 539, Pa. 620.

  "Malice" is wickedness of disposition, hardness of heart, cruelty, recklessness of consequences and mind regardless of social duty. *Green v. Pennsylvania Bd. Of Probation and Parole,* Pa.Cmwlth. 664 A.2d 677, 679.

  "Malice," in defamation cases, means that the defendant knows that the statement is false or that he has reckless disregard for determining whether it is true. *Century Management, Inc. v. Spring,* Mo. App.W.D., 905 S.W.2d 109, 113.

LIBEL AND SLANDER

Evidence supported jury's finding that veterinarian's inquiry of coworker as to whether former employee had drug or alcohol problem were slander per se, and were made out of "malice," rather than in "good faith," and thus were not protected by privilege; imputation of substance abuse reflected on former employee's capacity to perform duties of veterinary assistant, and veterinarian denied asking question when confronted by former employee, but during trial he claimed former employee had become unreliable. *Lara v. Thomas*, Iowa, 512 N.W.2d 777, 785.

In libel action arising from employer and employee relationship, actual "malice" means publication of statement with knowledge that it is false or with reckless disregard for whether it is false, and falsity coupled with negligence, failure to investigate truth or falsity of statement, and failure to act as reasonably prudent person are insufficient to show malice. *Maewal v. Adventist Health Systems/Sunbelt, Inc.*, Tex.App.-Fort Worth, 868 S.W.2d 886, 893.

"Malice," sufficient to overcome qualified privilege in defamation action, requires showing that defendant acted with knowledge of, or in reckless disregard of, falsity of publicized matter, that is that defendant in fact entertained serious doubts about truth of publication. *Mitre v. La Plaza Mall*, Tex. App.-Corpus Christi, 857 S.W.2d 752, 754.

"Malice" necessary to overcome qualified privilege in defamation action may be proven by evidence of personal ill feeling, exaggerated language or extent of publication. *Strauss v. Thorne*, Minn. App., 490 N.W.2d 908, 912.

Essence of "malice" in libel context is not lack of prudence, but actual awareness of probable falsity of published statement. *Weinel v. Monkey*, 5 Dist., 481 N.E.2d 776, 778, 89 Ill.Dec. 933, 935, 134 Ill.App.3d 1039.

Other West indexes also provide references to relevant articles in legal periodicals. Don't hesitate to ask librarians for assistance in using legal indexes to find cases, articles, and other sources.

Two excellent books will teach novice legal researchers to find cases, statutes, and articles by topic:

Cohen, Morris, Robert C. Berring, Kent C. Olson. *How to Find the Law.* 9th ed. St. Paul, MN: Westlaw, 1989. (See also Berring's abridged version of this book, entitled *Finding the Law.*)

Jacobstein, J. Myron, Roy M. Mersky, Donald J. Dunn. *Fundamentals of Legal Research*, 6th ed. Wesbury, NY: Foundation Press, 1994.

CITATIONS FOR CASES COVERED IN THIS CHAPTER

If you would like to follow up on cases covered in this chapter, here are the references. (See Hricik, page 742, on reading legal citations.)

The Maiden and the Pot of Gold: A Case of Emotional Distress

Nickerson v. Hodges. 84 So. 37 (1920)

The Ridiculed Employee: Another Case of Emotional Distress

Harris v. Jones. 380 A.2d 611 (1977)

The Overweight Nursing Student

Russell v. Salve Regina. 649 F.Supp. 391 (1986), 890 F.2d 484 (1989)

Assault and Battery on the Gridiron: A Case of Reckless Disregard of Safety

Hackbart v. Cincinnati Bengals. 601 F.2d 516 (1979)

Who Gets the Kids? Some Cases of Child Custody

Ashwell v. Ashwell. 286 P.2d 983 (1995)

Wood v. Wood. 190 Cal Rptr. 469 (1983)

Fingert v. Fingert. 271 Cal Rptr. 389 (1990)

In Re B.G. 523 P.2d 244 (1974)

In Re the Marriage of B.A.S. 541 S.W.2d 762 (1976)

Hot Coffee Spills

Harris v. Black. 204 S.E.2nd 779 (1974)

Pasela v. Brown Derby, Inc. 594 N.E.2d 1112 (1991)

Rudees v. Delta Airlines. 553 S.W.2d 85 (1977)

Nadel v. Burger King. 695 N.E.2d 1185 (1997)

The Felled Stop Signs: Some Cases of Homicide

State of Florida v. Miller. 2001 Fla App LEXIS 2081 (2001)

State of Utah v. Hallett. 619 P.2d 337 (1980)

Drag Racing and Death: Some Cases of Manslaughter

Commonwealth of Pennsylvania v. Levin. 135 A.2d 764 (1957)

Commonwealth of Pennsylvania v. Root. 170 A.2d 310 (1961)

Jacobs v. State of Florida. 184 So.2d 710 (1966)

RESEARCH TOPICS

1. Select a particular legal issue dealt with in this chapter (for example, emotional distress or drag racing) and research the book and periodical indexes to find some interesting recent cases. Use an index to legal periodicals if the library has one. Select one of these cases and report on its progress. Describe the facts of the case, identify the legal issues involved, describe and analyze the arguments on both sides, and discuss the case's outcome.

2. Using some of the Internet legal sites mentioned above, browse the Web until you find a topic that interests you (for example, tobacco lawsuits). Then, using the hyperlinks, research the topic as fully as you are able, online. (Remember to write down, electronically copy, or bookmark important URLs so that you can easily return to them.) Write a report *on the progress of your research,* rather than on the topic itself. Focus on what you were able to find, using Web

resources, and what you were unable to find. Explain your frustrations, as well as your high points of discovery. Indicate what other information—whether available online or in print—you would need to find before being able to complete a report on the topic.

3. Visit the county courthouse (if one is nearby) and sit in for a period of time on one or more trials. Report on your observations. Describe what you have seen and analyze the various aspects of the case or cases: the prosecution and defense lawyers, the defendant, the witnesses, the judge, the jury. What conclusions, from this limited observation, can you make about the legal process? What recommendations would you make to better achieve justice—or, at least, a higher standard of fairness or efficiency?

4. Research the legal system in a country other than the United States. Based upon your own experience or knowledge and upon what you have learned in this chapter, how does the process of criminal or civil cases in this other country compare to that in the United States? Which aspects of the other country's legal system appear superior to those of the United States? Which seem inferior? In your discussion refer to specific cases tried in the other country's legal system. You may choose to focus partially on offenses (such as criticizing the government) that are not crimes in the United States, but are in some other countries; however, focus primarily upon the ways that the legal system *works.*

5. There are many examples of feature films that focus on courtroom drama and other legal matters: *Young Mr. Lincoln* (1939), *Adam's Rib* (1949), *The Caine Mutiny* (1954), *12 Angry Men* (1957), *Witness for the Prosecution* (1957), *Anatomy of a Murder* (1961), *Inherit the Wind* (1960), *Judgment at Nuremberg* (1961), *To Kill a Mockingbird* (1962), *The Paper Chase* (1973), *The Verdict* (1982), *True Believer* (1989), *Class Action* (1991), *A Few Good Men* (1992), *Ghosts of Mississippi* (1996), *A Civil Action* (1998).

   View one or more of these films, then report on and draw conclusions from your observations. Using inductive reasoning, *infer* points of law and rules of courtroom procedure from what you see. Point out similarities and differences, where appropriate. For example, *The Caine Mutiny* deals (partially) with a court-martial, where the rules of procedure are somewhat different from those in civilian courts. *Judgment at Nuremberg* deals with war crimes tribunals in postwar Germany, and *12 Angry Men* deals with jury room deliberations, rather than with the trial itself. *The Paper Chase* deals with a tyrannical law professor attacking the "skullsful of mush" in his students' heads and goading them to "think like a lawyer!"

Credits

CHAPTER 1

Page 8: "The Future of Love: Kiss Romance Goodbye, It's Time for the Real Thing" by Barbara Graham, *UTNE Reader*, November/December 1996. Reprinted by permission of the author.

Pages 25–27: Figure 1.1: "Categories Used by American and Israeli Males to Screen Dating Candidates," Figure 1.2: "Categories Used by American and Israeli Females to Screen Dating Candidates," and Figure 1.3: "Comparison of Categories Used by American and Israeli Males and Females to Screen Dating Candidates" from "Choosing a Mate in Television Dating Games: The Influence of Setting, Culture, and Gender" by Amir Hetsroni, *Sex Roles*, 2000, 42: 1. Reprinted by permission of Kluwer Academic/Plenum Publishers and the author.

Page 29: Figure 1.4: "The (Un)Acceptability of Betrayal: A Study of College Students' Evaluations of Sexual Betrayal by a Romantic Partner and Betrayal of a Friend's Confidence" by S. Shirley Feldman, et al., p. 511, *Journal of Youth and Adolescence,* 2000, 29: 4, pp. 498–523. Reprinted by permission of Kluwer Academic/Plenum Publishers and the author.

Page 31: From "In Vitro Fertilization: From Medical Reproduction to Genetic Diagnosis" by Dietmar Mieth, *Biomedical Ethics: Newsletter of the European Network for Biomedical Ethics* 1.1 (1996): 45. Copyright © 1996 by Dietmar Mieth. Reprinted by permission of the author.

CHAPTER 3

Page 84: "Scenario for Scandal" by Mark Naison, *Commonweal* (January 2004). Copyright © 2004 Commonweal Foundation. Reprinted by permission.

CHAPTER 4

Page 99: "Instant Messaging Is In, Phones Out" by Ellen Edwards, *Seattle Times*, June 16, 2003: E4. Originally published as "Middle Schoolers, Letting Their Fingers Do The Talking," *Washington Post*, May 14, 2003. Copyright © 2003 by The Washington Post. Reprinted with permission.

Page 100: "Teens Bare Their Hearts with Instant Messages" by Stanley A. Miller II, *Milwaukee Journal Sentinel,* June 26, 2001. Copyright © 2001 by Milwaukee Journal Sentinel. Reproduced with permission of Milwaukee Journal Sentinel conveyed through Copyright Clearance Center.

Page 101: "Teens' Instant-Messaging Lingo Is Evolving into a Hybrid Language" by Stephanie Dunnewind, *Seattle Times,* April 12, 2003. Copyright © 2003 by Seattle Times Company. Used with permission.

Page 102: "Minding Your E-Manners: Over-use of Instant Messaging Can Be a Major Breach of Netiquette" by Michelle Slatalla, *New York Times*, September 25, 1999. Copyright © 1999 The New York Times Company. Reprinted with permission.

Page 106: "You've Got Romance! . . ." by Bonnie Rothman Morris, *New York Times*, August 26, 1993. Copyright © 1993 The New York Times Company. Reprinted with permission.

Page 107: "Online Dating Sheds Its Stigma as Losers.com" by Amy Harmon, *New York Times*, June 29, 2004. Copyright © 2004 The New York Times Company. Reprinted with permission.

CHAPTER 5

Page 137: "A New Start for National Service" by John McCain and Evan Bayh, *New York Times*, November 6, 2001. Copyright © 2001 by The New York Times Company. Reprinted by permission.

Page 138: "A Time to Heed the Call" by David Gergen, *U.S. News and World Report*, December 24, 2001, p. 60. Copyright © 2001 U.S. News and World Report, L.P. Reprinted with permission.

CHAPTER 11

CHAPTER 12

CHAPTER 13

CHAPTER 14

Index of Authors and Titles

CHECKLIST FOR WRITING SUMMARIES

- **Read the passage carefully.** Determine its structure. Identify the author's purpose in writing.
- **Reread.** *Label* each section or stage of thought. *Highlight* key ideas and terms.
- **Write one-sentence summaries** of each stage of thought.
- **Write a thesis:** a one- or two-sentence summary of the entire passage.
- **Write the first draft** of your summary.
- **Check your summary** against the original passage.
- **Revise** your summary.

CHECKLIST FOR WRITING CRITIQUES

- **Introduce** both the passage being critiqued and the author.
- **Summarize** the author's main points, making sure to state the author's purpose for writing.
- **Evaluate** the validity of the presentation.
- **Respond** to the presentation: agree and/or disagree.
- **Conclude** with your overall assessment.